# 1 MONTH OF
# FREE
# READING

## at

## www.ForgottenBooks.com

By purchasing this book you are
eligible for one month membership to
ForgottenBooks.com, giving you
unlimited access to our entire
collection of over 1,000,000 titles via
our web site and mobile apps.

To claim your free month visit:

www.forgottenbooks.com/free882564

ISBN 978-0-266-73932-6
PIBN 10882564

VOL. 85, NO. 1

287 Fourth Avenue, New York City
1436 Marquette Building, Chicago

PRICE TEN CE[NTS]

# The Outlook

## Saturday, January 5, 1907

# The Problem of Enormous Fortunes

### A discussion of the remedy involved in the proposed enactment by Congress of a progressive tax on inheritances

## By Philip S. Post, Jr.

# The Outlook

## SATURDAY, JANUARY 5, 1907

**Congress and the Brownsville Incident** — The suggestion is made by certain newspaper correspondents that Congress may attempt by law to reinstate in the army the members of the Brownsville battalion discharged from the service by the President, and a correspondent in the New York Times even suggests that the President has intimated that he would refuse to obey such a law if it should be passed, that the only remedy for the refusal would be impeachment, and that it is not likely that the House would go so far as to impeach him. All this is probably newspaper gossip; there is too much good sense in Congress to allow the passage of the law suggested by the fertile mind of the newspaper writer; and if such a law were passed, it would clearly be the duty of the President to disregard it. It is just as much a violation of the Constitution for Congress to usurp the functions of the President as it is for the President to usurp the functions of Congress. The President is made by the Constitution the Commander-in-Chief of the army, and if Congress were to attempt to execute the functions of Commander-in-Chief it would clearly be the duty of the President to resist the usurpation. Congress can by law determine the terms and conditions of enlistment; it can probably deprive the President in the future of the power to discharge enlisted men without trial, which he now possesses. But it cannot exercise the power of discipline over the army. It can no more discharge an officer or soldier, or reinstate an officer or soldier who has been discharged, than it could assume to direct military operations in the field in time of war, or promote or degrade officers, or direct the President whom to promote and whom to degrade. We do not deny the right of the Senate to investigate the Brownsville incident, or any other incident it wishes to know about, but we think it is a palpable waste of time for it to do so; for it can take no action as to what has been done, whatever may be the result of its investigation, and its opinion based on that investigation will have no legal authority, and no more moral authority than that of any other number of equally estimable gentlemen of National reputation. The President, and the President alone, is charged with the duty of maintaining discipline in the army, and the President is responsible to the Nation, not to Congress, for maintaining that discipline in a manner at once just and efficient.

**Insurance Officers Indicted** — While it was perfectly proper for the Grand Jury of New York City, in presenting indictments against Mr. George W. Perkins and Mr. Charles S. Fairchild on charges growing out of the Armstrong investigation, to point out that the policy-holders of the New York Life Insurance Company actually benefited by the transaction in question, and the men indicted did not personally profit by their act, nevertheless the conclusion should not be drawn hastily that for these reasons the illegal transaction was not morally reprehensible and contrary to public interest. If the facts are as stated in the indictments, there would be a fair parallel between this case and that of the executor of an estate who should by false affidavits save the estate from paying tax under a State inheritance law—that is to say, the executor could truly assert that those whose trust he held were financially benefited, and that he made no wrongful gain personally—yet the moral as well as the legal turpitude

1

of such an act is perfectly evident. The charges against Mr. Perkins, who was formerly the Vice-President of the New York Life Insurance Company as well as a member of the firm of J. P. Morgan & Co., and against Mr. Fairchild, formerly President of the New York Security and Trust Company, and at one time Secretary of the United States Treasury, are, in brief, that the New York Life Insurance Company was in danger of being refused permission to carry on business in Prussia because the Prussian authorities insisted as a prerequisite that insurance companies should hold only certain classes of investments. The New York Life held certain securities which did not come within the classification laid down by the Prussian Government. It went through the form of selling the securities in question to the New York Security and Trust Company, which was really subsidiary to the New York Life. On the books of the insurance company the transaction appeared as a sale, but on the books of the subsidiary company the same transaction appeared as a loan. To add to the evidence of subterfuge, it is pointed out that the note on which the supposed loan was based was signed by two totally irresponsible persons, financially speaking, one of whom was a colored employee of low grade. If these facts, which were alleged very plainly in the Armstrong investigation, are as above stated, and unless their significance is more favorably interpreted because of new evidence to be adduced, it seems plain that the officers who carried out the scheme were guilty of violating the laws of New York State for the purpose of obtaining a commercial advantage in Prussia which the company could not otherwise have had, and that therefore there was fraudulent intent within the meaning of the law. Technically, the charge is forgery. It need not be pointed out that an indictment is a very different thing from a conviction ; that all accused persons are entitled to a fair and full presentation of their defense before the courts ; that the men under indictment have held positions of great prominence in financial circles and have won the confidence of their associates and, in the case of Mr.

Fairchild, of the country at large ; and that public opinion should await their defense before passing judgment on them.

❧

**From Rodman to President**

Four weeks ago the country was shocked by the announcement of the sudden death of Samuel Spencer, President of the Southern Railway ; last week Alexander Johnston Cassatt, President of the Pennsylvania system, died almost as suddenly, though not by accident. The passing of Mr. Cassatt was possibly more pathetic ; whatever its proximate cause, its ultimate cause is believed by many to have been grief at the discovery of graft on the part of certain officials in his own company. For this Mr. Cassatt was not responsible ; but the discovery weighed on him as much as if he had been. Such a feeling was natural in one who had fitted himself thoroughly for his life-work. There was no financial necessity for Mr. Cassatt to choose any work ; he was born a rich boy ; he loved his pleasures quite as much as his books ; he could look forward to a life of ease. But an increasing number of rich Americans feel it incumbent upon them to choose a profession and to work at it as hard as though they were poor. Mr. Cassatt was one of these. He chose civil engineering. He was fitted for it at the Rensselaer Polytechnic Institute at Troy, and was graduated with honors when but twenty years old. He went to work in the lowest grade of engineering on a little railway line in Georgia, and the first year of the Civil War found him a rodman on the Pennsylvania system. From this position he rose through the various technical and administrative grades until, six years ago, he became President of a great system. No railway service, it is believed, has ever been more efficient. For Mr. Cassatt was not merely technically equipped for his task ; with faith in the future, with judgment both sound and swift, he was a signal example of broad-gauge energy. He was the first railway manager to take up the air-brake, to recognize the merits of the tank track, and to institute the six-track, long-distance system. Finally, with the courage of a true pioneer, he made his road first, among those that reach the metropolis by ferry, to secure entrance by expensive tunnels under the rivers. That the New York City terminal would involve the expenditure of a hundred million dollars did not check Mr. Cassatt. He borrowed that amount, and much more, for improvements on his road. He has made it, among the railways of the world, the first in value, as it is in diversified commerce. Mr. Cassatt was no ordinary financier, accidentally a railway president. When he thought of the Pennsylvania, he did not think of it as a sponge to be squeezed dry, nor as a property to be used for the benefit of Wall Street first and of its patrons only second. He was one of the most efficient officials the country has yet seen, because he tried to administer a great property for its own benefit and not at all for the benefit of the more or less temporary holders of its stocks and bonds. In his fidelity to this ideal Mr. Cassatt stood out in dramatic contrast to the disquieting spectacle of the financial speculators, not to say buccaneers, in control of certain railways. With these economic and moral ideals, and with an open mind for any suggestion, he had a statesmanlike grasp of the relations between the railways and the Federal Government. He was, if not the first, among the very first, to recognize the necessity of widening the Government's powers under the inter-State commerce clause of the Constitution, and, as a logical consequence, he recognized the right as well as the expediency of co-operation by the railways with the Government. His quiet force was felt to the full in the recent railway reform regulations. Uniting all these qualities, Mr. Cassatt also possessed a strong personal charm, which gave a compelling touch to his influence. It will be hard to fill Mr. Cassatt's place. Meanwhile men in similar positions will do well to study the aims and achievements of a man whose name promises to take historic rank among the constructive forces of an age of great achievements in engineering, administration, and finance.

**Sir Mortimer Durand's Retirement**

During the past week some silly stories in the daily press in connection with the retirement from his Washington post of Sir Henry Mortimer Durand, the British Ambassador, have aroused indignation among Sir Mortimer's friends. His diplomacy has been like his personal manner, dignified, simple, straightforward. He has a peculiar charm and worth to those who know him well. A man of wide knowledge and a close student of current events in two hemispheres, his observations have always been keen and incisive. He is also a literary critic of discrimination, as our readers will shortly judge upon the publication in The Outlook of an appreciation of Longfellow which Sir Mortimer has prepared at the request of the editors of The Outlook, in commemoration of the centenary of the poet's birth. In Lenox, Massachusetts, where the Ambassador has spent his summers, he has been held in enthusiastic esteem by all sorts of boys, because he welcomed them to his cricket field and taught them a game in which they quickly became proficient. Sir Mortimer is fond of all outdoor sports, especially of following the hounds and of big game shooting, his life in India having afforded many an opportunity for the latter pursuit. It was appropriate that he should enter the Indian service, as the son of the late Major-General Sir Henry Durand, whose history of the first Afghan War the son was later to edit, as well as to write the biography of his father. After a number of years of training in that service, in 1879, during the Kabul campaign, Sir Mortimer was made secretary to Sir Frederick, now Earl, Roberts. Later he became Foreign Secretary in India, a position which he long held. Towards the end of his term he conducted an expedition to the Amir of Afghanistan. In talking about India, its frontiers, people, government, society, literature, religions, Sir Mortimer conveys a more vivid notion of the problems there than do most English officials, and the world will be the gainer when he decides to put his Oriental reminiscences between covers. From India the Foreign Secretary was transferred as Minister to Persia, where he remained from 1894 to 1900, a critical period for England's relations with the Middle East. Had his Government followed its envoy's recommendations, its influence might have been intrenched for all time there; instead of that, it has been largely supplanted by Russia. Sir Mortimer wanted England to lend money to Persia on the security of the Gulf ports, a step without precedent. It was not approved by his Government, which was either unwilling or unable to follow his lead. Chagrined later by the results of its failure to follow Sir Mortimer's counsel, the Government promoted him to the Madrid ambassadorship. By this time he had completed a generation of Oriental service, which generally emphasizes any temperamental reticence. This quality, inculcated in the East as a cardinal virtue, had stood Sir Mortimer in good stead there. Nevertheless, in the West, despite a seeming shyness and diffidence, he made many friends, and after three years in Spain was promoted to the Washington embassy. During the three years that have elapsed since then, official and social Washington have learned to appreciate the value to society as well as to diplomacy of the British Ambassador and Lady Durand, people who represent refinement and old-fashioned domestic virtue. Their departure awakens keen regret. It is to be hoped that the rumor of a peerage in reserve for Sir Mortimer may prove true, for his Government owes him some such signal mark for long, loyal, yet independent service.

✸

*The English Situation* The adjournment of Parliament until February has created a lull in the political discussion in England, and has given both sides a chance to sum up the results of the session and to take account of gains and losses. On the whole, the session, under Liberal leadership, has been full of activity and accomplishment. Probably Parliament, with its infusion of labor members, has never kept itself so steadily to its task or taken itself so seriously as a legislative body. It is generally agreed that Mr. Balfour is responsible for the wrecking of the Edu-

cation Bill; and there are many, apparently even among the members of his own party, who believe that the temporary and technical advantage the Conservatives have gained by throwing out the chief measure of the Liberal Government is of small account as compared with the strong feeling against the Upper House which the rejection of this measure has created. There seems to have been, among many of the best men, a sincere desire to effect a compromise. To this end, it is reported, the King himself worked. The Duke of Devonshire and the Archbishop of Canterbury represent a considerable number of Conservatives who are anxious to avoid a sharp collision. The Prime Minister and the author of the bill were equally desirous of avoiding a collision between the two Houses. But Mr. Balfour, if report is to be trusted, carried the day against the more Conservative peers. The chief measure of the Liberal Ministry was defeated, with the result that a situation of a very serious kind is created for the House of Lords, and that Nonconformist England has been aroused in a very unusual way. Just before the adjournment of Parliament the Prime Minister announced that the Education Bill would be withdrawn, and declared that it was intolerable that the members of an Upper House should be the servant of the Conservative party when that party is in power, but should have it in their power to defeat the will of the country and thwart the policy which the English electorate had approved. He declared that the resources of the Constitution provided a remedy for the evil, and that the Cabinet would carefully consider the best means of preventing the House of Lords from nullifying the labors of the Lower House and defeating the will of the English people. It is reported that the Government will introduce, early in the next session, a purely secular education bill. In case that also is defeated by the Upper House, and all attempts at compromise thwarted, an issue will be created between the two Houses of the sharpest kind; an issue which, as The Outlook has pointed out, may be settled in one of two ways—by appointing a sufficient number of new peers to overcome the

Conservative majority; by popular agitation against the present constitution, and possibly against the continued existence, of the Upper House, and, if things go to the full length, an appeal to the country on the question whether the House of Lords can longer veto the popular will. If this issue were presented to the country, and the country decided by a great majority against the Lords, and the Upper House refused to recognize the popular decision, the House of Commons might itself, as it has done before, ignore the House of Lords, or resolve that it no longer possesses the veto power. None of these alternatives are likely to be necessary. If the House of Lords remembers, as it probably will, the precedents of its own history, it will make a strenuous fight to the last moment, and when it discovers that the Commons and the people are resolutely against it, it will make the best terms it can by way of compromise.

⊛

**The French Weekly Rest Act** Christmastide temporarily suspended the French Sunday-closing conflict, so far as Paris was concerned, for the Prefect decreed that retail shopkeepers be exempted from the obligation of the Act during the festive, busy three weeks of " Noël " and " Nouvel An." It is thought, writes a Paris correspondent of The Outlook, that with the New Year some welcome and seasonable compromise will be found to permit of the fuller application of the well-intentioned legislative effort, and terminate four months of sterile agitation in the retail trades of France. From the same correspondent The Outlook receives the following account of the provisions and working of the law: Passed on July 13, the Act nominally came into force on September 2. Its spirit is tersely and unmistakably indicated in its opening paragraphs, which provide that (1) no workman or employee shall be occupied more than six days per week in a commercial or industrial establishment of any kind; (2) that the weekly rest shall be for twenty-four consecutive hours; (3) that it shall be given on Sunday. It will be noticed that by omitting the word

" agricultural " the legislator releases one-half of the population of France (the powerful peasant electorate) from any obligations. It is fair to add that in this class the employers are almost as numerous as the employed. The main idea was to free the comparatively helpless mass of factory and shop workers from a week of uninterrupted labor. That such a rule must necessarily imply numerous exceptions was fully recognized; in fact, the eight lines embodying the principle are followed by eighty lines modifying or limiting its application. When it is proved that simultaneous Sunday rest of the whole staff would be prejudicial to the public or would compromise the normal working of an establishment, certain alternatives are specifically allowed: (1) a week-day holiday to the whole staff; (2) closing from Sunday noon to Monday noon (a long Sunday-closing struggle between Paris grocers and their clerks was settled on this curious basis); (3) Sunday afternoon and a half-holiday during the week by rotation; (4) the whole staff by rotation. A long list of excepted trades (*i. e.*, establishments authorized to adopt any of the above four systems without the Prefect's special sanction) follows: hotels and taverns, hospitals, drug-stores, baths, libraries, journals, means of communication, and trades handling perishable goods generally. Outside these trades exceptions are specifically provided for during the busy seasons prevalent in certain trades, and in other self-evident cases—Government arsenals working under pressure, outdoor callings subject to interruption by the weather, accidents and similar urgent matters.

⊛

**The Working of the Act** The weak points of the Act were evidently: (1) a tendency to leave the specific classification of certain trades to the Executive; (2) the omission of the provision of any special staff to insure the application of a measure of very wide scope. It was evidently a tentative text, calculated rather to gratify hopes and direct efforts than to secure prompt and full results. The fines provided for first offenses ($1 to $3 per employee) were slight; for repeated offenses ($3.20 to $20) hardly "exemplary." The decree putting the Act into force was merely a document providing that in the case of temporary or permanent exception from Sunday closing the "compensating holiday" should be duly fixed, and posted up in spots accessible to workers or inspectors. Gravest of all, the existing staff of factory inspectors was (over and above its ordinary and sufficient daily task) to insure the respect of the new law in the 825,000 "industrial or commercial establishments" of France. Under such conditions it is obvious that the actual effect of the Act would chiefly depend on the attitude of four classes—the employers, the employed, the police, and the magistracy—and, in cases of insufficiently defined professions, on the municipal councils and prefects, who were locally to study and decide such knotty points. Little difficulty arose in factories and wholesale establishments—the former already familiarized with Government inspection and control, the latter always apt to enjoy easier hours than retailers. The question was (and still is) whether Sunday shopping can be suppressed throughout France. That a loyal effort was made many can bear witness. Trades differed in their application of the letter of the Act, and even in their local preferences. Many classes of shops which could close on Sundays in the wealthier parts of Paris (barbers, etc.), preferred a week day in working-class quarters. Butchers and grocers felt that they must open a few hours on Sunday morning to allow their clients to buy the day's provisions. Compromises were thus frequent, but the tendency to respect the law was general, though not universal. Still, a feeling of uncertainty hung over the whole population. Small shopkeepers, conscientiously closing, saw law-ignoring neighbors summoned, but fined only nominal sums by hesitating magistrates—if, indeed, their cases were not remanded till an executive official had studied some technical issue. A few large central dry-goods houses tested the law frankly by remaining open. Many were closed, not by the authorities, but by the peaceable and dogged obstruction of the crowd of clerks from other establishments, who hung around their doors till business became impossible. The authorities, besieged by conflicting claims—the trade associations appealing for "exceptions," the shopmen's associations (with the moral and often active support of labor unions) demanding that "the law be respected"—temporize and seek a solution which will not alienate some powerful electoral class. So the holiday respite is welcome to all. That the action of the Act will be momentarily minimized there is little doubt. But the principle adopted by the nation's vote remains, to grow up gradually as the French conservative timidity towards change gives place to the second national characteristic—the sentiment of all-round justice and solidarity, which may be temporarily clouded by prejudice, but seldom fails finally to triumph.

❦

*Moroccan Affairs*    The United States Senate recently ratified the Algeciras agreement or convention of last April concerning Morocco, but also attached a declaration that the United States has no intention of interfering in European politics. Some Senators declare that this resolution is superfluous; it was apparently rendered necessary by the position of Senator Bacon, of the Committee on Foreign Relations, who was believed to be ready to rally the Democratic vote against the treaty unless such a resolution were adopted. The Foreign Ministers and Parliaments of France, Spain, England, and Germany had already discussed the determination of the two former Powers to send fleets to the Moroccan coast. In the French Parliament, despite the attack of M. Jaurès, the Socialist leader, M. Pichon, the Foreign Minister, carried the Chamber of Deputies with him in defending the Government. The Minister announced the note presented that very day to the Ambassadors of the Powers which participated in the international conference at Algeciras. He declared that the Government's aims in despatching a fleet to Morocco were only to carry out the terms of the Algeciras Convention to maintain order in Tangier, the chief port in Morocco, and to protect foreigners. The Chamber's confidence in the Government was shown by a majority of over three hundred ; it afterwards unanimously ratified the Algeciras agreement. On the same day, in the Spanish Parliament, Señor Perez Caballero, the new Foreign Minister, demanded the immediate ratification of the Algeciras Convention, and assured members that the Government was not supporting any policy of adventure in Morocco. As to England and Germany, their Foreign Secretaries have given assurances of approval of this plan to restore order in Morocco, so long as the action is kept within the terms of the Algeciras Convention. It is fortunate that the diplomats at Algeciras provided a system of international protection for foreigners in Morocco, and of international influence to check the misrule which for centuries has reigned there. While such intervention may be but the prelude to the closing act of the drama of Moorish independence, its independence has been purchased at a price which is an insult to civilization. In the early days of the Christian era Morocco, though mountainous in large part, was one of the world's granaries. There are to-day instead only abandoned and untilled fields, yet their soil rivals in fertility that of our prairie States. The population is given over to lawlessness. All this is due to a long succession of weak and lawless rulers. Though the various Powers have recently sent expeditions to the Sultan at Fez, his capital, any good intentions manifested by the monarch cannot be executed by his own military and civil agents because the whole country is infested with the agents of the pretender to the throne and of other rebel chiefs. The result is a condition of anarchy both for natives and foreigners, and this has impelled France and Spain, as the Powers immediately involved, to take appropriate military action.

❦

*Filling up the Canadian Prairie Provinces* Just before the snow comes the Immigration Department of the Canadian Government at Ottawa takes stock of its year's work.

Canada is eager for immigration; its Government spends a large sum of money on immigration propaganda; and from every point of view the stock-taking for the year was satisfactory. It showed that in the season of 1905–6, 189,000 immigrants arrived in the Dominion, as compared with 146,000 during the season of 1904–5. About the same time that these figures are compiled there are also compiled statistics of the harvest laborers carried into the prairie region beyond Winnipeg by the Canadian Pacific Railway Company. For the wheat harvest of 1906 the number was 22,850, an increase of 6,500 over the number who went in for the prairie harvest of 1905. Among immigrant and railway officials at Winnipeg it is estimated that forty per cent. of the men who go in as harvesters make their homes in the prairie provinces, and that in the next two or three years a large proportion of them will become homesteaders—will take up quarter-sections of Government land, or purchase land from the railway companies. During the twelve months which ended on the 30th of September, 50,000 homesteaders went into western Canada and possessed themselves of 12,500 square miles of farm land. Winnipeg is the clearing-house for most of this Western immigration ; and in these days, when the 250,000,000 acres of wheat land in Canada are being so rapidly peopled by immigrants from Great Britain, from the United States, and from the older provinces of Canada, its position among the larger cities of the North American continent is unique.

❦

*Municipal and Railway Development* In the immigration season Winnipeg has a transient population of from seventeen to twenty thousand ; while as a result of the immigration of the last three or four years the city has now reached the hundred thousand class. Other Western cities are increasing in population from the same cause ; but of all the Canadian cities Winnipeg is perhaps the best from which to form an idea of what the filling up of the wheat area of the Dominion means in the way of development. In Winni-

2

peg the increase in population has been so great that the municipal equipment of the city is in arrears, and extraordinary exertions and large outlays are now being made to bring the water supply, the sewerage system, and the street department up to the needs of the city. Even the railway companies, which are usually supposed to look far ahead, have found themselves behindhand and not quite ready for all the business—passenger and freight—which the rapid development of the prairie country is bringing to them. The new station of the Canadian Pacific Railway Company at Winnipeg is, as a station, almost as magnificent as Broad Street Station, Philadelphia. It was opened a few months ago, before it was fully complete. It still lacks a train-shed, and, large as it is, it has already been found too small, and the building of an annex is now to go on side by side with the completion of the main station. East of the city of Ottawa there is only a single track of rails; but the handling of the increasing grain crops—for the Canadian West now raises 85,000,000 bushels—has rendered necessary the double-tracking of the four hundred miles of railway which lie between Winnipeg and Fort William, where most of the grain is transferred from cars to steamers for conveyance down the Great Lakes to Canadian and American ports. So far, the Dominion Government has so organized its immigration propaganda as to bring into the country only people intending to settle on the land. Manufacturers have long urged that the Government should help them in recruiting skilled labor for the factories. The Government, however, will not change its policy; and consequently, at the annual convention of the Canadian Manufacturers' Association at Winnipeg, the Association decided to take this work into its own hands and begin at once a propaganda in Great Britain in the interest of the factories and workshops of the Dominion.

❦

**W.T.Grenfell, C.M.G.,** For the first time, **the Surgeon-Mariner** so far as we know, the King of England has given one of the "Birthday Honors" to a man as a reward for he-roic missionary work. It is true that the man could hardly be regarded as a conventional missionary; for Dr. Grenfell, who is now a Companion of St. Michael and St. George, fills many offices on the Labrador coast, as readers of The Outlook know. He is a surgeon, master-mariner, a magistrate, an agent of Lloyds in running down rascals who wreck their vessels for the insurance, a manager of a string of co-operative stores, a general opponent of all fraud and oppression, a fighter against the drink evil, which finds peculiarly helpless victims among the fisher-folk, an upholder of all good, and a friend and comrade to everybody who comes in contact with him. He takes his new honor with a characteristic spirit, for he values it, not as a tribute to himself personally, but as a sanction which will give him power in his struggle with unscrupulous traders, heartless dealers in rum, and all sorts of malefactors who find on that coast easy prey and safe quarters. He is now planning to introduce reindeer into that country. These animals will furnish food, clothing, transportation in place of dog-teams, material for manufacture, and consequently new opportunities for industrial development for all the people. Dr. Grenfell has already received several hundred dollars for this purpose. A hundred dollars will purchase and transport a deer. About five thousand dollars will furnish him a herd to begin with. The main part, however, of Dr. Grenfell's work is his bearing of health and strength to the sick and injured by means of medicine, surgery, and nursing. He has charge of four hospitals, and, by means of his hospital ship and his dog-teams, makes his rounds among the sparse and needy population, and everywhere he goes he carries with words, and, better still, by his life, the message of his simple, genuine, and untheological religious faith. Dr. Grenfell is now in this country, where he has many friends. Interest in his work has spread to many places. There is a committee for New England, represented at 14 Beacon Street, Boston, by Miss E. E. White. In New York there is the Grenfell Association, with a Board of Directors composed of representative men, of whom Dr. Henry van

Dyke is the President; the office of the Secretary of the Grenfell Association is at 287 Fourth Avenue; the Treasurer, Mr. Eugene Delano, 59 Wall Street, receives and acknowledges contributions. The friends of Dr. Grenfell are now planning to form a National organization, so that the support of his work may be unified. Dr. Grenfell is speaking in various cities; his visit will continue until some time in March. On January 15, in the evening, a meeting under the auspices of the Grenfell Association will be held in Carnegie Hall, New York City. Dr. van Dyke will preside, and Dr. Grenfell himself will give an account of his work, or, as he terms it, his " jolly good fun," in Labrador. He is not a martyr in any ordinary sense of the word; and his self-sacrifice is not of the kind that expresses itself in terms of affliction or deprivation. His spirit is that of the soldier who loves the battle. He ought to receive the heartiest and the most persistent kind of support.

⊛

*An Experiment in Scientific Christianity* Following quickly upon the report that a Western bishop would revive the mediæval ceremony of unction as a cure for illness, and incidentally as a counter-agent to Christian Science, comes the news of a significant enterprise at Emmanuel Church, Boston. The Rev. Dr. Elwood Worcester, rector of this parish, is endeavoring to put to humane, religious service the best results of scientific research in the treatment of spiritual and certain physical ailments by psychical means. To launch the project, Dr. J. J. Putnam and Dr. Richard Cabot, of the Harvard Medical School, joined with Dr. Worcester and his colleague, Dr. Mc-Comb, in speaking at two Sunday evening meetings in November at the parish rooms. These talks were preliminary to the formation of a class, the members of which may meet the rector and a medical specialist in neurology at the church on a specified week-day from this time forth. The consultations and treatment thus freely offered are, by a careful provision, to interfere in no wise with the work of the patients' own physicians,

if they are already under medical care. The purpose is rather to supplement and extend this work. Applicants for aid will receive the advice considered best for their special needs. A library of the most helpful books relating to suggestion and psycho-therapeutics in their more and less simple forms will be generously employed. Such obvious measures as setting the applicants to some unselfish work which shall bring them into healthier relations with their fellow-beings will form an impoitant element in the work Indeed, this lifting of the sufferer out of himself by the agencies of ambition, affection, and religion was pointed out by Dr. Cabot as one of the most effective means of cure. In this day of growing recognition of the close relation between body and mind it was to be expected that a concrete attempt would be made toward the intelligent yoking of the efforts of those who minister to the parallel needs of mankind. The scientific psychologist and the progressive clergyman can each bring so much to the other that the wonder is that they have stood so long apart. The distinctive note of the movement in Boston is the combination of sound religious teaching with sound scientific theory and practice. Both here and in England, where it has just been learned that a similar pioneer enterprise is on foot, the movement is worth watching. It is modestly and reverently undertaken, with a full realization that experiment alone can test its value.

⊛

*University Leadership* Soon after assuming the presidency of Yale, six years ago, Dr. Hadley in various addresses emphasized moral leadership as a proper and desirable function of universities as well as of churches. He gave practical illustration of this idea three years ago in his published lectures on the " Relation Between Freedom and Responsibility." These set forth the ethical basis of democracy, and the present low standard of public ethics as needing correction by the culture of a social conscience in the citizen, rather than by improving social machinery. In his recent lectures before the New Yale School of Philanthropy on the "Basis of Public Morals" he has again illustrated the same idea, in a discussion of modern ethical ideals, and the ethics of trade, of corporate management, and of political activity. In these lectures Dr. Hadley fully recognized the fact that there has been a betterment of business practices since the moral anarchy that set in subsequently to the Civil War. "The late insurance scandals," said he, "were a pious regard to the Ten Commandments, compared to the doings of that time in ' Erie.' " But while heroism and altruism remain the ideals of conduct in private life, he found their base opposites still common in business and political life. No legislative devices could be relied on to extirpate them, but only the moralization of the individual conscience by an interest for the common good in the light of common sense. The stress of every lecture was on the pernicious effect of all policies of self-interest, which is seen in the current evils that result wherever private advantage is preferred to fidelity to a public trust. These appear in the gambling and extortion observable when modern trade in its larger forms is perverted from its legitimate end of supplying public needs. They appear when corporations by selfish insistence on legal rights invite legal spoliation. They appear even in the National Legislature when parts of the country " extort constitutional blackmail " for not opposing National interests. The cure is not in new laws, but new minds, rational and unselfish ideals of good. The note of moral leadership has repeatedly come from Yale. Twenty years ago Professor Sumner in a little book declared it time to call out " all the moral reserves " to check the progress of moral decay. More recently Professor Ladd in another book gave warning of a moral crisis impending in the lack of moral energy in the churches. The keynote of President Hadley's inaugural address was fidelity to the moral ideals of democracy and Christianity. Since then he has kept the work of moral invigoration continuously in view by his addresses to the student community, as well as to other audiences. A conspicuous instance was his last baccalaureate, noticed as such by The Outlook at the time. It is hardly disputable that the churches need to do more than they have done in such endeavors to correct the low ideals of commercialism and industrialism. It is a wholesome example that the University sets them for the exercise of the moral leadership that is traditionally and naturally theirs.

❀

**The Pueblo School-House Plan** A new suggestion with regard to the school-house comes to us from Pueblo, Colorado. Its main object is health, but the educational features are by no means lost sight of. It is the application of the group system to educational facilities. Beginning with a central hall or auditorium, the needs of the community are met by the addition of new buildings on either side of this hall from time to time. A whole block is utilized, and the additions are made to meet the requirements of the situation. The number of school-rooms may be made always to meet the demand, which is not the case with a building of many rooms. The many-roomed building is usually ahead or behind the needs of the district ; there are vacant rooms intended for future requirements, or crowded rooms waiting for the school board to build. Under the new plan there is less waste room. There is less chance of fire, and in case of fire there is less chance for loss of property or damage by water, and the danger to pupils is reduced to a minimum. Light and ventilation may be obtained from any direction. There are no large hallways to accumulate dirt. There is less work for the janitor, and there is no sweeping of dust and other refuse from one floor down upon another. A recess may be taken out-of-doors at any time without disturbing other classes. There is a greater field for individuality on the part of both teachers and pupils. The view from the ground floor is more attractive to children, being nearer to nature. The artistic possibilities are greater. Those who advocate the Pueblo plan of single-story, detached school buildings ask, " If life, health, and economy be worth considering, is there any excuse for still erecting the four, eight, twelve, and sixteen-room buildings except the trouble of getting out of a rut?" The following extracts from letters of teachers in Pueblo who are teaching in one-room buildings will serve to emphasize the practical·value of the plan suggested:

Because of its being organized on the family plan, I prefer a cottage school. The teacher is able to take part in all the exercises, not only class exercises, but also games.

Each room can be independent in regard to discipline and recreation without disturbing others, thus giving teacher and pupil more outdoor life and exercise.

Children are less liable to be exposed to contagious diseases when the buildings are separate.

The plan makes it possible for the children to pass outside often for fresh air, rest, and nature study work, painting, or gardening.

Games, exercises, music, and other work can be given without being heard in the other rooms.

It gives better opportunity to study the individual child when you can be with him both in the room ánd on the grounds.

There is much less nervous strain upon the teacher in accomplishing the same amount of work.

❀

# What France Has Done

From week to week the readers of The Outlook have been informed of all the important phases of the great conflict which for the last four years has been going on in France.

Not since the French Revolution and the establishment of the Third Republic has France taken a step so important for her national life. The magnitude of the event can scarcely be overestimated. Great principles are involved which were long since settled in our own land, and we believe settled rightly and finally. No people are in a better position to judge dispassionately the situation in France than the American people, and none are more interested in knowing what has taken place. The value set upon American public opinion is seen in the efforts which are being made to influence it. France has been charged with persecution, spoliation, and robbery, with the violation of international obligations, with the repudiation of a national debt, with irreligion and blasphemy. How much of this is true? What has France really done? In answering this question some things must be kept clearly in mind.

In the first place, this conflict has not been a battle between Roman Catholics and Protestants. France is a Roman Catholic nation. There are thirty-six Roman Catholics to one Protestant. If Protestants had attempted to carry through this policy, they could have been overwhelmingly outvoted. The Jews likewise are few in number. This has been a battle of Catholics with Catholics. It is partly a battle between Catholics who have left the Church and Catholics who are still in it; it is still more a battle between the Catholic monarchists and the Catholic republicans, between Catholics at Rome and those in France.

Secondly, this question, so far as it has been decided for France, has been decided by the French people through their representatives in parliament. On the other hand, the final Catholic policy has been decided by one man—the Pope at Rome. Again and again the principle involved has been referred to the French people in general elections. In spite of the complications of French politics and the number and tendencies of French parties, the Separation Law has been sustained by overwhelming votes. The Catholics, on the contrary, have been much divided. Speaking generally, the monarchists have opposed the bill; the republicans have sustained it.

A group of twenty-three of the most eminent Catholics in France, among whom were Brunetière, Anatole Leroy-Beaulieu, and others of equal distinction in letters and law, in a letter over their own signatures, addressed the bishops of France, and, while deprecating the character and spirit of the law, urged the bishops to accept it and to organize under it. The fact that a number of eminent Catholic laymen should venture to influence the bishops in a matter of national importance made them the subjects of violent attack from the ultramontane organs;

they were dubbed "green cardinals," because so many of the signers were privileged to wear on their coat the green palm of the French Academy. The bishops, however, were not uninfluenced by this appeal. Some of them, like the Archbishop of Rouen, had independently upheld the law. It is probable that in the Assembly of Bishops, by a large majority, a decision was reached in favor of organizing under the new law. Thus if the question for the Catholic Church in France could have been decided by the suffrage of its most distinguished laymen or by that of the bishops, the vote would have been for submission. In France, however, while the affairs of the nation are settled by popular suffrage and by representative government, the affairs of the Church are settled by an appeal to the Pope, who has disregarded the bishops and the law.

A writer in the Catholic World, of New York, describing the situation before the Pope's decision, says : " The lay Catholics of France were then divided into two camps : on the one side there were those who were called ' submission-ists,' and on the other the advocates of resistance. The hierarchy and the clergy were equally divided." " So long as the Holy See had made no definite pro-nouncement concerning the policy which French Catholics ought to adopt, they were very much divided on the ques-tion, but unanimity instantly reigned on the day when Pope Pius X. formally indicated a definite policy."

This unanimity is not the unanimity of conviction, but of obedience. It is the unanimity with which soldiers obey a gen-eral even when they know he is wrong. A distinguished prelate of the Catholic Church in this country has publicly said that if Leo XIII. had been in the papal chair the deadlock would not have oc-curred. Another Catholic equally emi-nent has said that the present Pope knows nothing of international politics, does not understand France, and is guided by a small clique at Rome. It is not alone American Protestants who doubt the wisdom of governing a Church so that the ripest conviction of its most eminent men, both lay and clerical, is

set aside by the edict of one man in a foreign land ; many French Catholics have left the Church because they can-not be loyal to an authority that does not command their convictions. They refuse to accept the formula of M. Brune-tière to obey the Pope in the dark if they cannot obey him in the light. The most pathetic aspect of the religious situation in France is not due to the action of the Government, which has not closed the churches ; it is due to the fact that thousands on thousands of Catholics have left the Church because they decline longer to accept its dogmas or its authority. They are orphaned Catholics without a religious home. They cannot be recalled by decrees or anathemas.

Catholics, both regular and nominal, in France may concede the right of the Pope to decree as to vestments and doctrines, and to decide questions that are purely religious ; but a majority of the thirty-six millions of Catholics have decided that they will not longer main-tain a political alliance with the Pope or recognize in any official way the doctrine of his temporal sovereignty. Under this conviction, France has abolished the Concordat between the Pope and the State.

In doing this has France violated an international obligation ? It is not diffi-cult to answer this question both from the standpoint of ethics and of inter-national law. The Concordat was an agreement made between Napoleon I. and the Pope in 1801, with reference to the status of the Catholic Church in France. There is not a clause in it that indicates that it was in the nature of a perpetual contract. Indeed, there is a clause which indicates the contrary. It was provided that if at any time the successor of the First Consul should not be a Catholic, there should be a new agreement.

In refusing to regard the Pope any longer as a foreign potentate, France has taken a step which Garibaldi and Victor Emmanuel took for Italy years ago, in spite of Napoleon III. At the last Hague Conference the existence of the Pope as a sovereign was not even recog-nized. France may well claim that it could not recognize the sovereignty of the Pope, because every vestige of it is gone.

Has France repudiated a national debt? Upon what is the accusation based? Upon the assumption that the agreement to pay salaries in the Concordat was to be perpetual. The article of the Concordat reads: "The government assures a proper salary to the bishops and pastors whose dioceses may be included in the rearrangement." There was no contract as to how much should be paid or how long.

It has been said that France has actually done what the State of New York would do if it should seize and hold the property of Trinity Church. France has not assumed to-day in the new law the ownership of any buildings or churches which it has not owned for more than a hundred years under the Concordat. In that document the Pope formally renounced on behalf of the Church the title to the property acquired by the nation in the French Revolution. For instance, the ancient churches such as Notre Dame and the Oratoire, the former a Catholic and the latter a Protestant house of worship, belong to the French Government. For a hundred years France has allowed these religious bodies to use them. The new law does not confiscate them; it simply reaffirms the title to them which was declared in the Concordat. Nor has the State confiscated any church buildings erected since the Concordat and built by the individual offerings of pious Catholics. The law does not raise the question of their title. When there is any doubt on this point, it leaves the decision to the courts.

With reference to other property, real and personal, now held by the Catholic, Protestant, or Jewish churches, it requires that an inventory shall be taken of the same, and that it shall be legally held by associations or trustees formed from the representatives of these bodies. The law reads: "Conforming to the regulations of the general organization of the religious worship of which they propose to assure the exercise." The twenty-three eminent Catholics whose address to the bishops has already been referred to laid great stress upon this; they pointed out that the Pope had "the power to outline what are the general laws of organization for a Catholic association of worship." They completely answered the objection that such an association must be composed only of laymen, the rock of offense to the Pontiff. These eminent Catholics showed conclusively that the object of the law was to prevent non-religious associations from getting possession of the churches; they declare, "We are not hindered by the Law of Separation from believing what we choose, nor from practicing what we believe;" the hierarchy remains intact; "our churches, too, being allowed to remain at the disposition of organized associations and under the direction of the bishops;" and they point out the disastrous results of not organizing under the law.

The asperity of the discussion, and the evident desire of the extreme radicals to affront the dignity of the Pope and the Catholic Church, and even to scoff at religion itself, are greatly to be deplored, as is the violence of a few extremists, both clerical and secular, especially in the taking of inventories, a prudent measure in the law introduced at the demand of the Conservatives. It is to the credit of the great majority of Catholics, however, that they have refused to listen to the appeals of incendiary journals like La Croix; and it is to the credit of the Government that it has demanded, and in most cases secured, moderation on the part of its officials. These are matters incident to the enforcement of the law; they do not affect its underlying principle.

We have shown what France has *not* done. It is not difficult to understand what it *has* done. Omitting all unnecessary and minor details of the law, France has apparently decided:

That the union between Church and State shall be severed; that the Roman Catholic Church shall no longer be a privileged religion; that all sects shall stand on the same footing before the law; that liberty of conscience and freedom of worship shall be guaranteed to all; that the Government will no longer sustain official relations with the Pope;

that the State will retain the title to the cathedrals and churches that belong to it ; that it shall freely place these at the disposition of the different religious bodies ; that the property belonging to different sects shall be held by their legal representatives ; that no religion shall be salaried or supported by the State ; that the reduction of salaries now paid shall be gradual, and that pensions for life may be given conditionally to pastors and priests over forty-five years of age ; that the State shall no longer nominate ministers of religion to clerical offices, but they are restored to all their political rights.

❀

# Railway Rate Regulation: The Next Step

The New York Sun publishes a speech by Mr. M. H. Smith, the President' of the Louisville and Nashville Railroad Company, which, to use his own words, "sounds a pessimistic note." That note is, in brief, that the cost of improving and operating railways is constantly increasing, and that the people are demanding that the railways shall pay larger taxes and shall receive less sums in freight and passenger rates, and that if this process is continued indefinitely, the end must be bankruptcy. The cardinal mistake in this address, as it is with many if not most of the special advocates of the railways, is in the italicized portion of the following sentence: " A law has been enacted giving to a Commission mandatory power to fix rates, *the avowed purpose being to reduce the rates.*"

It is a mistake that the avowed purpose of the recent railway rate legislation was to *reduce* rates. Its object was, in some cases, to raise the rates—to some shippers. The objection of the American people to the railway rates was not that they were too high, but that they were unequal. The object of the American people was not to reduce the rates, but to equalize them. We repeat an illustration which we have used before : it would be better for the people of the United States to have a uniform rate of postage of three cents an ounce than to

have a general rate of two cents an ounce with a special reduction to a cent and a half to favored buyers. What the American people object to is not high rates, but special privileges. No doubt individuals can be found who complain that railway rates are too high. No doubt in some cases they are too high. But this is not the cause of the popular discontent. Very little has been said by President Roosevelt, who is the author of the railway rate regulation, about the prices being too high. Not much complaint was made on this score in the Congressional debates. The avowed purpose, we repeat, is not to reduce rates, but to equalize rates so that all shippers and all communities shall be treated alike. Public discussion to be of value must be discussion of the real question, not of an imaginary one.

There are two theories on which railway rates may be adjusted. The first is that the railway has something to sell, namely transportation, and that it may properly sell this transportation for the best price it can get, as a farmer does his apples, or a butcher his meat. The other theory is that transportation is not a piece of private property to be sold, but a public service to be rendered, and that freight charges are not a price paid by a customer for a thing purchased, but a toll paid by a trader for the use of a special kind of public highway. On the first theory the owner charges for the transportation which he has to sell whatever he thinks he can get for it—in other words, he charges all that the traffic will bear. On the second theory the toll is fixed by the State on equal terms to all who use the road, and this rate ought to be so adjusted as to pay a fair interest to those whose capital is invested in the road and a fair compensation to those who operate it, and no more. In old days we had turnpikes in some of our States and a toll-gate at either end. Our railways have been operated on the theory that the toll-gate keeper may charge any man who comes along whatever he can get out of him. The people demand that the toll be fixed by law, be charged on equal terms to all who use the turnpike, and be just alike to the traveler and the turnpike company. Some of our ablest railway officials recognize this distinction and accept the latter theory. The sooner all railway officials accept it, the farther we shall be on the road to a final settlement of the somewhat difficult question, On what principles shall we determine what rates are just and equal to the railways, to the shippers, and to the various communities?

All that we have done so far is to give the Inter-State Commerce Commission power, on complaint that particular charges are unjust and unequal, to order them made just and equal. This is a good first step, but not a final one. What we next want is an official recognition by law that freight charges are a turnpike toll, and a conference by representatives of the people appointed by the Government, and representatives of those railways only that accept that principle, in an endeavor to settle upon certain general principles to be universally applied by the Government in determining what the tolls should be.

⊛

# The Discomforts of New York

Americans have still a great deal to learn in the application of ideas and intelligence to the government of cities. Our notions on this subject have been largely rudimentary; we have treated cities as if they were mere aggregations of houses instead of vital organizations of community life, with a unity which can be expressed in legislation, in building, in the direction of affairs. We have thought of the government of cities as a kind of minor politics, involving the filling of offices, plans for raising money, collecting taxes, and gaining ground for the party. In Europe, as Americans have come to understand, many cities are studied as a whole and treated as unities, from the regulative, the administrative, the educational, and the æsthetic side; and to this point of view Americans are coming as rapidly as their preoccupations and prejudices will permit.

New York is becoming every year a more interesting place to live in; its cosmopolitan character increases and more sharply defines itself from decade to decade. Those who suppose that it is simply a business community know very little about it. Its life is many-sided; and the vast number of different peoples included within its boundaries present problems of the deepest interest. It is not, however, a comfortable city to live in; it is distinctly uncomfortable. In the rudimentary conception of the management of cities which has prevailed, small place was made for comfort; but comfort holds a great place in the life of any highly civilized community, and the success of the management of a city is very largely measured by the comfort in which its people live. The discomfort of living in New York is due to a considerable extent to its conformation, to lack of means and methods of transportation from point to point. At certain hours in the day every vehicle that runs on wheels and is open to the public, above or below ground, is crowded, not only beyond all comfort, but well beyond the line of decency. The scenes which take place, not only at the Brooklyn Bridge, but often at the stations of the Subway, are fast breeding a kind of savagery which will give the city in the end a very unenviable reputation. The logical outcome of the present tendency would be a free fight at the entrance to the platform of every car, and the opportunity of getting aboard to those who survive in the struggle. Women especially are subjected to familiarities which no woman, decent or otherwise, ought to bear, and the men who are eager to protect them are helpless under the pressure of the merciless horde which fights its way to a car platform. Public sentiment will do something when it is aroused; but final relief cannot come until the means of transportation are multiplied. In the meantime, and perhaps for all time in view of the conformation of New York and the fact that such a host of people are anxious to go in the same direction at the same time, the city needs to create a strong sentiment imposing restraint, patience, and courtesy on its citizens.

In many instances the trouble is due to the lack of application of ideas to the

tion. It is very hard, for instance,
layman to understand why the pro-
ns for transporting people across
York are so hopelessly inadequate.
ie foot of West Twenty-third Street
large railways have their city termi-
and pour in every day an army of
and women. To distribute this
over the city there is a single rail-
through Twenty-third Street. Be-
n four and six o'clock in the evening
.ccommodations for passengers who
to go to the ferries at the foot of
Twenty-third Street are hopelessly
equate; and in the morning, from
to ten, when the army of commuters
shoppers come in from the various
s across the Hudson River, they
m around the insufficient cars like
around a hive. The disproportion
een these commuters and travelers
the means of carrying them would
diculous if it were not exasperating.
e ought to be a conference of the pas-
er agents of the four railways that
terminals in West Twenty-third
et and the managers of the Twenty-
Street electric car line to provide
proper distribution of the multitude
is landed there every day and is
obliged to wait in the bitter winds
inter until a number of cars have
ed before it is possible to obtain even
room. To the lay mind the con-
ction of some kind of a loop at West
nty-third Street would seem imper-
e, or the building of parallel lines
ugh Twenty-second or Twenty-fourth
ets. Under any circumstances, the
ber of cars in use during the rush
s ought to be very largely increased.
nother source of discomfort in New
k is the multitude of unnecessary
es. The daily life of a modern city
not be conducted without a great
of noise, but probably two-thirds of
most irritating sounds that pierce the
of residents of New York are un-
essary. Mrs. Rice, who has organ-
the Society for the Suppression of
ecessary Noises, is in the way of
lering the public a great service if she
ceeds in carrying out the work which
has planned. She has interested a
ber of the most prominent men of
metropolis, and proposes, in the first

place, to secure relief for the hospitals.
She calls attention to the fact that the
street-car company that operates a line
of cars passing St. Vincent's Hospital
on Seventh Avenue agreed, at the time
of securing its franchise, that no bells
should be rung in front of the building,
and she asks very pertinently why the
same rule cannot be enforced in the
neighborhood of other hospitals. She
hopes to secure the co-operation of automobile clubs in order that, in passing
the hospitals, noises may be avoided.
She intends to ask that a policeman be
assigned on every block on which there
is a hospital. Several physicians in different hospitals who have been consulted
are agreed that street noises in the
neighborhood of these institutions are a
serious menace to the well-being of
patients, and one of them expressed the
opinion that two patients in the hospital
with which he is connected became insane during the year owing, partly, to
the constant noises prevailing about the
building. If Mrs. Rice is able to effect,
even in part, what she has in mind, she
will render a very important service not
only to the hospitals but to residents of
New York, and the movement may lead
the way to a marked diminution of one
of the most uncomfortable concomi-
tants of city residence. It is high time
to study the possibilities of diminishing
the discomforts of living in one of the
most interesting cities of America.

During the last few months residents
of New York have endured the discomforts of traveling across the Desert of
Sahara or over the alkali plains of Montana without securing novelty of surroundings or unusual scenery. Not in
the memory of this generation have the
streets of the city been in such a deplorable condition. In wet weather the
mud in many places is inches deep; in
dry and windy weather the streets are
filled with clouds of dust. The condition is deplorable; and unless circumstances exist which are unknown to the
public, it is unpardonable. What has
happened to the street-cleaning department? has it gone into the hands of a
receiver? It is giving New York the
reputation of being the dirtiest city in
America. Not many years ago, under

the leadership of Colonel Waring, jt was one of the cleanest cities in the world.

❋

# Self-Condemned

Last week a number of well-known men in New York assured the Secretary of State by letter of their conviction that for any measure he might adopt in order to give the European Powers the moral support of the United States in " any undertaking to secure conditions in the Congo that will not disgrace civilization," he would have their " earnest and urgent approval." The signers of this letter pointed to the fact that over a year has passed " since the report of the Commission chosen by the Chief Executive and virtual owner of the Congo to investigate conditions in that State was published," and that those Commissioners " felt constrained to report the existence of measures and practices of flagrant inhumanity." In view of the repeated assertions that the criticism of the Congo Government is based upon the tales of prejudiced missionaries and superficial travelers, it is important to remember that there is no occasion for looking any further for an indictment of the Congo Government than the report of these Commissioners. From that report were selected seven points for specific mention. One needs only to turn to that report to see how well established are those seven statements made by the writers of the letter. We here quote those seven points, and under each point certain portions of the report which substantiate the statement. We shall use the English translation of the report, published by G. P. Putnam's Sons, entitled " The Congo : A Report of the Commission of Inquiry." The numbers in parentheses refer to the pages of this edition. Readers of The Outlook who wish to follow this matter further will find these references useful. The measures and practices which the writers of this letter note are as follows :

The first point in this letter is, " The exaction of a labor tax so oppressive that many natives on whom it falls have little, if any, freedom." The Commissioners remark (p. 30) that " a labor tax,

as in the case of all taxes, should absorb only a small portion of the activities of the individuals ; it ought to supply simply the needs of the government, be in relation to the benefits which the contributors receive therefrom ; it ought finally, as we propose, be in harmony as far as possible with the principle of individual liberty, and we believe that within these limits it cannot be criticised." By decree of the King-Sovereign (p. 37) the total amount of the labor tax " cannot exceed during any one month forty hours of actual labor." As a matter of fact, however, what do we find ? In the first place (p. 39), it is not labor but produce that is exacted, and so great an amount of produce that in some cases the native has little or no time for anything but the toil of gathering it and conveying it to his taskmasters. Thus, concerning the collection of *chikwangue* (p. 46, 47, 48):

All of the witnesses who were heard by the Commission on this subject were unanimous in criticising the large amount that was imposed upon the women of certain villages, the continuity of the imposition, and the long journeys that had to be made. . . . The worst feature of this imposition is its continuity. As the *chikwangue* can be preserved only a few days, the native, even by doubling his activities, cannot at one time discharge his obligation extending over a long period. The imposition . . . becomes a sort of obligatory labor, since there is ever before the native the thought of delivery that must soon be made. . . . It is inadmissible that he should be obliged to travel 150 kilometers [over ninety miles] to bring to the place of delivery a tax which represents a value of about one franc and a half [about thirty cents]. . . . Following the rule that we have observed in vogue, the labor is thrown upon the weaker members of the family, so that it is the women, children, and domestic slaves who are forced to be the agencies of transport. This peculiarity, instead of attenuating the bad features of the system, rather increases them. For it is these who form the industrious element of the village, and if a great part of their time is taken up by the exigencies of the impost and procuring the means for their own subsistence, they have not, however great may be their desire, a chance to perform other labor ; hence the abandonment of native industries and impoverishment of villages.

So the report gives a similar picture of wretched conditions as a result of forced labor for porterage (p. 57 seq.):

Without doubt the form of impressed labor that weighs most heavily upon the natives is the service as porters. . . . Caravans of native porters could be seen in a constant stream carrying upon their heads innumerable articles that were impatiently awaited by the whites on the upper reaches of the Congo. . . . The caravan route where black and white, united in the same effort, had paid such a heavy tribute to fatigue and fever, the dark pathway holding in its keeping so many lifeless bodies, has been invaded by the plants and trees of the forest. In two days the trains now go from Matadi to Leopoldville and from the Pool to the lower river; the natives are born again to a new life. . . . But for every route which has disappeared, many others have been called into existence as the new regions have been opened up by the State.

The practical slavery of the native who is forced to gather rubber is thus described by the Commissioners (p. 63):

In the majority of cases he must make a journey every fortnight which takes two or three days, sometimes more, in order to reach that part of the forest where he can find in sufficient quantities the rubber vines. There, for a certain number of days, he leads an uncomfortable existence. He must construct for himself a temporary shelter; . . . he does not have the food to which he is accustomed; . . . he is . . . exposed . . . to the attacks of wild beasts. He must carry what he has gathered to the State post or to the company, and not until then does he return to his village, where he can tarry only two or three days before the time for the next delivery is close at hand. . . . The native . . . sees the greater part of his time taken up in the gathering of rubber.

The second point in the letter is the " Appropriation of land to such an extent that the natives are practically prisoners within their own territory."

The Commissioners explain that the State has ordained that to it belong all vacant lands, which means (p. 19) all the land except " those parts of the territory that are included within their [the natives'] villages or under their cultivation." The Commissioners continue (p. 19 seq.):

As the greater part of the land in the Congo has never been under cultivation, this interpretation gives to the State a proprietary right, absolute and exclusive, to almost all the land, and as a consequence it can grant to itself all the product of the soil and prosecute as robbers those who gather the smallest fruit and as accomplices those who buy the same. . . . It thus happens sometimes that not only have the natives been prohibited from moving their villages, but they have been refused permission to go, even for a time, to a neighboring village without a special permit.

Though the Commissioners hasten to add that agents have not rigidly enforced the law, they acknowledge that it *is* " the incontrovertible law," and they point out elsewhere (pp. 21 and 24) that it practically prevents the natives from profiting by the natural resources of the country, and from engaging in any trade.

The third point in the letter is " The employment under the authority of the Government as sentries of cruel, brutish blacks, chosen from hostile tribes, who murder, pillage, and rape the people for whose protection the Government is avowedly established."

These words of the Commissioners are sufficient to indicate the conditions of which the details would be too revolting to include even in their report (p. 71):

According to these witnesses, these auxiliaries, especially those who are detailed to the villages, abuse the authority committed to them, transform themselves into despots, demanding wives, food not only for themselves but also for a retinue of parasites and vagrants who, drawn by a love for rapine, become their associates and form a sort of bodyguard; they kill without pity those who make the least show of resistance to complying with their demands or caprice. . . . It is not possible for us to say, even approximately, how many abuses these sentries have committed. Several chiefs in the Baringa region brought to us a bunch of sticks, each one of which was said to represent a subject killed by the capitas [the less offensive of the two classes of sentries]. One of them declared that in his village one hundred and twenty had been killed during the past years. . . . None of the agents who testified before the Commission, or were present at the sessions, made any attempt to refute the charges against the sentries.

The fourth point in the letter is " The abuse of the natives by white representatives of officially recognized companies."

These are some of the things the Commissioners have to say on the subject (pp. 66, 67, 69, 144–5, 110):

In the absence of a specific law and precise instruction upon the subject, the agents charged with the exercise of coercion, applying the principle of solidarity which exists among those who are the subjects of the same chief, often trouble themselves but little to seek out the real culprit. The prestations were due from the village as a whole; when they were not forthcoming the chiefs were arrested and some of the inhabitants taken at random, often the women were held as hostages. . . . At the different posts in the Abir which we visited it was never denied that the imprisonment of women as hostages, the imposition of servile work on chiefs, the administration of the lash to delinquents, and the abuse of authority by the black overseers, were, as a rule, habitual. . . . The punishment most frequently used is the lash (chicotte). . . . The regulations fix fifty strokes as the maximum, and the convict cannot receive more than twenty-five in any one day. . . . Private parties, and notably the agents of the commercial companies, are not permitted to use the lash on their black employees. In spite of the restrictions imposed by law upon the use of the chicotte, it is often abused, either in resorting too frequently for slight offenses or in exceeding the limits prescribed. . . . Still. it is undeniable that the chiefs of stations are led to violate the provisions by the desire to inflict a punishment that will serve as an example. . . . These companies have done nothing in the interests of the natives nor improved the conditions in the regions occupied.

The fifth point in the letter is " The binding of little children to years of labor at uncertain wages by contracts they do not understand, and, even more serious, maltreatment of children supposedly under. the immediate care of the Government."

This is a part of what the Commissioners say on this subject (pp. 141, 142):

The unfortunate features of long engagements are especially noticeable in the case of children. It happens that the District Commissioners employ, particularly for the fields, children of seven and eight years who are bound for a period of several years by a contract whose provisions they probably do not thoroughly understand. . . . The average life of the native is much shorter than that of the white man. So that the term, which at the time of making the contract is not fully appreciated, will consume the greater part of his life. . . . It often happens that after a very short time the intrinsic value of the wage specified in the contract is not the same.

The Commissioners also (p. 122) call attention to the fact that the State itself often takes the children from their relatives—their natural protectors—and puts them into educational colonies in order to make out of them " excellent servants, good soldiers, and workmen of all sorts ;" and has thus been "forced to endure the reproach of 'recruiting,' under the guise of assistance. but against the wishes of those interested, the young people destined to fill the ranks of its constabulary." Later (pp. 125-129) the Commissioners refer to the abuse of

children in the missions which have accepted the authority of caring for certain children who have come under the guardianship of the State.

The sixth point in the letter is the " Great injustice in the administration of the courts, so that the natives dread the name of Boma, the place where the judicial system is centralized."

The Commissioners say (pp. 150-151):

Administrative agents . . . cannot . . . acquire a profound knowledge of the laws of the land. . . . It has therefore been found desirable to refer the most important civil and penal cases to the Boma court for trial. . . . But these long journeys are especially prejudicial to the blacks. It is a sad fact, verified by observation, the judges told us, that a large number of blacks who come down from the Upper Congo as witnesses never see again their native villages, but die during the trip they are forced to make. . . . The number of those who die has created a great impression upon the natives. The simple word " Boma " frightens them.

The seventh point in the letter is " The sending out of punitive expeditions, not for the purpose of establishing peace and order, but for the purpose of terrifying the natives into paying a tax which, as administered, even the Commissioners regard as inhuman."

Contrary to the law, companies send out such expeditions. This fact the Commissioners (pp. 96-98) say is established by documents and judicial reports as well as the reports of the commercial agents themselves. This is what the Commissioners have to say with regard to punitive expeditions :

During these irregular operations the greatest abuses have been committed ; men have been killed as well as women and children, often even when they were fleeing; others have been made prisoners and the wives taken as hostages. . . . The Government has, in fact, placed upon certain concessions a police force charged with the protection and supervision of the territory which is directly under the authority of the District Commissioner. The directors of the companies may summons them directly in case of extreme need. From what we could see it seems that these troops are devoted to the directors and agents, who call upon them every time the pecuniary interests of the company are involved.

This is but a fraction of what the King's own Commission have to say about the King's own government of the territory which has been given to him in trust. We wonder how long it will be before King Leopold will stop talking about the testimony of prejudiced missionaries and superficial travelers, how long before Belgium will stop debating and either accept or decline responsibility, how long before the people of America and of Europe will insist that their Governments interpose between their wards of the Congo and the rapacious guardians who are now over them.

❦

## The Spectator

It seems a thousand pities to the Spectator that the impression should be so widespread that New York is all given over to the mammon of haste and greed; that the very conditions of its life necessitate restless striving; that it knows no contemplation. On the contrary, what better conditions of repose can there be than a great sustaining sea of life and purposeful activity on which one may launch one's little bark, secure from molestation? That is the theory of the thing. Now, theory does all very well, but experience does better. And, luckily for the Spectator, it happened that, when he sallied forth to buy a new pad on which to transcribe his theory, he found experience. He will therefore let the theory go, and tell the little story.

❦

It was the tiniest shop imaginable, just off Broadway, on one of the side streets. The rush of the great thoroughfare, in its high noontide acceleration, was bewildering. Dodging people and horses and vehicles and rabbit-women and peanut-men and a dozen distractions else, the Spectator had worked his way along, watching for a stationer's sign, but watching so many other things too that very likely he passed half a dozen abodes of pads and bottles of ink. Finally he pulled himself up. If he was to find that pad! He looked about him, and, not fifteen paces away, he saw a modest sign: "Pens. Ink. Paper. Elastic Bands. All Stationers' Supplies." So then he spun away out of the vortex, descended a narrow flight of steps, and

opened a dusty door. It was almost more than the Spectator could do not to say, "Oh, I beg your pardon!" as he stood on the threshold of that little room. He had entered with all the contagion of the street's haste upon him, brusquely perhaps, and imperatively, his purse already half open to make his purchase and be gone. He was greeted with—pause and silence. A gray cat sat dozing upon the counter, her paws tucked neatly into her breast. An old man sat dozing beneath the window, a newspaper on his knee. On shelves along one side of the wall the advertised articles were arranged—piles of writing-pads, bottles of ink, a few books in a dusty row, some boxes of note-paper. But there was no sign of a customer, except the startled, arrested Spectator, and so little evident habit of one that neither the old man nor the cat stirred at the sudden entrance.

❦

A curtain at the end of the room lifted, and a woman came forward. She was evidently the wife of the man, some few years younger, but gray-haired, too, very portly and serene.

"They're both deaf," she answered the Spectator's mute appeal. "You can speak out. Did you want anything?"·

"I, oh, yes—" the Spectator stammered. He had forgotten what he did want, in his sudden revulsion of mood, his surprising shock of silence. "I should like a writing-pad, if you please."

"Yes. Well, if you will sit down here, I'll show you what we have."

It was going to be a pondered transaction, seriously and thoroughly done, that was evident. The Spectator settled himself on his stool to summon his best judgment. From one shelf and another the pads came down—thick pads, thin pads, ruled, unruled, glazed, rough—and he viewed them gravely.

"How about those?" he inquired at length, pointing to a pile yet untouched, on one end of the lower shelf.

"But those"—the answer came at once, with no doubt of its finality—"those cost ten cents."

The Spectator rose magnificently.

The comment was too obvious on his personal appearance.

"I will take six," he said.

❀

But the process of doing up his purchase gave him time to recover from his resentment. Little by little, he relapsed to his stool, leaned his elbow on the counter. and watched in a dreamy content. It was inconceivable that in New York, not fifteen paces from Broadway, a shop's supply of wrapping-paper should be kept folded up in a drawer and its string, more or less tangled, in a worsted bag.

"You're tired, sir," the good woman said, as she folded and tied, and began a search for the scissors.

"Yes; well," the Spectator admitted, moved to a sudden frankness which was the rebound of his late irritation, "I'm just back from the country, not used to the city yet."

It was a commonplace statement enough, but it touched a spring in the woman's mind. She laid aside the scissors, unused.

"You find it's peacefuller, then, in the country than in the city?" she asked, a little anxiously.

The Spectator thought of the theory which he had been fain to elaborate on one of his expensive new pads, and answered with interest, "No, not always." Then, involuntarily, "Why?"

❀

The woman sat down on a stool on her side of the counter. This seemed the most natural thing in the world, as if the bond between shopkeeper and customer was, in its nature, a social bond, conducive of conversation. The old man beneath the window stirred and settled himself more comfortably in his leather chair. The cat opened two large grave eyes, then went to sleep again. It was strange how the roar of Broadway without seemed but the accompaniment, the extraneous environment, of the central hush and calm of this shop where alone reality reigned.

"I guess maybe you're young yet," the woman affirmed, wfth a kindly, tolerant smile, "to care about peacefulness."

The Spectator assured her—though somewhat flattered withal—that such was not the case.

"Well, you ought to be, then,"· she rebuked him. "Jim and I was when we were your age. We kept a grocery-shop, and we were regular hustlers. Making money hand over fist. I tell you, those were days! In the shop every morning at six o'clock, never out of it till nine. Keeping up with all the new foods, all the whims and fancies. We made money; but 'twasn't living, 'twasn't living at all."

❀

The Spectator nodded his head. Not that he had ever kept a grocery-shop, or made any money, to be sure; but he had done other things enough to know the bane of over-action.

"I guess a person has to go sort of slow to know he's himself at all," the quiet voice went on. "I might have died just as well as not, in them days when I was hurrying so, and never have known the difference." A trenchant way of putting the case, which appears constantly the better, the more one considers it.

"I don't know as it's selfish, or unselfish, or what, to want quietness; but I guess it's natural after a while. Jim and I was just tired to death after fifteen or twenty years. It seemed to us as if we was just driving our lives on ahead of us and never catching up with them to see what they was like. I suppose it's very important that folks should have tea and breakfast foods; but Jim and I thought it was important, too, that we should live a little before it was too late. It's rather a serious matter, you know; for if a person don't get a good hold on his life while he has it here on the earth, what under the sun is he going to hang onto when he gets flung out into space?"

The Spectator caught his breath dizzily. True; what, in heaven's name?

"Of course we said we'd have a house in the country; all tired folks say that. I do just wonder who's first to blame for that idea that every one has, that a country life means peace. He's got a good deal to answer for; Jim and I can tell him that. We bought a place up in Connecticut, way off by itself, in a lonesome valley—the lonesomer the better, we thought, and we went there to live. Well—"

❀

The quiet voice broke off suddenly, while the portly form shook with chuckles of mirth, so that the gray cat stirred a little and stretched out one sleepy paw.

"I wish you could have seen Jim and me stranded on that farm! I never knew anything so funny, half pitiful, too, though it was. All them plans and hopes, all them expectations, all that happiness—and then! You needn't ask me what was the matter. 'Twould be shorter if I was to ask you what could help being the matter. I honestly haven't the least idea what people mean by talking about the simple life in the country. In order to do any one thing, you've got to do twenty-five other things first—if you call that being simple! However, that wasn't the worst difficulty. We had caught up with our lives now, sure enough. There they were, turning around on us, coming and sitting down in the parlor, and staring at us, and saying, 'Well?' That was just it: well? What was we going to do about it, now we'd found quietness?

"Only, of course, as a matter of fact, we hadn't found quietness. Quietness seems to be something inside you; it don't have nothing to do with woods and farm-houses. My feelings made more noise them days than a whole elevated road. We felt as if we was broken off, and didn't belong anywhere any more. The world went on without us.

❀

"We stood it just a year and a half. Yes, we stood it as long as that, because it didn't seem hardly decent to whop right around and go back on so many plans. We was pretty ashamed and disappointed, as we sat and talked on them winter evenings, with the snow-storms howling around us like mad. We had run away from New York to be quiet, and now New York seemed the quietest place in the whole wide world. Quietness—"

The good woman paused, caught in the throes of philosophy.

"Quietness comes from a lot of doing all taken together, I guess. Maybe no person alone can have it. It's like a river. The more water there is, the stiller every drop rolls along, and it's only the little brook that makes such a fuss and chatter."

Again there was a spacious pause. The Spectator tickled the head of the cat thoughtfully with his finger.

"They say," his hostess pondered aloud, "that God's the quietest thing there is. Well, then, I guess it's just because he has all the lives there ever was bound up in himself."

She cast philosophy to the winds, and returned to experience.

"We sold the farm and came back to the city, and bought this little shop. And now—well, I tell you, sir—"

A slow, contented light welled up in the placid eyes as they made the loving circuit of the little room.

"We're quiet now," she concluded.

There was really nothing more to be said. The Spectator understood that, and rose reluctantly.

"I wish I had a little shop," he observed involuntarily, as he tucked his package under his arm—his extravagant package!

"Oh, no, sir, not yet!" his hostess replied. And she shook her head at him.

❀

The rushing streets sang a brave song in the Spectator's ears as he made his way home that morning. Fullness of life and fullness of being, and therefore, under their noise of much doing, fullness of uttermost peace. For peace is what life is founded on, what life aspires to. And the proof of the wide beatitude of the common quest after quietness lies in the simple tale of this woman, who, searching for her soul's ultimate treasure, found it, not in seclusion and distance, but at the heart of the world.

Now, when the Spectator is tired, he leans back on the great city around him, and the million hands of his fellow-men lift him surely into peace.

# THE PROBLEM OF ENORMOUS FORTUNES

## A DISCUSSION OF THE REMEDY INVOLVED IN THE PROPOSED ENACTMENT BY CONGRESS OF A PROGRESSIVE TAX ON INHERITANCES

### BY PHILIP S. POST, JR.

YEARS ago travelers passing through the mountains of New Mexico saw from the car windows painted on a boulder in huge letters the words, " LIMIT WEALTH." Like the religious mottoes which in some parts of the country, blazoned on the roadside, tell the wayfarer to " Prepare to Meet Thy God," and warn him that " Death is Sure," so this inscription flashed into the eye of the passer-by some man's conviction that a limit would yet be placed upon individual wealth. No one seemed to know the painter. Few bothered themselves to fathom his meaning. Was he crank or prophet ?

On April 14, 1906, in a speech at Washington, President Roosevelt startled the country by declaring :

> It is important to this people to grapple with the problem of enormous fortunes. . . . I feel that we shall ultimately have to consider the adoption of some such scheme as that of the progressive inheritance tax on all fortunes beyond a certain amount, either given in life or devised or bequeathed upon death to any individual—a tax so framed as to put it out of the power of the owner of one of these enormous fortunes to hand on more than a certain amount to any one individual.

Notwithstanding the laconic comment of a distinguished Senator who characterized the suggestion as " rank Socialism," the President has, in his annual Message, renewed his advocacy of this system of taxation. " The problem of enormous fortunes " is thus officially recognized. The handwriting on the rocks has found an interpreter at the seat of power.

Taxes on inheritances, or succession taxes, are by no means uncommon. They are found in the Roman law, and they were adopted in England in 1780.

Nearly all the countries of Europe have some system of " death duties." As early as 1797 Congress imposed a legacy tax, and a similar Federal tax was put into force during the war periods of 1862 and 1898. Pennsylvania enacted such a law in 1826, and such taxes now exist in many States. The rates imposed by these laws are moderate. Bequests to lineal descendants are in several States taxed one per cent., while a higher rate is imposed on gifts to collateral relatives and to strangers in blood. Bequests to charity and education are generally exempt.

These State taxes have been enacted as revenue measures. The proposed Federal tax is advocated, not primarily for revenue, but to accomplish a sociological and economic result. It introduces into our revenue legislation the principle that a tax may be impose alone for fiscal purposes, but  th the definite object of dispersing property accumulated in the hands of a single owner.

The fact that this question may so become the subject of Congressional debate suggests a review of the arguments advanced against and for this system of imposts. The scope of the controversy and its fundamental character are revealed at the outset when it is found that the critics of the tax—and they have been able and vigorous—take their stand upon what are alleged to be certain " natural rights."

The first contention is that the principle of the inheritance tax destroys an essential and inherent quality in the nature of private property ; that the right of disposition is an incident of property, and includes the power to transmit property by descent or devise; that the State has no just power to take property from the private owner except as needed for governmental revenue; that when so taken, it is justifiable taxation; that when taken under the guise of taxation, but for the purpose of limiting the amount which may pass by descent or by will, then taxation has ceased and confiscation has begun.

It is contended that inheritance is one of the great natural and elemental rights; that, while not expressed in our Constitution, it is " a right born with our very institutions, a right which does not need to be expressed ;" and it is argued that · if the State may lawfully place a tax upon legacies and devises, it follows that the State has unlimited power over the property of deceased persons and "may, without any breach of natural law or denial of fundamental rights, take to itself all property."

It is protested that this is a "monstrous doctrine ;" that its application would have a most baneful effect upon civilized communities; that the family relation would be severed; that whatever. bond or duty the expectancy of property places on the child would be ·broken; that the. motive for parents to accumulate would be gone ; that thrift and industry would be paralyzed; that men will not work to gather property if it has no family perpetuation ; that the universal rule of the community would be, " Let us eat and drink, for to-morrow we die." Thus the tax has been styled "an infamous measure of taxation," " a penalty on death," "stealing from the estate by legislative authority," " an outrage that can find precedent only in Oriental autocratic governments."

It has been eloquently argued that American society is founded upon the American home, in which the father is both the protector of and the provider for the family ;' that it is his right and duty to make provision for his widow and children; that our social organization is built upon the idea that a man's children and kin shall take that which he has accumulated; and that, if this principle of the succession tax be accepted, the State has a right, if it sees fit, to step into every home desolated by

death and take from wife and children every dollar of property, not even leaving the heirlooms and the homestead hallowed by family associations.

It is not claimed that such drastic laws would in any human probability be enacted, but. it is insisted.that this arbitrary power over inheritances ought not to be countenanced; that the evil lies in the acknowledgment of the power·; that, once recognized, there is no protection against improvident and communistic legislation. It is asked whether it is possible, after all the care shown in centuries of Anglo-Saxon legislation in the effort to protect private property and individual rights, that the only thing which now stands between this country and an absolute state of Socialism is the passage of a law destroying the right of inheritance, a law which might be passed by a chance legislature carried into power upon the wave of some sudden and sporadic popular feeling.

It has been declared by no less an authority than Benjamin Harrison that the principle of the inheritance tax destroys the very foundations upon which our institutions rest. In his argument of the Illinois inheritance tax case—the last argument made by him before the Supreme Court of the United States— the ex-President pictured with solemnity and earnestness his view of the injustice and viciousness of this form of taxation :

From the dawn of history, in the earliest records, both these rights existed, the testamentary right and the right of inheritance. . . . These great natural and fundamental rights are both recognized; and though neither of them is written out on tablets of stone, they are both engraved on the fleshy tablets of every man's heart. . . . The statute of descents, as the courts have again and again said, is the expression of the legislature upon its conscience and duty as to what is the natural law—as to what should be the natural intention and desire of a testator. . . . The family relation and property rights have been built up and stand upon these two great natural rights. The legislature does not give them, it defines them. When they cease to be recognized as natural and fundamental rights, we shall have dissolved the basis upon which our society rests.

In the face of President Harrison's impressive plea, and of consequences as serious as these which have been predicted, it is evident that clear proof must be offered to convince the public mind of America of the necessity, justice, and wisdom of a Federal inheritance tax. What are the arguments in its favor?

First. There is no "natural right of inheritance." The right to dispose of property by will or receive property by descent is not an inherent quality of private property. These rights are the creatures of human law. Without the aid of statutes, the right of property dies with the owner. The State has the unrestricted right to control and restrict the disposition of the property left by a deceased person within its jurisdiction. As was said by Chief Justice Taney, "If a State may deny the privilege [of inheritance] altogether, it follows that when it grants it, it may annex to the grant any conditions which it supposes to be required by its interests or its policy."[1] In the eye of the law, all rights of inheritance depend upon express legislative enactment. "The right to take property by devise or descent is the creature of the law and not a natural right—a privilege, and therefore the authority which confers it may impose conditions upon it."[2]

Second. Since inheritance is not a right, but a privilege granted by the State, it follows that a succession tax is not a tax on property, but on the succession; in other words, on the privilege of receiving property by will or by descent. In this aspect it is eminently proper that the beneficiary should pay for the privilege which he can enjoy only by virtue of the State and the protection of its laws. From his standpoint, inheritance is a sudden acquisition of wealth without labor. His ability to contribute to the support of the government is increased. Only where the head of a family dies who is supporting wife, children, or kin has there been an economic loss to any one. If the estate goes to collateral relatives, or even to self-supporting children, there is an accidental addition to their means, and thus a gain in their taxpaying power. What class of property can be a more fit object of taxation than that which comes to an individual unearned by his own labor and often undeserved by any personal merits?

Third. Succession taxes are not inherently unjust. The deep-rooted prejudice as to the sacredness of testamentary rights arises from existing laws which lead us to forget that these rights are not natural rights, nor even the consequence of the right of property. No good reason can be offered for the operation of inter-State laws which not infrequently place property in the hands of distant relatives, whose existence was scarcely known to the deceased, and who very likely had far less affection for him and real interest in his welfare than many friends, employees, and servants.

Fourth. Inheritance taxes—particularly those which are progressive and place an increasing burden upon legacies as they increase in value—are no discouragement to industry and enterprise. It is not to be assumed that legislatures, because they have the power, will therefore enact laws dispossessing entirely the immediate family. Whatever may be the rates hereafter adopted, every enlightened government will suitably protect the dependent wife, children, and kindred. The passage of property, whether it be from a father to a son who is financially independent, or from an uncle to a grandnephew, or from an indulgent testator to the object of his bounty, is purely an artificial advantage in the struggle for existence. Without any exertion on his part, such beneficiary has been given a start over his fellows. In so far as the tax curtails this arbitrary advantage resting on the accident of birth, to this extent will there be an approach to the ideal of a greater equality.

Finally, the inheritance tax furnishes a plan by which to grapple with "the problem of enormous fortunes." Its advocates say that the method is wise, simple, and effective—wise, because it does not touch private property during the life of the owner, and thus places no burden upon business activity; simple, because the tax is easily ascertained and collected while estates are being administered in the Probate Court; effective,

---

[1] Mager vs. Grima, 49 U. S., 8 How. 493.
[2] Mr. Justice McKenna, in Magoon vs. Illinois Trust and Savings Bank, 170 U. S., 283.

because by the application of progressive rates any result in the direction of preventing the transmission of unduly large accumulations can be accomplished which the legislature shall from time to time deem advisable. Without some legislative regulation of this character there is no check upon the accelerating growth of wealth in the hands of the few; nothing to cause its distribution except the spirit of benevolence and the proverbial profligacy of the owners of inherited means. It is poor morality, as well as economics, to intrust the distribution of the world's wealth either to folly or philanthropy.

In this conflict of argument and opinion certain facts remain unchallenged. First, the legal power of Congress to impose a graduated inheritance tax has been sustained by the Supreme Court and is therefore not an open question. Second, progressive inheritance taxes have been tried with satisfactory results both in Australia and New Zealand, the region of experiments, and in England, the home of conservatism. With the constitutionality of the tax established and its utility tested by experience, it is clear that the question is largely one of the rates which should be fixed. Should small legacies be exempted? Should the tax be progressive? If so, what should be the scale of progression? Ought the highest rate to be five per cent. as now provided by some State laws, or fifty per cent. as was proposed by Edward Bellamy? Should the legislature adopt the views of Andrew Carnegie—reaffirmed in a recent utterance of exceptional significance—and exact from every large estate "a tremendous share, a progressive share"? What tribute might the Russell Sage millions properly have paid? What part of the colossal bequest held in trust for a grandson of Marshall Field and accumulating for his benefit, or injury, might the Government wisely have appropriated to the use of its citizens?

It is in the highest degree important that any such tax should be kept within conservative bounds, but what these bounds shall be—what is fair and wise, and what is unreasonable and confiscatory—must necessarily be left to the judgment of Congress. If it be argued against the tax that there is danger of unreasonable and radical legislation on the subject, such a contention, as was pointed out by Justice White in his scholarly and luminous decision upholding the Inheritance Tax of 1898,[1] "involves in its ultimate aspect the mere assertion that free and representative government is a failure."

In dealing with the problem of concentrated wealth, the progressive inheritance tax very naturally presents itself as a partial solution. Its sponsors have for years earnestly, but with indifferent success in attracting public attention, urged its adoption as a convenient method of raising revenue and an efficient means for reducing "swollen fortunes." By the sudden appearance of the President as its champion this proposition is now receiving that degree of public consideration which it well deserves. Why should it anywhere, even among the very rich, arouse fear and amazement? Is it not rather surprising that in democratic America the unqualified moral right to inherit regal fortunes should not long since have been assailed? How absurd now appears the doctrine of the divine right of kings, rulership over one's fellow-men, vested as a thing of private property in lineage, the grave responsibilities of the crown blindly intrusted to an unborn child! Yet power resides not alone in hereditary monarchs. The ownership of ten million dollars is a power greater than possessed by many a potentate. The use or misuse of such a fortune is fraught with far-reaching consequences, moral and economic, to whole communities and to thousands of human beings; yet without astonishment or doubt we have seen such fortunes, with all their latent possibilities of good or evil, pass to the heir-at-law, regardless of his capacity to administer the great trust. May not a future generation regard the present doctrine of unlimited inheritance in the same light with which men trained in democracy now view the transfer of the crown from the monarch to his next of kin?

In the light of considerations such as these, the progressive inheritance tax loses its destructive and ominous aspect.

[1] Knowlton vs. Moore, 178 U. S., 41.

Rather does it appear as a safeguard of private ownership. If our capitalists who "exhibit a singular stupidity in resisting every attempt to impose upon them their proper share of the public burdens" realized its ultimate effect, they would welcome this tax as a protection instead of viewing it as a threat. Let this tax limit, even in a slight degree, these gigantic fortunes, and compel them to contribute directly to the National revenue; let it thus become evident that the rich are bearing their proportion of the burdens of government, and the popular realization of this condition will be a bulwark to private property and vested interests.

Here is proposed a system of Federal taxation which must appeal strongly to the popular imagination. It adds no burden to the poor, but permits those who have much to contribute to the government somewhat in proportion to their ability to pay. It invades no natural rights. It violates no maxim of the law. It overleaps no constitutional barriers.

It weakens none of the sound timbers of our social structure. Rather does this proposed tax—with its ultimate purpose of a more equitable distribution of public burdens and private wealth—tend to strengthen and make firm the entire structure of the State. True democratic institutions need a broader basis than free and equal political rights; there must be at least reasonable economic freedom and equality. This tax aims to level up life's chances, to give every man a fairer start, to produce a greater "equality of opportunity," which, no less than equality of legal rights, should inhere in a republic as one of its essential attributes.

A reasonable inheritance tax, wisely imposed by Congress, under its ample powers, is neither revolutionary nor socialistic; it is, on the contrary, a measure of practical wisdom and of social justice. This tax has been styled "an institution of democracy." May it not indeed prove to be one of the head stones of the corner?

# INDUSTRIAL DEMOCRACY
## TRADE UNIONS AND POLITICS[1]
### BY JOHN GRAHAM BROOKS

UNTIL very recent years the trade union has been a bulwark against Socialism. That well-to-do people have not seen in the trade union one of the most powerful conservative influences shows unfairness. The attention has been fixed upon the points of friction with employers. Compared to the movement as a whole, this friction has been incidental and relatively unimportant. It has even been the source of innumerable labor-saving inventions from which society has received great advantage. But, wholly beyond the fighting line between employer and employed, the unions have done as much for education as any college. They have not only

[1] This is the twelfth article in the series on Industrial Democracy. A former article by Mr. Brooks, who is known to most of our readers as the author of the book "The Social Unrest," will be found in The Outlook of November 17 last, under the title "The Trade Union and Democracy."—THE EDITORS.

forced up and maintained their standard of living (which was as good for society as for themselves); they have carried on for a full century a system of group discipline that is educational in the highest sense.

The internal history of unions like those of the printers, cigar-makers, iron-molders, miners, shoemakers, is one long dramatic story of struggle to discipline the membership. It is strictly true that this inner conflict has been quite as severe as the conflict with the employer. To train millions of wage-earners to habits of submission to democratic organization; to inspire them to the continuous sacrifices necessary to this end; to train up such multitudes to that rare virtue in a democracy, *obedience*, stands for an immense educational influence. Even to create a local union, to make it conscious of common interests, to secure permanent committees and develop effective parliamentary procedure, is not only educational in the best sense, but it is precisely the kind of education those citizens most need. It is, however, when these locals begin to affiliate with State and National bodies that we see the full measure of this discipline. One of our ablest presidents of a National organization once told me, "It costs me far more time, anxiety, and tact to keep our local unions reasonable than all our differences with employers. I have much more to do in stopping strikes than in carrying them on. The local is so near the sources of trouble, there are so many green men and so many hotheads, besides no end of bitter rivalry in the organization, that our National body is on the strain all the time to keep the locals in order."

The single question of " jurisdictional fights " among different unions is of itself one of the most baffling problems with which the National body has to cope.

Perhaps one best of all sees the results of this long interior discipline by sitting two or three days in a convention of the Federation of Labor. I have heard very competent men assert that one saw there an average of parliamentary capacity which was distinctly above that of the best of our State Legislatures.

I repeat that so far as Socialism is thought to be a danger, this trade union tradition is not only conservative, but it has been the most active and sturdy exponent of Socialism in this country. The reason of this is that unionism practically accepts and co-operates with the competitive wage system. To uproot and cast out this system is of course one chief object of Socialism. That unionism should enter into partnership with the hated thing, should even make one of its highest aims the formation of joint agreements with employers, thereby making the partnership completer and more permanent, constitutes an offense which Socialists do not forgive. There is a body of Socialist literature containing far more bitterness of tone toward trade unions than toward the capitalists.

It is at this point that one of the most difficult as well as one of the gravest of labor and social questions arises. Has the wage system elasticity enough to retain its hold on organized labor? *Within* that system can labor continue to secure what it will insist upon—a rising standard of income in conformity to general progress? Or can a competitive system in a world market afford to *give* the income which labor will ask? In New Zealand and Australian colonies labor concluded that it could not get these advantages within the wage system as now constituted, and *therefore* it turned deliberately to the open field of general politics. When Sir Charles Dilke wrote his book on " Greater Britain," he was impressed by the fact that Australian trade unions had so long put their trust in the old political parties. This confidence assumes that the interests of labor are safe in the hands of politicians who represent the capitalistic interests of the time, as our own Republican party now does in this country. Sixteen years ago capitalism, backed by its own polities, inflicted upon unionism in Australia a defeat so humiliating that labor turned in solid phalanxes to form a party of its own.

After years of hesitation, a strong contingent in England now boldly adopts the same policy. The powerful unions in Belgium long since turned from the wage system to politics, with signal advantage to themselves. It is the only country where one is quite certain yet that it was an advantage.

Is labor in the United States to follow these tactics, or are we to work out policies of our own, still within the economic field marked off by the old wage payment?

That the world's business in different leading countries is every year being done more and more alike and more and more under pressure of vast currents common to all, would seem to mean that the United States cannot maintain a difference in labor method so sharp as this. Yet two facts of extraordinary significance will aid capitalism in holding labor to the wage system in something like its present form. The first is the fact of race variations, including the negro ; the second, the extent and significance of our immigration. This need not be left merely as theory. At hundreds of points one may now see the competitive ways in which these races, with fewer wants, are pitted against those with higher wants so as to check the demand of the union *except* for the stronger and more skilled worker. These are often deliberately selected and given a higher than the union wage, in order to cripple the men's organization. Strictly from the point of view of the average worker, it may become a terrible weapon, as one may see at the present moment in certain plants of the Steel Corporation, into which multitudes of South and East European laborers are being rushed. What this will mean in some future period of sharp and prolonged business depression suggests very ugly possibilities. But meantime, together with the growth of employers' organizations, it unquestionably tightens the grip of the wage system on labor and weakens the power of the trade union to act politically—to act politically in the new and not in the old sense. For two generations our unions have been in politics in the sense that they have been upon the field to secure specific benefits through legislation: shortened hours, prevention of imported contract labor, adequate factory and mine inspection, restricted child labor, and the like. They have again and again flirted with general politics, but invariably to their own undoing, as with the Knights of Labor, until the strongest of the unions united in keeping questions of party politics out of their councils.

Year after year the Socialists have fought the unions on this point, urging that the old parties in no sense represented the real interests of labor. The Socialists' glee at Mr. Gompers's apparent change of attitude is natural enough. A Socialist friend tells me with exultation, "We all knew the Federation of Labor would sooner or later get its lesson. President Roosevelt and Speaker Cannon have given it the first shock. When Gompers and his friends left that conference, they saw for the first time, what Socialists have all along known, that trade-unionism must break with the stupid tradition of avoiding politics.

For several years the fight has been hot between us on this point. The sleepers have at last got out of bed."

Is this unconcealed purpose of President Gompers and his followers the first momentous step in removing the barriers between Socialist and trade union policy in this country? My friend thinks it rather absurd to question this. He points gleefully to the obdurate facts, first, of accumulated defeats of labor legislation in Congress, together with injunctions that grow in number and severity, and, second, to the high enthusiasm inspired by triumphs of labor in the English Parliament.

Labor organization in that country avoided party politics until convinced that its economic existence was threatened by laws made too exclusively in the interests of capital. The recent Socialistic vote of two great bodies of miners, together with the uncompromising attitude of some thirty of the fifty-four labor members, has for the first time shocked English Liberals into some sense of the situation. That the politicians representing the employers should have shown no recognition of this seriousness has its partial explanation (as in our own country) in the current belief that Socialism is a bugaboo—a mere conjured specter casting its spell upon faddists and upon many queer and unsuccessful people here and there. That Socialism was to be thought of as an alternative to *anything* has not yet been really faced by the successful business man. He thinks the trade union an organization chiefly to create trouble and obstruct prosperity. Yet the contention of these unions has been to accept the present wage system, to co-operate with it, working out common agreements under which the two organizations of capital and labor could continue to do the world's work together. Here, then, capitalism itself has had a powerful if very irritating colleague, one ready to work with it along its own lines. Is this protection now to be withdrawn? For organized labor to "go into politics" in the sense now threatened by Mr. Gompers is to strengthen every revolutionary specific which Socialists have at heart. One of the hardiest and most seasoned of our politicians, commenting on the Speaker's snub to labor, said, "The old war-horse showed his usual sense. These labor mouthers are eternally bluffing about going into politics. They have scared us now and then just as the Prohibitionists have done, but the labor vote is as little dangerous to the old parties as Christian Science." The stubborn fact on the side of this scoffing politician is the past history of labor in general politics. But what of the future? We cannot decide with any confidence between the gay certainty of this Socialist and the grim cynicism of the party hack.

Since 1900, however, great things have come to pass in the United States. No event since the Civil War is half so momentous as the recent moral outbreak of indignant judgment against this same capitalistic politics in the United States. To make popularly known just what relations the various kinds of party boss sustain to speculative and privileged forms of business is the elementary achievement that will make reform both in business and politics at last possible. To do this, a form of moral and intellectual slavery has to be destroyed. It is the slavery of our stand-pat party politics. As its commercial alliances have strengthened, it has crippled the spirit of freedom in this country as effectually as did slave labor in the South before the war. That strong and enlightened men now cower before issues like that of reciprocity, which deals with specific monstrosities in the tariff, or are afraid to take sides against men like Quay and Penrose, gauges the intellectual subserviency. The extent of our revolt against this slavery measures also our hope of freedom and reform. That the people are waking both to the fact and the obligations which the fact implies may be seen at a score of centers just now in the United States.

That this situation offers a chance for organized political independence is too obvious for comment. It presents an issue as commanding and as distinct as that about which the Republican party drew its first inspiration and greatness. That the issues at present are so conspicuously economic is the reason why labor is likely to see its chance and

follow it. When John Mitchell published his book, "Organized Labor," he said cautiously that the *immediate* policy of the unions was to avoid politics, but the time might be near when they would be forced to act. The breathless succession of disturbing investigations since then reads like a cogent list of reasons why independent politics has at last become both a duty and good strategy. The saner heads in the labor movement had experience enough to know that the time had not come even to break ground for an independent party, for the sufficient reason that organized labor was too isolated and too weak in voting strength. The changes in the last few years have converted to belief in political action a formidable host from all classes, including the many modest business interests that may set themselves against political and business spongers as doggedly as labor.

Nor do I forget that the unions themselves sorely need purging. There is not a vice of our political and business tyranny which has left them unsmirched. But who has set before them the open and flaunting example of these vicious practices? Their first effective schooling was from the same alliance of privileged business and party politics. The most dangerous corruption of trade unions begins with City Hall affiliations, and here business and politics had long before set up their partnership of public exploitation. This is but another illustration of the common responsibility for these evils which lies so heavily upon every section of the community; most, perhaps, on those who do not vote at all.

The saying that we have not had a government by the people is now worn to a platitude. We have had government by professional political cliques working in sympathetic partnership with specific privileged interests. Practically every signal victory since the "awakening" has sprung from this new spirit of political independence. This new spirit is the strict measure of our achievement up to date.

Now, if labor organization be considered as a whole—Germany, France, England, Belgium, Australia, New Zealand— no influence matches it in bringing in this political independence, which surely is the first condition of a living democracy.

From the first there has never been a doubt about the main purpose of unionism toward democracy. The documentary evidence of this is complete; the union wants the referendum, the initiative, and primaries so revised that the people can act at the determining points of their political destiny.

Nothing will now permanently hinder the extension of these democratic agencies. The revolt is now on. It is on in Oregon, Missouri, Wisconsin, Ohio, New Jersey; indeed, in so many centers that it seems to beat with the pulse of the Nation. No class (if that word must be used) has so much at stake in all this as the wage-earners.

It is into this wholly new atmosphere that organized labor may enter upon its heavy task of leading the fight against a party tyranny that has become grotesque in its unfitness for the impartial, constructive service which society now awaits. To get the determination of political policies free from the clutch of privileged interests in every form is what the people have come to see as their

first task. There is no influence that can indefinitely postpone this task of enlarging the political motive so that it shall lie level with the common weal. To use local and National politics to hedge and coddle the speculative schemes of commercial cliques has been the occupation of the moneyed men of this country. They have secured the domain, the franchises, charters, and strategic privileges of every sort, while throughout the entire game party politics has been their lackey. All this could not have been avoided, because we, the people, ignorantly sustain them. What the new time has brought is common knowledge of these facts and a great wave of feeling which makes action possible. In the old days labor could not go into politics for utter lack of this popular insight and propelling sentiment.

These may now give to labor its opportunity. If it shows the valor to avoid the grosser errors of the monopolistic spirit, the strength of its legions will be redoubled by accessions from the multitude of electors whose passion for self-respect and independence makes them ready to take the field against the despoilers.

# SOURCES OF HOUSEHOLD WASTE

## BY CLARA G. BREWER

MANY writers from time to time give suggestions as to specific instances of waste. It is the purpose of this article to classify under broad heads the main sources of waste, with an example or two under each. If an intelligent housewife appreciates the force of a general proposition, she will be able more readily to recognize the specific violation when it arises in her household. It will be helpful for a reader to ask herself under what heads the errors of her establishment fall.

This article deals only with waste in household affairs, though many of its principles apply also to other expenditures; as dress, travel, amusements, entertaining.

Waste arises in buying, from lack of thought and good judgment as shown in

various ways. It is always wasteful to buy articles of inferior quality, as sleazy towels and tablecloths that have no wear in them, or loosely woven matting that soon pulls apart, or poor food that cannot be eaten. But it is equally wrong to pay extra prices for fancy stock. If fine large peaches can be bought for $2.50 per bushel, there is no merit in paying $3.50 for extra large ones. If a chair of artistic design, beautiful wood, and fine, plain finish can be bought for a certain price, it is folly to pay ten dollars more for some carving to catch the dust. Waste arises from failure to buy in quantities when it is advantageous to do so: as laundry soap and starch by the box, olive oil and molasses by the gallon, vinegar by the five gallons, matches by the dozen boxes. But, on the other hand, it is wasteful to buy in quantity if it is not advantageous. Sweet potatoes, very perishable, should be got in small lots. If carrots are six cents a bunch or two bunches for ten cents, there is no merit in buying two bunches if only one is really needed. Many women will buy two and finally throw away the second bunch.

Waste arises from failure to watch the market and buy at a favorable time. Twenty-five and fifty cents a ton may be saved by buying coal in the summer. Sugar usually goes up in canning time; the wise woman buys one hundred pounds in four twenty-five-pound bags before the rise. If one has established with a grocer the reputation of being a prompt payer and a fair-minded customer, arrangements can be made with him to let one know of special opportunities to buy to advantage. This can also be extended to other tradesmen.

It is wasteful to buy things because they are cheap, on a slender chance that they may sometime be used—as furniture polish, metal polish, and cement for broken dishes bought from persistent venders only to cumber the closet shelves; or to buy an article for which demand seems to exist without first seeing if something already on hand will not answer. The next day the hasty buyer says dejectedly, " Dear me! Why did I not remember that I had so and so! It would have done just as well as what I bought."

A source of waste to be strongly condemned is the growing custom of paying high prices for cooked food at bakeries and delicatessen shops in order to save one's self the trouble of home cooking. From five to six o'clock in the afternoon these stores are thronged by women who have been at the matinée, or shopping, or calling, and they hurry in to buy food already prepared which they can quickly set on the table, with small regard for its real food value. So they pay forty cents a pound for boiled ham, or thirty-five cents a pound for veal loaf, twenty-five cents for some potato salad, twelve cents a dozen for rolls, twenty cents for a pie, twenty-five cents for a small plain cake— and lo, a meal! If these things had been intelligently made at home, with

good management as to fuel, a saving of thirty-five to forty per cent. could be effected. The woman who daily loses money because she will not take the trouble to cook has probably another characteristic of a wasteful housewife— a contempt for small savings. One cent saved on a ten-cent purchase is a saving of ten per cent. just as truly as one dollar on ten dollars. A ten per cent. investment would be considered desirable by any business man. Much of the household savings must come from looking after the pennies.

To be condemned strongly is the growing custom of buying articles of food out of season when they are luxuries and the price is highest—strawberries at Christmas, " spring lamb " in January, and asparagus in February. It would be well if we could learn that there are better ways to entertain a guest than to impoverish ourselves in order to set before him some luxury out of season and probably lacking its real flavor. He who would enjoy fruits and vegetables at their best will be satisfied to eat them when they are at their perfection in his own climate.

One of the most serious sources of waste in buying is the practice of " running bills." It is useless to aver, " I never buy anything on credit that I do not really need." If one will steadfastly for six months hold himself rigidly to buying only what he can pay cash for, if he will keep his accounts carefully and at the end of the time honestly study the result, he will admit that he has cut off one serious source of former wastefulness. The merchant well understands the frailties of human nature, and he is eager to get you to " open an account," suggesting it in his advertisements, and even seductively soliciting it by letter.

Again, waste arises from misuse and neglect of materials after purchase. There is a loss of food through failure to care for it properly; milk is left standing in a hot kitchen to sour, or butter to melt; bread grows musty in a neglected bread-box; cheese is forgotten on the shelf and molds. The same tendency shows itself in failure to scrape clean the kettles, saucepans, and mixing-bowls, so that no food is left adhering to them. If only a tablespoonful of oatmeal is left on the sides of the double boiler each morning, it means quarts wasted in a year. A lack of good management of "left-overs" contributes to waste. It is one thing to get them eaten under protest so that they just escape being thrown away; it is another thing to use the "left-overs" so skillfully as to make attractive and palatable dishes, and so save the expense of providing new food. If the family does not like hash, there is no merit in using cold meat in this way and having it eaten "at the point of the bayonet," when, as croquettes, or filling for an omelet, or in shepherd's pie, the dish would be relished and praised. In this connection one is reminded that some woman said that the two most mysterious words in the English language to her were " stock " and " drippings." Until a housewife has come to be on familiar terms with the stock-pot and the drippings-jar, there is sure to be waste in her household.

Neglect as a source of waste is shown in a failure to care for each utensil and article of furniture so as to prolong its period of use. There is a right way to care for every article in household use, and by adhering rigidly to this right way it may be made to last from half as long again to many times longer than if used carelessly and ignorantly. If wooden tubs are left without water standing in them, it is not strange that the hoops fall off. If the boiler is not dried properly, of course it will rust. If brooms are always hung up when not in use, and if they are dipped in hot suds once a fortnight, their life will be doubled. If a couch is turned end for end each sweeping day, the springs will not sag and give way so soon. By changing the position of furniture in a room, the wear on the carpet is distributed. When money has been expended upon finished floors or hardwood floors, it is sensible to learn the best way to treat them and preserve their beauty. Failure to mend articles at the first sign of impairment is the guarantee of waste, for soon the article is in serious condition, if not entirely beyond repair. At first the cupboard door needed only a screw to tighten a hinge—any one could have put it in. Finally the door broke away from the hinges and a carpenter charged a dollar to mend it. Every house should have a kit of simple tools, nails and screws, and some member of the family should have interest enough and gumption enough to make little repairs. It is certainly wasteful to have to send for a man every time there is a leaky faucet to pack, or a shelf to put up, or a window-cord to mend.

A considerable part of daily loss comes from waste of fuel. This may arise from the use of an expensive fuel when cheaper is available, as artificial gas when coal is cheaper, or coal when natural gas is cheaper. Whatever the fuel be, most servants and some mistresses use it most recklessly. Often more fire is built than the nature of the work demands. Lena had a red-hot stove if she had only to boil an egg and make coffee. In using gas Katie would always turn on more than was needed, and it would blaze around the kettle in a beautiful but costly aureola. In vain did her mistress explain that the contents of a kettle would not cook one whit sooner because the water was in a state of violent ebullition. Katie only sniffed incredulously, turned down the gas with reluctance, and, when her mistress departed, triumphantly turned it on again full head. A common error lies in a failure to make a fire do as much work as possible. A careless ironer will make up a hot fire afresh when she is nearly done, and it burns on unused after she has finished. Or the gas oven is heated to bake a single dish, when by planning the menu carefully a whole meal might be cooked in the oven at the same time. Or the oven fire could be utilized to do extra cooking for the next day, as a dish of baked apples for breakfast or some custards for lunch; a pan of water also can be heated under the oven for dishwater.

Waste of lights occurs chiefly in not turning down gas when leaving bedrooms or bath-rooms. The men and boys of a household are the chief offenders here. The burning of a light in one's bedroom all night is a piece of wastefulness inexcusable in well persons.

A little investigation on the part of mistresses will disclose the fact that maids are apt to keep a light burning all night, and their excuse is that they are afraid to sleep in the dark.

Again, waste arises from allowing children to grow up with silly whims about eating, so that "Mary won't touch lamb," "John can't bear soft-boiled eggs," "George would rather starve than eat rice." Meals• cannot be economically served where special dishes must be prepared for notional people. In a family of four adults of my acquaintance there is such diversity of tastes that three meals must be prepared for each breakfast, lunch, and dinner. Except in rare cases, if children are managed in a kind and tactful but firm way, they can be brought to eat the articles of food commonly found on people's tables, thereby making them comfortable members of the household, and guests always welcomed by both mistress and maid.

A source of waste not always recognized is the common practice of ordering groceries and meat by telephone or from the man who calls for orders. Old-fashioned marketing seems to be dying out. "It is too much trouble," say the women. But the housewife who really cares whether she is economical or not will not begrudge the time or the trouble of marketing in person. Often on reaching the store she rearranges her menus, for she finds it advantageous to do so. The peas are not as tender as they should be, so she buys beans. She expected to get berries, but finds it advisable to purchase a pineapple instead. She not only gets the chops for dinner, but finds, for a small price, just the piece of meat for an Irish stew.

Waste arises from a lack of thorough knowledge on the part of the housewife of the whole round of housekeeping. If the mistress herself does not know how to buy, how to cook, how to use, how to save, the case is hopeless. But knowledge alone will not suffice—there must be vigilance and intelligent oversight. Poor Richard says, "The eye of the master will do more work than both his hands." Even competent servants will have no interest in true economy. No one but the mistress will see "the leak in the dike."

Lastly, a large part of household waste arises from moral cowardice—a fear of seeming stingy keeps people from being saving. Many a housewife is really afraid to say anything about economy lest her servant characterize her as "stingy" when the neighborhood servants gather for their nightly confabs. The disrelish of the average maid for economy or anything that looks in that direction is one of the serious phases of the problem. In possible explanation of this is the fact that many of the servants have come from the poverty of the Old World and so are inclined to call a family "rich" if they live in a comfortable house on a salary of $2,000; hence they say, "Why all this talk about economy?"

Moral cowardice brings on waste through a fear of being considered old-fashioned and queer in the appointments of the house. Furniture excellent in quality and correct in design must be sent to the attic or "traded in" at a low figure for the latest fashion as regards finish of wood and form. We would be ashamed to have the Murray-Hills visit us and find an old-fashioned sideboard in our dining-room when every one else has a buffet. And then think for a moment of the ignominy of being the only folks in our set without hardwood floors! When the friezes are too wide, or the drop-ceilings do not drop enough, or the wall-paper is light when every one else has tapestry papers, no course seems open to a self-respecting family but to cut down the subscription to the church and re-paper.

Moral cowardice impels to waste in providing too elaborate repasts when friends are entertained. There must be luncheons of eight courses when most of us are lucky to have two when we lunch alone. There must be show dinners with expensive place-cards, costly floral centerpieces, and such a succession of unusual and mysterious things to eat that we have to give up when we try to tell mother about it the next morning. As soon as a woman thinks of having a few friends to dine, she begins to cudgel her brain for novel ideas—there must be novelties in table decorations, novelties in food, novelties in the way of serving the food. We all know that the sweet grace of hospitality is stifled in this excess and flummery, but it is a rare woman who dares invite her friends to a simple meal suited to her purse and station. "Just think," she sighs, "of that perfectly elegant dinner the Schuylers gave! Why, I didn't know what I was eating half the time! How could I ask them to a simple dinner after that? I just couldn't do it."

I knew of a luncheon club of twelve young married women, one of whom each month entertained the others at lunch. As the months passed, the affairs became more and more elaborate, each striving to outdo the others. Soon the town resources were exhausted, and flowers, out-of-season delicacies, and fancy ices were ordered from the city. Some of the members could not afford this, and the others knew it. All felt that the affairs had gone too far and had become a burden to plan and most wearing to carry out, yet not one was willing to be the woman to assert her good sense and return to moderation. All honor to the woman who in the midst of a crooked and perverse generation dares to be simple and sane! If you are so blest as to know such a one, hasten to tell her how much you admire her, lest she too falter, lose her foothold, and be swept off by the waves of waste.

## SAINT THERESA

### BY FLORENCE EARLE · COATES

Weary and long the winding way;
    Yet as I fare, to comfort me,
Still o'er and o'er I tell the beads
    Of love's perfected rosary.

The fire that once hath pierced the heart,
    If from above, must upward flame,
Nor falter till it find at last
    The burning fountain whence it came.

O fire of love within my breast—
    O pain that pleads for no surcease—
Fill me with fervor!—more and more,
    Give me thy passion and thy peace!

O love, that mounts to paths of day
    Untraversed by the soaring lark,
O love, through all the silent night
    A lamp to light the boundless dark,

O love, whose dearest pangs I bear,
    This heart—this wounded heart—transform!
That all who seek its shelter may
    There find a refuge safe and warm!

Were there no heaven of high reward,
    Man's service here to crown and bless,
Were there no hell,—I, for love's sake,
    Would toil with ardent willingness.

And if—O Thou that pitiest
    The fallen, lone, and tempest-tost!—
If, Love Divine! Thou do but save
    Whom *I* well love, none shall be lost.

# TWO CHINESE HEROES

## I.—MAFU-CHANG, EX-SOLDIER

### BY FREDERICK McCORMICK[1]

WHATEVER attempts have been made to vindicate the Chinese soldier have attracted no attention. No doubt the cause of this is the estimation in which war is held by the Chinese. Confucian justice degraded the military profession and ignored the development of the art extolled by Cæsar, Alexander, Tamerlane, Genghis Khan, and even the Manchu Emperors.

No one has thought it worth while to inquire into the character of the Chinese soldier, much less to praise him, and the sterling qualities inherent in the race have never been suspected to pertain to the soldier even by the Chinese themselves. But when it is considered that the Chinese soldier is robbed and exploited by his superiors, facts of which he is perfectly well aware, his respect for authority is seen in this case to be purely accidental, and owes its existence to the filial training which the lowest Chinese possesses. War under such conditions is merely a personal adventure to the common soldier, who has been taught that the officials are responsible for the welfare of the people, and that China has no real enemies among the tributary barbarians visiting the borders. It is a fact that the Chinese soldier in an emergency delights to make sure his escape as well as to leave his superior in the lurch.

The old ideas regarding foreigners have, of course, been largely dispelled. Instruction in the art of war, as practiced by the West, has been carried on for many years in China, and those Chinese qualified for the profession of arms, acquainted with the geography of the world, the power of foreign enemies, and the consequences of battle with foreigners, have furnished an example of what a real Chinese soldier is. In 1900

the Chinese military students at the Tientsin arsenal defended first the walls of the arsenal, then, compelled to retire, defended the building, from which they retreated to their rooms, and died defending their bureaus.

The sterling qualities that have made the Chinese as a race so hardy appear unaffected by the political and moral degeneracy of which the nation has complained since the days of Lao-Tzu and Confucius.

The subject of this sketch may be taken as an eminent example of what the great body of the Chinese consist of, and something of what is possible in them. Chang is a man of the lower or peasant classes. He was one of a large family of children, and was noted in his neighborhood, but especially among his relatives, for his stupidity. When a young man, he became a soldier and served in the army of the Tartar general at Mukden, spending his time partly in the destitute barracks to which a Chinese soldier is consigned, and at intervals escorting prisoners and hunting bandits in the surrounding region. He was something over fifty years of age when he became my hostler, just preceding the battle of Liaoyang. On the last day of the battle I was taken in the Japanese lines, and Chang was obliged, with two animals and the baggage, to make the march during the Russian retreat of forty-five miles to Mukden, alone and unprotected. It is needless to say that an unprotected Chinese with a foreign army is theoretically helpless; especially during the retreats which the Russians made after their defeats, a Chinese was at the mercy of the soldiers. While *en route* to Mukden one of his animals lay down and died, but with the other he managed to save the baggage, but was thrown into prison, charged with being a spy, and remained for nine days in hourly danger of having his head taken off by an ignorant official who made no

[1] Mr. McCormick was the Associated Press correspondent on the Russian side during the Russo-Japanese War, and was for six years a newspaper correspondent in China.—THE EDITORS.

34

distinctions between suspects, and required little or no evidence in those days to execute them. He was released through the efforts of an Irish missionary, Mr. Fulton, who knew the family, and he returned to serve me through all the exciting adventures accompanying the last days of the Russian Grand Army. Most conspicuous were his courage and devotion in the flight from Mukden—the most alarming *débâcle* of the war. At seven o'clock on the morning of March 10, 1905, we were caught in the jam of artillery, including a number of fortress guns, and of baggage-wagons that were trying to get around the west wall of Mukden. The Mukden settlement was in flames, and we were just behind the rear guard, with the Japanese trying to cut the armies off several miles to the north. Chang was driving a Chinese cart containing the baggage, and was having great difficulty in managing the two animals—hitched tandem—by which it was drawn. Being a Chinese, he was frequently struck at by the soldiers. The baggage-wagons often attempted to crowd him from the road, and he was several times hit by the drivers. The situation was one in which protest was worse than useless, for in many cases the soldiers were going mad. When the sun got higher, the armies began to be heated, and it was very dusty. The Japanese were shelling with *brisants* that part of the roadway where we were marching, and at eleven o'clock two brisants struck just behind the cart. Chang was at the moment about to cross a gully, but quietly proceeded to repair the harness. Half a mile farther on he was attacked by an insane soldier, who first tried to bayonet him and then attempted to beat him off the cart with the butt of his rifle. Unable to reach the man, I appealed to an officer just behind him, but the officer refused to interfere, for he was himself in terror. But Chang's tact and presence of mind were fully equal to the occasion. By his coolness he brought the soldier to his senses, and after a few minutes, when the wave of excitement had abated, the soldier disappeared in the crowd.

About four o'clock in the afternoon the Pu River was reached, the scene of the greatest single disaster of the flight of the Russian armies from Mukden. There was a great congestion on the bank, which was steep and impossible for the artillery and wagons to descend except at one place. Being a Chinese, driving a Chinese vehicle, it was impossible to use this descent, where the Russians were striving among themselves to cross. Chang, who as a horseman was superior to any of the hundreds of Russian drivers who were plunging their horses down the embankment and trying to get out on the opposite side, took a perilous course to one side, and though struck at with sabers by the artillerymen on the bank as he passed, landed his cart safely in the water and ice below. He was received by an artilleryman who jumped off his horse and rushed twenty feet through the water to strike him. He passed quietly and indifferently down the stream behind a dozen caissons and wagons stalled in the mire of the north bank, and got out without difficulty. Half an hour before dark, when I thought we had passed the point at which the Japanese were cutting the army in two—though shells were still striking to the east of us—we stopped at a village to feed the animals, who had not been fed since dawn. Within a quarter of an hour we received a shower of bullets in the house and courtyard where we were resting, and a big fusillade began. The troops fled. The explosion of a few hand grenades across the road was now all that was necessary to complete their terror. From the gate of the compound the soldiers could be seen sweeping through the roadway of the village, until the dust became so thick that they were lost to sight and only their cries and terrified shouts could be heard above the fusillade. It was the point at which the rear of the Russian armies was cut off, and, thinking that it was almost certain death for him to leave the premises, I ordered Chang to remain in the house of the compound with the family of Chinese, where he would be safe, and where, being a native, he would be unmolested and might return to Mukden. But I saw that he could not understand, and while I was saddling my mare he was looking for bullets which were at the moment striking the trough where the animals were feeding, and the house. But fearing to be cut off, I again ordered him to remain, and rode away.

His subsequent adventures are as related by himself. The fusillade lasted about an hour, and it was quite dark when it ended. Under cover of the night he escaped from the village with the animals and baggage, and later on was able to join a Russian column making its way along the railway. Protected by the darkness, he marched all night unmolested, but when dawn came he was several times assaulted by soldiers and with much difficulty prevented the baggage from being looted and the animals taken. Toward noon he rested and then proceeded in the direction of Tiehling. Four native bandits, armed with swords and pistols, who had been in the service of the army and were fleeing with it, about the middle of the afternoon took possession of him and all of the effects. But he was able by threats and courage to compromise with them, and escaped by giving them one piece of baggage and half of the mess stores. Later in the day, however, they returned and took one of the animals. Chang employed a Chinese peasant, whom he met on the road, to follow the bandits, and when he arrived at Tiehling was able to locate them and the stolen animal at an inn. While the army was in heated flight, he induced the native magistrate to examine the case, which, in view of the fact that few Chinese officials could safely venture to interfere in any affair concerning an employee or follower of the army, was in itself an achievement. The animal was recovered and the robber thrown into prison, where he was afterwards, no doubt, decapitated according to Chinese law.

Later, at a time when I thought Chang safe in Mukden, I accidentally discovered him, nearly a week after, at Kaiyuan, seventy miles north of where we had begun the flight. He had, unarmed and without any protection, successfully withstood all the dangers of the flight, in which he was the best soldier that I saw, and for four days of the retreat proper, which began at Tiehling, he had successfully managed the distressed and importunate soldiers who were constantly trying to get possession of and loot the baggage. He was afterward presented with the cart and a fine mule, and I am obliged to say that he was amazed at the gift and sincerely ignorant of what he done to deserve it.

I have heard foreigners in China relate many similar stories, but I believe that in the present day they do not receive the publicity which they deserve, and which makes them of such peculiar interest at the present moment.

## II.—HIS EXCELLENCY HWANG

Chinese biography is not a study, outside of a few workshops where Western scholars are working out human history, which we pretend we have no time for, but which will be appreciated in another generation. We do not know the personnel of the Chinese Government. The main facts in the life of Confucius are understood, but the exact facts regarding the life of the present ruler of China, the Empress Dowager, are not known outside of China; and Li-Hung-Chang is the only Chinese statesman whose life attracted enough attention in the West to induce a publisher to consider a biography. The secondary officers of the Chinese Government, who became martyrs in 1900 because they opposed the anti-foreign schemes, are not known in America, although some of their names may be discovered in the State Department, and their memory among foreigners is cherished by the few resident in China.

The Chinese character needs no apology and no introduction to civilization. The history for many hundreds of decades of one of the most numerous of the races has filled its annals with illustrious names. In this great nation there are millions of competent men and not a few who may be called remarkable. There is no doubt that the veil of China's almost impossible language obscures much, especially in the national character, fo which the West, if it knew, would stand in awe and admiration. The following history is that of a relatively obscure man, already old, belonging to a circle many of whose members have been martyrs to the cause of advancement in China; some beheaded in disgrace, and others, after years of toil and sacrifice, dying in obscurity.

His Excellency Hwang was a boy of ten when the Taiping rebels took the city of Nanking on the Yangtse, in which he lived. It was the practice in those days, and is yet, for families to commit suicide rather than be subjected to the outrages practiced by soldiers in China. Following the example of the family, little Hwang and his brother hung themselves when the Taipings entered the city. He was saved by the soldiers, but his brother was already dead. Following their practice, which was to bring up children in the faith which they themselves professed, the Taipings carried him off, and during his career of two years with the Taiping army he added considerably to the knowledge which he possessed of his own language and acquired considerable proficiency in handwriting, which is a Chinese art. He was used by the rebels as a clerk and accountant. At the end of two years he escaped by way of the Yangtse River, which is the Mississippi of China, and floated down by the lumber rafts which from time immemorial have traversed that great waterway. He was kidnapped by a lumberman, but in the end approached the vicinity of his native city. In the environs of Nanking he learned that no members of his family had survived, and he consented to be adopted into the family of a farmer. On account of his knowledge of reading and writing he became a tutor, and later on the village schoolmaster. Self-taught, he aspired to literary honors, and while yet young he took his first degree. At intervals throughout the years following he advanced from one degree to another, which is the system in China by which a man becomes eminent, until he reached the highest honors possible for the province of Anhui, in which he resided, to confer. One literary distinction remained to him to acquire. This was the Hanlin Degree, conferred by the Emperor himself, in Peking. He was now about thirty-five years of age, and became what might be called the Senior Wrangler of the year. There is nothing like this distinction in other lands, for it carries with it honors that are conferred only by the State, and upon only one man in a year. The examination is nominally conducted by the Emperor himself, and on this occasion, according to the sacred practices of the Throne, the Emperor placed a robe upon Hwang's shoulders; the great middle Chien gate, reserved solely for the use of the Emperor, was opened, and the Emperor escorted him out of the Forbidden City, where the examination was held. The achievements of the little waif of the Yangtse had now entitled him to the highest emoluments of the Empire. The Emperor presented him with a home, and he was made a Censor, which, theoretically, is the most dignified position in the gift of the State. It carries with it the unqualified privilege of criticising all affairs pertaining to both individuals and men, as well as the conduct of the Emperor himself, who, according to the Chinese scheme of things, is regarded as the Son of Heaven. Mandarin Hwang devoted his influence as a public official and his money to benevolence and reform, attending to the responsibilities imposed upon him by his office, and relieving distress. One of his sons he sent abroad to acquire a knowledge of the outside world. On the occasion of a visit to a distressed village near Peking that had been nearly destroyed by a flood he was met by a little boy who had been sent out by the villagers with a list of persons in need of succor. Mandarin Hwang was so pleased with the boy that he took him into his own home, and later on sent him abroad for study; he spent four years in America and Europe, and is now, through the munificence of his patron, a student in Cornell University.

In 1900, when the Government of China was about to ally itself with the disgraceful Boxer organization, which brought the nation into ignominy, his Excellency Hwang, by the authority of his office and the courage of his convictions, memorialized the Throne against the Boxers, whose practices he denounced, saying that no State in such difficulties as were then harassing the Empire was ever saved by the devices proposed by the Boxers, or by the friends of the Boxers. Within two days a Boxer garrison appeared at his house, looted it, drove out his family, devastated the premises, and marched him off, a prisoner, to the palace of Prince Chuang. Here he was met by underlings, but Prince Chuang, who had been an old friend, refused to see him. He remained for two days a prisoner in Prince Chuang's hothouse cellar, where the old gardener, who had known him for years, smuggled food to him. Others were afraid to render him any assistance. At the end of two days he was placed in a chair and carried off to the Hsingpu, or State prison. A small, frail, mild, kindly gentleman, thoroughly Confucian in his abhorrence of brute force, his feelings may be imagined as he looked out of the windows of his chair and saw his countrymen decked out in red rags, carrying great brutal iron swords, and, with fierce looks, guarding him from escape and escorting him to prison.

The Government had fallen into the hands of the arch Boxer Prince Tuan, and Mandarin Hwang daily expected the sentence of death, and was prepared for execution. He had to bribe the jailer and the turnkeys in order that a few faithful servants might be admitted to bring him food and reports of his family. Soon after he was imprisoned, the foreign Legations, which were less than a mile away, were besieged, and he could by day and night hear every shot of the rifle and artillery and mine contest, able only to surmise what it was about, and entirely ignorant of the fortunes of the Throne and of his Emperor. At the end of forty days the foreign troops, which had entered Peking and relieved the Legations, threw open the doors of the prison, and his Excellency Hwang was turned loose into the street along with a miscellaneous crowd of prisoners. His home was broken up and his family scattered, but he gathered some friends about him and settled down in the Chinese city to assist the American troops, who were in charge of the district, in policing and governing it. During the occupation of Peking by the foreign troops he established an industrial and charitable institution, with the object of teaching useful trades to boys and educating them in the learning of the West. He was successful, owing to the support which a knowledge of his character attracted. At the same time his former enemies began to persecute him. It is due, I believe, to Mrs. Conger, the wife of the American Minister, who used in Hwang's behalf the rare influence which she enjoyed at the Chinese Court, that the Empress Dowager interfered to protect him; and he has now for several years enjoyed a measure of calm and prosperity, with his family about him. But his future is not at all certain, nor is that of any other Chinese reformer. Like the progressives of the past, and those for a long time to come, he is essentially a martyr, carrying his fortunes in his hand.

It is the fashion now, especially with the sentimentalists, to vindicate the Throne and the high members of the Government. Our magazines are open to these themes because they affect great personages. Men like Hwang are not inspired in their efforts by the hope of Imperial favor. Their efforts began long years before the Imperial family and the members of the Government made their final effort to exterminate Western influence and its missionaries. Their day will be brought nearer and their efforts will be more effective if the history of their deeds is cherished abroad.

# TWO BISHOPS' REMINISCENCES[1]

THE two professions that come into the most intimate relations with us all are, of course, the medical and the clerical, the body and the soul cure completing our lives, in ordinary. Notwithstanding the dreary triteness of remarks upon the gift for story-telling among clergymen, the truth remains that as a class they excel in this field, sometimes to the discomfiture of their hearers; but more often to their profit and entertainment. We know, having had it well drilled into our minds, that the proper study of mankind is man, and so we turn with pleasant anticipations to two volumes recording from widely separated view-points the impressions that " human warious " have made upon two *Bishops* of the Protestant Episcopal Church. Bishop Potter, in his " Reminiscences of Bishops and Archbishops," confines himself to men known more or less widely in England and America. He is able to indicate character by a stroke here or there, and the man stands before us, recalled by a good memory. As Secretary of the House of Bishops he had unusual advantages, and became intimately acquainted with men much his seniors, observing and narrating incidents in their lives. Ten portraits hang in the American room, and three English *Archbishops* are added. Bishop Whittingham, " precise and unimpeachable," exact in his knowledge and somewhat destitute of humor, is vividly described. He was tenacious of his episcopal rights, and once contended sharply with a certain rector as to his right to pronounce the Absolution. Curiously, after thought, both rector and Bishop reached the conclusion at the same time that the question was immaterial. "You may say the Absolution, Bishop, if you want to," said the rector, in the vestry-room. " But I don't want to ! " exclaimed the Bishop—quick to acknowledge the change in his convictions and generous in the acknowledgment. Bishop Williams, of Con-

necticut, had an influence and an affectionate following not bounded by the limits of his Church. To him are credited two witticisms that have been attached to other names. " The Puritans first fell on their own knees, then on the aborigines," he said. When some one was inquiring too inquisitively about the affairs of one of his clergy, and asked, " Has the Rev. Mr. —— said anything to you about ——?" the quick reply came, " Nothing to *speak of*, sir," and the gossip was silenced. A good story is told of Bishop Eastburn, whose style of preaching was ponderous. In describing the prayer of the rich man to Lazarus in Abraham's bosom and his request for a drop of cooling water, the Bishop added, " To this wholly inadmissible request the patriarch returned a negative reply." Upon the consecration of Bishop Huntington, of Central New York, in the presence of six bishops at dinner, the host, Bishop Eastburn, proposed the health of the new Bishop, saying, " I am the only man at this table who has the right to do it, for," running his eye around the table until it had included every bishop present—" I am the only born Churchman among you "—which was right. In the startled pause the fact was recognized that a Congregationalist, two Presbyterians, a Baptist, a Quaker, and a Unitarian had been transformed into Episcopal bishops. Bishop Clark, of Rhode Island, had a ready wit, an example of which is given. A presiding bishop, whose Christian name was Benjamin, became terribly involved when trying to explain a matter of discipline, and Bishop Clark, in passing the secretary's desk, threw a small roll of paper across the page. Upon it was written, to Dr. Potter's amusement, " But Benjamin's *mess* was five times as much as any of theirs."

Bishop Clark went abroad for six months, and wrote remunerative articles for the old New York Ledger. Dr. Potter asked what they were to be about. " On the moral uses of hairpins, and subjects of that character," said the Bishop. He was childlike and yet saw large

[1] *Reminiscences of Bishops and Archbishops.* By the Rt. Rev. Henry Codman Potter. G. P. Putnam's Sons, New York.
*My People of the Plains.* By the Rt. Rev. Ethelbert Talbot. Harper & Brothers, New York.

questions in a large light. Many stories could be related of Bishop Coxe, whose sensitiveness and dignity united to a fine frenzy often brought him into singular situations. A beautiful and pathetic scene in the life of Bishop Wilmer took place in New York City soon after the war. In his devotion to his high calling and forgetfulness of himself he entered the office of a great merchant, whom he had never met, and seriously spoke of the personal responsibility involved in great possessions. It was done in the spirit of his Master, and the merchant said later, "In all my life no one ever spoke to me like that!" The result was a large gift for the endowment of a cathedral—a result perhaps not so closely in the line of Christ's teachings as might have been expected. Bishop Potter supplements his personal recollections by many delightful sketches contributed by friends. A particularly pleasant reflection of Bishop Dudley is offered by the Rev. R. Grattan Nolan, who knew him all his life, He relates amusing tales of the negroes and their love and admiration for the Bishop. One awed waitress asked him, "King Dudley, will you have some cakes?" while another stood stiffly back, and, in reply to his mistress's whispered orders for more waffles, responded, "Huh! They ain't no mo'; he done had ten already."

Archbishop Temple has long been a fruitful source of stories; some, both new and old, appear in this volume. An old one is so good that it must be repeated. After the Archbishop's eyesight had failed, he was greeting his guests at a garden party at Lambeth. He said to one who approached him, "How do you do? How is your father?" The guest looked somewhat surprised and said, "My father is dead, your Grace." "And the widow, your mother, how is she?" said the Archbishop. "Thank you, she is quite well," somewhat stiffly. Afterwards the Archbishop asked some one, "By the way, who was that?" "That, your Grace," was the reply, with a spice of mischief, "was the Duke of Connaught."

Bishop Talbot for twelve years was associated with a different sort of men whom he calls "My People of the Plains"—rough, honest or dishonest, English or American, sturdy folk of our frontier. Among his friends he counted several Indians, and of one, Washakie, a Shoshone chief, he tells some excellent tales. General Grant sent Washakie a gift, which he received in silent emotion. Upon being urged to say some word of appreciation of the kindness of the Great Father, the old Indian said, "Well, Colonel, it is very hard for an Indian to say thank you like a white man. When you do a kindness for a white man, the white man feels it in his head, and his tongue talks; but when you do a kindness for a red man, the red man feels it in his heart. The heart has no tongue."

There are many diverting stories told of the way the sympathies of the cowboys and men of mining camps were enlisted in church work, and in several instances money was pledged to build a church, each man being "charged up according to his pile." The palmy days of the Rocky Mountain stage-coaches have passed away, disappearing before the advancing railway. In Bishop Talbot's time, in Wyoming and Idaho there were many thrilling adventures in stage travel. He recalls an epitaph which he says was found on an old gravestone:

> "Weep, stranger, for a father spilled
> From a stage-coach and thereby killed.
> His name, Jay Sykes, a maker of sassengers,
> Slain with three other outside passengers."

At one time Bishop Kemper was held up on a coach by a "road agent," who, on being informed that his victim was an Episcopal bishop, let him go, saying, "Why, that's the church I belong to! Driver, you may pass on."

In the Cœur d'Alene country, in the early days, Bishop Talbot's arrival was advertised in the following fashion on a green circular : "The Bishop is coming. Let all turn out and hear the Bishop. Services in George and Human's Hall to-morrow, Sunday, at 11 A.M. and 8 P.M. Please leave your guns with the usher." The charm was potent, the hall was packed, and a thousand dollars was raised to build a church. The men who went out as missionaries were of heroic character, and did much to preserve high ideals and insure the successful future of the new country. The Bishop often found well-educated Englishmen and Americans who had deliberately lost themselves in the West after throwing away opportunities at home. He declares he never met a professional gambler who defended his manner of life, yet, as a vice, gambling was the most hopeless to reform. There were not many colored people in the new country, but as a Missourian Bishop Talbot was interested in such of them as he met. At a meeting he attended Uncle Billy prayed that the good Lord would send down on the Bishop his " sanctum sanctorum." He afterwards explained, "I means dat I want de good Lord to send down on you jest de very best he's got on hand."

During the Western episcopate the Bishop went to England to attend missionary gatherings, and he tells some incidents that occurred during his visits. He stopped with several of the noted men of the Church of England, Archbishop Benson and Canon Farrar among others. In an address before a parish school he asked what a diocese was. A small boy, to the amusement of all, replied, " A diocese, my lord, is a district of land with the bishop on top and the clergy underneath." It is certainly true that even an American boy could not equal that. A strong plea is made for broad-minded treatment of the Mormons, and the Church is urged to provide churches and schools in every town and turn on light among these ignorant people. The Indians, too, are stoutly championed, and the story of our Nation's shame is told once more.

# Comment on Current Books

**The Adventures of Joujou** — " Joujou " is a piquant little heroine, and her love story is delightful—just as the pictures are—in a dainty, whimsical way. The hero is a marquis, and there are pretty scenes in the garden of an old French château. The volume is thoroughly attractive. (The Adventures of Joujou. By Edith Macvane. J. B. Lippincott Company, Philadelphia. $2.)

**Andrew Goodfellow** — A romance of love, heartless desertion, and the sea life of Nelson's time. The story is told in a frank, open-hearted way, with no subtlety and without much literary art. (Andrew Goodfellow. By Helén H. Watson. The Macmillan Company, New York. $1.50.)

**Another Book in Archaic Style** — Mr. Maurice Hewlett may have to look to his laurels. He is not the only author who understands how to write in cunningly archaic style. Mr. Edward Hutton is apparently running him a close second. If the incredulous Hewlett admirer does not believe it, he has but to look at the well printed and illustrated study of a fifteenth-century Italian despot just published by Mr. Hutton, namely, the interesting description of Sigismondo Pandolfo Malatesta, Lord of Rimini. Lovers of Italy, of Italian history, art, and literature, will welcome this volume. They will compare it, not so much with Mr. Hewlett's "The Road in Tuscany " or with any other

description of Italian scenery, as with such books as Mrs. Cartwright's "Beatrice d'Este " and " Isabella d'Este." Mr. Hutton professes to translate a contemporary chronicle written by a humanist, who was interested in art, namely, by one Pietro Sanseverino, with a sketch of the latter's life and an account of his meeting with Leon Battista Alberti. Let it be added that, despite this supposed translation, we find a number of very modern reflections and judgments. In the opinion of the fastidious, these, if not the narrative itself, might perhaps have been as well expressed with slightly less evident straining after effect. But this may be hypercriticism. (Sigismondo Pandolfo Malatesta, Lord of Rimini. By Edward Hutton. E. P. Dutton & Co., New York. $4, net.)

**Carolopolis** — It is doubtful whether many people have taken time to find out from whom the Carolinas took their names, and it is quite probable that most of us would say from Charles II. of England, who granted to the " Lord Proprietors " a large section of the territory known now as South Carolina. But the engaging writer of the history of Charleston reminds us that, a hundred years before this English grant was made, the French Huguenots sent out by Admiral Coligny claimed and named the new country for their king, Charles IX. of France. Beginning in 1679, this delightful chronicle of place and people leads us down to the close of the Civil War—in the saddened thoughts of her citizens, the period when the real Charleston ended. Mrs. Ravenel writes with loyalty, deep interest, and great care for important detail. She infuses into otherwise dry history the elusive charm of a vivacious and discriminating mind. Her magnetic quality collects exactly the items most interesting to the reader, and she often causes them to center about some piquant opinion of her own, or of some bygone character, with vivifying effect. Some of the most delightful glimpses are given of old Charleston society. For instance, a gentleman, being straitened in piazza room, always took his tea in summer on the broad sidewalk in front of his house. His friends would stop for a cup and a chat. "How did he manage with the people going by?" asked a modern son. "You surely do not suppose," said the astonished father, "that any one would intrude upon the old gentleman! Of course, when people saw him, if they were not his friends, they crossed the street and walked on the other side, not to annoy him!" Just this childlike unconventionality and delicate consideration for others were the dominant characteristics of old Charleston. Many in other parts of the country think it still exists, but to the real citizens of the old town it has long passed away. This criticism of Mr. Wister's "Lady Baltimore," exemplifying the old spirit, camé with the delicious Southern accent from the lips of a Charleston man: "Well, I read the beginnin'—far enough to find two men sittin' on a tombstone discussin' whether they were gentlemen 'or not—and that was enough. I didn't read any mo'." No real Charleston man or woman has any doubt upon such a subject. The illustrations by Vernon Howe Bailey are in full sympathy with the text. (Charleston, the Place and the People. By Mrs. St. Julien Ravenel. The Macmillan Company. $2.50.)

*The Colorado Desert* In two elaborately illustrated and finely printed volumes Mr. George Wharton James tells in detail of the picturesque features, natural characteristics, and history of that part of the Colorado desert which belongs to Southern California. The narrative includes a readable account of a journey by water along the overflow of the Colorado River which has resulted in the much-talked-of Salton Sea. This Sea, as our readers will remember from the story as told in The Outlook, threatened to become of such a size as to be injurious to the country in which it unexpectedly appeared; enormous sums have been spent in attempting to check this over-

flow and make the river return to its original channel, but newspaper despatches lately printed say that the elusive stream has once more foiled these efforts and that the Sea is again increasing in size. It need not be pointed out that Mr. James has in the general subject of his work a topic full of varied interest; and he is able to bring to its treatment knowledge of much that is absolutely unknown and strange to the average American reader, although it has to do with a part of his own country. Occasionally the reader feels that the author is giving a little too much detail, and is even inclined to question whether the material might not to advantage have been presented in a single volume. The same thing may be said of the three hundred pen-and-ink sketches made by Mr. Karl Eitel, who knows the desert in its pictorial aspects thoroughly; that is to say, while the pictures are capital in themselves, the work would not have suffered if there had not been quite so many. (The Wonders of the Colorado Desert. By George Wharton James. Little, Brown & Co., Boston. $5, net. Postage, 45 cents extra.)

*Christianity in the Modern World* It is refreshing to light upon a book of broad views, lifting one above the conflicting and eddying currents of the streets into the steady breeze above the housetops. Modern science, philosophy, and criticism have made havoc of the theology that.fitted well the comparative ignorance of past centuries. Many either rejoice or fear that the primitive faith is thereby doomed. As the lobster which has cast its old shell to put on a larger one is for the time more vulnerable to its foes, so is the case with religion in a time of transit from form to form of knowledge. But Mr. Cairns rightly sees in such a case " the modern *præparatio evangelica*" for a victorious advance of creative power. Whatever has become of the ancient dogmas fabricated to cope with the Hellenism of the classic and the barbarism of the mediæval age, the net result of the past century of historic research has been to lift into glorious pre-eminence the person of the Founder of Christianity, as the heavenly leader of human progress in all that tends to ideal manhood. A new manifestation of divine power unquestionably appeared in him. The impression he produced on his disciples, as reflected in their writings, can only be explained by a larger indwelling of God in him than in any other member of our race. Herein lies his moral authority for the conscience of mankind. How this is related to the twentieth century appears in the fact that this supreme authority is brought to bear upon the great powers of the world at a time when they have come into the closest relations of influence with all the backward and weaker peoples—at a time also when these great powers themselves are menaced by social tension and trouble within themselves, growing out of economic evils that are also moral wrongs. Thus has Christianity come through a century of preparation to face a task perhaps greater than any before, and religion, as in many previous crises both before and since the Christian era, may be confidently expected to bring to birth the new and better order of the future. The line of its hope lies in its power to moralize the selfishness of the individual by transforming private interest into the ideal of a common good. Precisely this is what Jesus effected in the apostolic age by his ideal of the kingdom of heaven. Rarely, if ever, has the subject of the book been better treated. (Christianity in the Modern World. By the Rev. D. S. Cairns, M.A. A. C. Armstrong & Son, New York. $1.50.)

*Diplomacy* Mr. Foster's competent pen has in successive publications performed good public service in popularizing knowledge of an important subject—the intercourse of our own with other Governments. He has already shown the beneficent influence of American diplomacy upon international law. He now describes the character, methods, and duties of our diplomatic service from its beginning until now, and records what it has attempted, together with its achievements, failures, and mistakes—all with sufficient detail to make the narrative historically valuable, as well as interesting to the general reader. Of instances humorous and serious, illustrating good form and bad, tact and indiscretion, there is no lack, and foreign diplomats come in for their share. The mooted points of practice in foreign relations, and also between the President and the Senate in regard to these, are clearly stated—some of them now settled, others still open. Treaties and other compacts, arbitration, and international claims, are amply and instructively treated. In the simplification and the moralization of international diplomacy the United States has evidently taken a leading part. It may be doubted whether any branch of the public service has so honorable a record, and yet it has been singularly starved by the parsimony of Congress from the beginning. On Congress also it still depends whether the character of our consular service shall be made as generally creditable to us as the higher grades have become. Such books as Mr. Foster's help toward this so far as they promote that compelling public opinion which Congress respects. (The Practice of Diplomacy. By John W. Foster. Houghton, Mifflin & Co., Boston. $3, net.)

*The Dogs of War* The illustrator of this little yarn, as well as its author, knows dog nature, and the characterizations are decidedly entertaining. The collaboration is quite perfect, and it is almost impossible to consider the story apart from the pictures. Possibly the drawings are a bit cleverer than the text, although there is much amusing matter in the dog biography and the account of "the greatest dogs' club in the world." (The Dogs of War. By Walter Emanuel. Charles Scribner's Sons, New York. $1.25.)

*Eight Secrets* We unhesitatingly pronounce this one of the best boys' books of the season, and note that it is particularly well adapted for boys who have an interest in invention and possess some share of the ingenuity which is often considered an all but universal American attribute. Apart from this, however, the tale has decided story interest and a capital plot idea in the house with its "eight secrets," which suggests the curiosity-stimulating title. Mr. Ingersoll is always to be depended upon for faithfulness to nature, and whether he deals with animals or with boys he gives us the genuine thing. The boy in this book is, to be sure, rather out of the common in his capacity for getting himself out of scrapes and for doing things in a wonderfully effective way; but while exceptional, he is by means impossible. (Eight Secrets. By Ernest Ingersoll. The Macmillan Company, New York. $1.50, net.)

*The Fair Hills of Ireland* "This book is written," explains its author, Mr. Stephen Gwynn, "in praise of Ireland." It is, in fact, obviously intended to play a part in promoting the "Irish revival," that literary and linguistic movement which aims to develop in the contemporary Irishman a greater interest in his native tongue and in his country's past glories, and thereby stimulate him to earnest endeavor to make the present more worthy of the past. What Mr. Gwynn has done is to write a topographical history of Ireland. He describes its ancient ruins, monuments, and relics, its famous rivers and towns, and its "fair hills," associating each with the period or event for which it is best known. In this way he contrives to incorporate in his pages an amazing variety of information—information historical, traditional, archæological, architectural, social, economic, and literary—and thus to appeal to a far wider audience than that composed of his fellow-Irishmen.

But it must be said that the wider audience will hardly be so interested as would have been the case had he hit upon a happier arrangement of his material. As it is, his book lends itself to desultory rather than consecutive reading. Its author wanders too rapidly and disconnectedly from theme to theme, indulges over-freely in allusion, and demands too great a previous knowledge of Irish history, legendary as well as authentic. Nevertheless, the book will be found well worth the pains necessary to read it, and should meet an especial welcome from prospective travelers in Ireland, who, we observe, Mr. Gwynn is quick to differentiate from "tourists." (The Fair Hills of Ireland. By Stephen Gwynn. The Macmillan Company, New York. $2.) ·

*The Flight of Marie Antoinette* With an incredible minuteness of detail the story of three tragic days in the life of the French Queen is told in a large illustrated volume translated by Mrs. Rodolph Stanell. A heroic figure surrounded by weak dependents, her children, and the slow-witted, foolish King, it is no wonder that she inspired romantic devotion in the hearts of a few brave men. Among these, Count de Fersen, a Swedish nobleman, takes the first place as the Queen's deliverer. On the 20th of June, 1791, the royal party left Paris at night, and, aided by a few faithful friends, escaped as far as Varennes. There they were overtaken and brought back prisoners. This brief tragedy, the opening scene to be followed by increasing dangers and tumults, is described, with each actor concerned in it. The volume may have a useful place among historical documents, but it will be found tedious and almost trivial in its exhaustiveness. It contains a large number of prints of places and people concerned in the affair. (The Flight of Marie Antoinette. From the French of G. Lenotre, by Mrs. Rodolph Stanell. J. B. Lippincott Company, Philadelphia. $1.50.)

*The Fortune of the Republic* We would commend this little volume of essays and addresses to the careful consideration of all who, by reason of the revelations of the past two or three years, are beginning to despair of the future of the United States. Rather, as Dr. Hillis in his sturdy optimism declares, should they rejoice in that these revelations bear witness to a public sentiment determined to rid the body politic of the germs of corruption and death. Searching further, as Dr. Hillis has searched in several years of travel through every State and Territory in the Union, the pessimists will find a wealth of evidence to dissipate their fears and convert them to his belief that "any darkness there is on the horizon is morning twilight and not evening twilight." This evidence is summed up in the growth of the religious spirit, the increasing popularization of education and culture, and the passing of sectionalism. Specifically, Dr. Hillis believes that everything points to a still greater America, greater in religion, in morals, in politics, in art, and, last though not least, in National unity. It may be objected that some of his generalizations are incapable of positive proof and are open to dispute, but nevertheless the candid reader must carry conviction from his pages, and with conviction the determination to play his part in realizing the ideals Dr. Hillis has set forth. In a word, his book makes for religious and intellectual betterment and for a whole-hearted, robust patriotism that must be up and doing. (The Fortune of the Republic. By Newell Dwight Hillis. The Fleming H. Revell Company. $1.20, net.)

*Guide to Preachers* Laymen who would qualify themselves to preach acceptably and effectively—and there is need of many such—will find this an eminently helpful book. It covers the whole subject—the Biblical, doctrinal, homiletical, rhetorical conditions of preaching and reasoning suitably to the needs of the modern world. Such subsidiary matters as language, literary style, elocution, and delivery receive proportionate treatment, and the important requisite of furnishing the layman with points helpful in his conflict with popular skepticism is not overlooked. There is no other book that so well meets the present want. The lists of books recommended are, with two exceptions, all British. Some excellent American substitutes should have had mention for the convenience of American students. (A Guide to Preachers. By Alfred E. Garvie, M.A., D.D. A. C. Armstrong & Son, New York. $1.50, net.)

*The "Imitation of Christ"* Every lover of this immortal book, the radiant product of a dark age, will be glad that it has found here a sympathetic and competent interpreter. A common misinterpretation of it is current; viz., that it is solely self-interested, concerned only for the good of the individual apart from his fellows. Though the distinguished name of Dean Milman is subscribed to this opinion, it is a strange misjudgment of one who wrote, "If you would be carried, carry another." That à Kempis was a thoroughgoing altruist, "in fact a socialist rather than an individualist," his commentator easily shows.

His aim must still be our aim—the Christianization of Christendom. Then atheism and lust defiled the Church. To-day self-interest in more refined forms of materialism has enervated it. Now, as then, great changes are impending. It was the wide upwelling of the mystic religious spirit, which has left its greatest memorial in " The Imitation of Christ," that produced a reformed Church, and so "made modern Europe possible." The same antagonistic principles, now as then, confront each other; the spirit of à Kempis has still further victories to win, and his book is a book for all time, until " The City of God," the dream alike of the Stoic philosopher and the Christian theologian, is realized on earth. The mooted question of its authorship is here critically discussed, and its authenticity fairly demonstrated; its structure is analyzed, and the various sources shown from which its author drew; lists and accounts of its manuscripts and printed editions are given; many fine illustrations, including some facsimile pages, are added; full recognition is shown to the work of Thomas's fellow-mystics. In short, it is a timely and helpful commentary upon a great recreative and reconstructive movement, the soul of which, in Thomas's little book, is still "marching on." (Thomas à Kempis. By J. E. G. De Montmorency, B.A., LL.B. G. P. Putnam's Sons, New York. $2.25, net.)

*Joyous Religion* An unpretentious but valuable little book is this, born out of an experience of hard trials. It invites to the way out of darkness and storm into light and peace. Its fundamental positions are true psychologically and ethically, as well as in the mystical religious life. It may be heartily commended to all who would reach the high levels of " the life that is life indeed," where no cloud or storm is that the sun does not quickly dissipate. (Rejoice Always. By Frank S. Van Eps and Marion B. Van Eps. Published by the Authors, New York.)

*Lord Acton's Lectures* Hitherto the general public has had scant opportunity to avail itself of the erudition of the late Lord Acton, celebrated as the most learned man in Europe; but now, it seems, some rich gleanings from his scholarship are at last to be given to the world. Of these the first installment is just to hand in a volume of lectures edited by Mr. John Neville Figgis and Mr. Reginald Vere Laurence. The lectures are those on modern history delivered by Lord Acton as Regius Professor of Modern History at Cambridge, and are doubly interesting as revealing the spirit in which he approached the study of history

and the idea underlying the monumental "Cambridge Modern History" which he planned, but in the execution of which he was able to take small part. To Lord Acton, it is very evident, history is the study of studies, and it is equally evident that he regarded as of most moment the history of the centuries intervening since the Renaissance and the Reformation. To him, too, the great thing was historical thinking rather than historical learning, "solidity of criticism" rather than "plenitude of erudition." For this he found all-sufficient reason in his view of history as the interpreter of the present. In this view, too, may perhaps be found the secret of the caution that so long kept him a student instead of a teacher of history. But, as these lectures amply demonstrate, once he began to teach he did not hesitate to formulate conclusions and pass verdicts. Modern history, as he presents it to us, is a vindication of general ideas, and for him, in his maturity at least, general ideas held no terrors. Take this pregnant sentence, expressing in a few words his conception of the salient feature, the central fact, of the historic cycles since the Reformation: " Beginning with the strongest religious movement and the most refined despotism ever known, it [the subversion of established forms of political life by the development of religious thought] has led to the superiority of politics over divinity in the life of nations, and terminates in the equal claim of every man to be unhindered by man in the fulfillment of duty to God—a doctrine laden with storm and havoc, which is the secret essence of the Rights of Man and the indestructible soul of Revolution." Sometimes, indeed, his generalizations must be held suspect, even in positive error. Thus, in the lecture on the American Revolution we must query his assertion that the colonists " were not roused by the sense of intolerable wrong," and that the Declaration of Independence "was too rhetorical to be scientific." But in the main there can be little question of the soundness of his views, the correctness of his attitude. And, what is not unimportant, the lectures show that, " scientific " historian though he was, he was keenly alive to the human element in history. Whether he is speaking of the discovery and exploration of the New World, of the Reformation, of the counter-Reformation, or of the Thirty Years' War, his thoughts center about some commanding figure, and through this figure reveal alike movements and forces and principles. (Lectures on Modern History. By the late Right Hon. John Edward Emerich, First Baron Acton. Edited by John Neville Figgis,

M.A., and Reginald Vere Laurence, M.A. The Macmillan Company, New York. $3.25.)

**The Master** " This book," says its author, the Dean of Faribault, "attempts to interpret Jesus Christ in the light of modern scholarship." It does this in the form of characterization, as Dr. Bushnell did long ago, rather than of narrative. The record of the Master's deeds may be called in question by critics ; but after scholarship has given all the light it can, and all documents and institutions have borne their testimony, the personal traits that are beyond controversy shine forth. The net result is that in Jesus Christ humanity is seen divinized and God humanized. Written from a conservative standpoint, the volume is free from dogmatism, while leading up to the teaching of the Nicene Creed. Its framers, as we know, did not believe with Dean Slattery that God and man are essentially of the same nature. But this view opens the question, *In what sense* was Christ " more than man " ? as the Dean concludes. He is content to accept it as a fact, and to leave it as a mystery. (The Master of the World. By Charles Lewis Slattery. Longmans, Green & Co., New York. $1.50, net.)

**A Modern Knight** The effect of municipal righteousness is demonstrated by Mr. George in this most modern of romances. The Knight rides forth to overthrow the giant called Graft, and he wears his lady's favor on his helmet. But the mystery and the misery appear in the train of the harmless double life of the lady—at home the devoted daughter of a railway king, and in the working world a young artist in stained-glass window designing. The Knight knows her only in the second character, until the forces of evil in a misgoverned city combine against him, and he almost loses both prize of honor and love of lady. While there are parts of the story that too thinly for artistic effect disguise the especial message that Mr. George feels himself commissioned to utter, the tale is well told and worth telling. The mixture of Scotch and Irish used by the district boss could be improved, and some unnecessary bad spelling might be eliminated to the advantage of the tale. (The Romance of John Bainbridge. By Henry George, Jr. The Macmillan Company, New York. $1.50.)

**Oxford** This is a new volume in the Langham Series of Art Monographs. Any one who expects to visit Oxford could do no better than to slip into his pocket this neat and handsome small volume. In many ways it would be vastly superior to the ordinary guide-book, and has also the advantage of presenting the beautiful university town and its colleges through photographs and drawings that are truly admirable. (Oxford. By H. J. L. J. Masse, M.A. The Langham Series. Charles Scribner's Sons, New York. $1, net.)

**Pardner of Blossom Range** A Western novel of average merit. (Pardner of Blossom Range. By Frances Charles. Little, Brown & Co., Boston. $1.50.)

**Paths to the City of God** Sermons by a widely popular preacher meet a wide welcome. In the present volume the Chicago pastor impresses one with a sense of asymmetry. He seems to give disproportionate attention to the " fall " of Adam with its alleged consequences, and the fall of Chicago, with its palpable consequences, from the moral ideals of all good citizens. He is at his best in " The Lessons of the Rainbow," " The Treasures of the Snow," " Religion and Art," " The Angel in the Sun." But in " Action and the Religious Life " he gives an essay in general terms, instead of a drum-beat to specific and neglected duties. Dr. Gunsaulus is gifted with a rhetorical power such as a successor of the Biblical prophets needs, and it is not exempt from the need of a chastening curb. The conditions which in our great cities call for prophets of the Biblical type present a field for the exercise of such a power in opening " paths to the city of God " which these sermons, except in a half-page, do not seem to recognize. (Paths to the City of God. By Frank W. Gunsaulus. The Fleming H. Revell Company, New York. $1.25, net.)

**Pauline Studies** A welcome greets this volume by the distinguished geographer and historian who published, a dozen years ago, the widely known work, " St. Paul, Traveller and Roman Citizen." Of the fifteen essays it contains nearly half are new or substantially new. The remainder, originally appearing in various magazines, have been thoroughly revised and improved. The critical study of early Christian history is not yet, as Professor Ramsay holds, duly influenced by the new learning of Roman Imperial history—a remark especially pertinent to critics of the Acts of the Apostles. Among the most interesting of these essays are two upon the Acts, whose Lucan authorship is vigorously maintained against Professor McGiffert. Another, the " Statesmanship of Paul," develops a view favored by many scholars, that Paul cherished the design of making the Roman Empire Christian : " Had it not been for Paul—if one may guess at what might have been—no man would now remember Roman and Greek civilization." That Paul fills so much of the New Testament is "because of his personal qualities and historical importance." A striking paper shows that the worship of the Virgin Mary at Ephesus took place at "a critical, epoch-making date in the development of Byzantine government and religion," as a substitute for the pagan cult of the virgin goddess Diana. Other important articles might be mentioned did space permit. Not only does Professor Ramsay bring fresh and valuable instruction from the field of his special study, but he renders good service as a judicious moderator of the schools of critics. (Pauline and Other Studies in Early Christian History. By W. M. Ramsay, Hon. D.C.L. A. C. Armstrong & Son, New York. $3, net.)

*A Romance of Old Wars*    "A Romance of Old Wars" has something of the quality of a fine old tapestry. The action takes place in the fourteenth century in France, during the reign of Charles VI. The story is well written—in the self-conscious, elaborate manner which is supposed to give historical perspective—and the plot is brought to an artistic close. But the writer, in common with all narrators but the very greatest, sees the past pictorially, romantically, showing the superficial pageant and leaving unexpressed that absolute humanity which makes it as real and living as the present. (A Romance of Old Wars. By Valentina Hawtrey. Henry Holt & Co., New York. $1.50.)

*Romola*    This is an elaborately "historically illustrated" edition in two volumes. The effort has been, in the words of the Introduction, "to apply the Röntgen rays of criticism to the fair form of 'Romola' in order to behold the historical skeleton divested of all clothing of romance." So we have facsimiles of the library slips by which George Eliot and Mr. Lewes drew books relating to Florence, every conceivable view of the historical monuments and architecture of Florence, and much else collected arduously, not to say painfully. And still Romola remains, a noble and beautiful romance. (Romola. By George Eliot. In 2 vols. A. C. McClurg & Co., Chicago. $3, net.)

*Salvage*    "Salvage" belongs to the class of light-weight novels, but it captures the interest at once and sustains it without lapse—a successful story of its kind, with no underlying philosophy or special motive, but good in plot and style. After an opening scene in London, which provides an element of mystery, the action continues in New York, where the various interests are subordinated to a well-managed love story. The characters are well conceived and ingeniously related. (Salvage. By J. Aquila Kempster. D. Appleton & Co., New York. $1.50.)

*Scotch Sermons*    The author of these discourses, the Principal of the United Free Church College at Aberdeen, is better known among American scholars and theologians than in our churches. In these, however, this volume of sermons on the Christian life will find a deserved welcome. Thoroughly evangelical, they are concerned with inward culture rather than with outward activities. They are not of the sort that in our country attract popular audiences, but of the kind that touch thoughtful hearers or readers in the meditative moments when, to understand ourselves, we must be by ourselves. (The Other Side of Greatness, and Other Sermons. By James Iverach, M.A., D.D. A. C. Armstrong & Son, New York. $1.50, net.)

*Some Irish Yesterdays*    A series of wordy and fragmentary attempts to depict Irish life and character. The book is seldom interesting, often dull, and sometimes almost unintelligible—and therefore not to be compared with the genuinely entertaining books of Irish sketches by these writers which have had great popularity. (Some Irish Yesterdays. By E. O. E. Somerville and Martin Ross. Longmans, Green & Co., New York. $1.50.)

*Soteriology*    In noting a fresh issue of Dr. Du Bose's well-known work it suffices to recall The Outlook's comment upon its appearance in a new edition in 1899: "It has been recognized as one of the strongest contributions that recent years have brought to the Catholic-orthodox teaching on the Scriptural doctrine of salvation." (The Soteriology of the New Testament. By William Porcher Du Bose, M.A., S.T.D. Reissue. Longmans, Green & Co., New York. $1.50, net.)

*Twenty Years of the Republic*    Something more than annals and something less than history—such is Professor Harry Thurston Peck's "Twenty Years of the Republic," which perhaps may be best described as an entertaining and in some respects illuminating account of the most significant events in the recent political, economic, and intellectual life of the United States. In these pages Professor Peck shows himself an acute observer and intelligent student of conditions obtaining in the world of affairs. A trained journalist, he appreciates the necessity of sustaining the interest and appealing to the imagination of his readers, and not once does the action lag in his story of the occurrences transpiring between the time of President Cleveland's inauguration in 1885 and the close of the McKinley-Roosevelt administration in 1905. His book, in fact, is a series of vivid word-pictures, clearly vizualizing events and *dramatis personæ*, and punctuated by anecdote. In method it is not unlike Mr. Herbert Paul's recently published "History of Modern England." But Professor Peck speaks his mind more freely than does Mr. Paul, and occasionally with undue warmth. Sometimes, too, he writes with an air of finality that is unwarranted in view of the fact that all the evidence is not yet at hand. And now and again his pen portraits are hardly fair to their historic subjects. For all of this, we have read his work with satisfaction, recognizing that in more than one important way it is soundly informative. Especially does it impress us as affording an excellent idea of the sources of the popular discontent that has made itself so strongly felt during the past few months. (Twenty Years of the Republic. By Harry Thurston Peck, LL.D. Dodd, Mead & Co., New York. $2.50, net.)

*Ye Gardeyne Boke*    This is a collection of instructive and sentimental quotations relating to gardens and garden-lore, tastefully decorated and beautifully printed. We may note also that this is one of a list of ten books put out in time for the holidays by a firm of San Francisco publishers who have, despite earthquake, fire, and business upheavals, "put through" this excellent achievement to the credit of their enterprise and literary judgment. (Ye Gardeyne Boke. Quotations Gathered and Arranged by Jennie Day Haines. Paul Elder & Co., San Francisco. $1.50.)

# Letters to The Outlook

## A SPLENDID EXAMPLE

[The following letter from General Robert E. Lee comes to us through a personal friend of the Lee family, and it is of extraordinary interest not only as throwing light on the scrupulous honor and personal modesty of the writer, but also as a singularly cogent example in these days of insurance scandals of the right attitude of companies and individuals toward their sacred trust. It will be remembered that General Lee wrote this letter only two years after the war, when he was broken in health and devoid of resources, with a family dependent on his efforts and upon his modest salary as President of Washington College.—THE EDITORS.]

Lexington, Va., December 23, 1868.

*Dear Mr. B——:—*

I am very much obliged to you for your letter of the 12th and the kind interest you have shown in my welfare. I approve highly of your views, and especially of your course, and feel satisfied that you will accomplish great good. I have considered Mr. F——'s proposition, and though I believe that the establishment in Richmond by the Universal Life Insurance Companies of a branch office, on the plan proposed, would be attended with much benefit, I do not think that I am the proper person for the position of Managing Director. The secure investment of the funds accruing from the Southern business in the present condition of our affairs, it seems to me, would be attended with great trouble, and should be managed with great care. In my present position I fear I should not have time, even if I possessed the ability, to conduct it. Life insurance trusts I consider sacred. To hazard the property of the dead, and to lose the scanty earnings of fathers and husbands who have toiled and saved that they may leave something to their families, deprived of their care and the support of their labor, is to my mind the worst of crimes. I could not undertake such a charge unless I could see and feel that I could faithfully execute it. I have therefore felt constrained, after deliberation, to decline the proposition of Mr. F——. I trust that the Company may select some better man for the position, for I think in proper hands it would accomplish good. For your interest in my behalf, and for Mr. L——'s kind consideration, I am very grateful. And with my thanks to both of you, and to Mr. F—— for his kindness, to whom I trust you to explain the reason of my course, I am,

Truly yours,

R. E. LEE.

## THE SOUL OF HONOR

The very magnanimous tributes to General Lee which have appeared in The Outlook—tributes the more interesting that they appear in a Northern journal which was for years under the editorial control of one of the great anti-slavery leaders, Henry Ward Beecher—remind me of an incident concerning General Lee which was told to me some years ago while visiting an old Southern family. The narrator of the incident was a fine example of the old-fashioned Virginia gentleman, tall, straight, upright in stature and bearing, with a strong, kindly face having in it a curious suggestion both of President Lincoln and of General Lee. Seated on the porch of his century-old mansion, he told this story with the charm of the accomplished raconteur and the simplicity and modesty of the old soldier who has fought on the losing side.

Just before the close of the war the Confederacy was in sore straits for transport animals. Sherman had struck into the vitals of the South, and they could not be obtained from Georgia or Alabama. The chief of transportation decided to send to Mexico to buy horses and mules. To get these it was necessary to send gold, not the depreciated Confederate currency. Trusted agents were each supplied with money belts containing five thousand dollars in gold, and ordered to proceed to Mexico for the purpose stated. Then came the break-up and the surrender. One of the transportation agents who had not started on his journey came to his superior, the chief of transportation, and returned the gold to him, though the former officer was of course now but a private citizen. Though without means for restoring his demoralized plantation to a profitable basis, this conscientious citizen had no thought of applying the windfall to his own necessities. He took counsel of various of his former associates as to what should be done with the money. One Confederate general said, "I am stranded. I can use some of that gold as a loan. So can So-and-so, and Such-a-one." Another said, "Divide it among the widows and orphans around you. Devote it to charity for the suffering survivors." He finally appealed to General Lee, who lived at some distance from his home. General Lee promptly said, "That money must be treated as captured property of the Confederacy, and surrendered as such to the Federal authorities." My friend took the money to Richmond, presented it to the astonished Provost-Marshal, took a receipt for it, and the incident was closed. I think this transaction reflects the highest credit on the conscientiousness and devotion to their sense of duty of both General Lee and the man who sought his advice. We do well to honor the memory of such men.

H. H. M.

### A PLEA FOR THE RIIS HOUSE

As we look about at the wonderful transformation in our shabby old houses at the Riis Settlement, and see their beauty and their fine equipment, and the new Theodore Roosevelt Gymnasium, the pride and joy of all our young people, and realize that they are all ours, without a penny of debt upon them, we can hardly believe it, and our hearts are so full of gratitude that a wonderful Christmas spirit pervades the building and inspires the groups of busy workers, all absorbed in preparations for the week of festivities that Christmas brings us.

First, there are those wonderful bundles to do up that go into the one hundred and thirty-five homes, with some remembrance marked for each member of the family, young and old; and then the stately tree that must bear beautiful fruit once, and often twice, each day, for the successive groups of the various clubs and classes—some fourteen hundred gifts in all to be provided. It is delightful work, and we wish those who have so generously given to make all this possible could share the joy with us.

The festivities will be over by the time these words pass through the press, but the Christmas spirit will remain to cheer many a humble home and overburdened heart. Only some of us will be reminded, with the opening of the new year, that enlarged buildings and fine equipment bring enlarged responsibilities and added expenses, for it takes a good deal of coal, gas, and electricity to keep our beautiful building warm and light, and up to the standard of higher living that it represents in this dreary neighborhood.

The regular demands of the kindergarten and all the club and educational work are already piling up bills faster than we can meet them, and we know that this bitter weather will bring sickness and suffering in the crowded, unsanitary homes, with many calls for relief. Our treasury is quite exhausted by the many little extras in finishing and furnishing the various rooms. This is all done now, and well done, but we need funds for the daily necessities of the work itself.

It will cost nearly six thousand dollars to carry us through to the first of May, when Fresh Air and summer contributions begin to come in. This is exclusive of the gymnasium support which is so generously provided by the boys and girls of eleven private schools, through the personal efforts of Mr. Riis. About two thousand dollars is due in pledges for the general work. Will not our kind friends among The Outlook readers, who have so often and so generously proved their interest in the Settlement, help us to raise the four thousand dollars necessary to make the winter's work a success, and to lift this last burden of anxiety from our grateful hearts?      CLARA FIELD, Treasurer.

Jacob A. Riis Neighborhood Settlement,
48 Henry Street, New York.

## THOSE LOST GARMENTS

Is there anything that you can do in the interest of art or mercy to check the painful illustrations of the stable scene at the time of the Nativity? Where, oh where are the nice thoughtful little garments that the sweet mother prepared in Galilee and carried with her in her anxious journey? Are we not especially told that she "wrapped him in swaddling-clothes and laid him in a manger, because there was no room for her in the inn"? There is nothing shocking in the thought of the fresh, free, cool cave where the cattle slept, or the little manger cradle. The shepherds stand about in adoring awe; but they are all clothed in sheepskins. Joseph, in a long, warm cloak, is leaning on his staff. The Virgin mother, wrapped up to the eyes in every kind of picturesque garment, sits enthroned in light, and at her feet or on her knees lies a poor little shivering baby—absolutely naked except for a halo of apparently electric light—quite devoid of any warmth or comfort!

There was one picture last year which went the rounds and was advertised in so many magazines that it was evidently much admired, in which the poor little pallid figure on the ground was so pitiful that the only text it suggested was, "Behold, I am a worm, and no man."

No woman paints these pictures. Her heart would forbid the cruelty. From the old masters down to their present very far removed successors, the greatly swathed Madonna holds a little naked Jesus and seems to be satisfied.

But where, oh where are the swaddling-clothes which the Bible tells us were used at the baby's birth, and which the Angel especially mentioned to the shepherds in giving directions as to their finding the Holy Child!

It puts Mary mother far off in sympathy from the other young mothers who spend their happy hours in making all possible soft, warm preparations for their own little ones, with prayers in their hearts for the blessing of the Holy Child Jesus on their coming joy.

Y.

## WOMEN AND WAGE-SPENDING

I ask for permission to write a few words concerning extravagant consumption by the laboring class. I have read with much interest both Mr. Cochran Wilson's article on "Women and Wage-Spending" and Mr. I. M. Rubinow's letter in criticism of Mr. Wilson. I agree perfectly with Mr. Rubinow that there is great need of statistical investigation of workingmen's budgets, and of the budgets of other classes also; for my observation tells me that there is much malconsumption among all classes. On the other hand, I think that Mr. Wilson, in spite of his contempt for statistics, has put forth a significant truth in declaring that workingmen's wives are given to unwise expenditures. As I understand Mr. Wilson, he pleads, not, as Mr. Rubinow charges, for lower expenditures, but for more rational and harmonious expenditures. Bulletin 65 of the Bureau of Labor throws no light whatever upon the question of how money is spent by workingmen within particular commodity groups. An expenditure of $107.84 per family for clothing may or may not be extravagant. It probably is not extravagant in so far as its nominal relations to the other items of expenditure are concerned; but the more important question is, What kind of clothes does the working family buy? Are they clothes that yield substantial, sensible utility, or are they merely, or in part at any rate, articles purchased in response to a foolish desire to emulate a higher social class or to maintain social competition with others of the same class? The expenditure of $326.90 for food may or may not involve extravagance. The important question is whether this food is such as will maintain health and economic efficiency, or whether in a considerable part it is food representing ostentatious consumption. An individual may spend his whole income for shelter and food, and still be extravagant. That he spends a small percentage of his income for tobacco, liquors, and amusements is evidence, as Mr. Rubinow intimates, that he is not extravagant. In America, where the emulation of a higher by a lower class is possible, and where there is less disposition than in Europe to accept a class status, there is bound to be much foolish spending, much unwise consumption. By all means we want to gain for the workingman higher wages, and encourage in him a development of more and more wants; but we want also to encourage him to make his consumption rational and harmonious, not only with respect to the relations between different groups of expenditure, but also with those groups.

RAYMOND V. PHELAN,

Assistant Professor of Economics and Sociology in Miami University.

Oxford, Ohio.

# Libby's
(Natural Flavor)
# Food Products

## Libby's Appetizing Soups

give zest to any dinner by their delicious, piquant flavor.
Made in the spotless Libby kitchens, by the well-known Libby chefs,

## Libby's Concentrated Soups

are recognized as the best of the ready-to-serve soups, and include Ox Tail, Chicken, Vegetable, Consomme, Tomato, Mock Turtle and Mullagatawny.

**Ask your grocer for Libby's, and insist upon Libby's.**

The new 84-page booklet, "How to Make Good Things to Eat," gives many delightful recipes for luncheons, dinners and evening spreads, that every housewife will appreciate. It is sent free on request.

**Libby, McNeill & Libby, Chicago.**

VOL. 85, NO. 2

287 Fourth Avenue, New York City
1436 Marquette Building, Chicago

PRICE TEN C

# The
# Outloc '

## Saturday, January 12, 1907

# Rome Against the Republic

## By Charles Wagner

Author of " Truth," " The Simple Life," etc., etc.

# The People and the Corporations

## By the Hon Peter S. Grosscup

Judge of the United States Circuit Court of Appeals

MADISON SQUARE GARDEN

It's A Packard,—
"Ask the Man Who Owns One"

Packard Motor Car Co.
DETROIT,          MICHIGAN

❊

**Secretary Taft's Letter** It may not be true that we are getting an absolutely new type of politicians, but a type radically different from the conventional is more in evidence than for many years past. The popular impression is that the man always seeks the office. There have been recently some striking illustrations of the office seeking the man, such as Mr. Roosevelt's nomination to the Vice-Presidency against his protest; Mr. Root's acceptance of his present position at great self-sacrifice, simply because it offered him an opportunity to render great service to his country; Mr. Hughes's reluctant acceptance of the nomination as Governor of the State of New York, forced upon him because he was the only person who could save the Republican party from defeat; the organization of a Third Term League to force a Presidental nomination on Mr. Roosevelt despite his pledge, though in this instance the League will find in that pledge and Mr. Roosevelt's persistent adherence to it an insuperable obstacle to their design. The most recent illustration of the office seeking the man is afforded by the letter of Secretary Taft published last week:.

For the purpose of relieving the burden imposed by recent publications upon some of my friends among the Washington newspaper correspondents of putting further inquiries to me, I wish to say that my ambition is not political; that I am not seeking the Presidential nomination; that I do not expect to be the Republican candidate, if for no other reason, because of what seem to me to be objections to my availability, which do not appear to lessen with the continued discharge of my own official duty; but that I am not foolish enough to say that, in the improbable event that the opportunity to run for the great office of President were to come to me, I should decline it, for this would not be true.

There are two veiled references here which we may venture to interpret. Mr. Taft's ambition, his friends have long known, is judicial, not political. He would rather be on the Supreme Court bench than in the White House. And he has thrice declined the desired judicial appointment solely because he will not voluntarily relinquish his present post until he has accomplished for the Filipino people what he set out to accomplish. As to his availability, his vigorous attack on the corrupt ring in Ohio may make his nomination difficult, but it would promote his election, since no virtue in public office appeals more to the American people than courage; his labor opinions would increase rather than diminish the labor vote for him, since workingmen want square treatment, not special favors; and while his public utterances in favor of tariff revision may concentrate against his nomination the politically influential representatives of favored interests, they would add to his popularity among the plain people. To-day Mr. Taft would be the strongest candidate the Republican party could put in nomination for the Presidency.

❊

**A Self-Evident Proposition** There is one action which the United States Senate ought to take, and take promptly, from the motive of self-respect if from no other. It ought to demand the right to debate and vote upon the Philippine Tariff Bill. A bill reducing the present Philippine tariff now and abolishing it altogether two years hence passed the House by an overwhelming majority. In the Senate it was referred to the Committee on the Philippines, and that Committee has refused to report it either with approval or with disapproval, or with neither approval nor disapproval. In other words, that Committee has refused to allow the Senate to debate and vote upon the bill. There are two ways of defeating legisla-

2

tion in the Senate: one is to smother it in committee; the other is to talk it to death in the open sessions. This bill could not be talked to death; public sentiment in its favor is too strong. The Senate ought not to allow it to be smothered in committee. There are some arguments which can be adduced against the bill, though they appear to us both feeble and fallacious, and the fact that the opponents of the bill dread discussion indicates that this is their belief now. But there is no argument for the position that a bill which is urgently called for by those most familiar with the conditions in the Philippines, which is supported by the representative press in both parties, and which has passed the House by nearly a two-thirds majority, shall not even be discussed in the Senate. If the Committee does not act of its own motion, we hope that some Senator will ask the Senate to call the bill out from the Committee and let the country see who favor a free debate and who favor a policy of stifling debate on the question of doing justice to the wards of the Nation.

❦

**The People vs. the Swindlers**  There is a movement in Congress to deprive the Post-Office Department of its present summary power to prevent by administrative order the use of the mails by fraudulent concerns to obtain, by means of seductive advertisements, the money of a too credulous public. The unprincipled lobby organized in the interest of such concerns could probably accomplish nothing were it not innocently supported by doctrinaires who believe that the powers possessed by the Post-Office Department are inconsistent with American ideas of liberty. It is true that there is no evidence that these powers have ever been exercised unjustly, that any man has been deprived of any other liberty than the liberty to cheat his neighbor and use the post-office in the operation; and there is abundant evidence that hundreds of fraudulent designs have been defeated. But there are not wanting in America very high-minded men who believe that an ounce of theory is worth a pound of

experience, and it is from such men that danger is to be apprehended. Under the present law, the Postmaster-General may upon adequate evidence issue an order refusing mail facilities to advertising matter of a fraudulent character. Under this law lottery schemes, guessing contests, turf-gambling enterprises, blind pools supposedly organized for speculating upon the stock market, sales of indecent literature and of medicines avowedly concocted for criminal purposes, have been broken up. The courts have held the law Constitutional; that is, they have held that the Government is not under a Constitutional obligation to carry any mail matter that may be offered, nor to wait until the courts, after tedious judicial proceedings, have passed upon the mail matter offered. The power of exclusion has been so cautiously exercised by the Post-Office Department that out of the 2,400 fraud orders issued an appeal to the courts has been taken in less than thirty cases. In all these appeals, with one exception in which no decision has yet been reached, the Department has been sustained. Under such circumstances it would be a great mistake to interfere with the present summary powers of the Department, lest in the future some innocent person should suffer injustice although no one has suffered injustice in the past. The opinion of the Postmaster-General on this subject is both cautious and conclusive:

If a single case could be shown in which injustice or wrong had been suffered by any honest man or woman in consequence of the exercise of authority contained in sections 3,929 and 4,041 of the Revised Statutes as amended, there would be good reason for demanding that similar occurrences in the future be strongly guarded against by legislation, but I am satisfied there has been no such instance. In my opinion, any such legislation now would be unnecessary and premature.

This is also the opinion of The Outlook. Yet there is some peril of such unnecessary and premature legislation under the combined influence of the lobby and the doctrinaire. Some one of those organizations which, in the interest of the people, are watching legislation would do well to watch the bill now before Congress, and, if its passage is seriously threatened, arouse public opinion to the peril and to the necessity of protesting against it. The object of legislation should be to protect the people against the swindlers, not to protect the swindlers against the protectors of the people.

❀

**Dr. Hall in India**
As Barrows lecturer of the University of Chicago, Dr. Charles Cuthbert Hall, of New York, four years ago gave a course of lectures in India which were most favorably received. He was reappointed, and is now giving another course of lectures in that country. The present is a most unpropitious time for an ordinary Christian lecturer to visit India. In fifty years there has not been such irritation and bias against the Government, and against most things from the West, as now. What this fact signifies in such a land is suggestively indicated by Mr. Bissell in his article published in this issue. The success of Japan in its war with Russia had powerfully quickened the desire of Indians to develop a more united and forceful national life. At this juncture Lord Curzon's Government forced a division of the Province of Bengal into two parts. This was bitterly resented by most Hindu Bengalis. Unfortunately, a spirit of opposition also to Christian missions and Christian thought, as well as to Western political authority and trade, was aroused. At such a time it is propitious that the Barrows lecturer is an American who had previously won the deep respect of India's leaders, and who is above all a most tactful Christian gentleman. An unprecedentedly cordial reception has been given to Dr. Hall and his message. The general subject of Dr. Hall's previous course was "Christian Thought Interpreted by Christian Experience." Under that general subject he attempted to show "that man as man, be he Oriental or Occidental, is bound to find in the essence of the Christian religion that which concerns him as a man and controls him as a man, through the reason, the conscience, and the affections." The general subject of the present course of lectures is "The Witness of the Oriental

Consciousness to Jesus Christ," and is "the outcome of reflections awakened by the study of Indian personality in its psychological relation to the most profound and the most lofty elements of the Christian religion." It is manifestly impossible to give any adequate summary in a brief space of a discussion which in its very nature calls for an Oriental subtleness of interpretation. Dr. Hall naturally emphasized the mystical element in the Christian religion. It is the mystical as opposed to the materialistic that the Orient values, and it is this quality that Dr. Hall told his hearers could be found in the religion of Christ. The popularity of Dr. Hall in India has been very marked. He has succeeded in no small degree in bridging the gap between the Orient and the Occident; and he has done this, not by refinements of philosophic speculation, but by direct appeal to the idealism of the Orient. Moreover, he has succeeded in impressing his hearers by his plea that the East should accept, not the ecclesiasticism and the theology of the West, but Jesus himself, the Asiatic teacher, interpret him for itself as the expression of the heart of God, and dedicate to him and his kingdom its own splendid gifts.

❀

**Dr. Hall's Reception**
Thus far Dr. Hall's few critics have been mostly from the minority of missionaries, who think that he has conceded too much to the value of the higher Hinduism. But many missionaries feel that, like the Greek philosophy, the truths of Hinduism should be treated as a preparation for the Gospel. Not the least interesting fact in connection with the lectures is that the men who have been chairmen of the various meetings have been representative of various elements in India. Hindus and English alike have given evidence of their hospitality and of their sympathy with the project. Dr. Hall began lecturing in the northwest of India. In Simla he lectured to a great company of men connected with the Government; in Lahore he lectured in the great hall of the Punjab University, the largest hall in India. Among the chairmen was a

Hindu judge of the High Court, an English judge of the High Court, the Governor of the Punjab, a distinguished Mohammedan of an ancient family, a native Christian Prince, and an eminent English banker. After Lahore he visited Lucknow, Allahabad, and Benares, and was cordially received. Till he came to Calcutta, which is now the boiling pot of unrest, it was uncertain whether the intense opposition to everything Western which pervades that city would interfere with the cordiality of his reception there or not. But he was welcomed as a brother by all the strong leaders of Bengal. His lectures were thronged, and were attended by many eminent Indians. With many of these he had constant personal intercourse. Calcutta is said to have more colleges and college students than New York City. In these colleges Dr. Hall received a cordial welcome. At the Metropolitan College, which is considered the most bitter against Government and missionaries, he was given a notable hearing. From Calcutta he went to Madras, and there also was received with the same enthusiasm. Even out-of-doors, under the stars, an immense audience in the Triplicane section of Madras listened with great respect to his persuasive message.

❦

*Sociology in Providence*      The hundreds of men and women who streamed through the campus at Brown during the holiday recess, while the college boys were away, represented the six different societies which met at that time in annual session—the Historic, the Economic, the Political Science, and the New England History Teachers' Associations, and the Bibliographical and Sociological Societies. Each of these had many representatives present, from all parts of the country. The Sociological Society was the youngest of them all, having been organized last year in Baltimore, but it had the optimism and the courage of youth, not to say its readiness to grasp everything that came to hand, for some of the speakers prophesied that the day would come when economics, philosophy, theology, and many other ologies would be absorbed by

sociology. With the generally accepted notion that theoretic sociology is the scientific side, and that philanthropy, or the effort to improve human conditions, is the applied science which rests on sociology, time was given to both. Social consciousness, social Darwinism, and the best way of teaching sociology were among the topics treated by the university men and women who took part in the discussion. Many subjects for investigation were presented, together with the results of some already undertaken, such as the birth-rate in this country. Those most strenuous for treating sociology as a purely scientific subject had to acknowledge that social betterment is not only united with it in the mind of the general public, but that the two must go together. Yet the amelioration of bad conditions will be more speedily accomplished if investigations as to the cause of the evils from which social groups are suffering are carried out in a scientific way. All social modes of activity must be studied, all the conditions and processes of the social relation. What men *do* must be learned as well as what men *are*. It was intimated by some of the speakers that the results of these studies and investigations would make a dreary picture of the many waifs and strays, degenerates and decadents, preserved through modern civilized measures, who under the more strenuous methods of olden times would have dropped like dead twigs from the human banyan; there was even one who held that possibly our present educational schemes hasten the evil days upon which we are about to fall; that the fact that there are as yet few grandchildren of college women argues ill for the higher education of girls; and that the decay of civilization will follow still faster when the tide of life and blood, of brains and brawn, with which the maws of the cities have been heretofore fed from rural districts shall fail because dried up at the source. It was refreshing after this dark foreshadowing to hear Dr. Lester Ward's bold declaration. He, too, was willing to acknowledge that the increase of population is inversely proportional to human intelligence, that there was a survival of the unfit through the interference of charitable work, and that the population must be always recruited from the great social masses below; but, said he, "we must do something to reach those masses. It is a great ultimate truth that of those 'groveling masses,' as they are called—the great proletariat, the working classes, the mountain folk, and all the rest—ninety per cent., viewed from the standpoint of their intellectual capacity, of their ability to be men and women, are our equals." Mr. Carl Kelsey, of the University of Pennsylvania, a strong advocate of a thoroughly scientific sociology, followed in the same brave strain, showing that mental capacity cannot be judged by social rank, and that the greatest genius may spring from the bottom of the social group; that the strong man or race is not supplanted by the weaker; that a well-planted people here need not fear races of less strength; that our ideals of education must be so changed that we can recognize that we may get culture from a sawbuck if we have but the right teacher, and that every man, rich or poor, high or low, must have an opportunity for self-expression.

❀

**Lady Burdett-Coutts**

Lady Burdett-Coutts, who died in London last week, was probably the best-known Englishwoman of the day outside the ranks of the writers. For many years her name has been a synonym for great wealth administered for the most generous ends, and, as a rule, in the most practical ways. Her association with the banking house which was regarded as second only in importance and resources to the Bank of England made her, on the death of her mother, one of the richest women in the world. No sooner had the vast fortune come into her possession than she made a careful study of many of the most successful charities of the day, which resulted not only in making her a generous patroness of some of them, but in suggesting a large number of original projects to her fertile mind. These projects she worked out along her own lines with uncommon sagacity and energy. She was devoted to the Church of England, and one form of her activities

was the building of churches and schools in poor districts in various parts of the country. The Church of St. Stephen's, at Westminster, with its schools and rectory, was one of the fruits of her generosity. The three colonial bishoprics of Adelaide, Cape Town, and British Columbia were endowed by her. She was profoundly sympathetic with unfortunate women, and her contributions toward helping fallen members of her own sex were conspicuously large. She established a sewing-school and a home in the slums of London, which became a most efficient means in rescuing young girls from the streets of that city. The English weavers, Scotch farmers, unfortunate Irish fishing people, who are sometimes the victims of severe winters, found in her a constant and ready helper, as did hundreds of destitute boys whom she put into the British navy. She built model tenements in London, endowed a model farm, and assisted many unfortunate people to emigrate. Her good deeds were, in fact, so many that she must herself have forgotten most of them. Twenty-five years ago she married William Lehman Ashmead-Bartlett, a Philadelphian by birth, who had long been associated with her in her charitable work. Her husband adopted the surname of Burdett-Coutts, and has represented the District of Westminster in the House of Commons for more than twenty years. Lady Burdett-Coutts had attained great age as well as great honors, for she was ninety-two at the time of her death. Many forms of recognition had come to her from different parts of the world. So long ago as 1871 Queen Victoria made her a baroness, and the following year the freedom of the city of London was presented to her. In an age when the making of colossal fortunes has been the chief concern, it was the special distinction of this woman that she distributed a vast fortune for the benefit of her kind.

❀

**Two Noble Gifts**

Two citizens of New York gave striking illustrations last week of the uses of wealth for the common good. Mr. William P. Letchworth has given to New

. York his great estate of one thousand acres lying on both sides of the cañon of the Upper Genesee River for . a distance of three miles north of Portage Bridge, and embracing the three Portage Falls. The American Scenic and Historic Preservation Society is to be the custodian of the property. Mr. Letchworth has ·been a lifelong servant of the State. Thirty years ago, when the Seneca Indians adopted him into their nation, they named him, with rare discernment, Hai-Wa-Ye-Is-Tah, "The Man Who Always Does the Right Thing." For twenty-five years a Commissioner of the State Board of Charities, Mr. Letchworth not only gave his time, talent, and strength to the State, but also paid his own incidental expenses. His work for the care of the insane and epileptics, the hospitality with which his estate has been thrown open to poor children, the creation of the museum of valuable Indian specimens, his intelligent and enthusiastic work for the development and preservation of scenic beauty, are crowned by this noble gift to the people of New York.——Evidently there is no cause which interests Mr. Carnegie more deeply or vitally than the propagation of peace, nor has he rendered a greater service to humanity than in the zeal, intelligence, and liberality with which he has striven by voice, by pen, and by the use of his wealth to forward this great cause. The Temple of Peace at The Hague will be not only a beautiful building, but a challenge in all times of international differences and controversy to try every ₒmeans of conciliation and adjudication before resorting to war. What he has done on the continent of Europe Mr. Carnegie now proposes to do in the Western world by a gift of $750,000 for the erection in Washington of a building for the Bureau of American Republics, which he believes will become a practical instrument for the unification of the Pan-American States. He would build an American Temple of Peace. The Government has already appropriated two hundred thousand dollars for the purchase of a site; the South American republics have subscribed fifty thousand dollars as their quota. Mr. Carnegie's gift will make it possible worthily and permanently to house a bureau which may prove the beginning of a permanent international brotherhood of peace in the Western world.

❦

*A French View* What is called "the smart set" has very much the same characteristics the world over, and usually develops itself in any city large enough to put sufficient money in the hands of people who are not accustomed to its use and to collect other people, long accustomed to money and social opportunities, who respect neither their privileges nor themselves. The people described in "The House of Mirth" are described by Balzac and Daudet in Paris and by every novelist who has dealt with the various phases of society in the great cities. Their characteristics are the same everywhere: lack of real interests in life, absence of the sense of dignity, the temptation to be what is called "fast" and to play about the edge of dangerous experiences for the sake of excitement, with a touch of vulgarity. Fast society in New York, like that in Boston, Chicago, Denver, San Francisco, London, Paris, and Berlin, shows these same characteristics. It is interesting, however, to get the side-light which a foreign observer sometimes throws on the fast society of a locality. Madame Blanc, who is one of the best informed and most intelligent women in Europe, has been expressing her opinion of Mrs. Wharton's story and of the people whom she describes. It is not a pretty picture as Madame Blanc sees it. "Men are capable of coveting other men's wives, but for that they must be under the excitement of cocktails or whisky; the women will be coquettish and easy on occasion, but when they compromise themselves it is only in order to pay the bills of their dressmakers if the natural banker, the husband, proves insufficient for the occasion." The fast woman in society in France compromises herself because she falls under the spell of passion; the fast woman in society in New York, on the other hand, compromises herself to pay for her bonnets and gowns. In this comparison the French fast woman has much the advantage of the American fast woman. They are both essentially vulgar, judged from the strictly social point of view. The men and women of the fast set always force the note. They overeat, overdrink, overdress, and overact their parts. They are to people in really civilized society what sensational journalism is to high-class newspaper work. They represent the " yellow " in morals, dress, manners, and style of life. It is a mistake to treat them too seriously. Irony, ridicule, and sarcasm are the only weapons that touch them. It is the stupidity of fast society that most impresses itself on other people ; the inanity of its interests and pleasures, its lack of invention, its general bad taste.

❈

**A Noiseless Bridge**   The new steel bridge recently in course of construction over the Sangamon River, near Springfield, Illinois, on the Chicago and Alton Railway, may be studied to advantage in various lines of work in our cities, if reports in regard to one of its qualities are true. It is said to be practically noiseless, the vibrations of the ironwork which cause the sound being practically eliminated. This has been accomplished, according to the Chicago Tribune, by laying upon a bed of steel eight inches of ballast, upon which the ties are placed, instead of directly upon the ironwork, which is the usual method of construction, with the result of reducing the noise of crossing the bridge to a negligible element. This experiment, if successful, ought to mark a revolution in a great many different lines of locomotion. If the method could be applied on a bridge, it could also be applied on the elevated railways, the noise of which, in certain sections of the city, is almost unbearable, and on summer nights must be an element of torture to a great many thousand people. Its importance where railway tracks are carried on elevated structures through the cities is also evident ; and it opens the way to the consideration of the elimination of noise as a practical and attainable result. It will be a great blessing when inventive genius is applied specifically to the reduction of noises ; for it will remove one of the most irritating and depressing of the many discomforts that diminish the joy and healthfulness of modern life.

❈

# A New Leader

Seldom has a gubernatorial or even Presidential message been so freighted with promise to American democracy as that which was sent last week to the Legislature of New York. By it Governor Hughes has made it clear that he is to be one of the leaders in that democratic movement of which Mr. Roosevelt is conspicuously the chief.

Governor Hughes's recommendations may be grouped under three general heads, which may be named, respectively, elections, corporations, and social welfare.

Concerning elections, his recommendations are in favor of measures which he believes will make the machinery of government a more sensitive instrument of popular rule. They are, briefly, that the courts be empowered, not only to authorize quo warranto proceedings to test title to office (a power now in the hands of the Attorney-General), but also in its discretion to order a recount ; that the present form of ballot, with party columns, be abolished, and a better form of ballot (which he describes) be substituted for it ; that the courts be empowered to review the action of State party conventions, and in their discretion correct such action, so as to prevent corrupt minorities from controlling the party organizations ; that the present law be amended so that any general committee of a party may make a trial of direct nominations instead of nominations by convention.

Concerning corporations, his recommendations are practically confined to the regulation of public service companies, and are in favor of measures which will more effectively bring them under public control. They are, briefly, that the present Board of Railroad Commissioners, which is inadequate, and the Commission of Gas and Electricity, with broad powers over gas and electric light and power companies, be abolished ; that in their place a new Commission be constituted to regulate and supervise the corporations now subject to the present Commissions; that the Board of Rapid Transit Commissioners, which supervises the New York City subways, be also abolished, and that in its place a new Commission, similar to the one he recommends for the State generally, be created, to have charge of gas, electric, and transportation companies within the city and immediate vicinity; that both Commissions be State Commissions, but that the acts of the latter be subject to the approval of the chief municipal body—the Board of Estimate and Apportionment.

Concerning social welfare, his recommendations are for a larger field of State supervision and assistance: agricultural labor, good roads, the labor department, child labor, pure food, etc., all receive attention.

Although there is in this Message no trace of political philosophizing, yet out of it one can readily frame an intelligible political philosophy. It might be framed thus: The machinery of government should be so constructed that the people may be able to understand public issues without being confused by the introduction of minor and irrelevant personal or party questions; that they may be able themselves to choose the men they wish to have as their representatives; that they may be able to record their decisions securely without fear of having their action nullified; and that they may be able to see their will incorporated into law. The government, made thus responsive to the people, should be sovereign over all its creatures; should exercise efficiently its mastery over all corporations and institutions, no matter how rich and powerful, not destroying them, but rather requiring them to serve the whole people. The government, so constructed and empowered, should be free not merely to act as policeman, but to promote industry, economic freedom, and happiness, and in fact to do anything which the people jointly can do better than any private concern. This view of government is not shared by the individualist who wishes to reduce government to a minimum, to rely upon the common law for justice and upon "natural laws," whatever they may be, for economic welfare. It is not shared by the Socialist, who would reconstruct society so that it might direct practically all human activities. It is shared, however, by a seemingly increasing number of Americans. It bears no party name or factional title, except that it has sometimes been called Roosevelt Republicanism; it has been assailed in vain on the one side by Mr. Parker and on the other by Mr. Bryan; during the recent years when it has prevailed it has been stamping a new character upon American democracy. We do not say it has been consciously adopted by Mr. Hughes; but it is the view which his recommendations have materially confirmed and strengthened. In the development of public opinion Mr. Hughes has thus, will he, nill he, made himself a leader.

Mr. Hughes has done more; he has become a leader, not merely of public opinion, but also in practical statesmanship. As we have said, there is no philosophizing in his Message; neither is there exhortation. Mr. Roosevelt has, with great effectiveness, used the Message as a sermon; Mr. Hughes, on the other hand, has made of his Message almost a schedule of desirable legislation. He even goes so far as to recommend a law for a recount of the votes of the last Mayoralty election in New York City, and thus exhibits the shrewdness of the honest man, which always makes the wisdom of the small politician seem as foolishness. Whether this and other particular measures which he recommends are advisable is another matter; the point is that he recognizes definite needs and urges the enactment of definite laws. Instead of recommending a general reform of the ballot, he distinctly advocates the adoption of that form of ballot "in which the names of the candidates for the respective offices appear but once grouped under the names of the offices." Instead of recommending vaguely governmental regulation of public service corporations, he urges the abolition of present boards of commissioners, and advocates the creation of other boards of a definitely described character. Instead of recommending undefined labor laws, he specifies how he would have the Legislature improve the Department of Labor and restrict the employment of children. He has not made a contribution to the abstract discussion of public questions; he has rather told the people and their legislators what he believes they are now called upon to achieve.

When he was elected, Mr. Hughes was known as a wholesale hater of iniquities, a keen inquisitor of shams and frauds, a friend of justice even when it was unpopular, a man high in integrity, sharp of wit, and capable of an incredible amount of work. Although he was known to be a Republican of the Roosevelt school, he had never held public office and had had no political experience. Most of his supporters, we believe, were satisfied to have elected an honest, aggressive, able man as Governor, and did not expect him to be a leader in a democratic movement. During his campaign he gave on the stump little evidence that he could or would be such a leader. He was busily engaged in another task—that of discrediting a political quack. How effectively he did his work the election figures have dramatically told. Now, confronting the task of directing the policies of a State, he has taken it up, not as the almost academic investigator, not as the merciless debater with an unscrupulous adversary, but as the constructive statesman. The people of New York State now know, what a few foresaw, that the man in the Governor's chair is to be a leader of the forces of real democracy.

❁

## Church and State

It is not a mere coincidence that the English people are making a determined attempt to free national education from ecclesiastical control; that the Emperor of Germany has dissolved the Reichstag in order to put an end to the dictation of the Clerical party in the Reichstag; that the Spanish Government has inaugurated a policy which can end only in the separation of Church and State in that country; and that the French people, with singular unanimity, have regis-

tered their determination that the union between the State and the churches of all kinds shall cease and that education throughout France, so far as it is possible, shall be secular. These are different phases of a movement which began with the Reformation, and which will not end until Church and State are everywhere entirely dissociated. This movement may mean, in the intention of some of its supporters, and in the apprehension of many of its opposers, the final separation of religion and government; it means, in the judgment of The Outlook, the drawing of a hard and fast line between politics and ecclesiasticism. It means ultimately the freedom of the Church; for the attempt of the Church, in various countries under various names, to exercise direct political control has done more to put the Church into chains, hamper its growth, check its influence, and dry up its power at the source than any other single condition which Christianity has faced since it began its westward march. This movement, though it may have an anti-religious appearance, is a manifestation of the deeper and broader religious spirit of modern times, and will result in a victory for religion rather than for secularism. The Church as an organization, in this country as in so many others, has lingered behind the Church as spiritually conceived by those of its members who in every generation are leading the way to a larger and nobler thought of the Incarnation and of the kingdom of God among men.

It is because of this spiritual conception of religion as opposed to a purely ecclesiastical conception that the majority of Englishmen of many faiths and creeds are determined that in English schools the dogma of no special Church shall be taught. It is not only the Nonconformist who is in revolt against the authority of the Established Church in English schools; it is also a large body of English Churchmen. When John Bright, years ago, took a distinguished American Bishop of the Episcopal Church into the House of Lords and semi-humorously shook his fist at the bench of Bishops, the American Bishop said to him, "I agree with you. They ought not to be there; their influence ought to be exerted in other ways." For this reason, and because the Established Church is becoming more and more penetrated with a sense of the impossibility of keeping the Church in organic relation with the Government, disestablishment, though ·it may be long deferred, will ultimately come. And it will be welcomed alike by the sacramentarian who revolts, as did the leaders of the Oxford Movement, from the control of the Church of God by any group of statesmen, however eminent; by evangelical Churchmen to whom the Church is above all an organized religious experience, and by the Broad Churchmen to whom the Church is a divine influence penetrating society from all sides through spiritual channels. When the Church of England is detached from the Government of England, it will become for the first time a free Church, and after a brief period of readjustment it will secure a spiritual authority which it has not possessed since the Reformation.

In Germany an electoral campaign is now in progress which turns, not upon the question of the policy of the Government in southwestern Africa, but on the great influence which the Clerical party has secured in the National Legislature. There is a very widespread protest against the policy in West and Southwest Africa, which has enormously increased the cost of the conduct of war during the last year. The Clericals in the Reichstag,, who · have hitherto been supporters of the Government, joined with the Socialists and defeated the appropriation for which the Emperor ·asked. The Emperor, who, in spite of some obvious mistakes, is an adroit politician as well as a statesman, has pushed aside this issue, and the campaign turns on the antagonism on the question of clerical rule. The fact that the Clericals have been willing to cast in their lot with the Socialists, whom they regard with abhorrence and terror, is looked upon as an indication of their willingness to work with any party and use any means to secure their own ends. It is not, the Government urges, a political party which it is fighting, but a group of sectarians representing less than one-third of the people of the Empire, attempting to dictate ,its internal and external policy. The phrase, " The political tyranny of the Ultramontanes has become intolerable," used by one of the National Liberal leaders lately, expresses what appears to be the sentiment of the German nation as a whole. What is called the " Rouge et Noir " combination—the union of the black and the red—has brought the nation face to face with a situation with which Bismarck was supposed to have dealt finally.

Spain has long been one of the centers of the Ultramontane element in the Roman Catholic Church ; a country in which there have been, as in every country, very noble examples of Christian effort and courage among the clergy, but in which there have been developed some of the most reactionary types of thought and policy within the Roman Catholic Church. The fact that the reactionary type has had, on the whole, the predominant influence explains the sharpness of the reaction which has brought into being in Spain, as in Italy, a group of the most radical Socialists and the most uncompromising Anarchists. Here, as in England, the educational question has come to the front, and the pressing necessity of enlarging the work and improving the quality of the public schools is generally felt. Between five and six thousand monks are engaged in the work of teaching Spanish children ; and the fact that there are in that country between three and four thousand monastic foundations has put into the hands of the Liberals a very strong argument, if not a positive grievance ; for the population of Spain is only about nineteen millions. The present Ministry, under the leadership of the Prime Minister, Dominguez, has adopted the policy of extending the action of the law passed in 1902, which provided for the civil control of religious associations in the general direction taken by the recently adopted French law ; the recognition of civil marriage as legal, whether accompanied by a religious ceremony or not, and the extension of municipal control over cemeteries. These are the preliminary steps in a movement for the separation of Church and State in Spain ; a measure which, in the judgment of many of the best men of all parties, will be even more beneficial to the Church than to the State.

The Outlook has given large space to the situation in France, because everything which the French do on a large scale is done dramatically, because of the intrinsic significance and importance to the country of the contest between the French Government and the Vatican, and because the general significance of what is happening in France is part of the larger movement that has embraced all western Europe, with the exception of Austria-Hungary. The account of recent happenings in Paris, prepared for The Outlook by M. Charles Wagner, which appears in another place, is significant as coming from the hand of a man who, although not a Catholic, is one of the most ardently and effectively religious men in the France of to-day. There, as in England and Spain, the immediate occasion of the struggle has been the endeavor to take education out of the hands of ecclesiastics and nationalize it. Beneath all subsidiary issues, and below all the confusion and irritability incident upon so vast a struggle, the French people, with extraordinary unanimity, annulled the Concordat with the Roman Catholic Church and have detached the State from association with all religious bodies. It is not the Roman Catholic Church as a Church that France, Germany, and Spain oppose ; it is not the Pope as the spiritual head of a church: it is rather the Vatican, which stands for a political policy and for what remains of the old union of Church and State throughout Europe. Nearly all the great mistakes of the Roman Catholic Church, its defects and disasters, have been due to its attempt to combine the functions of a spiritual society with those of a political organization. When the process which has been going on since before the Reformation is accomplished, and the Roman Catholic Church ceases to be identified with political organizations and to take part in party politics, it will enter upon a stage of influence and power which are likely to surpass anything that it has attained in those periods when its power was almost unassailable. Those who recognize, as

The Outlook does, its immense service to religion and to civilization, and who recognize also the great part which it plays and is to play in the religious and moral life of the modern world, will welcome even revolution, if through revolution the religious energy and power of the Catholic Church can be liberated to do purely religious work. The French people have acted not only for the State but for the Church in annulling the Concordat, in nationalizing education, in putting Church property under the laws of the State as it is in this country. They will make a great mistake if they attempt in any way to control or direct the form and manner of worship. Painful as the experience is for the Catholic Church with its traditions and the reverence with which it regards its places of worship and its religious houses, The Outlook believes, as a vast number of Catholics believe, that any movement which will take the Church finally out of political life, and conserve all its energies for its work, will bring untold blessings to it and to the world.

❀

## The Next Step

Several years ago, on a pleasant morning, a number of Americans were seated in a compartment in a train approaching the quaint old town of Nuremberg. Two of them were girls recently graduated from college and in the earlier stages of intense, eager American anxiety for knowledge. There happened to be a young Austrian in the same compartment ; when the train drew up at the station of a beautiful little village, suggestive of those walks through the woods which are one of the great resources of Germany, another train came down on the opposite side of the platform and poured out a crowd of people from Nuremberg. One of the American girls, on the *qui vive* every minute to observe and understand, turned to the young Austrian and said, " What goes on here ?" He answered quietly, " Nature."

Both the question and the answer were significant, the one of the prevalent American feeling that general interest is inexplicable from any other standpoint except that of some kind of action; the other, of the trained capacity of the German quietly to receive and deeply enjoy all forms of life and art within his reach. In Germany, as in many other parts of Europe, recreation, diversion, and pleasure are within the means of the poorest people at almost no expense of time, exertion, or money. Lovely views are made accessible at strategic points for observation; food and drink are to be had at the most moderate cost; the art of enjoyment is fostered and developed, and every arrangement is made to bring beauty and rest to the very doors of the humblest. Few things impress an American who gets out of the beaten highways of travel abroad more deeply than the capacity of people of all classes for simple pleasure; the obvious delight they find in the most inexpensive and humble amusements, their power of relaxation, of surrendering themselves without effort to the quiet, the beauty, and the repose of a stretch of trees or a bit of meadow. At certain hours on a summer day the roads in the Bois de Boulogne are thronged with carriages, and in the season the observer who likes to watch the procession of vehicles and persons goes there to see "the world go by," as he sits in front of the Café de Paris for the same purpose. But the happiest part of that world is not to be found in the moving mass of vehicles of all sorts and kinds, but under the trees, where numberless parties of men, women, and children, coming from the poorer sections of the city, are quietly lunching or playing games, or having an hour of talk in the heat of the day.

On the other hand, few things strike foreigners more forcibly in this country than the great expense of pleasure of all kinds, the distances which people have to go, the cost of transportation, the high price of admission to shows and spectacles, and the comparatively large cost for a very little and very often for very poor food. It is almost impossible to take a little excursion from any of our great cities without making an appreciable break in a five-dollar bill, even if one goes in the most modest way; and the country, as a whole, still remains uncharted and without paths, so far as access to commanding positions and beautiful views and lovely places of quiet are concerned.

We have in a way conquered the continent as the Romans conquered the Greeks, but the continent has taken its revenge, as the Greeks took their revenge on the Romans, by subjugating us. It has exacted so much toil that it has almost paralyzed our power of receiving pleasure from it. This statement is not inconsistent with the other statements, so often and so truthfully made, that the love of out-of-doors and the art of out-of-door living are steadily gaining ground among Americans. Every form of active, energetic life is steadily making progress; but there is another side of life which is still largely undeveloped. Men live quite as much by what they receive as by what they give, rest comes from repose rather than from action, and enrichment from opening the mind and heart to all the benignant and fruitful influences that flow from earth and sky. It is the power of passive enjoyment that Americans have still to develop, that capacity which lay behind the young Austrian's answer. In order to have pleasure and to be content, Americans, as a rule, must go where something "goes on." They are not satisfied and content to be with nature; to surrender themselves to the influences of a quiet hour and a secluded place. They are learning, with characteristic American energy, the names of the trees, the shrubs, the flowers, and the birds. One meets them tramping through the woods in every direction with popular handbooks under their arms, intent on being able to name everything in sight; but it remains true of a great many of these excellent people, who are doing an excellent thing if they do it in the right way, that they are not becoming acquainted with nature by this process, any more than they would become acquainted with flowers by learning their botanical names and the scientific method of analyzing them. The ability to name the animals, the trees, and the flowers adds greatly to the pleasure of out-of-door life, but it does not give us access to the heart of

the world. A man must know how to
let himself lie fallow, to empty himself,
so to speak, of his ambitions and energies, in order that nature may take
possession of him, to hear the birds sing
for the joy of it, as the lover of Shakespeare reads the play, not for the sake
of being able to give an exact scientific
description either of the song or of the
poem. We have conquered nature; it
is time now to win her confidence. As
she has helped · us with her colossal
energies, she stands ready to heal us
with those deep, vital, tranquillizing
currents in which her life flows.

●

# Railway Massacres

Last week, in two railway wrecks, sick-
ening in their horror, a hundred persons
were killed and many more were injured.
During the past fiscal year nearly ten
thousand people were killed in American
railway accidents and over eighty-six
thousand injured. These appalling totals
remind us that in regulating transportation there is an elemental governmental
duty, more insistent than that of freight-
rate supervision.

The financiers who control our railways seem to want, first, to get immediate cash returns from a particular property, and only secondly permanently to
equip that property. Their spirit of
gain has naturally been copied by the
actual physical operators of the property.
A callousness to the demands of humanity
sometimes results, as shown, for instance,
by this despatch in the New York Sun
concerning last week's fatal accident on
the Baltimore and Ohio road:

> The Coroner succeeded in getting from
> Chief Train Despatcher Dent the admission
> that orders had been given to allow a regular
> express train to pass by the scene of the
> wreck after the track had been cleared,
> before the relief train sent to bring in the
> dead was allowed to proceed. The relief
> train was thus delayed thirteen minutes. The
> object of the Coroner was to show that the
> railroad had had greater concern for the
> movement of its trains on schedule time
> than for bringing in the dead killed on its line.

Our railway disasters may be attributable to (1) the unreasonableness of the
hours of work required from railway
employees, and (2) the inadequacy of
present safety appliances.

As an example of the first cause, the
terrible destruction of life on the Rock
Island Railway in Kansas last week was
due to a wrong signal given by an
eighteen-year-old telegraph operator who
had been too long on - duty. We frequently hear stories of signalmen on
duty for twelve hours, and of engineers
under continuous strain even up to sixteen hours, and then with but inadequate
rest before their next runs. In one of
the reports of the Baltimore and Ohio
disaster we read:

> Commissioner Clements again questioned
> the engineer and his fireman, McClelland,
> closely on the subject of the amount of sleep
> they had had before beginning the run from
> Cumberland to Washington. It was brought
> out that they had both been on duty for
> forty-eight hours, with two intervals of four
> hours each for sleep. •

President Roosevelt's humane recommendation in his annual Messages on
this subject is now receiving deserved
attention in Congress: a bill to limit the
hours of railway employees is about
to be voted on by the Senate. Since
public attention has now been dramatically directed to this reform, one
would think that its principle, at least,
should be established by a unanimous
vote. Certainly the necessity for government regulation of inter-State railways, under the commerce clause of the
Constitution, has never been so evident.

But granted that the hours of railway
employees' service are to be reasonably
limited, there still remains the menacing
and more formidable second cause of
railway accidents, the inadequacy of
safety appliances. It has been said that
block signals, scrupulously followed, are
good enough. But they never will be
scrupulously followed, even by that road
which has just reported over sixteen
hundred search tests with not a single
failure, the penalty of dismissal attaching to any failure. However admirable these conditions of preparation, the
human factor, in actual attention to
signals, will remain human, exposed to
sudden ills or sicknesses or frailties in-
capacitating an engineer or operator
from duty. What then? Is a trainload
of precious human life always to be at

the mercy of one man ? In the Southern Railway disaster a month ago, in which the lamented Samuel Spencer lost his life, the company had furnished its road with the manual telegraph block signal system, but if its signal operators could not guard their own president, what chance have the road's patrons ? In last week's accident on the Baltimore and Ohio the road was also equipped with the block system, but the engineer could not see the light on account of a dense fog.

Though only twenty-two per cent. of our railways are protected by any block signal system, and less than five per cent. by an automatic device, the block system has done much to save life. But it does not go far enough. Its signal and switching appliances may either fall into neglect or those who work them may inadvertently or willfully allow more than one train on a single block. Indeed, a prominent authority declares that this has become a custom on our roads ! As long as railway companies give more attention to dividends and increased values of stock than they do to safe operation and the protection of their patrons' lives, just so long will there be indisposition to make use of the latest engineering discoveries and of the most expensive methods of operation which are independent of the human factor and its inevitable frailties. Such an up-to-date method is already in operation on the Boston and New York City subways. It should be applied, as far as weather conditions permit, to our trunk lines. The apparatus in question comprises an automatic block system of the type adopted by the Pennsylvania and a number of other railways, but with the addition of a short inclined plane alongside the track at the entrance to the block. This is interlocked by the mechanism which lights the red lamp at the entrance to the block whenever it is occupied by a train. The plane, when raised, touches a lever which depends from the second train, and this lever in turn applies the air-brake, bringing the second train to a standstill. Hence an engineer cannot run past the danger signal. This device is reported to be perfectly successful in operation, and is regarded as an absolute protection against the admission of a second train to the block already occupied.

Thus most of our railway accidents are preventable, since they are due to over-hours, or to inadequate appliances. Concerning the first cause, Congress, as noted above, is about to act, and concerning the second, Congress has acted. Under a resolution passed by it some time ago the Inter-State Commerce Commission has instituted, we are glad to say, an investigation of safety appliances in general and now particularly as to their working in the most recent disasters. In addition, a resolution has been introduced in Congress calling for an enlargement of the Commission's powers. Those powers should include, as they do in England, that of official investigation of all railway accidents, of adjudgment of responsibility for them, and of authority to order the installation of the best safety appliances. Whether we arrive at these results through the Commission or by the establishment of a special bureau in the Department of Commerce is a matter for debate. But debate ought no longer to be tolerated as to whether Congress has the right to exercise such supervision over American railways as shall make them at least as safe for travelers as the railways of the other civilized countries of the world.

# Through Man to God

In the title of his last volume, "Through Man to God," Dr. George A. Gordon indicates the change in the method of approach to God which distinguishes the new thinking. The Calvinistic theology proceeded in the opposite direction—from God to man. Its starting-point was a group of *a priori* assumptions respecting God—as that he is infinite in justice, purity, and truth, that he is omniscient, omnipresent, and omnipotent, that he is the absolute and unconditioned Sovereign of the universe. These assumptions being made, the Scripture was sought for proof texts to substantiate them ; but this was still from God to man, because the Bible was assumed to be, not the record of man's partial and imperfect experience of God, but the record of God's complete and perfect disclosure of himself to man. The gulf between God thus conceived and man as seen in actual life is enormous. To account for this gulf the doctrine of the Fall was conceived to be necessary; to bridge this gulf, certain views of revelation, miracles, atonement, mediatorship, were thought to be equally necessary.

Five converging lines of thought have brought about a radically different process of thought. Agnosticism has shaken, if it has not destroyed, the old *a priori* conceptions of God. Biblical criticism has changed the popular conception of the Bible. Anthropology has negatived the notion of a cataclysmic Fall. Evolution has traced man's gradual rise from a lower order of animal creation, and has measured humanity, not by an idealized picture of his early state of innocence, but by a scientific prevision of the goal toward which he is traveling. Depravity is no longer regarded as natural; it is religion and virtue that are natural; depravity is unnatural, contra-natural. Finally, for a search of the Bible for proof texts to sustain *a priori* theological assumptions has been substituted a study of the Bible as a collection of laws, history, and literature, especially a study of the earthly life of Jesus of Nazareth as it is recorded in the Gospels. The students, conducting their study from various points of view—the agnostic, the romantic, the Protestant, the Roman Catholic, the Jewish—have yet agreed in seeking to know exactly what that human, earthly life was, and in their conclusion that it was a life unique in the world's biographies. Dr. Gordon's description of Jesus may stand here as a statement, pictorially presented in exquisite miniature, of this conclusion on which substantially agree the world's students of every variety of faith and temperament :

Look at Jesus. Consider him simply as the perfect man. There is no higher name than that. The language of the creeds seems unreal in the presence of his spotless and sublime humanity. We gain one or two glimpses of his childhood, and how full of wonder and beauty it is! We have one clear glance into his boyhood, and we mark the thirst for knowledge, the reverence for authority, the flow of deep questions, and the high spirit that fill it with grace and -

charm. When we see him again, he has become a man, he has risen into the consciousness of his Father in heaven, into the consciousness of his Sonhood to God. We see him at the Jordan, accepting baptism as the sign of the new world that has risen into clearness in his soul. We follow him into the wilderness, and watch him under his great temptation. In trial he is so patient, so strong; and out of trial he comes so pure and mighty. We hear his teaching, we listen to his parables, we go with him in his errands of mercy, and try to count his countless acts of compassion and healing. We retire with him for prayer, we come again with him to the solemn business of living. We keep close to him while the great misunderstanding concerning him grows blacker and blacker, we are with him in the heart of the awful tragedy. We watch the supremely good, apprehended, tried, condemned, and crucified as the supremely bad, and in it all we behold comprehension so clear, pity so absolute, strength so victorious. This is man at his highest; this is our humanity carried to its best. This is the glory of human history. Nothing is wanting here that the wise and noble mind can ask for; everything is here that should be present in human character. And it is this perfect human reality that gives to Jesus Christ his unique influence over men, that lends to his character its endless interest for men. You may call him divine or semi-divine, God or the Son of God ; these are names, significant for some, insignificant for others. What you must note is that the sovereign soul of Jesus is his humanity; that is the reality, that is the truth of his being. Human nature, the greatest thing that we know, becomes in him the highest and best.

These concurring currents of thought, co-operating throughout the past century, have not merely changed theological opinions on certain doctrines ; they have not merely modified special articles in the ancient creeds ; they have not merely modified the point of view of the student—they have changed the method of approach to God. We no longer ask ourselves what God must be supposed to be, and deduce our conclusions concerning his dealing with men from such presuppositions. We ask ourselves, What is man ? we answer that question by asking another, What is the ideal of humanity toward which man is growing? and to that question we find our answer in the life and character of Jesus of Nazareth. Through this study, first of humanity as it is, next as it aspires to be, and last of all as it is exhibited in the realized ideal of humanity portrayed in the life of Jesus of Nazareth, we find our way to God. And this method gives us a fundamentally different conception of God from that furnished by the *a priori* conceptions of the old theology.

The skeptic may say that this method is also based upon a presupposition; that the faith that we are to find the likeness of God in ideal humanity is founded on the assumption that ideal humanity is made in the likeness of God. If religion were merely curiosity looking for an explanation of the riddle of the universe, this would be a just criticism. But it is not. Religion is aspiration looking for a model of character, and reverence looking for an object of worship. Neither is to be found in nature. The wind, the earthquake, and the fire may awake our awe, but never our reverence nor our love. These look for ideals to follow and objects to worship in the statesman creating a nation, in the patriot giving his life to its preservation, in the martyr scattering the seeds of a new revealing of truth through the ashes of his martyrdom, in the mother laying down her life in unrecognized service to her child; and back of all such deeds of heroism, and the type of them all, reverence and love find an ideal to follow and an object to reverence in the life of Jesus of Nazareth, and in the after-life of Jesus the Christ, manifested in the Christly lives of thousands who call themselves by his name and of other thousands who follow him without knowing that they do so; and back even of him and of the humanity he has inspired, inspiring their common life and guiding them to a common end, reverence and love dimly perceive the Spirit of purity and goodness and truth, and find in this figure, dimly as they perceive it, undefined and even undefinable though it be, the object of their quest, the One, interpreted to them by the life of idealized humanity but greater than all humanity, interpreted to them by Jesus Christ, the supreme object they have sought. Reverence and love have found God. And the evidence that they have found him is a mystic experience of his fellowship which they are powerless to impart to the unrevering intellect and which the unrevering intellect is equally powerless

to take away from worshiping reverence and love.

The Church to-day needs theologians who, frankly accepting this Biblical method of approach to God—for the method of the Hebrew people was always "through man to God"—and frankly discarding as theological material, without attacking, those creeds which were arrived at by a very different method, will interpret what may be known of God and his ways in a humanized theology. And it needs even more an apostolic ministry who, in the same spirit of frankness, will help humanity in this philanthropic age to find ideals for its life and an object for its worship through a humanized religion— a religion which will treat the spirit of humanity, not as a rival of religion, but as a teacher of religion and the guide of the soul "through man to God."

❀

# The Spectator

A third-class carriage in Switzerland is apt to be an international affair. When it is a carriage that is going on a pilgrimage to Einsiedeln, the "Swiss Mecca," it becomes a still more interesting epitome of mankind. The Spectator sat beside a white-haired peasant woman, brown and wrinkled and wholesome, and opposite him a voluble workingman, with a dog in his arms and a cage of birds in the rack above his head, was explaining to a stolid German, in a mixture of Italian and Swiss, how his pets disliked traveling. A pretty French-woman and her husband were in another seat with a couple of priests, and two peasant girls with quaint head-dresses were in a third. At the last moment, with a rush and clang, in trooped half a dozen soldiers, with guns and knapsacks, apparently off duty and somewhat exhilarated with beer. The birds in the cage twittered with fear; the dog barked; and altogether it was an animated scene, and reminded the Spectator of

"Kits, cats, sacks, and wives,
How many were going to St. Ives?"

❀

Certainly there was no more austerity about this part of the pilgrimage than the

Canterbury Pilgrims showed in Chaucer's day. One soldier produced a mouth-organ, and two others executed a jig in the aisle, while the old peasant woman smiled and nodded at them. The Spectator regretted his ignorance of patois, for a broad-shouldered, fair-haired young soldier entered into conversation loudly with the whole carriage, eliciting shouts of laughter. The Swiss soldier is for-ever associated with heroics and the Lion of Lucerne in the tourist's mind, but he appears to be a very simple, easy-going, and popular person in every-day life; and the two peasant girls ob-viously set their queer, wide-winged caps at him, and giggled tremendously at his evidently ardent compliments.

❀

If the train was crowded, Einsiedeln was more so. It was dark when the little mountain town, among its forested hills, was reached, but lights were mov-ing everywhere, and a band was playing in the great square in front of the abbey that dominates the place from its central height. Mine host of the Peacock had no rooms empty, though he boasts a hundred of them; but he had arranged with various outside lodgings to take the overflow, and the Spectator found himself in a tiny whitewashed chamber, with a bare floor, monumental feather bed, and a pitcher and basin the size of a teacup and saucer. The schedule of services for next day—the great pilgrim-age day of the year—hung on the door. Mass at half-past four A.M. began the list; but the Spectator mentally decided that he would not commence his devo-tions till later.

❀

However, he waked in time for it. Einsiedeln sees to that. The heavy clang of the abbey bells, so big and so close over the houses that they sounded as if on the very roof, would have waked the Seven Sleepers, even if not reinforced by the guns that were set off every two or three minutes for at least a quarter of an hour. The sound of hurrying feet began in the streets. All Einsiedeln was going to early mass. Thousands of pil-grims, with candles and without, were climbing the steep ascent to the great

3 A

church, answering the call of the insistent and persistent bells. The Spectator felt himself a renegade, but the morning was cold and the feather bed warm; and, besides, there were five more stated services that day. So he went to the half-past nine sermon instead, and was properly rewarded for his laziness, since the sermon was an hour long, and in German-Swiss, entirely beyond his com-prehension. The great church was so packed with men, women, and children that one could have walked on their heads. Some were French, some Italian; there were men with earrings in their ears, and girls in folded yellow kerchiefs on their braided hair, or bareheaded, with silver pins artistically stuck through the coils of their tresses. There were old and young, rich and poor—an extra-ordinary throng, but all serious and rev-erent, and nearly all armed with prayer-books and rosaries, which those who did not understand the sermon, like the Spectator, were diligently using in order to improve the moments.

❀

The Spectator had no such aids to independent devotion, so he slipped in and out through the crowd as he could, and barely managed, in the one hour of the sermon, to get from one end of the nave to the other, so dense was the crush. Einsiedeln has been a pilgrim center for over a thousand years, and consequently knows its business. The monks have handled these vast throngs of various nationalities so long that their system could hardly be improved upon. The great abbey church, to begin with, is full of gilding, frescoes, statuary, chapels, and shrines. It is one of the worst and most gaudy of eighteenth-cen-tury interiors, but its spaces are impress-ive and its great organ fine, and it lends itself to a continuous performance, so to speak, where all comers can find some-thing to suit them. While the preacher was haranguing an hour on end from a solid gilt pulpit with a flaring clock dial just over his head (a very good idea, indeed), a continuous mass was going on in the " Engelweihe " chapel, the original cell of St. Meinrad the hermit, which is built into one end of the nave very much as the Portiuncula of St. Francis has been preserved at Assisi. St. Meinrad flourished in 861 A.D., when the abbey hill was part of the " Dark Forest " of Einsiedeln. The son of a prince, he became a holy man of renown, and was murdered in his cell by two criminals whom he had befriended. They were followed, as they fled, by two ravens whom Meinrad had rescued from a hawk, and were pursued by the birds through the forest, and to a town where they were captured and executed for their crime. The shield of the abbey bears the two ravens, and the cell of the saint, now sheathed in stone, has become the nucleus of the abbey and town. It was dedicated, so the legend goes, by a company of angels—hence its name of *Engelweihe;* and it contains a wonder-working image of the Madonna and Child, as black as a coal, but clad in the stiffest cloth of gold, richly jeweled. A row of five silver lamps given by emperors and princes used to burn before this image, and sixteen silver candlesticks, one for each Swiss Catholic canton, stood on the altar. But Einsiedeln has been despoiled and restored over and over again in its long history, and these ancient things have vanished during the storms of war and politics, and are replaced by a great deal of copper-gilt bravery, red and white roses with gilt leaves, and electric lamps.

❀

Here, all morning long, the mass went on, one gorgeously robed priest succeeding another without a moment's cessation. A kneeling, praying crowd was twenty deep in front of it all the while. One pilgrim out of twenty carried a camp-stool, but the rest asked for no such luxury. At the smaller chapels lining the whole long nave, companies knelt and recited prayers together in French, Italian, and German, passing from one chapel to another. Then, as soon as the sermon was over, high mass began with the full choir and organ for which Einsiedeln is justly celebrated. The Spectator went off to lunch, and came back to find processions with robed choirs entering the chapel of St. Meinrad and singing the Salve Regina, kneeling, before the sacred image. After

that another sermon began. It had been raining in the morning; but now the sun shone, and the monks, some of them, were leading a procession of French pilgrims up the wooded hills to a cross half-way above the valley, singing as they went. It was all extraordinarily serious, reverent, devotional, emotional, and picturesque.

❀

But the great climax was in the evening—a dark, starless, chilly one, in which all the warmth and life seemed to radiate from the great church above, brilliantly lit, with wide-open doors, and with a double file of soldiery outlining a path down to the market-place. There a great platform, like a gigantic altar, hung with hundreds of tiny blazing lamps, faced the church, and down the stones to it came the last long procession of the pilgrims, each bearing a candle. There were young girls, all in white, with crowns of white roses; there were ranks of nuns, black-robed and white-coifed; there were priests and choir, dignitaries and bishop, and the Host borne under a canopy. Out in the night, under the flaring lights, a service was sung and chanted; and as the bishop lifted the Host, the whole throng fell on their knees on the stones, and there was a moment of awed and reverent stillness. Then the responses broke out afresh from the choir, the band joined in, the bishop and the rest marched up under the canopy, the pilgrim thousands crowded into the church doors again, almost sweeping away the lines of soldiers in their enthusiasm, and service, chant, and choral began again around the chapel of Meinrad, till at ten o'clock the Spectator left them still singing and came away. Down on the square a few pilgrims were drinking from the Virgin's fountain, going round from one to the other of its fourteen bronze spouts, as their custom is. The big bells were ringing yet, as they had rung practically all day long. They were the last sound the Spectator heard as he went to sleep, and they remain in his memory as the emblem of Einsiedeln's continual call.to the pilgrim, which has not failed for a thousand years.

# Rome Against the Republic

## By Charles Wagner

*When, a month ago, the conflict between Church and State in France came to an acute crisis, The Outlook by cable requested M. Wagner to furnish its readers with an account of the events of that crisis, and an interpretation of their meaning. The reply is the following article, which is, in our judgment, of world-wide interest because it presents the situation from the point of view of a patriotic Frenchman of high ideals and religious principles, who is not personally committed to either extreme in this struggle. Readers of The Outlook hardly need an introduction to the author of the article, who has contributed more than once to its pages. It will be remembered that M. Wagner, the author of " Youth," " The Simple Life," and other books that have left an impress upon this generation, is a Liberal Protestant pastor, and has participated in many enterprises for social and moral improvement without regard to sectarian questions.—THE EDITORS.*

WE had sincerely hoped—we Frenchmen of pacific tendencies who desire for every human being a place of his own under the sun of liberty—that the conflict between Church and State would terminate amicably. But the die is cast. War is declared. Not only is it declared, but hostilities have commenced. " We were not willing," said our Premier, M. Clemenceau, addressing an adversary, " we were not willing that you should fire the first shot." This first shot was the expulsion from French territory of Monsignor Montagnini di Mirabello, official delegate of the Pope.

Let us review here the first week of a fierce struggle whose consequences will long be felt. Before doing so, however, we shall find it of use, in gaining a clear comprehension of the circumstances, to supplement this review by a few reflections.

For several years the sectarian politicians of the Extreme Left had demanded the rupture of the Concordat. But wise Republicans felt that the hour for this had not yet come. We could, indeed, have lived for a long time still under the old régime had not Pope Pius X. raised such a protest as he did against the visit of President Loubet to the King of Italy— that famous protest with which the public is familiar. This tactless proceeding excited to indignation the entire democracy of France. Adroitly profiting by the situation, the Extreme Left demanded immediate separation. Rough drafts of laws were drawn up, but they were so drastic that public opinion remained unfavorable to them. An impulse toward Liberalism made itself felt in Parliament and through the entire country. Then the labor and travail of just minds bore fruit at last in the law of M. Briand. Through his policy, from which proceeded the main influence of the laical element, the law was made conformable to the spirit of the primitive Church, as well as to that of modern democracy. But it struck at the hierarchical philosophy of the Roman Church. The Vatican received it unfavorably. Our Catholic politicians, fiercely inimical to the democracy, encouraged resistance by spreading the report that the mass of French people were not in sympathy with the law. But the memorable elections of May 6, 1906, gave a formidable blow to the clerical and monarchical reaction. The Governmental majority was increased, and the separation law received an impetus. After the national conference a noticeable change of attitude took place among fair-minded Catholics—those who are attached to their religion from motives of piety rather than because of political considerations. After examining the law more closely they concluded that its observance would

65

be acceptable. Many priests, more Christian than clerical, were of the same opinion; and the bishops were quite ready, after a demonstration against the secular spirit of the law, to adjust themselves to it. They thus established harmony between Roman dogma and their own consciences as Catholics and Frenchmen on the one side, and on the other the *modus vivendi*, which they perceived had the great merit of conciliating all parties. The Government, for its part, seemed disposed to make all concessions compatible with its dignity and with respect for the law.

The intransigeants, however, waited and watched. Their evil minds saw a way in which to foment an agitation which, except for them, would have been purely indifferent and arbitrary, concerning the question of inventories. For the Government had instituted these inventories as a guaranty to the Church of its own interests. Those of us who have talked on terms of intimacy with a large number of curés know how sorely they were distressed by the disorders excited in the churches, contrary to their wishes, by the fanatical enthusiasts inspired by reactionary politics alone. Religion was in no way menaced. Every one familiar with affairs knew that to be a fact. But if things had taken place in an orderly fashion reactionary politics would have suffered a severe check.

After protracted silence the Pope spoke. His words were an anathema worse than the first. No longer could the organization of the "associations cultuelles " be dreamed of, even though their character were disguised. Our Catholic fellow-citizens, who had learned to hope for a peaceful solution, were thunderstruck. The desire to avoid extreme measures was nevertheless so strong that ecclesiastics and laymen united in an attempt to remedy the absence of "associations cultuelles " in the strict sense of the term. By the exercise of their good will and their ingenuity they invented methods based upon the text of the law. For this text was the last sheet-anchor. Far from discouraging this zeal, our Government outdid itself in evidences of the most open and conciliatory spirit. Conditions still gave

hope that an amicable settlement would be reached. An entire year of respite was promised, in order that the Church might adjust itself as well as possible to the law. But had these arrangements been consummated, no difficulties, no scandals, no persecutions, would have resulted, and the clerical and monarchical opposition would have lost an opportunity to resume its old attacks upon the Republic. Our clericals obtained, therefore, from Rome a proclamation which was a veritable defiance of Republican France, and which necessitated a policy of aggression and rebellion against the laws of the country; so that all hope of terminating the conflict by peaceful means vanished. The 11th of December was, therefore, a notable landmark. After that day every day was characterized by events of historic moment.

Let us note day by day the salient events of which we were the sad witnesses. For it must be conceded that, except for the parties of the Extreme Right and Left, the entire country has regretted the turn affairs took.

December 10.—After the Pope had forbidden bishops and curés to submit to the law of 1881 concerning public assemblies, the Minister of Public Education and Worship and the Keeper of the Seals drew up two circulars, one to the prefects, the other to the attorney-generals. M. Briand, in his circular to the prefects, said: " Just because the Government evinces in the application of the laws of 1881 and 1905 the most liberal spirit, it intends that the laws as they now stand shall be obeyed. Their character is imperative. There are no French citizens who, under any pretext whatever, wish to place themselves above the French law and to rebel against it. It is important, therefore, that if, at the expiration of the reprieve granted December 11, public worship is performed without previous declaration, the offenses committed by the curés and officiating clergymen shall be amenable to the law. I beseech you, therefore, to give at once the instructions which are necessary, so that all offenses shall be authenticated in public reports which you will refer to the tribunals."

The circular of M. Guyot Vessaique,

Keeper of the Seals, thus admonishes the attorney-generals: "Upon examination of the public reports drawn up your deputies should give the instructions necessary for the immediate suppression of the offenses."

The infraction of the law of 1881 was made punishable by a fine of from two to five francs, and a temporary imprisonment.

December 11.—This governmental measure evoked diverse criticisms. As a general thing the people were inclined to place the entire responsibility for the non-observance of the law upon the Pope. Opinion was not favorable to the imprisonment of refractory priests, for of course all priests would be refractory and all priests, therefore, would necessarily be sent to prison. Admitting that forty thousand delinquents mean forty thousand lawsuits, the results would be very complicated and would give to fanatical priests an opportunity to deliver innumerable harangues in which they would pose as martyrs.

In the meantime three curés of Paris were prosecuted for exciting the people to revolt. These were Abbé Richard, Abbé Jouin, and Abbé Leclercs. These three priests delivered on Sunday, the 9th of December, addresses of an extreme insolence while discussing the last Papal instructions. Monsignor Montagnini was implicated in these prosecutions. The Chamber of Deputies was much agitated by his expulsion. One of the Deputies, a member of the Right, interpellated the Government on the subject, and M. Clemenceau replied to him as follows:

"What did M. Montagnini do in Paris? We were in possession of documents from which it became evident that he received daily instructions from Monsignor Merry del Val, and transmitted them to the French bishops. We had known this for a long time, and we could have put an end sooner to this little international correspondence, but we all desired peace, conciliation, friendship.

"How have you responded to our conciliatory attitude? By a declaration of war. But do not entertain the delusion that you are going to continue this war on the same basis to which you have become accustomed—delivering your fire, that is, and receiving none. All is changed. We respect worship, but we shall fight without mercy the political action of Rome."

The Ministers, united in council at the Elysée, modified and adjusted a series of propositions presented by the Minister of Worship, and bearing on the four following points:

1. The suppression of board and allowance in the case of rebellious curés.

2. The immediate liquidation of the property of the public establishments of the Catholic religion.

3. The retaking by the State and the communes of presbyteries, bishoprics, and seminary buildings.

4. The rights of prosecution in behalf of the national safety.

On the other hand, the newspapers predicted that, the " associations cultuelles " not having been formed, all the young curés and seminarians, who have not been exactly amenable to military law, would be called into active service. Nearly five thousand five hundred of them were liable to this call.

December 12.—The people were for the most part calm and even indifferent. Everything seemed to go on as usual. Every one knew that religion itself is not in any manner threatened. Notifications having been given to the bishops and seminarists to evacuate the buildings occupied by them and belonging to the State and to the communes, there arose everywhere the stir and fracas of moving households. There was a rapid breaking up and moving out, carried on almost with ostentation. The streets were full of cabs packed with seminarists and their trunks. At the archbishopric of Paris archives and desks were cleared out. Cardinal Richard, who was ill, asked for a reprieve, and it was accorded him. He has, nevertheless, stated that he suffered military expulsion. At Nancy, the bishop, Monsignor Turinaz, always of a fiery temper, resorted to violence, and struck a policeman who was stationed in the street to preserve order.

Not much has been made public regarding the documents found in the apartments of Monsignor Montagnini.

But the Matin, generally well informed, declares on this subject: "We believe it to be a fact that certain of the articles seized are of great interest. They show conclusively that a very large majority of the French clergy had decided to submit to the law of 1881, and that only under imperative commands from the Pope did bishops and curés find themselves obliged to alter the intentions they had formed."

This we know; and we can cite the example of the Cardinal Archbishop of Bordeaux as illustrative of the small consideration paid by the Vatican to the sentiments and wishes of the French clergy. This Cardinal had adopted certain measures by means of which his diocese remained in harmony with the French law while yet obedient to the instructions received from the Pope. But the last interdiction in its succinct brutality destroyed the fruit of all his efforts.

What must intelligent prelates think at being thus disowned, when their methods were characterized by obvious wisdom and dictated by their sense of right as just men and good citizens?

December 13.—This morning mass was said in the seventy-one churches of Paris quite as usual and with no disturbance of the peace. The congregations were scarcely larger than on the preceding days, which is equivalent to saying that the churches were practically empty. Nevertheless, the services were considered as sixty-nine public meetings. Official reports of infractions were drawn up. It appears that in the two other churches declarations that a meeting for worship was to be held were made by two laymen of the parishes. This proceeding, executed, perhaps, without the curés' knowledge, was none the less valid. The friends of peace seized on this trifling occurrence as a last straw of hope. Might not laic intervention furnish the desired solution?

Billboards designed to instigate rebellion were posted in the neighborhoods of the churches. They were green, red, and yellow, and bore this motto: "Resist to the death."

It has been learned that the idea of having declarations made by the laity was the invention of Abbé Moineau, vicar of Saint Germain de Charonne, a dense quarter situated near the immense cemetery of Père la Chaise. Questioned by newspaper men, this vicar gave the following explanation:

"I thought only of avoiding the annoyances and the difficulties which would inevitably ensue. According to the law, it is not absolutely necessary that the curé of the parish should make his own declaration. The approval of two citizens is sufficient to make the declaration valid. That is why I selected two licensed tradesmen, with whom I am in relations, to perform the service.

"The curé, M. Montiton, summoned me this morning; but as each of us was hurried by a service, the interview was postponed till this afternoon. I was, nevertheless, able to see that his feelings were of a contrary character. I do not see in what manner the act could antagonize the ecclesiastical authorities. If you knew how many priests think as I do! But they do not dare to show themselves. They are afraid."

December 14.—Six churches of Paris have followed the example of the first two, where the declarations conformable to the law of 1881 were made by laymen. The Archbishop of Paris, consulted on the question, caused to be drawn up a written opinion, of which this is approximately the text:

"Do the declarations made by laymen constitute an act of disobedience to the Pope? No, seeing that they were made with the just and honorable intention of avoiding the difficulties which might result from anarchistic issues in the midst of which we live. No other method presented itself by which the good results desired could be attained. This method has, therefore, been employed as the only expedient possible to obtain this good result."

This defense was followed by a command from the Archbishop expressed in the following terms:

"The curés shall continue worship, abstaining from all new formalities."

Now this text applies only to curés, and the two citizens who made the declarations, not being amenable to ecclesiastical law, are left free.

Therefore there was no disobedience. Such a written judgment ` tells much concerning the effort made by men of intellect. It is to be hoped that a practical solution will suggest itself for the settlement of this question of public worship. Certainly it is essential that it should. The Government is elaborating a bill designed to terminate pending difficulties.

December 15.—M. Briand, Minister of Justice and Worship, has spoken to the Chamber upon the law announced. The bill is most moderate in character. Here is the article which will be of supreme interest to orthodox churchmen:

"In default of ' associations cultuelles ' to receive the estates and the interest accrued upon the edifices devoted to the exercise of worship, these edifices, as well as the furnishings and ornaments, shall continue to be leased, for the use of worshipers and ministers of worship for the exercise of their religion, until the time of the legalized disappropriation.

" After the promulgation of the present law the State, the departments, and the communes will resume control of bishoprics, archbishoprics, presbyteries, and seminaries which are their property, and the taxes on which have not been laid claim to conformably with the laws of 1905.

"The properties of the ecclesiastical establishments which have not been laid claim to conformably with the laws of 1905 will be attached to the communal institutions of charity, subsequent to the promulgation of the present law."

The reading of this bill was received with acclamation by the Republicans, but a dismal silence reigned on the Right.

Sunday, December 16.—This is the first Sunday following the expiration of the respite accorded by the law. Except at Amiens, at Rennes, and at Perpignon, where Catholics and anti-clericals made a few harmless demonstrations, the first Sunday of the new régime passed in a comparative calm quite unhoped for. All the excitement consisted in drafting official reports concerning the law of 1881.

Monday, December 17.—Cardinal Richard left his palace in the Rue de Grenelle. Four thousand Catholics accompanied him to the house of the deputy, Denys Cochin, who declared that he would shelter him as long as the Cardinal wished. " I am glad to be his porter," added M. Denys Cochin. The faithful unharnessed his equipage and then harnessed themselves to it.

The official residences of eight archbishops and twenty bishops, twenty-six seminaries, and sixteen small seminaries were evacuated. It was said that the palace of the Archbishop of Paris was to become the seat of the Minister of Labor, newly created, whose incumbent is M. Réné Viviani.

This, then, is the schedule of the first eight days.

In spite of the rallying and excitement of the clerical press, the country as a whole remained calm. A spirit of indifference was noticeable, which the intentional exaggerations of the reactionary journalists did not seem to dispel. The spirit of legislation has been so obviously liberal that it has broken up resistance. Neither the great mass of French Catholics, nor yet the clergy itself, understands the obduracy of the Pope.,

If we wish to gain an understanding of the situation created for the Catholic Church by its head, poorly counseled and poorly inspired as he was, we shall be obliged to recognize the following points:

When the adjustment to Republican law took place, the Church, which had always been in possession of the buildings devoted to worship—the presbyteries, the seminaries, the episcopal palaces—lost them without hope of appeal, unless, indeed, she had an enormous capital to invest in their recovery. She lost the estates of churches and cathedrals, and retained use of them only through the tolerance of the government, which did not, however, leave her in absolute control. Her estates are to be turned over to philanthropical institutions. The Pope has inflicted upon the Church of France a terrible ignominy, whose consequences will long endure. The losses we have recorded, however, are only material losses.

There are deprivations of a more serious nature. Recent events have shown to what an extent the Church of France has sacrificed her individuality, her seal of independence; and to what a spirit of indifference she has lapsed. The old error made by Roman Catholicism in drawing all the sap and juice of the Church into the priesthood has led that Church step by step into a blind alley. The faithful among the laymen are no longer of account. The clergy fears the laity, by whom alone it could be renewed and rejuvenated. The "associations cultuelles," by recalling the laity to the active councils of the Church, would have rejuvenated the spirit of Catholicism. But that which would have accomplished a return to the normal was regarded as an abomination. Inevitably one error engenders another.

It is easy to understand that if the people are of no account, the clergy, taken as a whole, is of no more account. The bishops count no more than the abbés, the archbishops no more than the bishops. They are consulted only to be contradicted. Their habit of humbling themselves before the god of the Vatican is such that they obey without protest being made publicly. And yet they know how greatly recent events are opposed to the interests of the Church and to the fulfillment of their own duties. Their efficiency, their experience of local conditions, their wisdom as shepherds of their flocks, combine to counsel an opposite course. It is, therefore, without conviction and without confidence that they follow their chief, and in the full knowledge that he has given them fatal orders, as he himself received fatal advice. What schism could be worse than this? A schism between the faithful and the clergy; a schism between the convictions of the episcopate and the orders given it; a schism between the supreme head of the Church and the leaders of the Church of France. And thus a system most massive and most logical, has led to incoherence through the exaggeration of authority. In olden times a council would have been called and light would have arisen out of discussion. To-day there is one individual who thinks for all the rest. And, as he is badly informed, he stands in the position of a blind man leading those who see clearly with their own eyes. No, never have the enemies of the Catholic Church done it as much harm as have its own institutions at this present crisis. All friends of the Church—and we are its friends—perceive this fact with sorrow and distress.

And the prayer of these friends is that the sufferings which have resulted from all these errors of administration will lead at last to a change of attitude and habit.

# IS THERE NO GOD?

### BY CHARLOTTE CHITTENDEN

There is no God?
Stand quiet there a space.
Let his love shine upon your face,
The whispering air stir soft your hair.
Let down the barriers of your will
Till light and faith dark spaces fill.
Why, all is God!

# THE CORPORATION AND THE PEOPLE: ARE WE ON THE RIGHT TRACK?

## BY THE HON. PETER S. GROSSCUP

*Judge of the United States Circuit Court of Appeals*

NO one doubts, I think, that but for the thing we call the "corporation," the relation . of the corporation to the people, and the questions that such relationship raises, there would have been no New York campaign last fall on the lines that the New York campaign followed, and no results so full of question marks.

Mr. Hughes stood in the State for what Mr. Roosevelt stands in the Nation—the policy of holding the corporations to a strict accountability to law; a policy chiefly carried out through the medium of lawsuits. True, some amendment to the law, as it heretofore existed, has been made, and other amendments are suggested; but the main proposition in the programme of the progressive wing of the Republican party is that the law, as it stands, is almost if not quite sufficient—that the chief thing needed is to compel the corporations, as they now exist, to obey the law.

Mr. Hearst stood for the same things, nominally at least, but with this addendum: That he was in dead earnest, while the Republicans were not—that, if successful, he would rescue government from corporation control, while the Republican party is so subject to corporate influence that it cannot rescue itself from corporate control. And on this issue, in the main, he pushed his canvass to a conclusion that brought to the ticket headed by him recruits enough from the Republican ranks to divide with the Republican ticket, almost equally, the vote of the great State of New York.

Now, with Mr. Bryan's announced policy, also before us, that the thing to do is to dig up the big corporations, root and branch—nothing different thus far being offered by any National political leader for the consideration of the people—the political weather for 1908 can be pretty fairly foretold. We may have a Presidential campaign not fought out on clear, high lines, on an issue upon which the people will be called upon to say aye and nay, but degenerated into a political mêlée, wherein the louder the denunciation of the corporation and all who are allied with it, the more likely will be the prospects of victory.

Thus confronted, is it not high time that the conservative intelligence and conscience of the country should look the situation squarely in the face? *Are we indeed on the right track?* Is reformation by denunciation the only cure? Is reformation by lawsuits the only cure, or the best cure? Is not the disease deeper, and must not, therefore, the cure go deeper into conditions as they exist to-day?

To answer these inquiries requires that we take a look backward, to the end, say, of the Civil War, which was the beginning, in a general way, of the new industrial era.

When the Civil War closed, we were still an agricultural people. The property of the country was still in a very large measure the land of the country. The farmer's boy still lived on the lands. Railways there were, but not the great railways of the present day; manufactures there were, but not the great so-called trusts; mercantile establishments, but not the great department store.

Since Lee's surrender to Grant all of this has been transformed. The farmer's boy is no longer in the country; he is in the great centers working for the corporation. The clerk in the mercantile establishment no longer looks forward to an individual career—he is the employee of a great corporation. The towns have grown, while the country has stood still; the corporation has grown, while individual careers in business and labor have become almost obsolete. During the period from 1865 to 1906 nearly every species of property, except land, has gone under corporate ownership and control.

I do not complain of this; I only put it before the reader as a fact. What I wish to set alongside of this fact, however, is the other fact—without which Mr. Hearst would have had no ground on which to build his appeal to human nature; without which Mr. Bryan and Mr. Roosevelt would have to rest their careers on other issues—the fact that the ownership and control of the property of the country, almost as fast as it passed into corporate form, passed away from the people. The causes I do not now discuss. I am only stating the fact. In the old industrial life, when agriculture was the largest interest of the country, the farms were owned by the people who occupied them. The farmer's boys remained at home until they married; then they became owners of farms of their own, either in the neighborhood or further West. Indeed, the one great ideal of the statesmanship of that day was to distribute the lands to those who would occupy them—to divide up the proprietorship of the land among those who did the farming. In the new industrial life into which we have come, the farmer's boy is in the towns, still contributing his help toward farming the lands, but from the machine shops and manufactories that turn out agricultural implements. And in these great industrial enterprises, all of them in corporate form, he has no interest as owner, and no prospect of such an interest. Through this channel alone—the draining of the farmer's boy into the towns—one-fourth of our population, perhaps, has been turned away from the institution of private property as a National interest that concerns *them.*

In the old industrial life the merchandising of the country was carried on by individuals and small firms—each man behind the counter either owning an interest in the business, or looking forward to the time when he would own an interest in a similar business. The small merchant is no more. The salesman looking forward to ownership is no more—another mighty army added to those already named, who have been turned away from private property as a National interest that concerns *them.*

In the old industrial life the artisan owned his shop, and the journeymen and the apprentices worked for the day when they, too, would be independent proprietors. That day has gone. There are now no proprietor artisans, no expectant journeymen and apprentices—another mighty army added to those who have been turned away from the institution of private property as a National interest that concerns *them.*

The savings of a people are their uninvested surplus—the sums that the depositors have gathered together for which they have not found a satisfactory investment. In the old industrial life these savings went into proprietorship of one kind or another. They created the new enterprises that became the competitors of the old. They constituted then, as they constitute now, almost the sole capital available for the purposes of competition. But in the new industrial life, though the savings have greatly increased, the people invest, *for themselves,* little if any of their savings; nor do the people exercise any influence on how such savings shall be invested. Depositing them in some local financial institution, the depositors give the matter no further thought. The deposits, of course, are not inactive. Put upon the financial streams that converge in the great money centers, these deposits constitute almost the sole capital available to start new enterprises—the difference between the old life and the new being that in the old this available capital was still at the call of competition, while in the new it is within the control solely of those who own the present enterprises and are therefore interested in keeping out competition. A mighty shift, this, from the ideals that lie at the basis of the institution of private property under republican institutions. A mighty strain upon the patience and patriotism to which alone we can look for the maintenance of that institution. So that when you ask me where Mr. Hearst got his following, my answer is that a large part of his following was ready made for him in the conditions I have just stated.

With this, the underlying effect of the transformation from the old life into the new, before us, and remembering that human nature cannot be repealed, let us ask ourselves again, What is the thing to be done? Mr. Roosevelt, thus far, has confined himself to the enforcement of the law as it now exists. He is aiming, unless it be indirectly, at nothing calculated to bring back the people into the ownership of the country's property —nothing calculated to counteract the system whereby the available capital of the country is placed at the disposition of those who already own the enterprises of the country. *Is that to be the alpha and omega of the present corporation agitation?*

Mr. Bryan follows closely along the same lines. To his vision the corporation does not loom up the necessary embodiment of the new industrial life—the form that in the very nature of things that new life was bound to take on. His vision, and the vision of those who see with him, is confined rather to the corporation as the embodiment of tendencies that necessarily must be oppressive. Governed by feelings like that, the corporation can never be made to be what it ought to be—a republican institution of republican government; an institution of the people, for the people. Governed by feelings like that, the corporation can never be made to be what our schools are, what our laws relating to real estate are, what our other institutions are—something that is ours, and that concerns us because it is ours. On the contrary, under that kind of perspective the corporation appears as an alien, an outsider, a stranger with whom the great body of the people can have no relation other than that of strangers with a stranger. Is that to be the beginning and the end of the great awakening? Is it to be the permanent policy of the country that the corporation shall be isolated—put under the ban, as a house where smallpox has broken out is put

under the ban? Or shall the house be cleaned up, remodeled, if necessary rebuilt on lines of conservatism, fidelity to trust, and honesty that will invite back into the new industrial life of the country the people of the country?

Will this policy of isolating the corporation—leaving it untouched except by denunciation or lawsuits—prevent monopoly? It has not thus far, in a single instance that I know of, broken up a monopoly. It has enjoined, by court decree, separate corporations from conspiring with one another to fix prices; but it has not prevented them from uniting in one large corporation, and in that way controlling prices.

Will this policy of isolation—leaving the corporation untouched except by lawsuits—restore competition? To restore competition there must be raised up competitors; and to raise up competitors requires that the capital of the country be available, not solely to those who already have the field, but to those who contemplate entering the field. Under the present policy governing corporations, the capital of the country is not thus available. Capital exists, exists in abundance, exists as the wealth, too, not of those whom we call the rich, but of the people at large. But it is not available to raise up competitors; for the competitor of the corporation must be itself a corporation, and under the free and easy, go-as-you-please present corporation policy of the country, the people at large do not directly invest their wealth in corporate enterprise of any kind. They prefer to intrust it rather to the financial institutions; and thus deposited, it flows to those who own existing corporations, and who on that account are interested, not in raising up competitors, but in suppressing them. No policy that keeps asunder the institutions that wield the capital of the country and the people who furnish it will succeed in restoring to industry the balancing effects of competition. To raise up competitors, the instrumentality that utilizes capital, and the people who furnish it, must be brought together.

Will this policy of isolating the corporation—leaving it untouched except by lawsuits—bring peace to our country; satisfy the human instinct that lies at the bottom of all this unrest? Here in America our aim has been to create as much as we can. To that end every incentive has been offered, and every protection thrown around, the creation of new property. Here in America our aim has been to divide with labor, as equitably as can be done, the immediate profits of enterprise. To that end we have protected our workers against the leveling effects of work done in foreign lands, and have legalized the organizations that enable the workers, in dealing with capital, to deal with the strength of united interest. But beyond that point, except in the case of the public lands, we have not gone. We have taken no pains to furnish the worker with any instrumentality through which he might, with reasonable safety, transmute a part of his day's profits into a permanent property interest. We have taken no pains to interest him as proprietor at all. We have done nothing to furnish the people at large with an instrumentality through which their individual capital might be transmuted into permanent property interests. We have done nothing in that direction at all. The one instrumentality in which the new industrial life embodied itself, and in the nature of things was compelled to embody itself, though State-created, has thus far been left a shell, under whose roof and behind whose walls every form of treachery and nearly every form of theft were given free rein.

Instinctively the American seeks the ownership of property. It was the prospect of a property independence that brought the first Americans over the sea. It is that instinct that took their children to the West. Congress appealed to that instinct in the homestead and pre-emption acts, and the appeal has been responded to by more than a million and a half of American families. A policy that leaves that instinct unsatisfied—that appeals, not to the individual, his hope and prospect in life, but solely to that quality in human nature that gets satisfaction out of making others, who happen to be more fortunate, obey the law, laudable as that kind of satisfaction is, will bring no lasting peace. There

can be in this country, permanently, no such thing as an exclusive proprietary class. Flesh and blood will not stand it. Intelligence and conscience rebel against it. The American voter, even now, in a blind way, is rising up against it. Sound economic judgment tells us that, compared with private enterprise, government ownership is a failure. Sound economic judgment tells us that, compared with private enterprise, government ownership would put skilled labor where neither organization nor skill would do the laborer much good; for let the labor market slip from those who possess it by organization and merit, to the wide expanses of politics, and all the advantages that organization and merit now hold would soon be leveled. Sound economic judgment tells us that the prosperity of America is due to the fact that the men who can invent *are* inventing; that the men who can think things out *are* thinking things out; that the men who can organize *are* organizing; that the men who can do the best things with their hands *are* doing the best things—each according to his individual gift; and that government ownership would upset all this—turn prosperity over to the keeping of pull or chance. But of what avail is sound economic judgment on this or any other subject when it runs counter to human nature? It is not because the wife in the market pays more than she has been accustomed to pay for the necessaries of life that the country is in a state of unrest. It is not because the husband gets less wages than he would like to get that this unrest exists. The unrest springs from that instinct in human nature that inspires every manly heart with an ambition to have some individual part in the achievements of his time; so that the question always remains, What will hold back the American people when they come to the point where they must choose, finally, between a system of private property in which they have come to feel they have no individual part, and property owned by the Nation of which they are a part? Will human nature suppress itself? Or will it be the institution, that no longer engages their interest, that will be engulfed?

The great Democratic party was

founded as guardian to the individual man. Why does it not accept, intelligently accept, the economic destiny that has created the corporation, turning its energies to such corporate reformation as would bring back into industrial life, in the full enjoyment of what was meant to be his appointed portion, the individual man ? The Republican party has shown its capacity to be a true friend of the people at the same time that it is a true friend of property—a true friend of property at the same time that it is a true friend of the people. It was the Republican party that put into the Constitution of the Nation the guaranty, the greatest that private property has to-day, that it should not be taken or abridged except under due process of law; along with the guaranty, the greatest that the humblest of our people have to-day, that life and liberty should ever be under the protection of National law. It was the Republican party that distributed the Western country into millions of farms, each the possession of some hopeful family of Americans; not fearing, however, to utilize the "corporation" to push through to the Pacific coast those bands of steel that, binding the old States into the new, made over these farms into populous States.

It is the Republican party that, through its tariff policy, claims to be securing to the worker with his hands the largest possible share in the division of the profits of enterprise. Why will not the Republican party, true to these inspiring ideals, put its mighty power behind the new ideal ?

But what, you ask me, can these parties do ? What can the people do to arrest the stream before it reaches the rapids—to substitute for the process that is now concentrating into the hands of the few the proprietorship and control of the incorporated life of the country, a process that will set out to widen and republicanize that life ?

My answer is: *Remove the causes.* Thirty years ago the German people went through corporation experiences much like our own. There, as here, the corporation, as originally designed, was a mere shell. There, as here, under the shelter of that shell, the property of the

country was being transferred from the German people at large, even the little they had, to the few. There, thirty years ago, as here now, great corporate scandals were exposed. And there, as here, the human nature that is everywhere behind civilization eventually began to recoil. It began there before it began here, only because conditions reached a climax there earlier than here, and because we as a people were too prosperous and too busy to look even a little way beneath the surface of things.

But when the work of reform did come there, it was a genuine reform. It did not content itself with indiscriminate denunciation, or with mere lawsuits. Nor did it die out, leaving the door still open to every character of corporation the cunning of men might conceive. Before a corporation can be organized in that country, it must prove, as in a court proceeding, its rightful title to a corporate existence. In the same way it must establish the amount and the character of the capitalization it is allowed to put out. When property is turned in, its value must be judicially ascertained. Upon officers and directors is not conferred supreme power; in the German corporation the shareholders' meeting is the counterpart of our New England town meetings—a genuine assembly intended to do something more than pass resolutions of approval. And every violation of trust. not merely to the public, but to the shareholder as well, is quickly punished with punishment that smarts. There is in the German corporation no room for one to do, with impunity, in his capacity as a corporation officer or promoter, what if done individually would land him in the penitentiary.

I am not holding up the industrial life of the Germans as an example of what our own should be, or their corporation as an institution to be followed, line by line, in our own work of reconstruction. We have found for our workman ways for increasing his share in the division of the profits of enterprise that the German workman does not enjoy. What the American in the ordinary walks of life could lay by for investment is larger, happily much larger, than anything the German can lay by. But the example is none the less valuable; for if, on such conditions, the German corporation could be reconstructed on lines that have successfully interested, as proprietors, to the extent of their means, the German people at large—resulting in the fact that it is not upon her corporate industries, but upon her unjust landed proprietorship alone, that the forces of German Socialism are directed—what may not be expected in America when the work of corporation reform, in the true spirit of reform, is undertaken and accomplished.

But while I am not attempting in detail to point out the exact structure of the American corporation as it should stand when reconstructed, some of the principles on which the reconstruction should take place can be particularized. The reconstructed corporation, for instance, must have no place in it for those schemes of spoliation that, *within or without*, plunder the people whose capital has created it and whose patronage must support it. In the reconstructed corporation the securities issued must be related in some way to the values actually put in. In the reconstructed corporation, not only must the officers be trustees of the stockholders, held to the strict accountability to which individual trustees are now held, and denied the privilege, as individual trustees are now denied, of making profit out of their trust; but the administration of the trust, as in the case of individual trustees, must be constantly kept under the eye of some tribunal of the Government. And in the reconstructed corporation tangible inducements ought to be given to the workman, the clerk, the employee of every kind, to secure proprietorship.

I shall not attempt to point out, in detail, how existing corporations shall be brought into the new régime. Considering, however, that existing corporations depend largely on the public, from time to time, to take their securities, especially their bonded securities, the probability is that, as a matter of self-interest—in many cases of life or death—existing corporations would be compelled to conform their organization to the reconstructed organization prescribed by

government; for otherwise they would brand themselves as suspects. Then, too, within the respective powers of the Nation and States, to prescribe the kind of collateral that banks, insurance companies, and savings institutions shall *not* take for loans, the Nation and States could exert a leverage toward the new order of things that could not be resisted; for nearly every great corporation is a heavy borrower from these financial reservoirs of the people's wealth.

But the purpose of this article does not require that I go far into details. That is not the first task to be accomplished. The first duty and the first task is to get the thought of the country turned from the by-roads of corporate reform to the main road—from aims that lead nowhere to a determined aim that will lead to practical results. No one who has observed carefully the workings of public ownership wishes public ownership, at least to any widespread degree; in no other way could the prosperity of the country—the individual prosperity of every man and woman of the country—be so quickly sunk. No help is in sight, as the Wisconsin Commissioner of Labor has just pointed out, from the so-called " co-operative " undertakings; the plain reason being that in this, as in public ownership, the undertakings are never conducted on business principles—never suitably manned. To be conducted on business principles—to be suitably manned—a business undertaking must start and grow in the natural order of things—manned usually by the men who build them up, or by men who, in the natural order of business selection, must come to take their places.

The *corporation*, indeed, is the only form of proprietorship in sight in which our great new industrial life can embody itself, *and maintain its vitality*. But the corporation itself, as now constructed, looked at as I have tried to point out, from the standpoint of universal human nature (and by that standard it is bound to be judged), is built upon the sands. The duty and the task of this generation of Americans is to put it on the solid ground of human interest—to so rebuild it that, as the antithesis of public ownership, it will present also a countenance that is human—to make for our incorporated industrial life a name that, along with the other great names of American achievement, can be put on our flag in the contest that is bound some day to come between the civilization of to-day, the product of what has been best in the exertions of mankind, and a civilization that would sink us to the level of what is the worst that mankind can endure. And some day, to some man, will be given the strength successfully to summon to this great task the good sense and the conscience of the American people.

# INDIA'S AWAKENING
## FROM AN AMERICAN POINT OF VIEW
### BY H. G. BISSELL

The writer of this article has gained his knowledge of India at first hand as a representative of the American Board of Commissioners for Foreign Missions. His article illustrates the broad spirit which is actuating an increasing number of missionaries ; his picture of India is that of a cosmopolitan. In a forthcoming issue The Outlook will print an article on India's Awakening from an Indian point of view.—THE EDITORS.

THERE are more races crowding the great plains and huddling among the hills of Hindustan than one can count on the continent of Europe. The Mohammedans alone outnumber all the world's Mohammedan population besides. These peoples differ in race and voice, color and costume, occupation, literature, philosophy, and religion. Added to these racial barriers, which have some natural sources, are the social and religious barriers of caste among the Hindus.

The people say that the god created men in layers. Some came from his feet, some from his body, some from his arms, and some from his head. But, not satisfied with these four, the Hindu's imagination seems to have run riot with him till every trade is a separate caste. It is a rigid, frigid, petrified system. It compels the son always to follow his father's trade, and weds the daughter only to a man of the same caste. The average Hindu probably would rather omit the worship of his gods than break caste by certain associations with a lower-caste man, such as drinking out of the same cup with him or sharing his lunch. A score of Hindus in all India could not number for us these accursed caste circles.

India is not a nation. It has no national life. It has no flag as an emblem of national life. For centuries together, political differences, defended and forced by weapons, have existed among those hoary people. Internal civil strife, racial and political uprisings, cruel invasions, siege and bloodshed were common occurrences. These differences cannot be obliterated in a single century of peace enforced by a conquering neutral nation. The interests of the Indian people are still more or less divided into and confined by States—British and Native States. Great Britain's paternal colonial government has by no means yet passed the stage of governing by arms. The amalgamation of such peoples, the centralizing of their interests, the welding into one of their political ambitions, is a task the magnitude of which is ill appreciated by onlookers or casual visitors. Why will not England give India larger representation in Parliament ? Because India does not yet produce large-hearted men who will look far beyond kith and kin and kind, and take into consideration disinterestedly the welfare of all India. That populous empire has had many noble reformers in the interests of religion, society, and politics, but circumstances have always limited their vision and the reach of their influence, and the effect of their best work has been confined to sections of the country and only parts of the people. India's real political interests have as yet scarcely been molded into definite shape, let alone their being the uniform passion or pursuit of the people.

India's economic life helps on this division of interests, and emphasizes the lack of unity among the people. A man's trade determines his social and largely his religious standing. What sympathy has the higher with the lower? What ambition has the lower to rise? The man who prepares leather for shoes and sews them for the Brahmin is abhorrent in the wearer's eyes. The bearer of messages and money from town to town, the Mahar, would never be admitted into the house of the writer or receiver of the same. He is the serf. The countless lower castes are forbidden the temple precincts in India; are forbidden to hear the sacred scriptures when read, for it would be sacrilegious, because they make ropes with which the farmer ties his cattle and draws water from his deep wells for his rich fields, because they make brooms with which the temples are swept and mattings of the date-palm or aloe on which all higher-caste people are glad to sleep at night. The man who weaves the warm goat's-hair blanket is excluded from higher circles of society, while his blankets are bought by all alike. What a hopeless task is this to bring these hearts together as common sons of a common father, as brothers in a family! The enormity of the problem is the measure of the necessity of its solution.

What of the dividing lines of the religions in India? It may be enough perhaps simply to say that all the great religious systems of Asia have first and last had their temple homes in India. A half-dozen of these religions are still there, each restless because of the others; perhaps all well-nigh resistless before the twentieth century's best Christian message. Religion is on the ground early and late, first and last and always; tenfold more elaborate religious codes than the Jews ever possessed. Building a house, digging a well, preparing for marriage, casting up accounts, beginning his spring plowing, sowing his seed, gathering the harvest, and all that one can conceive of his doing, a man does with some religious ceremony. The zeal of the people in expressing their devotion to their gods goes to the extreme of self-abnegation and self-denial, unheard of among the most zealous of Western Christians.

Among the one-third of the human race who are the followers of Buddha must be counted India's contributions. That prophet had a great soul. Like Christ, he thought out the problems of life in the mountains alone; like him, he left no writings in prose or poetry. He lived, he thought, he died. The system which bears his name is not all contradictions and falsehoods, but it does lack the dynamic force of an ever-present and all-powerful personality.

Mohammedanism is a force upon which India and many other lands have had to count for centuries. Mohammed fought against idolatry. He taught submission to the one personal God; he acknowledged Jesus as the Messiah, though not as divine. The Koran he believed to be the last stage of God's revelations to man. He has ninety-nine names for God. Shall we go to his followers with the hundredth and crowning one of Father? Among the Mohammedans woman is man's slave. Crime or immorality will not excommunicate a Mohammedan. Church and State are one. Sensuality and lust run in the Tartar blood. Its fatalism is fatal to its own healthy development. Mohammedanism needs to put Jesus supreme. It needs the love of righteousness. It needs the conception of God as love and of religion as a life with God, a life of love and of holiness.

The followers of Zoroaster, the Parsees from Persia, have been in India for five hundred years. Zoroaster was one of the great teachers of the East. An echo of his own moral struggles is heard in his teachings of dualism. The Parsee adores the sun, the source of so much blessing, giving life and light and having such cleansing power, being, too, the largest body symbolic of the source of all such power. The Parsees are devout. They do not proselyte. Their temples are exclusive. Sins of lust and passion are regrettably noticeable among them. Charities abound, but are promoted by mixed motives. Zoroastrianism suffered its first blow at the hands of Mohammedans in the seventh century. It will never recover itself. It lacks a vital motive to live and to do.

Then there is Hinduism, ancient and modern, the strongest, the oldest religion in India. There is a certain prestige about old age. Hinduism has gained no small share of its power by its openness, in a way, towards other faiths. Probably for this reason very few Hindus could be found in all Hindustan who could define Hinduism. This ancient, elaborate philosophy is professed by 190,000,000 people. Nature-worship is its backbone, mystery its watchword. The Hindu connects all unusual phenomena with Deity. The Vedas are selections made from the ancient scriptures, and are not the daily thought of those former pastoral people. Hinduism, ancient and modern, is a conglomerate, colossal mass of philosophies and systems hopelessly interborrowed. What of truth is in it is from God. Its teachers and its writings have gripped the people as few other religious systems have ever done. Still, religions must be judged, not by their roots, but by their fruits. Hinduism is not sufficient to the task of saving men from sin, nor does it incite to unselfish service for one's fellowmen. The caste system of the Hindus is unyielding and intolerable. Preservation of life is the cult of some sects, while animal food is freely used by people of others. The custom of early marriages with all its attendant evils, the abuse of widows to limits of cruelty and sensuality inconceivable, and the opposite of this, namely, widow remarriage and postponement of weddings to maturer life, are observed together in almost any city or town. Religious opposition so easily develops fanaticism and bursts out into intolerance. Hence the active dislike of these people of differing religions in India for one another, and the open riots, in some cases suppressed with difficulty by the police and the standing army. The thin crust of consent to live in peace, because compelled to, all too often breaks through with real volcanic explosion and disaster. Here is a problem for the peace-loving Christian.

The extreme conservatism of the East often baffles the most ambitious hustler of the West, and makes him side with Kipling in the conclusion that the race is not for the swift. The East will simply not race. The leisurely life of the Orient is no doubt due partly to the enervating climate, partly to the general fertility of the soil, which with a little coaxing has for centuries supplied the limited material wants of millions of humanity, partly to the predominating fatalistic philosophy of the people, and possibly more than all to the semi-superstitious and religious beliefs of the people, which still have a firm grip on most of them. A single illustration will suffice. A few years ago, Ahmednagar, one hundred and fifty miles east of Bombay, with a population of thirty-eight thousand, experienced its first siege of the ravaging plague. That disease has in the last decade carried off two million people in India alone. Upon the spread of the disease Government medical authorities planned rigorous measures for the daily inspection of the city; the segregation of families where patients were found and the removal of the patients to temporary hospitals were ordered. An old priest started the story that the Queen of England was dying of old age, and that her physicians had prescribed for her a diet of human hearts, and all these plague regulations were a subterfuge on the part of the Government authorities to secure human hearts; the patients once taken to the hospital would be drugged and then the hearts removed and forwarded to the Queen. The story was widely believed, especially by those who yield to priestcraft, and the result was that people hid their sick, buried their dead secretly in wells or under their houses, or, deserting both sick and dead, locked them up in their houses and moved away. The death-rate reached seventy a day.

If it is true that religion permeates all the activities of the Hindu, it is also true that such superstitious beliefs are inseparable from his religion. The control the priesthood has of the ignorant people is probably without parallel. The priests are the interpreters of the scriptures, the revealers of the gods' wishes, and are often worshiped as gods. I have seen even the ordinary Brahmin, laying no claims to being a priest, stop on the crowded streets of our city while some of the people poured water on his feet and then drank it as a special cup of blessing. Certain classes of priests determine the lucky days for weddings. Large parts of the year are altogether excluded from these chosen days. The farmer sows his seed in certain phases of the moon declared by his priests to be lucky, while signs of all kinds control devotees starting on pilgrimages. Will the truth appeal to such minds? Will these people who live in the past be easily reached by the Christian's message, taken to them barely a century ago? It is not easy to say yes, but not possible to say no. In a large measure all this is due to the dense ignorance of the populace. One woman in about seventy can sign her own name, and one man in about twenty. There are scores of villages in the Bombay State alone with no schools of any kind.

Are there any redeeming features in this situation outlined above?

There are the great ports and centers of industry, like Bombay, Calcutta, Madras, Karachee, and Colombo, among the busiest cities in the world. The first two furnished last year a commerce worth five hundred million dollars to the Western world, while the entire foreign commerce of America was worth to her only a billion dollars. The world's commercial interests are bringing India into line with better nations. This will bear fruit in more than simply economic lines.

There, too, are the men caught by the ambition of learning who are in the half-dozen universities established by the British Government, and sustained at millions of dollars of annual expenditure. Or, with a larger ambition still, they will cross over to Cambridge or Oxford, or to Germany, or to the United States, whence scores of intelligent young men are returning, with their B.A., M.A., or LL.B. and M.D. proudly attached to their names. Many such will already be found in India occupying judges' benches, practicing as lawyers and doctors, acceptably filling civil offices of legal, judicial, and financial responsibility. They may be found as officers in the standing army, in the forestry and the engineering departments. Some of them are heads of large business firms and managers of factories. All this is but a beginning, when the country is considered as a whole, but a good beginning, and it is significant. Under Lord Curzon primary education received a great impetus. It is being encouraged under his successor. Much as one may often regret the religious neutrality of Government schools, or decry the great predominance of Hindu literature used, which makes the way easy for the teachers, almost without exception themselves strong Hindus, to refer to Hindu mythology and to the Hindu scriptures—in short, to teach Hinduism—and little as this educational system may reach the most neglected classes, since it is against the social and religious instincts and customs for a higher-caste teacher to associate with lower-caste pupils, yet the Government schools educate. They prepare for higher education. They start ambitions for learning, and are helping boys, and girls too, to more knowledge. This opens the way for better influences to come into their lives. The horizon is broadened. The past and the environment of the present become unsatisfactory. The desire for better things is started.

The mingling and commingling of these diverse peoples is brought about by such agencies as railways. Travelers must sit together in the trains. If they travel all day, they must converse somewhat, and they have their lunches with them. Irrespective of caste or creed, they must become acquainted with one another. There are thousands of miles of railway in India. More are added every year. The interests of the people in other classes and places than theirs are stimulated by the newspapers, English and vernacular, now found in all cities of twenty thousand or thirty thousand and over. Disasters or developments anywhere are crowded on to the notice of all who can read. People are compelled to think about one another, and to take a slight interest at least in the welfare and the woe of others. The wider acquaintance with foreign lands, too, is increasing. The desire to travel abroad, to pursue studies in Western lands, the visits of leading men to our countries, merchants and kings and students coming to America to study the economic, the social, and the educational conditions and institutions, have many good results.

The pathos of idolatry or polytheism anywhere is the restlessness of the soul seeking for God and for help somewhere, doing everything or anything, calling anything, all things, God, leaving nothing untried to find satisfaction at last. All modern influences which in any way have come to affect India's people simply conspire to bring out this uneasiness. The theistic movements under the name of Samaj are all the outcome of Christian influences. These systems postulate that there is one God; that all men are brothers. This is expressing strong convictions against idolatry and the caste system. Leaders in these Samaj churches (for they are churches in some sense) have lately urged the practical method of testing the tenets of Samaj followers by calling together people of various creeds and castes—Mohammedans, Hindus, Christians, Samajists, and others of whatsoever origin—and asking all to share in a common feast. Such gatherings are to be the regular features of the Samaj national gatherings in many parts of India. The followers of Zoroaster, Krishna, Mohammed, Buddha, and Christ are comparing notes as never before. The Hindus, and others too, are eliminating from their religious festivities many immoral and distasteful features. Other festivals are being remodeled. Many public teachers and priests are attempting to restate Hinduism in more Christian terms. They are trying to find similarities between Hinduism and Christianity and to prevent converts from leaving the old faith. To be sure, these efforts may not be as widespread as one might like to see, but spreading they are. In many instances the native non-Christian press is urging that the Christian be given a standing according to his intrinsic value, just as any other man should be.

From the political point of view, something encouraging is observed also. The desire to have national gatherings to discuss reforms such as child marriage, female education, widow remarriage, etc., has already borne fruit. The interests of the common classes and kindred subjects are discussed. Gatherings are convened to articulate the immediate political interests of India, to discuss India's representation in Parliament, or the starting of national universities, or to petition the British Government to allow equal competition between natives and foreigners for appointments to civil offices of all kinds. The discussing of India's natural resources and her indigenous industries with a view to improvement—in short, attempts to formulate national life and urge patriotism upon the Hindu as a lofty sentiment—are coming to be a feature of India's activities, although for the present only a limited number of leading men seem to be moving in these lines. No small amount of encouragement to all this was given by a recent deputation sent to India by Japan. The enterprise and activity of that little Asiatic nation, deserving rather the adjective great, are mightily influencing all neighboring Asiatics.

The serious features of the problem and some redeeming features of it lead to a consideration of the question of solution.

The solution is imperative and not impossible. So far as it lies with the missionary, I believe that he must go more and more with these three ideas dominating his policy and all his effort. In the first place, he must be conscious of the fact that centuries before the first preachers from the West ever landed among these people, God was busy with them, revealing himself to them according to the capacity they had to receive. The preacher must go in the spirit of Jesus, desiring and working, not to destroy the law and the prophets that already exist among them, the ideals they may have, but trying to fill in where they need more light and more effectual help from sin. The iconoclast who says, " Away with all this you have here! it is all falsehood and superstition and empty liturgies, dishonoring God and a curse to men; I have what you want; this is the truth, take this," will find little response in India, as he will anywhere in God's world. Woe to him who destroys another man's ideal! Let him rather build upon the good to be found and bring it to the best development with the larger help offered through the daily companionship of Jesus of Asia.

In the second place, the missionary must interpret in a larger way the words of Jesus, "Go into the whole creation and preach the gospel." He must believe that that means more than geographical extension; it means go with the Gospel and permeate all the departments of men's lives. Man lives but one life. There is no secular and religious distinction to the Christian; he does all things for the love of God, for the love of man. Man must be lifted symmetrically. His economic condition, the indigenous pursuits of his country, any special resources in his land, his social life in the home and among outer circles, his educational needs, proper sanitation for his dwellings and towns, effective medical care for his body, and his religious needs—all these sides of the man's life need the Gospel's help. Giving him the right kind of help along these lines is giving the whole Gospel to help the whole man. This the missionaries are trying to do just as fast as we back them up with something to invest in such enterprises.

In the third place, the missionary must go desiring most to take to the non-Christian people the essential message of Christianity, and not in the boastful spirit which bombards the heathen in his blindness with a storm like this: "You take the Lord Jesus in your heart and put all this elaborate church paraphernalia, which we have prepared in the West under certain peculiar needs and conditions, and put them on your back, brother, and God bless you!" Why, the thoughts and deeds of the Orientalist are all alive with religion! Let us say to him, "My brother man, you and I can walk in daily touch with God every day; Jesus will teach us how to do it; he did it himself, he knows what help man needs. By his daily companionship with them he can help men to know God better, and to walk nearer to him. Shall I tell you about Jesus?" What else besides this do we wish the Orientalist to take from the message that Christianity has for the world?

Multiplied organization does not run in the Hindu's life, but the people do possess a genius for religion. They have their own countless ways of expressing their inner faith, imperfect, distorted often, to be sure, but I believe the Hindus need far less than we think the externalities of Western Christianity. Heaven save the Orient from the havoc of isms! The religious instinct, the devotion and abundant religious activities, are already the Orient people's possession. Add to these the power of truth, righteousness and love personified in the God-man, and the church of the East will be the greatest church we know. I will go further than that and say that God's complete orb of truth is so great, so much greater than any of us think, that we of Christendom will never know it all till men everywhere made in God's image and feeling after him have experienced the Father's saving presence in Jesus the Saviour, and have brought in their contributions to the interpretation and the understanding of God's truth. We are people of one world. None of us liveth unto himself, and no one part of the human family can do the thinking for all the rest. With the multitudes and varieties of peoples, their religious activities, the contributions of many good thinkers, and with the mistakes and successes of the Western church, and the ripest results of our best scholarship in science, in speculation and religion in view, India's millions will one day rise to the position of a great church power, and take their full share in the work of the world's redemption.

# THE NEW SPORT OF REAL-ESTATING

## BY BERT LESTON TAYLOR

**Real Estate.** *n*. Land for which real money is asked and on which taxes are required to be paid.

**Real-estate.** *v*. To investigate, explore, and consider land with a view to purchasing, but without necessarily having the purchase price.

—*Twentieth Century Dictionary*.

REAL-ESTATING as a recreation is not so new as solitaire whist, but it is only within recent years that it has become popular as a sport and taken its place beside motoring and golf. It is with golf that one naturally compares it; and the two diversions have these points in common : They take one into the open air ; they compel mild exercise; they may be pursued when one has become too stiff for tennis.

But to golf one must belong to a club, or negotiate an invitation from a member ; one must foot it to the links or pay to be transported thither ; at the club, too, one may easily fall into habits which one's wife would hesitate to approve, except on ladies' day. On the other hand, in real-estating—

"It is a pleasant day," I remark to Arethusa; "suppose we go real-estating."

She assents, and I telephone to a real estate sharp of my acquaintance : "Hello, Higgins ! If you have any bargains in country property, I would like a look at them this afternoon."

"I'll be around with the auto in about an hour," he replies.

And an hour or so later we are chugging through the landscape in the pleasant sunshine, and Higgins is pointing out the various properties for sale along the way.

"This," he remarks, signaling the chauffeur to stop, "this is my best bargain ; grand old house, built in 1798, good barns and outbuildings, and seventy acres of as fine land as ever lay out-doors."

"How about neighbors ?"

"Best ever. You are sandwiched in between two magnificent estates." He mentions the names of two well-known members of the plutocracy.

"And the price ?" I inquire, carelessly, as if I were buying a grapefruit or a dog collar.

"Twenty-eight thousand. Might shave it a little."

I glance at Arethusa : not an eyelash has quivered ; she is an even better real-estater than I am. We descend from the auto.

"Here is the best look-off," says Higgins, leading us to an eminence commanding a million dollars' worth of view.

"This is the place for the house," I remark.

"We will move it here," my wife decides promptly.

The question of outlook disposed of, I inquire whether there is a stream on the place, and learn that a perfectly good brook crosses the lower end of the homestead. Leaving Arethusa to explore the house (old houses are her dearest fad), Higgins and I walk over the seventy-acre tract, discussing its comparative cheapness when compared with contiguous property, and its probable appreciation within a very few years.

Arethusa bubbles with enthusiasm over the house. It is nearly all handmade, and is unspoiled by modern conveniences. There are fireplaces upstairs and down—one with a crane—and an old-time smoke-oven aloft. The mantels are hand-carved, the door hinges and latches hand-wrought, the window-glasses are somewhat larger than dominoes, and all the floors run uphill. In the attic are innumerable copies of Godey's Lady's Book and Peterson's Magazine. "And I found a spinning-wheel and a hoopskirt," says Arethusa, excitedly. "I shall bring those downstairs and put them in the hall or the den."

83

We withdraw to discuss the sordid financial end of the enterprise.

" Twenty-eight thousand dollars is a good deal of money," I observe, tentatively.

" Mr. Higgins said they might shave it a little," my wife reminds me.

" Well, say twenty-five. Where in the world are we to get twenty-five thousand dollars ?"

" They wouldn't want it all at once, would they ? Don't you suppose they would take two thousand down and the rest on mortgage ?"

" Assume for the sake of the argument that they would ; where can we raise the *two* thousand ?"

Arethusa's forehead wrinkles, and then as suddenly smooths.

" Perhaps Aunt Jane would lend us the money," she says. " We might just as well pay interest to her as to a bank."

" To be sure. That will keep part of the mortgage in the family," I reply, and we return to the auto.

During the afternoon we inspect a dozen properties. Some of these we merely glance at, others we explore ; but we find nothing we like so well as the sevenry-acre tract with the house built in 1798. We tell Higgins that we will come to a decision within a week, and thank him for a profitable and a pleasant afternoon. We have motored some twenty-five miles and have walked the equivalent of eighteen holes at golf, or better, through grassy lanes and smelly orchards and woodland murmurous with brook water ; we have exercised, not only our limbs, but our imaginations, enjoying all the pleasures of property-owning with none of its pains ; we have, in a word, had a most delightful excursion, and—it has not cost us a penny.

Of course the gentle reader understands that real-estating must be pursued in perfect good faith, for otherwise an honest sport becomes an ignoble scheme for obtaining entertainment under false pretenses. One must really wish to buy " a place in the country," however humble, and it is the property within one's means that one actually quests for ; but imagination is untrammeled, and is indispensable to real-estating. It is indispensable because, first, it enables one " to investigate, explore, and consider land with a view to purchasing, but without necessarily having the purchase price ;" and, secondly, it enables one to reform, before the mind's eye, the most abandoned farm, and make its desert acres blossom as the rose.

Given imagination, nothing stimulates it more than real-estating ; nothing, again, leads one, educationally, more widely and pleasantly afield. Latent talent for landscape gardening, architecture, interior decoration, is developed in a surprising degree ; and, pursuing these things, one is brought into contact with interesting, often fascinating, people. Real-estating also enables one to get into houses which are barred against the merely curious, and enlarges one's knowledge of how " the other half " gets on. Every seasoned real-estater has remarked to himself or his wife, " Isn't it funny how some people live ?"

Golfers chatter of their scores, real-estaters of their " finds " and narrow escapes from property-owning.

There is my friend Atwater, who, in prowling around the New England village of Red Brook, stumbled on the most beautiful Colonial house imaginable.

" Its only occupant," he relates, " was an aged dame named Scofield, who coldly informed my wife and me that the place was not for sale, and refused even to permit us to view the interior of the house. We inquired a bit, and learned that the old lady had a lot of wonderful furniture and china, and had been pestered by curious summer visitors. We learned, too, that a man named Hornbeak held a mortgage on the property, and claimed to own it.

" We approached Hornbeak. He professed to be willing to sell, but it made his heart bleed to think of depriving Dame Scofield of the only home she had in the world. You could tell at a glance that Hornbeak was as soft-hearted as a grindstone, and we wondered what his game was until he hitched up and carried us two miles uphill to look at a piece of land for which he claimed the finest view in the State. It was an entirely satisfactory view, but there was nothing

Colonial about it, and we told Hornbeak that we preferred to figure on the Scofield place, much as it would grieve him to turn the old lady out. He was disappointed, and on the way down the mountain tried to sell us his horse. But again we demurred. There was nothing Colonial about Faithful Billy; he was nearer Gothic.

" Meanwhile Dame Scofield had got wind of our dickering with Hornbeak, and sent word to us that she was the only, original owner of the property. We hurried over, and this time were cordially received. While my wife rummaged the house and pawed over the china I arranged with Dame Scofield to lift Hornbeak's mortgage and pay her a few hundreds in addition. In the enthusiasm of the moment I quite forgot that the old lady had no other home to go to, but my wife spoke of it on the way back to the city, and we began to see what a shame it would be to turn Dame Scofield adrift. We pictured her tottering away in tears from the ancestral porch, and dear old Hornbeak trying to comfort her, and—well, we simply didn't have the heart to do it. That," concluded Atwater, " was the narrowest escape I ever had."

Not all real-estaters are so lucky. Accidents happen to the best of them. There was my friend Bentley—we speak of him in the past tense, as one dead. Bentley lost his head completely and actually *bought* a property. Poor chap! he feels pretty sheepish about it, and blushes painfully when I ask him whether his roof leaks, and how he likes seesaw floors, and what train he usually doesn't catch to the city.

I myself have had some close shaves. September last I heard of a bargain in a happy valley some six miles off the railway. The town clerk at the county seat, who had the selling of the property, hired a handsome turnout and drove us over the hills. And from the moment the house came into view Arethusa and I yearned to possess it.

It was a grand old mansion, with a vast hall amidship, an old-fashioned kitchen big enough to give a ball in, half a dozen fireplaces—everything we had dreamed of. The ninety-odd acres were ideally divided into pasture, mead-ow, and woodland, and at the rear of the house ran the indispensable little river.

Left to ourselves for a few minutes, Arethusa and I exchanged significant glances.

" At last!" she sighed.

" Yes; fairly caught," said I. " The price is absurd—nine hundred dollars."

" There doesn't seem to be a single defect—nothing that we can object to."

" Not that I can see."

" There are no mosquitoes?"

" It is September, my dear. Still, this is not a mosquitoish locality."

" Then we shall have to buy it."

" I am afraid so."

We walked along the bank of the river.

" I wonder," said Arethusa, suddenly, ".what makes the water so dark?"

" It *is* dark," said I, " almost black; and the river bed is sandy."

" Ask that man going by," said Arethusa. " He may know."

He did. It appeared that a paper-mill was located two miles upstream, and that the refuse and chemicals from this mill were dumped into the river. "Smells awful bad in summer," said our informant.

Of course that settled it. The town clerk agreed with me that so long as the farmers in the valley tolerated the polluting of the stream they could not hope to interest " city folk " in their property. He was ignorant of the fatal drawback, he averred, and regretted that we had wasted our time to no purpose. But we assured him that we had enjoyed the drive, and had spent a very pleasant afternoon.

Speaking of mosquitoes, a topic inseparably connected with real-estating, Atwater relates an experience with Higgins. Higgins had taken him to one of his bargains, and was expatiating on the view, when Atwater observed a large mosquito light on the agent's forehead.

" By the way," said Atwater, carelessly, " are there any mosquitoes here?"

" Never heard of any," replied Higgins, with admirable nerve.

Atwater looked him in the eye. The mosquito meanwhile was boring in.

" Are you quite sure ?"

The mosquito drilled to the limit. Higgins smote the insect flat.

" Oh, well," he said, " there may be one occasionally."

POSTSCRIPT: Arethusa has just come in with news of a glorious Colonial house that may be had for the foolish sum of fifteen thousand dollars. "The only drawback," she says, " is that it, the house, is too near the street."

I suggest a ten-foot brick wall. But it may be cheaper to move the house back a few hundred feet. I shall inquire of a contractor to-morrow.

# THE BEATITUDE OF PROGRESS

## BY PERCY H. EPLER

*I. Progress—the Beatitude of the Nation.*

Equality is the equal right of every man everywhere to progress.

Troubled by the statement that there is no such thing as equality in America and that the Declaration of Independence is mere bombast and fustian, I light upon this air-clearing definition, rediscover our National birthright, point it out to others, feed upon it myself with joy, become a patriot with a reason.

By it I see the advance of our constitutional freedom upon the lesser liberties of Old World monarchies. There classes are petrified into castes. Here they are not. There a man cannot easily pass from one level to another, and it is not meant that he should. Here it is meant that he should, and he does. Such equal chance to progress generates our native-born equality and breathes out a beatitude of hope which is distinctly atmospheric of America.

My conscience and Christianity have sometimes been challenged by the extreme Socialist's demand, for equality's sake, of an equal distribution of wealth and a leveling of fortunes. But, in face of this illuminating definition of equality, I see that such a course would be fundamental inequality, for it would destroy the equal chance of every man everywhere to progress according to his individual ability, a thing different in every person. Such apparent inequality would be basic inequality—a slavery worse than any that ever shackled humankind. It would reduce every man to mediocrity, prosperity to penury, and progress to paralysis.

But whosoever, poor or rich, that threatens and destroys the equal right of every man everywhere to progress is equally an enemy of the Republic. My brother the social extremist troubles me no more than the kind of money king that advances only by crippling and defying his fellow-man's right of way independently to go on. Such a blockade-runner of progress's equal right is being exposed to-day as our most dangerous foe. His exposé brings to an American heart satisfaction and assurance. Our right to progress—it is being battled for and saved !

Once confused by the negro problem, I am by this idea of equality made clear. Four decades ago mere nominal political liberty granted the African was grand, but it did not make him free, as men then thought. For it did not wholly put him on the equal right of way, ethically, educationally, and industrially, to progress. This new liberty is what is being found for him to-day—a freedom not of form but of substance, where " an inch of progress is worth a yard of fault-finding."[1] Therefore hope ! The negro is on his way to a deeper equality. A new beatitude in view of this dawns upon the black.

Our colonial questions pestered me, and I was troubled when my friend the Boston minister exclaimed, on his embarkation for Europe, "The Republic— the Republic is dead !" I was tempted to fear. But peace comes in the light of this working idea of equality, and I see our colonies on the way to just this— the growing equal right of every man to progress, educationally, industrially, and

[1] Booker T. Washington.

ethically. So I say, " Amen." They are getting the substance of liberty in preparation for the form thereof. Such a fact brings, not perturbation, but a National beatitude.

Equality—the equal right of every man everywhere to progress. Quaking at the tread of herds of Europe's masses at Castle Garden, in this I find peace. I go down to the alien's home which he so fast acquired. In broken English I hear the father say to his son : " My boy, I want you to have a better education and career than I had. And you can, and you will "—and he does. I hear the mother say to her girl, " My daughter, I wish for you a better home than I've had, and you can get it, and you will "—and she does. It is so all along the line.

The consciousness of progress is the beatitude of the new industrial millions and is what makes them happy. It is a new and blessed assurance of equality— an equality which knows no petrifaction of classes, but says to every man, " Come up."

Prince Henry, surrounded by his German cuirassiers and accompanied by his princely staff, was asked, after his visit to America, his conclusions. And what a climax to what we have said was his reported reply when he made answer that the greatest revelation in the American people was this : *The hope that lit the upturned faces of the multitudes that banked the highways, in contrast to the sodden hopelessness that sat heavy upon the peasantry of Europe.* And from what did the hope that lit their faces spring ? It sprang from the glad sense of the equal right of every man everywhere to progress—America's God-given birthright.

II. *Progress—the Beatitude of the Individual.*

The confusion which is everywhere routing men's minds to-day is due to a lack of personal independence, which might be had if, instead of losing his head and being carried off his feet by what other men are thinking and saying and getting and doing, a man should look to and stand by his own sense of progress.

Starting with what the Almighty has given *me*, be it ever so little, and though my advance be away behind some other man's starting-point—am *I*, a law unto myself, progressing ? That is the point ! Let me feel that I am, and I will have a blessed sense of independence. I shall not care if others are ahead. I am doing my best—not another man's best, but my best. I am filling my place—not another man's place, but my place. I am doing my work—not another man's work, but my work. I am running my race—not another man's race, but my race.

" Not in the clamor of the crowded street,
   Not in the shouts and plaudits of the throng,
   But in ourselves, are triumph and defeat."

I am to use, as the stage by which I gauge my progress, not some other's stage of life, but the previous one in my own. If I can look back and say, " I have advanced over that "—it may not be very illustrious, it may not be very great, the world may think little of it— yet be it advance over my former levels, then a new happiness arrives in my soul ; I am enabled to get up and go on ; and in a world of my own, independent of any other man's world, I feel God's commendation there. I am advancing along lines and within limits set me by the Almighty. I am in harmony with myself, my fellows, and the universe ; and, unconfused, unhumiliated because I have not come up to some other man's goal, I am as independent as a king and as kingly as a son of God.

" Ask thy lone soul what laws are plain to thee—
   Thee and no other ! Stand and fall by them,
   That is the part for thee."

When disheartened, then, by what others are saying and thinking and getting and doing, I can fall back for my beatitude of peace upon this—my own soul's sense of progress.

Phillips Brooks, disquieted by a cartoon which made light of the defects of his qualities, whipped it over and wrote on the back—

" Is this then the way he looks ?
A tedious creature, Phillips Brooks.
Well, surely, if 'tis thus he looks
The world well doubts this Phillips Brooks.
Yet, if he knows himself, he'll try
To give those doubtful looks the lie.
He'll walk the path that shall be shown,
He'll trust a strength that's not his own,

Till men, when laying him to rest,
Shall say, ' At least, he did his best.' "

Nothing can throw a man off his equilibrium and equipoise if he but have the balance-wheel of progress.

Criticism cannot; neither can even sin or age.

David committed a sin whose penalty cursed his family and rotted the family tree; cursed the kingdom and displaced the crown; cursed the temple and violated the very stones. Even then he met God with it. He subjected it to His breath, and though his outward life plans were lost, God made him through his psalms of penitence and praise a Temple, if not for his age, for millenniums; a Priest, if not for his day, for all days—a Priest to whom all penitent souls in the stained temple of life may go for consolation.

Meet God with your sin. Subject it to his breath. He can make you like David, a temple, if not for a multitude, for one; a priest, if not for a host, for another. In this, as with the fallen king, may be your greater glory—in this your masterpiece.

Here comes a man who grants even that, yet says, " But age has thrown me from the track of progress. I am growing too old."

I confront such a man with his faith which he has yet unfathomed. I charge him with its uncaught message.

Hast thou not known? hast thou not heard, that the everlasting God, the Lord, the Creator of the ends of this earth, fainteth not, neither is weary? He giveth power to the faint; and to them that have no might he increaseth strength. Even the youths shall faint and be weary, and the young men shall utterly fall: but they that wait upon the Lord shall renew their strength; they shall mount up with wings as eagles; they shall run, and not be weary; and they shall walk, and not faint.

No! An old man has not lost, but extracted, the essences of life. The realities are his, stripped of husks and forms.

" The soul's dark cottage, battered and decayed,
    Lets in new light through chinks which time has made;
Stronger by weakness, wiser men become
As they draw near to their eternal home."

The brilliant mistakes of to-day are the mistakes of young men who in the enthusiasm of shooting have not seen where bullets hit; who have mistaken form for realities and have never been disillusioned. The voice of the old man, pushed aside as good for nothing, is a great need to offset their rashness. It needs to be lifted from oblivion again. It needs to be elevated at the city's gates—for it is true yet that we need " old men for counsel and young men for war." A man is never unneeded.

Age cannot throw him off the track of progress, nor dislodge him from its beatitude. Nothing can. There is no exception. It is a universal principle, true for all time. Hence no other one thing in the universe can give a greater sense of joy and peace than the consciousness of progress. It is indeed everywhere the beatitude of the individual.

We have heard it said, " I smile when I see God's completeness round about my incompleteness, and round my restlessness his rest." It is beautiful, but not wholly true. We smile when we see our incompleteness progressing towards his completeness, and, progressing towards his rest, our restlessness. The progress of the Spirit is the smile of the soul.

### III. Progress—the Beatitude of God.

He progresses in his physical worlds.

Such is the depth of the immensity of space that the farthest star's light, though traveling 186,000 miles a second, takes 800,000 years to reach the earth, and the nearest star's light takes no less than four years. But in this immensity of space new worlds are forming before our eyes. Fire-mist and star-dust are seeable wheeling about a central core in all the stages of formation of new globes, forming as this globe formed ages ago. The spectra of the spectroscope, which catches their rays and splits them into prismatic bars, finds such bars identical with the bars which known elements on this earth, when set afire, burn—a fact that proves that those starry worlds are forming out of the same elements as this planet.

There they are—being created in unimaginably larger proportions than our globe, but in like stages of construction ! There still is enacted the divine fiat, " Let there be light !" There still the morning stars sing together, and all the sons of God shout for joy! There " His arm is stretched out still!"

Instead of " the eternal silence of the infinite spaces, where the intolerable vastness bows him down and the awful homeless spaces scare his soul;" instead of "the cold, pitiless, passionless eyes, cold fires, yet with power to burn and brand His nothingness into man;" instead of " a ghostly eyesocket that stares at us where an eye should have been," the seer detects the living God—God, moving, acting, progressing!

God is also progressing in his Truth. The Bible is a progressive revelation. Troubled by the discovery in the Bible of outworn standards and lower levels—scientific, literary, historical—I have in this definition, all stumbling-blocks removed, an increasingly enlivened Bible, and the recovery for myself and others of the experience that the blessed "secret of Christian rejuvenation is a bath in the original sources."

The revelation of God has always been commensurate with the capacity of man to receive it. God is " the Father of Lights, with whom is no variableness, neither shadow of turning." The variable quantity has not been God, but man. Man, being the medium of that revelation, and man's mind having varied, the received revelation has varied. Light has always been the same. The changeable factor has been the medium.

It is like physical light and the eye. Science knows that once the light shone and that there was no organism of the eye to receive it. But light beating on the rind of the creature's skin finally developed a crude organ. Then, still shining, more and more it refined, developed, and enlarged the organ, till its retina caught more and more of the light ray. The sunlight was the same but the medium differed. The light came to the creature gradually through the gradually developed eye. The Creator made the eye as well as the light, and therefore determined the gradual and progressive reception of the light. Just so, it is not to disclaim God and to say that only man made the Bible when we call it a progressive revelation, with truths, standards, and levels at first imperfect and lower, then advancing commensurately

with the capacity of man to receive it, till in " the path of the Just it is as the shining light, that shineth more and more unto the perfect day."

It is like the evolution of the window-pane. The sunlight has always been the same. But once the window-pane was of oiled skin, and the light that shone through into human dwellings vague and darkling. Then the window-pane was of oiled paper, and the light that fell through was brighter but still vague. Then the window-pane was of crude, rough, coarse glass, and the light that fell through was brighter, yet still discolored. Finally the window-pane was of melted white sand, pure as crystal, and the light that illuminated the dwelling was absolutely clear and brilliant.

So with the Bible—the light of God is eternally the same. In Genesis, as through oilskin, it fell through the child-mind of primitive man, and the resultant light recorded was real but vague. In the Kings it permeated the oiled paper, as it were, of the minds of that day, and the reflection was brighter but still vague. In the Prophets it passed through the raw, crude glass of the prophets' mind, and the light that shone through was radiant and roseate, realer than ever before, but not yet clear. Finally, in the mind of Christ came the crystal-pure medium, and we see in it " as in a glass—the glory of the Lord."

To detect God thus in his truth, moving, progressing, through man to man, medium to medium, age to age, is to see in the old dead Bible the Living God. Instead of making us throw the Bible away at the discovery of lower levels, it will make us cry, " Surely the Lord is in this place ; and I knew it not."

God progresses not only in his worlds and in his truth, but in his love!

The love of God reached its high tide in Christ on Calvary. There was its extension into time and space. Christ on Calvary was the fountain head on earth of the underground stream of the atoning love of God. There was the nativity, not of the Christ-babe, but of Love, full-born, not of Mary at the incarnation, but out of the travail of God's heart when Christ cried, " It is finished." There, at Calvary, the love of God first reached high tide    Yet it did not end there. In height Love's high tide was reached. In breadth it was not.

Is it high tide when out in mid-ocean the water rises to full sea? No; it is not high tide till it sweeps over the surface of the intervening seas, uplifting their level to its level, surging earthwards till it fills every empty channel and lifts every listed ship. Not till then is the tide high and the sea full. So the love of God that reached its blessed

height in Christ on Calvary did not end there. It is still progressing. We are in a stage of that progress now. Starting from that point in the mid-ocean of time, at the crucifixion, it still goes sweeping over the intervening seas of humanity, lifting their levels to its level, surging earthwards, till it fill every empty channel and lift every listed ship. Yes, God's love is still progressing! There's no question about that. The only question is, *Are we progressing with it?*

# GEORG BRANDES: SOME CHARAC-
# TERISTICS

## BY PAUL HARBOE

THE Macmillan Company have just issued Georg Brandes's " Main Currents in Nineteenth Century Literature " in a new illustrated edition. This monumental work is now completely accessible in English. The six volumes bear the following titles: I. The Emigrant Literature; II. The Romantic School in Germany; III. The Reaction in France; IV. Naturalism in England; V. The Romantic School in France; VI. Young Germany. It is only fair to say parenthetically that the arduous task of translating Brandes's pure, flexible Danish into our language has been admirably done.

In his introduction to the second volume of the series the Danish critic makes these statements: "I shall endeavor . . . to treat the history of literature as humanly as possible, to go as deep down as I can, to seize upon the remotest, innermost movements which prepared for and produced the various literary phenomena. . . . By preference, I shall always. when possible, embody the personal in the abstract. . . . Drawing-room history of literature, like drawing-room poetry, sees in human life a drawing-room, a decorated ball-room—the furniture and people alike polished, the brilliant illumination excluding all possibility of dark corners. Let those who choose to do so look at things thus. It is not my point of view."

From the attitude these lines denote (they were written over thirty years ago) Brandes has never departed. In a certain sense and to a certain extent his development has taken place along a straight course. To the best of my knowledge, his life has been shaken by no such phenomenon as a spiritual reaction. The difference between Brandes at thirty and the same man at sixty-four is mainly one of stature. The years have left his early convictions, beliefs, principles, practically unchanged. He knew and accepted himself, stood erect and strong in the light of his assurance, at an age when most men are still groping in the dark of moral trepidation, surrounded with phantoms of multiform questions, riddles, enigmas. Once having recognized his own particular genius in that of the man who taught him the very rudiments of modern criticism— Hyppolyte Taine—the pupil was never to renounce his first and chief master. What wonder, then, that here and there throughout Brandes's many books we should hear, as it were, the echo of the great Frenchman's voice?

A journey with the subject of this little sketch is not so much a journey among books as an intercourse, a companionship, with men. His interest in what certain writers have said is, indeed, sometimes even subordinate to his curiosity as to what they have done or how they have lived. It seems trivial (for the obviousness of the thing) to observe that there is nothing of the traditional Easy Chair atmosphere ·in his· writings, nothing suggestive of the familiar-talks-in-a-library style of literature. As discursive as any contemporary, he yet never chats with you good-humoredly, reminiscently, about this or that situation, character, or subject. It is apparent that the Gentle Reader type is not, with him, a favorite presence.

The revolutionary spirit has always exercised a strange charm upon Brandes. Hence the men in whose company he himself appears most impressive are Shelley, Byron, Börne, Hugo, Heine, Ibsen, etc.—men at war with conventional society, all forms of authority— dramatic figures, iconoclasts. With those writers who seem screened behind their writings or who stand obscure, remote, timid, in the background of their stage he has scant patience. Beauty to Brandes is in a large sense inseparable from strength, strength equally so from passion, and passion from the fighting spirit, the latter quality being essentially indicative of personality. We have had too many harmless, soft-speaking, polite poets, he seems to contend. The sea of literature is altogether too calm and the crafts that sail it too gorgeous, too fashionable-looking. Let us have more open boats with fearless, viking-like commanders at the helm. The pen, like the sword, is a weapon to fight with, not a mere brush to splash colors. Be rebellious, Brandes further seems to exhort the young writer—audacious, fiery, determined, human· or dæmoniac, but, above all, be fearless. Let your books be strong with the strength of your struggles, let them have the taste of the battles you won— or lost. Learn the lesson of the great individual, the great personality, whether intellectual aristocrat or spiritual democrat, and in his deeds you shall discover the secret of all human glory.

If there be any living critic greater than Georg Brandes, there certainly is none like him ; none, that is, comparable to him for power of persuasiveness, eloquence, and stimulation. For one who has had occasion to acquaint himself with the story of his remarkable career it is impossible to read Brandes without feeling that he appeals most forcibly to youth, or, more properly, to the spirit of youth, which he has ever championed, and whose fire has never ceased to burn within his own bosom. Youth, and all that that grand word implies, represents to him the superb fundamental pregnant influence in human life. Without its devoted admiration, its passionate enthusiasm, what shall a man's endeavor avail? But if he can animate, arouse it, focus and harness its immeasurable resources of will and courage, he shall conquer empires.

In cultivating his critical faculty and storing his mind with myriad knowledge, Brandes has· yet effectually guarded himself against the deadly affliction of staleness—to speak with the athletes. He has read tons of books and spent thousands of hours in libraries; but of equal significance is the fact that he has known thousands of men and women, and lived the life of a man of the world, constantly in touch with his environment, with the various manifest movements of his time, and forever "on the lookout" for the appearance of some new formidable gladiator in the arena of civilization. It was Brandes, we may recall, who first interpreted to Scandinavians the message of such men as John Stuart Mill, Henrik Ibsen, and Friedrich Nietzsche. And how he welcomed, how he celebrated, how he rejoiced in their achievement !

Brandes has been reproached in certain quarters on the score of his field of' endeavor being cosmopolitan. ·It is true, of course, that his chief works treat of foreign subjects. He has written a large volume dealing with the city of Berlin, biographies of Lassalle, of Disraeli, numerous studies in the French, German, and English literature, books on Russia and Poland, etc. However, it seems to me unjust to accuse the author of "William Shakespeare" of having neglected home product. For many years he acted as touchstone to countless young writers, encouraged and guided them, read their manuscripts, pleaded their case with those whom it concerned. He did all this at a great sacrifice of energy and time, and to a certain extent he does so even to-day. Besides, it should not be lost to view that quite apart from his sympathetically admirable monograph on Sören Kierkegaard he has appraised the fictions of practically every modern Danish novelist of any importance whatever, and published appreciative essays on every representative exponent of the school that came into existence with J. P. Jacobsen's "Marie Grubbe" in 1876. However, for certain revered Danish classics he has had few words of praise and many of disparagement. Herein lies one reason why he will not for many years to come (if ever the miracle transpires) grow dear to the hearts of his fellow-countrymen. Another may be found in the circumstance, I believe, that his eye has never opened to the splendid greatness of Grundtvig as a moral force. But there are many other explanations, and this is scarcely the proper occasion for enumerating them

During the last decade his fame has flown far abroad. In most Continental cities he is admired not only as an illustrious critic but as a defiant, impassioned man of ideas, the aggressive enemy of hypocrisy, ignorance, and oppression. Public dinners in his honor have been given at Paris, Berlin, Vienna, Stockholm, Prague, and other places. I have seen him referred to by Polish, Russian, and Finnish newspapers as "that loyal friend of our people." I mention this as an illustration of the effect of what has been called rather scornfully his "political purpose." Time alone, of course, will show whether Anglo-Saxon civilization is at all amenable to the doctrines he inculcates. Verily there are vast gulfs between the ground he stands upon and that upon which we have been and are continually being taught to build our houses of life. But, all his "doctrines" apart, Brandes has produced several critical masterpieces that no student of literature can afford to disregard. He is certainly, it seems to me, one of the most inspiring, most definite and brilliant of living critics.

## Comment on Current Books

**Abyssinia**　　Mr. Robert P. Skinner is one of the most energetic men in the American consular service. Stationed at Marseilles, his acute observation is by no means bounded by the limits of his immediate consular district, important as is that district. The ships which come into the port of Marseilles fly many flags—indeed, scarcely any of the world's ports shows a more varied assortment. The particular function of Marseilles has always been its connection with the Orient. From this port in every epoch travelers from Europe have set forth to Asia and Africa. Within the past few years a special interest has attached to African commerce. The vast continent is overwhelmingly occupied by colonizing powers, as we know, France and England having absorbed most of it, but leaving Germany, Belgium, and Portugal in the possession of regions more or less interesting and valuable. Two native States still enjoying marked prominence because of their independence and individuality are Morocco and Abyssinia. The latter has long been enviously regarded by certain Powers, but has remained ruggedly independent. A chief reason for this is, we suppose, ethnological—at all events, those who suspect the Abyssinian type of representing negro blood and negro qualities, physical and mental, would do well to read Mr. Skinner's excellent book. Racial differentiation must have led the inhabitants of the African highlands in all ages to be independent and self-sufficient in trade as well as in politics and religion. Mr. Skinner's attention was early attracted to the Abyssinian field as affording a further outlet for American commerce, and finally, three years ago, on his initiative, our Government sent an expedition to East Africa and appropriately put Mr. Skinner himself in charge. An interesting evidence of Abyssinian self-sufficiency is that, though the country represents but a small part of the ancient Ethiopian Empire, the Abyssinian court is still significantly known to the inhabitants of East Africa as the court of Ethiopia, or "The Court of the King of Kings." Most interesting of all to us is Mr. Skinner's account of the ancient Ethiopian Church, which upholds the monophysite doctrine, namely, the doctrine that Christ has but one nature, partly divine and partly human, in contradistinction to the doctrine that by the Incarnation two complete natures, the divine and the human, were united without confusion. Thus every thing in Abyssinia seems unusual, individual, and characteristic, as well may be when we realize that we have to do with a hoary civilization which drew its inspiration from Solomon, and for very many centuries has been cut off from the outside world; indeed, in its essential aspects, Abyssinian civilization to-day is the same as that which prevailed in Palestine two millenniums ago. (Abyssinia of To-Day. By Robert P. Skinner. Longmans, Green & Co., New York. $3.)

*Cap'n Chadwick* This posthumously published book furnishes a vivid picture not only of its subject, Captain Chadwick, Marblehead skipper, shoemaker, and storekeeper, but incidentally of the antecedents and early environment of his son, John White Chadwick, who became one of the foremost of American Unitarian preachers and writers. Captain Chadwick was a man of heroic mold; this simple story of his life is good to read in pessimistic hours when the lament comes to mind that " wealth accumulates and men decay." At the tender age of seven he began his toilful industrial career; he early took to the sea, was for many years captain of a Marblehead schooner, and one of his proudest achievements was the bringing of his vessel and crew safely out of the Great September Gale of 1846; he was a man of marvelous memory, of remarkable physical power, and of sterling personal qualities. As a portrait of the rugged yet tender, courageous and faithful New Englander of the older days, who filled his humble station with a fine ethical ideal and with real greatness of soul, this little biography will be treasured not alone by those who revere its author's memory, but by the wider public who will find in it a sympathetic yet discriminating characterization of a life well worth telling about, but of a kind not often described outside of fiction. (Cap'n Chadwick. By John White Chadwick. True American Types Series. American Unitarian Association, Boston. 60c., net.)

*The Decade Before the War* Few volumes in the " American Nation " serial history of the United States have proved so thoroughly satisfactory to us as has Professor Theodore Clarke Smith's study of the exceedingly difficult decade preceding the outbreak of the Civil War. It was a decade in which, as the historian must always recognize, the supreme fact was the final breakdown of the effort to solve the slavery problem by compromise. But this was by no means the only fact of the decade. Side by side with the developments in the struggle over slavery ran other currents—social, economic, and intellectual— that left an enduring impress on the life of the United States. Most historians have taken these currents into account, but usually, it must be said, they have laid such emphasis on the sectional controversy that their readers have failed to grasp firmly the real significance of the non-political movements and occurrences of the decade. Into this error Professor Smith does not fall. He pays due regard to the slavery issue, tracing its ramifications in the North, in the South, in Kansas, and at Washington, and unfolding the sequence of stirring events in a most lucid way. But he is equally careful to instruct the reader in those other important facts of the period—the industrial and commercial expansion due to the railway " mania;" the disastrous after effects of that same mania; the contrasting social and economic conditions in the North and South; the complications in the foreign relations of the United States; the wonderful literary activity of the decade, and the unrest that found vent in the spread of "isms," from spiritualism to the crusade for "woman's rights." All this stands clearly revealed, and in proper perspective, in his pages, the tone of which, moreover, is eminently praiseworthy. So that, although Professor Smith seems to have delved into original sources with less assiduity than some of his colaborers, the conscientious student cannot fail to derive from him assistance to the better understanding of conditions as they existed throughout the Union in the years just preceding the great war. (The American Nation. Vol. XVIII. Parties and Slavery. By Theodore Clarke Smith, Ph.D. Harper & Brothers, New York. $2, net.)

*An Early American Document* With the publication of the "Court Book" of the Virginia Company" the National Government places within the reach of every student of American history what has long been regarded as one of the most precious manuscript treasures in the United States. As is well known, it was the Virginia Company that planted the first successful English colony in America, and— what is not so well known—it was by this same Company that the seeds of self-government were first sown here. When in the passage of time King James the First determined to revoke the Company's charters and resume the government of Virginia for himself, the secretary of the Company, fearing the destruction of the official records, caused a transcript of them to be made. His fears were justified to the extent that the original documents have long ago disappeared; but his transcript, as fate would have it, was preserved to become the property of the United States. And this it is that has now been put into printed form under the most careful editorial supervision and with faithful adherence to the quaint spelling and diction of the seventeenth-century makers of America. It does not tell the story of the Virginia Company from its beginnings in 1606—the records of the early years have gone no man knows where—but it does tell it from 1619 onwards, and from its pages the student will be able to gain for himself a clear idea of the motives and ideals of the Virginia "adventurers" and of the part they played in determining the future trend of government in America as well as in their own land. From the student's standpoint, too, the value of the present publication is increased by Miss Kingsbury's elaborate expository and critical introduction discussing the character and achievement of the Virginia Company and the various known sources for study of the Company's affairs. (The Records of the Virginia Company: The Court Book, 1619–1624. Edited by Susan Myra Kingsbury, A.M., Ph.D. Government Printing Office, Washington. $4 per set of two volumes.)

**The Fairy Ring** A new collection of the most readable fairy tales, by two editors, Kate Douglas Wiggin and Nora Archibald Smith, who are not only familiar with the literature of the subject, but—what is quite as important—are also familiar with the tastes of children and know the stories that specially appeal to them. The volume is supplied with a characteristically vivacious introduction and is very prettily made. (The Fairy Ring. Edited by Kate Douglas Wiggin and Nora Archibald Smith. McClure, Phillips & Co., New York.)

**The Friendly Town** A charming little volume of selections in prose and verse, prepared, as the subtitle tells the reader, "for the urbane," and compiled by Mr. E. V. Lucas, whose recent books, "A Wanderer in London" and "Listener's Lure," have proved him to be a writer of sentiment and quality. These selections, which have to do with friends, the table, music and painting, the courtly poets, the wise men, and kindred themes, show on almost every page the taste of the cultivated lover of good literature. (The Friendly Town: A Little Book for the Urbane. Compiled by E. V. Lucas. Henry Holt & Co., New York. $1.50.)

**Lane's Arabian Nights** A new edition in four volumes of convenient size of Lane's well-known translation, edited by Stanley Lane-Poole, with slight modifications. This edition reproduces the text of the edition of 1859 with its notes, to which brief additions have been made. Two stories not included in Lane's translation, on account of their wide popularity, are added to the tales in this form. (The Thousand and One Nights: The Arabian Nights. Vols. II. and III. Translated by Edward William Lane. Edited by Stanley Lane-Poole, M.A., Litt.D. The Macmillan Company, New York. $1, net, per vol.)

**Literature and Life in School** This title exactly describes the scope of Miss Colby's book, which is intended for teachers, and aims to show that literature should be made a vital part of school life—not merely in the formal instruction, but in many incidental ways and in a spontaneous rather than a conventional fashion. The book is very well worth reading, not merely by teachers, but by all who have an interest in the development of the child mind and in the advance of good taste and right standards in literary study. An appendix gives in condensed form suggestions for class and outside reading. (Literature and Life in School. By J. Rose Colby, Ph.D. Houghton, Mifflin & Co., Boston. $1, net.)

**Looking Forward** This is a conspicuous contribution to what may be called the literature of impractical reform. Not for one but for many vital problems in the contemporary life of the United States does Mr. Cirkel proffer a solution. In turn he takes up and with remarkable ease disposes of the issues raised by the growing power of corporations, by the railway companies, by the insurance revelations, by the relations between capital and labor, by the spread of the socialistic movement, and by the necessity of securing an "elastic currency." Always, however, it is only too evident that he has developed his suggestions without due regard to two fundamental questions—Will they, if given effect, bring about the results anticipated? and Can they be given effect? It is quite true that there is a good deal in his pages to stimulate thought. But this is far overbalanced by the visionary character of the author's principal proposals and by the extremism of many of his views. (Looking Forward. By August Cirkel. The Looking Forward Publishing Company, Chicago. $1.25.)

**Modern English Literature** A new and revised edition, enlarged, Mr. Gosse tells his readers, to receive for the first time a collection of the portraits of the principal writers discussed in it. The list of illustrations fills two pages, and the title of the book must be translated in the largest possible terms; for under the title " Modern English Literature " the book endeavors to show the movement of that literature from the time of Langland—the age of romance and chivalry—to that of James Anthony Froude and of Dante Gabriel Rossetti. (Modern English Literature. By Edmund Gosse, M.A., LL.D. Frederick A. Stokes Company, New York. $2.50, net. Postage, 18 cents.)

*Napoleon's Life in Elba* The story of Napoleon's ten months of exile in Elba has been told before, notably by his confidant Pons de l'Hérault, but there is ample room for a narrative such as has been written by M. Paul Gruyer, who brings together the wealth of information contained in scattered and forgotten sources, and presents it in an eminently readable form. Beginning with a vivid description of the Elba of to-day, and thus providing a realistic background for the events of 1814-15, he follows those events in chronological sequence and in full but never wearisome detail from the moment of Napoleon's arrival to the hour of his escape, bent on fresh conquests and the rehabilitation of his prestige. The point of view is to a surprising extent that of a participant in the once mighty Emperor's fallen fortunes—a point of view, we need hardly say, attained by the most painstaking study of the contemporary records. We see Napoleon alternating between hope and despair, we see him in his days of lethargy and in those other days of feverish excitement, passing from town to town, drilling his toy army, superintending public works, lording it over his tiny court. And always we are made to feel that he was in reality playing a stupendous part, lulling his enemies into misplaced confidence, and biding his time, if impatiently, against the moment when he could strike once more. Not, be it noted, that M. Gruyer is a Napoleonic idolater. He has too clear a perception of his hero's faults. But he sees his hero as a man, and, thus seeing him, presents him as we must believe he really was during those weary months of waiting on the rock-held island in the Mediterranean. (Napoleon, King of Elba. From the French of Paul Gruyer. J. B. Lippincott Company, Philadelphia. $3.50, net.)

*New Edition of Murray's " Japan "* A good deal of new material will be found in this edition of the late Dr. Murray's well-known and exceedingly useful work on Japan. Mr. Albert White Vorse contributes supplementary chapters continuing the narrative history through the periods of the Chinese and Russian wars, and the Baron Kentaro Kaneko, who has been in confidential relations with the Government of his native land, undertakes to set forth for American and British readers the policies and ideals of modern Japan. Writing at considerable disadvantage, the outcome of the war with Russia being still uncertain when he was penning his lines, he is nevertheless really informing, and his statements may be accepted with few reservations. He scouts the idea that the nations of the West are in danger of a " Yellow Peril," depicts Japan as the Oriental champion of the Anglo-Saxon civilization, insists that her national policy is based on truly liberal principles, and asserts that in her international dealings she will be found no less liberal. Of Mr. Vorse's contribution it need only be said that the author fully appreciates the importance of the great wars of 1894-95 and 1904-5 as establishing Japan's place in the family of nations, and that if his presentation of the subject matter hardly attains the standard set by Dr. Murray, it has the merit of being compact and lucid. (Japan. By David Murray, Ph.D., LL.D. G. P. Putnam's Sons, New York. $1.50, net.)

*Pardonable Indiscretions* Italy and its wonderful climate have always contributed to indiscretions. No one can fall under the spell of that country and be quite the same impassive, unresponsive human being who gets along fairly well in America or England. The physical, mental, and social atmosphere of Italy contributes to expansiveness. We see this in the writers who have described Italian scenery and structures and statues and pictures; they have used more glowing language than their usual custom—to take some names at random, Gautier, Dumas, Taine, Bourget, among Frenchmen, and Ruskin, Carmichael, Maurice Hewlett, and Arthur Symons among Englishmen. If this is true as to nature and art, it is certainly true as to society. Writers on that subject are apt to describe more than might be expected as to the Italians of distinguished rank whom they may meet. In her delightful " Roma Beata " Mrs. Maud Howe Elliott gave us a good example of what might be termed high-class and worth-while gossip. In her just published volume, Tryphosa Bates Batcheller excels Mrs. Elliott in certain charming indiscretions and in naïve self-revelations; but the personal tone is so strenuously evident throughout that it becomes wearisome. The book is ingenuously written. The interest of the author is apparently in herself first of all, secondly in the exalted personages whom she has been able to meet, and only thirdly in the grand old nation with its historic associations and its marvelous evidences of art on every hand. Nevertheless, to those who would gain some gossiping knowledge of Italian society and do not mind occasional misstatements, such a book has undoubted merit, and to its readers any emotional egoisms and indiscretions may seem pardonable. (Glimpses of Italian Court Life. By Tryphosa Bates Batcheller. Doubleday, Page & Co., New York. $4.80.)

*Pocahontas Again* Mr. Boyd Smith's "Story of Pocahontas and Captain John Smith" should have prominent place among picture books of the year. As a bit of decoration in page and print and illustration and cover the book seems unique. Its text is apparently historically correct. The story is told vividly and reinforced emphatically by the three-color process pictures. The publication has special timeliness, for the celebration is not far distant of the three hundredth anniversary of the settlement of Jamestown. (The Story of Pocahontas and Captain John Smith. Told and Pictured by E. Boyd Smith. Houghton, Mifflin & Co., Boston. $2.50, net.)

*The Political History of England* The period allotted to Professor Oman in the Hunt-Poole "Political History of England" is one that has been pretty generally neglected by historians, probably because of the inaccessibility of much of the material for its study. But it is a period of first-rate importance, covering as it does the warring fortunes of the Houses of Lancaster and York and the rise of Parliament to a pre eminence from which it was to be only temporarily dislodge1 by the absolutism of the Tudors. It is, therefore, a pleasure to find that Professor Oman has explored it with a thoroughness in no way inferior to that achieved by any of his fellow-contributors to this co-operative history; and that he has surpassed most of them in point of readability. Especially is this latter feature of his work conspicuous in his handling of the French wars and the several insurrections—notably the great rebellion of 1381, the rebellion led by Wat Tyler and John Ball—that disturbed the peace of the realm from the early years of Richard II. to the closing years of Richard III. He is less fortunate in his treatment of some of the leading historic personages of the period—for example, Henry V. and Warwick—who seem very remote indeed in his interpretation. But the general result of

his labors must be to stimulate a greater interest in this transition era in the history of England, as well as to increase the student's knowledge of it. And, as always in the several volumes of this work, a comprehensive bibliography is included to facilitate independent research. (The Political History of England. Vol. IV., 1377-1485. By C. Oman, M.A. Longmans, Green & Co., New York. $2.60, net.)

*Primitive Christianity* In this revised and enlarged edition a veteran theologian has availed himself of the latest fruits of learned research. The present volume, after a chapter on the first Christian community, is occupied with the Apostle Paul, his writings, and his theology. Paul's theology may be represented by the figure (not used by Dr. Pfleiderer) of an ellipse, whose two foci are his doctrine of atonement, in which Hebrew thought predominates, and his doctrine of the Spirit, more cognate with Greek thought. Seneca, his Stoic contemporary, conceived of a "holy spirit," given from above to good men. "Paul's ethic," says Pfleiderer, "is an autonomous idealism, nearly related to that of the Stoics, but on a more religious foundation." A central point in his theology is given in his saying, "The Lord is the Spirit, and where the Spirit of the Lord is, there is liberty" (2 Corinthians iii. 17). This identification of the principle of religious enthusiasm—the Spirit—with the historical personality of the Lord Christ "satisfied equally," says Pfleiderer, "the two needs of that age, its mystical longing for revelation and self-surrender, and its effort after a National ethical ideal," a problem which has exercised the best thinkers of the Gentile world. In his conception of the self-incarnating divine principle as the Spirit, which he identifies variously both with God and with Christ, Paul is more akin to the modern mind than John in his conception of it as the Logos. Professor Pfleiderer is not *persona grata* to disciples of the old orthodoxy. He does not conceive of Christianity as miraculous, but "as the necessary outcome of the development of the religious spirit of our race." In this view, he contends, is to be found "the most solid and imposing Apology for Christianity which it is possible to conceive." (Primitive Christianity. Vol. I. By Otto Pfleiderer, D.D. Translated by W. Montgomery, B.D. Edited by Rev. W. D. Morrison, LL.D. G. P. Putnam's Sons, New York. $3.50.)

# Letters to The Outlook

## QUEEN MARY'S PRAYER

My attention was recently called to an article in The Outlook giving the Latin verses written in the Prayer-Book of Mary Queen of Scots, and generally attributed to her; together with a very admirable metrical translation signed " J. C. Crowell."

The translator remarks, in reference to the original, that in no edition of Latin hymns, ancient or modern, has he been able to find another metrical version in English.

It may interest Mr. Crowell, and your readers, to mention that this prayer was most gracefully and pathetically expressed in English verse by Arthur Cleveland Coxe, who later became Bishop of Western New York. This version was among his earlier poems, and is included, if I remember aright—though I have not a copy of that book at hand—in his "Christian Ballads." It is entitled "The Lament of Mary Queen of Scots," and is as follows :

"O Blessed Redeemer, I've trusted in Thee.
O Saviour, my Jesu, now liberate me !
In horrible prison
And gloom have arisen
My sighs, O my Jesu, incessant to Thee.
But O, on my sorrow
Hath brightened no morrow,
Yet hear me, my Jesu, and liberate me !

O Blessed Redeemer, I've trusted in Thee !
And still will I trust Thee to liberate me.
And so, while I languish,
I cry in my anguish,
Adoring, imploring, and bending the knee.
In sorrow and tremor,
O Blessed Redeemer,
Smile on me from Heaven and liberate me !"

WILLIAM J. SEABURY.

New York City.

## THE GENTLE ART OF KILLING FISH

I have been surprised and disappointed that Mr. McFarland's vigorous protest against fishing for "sport" has not aroused more discussion. This protest has a significance far beyond the particular phase of nature-attitude that he discusses. In the original article, and in the one reply to it, much is made of the question as to whether the fish does or does not suffer in the protracted process of killing; but it seems to me that the real question is a human one, and that it is to be answered by personal feeling rather than by argument. Every one has a right to his personal feeling, and therefore I had hoped for a somewhat full expression, as giving us some clue to current opinion in this time of awakened nature sympathy.

Two features of killing for sport are to be distinguished : (1) Is this sport worthy a man and worth the while? (2) What relation has it to the ethics of fair play? These questions go deeper than mere sentimental sympathy with dumb animals that we assume to be suffering. The question of fair play seems usually to be overlooked. The hunter or fisherman has every advantage of knowledge and invention; he usually attacks a defenseless, unsuspecting, and harmless creature ; he ordinarily exposes himself to no danger or risk. He employs every means of stealth and has every vantage of long-range weapons and of position. It is said that the hunter matches his skill against the animal's cunning ; but the animal is usually unaware of the game until too late.

I have no desire to pass judgment, nor even to express a general opinion; I wish only to state my own feeling, hoping that others may do likewise : the books and periodicals that make much of killing for sport are distasteful, although I am not wholly out of sympathy with hunting and fishing. Emerson's attitude appeals to me :

"He goes to the river-side—
Not hook nor line hath he;
He stands in the meadows wide—
Nor gun nor scythe to see."

Ithaca, New York.          L. H. BAILEY.

## THE INQUISITION: AN INTERPRETATION

Will you allow me to suggest two brief lines of thought apropos of the short review of Dr. Lea's "Spanish Inquisition" in your number of November 10 ?

1. All scholars of whose books I have any knowledge hold that the Inquisition in Spain was never a purely religious institution. Some authors hold that it was a mixed tribunal—partly political and legal, and partly religious. Others hold that it was purely and exclusively a civil institution. In these last months the History Professor at our University here has been lecturing on the bibliography of this question, and the amount of the literature on the subject is enormous. I have not been able to look into all the books personally, but, so far as I know, not one of those scholars, of any reputation, has ever considered the Inquisition to be purely a Church court. If the historical student can regard the Inquisition, not from a religious, but from a legal and political point of view, he will not be so liable to break out into

97

denunciations which do no one any good, and but perpetuate historical mistakes.

2. The ordinary run of readers know very little about the mediæval conceptions of law, and therefore they judge the Inquisition from the point of view of the Church instead of from that of the State. The law of the Middle Ages considered the Church as that power, above the State, which lent to the State its claim on man's obedience and loyalty. The old simile was that of sun and moon. The State was the moon, which shone with the reflected light of the Church, the sun. All civil rights were thus bound up with membership in the Church. Only as a member of her higher order did the individual have any civil rights at all. So soon as he cut himself off from the Church by unbelief he lost immediately all his civil rights. He was an utter outcast. Whether this was a just conception or not is beside the question. But such was the teaching of all the great judges and legal experts of the time. Thus the heretic, without civil rights, was also a traitor to the State. He had struck at that source from which the State derived all its power. And as such he was a public menace. But, having forfeited his civil rights, he could be proceeded against summarily, and it was considered rather merciful of the State to allow him any trial at all. Hence in the Inquisition courts (which were predominantly civil, not religious) the main point was to prove the accused's heresy. If that were proved, the rest was simple. The court could proceed against him as a man outside the law, who was endeavoring to overturn the very foundations of society. He was the "Anarchist" of his age. If he had held any civil or ecclesiastical position, he was publicly degraded, to show to a people, who had to be taught by symbolical acts, that he had forfeited all rights which his position had conferred upon him. It was like the modern ceremony of military degradation of an officer who has sold information to the enemy. The officer's sword is broken, his insignia, even the buttons of his uniform, stripped away. He is an outcast, and, before martial law, has not rights at all any more.

Of course as this old mediæval conception of the relation of Church and State fell away there followed a period of clouded legal conceptions, from which the idea of the modern State only gradually emerged. But that was long after the Spanish Inquisition had passed out of its powerful position.

For a clear statement of these legal facts I can recommend your readers to Prince Hohenlohe's Memoirs, which have made such a sensation in political Germany in these last weeks. In the first volume, dealing with the Prince's activity as Bavarian Prime Minister, the mediæval and the modern conception of the State are very clearly illustrated in the political differences between the liberal and ultramontane parties in Bavaria and Austria. Also the Prince's struggle against the Vatican Council and the letters from his brother, Cardinal Hohenlohe, who opposed the Infallibility decision, give very helpful side-lights on the whole question.

If one can consider the painful story of the Spanish Inquisition from these two suggested points of view, one will be spared the hopeless endeavor to apologize, if one is a Catholic; and if one is a Protestant, there will be less ground for galvanizing into life the old spook of Roman Catholic intolerance and cruelty. I quite understand, of course, that the vast majority of The Outlook's readers are Protestants, and that a Catholic must be willing to accept many unintentional misrepresentations of those historical facts which have been the war-clubs with which Protestantism has belabored Catholicism for centuries. But none the less I think that both sides ought to seek out those points of view which will enable them to judge their opponents with the widest justice, for the sake of the common pride in our European civilization.

JOHN OLIVER.

Innsbruck, Austria.

## HAS MAN A SOUL?

Your comment, "Have We Souls?" on Dr. Thomson's book in The Outlook for December 15 interested me greatly. If it be not impertinent, however, I should like to ask if the burden of proof does not rest with the materialist who asserts that a *thing*, brain, produces a *process*, thought, as a *thing*, liver, secretes a *thing*, bile. Is not the analogy false?

But, what is more important, the fact of our consciousness is the most certain knowledge we have. It is here that Des Cartes began his philosophy, and others later have shown that all other knowledge depends upon a process of deduction and stands or falls with the validity or invalidity of thought. But we have every reason to believe that even an idiot knows he is, for we are often conscious when irrational. How then shall one presume to say that this greatest certainty is the product of that which by the laws of thought may be proved an uncertainty? If we are to reason, it must be by the laws of thought. The materialist does not even know there is a brain by any other means.

J. C. NICHOLSON.

ROYAL Baking Powder is indispensable to the preparation of the finest cake, hot-breads, rolls and muffins.

The very essence of grapes, the delicate and healthful acid of their juice, is the chief ingredient in Royal Baking Powder. Is there any wonder that it makes the cake and biscuit superlative in flavor and taste?

In buying baking powder ask for and be sure to obtain the Royal. Buy only a baking powder whose label shows it to be made from cream of tartar. Alum baking powders are injurious to health.

ROYAL BAKING POWDER CO., NEW YORK.

# The Outlook

## Saturday, January 19, 1907

OSCAR II., KING OF SWEDEN

ROYAL Baking Powder is indispensable to the preparation of the finest cake, hot-breads, rolls and muffins.

The very essence of grapes, the delicate and healthful acid of their juice, is the chief ingredient in Royal Baking Powder. Is there any wonder that it makes the cake and biscuit superlative in flavor and taste?

In buying baking powder ask for and be sure to obtain the Royal. Buy only a baking powder whose label shows it to be made from cream of tartar. Alum baking powders are injurious to health.

# The Outlook

*Saturday, January 19, 1907*

OSCAR II., KING OF SWEDEN

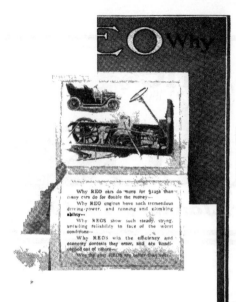

SATURDAY, JANUARY 19, 1907

❀

**The Usurpations of the President** There has been a great hue and cry raised by some politicians over the President's alleged usurpations of the authority and functions of other departments of the Government. He has been accused of endeavoring to unite in himself the various offices of the executive, legislative, and judicial powers. The Senate especially is deeply stirred by the bogie of a usurping President, and has been vigorously assaulting this creature of its own imagination. When a President contents himself with simply executing the will of Congress, he is criticised because he does nothing; and when a President of energy and initiative endeavors to achieve results and to do the normal work of a President as one of the leaders in American public life, he is denounced as having hidden purposes which look to the subversion of the Government. There is a touch of humor in the sensitiveness of the Senate in this matter. Those who recall a paper by that very careful and intelligent observer Professor Henry Loomis Nelson on "The Usurpation of the Senate," which appeared in Harper's Magazine a few years ago, will wonder whether the apparent gravity with which the Senate regards the usurpations of the President is not an official form of the great American joke. For many years past the Senate has steadily pushed its power in every direction, checking the President here and there, reducing the House of Representatives to a subordinate body, and making itself, as a distinguished member of Mr. McKinley's Cabinet said, "a group of gentlemen who spend their entire time in extending their privileges." The report that a joint resolution is being prepared, by the terms of which the President of the United States will be required to file with Congress a copy of every Executive order, and which provides also for the creation of "a commission of distinguished lawyers to report on the President's acts and orders," must be counted among the humors of the session. It is impossible to believe that even the Senate could discuss these propositions with a grave face.

❀

**A Measure for Public Safety** If any one should doubt whether the regulation by law of the number of hours in which railway employees should be engaged in labor is of concern to others than the employees themselves, let him read the article published in The Outlook last summer called "Asleep at His Post," or read the evidence, referred to last week in The Outlook, taken in connection with recent railway massacres. The public, therefore, as well as railway workers, may be congratulated that the Railway Hours Bill passed the Senate last week by a vote of seventy to one. That the bill, with its sixteen-hour limit of work, may not be exactly what a final and thorough dealing with the subject demands is indicated by the fact that an English locomotive engineer, in a frank and good-natured letter to the New York Times describing his experience in New York, says that he found that railway men are worked harder and longer here than in England, and adds: "We are not so well paid in England, but then we work only ten hours a day and have two hours off for meals." He notes also that there appears to be less good feeling between railway employees and the traveling public in America than in England. Yet the bill is of substantial value, and Senator La Follette showed his good sense by adopting many suggestions made by colleagues in criticism of the original bill, so that the bill actually passed was in fact a substitute for the original.

Briefly stated, the bill as passed prohibits railways engaged in inter-State and foreign commerce from requiring or permitting those of their employees who have to do with the movement of trains to work more than sixteen hours consecutively, or more than an aggregate of sixteen in each twenty-four hours, and requires that when an employee shall have worked for sixteen hours there shall follow a period of rest of not less than ten hours before he shall resume his duties. Certain exceptions are made to provide for accidents, the failure of trains to make their regular schedules, connections, etc. Violation of the act is declared to be a misdemeanor punishable by a fine of from $100 to $1,000, and the Inter-State Commerce Commission is charged with the duty of enforcing the law, and all authority necessary to do so is given it. A touch of the burlesque was added to the vote on the bill by the explanation given in the newspapers for the single vote cast in opposition. This one Senator out of seventy-one who could not conscientiously vote in favor of the bill was Mr. Pettus, of Alabama, and we are told that this was because he is a constant opponent of all legislation regulating railways, since he is convinced that any such legislation is and must be a violation of the rights of the States. Evidently Mr. Pettus is one of those who believes, not that the United States is a Nation, but that the United States are a Nation.

❦

*Coroners' Investigation of Railway Accidents* Last week the investigation of the railway accident on the Baltimore and Ohio road at Terra Cotta, D. C., ended. The coroner's verdict was that the deaths were caused by impact due to the act of an operator in displaying an improper signal, and also to the engineers, conductors, train despatcher, and division operator involved. It is a special satisfaction to note that the jury arraigned the block system on the Baltimore and Ohio as not affording satisfactory protection to the lives and property of its patrons; arraigned the system of wages paid to the operators and signalmen; recommended

that all block signal stations be kept open twenty-four hours a day, and that no additional duties be given to the operators aside from working the signals and attending to their telegraphic duties. Many coroners' investigations seem farcical; this one, spurred by the Inter-State Commerce Commission, has been not only apparently thorough in fixing the blame, but, what is far more important, has recommended some safeguards in the effort to prevent future accidents. The inquiry, published day by day in detail, has sufficiently shown that young men characterized by their fellow-operators as "incompetent, wild, and reckless" ought never to be given opportunity to display a possible wrong signal; that for an engineer to run past a signal, the situation of which is known and expected by him, simply because it is obscured, is as reprehensible as for him to run into a train showing red lights a hundred feet ahead; that any but an automatic block signal system is untrustworthy; finally, that in most railway disasters the ultimate fault lies not so much with operators and engineers, or with superintendents and presidents, as with those in financial control of them and the road, who are prone to manage the property not so much from the operative as from the speculative side.

❦

*Railway Investigation of Railway Accidents* Most railway accidents are preventable, since they are due to defects in signaling systems or in track or train apparatus, to negligence of train despatchers or engineers, or to unreasonably long hours of work. But accidents never will be prevented so long as the railway companies themselves, or even coroners' juries, conduct the investigation. After every serious accident the company involved immediately announces that it will promptly hold an investigation, and this doubtless means as thorough an inquiry as the operating officers can make. But what assurance or comfort is it to the relatives and friends of the killed and to the maimed to know that the railway company, an interested party, is to conduct an investigation? Such investigations are not only partisan; they are secret, because, for one reason, too much information might be furnished for damage suits. Railway patrons have now for the most part lost patience with such partisanship and secrecy. What do the patrons of the Lake Shore road, for instance, know of its investigation of the awful and unnecessary Mentor disaster—the direct result of the use of facing switches on a double-track railway?—a use which ought long ago to have been prohibited by law. What do the Pennsylvania's patrons, for instance, know of its investigation of the more recent disaster near Atlantic City, when scores of passengers on one of its subordinate lines were suddenly hurled from a bridge into the water and drowned like rats? What do the Southern Railway's patrons know of its investigation of the Thanksgiving Day disaster, when the President of that road and other prominent men lost their lives? Even if the public has already established the blame as to the cause of these disasters, does it see any very immediate effort on the part of the railways to prevent a repetition? Has it learned that on the Lake Shore there are any fewer facing switches? that on the Pennsylvania bridges there are more inside steel guard-rails and complete interlocking systems? that on the Southern there has been a tardy installation of mechanical checks to prevent operators from giving wrong signals? If not, dividends might better be withheld until these things are done. The railway's recommendations to itself are not published, and if, in the very rare case that a coroner's jury, as last week, presumes to make recommendations, it cannot enforce them. What is needed is something thorough, public, and mandatory.

❧

*Government Investigation of Railway Accidents* In England, when any railway accident occurs, the law has for many years required an investigation, not only by the company involved, but also by the Bureau of Railway Accidents, a department in the Board of Trade, and thus under the ultimate charge of a Cabinet officer. The non-partisan, public, government investigation fixes the blame, and the Bureau decides what preventive remedies should be used, its recommendations having the force of law. With regard to accidents on our railways engaged in inter-State commerce, it is a pity that the Inter-State Commerce Commission has not sufficiently broad powers, or that they are not lodged in a special bureau to be created in our Department of Commerce. Such a Bureau of Railway Accidents, composed of the most eminent experts, is needed to investigate disasters, independently of the companies or the coroners, to employ the power of the Federal courts in compelling the attendance of witnesses and the production of papers, to fix the responsibility, and to decide upon methods for the avoidance of further accidents. Its recommendations should be mandatory. Nor should it be forgotten that the moral effect of the thoroughness, publicity, and authority of such a system would operate upon our railway companies, as it has in England, in the prevention of disasters. Does not Congress realize that railways are highways, and that while they transport inter-State traffic the authority of Congress over them is exclusive? Does not Congress appreciate the fact that its action in establishing Federal investigation of railway accidents would elicit approval from the executive branch of the Government, as from all thoroughgoing railway officials and from all railway passengers? How many more disasters are necessary before Congress will act?

❧

*Governor Hughes and Party Hacks* The hack politicians of both parties in New York State seem to be acting as if the last election were a mandate for them to do as they please. The popular interpretation of the election is quite the contrary. It would be hard to imagine an election by which the voters could more clearly express their dissatisfaction with machine politics. They rejected the candidate for Governor who owed his nomination to intrigue, and chose the candidate who was nominated for his personal qualities alone; at the same time they defeated those State officials who, justly or unjustly, had come to be regarded as the representatives of a well-intrenched party organization, and put in their places untried men whose political obligations were at least somewhat less obvious. They defeated a number of legislators who had been zealous servants of political managers, and, with scarcely an exception, they returned to the Legislature men who had exhibited independence in the service of the State. In spite of this fact, both party machines are acting as if they had been granted a new lease of life. The Republican leader of the State Senate has made up the Senate committees so that well-tried agents of boss rule are in places of power, and men who have shown independence with party loyalty are for the most part where they can exercise little authority. The pretense that these committees have been formed on the principle of seniority is not supported by the facts. It might be supposed that the Democratic party would see in this situation its opportunity. Instead of that, it seems to regard it as a challenge to compete in obstinacy. It has accepted the challenge and proved its own resources in folly. Charles F. Murphy, the notorious Tammany boss, has visited Albany and assumed the place of State leader; in the lower house of the Legislature the Democrats have chosen as their party leader "Paradise Park Jimmy" Oliver. Incidentally the Independence League, in spite of the treatment it received at the hands of its creator, Mr. Hearst, has chosen him its State Chairman. There are, on the other hand, a number of honest, able men in the Legislature whose character alone will give them power. These are the men, whatever their official positions, who really represent the present determined temper of the voters. In the meantime Governor Hughes is conspicuously the man to whom the people look as their champion against special interests and party bosses. It remains to be seen whether these special interests and party bosses will have the audacity to invite popular anger by engaging in a contest with Governor Hughes.

*An Election Fourteen Months Long*

Proceedings to oust Mayor McClellan, of New York City, from his office and to put William Randolph Hearst in his place have been renewed. The Attorney-General of the State, elected last fall on the Hearst State ticket, himself a pronounced supporter of Mr. Hearst, a pupil learned in the phraseology of Hearst journalism, and a protégé of one of the least respectable bosses of the State, has served, in the name of the people of the State, a summons and complaint upon Mayor McClellan. In the complaint the charge is made that in the mayoralty election of 1905 Mr. Hearst was "duly and legally elected Mayor," that in "each and every election district" in the city Hearst ballots and void ballots were counted for McClellan, that returns were illegally made, and that "the defendant, George B. McClellan, has usurped and intruded into and now unlawfully usurps and holds said office of Mayor of the said city of New York." After obtaining a court order from a Supreme Court Justice, the Attorney-General, Mr. Jackson, by his representatives, who are said to have been Hearst inspectors of election in the mayoralty campaign, made a raid at two o'clock at night on ballot-boxes in storage, seized them, and sealed them. As a consequence the evidence concerning Mr. McClellan's election is now, a year and two months afterwards, in the virtual possession of his opponent. In the meantime bills for a recount of the ballots have been introduced into the Legislature, and the Governor recommends that some measure of that sort be passed. The whole situation borders upon the ridiculous; it reminds one of the kind of political methods that have made Cuba once more a dependency and have cursed such a country as Venezuela. The stability of democratic institutions depends upon the acquiescence of all the people in the determination of a contest at the polls. If that contest is to be indefinitely prolonged by legal processes, stability of government is at an end. The defect in this case is partly in the disposition of Mr. Hearst, who is a "bad loser." It is also partly in the law. There ought to be some reasonably accurate and speedy method of determining the result of an election, and a provision that when the result by that method has been secured the evidence be destroyed.

❀

**Direct Primaries**   Public sentiment in favor of a more direct participation by voters in the machinery of government is growing stronger. Last week it found expression in the Message of Governor Stokes, of New Jersey. He recommended to the Legislature a law to provide virtually for the popular election of United States Senators. The Federal Constitution, it is true, provides that the members of the United States Senate be elected by the Legislatures of the several States; but it also provides that the President be elected, not by the people, but by a college of electors. As, however, each elector is chosen with the unmistakable understanding that he is to vote for a definitely designated Presidential candidate, so each legislator may be chosen with an equally unmistakable understanding that he will cast his vote for a definitely designated Senatorial candidate. Although the cases are not quite parallel, since the electoral college has but this one duty, while the Legislature has many duties, yet several States have succeeded in bringing about by this means what is in effect a popular election of Senators. As Governor Stokes declares, the popular election of Senators, as thus secured, is in conformity with the practice in electing the President and Vice-President; and he suggests that it embodies, in a regular way, the desires of the voters. "Whatever may have been," he says, "the theory of our forefathers in vesting the election of the United States Senators in the Legislatures of the several States, the presumption to-day is that the members of the Legislature, in performing this duty, voice the sentiment of their various constituencies." What makes Governor Stokes's recommendation the more significant is the fact that it comes from the by no means radical Governor of a conservative State. The people of New Jersey, however, have been roused by the candidacy of Senator Dryden for re-election; they know that he would never have been Senator except for his connection with the enormously powerful Public Service Corporation and a large and very influential insurance company. A great many people of New Jersey do not relish that fact. Governor Stokes is, therefore, sowing in prepared ground. The difficulties of drafting a praticable law for the popular election of Senators in a State such as New Jersey, which is nearly equally divided between the two great parties, are much greater than in a State, such as South Carolina or Arkansas, where one party is in the ascendency. Governor Stokes indicates these difficulties; he recommends, nevertheless, that the county, as the unit of representation in New Jersey, be legally entitled to express at the primaries its choice for Senator. This recommendation was followed in two days by the recommendation of Governor Woodruff, of Connecticut, that the Legislature of that State carefully consider the report of a legislative commission in favor of a direct primary. This movement on the part of the voters to take the selection of their representatives more and more into their own hands ought to be borne in mind at the same time with the movement toward granting the Federal Government greater powers. Both movements are equally characteristic of the present development of American political institutions.

❀

**Progress in Forestry**   Last week at Washington the annual meeting of the American Forestry Association took place. It was, first of all, a celebration, for, as Dr. Will, the Association's Secretary, said in his report, in the entire history of the forest movement in America the year 1906 was the most notable, in its rapid expansion, National and State, in the strengthening of forest education, and particularly in the activity of the American Forestry Association, which during the year gained twenty-seven hundred new members! In his address the Association's President, the Hon. James Wilson, Secretary of Agriculture, brought out the imperative need of forest preservation and extension, showing that the scarcity of wood to-day compared with the quantity available in the past is beginning to be felt by every one throughout the country. The steadily increasing general demand outruns production. The disheartening results attending some attempted National legislation moved him to urge upon the separate States to make more of forestry as a State issue, inasmuch as it would redound to their respective interests in the future. These remarks were confirmed by Dr. Edward Everett Hale, who showed how the national income of certain European countries has been wonderfully increased by a proper State investment in forestry, and then, turning to the other extreme, instanced Syria, where abject poverty exists principally because the land is deforested. After listening to other addresses of an equally important character, the Association put itself on record by recommending to Congress to loan to the Forest Service the sum of five million dollars as working capital for the development of the forest reserves, a loan also recommended by President Roosevelt in a recent Message; next urging upon Congress the repeal of the Timber and Stone Act, so long a source of fraud and loss to the Government, and the substitution therefor of legislation providing that land more valuable for timber than for other purposes shall hereafter not be subject to entry of any kind; thirdly, warning investors, irrespective of locality, of the danger of loss in their investment unless the Government safeguards forest conditions—a novel but necessary appeal, since the general welfare is being injuriously affected by the increasing scarcity and cost of wood materials, and many savings are invested in various enterprises dependent on water-power, which would be ruined by forest destruction.

❀

**The Appalachian and White Mountain Reserves** But the most strenuous of all the resolutions passed at the meeting of the American Forestry Association was that concerning the proposed Appalachian and White Mountain reserves. In the West more than a hundred million acres of reserves have thus far been secured. The East has no similar reserves, yet they are no less needed for the preservation of timber and the prevention of drought. The White Mountain forest range regulates the flow of the five principal New England rivers; the lower Appalachian range regulates the flow of all the largest rivers south of the Ohio and east of the Mississippi. The two ranges thus hold one of the chief sources of the wealth of thirteen States—their water-power. The bill to establish the Appalachian and White Mountain reserves, when first proposed, was opposed by those who declared that each individual State should attend to the matter for itself, following New York State's example in the Adirondacks. But the States concerned in the proposed reserves are pecuniarily unable to do so. Again, the creation and maintenance of a reserve often concerns other States than that or those in which the proposed reserves would be. Finally, Federal control is more efficient than State control. Hence, the bill to establish Appalachian and White Mountain reserves ultimately passed the Senate without dissent, and was unanimously reported to the House of Representatives by its Committee on Agriculture. A majority of the House is understood to favor it; yet it may not be permitted to come to a vote. Why? Because the Speaker of the House, influencing the Committee on Rules, blocks the way. He says that if the proposition included only the White Mountains, a park there might be feasible; but that "to buy up half the Southern States" is "too big." When we remember that the floods in one year, 1902, caused a loss in the Southern States of eighteen million dollars, sweeping away cotton and saw mills and distributing silt from the mountains over farms through a wide region to its ruin, one wonders how Mr. Cannon can oppose such a measure, especially one likely to lessen the swollen River and Harbor Bill. How is it that, when a bill has passed the Senate and been recommended to the House by one of its largest committees, has beforehand the President's approval, with the active support of every Governor and of prominent business men in many States, one official may prevent the National House of Representatives from considering it? The Outlook reader who is interested in this admirable work can help it on by writing to his Representative in Congress, asking him not only to vote for this measure if it comes up, but also to see that it does come up for action.

❦

**The Increasing
Appreciation
of Good Architecture**

Last week the American Art Institute kept its fiftieth anniversary in Washington—an occasion fitly celebrated by the completion of the fund to purchase the famous Octagon House. That picturesque residence was built in 1798, from the plans of Dr. William Thornton, the successful competitor for the position of architect for the United States Capitol. Thornton, no less than his patron Thomas Jefferson, had a wide knowledge of classic architecture, and stamped its character upon our capital city. When completed, the Octagon House was occupied as a residence by Colonel John Tayloe, one of President Washington's close friends. The President often visited the building, which was then one of the handsomest houses in the country. After 1814, the British having burned the White House, President Madison occupied the Octagon House. During this occupancy the Treaty of Ghent, which closed the second war with England, was signed by him in the famous circular room, now used as the office of the Secretary of the American Institute of Architects. It will be a satisfaction not only to all architects, but to all Americans, to think that this fine old residence is now to become the permanent home of the American Institute. At a reception there a chief figure of interest was Sir Aston Webb, the restorer of St. Bartholomew's, that oldest of London churches, and the architect of several Government buildings. He was later the recipient of the Institute's gold medal for distinguished achievement in architecture. That the first bestowal of this medal should be given to an Englishman is a recognition of the indebtedness of American architects to England. As Mr. Day, President

of the Institute, remarked, our early settlers brought the wholesome tradition of English architecture with them, and as each wave of immigration reached our shores, there came not only a larger knowledge of English art but a stronger impulse to build wisely and well, as the English do; we learned this lesson, as may be shown by buildings at such widely separated places as Newport, Annapolis, Charleston, and the James River region. Thus, concluded Mr. Day, not only did the traditions of Inigo Jones and Sir Christopher Wren give vitality and character to our colonial buildings, but, at a later time, the classical revival which swept over Europe was especially evident in the work of William Thornton. As was expected, the Institute did not adjourn without urging the passage of the bill now before Congress providing for the appointment of a commission to supervise the erection and improvement of all buildings that are Government property, throughout the United States. This measure also covers the establishment and improvement of Government reservations, army posts, and highways. Thus the bill is not merely an architectural project, but its application to reservations and highways should strongly operate for the preservation of natural scenery.

❦

**Savings Bank
Insurance**

In the recent investigation and discussion of insurance matters the fact was brought out conspicuously that the cost of what is called industrial insurance is far greater than it should be, even when full allowance is made for its peculiar character. In other words, the very poor man pays far more for his insurance than any one else, both absolutely and relatively. One method proposed to better this is that of savings bank insurance, and to this end a bill has been introduced into the Massachusetts Legislature, and we believe similar movements are on foot elsewhere. In Boston Mr. Louis D. Brandeis, who is the leading advocate of the Massachusetts measure, pointed out that the workingmen of the State in fifteen years have paid over $61,000,000 to

2-a

industrial insurance companies, and have received back about $21,000,000, with an accumulated reserve of only $10,000,-000, so that more than half of what has been paid in (to say nothing of interest) has gone for expenses and dividends to stockholders. He avers that the holder of an industrial policy pays from two to eight times as much as the holder of an old-line policy. As to the enormous profit of industrial companies, he says that one of them pays 219 per cent. on the cash capital actually paid in, while the stock is in comparatively few hands. The whole machinery of industrial insurance is enormously expensive, for it combines all the disadvantages of the small installment selling plan for any commodity, besides a tremendous loss from lapsed policies. What is the remedy? Government insurance and savings bank insurance are two proposals very wide apart, and there are undoubted arguments of force against both. No one suggests that the present companies should be abolished, but, says Mr. Brandeis:

· It seems to me the State is called upon to provide some way in which workingmen can have such insurance without making such terrible sacrifices. We encounter first of all the argument that unless you have such a system people won't insure—that you must have the solicitor hounding people in the first instance or they won't take out insurance, and weekly domiciliary visits afterwards or they won't pay. That may be true for a certain portion of the community, but there is a large class of intelligent and thrifty citizens who would avail themselves of a better system. Life insurance is only at the beginning of its development, and it is our duty to provide the best means for its future growth.

The special advantage of the savings bank plan, in Mr. Brandeis's opinion, is that the officers and directors are peculiarly suited to act as trustees, as they are emphatically trustees now. Thus they could carry on with economy and care the insurance business with the same methods, spirit, and purpose as they do the management of savings. Moreover, this increased usefulness would work through an established plant, and instantly information and urgent advice to insure would be conveyed by the banks to their 1,880,000 depositors. Heavy initial expense

would be avoided. Again, Mr. Brandeis thought that people would welcome an opportunity to do business at home with men they know rather than to send to great financial institutions in distant places. His scheme includes provision for payment of premiums from the savings bank account of the insured, so that their money would draw interest until it was actually applied to the insurance. There might also be a central reserve fund between the savings banks as a guarantee. To the objection that this plan would benefit the thrifty only, Mr. Brandeis replied that his idea was to make every citizen thrifty. The Outlook here simply reports the interest shown in trying to find some way to give the poor man plain and simple insurance at moderate cost. The future will bring out detailed discussion of various possible plans. But as to the pressing need of some plan no one can doubt.

❀

*Judge Landis's Decision*

The suit against the Standard Oil Company for accepting preferential rates of oil shipments has been decided in the Government's favor by Judge Landis at Chicago. The charge was that the Standard Oil Company obtained railway transportation at rates less than those named in the published schedules. This violated the Elkins Law, the offenses being committed prior to the enactment of the Railway Rate Regulation Law last June. The defendant contended that the Elkins Law did not prohibit a shipper from taking directly from a carrier a less rate than the published tariff, the claim being made that the law's purpose was merely the prohibition of indirect methods, or of inventing fraudulent devices to obtain preferential treatment. But Judge Landis said:

Until this argument was advanced here, the Court had supposed that everybody agreed that what Congress was trying to do was to secure uniform freight rates, and that the various prohibitions and penalties were imposed to accomplish that result. I had never heard an intimation to the contrary from any quarter, and have heard nothing in this argument to change the Court's mind on this proposition. It is written in every section and line of the law that the thing sought by Congress was a fixed rate, absolutely, unvaryingly uniform, to be adhered to until publicly changed in the manner provided by law. The thing prohibited was the departure from that rate by any means whatsoever.

The defendant had also urged that to require a shipper to adhere to a fixed published rate defeats the ultimate object of inter-State commerce legislation, that object being the transportation of property for a reasonable compensation. Judge Landis no less quickly brushed this aside. What Congress wanted to bring about, he declared, was a reasonable rate for *all* shippers, not simply for some shippers. Congress knew that, as an essential prerequisite, preferences would have to be abolished. To abolish them the published rate must be the only lawful rate. This does not mean, said he, that a rate once fixed shall never be changed, but it does mean that when the change is made it must be in the way provided by law, namely, by publication, so that the new rate may be available to all shippers at the same time on equal terms. Thirdly, the defendant urged that some of the indictments are bad because they allege that the defendant procured its property to be transported for less than the published rate from or to points beyond the carrier's own line. Judge Landis's words are again worth quoting :

The Court does not understand this to be the law. The shipping public is no more concerned with the question of whether the carrier owns the roadbed through to destination than it is with the question whether the carrier owns the car in which the property is transported. In such case the law regards such carrier so publishing its rate as thereby announcing that it has facilities for the transportation of property between the points mentioned in the schedule. Whether part of the distance is covered by lease, license, or some species of traffic arrangement is wholly immaterial. The rate once published, until publicly changed according to law, is no less binding upon all parties than it would be if the carrier owned outright the entire line.

❀

*A Supposed Advantage No Advantage*

The Elkins Law was superseded by the Railway Rate Regulation Law, which was approved by the President June 29, 1906. Congress adopted a joint resolution, approved June 30, providing that the law should take effect sixty days after its approval by the President. But the Standard Oil Company claimed that by the President's signature the new Rate Law went into effect on June 29, and that indictments under the Elkins Law could not therefore be returned in August. Judge Landis decides that the new law was effective in June, but that the indictments found under the old law are nevertheless good, and for the following reasons : Under common-law rules of construction, Judge Landis concedes that the repeal of a penal statute operates to wipe out all offenses against such repealed law, unless there is a statutory provision expressly authorizing their future prosecution. But offenses against the Elkins Law are kept alive for future prosecution by the statute of 1871, which provides that " the repeal of any statute shall not have the effect to release or extinguish any penalty, forfeiture, or liability incurred under such statute, unless the repealing act shall so expressly provide." Thus the repeal of the Elkins Act would not exculpate any one who had violated that act and escaped indictment. The Elkins Law had failed to establish uniform and reasonable railway rates, and hence was strengthened by the creation of additional and severe penalties. For instance, for the Standard's offenses, the Elkins Law prescribed punishment only by fine ; the new law authorizes the additional penalty of imprisonment. Furthermore, as Judge Landis added, it is inconceivable that Congress, drafting a law the object of which was to secure to all fair treatment in the transportation of property on the basis of absolute equality, could say to prior offenders that those indicted should be punished and those who had avoided the Grand Jury should be pardoned. Judge Landis's opinion upon the Standard Oil's demurrers to the indictments thus constitutes a notably sweeping decision on the subject of corporate control and methods.

❀

*An Instructive Typhoid Epidemic*

For four weeks the city of Scranton, Pennsylvania, has been in the grasp of a severe epidemic of typhoid fever. In spite of the prompt

adoption of the most thorough and drastic methods to prevent its spread, the
number of cases has exceeded one thousand and the number of deaths eighty.
Early in December the Bureau of Health
discovered that an unusually large number of cases existed in the city. A prompt
investigation led them to believe that the
source of the disease was the water from
one of the reservoirs which supply the
city. The water from this reservoir was
cut off, and that of another substituted.
For three weeks the number of cases
increased rapidly, almost entirely in the
part of the city that had been served from
the suspected source, and then a distinct
lessening in the daily average of cases
began to be observed. The co-operation
of the State authorities was asked by the
Mayor, as they have jurisdiction over the
parts of the water supply system which
are outside the city limits. An analysis by
the State officials of the water from the
reservoir in question resulted in the discovery in it of the typhoid bacillus, a result
of rare occurrence in the case of water
supplies ; the isolation of the bacillus
in such large quantities of water seems
to be almost entirely a matter of chance.
A thorough and painstaking examination
of the entire watershed was made by both
State and city authorities. While certain
nuisances, which have been in existence
for years, were found, all their efforts
failed to locate the case of typhoid from
which the infection proceeded. It must
be remembered that the mere presence
of sewage contamination in water is not
a sufficient cause of typhoid infection.
Actual bacilli from a typhoid patient
must be present before the disease can
be communicated. The fact that the
source of the Scranton infection cannot be
localized, in spite of the existence of these
undoubted nuisances, calls attention to a
possible source of danger to water supplies
too seldom considered by communities.
The complete elimination of nuisances
such as have existed in the Scranton watershed for many years is a duty of such
primary importance that it ought hardly
to need to be stated. But beyond these
permanent possibilities of pollution are
the occasional possibilities arising from
the presence on a watershed or near
a reservoir of hunters, trampers, pic-

nickers, or casual visitors. In the case
of Scranton a not impossible source
of infection was the passing trains on
the Lackawanna Railway, which runs
for a considerable distance close to the
contaminated reservoir. This source of
danger is now done away with by an
arrangement with the railway by which
the toilet-rooms on all trains are locked
while passing through the watershed.
The land around certain of the Scranton reservoirs is laid out with a network of beautiful roads, which form the
main pleasure drives and walks of
the people of the city. The work has
been done by the President of the water
company, Mr. W. W. Scranton, with the
most praiseworthy intention. The result has been to encourage approach to
the vicinity of the reservoirs and the
sources of the water supply rather than
to make it difficult. This condition is
common throughout the country. Almost universally, approach is virtually
invited, not forbidden. The presence
of a single victim of walking-typhoid or
a single typhoid convalescent may produce widespread disaster. The case of
Scranton carries warning for every community. A city which prided itself on
its good health, in especial its freedom
from typhoid, and on its fine water supply, suffers because its precautions have
not gone far enough. Typhoid epidemics
are absolutely preventable ; but only by
the most thorough system and the utmost
vigilance.

❦

*Anarchy Against
Anarchy*

The assassination in
St. Petersburg last
week of General Pav-
loff, the Advocate-General, like that of
the Prefect of Police, General von der
Launitz, the preceding week, and like
that a few days later of Colonel Andrei-
eff, chief of gendarmes in the Lodz
district, illustrates most forcibly an
underlying truth of the present condition in Russia, already pointed out as
such by The Outlook—namely, that revolutionary anarchy is contending against
governmental anarchy. The concerted
and deliberate attempt of the fighting
section of the revolutionists to terrorize
the Government by assassination is
avowedly largely based on the lawless

and arbitrary acts of the Government in seizing and executing suspected persons without proper trial. Thus anarchy fights anarchy. It is as truly terrorism for the agents of the Czar to prevent citizens from meeting in peaceful assembly to select candidates for seats in the new Duma as it is for the political assassin to throw a bomb or fire a pistol in the streets of St. Petersburg. Take, for instance, the case of General Pavloff. He was hated not merely because of the extreme measures he took as a public prosecutor, but most of all because it was believed that he had waved aside all semblance and pretense of acting under the law. In the early days of the first Duma, when he was called upon to appear and explain the frightful summary court martials and executions without court martial in the Baltic provinces, he showed such cold-blooded contempt for law that he was driven from the rostrum amid cries of " Murderer !" "Assassin !" and "Hangman !" and from that time on he was commonly known as " Hangman Pavloff." There seems to be no reason to doubt—to take a single instance— that he deliberately suppressed an order from the Czar countermanding the execution of certain prisoners, and on his own responsibility allowed the executions to proceed. If he did so, he committed murder, and ought to have been legally tried, and, if found guilty, executed. Instead of this, he was promoted, and thereby the Government went far to assume his guilt. It is in no way a commendation of assassination to point out that no Government can be continuously carried on in safety if it ignores law and justice. General von der Launitz, on the other hand, it is said, was not personally execrated, and for the very reason that, although he acted with continuous severity against the revolutionists, he showed a disposition to preserve the forms of law. But his position made him peculiarly the impersonation of the Government's system of widespread repression and wrongful interference with political rights. Thus, it is significant to note that under him the so-called flying section of the secret police made five hundred and eighty-eight arrests in St. Petersburg during

three days in the latter part of December last. The charges were " revolutionary activity and illegal agitation "—a general phrase which might include almost anything, and which certainly was made to include the simplest and most natural exercise of the political liberty granted under the Czar's own rescript. The recent assassinations, and others which preceded them, have created a powerful impression, because the assassins undertook their work without the slightest expectation of escaping death, and because it is evidently perfectly easy to supply their places as fast as they are executed. Thus the terrorists have not merely threatened, but are actually carrying out, the tragic and dreadful design of destroying, one by one, the Czar's trusted and efficient agents in the work of repression. While it would be suicidal for the Government to yield to threats, it is perfectly clear that the only hope for internal peace and prosperity in Russia is the firm establishment of a true system of representative government. Unhappily, at the present moment all the indications are that the new Duma will either be a mere tool in the hands of the bureaucrats, or, if the popular will is strong enough to elect members of the Duma who shall really represent the people, that the Czar may again dismiss the legislative body which his own act created.

                ❀

**The Pope's Encyclical**    The Third Assembly of French Bishops is to be held this week in Paris, and it has been the hope of moderate people of all parties that the way would open for some working arrangement between the Government and the Catholic Church. It looks, however, as if the Pope's Encyclical to the French Church, as published in the Osservatore Romana, which is regarded as the official organ of the Vatican, last week, makes compromise more difficult. The Encyclical was evidently prepared with great care as a definition and defense of the position of the Vatican. It explains at some length the reasons for the Pope's refusal to permit the Church to avail itself of the associations cultuelles or of the opportunity of using church buildings by filing an annual declaration under the law of 1881. The Pope says the acceptance of the associations was impossible because under the law they were not only given authority over the possession and administration of church property, which belongs under canon law to ecclesiastic authority, but power over the exercise of worship, the associations being put entirely under civil authority. The Encyclical points out that the Pope's position toward Prussia is radically different from that toward France, because Prussian law recognizes the Catholic hierarchy, as does the law in Great Britain and in this country, while the French law ignores it. In this country and in Great Britain the management of Roman Catholic affairs is left entirely in the hands of Roman Catholic clergy. The Pope states as his reason for objecting to the use of an annual declaration of an intent to hold meetings for public worship that M. Briand in making this offer used his own discretion, and that the offer might be withdrawn by one of his successors; it has, therefore, no element of permanence. The Pope describes the law enacted three weeks ago to meet the situation created by the refusal to form associations cultuelles as the culmination of a general campaign of spoliation. Church buildings are set apart for religious purposes; but if a case should arise in which a part of the laymen in a parish accepted ecclesiastical authority and part refused it, the decision as to which faction should use the church would be left for the municipality to decide; in a number of cases, the Encyclical declares, such associations have been formed in the face of the Pope's prohibition, and the law of January 2, 1907, will induce anarchy. The Encyclical contains no definite direction as to the attitude of the clergy towards buildings which under the law of January 2 may be occupied by Catholics; that, apparently, is to be left to the bishops to decide. If these privileges are rejected, the Catholics will be driven to private dwellings as places of worship. There is good reason to believe that the two previous assemblies of bishops were ready to accept the law authorizing the making of declarations, but were turned

from this course by orders from the Vatican. It seems probable that a majority of the French bishops still favor this attitude, but they will obey orders from Rome and condemn any effort at schism or secession.

❧

**Raisuli Once More** — Three years ago people who are interested in such matters were following the story of the kidnapping of Mr. Perdicaris from his home on the outskirts of Tangier by Raisuli, his perilous and exhausting ride to an almost inaccessible part of the mountains, and his detention there as a hostage; and readers of The Outlook have not forgotten John Hay's characteristic phrase, much quoted at the time— "Raisuli dead or Perdicaris alive!" The American Government sent a fleet to Tangier, and Mr. Perdicaris recovered his liberty on condition that Raisuli should be appointed by the Sultan Governor of all the districts in the neighborhood of Tangier; that the existing Governor, who had betrayed him, should be deposed; that he, Raisuli, should receive $70,000 in money; that all his enemies should be imprisoned, and all his friends released from prison. These terms being granted, Raisuli became the most important factor in the situation in Morocco, and for a time governed with an iron but just hand. He could not resist, however, the temptations of unrestricted power. After the old Oriental fashion, he began to squeeze money out of his subjects; he threatened, levied, and blackmailed in every direction; and, instead of being the protector, became the tyrant of the districts about Tangier, up to the very gates of the city. He made the mistake of interfering with the privileges and subjects of foreign Governments; he flogged protected natives; he deprived people of electric light; he blackmailed Europeans; and a fortnight ago the representatives of the Powers sent a collective note to the Moorish Minister of Foreign Affairs demanding that this state of things be brought to an immediate end. All the available forces of the country were directed against Raisuli, and he was compelled to flee the country, putting himself, according to the latest reports, in the hands of his brother-in-law, and now his brother-in-law offers to sell him for a large sum of money. To this unhappy position has come a man in whose veins is some of the most aristocratic Mohammedan blood ; for he is a Shereef, or direct descendant of the Prophet. Even the blood of a prophet, however, will not save a man who begins by carrying off cattle and ends by becoming a blackmailer, nor can this kind at least of plunder through politics be continuously successful.

●

# The President and Prosperity

Pearson's Magazine for January contains an article by Mr. James Creelman on the personality and policy of President Roosevelt which deserves and probably will have a wide reading throughout the country. It may be thought that the subject has been pretty well exhausted by the magazines and newspapers, but Mr. Creelman has succeeded in giving a description of the President and his work which is vivid, fresh, and absorbing in interest. The title of the article, "Theodore the Meddler," is in itself so sensational that the man who knows how these things are often done in our modern newspaper-magazines is inclined to wonder whether the author has not let his journalistic sense get the better of his sense of accuracy. It is so much easier in a newspaper office to make your facts fit your headline than your headline fit your facts. · The Outlook, however, has taken the pains to make some inquiry into the character of the article and is convinced of its substantial accuracy. Its purpose is to show that the President and his administration are not attacking thrift, industry, the material development of the country, or the accumulation of wealth. The President is not a meddler with the rights of capital nor with the progress of prosperity ; he is a meddler with the wrongs of capital and with the doctrine that the Government of the United States is a Government for Prosperity rather than a Government for equal rights under the law. The follow-

ing incident related by Mr. Creelman is a striking illustration of the conflict between these two theories of government :

The Governors of six Northwestern States appealed to the President for relief from the Northern Securities railroad merger, which destroyed competition between the Great Northern and the Northern Pacific lines. The President referred the matter to Attorney-General Knox with instructions to deal with the case without fear or favor. The Attorney-General reported that the merger was a clear violation of National law. He was ordered to bring suit at once.

Representatives of the Morgan-Hill merger interests went to the White House. Attorney-General Knox was present with the President.

"You should have given private notice before filing a bill in the courts against the Northern Securities Company," said one.

"Why?" asked the President.

"We were taken by surprise and the action of the National Administration suddenly knocked the prices of our stocks to pieces in the market. You should have given notice for the sake of the innocent widows and orphans whose money was invested in the stock."

"I would like to ask you," said Attorney-General Knox, heartlessly, "whether you gave advance information to the widows and orphans when you cornered Northern Pacific stock?"

Again the President showed his teeth.

"The Government doesn't give notice," he said. "When it believes that a man has committed a crime, it arrests him, and then notifies him of what he is accused. Why should the Government give notice to one man and not to another?"

"But you might at least have notified five or six of the biggest men in Wall Street."

The President smiled and rubbed his hands together softly.

"I'm afraid that the little men would not have appreciated it," he answered, with cruel gentleness.

"I'll say this for the President," exclaimed the Attorney-General, leaning back in his chair. "There is no stock ticker in the White House. That might as well be understood right now."

We occasionally receive letters from correspondents in which The Outlook is criticised as being a thick-and-thin supporter of President Roosevelt. To all such critics—all of whom no doubt have been entirely sincere, and most of whom have been entirely courteous—we commend Mr. Creelman's article as an exposition of those qualities in the President which command the support of The Outlook in the great political conflict which is now going on in this country. This conflict is deeper and more lasting than any policy of any President. It is a conflict between Equal Rights and Special Privilege, not a conflict of the forces of anarchy and disorder against the forces of industry and thrift, as many men actively engaged in the industrial and financial world mistakenly although sincerely believe it to be.

A well-known New York banker, whose public spirit and genuine patriotism are unquestioned, who, although a Republican, profoundly believes that President Roosevelt is an irritating and obstructive " meddler," put the case for special privilege very clearly in a recent discussion in these words: " The corporations, it is true, must be made to obey the law; but the law must allow the great captains of industry discretion as to how the country is to be developed. For example, a great tract of timber lies five hundred miles west of St. Paul. A capitalist proposes to build mills, to establish a village, to promote immigration, to open up a great territory, and thus to add greatly to the developing of the welfare of the entire country by the manufacture of this timber into shingles. He says to Mr. Hill, of the Great Northern Railway, ' I will do all this if you will give me a rate of five cents a thousand on shingles.' The small shingle-makers along the road between this point and St. Paul are paying ten cents a thousand. ' All right,' says Mr. Hill, ' I will give you this special rate in view of the great business you are promoting.' This, of course, destroys the small shingle-makers, who have to pay ten cents a thousand. It is painful, sometimes even pathetic, but the small manufacturer must submit to the law of the survival of the fittest, and Mr. Hill must be allowed to make the special rate, because if he does not make it our frontier will remain a vast wilderness and capital will have no incentive to develop new country, build new railroads, open new mines, and thus continue the greatest era of material progress and prosperity the world has ever seen."

This economic theory is advocated by some men with perfect honesty and sincerity, and is taken advantage of by some others for purposes of graft and corrupt profit. In either event it is dangerous because it is destructive. It is better that the small shingle-maker should have his rights and the country develop slowly than that the large shingle-maker should enjoy special personal privileges, even if they are granted to him for the purpose of rapidly developing the wealth of the whole country. The contest is a very much broader and deeper one than a conflict between the President and a group of leading financiers. Those men, like the banker whom we have just quoted, or those newspapers, like Harper's Weekly and the New York Sun, who imagine that if it were not for President Roosevelt Special Privilege could go on its way undisturbed, are not clearly reading the signs of the times.

❦

# Railway Rate Regulation

## A Conference Wanted

The law passed by the last Congress gives to the Inter-State Commerce Commission authority on complaint to declare a freight rate unjust and unequal and to prescribe in its place one that is just and equal. This was a necessary first step in the process of bringing the highways of the country under governmental control. But it is not final. It is at once too little and too much for a finality. It is too little because it does nothing to determine by what principles the Commission shall be guided in determining what are just and equal rates. It is too much because it gives the Commission practically unlimited power to determine what is just and equal without furnishing any standard by which it is to be guided. The courts have no such unlimited powers. They are controlled in their decisions, first by the Constitution of the United States and of the various States, secondly by the laws of the United States and of the various States, thirdly by the common law of the United States and the several States, and lastly by the body of past judicial decisions. The Inter-State Commerce Commission has no such body of doctrine to guide it. The railways have, therefore, some ground for their apprehension in the gift of such power of almost arbitrary decision upon that Commission.

It is a mistake to suppose that the railways are the enemies of the people, or that railway officials are exceptionally hard, unreasonable, or corrupt; though doubtless in some cases railways, acting on the principle that it is right to charge all that the traffic will bear, have dealt hardly and unjustly with special shippers and with special localities. It is also a mistake to suppose that the people are inimical to the railways or begrudge a fair profit to the owners and administrators of the railways for the services they render; though doubtless in some localities the people have made unreasonable demands and imposed unreasonable regulations on the railways. What is now wanted is that some fair-minded, public-spirited representatives of the railways should meet in conference with some fair-minded and broad-minded representatives of the traveling and shipping community, and endeavor to come to an agreement as to certain general principles to be applied in determining what are just and equal rates. The definition of those principles ought not to be left to be determined by the railways without taking account of the community's interests, nor by representatives of the community without taking account of the interests of the railways; nor should it be left to be determined by the Inter-State Commerce Commission by the very slow process of decision as to what is just and equal in special cases brought before the Commission by special complaints.

If such a conference as is here suggested could be held, in which the railways were represented by such men as the late Mr. Cassatt, and the Government, that is the people, were represented by a man of the judicial quality of Secretary Taft or Secretary Root—and such men not already so engrossed in public affairs can be found—it is not impossible that an agreement could be reached as to the fundamental principles

of just and equal railway administration. If such an agreement were reached, Congress could be depended upon to enact it into law. And a law thus arrived at would be more likely to be just and equal than one obtained by a victory of the shippers over the railways, or by a victory of the railways over the shippers, or by a compromise between the railways and the shippers after a hot controversy between the two. And it would be more speedily reached than by waiting for the slow process of complaint before the Inter-State Commerce Commission, its decision on such complaints, appeals to the courts, and their final elucidation of the principles as the result of such appeals.

In a subsequent article we may point out by way of illustration what appear to us to be certain principles which such a conference might be expected eventually to reach, and Congress, as a result, to embody in legislation.

❋

## *Persia and Its Shah*

A few years ago the death of the Shah of Persia would have caused great uneasiness in Europe, but now the loss of Muzaffer-ed-Din, who succeeded his father on the assassination of the latter in March, 1896, will probably not check the increasing stability and constitutional development of that country. The late Shah, who was selected by his father under the Persian law as his successor, came to the throne in middle life, after having served as Governor of Tabriz, the second city of importance in the country. He promptly reduced taxes on food, introduced a merit system for appointments in public offices, and announced that he would be his own Grand Vizier and the President of his Cabinet. Seven years ago he visited Europe and was entertained in the principal capitals of the Continent, barely escaping assassination at the hands of an Anarchist in Paris. He subsequently made two other European trips, and it was while he was in Paris in July, a year ago, that he was overcome by the heat. He seems never to have been well since that incident. He was a man of very considerable intelligence, and had made a careful study of Western institutions, with the intention of adapting them, so far as possible, to Persian conditions ; he was thrifty and foreseeing, and consistently developed the resources of the country, strengthened its political and social institutions, and maintained freedom and security of person and property. His attitude towards the Mohammedan priests was reverential, but he was a firm believer in the supremacy of the civil over the religious power. Foreigners who had opportunities of meeting him agreed in ascribing to him intellectual abilities of an unusual order and a very agreeable and interesting personality. While on his visits to the Continent and in England he was tactful in maintaining the dignity of his position, while yet giving himself the freedom of a private person. Visitors at Carlsbad often saw him at close quarters ; and the sole objection to his presence seems to have been his insistence on using a room in the hotel in which he was staying as a slaughter-house for the preparation of his food under the conditions required by the rules of the Mohammedan faith. When his father visited London in the time of Queen Victoria, he was given a very beautiful reception at Stafford House, the London home of the Duke of Sutherland. The Persian Shah was so impressed by the magnificence of the house and the splendor of the company that he called the Prince of Wales aside during the evening and asked him about the owner. He was told that the Duke was one of the foremost noblemen in England. The Persian ruler thereupon advised the Prince of Wales at once to decapitate him, declaring that, as a result of the long experience of Persian rulers, powerful subjects were dangerous, and that the Duke of Sutherland was not a person to be tolerated by a reigning monarch.

The late Shah was too much in touch with the modern world to cherish the illusions of old-time Oriental authority ; he was too familiar with the political and social conditions in the modern world, and he ruled a people who, with the Japanese, stand for individual initiative and force of character among Ori-

entals. The country of Cyrus and Zoroaster, whose ancient education consisted in teaching its boys to ride well, to shoot straight, and to tell the truth, has never entirely lost its vigor. Strongly religious and producing every devotional type from the most advanced mystic to the most practical religious reformer, Persia has not undervalued modern opportunities nor been blind to the value of commercial success. The ancient home of poetry, having a list of poets numbering, according to Persian statistics, between ten and twelve thousand, and including such charming singers as Hafis and Saadi, such a poetic historian as Firdusi, such a master of agnostic philosophy in poetic form as Omar Khayyám, Persia has never lost the capacity for dealing strongly with realities. Coveted by more than one great Power, she has succeeded in maintaining her political integrity, and seems to have now entered upon a new period of political and commercial development.

The Outlook reported not long ago the granting of a constitutional government to the Persian people, providing for a Senate of sixty members, thirty being elected and thirty appointed by the crown ; the Assembly to have control of the finances of the country, both local and foreign, of commercial treaties, of the initiation and management of public works, and of the organization of companies for the construction of railways. The power of the sovereign is limited by a provision that the Lower House cannot be dissolved without the consent of the Ministers and two-thirds of the members of the Senate. This work of a progressive and open-minded Shah will undoubtedly be carried on by his successor, Mohammed Ali Mirza, who has repeatedly expressed his approval of the great political changes made by his father. The new Shah begins his reign in his thirty-fifth year, has had an excellent education, and is in many ways exceptionally well fitted to conduct the affairs of Persia in what promises to be a critical period in her growth. He speaks several languages, has studied European politics, and is familiar with European affairs ; he is said to be a keen sportsman, is devoted, as were his remote ancestors, to hunting, and is skillful in motoring. He has passed through all grades in the army, from lieutenant to field marshal. Bordering on the Caspian Sea, with access to almost all Russia through the Volga River; touching Turkestan, Armenia, and Mesopotamia; with British India at the east, Persia has great advantages of position, and exceptional opportunities of regaining something of her old influence and prestige.

❀

## *The Spectator*

The Spectator confesses to an unmanly weakness for tea. Not the tea of the drawing-room, be it understood, that implies social amenities and an acrobatic style of chit-chat for which the Spectator has no sort of genius. What he wants when he is jaded, body, soul, and spirit—when the day is glowering into the unsympathetic twilight of early winter, and he has before him the long journey into Suburbia—is the soothing effect of the fragant cup sipped solitary, or with only a good companion who knows the mercy of silence. If his office were only in London, now, he could despatch the office-boy to the nearest " A. B. C." for a steaming pot, a plate of paper-thin bread and butter, jam, and perhaps a buttered scone. Imagine the result should he send the Outlook's Billy, or James, or Jonathan on such an errand! What is there disgraceful about tea? The Spectator supposes that he could step out and get a cocktail without forfeiting the office-boy's respect. But he doesn't like cocktails. They fret him instead of soothing. Indeed, there are times when he fancies that the nervous tension of New York business life is founded upon the cocktail, and that if we could substitute the English teacup we should accomplish as much and wear out less rapidly.

❀

Perhaps the tea-table of the drawing-room is the entering wedge. Mrs. Spectator reports a growing tendency among the men who drop in of an afternoon to look upon the tea she offers as something more than a compliment well meant but embarrassing. But we have by no means come to realize the full value of the Boon

of the Orient. The Spectator had this forcibly borne in upon him not long ago when business called him to the little town of Peabody, Massachusetts, a suburb of Salem. The afternoon was chill and gloomy with fine rain. Trains are sixty minutes apart at the little Peabody station, and the Spectator's business detained him so that he caught just a glimpse of the departing four o'clock express. Fresh from an English summer, he at once bethought him of consolation to be found in some cozy tea-room where the hour might be idled away pleasantly enough. A glance up and down the dull little street banished abruptly his dream of consuming toothsome cakes by the glow of a leaping fire. This was not England. Still, the Spectator fancied the automobile might have developed some nice private refectory where he might stay the cravings of the inner man. He inquired. " A tearoom? Oh, yes. There was Banning's, with the blue sign." The Spectator sought out Banning's. But alas for his comfortable anticipations! A fly specked window coldly warned him. Inside a dingy, two-by-twice shop, dense with the odors of untold successions of ill-cooked meals, was a bald lunch counter set forth with slabs of unspeakable leaden pie. A tea-room indeed!

❀

The Spectator ultimately discovered little cakes of bakerish suggestion at a confectioner's, and beef-tea at a soda fountain. But as he sat bolt upright on a revolving stool and consumed the hot and so far comforting beverage, he could not help thinking how much the poetry of the exercise was dissipated by the surrounding drugs and nostrums, nor how cozily the kettle simmers, for native and stranger alike, in a thousand bright, clean little shops scattered through the tiniest villages of Old England.

❀

For the matter of that, it's not in shops alone that you find the cheering cup. Does it not invite you, hot and fragrant, at the very door of your railway compartment every time the train stops? Do not the coaches upon the post-roads of Devon, Cornwall, and, for aught the Spectator knows, the Lakes, draw up at tea-time at some posting-house, that the passengers may perform the graceful rite without which no English day is complete ? The Spectator will not soon forget an October drive from Porlock over moor and forelands to Lynton. The hunt was out, the posting stations noisy with riders dashing in for fresh mounts, the whole countryside thrilling with the music of the horns. From all this heartening bustle the coach climbed up to the solitude of the moors. The sun dropped into a deep bank of cloud, a " nipping and eager air " awoke on the moor, and the Spectator began to find himself, as the guard said, " perishin' cold." It was after hours of brisk cantering over the long, red Devonshire road, when the Spectator's blood was congealing in his veins, that the coach drew up at a crossroads. And there, apparently miles from any house, sat a little old woman nursing a tea-tray ! Off came a deep-padded cozy, and wreaths of beneficent steam began to rise on the frosty air. Nobody asked the Spectator whether he would have a cup of tea, and as he was perched on the highest seat of all, and the ladder was not forthcoming, he began to despair of getting any, when the guard came clambering up, dexterously balancing a full cup. And even now he did not ask if the Spectator would take it, merely demanding sixpence as if it were part of the road-fare. From his point of view it would have been as incomprehensible that a sane man should refuse tea as that he should profess to scorn bed and breakfast. Never shall the Spectator forget the genial glow that pervaded his whole being as he plied himself with bread and butter and piping-hot tea, nor the doze of dreamy contentment in which he passed the remainder of the drive until the lights of Lynton appeared, gleaming like a swarm of fireflies on the shoulder of the cliff. He thought then that he understood the cult of the tea-leaf.

❀

But he had still something to learn. A week or two later he and Mrs. Spectator attempted to travel to the little town of Broadway. At Evesham they were stayed by the absence of any sort of conveyance except a funereal-looking carrier's cart, the electric train having departed a few minutes before. They set out, therefore, to trudge the six miles afoot. The way was lovely enough, the placid Warwickshire country swimming in the golden afternoon light. But the way was long. Mrs. Spectator's courage failed her when Broadway was yet three miles away, and down she sat her, with an air of hopeless exhaustion, on the long grass beside the road. " Mr. Spectator," she gasped, " I would sell my soul for a cup of tea !" The words were scarcely out of her mouth when her jaw fell. She looked as if she had seen a ghost. Then she began to laugh hysterically. " Is it "—she pointed with a shaky finger—" is it *real ?*" The Spectator looked behind him. Tiptoeing across the road came two little English girls in pinafores, bearing—yes, it *was* real—bearing cups of smoking tea. " Mother said," began the elder, shyly, " would you like some tea ? She was just pouring hers, and she thought you looked tired." Mrs. Spectator declares that hereafter, whenever the tea craving seizes her, she shall simply recline upon the landscape and tea will be brought to her. So much for the humanizing influence of the cult.

❀

The Spectator has been told that there is an economic side to all this which is not so bright. They say, though for this he cannot vouch, that in England day laborers and field hands insist upon thrusting a tea-time recess into their already diminished working day. This must be very embarrassing for employers, but doubtless it is beneficial enough to the workers. For the virtue of afternoon tea is in the relaxation that goes with it, the little oasis of quiet in the midst of the busy day. If we Americans could only learn to interject such a period of repose into our rush, it would matter little what the excuse for it was, whether malted milk, or popcorn, or confectionery. The pause is the thing. And the Spectator maintains that the American soda fountain does not provide it. Who lingers over the phosphate glass ? Indeed, who *can* linger, with a dozen other thirsty souls chafing to possess themselves of his seat ? New York has tea-rooms and so has Boston, artistic places, but fearfully popular. The cheerful chatter dissipates that quietness of spirit which belongs to the little tea-and-cakeries of Old England. There no eagle-eyed waitresses hover about, fretting to clear away the tea-things, no ostentatious check keeps the monetary part of the ceremony always in view. You may dawdle as long as you please, and the discreet little tea-maker will keep herself out of the way till the moment of your voluntary departure, when she will look thriftily after the shillings.

⊛

When the Spectator wants to dine out and enjoy the full luxury of the experi-ence, it is rarely to an American hotel or restaurant that he goes. The little foreign cafés, these provide brisk service when service is wanted, and complete obliviousness when it is not. The Spectator knows a little French place in Boston where this principle is understood to perfection. You may dine at six and smoke till ten, and not a waiter will cast an envious eye upon your table. It is this that as a nation we must learn—the fine art of idleness. It is for this reason that he advocates the teakettle in the counting-room, and inscribes upon his banners those memorable words of Colley Cibber's: " *Tea !* thou soft, thou sober, sage, and venerable liquid, smile-smoothing, heart-opening cordial, to whose glorious insipidity I owe the happiest moments of my life, let me fall prostrate !"

# THE INDIANS AND OKLA-HOMA

## BY HENRY S. BROWN

TO have carved out of a wild prairie a new State with an area equal to that of New York, New Jersey, Massachusetts, and Connecticut combined, which starts off with more than a million inhabitants, and enters Congress with five Representatives in the popularly elected branch, is something which a man may well be proud to have to his credit. To have done this work without serious scandal, to have safeguarded the interests of all, and to have brought about great reforms in disposing of Indian lands and regulating the making of homes in the wilderness, is something of a test of administrative ability.

Mr. E. A. Hitchcock, the Secretary of the Interior, has really seen the new State of Oklahoma grow from a desert into a great commonwealth. It is true that when he entered the Department early in 1899 the movement of settlers had been going on for about ten years, but it had been in progress spasmodically and almost without regulation. Outlawry was rampant, and the revolver and the bowie-knife the arbiters of disputes. Unscrupulous adventurers had flocked into the Territory, bad methods were in operation, and a strong hand was needed.

The following is a plain story of some of the things that were done by the Secretary of the Interior. As he has been praised sometimes where he did not deserve particular praise, and blamed many times when he deserved nothing but commendation, it will be interesting to point out some of the events which have marked his administration.

It will be recalled that in all of the openings of new " strips " and reservations prior to about eight years ago there was a sensational rush of home-seekers. Before the day set for the opening the homesteaders would encamp on the border. Men, and women too, mounted on swift horses would be waiting for the signal for the crossing of the strip.

When the signal was given, each home-seeker would dash across the line and make for some favorable point, when the land claim would be staked out. In many instances there was bloodshed between rival claimants, and men, women, and children were injured in the scramble. In addition to this, it was apparent that there was nothing fair in the arrangement, and that many persons, posted in advance through visiting the country quietly, would have a great advantage.

Secretary Hitchcock decided to make a change which would give each person an equal chance. He devised a plan whereby the land was divided up into quarter-sections. Numbers for as many quarter-sections as there were in the territory to be opened were put into a wheel, and on a given day a drawing took place. The man or woman who drew the first number had the first chance, and located his or her claim, and, after having it registered at the nearest land office, entered upon the property. There was a great outcry on the part of many persons because the Secretary of the Interior was conducting a lottery for the Government, but the system was continued, and there was as fair a deal in picking out homes in Oklahoma as it was possible to devise.

It has been during the management of the Interior Department by Secretary Hitchcock that the important question whether Congress or the Indians had the right to dispose of Indian lands was settled. This came about through the great suit of Lone Wolf against Hitchcock, over the opening of Kiowa, Comanche, and Apache reservations within the precincts of Oklahoma. A law had been passed by Congress in 1901 opening up to settlement a tract as large as some of the Eastern States. An allotment of land had been made to the Indians, and arrangements had been made for the sale of the remainder. Lone Wolf, a chief of the Kiowas, who had in a measure lost his influence with his tribe, set about an agitation against the opening of the country, with every prospect that he might rehabilitate himself with his people. With the assistance of the Indian Rights Association and others he obtained an injunc-

tion restraining the Secretary of the Interior from carrying out the provisions of the law, on the ground that the consent of the Indians had not been obtained. The Secretary fought this case through the courts, and obtained a decision from the Supreme Court of the United States as to the constitutionality of the law. It was the first time that the question had ever been brought up. If the Indians had the right to control their own land, then the titles of tens of thousands of homesteaders were in doubt. The Court held that the Indians had only the right of occupancy to the lands, that Congress had the right to dispose of them, and that it was to be assumed that Congress would throw safeguards around the disposal of those lands which were not needed by the Indians.

When this case was decided, the greater part of the new State of Oklahoma, which is now dotted with fertile farms, was a trackless waste. Where the thriving town of Anadarko now stands was then a corn-field. It is the outlet to-day of a great and prosperous section that was then not cultivated. Secretary Hitchcock and the Government were criticised for the course pursued in this matter, but it was a question that had to be settled and should have been settled earlier; but the time was coming when Mr. Hitchcock would be criticised by those who supported him in this matter and praised by those who blamed him.

The Secretary held that the Indians were not receiving sufficient money for their lands. He had kept his eye pretty steadily on the land speculators and schemers who sought to get the lands for a mere song and dispose of them at enormous profits. Throughout the Territory there was a band of human wolves with whom the Secretary was to try conclusions.

This test came over the question of the appraisal of Indian lands and their sale to the highest bidder, in case only that the highest bid came up to the price of the appraisement. The Department decided that this was the only fair way to dispose of the lands of the Indians, and this was adopted. It became the policy of the Department only after a hard fight in Congress. The Territorial land ring, the speculators, and the adventurers opposed any departure from the old scheme of having the lands disposed of at about $1.25 an acre. A bill was finally passed in connection with the disposal of 480,000 acres of Kiowa lands, which had been for years rented as pastures, and 25,000 acres of woodland. There was a stubborn contest in Congress, the Secretary holding that these lands were worth at least five dollars an acre and some of them worth much more than that. In committee meetings and on the floor of Congress it was asserted that the land would never be taken up by settlers if they had to bid for it; but the arguments of Secretary Hitchcock and the Indian Commissioner finally prevailed, and it was decided that there should be bidding for the land in homestead tracts, and no bid would be accepted that did not at least come up to the appraised price.

At the present writing these bids are being received. Under the terms several alternate bids can be received from each person, so that if the bidder cannot get the land that is his first choice he can also have an option on other land. This plot contains in pasture or farming lands three thousand quartersections of one hundred and sixty acres each; in other words, three thousand farmsteads. Instead of the scheme being a failure, there have been seventy-six thousand bids already received; one hundred clerks are kept busy opening them, bids are coming in at the rate of four hundred a day, and it is estimated that by the time the bids are all in there will be, including alternate bids, two hundred and twenty-eight thousand applications for land at the rate of five dollars an acre and upwards.

In connection with the sale of Indian lands there is a notable incident which will illustrate the difficulties of the Secretary of the Interior and his peculiar indifference to public criticism where he knows he is right. It will be recalled that at the last session of Congress the Committee on Appropriations of the House of Representatives professed to have discovered a startling instance of the disregard of the law by the Secretary.

It was disclosed by the Committee on Appropriations that the Secretary had sold town lots in Hobart, Anadarko, and Lawton, county seats of three counties; had realized the sum of $730,000, which, instead of turning into the treasury, he had deposited to his own account, and had arbitrarily expended this sum without warrant of law. The obvious intent of these representations was to make it appear that the Secretary had violated the law and had misappropriated $730,-000.

The fact is that the law provided that the proceeds of this sale, after paying the expenses of surveying, etc., were to be expended, under the discretion of the Secretary, in the construction of public improvements, such as court-houses, school-houses, jails, bridges, and roads. This was done, but, so far as known, the Secretary has never taken occasion to reply to his Congressional critics; and the developments subsequent to the sale show that it was a very wise provision which placed the disposal of the money in the hands of Mr. Hitchcock. The sale over, a great clamor rose as to how the money should be expended. The inhabitants of each locality wanted the cash apportioned and deposited in the respective county treasuries. Instead, the Secretary had the money deposited in the Sub-Treasury at St. Louis to his credit as trustee of the various town site funds. This led to a great criticism on the part of local politicians who wanted to expend the money.

In the beginning the Secretary attempted to operate, in the disbursement of the funds and the construction of the improvements contemplated, through the local county organizations, with the approval of the Governor of the Territory. In one of the counties, however, the county commissioners proceeded to such a point as to advertise and let a contract for the construction of a court-house, without the Secretary's knowledge. An inspector was sent down to investigate. He found a vast amount of material on the ground, the foundations in, and the walls partly up. He had no difficulty, however, in pushing the walls over with his foot, with a very slight shove.

Subsequently it was ascertained that

in this same county bridge piers had been authorized, accepted, and payment ordered, although the piers had never been built at all! An investigation resulted in the flight of the commissioners. They were, however, indicted, in company with the contractors, and brought back for trial. Although the evidence was very direct, public opinion against Secretary Hitchcock was such that the men were acquitted.

The Secretary went quietly on his way, taking the expenditure of the funds out of the hands of local authorities, and organized a construction corps. With the assistance of the engineers of the Reclamation Service and the Geological Survey, he gave to the Territory all the improvements contemplated by the act, and he gave it the worth of the money. He built roads, bridges, water-works, sewers, jails, school-houses and court-houses. All of them are models of their kind, and, notwithstanding the scarcity of labor and the increase in the price of material, each one of these improvements, including the cost of supervision, was constructed within the contract price, and a balance was left in each fund.

In straightening out the tangled affairs of the Territory, the Secretary rendered no greater public service than in connection with the handling of the coal and oil leases. The discovery of great deposits of bituminous coal, and subsequently petroleum and gas, on the Indian lands had led many persons to invade the Territory and obtain leases. These were subsequently sublet, and accumulated in the hands of single persons or corporations, and in time the Secretary found himself confronted with a situation under which practically the entire oil output of the Territory would soon be concentrated in the power of companies allied with the Standard Oil Company. The Prairie Oil and Gas Company had laid a pipe through the Territory, and it was shown to be an ally of the Standard. This finally led the Secretary to make regulations providing for pipe lines in the future in Indian Territory. These provide that no pipe line shall have any further extensions unless it agrees to abide by the

rules of the Department, and the effect of this will be to prevent the Standard Oil from maintaining a monopoly and transporting the oil of favored producers only. No exclusive franchises will be granted hereafter; in case of disputes the Secretary of the Interior shall have the power to fix rates, and may compel the extension of a trunk line or lateral lines to new oil-fields; and no independent line may consolidate in the future without the express approval of the Secretary of the Interior.

So, too, with the coal leases. The Secretary made his influence felt in these matters. Mr. Hitchcock is an old coal-miner, and knew all about the business. A very brief investigation on his part convinced him that the Indians were in danger of being cheated by the coal companies under the terms of the lease, which required a royalty on the net ton. This meant that only the coal adhering in large lumps paid a royalty, while that was a small part of the coal actually mined and marketed. The Secretary made the rule that the rate of payment should be on the gross ton, and, while the amount was dropped from ten cents a ton to eight cents a ton, the Indians are now getting a proper return and a payment on all coal mined.

Thus have been hurriedly sketched some of the important reforms wrought by the Secretary of the Interior in the great State which has grown up almost like magic in the Southwest. His influence has been felt by the population, which, looking to the future, is at this time preparing for the holding of all mineral lands not now occupied by settlers for the benefit of the State. In the same way his influence is being shown in the plan proposed by Mr. Francis E. Leupp, Commissioner of Indian Affairs, to safeguard the rights of the red men to their mineral lands by organizing them into a company, in which each Indian will be a stockholder, and at the head of which will be the White Father at Washington. Thus Oklahoma may in a short time be the home of two of the most interesting experiments in social economy in modern times—a State owning its coal mines and a Nation constituted as a joint stock company.

# KING OSCAR OF SWEDEN

## BY PAUL HARBOE

IN the course of a visit to Stockholm a year and a half ago—a long, delightful visit—I found myself face to face repeatedly with a phenomenon whose aspect, I was very sure, I had observed in no other Continental capital. At first the mystery was evasive enough, but little by little, as my impression of the town continued to deepen in tone, its more intangible parts began to simplify themselves and loom appreciably distinct. Finally, for my curious sense, there was no escaping some sort of interpretation, the last stage of which unconscious process developed on the day of my departure. For it was then I felt, irresistibly, that, though I had had but the merest glimpse of him in the flesh, I was yet familiar with the *spirit* of the King. I knew now that I had seen reflected in so many things, material and immaterial, fruits of the will and the work of a beautifully human monarch. By these signs I could recognize the subtle sensibility, the educated conscience, the generous knowledge and large nature of Oscar II. of Sweden, And I recall hearing myself mutter, not, I confess, without emotion : " This king at least has a soul."

Oscar Fredrik, third son of the then Crown Prince Oscar (afterward Oscar I.) and Princess Josephine, was born at Stockholm January 21,1829. From his grandfather, Carl XIV. Johan, he received the title of Duke of Östergöthland. This title he bore until 1872, when, having become heir apparent by reason of the deaths of his brother Gustaf and the infant Crown Prince Carl Oscar, he succeeded Carl XV., whose demise occurred September 19 of the above year.

Prior to this period Oscar had taken little or no active interest in affairs of state. Only in an abstract way, through the medium of temperament perhaps, did he appreciate the import of administrative matters, politics, diplomacy. Of course it was inevitable that he should mingle with courtiers and hear more or less of the hum of the monarchical machinery. But his heart dwelt elsewhere. One cannot read the record of his apprenticeship in the navy (which began when he was but ten years of age), or the even more illuminating story of his career as amateur traveler, poet, historian, scholar, without being struck by the truth of this. For a long time, however, he cherished but one prime aspiration—to see himself the commander of a fleet. He learned to love the sea with an intelligence of instinct and a fervor of passion consummately wonderful. For the heroes of his boyhood and early manhood he had an affection and admiration, the best accessible proof of which may be found in his verses to such daring Swedish sea-fighters as Claes Uggla, Jonas Hökenflykt, and Nils Ehrensköld. Many pages of King Oscar's "Ur Svenska Flottans minnen " (Out of the Story of the Swedish Navy) are devoted to a glorification of their deeds. The same book of poems, anonymously submitted, was awarded a prize by the Swedish Academy in 1857, and contains what must be considered the author's finest poetic effort, the melodious, virile stanzas to the Baltic. Very fair translations of this poem exist in German and French.

Wandering through the published writings of Oscar Fredrik (as he always signs his productions), I one day found the following bit of sentiment :

More than life itself to many a youth is a flower to adorn the bosom of his love; and well it is that this be so.

If we regard the quaint little aphorism in the light of the most beautiful event in King Oscar's personal life, or apply it thereto, it will have twofold significance. I refer to his courtship with Princess Sophia of Nassau, at Monrepos Castle, near the banks of the Rhine, in Koblenz, where the young couple first met. She was then twenty, he twenty-seven. Beautiful, lovable, dearly fond of many of the very studies to the pursuit of which he was greatly devoted—history, languages,

119

music—Oscar Fredrik soon saw in the German Princess the woman of his dreams. September 26, 1856, they announced their betrothal, and, in commemoration, immediately afterwards they cut their names in the trunk of a giant oak, benign witness to their troth. Likewise, the lovers planted a few of its acorns, one of which sprouted and became in the course of a year a two-leaved tree. This they transplanted in a flower-pot and brought with them to Stockholm to set it out in the idyllic gardens of Drottningholm Castle. Eight or nine years later, when Hans Christian Andersen was visiting the royal family there, Prince Oscar gave him a branch of the memorial tree, which, as the story-teller remarks, was even then taller than he. It is to-day one of the sturdiest of all the oaks on the grounds.

After his marriage to Princess Sophia the heir apparent cultivated his literary talent with renewed zeal. Such was the quality of his interest that it was no rare occurrence with him in those days to sit up till dawn discussing Runeberg, or Tegnér, or Goethe, with some congenial companion. Strangely enough, however, he had no liking for the representatives of the New School (so called), a reactionary party that championed " the rights of fancy and feeling within the domain of poetry " and deprecated and opposed the prevailing French standards and tastes in arts and letters, as instituted by Gustavus III. In 1859 he published a translation of Herder's version of "Poema del Cid," sumptuously illustrated and dedicated to his brother, the Crown Prince, likewise an amateur man of letters. Two years later, at his wife's initiative, he had rendered Goethe's " Torquato Tasso " into Swedish. As an aid to the perfecting of her knowledge of the language, Princess Sophia copied the translator's manuscript, of many revisions and blurs, in an elegant hand, from which it was ultimately typed. The production is dedicated to her.

Few, if indeed any, of King Oscar's predecessors equal him as an orator. His eloquence has on more than one occasion proved a power by which he has been enabled distinctively to assert his royal position and authority. Sono-

rous, rich, musical, his voice is in itself a splendid artistic force. During the crisis with Norway, in June, 1904, I had the pleasure of hearing him address ten or fifteen thousand loyal subjects who had gone to his country seat, Rosendal, on the outskirts of the capital, to express their approbation of his attitude and their affection for their king. He spoke very briefly, perhaps not more than two hundred words. But there was a tremor in his voice, and an indefinable something about his bearing, his gestures, from whose haunting appeal it was impossible to escape. It was a most impressive spectacle. I shall never forget the sight of the venerable monarch standing there on the balcony, surrounded by his children and grandchildren, in the failing light, facing the multitude. Not like a crowned ruler did he look to me; I could distinguish only the man who, deeply conscious of the responsibilities of his office and the solemn significance of the particular hour, recognized above all the reciprocity of the issue, and, recognizing it, seemed indeed to be *of* the people that were doing him homage.

With his ascendency to the throne his literary activities virtually ceased. He surely must have found it a somewhat awkward journey, the transit from the quiet haunts of private life to the inviolate halls of sovereignty. In the beginning, extreme caution characterized his official acts. He spared no effort to continue as nearly as possible the administrative policy of his predecessor, Carl XV., than whom there never was a more popular regent in the Kingdom of Sweden. It may be mentioned that the people were slow to approach the new king. They mourned the loss of his brother very much as the Danes had grieved over the death of their Frederick VII. about ten years previously. For quite a long time the nation showed either a lack of inclination, or sheer inability, to reconcile itself to the change. At least a decade was to pass before Oscar II., thanks in large measure to his wise dealing with public questions, his patriotism, his keen sympathies with national ideals and prompt appreciation of the urgent need of certain reforms, completely won the people's hearts.

The progress of the country in commerce, industry, agriculture, education, etc., during his reign, has been gradual and sure. In 1875, for instance, Sweden had 2,516 factories, employing altogether 52,207 hands and producing material to the value of 143,000,000 crowns. In 1895 the number of factories had increased to 5,083, that of the employees to 140,776, and the value of the output to 418,000,000 crowns. Since his coming into power over one hundred new railways have been constructed and thrown open for traffic. In 1875 about 6,400,000 acres of soil.were under cultivation; in 1895 almost 9,000,000. All the institutions of learning owe much of their present prosperity directly to the King's interest. The splendid International Exposition held at Stockholm ten years ago testified eloquently to Sweden's eminence in the matter of national efficiency.

The gravest period of his reign came in the summer of 1904. Norway had again made the consular question a crucial issue. The attitude of the heads of her Government, Berner, Lövland, Michelsen, was almost aggressively defiant. A now-or-never spirit of determination marked their whole *modus operandi.* Would King Oscar at last sign the bill (unanimously passed by the Storthing) giving the Norwegians the right to appoint consuls of their own and cease to recognize those named by Sweden? There were many days of suspense. Then suddenly the " Extras " announced that the sovereign's answer was a veto. From that moment events moved with great celerity, and on June 7 Oscar II. was King of Sweden only. A less peace-loving monarch than he would never have gone through that crisis without bloodshed. As it was, war was narrowly averted. Had the Norwegians been dealing with Crown Prince Gustavus, the result would probably have been different.

Returning to the personal side of the King, mention should be made of his annual summer excursions to Marstrand, on the western coast. For at least a generation Oscar II. has spent a month or more of each year at that resort. Naturally, the little place is crowded to overflowing during his visits—the fair sex predominating. At Marstrand the monarch meets old friends, classmates at college, fellow-officers of the navy; he participates in social functions, revives ancient sea memories, swims, sails, and mingles freely with the hardy inhabitants. For him it has become a place of reunions, a treasure-room of fond reminiscences. It is not too much to say that in its welcome to the royal visitor Marstrand somehow embodies the heart of the entire nation. Those sojourns in the historic town, through whose quaint streets sometimes blow the winds of the near North Sea, have contributed largely to disseminate a broader knowledge of King Oscar's personal attributes among the people.

As a patron of art, the Swedish monarch's name will be coupled by posterity with that of Gustavus III. It is a rare artistic delight to wander through the halls and corridors of Drottningholm Castle, where the monarch spends most of the summer. Since the elaborate renovation and reconstruction of its interior, begun in 1885, and carried out under the King's personal supervision and measurably at his own expense, it has become one of the most beautiful royal residences in the world. Every object bespeaks fastidious selection. The arrangement of the paintings, the architectural effects, the form of the furniture, the floors, ceilings, windows, all add essentially to the general harmonious beauty of the place. To see it is to be convinced of King Oscar's intelligent appreciation of art, especially when you know that the work bears the marks of his own hand.

The Swedish sovereign was ever a devoted theater-goer and admirer of good acting. Few foreign players of distinction have appeared in Stockholm without being honored by an invitation to meet the King. Some years ago, actuated by his love of the stage, he established a new order, or roll of honor, entitled "Litteris et Artibus." He himself makes the awards; and though the decoration is intended chiefly for worthy representatives of the histrionic profession, literary men, scientists, and musicians are, I believe, also eligible.

Among famous theatrical folk who have received it are Sarah Bernhardt, Eleonora Duse, and Christina Nilsson.

No one could testify with greater authority to King Oscar's interest in science than Dr. Sven Hedin, author of "Through Asia." It is a matter of simple fact that Hedin's first great journey of exploration was very materially backed by his royal patron. When the scientist returned, having penetrated wildernesses and traversed deserts never hitherto trod by a white man's foot, the venerable King embraced him like a father, calling him "my son." Sven Hedin is again in Asia, and a large fraction of the money that made possible his second expedition was likewise contributed by Oscar II.

It is not generally known here that the monarch's youngest son, Prince Eugene, takes rank with the leading artists of his country—with Norström, Berg, and Zorn. Nor are very many Americans aware of the not uninteresting fact that Crown Prince Gustavus is an inveterate if not an invincible tennis-player. Every season he enters open tournaments, and though he does not always prove a winner, there are but three or four men in all Sweden who may be called his superiors. His passion for sport Gustavus inherited doubtless from his father. From time to time, throughout a long span of years, King Oscar has distinguished himself as a follower of many branches of outdoor pastime. As recently as 1895, at the army maneuvers at Nerike, he surprised every one by his daring expert horsemanship. In 1893, at the races of the Royal Swedish Yacht Club, he personally sailed one of the competing boats to victory. He is a patient, lucky fisherman, a sure shot, a reliable bowler and curler, and was not so very long ago a "rattling" ski-jumper and a first-rate swimmer.

Greater kings have occupied the throne of Sweden; more efficient rulers too, perhaps, and stronger men. Not with Gustavus Wasa, Gustavus Adolphus, or Charles XII. will be the place of Oscar II., round whose name no lustrous historical glories can ever cluster. His was a reign of peace. The mention of his name will have no echo of cannon-thunder or battlefield horror. But it shall be said of him, with truth, that he served his country well. It shall be said of him that never did he stand unmoved, haughty, cold, before any prayer of his people. He has striven conscientiously and to the utmost extent of his powers to fulfill not merely the official but the human duties of his exalted position. Sincerity of purpose, unselfishness, energetic pursuit of the intellectual ideal—by such virtues shall posterity recognize the moral greatness of Oscar II., one of the most human, most intellectual, most lovable royal personages of modern times.

# PROBLEMS OF MODERN FREIGHT HANDLING

## BY EARL MAYO

THE head of the greatest milling company in the country said some time since that he could ship a barrel of flour from his mill in Minneapolis to London for fifty cents, or exactly the cost of delivery in the suburbs of the city. This is a striking illustration of the measure of perfection to which the long-distance shipment of merchandise has been developed. It is no less instructive as showing that the problems of the local handling and transshipment of freight have not been solved in any such satisfactory manner. While the price of railway transportation has been reduced forty per cent. in the past twenty-five years, the cost of transshipment and local distribution, even in our largest cities, is practically the same as it was a quarter-century ago, while, broadly speaking, there has been little improvement in the agencies performing this part of the work of transportation.

In these days, when competition is a struggle between localities rather than between individuals, small economies in the handling of business become important factors in determining the commercial position which a city shall occupy. Boston, New York, Philadelphia, Baltimore, Norfolk, New Orleans, Galveston, and other ports are all competitors in handling the products of Western farms for export. All of these, as well as Chicago, St. Louis, and others of the more advantageously situated cities of the interior, are competitors for the manufacturing and distributing trade of the country. Trade follows the channels of least resistance, just as surely as do the forces of nature, and, since the reduction in railway freight rates has made terminal and transshipment charges a large proportion of the total cost of reaching a given market, the city which can do this part of the business most cheaply and efficiently has a decided advantage in the struggle for trade.

A lively appreciation of the importance of this fact is causing the big cities to give attention to their equipment in this particular, with the result that some very ambitious and comprehensive plans for cheaper and more rapid handling of merchandise are being carried out in different parts of the country. It is in this direction that attempts to introduce further economies into the business of transportation are likely to be most successful in the near future. At present the cost of moving a hundred pounds of grain by rail from Chicago to New York —a thousand miles—is ten cents, while the cost of moving it from car to ship by lighter—two or three miles—is three cents. Manifestly the railway charge is low out of all proportion to the lighterage charge, considering the enormous investment required for railway as compared with water transportation. Many similar illustrations exist to indicate that warehousing and transshipment facilities must be greatly extended and cheapened to keep pace with the demands of modern business.

Naturally the situation and the requirements of each trading center are peculiar to itself, so that the methods of meeting these must be diverse. Naturally, too, different cities have been particularly successful in handling different phases of the general problem. The seacoast cities, for example, have been especially concerned with the improvement of their means for handling export and import trade, and have dealt more especially with the problem of transfer from ship to rail or *vice versa*; while, of the interior cities, Chicago and St. Louis have given particular attention to the transshipment of goods between local business houses and the railways.

For the handling of wholesale and jobbing business, St. Louis has in operation a highly efficient system, combining the warehousing and shipping requirements of the city's great trade in the Southwest. This is accomplished by bringing together in a series of great buildings—collectively called Cupples Station—under one administration, a large part of the city's wholesale business. The various railway lines entering St. Louis are connected by what is known as the Terminal Railway, so all freight can be moved over a single series of tracks. Alongside these tracks are erected the great brick buildings of the regulation warehouse type which compose Cupples Station. Spurs and switches extend into each of the buildings. Freight destined for any of the various firms occupying space in the buildings is unloaded from the car upon trucks which are run upon powerful hydraulic lifts, raised to the floor which the firm occupies, and delivered to the consignee at one handling. Similarly the outgoing shipments of the various firms are placed upon trucks at their doors, are moved down to the car platforms, and placed in the cars by the employees of the station management, who also attend to all such matters as making out bills of lading and other details of shipment. In this way the slow and costly method of team cartage is eliminated entirely, except upon local business.

The advantages of the plan embodied in Cupples Station are numerous, aside from the saving in time and expense through the elimination of cartage. The shipping business of all the firms occupying quarters in Cupples Station is conducted practically as though it were that of a single firm. All the loading, unloading, and handling of freight is done by a single force of employees, and consequently is done in the most economical manner. Incoming freight is received and unloaded during the night, and outgoing freight is loaded and shipped during the day. Each road has a scheduled hour for pulling its train, and the various firms assort their orders and get out their shipments to conform as closely as possible to these schedules. Shipments are made in carload lots, and it is as easy for a firm to ship a single package as a carload. The expense of freight handling and shipment is assessed pro rata among the tenants of the various buildings.

Two thousand employees are required to handle the business of Cupples Station, and while there is a great saving to the various tenants over the cost of conducting their trade in sèparate and detached buildings, the station itself pays handsome dividends. The property now belongs to Washington University, having been presented to the institution by Mr. Samuel Cupples and Mr. Robert Brookings, the original owners. The various buildings of the station occupy an area of over thirty acres, with a floor space of over a million and a half of square feet. Its thirty tenants do a yearly business running well up toward $100,000,000. If the various economies introduced by this concentration of business amounted to only one per cent., it would represent, therefore, a saving of a million dollars yearly. Actually it is probably three or four times this amount.

In Chicago the problem of handling the goods traffic within the city by the slow and costly system of trucking became so difficult on account of the congestion of the streets and freight terminals that five years ago the construction of a freight tunnel, running through the main business section and connecting with the railway terminals, was begun. This tunnel was opened for business in January, 1905, and at present is thirty-four miles in extent, with a capacity of 30,000 tons of freight per day, and represents an investment of $15,000,000. It is intended ultimately to extend the system to the outlying districts of the city. Another feature of the plan is the proposal to bring together all the railway lines entering Chicago in a common

terminal station, with the underground road acting as the collector and distributer of freight between the railways and wholesale houses.

The peculiarity of the underground Chicago railway is that it carries only freight, no passengers. Its stations are platforms connecting with the basements of the great business houses at a level of from twenty to forty feet below the street. The difficulty arising from the fact that not all the business structures were built down to the level of the roadway has been met by the construction of elevators by which cars are lifted up to the loading platforms, thus doing away with the necessity of a double handling of goods.

Most of the merchandise handled by this underground railway goes direct from the store of the shipper to the railway, but the company maintains warehouses where goods may be stored if necessary. Incoming freight is distributed to the various houses for which it is destined at night, while outgoing traffic is collected and moved to the railway freight stations by day.

Taking into account the greater cheapness of this method of handling freight, and the saving in time over the movement of goods by team through crowded streets, and in the orderly delivery at freight depots as compared with the confusion and delay that prevail when the approaches to these stations are crowded with teams, it will be seen that this system presents tremendous advantages for a city with business houses distributed over an extended area, and with congested streets in which it is practically impossible to keep traffic moving steadily and freely. It is inevitable that in the course of time most of the larger cities of the country will have freight subways or tunnels for the handling of heavy goods traffic on a plan somewhat similar to that adopted in Chicago.

The problem in port cities presents special features in addition to those indicated in these inland trade centers. Here are necessary not only a close and convenient connection between business houses and railways, but also one between railways and ships for the handling of the great volume of export and import trade. In the ports of recent development, such as Norfolk and Newport News, as well as in some of the older ports which have undertaken improvement work on a comprehensive scale, such as Boston, this problem has been met with fair efficiency. In these cities, for example, ships can dock on one side of grain elevators while freight cars run up to the other side, and the grain passes through the elevator from car to ship with the greatest speed and the minimum cost.

New Orleans may be cited as an excellent example of economic handling of export grain traffic, both because it has an enlightened and liberal system of port administration, and because it has one of the most complete and efficient systems of docks in existence. These are the Stuyvesant docks of the Illinois, Central Railroad, which were destroyed by fire about a year ago, but have now been rebuilt, and present a perfect example of an up-to-date system of transshipment from rail to water. The principal item in the export trade of New Orleans is the shipment of grain, in which it is rapidly coming to be the first port of the country. The system of handling grain on these docks is typical of the latest and most efficient development of this business, although it does not differ radically from that in vogue in various other ports.

The tracks of the Illinois Central run directly along the river front, and a part of the dock equipment consists of two immense grain elevators. Switches from the main freight tracks run directly into the elevators, and the opening of the car door allows the grain to run through gratings upon belts which elevate it. Another series of endless belts convey it through a long aerial passageway to the edge of the docks, where it is discharged through a boot directly into the steamer's hold. Thus the grain is conveyed from car to ship by automatic machinery in the most rapid and economical way possible. As the docks are the property of the railway, there is no charge upon steamers for the use of docking facilities. Thus New Orleans is a free port so far as the grain trade is concerned. The steamers avoid not only the high pier rentals charged in

New York, but also the moderate tonnage taxes which are imposed in most other cities and the low tonnage tax charged at the State-controlled piers in New Orleans. It is this fact, in connection with the enlightened and progressive policy of the railway company in its competition for grain trade, that has done more than anything else to build up the wonderful grain business of the Crescent City.

When one turns to the methods of handling business in the greatest port of the country, he is struck by the fact that it has lagged behind other cities of America and Europe in the improvement of its facilities. The very advantages which caused New York to become the commercial headquarters of the country are in part responsible for the handicap under which it labors in the transshipment of freight. Being an island, New York has never been able to transfer freight direct from cars to ships, or *vice versa*, as is done in other cities, thus bringing about one of the great causes of excessive port charges, the expense resulting from lighterage. Most of the freight that enters or leaves the city must be transferred by lighters to or from ships, or by car floats or ferries across one or both rivers.

The high lighterage charges and the double handling of freight result in part from inadequate or inconvenient dock and warehouse facilities. The inadequate facilities in turn result from the topography of New York, which has brought about congestion in a small section, enhancing to enormous figures the value of New York real estate. Further, the docks of the city are to-day a source of revenue approximating $2,000,000 annually from rentals and other charges, and the value of a policy which makes them such a source of income is becoming more and more questionable in view of the beneficial results which English ports enjoy from free docks. The city, instead of securing a huge return from her docks, could well afford a tax for a number of years which would make for her ultimate prosperity by attracting increased freight, and, as a result, still further increasing the value of her real estate.

So long as the present inadequate dockage facilities continue, so long will one great obstacle to New York's commercial supremacy—excessive port charges—remain in her path. Liverpool, with a population of 600,000, has spent $200,000,000 on terminals and docks, and Marseilles, with only 400,000 inhabitants, has disbursed an equal sum. The New York Commerce Commission, appreciating the wisdom of such a policy, recommended that the conveyance in perpetuity of any land under water within the limits of the city of New York be prohibited, and that the city, with the aid of the Legislature, should strive rapidly to provide New York with modern piers with which to meet the demands of commerce.

Again, aside from the handicap of inadequate dockage facilities, New York, on account of her closely centered population, finds the struggle against freight congestion in the handling of cars a severe one. The same policy that would benefit the handling of water traffic would, on account of the interdependence of the various factors, aid very materially in every way in the solution of the problem which New York is facing. When freight can be moved directly from car to vessel, both land and water transportation will be benefited.

"The purposes of a terminal," says the New York Commerce Commission, "are three: three purposes are served; the first is receipt, the second storage, and the third shipment. Where these are united, as in Newport News, Baltimore, and New Orleans in the South, and at Montreal, Boston, and Portland in the North, a perfect terminal exists; but in the proportion that they are separated, as they are in New York, that is an imperfect terminal."

The greater part of New York's incoming rail freight is received on the Jersey shore. That which it is necessary to store is held in Brooklyn, and nine-tenths of the outgoing freight moves from New York. In other words, the three functions of a terminal being widely separated, New York's commerce is bound to suffer as a result. Ships being loaded in New York with grain for foreign ports are forced to receive that grain from a lighter, since they cannot lie alongside docks and receive it direct as in other cities. In Boston, for example, grain going from an elevator where it has been stored, to the piers where the boats are lying, after having been unloaded at the elevators from the cars, is discharged directly into the holds of the steamers on a belt inclosed in an aerial gallery.

In New York, freight, if it is to be stored, must be moved from the car in various complicated and expensive manners. That which is to be stored up and down town in the city is handled by a system of drayage so vast that estimates of its cost place it at $35,000,000 annually. So large is this system that it has been said that if all the drays in the city were put into a single line the shouts of the drivers could be heard from New York to San Francisco. In contrast to this inefficient system may be instanced Chicago's freight subway, which is planned to connect with every terminal and with practically every important shipping house in the city, and to collect and distribute freight unimpeded below the level of the city streets. Everywhere in New York one may see the workings of this drayage system. Everywhere on the river may be seen examples of the lighterage and car-float system, which altogether cost the city, at a conservative estimate, $50,000,000 a year.

The great bulk of incoming freight, when it arrives at the western side of the North River, where the freight terminals are located, must either be floated across the river to Manhattan and distributed by drays, or must be taken by floats or lighters down the North River, through the bay, and across to Brooklyn, or up the East River—a long voyage on probably the most congested waters of the world, which naturally results in an increased expense in handling. All this expense can be remedied only by centralizing receipt, storage, and shipment points of freight.

The improvement which is so urgently needed to enable New York to handle her vast volume of goods transportation efficiently must come from the adoption of the policy which is now definitely settled upon to solve the problems of passenger transportation—the construction of tunnels. Underground systems of transportation have proved their superiority to bridges, surface and overhead systems in the handling of human freight. In the movement of goods the latter are totally inadequate under the conditions of congestion and high land values that obtain in New York.

At present the energies and resources both of the city itself and of the great transportation systems serving it are being devoted to the work of providing for the adequate handling of passengers. As soon as the comprehensive plans for the provision of such facilities are determined upon, equally intelligent effort should be directed to the matter of extending similar advantages to the freight business of the port. Two things are necessary for this—the construction of freight subways, either as a municipal enterprise or by private capital, and the building of freight tunnels under the rivers by capital supplied or supported by the transportation lines centering in New York. These measures, in connection with a new system of dock administration, will make it possible to combine the three functions of receipt, storage, and shipment far more closely and effectively than at present, and will do more than anything else to maintain New York's prestige as the commercial metropolis of the country.

Meanwhile, as a direct advance toward greater expedition and lessened cost of transshipment of freight, important plans are now in progress which will result in more direct connection between Western trunk lines and the railways that serve New England and Long Island. These plans will do away to a great extent with the tedious and indirect shipment of freight by boat from Jersey City terminals across the North River, around the lower end of Manhattan Island, and up the East River to Harlem for the New England roads, and to Long Island City and Brooklyn for the Long Island traffic. The new plans provide for a short ferriage across the unobstructed waters of the upper bay from terminals located on its western shore, and then from the landing-point in Bay Ridge for rail connection with the New England and Long Island roads. Probably—indeed, we may say inevitably—the ferriage will be done away with in the course of time by means of the projected tunnel under the bay, which will make possible an all-rail route via New York for traffic to the East from Western points.

The details of the plan now in execution show how vast are the improvements already under way. The New York, New Haven, and Hartford Railroad is enlarging the capacity of its freight yards in the Bronx, and, slightly below them, has acquired over eight hundred acres of ground which are now receiving an equipment that will make this property one of the finest yards in the country. The old yard will continue to handle local freight, while all through traffic will move in the future through the new yards. On the Jersey side the plans of the Pennsylvania road call for a new and tremendous freight terminal, not opposite the island of Manhattan, as at present, but nearly two miles further south— that is, at about the central point of the west shore of the upper bay. Almost directly opposite these terminals the Pennsylvania and Long Island Railroads are to prepare another set of freight yards. From this point the lines of the Long Island Railroad, running north, are to carry freight to a point near its Long Island City terminal, where it is to connect with the newly franchised New York Connecting Railway. The tracks of the new road will cross the East River by a bridge via Randall's and Ward's Islands to the Bronx terminal of the New York, New Haven, and Hartford.

Simplicity is one of the prime requisites in freight handling, and the railways having these improvements in hand doubtless see ample returns for the great outlay which these projects require, while the business of the city as a whole must inevitably respond by a proportionate increase.

Another item in New York's commercial reorganization as a shipping center is the still indefinite project for a freight tunnel parallel to the river front on the west side of the island of Manhattan—a tunnel to collect freight from all parts of the city, connecting with all the various tunnels and terminals, to deliver it for further shipment. Transfer yards under the city itself are by no means an undreamed possibility, since Chicago's freight subways have shown what may be done along these lines.

Then, too, the projected vast new terminals of the New York, New Haven, and Hartford, and the Pennsylvania, will afford better facilities for the loading and receiving of transatlantic cargo. Thus the plans already under way will make for the unification of terminal purposes ; but these improvements, important as they are, are merely the first steps toward the adequate and finally satisfactory solution of New York's transportation problem.

The importance of these improvements in different parts of the country, in which hundreds of millions have been or are being invested, is to be measured only by the vast volume of our foreign and domestic trade. The saving of a quarter-cent in the handling of each bushel of grain or each bale of cloth on its way to market means a saving of millions in the course of a year. The achievement of the same relative speed, cheapness, and efficiency in the collection, delivery, and transshipment of ·merchandise at terminal or shipping points that has been realized by American railways in the transportation of this merchandise over long distances means a great step forward toward the commanding position in the markets of the world.

# MY BOYHOOD'S BLACK FRIEND

## BY JACOB A. RIIS

IT doesn't seem as if a man could go away from home, these days, leaving everything snug, without some one coming along, before his back is fairly turned, and "exposing" something or somebody to which he had pinned his faith without question. It is bad enough that it has got to be so that one hates the sight of a bank, and pays his insurance premium with an inward turn at the suggestion of champagne suppers and campaign corruption which it will bring up. But when, the other day, traveling way out West, I picked up a paper and found the European starling posted as the worst, most immoral of recent immigrants, a thief, a marauder who ought to be deported without a hearing, I own that the limit of my patience was reached. I don't know what the poor bird had done. The man who wrote the story was so busy piling up wrath against him that he had no time to bring forward his evidence. I should like to see it. The one charge I made out was that he ate fruits of a kind he didn't specify, but of which it was said there weren't any in the neighborhood of New York, where the starling, so the story said, is becoming numerous. I expect it is all of the same kidney, poor stuff. The starling was my boyhood's friend, and I should think myself a poorer stick than his maligner if I did not speak up for him, now that he is in trouble.

I did not know that he had crossed the sea. I have longed for him often, and the news moved me more than your readers can perhaps easily understand. You see, we grew up together. Almost the earliest thing I remember is the box by my bedroom window which the first rays of the rising sun struck in early spring. Then, as soon as ever the winter snows were gone and the daffodils peeped through the half-frozen crust, some morning there would be a mighty commotion in that box. Black shadows darted out and in, and a great scratching and thumping went on. And while I lay and watched, with heart beating fast —for was not here my songster playmate back with the summer and the sunlight on his burnished wing?—out he came on the peg for a sidelong peep at my window, and sat and whistled the old tune I loved, nodding to the bare trees he knew with his brave promise that presently Jack Frost would be banished for good, and all would be right. Was he not there to prove it ? And it was even so. The summer was right on his trail always.

The weeks passed and the Old Town lay buried in a dreamy sea of blossoming elders. In field and meadow the starling was busy from early dawn till the sun was far in the west; for his young, of whom there was always a vigorous family—and oh! the glorious blue eggs we loved to peep at before Mrs. Starling had taken them under her wing—had a healthy appetite and required worms and grubs in countless numbers. But whether they went to sleep early, or he thought they had had enough, always when the setting sun gilded the top of the old poplar he would come with all his friends and sing his evening song. In the very top branches, swaying with the summer wind, they would sit and whistle, the sweet clear note in the minor key that comes across all the years to me, when I am worn and tired, with the promise that some day it will all come back, even my black playfellow of the young days. Near New York the article said he was. Then he may be near my home on Long Island, and I shall put up boxes in the spring.

That was the first labor of love I turned my boyish hand to, just an empty starch-box. Later on, when I learned carpentering, I made him a more substantial home, a tenement with flats for three, and it hung by my window many years after I knew it no more. I had long been absorbed in the fight with tenements made for human kind by builders with no such friendly feelings, when my father wrote that the winter storms had blown down the box and broken it, and that written inside in my boyish hand they had found this legend:

This box is for starlings, but, by the great horn spoon, not for sparrows.

JACOB RIIS.

I suppose it was the near approach of his going away, with the stork and the swallow, to leave us in the grip of the long winter, that made me in desperation try to cage him once. How I could I don't know. Boys are boys everywhere, I suppose. I made the cage with infinite toil, caught my starling and put him in. But when I saw him darting from side to side, struggling to get out to the trees and the grass and the clouds, my heart smote me and I tore the cage apart and threw open the window. It was many days before I could look my friend in the eye, and I was secretly afraid all winter that he would not come back. But he was a generous bird and bore no grudge. Next spring he was there earlier than ever, as if he knew.

It must be almost fifty years since, but I have not forgotten it. It is to me as vivid as if it were yesterday, that black day when, with the instinct to "kill something" strong in me, I had gone out with my father's gun, and, coming through the willows, met a starling on joyous wing crossing the meadow on the way to his nest. Up went the gun, and before I knew I had shot him. I can see him folding his wings as he fell at my feet. I did not pick him up. I went home with all the sunlight gone out of the day. I have shot many living things since, more shame to me, but never one that hurt as did that. I had slain my friend.

There was a story abroad in my childhood that young starlings were good eating. I cannot say how true it is; it was like the theory as to squabs. I once kept pigeons on purpose, but gave it up, without finding out. How can one kill one's own pigeons? But I can testify that young sparrows are good. I have eaten many without a pang of conscience. We used to borrow the cook's long stocking, and go out to the straw-thatched barn by night and dig into the nests in the thatch which we knew of. When the stocking was full we had enough for a good meal.

The sparrow we scorned. He was a cheeky tramp without redeeming qualities. The starling was good company, and more than paid with his song for the house-room we gave him. I guess he has not changed. It is perfectly easy to prevent his disfiguring houses and trees with his nest by just taking him into the family. In that he is just human and a type of the boy we sometimes bewail as bad. Just treat him with kindness and see what he will do. And the outlay in time and trouble is such a trifle compared with the return in the case of both.

In Denmark the starling had long been protected, when I saw him last, because of the service he renders the farmer. And I can well believe it; for I have seen an innumerable host of them moving across a meadow, like an army, and with something of the precision of it in its way of progress, leaving no wriggling thing behind. Because of the protection he has enjoyed he has multiplied almost beyond belief. A dozen years ago, when I spent a summer in Denmark, we used to drift down the river in our rowboat after a day's fishing. In the twilight the chatter of these birds in the reeds, where they were settling for their night's rest, and settling the day's disputes at the same time, as it seemed, was deafening. Suddenly getting on our feet, we would shout and clap our hands. Then the flocks would rise and rise, and keep rising farther and farther down the river until the sky was darkened and the twilight became night, while the noise of the million wings sounded like rolling thunder. We stood, open-mouthed, and watched the marvelous sight, while the children crowded up close, half afraid. Yet I do not remember hearing any one complain of the starling as a nuisance.

To be sure, they ate the elderberries when they were ripe, and the town that was white in spring became purple from their droppings. But we could not find use for all the berries in the soup which Danish housewives know how to make so well, and were glad to share with them. That, so far as I know, was the starling's only lapse from a meat diet—in Denmark. There was an interval between the blossoming and the berrying of the elder, when he disappeared from our fields with his young brood, then full grown. It was reported that during those weeks he made a raid upon the olive groves of southern France, and that there they gave him an evil name and hunted him as a malefactor. I don't know about that. Since I have tasted the raw ripe olive in southern California I have my opinion of any one who would choose such a· diet—but no! I am speaking of my friend, and I have set out to defend him. Anyway, it is hearsay evidence upon which a jury would not convict a known thief—certainly not I my boyhood's friend and companion. If America never gets a worse emigrant, I think we can rest easy. I shall want more than the evidence of a grouty newspaper correspondent before I shall be convinced that he is not entitled to come in and be heartily welcomed as a lovable, companionable bird and a singer, or perhaps rather a whistler, such as we have not the like of, unless it be the mocking-bird of the South.

# INDIA'S AWAKENING: THE SWA-DESHI MOVEMENT[1]

## BY YOTRINDA MOHAN BOSE

LORD MACAULAY said, "The heaviest of all yokes is the yoke of the stranger." India, with a population of about three hundred millions, is under the yoke of a stranger. Nearly all that is known in this country about India is that it is a country full of snakes and wild beasts, where widows are oppressed, and that it is yearly ravaged ·by famines, plagues, and other kinds of pestilences. Because of these horrible calamities you Americans with kindness send timely help and you also send missionaries to "save" the people. Yet hardly any of you know or care to know the causes that underlie almost all these evils. But at present I shall confine myself to telling something about the present new spirit afloat in India, called the "Swadeshi Movement." It aims to work out our own salvation, and very little is known about it in this country. The London Times calls

[1] Last week we published an article by Mr H. G. Bissell on India's Awakening from an American point of view. This article discusses the subject from an Indian point of view.—THE EDITORS.

it "the rise of a new political power in India," and its own correspondent writes about it as follows: "However much we may deplore that so much of the Westernized intelligence and energy of India should be devoted to purely political purpose and propaganda, nothing can be gained by blinking that fact. The spirit of revolt against authority, which, as I said in my last letter, the Western education has itself produced, has taken the shape of a revolt against British political authority—not against the supreme authority of the British Crown, but against the form in which the supremacy is exercised. The National Congress party controls almost the whole of the vernacular press and not a few English papers in India; it controls a large section of the native teachers and professors who are molding the minds of the rising generation; it reckons among its stanchest supports the vast majority of liberal professions, and notably the large, influential army of pleaders and barristers. . . . These are powerful forces, which it is unwise as well as unfair to underrate. For, if they comprise many elements of prejudice, jealousy, and ignorance, they comprise many worthy elements, a great deal of unselfish devotion and patriotism, however misguided and misapplied these qualities may seem to us. There are men amongst the leaders of the National Congress party whose single-mindedness of life must command the respect of Englishmen as fully as they command the admiration of their fellow-countrymen."

Before describing what this new spirit means it may be desirable to explain briefly about the past British policy in India, in order to realize the situation more clearly. In discussing the Reform Bill of 1833, Lord Macaulay said in the House of Parliament, "We are free, we are civilized, to little purpose, if we grudge to any portion of the human race an equal measure of freedom and civilization. Are we to keep the people of India ignorant in order that we may keep them submissive? Or do we think that we can give them knowledge without awakening ambition? Or do we mean to awaken ambition and to provide it with no legitimate vent? Who will

answer these questions with the affirmative? . . . I have no fears. The path of duty is plain before us. . . . It may be that the public mind of India may expand under our system till it has outgrown the system. . . . They may in a future age demand European institutions. Whether such a day will ever come I know not. But shall I attempt to avert or retard it? Whenever it comes, it will be the proudest day in English history."

In that Reform Bill it is said: "And be it enacted that no native of the said territories, nor any natural born subject of his Majesty resident therein, shall, by any reason of his religion, place of birth, descent, or color, be disabled from holding any place, office, or appointment under the said company" (East India Company). If the modern British high officials had followed this act fairly, then by this time the Indians would have been able to serve as governors of their own country. Mr. Macaron (a civilian), while giving evidence before the Commission of 1852, said: "Not a single native that I am aware of has been placed in any better position in consequence of that clause in the statute [of 1833] than he would have been in if no such clause had been enacted."

Moreover, in India the English officers are so expensive that the income of about seventeen hundred natives is spent in maintaining one of them, and the result is expressed by Mr. R. N. Stock: "There is a constant drawing away of the wealth of India to England, as the Englishman grows fat on accumulation made in India, while the Indians remain as lean as ever." -

From the time of the opening of the India National Congress in 1855 by the Indian leaders, with the advice and help of some benevolent Englishmen, such as Sir W. Wedderburn, Mr. Hume, and others, we have been sending suggestions and resolutions to the Government of India for reformatory changes, but very seldom has any sympathetic attention been paid to the people's wishes. Yet the work has been diligently followed by the educated Indians for the last twenty years, and though no visible gain came out of this continuous agitation, we slowly acquired that determined strength, the outcome of which is the "Swadeshi Movement" in India, which surely has come to stay and grow.

The British are of the opinion that the Indians are not yet ready for self-government. They often say, "Deserve before desire;" that is, let the Indians be competent in the management of their government before the self-government is granted to them. In other words, it is just the same as to expect anybody to learn swimming before entering into water. They also say that the percentage of the educated population in India is too small to allow any self-government. But in England the House of Commons was established two hundred years ago, when the percentage of education was even less than that found now in India. And whose fault is it that only ten per cent. of the Indian population is educated? Compare the facts that the Indian Government has created an income of $27,000,000 from the sale of liquor, opium, and other intoxicating drugs (as these are a Government monopoly), and has an army expenditure of $90,000,000, with the fact that only $7,000,000 is spent on education in all India. I cannot here explain in detail how, instead of sufficient arrangements being made for education, the Government tried its best to demoralize the people of India by forcing the intoxicating drug habit, to increase the revenue.

Mr. Gladstone said, "It is liberty alone which fits men for liberty." Another high-minded Englishman said, "Liberty is the best educator. Its atmosphere is pure and bracing, through which the lark of genius soars high beyond the reach of the shafts of despotism and clouds of ignorance."

In 1872 Sir Charles Trevelyan (late Governor of Madras) recommended this course to the House of Parliament: "Give them the raising and spending of their own money, and the motive will be supplied, and life and reality will be imported into the whole system. All would act under real personal responsibility, under the eye of those who would be familiar with all the details and would have the strongest possible interest in maintaining a vigilant control over them.

And it would be a school of self-government for the whole of India, . . . the longest step taken towards its 200,000,-000 of people governing themselves, which is the end and object of our connection with that country." But instead of allowing any hand in the government, the revenue of the country is arbitrarily spent regardless of the people's interest, and the tax is laid without any representation.

Compare, on the other hand, India with Cuba and the Philippines, the people of which countries are in no way more competent than the Indians. In a few years' connection with "Uncle Sam" they got ready for at least some measure of self-government; while India is not yet ready after one hundred and fifty years' connection with England. Mr. Moorfield Storey, of Boston, once asked Sir Andrew Clark, "Have these centuries of British rule brought the Indian people any nearer to self-government than they were when the British began?" The reply was, "Not a bit." Yet the British government in India is "successful."

In brief, the following are the main causes which gave rise to this new spirit, which Mr. Morley referred to in his budget speech: 1. Lack of flexibility in the administration. 2. The reluctance as to adjustment of the system to changing conditions. 3. The growing lack of touch between government and people. 4. The fact that the people have no share in making their own laws for their own benefit. 5. The aspiration induced by the dazzling rise of the New Japan.

Every act of despotism has its limits. That limit is now reached in Russia, and its result is vividly shown in an Occidental way. And that limit was reached in India when Lord Curzon, in spite of popular protests, divided the province of Bengal on the 16th of October, 1905. I am unable freely to discuss this act, for want of space; but its direct result is the rise of the "Swadeshi Movement" in India. The main underlying objects of this partition scheme are very concisely stated in an Anglo-Indian paper of Calcutta, The Statesman, to be as follows : "The objects of the scheme are, briefly, first, to destroy the collective power of the Bengali people; secondly, to overthrow the political ascendency of Calcutta; and, thirdly, to foster in East Bengal the growth of a Mohammedan power which it is supposed will have the effect of keeping in check the rapidly growing strength of the educated Hindu community."

There were held about six hundred public meetings in different parts of the province, and from ten to forty thousand people attended each meeting and protested against the partition scheme. On the 7th of August, 1905, there was an immense public meeting in the Town Hall of Calcutta, where about twenty-five thousand educated people of Bengal assembled to protest against the partition scheme. It was resolved in this meeting that if the partition scheme were not withdrawn, the people would not use any British goods, and would keep this as a sacred vow until the act were undone.

But nothing could avail them against Lord Curzon's waywardness. On the partition day (October 16, 1905) there was an unprecedented sight in the city of Calcutta, where all native shopkeepers closed their shops; in fact, almost all the business of the city was suspended. No fire was lighted in any house to cook anything, all wore their respective mourning costumes, and the day was considered as a general mourning day in memory of the partition. It was a grand sight to see the legions of people with solemn countenances and barefooted (as a sign of mourning) flowing down the streets of Calcutta to attend public meetings. There were twenty or more public meetings in the different parts of the city; in one about one hundred thousand people attended, and here, after various inspiring speeches, the late Mr. A. M. Bose laid the foundation of a public hall to be called the "Federation Hall," where public meetings are to be held in the future and a museum of Indian products will be kept. At the end of the meeting an ancient custom call "Rakhi" (a silk thread tied round the wrist of a fellow-man as a sign of lifelong friendship and to share equally weal or woe) was revived among both the Hindus and the Mohammedans, meaning, "Brother to brother, side by side."

Then in procession the people went to the Ganges to take a holy bath, shouting on their way, "Bande Mataram!" (Hail, Motherland); and everybody took a solemn vow that the day should be kept as a memorial mourning day till the partition is undone, and to keep this national cry of "Bande Mataram" sacred to his heart for his life long. From this day India (not Bengal alone) is initiated into that aspiration which will undoubtedly bring back within a measurable future her past glory.

Again, on the 1st of November, 1905, the following proclamation was issued from the people of Bengal:

Whereas, the government has decided to divide Bengal in spite of the protest from the people of Bengal, so we the people of Bengal, to avoid any ill results of this divide-and-rule policy, and to keep the unity of the whole nation, hereby promise to apply our conjoint forces. . . . May God help us.

Long before this there had been a spirit gradually rising in India to use more of its country's products even with loss and inconvenience, and this at once broke into flame at this moment of agitation. The people of Bengal asked the help of the Manchester Chamber of Commerce to use its influence in the House of Parliament to undo this partition, but it refused to do so, calling the agitation ungrounded. Consequently forthwith they boycotted the British goods, and took a sacred vow at the temple of Kalighat in Calcutta to keep that vow religiously till the partition should be undone; for they could perceive that the way to touch the British public was through its pockets.

The partition question now took the shape of the "Swadeshi Movement" (national movement), and the people of Bengal have gone almost into partial fanaticism to attain their object, not caring for the partition only, but for a higher ideal of self-government, which they are bound to realize within measurable future. For the attainment of this they have formed a National Council of Education and chartered a national university to educate the rising generation on national lines and in that spirit of freedom-loving which made America so great. From Bengal this Swadeshi Movement has now spread all over India, and in our last National Congress (December 26 to 28, 1905) the president said that "From evil cometh good. . . . The popular spirit that is expressed by this agitation will be remembered in our national history."

It was possible for the British administrators of India to have converted these new forces, which in genesis are Western and in aspiration freedom-loving, into strong allies of the Government, but they have unfairly been drawn into a position of acute antagonism, due to lack of sympathy. Never was the blundering policy of the modern rulers of India so apparent as in the treatment of the aspiration of the educated community of India. Seventy years ago Macaulay declared from his place in Parliament that that would be the proudest day in the annals of England when Indian subjects of the King, trained in the Western methods, should crave for Western institutions. That day has now arrived, but to the modern rulers of India it is a day of trouble and tribulation. The history of the last fifty years has been, with bright intervals here and there, a record of broken promises, tempered by most unsympathetic treatment of Indian public opinion and outrageous disregard of the constitutional rights of the people. The climax was reached under the reactionary régime of Lord Curzon, when the partition of Bengal was carried out against the protests of the people; and the people had to reap the bitter fruits of the partition in the Russian methods of rule introduced into the new province.

The Government of the new province undoubtedly adopted a policy of repression, and relentlessly pursued it, apparently with no other object than to kill the agitation and to stifle and strangle the Swadeshi Movement. Circulars were issued everywhere prohibiting the right of public meeting and suppressing public processions. It was because of these circulars that the police dispersed with inhuman assault the Provincial Conference of the Indian National Congress at Barisal. Government lawyers and schoolmasters were removed from their offices for their connection with the Swadeshi Movement. Then there was a

crusade against the school-boys. They have been hunted out of the schools, rusticated, and some sent to jail. Even the very schools they attended did not escape. Some of these were deprived of the "grants-in-aid" they have been receiving from the Government, others were excluded from the privilege of competing for the Government scholarships. Military and punitive police have been stationed at places to terrorize the meek masses and break the back of the agitation. Mr. Morley's "sympathetic policy" has withdrawn these circulars, but the spirit which inspired the circulars is still in force.

The despotism of the Governor of the new province at last reached its limit, and on August 6, 1906, he was forced to resign his position, after being asked by Lord Minto, the present Viceroy of India, through the advice of Mr. Morley, to withdraw his arbitrary order of disaffiliation of certain schools from the University of Calcutta. The next day, the 7th of August, was the anniversary of the partition-protest meeting at Calcutta, and this resignation was taken as a practical result of the agitation, and great popular satisfaction was shown throughout India. In the anniversary meeting renewal of the vow for the Swadeshi Movement took place, with great applause of " Bande Mataram !" (Hail, Motherland).

The practical result of the Swadeshi Movement is not yet apparent, as the time that has elapsed is too short, and, moreover, we are under the constant pressure of the British bureaucracy. But it can safely be stated that in ten years from now Old India will be a New India, and we only want from the outside world kind and sympathetic wishes to strengthen us to work out our own salvation.

The following few lines from the pen of Miss Noble, of the Irish Unionist party, will show how deep-rooted is this Swadeshi Movement in India:

"All India is watching to-day the struggle that is going on in eastern Bengal. Scarcely a word appears in the papers, yet the knowledge is everywhere. The air is tense with expectation, with sympathy, with pride in those grim heroic people and their silent struggle to the death for their Swadeshi Movement. Quietly all India is assimilating their power. Are they not a farmer people engaged in a warfare which is none the less real for being fought with spiritual weapons ? But let him note who stands in the path of right, and beware. We cannot fail, for all these forces of the future are with us. The Swadeshi Movement has come to stay and to drive back forever in modern India the tides of reaction and despair. Of Calcutta it may be said that in all directions small industries have been springing up like flowers amongst us. Where before there were only despair and starvation, we see to day glad faces and feel an atmosphere of hope.

" Is the Swadeshi Movement an integral part of the national righteousness ? The Mother Church at last has spoken in no uncertain voice. . . . Throughout the whole country is heard the fiat issued at Puri (one of the most important holy places in India). Henceforth it would be held a sacrilege to offer foreign wares in worship. . . . " These extracts are taken from the Indian Review of March, 1906.

Whether Mr. Morley and Lord Minto will rise to the height of the situation remains to be seen. But the problem which confronts them is one of the gravest that any Indian statesman has had to deal with.

# THE NEW PLACE OF THE BIBLE IN THE AMERICAN COLLEGE

## BY HENRY T. FOWLER

IN 1886 Yale University called to her new chair of Semitic Languages a young teacher from a Western theological seminary who, in addition to the regular work of this position, undertook the Hebrew instruction of the Divinity School. Soon it was noised about in the University that the theological students were working as they had never worked before, and, what was more, they were enjoying the Hebrew grammar and vocabulary ; they were eagerly mastering the elements of the language, inspired by one who led them to realize their value in opening the mysteries of Hebrew thought and the beauty of its original expression. It was not long before the friends of Yale and the Bible saw the opportunity. This young professor, who had roused such enthusiasm in the Divinity School, might awaken similar interest in Hebrew literature among undergraduates. The money was subscribed, the Woolsey chair of Biblical Literature was established, and the zealous instructor was offered its duties, in addition to those of the University chair of Semitic Languages and the Hebrew professorship in the Divinity School. How royally he welcomed this, as every

opportunity to advance a more thorough study of the Bible, his students have tried to show in their recent tributes to William Rainey Harper, prince of teachers.

This professorship of Biblical Literature at Yale, established in 1888, marks the first free and unhampered attempt to teach the Bible to undergraduate students with the combined resources of modern archæological, historical, literary, and linguistic knowledge.

So sharp is the contrast between the type of work thus inaugurated and the forms of Biblical study which had existed in the early days of American collegiate education, that a review of the earlier study and of the causes which led to the change is essential to an understanding of the present place of the Bible in American colleges and universities.

At Harvard, down to the year 1787, Hebrew was a prescribed study, and for thirty years more a Hebrew part appeared on Commencement programmes. For some years longer that language was specified as a junior course, for which, however, mathematics or another language might be substituted ; then it ceased to appear as a regular study and was announced as " taught to those who desire it." Afterwards, provision for Hebrew temporarily lapsed, to be restored, subsequently, " for those who desired it," and again dropped, until in 1872 the language reappeared as a regular senior and junior elective course. In 1825, when the college catalogue first contained a statement of requirements for admission and of the college course, a candidate for the freshman class was required to " be able properly to construe and parse any portion of the following books : Jacob's Greek Reader, the Gospels in the Greek Testament, Virgil, Sallust, and Cicero's Selected Orations." The student, thus admitted, continued the study of the Greek Testament during a part of his college course. A little later this subject was relegated entirely to the preparatory years, save that specified classes of undergraduates were required to attend lectures on the New Testament, for which eventually lectures " on the means of preserving health " were substituted ! In 1843 the four Gospels disappeared from the requirements for admission.

With changes in details, the history of the study of the Biblical languages at our oldest institution of higher learning is the history at many other of our older colleges. Work in the Greek Testament at Yale, as a requirement for admission, was given up a year before its abolition at Harvard. In 1858 Hebrew disappeared from the list of college optional courses and practical surveying took its place ! In Princeton, however, Biblical work, consisting in part of reading from the New Testament in Greek, was required of freshmen and sophomores until quite recent years. The English Bible, if taught at all, was usually assigned to some Sabbath hour, under charge of the president. Rutgers students of the fifties kindle into eloquence when they recall the Bible class of President Frelinghuysen, which every student was expected to attend before the Sunday morning preaching service. Similarly, at Brown, the Sunday class of President Robinson left its deep impression. Bible study in our American colleges was thus generally limited to two phases—the study of the Biblical

languages provided for in the curriculum, and the devotional study of the Sunday Bible class.

Clearly, sound judgment was shown by those who finally substituted classical authors for the New Testament as an admission requirement in Greek ; the reason for dropping the reading of the Greek Testament from the programme of college studies is not so manifestly sound, yet it is not difficult to see how, before the modern elective system made room for many things, the wealth of classical Greek literature drove out a subject which had no especial instructor and must be taught by one whose chief interest lay in other departments of his field. In the increasing proportion of students preparing for other callings than the ministry is doubtless to be found another reason for the gradual elimination of the Biblical languages from the general academy and college courses.

While this work was being crowded out of the old rigid American college curriculum, there were developing, in the world of scholars across the water, methods, material, apparatus, and a new point of view towards the Bible, destined to produce the different type of Bible study which has come to American institutions of higher learning and has found in them, changed marvelously from their former organization and spirit, a fertile field for a new, characteristic American growth. The sources of this new type of Bible study are to be found in the whole movement of modern thought which has submitted the records of all past civilization, as well as the phenomena of nature, to searching examination. Time-honored institutions, as well as traditional beliefs in science and history, have been required to show their validity. The most imposing of these, the infallible church, was roundly questioned and widely rejected early in the history of modern thought, but the Bible seemed long to lie above and beyond all questioning. Luther, indeed, did not hesitate vigorously to comment on some parts of it as below the level of other parts, or even contradicting them ; but he grounded his fight against the Papacy on the Bible, and his followers, less bold, forgot his criticisms, and, having given up their soul's rest in an infallible church, fell back upon the dogma of an infallible Bible. The opponents of Protestantism early attacked this dogma on the ground of the variant readings of the Biblical manuscripts.

Problems concerning the Bible, once started, were not limited to those growing from the obvious variations of manuscripts. The late seventeenth and the eighteenth centuries discovered many other objections to long accepted views. In the advance of human thought, questions as to when, how, by whom, the books themselves were composed were just as inevitable as the earlier textual study. The early church had fixed upon twenty-seven books, which, in conjunction with the Jewish sacred writings, composed its authoritative canon; the church of the Middle Ages had fenced in these from free investigation; the Reformation demanded that the individual should have the right to study and interpret these documents. Given the open Bible of the Reformation and the modern thirst to know things back to their very roots and then back to the composition of the soil out of which the roots draw their sustenance, the free investigation of the Bible could no more be stopped than the progress of natural science.

It happened that when the thoroughgoing examination of the books of the Bible was begun, there was in use among students of ancient literatures a name for such investigation—the "higher criticism." Naturally enough, one of the scholars of the late eighteenth century, Eichorn, a man trained in classical study and an intimate associate of men of letters, used the term familiar to humanists of his time to describe this process of investigating the inner nature of the writings of the Old Testament. The term has given offense to many who are unaware of its origin. Scholars have now largely dropped it, not because of ignorant carping at a supposed claim to higher light, but because the term is no longer the most accurate one. The process of analyzing a book into its earlier and later elements, to which the term was originally applied, is but one part of the work of present Biblical

scholarship; the larger process is better termed historical criticism.

Soon after the earlier literary (or "higher") criticism of the Bible began to be widely felt, laborers in other fields unearthed treasures which gave the open-minded Bible student materials before undreamed of. At the beginning of the nineteenth century the decipherment of the hieroglyphs brought to light the ancient civilization of Egypt, with which early Israel once and again came into contact; in the heart of the century explorers and translators made the long-buried life of the Tigris-Euphrates valley move again before our very eyes; in the second half it became possible to read the history of ancient Israel as an integral part of the world's early civilization. Her national traditions trace her origin back to that same Tigris-Euphrates valley; Babylonian influences are clearly manifest in her traditions of prehistoric times—as in her narratives of the creation and the flood—and the kinship of her laws with the code of Hammurabi. In the same eager nineteenth century the coating of mediæval, worthless geographical tradition was torn from the hills and valleys of Palestine. An American, Professor Edward Robinson, of Andover, has been styled "the pioneer and father of modern Biblical geography." Prior to his work, cut short by his death in 1863, it had not been possible to picture Biblical history on its true background. Such agencies as the Palestine Exploration Fund have made their contribution by unearthing coins, pottery, inscriptions, and ruins. Side by side with all this work, the free internal study of the Bible steadily pressed forward. Even when it went to extreme limits and adopted one-sided methods, it rendered service by forcing conservative students to adopt historical methods in Biblical study.

The stage reached in Bible study in the last quarter of the nineteenth century may be summarized as follows: (1) The passion to know things as they are led a rapidly growing body of trained scholars, through a century of cumulative effort, to go back of Jewish and Christian traditions about the Bible, and fearlessly to question the books themselves, as to their origin, growth, purpose, and meaning. (2) The methods adopted in this questioning were the inductive methods developed by the natural scientists and already in use by qualified students of other ancient histories and literatures. The application of these methods to the Bible would have accomplished something in itself, but (3) in addition, investigators throughout the century poured into the field of the Bible student new facts from the Nile valley, the Tigris-Euphrates valley, and from Palestine itself.

The colleges and universities of Britain and America were little touched by all this development, in its early stages. At the fortunate moment, however, new ideals in the whole spirit and method of higher education in America were already in the air, or in actual process of realization. Harvard was making earnest efforts to develop non-professional graduate study. Cornell, with its liberal ideals, was completing its first decade of history. Johns Hopkins, first to prove graduate courses a success in America, was only a year in the future. The phrase "university spirit" began to be a term with content in our institutions of higher learning. In some cases a genuine spirit of research entered the cut-and-dried courses of professional schools. The old rigid undergraduate curriculum, in some instances suddenly, in others gradually, was replaced by a programme of elective courses. With this rapid development of opportunity for free investigation in every field of human interest, the claims of Semitic history and literature could not long be ignored. The subject was even winning great popular attention because of the discovery and decipherment of the fascinating inscriptions and relics. Our stronger institutions began to establish Semitic chairs. Now Harvard, Yale, Columbia, Princeton, Pennsylvania, Johns Hopkins, Cornell, Chicago, California, all have their Semitic instructors, chairs, or departments with several instructors.

We have now traced, as rapidly as possible, some of the streams of influence which, united, made that Woolsey chair in 1888 possible. One other must not be overlooked; four years earlier the entire Bible had been issued

in an English translation sufficiently accurate to enable students to do worthy undergraduate work without taking the time necessary to read the Biblical books in their original languages. What was wrought at Yale in the eighties has been accomplished elsewhere. A department of Oriental history and Semitic languages, established at Brown in 1890, developed five years later into a department of Biblical literature and history. In the majority of universities, though, the Biblical courses are treated as a phase of the Semitic department.

But the new place of the Bible is not to be found only in the universities. These can afford full instruction in Semitic literature and history and, as we have seen, provide adequate courses in the English Bible, as a part of this. In separate colleges the strength of the position is keenly visible. These are increasingly providing full courses in the English Bible, under trained specialists. College Bible study under the old conditions ran its course, died its natural death; under the new the subject is an organic part of collegiate education. Especially conspicuous are the women's colleges for their provision in this direction. Wellesley, Smith, Vassar, Bryn Mawr, all have their Bible chairs. Among colleges for men, Amherst can well claim leadership, since she had a quaintly defined "professorship of Biblical history and interpretation and of the pastoral care," established in 1864. The scholarly men who have filled this chair with distinction have labored under great difficulties, because their pastoral relation put their instruction on a different basis from that of other departments—a hampering combination of functions now happily abolished.

The catalogues of American colleges show the wide sweep of the new departure and its influence even in the smaller institutions. Alfred University, in western New York, announces Biblical instruction for its college students "from a literary and historical point of view." Allegheny College, Meadville, has a combined professorship of the English Bible and the philosophy of religion. The catalogue announces that the Biblical instruction is intended "to familiarize the student with the history of the Hebrew people, their civilization, and their influence on the world; and to lead to the critical study of the spirit and form of Hebrew literature as it is shown in the English version." Beloit College, Wisconsin, has established a professorship of Biblical Literature and Religious History within the last two or three years, while out in the little University of Southern California we note the Hazard professorship of the English Bible, with, apparently, a well-planned department on the modern basis.

With all this provision in the curriculum, the place of the old devotional Sunday classes has not been left empty. It has been filled by voluntary Bible study, under the fostering care of the Intercollegiate Young Men's and Young Women's Christian Associations. Last year thirty-three thousand young men in American institutions were enrolled in groups and classes for Bible study. Alumni are organized into local committees to encourage this work and secure for it continuity and strength. The intercollegiate officers in charge of the movement are seeking close touch with those who teach the Bible on college and university faculties. They are advising with these men and inviting them to write text-books for the college Bible courses that form no part of the curriculum. There is happy omen in this growing union between those who are developing college Bible study from the standpoint of the student Christian associations and those who are directing it from the standpoint of the faculties of instruction. It is recognized that the two standpoints are not opposed.

The thoughtful student must pursue his devotional study with a sound intellectual basis, or the Bible ceases to command his respect. College teachers of the Bible rejoice in contributing to the progress of the Association classes, knowing that the historical study of the Bible, to which their lives are devoted, renders high service when it forms the basis for a new confidence and freedom in the devotional and practical use of the Scriptures. In coming to its new place in the modern college and university discipline, the Bible, better understood, comes anew to its old place in the personal life.

# ANCIENT MASTERS FOR MODERN TIMES[1]

MANY years ago the present writer asked a better-informed friend to name the best work on political science. He replied, " Read Aristotle." To-day he might with good reason recommend the present volume as one than which there is no better. Aristotle was the critical disciple of Plato, and gives us a reconstructed Plato at a date when Greek political wisdom had reached its acme on the verge of the great transition effected by Alexander of Macedon from city politics to world politics. Mr. Barker's work is no mere translation, it is a masterly exposition of the two chief constructive thinkers of ancient civilization. Plato and Aristotle have been put to larger use in other fields than that which is opened here.

It is timely to turn to this. The same causes which turned them to political studies—the evils, resulting from political selfishness and the clash of classes, that finally broke down the Greek city-state—are to-day producing the conviction that modern democracy, like the ancient, is on trial. The ancient democracy differs in form from the modern. It was direct; ours is indirect, administered through representatives. It was unlimited by wholesome checks; ours is limited by constitutional safeguards. But the conception of the State bequeathed to us by Greek idealism must be our cynosure. It is essentially an organization for moral interests, for the realization of a good life. Plato and Aristotle agree in this fundamental conception, though Aristotle is nearer to modern modes of thought in working it

[1] *The Political Thought of Plato and Aristotle.* By E. Barker, M.A. G. P. Putnam's Sons, New York.

out. They agree that the virtues of the State are simply the virtues of the individual writ large, and that the essential thing is to moralize the individual. We still find it needful to emphasize this ancient lesson, though we have learned to rely less on external means for making men good. At the same time we must recognize in Plato's idea of abolishing spiritual evil by abolishing the material conditions that foment it a conception that practical Christianity cannot dispense with.

Such ideas as that property is a thing to be held in trust for virtue, and that in the ideal State wealth will be used only for moral ends, are regarded to-day as of Christian or Hebrew origin, and the product of religious thought. They are also Aristotle's own. There is a striking similarity between his view that private property is right when, and in so far as, it subserves the moral end for which the State exists, and Wiclif's view, now being revived by Christian thinkers, that there is no moral title to wealth except as morally employed. In this line of thought, as Mr. Barker shows, Aristotle's ideal State, as a real commonwealth, secures the good of communism while avoiding its evil. Aristotle teaches that common ownership by itself will not produce common-mindedness, but only the devotion of private property to the public service will do this. His formula, "private possession with common use," expresses just what appears to have been the practice of the primitive Christian society at Jerusalem, often misrepresented as communism. The reformed political economy to-day, in its insistence that the proper sphere of economics is that of housekeeper and steward to ethics, is simply repeating Aristotle's lesson. In his time the unchecked democracy of Athens had become "a government of the poor by the poor." We, in a democracy constitutionally limited, have what Aristotle thought of as the ideal form. But we still need his teaching, that liberty consists, not in absolute freedom, but in freedom to do what one ought; that the essence of law is in the law-abiding disposition of the citizen; that it is not a specific form of government—monarchy or democracy—that a nation needs, so much as the right moral habit of mind; in short, to use Mr. Barker's expository phrase, "that it is a cleansing of the heart, not of garments, that the world requires." This accords with the great word that stands first in Jesus' preaching of the kingdom of heaven—"Change your minds." It is the great word to be spoken first to a democracy whose industry, trade, and politics are dominated to-day by self-interest, and which is casting about for new laws to stop the mischief of it.

Two most desirable qualities appear in Mr. Barker's exposition—a just perception of parts as related to the whole, and insight into the spirit within the letter. Certain objections are thereby mitigated which are often made, especially to Plato's scheme for community of wives in his ideal State, and to Aristotle's approval of slavery. In each case Mr. Barker finds a moral interest, however misdirected or imperfect, dominating. Plato's aim, for which he would sacrifice even the family, was a more unselfish patriotism, and a larger freedom to serve the general welfare. Likewise it was for its moral benefit to the slave, conceived of as an inferior being, that Aristotle justified the mild form of slavery which he approved. Each, indeed, exaggerated the effectiveness of laws in molding men—an error not uncommon even now. But each of them combated the exaggerated individualism and sectionalism which is still the bane of American democracy. Each insisted that the ship of State will capsize "if not well ballasted with a social spirit and rational self-control." The spring of wisdom thus opened by sages too late to save the Greek city-state, and the other like it, opened centuries earlier by prophets too late to save the Hebrew monarchy, are the classic sources for the highest political wisdom. The universities to which we look for future statesmen may be congratulated on the addition of this volume to their apparatus for political studies.

# Comment on Current Books

**The Apostles' Creed**

For clear religious insight and for warm religious feeling the author of this series of short expositions of the Creed is deservedly and widely esteemed. Like his other books, this is characterized by these qualities, preeminently desirable for the exposition of a creed designed especially for use in worship. As an interpreter of Scripture Mr. Meyer's work is occasionally marred by a literalism which mistakes poetry for prose, and fancy for reality. Traces of this have to be overlooked in his present work as in others. (The Creed of Creeds. By F. B. Meyer, B.A. Fleming H. Revell Company, New York. $1, net.)

**The Cassowary**

A group of crude short stories, supposed to be told by passengers gathered together in the "Cassowary," the most comfortable car on a train snow-bound somewhere near the base of Pike's Peak. (The Cassowary. By Stanley Waterloo. Monarch Book Company, Chicago.)

**Christianity in the Apostolic Age**

This is a proper sequel to the "Constructive Studies on the Life of Christ" by Professors Burton and Mathews, and by an equally competent scholar. That work was based on the Gospels; this is concerned with the remainder of the New Testament. Its successive portions first narrate events and comment upon them, then propose questions and suggestions for study, with supplementary topics and references to literature. Questions of critical scholarship and matters of detail, more suited to teachers and mature students, are distinguished by smaller type. Four pages are thus devoted to the origin of the Epistle of James and 1 Peter. The important question about the apostolic letter in Acts xv. 23–30 is dismissed more lightly, without notice of the probability that it had, as Professor McGiffert has shown, another origin than the Jerusalem conference. The volume is finely illustrated. (A Short History of Christianity in the Apostolic Age. By George Holley Gilbert, Ph.D., D.D. The University of Chicago Press, Chicago. $1.)

**The De Witt Clinton Book**

This little book is of peculiar interest in that it is the work of the pupils, the teachers, and the friends of the De Witt Clinton High School in New York City. Having adopted as the name of the school that of a famous statesman, all who have to do with this school naturally feel a certain sense of responsibility in molding the character of scholars in accordance with the achievements and qualities of one of the greatest historical figures of New York City and New York State. Accordingly, the school carries on a Clinton Memorabilia Society, which collects and preserves material of all sorts bearing on the history of the school, and also aids in bringing about a more extensive knowledge of the varied activities of Clinton's eventful life. The present booklet is the first of a series which this Society plans to publish. It has the High School song beginning, "When Clinton was the Governor in 1824." It has also the Clinton coat of arms beautifully reproduced in color, and the book is inscribed to the grandniece of Clinton, Marie Clinton Le Duc. There are also a chronology of the events in Clinton's life; chapters on his boyhood and political life; an account of his work as a naturalist; the story of his connection with the Erie Canal, and, most important of all, of his connection with the New York public schools—all followed by an interesting sketch of New York City in Clinton's time. The De Witt Clinton Book. Edited by Frank Bergen Kelley. Brentano's, New York.)

**Dr. George A. Gordon's Sermons**

This volume of sermons is well worth reading by thoughtful laymen and well worth study by thoughtful preachers. Dr. Gordon easily ranks among the first dozen preachers in America. In this book certain secrets of his power are easily discernible. He is both philosopher and poet—not a philosopher who, having reached conclusions, clothes them in poetic form in order to commend them to those who are less philosophically-minded than himself, but a philosopher who sees truth in images, who thinks in poetic forms, a philosopher of the type of Plato rather than that of Aristotle. His mind is characterized by another contrast: it is thoroughly modern but not critical. He is sympathetic rather than analytic, constructive not negative, and therefore at once a man of free thought and of positive faith. He is always rational but never a rationalist. There is yet another characteristic to his preaching as it is exemplified in this volume of sermons. The logical preacher has been much praised in the schools, and "he is not logical" has been counted in certain quarters the final word of

141

condemnation. Dr. Emmons was a fine specimen of the logical preacher, with nine-tenths of his discourse devoted to proving certain propositions and one-tenth to pointing out certain practical conclusions or "appli-cations." At the other extreme is the horta-tory preacher, the extreme being found in the Salvation Army exhorter. There may be a slight basis of fact or philosophy or Scripture as a pedestal, but the exhortation is the statue, and sometimes there is no pedestal. Between these two is the preacher who sets forth certain truth, but always with the moral purpose animating him. He does not exhort, but the truth is so presented as to exhort for him. Of this type Phillips Brooks is the finest of modern examples. To this type belongs George A. Gordon. His preaching carries with it a moral impulse. Clearer in definition, he is less powerful in impulse than Phillips Brooks; his enthusiasm is more intellectual, less human, more an enthusiasm for truth, less an enthusiasm for humanity. But they both belong to the same school, the school that uses truth for moral ends, and whose sermons therefore are warm with a suggested rather than an expressed emotion. For all these reasons—for their philosophic grasp, their modern view, their poetic vision, their vigorous faith, and their sane and tender feeling—we commend this volume of sermons both to the thoughtful reader and to the homiletical student. (Through Man to God. By George A. Gordon. Houghton, Mifflin & Co., Boston. $1.50.)

*Gabrielle* The most attractive feature of this rather improbable romance is the deserted garden which serves as a trysting-place for Gabrielle, the innocent child wife of a French nobleman whom she has never known, and an Eastern prince who has fled to New Orleans to escape the tyranny of the Sultan of Turkey. The given plot could be handled with some deli-cacy, but there are offensive touches, and the simplicity of Gabrielle is not presented with fine feeling. (Gabrielle: Transgressor. By Harris Dickson. J. B. Lippincott Com-pany, Philadelphia. $1.50.)

*Is Mars Inhabited?* The question whether Mars is inhabited has not been taken up very seriously by the great body of astronomers. Perhaps this is be-cause scientists are quite as conservative in their way as theologians and quite as un-willing to tackle a really new problem, per-haps because their interest is in the material side of astronomy, not in a human question like this, which they regard as out of their beat. However that may be, we are very glad that some scientific astronomers have taken it up and are investigating it with

promise of results. Prominent among these is Mr. Percival Lowell, and the latest, and we are inclined to think the fullest and best, contribution to its solution is this remark-able volume, written in a very clear style, free from scientific technicalities, and illus-trated by maps and diagrams, so that the non-expert layman can understand it. As Mr. Lowell has promised The Outlook to give at no distant day to our readers his con-clusions in a special article, we shall not here anticipate him further than to say that we took up his book with some prejudice against the conclusion which he had reached, and that we have laid it down convinced that the hypothesis that the planet Mars is inhabited is sustained by cumulative evidence which makes it at least a probable hypothesis. But Mr. Lowell's investigations, coupled with those of other earlier investigators, indicate much more than this: they indicate that the inhabitants of Mars are carrying on a sys-tem of irrigation for agricultural purposes on an immeasurably larger scale than has ever been dreamed of on our planet, that they possess a high degree of agricultural and mechanical intelligence, and a degree of moral development so far in advance of any we have yet reached that in all probability war is among them wholly unknown. For the reasons by which this opinion is sustained the reader must be referred to the book. (Mars and Its Canals. By Percival Lowell. The Macmillan Company, New York. $2.50, net.)

*Jeremiah* Involved in the tragedy of a dying State, and spending his life in the hopeless task of striving to avert its extinction, the lot of Jeremiah seems as pitiful as that of any patriot known to his-tory. On the other hand, in his appeal from such a situation to the Eternal Righteous-ness, his utterances reveal a larger piety than appears in the earlier prophets. These two elements of his experience make him an object of peculiar interest among Biblical characters. The present volume will enable readers of ordinary education to read appre-ciatively the book which bears his name. The translation, divided into sections and paragraphs with headings summarizing their contents, is that of the Authorized Version, modified so far as required for clearness and accuracy, and is accompanied by a sufficient minimum of explanatory notes; the literary form and historical setting receive treatment in an introduction. The name of the distin-guished editor evinces the worth of the work. (The Book of the Prophet Jeremiah. A Re-vised Translation by Rev. S. R. Driver, D.D. Charles Scribner's Sons, New York. $1.50, net).

**Jewel Weed** The action here takes place in a small Western town, and a mystic Hindu character serves as a touch of color and complicates the plot. But the book is too full of reflected culture, and lacking in realism and vitality. It is weak fiction. (Jewel Weed. By Alice Ames Winter. The Bobbs-Merrill Company, Indianapolis.)

**A Maid in Arcady** This is a commonplace little volume which strives to be idyllic. The story and the marginal photographs are equally inartistic and lacking in suggestive quality. (A Maid in Arcady. By Ralph Henry Barbour. J. B. Lippincott Company, Philadelphia. $2.)

**Mental Development** This work has been translated into French and German, with improvements by the author which are embodied in this third revised edition. The contention, advanced long ago by some evolutionists, that where life is, however lowly, there is consciousness, however rudimentary, appears here in more defined terms. Biologists are coming to the view held by Professor Baldwin as a psychologist, that the physical basis of pleasure-pain consciousness originates in primitive organisms rather than in subsequently developed particular organisms. In other words, the "physiological analogue" of pleasure and pain appears at life's beginning, in the heightening of central vital processes, and its effect. Under this stimulus life then and thereafter adapts itself to its environment. All stages of mental accommodation and development are thus included with all the phenomena of organic adaptation under the terms of a single concept. This is the main thesis here unfolded and maintained in elaborate studies of methods and processes. The work is largely a record of the refined research and results of experimental psychology, especially in the study of infant and child life in the author's own family. With the interest these have for specialists in his science goes an interest for teachers, writers on education, and parents in the practical lessons resulting therefrom. The misfortune of being "an only child," who "has only adult 'copy,'" is plainly shown; so is the narrowing tendency of exclusive friendships; so is the folly of fathers who "know every corner of the house familiarly, and what is done in it, *except the nursery*." Certain points are more fully treated in the author's other works, and are duly referred to wherever occurring. As a book of genesis, biological and psychological, the present work is of distinctive and permanent value. (Mental Development in the Child and the Race. By James Mark Baldwin. Third Edition, Revised. Seventh Printing. The Macmillan Company, New York. $2.25, net.)

**The Pope and the Pentateuch** The Outlook reported, August 25, 1906, the conclusions of the Commission appointed by the Pope to pronounce upon the opinions of the higher criticism concerning the Pentateuch, and characterized them as "a distinct and emphatic repudiation" of those opinions. Soon afterward Professor Briggs, of New York, and Baron von Hügel, his Roman Catholic friend, and his peer in Biblical scholarship, exchanged letters on the decision of the Pontifical Commission, which are given to the public in this small volume. They agree that scholastics, not scholars, are in the saddle again, and that the decision now approved by the Pope tends to alienate from the Church educated men and women, but they deem it reversible by the persevering co-operation of Biblical scholars. The succinct statement of the scholars' case against the scholastics which these letters contain gives them an interest for all who regard it as doubtful. (The Papal Commission and the Pentateuch. By Rev. Charles A. Briggs and Baron Friedrich von Hügel. Longmans, Green & Co., New York. 75c., net.)

**The Princess of Manoa** A slender volume, original both in its material and its form. It contains nine Hawaiian folk stories very simply and sympathetically told, and in excellent taste. The volume is printed in black type on paper of a dark brown hue, and there are ten pictures by Mr. D. Howard Hitchcock, which are not simply decorative, but also highly illustrative. In more than one instance they are distinctly striking. (The Princess of Manoa and Other Romantic Tales from the Folk-lore of Old Hawaii. By Mrs. Frank R. Day. Paul Elder & Co., San Francisco.)

**The Queen's Museum** This selection from among the most characteristic of Stockton's stories for younger readers is a fascinating piece of book-making, with a cheerful dragon on the title-page which would have charmed the genial author, and with illustration in color and gold by Frederick Richardson which will be a source of joy to the fortunate children into whose hands the volume falls. (The Queen's Museum, and Other Fanciful Tales. By Frank R. Stockton. Charles Scribner's Sons, New York. $2.50.)

**Religion and Experience** The gifted British essayist, whose volumes have followed one another with remarkable frequency, evidently, as the present volume like its predecessors shows, reaps a rich-soiled field. Literature and history, science and philosophy, serve him nimbly while he weaves his thought into a texture both strong in substance and graceful in form. The brevity of his essays, rarely exceeding eight pages, commends them to a world that prefers short sermons, and to preachers who would learn to say in fifteen or twenty minutes much that will both hold the attention and stick in the mind afterwards. The standpoint is that of a devoutly Christian thinker fully responsive to the intellectual demands of the modern world. The Introduction compresses into a short statement, clear and simple, the modern argument for experience as the test of reality, whether in science, philosophy, or religion. (Religion and Experience. By J. Brierley, B.A. Thomas Whittaker, New York. $1.40, net.)

*A Reply to Ignoramuses*    It is regrettable that public men, from the President downward, are attacked by constant volleys of ignorant criticism. Nothing has shed more luster on the American name than the work of American missionaries among the backward nations. Yet these workers are still a favorite target for ignorant ridicule or calumny in a large portion of the daily press, including some of high pretensions to veracity. The present volume is of the sort that should give a quietus to all who in ignorance or malice "deblatterate" (as Robert Louis Stevenson said) on its subject. It deserves a place among the books of reference found in every well-furnished editorial library. Its chapters, after briefly describing the missionary in contact with the various conditions and classes of persons in his environment, conclude with illustrative testimonies by men of high rank in government, science, literature, journalism, and the public service, Americans and foreigners, hundreds of whom, Christian and non-Christian, tell what they have seen of the praiseworthy facts. It is not only an enlightening but a thoroughly interesting book, and greatly needed also. (The Missionary and His Critics. By Rev. James L. Barton. Fleming H. Revell Company, New York. $1, net.)

*Washington Etiquette*    While books of etiquette are generally considered a negligible quantity, they would not be published if they were not needed. The present well-printed small volume by Florence Howe Hall on Washington well covers not only the more or less fixed etiquette of official service, but also the social "departures" which have recently characterized more general society. (Social Usages at Washington. By Florence Howe Hall. Harper & Brothers, New York. $1.)

# Letters to The Outlook

### THE BIBLE IN THE OLD-FASHIONED HOME

I also was brought up after the manner of the Puritans, with the strict ideas of Sunday observance and of reading the Bible described in a recent article entitled "My Fetish Bible." But I feel that the author does great injustice to the majority of the children reared under those conditions. I was a merry, fun-loving boy, with a genius for mischief, yet the strict Sabbath-keeping of my early home has for me only the sweetest recollections. Even in my boyhood days the Bible was most fascinating to me. Story-books were few and highly prized, but the Bible stories were far more interesting, and they have never lost their charm. There are those even in this cynical age who cannot hear the story of Joseph and his brethren without tears, and still others who cannot read the account of David's magnanimous treatment of King Saul without a choke in their voice.

I have heard many of the most eloquent public speakers on both sides of the sea, and I have observed that nothing stirs their audiences more profoundly than the old Bible stories well told.

I, together with many of your readers, committed to memory numerous Scripture verses during those quiet old-fashioned Sundays, and now they are more precious to me than all the treasures of secular literature. To thousands of others the Bible is a mine of spiritual knowledge, from which they have ever been digging new and precious thoughts; and it is not a rare thing for them to speak enthusiastically to one another of some new meaning which they have found hidden away under the dear old words. We need no better proof that the old Puritan Sunday and Bible study were great blessings than the fact that most of the children trained under such influences grew up to be godly men and women, a credit to themselves, their parents, and their country. And they in turn raised families of God-fearing and God-serving children who have won honor in every sphere of social, intellectual, and commercial life. H. H.

### CONDITIONS IN TURKEY

We are. as I write, in the midst of the sacred Mohammedan month of fasting, Ramazan. Not only must no food or drink pass the lips from before daylight till after sunset, but the Koran must be read through, there is daily preaching in the mosques, more time is given to prayer, and in other ways past offenses are to be atoned for and good works laid up in credit for the time to come. Yesterday, in a call upon our Vali—Governor-General—I told him that I had heard that he had directed that the preachers should give their attention to practical affairs. He replied, " Yes, I have told them that we know all about heaven and hell and the future life, but we need to be taught how to conduct ourselves in this life, how to be good citizens. Instead of prosy exegeses upon the Koran, we need to be taught how to behave toward one another and toward the Government." I told him that this is what President Roosevelt is preaching on all occasions. The Vali himself is a faithful attendant upon all the preaching services in the mosque near his residence.

It is not customary for Christians to attend the mosque services, as they have the impression that it is not agreeable to the worshipers there. I listened to a sermon in a mosque many years ago, which was upon the duty of the Pilgrimage to Mecca, and I had a curiosity to hear a sermon of the kind that our good Vali was demanding, so when the muezzin gave the call to the mid-afternoon prayer, I took a native friend with me and entered the mosque. There was a large congregation, and they were engaged in prayer, all facing the south, toward their sacred temple at Mecca. Until this part of the service was finished we stood at the back of the congregation. This is an interesting sight, although I tried to lift up my own heart in prayer for a blessing upon the service, even though, to the most of those who were engaged in it, it was a matter of form, probably. The prayer was mostly ejaculations in Arabic, uttered in a loud voice by the leader, while all followed him in kneeling, bowing with the forehead to the floor, retaining that position for a considerable time, then at another utterance rising to their feet, and again prostrating themselves. As it is Ramazan, this service is prolonged beyond the usual time. The most common ejaculation was " Allah Akbar "—God is great—and with each utterance the position of the body was changed. The congrega-

tion was seated in rows, and it is an impressive scene when several hundred people prostrate themselves in worship, even though it may be a formality.

The pulpit is of masonry at the side of the mosque. The preacher, who is the most prominent member of his profession in this district, climbed into it at the close of the prayers, while a Dervish chanted an Arabic hymn. After a prayer in Arabic by the preacher he read an Arabic text, and he proceeded with his sermon. There was very little in it to which I could not say Amen. My companion thought that the sermon received its shape somewhat from the preacher's seeing me among his auditors. He said that their religion demanded that Christians should be treated in all kindness, that along with the Koran they accepted the Old Testament and the New, that the motive determines the quality of the act, that eating in secret while professing outwardly to keep a fast could not be accepted, that God had two books for sins, one for those committed in secret, which were of less harm than those which were committed before others to their being led astray, and these were recorded in the other book, etc., etc. The sermon lasted for more than an hour. It rambled, of course, but it touched upon almost every matter of practical morality, so that after we left the mosque I said to several officials that if they would practice what they had just heard the country would be reformed at once. " That is a different matter," they said; " we understand what is right, but no one of us does it." The preacher also confessed that " we who preach don't practice what we preach." It is a good thing, however, to have the attention called to the essential principles of true morality. I was surprised at the emphasis put upon the motives which lie back of the outward act, for I have been told by Moslems that we are judged by what we do, and not by what we think. The preacher repeated several times, " You can't deceive God."

I have recently been looking through my letter copy-books, and I find that in letters written nearly thirty years ago to The Outlook—it was The Christian Union then—I spoke of the poverty of the people, of official corruption, of the promise of " reform," and it seemed then that matters had reached an extreme limit, and that the process of decline and disintegration could not go on much longer. But there has been a steady increase of poverty since, the long-promised reforms are spoken about no more, and while there are a good many officials who are trying to stem the tide of corruption, it exists in every department, high and low, according to the confessions of officials themselves; and as to poverty, it is absolutely appalling. Years ago the people were very poor, but the opportunity to go to America and return brought a good deal of money into the country; but that door has long been closed. Now and then an Armenian smuggles himself into the country from America, but if the Government catches him he is hustled out of the country without any ceremony, and that by Imperial order. Fifteen innocent villagers who had recently come to their homes have been sent away this week' under guard, and without the privilege of taking their families with them. A good many still manage to steal out of the country by the payment of bribes, but the most of them make no provision for the payment of their taxes, and they send no money, so their going adds to the burdens of those who remain. There is a steady increase of taxes of every imaginable kind.

Then, too, came the terrible massacres of eleven years ago, with their. burning and plunder. Even from the standpoint of the Government it was an insane blunder. Turks who engaged in the general robbery confess that it was a disaster even to themselves. They say that they gathered up the property of others, but that in the general impoverishment they are suffering serious loss. The Armenians have wonderful recuperative power, but the majority of them were so completely crushed in the events of 1895 that they can never recover their former condition. There is little or no enterprise. Able-bodied men seek work in vain. It is a year of high prices, and there is little money in the country.

While physical conditions are thus dark almost to blackness, there is a brighter side. The churches do not lose heart and hope. Earthly trials help them to look to the life beyond, and this is their chief joy. Economic conditions delay complete self-support, but great self-denial is practiced in maintaining their own institutions—the churches and schools. Euphrates College is crowded. In the college proper there are one hundred and sixty male and eighty-two female students, while the whole number of pupils, including the primary departments, is well on towards a thousand. The Industrial Department, including the work done by the orphans, is not only teaching important trades, but it helps many poor pupils to pay in part for their own education. The orphan girls make a superior quality of gingham, and the rugs which they make are of superior quality and bring, an extra price. The Vali, a few days ago, paid a long visit to' these different departments, educational and- industrial, and he expressed much surprise at the progress made here, and he dictated a long article for the local paper in praise of what he had seen. He also asked to have a quantity of the orphan-made rugs sent to him, and from them he selected and paid for nearly $400 worth. The college needs a few thousand dollars for enlargement, while Miss Emily Wheeler, in Worcester, will be glad to welcome additional helpers for our important orphan work.

The Medical Department here has great possibilities, but it is hindered for the lack of a hospital. Some friends have generously started an endowment for an Annie Riggs Memorial Hospital, but only about half of the needed $10,000 has been secured. Help along these lines will increase the light that is struggling with the darkness, and it will wonderfully hearten the workers. Mr. Wiggin, of the American Board, is always a cheerful agent for the passing on of such funds.                HERMAN N. BARNUM.
Harpoot, Turkey.

## BELLAMY'S "LOOKING BACKWARD"

When " Looking Backward" was published, twenty years ago, so impossible did its ideals seem that it received little serious attention. Of the many indications of a considerable advance in sentiment towards those ideals a striking one is the interesting article by H. G. Wells, in the November Fortnightly Review, on "Socialism and the Middle Classes." In practically every point set forth there Mr. Wells is at one with Mr. Bellamy. The disappearance of the lower classes and of the "governing class with means," the avoidance of the present social incoherence and waste by extended public control, the economic independence of women, and the transference of the responsibility for the support of children from the parents to the State, are a few of the points on which stress is laid by both.

Not alone in conviction, but in actual accomplishment, we seem much nearer Bellamy's Utopia. There is the rapid growth, on the one hand, of the great combinations, and, on the other hand, of the idea that public control of them is possible. Municipal control of public commodities finds increasing favor. And in England we notice the attitude of the present administration in regard to feeding school-children and the promise of old-age pensions.

Might not some of those who twenty years ago read Mr. Bellamy's book only to smile at its enthusiasm find it to their profit to read the book again in the light of recent events?
                                E. D. WALKER.
Stellenbosch, South Africa.

BRUARY

1100

ILLUSTRATED

The Quarterly Journal of Economics

# The Outlook

## SATURDAY, JANUARY 26, 1907

⊛

**The Causes of the Kingston Earthquake** The fact that the terrible disaster on Monday of last week at and near Kingston, the capital of Jamaica, followed similar calamities at San Francisco and Valparaiso and was both preceded and followed by reports of earthquakes in the Pacific, in southern Russia, and elsewhere, has led many people to imagine that all these devastating earth-tremblings have had some common and general cause. But Professor Pirsson, of the Yale department of physical geology, points out that the idea of a "seismic epidemic" is quite unscientific. "There is probably," he says, "an earthquake somewhere on the earth every day. The recent ones have just happened to hit inhabited regions. . . . There are earthquakes every bit as severe as that of Kingston occurring every day which are never heard of." The most received modern theory as to causes of earthquake is that the vibrations come from the sudden slips of great masses of rock where geological "faults" exist; and that these slips are caused by tremendous pressure. The pressure in its turn comes sometimes from volcanic action (and Jamaica has at least one long-extinct volcano), sometimes from changes in sea-level and consequent shifting weights from above, sometimes from hardening or softening of great tracts of earth or rock. As the vibrations approach the surface they increase in their intensity, and when, as at Kingston or San Francisco, a populous city stands over the line of most violent disturbance, the calamity ensuing is of the most appalling class known in human history. In Kingston, as in San Francisco, devastating fire followed the destruction by shock, and to the spread of the fire and the cutting off of the water supply by the breaking of the mains are to be attributed the ruin of a large part of the city, including most of the business and public buildings. It is now two hundred and fifteen years since Jamaica was visited by a severe earthquake; in 1693 the old town of Port Royal was thus destroyed.

⊛

**The Loss of Life: Relief Measures** The estimates as to the loss of life differed widely even several days after the disaster. The Governor of Jamaica, Sir Alexander Swettenham, in a despatch on Thursday of last week to the British Colonial Office, stated that the burials up to that date were 343, and that "a few bodies are still covered by the ruins." But other despatches estimate the number of people killed at from five to twelve hundred—perhaps six hundred would be a fairly correct statement. About five hundred wounded and injured people have been treated in the hospitals and on board ship. The horror of the calamity and the intense suffering of the victims are indicated by such incidents as that one hundred and twenty employees were killed in the collapse of a cigar factory, and that seventy-nine amputations were performed on board the Arno, one of the vessels used as a hospital ship. Refugees who fled to Cuba say that twenty-five square blocks of the city were destroyed by fire, that most of the hotels were demolished, and that the electric power-house was overthrown and many persons lost their lives by coming into contact with charged electric wires. The condition of the homeless people was pitiable in the extreme. So far as known, no travelers or visitors from the United States were among the killed. The first and severest shock was felt at 3:30 on January 14; a number of slighter shocks followed. Rumors of a huge tidal wave and of the gradual subsidence of the city were not confirmed. As might be expected, our Government took prompt measures to render assistance, and two battle-ships which were comparatively near by were at once ordered to Jamaica, and their marines were landed to aid in enforcing order. A supply-ship followed. Congress authorized by joint resolution the use of naval supplies for immediate relief, and the offer of any assistance needed was made by cable to the British Foreign Office. But Governor Swettenham, annoyed by a trivial misunderstanding about a salute, and apparently resenting the landing of American parties to guard the United States consulate and to aid in helping the distressed and preserving order, wrote a letter to Admiral Davis in terms which the London Express calls "peremptory and cutting," while the London Mail terms the Governor's action "a deplorable blunder." Admiral Davis at once left Kingston with the battle-ships. The National Red Cross, under its new systematized and thorough organization, was prepared to act at once, and issued orders for supplies to be shipped instantly from New York. Contributions from individuals for the Jamaican sufferers may be made through State branches of the Red Cross, or by sending check or money-order directly to the Treasurer of the American National Red Cross at Washington.

❀

*Secretary Root on the Tariff*    The Secretary of State, Mr. Root, rarely makes a speech without furnishing a topic for serious thought and public debate. Whether one agrees with him or not, one must reckon with him. His latest speech, delivered before the National Convention for the Extension of Foreign Commerce in Washington last week, advocated a form of tariff revision which is not novel, but has not heretofore been generally discussed. He said: "In my judgment, the United States must come to a maximum and minimum tariff. A single straight-out tariff was all very well in a world of single straight-out tariffs, but we have passed on during the course of years into a world, for the most part, of maximum and minimum tariffs, and with our single-rate tariff we are left with very little opportunity to reciprocate good treatment from other countries in their tariffs and very little opportunity to defend ourselves against bad treatment." There are three tariff policies before the country : (1) Tariff for revenue only, which it is certain the country would not adopt; (2) the maintenance of the present protective tariff, formed to exclude all foreign competition with home-made goods, of which it is certain the country is growing very tired; (3) some form of reciprocity, for the double purpose of admitting some measure of foreign competition into America, and of promoting commerce with other countries by America. But past experience has indicated that no reciprocity treaty will get through the Senate. The special interest threatened by reciprocity will rally to its support many other special interests, and two-thirds of the Senators cannot be forced to agree to any scheme of bargain which does not give all the advantage of the bargain to the United States. The maximum and minimum tariff would enable the President by executive order to reduce the tariff to a specified minimum or to raise it to a specified maximum, as in his judgment the commercial interests of the country might require. In brief, it would give him a limited power of attorney for the purposes of conducting commercial bargains with other countries. This is not, in our judgment, all the tariff reform that is needed; but it looks as if it were all the tariff reform that can be secured at the present time from the Republican party, and as such it may well be welcomed by those who agree with The Outlook in desiring tariff reductions of a much more radical character.

❀

*A French View of American Colonial Government*    Those who, with The Outlook, believe that the people of the United States have treated the people of the Philippine Islands, not as the subjects of imperial conquest, but as brothers and neighbors in need of a helping hand, will be interested in a letter by Dr. David P. Barrows which is published in the Manila Times. Dr. Barrows is Director of Education in the Philippines, and his letter is a digest of a paper published in Paris in which the French colonial expert M. de Lamothe discusses the American colonial policy in the Philippines. M. de Lamothe has spent thirty years in the colonial service of the French Government, having in that time been Governor of two colonies in America, two in Africa, and two in the Far East, and he " was commissioned by the Governor-General of Indo-China to visit the Dutch, English, and American possessions in Malaysia with a view of reporting upon their administration for the instruction of French colonial officials." Dr. Barrows points out that Governor de Lamothe is distinguished from other foreign critics of the Philippine administration by the fact that he has actually dealt with colonial problems himself in a responsible official position. M. de Lamothe is struck with the fact that the Philippine archipelago is an area almost three-fifths the size of France and contains a population of nearly 8,000,000 natives of diverse tribes and tongues. The difficulties and the expense of administering such a territory have created a strong opposition at home, but the people of the United States have persisted in their difficult task because to abandon it " would risk not only throwing into anarchy the eight millions of Filipinos, but provoking the jealousy of foreign powers which would endanger the peace of the world." And "these moral reasons for the American domination in the Philippines have determined its character." The school system he considers the most important phase of the work, because it is the " corner-stone of the entire political system of the Americans in the Philippine archipelago." During the three hundred and fifty years of their domination in the islands the Spaniards had not succeeded in making their language the common language of the people, as in Mexico. " Out of the 7,500,000 inhabitants, at the most, according to generally accepted estimates, 300,000, or, according to the most optimistic, 500,000, could so much

as converse poorly in Spanish, while only 100,000 at the most possessed in that language an instruction corresponding with us." The Americans, on the contrary, have begun at once to teach the people in a systematic and comprehensive way the English language. " They have brought from America nearly a thousand teachers, men and women ; not pedagogues of an inferior category with certificates of an elementary character— as has too often been done in our colonies, and especially in Indo-China—but graduates holding accredited diplomas from the universities of the United States." Not only has this been done, but in less than four years a considerable and influential body of native teachers has been formed. In four years' time four hundred thousand young Filipinos were regularly, although voluntarily, attending the American schools, while under Spanish rule in 350 years there were enrolled hardly 200,000 pupils, "with a very mediocre average of attendance." The American teacher " is truly the friend of all, the representative of the idea of progress. He has known how, in introducing entirely new pedagogic methods, to interest in study the pupils who experienced nothing but *ennui* in the schools of the Spanish régime." As a Frenchman, M. de Lamothe is particularly struck with the success in a Roman Catholic country, accustomed to Spanish forms of social etiquette, of " the audacious innovation of co-education." The final conclusion of M. de Lamothe is that the American policy of partnership in colonial administration ought to be substituted for the general policy of domination adopted by France, England, and the Netherlands, in the " splendid territories " lying about the China Sea, and populated by more than sixty million men and women.

❦

The Debate on the Brownsville Affray

The useless debate on the Brownsville incident continues in the Senate—useless because it is morally certain that the Senate will not come to any unanimous decision upon the case, and any judgment which lacks unanimity will have less influence on public opinion than the unanimous reports of the two investigations which have already taken place and the judgment of the Secretary of War based upon the evidence therein given. It is only for its effect on public opinion that the Senatorial investigation is proposed. The Senate has no Constitutional right to interfere with the action of the President as the Commander-in-Chief of the army. If he has exceeded his Constitutional powers, the only remedy is impeachment, and the Senate cannot initiate impeachment. Senator Foraker's opposition to the President's action is based on the false assumption that a soldier's position in the army is a right of which he can be deprived only as a punishment after trial. It is on this ground that he insists that the investigation should have been a public one and the witnesses cross-examined. In fact, if complaint is made against an Indian agent, a postmaster, or other subordinate official, the usual course is to send an inspector and investigate the case, and if, on the report of that inspector, the President is satisfied that the good of the service demands a discharge, the discharge follows. It would be impossible to conduct even the civil administration of the country if the head of the Government could never discharge a subordinate except upon legal evidence of crime and a formal trial. One aspect of the President's order gave to it an appearance of punishment—that which debarred the discharged soldiers from employment in the civil service, and this portion of his order the President has rescinded in the following words: " I am now satisfied that the effect of my order dismissing these men without honor was not to bar them from all civil employment under the Government, and therefore the part of the order which consisted of a declaration to this effect was lacking in validity, and I have directed that such portion be revoked." We do not say that this Senatorial debate has been provoked by the desire to gain a factional advantage in the Republican party, but it has had all the disadvantages it would have had if this had been the animating purpose. A tournament involving the

race issue between two knights errant of the character of Senator Foraker and Senator Tillman is of distinct disadvantage to the negro race and of no advantage to the rest of the people.

❧

*Will Congress Pass a Citizenship Law?*    Mr. Hay's policy in the direction of naturalization and citizenship is being vigorously pursued by Mr. Root, his successor as Secretary of State. Two years ago Mr. Hay's report on naturalization was sent to Congress, setting forth the faulty laws under which we had been living and the careless character of their administration. During the recess of Congress a Naturalization Commission was appointed by the President. Its exhaustive report was the basis of a comprehensive bill passed at the last session. The measure settled the question of naturalization, but did not touch certain unsettled questions of citizenship, expatriation, and protection abroad which have brought upon the State Department a great amount of unnecessary and intolerable imposition, from which it should long ago have been relieved. Congress was asked to provide for a commission to report on these questions, and the Senate passed a joint resolution favoring it. The House Committee, however, suggested instead that the report be made by the Department, whereupon the Secretary created a Commission consisting of Mr. James B. Scott, the Department's Solicitor, Dr. David Jayne Hill, American Minister at The Hague and formerly Assistant Secretary of State, and Mr. Gaillard Hunt, Chief of the Passport Bureau; the last named had also been a member of the Naturalization Commission. The conclusions reached by this Commission were published a fortnight ago. They consist of recommendations for constructive and declaratory legislation and for executive regulations. As to constructive legislation, one of the recommendations concerns those who have declared their intention to become American citizens, who have not yet been admitted as such, but who find themselves on a visit abroad without the protection of their native or their adopted country; without the first, since they have formally declared their intention to forswear their allegiance; without the second, because they are not yet our citizens. The Commission recommends that qualified passports be issued to such persons, if they go abroad for a stay so brief that it will not interrupt the real continuity of their American residence, the passports not to be effective, however, in the country of the declarant's origin. As to declaratory legislation, since Congress has, strangely enough, never defined how Americans may lose their citizenship, the Commission recommends the passage of an act declaring that expatriation of an American citizen may be assumed when he obtains naturalization in a foreign State, or when he engages in the service of a foreign State, such service involving the taking of an oath of allegiance, or when he becomes domiciled five years in a foreign State without intention of returning. This upsets the old theory, Once an American citizen always an American citizen. Furthermore, Congress is asked to declare that an American woman marrying a foreigner thereby becomes a foreigner. Upon the dissolution of her marriage, however, either by the death of her husband or by divorce from him, she may, if she choose, revert to her original citizenship. As to children, according to existing law, those born in this country, except in foreign legations, are American citizens. Concerning children born abroad of alien and non resident parents, one of whom has since been naturalized, the Commission recommends that the naturalization of the father shall confer citizenship upon minor children only if they come here actually to reside. These recommendations ought to be established by legislation. They will be if the House of Representatives and the Senate pass the Citizenship Bill favorably reported last week by the House Committee on Foreign Affairs.

●

***Not Cheapness but Equal Rights*** The New York Sun last week laid a weighty load on the conscience of President Roosevelt. In one of those infrequent editorials in which the Sun appears to be serious, almost tearful, it exclaims over the Pres-

ident: "He is responsible for the general insanity on the subject of railroads which all sorts of communities betray everywhere throughout the country." In what does this insanity consist? Let the Sun diagnose the case: "On all sides there is an insistent clamor for lower rates for all classes of transportation." The Sun, moved by profound pity for the "thrice unhappy railroad executive," recites as alarming symptoms the laws which are being enacted. We shall, it seems, have to turn our insane asylums into refuges for the few remaining sane, who can then in security mournfully view the destruction on which the populace is intent. No wonder it is led to inquire with fear, "What is going to come of it all?" This brilliant journal, which sees humor in everything except its own comically serious moods, takes its cue from the new President of the Southern Railway, Mr. W. W. Finley. In a published statement he showed how the cost of railway operation had advanced. Bridge timber, cross ties, steel rails, locomotives, passenger coaches, freight cars, coal cars, labor, taxes—all have increased in cost; and besides there are "excessive verdicts of juries in personal-injury cases" and the heavy penalties which many States impose on carriers for failures of service. At the same time there is a growing demand for additional track capacity, and there is need for improvement in safety appliances. It is a serious dilemma in which Mr. Finley thinks that he and his fellow railway managers are placed. This is the way he describes it:

As bearing upon the capacity of the railroad companies to obtain the means to make necessary additions to their facilities and to provide the most approved safety appliances in operation, the public should give fair business consideration to the situation which confronts the carriers.

The present situation is:

An immense increase in all expenses, without any increase in rates—in fact, with the proposition almost universally made to decrease rates by legislative action.

The real difficulty is that the Sun and Mr. Finley, and other journals and railway managers that argue like them, are in terror of a creation of their own rhetoric. It is not the American Nation that is going crazy; it is rather they who seem to be the victims of a " fixed idea." The laws for the regulation of railway rates do not embody "a proposition almost universally made to decrease rates by legislation;" they have not been enacted in consequence of "an insistent clamor for lower rates for all classes of transportation." To characterize railway rate regulation in these terms is like declaring that the American colonists fought England in order to get cheap tea. What the American colonists resented was not heavy taxation, but taxation levied unjustly; and what the people of the United States now resent is not exorbitant railway rates, but rates exacted arbitrarily and unequally. The American people are saying, not, "We want goods carried at lower cost," but, "We insist that goods shall be carried on terms equally open to 'all." Because the railways have been either unable or unwilling to make sure that no shipper and no locality should have any advantage in rates over any other shipper or locality, for the same service, the people " everywhere throughout the country " (to use the Sun's phrase) are demanding that the Government fix the rates. Better than special rates to favored shippers would be higher rates to all. But, higher or lower, let the rates be fair. That is the purport of this "clamor." That is the nature of this "proposition almost universally made." In the matter of freight rates the American people are determined to secure, not cheapness, but equal rights.

⊛

**Are We Too Prosperous?** What the increased demand is for transportation facilities, of which Mr. Finley speaks, was impressively described in a letter addressed to Governor Johnson, of Minnesota, by Mr. James J. Hill, President of the Great Northern Railroad. He declares that ' it is not by accident that railroad building has declined to its lowest within a generation, at the very time when all other forms of activity have been growing most rapidly." He then utters a part, at least, of the same complaint which Mr. Finley put forth. Railways have been made unpopular by legislation; they have been unduly taxed; investors have been frightened; consequently, while wealth has increased, facilities for transporting that wealth and making it available have almost stood still. " Within the past ten years," says Mr. Hill, "the volume of railroad business in this country has increased over 110 per cent." With that statement he contrasts the recent very moderate increase in mileage. To take care of a traffic growing at an average of eleven per cent. a year (for the past ten years), there is a mileage which has grown since 1904 only at the rate of 1½ per cent. a year. There are plenty of cars, but they cannot be moved because there are not enough tracks. Within the next five years the railways, he argues, ought to build fifteen thousand miles of track each year. In order to do this, the railways would require each year two million tons of steel rails, which is nearly two-thirds of the annual product of all the rolling-mills in the United States. This and the other necessary items would cause an annual expenditure of over a billion dollars. All this just to keep pace with the growing business of the country. These figures appear to us to emphasize the need of a greater unification of our railway system, and therefore of some settled measures of Federal control. It is not, as Mr. Hill seems to think, unjust legislation that has produced the conditions of which he complains; it is the uncertainty growing out of the unrestricted manipulation of railways by men who have not been held sufficiently accountable to the people who use and support the railways. Surely, in the face of Mr. Hill's figures, there is some reason for the Nation to be frightened at its own prosperity, and stand in awe at the problem of seeing that its enormous wealth is justly distributed among those who have really created it.

⊛

**An Autocratic Rule** The New York State Senate has imitated the fabled action of the ostrich, which is said to hide its head in the sand and so imagine that it can escape the eye of the hunter. It has adopted a rule empowering the Clerk to withdraw, without special authority from the Senate, the license to any press representative to have all of the usual press privileges in the Senate in the discharge of his professional duties. The excuse for this action is that some newspapers have treated some Senators with great disrespect; the real reason for the action is probably correctly interpreted by the New York Times:

All candid and right-thinking men will admit that the presence of a vigilant body of correspondents is a constant source of danger to legislative measures involving jobs and steals. If the Senate Chamber, as some observers predict, is to be made this winter the graveyard of Governor Hughes's policies, anybody can understand that the grave-diggers would feel more free and comfortable if the reporters, or certain reporters, were out of the way.

That Senator Raines and Senator Grady should have advocated this measure is not strange; the people of the State are not accustomed to look to these political leaders for statesmanlike views or policies. But that Senator Armstrong should have voted for it is both a puzzle and a disappointment to his best friends. The law should protect the right of a man to his reputation as well as to his purse, but both rights should be protected by the same method. There would be something to be said for a law providing for more summary proceedings against irresponsible newspapers · for libelous attacks, but there is nothing to be said for a resolution which gives to the Clerk of the Senate autocratic power to determine what papers shall be given and what papers shall be denied special privileges in reporting to the public the proceedings of the State Legislature.

❧

*Race-Track Gambling*　For eleven years the State of New York has been in a humiliating position in regard to race-track gambling. All kinds of gambling are alike expressly and positively prohibited by the Constitution of the State, as revised in 1894. Other forms of gambling, and even betting on horse races, when the betting is done outside the limits of a race-course, are recognized as crimes by the State laws, to be suppressed by the police forces of the communities of the State, and pun-

ished by the courts. By a deliberate act of the Legislature, in direct defiance of the Constitution, the one act of betting on a horse race *within the limits of a race-track* has been practically legalized. The Constitution, after prohibiting all forms of gambling, provided that "the Legislature shall pass appropriate laws to prevent offenses against any of the provisions of this section." In pursuance of the duty thus imposed, the Legislature of 1895 passed the Percy-Gray Law, which prohibited betting on race-tracks, and provided as a penalty that the loser of a wager might sue the winner and recover twice the amount of his bet. The law further provided that this should be an exclusive penalty for the offense. The ridiculous inadequacy, the utter futility, of the penalty is so obvious as to require no comment. The intent of the framers of the law to evade the positive prohibition of the Constitution is undisputed. The effect of the law has been to work a flagrant injustice. Betting on a race within an inclosure may be done with impunity, subject only to a ridiculous penalty which no one would ever think of trying to inflict. Betting on a race ten feet away on the other side of a fence is a crime punishable by not less than a year's imprisonment. For ten years Legislature after Legislature has acquiesced in the utterly immoral act passed in 1895. One reason for their callous indifference to their oaths of office, which bound them to support the Constitution, and to principles of simple right and justice, arises from the astute action of the framers of the Percy-Gray Law. The law contains a provision that five per cent. of the gross receipts of the racing associations shall go to the State for the encouragement of agriculture. This money has been divided among the agricultural societies to provide prizes for county fairs. In the words of ex-Governor Higgins, "the largess of a quarter of a million dollars a year distributed annually among agricultural fairs throughout the State has created a selfish and unnatural community of interest [with gamblers] which is to be deplored." All efforts in past years to influence the Legislature have been of no avail. Now District Attorney Jerome has taken up the fight and promises to wage it with all his characteristic energy and fire. He has prepared three bills, which have been introduced in the Legislature. One amends the Percy-Gray Law so as to put racetrack gambling in the same category as any other form of gambling. A second appropriates $210,000 for distribution among the agricultural fairs. This provision will deprive the agricultural interests of any possible reason for opposing the amendment. The third amends the Penal Code so as to make gambling a misdemeanor rather than a felony. The reason for this is that the penalty for committing a felony is so severe that it is practically impossible in the present state of public sentiment to secure convictions in gambling cases. In Mr. Jerome's opinion, it will greatly aid the District Attorneys of the State in suppressing gambling to have this amendment passed. At a meeting in New York last week of a committee of ministers of the different denominations in the city and representatives of the National Federation of Churches, Mr. Jerome secured the promise of their co-operation in his fight. The National Federation will undertake the work of arousing the churches of the State to the importance of the repeal of the vicious law. The fight will be a hard one. It will need the co-operation of every decent element in the State. The gambling element is powerful; what is more, it is fighting for its life. A united public opinion is the only weapon that can prevail against it.

❀

*The Fare to Coney Island*    The Court of Appeals of the State of New York has rendered a decision which has been misinterpreted by newspapers that ought to be intelligent enough to understand it. Last summer a trolley line running from Brooklyn to Coney Island charged each passenger ten cents for the trip. This was in direct defiance of a court decision which declared that the company had no right to charge more than half that sum. For several days the patrons of the road, the employees

of the company, and the police engaged in an altercation which at times became riotous. Finally the company, pending a decision by the highest court of the State, gave each passenger a receipt entitling the recipient to a rebate of five cents if the decision finally proved adverse to the company. The Court of Appeals has now handed down its decision. This is, in brief, that the law forbidding a railway to charge more than one fare within the limits of any city or village applies only to street surface railways, and therefore does not prohibit the Brooklyn Rapid Transit Company from charging an additional fare over what was originally a steam railway. This reverses Judge Gaynor's decision— though in a different suit—that the Rapid Transit Company had no right to charge such double fare, but it does not make it any less true that Judge Gaynor's decision was law until reversed by a higher court, and that the Rapid Transit Company was lawless in its disregard of that decision. What that court decided was for the time being law, and that decision, rendered in favor of one individual passenger, was applicable, until reversed, to all passengers. It is only on this principle that order can be maintained in organized society.

❀

*Child Labor : What Has Been Gained*    Lack of uniformity in all the essentials of child labor laws—in age limits, hours of labor, school attendance, educational requirements, briefly, in all protection— this is what emerges most prominently from a study of the Handbook of Child Labor Legislation issued by the National Consumers' League. The Handbook, originally published as a four-page leaflet in 1902, has expanded to a sixty-four page pamphlet, issued this year as the January Supplement to the Annals of the American Academy of Political and Social Science. During 1905 a compulsory education law was enacted for the District of Columbia, and seven States changed their child labor laws— Georgia, Iowa, Kentucky, Louisiana, Maryland, Massachusetts, and New York. Of these most interest attached to the

Georgia law, since it removed Georgia from the blacklist of States and Territories which have no protection whatsoever for working children. The District of Columbia still remains in that list, Congress at its last session having failed to enact the District Child Labor Bill. The new Georgia law, like the laws of the other industrial States of the South, will afford only a minimum of restriction upon employment of very young children, until provision is made for factory inspectors, truant officers, and effective registration of births. Notwithstanding the gradual legislative gains of each year, uniformity has not yet been secured even in the laws fixing the age at which children may begin to work. While the number of States slowly increases which set fourteen years as the minimum age, four States still permit children to work at ten years—Nebraska (in vacation), Alabama, Georgia, and Arkansas—if they are children of widows or of disabled fathers. In the North three States, which have cotton-mills employing children—Maine, New Hampshire, and Vermont—still permit children to work at twelve years of age. This is nominally only in vacation, but the return of children to school after the summer is obviously almost impossible to enforce. In addition, two glass-manufacturing States —Maryland and West Virginia—still allow children to work at twelve years, and eight mining States allow children of the same age to work in mines. Uniformity is lacking also in the laws restricting children's hours of labor. Here the most hopeful showing is made by the growing list of States that set an early closing hour for children to the age of sixteen years. This includes Illinois, Kentucky, Michigan, New York, Ohio, and Oregon. Illinois, in addition, leads all the States in having and enforcing an eight-hour day for minors under sixteen years. But, on the other hand, the District of Columbia and twenty-nine States and Territories have set no legal closing hour after which children may not be employed. Without this invaluable provision, laws restricting hours of labor by the day or by the week are practically non-enforceable. No law affords real protection against night work—the

greatest menace to the children—unless it fixes a definite end of the working day.

❦

*Child Labor a National Question* — In contrast to this hodge-podge of State laws on ages and hours (and the diversity is as great regarding educational requirements, dangerous occupations, etc.) the Handbook includes the text of the Beveridge-Parsons Child Labor Bill, introduced in the United States Senate in December. This proposes to exclude from inter-State commerce all products of mines and factories which employ children under the age of fourteen years, thus setting the minimum standard for all the States of the Union. The bill marks an epoch in the history of Federal legislation. For the first time, the principle is embodied in a proposed law that children in Georgia, Florida, or Alabama have the same rights to childhood as children in Oregon or Illinois; that the Nation accepts the task of safeguarding its future citizens against overwork in childhood, as it already protects consumers against the transportation of poisons and adulterations in their foodstuffs. National interest in the fight against child labor is further illustrated by the fact that there are now pending before Congress, besides the Beveridge-Parsons Bill, the Lodge Child Labor Bill, the bill for the Children's Bureau in the Department of the Interior, the District of Columbia Child Labor Bill, and the bill for the investigation of the work of women and children. The vital importance of court decisions on child labor laws was exemplified during the past year in Pennsylvania, where the admirable law of 1905 was declared unconstitutional by two courts. Under these rulings, the two most valuable provisions of the Pennsylvania law are void, those requiring documentary proof of age and an educational qualification, before beginning to work, for children under sixteen years of age. The only proof of age now required in Pennsylvania is the affidavit of parent or guardian. Experience has shown that this is valueless as proof and merely places a premium on perjury. In contrast to the Pennsylvania decision, the decisions of the

Supreme Courts of California and Oregon (the texts of which are included in the Handbook) upholding the 1905 child labor laws of those two States are of particular interest. Even the most ardent believers in the right of the separate States to regulate social conditions within their borders must be convinced by the facts presented in this admirable handbook of the almost hopeless confusion that has resulted from the attempts to regulate the abuses of child labor by State legislation.

❦

*Justice for the Blind*   If Boston is the Athens of America, New York City is its Corinth. But if all the Bostonians do not " spend their time in nothing else but either to tell or to hear some new thing," neither are all New Yorkers engaged in nothing else than in making money and spending it in luxury and ostentation. Two remarkably successful meetings held last week evidenced the interest that is felt among the wealthier classes of the latter city in philanthropic and missionary movements, if sensibly conducted and effectively presented. On the same evening an audience of twelve hundred filled the large audience-room at the Waldorf-Astoria to hear of a comparatively new movement to help the blind to help themselves, and an audience of about three thousand packed Carnegie Hall from the floor to the upper gallery, gathered to hear Dr. Grenfell tell of his work in Labrador. The blind have long been an object of charity—and injustice. The State teaches the seeing to read and write, and it equips them with the training necessary to enable them to earn their livelihood, while the blind it has generally treated as it treats the insane, housed them, fed them, and clothed them in asylums—and in idleness, or furnished them with such play-industry as bead-work, which, to quote Helen Keller, could " be looked upon only with the eye of pity." The new movement demands that the community do for the blind what it does for the seeing —teach them to read and write, and equip them for self-support by training them in those industries in which expe-

rience has proved they can become proficient. That this is possible the meeting at the Waldorf-Astoria abundantly demonstrated, not merely by the facts reported, but by the facts actually witnessed by the audience. They listened to a blind violinist whose skill evoked admiration, not pity, and to a blind lecturer who explained stereopticon pictures which he could not himself see; and they witnessed moving pictures of the blind bicycling, running races, playing games, and performing extraordinary athletic feats. But the interest of the evening was centered on Helen Keller, blind, deaf, and dumb, and yet graduated on equal terms with the seeing from Radcliffe College. To see her lifelong companion and friend, Mrs. Macy, by the play of her fingers on Miss Keller's hand interpret to her what the speakers were saying, to see the interest depicted on a countenance that was anything but dumb, to see her applaud with enthusiasm and laugh with hearty appreciation at happy hits, and then to hear her speak in a well-tempered plea for justice for the blind, in a speech wonderfully clear in enunciation, and to realize that she could not hear a word of what she was herself saying, while Dr. Graham Bell, holding her hand, and speaking with her every now and then by the sign language on her hand; interpreted her for the benefit of the remoter listeners—this furnished a picture never to be forgotten, and constituted a more earnest plea for imprisoned souls than any words, however well chosen, could furnish. For information as to this movement, address Miss Winifred Holt, 44 East Seventy-eighth Street, New York City, or C. F. F. Campbell, 678 Massachusetts Avenue, Boston, Massachusetts.

❦

*A Modern Missionary*   Those who fear that the nerve of missions has been cut by the new theology, and that the age is becoming less altruistic as it is becoming less theological, might have found some abatement of their fears had they attended the other meeting held that same evening, the Grenfell meeting at Carnegie Hall, where an enormous audience filled one of the largest auditoriums in New York City to hear a missionary story. They were told that if they did not get there early they could not get in, so they got there early and sat patiently in their seats until Dr. Grenfell's lecture should begin. There was no orchestra, no flowers, no array of distinguished speakers—nothing but an empty stage, two chairs, and a large white screen upon which some lantern pictures illustrating the lecture were to be thrown. No such audience would have gathered to see the same pictures accompanied by a description, no matter how eloquent, of a journey of exploration and adventure. They came because they wanted to hear the man, genuine, simple, vigorous, and masterful, tell what he was doing in Labrador to carry out Christ's mission as Christ himself defined it—preach glad tidings to the poor, heal the brokenhearted, and set at liberty them that are bruised—to make men more healthy, more intelligent, more hopeful, and therefore happier, more useful, and more virtuous. Dr. Grenfell is so genuine a man himself, so modest, so absolutely unconscious of any of the arts of the emotional religious orator, that his hearers, while they listen to him with the keenest interest and with an awakened desire to become his helpers and co-workers, are not likely to appreciate how great a man he is. He is the master and navigator of a small steamer which cruises about that rock-bound, unlighted coast in a way that astonishes even the Labrador fishermen themselves, and they are among the most fearless sailors in the world; he can amputate a leg, contract the walls of a pleuritic lung by shortening the ribs, or cure, by the use of modern methods but with home-made appliances, a man suffering from a certain form of paralysis of the lower limbs; a hundred and fifty miles from a shipyard he can raise the stern of his little iron steamer out of the water by the rough application of the principles of hydraulics, and repair her propeller; he can handle dynamite, and blast out an excavation under one of his simple hospital buildings in which to place a heating apparatus; he can start a lumber-mill and teach the starving inhabitants of lonely Labrador not only how to handle a saw, but how to

sell the product for a living wage; he can establish co-operative stores, and, what is better, make them pay, so that those fishermen who have practically been slaves to unscrupulous traders, never seeing the smallest piece of silver from one year's end to another, can accumulate their little savings in cash; and he has a "muscular Christianity" that enables him to knock down and drag out the human beast that comes into Labrador to add the illicit whisky-bottle to the other sources of the suffering which the inhabitants have to endure. Sailor, surgeon, engineer, industrial leader, manufacturer, explorer, and policeman, as well as teacher and preacher, he combines in one person all, or nearly all, the activities that make the best modern missions a center of civilization and a bringer of life wherever they are established. And one has but to talk to him and live with him to know that all his activities spring from the most profound and yet the most simple and unostentatious religious spirit. Any one who desires to know more of him and his work may address Ernest Hamlin Abbott, Secretary of the Grenfell Association, 287 Fourth Avenue, New York.

❦

**The French Bishops**

The meager reports of the action of the French bishops at the council held in Paris last week throw very little light on the real attitude of the official leaders of the French Church towards the policy of the Vatican in that country; and it is impossible, at this distance and with such imperfect knowledge, to determine whether the conclusions reached by the bishops recorded their own opinion of what was wise and best for the Church, or whether they acted in submission to the sharply defined policy of the Pope. It is probable that certain matters were practically taken out of the range of discussion at the very start, and among these the continuation of public worship, the Pope having declared that public worship must be maintained. The address to the Pope, framed by the council, expresses the gratitude of the French people for the Encyclical reported in The Outlook last week, and puts on record the absolute obedience of the Church in France. It declares that the Church cannot accept the attitude of the Government in refusing to recognize the hierarchy and the inviolability of the property and liberty of the Church; it also protests against the charge that the Pope has been influenced by considerations other than the peace and prosperity of the French Church, and that the French bishops are following the Pope as a matter of arbitrary obedience rather than by conviction. The significance of this address depends on the spirit in which it was framed; its practical effect may be to fasten the policy of the Pope on the Church in France, though that is not yet certain.

❀

# Centralized Democracy

Sometimes one does not know whether to take Mark Twain seriously or not. Does he really fear that a monarchy is coming in this country, or is he only chaffing when he writes in the North American Review:

I suppose we must expect that unavoidable and irresistible Circumstances will gradually take away the powers of the States and concentrate them in the central government, and that the Republic will then repeat the history of all time and become a monarchy;. but I believe that if we obstruct these encroachments and steadily resist them the monarchy can be postponed for a good while yet.

Whether Mark Twain is afraid of a monarchy or is only poking fun at those who fear it, there is no doubt of the solemn seriousness of the editor of the North American Review:

The present proposal, therefore, to "obliterate State lines," even to the "extinction of State authority," involves a complete reversal of our basic theory of government, and strikes at the very root of personal freedom.

It is our firm conviction that we are at the beginning of such a struggle now, and that, as solemnly adjured by Daniel Webster, we must "not wait till great public mischiefs come, till the government is overthrown, or liberty itself put into extreme jeopardy," if, in the words of Thomas Jefferson, we would retain "our peculiar security in the possession of a written constitution, not made a blank paper by *construction*."

The Providence Journal in a thoughtful editorial furnishes a complete answer to these nightmare apprehensions, and points out the real dangers to liberty, the remedy for which is to be found in what we venture to call a "Centralized Democracy:"

The motive behind the magnifying of the Federal power is essentially and wholesomely democratic. The people have seen the baronial influence in America waxing great in spite of the "beneficent balance" established by the framers of the United States Constitution—to some extent, indeed, because of this "balance." The inter-State trusts have had their rise because no one State was powerful enough to keep them down—and because some States were distinctly favorable to them. They have grown fat and arrogant on "State sovereignty," as slavery prospered upon it two generations ago. And not the least danger to democracy at the present moment consists in the venality or subservience of State legislatures that send to the upper house of Congress multimillionaires of the familiar contemporary type.

We may differ among ourselves as to the seriousness of the Federal menace that threatens the boundaries of the individual States, but it is foolish to magnify the trend toward "centralization" into a drift toward monarchy, when it is chiefly through the agency of the States that our new American oligarchy is fastening its grip on the law-making power. The "centralizers" are nearer to the people than the "barons" are. They have emphasized the Federal power, if at all, because of the undemocratic tendencies of the States.

We said some years ago—we quote from memory—that if the time should ever come when one small body of men controlled the lights, and another small body controlled the fuel, and another the meats, and another the lumber, and another the transportation, and another the currency, we should be perilously near a despotism. For whenever an oligarchy controls the necessities of life, it controls the life, whatever the political forms may be. That peril America confronts to-day. The danger to personal freedom in America is from a real plutocracy, not from an imaginary monarchy; from money kings, not from an autocratic President and Cabinet; from the Goulds and Vanderbilts and Harrimans and Rockefellers, not from the Roosevelts, the Roots, and the Tafts.

And the only way in which the American people can reach and overcome that peril is by a Centralized Democracy. Centralized capital is more than a match for decentralized political power. Concentrate the capital of the Nation in the hands of a score of men and scatter the political power of the Nation among more than a score of States, and it needs no prophet to foretell the result. We may expect for the next decade that great capitalists will be warm advocates of States' rights. They will be supported by doctrinaires who dread the ghosts of long dead and buried perils more than perils that are armed and very much alive. Perils of monarchy! Roots of personal freedom! What has given Mr. Roosevelt his political power? What has, in fact, threatened the freedom of the American citizen?

No doubt Mr. Roosevelt has exercised a greater influence over legislation than any President in the last half-century. But how? By a display of military power? Has there been in sight any possibility of an American Cromwell dispersing a recalcitrant House of Representatives? No one imagines that. Has he then dragooned or bribed the House by his use of patronage? No man since Jackson's time, not even Grover Cleveland, has used patronage so little for political ends. The same critics who condemn him for the exercise of autocratic power condemn him for relegating appointments to the Congressmen. He has seen a public injustice; he has felt the rising but unexpressed public indignation; he has helped to form the public will; he has given voice to that indignation and that will. And Congress has passed the Railway Rate Regulation Bill, not in response to the demand of the President, but in response to the demand of the people interpreted by a President who understood them and spoke for them. This is not autocracy; it is Centralized Democracy, and in this Centralized Democracy is the hope, not the peril, of America. Money kings it is very difficult to dethrone, but the President and his Cabinet can be relegated to private life at the next election if they do not rightly interpret and justly and efficiently carry out the public will.

And personal freedom! Is it threatened by a law that compels the railways to charge all customers and all communities just and equal rates? Is the personal freedom to charge unjust and unequal rates one which it is necessary for the American people to safeguard? Or is personal freedom threatened by unregulated railways giving such favored rates to favored customers and favored communities as build up a few multi-millionaires and strangle scores of independent competitors? Is the "root of personal freedom" struck at by a law which forbids inter-State railways from carrying the products of factories and mines where little children are employed? Is the right to rob childhood of its playground and its school-room a right that the American people wish to safeguard? Or is the root of personal freedom threatened by an unregulated traffic which leaves unscrupulous men to grow rich on the wasted lives of little children and compels more scrupulous men to follow their infamous example against their will or go out of business?

The peril to American institutions is not political autocracy; it is an ungoverned and ungovernable plutocracy. The hope for American institutions is not in the maintenance of State sovereignties and a jealous dread of Federal sovereignty; it is in a Centralized Democracy, strong enough to give protection to lawful and honest wealth and to govern the wealth that is lawless and dishonest.

●

# Railway Rate Regulation

## What is Just and Equal

The country is passing through a transition in railway administration, the full significance of which is not anywhere understood. We are passing from a condition in which the railways are treated as private property, and transportation as a commodity which the railway corporation may sell for the best price it can get, to one in which the railway is treated as a public highway, the railway corporation as a public servant who has special rights in and responsibilities for the operation of the highway, and freight as a toll which he charges for his service. In the first case he may charge whatever the traffic will bear. In the second case he may charge only a just and equal rate, and the Government is to determine, in case of dispute, what is a just and equal rate.

The Outlook believes that there are certain general principles which should be applied in determining what are just and equal rates; that, if possible, an agreement should be reached between the railway and the Government in determining what these principles are; and that they should be enacted by Congress into law and should govern the Inter-State Commerce Commission in its decision upon specific cases brought before it. We here state by way of illustration four of these general principles. Further discussion might lead us to modify some of these statements. We are not so much concerned to advocate particular principles as we are to make it clear that there are principles which can be and ought to be enacted into law and applied practically in determining what rates are just and equal.

I. The first is the principle already enunciated: Transportation is not a private property to be sold, but a public service to be rendered, and the public are finally to determine what shall be paid for such service. To this principle the public have come; from it they will not retreat; and it is recognized as a sound principle by an increasing number of able railway experts and officials.

II. The same rates should be paid for the same service. There should be no favored individuals and no favored localities. No railway should be allowed, under guise of real or supposed economies, to grant better terms for the same service to one shipper than to another shipper; or, under guise of building up traffic, to grant, for the same service, better terms to one community than to another community. The same charge should always be made for the same service, under the same conditions.

III. The service differs with the character of the goods transported. There is one fixed price for a two-horse team

that crosses Brooklyn Bridge. The two horses may draw a victoria with one lady for passenger, or it may draw a ton of coal and two men on the driver's seat: the charge is the same. It is evident that this principle cannot be applied to railways. The public cannot demand that the railway shall carry a ton of furniture for the same price that it charges for a ton of coal. There must be a classification of freights. There is such a classification now. But the classification ought to be the same in all parts of the United States and on all railways; it ought to be determined by the Government, or determined by the railways subject to the approval of the Government; and it ought not to be subject to change except with the approval of the Government; and having been once fixed, it should be applied equally to all shippers and in all localities.

IV. There should be some established unit of wholesale. It is evident that a railway can afford to carry a car-load of furniture for less than double its charge for half a car-load; because the cost of packing and transshipping is not twice as great in the case of a car-load as of half a car-load; indeed, it may be less. Perhaps it can afford to take a train-load of ten cars for less than ten times its charge for one car-load. We are inclined, however, to the opinion that a car-load should be the unit of wholesale; that is, that no railway should be allowed to charge for ten cars less than ten times what it charges for one car. This would be of distinct advantage to the small shipper. And there is much to be said for the contention that public interest demands that the smaller shipper be favored; that, for example, the farmer who can ship one load of grain should have all the advantage that can be given to the middleman who ships by purchase hundreds of car-loads. At all events, some unit of wholesale should be adopted by law, and all railways required to conform to it.

V. No railway should be permitted to charge one locality more than another locality for the same service; therefore no railway should be permitted to charge more for a shorter haul between the same termini and over the same road than for a longer haul. It is now contended by the railways that this principle does not apply where the conditions differ. Thus, there is both railway and steamship communication between New York and Charleston. It is contended for the railways that steamship competition makes it necessary to charge an exceptionally low rate to Charleston, therefore the railway ought not to be required to carry goods to a point a hundred miles nearer New York for the Charleston rates. If the railway is private property, and transportation is an article of commerce which the owner of the railway may sell for whatever price he can get, there is much force in the contention of the railway. But if the railway is a public highway, and freight is a toll charged for service rendered, there is no force in that contention. Either the railway can afford or it cannot afford to carry a car-load of merchandise to Charleston at its announced rate. If it can, then it can afford to carry it for that rate a hundred miles shorter distance over the same road. If it cannot afford to carry it to Charleston at its announced rate, it is not just and equal for it to carry the freight to Charleston at less than it can afford, and recoup for the loss by charges to shippers at other points along the line.

We believe that the particular principles as here stated are sound, but whether they are sound or not, what we want to see is a conference of representatives of the railways who believe that transportation is a service and the freight a toll, with representatives of the Government, that is, of the people, for the purpose of reaching an agreement as to a few fundamental principles which can be enacted into law to govern the Inter-State Commerce Commission in its decisions respecting special rates in such special cases as may be brought before it. Such a conference for such a purpose might go far toward settling our perplexing railway problem, toward taking it out of politics, and toward reducing to a minimum the present state of uncertainty, perplexity, and often wholly needless hostility between the railways and the shipping and traveling public.

# The Presence of God

There is a phrase quoted by Mr. Shorthouse which has a strange and almost alien sound in our busy age— "The Practice of the Presence of God." Men and women of to-day are not less earnest or high-minded than their ancestors of three or four hundred years ago; but their interests and occupations have been multiplied many times. In what are sometimes called the religious ages the major interests of life were few; science, politics, political economy, social questions, education, literature, and travel, in their modern scope, were practically non-existent. The author of the Book of Job felt the fundamental mystery of life profoundly, not only because his imagination had great capacity and range, but because none of the diversions of modern life touched him. Face to face with nature, in the quietness of a nomadic life, he was continually in the presence of the mystery that enfolds us all.

In the Middle Age life in city and country was full of perplexity, but it was concentrated and essentially simple; the social order was not the concern of every man, however obscure and uneducated; occupations were fixed and limited; philosophy was the business of a little group of students; thinking was delegated to a small class of experts; the cathedral, towering over the town, was not only a noble symbol and a place of refuge from the sorrows of life, but it was also school, hospital, charity, library, social center. To-day concentration of thought and interest is the result of a powerful action of the will; five hundred years ago it was imposed by the conditions of life. Men and women to-day are not less thoughtful than their ancestors, but the objects of thought have been multiplied a hundredfold; they are not less devout than were their ancestors, but the emphasis of religion has been shifted from worship to service.

These changes have come about in the order of development; society has grown complex by the law of its growth; interests have multiplied by the opening of the world to thought and action on every side. To hold men responsible for not standing where their fathers stood and doing what their fathers did is to ignore the living energy inherent in the universe as the God of the fathers made it.

The earlier ages had their temptations which grew out of the conditions in which men found themselves, and our age is tempted by the very opportunities and duties that have come to it through its energy and power. It is in grave danger of putting the work of its hands in place of the life of its spirit, and of becoming so absorbed in the doing of things as to forget the ends for which things are done. To live continually under the pressure of a thousand interests, no matter how noble, is to cease living consciously in the presence of God. He is always present in all duties and works; whether we take account of him or ignore him, we are moment by moment in his hand and under his will. But we do not live in and with him unless we keep ourselves in his presence by continual thought of him. When Christ said, "The Father and I are one," he touched the source of his unique power and authority. God was not an abstract principle, an impersonal force, to the teacher who spake as man never spoke before and has never spoken since; he was a divine personality to whom one could speak and listen, with whom one could live in hourly intimacy. Christ practiced the presence of God.

We are always in God's presence, but that presence does not touch our souls, strengthen our wills, help us to overcome our faults, companion us in loneliness, and console us in sorrow, unless we open ourselves to its influence. The Father of our spirits is always ready to give them shelter and peace; it is not even necessary that we should go to him; he is nearer than our closest friend, more ready to help than those who are dearest to us. But he cannot force himself upon us; we must open the door to him. The secret of living with God lies in continually directing our thoughts to him; the practice of his presence is simply keeping consciously with him in all times and places. In this busiest of ages there are men and women who live with God in the rush and tumult as truly as

the men of religious mind lived with him as, long ago, they watched their flocks in the stillness of the far Eastern night. These men and women, when the moment of freedom comes, have so trained their thoughts that they turn instinctively to Him in whom is the fullness of life. When the mind is disengaged, thought either wanders or goes by a familiar path to persons or things in which we are deeply interested; when one has learned how to practice the presence of God, there is a well-worn path between him and the Father, and along that path thought goes simply and joyfully home to Him in whose will is our peace.

●

# A Golden Book of Friendship[1]

Mrs. Brookfield's "Cambridge 'Apostles'" ought to be issued in a special edition and sent to the unfortunates who live in the many chambers of the House of Mirth, in order that those benighted persons may get a glimpse of really good society and an idea of the pleasures of life where living is a matter of brains as well as of instincts and appetites. A more interesting and witty book has not come from the press for a long time. It is in no sense original; it is not particularly well written; its chapters have no special sequence; but it is a record of the talk and a study of the character of a large group of gifted people who enlivened their intercourse with one another with unfailing gayety of mood and unflagging humor. High spirits and abounding wit are generally found in the company of men of genius; and the madness theory of Nordau is set at naught by the sanity and love of fun of the "Apostles" who gave the University of Cambridge distinction between 1830 and 1840. Tennyson, it is true, had his moods; FitzGerald was shy to an abnormal degree; and Carlyle, who was the chosen friend of many of the "Apostles," had a habit of growling up the chimney and declaiming, with a won-

[1] *The Cambridge "Apostles."* By Frances M. Brookfield. Charles Scribner's Sons, New York.

derful mixture of humor and passion, against modern ways and men; but the moodiness of Tennyson, FitzGerald, and Carlyle was the sublimated soul of good sense compared with the banal eccentricities of conduct and taste of many so-called self-made men, who have fashioned themselves of gold, silver, hay, stubble, and such like material.

In the year 1820 a group of exceptionally promising undergraduates at St. John's College, Cambridge, eager for more nourishment for brain and heart, for a deeper and richer intellectual life than the University offered them, banded themselves together to pursue truth with the free foot of youth rather than the leaden foot of academic routine. They shared the rising tide of emotion and thought of their period, and they were determined to live boldly in the nineteenth century; the University lagging, as has often been the case, a century or two behind. They handicapped themselves at the start by adopting the awkward title of " Cambridge Conversazione Society;" but they were speedily relieved of this burden by the kindly badinage of their fellow-students, who dubbed them the " Apostles " in recognition of their zeal and enthusiasm. They accepted the more familiar title with modest assurance; added to their number the elect from other colleges; held meetings in one another's rooms every Saturday night; " sported the oak;" ate anchovies on toast; drank generous quantities of coffee; read essays and talked without limit on religion, philosophy, literature, art, politics, and all other matters of interest in heaven or on earth.

All this would have meant little if they had been average men; but they were perhaps as notable a group as ever were gathered at one time in a university: among them were Alfred and Charles Tennyson; Arthur Hallam; John Stirling, whose life Carlyle wrote with such tender and compassionate insight; Alford, who became Dean of Canterbury and a profound scholar; Spedding, the editor of Bacon; Merivale, the historian of the Cæsars; Maurice, one of the most influential of modern religious thinkers; Kinglake, the historian of the Crimean War; Thompson, afterwards Master of

Trinity; Trench, the famous Archbishop of Dublin; Brookfield, a master of noble eloquence and delightful wit, and one of the best-beloved men of his time; Milnes, better known to this generation as Lord Houghton, whose breakfasts became famous by reason of the catholicity of the invitations, and of whom Carlyle said that he ought to be president of a society for the amalgamation of heaven and hell; and other men, like Buller and the Lushingtons, whose names are part of the literary history of the time. In later years equally illustrious names were written in the books of these " Apostles " of free thought and the joy of untrammeled talk.

These men were full of the gayety and abounding vitality of youth, and were untouched by that blasé spirit, that satiety with a world of which they know nothing, which led one of the great spirits of our time to say of a certain group of men in his own university that they were inaccessible alike to God and man! The " Apostles " were as free on all sides as men of genius must be; they were radiant with hope and enthusiasm, as normal youths always are; the air of greatness hung about them, a fine generosity ran through all their relations, and when they had become old and famous they held together with a manly loyalty which is in striking contrast to the shabby egotism and petty jealousy that are often supposed to blight the companionships of gifted people. Nearly all of them were celebrated in song, for they were all poets on occasion; and a golden rosary of their qualities might be made from the English poetry of their time. Of the many expressions of the love that held these friends together every reader of Tennyson will recall the poet's invitation to Maurice when the latter offended his ecclesiastical superiors by doing a little thinking for himself:

" For, being of that honest few
Who give the Fiend himself his due,
Should eighty thousand college councils
Thunder ' Anathema,' friend, at you;

Should all our churchmen foam in spite
At you, so careful of the right,
Yet one lay-hearth would give you welcome
(Take it and come) to the Isle of Wight."

These ardent young explorers of the field of knowledge might have become oppressive if they had not been so generously endowed with humor. "The world is one great thought, and I am thinking it," said John Kemble, one of their profoundest philosophers. The most tremendous discussions were mitigated by wit, and when seriousness became portentous it was dispelled by an outburst of fun. At a breakfast-table around which sat Rogers, Spedding, Milnes, Thirlwall, Sydney Smith, and Gladstone, W. H. Brookfield reports that Sydney Smith said of a certain bishop: "He is so like Judas Iscariot that I now firmly believe in the Apostolical Succession." Brookfield and Thackeray were always together, and each evoked the humor of the other, peals of laughter invariably betraying their presence to other people. "In irresistible humor none of the Apostles rivaled Brookfield," said Venables; and Kinglake added: "I never heard him say a bitter thing." On one occasion, when Brookfield had failed to keep an appointment, he said: "I covered my shame with the fig-leaf of a humorous note, and am now once more a punctual man." Like Matthew Arnold, Brookfield was for a time an Inspector of Schools, and gave even that serious business a touch of fun. "A gentleman informed me," he writes, "that in anticipation of my visit to Morden the schoolmaster there had hanged himself;" adding, politely, "This shows the value of inspection." He reports some one saying, at a dinner at the Oxford and Cambridge Club, that Sydney Smith remarked on his death-bed: "Ah, Macaulay will be sorry, when I am gone, that he never heard my voice. He will wish sometimes he had let me edge in a word." When Brookfield went to St. Paul's as a "special preacher," he was told that the warming of the cathedral for special preachers had produced certain injuries to the roof. "Was it not dry rot?" he asked.

The deepest interest in Mrs. Brookfield's book springs from the warmhearted friendship that bound together for life the men who laid the foundations of their fellowship in the generous aspirations of youth. In all literature there is no finer memorial of the love of man for man than "In Memoriam," which will remain the lasting monument of the companionship of the "Apostles." In 1832 Hallam wrote: "I am now at Somersby—not only as the friend of Alfred Tennyson, but as the lover of his sister;" and with him were Spedding and Brookfield.

> " O Bliss, when all in circle drawn
>   About him, heart and ear were fed
>   To hear him, as he lay and read
> The Tuscan Poets on the lawn,"

and morning came upon them unawares after the intoxication of their talk, and they climbed the hills to meet the sunrise. Tennyson's occasional moods were sometimes challenged by his friends. Visiting Aubrey de Vere in Ireland, he began one evening to declaim against dancing. "How would the world get on," briskly answered his hostess, "if others went about growling at its amusements in a voice as deep as a lion's? I request that you will go upstairs, put on an evening coat, and ask my daughter Sophia to dance." When Tennyson caricatured a brilliant fellow-student at Cambridge in an early poem, and the victim was told that he was the study for "A Character," he said, "Oh, really, and *which* Tennyson did you say wrote it? The slovenly one?"

But these touches of acerbity or impatience are only passing shadows that bring out the massive lines of the Laureate's great nature. "It is a warm and glowing picture," writes Mrs. Brookfield, "the end of Tennyson's life. The splendid old bard, his Bible at his side, with his beautiful surroundings, fading into the sunset; his great achievements like banners around a cathedral, his noble poetry resounding his own Requiem. Did he not sing, when his first child died:

> "'Hallowed be Thy name—Halleluiah!
>    Infinite Ideality!
>    Immeasurable Reality!
>    Infinite Personality!
> Hallowed be Thy name—Halleluiah!'"

# JULIA WARD HOWE

## BY THOMAS WENTWORTH HIGGINSON

MANY years of what may be called intimacy with Mrs. Julia Ward Howe do not impair one's power of painting her as she is, and this for two reasons: first, because she does not care to be portrayed in any other way; and, secondly, because her freshness of temperament is so inexhaustible as to fix one's attention always on what she said or did this morning. After knowing her more than forty years, and having been fellow member or officer in half a dozen clubs with her, first and last, during that time, I now see in her, not merely the woman of to-day, but the woman who went through the education of wifehood and motherhood, of reformer and agitator, and in all these was educated by the experience of life. She lived to refute much early criticism or hasty judgment, and this partly from inward growth, partly because the society in which she moved was growing for itself and understood her better. The wife of a reformer is apt to be tested by the obstacles her husband encounters; if she is sympathetic she shares his difficulties, and if not, is perhaps criticised by the very same people for not sharing his zeal. Mrs. Howe, moreover, came to Boston at a time when all New Yorkers were there regarded with a slight distrust; she bore and reared five children, and doubtless, like all good mothers, had methods of her own; she went into company, and was criticised by cliques which did not applaud. Whatever she did, she might be in many eyes the object of prejudice. Beyond all, there was, I suspect, a slight uncertainty in her own mind that was reflected in her early poems.

From the moment when she came forward in the Woman Suffrage Movement, however, there was a visible change; it gave a new brightness to her face, a new cordiality in her manner, made her calmer, firmer; she found herself among new friends and could disregard old critics. Nothing can be more frank and characteristic than her own narrative of her first almost accidental participation in a woman's suffrage meeting. She had strayed into the hall, still not half convinced, and was rather reluctantly persuaded to take a seat on the platform, although some of her best friends were there—Garrison, Phillips, and James Freeman Clarke, her pastor. But there was also Lucy Stone, who had long been the object of imaginary disapproval; and yet Mrs. Howe, like every one else who heard Lucy Stone's sweet voice for the first time, was charmed and half won by it. I remember the same experience at a New York meeting in the case of Helen Hunt, who went to such a meeting on purpose to write a satirical letter about it for the New York Tribune, but said to me, as we came out together, " Do you suppose I could ever write a word against anything which that woman wishes to have done ?" Such was the influence of that first meeting on Mrs. Howe. "When they requested me to speak," she says, " I could only say, I am with you. I have been with them ever since, and have never seen any reason to go back from the pledge then given." She adds that she had everything to learn with respect to public speaking, the rules of debate, and the management of her voice, she having hitherto spoken in parlors only. In the same way she was gradually led into the wider sphere of women's congresses, and at last into the presidency of the woman's department at the great World's Fair at New Orleans in the winter of 1883–4, at which she presided with great ability, organizing a series of short talks on the exhibits, to be given by experts. While in charge of this she held a special meeting in the colored people's department, where the " Battle Hymn " was sung, and she spoke to them of Garrison, Sumner, and Dr. Howe. Her daughter's collection of

JULIA WARD HOWE

Drawn from life for The Outlook, December 20, 1906, by Kate Rogers Nowell

books written by women was presented to the Ladies' Art Association of New Orleans, and her whole enterprise was a singular triumph. In dealing with public enterprises in all parts of the country she soon made herself welcome everywhere. And yet this was the very woman who had written in the "Salutatory" of her first volume of poems:

" I was born 'neath a clouded star,
More in shadow than light have grown ;
  Loving souls are not like trees
That strongest and stateliest shoot alone."

The truth is that the life of a reformer always affords some training; either giving it self-control or marring it altogether —more frequently the former; it was at any rate eminently so with her. It could be truly said, in her case, that to have taken up reform was a liberal education. Added to this was the fact that as her children grew, one by one, they filled and educated one side of her life. One of her most attractive poems is that in which she describes herself as going out for exercise on a rainy day and walking round her house, looking up each time at the window where her children were watching with merry eagerness for the successive glimpses of her. This is the poem I mean:

THE HEART'S ASTRONOMY

This evening, as the twilight fell,
  My younger children watched for me ;
Like cherubs in the window framed,
  I saw the smiling group of three.

While round and round the house I trudged,
  Intent to walk a weary mile,
Oft as I passed within their range,
  The little things would beck and smile.

They watched me, as Astronomers,
  Whose business lies in heaven afar,
Await, beside the slanting glass,
  The reappearance of a star.

Not so, not so, my pretty ones !
  Seek stars in yonder cloudless sky,
But mark no steadfast path for me,—
  A comet dire and strange am I.

And ye, beloved ones, when ye know
  What wild, erratic natures are,
Pray that the laws of heavenly force
  Would hold and guide the Mother star.

I remember well that household of young people in successive summers at Newport, as they grew towards maturity ; how they in turn came back from school and college, each with individual tastes

and gifts, full of life, singing, dancing, reciting, poetizing, and one of them, at least, with a talent for cookery which delighted all Newport ; then their wooings and marriages, always happy ; their lives always busy ; their temperaments so varied. These are the influences under which "wild erratic natures" grow calm.

A fine training it was also, for these children themselves, to see their mother one of the few who could unite all kinds of friendship in the same life. Having herself the entrée of whatever the fashion of Newport could in those days afford ; entertaining brilliant or showy guests from New York, Washington, London, or Paris ; her doors were equally open at the same time to the plainest or most modest reformer—abolitionist, woman suffragist, or Quaker ; and this as a matter of course, without struggle. I remember the indignation over this of a young visitor from Italy, one of her own kindred, who was in early girlhood so independently un-American that she came to this country only through defiance. Her brother had said to her after one of her tirades, " Why do you not go there and see for yourself ? " She responded, " So I will," and sailed the next week. Once arrived, she antagonized everything, and I went in one day and found her reclining in a great armchair, literally half buried in some forty volumes of Balzac which had just been given her as a birthday present. She was cutting the leaves of the least desirable volume, and exclaimed to me, " I take refuge in Balzac from the heartlessness of American society." Then she went on to denounce this society freely, but always excepted eagerly her hostess, who was "too good for it ;" and only complained of her that she had at that moment in the house two young girls, daughters of an eminent reformer, who were utterly out of place, she said— knowing neither how to behave, how to dress, nor how to pronounce. Never in my life, I think, did I hear a denunciation more honorable to its object, especially when coming from such a source.

I have never encountered, at home or abroad, a group of people so cultivated and agreeable as existed for a few years in Newport in the summers. There were present, as intellectual and social forces, not merely the Howes, but such families as the Bancrofts, the Warings, the Partons, the Potters, the Woolseys, the Hunts, the Rogers, the Hartes, the Hollands, the Goodwins, Kate Field, and others besides, who were readily brought together for any intellectual enjoyment. No one was the recognized leader, though Mrs. Howe came nearest to it; but they met as cheery companions, nearly all of whom have passed away.

England, and herself a lover of all things intellectual, came among us.

It was in the midst of all this circle that the " Town and Country Club " was formed, of which Mrs. Howe was president and I had the humbler functions of vice-president, and it was under its auspices that the festival indicated in the following programme took place, at the always attractive seaside house of the late Mr. and Mrs. John W. Bigelow, of New York. It was modeled after the

FROM REMINISCENCES, BY JULIA WARD HOWE. HOUGHTON, MIFFLIN & CO.

JULIA WARD AND HER BROTHERS SAMUEL AND HENRY

From a miniature by Anne Hall

One also saw at their houses some agreeable companions and foreign notabilities, as when Mr. Bancroft entertained the Emperor and Empress of Brazil, passing under an assumed name, but still attended by a veteran maid, who took occasion to remind everybody that her Majesty was a Bourbon, with no amusing result except that one good lady and experienced traveler bent one knee for an instant in her salutation. The nearest contact of this circle with the unequivocally fashionable world was perhaps when Mrs. William B. Astor, the mother of the present representative of that name in

Harvard Commencement exercises, and its Latin programme, prepared by Professor Lane, then one of the highest classical authorities in New England, gave a list of speakers and subjects, the latter almost all drawn from Mrs. Howe's ready wit.

Q · B · F · F · F · Q · S
Feminae Inlustrissimae
Praestantissimae · Doctissimae · Peritissimae
Omnium · Scientarvum · Doctrici
Omnium · Bonarum · Artium · Magistrae
Dominae
IULIA · WARD · HOWE
Praesidi · Magnificentissimae

Viro · Honoratissimo
Duci · Fortissimo

, In · Litteris · Humanioribus · Optime · Versato
Domi · Militiaeque · Gloriam · Insignem · Nacto
Domino
Thomae · Wentworth · Higginsoni
Propraesidi · Vigilanti

[ Necnon · Omnibus · Sodalibus
Societatis · Urbanoruralis
Feminis · et · Viris · Ornatissimis

Aliisque · Omnibus · Ubicumque · Terrarum
Quibus · Hae · Litterae · Pervenerint
Salutem · In · Domino · Sempiternam

Quoniam · Feminis · Praenobilissimis
Dominae · Annae · Bigelow
·Dominae · Mariae · Annae · Mott
Clementia· Doctrina· Humanitate· Semper· Insignibus
Societatem · Urbanoruralem
Ad · Sollemnia · Festive · Concelbranda
Invitare · Singulari · Benignitate · Placuit
Ergo
Per · Has · Litteras · Omnibus · Notum · Sit · Quod
Comitia · Sollemnia
In · Aedibus · Bigelovensibus
Novi Portus
Ante · Diem · VIIII Kalendas · Septembres
Anno · Salutis · CIƆ · IƆ · CCC · L XXXI
Hora Quinta Postmeridiana
Qua · par · est · dignitate · habebuntur

*Oratores hoc ordine dicturi sunt, praeter eos qui*
*ualetudine uel alia causa impediti excusantur.*

I. Disquisitio Latina. "De Germanorum lingua
et litteris." Carolus Timotheus Brooks.
II. Disquisitio Theologica. "How to sacrifice an
Irish Bull to a Greek Goddess." Thomas Wentworth
Higginson.
III. Dissertatio Rustica. "Social Small Potatoes;
and how to enlarge their eyes." Georgius Edvardus
Waring.
IV. Thesis Rhinosophica. "Our Noses, and What
to do with them." Francisca Filix Parton, Iacobi
Uxor.
V. Disquisitio Linguistica. "Hebrew Roots, with

a plan of a new Grubbarium." Guilielmus Watson
Goodwin.
VI. Poema. "The Pacific Woman." Franciscus
Bret Harte.
VII. Oratio Historica. "The Ideal New York
Alderman." Iacobus Parton.
Exercitationibus litterariis ad finem perductis, gradus
honorarii Praesidis auspiciis augustissimis rite con-
ferentur.

Mercurii Typis

I remember how I myself distrusted
this particular project, which was wholly
hers. When she began to plan out the
"parts" in advance—the Rev. Mr.
Brooks, the foremost of German translators, with his Teutonic themes; the
agricultural Waring with his potatoes;
Harte on Pacific women; Parton with
his New York aldermen, and I myself
with two recent papers mingled in one—
I ventured to remonstrate. "They will
not write these Commencement orations,"
I said. "Then I will write them," responded Mrs. Howe, firmly. "They will
not deliver them," I said. "Then I will
deliver them," she replied; and so, in
some cases, she practically did. She
and I presided, dividing between us the
two parts of Professor Goodwin's Oxford
gown for our official adornment, to enforce the dignity of the occasion, and
the *Societas Urbanoruralis*, or Town and
Country Club, proved equal to the occa-

FROM REMINISCENCES, BY JULIA WARD HOWE.   HOUGHTON, MIFFLIN & CO.

THE HOWE HOME AT NEWPORT
From a photograph by Briskham & Davidson

sion. An essay on "rhinosophy" was given by "Fanny Fern" (Mrs. Parton), which was illustrated on the blackboard by this equation, written slowly by Mrs. Howe and read impressively:

$$Nose + nose + nose = proboscis$$
$$Nose - nose - nose = snub.$$

She also sang a song occasionally, and once called up a class for recitations from Mother Goose in six different languages; Professor Goodwin beginning with a Greek version of "The Man in the Moon" and another Harvard man (now Dr. Gorham Bacon) following up with

> Heu! iter didilum
> Felis cum fidulum
> Vacca transiluit lunam
> Caniculus ridet
> Quum talem videt
> Et dish ambulavit cum spoonam.

The question being asked by Mrs. Howe whether this last line was in strict accordance with grammar, the scholar gave the following rule: "The conditions of grammar should always give way to exigencies of rhyme." In conclusion, two young girls, Annie Bigelow and Mariana Mott, were called forward to receive graduate degrees for law and medicine; the former's announcement coming in this simple form: "Annie Bigelow, my little lamb, I welcome you to a long career at the ba-a."

That time is long past, but "The Hurdy-Gurdy," or any one of the later children's bocks by Mrs. Howe's daughter, Mrs. Laura Richards, will give a glimpse at the endless treasury of daring fun which the second generation of that family inherited from their mother in her prime; which last gift, indeed, has lasted pretty well to the present day. It was, we must remember, never absolutely out of taste; but it must be owned that she would fearlessly venture on half a dozen poor jokes for one good one. Such a risk she feared not to take at any moment, beyond any woman I ever knew. Nature gave her a perpetual youth, and what is youth if it be not fearless?

In her earlier Newport period she was always kind and hospitable, sometimes dreamy and forgetful, not always tactful. Bright things always came readily to her lips, and a second thought sometimes came too late to withhold a bit of sting. When she said to an artist who had at one time painted numerous portraits of one large and well-known family, " Mr. ——, given age and sex, could you create a Cabot?" it gave no cause for just complaint, because the family likeness was so pervasive that he would have grossly departed from nature had he left it out. But I speak rather of the perils of human intercourse, especially from a keen and ready hostess, where there is not time to see clearly how one's hearers may take a phrase. Thus when, in the deep valley of what was then her country seat, she was guiding her guests down, one by one, she suddenly stopped beside a rock or fountain and exclaimed —for she never premeditated things— " Now, let each of us tell a short story while we rest ourselves here!" The next to arrive was a German baron well known in Newport and Cambridge—a great authority in entomology, who always lamented that he had wasted his life by undertaking so large a theme as the diptera or two-winged insects, whereas the study of any one family of these, as the flies or mosquitoes, gave enough occupation for a man's whole existence—and he, prompt to obedience, told a lively little German anecdote. "Capital, capital!" said our hostess, clapping her hands merrily and looking at two ladies just descended on the scene. " Tell it again, Baron, for these ladies; *tell it in English.*" It was accordingly done, but I judged from the ladies' faces that they would have much preferred to hear it in German, as others had done, even if they missed nine-tenths of the words. Very likely the speaker herself may have seen her error at the next moment, but in a busy life one must run many risks. I doubt not she sometimes lost favor with a strange guest, in those days, by the very quickness which gave her no time for second thought. Yet, after all, of what quickness of wit may not this be said? Time, practice, the habit of speaking in public meetings or presiding over them, these helped to array all her quick-wittedness on the side of tact and courtesy.

Mrs. Howe was one of the earliest

contributors to the Atlantic Monthly. Her poem "Hamlet at the Boston" appeared in the second year of the magazine, in February, 1859, and her "Trip tions were suspended. Several more of her poems came out in Volume VIII. (1861), and the "Battle Hymn of the Republic" in the number for February,

JULIA WARD HOWE WHEN THE "BATTLE HYMN OF THE REPUBLIC" WAS WRITTEN

From a photograph by J. J. Hawes

to Cuba" appeared in six successive numbers in that and the following volume. Her poem "The Last Bird" also appeared in one of these volumes, after which there was an interval of two and a half years during which her contribu- 1862 (IX., 145). During the next two years there appeared six numbers of a striking series called "Lyrics of the Street." Most of these poems, with others, were included in a volume called "Later Lyrics" (1865). She had previously, however, in 1853, published her first volume of poems, entitled " Passion Flowers ;" and these volumes were at a later period condensed into one by her daughters, with some omissions—not always quite felicitous, as I think—this definitive volume bearing the name " From Sunset Ridge " (1898).

Mrs. Howe, like her friend Dr. Holmes, has perhaps had the disappointing experience of concentrating her sure prospects of fame on a single poem. What the " Chambered Nautilus " represents in his published volumes, the " Battle Hymn of the Republic " represents for her. In each case the poet was happy enough to secure, through influences impenetrable, one golden moment. Even this poem in Mrs. Howe's case was not (although many suppose otherwise) a song sung by all the soldiers. The resounding lyric of " John Brown's Body " reached them much more readily, but the " Battle Hymn " will doubtless survive all the rest of the rather disappointing metrical products of the war. For the rest of her poems, they are rarely quite enough concentrated ; they reach our ears attractively but not with positive mastery. Of the war songs, the one entitled " Our Orders " was perhaps the finest—that which begins,

"Weave no more silks, ye Lyons looms,
  To deck our girls for gay delights !
The crimson flower of battle blooms,
  And solemn marches fill the night."

" Hamlet at the Boston " is a strong and noble poem, as is " The Last Bird," which has a flavor of Bryant about it. " Eros has Warning " and " Eros Departs " are two of the profoundest ; and so is the following, which I have always thought her most original and powerful poem after the " Battle Hymn," in so far that I ventured to supply a feebler supplement to it on her last birthday.

It is to be remembered that in the game of " Rouge et Noir " the announcement by the dealer, " Rouge gagne," implies that the red wins, while the phrase " Donner de la couleur " means simply to follow suit and accept what comes.

### ROUGE GAGNE

The wheel is turned, the cards are laid ;
The circle's drawn, the bets are paid :
I stake my gold upon the red.

The rubies of the bosom mine,
The river of life, so swift divine,
In red all radiantly shine.

Upon the cards, like gouts of blood,
Lie dinted hearts, and diamonds good,
The red for faith and hardihood.

In red the sacred blushes start
On errand from a virgin heart,
To win its glorious counterpart.

The rose that makes the summer fair,
The velvet robe that sovereigns wear,
The red revealment could not spare.

And men who conquer deadly odds
By fields of ice and raging floods,
Take the red passion from the gods.

Now Love is red, and Wisdom pale,
But human hearts are faint and frail
Till Love meets Love, and bids it hail.

I see the chasm, yawning dread ;
I see the flaming arch o'erhead :
I stake my life upon the red.

This was my daring supplement, which appeared in the Atlantic Monthly (Contributors' Club) for October, 1906 :

### LA COULEUR

"I stake my life upon the red !"
With hair still golden on her head,
Dame Julia of the Valley said.

But Time for her has plans not told,
And while her patient years unfold
They yield the white and not the gold.

Where Alpine summits loftiest lie,
The brown, the green, the red pass by,
And whitest top is next the sky.

And now with meeker garb bedight,
Dame Julia sings in loftier light,
" I stake my life upon the white !"

Turning to Mrs. Howe's prose works, one finds something of the same obstruction, here and there, from excess of material. Her autobiography entitled " Reminiscences " might easily, in the hands of Mr. M. D. Conway, for instance, have been spread out into three or four interesting octavos ; but in her more hurried grasp it is squeezed into one volume, where groups of delightful interviews with heroes at home and abroad are crowded into some single sentence. Her lectures are better arranged and less tantalizing, and it would be hard to find a book in American literature better worth reprinting and distributing than the little volume containing her two addresses on " Modern Society."

In wit, in wisdom, in anecdote, I know few books so racy. Next to it is the lecture " Is Polite Society Polite ?" so keen and pungent that it is. said ' a young man was once heard inquiring for Mrs. Howe after hearing it, in a country town, and when asked why he wished to see her, replied, " Well, I did put my brother in the poorhouse, and now that I have heard Mrs. Howe, I suppose that I must take him out." In the large collection of essays comprised in the same

to the occasion, and her fortunate memory for words and names is unimpaired at eighty-six.

Since I am here engaged upon a mere sketch of Mrs. Howe, not a formal memoir, I have felt free to postpone until this time the details of her birth and parentage. She was the daughter of Samuel and Julia Rush (Cutler) Ward, and was born at the house of her parents in the Bowling Green, New York City, on May 27, 1819. She was married on

THE HOWE HOME IN SOUTH BOSTON

From a painting in the possession of M. Anagnos

volume with this, there are papers on Paris and on Greece which are full of the finest flavor of anecdote, sympathy, and memory, while here and there in all her books one meets with glimpses of Italy which remind one of that scene on the celebration of the birthday of Columbus, when she sat upon the platform of Faneuil Hall, the only woman, and gave forth sympathetic talk in her gracious way to the loving Italian audience, which gladly listened to their own sweet tongue from her. Then, as always, she could trust herself freely in speech, for she never spoke without fresh adaptation

April 14, 1843, at nearly twenty-four years of age, to Dr. Samuel Gridley Howe, whom she had met on visits to Boston. They soon visited Europe—the first of six visits—where her eldest daughter, Julia Romana, was born during the next spring. This daughter was the author of a volume of poems entitled " Stray Clouds " and of a description of the Summer School of Philosophy at Concord entitled " Philosophiæ Quæstor," and was the founder of a metaphysical club of which she was president. She became the wife of the late Michael Anagnos, of Greek origin, her father's suc-

Battle-Hymn of the Republic.

Mine eyes have seen the glory of the coming of the Lord:
He is trampling out the vintage where the grapes of wrath are stored;
He hath loosed the fateful lightning of His terrible swift sword:
    His truth is marching on.

I have seen Him in the watch-fires of a hundred circling camps,
They have builded Him an altar in the evening dews and damps;
I can read His righteous sentence by the dim and flaring lamps,
    His day is marching on.

I have read a fiery gospel, writ in burnished rows of steel:
"As ye deal with my contemners, so with you my grace shall deal;
Let the Hero, born of woman, crush the serpent with his heel,
    Since God is marching on.

He has sounded forth the trumpet that shall never call retreat,
He is sifting out the hearts of men before His judgment-seat:
Oh! be swift, my soul, to answer Him! be jubilant, my feet!
    Our God is marching on.

In the beauty of the lilies Christ was born, across the sea,
With a glory in his bosom that transfigures you and me:
As he died to make men holy, let us die to make men free,
    While God is marching on.

    January 7th 1907.    Julia Ward Howe.

**THE BATTLE HYMN OF THE REPUBLIC**
Written for The Outlook by Mrs. Howe, January, 1907

cessor in charge of the Institution for the Blind, and her early death was received with general sorrow. Mrs. Howe's second daughter was named Florence Marion, became in 1871 the wife of David Prescott Hall, of the New York bar, and was author of "Social Customs" and "The Correct Thing," being also a frequent speaker before the women's clubs. Mrs. Howe's third daughter, Mrs. Laura E. Richards, was married in the same year to Henry Richards, of Gardiner, Maine, a town named for the family of Mr. Richards's mother, who established there a once famous school, the Gardiner Lyceum. The younger Mrs. Richards is author of "Captain January" and other stories of very wide circulation, written primarily for her own children and culminating in a set of nonsense books of irresistible humor illustrated by herself. Mrs. Howe's. youngest daughter, Maud, distinguished for her beauty and social attractiveness, is the wife of Mr. John Elliott, an English artist, and has lived much in Italy, where she has written various books of art and literature, of which "Atalanta in the South" was the first and "Roma Beata" one of the last. Mrs. Howe's only son, Henry Marion, graduated at Harvard University in 1869 and from the Massachusetts

Institute of Technology in 1871, is a mining engineer and expert, and is a professor in the School of Mines at Columbia University. His book on "The Metallurgy of Steel" has won for him a high reputation. It will thus be seen that Mrs. Howe has had the rare and perhaps unequaled experience of not merely being herself an author, but the mother of five children, all authors. She has many grandchildren, and now a great-grandchild, whose future career can hardly be surmised.

There was held in honor of Mrs. Howe's eighty-sixth birthday (May 27, 1905) a meeting of the Boston Authors' Club, including a little festival whose plan was taken from the annual Welsh festival of the Eistedfodd, at which every bard of that nation brought four lines of verse—a sort of four-leaved clover—to his chief. This being tried at short notice for Mrs. Howe, there came in some sixty poems, of which I select a few, almost at random, to make up the outcome of the festival, which last did not perhaps suffer from the extreme shortness of the notice:

### BIRTHDAY GREETINGS, LIMITED

Why limit to one little four-line verse
  Each birthday wish, for her we meet to
    honor?
Else it might take till mornrise to rehearse
  All the glad homage we would lavish on
    her!
             *John Townsend Trowbridge.*

### THE "NONNA" OF MAGNA ITALIA

Within the glow shed by her heart of gold,
  Warm Southern sunshine cheers our Northern skies,
And pilgrim wanderers, homesick and a-cold,
  Find their loved Italy in her welcoming
    eyes.
             *Vida D. Scudder.*

### FIVE O'CLOCK WITH THE IMMORTALS

The Sisters Three who spin our fate
Greet Julia Ward, who comes quite late;
How Greek wit flies! They scream with
  glee,
Drop thread and shears, and make the tea.
             *E. H. Clement.*

Hope now abiding, faith long ago,
  Never a shadow between.
White of the lilacs and white of the snow,
  Seventy and sixteen.
             *Mary Gray Morrison.*

In English, French, Italian, German, Greek,
Our many-gifted President can speak.

Wit, Wisdom, world-wide Knowledge grace
  her tongue
And she is *only* Eighty-six years young!
          *Nathan Haskell Dole.*

How to be gracious? How to be true?
Poet, and Seer, and Woman too?
To crown with Spring the Winter's brow?
Here is the answer: *this* is Howe.
          *Mary Elizabeth Blake.*

If man could change the universe
By force of epigrams in verse,
He'd smash some idols, I allow,
But who would alter Mrs. Howe?
          *Robert Grant.*

Lady who lovest and who livest Peace,
  And yet didst write Earth's noblest battle
    song
At Freedom's bidding,—may thy fame increase
  Till dawns the warless age for which we
    long!
       *Frederic Lawrence Knowles.*

Dot oldt Fader Time must be cutting some
  dricks,
Vhen he calls our goot Bresident's age
  eighty-six.
An octogeranium! Who would suppose?
My dear Mrs. Julia Ward Howe der time
  goes!
  *Yawcob Strauss (Charles Follen Adams).*

You, who are of the spring,
To whom Youth's joys *must* cling,
May all that Love can give
Beguile you long to live—
  Our Queen of Hearts.
       *Louise Chandler Moulton.*

H ere, on this joyous day of days,
O  deign to list my skill-less praise.
W hate'er be said with tongue or pen
E xtolling thee, I cry "Amen."
         *Beulah Marie Dix.*

Mrs. Howe was not apprised of the project in advance, and certainly had not seen the verses; but was, at any rate, ready as usual, and this sketch may well close with her cheery answer:

### MRS. HOWE'S REPLY

Why, bless you, I ain't nothing, nor nobody,
  nor much,
If you look in your Directory you'll find a
  thousand such,
I walk upon the level ground, I breathe upon
  the air,
I study at a table and reflect upon a chair.

I know a casual mixture of the Latin and the
  Greek,
I know the Frenchman's *parlez-vous,* and
  how the Germans speak;
Well can I add, and well subtract, and say
  twice two is four,
But of those direful sums and proofs remember nothing more.

I wrote a poetry book one time, and then I
    wrote a play,
And a friend who went to see it said she
    fainted right away.
Then I got up high to speculate upon the
    Universe,
And folks who heard me found themselves
    no better and no worse.

Yes, I've had a lot of birthdays and I'm
    growing very old,
That's why they make so much of me, if
    once the truth were told.

And I love the shade in summer, and in win-
    ter love the sun,
And I'm just learning how to live, my wis-
    dom's just begun.

Don't trouble more to celebrate this natal
    day of mine,
But keep the grasp of fellowship which
    warms us more than wine.
Let us thank the lavish hand that gives world
    beauty to our eyes,
And bless the days that saw us young, and
    years that make us wise.

# *A PICTURE*

### *BY HELEN FIELD FISCHER*

Gray skies, gray streets, and dreariness,
A tired woman and a fretful child;

A crimson leaf whirled by a vagrant breeze,
A breath of something fresh and sweet and wild!

A woman smiling through her weariness,
A little child with happy laughing eyes:

How close is heaven when a crimson leaf
Can open thus the gates of paradise!

# A SOUTH AMERICAN
# METROPOLIS
## BY SYLVESTER BAXTER
### Special Correspondent of The Outlook in South America

BIG Pacific liner is bound through the straits for Valparaiso. At evening, waiting in the quiet bay to finish discharging the Rio cargo, the scene on the wide decks has the distinctive social charm of ocean life found on scores of such ships as they course the tropical seas. Men and women, youths and maidens, lounge about the decks in the calm warm air, all in evening dress. A small band, led by a pale-faced hunchback, a poetic sensitiveness in his clean-cut profile, is playing, and there is dancing. The piano is kept always on deck, housed in a water-proof box; there is another piano in the music-room, another in the second cabin. Forward four gentlemen—one an old boy with a monocle—are playing bridge about a table in the open air. These ships are the ocean equivalents of express trains—" trains de luxe," if we can fancy them immensely expanded and combined with huge freight trains. They stop at various great stations along the way in France, Spain, Portugal, Brazil—dropping and taking on passengers and cargo. Such are the ties that bind Europe and South America; dozens of such steamers, big and luxurious, heavy with freight, crowded with passengers, ever coming, going; numerous lines, British, German, French, Spanish, Italian, Austrian. And to and from the United States only two small passenger-boats worthy of the name! Is it to be wondered that South America knows so little about us, and cares less?

It is almost dawn when the donkey-engines stop their clatter and the ship's silent gliding seaward wakens me. From my window I watch the farewell procession of the lights of Rio passing in splendid retreat under the familiar mountain profile, mysterious in luminous shadow under the perfect moonlight.

The last of moonlight, the last of ideal tropical voyaging for this trip! A day of boisterous weather, then the next morning we are at Santos, winding up the narrow, river-like harbor with pictorial shores rising into rugged mountains. The greatest of coffee ports! More than half of the world's coffee supply is shipped from here. The building of the port works, the "docas de Santos," has converted Santos from a fever-ridden hole into a healthy city. That alone was worth the cost. But it seems strange that the progressive, enlightened state of São Paulo should have practically given the concession away and not have profited thereby itself. It was a comparatively easy thing to build a long sea-wall, fill in behind with suction-dredging from the harbor, and then build a line of warehouses and railway connections. The company is practically owned by two men, who get a revenue, it is said, of several hundred thousand dollars a month from the double charges for wharfage and warehouse. There are no wharves or piers; the vessels lie along this quay for a mile or so, often two abreast. Eighteen ocean steamers were in port that morning, and we met a big North German Lloyd boat just going out. And all nothing but coffee!

"That is all there is to Brazil," says some one. Well, there are also rubber, and sugar, and a few other things. But still coffee is the main product. It seems strange that so vast a country should find its chief dependence in the production of a beverage, and that mainly in one State. But other staples will increase their proportions. A concession for great port works at Rio Grande do Sul has just been arranged for. That will make possible the production and export of grain, cattle, hides, etc., on a great scale; will induce extensive immigration; will make a second Uruguay of that part of Brazil.

The second day out from Santos we skirt the mountainous coast of Paraná, the Serras do Mar, grand and noble contoured, extending up and away inland, range piled upon range to dim distances, an average height of 1,500 meters—something over 5,000 feet. When we think of tropical Brazil, we usually overlook the fact that perhaps half the country is turbulent with mountains, raised in high tablelands where the climate is temperate, even cool for much of the year, well adapted to habitation by the white race.

Raw, wet weather and fog! Then we awake quietly at anchor. The ship is quiet, not the sea. A *temporal* blows in heavily from the south—wet, raw, bonechilling. The yellow water, thick like pea-soup, washes past in big rollers with creamy crests. Occasionally the mist shoreward lifts and reveals the Cerro of Montevideo, the great landmark at the mouth of the Rio de la Plata, a flattened cone like a big ant-hill, fortress-crowned. We also see the large city, spreading wide; monumental buildings and church towers in evidence. In this sea the health officer, the port doctor, dares not venture out; we are three miles from land, and the big steamer can get no nearer. We wait impatiently and shiver. Another night on board. In the morning it blows worse than ever. Along in the afternoon there is a lull; the sun appears; a little steamer with a yellow flag labors out towards us; at last the doctor clambers on board, pallid and seasick.

So we get to land, finding blessed relief as we suddenly pass behind the breakwater into the calm water of the harbor. Here lie many ocean steamers of lesser draft than ours, and the shores are crowded with boats, fishermen, and coasting craft. Extensive port works are under construction by a French company, and the harbor is to be dredged deep enough for the biggest liners. But now all foreign cargo has to be lightered ashore.

Montevideo is a large, important-looking city, growing steadily, and now well past the quarter of a million mark—a city of the Cincinnati or New Orleans rank, or comparing with its big neighbor up the river much as Baltimore compares with New York. It is pleasant to stroll through its cleanly streets and

the trolley-cars are only two months away.

Montevideo is a city certain of a fine future—the live capital of a curious little country full of strange contradictions. But now it is near sundown, and we must take the night boat for Buenos Aires—a river boat, and the river spreads like Lake Erie! Fancy going out in a rowboat to take one of the Fall River steamers! The Venus is a large paddle-wheel craft without guards, Glasgow-built. She seems a cross between an

THE DOCKS OF BUENOS AIRES

well-groomed public gardens, bright with the springtime bloom of mid-September. A thoroughly Spanish-looking city, where antiquity and modernity touch hands, is Montevideo. The Brazilian cities are Iberian, but not of the Spanish type one knows from Mexico ; Havana, however, is closely akin to Rio in general plan and architectural quality. At Montevideo swarms of mule-cars—sisters in shabbiness to New York's cross-town lines—straggle through the streets, their sides covered with disreputable-looking patchworks of advertising. But they are now electrifying the lines, and

English Channel steamer and one of the big passenger-boats of the Rhine. Beside her lies anchored, also sparkling with lights, another large river steamer ready to start for Concepcion in Paraguay, a thousand miles up the great streams La Plata, Paraná, and Paraguay.

On the two smokestacks of both these steamers stands the letter " M "—an initial to be seen in a corresponding place on four hundred or more other river boats in these waters. It tells of the opportunity that often awaits enterprise in this part of the world. It means that all this enormous fleet—passenger-boats, cargo-boats, tugs, barges—is owned by one man, Nicolas Mihanowich, a millionaire many times over, one of the magnates of Buenos Aires. Mihanowich is a Hungarian Slav. He came penniless from Buda-Pesth many years ago, and started his New World career as an ignorant boatman, rowing people ashore from the ocean and river steamers. Thrift and opportunity did the rest. Somehow he contrived to succeed where others, big navigation companies even, had failed. Now he practically monopolizes the entire trade of the Rio de la Plata and all its affluents—the Uruguay, Paraná, Paraguay, and dozens of their tributaries, far up into Argentina, Uruguay, Paraguay, Brazil, Bolivia.

The trip from Montevideo to Buenos Aires is 120 miles up the river, as from Boston to Portland; but out of sight of land on fresh water. The practice is that of an ocean steamer, the passage-money including meals and stateroom. But, if traveling alone, one is liable to have a stranger roommate thrust upon him—possibly an undesirable one. An excellent course dinner is served in good style, including two sorts of wine, Chianti and a red wine from Uruguay.

Our respite of bright weather is short. The *temporal* sets in again worse than ever. The wind blows abeam with a choppy sea; our craft rocks with short, vicious rolls; before dinner is half over there is a continual crashing of crockery from the rackless tables, and much spilling of good wine. The rain drives in sheets; the decks are sloppy; sleep is scanty.

At daylight the storm is over. Land is not yet to be seen. But the shoreless river is populous with all sorts of craft, both steam and sail, down to queer little square-riggers, bluff-bowed, bobbing down stream, and looking as if they might have stepped out of the eighteenth century in Massachusetts Bay. A line of big steam-dredges ever at work marks out the path of the mighty commerce that makes for Buenos Aires and beyond.

At last we sight the wide, low line of the great city before us—grain elevators, factory chimneys, warehouses; it might easily seem Chicago were it not for the absence of sky-scrapers. We aim for a gap in a long sea-wall, and are soon picking our way along a stream that suggests the Chicago River—crowded with shipping of all sorts. It is the Riachuelo, or Rio Matanzas, recently dredged and canalized far up into the city and connected with one end of the magnificent series of dock basins—one of the many wonderful transformations that have come over this big metropolis in the past few years. It was not long ago when all the ocean liners had to lie many miles from shore far down the river, putting their passengers off in rowboats whence they had to complete their landing in carts backed into the water. Now the new dock system, although calculated to serve the needs of the next half-century, has already reached its capacity in five years, and enormous extensions have been determined upon. The docks here are real docks, great basins like those at Liverpool and London.

On shore and driving into the town—the first impression is of the tremendous extension of the place. One drives on and on and on, through long streets, straight and narrow, of interminable perspective. In many respects it seems a repetition of Mexico; the same rectangular lay-out, the same narrow thoroughfares, narrow sidewalks. But it is a Mexico sobered and subdued, without its color, its warm·sunshine, its splendid churches. But also without its squalor, its ragged "pelaos," its wretched substratum of miserable *indigines*, drunken, pulque-soaked. There is a suggestion of Philadelphia—much the same city plan, in the old part the same narrow streets, the street-car lines going one way in one street and returning in the next. Take Philadelphia, soak the Quakerism out of it and then saturate it in Spanish-Colonial, replacing red brick with the gray and the buff of universal stucco, garnish it liberally with a Parisian Renaissance of the latest mode, and you have a suggestion of Buenos Aires. But thereto must come a most liberal provision of public grounds, and beyond the old town on all sides most admirable extensions of wide avenues and boulevards, providing liberally for future growth. It is a city of vast

AVENIDA DE MAYO

THE CATHEDRAL

expansion, spreading in every direction over the pampas, the level plains—a city, almost everywhere outside of the center, built of one-story, flat-roofed houses, ample in plan.

The newcomer is immediately struck by two things—the large, strong, sleek horses, plump from their diet of green alfalfa all the year round; the vigorous-looking, well-fed, well-dressed population, active in movement and with a certain alert air that one instinctively notes as "American." Indeed, it seems surprising that almost everybody should be talking Spanish. But it is not "American" of our sort after all, though cognate. In the alembic of the New World's southern hemisphere the fusion of human races is producing new blends, resulting in types distinctively "Argentino," as with us they are distinctively American. One of these types, for instance, gives us young men stalwart-framed, placid-faced, a calm-eyed ruminant look that suggests kinship with the great herds of the "camp"—a gaze wonted to vast expanses of earth and sky or to wide-spread city levels. Great reserves of energetic life, possibilities of illimitable prosperity, are what strikes the observer in a land that is only just beginning to realize the potentialities of inexhaustible riches. The results of the twenty-five per cent. or so of Italian blood in its population are evident on every hand. It is first-class Italian stock for the most part—the shapely North Italian peoples rather than the "sawed-off" little folk from the South. Hence, because of this and other felicitous blends, the Argentinos—men, women, youths, and children—are altogether the handsomest people I have ever seen, with perhaps the single exception of their cousins, the Uruguayans, where the blend appears to have been somewhat different in its Creole elements.

The famous central avenue cut through the midst of the old town in 1893, the Avenida de Mayo, seems an exact reproduction of one of the great Parisian boulevards in all its gayety and animation—architecture, cafés with their little tables on the wide sidewalks, kiosks, public conveniences, and incessant street traffic. Indeed, the constant movement of carriages and automobiles here quite surpasses that of Fifth Avenue.

This Avenida de Mayo, however, is phenomenal as a thoroughfare only by virtue of its central location. In scale it is not only matched, but frequently surpassed, by numerous other avenues, promenades, and boulevards so liberally provided for in the newer sections. Many of these have central garden-spaces astonishingly prodigal in their effect of elegant elaboration. The Avenida de Mayo is distinctive, however, in its relation to an admirable civic grouping of monumental buildings—at one end the handsome Plaza de Mayo, where, beside the cathedral and other monumental buildings, national, municipal, and mercantile, the Government House (executive departments) overlooks the waterfront, with a wide fringe of embellished promenades and the docks and warehouses beyond; at the other end the avenue the new Legislative Palace under construction, its dome on the axis of the thoroughfare. The tree-planting of the Avenida and all the streets is done by the city, according to a comprehensive system, as in Paris—the trees set close and kept trimmed low, giving shade but not obscuring the architecture.

The climate is semi-tropical, much like southern Georgia or southern California—long, hot summers, winters when the temperature occasionally falls below the frost point, though not far enough to blight the roses that persistently bloom. But how cold a semi-tropical winter can feel! The incautious stranger takes it for granted that well along in September he will find the ethereal mildness of his own northern spring at its best. The latitude, about 35° S., seems to vouch for that. But now he wonders that the palms do not wear mittens! He concludes that tropical vegetation must be of insensitive temperament, it all looks so nonchalant. so smilingly verdurous, so happily indifferent to the shivering atmosphere. The hardier vegetation, imported from rigorous climates, knows better; it appreciates what cold is. The plane-trees on the Avenida know that spring is at hand. Inherited experiences have taught them. So here and there they cautiously thrust out little pale-green leaves, like timorous finger-tips to test the feel of the air. Curious how the palm-trees trust it and the plane-trees refuse to confide!

The south wind hangs on; it blows gently enough now, but with a chilling torpor, an unfriendly caress as of invisible cold hands that, as they stroke us, convey all the heat from our shivering bodies. Thus it is the while the south wind blows. South America tapers down into the seas of the high latitudes; hence the Argentina climate is more insular

shine, to lower the awnings over the café sidewalk-tables where one would expect to find the multitude trying to bask, like sensible cats and dogs. The dwellings and the hotels are built with inner courts, or patios, as in Mexico. Sleeping-rooms open on these, rooms where sunlight never enters, daylight hardly. They are chill and sepulchral.

This is the greatest drawback to enlightened progress in this otherwise most progressive metropolis. The great sanitary improvements carried out in the

A SUBURBAN QUINTA OR VILLA

than continental, and the south wind brings its humid breath from the ice-floes beyond Cape Horn. The sun shines deceptively: it lures the plane-tree leaflets out—the few that volunteer for picket duty. But it is heatless sunshine, almost as cool as moonlight. Nevertheless the traditions of warmer ancestral lands bred in the Argentinos the habit of chimney-less houses. It is almost hopeless to attempt to find warmth, indoors or out, in the cold weather, anywhere except in bed, with a hot-water bottle at one's feet. And the same traditions lead them to draw the blinds to keep out this chilled sun-

past decade, with perfect systems of sewerage and water supply, have made Buenos Aires the second healthiest great city in the world, ranking next after Berlin. These improvements have reduced the death-rate more than one-half. But it is no wonder that tuberculosis is still prevalent; that it is the worst, most deadly, of all diseases. The population, almost universally, continues to sleep in these tomb-like chambers, close-sealed from the outside air. Moreover, the lower classes huddle themselves many in a room. Only the circumstance that by daylight their family life passes

IN A BUENOS AIRES PARK

so largely outdoors, where the poor people cook and eat, as a rule, even in the winter, prevents tuberculosis from being a frightful scourge. Fortunately, as in Italy and Spain, the population seems to be comparatively insensitive to winter cold.

As to water supply and sewerage, it should be mentioned that the national government is keenly alive to their importance. Although Argentina began as the most loosely tied of South American States—the United Provinces of La Plata—it is now the most highly centralized and correspondingly the most efficient. The national government, therefore, looks out for municipal sanitation itself. Having provided its capital with the best possible sewerage and water supply, it is now doing the same for all the other leading cities.

In this connection it should be mentioned that Buenos Aires streets are kept scrupulously clean. Of our great cities, Washington is the only one that can compare with it; no other can remotely approach it in this respect; and Buenos Aires is a commercial metropolis with an exceptional street traffic.

The policing, too, is admirable. It is the old Spanish system, as in Mexico—an officer stationed at every street corner; at night his lantern at the intersecting point indicates that he is close by—and never in a neighboring barroom! The policemen look businesslike—always neatly uniformed and trim. They seem to be recruited from one class, so uniform is the type—a blend of Indian with the south Spaniard, hardened by the vigorous life of the *campo*. They are muscular and stocky—about five feet high almost invariably—never approaching the burly corpulence of our typical American patrolmen, never moving with the sauntering, lagging gait of the "cop." Their step is alert, their air vigilant, never insolent. They wear helmets of the German police pattern.

The Argentino military air is also strongly German, naturally, for German army officers are the instructors—notable in the efficient-looking rank and file, the neatly uniformed, well-set-up officers —all of German carriage, the horn-like up-twisted mustache of Kaiser Wilhelm's lately abandoned style universally imitated. In army aspects the observer is likely to note many things in which the comparison favors Argentina as against Brazil, where French traditions—perhaps obtaining through Portugal—are followed in the showy but more tinsel-like uniforming.

One notes in Buenos Aires a general aspect of public order. Intoxication is almost never seen in public; whenever it is, I am told, the person is pretty certain to be a foreigner of a race in which the vice is common. American and English residents with whom I have talked all agree that, whatever the faults of the Argentino, drunkenness is not among them; that even an approach to intoxication is regarded as a social disgrace well-nigh unpardonable. Yet the drinking of light wines at meals is universal. Aside from wine—and maté, Paraguay tea, among the common people—milk is said to be the favorite beverage.

The south wind subsides; soft airs set in from the north; everything outdoors takes on an aspect so friendly that the visitor revises his harsh judgment of the climate. For the better part of the year this is a warm country, after all, and correspondingly agreeable. But the average Northerner, wonted to domestic comfort, would do well to make his visit to Argentina between September 25 and May 1. The palms are in keeping now. There are palm-trees, palmettos, oranges —a rich flora that suggests southern California. The luxuriance of vegetation in the beautiful public grounds otherwise suggests that of Washington under similar conditions. But how the springtime flora, which at home blossoms in a fixed order, a procession with stated precedences, leaps into bloom in joyous simultaneity! A few days ago dandelions were spangling the grass under the palms. Forsythia and the daffodils are also past. Now we have about everything else that is scheduled for springtime flowering all at once. The white spirea, the bridal-wreath kind, is everywhere in garden and field—hedges of it with spray-like flowers, a national adoption, like the privet and the English barberry in eastern Massachusetts. Amidst this a blaze of the pyrus japonica, the Japanese quince, offers an ardent contrast; daisies and pansies galore; long borders of delicate white iris. Freesias

HOME OF THE NATIONAL EDUCATION COUNCIL

are prodigiously abundant; like our trailing arbutus, their northern odor of exquisite purity is a token of spring in the cool southland. But with it is wafted a tropical breath; out of many a garden gate the air flows laden with the saturating scent of orange blossoms.

An American friend takes me out to his *quinta* in the growing quarter of Flores, five or six miles from the center. We speed quickly along over the magnificent Rivadavia Avenue in an electric cab. One of the great tramway companies has established an excellent service of motor-cabs. The surplus current from the power stations is thus utilized. In a way, therefore, the extra motive-power required for the cabs costs the company nothing. Patrons find the electric vehicles cheaper than the horse cabs for long distances, inexpensive though horse-feeding is in this land of plenty. My friend's *quinta* (Spanish for villa) is what remains of an old rural estate. The house and grounds occupy an entire block, and the expanding great city has built up compactly all around it. The place makes a lovely verdurous island in an urban sea—a Spanish country-house transformed with New England comfort and filled with treasures found in the local antiquarian shops. In the grounds a wonderful variety of trees and shrubs represents many a land and climate; the flowers are bewildering in beauty and mass; hosts of roses—the most delicate greenhouse sorts here robustly blooming in the open—carry the early Argentine spring forward to the equivalent of our June and July. Then the fruits, present and prospective: there are guavas and quinces, almonds and peaches, figs and cherries; the tropics and the high latitudes stand shoulder to shoulder; luscious ripe mandarin oranges hang over a bed where the sweetest of strawberries keep on ripening for months at a time.

Particularly delightful is a ramble in the charming Paseo de Julio that follows the line of the bluff where the city takes a drop of fifteen or twenty feet to the water-side levels. The wide avenue of the paseo runs between the littoral belt of docks, warehouses, and their connecting railway lines, and the great mass of

the city. On the inner side of the avenue a broad arcaded sidewalk of the characteristic Spanish style *(portales)*, and similar to that of the Rue de Rivoli in Paris, runs beneath substantial great business structures for a long distance— perhaps a mile or more—making an imposing architectural feature. Through the center of the paseo runs a long belt of gardening embellished with picturesquely grouped trees, shrubbery, flowers, fountains, and statuary. This makes a beautiful interlude between the prosaic commercial water-front, with its shipping and its bustling traffic, railway and maritime, and the more architectural and monumental features of the great city. The glimpses of the vast river spreading beyond the docks like the ocean itself are impressive. In its shallow immensity it lacks the majesty of the salt sea. It has its own aspects of beauty under certain lights, at certain hours of the day. But ordinarily its tawny expanse, spreading to an unbroken horizon, suggests a vast plain of newly plowed ground.

The marvelous growth of Buenos Aires has wrought quick transitions. Even six years ago the typical aspects of old Spain, of Italy, characterized the mercantile districts. The open shop-front was universal. The breezes blew in without hindrance, often working their will with the goods and with the skirts of customers. Then came the first plate-glass window. It made the little "Yankee-notion" shop that imported it the talk of the town. Now every shop has its plate-glass front, and the window displays compare with what may be seen in any great city.

The electrification of the street railways was only lately taken in hand. Some of the lines still have animal traction. The narrow streets, the marvelous growth of the city, the phenomenal vehicular movement, make inevitable for the near future an unbearable congestion of traffic in the central districts. A wide north-and-south avenue, soon to be cut through the old town, bisecting the Avenida de Mayo, will give much relief. Two great diagonal avenues radiating outward from the new House of Congress, with vistas of its dome, are also to be built.

Two subway systems are projected for the near future. The great Western Railway Company, whose terminal is now a long distance from the center, is to build subway routes for freight and passengers connecting with the waterfront and the docks. Another subway concession is for purely local traffic. A liberal percentage of the gross receipts is to go to the government, and at the end of fifty years the entire property reverts to the municipality.

Trips to Adrogúe, a favorite residential suburb half an hour out on the Southern Railway, and again by express train to the city of La Plata on another branch of the same line, give a good idea of the general character of rural Argentina in its older sections. Everywhere are level plains.

All around Buenos Aires trees are very general. Probably they would flourish everywhere. The fat black soil, the vast and verdant reaches dotted with farmsteads where windbreak groves accent the landscape like islands rising from the sea—all this seems exactly like a railway trip across the prairies of Illinois or Iowa. There are differences in detail, of course—houses of masonry, for instance, instead of wood, from the box-like cottages of the small farmer to the lordly dwellings of the great estancias. The trees are eucalyptus for the greater part, attaining giant size in a few years.

The life of the "camp" of the vast plains has many interesting aspects, more picturesque than that of our own Far West, so much depicted in recent fiction. In the streets of Buenos Aires the young Gaucho, cousin to our cowboy, and of divers blends of Creole-Spanish and Indian stocks, is a familiar figure. He is frank-faced, the free repose of the pampas in his clear eyes. His clothing is brownish or buff, and the hue of his blanket—his poncho carried folded over his shoulder—is the same. He keeps his head, and is not addicted to " shooting up the town."

One sees in the outskirts much of the big carts from the country, always of Spanish type, with two high wheels, at least six feet high. In Uruguay I saw carts of ten-feet gauge, with three or four mules abreast. In remoter districts of Argentina there are carts with wheels ten feet high, and carrying as much 'as two hundred sacks of grain. One who has traveled all over Argentina tells me that something near half the farming population are Italians.

The immense pampas are known as the most distinctive and valuable feature of Argentina. But there is much besides. Between the Chaco and the Misiones in the tropical north and the cool Patagonian territories in the far south there are great diversities and great riches— noble mountains, beautiful lakes, splendid rivers. Brazil is so overwhelming in size that we hardly consider that Argentina is itself a big country. A land more than one-third the size of the United States makes a large slice of South America. We think of Mexico as a country of imperial proportions. But Argentina, comprising one-sixth of South America, is larger than Mexico was before we despoiled her. Her map, laid upon that of North America along the Pacific, would extend from the Canadian line down to the southern extreme of Mexico. The area would make either twenty-five Pennsylvanias, or seven Californias with nearly half of New York added. In the north Argentina's width would extend east from Puget Sound about as far as Bismarck, North Dakota, or the distance from New York to St. Louis ; in the south it would be about that of Mexico at the Isthmus of Tehuantepec. The length of the country north and south is equal to the distance from the center of Hudson Bay to the extreme of Florida. The coast line would not only take in the entire Atlantic littoral of the United States from Key West north, it would also include that of Canada's maritime provinces as far as Halifax.

This great country practically commands the mouth of the second largest river system in the world. In volume the Rio de la Plata is eighty-four per cent. greater than the Mississippi. The vast traffic of these waterways, existing and potential, including enormous areas of Brazil and Bolivia, much of Uruguay, and all of Paraguay, is tributary to the Argentine metropolis, where

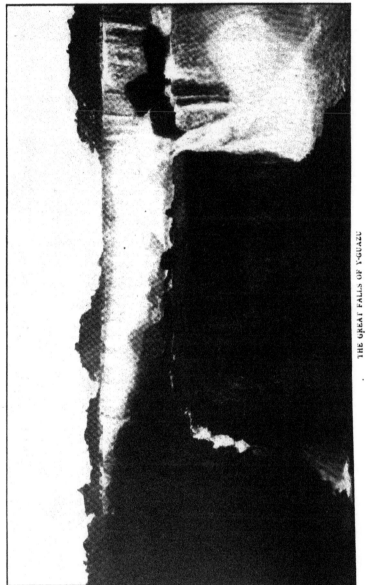

THE GREAT FALLS OF Y-GUAZÚ

the distance across the river to the nearest point on the opposite shore, quaint La' Colonia in Uruguay, is about thirty-five miles. Imagine Nantucket Sound a stream of fresh water !

Argentina's political and economical development—her present standing before the world and her brilliant prospects—justifies her heroic history. To call her the mother of South American liberty is no exaggeration. In thwarting with her splendid valor England's covetous designs upon the Spanish provinces of La Plata she was the first to say to Europe—as later the Monroe Doctrine made us say for all America—"Hands off ! No trespassing !" In San Martín she gave to the world not only one of its greatest soldiers, but one of the three great constructive patriots of America's revolutionary period. San Martín alone —noble, unselfish, pre-eminent in generalship—can take rank beside Washington and Hamilton. He was the true redeemer of his continent. Without his wonderful campaigns, planned throughout with marvelous sagacity, the magnificent struggle of Bolívar in the north— Bolívar the ill-balanced; ambitious, vain, selfish, cruel, treacherous, and yet a splendid general—must have come to naught. ·It is hardly to our credit that we Americans, the first free people, should not only be so ignorant of the superb struggle for South American independence, but should misinterpret its significance, depreciate its results ; viewing it as a disorganized series of unrelated insurrections whose final outcomes in tyranny and misrule only made lamentable their success. The 'truth is that in heroic qualities and in able, devoted leadership the history of that struggle is comparable with our own ; that its ultimate fruitions will justify it, like the French Revolution, because it was the inevitable outcome of that of North America, accomplishing for the rest of the New World what the French Revolution did for Europe.

In a nation with such a history there naturally is much talent for statecraft. In the past, as in most other countries, there has indeed been no lack of defective leadership, much stumbling in the dark, no little going astray upon the road onward. But from Pueyrredon and Rivadavia down to Mitre and Sarmiento, to Calvo and Drago, the landmarks in statesmanship have been continuous, and the proportion of high-minded, patriotic men—determined, able, scholarly men who are giving their best thought to the gravest problems of their country and their age—vouchsafes that they will continue.

The population is small as yet—considerably less than 6,000,000, all told. Mexico's 15,000,000 or so within a much smaller area looms large in comparison. But when it comes to quality the comparison is the other way. Mexico is an extraordinarily rich country with a magnificent future fully assured. But something like eighty per cent. of the population is Indian, including the purely indigenous and the variously blended elements.

In purchasing power, in the development of wants to be supplied by trade and commerce, the Argentine population ranks phenomenally high. According to excellent observers, the 5,000,000 odd are in this respect the equivalent of twice Mexico's 15,000,000. Something more than forty per cent. of the Argentine population lies in cities—over a million in Buenos Aires. There is more than that number in the greatest and richest province, bearing the same name. Metropolis and province together comprise nearly half the population of the nation. In the cities the proportion of well-clothed, well-fed people is greater than in our own ; the slums are smaller and the " submerged " classes less in proportion. I took pains to talk with many competent observers, able men in various branches of business, American, English, German. They regarded the country and its people from various points of view. But all agreed unanimously in one thing : That the resources of Argentina were marvelous, that its growth in wealth was practically limitless, that relatively its development was hardly beyond its early beginnings. In the past ten years Argentina exports have more than doubled. The country has already a tremendous purchasing power, and the climate is such as to make a high demand upon manufacturing nations.

THE CAPITOL FROM AN ISLAND IN THE SUSQUEHANNA

# A Costly Triumph

## By Harold J. Howland

*Illustrated by the J. Horace McFarland Company and William H. Rau*

"FOR four years I have been living in a dream," was the first of two significant statements made by Mr. Joseph M. Huston, the architect of the Pennsylvania Capitol, as we were looking over a collection of photographs of the newly completed building in his Philadelphia office. The words were suggestive of the spirit in which he had conceived his great work and carried it out. He is essentially a dreamer, an artist, an idealist. The opportunity came to him, first to plan and build the structure which should be the center of the public life of his native State; and then, by an unusual combination of circumstances, to complete the work by decorating and furnishing the building in harmony with his ideal for it. For four years he gave himself up to his dream, a dream of a Capitol which should be a worthy monument to the greatness, the wealth, the pre-eminence of the State, and which should contain in its various parts an epitome of Pennsylvania's history. He never spared himself, his time, his strength, or his money. He worked with the builders, the artisans, the artists, and infused them with some of his own idealism, so that the completed structure is full of craftsmanship, of work done for the love of it, and, above all, of a unity that shows one master mind informing the whole. When the building was almost ready for the dedication, two pedestals at the foot of the main staircase, intended to receive angelic figures bearing in uplifted hands globes of light, and typifying Aspiration, stood vacant; the appropriation for the figures had been withheld. When the day of dedication came, the figures were in place, paid for by the architect himself.

So much for the architect's dream.

His second statement was no less significant. "It was my first public building, and, please God, it will be my last." It showed the sensitive spirit of the artist, hurt to the quick by harsh and, as they seemed to him, unwarranted attacks upon the methods by which the work had been accomplished, by accusations of dishonesty and fraud. A dreamer who had dreamed and seen his dream take permanent form, he found himself robbed of credit for a noble and in some respects unprecedented achievement, and looked upon with suspicion and distrust.

In considering the new Capitol, there are several quite distinct questions which should not be confused. First, is it a good Capitol, one that the people of Pennsylvania and of the country may be proud of—a practical and artistic success? Second, were the methods by which it was built and furnished legal? Third, were those methods fair to the people of Pennsylvania, who were paying for the Capitol? Fourth, were the building, decorating, and furnishing honestly done? Did the State and the people of the State get their money's worth?

The first question, in my judgment, ought to be kept entirely separate from the others, and considered without reference to them. What Pennsylvania wanted

193

THE CAPITOL FROM THE PARK

was a worthy Capitol. If the finished building was inadequate, or poorly built, or ugly, the State had not accomplished its purpose, no matter how scrupulously honest and painstaking its designers may have been. If, on the other hand, the structure was well built, suited to its purpose, and beautiful, the State had got what it wanted—the methods by which the result had been accomplished were another matter, to be searchingly inquired into, if necessary, but having no bearing on the main question.

The first thing to be considered is, then, What kind of a Capitol has Pennsylvania built?

The Capitol Park occupies an oblong seventeen acres in the center of Harrisburg, two blocks from the Susquehanna River, the city's western boundary, and parallel to it. The ground in the Park rises gently from three sides toward the middle of the third, the eastern, side. The slight eminence so formed is the site of the Capitol, which is surrounded on three sides by the tree-covered slopes of the Park, and on the third (fortunately the rear) by an ill-favored dwelling-house district, extending to the main line of the Pennsylvania railway, and showing Harrisburg at its worst. A strong movement to have this slum region cleared out by the State and added to the Park is under way. It needs only this to make the surroundings of the new Capitol worthy of the building itself; for, in comparison, this great structure is far more closely hedged in than either the Providence or the St. Paul buildings, recently erected. If Pennsylvania should thus give her Capitol a dignified approach from the east, travelers on the railway would have opportunity to see the building as favorably as the Connecticut and Rhode Island capitols may be viewed.

The exterior of the Capitol has no especial claims to pre-eminence. Its lines, however, are dignified and substantial, culminating in a dome modeled on that of St. Peter's in Rome. The material of the exterior is Vermont granite, of a gray tone which gives an impression of solidity and strength.

The main entrance, in the center of the western façade, is closed with a richly decorated pair of bronze doors. Each leaf of the doors, which weighs a ton and yet is so nicely balanced that it swings noiselessly under the lightest pressure, was cast in a single piece. The process employed was one demanding not only skill and delicacy of manipulation on the part of the founder, but boldness on the part of the designer, for he must stake all on a single throw. It is called the "cire perdue" or lost wax process; in it the modeling of the details of the design is done in wax to secure sharpness and fineness of outline. The mold is made over the wax, which, when the casting is done, is driven out by the molten metal, thus destroying the only model of the design. In case of a mistake or an accident in the casting the whole work goes for nothing, and the modeling must be done again from the beginning. The leaves of the doors bear four panels and two medallions. The panels illustrate the signing of the Declaration of Independence and the Constitution, and the mineral and agricultural wealth of the State. The medallions symbolize History and Education.

While the exterior of the Capitol needs no apology, but, on the contrary, worthily fulfills its purpose, it is the interior by which its claims to pre-eminence among American public buildings (if such pre-eminence is to be successfully maintained) must be supported. There are five features or parts of the building in which interest centers and each of which, taken as a whole, has great beauty and distinction. They are the rotunda and dome, the Senate Chamber, the Chamber of the House of Representatives, the Governor's Suite, and the Supreme Court Room. The rest of the building is divided into offices, committee or meeting rooms, and workrooms, larger or smaller as use requires, the total number of rooms reaching four hundred and seventy-one. All of these are designed and furnished with unusual richness, extending far beyond the requirements of the mere transaction of business, but giving to the entire building unity of conception and treatment.

From the main entrance a vestibule leads into the rotunda. Directly before you the grand staircase of Vermont and Italian marble leads by an easy flight to a broad landing on the mezzanine floor, and thence by two flights following on either side the curve of the walls of the rotunda to the gallery on the second floor. The marble rail of the staircase flows in a continuous and graceful line into the balustrade of the gallery. As seen from a point above in the dome, the noble curve of this balustrade, uniting balcony and

the lateral corridors stand three great Doric columns of white Vermont marble. Their massive strength and simplicity are appropriate to their position at the base of the dome which rises above them. The first impression of the rotunda is one of dazzling brilliancy from the pure white of columns and staircase; but it is relieved from any hint of coldness by the rich warm red of the floor.

Before looking up into the dome this floor is worthy of study. It is composed

THE MAIN CORRIDOR LOOKING TOWARD THE ROTUNDA

staircase, was to me the most distinguished single feature of the building. The figures of Aspiration on the posts at the foot of the balustrade, already mentioned, give a superb finish to the staircase. When illuminated from within, the balls of crystal float in their upstretched fingers like giant bubbles of imponderable light.

From each side of the rotunda a long corridor leads through the main body of the building to the north and south wings. On either side of the entrances to the rotunda from the main door and

of small tiles, whose smooth unevenness is particularly pleasing to the foot. At intervals are interspersed larger tiles, bearing in quaint designs of strong, simple lines figures and scenes reminiscent of Pennsylvania's history, its animals, birds, and plants, and the life of the people. The spinning-wheel, the emigrant wagon, the turkey gobbler, the bumblebee, the churn, the bear, the loon, the automobile, Indians, and old Dutch settlers are some of the four hundred subjects scattered through the pavement of rotunda and corridors. The

**MORAVIAN TILES**

tiles were made by Henry C. Mercer, at Doylestown, Pennsylvania, in the manner of the pottery tiles introduced into the State by the early Moravian settlers from their Austrian home. It is interesting to note that one not altogether fanciful purpose of the use of the tiles here is to provide an imperishable record of Pennsylvanian life for future ages, as the hieroglyphs have furnished our records of ancient Egypt.

The impression conveyed by the dome as seen from below is indescribable. Effects of space and height, of nobility of proportion, of richness of decoration, of the soft blending of colors into a pleasing harmony, all combine to give a feeling of majesty and beauty. Especially fine is the effect at night, when thousands of hidden lights emphasize the beauty of line and color, leading the eye to the central opening into the cupola, whose background of blue studded with golden stars gives a faithful counterfeit of the canopy of the heavens.

The north and south corridors are lined with pilasters, the lunettes between them above the wainscoting being filled with mural decorations. In the south corridor the paintings are by W. B. Van Ingen, and represent the many religious sects to be found in Pennsylvania. The spaces in the other corridor will be filled with paintings by J.W. Alexander, representing the changes in the physical characteristics and material resources of the State throughout its history.

From the north and south sides of the rotunda gallery handsome doorways lead through the appropriate anterooms into the Chambers of the two Houses of the Legislature. Each of these halls has its distinctive color scheme and style of decoration —the Senate green and gold, with its columns and pilasters of the Doric order; the House blue and gold, and Corinthian in style. The House is the more ornate, but the Senate is the more dignified and, to my taste, the more beautiful.

As one enters the

THE SENATE CHAMBER

House the eye is first caught by the wainscoting, which, varying from six to nine feet in height as the floor slopes toward the Speaker's desk, is composed of marble from the French Pyrenees. In color it is a blend of cream and buff, clouded with spots of rose and gray and black. The marble has been cut in leaves, and the adjoining slices opened out like the leaves of a book, and placed side by side. This process produces in each pair of slabs curious and interesting patterns, here a great butterfly, there a turtle, in another place a phantom head. Above the wainscoting rise Corinthian columns in creamy yellow and gold, which support the main beams of the ceiling through the broad ribs of the cove, or half vaulting. The richest part of the decoration is above the line of the columns. The ceiling is divided by immense beams, covered with elaborate carving and gilding, into deep spaces, the central one circular, the others rectangular. The central space is to be filled with a mural painting, representing the twenty-four hours, by Edwin A. Abbey, who will also decorate the mural spaces behind the Speaker's desk with paintings illustrating the history of the Commonwealth. The other spaces in the ceiling are covered with rich ornamentation in deep blue and gold. From the intersections of the beams hang immense chandeliers. These chandeliers are each eighteen feet in height, and massive creations of elaborately wrought bronze gilt and cut glass. Between the ribs of the cove are round stained-glass windows designed by W. B. Van Ingen. The colors in these windows are deep and brilliant, giving them the appearance of jewels set in the rich gold ornamentation around them. The subjects represented are Education, Abundance, Steel and Iron, Religion, Printing, Liberty, Bridge Building, and the like, each typified by a single figure with appropriate symbols. The furniture of the Chamber is of mahogany, giving a quiet but rich foundation for the ornate decoration above. Like the dome, the House is seen to the best advantage by artificial light. The colors and the gilding are softened and blended, while the lights bring out the wonderful beauty of the chandeliers.

COPYRIGHT, 1906, BY S.C. HUSTON

THE HOUSE

These have lights not only within, behind screens of shimmering cut glass, but dozens of electric bulbs without, which shine like stars.

In the Senate Chamber the wainscoting is of green Connemara marble, reaching to the sills of the long windows. The ceiling is divided by profusely carved and gilded beams into square recesses, each with a gold rosette in its center. The spaces between the ribs of the cove are covered with richly gilded decoration, forming again frames for stained-glass windows by Van Ingen. The chandeliers are less elaborate than in the House, but have more delicacy of outline and ornamentation. In this Chamber, too, wall spaces, now bare, will be filled with mural paintings by Mr. Abbey. It only needs the brilliant color which his paintings will doubtless supply to make this a room unsurpassed for beauty of design and decoration.

There are two principal rooms in the Governor's Suite, the reception-room and the Governor's private office. The reception-room is seventy-two feet long and twenty-seven feet wide, and is lighted by three tall French windows on one side. The walls are wainscoted to a height of nine feet in dark oak. The broad plain panels, unadorned with carving or decoration and separated from each other by simple pilasters, show remarkable beauty of grain and color. Above the wainscoting and extending to the ceiling around the entire room is a frieze of mural paintings by Miss Violet Oakley, representing "The Founding of the State of Liberty Spiritual." The paintings "take up the thread of this struggle [for absolute individual, spiritual, and religious liberty] in the mother country in the days of the wider dissemination of the Bible (in English) after the invention of printing, and follow it through the conflict of human wills and human opinions in regard to Truth, one against another, until we come to a State built upon the broad foundation of tolerance." The subjects begin with William Tyndale printing his translation of the Bible into English at Cologne, include the smuggling of the first copies into England, the burning of the Books at Oxford, the execution of Tyndale, and the granting by Henry VIII. of permission for the free sale and reading of the

7

199

translation; the death of a typical martyr to the Truth, Anne Askew; the culmination of intolerance and persecution in the Civil War; the vision of George Fox at the beginning of his ministry; and scenes in the life of William Penn, ending with his first sight of Pennsylvania. Miss Oakley's style in the paintings of the frieze is peculiarly the decorative, not only in color but in drawing. Her figures and faces are lacking in the quality of character delineation which is found to such a remarkable degree in Mr. Abbey's frieze of the Holy Grail in the Boston Public Library; but in fidelity to detail, artistic feeling, and purely decorative quality they are on a high plane of performance.

The private office of the Governor is comparatively small, but sumptuous in its decoration. The richly carved oaken wainscoting, reaching three-quarters of the way to the ceiling; the frieze of portraits of the Governors of Pennsylvania, set in oak panels which continue the wainscoting; the ceiling of buff with cream and gold ornamentation; the carved fireplace and mantel of red Numidian marble, with a high overmantel of oak inclosing a beautiful clock; the chandeliers, designed on charmingly graceful lines and set with ropes and panels of crystal drops, are features that make this room in some respects the gem of the entire building.

The Supreme Court Room is fittingly designed in a spirit of dignity. The pure Greek Ionic style is used throughout, the proportions and details having been suggested by the Erechtheum, the beautiful Ionic temple at Athens. The wall is wainscoted in mahogany for a third of its height, and the panel spaces above are to be filled with paintings by Mr. Abbey representing the development of Law from the unwritten tradition to the codified system. The main feature of the room is a low dome, made of opalescent glass in shades of amber, pearl, and gray, with green scroll-work decoration. The proportions of the dome heighten the impression of dignity made by the whole design of the room, while the warm, mellow light shed by its translucent glasses gives the chamber a distinctive atmosphere.

As a whole the Capitol is a wonderful product of the art of the architect, the sculptor, and the painter, the work of the builder, the carver in wood and stone, the artificer in metals and glass, the decorator and the furniture-maker. One may quarrel with the architect's conception of the building; one may question (and with good warrant, in my opinion) whether a building in the ornate style of the Italian Renaissance is a fitting center for the public life of a democratic State, especially that State, of all others, which was founded by a Quaker. But granting, for the moment, that the architect's conception is the true one, or as good as another, it must be admitted that it has been carried out ably, consistently, and with wonderful artistic feeling. The building has unity, dignity, strength, and, above all, beauty.

If I may say a word of personal experience to the reader who, since he may not go to Harrisburg himself, must see through my eyes, I went to the Capitol strongly averse to over-elaboration and ornateness, and prejudiced against the building itself because of what I had heard of it. I tried not to like it, but I could not help myself. The building is beautiful, and I had to admire and praise it.

The answer to the first question in regard to the new Capitol—as to its worthiness—I have indicated, in so far as my personal judgment, which is frankly that of a layman, is concerned I may say, however, that this judgment, in its essential points, is concurred in by every one with whom I have talked on the subject who has seen the building.

The other questions of the legality, the honesty, and the fairness of the methods by which the building and adornment of the Capitol were accomplished must in the final event be answered by investigation of the proper authorities. A statement, however, of certain facts in connection with the work, and of certain points where inquiry seems necessary, can even at this time be fairly made.

On July 18, 1901, the General Assembly of Pennsylvania appropriated four million dollars for the construction of a

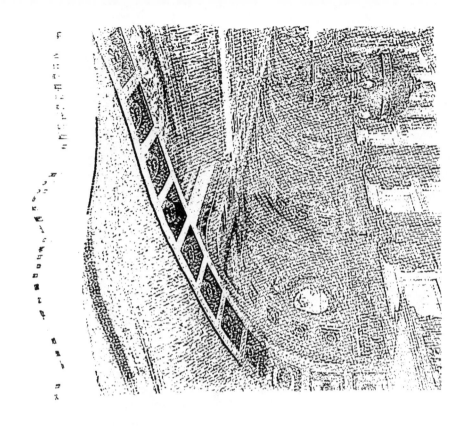

THE MAIN STAIRCASE

capitol. A Commission was appointed, composed of Governor William A. Stone, William H. Graham, of Allegheny, W. P. Snyder, of Chester County, N. C. Schaeffer, of Lancaster, and Edward Bailey, of Harrisburg. This Commission was authorized and empowered to "construct, build, and complete the State Capitol Building at Harrisburg," which building should be completed in all its parts, ready for occupation, on or before January 1, 1907. The Commission, under the expert advice of Professor W. R. Ware, a professor of architecture in Columbia University, selected from a group of competitive plans those of Mr. Joseph M. Huston, of Philadelphia, and proceeded to let the contract for the construction of the building in accordance with those plans. The work of the contractors and the Commission was completed within the specified time, within the specified appropriation, and, so far as I can learn, to the satisfaction of all concerned.

It should be noted here that the Building Commission conceived it to be their duty to deliver to the State a completed building ready for occupancy. At the dedication of the Capitol the President of the Commission, in presenting the building to the commonwealth, made this point perfectly clear. He said also, "We found that in addition to the money necessary for that purpose [the completion of the building] we could spare one hundred and ninety thousand dollars for decoration. Contracts were made with Miss Violet Oakley, George Gray Barnard, and Edwin A. Abbey for mural paintings and sculpture." It seems evident, therefore, that the Building Commission believed it to be right and proper for them, as far as the money at their disposal permitted, to decorate the building as well as merely to construct it. The Legislature, in authorizing the building of the Capitol, made no specific provision for furnishing. This part of the work had been taken care of in another way. There is in Pennsylvania, established by the Act of June 18, 1885, a permanent Board of Public Grounds and Buildings. This Board consists of the Governor, the Auditor-General, and the State Treasurer, and has "entire control and supervision of the public grounds

and buildings . . . and all the repairs and improvements made, and all work done or expenses incurred in and about such grounds and buildings, including the furnishing and refurnishing of the same." On this Commission naturally devolved the duty of providing furniture for the new Capitol. In addition to the task of furnishing the Commission took it upon itself to further decorate and adorn the Capitol. To plan and supervise this work, as well as to design the furnishing, the architect of the building, Mr. Joseph M. Huston, was employed by the Commission. From this double employment—by the Commissions charged with building and with decorating and furnishing the Capitol—arose the architect's great opportunity to realize his dream as a whole, to give it unity and consistency throughout.

The cost of the furniture provided by what we may call, for the sake of conciseness, the second Commission, was given by Governor Pennypacker, the chairman of the Commission, in a letter to the Attorney-General on December 28, 1906, as $876,066.44. In a statement issued September 26, 1906, the Governor stated that the entire amount expended in both furnishing and decorating the Capitol, when material ordered but not yet paid for was included, would be $8,601,922.18. From these figures it appears that the cost of the decorations alone provided by the second Commission was $7,725,855.74. The cost of the building as constructed by the Building Commission was given by former Governor Stone as approximately $3,970,000. The total cost of the Capitol, therefore, completed and decorated, but without furniture, was approximately $11,685.855.

In considering the question of the legality of the action of the Board of Public Grounds and Buildings three facts should be noted: First, the work done by the contractor under the second Commission in a number of cases replaced, in more ornate and elaborate fashion, work already contracted for by the first Commission in carrying out its conception of "a completed building, ready for occupancy." For instance, the first Commission had naturally provided for floors throughout the building. In many places the second Commission substituted elaborate and costly tiled floors for the simpler forms contemplated by the first. Second, the Public Buildings Commission expended the sum ·of $303,695.14, as Governor Pennypacker states in his letter of December 28, " in preparing the eighth story of the Capitol for the use of departments not in existence when the Capitol Commission made its contract." Third, in the General Appropriations Act of 1905, one section of which appropriated whatever money was necessary for the carrying out of the duties imposed upon the Board of Public Grounds and Buildings, a distinct provision was inserted " that expenditures allowed

THE DOORWAY OF THE SUPREME COURT ROOM

under this section shall not be so construed as to authorize the Commissioners of Public Grounds and Buildings to complete the present Capitol building."

A question of this kind can of course be definitely settled only by the courts, but it seems to me that the question may be pertinently raised whether the action of the second Commission in providing from its appropriation parts of the building which the first Commission in the natural course of events would have provided, and as a matter of fact had authorized its contractor to furnish, did not, in effect, amount to completing the building in the sense of the Act quoted above. Its action in finishing for occupancy the eighth story seems to me to come even more clearly within the prohibition of that Act.

A still broader question might be raised, and in fact has been raised by critics of the activities of the second Commission. It is whether the law that gave that Commission " entire control and supervision " of public buildings and authority to undertake all " repairs " and " improvements " and "furnishing," gave the Board any warrant whatever to expend the money of the State for the " decoration " of the Capitol.

Whatever may be the ultimate decision as to the legality of the actions of the Board, I feel strongly that the way in which the work was carried on was unfortunate, ill-advised, and above all, unfair to the people of the State. The two Commissions acted in absolute independence of each other, although one man was a member of both Commissions and the same architect was employed by both. I was informed by a prominent member of the Building Commission that he and his associates (with the exception of course of the man mentioned above, whose silence has not yet been explained) were unaware of what the other Commission was doing until the close of their work was at hand and they found that parts of the building for which they had contracted were being replaced with more elaborate designs and more costly materials. Indeed, it was this very lack of co-ordination between the two bodies which was the cause of the first outburst of criticism. In Au-

gust of last year the announcement was made that the Capitol had been completed not only within the specified time, but within the appropriation of four million dollars, a fact which was proclaimed as being almost unprecedented in the

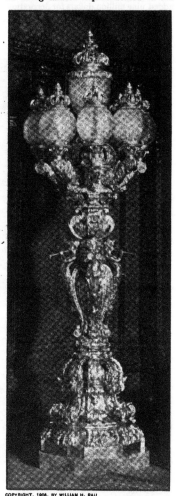

A STANDARD IN THE GOVERNOR'S
RECEPTION-ROOM

history of public construction. The people of the State had congratulated themselves for several weeks on the result before the announcement was made that to the four million dollars which the building of the Capitol had cost must be added nine million dollars for decoration and furnishing. The only defense which I have heard of the secret way in which the spending of the additional money was done is that if the people of the State had known that they were to pay thirteen millions of dollars for their Capitol instead of four millions there would have been such an outburst of protest that the work could not have been completed, and the State would not have had the magnificently artistic and beautiful Capitol which it now has. If the people of the State would not have been willing to spend thirteen million dollars for the Capitol if they had known that it was

THE GOVERNOR'S PRIVATE OFFICE

THE GOVERNOR'S RECEPTION-ROOM

being done, what argument can justify the action of men who, because they believed that the people ought to want to spend so much money for so fine a building, arbitrarily and secretly compelled them to do so?

The question of the honesty of the charges and payments for the work of decorating and furnishing has been raised by the State Treasurer, Mr. William H. Berry. Mr. Berry took office last May, and the first thing that he found, as he told me, was that the posting of the books of his department was far in arrears. As soon as the books had been brought up to date he discovered, what had not up to that time been revealed, that the cost of the new Capitol would be nearer thirteen million dollars than four. His subsequent announcement was the first intimation that the people of the State had of this fact. His suspicion was first aroused as to the fairness of the prices which were being paid for decoration and furnishing, he told me, by a bill for ninety thousand dollars for parquetry flooring. From personal observation he knew that this flooring had been laid by a gang of about fifteen men in about two weeks, and, as he said, he "knew that there weren't fifteen men in the world who could lay ninety thousand dollars' worth of parquetry flooring in two weeks." He determined then to take the rooms of his own department and find out what the decorating of them had cost and to compare the prices with liberal estimates which he would obtain from other sources. He found that the ceiling of his private office, a comparatively small room, could be duplicated by a responsible decorator for five hundred and fifty dollars. It cost the State $5,500. He took up also the cost of the oak wainscoting of his room. "The highest estimate," he told me, "that any one was willing to give me by stretching his conscience was $1,800. That wainscoting cost the State $15,500. The same scale —ten prices—runs through the decorating of this whole building. The State has paid five million dollars more for this Capitol than it should have paid." He then explained how, in his opinion, it had been made possible for such excessive prices to be charged. A special schedule for "furniture, carpets, fittings, and decoration" was prepared by the architect. This schedule contained

various items on which bids would be received from contractors. On each item a maximum price was set, above which no bid would be received; the contractor was required to make his bid by stating the per cent. below the maximum price for which he would be willing to supply the item. Here are several sample items from this schedule showing the maximum price. and the per cent. below this price bid by two contractors:

| Description of Articles. | Maximum Price. | International Mfg. Supply Co. | John H. Sanderson. |
|---|---|---|---|
| 1. Bookcases and wardrobes (mahogany), Series F, per lineal foot............... | $37.00 | 40 | 58 |
| 2. Leather-covered easy armchairs (mahogany), Series F, each................. | 55.00 | 25 | 37 |
| 3. Leather-covered swivel armchairs (mahogany), Series F, each................. | 40.00 | 25 | 28 |
| 22. Designed furniture, fittings, furnishings, and decorations of either woodwork, stone, marble, bronze, mosaic, glass, and upholstery, Series F, per foot........ | 20.00 | net | 8 |
| 31. Designed special finished bronze-metal gas and electric fixtures, Series E-F, each.................... | 225.00 | .. | 14 |
| 32. Designed bronze-metal for gas and electric fixtures, hardware, and ornamental work, mercurial gold finish, hand-tooled, and rechased, Series E-F, per pound.................. | 5.00 | 20 | 3 |

It was found that John H. Sanderson, of Philadelphia, had, on the whole, made the best bid for the entire schedule, and he was therefore awarded the contract.

Mr. Berry called my attention to the chair in which I was sitting, which he said was one of the chairs described in item No. 2. For a chair of this sort the contractor had bid $34.65. When, however, the chair came to be paid for, it was billed under the omnibus item No. 22, on which a bid of $18.40 per foot had been made. It was determined (by just what process has not been made clear) that the chair contained eight feet, and the price accordingly was $147.20. Similarly, the chandelier in the room was one of those contemplated in item No. 31. The estimated price for such a chandelier was $193.50. It was, however, billed under item No. 32, at $4.85 per pound, making the price about $2,500. These examples will serve to indicate the methods which

THE CEILING OF THE SENATE CHAMBER

Mr. Berry charges were used to defraud the State.

He told me of another instance which he had carefully investigated, and of the correctness of which he was convinced. Around the drum of the main dome are quotations from the writings of William Penn in mosaic. This mosaic work was planned by the Building Commission and included in their contract. Later, however, they decided that it would be better to omit this particular decoration and use the money in some other way; they accordingly obtained an allowance from the contractor for the omitted work of eight dollars per square foot. Mr. Berry had found that the work, which was to have been of imported favrile mosaic, would have cost the contractor five dollars per square foot, giving him a profit of three dollars per square foot, which was perfectly proper. Subsequently the second Commission determined to have the inscriptions put up as originally planned. The work was done by their contractor, and charged for under item No. 22, at $18.40 per square foot. Mr. Berry states that he has found the man who actually did the work for the contractor, and has discovered that the work is of inferior quality and cost three dollars per square foot. The contractor's profit was, therefore, $15.40 per square foot.

It must be remembered that thus far these accusations of fraud and graft are merely accusations. This phase of the matter is being investigated by the Attorney-General of the State, and will probably be the subject of a legislative investigation. The public cannot do otherwise than to suspend judgment of the proof or falsity of the charges until the results of the official investigation are reached. No public reply has been made to the various specifications in the charges by those who have been accused. The general position, however, has been taken both by the architect and Governor Pennypacker that in considering the cost of the Capitol. the building should be taken as a whole; its entire cost should be compared with that of other public buildings. The question whether the people of Pennsylvania have got their money's worth should be determined by such a broad view and such a comparison. In an article by Isaac A. Pennypacker in Harper's Weekly thé comparison is made as follows:

The cost per cubic foot of contents, which is the usual architectural way of estimating, is $1.04, inclusive of all the furnishing and decorating. Compare with this the cost for construction alone of the following buildings which are on a similar scale:

| | |
|---|---|
| Capitol at Washington, per cubic foot............ | $1.10 |
| "    at Albany   "   "   " ............ | 2.00 |
| William C. Whitney's residence, per cubic foot | 2.55 |
| Knickerbocker Trust Company, New York, per cubic foot.................................... | 1.30 |
| New York Hall of Records, per cubic foot....... | 1.25 |
| Hotel St. Regis................................. | 1.10 |

It is said also that the reason for the high cost of many of the items is that the elements of art and craftsmanship enter so largely into their construction. In the case of the chandeliers, for instance, special designs were made, the finishing was done by workmen who are more than mere artisans, and the molds were broken when the work was done so that no piece can be duplicated. It of course goes without saying that such work commands a higher price than ordinary stock designs mechanically finished would bring. It might be asked, however, how, in the case of work in which those elements were so prominent, the price could be properly fixed on a basis of mere weight.

In conclusion, I want to emphasize the point of view from which Pennsylvania's new Capitol should be judged. The building is a wonderful achievement of art and craftsmanship, a worthy monument to a great State; but that important fact carries with it no palliation of any illegal or dishonest methods that may have been used in building and furnishing it. On the other hand, the fact that grave charges have been made in connection with the work of decoration and furnishing should not be allowed to obscure the realization of the magnificent character of the Capitol itself. Each question should be judged on its own merits. Good work should receive its due reward of praise; accusations of dishonesty should be untiringly investigated, and if any are found guilty, they should be relentlessly punished.

# MERIT AND DIPLOMACY
## SOME PERSONAL IMPRESSIONS

"TO the victor belong the spoils." To the victorious political party belong the offices. These spoils go to him who has rendered his party service; whether he is qualified for any particular office is quite another consideration. Time was when these ideas ruled in our Government service at home and abroad. But twenty-five years of civil service reform have had their effect. The spoils system seems actually getting shaky.

This has been especially marked during the present administration, and particularly so with regard to our representation abroad. Merit—that is, character,

attainments, and proved efficiency of service—has been increasingly emphasized by President Roosevelt's foreign appointments and by all those suggested by his two Secretaries of State, John Hay and Elihu Root. Indeed, such a principle was essential if proper effect was to be given to the frankness, straightforwardness, and courage distinguishing the John Hay and Elihu Root diplomacy from that of many of their contemporaries.

More than passing notice, accordingly, is demanded by the recent nominations of Messrs. White, Riddle, Griscom, and Dudley to be Ambassadors to France, Russia, Italy, and Brazil. While each is an example of what may be accomplished in the diplomatic service by a

JOHN WALLACE RIDDLE
Now Minister to Rumania and Servia; to be Ambassador to Russia

man of tact and sense, the chief thing to be noted is that each was promoted for merit and not for any "pull" of political influence.

One of these four men is in the prime of life; the others are younger. Mr. White is fifty-six years old, Mr, Dudley forty-five, Mr. Riddle forty-two, while Mr. Griscom is only thirty-six.

Mr. White and Mr. Riddle were educated in this country and France, the history of diplomacy and in international law, in history and politics, and, above all, in that intimate knowledge of foreign countries which can best be obtained by a knowledge of their languages. Harvard and Columbia were supplemented by the École des Sciences Politiques and by the Collége de France. Mr. Riddle speaks fluently French, German, Italian, Spanish, Russian, and Rumanian.

Of the four appointees Mr. White is

COPYRIGHT, 1903, BY J. PURDY

HENRY WHITE
Now Ambassador to Italy; to be Ambassador to France

latter being a Harvard and Columbia Law School man. Mr. Griscom is a University of Pennsylvania graduate, both of the collegiate and law courses. Mr. Dudley is a graduate of Kenyon and of the law department of Columbia University. While the active practice of the law may first have attracted many of those who afterwards became clever diplomats, Mr. Riddle is one of the few men who from the first have resolutely set about fitting themselves for a diplomatic career. Long before he became a diplomatic agent he had grounded himself in the the oldest, the most experienced, the most distinguished, and perhaps the wealthiest. In his case no financial necessity could have greatly moved him to take up a livelihood. But many a rich American, as we may all be proud to recognize, feels it incumbent upon him to work at some profession, and to work as hard at it, too, as if he were dependent on it. Such energy has been so characteristic of Mr. White that none of his friends can think of associating the idea of money with him. For he knows and they know that his advancement has rested on no campaign contribution, nor is it supposed that he ever influenced a campaign contribution. When we consider that such financial evidence of party loyalty has sometimes formed the sole qualification of a candidate for diplomatic or consular honors, we may gratefully note its absence in this latest list of preferments.

With their respective records for service in mind, Henry White's promotion surprises no one; the others are surprises, more or less. Few have associated the Brazilian Embassy with Mr. Dudley's name; hardly any one could have thought of so young a man as Mr. Griscom stepping into the shoes of George P. Marsh; and certainly no one supposed that the time had quite come for Mr. Riddle's promotion to a post which he is certainly fitted to adorn. But last year the Secretary of State circumnavigated South America, and among the Ministers representing us on that continent he found more than one de-

serving reward. Hence we see John Barrett's efficient service at Bogotá recognized in a promotion to the headship of the International Bureau of American Republics, now to be a far more influential body than ever before; and we see Irving Bedell Dudley, who had been active in acquainting the Department of State with the exact situation in South America, invited to step up from ministerial rank at Lima to ambassadorial rank at Rio de Janeiro. Lloyd Carpenter Griscom, the retiring Ambassador at Rio, was a favorite of Mr. Hay's and enjoys the consideration of the present Secretary of State. He is rewarded by more exalted rank. He had his introduction to the diplomatic service as private secretary to Mr. Bayard when that statesman became first American Ambassador to England. It is believed that Mr. Griscom's record as Secretary at Constantinople, Minister at Teheran and Tokyo, and Ambassador at Rio will be consistently carried out at Rome. As to

PHOTOGRAPH BY R. MARUKI, TOKYO

LLOYD CARPENTER GRISCOM
Now Ambassador to Brazil; to be Ambassador to Italy

John Wallace Riddle, a comparatively poor man, with no great political backing, no one has associated him with any immediate appointment to an embassy where his predecessors have probably spent their entire salary in house-rent alone. Most patently this appointment rests on no campaign contribution nor any financial influence. If Mr. Riddle cannot vie with his predecessors in display of wealth, he can equal their personal service in a position which perhaps almost more than any other has required the exercise of infinite patience, tact, spirit, resource, and firmness. While he was serving as Secretary at the St. Petersburg embassy some years ago, having been promoted from the Constantinople secretaryship, his first office, the oppression of the Jews at Kishinev and other Russian cities attracted Colonel Hay's attention and indignation. The result was a message, including a petition in behalf of the Jews, from the President to the Czar, which, in the American Ambassador's absence, Mr. Riddle was to deliver personally to Count Lamsdorf, the Russian Foreign Minister. Mr. Riddle promptly went to the Foreign Office and read the entire despatch to Count Lamsdorf, including the petition, and *then* asked whether the Russian Government would be pleased to receive it. The Foreign Minister peremptorily declined, but Mr. Riddle had accomplished the object for which the President and his Secretary of State had striven. When Mr. Riddle left St. Petersburg, it was to go as Agent and Consul-General to Egypt, where he remained until he became Minister to Rumania and Servia, his present position. Mr. Riddle represents real, potent worth as do few.

Of course Henry White's is the longest and most distinguished record. He has been in the American diplomatic service over twenty years. He was, first, a Secretary at Vienna, then Second Secretary at London, and then First Secretary, a position which he held so

IRVING BEDELL DUDLEY
Now Minister to Peru; to be Ambassador to Brazil

long as seemingly to have a life tenure. He repeatedly acted as Chargé d'Affaires, and was also our representative at the International Conference for the Abolition of Sugar Bounties. Two years ago Mr. White became Ambassador to Italy. His Roman service has been characterized by the same broad grasp of subject and thorough attention to detail that characterized his London service. As regards long experience, knowing and appreciating the qualities of many men representing many social and political shades, Mr. White is emphatically an all-round diplomat. His aptness in correctly judging the persons with whom he is brought in contact is a quality which we like to think peculiarly American. It has been called a Yankee shrewdness, and so it is, but it is characteristic of many men born outside of Rudyard Kipling's pie-belt, as is seen in the present instance. If Mr. White is a born judge, he is also an entire democrat. Although accustomed to move everywhere in aristocratic circles, he is absolutely free from "a certain condescension," and has always served the poor man and the nobody as well as he has the rich man and the somebody. No one who has ever seen him in the official discharge of his duties at London or Rome can regret his appointment to a position where the demands upon him will be even greater, for, despite his long foreign sojourns, no more whole-souled American represents America abroad.

During the past twelvemonth Mr. White has enjoyed one distinction perhaps as great as any which may come to him in his new station, namely, participation in the International Moroccan Conference at Algeciras, Spain, as Special Ambassador from America. In the discharge of this duty Mr. White found himself in a peculiar position. He represented a country the interest of which in Morocco was almost entirely commercial. When the issue between France and Germany regarding that corner of Africa became acute, and even war was talked about by alarmists, Mr. White was the one, more than any other Ambassador at Algeciras, to whom the representatives of those two Powers turned as to an umpire. Largely, perhaps chiefly, through his efforts, an agreement was reached, hardly attainable otherwise. It is not too much to say that when the position of American Ambassador at London becomes again vacant there will be no more deserving candidate than Henry White.

In 1900 John Hay, alone of Foreign Secretaries, pursued a policy respecting China which was first scorned and scouted by the others, and finally adopted by them. Mr. Hay's clear prevision, resource, and frank courage placed America in the diplomatic world where she had never been before.

In 1905 Theodore Roosevelt, by the exercise of a diplomacy as persuasive as it was strenuous, brought together in a peace treaty the combatants in the greatest and fiercest war of modern times. Had there been any doubters as to America's diplomatic leadership, that leadership was then positively confirmed.

As we think of those two events, we Americans must also feel that the future may bring events in which it may be our privilege and our duty also to play a leading part. We shall always be ready with agents for that part if, in our Government service at home and abroad, we cast off whatever remains of the spoils system and perfect the merit system.

# THE DOGS OF WAR

## BY W. G. FITZ-GERALD

ITALIAN AMBULANCE AND SCOUT DOGS

E know the dog as policeman in Central Europe; as life-saver he has worked in the Alps for a thousand years. But the dog regularly enlisted in every great army of the world—whether in the Red Cross Department, or as scout and despatch-bearer—is surely something of a novelty.

In the Franco-Prussian War, out of 129,000 casualties, 13,000 were returned as "missing;" and who shall say what agony those unfortunates suffered? Every war of the future, however, will see the dog mitigating its horror. In Germany the education of the war dog is at this moment undertaken by a voluntary society with nearly two thousand members, among them some of the most distinguished officers in the world's greatest army.

The idea is not new. Xenophon tells us of Spartan dogs that wore huge spiked collars, and were probably used much as we used bloodhounds years ago against the once powerful Seminoles and Sioux. Again, there were the mastiffs that followed the Knights of Rhodes and scented out Turks miles away. The Dutch used them also in their age-long war with the Achinese, both as ambulance dogs and as dogs of war.

For there is a difference. The war dog proper is used for sentry, messenger, and scouting service; while the ambulance dog's training impels him only to scour the battlefield in search of the wounded and missing. That it is unsafe to use one dog for another's work was seen in the recent great German maneuvers, when an ambulance dog was sent on a message, and, having found a man really wounded, through being dismounted and trampled in a cavalry charge, he remained pathetically behind with him, and forgot all about the real business upon which he had been sent!

The exigencies of modern warfare not only necessitate an enormous extension of the battlefield, but also compel the troops to take every possible advantage of natural cover. This and the fact that wounded men will use their last strength to seek protection from artillery fire, cavalry charges, and the wheels of galloping guns, in such places as thick bushes, ditches, and natural holes, will show how difficult it is for the overworked stretcher-bearers of the Red Cross Department to notice prostrate figures not readily seen. Moreover, it must be borne in mind that modern warfare is carried on very largely by night attack, and at night, too, the wounded have to be collected.

The clever modern electric and acetylene searchlights are useful only for open country; and in broken ground the brighter the light, the darker are the shadows thrown. The ambulance dog, however, is entirely independent of artificial light, and relies only on his extraordinary power of scent. Last year, during the great Austrian maneuvers, two hundred men were left lying on the field to represent the wounded; and the stretcher-bearers, working against time, overlooked thirty-eight of these. Within twenty minutes the Viennese dogs had discovered them all.

Each dog carries about his neck a flask containing brandy or soup and also a roll of bandages. The wounded man, having made what use he can of this relief, gives the dog his cap or belt, and the intelligent creature at once races off with it to the ambulance attendants, whom he conducts to the rescue with all speed.

A great authority on the dogs of war, like Surgeon-General Haecker or General von Herget—both of the German Staff—can tell marvelous stories of the dogs which the Allied Troops took with them to China for the suppression of the Boxer rebellion. The Italian dogs especially distinguished themselves, having had great training on the mountains of Savoy; they were collies chiefly, and had long been employed with the Bersagliere troops in their operations on the Italian side of Mont Blanc. These dogs had frequently rescued soldiers who had tumbled into crevasses or had fallen frostbitten on the march.

Some of them, by the way, took a very active part in the mimic warfare, for they carried a canvas satchel connected across their loins with a belt of light bent-wood, intended for the conveyance of ammuni-

TEACHING A NEW CANINE RECRUIT THE IDEA OF "SEARCH"
A man is lying prostrate within

tion to the firing line. The French in Algeria have also used dogs in this way in their warfare with the Arabs. One canine favorite with the Oran garrison was three years ago decorated with the stripes of a corporal, and has just been raised to the rank of a full "sergeant" on account of his preternatural sagacity! He is one of those rare dogs who can be used indifferently as scout, sentry, despatch-bearer, or seeker for the wounded on the battlefield.

His name is "Toto," and his education commenced at the age of eight months. He is a Russian Borzoi, and he and his inseparable mate, a German boarhound, are considered among the most valuable members of the garrison. They do not even mind being harnessed to light ambulance carts and assisting to haul the wounded to the hospital tent or wagon, after they have found them prostrate on the field.

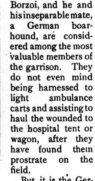

But it is the German army authorities who have adopted war dogs on the largest scale, and thus stamped the institution with the seal of permanent value.

General von Herget, speaking after a series of experiments with ambulance dogs, remarked: "However great the progress made in the Army Medical Department in the treatment of wounded, the comforts of science can only be applied when the wounded have been found; and this question is an exceedingly difficult one in modern war, with a vastly extended battle-front, night attacks, and the imperious necessity for taking cover. Indeed, in many cases the rendering of aid to missing wounded is impossible without some special help such as is ideally afforded by these dogs."

Austria, Switzerland, Great Britain,

RED CROSS SEARCHERS FOR THE WOUNDED AND MESSENGERS OF THE BRITISH ARMY

Holland, Italy, and France followed the greatest of military powers in this matter; and now the dog is thoroughly established in the battlefield as a unit of high value. It is realized that hundreds if not thousands of men may owe their lives to canine searchers, or at least the mitigation of terrible suffering, such as the dreadful thirst resulting from loss of blood.

The Russian army in Manchuria employed hundreds of specially trained collies, and Captain Persidsky, of the late Count Keller's staff, reported to his chief: "In finding the missing and wounded with which the millet fields were strewn, nothing even approached our pack of seven English dogs. In our last engagement fifty-three men were found more or less badly wounded in utterly unsuspected places, where the stretcher-bearers and the surgeons would never have even dreamed of looking."

On another occasion with the Russians all the wounded were found by the dogs in places where otherwise they could not have been discovered at all, but would merely have been reported "missing." In the most recent German maneuvers, when the Emperor himself commanded a division of thirty thousand troops of all arms, with its due complement of dogs, the officers of the Prussian Jaeger regiments found the performance of the ambulance dogs beyond all expectations.

Under most unfavorable conditions— a broiling sun, among total strangers, in close, overgrown country unknown to the dogs, and with an entire lack of scent except that of numerous foxes and other game—they carried out their work of finding the "wounded" with unerring

zeal. Prince Adolf, of Schaumburg Lippe, had a night trial at Bonn, when the dogs discovered casualties which could not be found at all by even the most experienced of the ambulance men. Similar trials were carried out by Captain Cistola, head of the Ambulance Dog Establishment in Rome, which has been subsidized by the Italian Government, with surprising results.

As to Great Britain, every year her War Office authorities carry out exhaustive tests of war dogs, both at Aldershot and in the great territory recently acquired for military purposes on Salisbury Plain. The scene during one of these night trials is most weird and impressive.

Long shafts of dazzling light thrown by portable searchlights sweep the entire range of rugged, boulder-strewn common, and under these rays the engineers and dogs glide silently through bracken and undergrowth seeking for men supposed to have been wounded

ONE OF THE POWERFUL BELGIAN HOUNDS USED BY THE RUSSIANS AS SENTRIES AND SCOUTS IN MANCHURIA

in a battle just fought, with a front extending over fifteen miles. The dogs had been specially trained in Forfarshire, Scotland, by Major E. Hautonville Richardson, of Carnoustie; and the way in which they corrected the human searchers by bringing to light supposed casualties in out-of-the-way places had to be seen to be believed.

As the bearer sections advanced, with the Major and his dogs, the collies would be loosed from their leash with the sharp words, "Seek, laddie!" Instantly the eager and powerful animal would spring into the undergrowth, nosing silently and swiftly among the bushes and long grass, ever searching and racing, and covering more ground

TRAINING A DOG TO ATTEND A WOUNDED MAN ON
THE FIELD OF BATTLE—GERMAN ARMY MANEUVERS

in one minute than one of the ambulance-bearers would in a quarter of an hour.

Jangling bells about the dogs' necks enabled them to be followed easily by the stretcher-bearers. After a few thrilling minutes in the darkness, with the vast blinding beams from the searchlights playing this way and that, a bell that had been carefully followed would suddenly cease ringing, and a low, piercing whine from the collie would proclaim a " find."

Hurrying to the spot, the officer and his stretcher-bearers would find the soldier lying collapsed and prostrate on the ground, feigning to be very far gone indeed. He was lifted tenderly on to the canvas stretchers, while his savior gave a series of low delighted barks and wagged his tail as the Major rewarded him with kind words and caressing hand.

The dog immediately resumed his search for the next casualty; and soon the cry of " Bearer company " from out of the darkness would bring the stretcher men up at the run. After this, for some time, the dog searched over a large area

in vain. Suddenly he plunged into a dense growth of bracken on the left flank of a hill. Major Richardson judged that this was too far away for any wounded men to be found, and called him back.

But the dog ignored him, and, as no bell could be heard, the eager creature was followed, and found standing over two prostrate " wounded " almost wholly buried in ferns and bushes.

In Germany the war dog plays many parts besides searching for the wounded. Thus he guards baggage, and will carry despatches at great speed and with many wiles, escaping rifle-shot and bursting shell (he is thoroughly accustomed to both), and getting through an enemy's lines where cavalryman or trooper would merely court inevitable destruction.

The training of the dogs is by no means easy, and calls for sympathy, insight, and immense patience. They vary in intelligence, just as human beings do; and some of them readily see what is required of them and take to the work with great zest. As regards their equipment, the great military na-

220

tions have various systems. Bungartz, in Germany, equips his dogs with a saddle which has several pockets, in which are placed neat bandages and surgical dressings; while round the animal's neck is a small barrel with brandy or other stimulant.

Captain Cistola, the Italian authority, places his flask in the pockets of the saddle. Colonel Malentieff, the Russian staff officer charged with the instruction and maintenance of war dogs, provides his four-footed soldiers with lanterns. Major Richardson, however, the English military trainer, considers that the equipment should be as simple as possible. He thinks the bandages and stimulant unnecessary, since British troops carry all their "first aid" dressing on their person. Also, he points out that if a wounded man were able intelligently to take the bandages and stimulants from the dog, he would surely be in a fit state to call out for the stretcher-bearers. Undoubtedly the extra weight of these articles hinders the action of the canine scout.

"My own dogs," he told the writer, "wear a very light canvas saddle with no pockets, but with the Geneva Cross on flaps at either side. Each wears a leather collar and a loud bell. They are attached in relays to the bearer companies of the Ambulance Corps; also to companies of the Royal Army Medical Corps, and to volunteer bearer companies."

Their real use is now internationally acknowledged, as we have seen; and this is especially felt after a battle, when the searchers have collected all the wounded that are visible, and yet it is known from the roll-call that many are still "missing." The great difficulty lies in having dogs trained and ready in sufficient numbers. For it is utterly useless to take untrained dogs into the field in time of war.

A model establishment is, perhaps, that of Italy, where, in the Roman military headquarters, there is a regular training establishment for the "dogs of war," and a large stud of dogs are kept in constant training in peace time. And hither officers come from all parts of the country, from the Alps to Mount Etna, to get practical instruction in the value, selection, and education of the dogs.

ONE OF THE WAR COLLIES OF THE BRITISH ARMY RETURNING WITH A MESSAGE IN HIS POCKET. HE HAS TRAVERSED SIX MILES OF COUNTRY

HENRY CHURCHILL KING

# CREATIVE AMERICANS

## HENRY CHURCHILL KING

### LEADER IN THEOLOGICAL THOUGHT

#### BY WASHINGTON GLADDEN

R. Drummond says that while the New Jerusalem was the proper object of John's faith, because the old Jerusalem was John's city, the vision which should kindle our enthusiasm is not of the new Jerusalem, but of the new Glasgow, the new Boston, the new Chicago, the new Columbus, or whatever city or town may be our home. The new Chicago is waiting in the heavens above the old one—waiting to come down to earth as soon as the people on the ground get ready for it and call it down.

Other cities, great and small, have experienced this transformation. Some of the worst are much less bad than once they were, and some of the best are a great deal better.

It may not have been widely published, but it is a fact that there is a new Oberlin. It has been coming down out of heaven from God for a number of years, but of late the descent has been more rapid and notable. The Oberlin of to-day, in its physical features, in its intellectual attitude, is quite a different community from that of fifty years ago, or even of twenty-five years ago. I do not think that the fundamental moral convictions or tendencies have greatly changed, but the horizon has been extended and the outlook has widened. More than one hand has helped to lay the foundations on which the new Oberlin has been descending out of heaven from God; that calm and courageous thinker, James Fairchild, had much to do with them; that seer and master of assemblies, Edward I. Bosworth, has been busy

upon them. But the master builder of the new Oberlin is its present President, Henry Churchill King.

Of the place which President King holds in the hearts of the new generation of Oberlin men and women I have had some opportunities of judging. A few years ago, when he was teaching philosophy in the College, it was my privilege to hear him deliver a "Thursday Lecture" to the students in the chapel. The old building was packed to the doors, and the welcome which the students gave him when he rose to speak was itself a revelation. The lecture was a rather stiff scientific discussion of the psychological principles underlying conduct; it was unsparing as surgery, but it was tender as maternity, and it was good to look into those students' faces and see how this serious appeal in which there was never a tone of "jollying" held their thought and gripped their consciences. When the hour's address was ended, the volley of sustained applause was a tribute that did equal credit to speaker and hearers. From that hour I had no doubt who ought to be the President of Oberlin.

Three years ago, at his inauguration, I had the honor of walking with President King in the procession to the church, and when the long line opened order and let us march through, the greeting that he received was something to remember. The faculty and the alumni, especially the later ones, were enthusiastic enough, but the undergraduates—what a passion of loyalty, of admiration, of affection, it was that shone from their eyes and rang in their voices! To have won such regard as this from thousands of young men and women is a greater

223

service to education than to have created half a dozen quadrangles or to have gathered ten millions of endowments.

There is no mystery about the method by which Henry King has won for himself, and for the things for which he stands, the allegiance of his students. He is willing to know the truth, and he is willing that they should know it. He treats them with the utmost candor. He is not afraid of facts. I remember hearing him describe a meeting at which a great body of young Bible students had been misled by a cowardly and disingenuous obscurantism. "I determined," he said, "that the students at Oberlin should not, if I could help it, go out into the world without knowing the truth about the Bible. It is safe for them to know it, and it is not safe for them to be ignorant of it." President King believes in the "square deal" in the class room, even when theology and criticism are under discussion. And yet he is as far as possible from being an iconoclast. His reverence for old truth is as tender as his hospitality to new truth is cordial. He is too good an evolutionist to be a despiser of the ways in which the Spirit has been leading the churches. And while it is always fresh truth that he gives you, you know that it is vitally related to the life of the past generations.

Dr. King has been closely identified with Oberlin from an early age. He graduated from the College in the class of 1879, and from the Seminary in 1882; taught Latin and mathematics for several years in the Academy; occupied the chair of mathematics for six years in the College, and that of philosophy for about the same period; and since 1897 has been the professor of theology in the theological seminary, carrying that burden along with the presidency of the University since 1902. But for a year or two of post-graduate study at Harvard and a similar period at Berlin, his scholastic life has all been spent at Oberlin. Strong influences have sought to remove him to other positions of honor and usefulness, but they have not greatly tempted him. Yet his influence is by no means confined to the lines which proceed from Oberlin. Thinking men of all sects and sections are his debtors; he is distinctly

one of the stimulating forces of theological and sociological thought at the beginning of this century.

The four volumes in which President King has challenged the attention of his contemporaries are: "Reconstruction in Theology" (1901); "Theology and the Social Consciousness" (1902); "Personal and Ideal Elements in Education" (1904), and "Rational Living" (1905). The third of these is a collection of addresses; the other three are consecutive treatises on the themes indicated in their titles.

The first of these books frankly confronts the demand for a thorough restatement of theological theories. Twenty-five years ago there arose in Oberlin a demand for the reshaping of the theology of the Congregational churches. Those who gave voice to this demand pointed out that the only body of doctrine to which the Congregationalists of this country had ever committed themselves was the Savoy Confession, and that the churches had, undeniably, moved far away from that, and ought not to be under the suspicion of adhering to any such antiquated symbol. Their contention prevailed to this extent, that the National Council appointed a Commission who prepared and published, on their own authority, what was known as "The Creed of 1883." That was regarded as a great improvement. It was, indeed, free from many of the fatalistic and unethical elements contained in the elder symbol, but its constructive idea was still that political or monarchical conception by which the whole of Western theology has been shaped since the days of Augustine. This forensic figure has more than served its time; it is wholly out of harmony with the prevailing modes of thought; and President King has helped us to see the need of setting it aside and substituting for it a more spiritual conception of our relation to God.

The most important contribution which President King has made to theology is in the clearness and power with which he has set forth the fact that religion is purely a personal relation, and not in any but a very subordinate sense a political or legal relation, to God; and that all our explanations of the religious life must be given in terms of this ruling idea. "Such a personal relation," he says, "when adequately conceived, has no need to be supplemented by any other notion, as of government. It contains in itself the whole truth. The fact is not that we are in personal relations to God and *also* in relations to his government; we are in relation to the government of God because, and in that, we are in personal relation to God."

Such a conception wonderfully simplifies our theological problems. We see at once that most of our difficulties have arisen from our attempts to adjust the schemes of political and juridical machinery which we have constructed out of our own heads for the divine administration.

It helps us, also, to put into a perfectly intelligible statement the facts of the religious life. For, if religion is a personal relation to God, "it means that all the experiences of the Christian life may best be brought under the phenomena of friendship; that its highest possible attainments may be best considered as a deepening friendship; that the conditions may be best known and best definitely formulated as conditions of a deepening friendship. This conception of the Christian life as friendship is fundamental and thoroughgoing, with wide implications. It has often been used in an illustrative way as an analogy; but, so far as the writer knows, it has never been carried thoroughly through in all the aspects of Christian life and experience and thinking as the nearest approach man can make to the final realities of religion. It is far more than an analogy; it is a fact; our relation to God *is* a personal relation, and its laws must be those of personal relations. To say so is only to interpret religion by the very highest in ourselves, and this is our best and only adequate key."

Following this light, we readily see that sin is the violation or the loss of this friendship with God; that redemption or salvation is the restoration of this friendship. And when we comprehend how much it sometimes costs the friend who has been sinned against to repair the broken bond, we have some hint of the nature of what we call atonement. Redemption, in such a case, must always mean the cost "of reverently, patiently, to the bitter end helping another to conquer himself—the inevitable suffering of all redemptive endeavor for those whom one loves. This involves suffering in contact with sin, suffering in the rejection of those sinning, and, most of all, suffering in the sin itself of those one loves because one loves them—suffering which is the more intense the more one loves."

Not only on the side of redemption is this conception fruitful, but it is especially so on the side of sanctification or growth in grace, as shown in the lucid setting forth of the conditions of a deepening friendship with God.

The second volume of the series I have named, "The Theology of the Social Consciousness," makes large use, also, of this personal element. The social consciousness, in President King's view, is a profoundly interesting fact, as it must be to any theologian who believes that God is always in his world; and it must furnish at once the source and the test of the true theology. Dr. King defines the social consciousness simply as the "growing sense of the real brotherhood of men," and he finds in it five elements—"a deepening sense (1) of the likeness or like-mindedness of men; (2) of their mutual influence; (3) of the value and sacredness of the person; (4) of mutual obligation, and (5) of love." The presence of these elements among the ruling ideas of our time cannot be doubted, and their significance for religion and for theology this book most luminously sets forth.

The "deepening sense of brotherhood" is the same phenomenon which Benjamin Kidd describes as the accumulation of "a great fund of altruistic feeling" in the social consciousness; and such a fact will have consequences for theology. Not a few of the old conceptions will find it impossible to live in such an atmosphere. Just how it is affecting dogmatic theology President King points out.

Take the elements into which he analyzes the deepening sense of brotherhood, and apply them to the problems of theology. The conviction of "the like-mindedness of men" is the first of these. This, according to Professor Giddings, is the fundamental reason for society. Men are associated because they possess this "consciousness of kind;" it is this that holds them together. This means that deeper than all the differences are the unities of human nature, that in the fundamental interests of life we are alike. Burns's "A man's a man for a' that" is the voice of this conviction. "The uniform experience of social workers, that really knowing 'how the other half lives' brings increasing sympathy, also affirms the fundamental likeness of men."

A generation imbued with this notion can never believe that there are any "prime favorites with God," and thus the old partialism goes glimmering into the outer darkness where it belongs. "We are slowly learning to see the likeness under the differences, and so to transcend the differences even between Occidental and Oriental. And this means much, not only for our practical missionary putting of the truth, but also for our final theological statements. They will inevitably grow simpler, larger, more universally human, and at the same time more deep and solid." The missionaries are finding this out; it was the note struck most often and with deepest conviction at the Haystack celebration.

This conception makes room for a larger belief in men, and a stronger hope for them, and enables us to discern, even beneath theological disagreements, an essential unity. "There is doubtless much 'unconscious Christianity,' much 'unconscious following of Christ.' And we are only following Christ's own counsel when we refuse to forbid the man who is working a good work in his name, though he follows not with us. Certainly, if we accept the witness of a man's life against the witness of his lips when the witness of his lips is right, we ought to accept the witness of his life against the witness of his lips when the witness of his lips is wrong."

The second element in the social consciousness, the growing sense of "the mutual influence of men."—of the fact that they are "members one of another"—produces also its theological consequences. "That we are bound up in one bundle of life with all men and cannot live an isolated life if we would; that we do influence one another whether we will or not, and tend unconsciously to draw others to our level and are ourselves drawn to theirs; that we joy and sorrow together whether we will or not, and grow or deteriorate together," that this is the way we are meant to live, and that the good of life, if we ever win it, will be won through this mutual influence—all this must be taken into account when we frame our theological theories. That character is made only in this way, and that salvation is character, is the fundamental fact. Our explanation of God's ways of winning and saving men must recognize this fact. Our soteriology must make room for this principle. "All the realities in the problem of redeeming a man from sin to righteousness are intensely personal, ethical, spiritual." "Christ saves us, in the only certain way we know that any man is ever saved to better living, through direct contagion of character, through his immediate influence upon us." "The self-giving on the part of one trying to win another into character must precede the self-giving of the sinner; for the sinner's own willingness to yield himself to the influence of the character of the other must first of all be won. This initial winning of the co-operative will of the other is the heart of the whole battle."

The third element of the social consciousness, the growing sense of the sacredness of the person, is perhaps the most potent of all in its effect upon theology. This is enforced by President King in many impressive ways. It helps us to hold fast to the real personality of God; not things, nor forces, nor systems, but persons, are of prime importance: for them all things are and were created; and the Creator who has put such honor upon persons can hardly, himself, be less than a Person.

This reverence for the person which the social consciousness emphasizes falls in with all Christ's methods of dealing with men, and we are beginning to understand his methods and to interpret

God in accordance with them. "That glimpse which the Revelation gives us of Christ standing and knocking at the heart's closed door is a true picture for evermore, not only of the attitude of Christ's earthly life, but of God's eternal relation to us. Men may override and outrage us, and even think that they show the more love thereby; God never. . . . The definite bestowal of the fateful gift of moral freedom, with the practical certainty of sin—the creation of beings who could sin against him— shows how deeply implanted in the very being of God is this principle of reverence for the person."

The principles of morality cannot change when spirits pass from one life to another. The sacredness of the person will be respected in all worlds. There will be no withdrawal of the freedom once given, and no doors will ever be shut against the returning prodigal. "If, then, the abstract possibility of endless resistance to God cannot be denied, so neither can the possibility—perhaps one might even say the practical probability—be denied that God, in his infinite love and patience and wisdom, may finally win them all out of their resistance. And the eternal hope is at least open; but it is open, it should be noted, only upon the fulfillment by men of those moral conditions which hold now in the earthly life, and which ought now to be obeyed. There will never be an easier way to God. It is shallow thinking which supposes that if there be any possibility of turning to God in the future life it is of small moment that one should now put himself where he ought to be. The full results of our evil sowing we must receive. The utmost that on any rational theory, then, can be held out to men is the hope that, facing a greater heritage of evil than now they face, they might return to God under the same condition of absolute surrender that now holds and the fulfillment of which is now far more easily possible to them."

Such are a few examples of the reaction which President King has traced of the social consciousness upon theology—of the modifications which the Zeitgeist is making in our philosophy of religion.

One might question whether it is safe to permit the social consciousness thus to reconstruct theology. Safe or unsafe, the thing is going on and we are not likely to stop it. We may reassure ourselves by the reflection that all these changes are in the direction of a more Christian conception of God and his relation to man. The social consciousness is more Christian than theology is; it is the Christian elements in the social consciousness that are getting themselves incorporated into theology.

The fact seems to be that the living Christ finds his way into the thoughts and lives of men more readily than into the theological systems. Thus the sentiments and feelings of the people become more thoroughly Christianized than are the philosophical theories of religion; and the social consciousness reacts upon theology and shapes it according to the mind of Christ. This is the history of doctrine; all the great changes have been the result of a purified ethical sentiment. Dr. King is looking in the right place for his causes; his method is scientifically accurate.

The other two books, of which I have little room to speak, are full of very stimulating reading. The closing address of the volume entitled "Personal and Ideal Elements in Education" is upon the question "How to Make a Rational Fight for Character." It is a masterly handling of this great theme. I know of nothing finer in the language in the way of practical counsels to young men.

The volume entitled "Rational Living" follows, somewhat, the lines of this address, but extends and deepens them. It takes up the four great inferences from modern psychology—"Life is complex; man is a unity; will and action are of central importance; and the real is concrete"—and undertakes to apply them to the practical problems of conduct. The freshness and vigor of these discussions are notable. Last summer I took this book into the midweek service of my church, and read the greater part of it, on the Wednesday evenings of July and August; and the attendance on those midsummer evenings was larger than it is apt to be in the cooler months. The interest of the people in these practical applications of the new psychology to the problems of the Christian life deepened to the end of the readings. That may serve as an indication of the manner in which this teacher is able to popularize great themes.

President King is yet a young man; he was born in 1858. The contribution which he has already made to theological and ethical science is very valuable; let us hope that the administration of his great university will leave him time and strength for larger tasks in the coming years. In few of our teachers is there a happier blending of courageous intellect, irenic femper, moral thoroughness, and religious earnestness. The splendid body of young men who are just now coming to the front in all parts of the land as teachers and preachers and journalists will find in him a brave and safe leader.

## LYRICS UNSUNG

### BY EDITH M. THOMAS

Oh, believe not those who say,
Song hath had its Perfect Day !
Tones of infinite sweet change
Tremble past our hearing's range;
Rays beyond the violet
Eyes of ours behold not yet !
Here a gage will I throw down—
*We are not the ages' crown :*
After us are coming those
To whose senses shall unclose
Beauty hidden from our sight
In a fold of common light—
Music, shut in Eol's cell,
Sweeter far than Arion's shell
Touched to soothe the savage sea !

Who will answer this to me,
When I ask if any deem
That the poet's song and dream
Have not reaches unexplored—
Deeps unsounded—heights unsoared?
Nay ! To every race and tongue
There are lyrics yet unsung !
For this life of man keeps pace
To a Mighty Step in space ;
And the mists that round us drift
Ever more and more uplift !
Oh, the Father still creates ;
And the child in wonder waits,
Ready, new delights to find
Where, before, the eyes were blind—
Where, before, the ears were dead !
So, I say, as I have said :
There are lyrics yet unsung—
Unto harps as yet not strung '

WILLIAM AUSTIN

# PETER RUGG, THE MISSING MAN

### BY WILLIAM AUSTIN

#### WITH AN INTRODUCTION BY HAMILTON W. MABIE

**T**HE opinion that Americans are materialists, so widely held in Europe and so often enforced with more heat than light by a small group of our own writers and a larger group of Americans resident in foreign parts, will strike students half a century hence as one of those curiosities of partial observation and mistaken judgment which furnish the pages of history with innumerable warnings. The most casual acquaintance with American literature shows how misled and misleading this opinion is; how strikingly American prose and poetry have revealed, from the beginning, an idealistic temper. The early New England writers were much more concerned with the safety of their souls than with the comfort of their bodies; Freneau, Hopkinson, and Woolman, in the section now known as the Middle States, were intensely preoccu-

229

pied with the struggle for independence or the direct communion of the spirit with its Maker; Smith, Byrd, Beverley, in Virginia, wrote of strange adventures in a new world, of men and affairs, with the wit, intelligence, alertness, of accomplished men of the world, or of historical occurrences with a grave reserve and sometimes with a sober eloquence. "The next favor I would ask of him," wrote Robert Beverley in a half-serious address to his reader, "should be not to criticise too unmercifully upon my style."

The background of the supernatural against which life in New England moved for many decades, and of the marvelous and mysterious in nature which deeply affected the imagination of the Southern colonists, or of the adventurous settlers who crossed the Alleghanies or advanced up the Mohawk Valley, tinged a good deal of early writing with a sense of wonder, and fostered the love of the marvelous and the unseen. Of this kind of writing, which Hawthorne and Poe were to carry close to the line of perfection, "Peter Rugg, the Missing Man," is a very interesting though very little known example. Its author, William Austin, was an important figure in his own time, though his name does not appear in the indexes of many books on American literature. He belongs to the earliest period of the first considerable literary movement in this country; for he was born in Charlestown, Massachusetts, in March, 1778, three years after the battle of Lexington. He was graduated from Harvard twenty years later and began the study of law. He appears, however, to have been as deeply interested in his avocations as in his vocation, and foremost among these was the writing of books. His activity in politics is suggested by the fact that early in the last century he was wounded in a duel, the culmination of a political quarrel. Among the publications which bore his name were a collection of "Letters from London," an "Oration on the Anniversary of the Battle of Bunker Hill," "The Late Joseph Natterson," and an "Essay on the Human Character of Jesus Christ."

None of these attracted the attention or gained the popularity of "Peter Rugg, the Missing Man," which appeared in the New England Galaxy about 1824, and which is reprinted in the very useful "Library of American Literature" edited by Mr. Stedman and Miss Hutchinson (now Mrs. Royal Cortissoz). It is probable that the story in the form in which it was originally written was identical with that which The Outlook gives its readers this week as the second of the twelve short stories of permanent interest to appear in the twelve Magazine Numbers for 1907; and that its popularity led Austin to write a kind of sequel, describing Peter Rugg's journeys as far south as Virginia, and his final return to Boston. This addition, which weakens rather than deepens the impression of the mysterious and fateful which the story conveys, will be found in "The Library of American Literature."

The motives of "Peter Rugg"—for it has two motives—are very old; the man who is driven on to a destination which he never reaches, and the man who loses the consciousness of time and awakes to find his world wholly changed, are familiar figures in the legends of many countries. In many of these stories the offense which brings down the penalty is, as in this story, the audacious assertion of the will against the higher powers. In the changed Boston to which Peter Rugg returns in the sequel there is a suggestion of "Rip Van Winkle," which appeared in "The Sketch Book" in 1819; but the story has the spirit of Charles Brockden Brown, of Hawthorne, and of Poe, rather than of Irving, whose genial feeling invested with perennial charm the career of the lovable vagabond, and gave his awakening on the lonely slope of the Catskills a touch of humor. "Twice Told Tales" did not appear until more than a decade after the publication of "Peter Rugg;" the earliest of Poe's stories of mystery and terror was not published until 1831. It is evident, therefore, that neither Hawthorne nor Poe influenced the author of "Peter Rugg." Charles Brockden Brown, the first American who followed Letters as a profession, and whose tales turn largely on mysterious persons and happenings and deal in somnambulism, ventriloquism, various forms of insanity, presentiments and dreams, died in 1810, and "Arthur Mervyn," "Ormond," "Edgar Huntly," and "Wieland" were probably in the hands of William Austin, and may have had something to do, by way of suggestion, with the single story that is likely to survive the oblivion which has overtaken the "Letters from London." It is too late to settle this question, and it is of slight importance. The story of the man who was driven relentlessly on through storm and time remains an interesting and significant achievement of our early literature.                                    H. W. M.

## FROM JONATHAN DUNWELL OF NEW YORK, TO MR. HERMANN KRAUFF

SIR,—Agreeably to my promise, I now relate to you all the particulars of the lost man and child which I have been able to collect. It is entirely owing to the humane interest you seemed to take in the report, that I have pursued the inquiry to the following result.

You may remember that business called me to Boston in the summer of 1820. I sailed in the packet to Providence, and when I arrived there I learned that every seat in the stage was engaged. I was thus obliged either to wait a few hours or accept a seat with the driver, who civilly offered me that accommodation. Accordingly I took my seat by his side, and soon found him intelligent and communicative.

When we had traveled about ten miles, the horses suddenly threw their ears on their necks, as flat as a hare's. Said the driver, "Have you a surtout with you?" "No," said I; "why do you ask?" "You will want one soon," said he; "do you observe the ears of all the horses?" "Yes, and was just about to ask the reason." "They see the storm-breeder, and we shall see him soon." At this moment there was not a cloud visible in the firmament. Soon after a small speck appeared in the road. "There," said my companion, "comes the storm-breeder; he always leaves a Scotch mist behind him. By many a wet jacket do I remember him. I suppose the poor fellow suffers much himself, much more than is known to the world." Presently a man with a child beside him, with a large black horse, and a weather-beaten chair, once built for a chaise body, passed in great haste, apparently at the rate of twelve miles an hour. He seemed to grasp the reins of his horse with firmness, and appeared to anticipate his speed. He seemed dejected, and looked anxiously at the passengers, particularly at the stage-driver and myself. In a moment after he passed us, the horses' ears were up and bent themselves forward so that they nearly met. "Who is that man?" said I; "he seems in great trouble." "Nobody knows who he is, but his person and the child are familiar to me. I have met them more than a hundred times, and have been so often asked the way to Boston by that man, even when he was traveling directly from that town, that of late I have refused any communication with him, and that is the reason he gave me such a fixed look." "But does he never stop anywhere?" "I have never known him to stop anywhere longer than to inquire the way to Boston; and, let him be where he may, he will tell you he cannot stay a moment, for he must reach Boston that night."

We were now ascending a high hill in Walpole, and as we had a fair view of the heavens, I was rather disposed to jeer the driver for thinking of his surtout, as not a cloud as big as a marble could be discerned. "Do you look," said he, "in the direction whence the man came, that is the place to look; the storm never meets him, it follows him." We presently approached another hill, and when at the height, the driver pointed out in an eastern direction a little black speck about as big as a hat. "There," said he, "is the seed storm; we may possibly reach Polley's before it reaches us, but the wanderer and his child will go to Providence through rain, thunder, and lightning." And now the horses, as though taught by instinct, hastened with increased speed. The little black cloud came on rolling over the turnpike, and doubled and trebled itself in all directions. The appearance of this cloud attracted the notice of all the passengers; for after it had spread itself to a great bulk, it suddenly became more limited in circumference, grew more compact, dark, and consolidated. And now the successive flashes of chain lightning caused the whole cloud to appear like a sort of irregular network, and displayed a thousand fantastic images. The driver bespoke my attention to a remarkable configuration in the cloud; he said every flash of lightning near its center discovered to him distinctly the form of a man sitting in an open carriage drawn by a black horse. But in truth I saw no such thing. The man's fancy was doubtless at fault. It is a very common thing for the imagination to paint for the senses, both in the visible and invisible world.

In the meantime the distant thunder gave notice of a shower at hand, and just as we reached Polley's tavern the rain poured down in torrents. It was soon over, the cloud passing in the direction of the turnpike towards Providence. In a few moments after, a respectable-looking man in a chaise stopped at the door. The man and child in the chair having excited some little sympathy among the passengers, the gentleman was asked if he had observed them. He said he had met them; that the man seemed bewildered, and inquired the way to Boston; that he was driving at great speed, as though he expected to outstrip the tempest; that the moment he had

passed him a thunderclap broke distinctly over the man's head and seemed to envelop both man and child, horse and carriage. "I stopped," said the gentleman, "supposing the lightning had struck him, but the horse only seemed to loom up and increase his speed, and, as well as I could judge, he traveled just as fast as the thunder cloud." While this man was speaking, a peddler with a cart of tin merchandise came up, all dripping; and, on being questioned, he said he had met that man and carriage, within a fortnight, in four different States; that at each time he had inquired the way to Boston, and that a thunder shower like the present had each time deluged him, his wagon and his wares, setting his tin pots, etc., afloat, so that he had determined to get marine insurance done for the future. But that which excited his surprise most was the strange conduct of his horse, for that, long before he could distinguish the man in the chair, his own horse stood still in the road and flung back his ears. "In short," said the peddler, "I wish never to see that man and horse again; they do not look to me as if they belonged to this world."

This is all that I could learn at that time; and the occurrence soon after would have become with me like one of those things which had never happened, had I not, as I stood recently on the doorstep of Bennett's hotel in Hartford, heard a man say, "There goes Peter Rugg and his child! he looks wet and weary, and farther from Boston than ever." I was satisfied it was the same man that I had seen more than three years before; for whoever has once seen Peter Rugg can never after be deceived as to his identity. "Peter Rugg!" said I, "and who is Peter Rugg?" "That," said the stranger, "is more than any one can tell exactly. He is a famous traveler, held in light esteem by all inn-holders, for he never stops to eat, drink, or sleep. I wonder why the Government does not employ him to carry the mail." "Ay," said a bystander, "that is a thought bright only on one side. How long would it take, in that case, to send a letter to Boston? For Peter has already, to my knowledge, been more than twenty years traveling to that place." "But," said I, "does the man never stop anywhere, does he never converse with any one? I saw the same man more than three years since, near Providence, and I heard a strange story about him. Pray, sir, give me some account of this man." "Sir," said the stranger, "those who know the most respecting that man say the least. I have heard it asserted that heaven sometimes sets a mark on a man, either for a judgment or a trial. Under which Peter Rugg now labors I cannot say; therefore I am rather inclined to pity than to judge." "You speak like a humane man," said I, "and if you have known him so long, I pray you will give me some account of him. Has his appearance much altered in that time?" "Why, yes; he looks as though he never ate, drank, or slept; and his child looks older than himself; and he looks like time broke off from eternity and anxious to gain a resting-place." "And how does his horse look?" said I. "As for his horse, he looks fatter and gayer, and shows more animation and courage, than he did twenty years ago. The last time Rugg spoke to me he inquired how far it was to Boston. I told him just one hundred miles. 'Why,' said he, 'how can you deceive me so? It is cruel to deceive a traveler. I have lost my way. Pray direct me the nearest way to Boston.' I repeated it was one hundred miles. 'How can you say so?' said he. 'I was told last evening it was but fifty, and I have traveled all night.' 'But,' said I, 'you are now traveling from Boston. You must turn back.' 'Alas!' said he, 'it is all turn back! Boston shifts with the wind, and plays all around the compass. One man tells me it is to the east, another to the west; and the guide-posts, too, they all point the wrong way.' 'But will you not stop and rest?' said I; 'you seem wet and weary.' 'Yes,' said he, 'it has been foul weather since I left home.' 'Stop, then, and refresh yourself.' 'I must not stop, I must reach home to-night, if possible, though I think you must be mistaken in the distance to Boston.' He then gave the reins to his horse, which he restrained with difficulty, and disappeared in a moment. A few days afterwards I met

the man a little this side of Claremont, winding around the hills in Unity, at the rate, I believe, of twelve miles an hour." "Is Peter Rugg his real name, or has he accidentally gained that name?" "I know not, but presume he will not deny his name; you can ask him, for see, he has turned his horse and is passing this way." In a moment a dark-colored, high-spirited horse approached, and would have passed without stopping, but I had resolved to speak to Peter Rugg, or whoever the man might be. Accordingly, I stepped into the street, and as the horse approached I made a feint of stopping him. The man immediately reined in his horse. "Sir," said I, "may I be so bold as to inquire if you are not Mr. Rugg? for I think I have seen you before." "My name is Peter Rugg," said he; "I have unfortunately lost my way; I am wet and weary, and will take it kindly of you to direct me to Boston." "You live in Boston, do you, and in what street?" "In Middle Street." "When did you leave Boston?" "I cannot tell precisely; it seems a considerable time." "But how did you and your child become so wet? it has not rained here to-day." "It has just rained a heavy shower up the river. But I shall not reach Boston to-night if I tarry. Would you advise me to take the old road, or the turnpike?" "Why, the old road is one hundred and seventeen miles, and the turnpike is ninety-seven." "How can you say so? you impose on me; it is wrong to trifle with a traveler; you know it is but forty miles from Newburyport to Boston." "But this is not Newburyport; this is Hartford." "Do not deceive me, sir. Is not this town Newburyport, and the river that I have been following the Merrimac?" "No, sir; this is Hartford, and the river the Connecticut." He wrung his hands and looked incredulous. "Have the rivers, too, changed their courses as the cities have changed places? But see, the clouds are gathering in the south, and we shall have a rainy night. Ah, that fatal oath!" He would tarry no longer. His impatient horse leaped off, his hind flanks rising like wings—he seemed to devour all before him and to scorn all behind.

I had now, as I thought, discovered a clue to the history of Peter Rugg, and I determined, the next time my business called me to Boston, to make a further inquiry. Soon after I was enabled to collect the following particulars from Mrs. Croft, an aged lady in Middle Street, who has resided in Boston during the last twenty years. Her narration is ·this : The last summer a person, just at twilight, stopped at the door of the late Mrs. Rugg. Mrs. Croft, on coming to the door, perceived a stranger, with a child by his side, in an old, weather-beaten carriage, with a black horse. The stranger asked for Mrs. Rugg, and was informed that Mrs. Rugg had died, at a good old age, more than twenty years before that time. The stranger replied, "How can you deceive me so? do ask Mrs. Rugg to step to the door." "Sir, I assure you Mrs. Rugg has not lived here these nineteen years; no one lives here but myself, and my name is Betsey Croft." The stranger paused, and looked up and down the street, and said, "Though the painting is rather faded, this looks like my house." "Yes," said the child, "that is the stone before the door that I used to sit on to eat my bread and milk." "But," said the stranger, "it seems to be on the wrong side of the street. Indeed, everything here seems to be misplaced. The streets are all changed, the people are all changed, the town seems changed, and, what is strangest of all, Catharine Rugg has deserted her husband and child." "Pray," said the stranger, "has John Foy come home from sea? He went a long voyage; he is my kinsman. If I could see him, he could give me some account of Mrs. Rugg." "Sir," said Mrs. Croft, "I never heard of John Foy. Where did he live?" "Just above here, in Orange-Tree Lane." "There is no such place in this neighborhood." "What do you tell me! Are the streets gone? Orange-Tree Lane is at the head of Hanover Street, near Pemberton's Hill." "There is no such lane now." "Madam! you cannot be serious. But you doubtless know my brother, William Rugg. He lives in Royal Exchange Lane, near King Street." "I know of no such lane; and I am sure there is no

such street as King Street in this town." "No such street as King Street? Why, woman! you mock me. You may as well tell me there is no King George. However, madam, you see I am wet and weary. I must find a resting-place. I will go to Hart's tavern, near the market." "Which market, sir? for you seem perplexed; we have several markets." "You know there is but one market, near the town dock." "Oh, the old market. But no such man as Hart has kept there these twenty years."

Here the stranger seemed disconcerted, and muttered to himself quite audibly: "Strange mistake! How much this looks like the town of Boston! It certainly has a great resemblance to it; but I perceive my mistake now. Some other Mrs. Rugg, some other Middle Street." Then said he, "Madam, can you direct me to Boston?" "Why, this is Boston, the city of Boston. I know of no other Boston." "City of Boston it may be, but it is not the Boston where I live. I recollect now, I came over a bridge instead of a ferry. Pray what bridge is that I just came over?" "It is Charles River Bridge." "I perceive my mistake; there is a ferry between Boston and Charlestown, there is no bridge. Ah, I perceive my mistake. If I was in Boston, my horse would carry me directly to my own door. But my horse shows by his impatience that he is in a strange place. Absurd, that I should have mistaken this place for the old town of Boston! It is a much finer city than the town of Boston. It has been built long since Boston. I fancy Boston must lie at a distance from this city, as the good woman seems ignorant of it." At these words his horse began to chafe, and strike the pavement with his fore feet; the stranger seemed a little bewildered, and said, "No home to-night," and, giving the reins to his horse, passed up the street, and I saw no more of him.

It was evident that the generation to which Peter Rugg belonged had passed away.

This was all the account of Peter Rugg I could obtain from Mrs. Croft; but she directed me to an elderly man, Mr. James Felt, who lived near her, and who had kept a record of the principal occurrences for the last fifty years. At my request she sent for him; and, after I had related to him the object of my inquiry, Mr. Felt told me he had known Rugg in his youth; that his disappearance had caused some surprise; but as it sometimes happens that men run away, sometimes to be rid of others, and sometimes to be rid of themselves; and as Rugg took his child with him, and his own horse and chair; and as it did not appear that any creditors made a stir, the occurrence soon mingled itself in the stream of oblivion; and Rugg and his child, horse and chair, were soon forgotten. "It is true," said Mr. Felt, "sundry stories grew out of Rugg's affair, whether true or false I cannot tell; but stranger things have happened in my day, without even a newspaper notice." "Sir," said I, "Peter Rugg is now living. I have lately seen Peter Rugg and his child, horse and chair; therefore I pray you to relate to me all you know or ever heard of him." "Why, my friend," said James Felt, "that Peter Rugg is now a living man I will not deny; but that you have seen Peter Rugg and his child is impossible, if you mean a small child, for Jenny Rugg, if living, must be at least—let me see—Boston Massacre, 1770—Jenny Rugg was about ten years old. Why, sir, Jenny Rugg if living must be more than sixty years of age. That Peter Rugg is living is highly probable, as he was only ten years older than myself; and I was only eighty last March, and I am as likely to live twenty years longer as any man." Here I perceived that Mr. Felt was in his dotage, and I despaired of gaining any intelligence from him on which I could depend.

I took my leave of Mrs. Croft, and proceeded to my lodgings at the Marlborough Hotel.

If Peter Rugg, thought I, has been traveling since the Boston Massacre, there is no reason why he should not travel to the end of time. If the present generation know little of him, the next will know less, and Peter and his child will have no hold on this world.

In the course of the evening I related my adventure in Middle Street. "Ha!"

said one of the company, smiling, "do you really think you have seen Peter Rugg? I have heard my grandfather speak of him as though he seriously believed his own story." "Sir," said I, "pray let us compare your grandfather's story of Mr. Rugg with my own." "Peter Rugg, sir, if my grandfather was worthy of credit, once lived in Middle Street, in this city. He was a man in comfortable circumstances, had a wife and one daughter, and was generally esteemed for his sober life and manners. But unhappily his temper at times was altogether ungovernable, and then his language was terrible. In these fits of passion, if a door stood in his way he would never do less than kick a panel through. He would sometimes throw his heels over his head, and come down on his feet, uttering oaths in a circle. And thus, in a rage, he was the first who performed a somerset, and did what others have since learned to do for merriment and money. Once Rugg was seen to bite a tenpenny nail in halves. In those days everybody, both men and boys, wore wigs; and Peter, at these moments of violent passion, would become so profane that his wig would rise up from his head. Some said it was on account of his terrible language; others accounted for it in a more philosophical way, and said it was caused by the expansion of his scalp, as violent passion, we know, will swell the veins and expand the head. While these fits were on him, Rugg had no respect for heaven or earth. Except this infirmity, all agreed that Rugg was a good sort of a man; for when his fits were over, nobody was so ready to commend a placid temper as Peter.

"It was late in autumn, one morning, that Rugg, in his own chair, with a fine large bay horse, took his daughter and proceeded to Concord. On his return a violent storm overtook him. At dark he stopped in Menotomy (now West Cambridge), at the door of a Mr. Cutter, a friend of his, who urged him to tarry overnight. On Rugg's declining to stop, Mr. Cutter urged him vehemently. 'Why, Mr. Rugg,' said Cutter, 'the storm is overwhelming you; the night is exceeding dark; your little daughter will perish; you are in an open chair, and the tempest is increasing.' ' *Let the storm increase,*' said Rugg, with a fearful oath, ' *I will see home to-night, in spite of the last tempest! or may I never see home.*' At these words he gave his whip to his high-spirited horse, and disappeared in a moment. But Peter Rugg did not reach home that night, nor the next; nor, when he became a missing man, could he ever be traced beyond Mr. Cutter's in Menotomy. For a long time after, on every dark and stormy night, the wife of Peter Rugg would fancy she heard the crack of a whip, and the fleet tread of a horse, and the rattling of a carriage, passing her door. The neighbors, too, heard the same noises, and some said they knew it was Rugg's horse; the tread on the pavement was perfectly familiar to them. This occurred so repeatedly that at length the neighbors watched with lanterns, and saw the real Peter Rugg, with his own horse and chair, and child sitting beside him, pass directly before his own door, his head turning towards his house, and himself making every effort to stop his horse, but in vain. The next day the friends of Mrs. Rugg exerted themselves to find her husband and child. They inquired at every public house and stable in town; but it did not appear that Rugg made any stay in Boston. No one, after Rugg had passed his own door, could give any account of him; though it was asserted by some that the clatter of Rugg's horse and carriage over the pavements shook the houses on both sides of the street. And this is credible, if, indeed, Rugg's horse and carriage did pass on that night. For at this day, in many of the streets, a loaded truck or team in passing will shake the houses like an earthquake. However, Rugg's neighbors never afterwards watched again; some of them treated it all as a delusion, and thought no more of it. Others, of a different opinion, shook their heads and said nothing. Thus Rugg and his child, horse and chair, were soon forgotten; and prob-ably many in the neighborhood never heard a word on the subject.

"There was indeed a rumor that Rugg afterwards was seen in Connecticut, between Suffield and Hartford, passing through the country like a streak of chalk. This gave occasion to Rugg's friends to make further inquiry. But the more they inquired, the more they were baffled. If they heard of Rugg one day in Connecticut, the next day they heard of him winding around the hills in New Hampshire; and soon after, a man in a chair, with a small child, exactly answering the description of Peter Rugg, would be seen in Rhode Island, inquiring the way to Boston.

"But that which chiefly gave a color of mystery to the story of Peter Rugg was the affair at Charlestown bridge. The toll-gatherer asserted that sometimes, on the darkest and most stormy nights, when no object could be discerned, about the time Rugg was missing, a horse and wheel carriage, with a noise equal to a troop, would at midnight, in utter contempt of the rates of toll, pass over the bridge. This occurred so frequently that the toll-gatherer resolved to attempt a discovery. Soon after, at the usual time, apparently the same horse and carriage approached the bridge from Charlestown square. The toll-gatherer, prepared, took his stand as near the middle of the bridge as he dared, with a large three-legged stool in his hand. As the appearance passed, he threw the stool at the horse, but heard nothing except the noise of the stool skipping across the bridge. The toll-gatherer on the next day asserted that the stool went directly through the body of the horse, and he persisted in that belief ever after. Whether Rugg, or whoever the person was, ever passed the bridge again, the toll-gatherer would never tell; and when questioned, seemed anxious to waive the subject. And thus Peter Rugg and his child, horse and carriage, remain a mystery to this day." ●

This, sir, is all that I could learn of Peter Rugg in Boston. . . .

# Comment on Current Books

**Comedy Queens**

Kitty Clive, Peg Woffington, George Anne Bellamy, "Perdita" Robinson, Mrs. Jordan— such are a few of the names that come to mind when one thinks of the stage in the days of the Georges. All these, and others less known to students of the period, are described by Mr. Fyvie with animation and abundant anecdote. We might perhaps have been spared a little of the scandal, and one would prefer, as a matter of proportion and taste, that there should have been less about these actresses' private lives and more about their public careers and their manner of acting. There is sometimes also displayed a not altogether good-natured spirit. The book will not rank with the recent memoirs of David Garrick by Mrs. Parsons. There are many portraits, and the book is handsomely made. (Comedy Queens of the Georgian Era. By John Fyvie. E. P. Dutton & Co., New York. $4, net.)

**Christ and the Human Race**

In these lectures on the attitude of Jesus Christ to foreign races and religions Dr. Hall, now returning from his second series of lectures in India, is concerned with the proper attitude of a Christian man toward the non-Christian religions. "The large fact" for those to consider who would sympathetically study the religious life of Orientals he finds in "the age-long struggle for philosophical monotheism. . . . The outcome promises to be the most profound mystical conception of a personal Deity to which man has yet attained." Both Christianity and culture demand the discarding of race prejudice, together with provincial disdain of ways which are not our ways, that we may see how God fulfills himself in many ways. There is no quarrel of the Orient with Christ. Its opposition to missions from the Occident springs from its "scorn and distrust" of the hostile Powers of the West. But if the East, as we believe, needs the West, so does the West need the East. The monotheism which culminates in the religion of Jesus Christ has, says Dr. Hall, "a vastness of design, a universality of content, a mystical depth, by which it exhausts the Western power of interpretation, and demands the prophetic insight of the East also. . . . As our knowledge of religious insight and experience outside of Christianity increases, . . . we become conscious of depths in that religion which can be sounded only by those who have the mind and temperament of the East

by birth or by sympathetic assimilation." To-day, he affirms, "the East denounces Western Christendom, yet in spirit approaches nearer and nearer to the worship of Christ." Thus far have the leaders of Christian thought advanced from the recent grouping of all religions but their own as "false religions." In conclusion Dr. Hall gives the standpoints now to be taken by the Christian educator, physician, and minister in the East. What he says of the minister in the East must be pondered by the minister here. "He must take the position that, as yet, Christ has been but partially interpreted through the evolution of the Western religious consciousness." (Christ and the Human Race. Being the Noble Lectures for 1906. By Charles Cuthbert Hall, D.D., LL.D. Houghton, Mifflin & Co., Boston. $1.25, net.)

**Costume and Fancy Dress**

Not so much the decrees of modern fashion in woman's dress and adornment as the singularities, beauties, and monstrosities of old times, the typical costume of races and nations, receive attention here. Fancy and theatrical garb and peasants' dress also receive careful attention. The book would certainly be of great use to any one designing stage or ball costumes in securing correctness and uniformity of plan and preventing the too common anachronisms. The author has sought faithfully for material and gives elaborate and detailed information, while the artist, Mr. Percy Anderson, gives us many attractive colored plates and drawings in monotone. (Costume: Fanciful, Historical, and Theatrical. Compiled by Mrs. Aria. The Macmillan Company, New York. $2.50, net.)

**The Enemy at Trafalgar**

The English author of this narrative of the battle of Trafalgar thinks that attention has been heretofore too exclusively centered on Nelson. He aims therefore to describe the "enemy's side" through the words of French and Spanish eye-witnesses and participants in the fight. One special advantage of this method is that it allows of an extremely interesting account of the fate of the captured ships and the adventures of the prisoners. Altogether it is a novel idea, and its manner of execution throws light on the last great naval combat between France and England. (The Enemy at Trafalgar. By Edward Fraser. E. P. Dutton & Co., New York. $3.50, net.)

237

**The Foolish Almanak**
The calendar stars various days with jokes and "grinds" more or less witty. Thus, for the first Wednesday in February:

(1781) "Battle of Cowpens." British defeated by Morgan.
(1906) Second "Battle of Cowpens." Packers defeated by O'Neil and Reynolds.

Besides many other good specimens there are also many unsuccessful attempts at wit. (The Foolish Almanak 2d. John W. Luce & Co., Boston. 75 cents.)

**Geology and the Bible**
For more than forty years the veteran Oberlin professor has been an assiduous student of geology as well as of theology, and has traveled widely in that interest. This volume embodies the results of his latest investigations besides those found in his former writings. They show, what other investigators have held, that certain occurrences recorded in the Old Testament as miracles—the deluge, the destruction of Sodom, the Hebrews' fording of the Red Sea and the Jordan, the overthrow of Jericho—belong to the history of the natural operation of geological causes. These natural causes, however, Dr. Wright holds to have been touched off by the direct act of God to meet the occasions, as really as the hunter fires his gun. It is more surprising that he apparently regards the legend of "Lot's wife" as credible history. Whether in the Old Testament or the New, Dr. Wright is uncompromisingly opposed to the conclusions adopted by the majority of Biblical scholars. He is also opposed to anthropologists in his belief that the entire human race except the family of Noah perished in the deluge. Geology is his forte, and the value of the present volume comes from his researches in that field. (Scientific Confirmations of Old Testament History. By G. Frederick Wright, D.D., LL.D. Bibliotheca Sacra Company, Oberlin, Ohio. $2, net.)

**Hero Tales**
The characters sketched in this volume are all illustrious in the history of the Congregational churches for nearly three centuries. As pioneers of religion and civilization, and as builders of institutions, their names have gone into our National history, and their lives deserve the commemoration here bestowed. It is intended especially for adolescent readers, and is effectively illustrated. (Hero Tales of Congregational History. By Grace T. Davis. The Pilgrim Press, Boston. $1.25, net.)

**In Uganda**
It is the northern part of Uganda here described by an English missionary—a section of Africa now fairly well known to geographers and eth-nologists. As a record of travel, sport, and adventure the book has considerable interest, and the author gives a clear idea of the customs and superstitions of the natives. There are many pictures of but moderate interest. (Uganda to Khartoum. By Arthur B. Lloyd. E. P. Dutton & Co., New York. $3, net.)

**Poems of W. B. Yeats**
The first of two attractive volumes in which Mr. Yeats proposes to put all his poetry which he cares to have preserved. This volume contains selections from his early poems: "Ballads and Lyrics," "The Wanderings of Oisin," "The Rose," "The Wind Among the Reeds," "In the Seven Woods," "The Old Age of Queen Meave," and "Baile and Aillinn." The second volume, which will be issued later in the season, will contain Mr. Yeats's dramas in verse. (The Poetical Works of William B. Yeats. Vol. I. Lyrical Poems. The Macmillan Company, New York. $1.75, net.)

**The Story Book Girls**
A very interestingly planned and well-executed book, with a delightfully fresh plot, in which a group of English girls attempt to conduct their lives according to story-book ideals. The difficulties in the way are innumerable, but the faith is great, the rewards are many, and the story moves with a lively step through a great many entertaining scenes. The characters are well drawn, clearly contrasted, and the talk very bright. Altogether this must be counted not only an interesting book for older girls, but also a very promising piece of work. (The Story Book Girls. By Christiana Gowans Whyte. The Macmillan Company, New York. $1.50.)

**Styles in Furniture**
If furniture-makers get hopelessly mixed up in attempting to define to their patrons just what furniture belongs, in style, to the ages of Louis XIV., XV., and XVI., the general public is apt to get still more mixed. It is indeed time that we should have such a popular book as the present, clearly defining that which really distinguishes each of these styles; and not only these, but also defining differences between the Elizabethan and Jacobean styles, and between the Queen Anne and the Chippendale. Furniture-makers should be grateful to Helen Churchill Candee's well-printed and interestingly illustrated book, for it will increase popular knowledge and appreciation of their goods. But the buying and "looking" public may have greater cause for gratitude. (Decorative Styles and Periods in the Home. By Helen Churchill Candee. Frederick A. Stokes Company, New York. $2, net.)

Every woman in the home comes under the influence of snowy white

## "Standard" Porcelain Enameled Ware

Its absolute sanitation makes it impervious to the accumulation or absorption of dirt and is a constant guarantee of domestic health. The pride of possession and satisfaction of daily usage alone repay the cost of installation, and its indestructibility makes it the most economical bathroom equipment you can install.

Our Book, "MODERN BATHROOMS," tells you how to plan, buy and arrange your bathroom, and illustrates many beautiful and inexpensive as well as luxurious rooms, showing the cost of each fixture in detail, together with many hints on decoration, tiling, etc. It is the most complete and beautiful booklet ever issued on the subject, and contains 100 pages. FREE for six cents postage and the name of your plumber and architect (if selected).

The ABOVE FIXTURES, No. P-26, can be purchased from any plumber at a cost approximating $101.00—not counting freight, labor or piping—is described in detail among the others.

CAUTION: Every piece of *Standard* Ware bears our *Standard* "GREEN and GOLD" guarantee label, and has our trade-mark *Standard* cast on the outside. Unless the label and trade-mark are on the fixture it is not *Standard* Ware. Refuse substitutes—they are all inferior and will cost you more in the end. The word *Standard* is stamped on all our nickeled brass fittings; specify them and see that you get the genuine trimmings with your bath and lavatory, etc.

Address **Standard Sanitary Mfg. Co.**, Dept. 22, Pittsburgh, U. S. A.

Pittsburgh Showroom, 949 Penn Avenue

Offices and Showrooms in New York: *Standard* Building, 35-37 West 31st Street
London, England, 22 Holborn Viaduct, E.C.    New Orleans, Cor. Baronne & St. Joseph Sts.
Louisville, 325-329 West Main Street    Cleveland, 208-210 Huron Street

85, NO. 5

287 Fourth Avenue, New York City
1436 Marquette Building, Chicago

PRICE TEN CE

# The Outlook

## Saturday, February 2, 1907

# Race Riots and Lynch Law

## I. A Southern Lawyer's View
### By Hooper Alexander

## II. A Northern Professor's View
### By J. E. Cutler

# The Church Question in France
## By Goldwin Smith

# New
# Victor Records

## On sale January 28th at all Victor Dealers throughout America.

All songs are with orchestral accompaniment.  8-in. 35c; 10-in. 60c; 12-in. $1.00.

| No. | | In. |
|---|---|---|
| **United States Marine Band** | | |
| 4943 March Comrades | Wagner | 10 |
| 4944 Semper Fidelis March | Sousa | 10 |
| 31579 Manilla Waltz | Choper | 12 |
| **Arthur Pryor's Band** | | |
| 31600 Monsieur Beaucaire—Incidental Music | | 12 |
| 31603 Plantation Echoes | Conterno | 12 |
| **Victor Concert Orchestra** | | |
| 4978 Juliet's Slumber—Romeo and Juliet | Gounod | 10 |
| 31604 Hungarian Lustspiel Overture | Keler-Bela | 12 |
| 31605 Rosamunde Overture—Part 1 | Schubert | 12 |
| 31606 Rosamunde Overture—Part 2 | Schubert | 12 |
| **Victor Dance Orchestra** | | |
| 31602 La Barcarolle Waltz | Waldteufel | 12 |
| **Cornet Solo by Emil Keneke** | | |
| 4952 The Rosary | Nevin | 10 |
| **Banjo Solo by Vess L. Ossman** | | |
| 4943 Silver Heels | Moret | 10 |
| **Violin and Flute by D'Almaine & Lyons** | | |
| 31598 Dream of the Mountains—Idyl | La-Itzky | 12 |
| **Soprano Solo by Miss Ada Jones** | | |
| 4969 Fancy Little Nancy (Soubrette Song) | Baines | 10 |
| **Comic Song by Miss Helen Trix** | | |
| 4946 The Next Horse I Ride On  Murray-Everhard | | 10 |
| **Contralto Solo by Miss Corinne Morgan** | | |
| 4976 Forever and Forever | Tosti | 10 |
| **Tenor Solo by Harry Macdonough** | | |
| 31601 The Palms | Faure | 12 |
| **Baritone Solo by J. W. Myers** | | |
| 4968 The Bowery Grenadiers | Kelly | 10 |
| **Songs by Billy Murray** | | |
| 4949 Sweet Anastasia Brady | Jerome-Schwartz | 10 |
| 4974 Cheyenne Parody | | 10 |
| **Records by Burt Shepard** | | |
| 4922 The Old Brown Hat | Gorman-Lowan | 10 |
| 4965 Matrimony (Talking Record) | Kendall | 10 |
| **Coon Song by Arthur Collins** | | |
| 4947 Moses Andrew Jackson, Good Bye | | 10 |
| **Duet by Collins and Harlan** | | |
| 4972 I'm Keeping My Love Lamp Burning for You | | 10 |
| **Duets by Miss Jones and Mr. Murray** | | |
| 4951 Wouldn't You Like to Flirt with Me ?  Rogers | | 10 |
| 4975 Don't You Think It's Time to Marry? Edwards | | 10 |
| **Duet by Miss Trix and Mr. Quinn** | | |
| 4953 Fol de Iddley Ido | Bratton | 10 |
| **Trio by Miss Jones, Mr. Murray and Mr. Kernell** | | |
| 4970 Whistle It  from "The Red Mill" | | 10 |
| **Trinity Choir** | | |
| 4971 Jesus, Meek and Gentle | Ambrose | 10 |
| **Male Quartets by the Haydn Quartet** | | |
| 4967 When the Flowers Bloom in Springtime, Molly Dear, | Von Tilzer | 10 |
| 4966 When Her Beauty Begins to Fade | Morse | 10 |

| No. | | In. |
|---|---|---|
| **Yankee Stories by Cal Stewart** | | |
| 4979 Uncle Josh and the Labor Unions | | 10 |
| 498c Uncle Josh's Second Visit to the Metropolis | | 10 |
| **Descriptive Specialties by Miss Jones and Mr. Spencer** | | |
| 4973 Rosie and Rudolph at the Skating Rink | | 10 |
| 31597 Down on the Farm | | 12 |
| **TWELVE 8-INCH RECORDS** | | |
| **United States Marine Band** | | |
| 4911 Maple Leaf Rag | Joplin | 8 |
| **Victor Orchestra** | | |
| 4962 Traumerei | Schumann | 8 |
| 4965 Popular Waltz Medley | | 8 |
| **Contralto Solo by Miss Corinne Morgan** | | |
| 4904 O Promise Me | De Kovea | 8 |
| **Soprano Solo by Miss Ada Jones** | | |
| 4 73 The Bullfrog and the Coon | Nathan | 8 |
| **Coon Song by Arthur Collins** | | |
| 4951 I'm Going Right Back to Chicago | | 8 |
| **Duet by Stanley and Macdonough** | | |
| 4917 Almost Persuaded | Bliss | 8 |
| **Duet by Collins and Harlan** | | |
| 4960 Arra'h-Wanna | Morse | 8 |
| **Male Quartet by the Haydn Quartet** | | |
| 2528 Rocked in the Cradle of the Deep | | 8 |
| **Recitation by Edgar L. Davenport** | | |
| 4949 The Seven Ages | Shakespeare | 8 |
| **Descriptive Specialty by Miss Jones and Mr. Spencer** | | |
| 4363 "Pals" (Introducing "He's My Pal") | | 8 |
| **Yankee Talk by Cal Stewart** | | |
| 2575 Uncle Josh and the Fire-Department | | 8 |
| **Baritone Solo by Senor Francisco** | | |
| 4937 La Marseillaise | | 10 |
| **German Solo by George P. Watson** | | |
| 4953 Life in the Alps (with yodel) | | 10 |
| **Duet by Miss Carlson and Mr. Herskind** | | |
| 4977 Gobble Duet  from La Mascotte | Audran | 10 |
| **NEW RED SEAL RECORDS** | | |
| 10-inch, $2.00;  12-inch, $3.00 | | |
| **Johanna Gadski, Soprano** | | |
| 87002 Walkure—Brunnhilde's Battle Cry | Wagner | 10 |
| 88038 Lohengrin—Elsa's Traum | Wagner | 12 |
| 88039 Ave Maria (violin o ligato) | Bach-Gounod | 12 |
| 88040 Aida—"O patria mia" (My Native Land) Verdi | | 12 |
| 88040 The Erlking (with piano) | Schubert | 12 |
| 88041 { (a) Verborgene Wunden } with { (b) Like the Rosebud } piano | LaForge | 12 |
| **Emma Eames, Soprano** | | |
| 88045 Faust—"Le Roi de Thule" | Gounod | 12 |
| **Violin Solos by Mischa Elman, $1.50** | | |
| 74051 Souvenir de Moscow | Wieniawski | 12 |
| 74052 Nocturne in Eb | Chopin | 12 |
| 74053 Melodie | Tschaikowsky | 12 |

The list of Victor Records never stops growing. Go to your dealers the 28th of every month

## Victor Talking Machine Co., Camden, N. J., U. S. A.
### Berliner Gramophone Co. of Montreal, Canadian Distributers

❀

**Federal Prohibition of Child Labor**

The Outlook has already given some account of the bill prepared by Senator Beveridge, of Indiana, for regulation of child labor by the Federal Government. The bill has been introduced in the Senate by Senator Beveridge and in the House by Congressman Parsons, Chairman of the New York County Republican Committee. It has been indorsed by the National Child Labor Committee, and some Southern Senators and Representatives have expressed sympathy with its general purpose in spite of their reluctance to see any further extension of Federal power as opposed to the doctrine of States' rights. Senator Lodge has introduced a similar bill in the Senate, although it is expressed in somewhat simpler terms than that drawn by Senator Beveridge, and does not apparently provide so efficient a machinery for carrying the provisions of the bill into effect. There is undoubtedly at the present moment a danger of calling too loudly on the Federal Government to right wrongs or amend abuses which the State governments have neglected. The Outlook's belief in home rule or local self-government is unshaken, but this principle should be applied only to those affairs which concern the local community. New York City should maintain, regulate, and control its own police force, for the condition of its police force affects, generally speaking, the welfare of the city only. But the State Legislature should have authority to determine what is to be done in New York City to control, mitigate, and if possible eradicate, tuberculosis. For if the people of the city of New York, through indifference, ignorance, or vice, do not use the most modern and most scientific means of fighting tuberculosis, it may spread and ravage the whole State. The abuses of child labor

by this reasoning constitute a National evil, which, if ignored or neglected, is likely to have a far-reaching and dangerous effect upon the life of the whole people.

❀

**The Effects of Child Labor on National Life**

It is this phase of the question which appears to us to make Senator Beveridge's arguments in favor of National legislation, supported by an array of facts and figures marshaled from all sorts of workrooms and communities, unanswerable. "The census," says Senator Beveridge, "shows that nearly two million child breadwinners under fifteen years of age are now at work. Of these, almost seven hundred thousand are engaged in work other than agriculture. Child labor on the farm is good. This bill does not strike at that. It strikes only at child slavery in factories, mines, and sweatshops." One of the most striking portions of Senator Beveridge's speech is found in his description of the experience of Great Britain in dealing with this same problem. Early in the last century the philanthropists and larger-minded statesmen of England found that the people were slowly but surely suffering from physical degeneration, which could be directly traced to the malign effects of mine and factory labor upon children. At the time of the Boer War, when it was necessary to raise an army from the forty millions of population of England, Ireland, Scotland, and Wales to meet twenty-eight thousand Boers who lived the healthful outdoor life of a farmer, "an average of thirty per cent. of all recruits were rejected for reasons of physical and nervous inferiority. The Inspector-General reported that from forty to sixty per cent. of the recruits were unfit for military duty. Undersize, narrow chests, bad teeth, decayed nerves, bad vision, and all the other evidences of race inferiority were the causes of rejection." A large part of this physical inferiority, which of course means also mental and moral inferiority, may be directly traced to conditions of factory and mine labor; and the English Government is now endeavoring vigorously to suppress the evil. Senator Beveridge, who is one of the hardest-working and most faithful members of the Senate, deserves the highest credit for the tireless investigation which he has made of this important question. The stand which he has taken has brought the subject to the attention of the people of the country with an effect which no committee of philanthropists (more is the pity) could have hoped to produce in .years of agitation. And even if, on debate and consideration, it should be found wise to modify his bill in some of its minor details, its main spirit and object should have the hearty support of the entire country, irrespective of partisan or pocketbook interests.

❦

**A Wise Decision** The Secretary of War has rendered his decision on the applications for permission to use water from Niagara Falls for power purposes, and to import electric power from Canada. By the terms of the Burton Act, approved last June, the Secretary of War is authorized to grant permits for the diversion of water for the creation of power to an aggregate amount not exceeding 15,600 cubic feet a second, and to grant permits for the transmission of power from Canada to an aggregate quantity not exceeding 160,000 horse-power. Secretary Taft has given the most careful consideration to the question in the light afforded by the statements of the representatives of the power companies, of those interested in the preservation of the scenic grandeur of the Falls, and of the engineers of the War Department. He has granted permits for the diversion of the maximum amount of water under the act and for the admission of the maximum quantity of power. At the same time he records his conviction that the purpose of the law is to preserve the Falls from encroachments which will injure their beauty, and by the tone of his decision he makes it plain that he feels himself intrusted with their protection. At the hearing on this question Secretary Taft stated that it is his intention during his term of office not to authorize the diversion of any further amounts of water or the admission of any more power from Canada, although the Act leaves it in his discretion to do so after six months have passed. In reporting his decision Mr. Taft explains why he believes that the diversion authorized may be made without harm to the Falls:

I have reached the conclusion that with the diversion of 15,600 cubic feet on the American side and the transmission of 160,-000 horse-power from thè Canadian side, the scenic grandeur of the Falls will not be affected substantially or perceptibly to the eye. With respect to the American falls this is an increase of only 2,500 cubic feet a second over what is now being diverted and has been diverted for many years, and has not affected the Falls as a scenic wonder. With respect to the Canadian side, the water is drawn from the river in such a way as not to affect the American falls at all, because the point from which it is drawn is considerably below the level of the water, at the point where the waters separate above Goat Island, and the Waterways Commission and Dr. Clark agree that the taking of 13,000 cubic feet from the Canadian side will not in any way affect or reduce the water going over the American falls. The water going over the Falls on the Canadian side of Goat Island is about five times the volume of that which goes over the American falls. . . . If the amount withdrawn on the Canada side for Canadian use were 5,000 cubic feet a second, which it is not likely to be during the three years' life of these permits, the total to be withdrawn would not exceed ten per cent. of the volume of the stream, and, considering the immense quantity which goes over the Horseshoe Falls, the diminution would not be perceptible to the eye.

Mr. Taft has further appointed a committee consisting of Mr. Charles F. McKim, Mr. Frank D. Millet, and Mr. F. L. Olmsted, to advise him what changes can be made by the Niagara Falls Power Company at the point where its tunnel discharges to "put the side of the canyon at this point from bottom to top in natural harmony with the Falls and the other surroundings, and . . . conceal, as far as possible, the raw commercial aspect that now offends the eye." He implies that the carrying out of the plans of the committee will be made a condition of granting a permit to the company. Secretary Taft's decision seems to The Outlook to be eminently wise, insomuch as it has satisfied the defenders of the Falls as an object of natural beauty, and has satisfied, at least for the present, the power companies. The exploitation of the Falls has been stopped before the effect on their beauty and grandeur has become apparent to the eye. It has been stopped without doing injustice to the companies that have made large investments in power plants. The question has been settled for three years, which covers the life of the present permits; it remains for the American people to insure that any further exploitation shall be rendered impossible.  .    ·

❀

**The Panama Canal**    The resignation of Mr. Theodore P. Shonts as Chairman of the Isthmian Canal Commission has been accepted by the Government with expressions of appreciation of the excellent work of Mr. Shonts during the past eighteen months. The resignation was evidently made after full consultation and without the slightest friction. Mr. Shonts will become President of the Interborough-Metropolitan Company of New York, and Mr. Roosevelt in his letter accepting the resignation says : "I hardly know whether most to regret the fact that the National Government is to lose you or most to congratulate those who are to profit by your services in your new position." As we understand the matter, Mr. Shonts, who has had large experience in railway management, was asked to undertake the work he has just laid down not as an engineer but as an organizer. This was the prime, pressing need of the Canal project at its outset, but Mr. Shonts rightly says: "The Panama Canal work has passed the creative stage—it is qrganized—it can and will go right ahead successfully under the direction of Mr. Stevens, the chief engineer." Mr. Stevens has had the enthusiastic indorsement of all the writers and engineers who have studied the question on the ground, and his immediate appointment to succeed Mr. Shonts as the head of the Commis-

2   ,

sion is without dissent accepted as the best possible. If a single Commissioner shall take the place of the present Commission, as the President has recommended, there can be no doubt that Mr. Stevens will fill the office. Meanwhile the question of placing a large part of the work in the hands of a contractor seems to be approaching a practical result. The bid made by Mr. William J. Oliver was the most favorable of those submitted at the recent competition; it offered to accept as compensation a percentage of 6.75 on the cost. But one of the requirements of the contract was that at least two contractors 'or firms should be associated in this enormous undertaking, and the proposition first made by Mr. Oliver was not acceptable to the Government in this particular. The next most favorable bid put the percentage nearly twice as high, and the Government found it wise to give Mr. Oliver ten days in which to find two associates who should be satisfactory in financial standing and responsibility. The contract is an unusual one in its form, and it is practicable only because an elaborate system of checks, limitations, and requirements makes the contractors responsible to furnish actual results in work done proportionate to the cost upon which their percentage of profit is charged.

❀

**New Senators**    The elections, during the past fortnight, of United States Senators have been of peculiar interest, first, because of the number of well-known men who have been chosen to succeed themselves for six years. Among such are Messrs. Frye, of Maine, Burnham, of New Hampshire, Crane, of Massachusetts, Bacon, of Georgia, Bailey, of Texas, Elkins, of West Virginia, Nelson, of Minnesota, Morgan, of Alabama, Cullom, of Illinois, Warren, of Wyoming, Simmons and Tillman, of North and South Carolina. Deadlocks persist in the Rhode Island and New Jersey Legislatures, where Messrs. Wetmore and Dryden are candidates to succeed themselves. They have met with strongly intrenched and obstinate opposition. Among the new men in the

Senate are the able and distinguished Congressman William Alden Smith, of Michigan, a Republican, succeeding the late Senator Alger, a Republican ; Congressman Charles Curtis, a Republican, from Kansas, the first Senator of Indian parentage, succeeding Senator Benson, a Republican ; Congressman Joseph M. Dixon, a Republican, from Montana, only thirty-nine years old, succeeding the well-known mining multi-millionaire Senator W. A. Clark, a Democrat ; Simon Guggenheim, a Republican, from Colorado, succeeding Senator Patterson, a Democrat. Mr. Guggenheim is a member of the well-known Hebrew family who control the American Smelting and Refining Company, generally known as the Smelting Trust, and will share with Mr. Dixon the distinction of belonging to the youthful class in the Senate, both men having been born in the same year. Mr. Guggenheim is a native of Pennsylvania, but has been a resident of Colorado since 1889. Some years ago he was nominated for Lieutenant-Governor by the Silver Republicans of that State ; he declined the nomination, although the ticket was elected. Later, in 1898, he was nominated by the same party for Governor, and indorsed by the People's party, but withdrew from the ticket. In 1904 he was chosen as a Presidential elector from Colorado. Although the representative of vast financial interests, and doubtless owing his election largely to his power as a financier, Mr. Guggenheim has resigned from all his business positions, and has declared that his one work in life will be worthily to represent the State of Colorado in the Senate. His friends, placing implicit confidence in his integrity, expect the fulfillment of this promise to the letter. Mr. Guggenheim's election, generally regarded as the latest striking example of the power of campaign contributions, was in strong contrast with that of less wealthy candidates, for instance Mr. Smith, of Michigan, and Mr. Curtis, of Kansas (both of whom began life as newsboys), whose Congressional experience leads observers to anticipate even greater distinction than that which they have won in the House of Representatives. Turning to the South, we find in Arkansas the dema-

gogic Governor Jefferson Davis, Democrat, succeeding, to the general regret, one of the most picturesque and respected figures in the Senate, James H. Berry, Democrat. In Tennessee the able Senator Carmack, Democrat, is succeeded by Governor Taylor, Democrat. In Kentucky another Governor, J. C. W. Beckham, Democrat, replaces Senator Blackburn, Democrat ; and in Delaware Harry A. Richardson, Republican, - succeeds Senator Allee, Republican ; Messrs. Beckham and Richardson will be the youngest Senators, being each only thirty-seven years old. In Nebraska Senator Millard is succeeded by Senator Brown, who may also be regarded as belonging to the "juveniles," being but forty-four years old ; and in Montana Senator Borah, Republican, replaces Senator Dubois, Democrat. Finally, in Oregon, Messrs. F. W. Mulkey and Jonathan Bourne, Jr., both Republicans, succeed Senator Gearin, Democrat, and Senator Fulton, Republican. Of the above elections, that in Oregon is the most notable, since, by the successful use of popular elective methods, the will of the people seems to have been registered more directly than has been the case in any other Senatorial election in our history. The Oregon methods might well be copied by every State in the Union.

⊛

*In Congress* While it required a certain degree of moral courage for Congress to pass a bill increasing salaries of Senators and Representatives from $5,000 to $7,500, we have not noted that the action has incurred reprobation from either people or press. The United States can do one of three things in this matter of compensation to its legislators : it can ask them to serve without pay, as do the members of the English Parliament ; it can offer them a small honorarium not based on the value of services ; or it can pay salaries which may fairly be regarded as compensation. The amounts now fixed certainly cannot be considered excessive in view of the recent increase in the cost of living and in comparison with the sums earned by lawyers and other professional men of no greater ability than that which the average Congressman should at least be supposed to have. The Outlook now, as always, favors not only reasonable but liberal compensation to those who serve the Government in important offices. The bill carries also an increase of the salaries of the Vice-President, Speaker of the House, and members of the Cabinet from $8,000 to $12,000. In the debate Senator Lodge pointed out that the traditional system of England in not paying its members of Parliament, while it worked well in certain ways, had also its weak points, in that the poorer Irish members and the labor members were partly supported by contributions collected from their constituents—a palpably bad method. Mr. Lodge also pointed out as an example of the defects of our own system of inadequate pay that his late colleague, Senator Hoar, one of the ablest men who ever entered public life, had devoted himself to the service of the people, giving up a lucrative practice at the bar, and that in consequence he had been constantly under disagreeable financial pressure.——Another important bill which has now passed both Houses is that making it unlawful for any National bank or corporation organized by authority of Congress to contribute money in connection with any political election, or any corporation whatever to contribute money in connection with a Federal election. To the penalty of a fine, imposed in the Senate bill, the House has added the penalty of imprisonment. We hope that in conference the bill will be even further strengthened.——Still another measure of general interest which has passed both Houses is the joint resolution calling on the Secretary of Commerce and Labor to investigate and report on the condition of child and women workers in the United States. It is greatly to be regretted, however, that this bill contains no appropriation to carry out its own provisions. As the advocates of the bill point out, it is impossible to discuss rationally or to treat wisely the many problems involved without a basis of carefully gathered facts and figures relating to the social, sanitary, moral, physical, and economical conditions under which women and children

work. The present Commissioner of Labor, Mr. Neill, is anxious that his bureau should make such an investigation as would leave in its records material of great value and in a wide field. Surely Congress should either declare its opposition to this measure as unnecessary or unconstitutional, or, if it approves it, as the passage of the bill implies, it should furnish—and furnish liberally—the means to carry it out.——The General Pension Bill now before the House of Representatives carries a total of about $2,000,000 less than for the previous year, and there is a net reduction of about 12,000 names in the pension roll, leaving the total, however, at 988,-000. The number of pension agencies is reduced by one-half. A separate bill (the McCumber bill) provides what may be called an old-age service pension— $12.a month for veterans of sixty-two, $15 a month for those of seventy, $20 a month for those of seventy-five. This is simply an enlargement of the present law, which fixes the attainment of the age of sixty-five as *prima facie* proof of pensionable disability.

❀

*Railway Disasters*   On one day last week eight railway disasters were reported. During the week there were as many more. Two of them occurred on the "Big Four" railway in Indiana; in one case, in a disaster memorable in the notorious record of American railways, twenty-three persons were killed and twenty-five injured; in the other the explosion of a car of dynamite standing alongside a passenger train caused an even more tragic and terrible massacre. Another disaster occurred on the Lake Shore, and from the cause which precipitated the awful Mentor accident a few years ago—an open switch; the system of open or facing switches should long ago have been prohibited on all double-track roads. The other accidents were caused by locomotive explosions, derailments, and head-on collisions. With such a record as last week's the public is becoming increasingly and deservedly restive. We should like to know how many of the above-mentioned disasters are not ultimately due to the unduly long hours demanded of railway employees. It will be of public interest to give some of the cases as described by Senator La Follette in presenting his bill limiting the number of hours in which employees on inter-State railways may be employed:

In one of the first or earlier cases reported in this table I find this entry: "Collision. Engineman asleep; hours on duty,17; hours of rest preceding the service"—which was interrupted by this accident—"hours of rest, 2." That is, this engineer who fell asleep upon his engine had been seventeen hours on duty, and had gone on duty—had been called by the company to go out upon his engine—after having had only two hours to rest following the preceding service.

Another: "Collision Train not under control" is stated as the cause of this collision. "The hours on duty, 42."

Another: "Collision. The engineman dozing; 17 hours on duty," and with only six hours' rest immediately preceding his call to this service.

Another, resulting in the killing of one man, the cause being stated as follows: "Signalman went back to flag; fell asleep; 20 hours on service."

Another, resulting in collision: "Engineman asleep; 20 hours on service."

Another case, resulting in collision; cause reported by the railway company: "Flagman neglected to flag; hours on duty, 19."

Another, resulting in collision: "Engineman dozing; 20 hours on service."

Another, resulting in collision: "Engineman mistaking signals." Twenty-seven hours on duty.

Another, resulting in collision: "Engineman going to sleep;. 15 hours on duty, with 5 hours of rest immediately preceding the call for that service."

❦

*Causes*  But this is not the only cause of railway disasters. Even with men who are employed a proper number of hours defective discipline is only too much in evidence. Railway discipline has now sunk to a low condition even among those who are adequately provided for by the roads; and the present condition is due, not only to shiftlessness on the part of superintendents and other officers, but to the growth of a certain trade union idea which would demand employment for any man whether he is worthy or not; for instance, an engineer was recently discharged for drunkenness, but his union persisted in their demand for his reinstatement despite his fault. Another and equally noteworthy

element leading to the present condition of lax discipline is the tremendous demand for employees; in consequence, many of them are no longer anxious lest they shall lose their jobs; they have grown indifferent, lost their sense of duty, and have also lost respect for authority. Then, as a further contributory cause, comes the question of inadequate safety appliances, to which The Outlook has already referred with recommendations for their betterment. Finally, however, and perhaps chiefly, the fault as to the number of railway accidents lies ultimately with some of the great financial powers controlling the railways. These powers have narrow views of their responsibility, as of their own real interest and certainly of the interest of society. It is a satisfaction to note the declaration at a recent meeting of the American Railway Association of a distinguished officer that an impending calamity lay in the drifting of the control of railways from the hands of professional and technical men into the hands of those financiers who regard railways not so much as transportation machines as opportunities for speculators to make money. But no matter what the causes of American railway accidents, the American people have only themselves to blame so long as they ignore a perfectly evident means of diminishing them. For thirty years England has made travel comparatively safe by the governmental investigation of railway accidents through a Bureau in the Board of Trade. Will not Congress establish a similar Bureau in our Department of Commerce?

❦

*A Notable Automobile Show*  New York's second automobile show of the season brought together in the Madison Square Garden the products of thirty-two American manufacturers of gasoline cars, seven importing concerns, and several makers of electric vehicles. For a week the Garden was thronged with owners of cars anxious to keep informed on the progress in automobile-making, prospective buyers comparing the merits of the various makes, and the general public, brought by curiosity or real interest. As in the earlier show, described in The

Outlook a few weeks ago, the higher priced and more luxurious cars were the most prominent features. Strictly low-priced cars, costing from five hundred to eight hundred dollars, were conspicuous by their absence. A single exception was a simple buckboard fitted with a one-cylinder engine and selling for about four hundred dollars, and in somewhat more elaborate and powerful forms for slightly higher prices. The demand for touring-cars at medium prices, say from $1,500 to $3,000, and for the more luxurious and high-powered cars, has increased so rapidly that the manufacturers can hardly keep pace with it. There is little or no incentive for them, therefore, to devote their attention to cars for the man of modest income. One firm, indeed, whose first reputation was made on a low-priced car of unusual excellence, now makes that style only on order and does not exhibit or generally advertise it. It is now turning out higher-priced cars, of which, as a representative said, " we can sell all that we can make." It required only a casual observation of the exhibits to force the conclusion that in the points of beauty of form and finish and of comfort and convenience for passengers the American manufac-turer has set himself a high standard. Many of the cars need fear no ·com-parison with cars of foreign makes noted for their excellence in these particulars. The more fundamental question of me-chanical design and construction cannot be determined by so casual a study or by an untrained observer. It is, how-ever, probably unquestioned that this exhibition shows a marked and important advance in this direction as well. What is practically (as far as general use is concerned) a new type of car has ap-peared this year. It is the high-powered runabout, intended for road-racing or speeding.

❀

*The Automobile on the Highway*    The popularity of the new type, which would seem to have no other reason for being than the ability to attain high speeds, emphasizes again the need for more efficient measures for control-ling the movements of automobiles on the highways. A correspondent has called to our attention· the law in force in the island of Jamaica. It is simply this :

No person shall drive a motor-car on a public highway recklessly, or negligently, or at a speed or in a manner which is danger-ous to the public.

The wisdom of such a provision, as op-posed to one which sets a maximum speed limit for different parts of the high-way, is upheld by the statement of the Commissioner of Motor Vehicles for New Jersey in his annual report to the Governor. He shows that in almost every instance of an accident the auto-mobile was not exceeding the speed limit ; the accidents occurred at inter-secting streets, at sharp turns, or where the traffic was heavier than to justify the speed at which the car was being driven. The Jamaican law, which is similar to those in force in European countries, puts the responsibility for caution on the driver. It leaves to judicial interpretation what, under each set of circumstances, constitutes reckless or dangerous driving. It simplifies the detection of violations of the law, substituting a broad consider-ation of conditions for an accurate deter-mination of speed, a task requiring the expert use of a stop-watch, with the result always open to dispute. ·A simplification of the automobile laws in this direction would, in the opinion of The Outlook, make for the better restraint of the selfish driver and the greater safety of both auto-mobilists themselves and the general pub-lic. In the final event, however, the laws, however wisely drawn, must be rein-forced by the sentiment of automobile users themselves to be really effective. A promising indication of the growth of such a sentiment was given by an occur-rence last week. Mr. Colgate Hoyt, President of the Automobile Club of America, and four ex-Presidents of the Club, were made special officers of the New York police force. Their purpose is to detect and secure the punishment of violations of the highway laws. Whether they succeed in accomplishing· much in the direct performance of their police duties, this expression of respect for the rights of the public by leaders among automobilists can hardly fail to have a wholesome effect.

**The Coming Hague Conference**

During the past fortnight there have been three indications of official and popular interest in the coming Peace Conference at The Hague. The most important has been the action of the Emperor of Russia, who is to issue the call for the Conference. He has sent, as Special Envoy to the Powers, Privy Councilor Frederick de Martens, Professor of International Law at the University of St. Petersburg and a member of the first Peace Conference; he was also the legal adviser to the Russian Ambassadors at the Russo-Japanese Conference at Portsmouth a year and a half ago. It is interesting to note that Professor de Martens proceeded directly from St. Petersburg to Berlin, where he discussed the plans for the coming Conference with Mr. Tower, the American Ambassador. In the limited time at the Russian Envoy's disposal he could not go to Washington, and our Government, therefore, has authorized Mr. Tower to confer on the matter, submitting to Washington, however, for approval or disapproval, any proposition made by the Russian Envoy. It is understood that our Government also represents the views of the Central and South American States. Some of the Powers would welcome May 18 as a date to mark the opening of the second Peace Conference; historically because the Conference of 1899 convened on that date, and practically because, in view of the number of subjects to be considered, the Conference may be a long one, and the date of meeting should be put as far in advance as possible. A second indication of the general sentiment concerning the necessity of another conference was shown at a meeting in New York City, addressed by a number of speakers, among whom Mr. Edwin D. Mead, of Boston, was prominent. He declared that our people should stop thinking themselves Americans first, last, and all the time; they must consider themselves citizens of the world first and citizens of America afterwards. Attention was also called to the fact that the American Government is being increasingly recognized as a model, men everywhere seeing in the Federal control of our States by the Federal courts a model for the federation of all nations by a central and controlling body. Hence the proposition of the Interparliamentary Union at London last summer, that the Hague Tribunal should ultimately constitute the Upper Chamber and the members of the Interparliamentary Union the Lower Chamber of a new International Parliament, will, we think, receive deserved attention at The Hague. As the first Peace Conference established an international tribunal, so the second Conference may establish an international legislature.

❋

**The Code Duello**

In addition, the principal subjects for discussion at The Hague are: (1) the payment by the Powers, proportionately to their population, of ample salaries to the judges of the Hague Court, such judges to hold no political position of any kind during their term of office; (2) the protection of private property at sea in time of war; (3) the rights and duties of neutrals; (4) the codification into international law of the principles of arbitration and mediation; (5) the Drago Doctrine as to the collection of debt; (6) action on the matter first urged by Russia as a reason for a peace conference, namely, some agreement towards disarmament; and (7) finally, also action on a matter now suggested by Russia, namely, a definition of the methods hereafter to be followed in opening hostilities. Concerning the further action on mediation, Mr. W. T. Stead, editor of the London Review of Reviews, has undertaken a personal pilgrimage to the different Powers to induce them to make obligatory the article of the Convention of 1899 which provides that, in case of a conflict being imminent between two nations, a third Power may exercise the right to offer its mediation without either of the two possible belligerents being able to take offense. Mr. Stead hopes to induce an agreement among the Powers, before the second Conference meets, looking toward the reinforcement of this article to the effect that, in the case of failure to receive mediation, neither country shall open hostilities until a period of fifteen or twenty days shall have elapsed. Mr. Stead would thus sensibly apply to quarreling nations the " code duello."

❀

**Who Will Help ?** Americans do not yet realize that the present actual suffering in China from famine is much greater than that caused by earthquake and fire in San Francisco. Last summer heavy rains flooded much of the country along the Grand Canal from knee-deep to waist-deep, while in some places people had to wade through places with water up to their necks. The floods have widened and deepened until what was formerly a fertile plain west of the canal, covered with good crops and prosperous villages, is now a vast lake. The villages and hamlets which rise above the sheet of water can be reached only by boats. The people are destitute. In an area of forty thousand square miles the crops have been almost totally destroyed, and in the country beyond only partial crops have been saved. From ten to fifteen millions of people live in the affected region. At least a third of them are on the verge of starvation. In addition, the reeds which constitute fuel have been destroyed by the floods. Thousands of houses have also been destroyed. There is no hope of relief before the ripening of the crops next June, and even for that farmers have no wheat to plant and are forced to sell their work animals to buy food. The American National Red Cross, true to its motto of neutrality and humanity, has been quick to note the need in China. It has appointed Mr. J. L. Rodgers, United States Consul-General at Shanghai, Special Red Cross Agent to receive and superintend the distribution of supplies, and has appealed to the American people for funds with which to buy supplies. President Roosevelt has issued a special message on this subject. If only our people realized that for every dollar sent to the Red Cross a fifty-pound sack of flour can be delivered to the suffering, we think the response would be specially prompt and liberal. The delivery of so much flour for so little money has been made possible in part by the generosity of

Mr. Harriman, President of the Pacific Mail Steamship Company, in offering to transport supplies without charge. Moreover, bids are asked, that the flour may be bought at the cheapest possible rate. Flour, corn-meal, and seed-wheat have been specially asked for, the seed-wheat being needed for planting. Money may be sent to the local treasurers of the Red Cross—Mr. Jacob H. Schiff, 500 Fifth Avenue, New York City, being the treasurer of the New York State branch—or, simply to the Red Cross, War Department, Washington, D. C. As the Hon. William H. Taft, Secretary of War and President of the National Red Cross, said last week at a special Red Cross meeting in Charleston, South Carolina :

> In the matter of fraternal brotherhood, in the matter of friendly feeling of one man toward another, of one woman toward another, it is necessary, if that feeling is to be given . . . practical effect, that machinery should be developed so that all the tears of sympathy that any misfortune awakens shall be gathered together in a flood, which, carried on, shall give force—a force in one blow to do something practical for the good of the person whose misfortune has awakened sympathy. That is the machinery which the Red Cross proposes to furnish, so that those who have a feeling for five minutes—and sometimes the feeling does not last longer than that—may know that if in that five minutes it occurs to them . . . to put ten dollars in a fund to help the Chinamen in China, or the negroes in Kingston, or our own people in San Francisco, they . . . can do it, because they know that there is a machinery through which it can be done efficiently, practically. That is the object of the Red Cross.

❀

**An Unhappy Humorist** As a test of the good understanding between this country and Great Britain nothing could have been more fortunate than the ridiculous letter of Governor Swettenham, of Jamaica, to Rear-Admiral Davis. The folly of the foolish is sometimes overruled for more efficient service than the wisdom of the wise. The facts appear to have been that, through a misunderstanding, Admiral Davis did fire a salute in the Governor's honor, although the Governor had requested that no salute be fired ; that without invitation he did land six marines to protect the American Consulate, but that immediately afterward he was asked by the authorities of the island to land fifty marines to assist in the work of protection and restoration, which he promptly did. It would seem as if the larger request condoned the smaller offense. It was, however, Governor Swettenham's unhappy idea that he was a humorist that led him to commit a gross discourtesy under the impression that he was making himself agreeable, and he could hardly have been expect 1 to recognize in things that humor which he failed to discover in himself. The incident was instantly understood in this country, and no importance whatever was attached to it. Americans accepted the fact that the Governor of Jamaica was one of those malaprops who sometimes turn up at the wrong moment in diplomatic service, and refused to accept him, as they would have done two decades ago, either as a typical Englishman or as expressing the spirit of his Government. In England, however, the indignation appears to have been very general, and the promptness with which the American fleet acted as a neighbor in a moment of great need has been universally appreciated. The Government of the United States has wisely ignored the whole matter. It only remains for the British Government to settle with Governor Swettenham. Among other beneficent results of the incident is an expression of opinion from Mr. George Bernard Shaw, who is almost always successful when he essays humor:

Rear-Admiral Davis evidently is not accustomed to the manners of the English official classes. Governor Swettenham would naturally regard an American admiral with a certain suspiciousness, first, as a foreigner and a dissenter; second, as a member of a naval branch into which the sons of clergymen and other professional persons enter freely; and, finally, as an officious intruder whose action implied that England could not cope with an earthquake without assistance. The Governor probably conceived himself as acting with studied politeness under circumstances of most presumptuous provocation.

The Archbishop of Jamaica's reported interpretation of Governor Swettenham's action also deserves to be reproduced as a specimen of perhaps unconscious humor:

It was merely a result of the dictatorial character of the Governor. His imperious manner, his frequent abuse of subordinates, and his discourtesy to citizens have earned him great unpopularity, although otherwise he is regarded as a comparatively conscientious official.

❀

**The Lee Centennial** The one hundredth anniversary of the birth of General Robert E. Lee was observed in many places, but interest centered in the celebrations held in the Lee Memorial Chapel of Washington and Lee University, at Lexington, Virginia, and at Willard's Hotel, in Washington. Speaking at Washington and Lee University, Mr. Charles Francis Adams said:

Speaking advisedly and on full reflection, I say that of all the great characters of the Civil War, and it was productive of many whose names and deeds posterity will long bear in recollection, there was not one who passed away in the serene atmosphere and with the gracious bearing of Lee. From the beginning to the end those parting years of his will bear the closest scrutiny. There was about them nothing venial, nothing querulous, nothing in any way sordid or disappointing. In his case there was no anticlimax, for those closing years were dignified, patient, useful, sweet in domesticity, they in all things commanded respect.

At the meeting in Washington addresses were delivered by Senator Berry, of Arkansas, Justice Brewer, of the United States Supreme Court, and Representative Williams, of Mississippi; but the most striking feature of the occasion, and indeed the most significant feature of the celebration anywhere in the country, was a letter from the President of the United States, in which he said:

General Lee has left us the memory, not merely of his extraordinary skill as a general, his dauntless courage and high leadership in campaign and battle, but also of that serene greatness of soul characteristic of those who most readily recognize the obligations of civic duty. Once the war was over he instantly undertook the task of healing and binding up the wounds of his countrymen in the true spirit of those who feel malice toward none and charity for all; in that spirit which from the throes of the Civil War brought forth the real and indissoluble Union of to-day. It was eminently fitting that this great man, this war-worn veteran of a mighty struggle, who at its close simply and quietly undertook his duty as a plain, every-day citizen, bent only upon helping his people in the paths of peace and tranquillity, should turn his attention toward educational work, toward bringing up in fit fashion the younger generations, the sons of those who had proved their faith by their endeavor in the heroic days.

The President also commented on the spirit in which General Lee, at the close of the war, accepted a salary of fifteen hundred dollars a year as President of Washington and Lee University, in order that he might do some good work for the young men of the South ; devoting his great powers to two objects—the reconciliation of all his countrymen with one another, and the fitting of Southern young men for the duties of a lofty, broad-minded citizenship ; and the President expressed his hope that advantage would be taken of the anniversary to appeal to the people of the whole country to commemorate General Lee's spirit and life by the establishment of a permanent memorial at one of the representative educational institutions of the South. The prediction in The Outlook that the occasion would mark in the most striking way the moral miracle of reconciliation, and that it would evoke widespread admiration for General Lee's spirit and life, has been more than fulfilled.

❦

*Ancient Writings* The German scientific expedition under the direction of Dr. von Lecoq, which has been at work in the Jaxartes Valley, according to a report in the New York Tribune, has made a very interesting discovery in the form of a store of literary and artistic treasures, including a large group of manuscripts on paper, leather, and wood in ten languages and a number of dialects. Two of the languages have been hitherto practically unknown ; the third has been known only through a few rock inscriptions in Tibet; the existence of the fourth has never been suspected. The collection is said to equal in volume the entire mass of Middle Persian writings hitherto known to exist. Other manuscripts are in Chinese, Tibetan, Syriac, Uighur, and the primitive Turkish language, the alphabet of which is said to bear a curious resemblance to that of the ancient Norse. The country in which these manuscripts were found lies between the Oxus and the Irtish, and, as readers of Firdusi will remember, was at one time a kind of cosmopolis of Asia,

where many tribes and nations met. Persian, Mongol, and Tartar came together at that point ; China, Persia, and Hindustan finding in it a common meeting ground. The Tribune ventures the suggestion that the German explorers have found what was once a kind of Carnegie library, or reading-room annex. The possibilities of the discovery are very great; in so large a mass it is highly probable that many important writings are included. Such a discovery also strengthens the hope that repositories in Europe are still to be brought to light, and some of the ancient writings known to have been lost may possibly be recovered.

❦

*A French Estimate of Greatness* No recent happening in France shows more clearly the change of national ideals and standards of greatness than the results of a plebiscite which the Petit Parisien, one of the most widely circulated journals in France, has been taking to secure popular selection of the greatest Frenchmen of the nineteenth century. It is significant also of the interest which the French people feel in such matters that more than fifteen million votes were cast, and that a number of men received more than a million votes each. This device for discovering the state of popular opinion has often been tried, and sometimes very seriously, by newspapers in this country, but the results are not, as a rule, very enlightening, because readers do not generally respond by expressing their opinion. Until within a very few years there could have been no doubt as to the name which Frenchmen, almost by acclamation, would have put at the forefront; and the change of standards of achievement indicated by the fact that the first name on the list, instead of being that of Napoleon, was that of Louis Pasteur, who received 1,338,425 votes, is one of the most radical and extraordinary things in contemporary history. Victor Hugo, who received 1,227,103 votes, came second on the list—a result which might have been anticipated ; for Victor Hugo, whatever his defects, is one of the foremost lyric poets that France has produced, one of its most impressive and widely read novelists (though his vogue has passed, probably never to return), and one of the most picturesque figures in the political history of the country; an ardent lover of liberty, and the victim of the latest rule of imperialism. Not until the third name, Gambetta, is reached, does a public man in the old sense of the word come to the front, and Gambetta was much more than a statesman. He was an orator whose eloquence had the impassioned vividness characteristic of the men of southern France, which appealed to men of every section of the country. The histrionic element in him was excessive, as it is in the striking monument which commemorates him in the court of the Louvre; but he was a man to touch the enthusiasm of a generous people as well as to command their following. Napoleon came fourth, and Thiers, who was a writer as well as a statesman, and who was identified with the terrible months following the fall of the Empire and with the laying of the foundations of the Third Republic, fifth. Later one finds the names of the discoverer of radium, of a great electrician, of the man who discovered the antidote for diphtheria, of an explorer, of an actress, of the builder of the Suez Canal, of the inventer of the loom. This is a remarkable list, and shows, not only how the spell of military glory has been broken in France, but how wide a conception of what constitutes greatness has taken its place. It is doubtful if Americans would have shown so much intelligence and breadth of view in such a contest.

⊛

*Dr. Henry M. Field*   Dr. Henry M. Field, whose death was announced last week, was the last survivor of a remarkable family. It is very rare for four brothers to occupy each so unique a place and render each in his own way so unique a service as the four brothers, David Dudley, Stephen J., Cyrus W., and Henry M. Field. The first developed, if he did not create, the scheme of a codification which has revolutionized law as a practical art if not as a true science in the State of New York

and in other States which have followed its example; Stephen J. Field occupied an honored position on the Supreme Court bench, and ranks among the eminent jurists of American history; to Cyrus W. Field we owe the Atlantic cable, which has done more than treaties to bind the Old and the New World together and to make peace easy and war difficult; Henry M. Field takes rank as one of the foremost religious journalists of America at a time when the influence of denominational journalism was at its height, and by his personal ability maintained The Evangelist as a personal journal after personal journalism had almost ceased to be a force in America, and this victory he achieved by maintaining a denominational journal that was not sectarian and a personal journal that was broadly and generously human. His death came in the eighty-fifth year of his age, after a period of seven years of retirement from active life. Dr. Field was a true representative of Berkshire County, which has given many men of note to Massachusetts and to the Nation. He was not only a man of great intellectual activity, but of a very genial and companionable nature, a vivacious talker and an attractive speaker.

⊛

# The Executive and the Senate

Government in the United States is divided into three Departments: the legislative, the judicial, and the executive. It is the function of the first to enact law, of the second to interpret law, of the third to execute law. On the careful maintenance of these Departments, which we have inherited from our ancestors and share with all free peoples, the preservation of our liberties depends. Whenever the three functions are united in one body, whether a single person like Cæsar or a Council like that of Venice, the inevitable result is despotism. The American people are right, therefore, to guard jealously any usurpation by one Department of the authority belonging to another Department.

But the line between these Departments is not and cannot be sharply drawn. Each sometimes exercises functions which in an academic classification would belong to another. The appointment of officials is an executive function; but the courts appoint receivers who exercise very large powers. The enactment of law is a legislative function; but the President is explicitly authorized by the Constitution to veto acts of Congress and is instructed by the Constitution to recommend legislation. In passing judgment on patent claims, land claims, pension claims, and the like, the Executive Departments exercise judicial functions. The advice and consent of the Senate are required for appointment to office in a great number of cases, the Senate thus sharing with the President in executive functions; and in being made the sole judge of Congressional elections Congress is invested with judicial powers. Indeed, it is sometimes difficult to tell whether a particular function is executive, judicial, or legislative; the question how the Inter-State Commerce Commission is to be regarded was hotly debated by Constitutional lawyers in the Senate. Since, thus, these Departments do in a measure overlap, and since each Department does of necessity sometimes exercise functions which, strictly speaking, seem to belong to a different Department, it is not at all strange that questions should continually arise between the different Departments as to their respective rights and duties, nor that each should be jealous of real or fancied encroachments upon its peculiar field.

Recently this question has arisen between the Senate and the Executive in two rather important instances—the Brownsville incident and the withdrawal by executive order of certain lands from sale and settlement.

The Constitutional and legal right of the President to discharge enlisted men without trial appears to The Outlook to be unquestionable. The Statutes of the United States provide that " no enlisted men, duly sworn, shall be discharged . . . except by order of the President, the Secretary of War, the commanding officer of a department, *or* by sentence

of a general court martial." It would be quite clear from the language of this statute that a court martial is not legally necessary in order to a discharge, even if there were no practice to interpret the statute. But there is such practice, which is thus summarized by the Judge-Advocate General of the United States Army, who cites in notes his authorities for his summary : " Although the engagement of the soldier under his contract of enlistment is for a term certain, the Government is under no obligation to retain him in service to the end of the stipulated period, and, under the authority conferred by this Article, may 'terminate at pleasure an enlistment without regard to the soldier.' " That the President was clearly exercising a Constitutional and legal authority in discharging the Brownsville battalion is no longer questioned by the Senate. Senator Foraker could not get that body to adopt a resolution to investigate the incident without first accepting as an amendment the phrase, "without questioning the legality or justice of the President." Whatever the Senate may do in the future, it does not now question the legality of the President's act. What business it has to investigate an act the legality of which it does not question it is not easy to see. Suppose the Senate should expel Mr. Smoot, and the President should thereupon appoint a Commission to investigate the facts respecting Mr. Smoot's connection with the Mormon Church—what would the Senators say to such a proceeding ? Would their opposition be appeased by the President's declaration that he did not question the legality of the Mormon Senator's exclusion ? In the Brownsville incident the Senate is clearly infringing upon the functions of the Executive, whose exclusive duty it is to determine whether the good of the service requires the retention or the discharge of the Brownsville battalion.

In the other incident the legal issue is equally clear, and, we regret to say, the motive for the action of the Senatorial Committee is clearer.

By acts passed in 1898, 1902, and 1906 Congress opened the Indian Territory to settlement, provided for the allotment of land to the Indians in severalty, for the reservation and leasing of certain mineral and coal lands, and for the sale of the land not allotted or reserved. The provision for such sale in the latest of these statutes was in the following words : "When allotments as provided by this and other Acts of Congress have been made, . . . the residue of lands in each of said nations, not reserved or otherwise disposed of, shall be sold by the Secretary of the Interior, *under rules and regulations to be prescribed by him,* and the proceeds of such sales deposited in the United States Treasury to the credit of the respective tribes." No time was fixed within which the sale must be completed. Congress had previously, in 1891, authorized the President to " set apart and reserve in any State or Territory having public lands bearing forests, . . . public reservations." The Secretary of the Interior has withdrawn from sale certain of the forest lands in the Indian Territory, instead of pushing forward the sale of all the lands as expeditiously as possible. He has done so avowedly only temporarily and until Congress can direct what action shall be taken.

In support of this withdrawal are cited the Secretary's definite authority to prescribe rules and regulations for the sale of the unallotted lands ; the past action of the Department in many cases where executive action has been suspended by executive order to await Congressional reconsideration; the policy of the Government, already approved by Congress in its legislation authorizing withdrawal of forest lands from sale ; a special request of the Department of Agriculture for the withdrawal of these lands ; the importance of their withdrawal to protect lower lands from the disastrous floods which are characteristic of the Red River, along which great sums of money are being expended by Government in the construction of levees to protect the bottom lands from such floods ; the report of a special Federal inspector, from the field, that the sentiment of the Indians, the judgment of their chiefs, and the opinion of the prominent men in the Territory, excepting only the lumbermen who were purchasing the

allotted lands from the Indians, were favorable to the policy of forest reserve in the proposed area. These lumber interests appear to outweigh in the Senate Committee all other considerations, for the report presented by Senator Clark, of Wyoming, declares that the action of the Secretary of the Interior is illegal, but presents no argument whatever in support of this conclusion except the following sentence : "The agreement with the tribes and the act of Congress approved July 1, 1902, authorized and directed the allotments to be made as soon as practicable, and that law the Committee believe cannot be set aside, impeded, or nullified except by act of Congress repealing or changing the original statute."

A very conscientious boy once promised his father that at four o'clock he would surely water the garden. At a quarter before four a thunder-storm arose, and at four the rain was pouring down in sheets. The conscientious boy put on his rubber boots and his mackintosh, took an umbrella, filled his waterpot, and went out in the pouring rain to water the garden. That is not the kind of person Americans want for President. He is sworn to administer the laws faithfully—that is, in good faith. If, after a law has been enacted, new conditions arise or new facts are brought to his knowledge which make it clear that the execution of the law will be injurious to the public welfare and contrary to a public policy which Congress has already adopted, while delay in the enactment will imperil no public interest, good faith requires that he should postpone the execution and give Congress an opportunity to reconsider its action in the light of the new knowledge. This is what the Secretary of the Interior has done. His action, approved by the President, temporarily reserving from sale forest lands in the Indian Territory, was clearly Constitutional, and was apparently a necessary protection of the public interests against private rapacity.

In the Brownsville incident the Senatorial critics of the President are going outside their proper function in pressing upon the Senate an investigation into a,1 act of the Executive, the legality and justice of which the Senate has explicitly said it does not question; in the land incident they are attempting to make an automaton of the Executive Department in order to promote private interests which the best expert judgment indicates to be injurious to the public welfare. The peril to the country is not from an executive usurpation of legislative functions; it is from a Senatorial encroachment upon executive functions. It is the Senate, not the President, that the country needs to watch.

❦

# The Medicine for the Mob

Nothing is more irritating than the tone of superiority in an ignoramus. The people of the South have had to endure a great deal of dogmatic counsel and even submit to authoritative commands from folk who knew nothing of the Southerners' problems. The effect of the so-called Reconstruction Period was not such as to justify complacent theorists.

Nevertheless, the problems of the South are the problems of the Nation. This is true not only because what concerns civilization in one section affects civilization throughout the country, but also, as has been proved by recent events, because conditions which have been acute in the South may arise in any section. The very fact that these problems are in the last analysis National should liberate every American who discusses them from the imprisoning spirit of condescension.

Race riots and lynchings are a product of imperfect, and sometimes unhealthy, social conditions. In another part of this issue a Southern lawyer and a Northern professor discuss the cause and the cure of these disturbances. Although the diagnosis and the prescription of one differ from those of the other, they agree in this—that the disease will not be cured by trying to prevent the symptoms. Mr. Alexander finds the disease chiefly racial and political. He contends that the negroes are an essentially inferior people; they have been treated politically as if

they were not; a political system founded thus on a falsehood causes turmoil and confusion. Allow the people of the Southern States discretion in forming their political system, he urges, and the symptoms will cease. Proof: before the Civil War, when the negroes were excluded from the political system, they were docile and contented; now that they have a part in that system, they are turbulent and discontented; moral: let us, so far as the political (not the industrial) system is concerned, return to the conditions that prevailed before the war. This is the substance of Mr. Alexander's argument.

In considering this it should be borne in mind, first, that it ought not to be called "the Southern view." It is a view which many Southerners would hasten to disavow. Second, that it assumes several things that are controvertible; for instance, that the negroes are in a worse state now than ever before. Third, that the remedy it suggests would have no practical effect in those Northern States where lynchings and race riots have occurred. Fourth, that it supposes that a restoration of a former political system without a restoration of its concomitant industrial system would bring again that tranquillity which was insured by the industrial as well as the political domination of the whites.

Mr. Cutler attributes the disease to conditions which are much more general, less sectional, than those which Mr. Alexander cites. Analyzing the causes he mentions, we find them to be these: First, to some degree, but not largely, a faulty procedure in the courts; second, ill-trained and unfit court officers; third, inefficient and timid officers of the law, such as sheriffs and constables; fourth, the lack of an effective police for rural districts; fifth, and most important, unhealthy and immoral social conditions. The cure he suggests is greater responsibility in the selection of administrators of justice, the establishment of an adequate constabulary for the prevention of crime, and the cleansing of foul communities by the application of sanitary and social reforms.

In so far as the evil of lynchings and race riots is due to the existence of negroes in America, it calls for an intelligent treatment of the negroes' racial characteristics. The negro is a child race. In that sense it is inferior. Difficulties arising from such inferiority cannot be remedied by treating the negroes as if they were all racially mature; neither can they be remedied by repressing the negroes and making sure that their inferiority will be perpetual. They can be remedied only by instituting processes of education which will promote the progress of the race as a race, and then by rewarding those individuals who rise above the childhood level of their fellows. This is what most of the Southern States are doing.

In so far as the evil of lynchings and race riots is a consequence of imperfections in the machinery of government and disease in the social body, it calls for measures of governmental and social improvement. With such improvement, not only these but other disturbing symptoms, such as intemperance, vagabondage, strikes, diseases, and even such remotely connected troubles as railway accidents, will diminish.

The charge of the judge is ended. We leave the case to the jury—our readers.

⊛

# Ecclesiasticism vs. Christianity

Dr. Goldwin Smith presents on another page admirably the contrast between the Catholic Church and the Papacy, a contrast which both loyal Catholics and Protestant critics never should but often do forget. To his presentation of that difference between the two we can add nothing; but it is legitimate to remind our readers that a similar difference, though sometimes in less striking manifestations, is to be seen in the history of the Church universal.

For Christianity and ecclesiasticism are not identical; they have often been real foes even when apparent allies. Indeed, there is some ground for saying that the spirit of ecclesiasticism has been the worst foe that the spirit of Christianity has had to encounter. Christianity

is the liberty of the children of God, ecclesiasticism is the servitude of bondsmen to a bureaucracy; Christianity is a fellowship, ecclesiasticism breeds sectarianism; the inspiration of Christianity is charity and humility, the inspiration of ecclesiasticism is ambition and pride.

This contrast is most clearly seen in the most highly organized churches; but it is not confined to them. Dr. Goldwin Smith's object—to interpret the present conflict in France—required him only to indicate the conflict between Christianity and ecclesiasticism as it appeared in European history in the mediæval Church; but a complete history of that conflict would include the story of the Episcopal Church in the time of Laud, of the Presbyterian Church in the time of Knox, of the Puritan Church in the time of the Mathers, in truth of all Churches, past and present, Jewish, Greek Catholic, Roman Catholic, and Protestant, wherever the ambition for power and the aspiration for influence have been seen in contrast, if not in open conflict.

Ecclesiasticism crucified Christ in the name of religion; and it has never been more friendly to him since. Dr. Goldwin Smith's article, read aright, should lead the Protestant to regard with discriminating appreciation the spirit of Christianity in the Roman Catholic Church, and with inveterate hostility every manifestation of the spirit of ecclesiasticism in his own.

⊛

# Public Rights in Street Railways

Students of questions of municipal government will read with interest an article, printed elsewhere in this issue of The Outlook, entitled "Private Rights in Street Railways." Professor Garfield, the author of this article, who, our readers will remember, is a son of the late President Garfield and a brother of Commissioner James R. Garfield, the incoming Secretary of the Interior, is a lawyer of attainments, public spirit, and of the highest character. For many years he was a resident of Cleveland, and his summer home is still in that immediate neighborhood. His well-known sympathy for all genuine movements in behalf of popular rights, his knowledge of the legal questions involved, and his intimate acquaintance with the community of Cleveland entitle what he has to say upon the street railway controversy of Cleveland to careful and .respectful consideration. Nevertheless, while The Outlook is glad to present through the medium of Mr. Garfield's article the position and arguments of those who are arrayed against Mayor Johnson, in its opinion their arguments are not convincing and their position is not impregnable, for the following reasons :

On the surface the Cleveland conflict appears to be a local and temporary one in which the people on the one side are clamoring for cheap fares and a great street railway corporation on the other is struggling in the courts to preserve the just and reasonable rights of invested capital against the attacks of selfishness, envy, and demagoguery. In reality the conflict is very much deeper and more elemental. It is a pivotal battle in a great general campaign that is now going on in this country—a campaign which is to settle this question : Shall the streets of a municipality and the traffic thereon be controlled by the people of the municipality or by private corporations who have received from the people special and profitable privileges for the occupation of those streets?

A. private street railway company, whose history in the past, however honorable it may be to-day under the management of Mr. Andrews, is admitted to be spotted with corruption, has controlled the streets of Cleveland ; it has sought by the exercise of every expedient known to legal and financial skill to retain that control. It is inadequate to argue in defense of this corporation that its present managers are honorable and high-minded men, although this is undoubtedly a fact. The corporation is judged and condemned, not by its present character, but by its past record and by the unsavory history of street railways in this country for the last twenty-five years. The people of New York, Philadelphia, Boston, Chicago, and San Francisco have suffered too much from the lawless encroachments of the street railways, these cities have been too terribly burdened by municipal councils and State legislatures with unpaid for and perpetual franchises, they have been too exasperated by the obstacles thrown in the way of their obtaining even their commonest rights, to be much affected by Mr. Garfield's main argument. This is, as we understand it, that Mayor Johnson's record in the past as a street railway man is open to the greatest suspicion ; admitted : that the consolidated railway of Cleveland is now managed by Mr. Andrews, who is a man of the highest probity and is a vigorous and consistent opponent of corporate and political corruption; admitted : that therefore the people of Cleveland ought to trust their interests to Mr. Andrews and his colleagues rather than to Mayor Johnson and his associates ; not admitted.

The Legislature of Ohio, at the instance of private owners of street railways, has forbidden municipalities in that State to own street railways. No arguments can convince the average citizen that this is anything more than an attempt, in perfect harmony with the whole history of street railways in this country, of private capital to control the public streets. Mayor Johnson professes to believe in the public control of public streets; as an expert street railway man he asserts that street railways properly capitalized—that is to say, with the water squeezed out of the stock—can be run in Cleveland profitably at a three-cent fare. The consolidated company bitterly opposed the three-cent fare, and it is quite possible that with inflated capital they cannot pay dividends from a three-cent fare. The municipality could not, under a law passed for the benefit of the street railways, own its own tracks and lease the route to a company willing to charge only three cents. Mayor Johnson thereupon devised an ingenious scheme for providing the city with low fares and proper accommodations, and one which should at the same time conform to the law. He organized a new railway company and proposed to the city that if it would grant franchises to this new company it would be managed by a board of trustees who would act on behalf of the public as semi-municipal officers. These trustees, if they perform their duties as Mr. Johnson proposes that they shall, will bear the same relations to the people of Cleveland that the trustees of a museum, a hospital, a park, or a savings bank maintain. For our part, if we were citizens of Cleveland, we should say to Mr. Johnson, "This may be quixotic; it may be that, as an astute ex-street railway capitalist, you are trying to get hold of our street railways for your own personal profit; but you can't be worse than the Consolidated Road has been in some previous periods of its history; and if on trial you prove faithless to your promises and professions, we will deal with that question when it arises." This is practically what the people of Cleveland have done. They have indorsed Mayor Johnson and his plan on numerous occasions; and as the Supreme Court of the United. States has decided that franchises which the Consolidated Road had been trying to prolong perpetually have in effect expired, that corporation has now practically given up its contest and is trying to make the best terms it can with Mr. Johnson. There is every prospect that Mayor Johnson's plan of a holding company, which shall administer the street railways at three-cent fares for the benefit of the people, will be given a fair trial. Citizens of New York who remember how the street railway managers of that city obtained the enormously valuable Broadway franchise in the days of " Jake " Sharp, how they maintained four tracks in Amsterdam Avenue against the protests of citizens and municipal officers, how different companies fought tooth and nail the introduction of such improvements as vestibuled platforms, the abolition of the steam locomotive, the introduction of the proper lighting of the cars; and Philadelphians, Chicagoans, and San Franciscans who know how their street railway managers have persistently opposed, step by step, the introduction of reforms or improvements, will feel that even the failure of Mayor Johnson to carry out the public trust which he has assumed will in no wise affect the general principle for which the people of the city of Cleveland have been con-tending—namely, the fundamental doctrine of municipal politics, that the public streets shall be controlled by the public.

❀

# The Situation in Germany

The German Reichstag was dissolved by the Emperor on the 13th day of December; under the provisions of the German constitution it was necessary that the election of members to the new Reichstag should be held before the 11th day of February, and that the Reichstag should meet before the 13th day of March. The elections took place on Friday of last week. The issue between the Emperor and the Reichstag was on the question of voting a supplementary appropriation for the conduct of the war in southwestern Africa, the expenses of which exceeded by a number of millions the original estimates. The Socialists, who, with the Centrists or Clerical party, numbered two hundred members in the Reichstag, united to defeat the appropriation. The dissolution was promptly followed by a sharp alignment of parties and a vigorous discussion of the issue, which at once took the form of a conflict between the Clerical party and the Government. It was declared by the supporters of the Emperor that the Centrists, or clerical group, represented an unpatriotic policy, were introducing into German public affairs a foreign influence, and were showing by the alliance with the Socialists that they were ready to join hands with any one who would forward their interests. Later the issue broadened, largely through the declarations of Chancellor von Bülow, and the battle was waged on the question of the colonial policy of the Emperor as a whole.

That policy found early definition in the mind of the Emperor, and has been growing more important and comprehensive in his mind and action from year to year. When William II. became Emperor, the Empire was in many ways in a very strong position, but without adequate means to support that position. With a sagacity and foresight with which even his bitterest enemies must credit him, the Emperor turned his attention to the commercial development of the country, and by the application of statesmanship to commercial conditions and problems, by a study of the resources of the country and their development, above all by a broad-minded and far-seeing alliance between education and science on one hand and manufactures and commerce on the other, Germany has come into the front rank of commercial nations. Part of the Emperor's plan has involved an increase of colonization for commercial purposes. It must be remembered that Germany has only two notable harbors on the North Sea, Hamburg and Bremen; she is hampered, therefore, somewhat as is Russia in freedom of access to the sea. The policy of the Emperor has been to develop the commercial power of Germany to the very highest point, to plant colonies in different parts of the world, and to secure space and freedom for growth. Whatever may be thought of the wisdom of this policy, it has been consistently followed at a very large expense, and the burden of this expense and the question as to the effect of the reaction of the policy on the German people have called into being a vigorous opposition.

The members of the Reichstag, which bears to Germany the same relation that the House of Representatives bears to the United States, are chosen by secret ballot upon a basis of direct universal suffrage. Every male person of twenty-five years may vote, unless disqualified by pauperism or active military service. The electoral districts are so arranged that every State in the Empire elects at least one representative. Originally each electoral district numbered at least one hundred thousand inhabitants, except in the smaller States. In thirty years there has been no change in this system, but there has been great growth, in the larger cities especially, so that striking inequalities of representation exist to-day. In proportion to its population, for instance, Berlin ought to have at least twenty members; it has six.

The Reichstag consists of 397 members. In the election four years ago

3

three million voters stayed at home, which shows that this class of indifferent citizens is as well represented in the Old World as in the New. The Socialists captured seventy-nine constituencies, having increased the number of their members in every election for the past twenty years, and prophecies were freely made that the new Reichstag would include at least one hundred Socialists. There are still a number of re-elections to be made, but at present the Socialists have met a net loss of nineteen seats, and will probably number less than fifty in the new Reichstag. The party of the Center, or Clericals, which numbered one hundred and two in the last Reichstag, will probably number about ninety-five in the new Reichstag; the National Liberals, who numbered fifty-two, will probably have about seventy; and the Radicals, divided into two groups, who elected only thirty-six members in 1903, will now probably have more than forty.

The result of the elections, therefore, is a practical victory for the Emperor. The Government guns were turned on the Clericals, but they appear to have played havoc with the Socialists. The Clericals lose only five or six seats, but their alliance with the Socialists has very seriously diminished their prestige in Germany, while the loss of seats by their allies has turned the balance of power over to the supporters of the Government. A strong appeal was made to the voters who stayed at home in the last election, and their activity appears to have determined the result. After the second ballotings have been held and the new Reichstag has convened, the Government will undoubtedly secure the passage of a supplementary appropriation for carrying on its work of conquest in West Africa. Chancellor von Bülow must now keep himself in power by securing the co-operation of the National Liberals, the Radicals, and the Conservatives. The unnatural alliance of the Clericals and the Socialists has been defeated, and both the Emperor and the Chancellor have attained their ends in the dissolution of the Reichstag; but the task still devolving upon Chancellor von Bülow will demand his highest self-restraint, tact, and good judgment.

## The Spectator

Kingston—poor, sorely afflicted Kingston—lying only a short night's run from Santiago de Cuba and offering a haven half-way between Havana and Ponce in Porto Rico, has of late years been threatened with an American invasion. Not long ago the Spectator was himself one of the invading horde. Unlike many West Indian ports, Kingston, it seemed to the Spectator, really invited the stranger to tarry and rest a while, although some of the towns on the neighboring islands were so crude and primitive that they clearly offered little more than quaint pictures and positive discomforts to a person venturing more than the briefest visit of inspection.

❈

The commercial relations between the United States and Jamaica would alone be sufficient to arouse the keenest interest in the Kingston catastrophe. The Boston Fruit Company has established itself on the north shore of Jamaica, and, with its regular steamship service, is the leading business venture of the place. The industry is carried on in a broad American way which has made a fearful and wonderful impression on the natives, black and white. They speak of the Boston Fruit Company as Americans do of the Standard Oil.

❈

The use of brick as a building material was strikingly more common here than elsewhere in the West Indies; brick walls and brick houses looked very substantial compared to mud huts and flimsy frame dwellings. Window-panes of glass were also frequently seen—were, in fact, almost universal in the better houses. One might almost say that these two luxuries differentiate Jamaica and English colonies generally from those of other nationalities. The Kingston homes all had front yards full of flowers and shrubs. The hibiscus plant seemed to enjoy local approval if not admiration, for it was here considered a utility plant like cabbage or cotton, its local alias being "shoeblack," and prejudice ran so strongly in its favor that the Spectator greatly doubted if any recommendation or advertising would launch with profit a legitimate polish on the Kingston market.

❈

It was a great satisfaction to start on a country drive in any direction and feel absolutely sure of perfect roads, smooth and hard as park boulevards, but more verdant and picturesque than any park drive could possibly be. Kingston was well supplied with hacks—"buggies" they are called in Kingston—at seventy-five cents an hour, and the horses were better than they looked. There was also a car system with a belt line making a circle of the town and passing most of the large buildings that have been reported destroyed, including the two hotels best known to Americans—the Park Lodge, and the Myrtle Bank Hotel, which resembled a red brick factory building, but which overlooked the water and was exceedingly habitable and airy.

❈

The Spectator undertook one morning to find some characteristic souvenirs of his visit, and drifted into a little sweetmeat shop on Harbour Street—a kind of tropical delicatessen store. There was Jamaica ginger for sale, of course, but most of the other preserves had quite unfamiliar names—cocoa plums, guava dolce, mangolina, cashew apple, tamarinds, cherimelias, nasberries, grenadilla. The pickled dainties sounded quite as interesting if less inviting—calabash, chippolata, and turtle eggs. There was a Woman's Exchange, called, of course, Lady Somebody's Industrial Bureau, where a few odd things were found—fiber doilies, filmy as cobwebs and really exquisite; but the market-place merchandise was more varied and surprising. There were tiny fagots of sweet-smelling twigs, pottery lamps, coal-pots, chickens for sale alive with their feet tied and doves sprawling on banana leaves, grapes, grapefruit, shaddock, mandarins and tangerines galore. The turtle-shell shops were filled with a great variety of articles made of the beautiful transparent shell. Turtle soup, indeed, passed simply as a by-product, and the

Spectator turned from it gladly to chilled watermelon on those hot February days !

❁

The Jamaican market women are quite beyond compare. On Saturday morning one could see them trooping into town, a stalwart procession of mammies, all of them quite black and most of them ugly, cleanly dressed but barefoot, tramping erect with their baskets on their heads. The Spectator had heard of the incredible distances these women walked to barter their dozen oranges or hand of bananas for a fish or a kerchief, and had refused to believe the twenty-mile yarns, as they seemed, but he soon verified these claims by his own observation. The railway, by which he was making a comfortable excursion, ran parallel to the highway on which the negresses were forging along, market bound. Mile after mile he watched them from his car window—a healthy, happy, stupid-looking set, stepping smartly along with that pronounced swing of the hips that comes of carrying burdens on the head.

❁

Sunday morning sweeps a British community—and the stranger within its gates—into the sanctuary. The big edifice of the Church of England was packed, and its packing was mostly black—a neat, self-respecting, earnest congregation. There were a few whites in the choir, but the procession of choir-boys was all black. There were some whites in pews of their own, and a few odd whites, like the Spectator, in pews with black neighbors, all one before the face of the Lord. The service was intoned, and the mellow negro voices were remarkable in the chants and responses

❁

The Spectator remembers the Kingston park with delight. Hope Gardens is a lovely spot, and a most valuable botanical station into the bargain. There were patches of test plants, seedlings of new varieties, slips to be tried in various localities ; and all the flower-pots were transverse sections of bamboo stalks, artistic, glossy, and cheap where the rustling, crackling bamboo is so plentiful. There was a fine orchid house and a more charming orchid avenue where air-plants and orchid boxes hung from the trees. Here to the Gardens comes the holiday crowd on Sunday afternoon—negroes and well-starched negresses, white colonials with more than British lack of " chic," and showy zouaves with their best black girls. The Spectator had seen a company of these soldiers swing by at the Up Park Camp, and what a picture they made ! One white man in command, the rest all black as the ace of spades. They looked ready for a fancy dress ball or a light opera chorus drill, gaitered and turbaned and bloused, a rolling cloud of scarlet and white. There was no more rollicking dash in the West Indian color scheme than the black zouave soldier man, and the Spectator hoped that the War Office in London would make no such fetish of common sense as to declare in favor of khaki for Jamaican troops.

❁

In the little Kingston museum the Spectator saw an iron frame or human cage, a rough device for torturing and squeezing a person to death. The cage a few years ago was washed to the surface after heavy rains. Its story is unknown, but it is not hard to reconstruct it in the light of early West Indian history—the expulsion or annihilation of the Caribs and the Arawaks by the explorers, the settlers' own fierce rivalry among themselves in their greed for gold, their fiendish brutality toward imported slaves. The Spectator has been thinking a great deal about that cage during the past week or so. As one dire report after another has brought the news of fire and flood and earthquake, his mind has pictured the iron instrument of torture, with all the horrors it symbolized, horrors gross and wanton, the coarsest form of man's inhumanity to man, and has turned with some degree of patience, if not with peace, to the suffering and loss that have come through the orderly working of some stern law of nature after which we may make bold to grope.

# PRIVATE RIGHTS IN STREET RAILWAYS[1]

## BY H. A. GARFIELD

### Professor of Politics in Princeton University

THE Cleveland Traction struggle, as described by Mr. George S. Sikes in The Outlook of November 17, hardly inspires one with hope for the American city. The reader is led to believe that Cleveland is engaged in a struggle with a corporation which seeks by every means short of direct bribery to wrest the control of the streets from the people, that Mayor Johnson is entirely disinterested in his opposition to this attempt, and that, if he is beaten, public utility corporations everywhere will be encouraged to strive for the mastery.

The allegation of selfishness and greed made against the Cleveland Electric Railway by Mr. Sikes, and the inference that even under the leadership of a man as principled against bribery as Mr. Horace E. Andrews, President of the company, is conceded to be, the profit-making street railway corporation still finds it in its soulless heart to worry and browbeat the public, and block all attempts of the city administration to carry out any constructive programme whatever, are condemnatory of the American policy of private initiative as the best means of securing equal opportunity to all before the law, so far, at any rate, as public utilities are concerned.

Mr. Sikes's study of the Cleveland situation leads him to conclude that the advocate of regulation and control must consider himself beaten, and that the only salvation for the American city lies in eliminating the private corporation and extending municipal functions so as to include the ownership and operation of street railways. Scarcely has Mr. Sikes's article appeared when the value of his conclusion is seriously disturbed by a decision handed down by the Common Pleas Court at Cleveland, on a demurrer by the city to a petition filed by the Cleveland Electric Railway.

The Court held that "the relations which Mayor Johnson sustained toward the city and toward the street railway enterprise were in direct antagonism. As Mayor of the city he was officially a party to the several contracts with the railway company, and fidelity to the city forbade his being personally interested, directly or indirectly, in the welfare of the company, in the obtaining of privileges from the city. That he was so interested the facts here admitted can leave no doubt."

The following were the facts found by the Court: Mayor Johnson "conceived, initiated, and promoted the whole scheme of building and operating a system of three-cent-fare railways in this city. He procured a Mr. Green to make application for a grant from the Council. He procured the Council to make two successive grants to Green. He procured the incorporation and organization of the Forest City Railway Company, and then procured Green to assign his rights to that company. He procured the Council to make further grants to that company. He assumed secondary liabilities for payment of rails, cars, and other equipments for the road. . . . He procured the incorporation and organization of the Municipal Traction Company, to which the road has been leased." The Court also found that Mayor Johnson had joined in a written undertaking indemnifying subscribers to the Forest City Railway stock against loss, and agreeing to purchase their stock within a fixed period at the option of the subscribers.

The principle invoked, and against which Mayor Johnson has offended, is well stated by Judge Phillips, who rendered the decision. He said: "In the whole realm of jurisprudence no principle is better established or rests on a firmer foundation than the one which forbids one occupying a fiduciary relation from pledging himself in any degree

[1] See editorial comment on another page.—THE EDITORS.

in antagonism to his trust. A public officer is one to whom is delegated some of the sovereign functions of government, to be exercised by him for the public benefit. He acts only for the public; and the public are represented, in this instance, only by him; and the theory upon which his acts bind the public is that his acts have the public sanction, because they are exclusively in the interest of the public."

Mayor Johnson cannot expect the public to suspend judgment until the facts are formally proved at the trial of the case, because he has already furnished a statement over his own signature which is conclusive. During the month of June, 1906, the printed prospectus of the Forest City Railway was issued. In it was published a letter from Mayor Johnson, in the course of which he said: " I have in the past a number of times, when requested, become liable as surety on bonds and guaranteed the payment of obligations of the Forest City Railway Company. . . . I shall do all in my power to further the success of the Forest City Railway and the Municipal Traction Company. . . . This enterprise shall have my hearty support, and I confidently invite the support of the public, both as citizens and investors." This statement ought not to have escaped the attention of Mr. Sikes. It acknowledges the existence of a relation obviously antagonistic to the city's interest, as the Court has since declared.

The conflict is not, then, between the city and the Cleveland Electric Railway, but between that company and the Forest City Railway. The former of these, the old company, desires to maintain its control of the streets, but refuses to buy the privilege. The new company seeks to displace the old, and relies on the Mayor for success. All the vast powers of the office of Mayor have been arrayed against the old company, and the man who, for the time being, is intrusted with the exercise of those powers is financially interested in the company he supports. Manifestly, this is not competition, and it is in violation of the rules governing the conduct of public officials.

Mayor Johnson's relation to the Forest City Railway is a sufficient explanation of his opposition to President Andrews's request that the offer of the Cleveland Electric Railway be submitted to popular vote, and of the Mayor's undue haste in tearing up the tracks of the old company in the face of the Court's injunction, in order that the tracks of the Forest City Railway might be laid; it gives weight to the opinion, frequently expressed in Cleveland, that Mayor Johnson will consent to no settlement with the old company which fails to provide for the Forest City Railway; it vitiates every grant to the three-cent-fare enterprise, and defeats the usefulness of the non-profit-sharing plan devised by Mayor Johnson and his associates.

Because the Mayor of Cleveland is financially interested in one of the companies included in the so-called holding company plan, the city is made party to an experiment which, though lawful to private individuals or companies, is clearly beyond the scope of the powers of an Ohio municipality. To the inquiry whether a municipality should be permitted to enlarge the scope of its powers or otherwise modify a policy duly and constitutionally prescribed by the State Legislature for the government of cities the answer is obvious. Yet this is in effect what Mayor Johnson, with the co-operation of the City Council, is undertaking to do. Consistently, from the beginning, the State of Ohio has adhered to the policy of leaving the development of transportation facilities to private enterprise. Cities have not been permitted to own or operate their street railways. By refusal to pass bills granting such permission, the Legislature has declared for the policy of regulation and control and against the policy of municipal ownership.

Understanding the limitation thus imposed upon the city, Mayor Johnson and his associates, by means of a non-profit-sharing holding company, seek indirectly to reverse the State's policy, and involve the city in the street railway business. As stated by the Vice-President of the Municipal Traction Company in a letter laid before the City Council last August, they seek " to make of the city a full partner in the enterprise." To this proposal Mr. Johnson and the members of the City Council raised no objection. On the contrary, they have on many occasions expressed their entire accord with it, and have voted grants to the Forest City Railway in furtherance of the plan.

Mayor Johnson's friends reply hotly to this line of reasoning. In effect, they protest against the application of the rule that public officials may not do many of the things permitted to private citizens. On the theory, "No matter what you do if your heart be true," they brush aside Mayor Johnson's interest in the Forest City Railway as of no importance. It was entered into with a right motive, they say. But men's motives must be judged in the light of their conduct, and the lawlessness displayed by Mayor Johnson casts a doubt upon the claims of his friends.

The whole difficulty arises out of the Mayor's financial interest in the Forest City Railway. It is this fact that gives reality to the proposed "partnership," and would in effect involve the city in the street railway business. The case would, of course, be different if the stock of Mr. Andrews's company were held by the Municipal Traction Company, because the Mayor has no prejudicial interest either in the Cleveland Electric or the Municipal Traction.

It is in this direction that hope lies. On the 7th of January the Supreme Court of the United States handed down a decision which was both a victory and a defeat for Mr. Johnson. The Court held that the franchise of one of the branch lines of the Cleveland Electric Railway had expired, but refused to permit the city to take possession of the rails, poles, and other property of the road necessary for its operation. The inconvenience to the public which would have resulted in stopping operation on this branch altogether, and the necessity of opening negotiations for the purchase of the rails, poles, and wires, presented an opportunity to reopen the whole question for settlement. The contending companies therefore agreed to suspend hostilities for thirty days. During this period the old company agrees to charge only three cents on this branch line, and to allow the Forest City Rail-

way to run its cars into the public square over the tracks of the Cleveland Electric Railway, it being expressly provided that if at the end of the thirty days no settlement is reached, the Forest City Railway will at once cease operating its cars over the tracks of the Cleveland Electric, and that each party shall stand exactly where it stood prior to the 11th day of January, which was the date of the agreement.

On Monday, the 14th of January, the old company addressed a letter to the City Council, saying that while it still believed that its offer of seven tickets for a quarter and universal transfers was best for the city, it realized the people's desire to have the question settled, and hence was willing to confer, with a view to leasing its property to the Municipal Traction Company under the holding company plan, at the same time reiterating its belief that the property cannot be efficiently operated on a three-cent cash fare basis. The Council received the letter, and Mr. Du Pont, President of the Municipal Traction Company (controlling the Forest City Railway), was authorized to negotiate. It is generally conceded that the chief stumbling-block in the way of settlement is the price at which the property may be acquired by the city, if at any time the Legislature reverses its policy and permits municipalities to own the tractions.

I have no disposition to detract from the credit due Mr. Johnson for his determined fight for lower fares. My whole contention rests upon the method he has pursued—a method not only discreditable in itself, but which has, I believe, unnecessarily postponed a settlement of the question. Furthermore, we should not lose sight of the fact that if a settlement is reached, the Forest City Railway will have to be taken care of, and that the roads cannot for a long time to come be actually operated on a three-cent cash fare basis. I do not mean to associate these two facts as cause and effect, but as important items which one may be tempted to lose sight of, if called upon to applaud Mr. Johnson for winning a "three-cent fare victory." We ought to hate unfair fighting even in a good fighter.

# Race Riots and Lynch Law: The Cause and the Cure[1]

## I.—A SOUTHERN LAWYER'S VIEW

### BY HOOPER ALEXANDER

*Of the Georgia Bar*

ALTHOUGH comment has been abundant on the subject of the race riots which occurred in Atlanta in September, the fact seems to have wholly escaped observation that they indicate the advent of a new phase in the negro problem. What is called lynch law has been so prevalent in the entire South of late years, and the phenomena of lynch law and race riots are, on the surface, so very much alike, that they have been confused in the public mind. The truth is that they are quite distinct and spring from different causes.

Lynch law is generally provoked by some specific crime, and is simply an effort to inflict extra-legal punishment on the wrong-doer. A general state of criminality among the negroes was in some measure, perhaps, the immediate provoking cause of the Atlanta outbreak, but the rioting did not in any sense spring from any particular crime, or any purpose to punish crime, and was a mere series of brutal and murderous assaults on every negro in sight, without reference to his guilt or innocence, and was nothing more than a symptom of racial animosity.

Outbreaks of a similar character have occurred during the past few years in a number of Northern cities, and this has not been surprising, because there never were in the North any old ties of asso-

ciation and kind memories between the races to mitigate the natural antagonism of species. In the South, however, the surviving but diminishing residuum of good will that has come down from a former era has heretofore sufficed to prevent such indiscriminate brutalities.

Aside from the fact that the Atlanta incident probably marks the turning-point of the balance between the old and new influences, it is the more ominous because the acts of violence emanated from the wholly irresponsible elements of society. Lynch law, so called, has been, in the main, administered by men of at least comparative prominence in their several communities—men who at least believed they were establishing order, and so discharging a public duty. The Atlanta riot was wholly wanting in responsible leadership, was lawlessness pure and simple, with no redeeming motive, and sprang from an unmitigated race hatred. There is in the community an instinctive but undefined apprehension that the affair is the beginning of a graver era in the development of the negro problem.

There are more negroes in Georgia than in any other State. The State is admonished by the census that they are moving southward into her borders in increasing numbers. Georgia will in all probability be the center of the theater in which the settlement and solution of the negro question will have to be worked out. In Georgia, therefore, the subject can be studied to better advantage than elsewhere, because Georgia is typical of all the South. It cannot be studied without a broad view of the historical aspects

[1] In President Roosevelt's recent Message to Congress special stress was laid upon four subjects as of vital and paramount importance. Under the title "The Problem of Enormous Fortunes," a discussion of the inheritance tax by Philip S. Post was printed in The Outlook for January 5; "The People and the Corporations," by Judge Grosscup, appeared in The Outlook for January 12. The third of these four subjects is here treated in two articles. The fourth, "The Income Tax," will be discussed by Mr. Post in the near future.—THE EDITORS.

and successive stages of the question, passing by the petty animosities and less important matters that have at every period beclouded and concealed the larger movements.

The presence of the negroes in Georgia is attributable chiefly to the commercial and State policy of England during the seventeenth and eighteenth centuries; next to the navigation interests and commercial policy of her maritime colonies in America; and lastly to the individual desires of a small minority of the Georgia colonists themselves, and the complaisance of a few others who, as citizens, would have opposed the introduction of slaves, but were willing to take individual advantage of a practice that had the sanction of authority. The majority of the people of the colony, and afterwards of the State, were opposed to the introduction of negroes, either bond or free, and their sentiments were, as far as possible, reflected in their legislation.

The fundamental principles underlying the legislation of Georgia, both as a colony and a State, were, first, that, no matter whose fault it was, the negroes were here and that their presence raised a condition with which it was necessary to deal; second, that the negroes were incapable of self-control, and, *a fortiori*, of self-government, and unsuited to become a constituent part of organized society; third, that, both for their good and for the good of society, it was necessary to govern and control them—with such measure of kindness, indeed, as was possible, but, in any event, with all necessary firmness. The resultant system was a sort of patriarchal or feudal government operating within an organized democracy and restrained and supervised by it. The system thus evolved differed in many important particulars from a pure slavery, and was much milder and more humane, but was commonly known as the institution of domestic slavery. The designation was perhaps as accurate as could be expected, but the name was misleading.

Whether domestic slavery was or was not the wisest and most humane system that could have been worked out to meet the situation, it represented the best judgment of which the people of Georgia

were capable under all the circumstances, and was at least an improvement on the former condition of the negroes in Africa, as well as upon their original enslavement prior to the recognition and regulation of slavery by law.

At the time of the abolition of the system, the negroes in Georgia were an unusually law-abiding people, highly trained in the elementary knowledge of productive industry and skilled in handicraft, and a peculiarly happy and cheerful race. Their docility under the system was considerable, and the virtues of personal affection and fidelity were more marked among them than among any other race or people of any age. They were in the receipt of a substantial wage of labor, paid mostly in kind, but larger in value than was then paid to labor in most countries, and by law were in receipt of old-age pensions. There were some hardships incident to the system, but on the whole the negroes were content.

During the first six decades of the nineteenth century there grew up in the Northern States a considerable opposition to the Southern system, the causes and growth of which need not be here examined. Intense sectional animosities resulted, which brought on civil war, at the end of which the Northern opinion prevailed, and domestic slavery was abolished by force of arms, together with the incidents of its allied code.

Without any useless caviling over the wisdom or unwisdom of this policy, the people of Georgia reluctantly but sincerely acquiesced in the result, and themselves prohibited slavery by Constitutional enactment, assenting also a little later to a similar amendment to the Federal Constitution.

The abolition of the system left the negro without any established legal status. In this condition of affairs, it was the judgment of the people of Georgia that some kind of new status should be established, conforming, indeed, to the edict of emancipation, but still predicated upon the original theory that the negro was unsuited for citizenship, must of necessity be controlled kindly but firmly, and that he should, both for his own and the common good, be assigned to some subordinate position of tutelage defined and established by law. What sort of system would have been evolved if the people had been permitted to work out the problem for themselves is by no means clear. As a matter of fact, however, the entire subject was withdrawn from their jurisdiction, and the task was undertaken by the dominant section operating through the machinery of the General Government.

The fundamental principles underlying the work done by the Northern States were exactly the opposite of those previously acted on by Georgia. It was assumed as a basic doctrine—first, that the negroes were capable of self-control and self-government; second, that they were suited for co-equal citizenship under the laws and institutions which the people of Georgia had worked out for themselves; third, that of right they should be incorporated into the body politic as an integral part thereof, and that such course was not only wise, but necessary for the protection of the negroes; and that it was further necessary to compel the State to bestow the franchise of suffrage on the new element. These views were crystallized into the Fourteenth and Fifteenth Amendments to the Federal Constitution.

After forty years' experience under the new system, the situation of the negro is not satisfactory, and the consensus of opinion in the South is that it is worse than it was under the old system. As a productive unit, the negro has neither the skill nor the industry for one-half his former productive capacity. As a race the negroes have become idle, ignorant, irreligious, and criminal. There is among them a steadily growing hostility to the people and government of Georgia. They enjoy exact justice in the court-house, but really receive less actual protection from the law than in their former status. The aggregate wage received by them is less than formerly, and their old-age pensions have ceased. The increasingly sharp competition of white labor and the increasing indisposition of the negroes to do steady work have already narrowed their possible field of activity, and will do so further. The former joyousness of the race has wholly

disappeared, and has been superseded by a customary moroseness, with intervals of joyless boisterousness.

The personal affections growing out of the old patriarchal system have in the natural order of things almost entirely disappeared. There was an aggregate affection and attachment between the races, growing out of the personal relations, which was not quenched even by the interventions of the reconstruction period. This also is passing away and being superseded by an increasing antagonism which promises to aggravate the situation.

Atrocious crimes committed by negroes on helpless women and children, and other crimes almost as grave, provoke with increasing frequency summary extra-legal punishments. Very recently, as in the Atlanta riots, a tendency has appeared among the less responsible classes to inflict indiscriminate violence and murder upon peaceable and innocent negroes, in a way similar to outbreaks that have occurred in Northern cities where there never were any personal ties between the races. These conditions are of course very dangerous to organized society, and tend to produce a decline in public and private morality.

The people of Georgia have not until recently felt or shown any inherent personal or racial animosity toward the negroes. They do object and have always objected to the negro as an equal and a citizen. Language employed by Mr. Toombs in his Boston lecture on the 24th of January, 1856, and similar language used by Mr. Lincoln at Charleston, Illinois, September 18, 1858, so exactly describe the attitude of the people of Georgia on the subject as to warrant reproduction here.

Mr. Toombs said:

I maintain that so long as the African and Caucasian races co-exist in the same society, the subordination of the African is its normal, necessary, and proper condition, and that such subordination is the condition best calculated to promote the highest interest and the greatest happiness of both races, and consequently of the whole society; . . . that the white is the superior race and the black the inferior, and that subordination, with or without law, will be the status of the African in this mixed society, and, therefore, it is the interest of both and especially of the black race, and of the whole society, that this status should be fixed, controlled, and protected by law.

Mr. Lincoln said:

I will say, then, that I am not nor ever have been in favor of bringing about in any way the social or political equality of the white and black races—that I am not nor ever have been in favor of making voters or jurors of negroes, nor of qualifying them to hold office, nor to intermarry with white people; and I will say in addition to this that there is a physical difference between the white and black races which I believe will forever forbid the two races living together on terms of social and political equality. And inasmuch as they can not so live, while they do remain together, there must be the position of superior and inferior, and I, as much as any other man, am in favor of having the superior position assigned to the white race.

The present system was a mistake. It attempts the impossible, and has produced the evil consequences of the present day because it is founded upon an elementary premise that is false. The present conditions have constantly been foreseen and foretold by nearly all the Southern people. It is also now foreseen that they will become a great deal worse; and, so long as the disturbing cause persists, it is difficult to see how any human authority or code can correct the increasing evil. It is, therefore, the duty of the dominant power in the United States to re-examine the original premises and correct the error. The only possible way to make the correction will be found, upon examination, to be in striking from the Federal Constitution the Fourteenth and Fifteenth Amendments, leaving the question of the negro's status and government, as it was left by the founders of the Republic, in the hands of the people of the several States, to the end that authority may co-exist in the same hands with responsibility.

The correction of the error by Constitutional amendment will be very difficult, for the reason that one-third either of the House or Senate or one-fourth of the States can prevent it. Nevertheless, if an overwhelming public sentiment should demand the correction, it will probably be made by judicial decision. It is undeniable that neither the Fourteenth nor the Fifteenth Amendment was put into the Constitution in the way pointed out by

that instrument for its own amendment. Both were revolutionary enactments accomplished by revolutionary methods, and, while the Supreme Court would no doubt uphold them in the present condition of public sentiment, it is entirely likely that it would not do so if public sentiment realized the imperative necessity for getting rid of them and cried out against the methods by which they were adopted. The Court has never yet been called on to consider the question of their validity.

The people of Georgia are entirely capable of governing the negro effectively, and without any failure either of kindness or justice, and will do so when permitted, protecting him in life, liberty, and property, and eventually restoring him to a condition of morals and industry as good, and an enjoyment of the personal virtues as complete, as were his in 1865. There is no trouble whatever in so doing, and the only reason it is not done lies in the fact that there has been withdrawn from the people of the State a certain and a necessary part of their originally reserved autonomy. When that is restored, they can and will promptly take up the task and work out a solution.

If the negro continues to remain in America, this reform will come about, because it will have to come. Conditions will grow so much worse as to challenge the common sense and humanity of the country and override all obstinacy of opinion by forcing on the civic conscience a recognition of its imperious necessity. Nevertheless, it is highly probable that the reform will be so long delayed as to force upon the people of Georgia the necessity for adopting some expedient for temporary relief against conditions which will otherwise become morally intolerable.

So far as concerns the evils entailed by the Fifteenth Amendment, the evolution of such an expedient has already progressed far enough to indicate the general character it will take on. The so-called "Grandfather" constitutions are no essential part of the system, though they constitute a very important adjunct as a sort of outer fortification to fall back on in any temporary emergency.

They have in themselves a potential rather than an actual value as a factor in the problem. The reliance of the people for actual use is in the institution, not yet perfected anywhere, but more highly developed in Georgia than anywhere else, known as the white primary. In its essence and philosophy the white primary is a State within a State—not a legal or official government, and not supported by any sanction of law, but, none the less, the real government of Georgia, in fact, the State. It is as complete a protection against what is called "boss rule" as can be devised, preserving a genuine democracy among the people of the State, and at the same time absolutely and completely excluding the negro from participation in the government, and by methods which are beyond the possibility of criticism as violating either the Constitution or any statute.

While it was more immediately necessary thus to devise a highly evolved supplementary governmental system for escaping the evils of the Fifteenth Amendment, it is, in the ultimate outcome, even more important to the peace and stability of the State to work out a method for legally and peaceably escaping the consequences of the Fourteenth. Thus far its operations have been productive of violent and extra-legal attempts to mitigate the evils entailed by it—attempts wholly unpremeditated, except in the case of the Ku Klux, and not co-ordinated into any system—just as, in the first two decades after the Civil War, the suffrage amendment produced sporadic violence and varying illegal methods for controlling elections, until a system was finally worked out for its complete nullification by perfectly legal methods.

The Fourteenth Amendment, being in its nature largely self-executing, will be much more difficult to escape from by legal methods than the Fifteenth. Nevertheless, all experience teaches that evils of such magnitude as have been brought about by this attempt to incorporate an impossible element into the body politic are certain in time to produce their own remedy, just as the stomach will throw off unwholesome food or nature encyst a foreign substance embedded in the muscular tissue. It is quite likely that the remedy finally worked out will be analogous to the white primary; that is to say, some sort of purely voluntary government within a government will be developed. It may possibly be connected with the white primary system, by some sort of unofficial white legislative body, operating through the voluntary consent of its constituents, and so regulating and directing their conduct, upon strictly legal principles, as to bring into play through them a strong individual persuasion on the negro race in connection with contractual relations.

The possibilities of such a plan in the hands of a capable people are almost limitless. And the people of the Southern States have more skill in the science of government and more of the genuine spirit of democracy than any other people on earth.

## II.—A NORTHERN PROFESSOR'S VIEW

### BY J. E. CUTLER

*Assistant Professor of Political Economy at the University of Michigan; author of the book entitled "Lynch Law"*

THERE exists, unquestionably, a conviction, which is widely held, that the *lynching* of a suspected criminal is never right and never really justifiable, no matter what the circumstances. It must be admitted, however, that this conviction is most widely and most firmly held in those sections of the country where conditions are such that occasions for lynching rarely arise; elsewhere it has barely strength enough to find a feeble and ineffectual utterance as an aftermath of lynchings—there is practically no effective power in it for the prevention of lynchings. A public opinion that merely condemns lynching in the abstract, or, owing largely to remoteness, condemns the practice without real knowledge of the circumstances and conditions which foster it, avails little.

The task to be accomplished, therefore, is the development of an intelligent public opinion, in all sections of the country, which shall condemn absolutely and unequivocally the practice of lynching, and at the same time shall have the wisdom to profit from the experience of the past and the foresight to accept and act upon the dictum that prevention is better than cure. There are several measures, preventive of lynchings, for the adoption of which the support of public opinion may be sought with some degree of confidence, and which may therefore be regarded as practicable.

One other test of practicability must not be overlooked, however. Any measure that is preventive of lynchings must be applicable to local conditions. A lynching in its inception is a purely local affair. Every occasion for a lynching is the direct outcome of conditions which have come to exist in a single community. Lynchings do not occur simultaneously at a number of points in a given section of the country as the result of some common factor to be found in the social conditions prevailing over that area. The extent to which the genesis of lynchings is local in character is revealed by a study of the distribution of lynchings by counties in those States where the greater number has taken place in the last twenty or more years. It has been commonly assumed that the presence of the colored race, because of the nature of the crime which negroes are believed frequently to commit and the resulting racial animosity, is alone responsible for the occurrence of lynchings; but no distinct correlation can be traced between the distribution of lynchings and the percentage of negroes in the population. It is only the proportion of whites lynched to negroes lynched that seems to bear any relation to the proportion between the white and colored elements in the population. No tendency is shown for the percentage of lynchings to increase where the percentage of foreign-born in the population is large. Neither does the degree of illiteracy, as shown by the census, have an appreciable influence on the distribution of lynchings. Measured by the test of the percentage of illiterates in the

population, it may be said that lynchings are not confined to backward or degenerate communities. Neither are lynchings confined wholly to any one section of the country. Only New England has escaped altogether from appearing in the record in recent years, although there have been threatened lynchings in this section—notably one on the night of October 17, 1904, when "rum-crazed" Henry Boles, living at 88 Bolyston Street, Brookline, Massachusetts, shot and killed his wife, and also killed a popular and fearless policeman, the threatened mob violence being prevented only by the prompt arrival of a patrol wagon and a squad of policemen. And there have been whippings and other forms of corporal punishment administered by White Caps—notably on the night of February 14, 1906, when a band of White Caps took a man from a house in Granby, Connecticut, and, with some violence, escorted him over the State line into Massachusetts, a proceeding in which a deputy sheriff took part, who, by his own confession, was "a member of the 'bouncing' party as a private citizen and not in his capacity of sheriff," confident that he "understood the sentiment of Granby." "Prosecute me? Well, I ain't afraid of it. I tell you the people glorify in what was done. I ain't the only man that is willing to say that he was in the party."

In the consideration of what is practicable for the prevention of lynchings, therefore, at least two tests of practicability should be kept in mind—first, the extent to which the proposed measures can enlist the support of public opinion, and, second, their applicability to local conditions, the extent of their serviceableness to local districts, to communities as such.

Some writers and public speakers have urged specific changes in the judicial procedure, such as, for example, the abolition of the right of appeal in criminal cases. This change has been urged in the belief that the courts give so much weight to mere technicalities that, through the exercise of the right of appeal, justice often is, if not entirely defeated, at least flagrantly delayed and perverted. To the ordinary private citizen the courts often seem to be much more concerned about conformity to precedent and stated rules of procedure than about the administration of justice, speedily and effectively, in particular cases; and it is quite impossible for members of the legal profession to convince laymen that technicalities have not, in the administration of the criminal law in this country, all too frequently, and indeed unnecessarily, defeated the ends of justice. It is true that the lawyers criticise the jury system, and point out that the average juryman in the criminal courts cannot be depended upon to render a just and discriminating verdict. Undoubtedly a higher grade of citizenship is demanded in the jury-box. Men of character and standing in the community should be less frequently excused from jury duty. But this is aside from the point under consideration. A prominent excuse for lynching is the law's delays and the uncertainty of the result of legal procedure, for which there is, it is admitted, some basis in fact. Must the right of appeal in criminal cases, therefore, be abolished, or some other equally radical change in legal procedure be brought about, in order to invalidate this incentive toward lynching? Such a measure, if adopted, would probably overreach the desired end; its effect would be so far-reaching as to produce unforeseen consequences, more undesirable, perhaps, than the delays and uncertainty that now exist. Furthermore, public opinion is not likely to support such a measure. Nothing less than full opportunity to every man accused of crime to prove his innocence, if he is innocent, will satisfy public opinion.

The truth of the matter is, the basis for the complaint of the law's delays and uncertainty is to be found, not in any radical defect in the established code of criminal procedure, but in the low professional standard of the criminal lawyers and the legal incapacity, the utter incompetence often, of the prosecuting attorneys and trial judges. In the course of most criminal trials it is apparent that the defendant's counsel seeks, if he cannot secure an acquittal, to obtain in one way or another adequate ground for an appeal to the higher courts. The more

desperate the case—the more evident it is that the accused is guilty of the crime charged—the greater the effort on the part of the defendant's counsel to secure a basis for an appeal; that is his only hope of ultimately winning the case. Whether he succeeds or not in his purpose depends upon the ability, the legal knowledge, and the skill of the prosecuting attorney and the judge on the bench, officers into whose hands the people have committed the duty of determining justice and meting out punishment. The records of the appellate courts furnish abundant evidence of the fact that the ability of the bar is inadequately represented in the office of prosecuting attorney and on the bench of the trial courts. There is urgent need in this country of a speedier conclusion to trials, and of criminal courts which will command greater respect and confidence on the part of the citizens; but the responsibility for improvement should be placed where it belongs, that is, on the people themselves. Abler prosecuting officers and judges can remove from the law much of its delay and uncertainty, and it behooves American citizenship to see that only men of the highest standing at the bar shall occupy these responsible positions. It is time to recognize the absurdity of putting comparatively incapable and inefficient men into office for the purpose of conducting the trial and punishment of criminals, and then of complaining that the ordinary judicial procedure is so open to delay and uncertainty that criminals must be dealt with by summary and illegal methods for fear that justice may miscarry.

Numerous cases might be cited in illustration. Reference need here be made only to three cases, all of which have attracted general attention, and one of which is in marked contrast to the other two.

It was on December 30, 1903, that the whole country was shocked by an unparalleled loss of life at a theater fire, and by the evidence of the criminal violation of law which had been permitted in Chicago. A year later there appeared in the editorial columns of the Chicago Tribune (the issue of December 31, 1904) the following comments: "When Judge

Kersten spent a week hearing arguments with regard to a change of venue in the Iroquois fire cases, something was wrong either with the Judge or with the system under which he was obliged to work. Justice was frivolously delayed, the time and money of the State of Illinois were squandered, and a feeling of suspicion and of disrespect for law was fostered among the people of the city of Chicago. . . . When a whole year passes after such a catastrophe as the Iroquois fire and neither acquittal nor punishment has been secured, the people are justified in demanding that their judges, their lawyers, and their legislators bestir themselves in the direction of change and improvement. If improvement does not 'come, the judges may expect themselves to be held responsible for a condition which they now attribute to the sys tem." Not until the latter part of January, 1906, was it even decided that the manager of the burned theater must go to trial.

In New York City on September 23, 1900, an aged millionaire died from poison which had been given him with murderous intent. In April, 1901, Albert T. Patrick was indicted for the murder, and at his trial was found guilty and sentenced to die in the electric chair in the week of May 5, 1902. Numerous appeals and pleas based on technical errors were then brought forward from time to time, with the result that the sentence remained unexecuted for more than four years, until on December 20, 1906, Governor Higgins commuted the death sentence to life imprisonment.

In contrast to these two cases, the history of the Tucker case in Massachusetts is worthy of note. Charles L. Tucker was arrested for the murder of Mabel Page April 9, 1904. On June 9, 1904, the Grand Jury found an indictment against him. Six months later he was brought to trial by a prosecuting attorney of marked ability before a carefully selected jury, and, chiefly on circumstantial evidence, he was convicted of the crime. Tucker's counsel at once filed a motion for a new trial, which motion was denied. Thereupon his counsel filed various exceptions to the rulings of the presiding judges. These

were considered by the supreme judicial court of the Commonwealth and were overruled. A second motion for a new trial was then made by his counsel. This motion was likewise overruled January 22, 1906. An application for a writ of error was then made to the Supreme Court of the United States. This application was also denied. Finally an appeal was made to the Governor of the Commonwealth. In his decision, rendered after an exhaustive investigation and after highly commendable deliberation, Governor Guild used these words: " Neither, therefore, on the ground urged that the verdict was unwarranted by the evidence, nor on the ground usually urged, can I interfere with the execution of this just sentence. Every citizen must sympathize and sorrow with this unhappy man's afflicted family, but of more importance than the life of any one citizen is the protection by government of the life of every citizen, is the safeguarding of woman's chastity in the lonely farm-house as well as in the patrolled streets of the city, is the assurance to the people that the ordered action of their courts is to be respected, and that irresponsible agitation cannot be substituted for law and order in this Commonwealth." The sentence of death was carried into execution but little more than two years after the crime had been committed, and the forces of law and order were immeasurably strengthened in the Commonwealth of Massachusetts by reason of the ability and conscientious work of the men whose duty it is to administer and execute the law.

The right of appeal in criminal cases need not necessarily be abolished, nor other radical step taken of a similar nature, in order to secure expeditious trials and inspire greater confidence in the work of the criminal courts. A more careful and a wiser selection of men for the offices of prosecuting attorney and judge will bring about the desired result without any radical change in the code of criminal procedure. The system should not be blamed for the inefficiency of the men selected to carry it on. An effort may wisely be made in every judicial district in the country to improve the personnel of the judiciary and to maintain for it a higher standard of efficiency, and this is a practicable measure that will be preventive of lynchings.

In every community where the white and the colored races live in close proximity an intelligent, conscientious, and efficient judiciary is indispensable. When crimes are committed that cross racial lines, as is often the case, the difficulty of securing an invariable observance of due process of law is greatly increased. Nowhere is there a greater demand, nowhere a necessity that is more urgent, for wisdom and intelligent action on the part of the judiciary than in those sections of the United States where there are strong racial contrasts in the population. Likewise there is need, under such circumstances, of men who are efficient and conscientious in the discharge of their duty, to control that part of the legal machinery which has to do with the apprehension and protection of suspected criminals. Numerous cases of lynching have evidenced a criminal neglect of even ordinary duty on the part of sheriffs and constables. In a number of cases, too, where there has been some reason for doubting that the person lynched was guilty of the crime charged, the authorities have made not the slightest effort to apprehend the real culprit and fix beyond the peradventure of a doubt the responsibility for the crime.

By far the most important measure, however, that is practicable at the present time for the prevention of the lynching of negroes is a wider exercise of the police power, with the end in view of controlling the criminal elements in both races and preventing the commission of crimes likely to excite lynchings. If men and women are permitted to live in generally unwholesome and immoral surroundings, criminal tendencies will become dominant and crime will result inevitably. Many cities contain negro sections which are utterly neglected and may rightly be characterized as breeding-places of crime. What has happened at Springfield, Ohio, and at Springfield, Missouri, within the last two years is sufficient proof of the folly of this let-alone policy. In both these cases the inevitable has happened: negroes committed deeds of violence which aroused a spirit of vengeance in the community, and mobs quickly formed, which, after lynching the individuals suspected of the crime, went through the negro quarter of the city, burning and destroying property and terrorizing the inhabitants—"cleaning out" the district, it was called. The effects of such occurrences do not cease with the restoration of order and outward tranquillity through the calling out of the militia; a rankling animosity is felt long after the departure of the troops. The preventive means to be employed are streets open to the sun by day and studded with arc lights by night, close surveillance of saloons, dance halls, and disreputable resorts, model tenements, no overcrowding—in short, the strict enforcement continuously of all the sanitary, public health and public welfare regulations in the negro quarter as well as in other sections of the city. There should be no excuse whatever, no shadow of a justification, for such raids and such orgies of "cleaning out" by mob violence as have taken place at Springfield, Ohio, and Springfield, Missouri.

In many rural districts in the South the criminal element among the negroes is large. Professor Du Bois, of Atlanta University, has made the positive statement that at least nine per cent. of the country black population in the Black Belt are thoroughly lewd and vicious. If crimes are to be prevented and the virtuous protected from criminal attack in such districts, only an efficient and thoroughly organized constabulary police force can bring it about. Several of the Governors of Southern States have been able to use the State militia effectively to prevent threatened lynchings, as, for instance, at Roanoke, Virginia, in February, 1904, when Governor Montague ordered out a large body of militia from Richmond, Petersburg, Lynchburg, Suffolk, and other towns, and sent them to Roanoke by special train to protect a negro prisoner who had entered the house of a white man and made a fiendishly brutal assault on his wife and little daughter. Under the protection of the militia a jury was empaneled and the perpetrator was tried and sentenced, within a few hours, to be hung on a date six weeks after the crime had been committed. Obviously, however, it is impossible to use the State militia to prevent the commission of a crime such as the one that threatened a lynching at Roanoke. The establishment of a constabulary system of patrol and protection in many districts in the South seems to be a practicable and most desirable measure, and certainly it is one that will be preventive of lynchings. In this connection the experiment which Pennsylvania is making with a State constabulary, organized for the purpose of maintaining order in the mining region, may be watched with interest and doubtless with much profit.

The racial discrimination involved in many of the anti-lynching measures that have been proposed is a fatal objection to them. In employing a wider and fuller exercise of the police power for the prevention of lynchings, racial discrimination may be entirely avoided. Afro-Americans, newly arrived immigrants, native whites, all who inhabit those sections of a city in which conditions are such that crime is fostered, and which are a menace to the welfare of the community, may receive the same and equal treatment with advantage to the community. In the rural districts of the South the work of a constabulary force need not be confined to the control of the criminal classes among the negroes alone. The end always to be kept in view is the control and improvement of conditions which are a menace to a community, which tend to make life and property unsafe, and which at the same time promote racial antagonism and lynchings.

For the prevention of lynchings in this country neither additional legislation directed specifically against lynching, nor any very radical change in the established code of criminal procedure, is seriously needed. The great preventive and reforming force is an opposing public opinion, intelligent, active, vigilant, and effective. American citizenship is confronted with a crucial test of its quality and its wisdom, of its capacity to meet, more adequately than in the past, the exigencies of existing conditions and the civic responsibility which our form of government requires of the citizens.

# THE SHIP THAT COMES

### BY MARY BALDWIN

Oh, the ships that come and the ships that go,
Bearing their burden of weal or woe!

And some sail far 'neath the wide world's rim,
And faint grows the heart as the ship grows dim.

But the ship of hope that goes down to the sea
Gives eyes and ears to the heart of me—

A tiny craft with a trembling sail,
Pale as a moonbeam, gossamer frail,

Fearlessly following God as a star,
For trackless the paths of Eternity are;

My heart through the mist of the evermore drawn
On and on to a coming Dawn,—

To a coming dawn, to a full-tide sea,
And a little new Life safe anchored by me.

# THE CHURCH QUESTION IN FRANCE

## BY GOLDWIN SMITH, D.C.L.

THE Catholic religion is one thing, the Papal theocracy is another. From what is now passing in France, in some measure also in Spain, there is reason to surmise that the liberation of religion from the Papal theocracy may be at hand. It seems strange that the distinction between the religion and the theocracy, being as it is of the highest importance, should not have been more clearly seen. The Catholic religion, with all its special doctrines and features, its sacramentalism, its sacerdotalism, its asceticism, its belief in miracles and relics, is the religion of the post-Apostolic times, of the Latin Fathers and the Latin Church, down to the eleventh century, when the ambition of Hildebrand, taking itself for spiritual aspiration, founded the Papal theocracy, a power not the less temporal or the more moral in that it was based, not directly on force, but on religious superstition which placed force at its command.

Christianity, going forth to convert human nature into the image of its Founder, encountered adverse influences of different kinds: that of Paganism, in the way both of persecution and of infection; that of Alexandrian metaphysic, which framed and imposed the yoke of dogma; that of Eastern asceticism, which perverted the ideal of character; that of Byzantine imperialism, which entailed bondage to the power of the court and subjection to intolerant legislation. But the most fatal of all the influences in its consequences was the theocratic.

Marked as was the ascendency of Gregory the Great in the sixth century, there was on his part no claim or visible desire of the temporal power. Head of the Western Church, its center, and its best protector amidst the cataclysm of barbarian invasion, the Bishop of the Imperial city naturally was; and his authority would be all the greater because it was not, like that of his rival at Constantinople, overshadowed by the presence of the court. But his authority was still spiritual, not temporal. If, while he denounced as an impious assumption the title of Universal Bishop, he showed a tendency to claim universal pre-eminence, it was ecclesiastical pre-eminence alone. If he rebuked a minister of the State for misuse of power, it was not as a civil superior, but as Ambrose had rebuked Theodosius for the massacre at Thessalonica. If he, very wrongly, and to his great discredit, applauded the usurpation of the empire by Phocas, it was in the general interest of the Church, and there mingled with his approval no note of a suzerain's confirmation. Of the city of Rome a Pope was naturally the temporal ruler. But his title came simply from the need of a local governor and protector. Over missions, such as that of Augustine in England, he would of course exercise plenary authority, without, however, supplanting or overriding that of the Saxon King.

From Hildebrand really dates the claim to temporal power, with all its fatal consequences to the Church and Christendom. In the mind of that aspiring and stony-hearted monk was begotten the idea of a theocracy; that is, of an autocracy, temporal, but founded on superstition, putting the powers of the world under its feet by its anathemas, and using them as the agents of its despotic will. A celibate clergy cut off from domestic affection and gentle influences was the well-chosen instrument of such a power. It is strange that historical philosophy should be prone to regard with complacency the ascendency of superstition as an influence more moral than force; when in fact it is more profoundly immoral, and moreover always has to suborn force as the instrument of its designs. Charity may plead that

269

Hildebrand was so far self-deluded as to believe that his dominion was the ascendency of the spiritual over the carnal, and of the authority of God over that of the powers of the world. But of what crimes and calamities has self-delusion not been the source?

To establish the supremacy of the spiritual power over the powers of the world, and inaugurate the kingdom of God, Hildebrand allies himself with the piratical Normans, who, combined with a contingent of Saracens, come to Rome for his protection and fill the sacred city with massacre and ruin. In Germany, to put the Empire under his feet, he stirs up rebellion and civil war, the commencement of a train of the same calamities brought on with the same motive by heirs of his aspirations. He shows himself the true successor of the meekness of the Founder of Christendom by trampling on the vanquished Emperor at Canossa. He bestows his blessing on the buccaneering invasion of England by William the Norman, and his sacred banner is carried by the invader at Hastings. One of his successors sanctifies the Norman invasion of Ireland, proclaiming it as a well-established truth that all islands are the property of the Holy Sea, while he reserves to himself the suzerainty, with an annual tribute. Hildebrand would have made himself suzerain of England. But for this his Norman accomplice was too strong. With the weak John another Pope succeeded better, making himself for the time suzerain of England and drawing from her a feudal tribute, to which was presently added an enormous appropriation of her ecclesiastical patronage and revenues. A Papal excommunication of the authors of the Great Charter was an incident of the struggle, and presents itself as a text for those who imagine that Papalism was an antidote to feudal oppression. The Papacy got on very well with Philip II., with other despots, and with despotism in general, however oppressive, in after times.

In the case of the Norman and Hildebrandic invasion of England real Christianity was not without a witness. Guitmond, a monk, and Gulbert, a Norman knight, refused to share the booty; the monk saying that he would as soon touch fire.

A Pope could, on occasion, appeal to the people through his creatures and agents, the mendicant orders. But it was to get help for himself, as he effectually did, in his struggle with the higher political powers, not that he wanted to elevate or did elevate the people.

The False Decretals of Isidore and the fictitious grant of Constantine, palmed upon the Christian world, were congenial title-deeds of theocratic usurpation.

The consequences followed : civil war after civil war in Germany to put the Empire under the Pope's feet; the extermination, with hideous massacres, of free thought in the South of France under the fanatic and brigand de Montfort; similar massacres in other districts; the Inquisition, burning fifteen hundred victims in Spain in a single reign; Alva's tribunal of blood in the Netherlands; the massacre of St. Bartholomew, hailed with ecstasy and glorified by Rome; the institution of the Order of Jesus, strangely misnamed, as the intriguing pioneer of Roman ambition, a part which the Order is still playing.

What was the theocracy in France, the present scene of the struggle? We see the pious Francis I. and his court showing their loyalty to Rome by witnessing heretics swung in chains over the fire. At a later date a "Council of Conscience" is sitting at Versailles. At its head is the King, a notorious adulterer. Present are Louvois, the ravager of the Palatinate, the Jesuit Père La Chaise representing the Papacy, and Harlay de Champvallon, Archbishop of Paris and Primate of the French Church, the profligacy of whose life is notorious and is the theme of epigram. This Council decides, for the greater glory of God, to break the solemn covenant with man embodied in the Edict of Nantes, under which the Huguenots worshiped in peace. There follow the Dragonnades. The worthiest and most industrious people of France are visited with a persecution as cruel as any ever inflicted by paganism upon the Christians; their worship is suppressed, their churches are destroyed, their homes are rifled, their pastors are sent to the galleys; such of them as are driven into exile are forbidden to take their children with them. Everything, says the French historian Martin, was permitted to the soldiery saving rape and murder, and even that restriction was not always respected; many victims died or were maimed for life in consequence of the treatment they had undergone, and the obscene tortures inflicted on women differed from the last outrage only in refinement of cruelty. All the diabolical inventions of the brigands of the Middle Age to extort gold from their captives were in some cases renewed to enforce conversions. The persecutors put fire to the feet of the victims, racked them, hung them up by their extremities. They tied young mothers to the posts of their bed while their sucking infants writhed with hunger. Leading men were thrust into noisome dungeons, in one of which died a brother of Bayle, not without consequences to the murderers. (See Martin, " Histoire de France," XIV., 50.)

For none of this was Christianity, or, rightly speaking, the Catholic form of it, to blame. Spiritual Christianity was all the time struggling in different places and in various forms—some of them, it is true, rude, wild, and fanatical enough—to get loose from the theocracy and worship God in its own way. The discontent seldom slept which in the end produced Savonarola, Huss, Jerome of Prague, and Wycliffe. Witness was borne to Catholicism as Christianity by such characters as that of the author of the " Imitation of Christ," afterwards of Blaise Pascal and Fénélon; as it has been in our own day by the opponents of the Jesuit and of the Council of Rome.

As a great light of morality the Papacy has never shone. The Popes, generally speaking, were men whose passions had been chilled by old age. Yet the lives of some of them, such as John XXIII. and Alexander VI., were very bad even on the throne. Italy, in which the Papacy had its seat, was more eminent in art and culture than in virtue. Ambition of the most worldly kind actively engaging in all the intrigues and plottings of Italian politics, not seldom in wars, was a curious representation of the

Founder of Christendom. An Italian, native or by adoption, the Pope, as a rule, had, and still has, need to be. Christendom is universal; Catholicism is universal ; Papalism, a temporal power though pretending to be spiritual, is Italian.

The corruption of the Curia and the whole Papal administration was notorious, and the history of Thomas à Becket tells us that it had commenced in the twelfth century. The nepotism was shameless. The jubilees and dispensations by which the Papacy swept enormous sums of money into its coffers were worse than naked bribery or peculation, worse than the exactions of feudal kings or barons, because they profoundly falsified the conscience of Christendom. The nepotism adorned Christianity with the character and career of Cæsar Borgia.

That it was through the Church that in the feudal age men of lowly birth rose to commanding positions is true; but through the Church it was, not through the Papacy. Nor was feudalism much tempered by their rising. Unfortunately, when they had risen they became agents of Papal obscurantism and for centuries kept back the intellectual and scientific progress of the world. It was at Rome that Galileo was condemned as a heretic. In the flower market of Rome stands the statue of Giordano Bruno there burned for foreseeing the age which now erects to him that statue.

Italy, the seat of the Papacy and the center of its influence, was in fact rather more pagan than Christian. A grand product of mediæval religion was Gothic art, through the works of which, cathedrals and churches, it still has a powerful hold on the religious world. But in Italy Gothic art was comparatively weak. There is scarcely a relic of it in Rome. The theocracy showed its character when it pulled down the Catholic Basilica and reared in its stead St. Peter's, a magnificent product of classic art, but alien to Catholic religion. How, indeed, could Leo X. have performed his ceremonial in a Christian fane?

The Papacy may say that it led Christendom in the conflict with Islam. It did, but with equivocal results. The leadership was senile, unsteady, passionate rather than politic, crossed and marred by ecclesiastical ambition. The Empire would probably have done the work better. The behavior of the Papacy to Frederic II. was insane. Papal pretensions divided the forces of Christendom and fatally prevented effectual aid from being lent to the Eastern Church at Constantinople against the Turk.

Credit is claimed by the Papacy for having upheld the sanctity of marriage. Innocent III. did forbid his enemy, Philip of France, to change his wife, but he had not forbidden John of England, on plea of consanguinity, to exchange a lowly for a higher marriage on his succession to the throne. Napoleon was allowed to put away Josephine and marry an Austrian princess, though his marriage with Josephine had been repeated with full ecclesiastical forms at the special instance of the Pope. The Pope, it is true, was in duress at the time, but he must have known what his priests were doing. Never was divorce easier than it was when the theocracy was at its zenith, under the pretense of dissolution of marriage on the ground of consanguinity or pre-contract, for the class who could afford to pay their fees.

The State Church of France was wrecked in the Revolution. It was restored as a necessary complement of political despotism by Napoleon, who was himself absolutely without religion and in Egypt had affected conversion to Islam. In return for this the Pope goes in person to crown Napoleon shortly after the murder of the Duc d'Enghien.

Against the French Republic the Papacy, represented by the Jesuit and the Ultramontane priesthood, has been carrying on a standing conspiracy. More than once the Republic has been brought to peril largely by its machinations. The present measure is one, not of religious persecution, but of political and social self-defense. In the Syllabus, the latest manifesto of the Papacy and the Jesuit, with general antagonism to religious liberty, freedom of thought, and the spirit of a liberal and scientific age, there is a distinct assertion of the claim of the Church to temporal power.

Lord Acton, a devout Catholic to the end of his days, said of the Council of Rome, which gave infallibility to the Pope, "We have to meet an organized conspiracy to establish a power which would be the most formidable enemy of liberty as well as science throughout the world." "The scheme adopted by the Council," he says, "makes civil legislation on all points of contract, marriage, education, clerical universities, mortmain, even on many questions of taxation and common law, subject to the legislation of the Church, which will simply be the arbitrary will of the Pope." "Most assuredly," he adds, "no man accepting such a code could be a loyal subject or fit for the enjoyment of political privileges." Most assuredly, with Lacordaire, Montalembert, and all that body of Catholics who seceded or stood aloof from the Ultramontane and Jesuit Council of Rome, Lord Acton would now be on the side of the State and the civil government of France.

"A speculative Ultramontanism separate from theories of tyranny, mendacity, and murder, keeping honestly clear of the Jesuit with his lies, of the Dominican with his fagots, has not yet been brought to light," so says the good Catholic Acton. Nor is it at all likely that such an Ultramontanism will be found. But Catholicism, such as Acton's was, existed for centuries before Ultramontanism or the theocracy, and when rid of it, as it seems now not unlikely to be, may again play its own part and do whatever is in it to do for Christendom and mankind.

We in Canada have just had a specimen of theocratic influence dividing the citizen's allegiance in the shape of the "Autonomy Act" of the last session of the Canadian Parliament, forcing sectarian education in the interest of the Papacy on the new Provinces of the Dominion. The measure, clearly against the bent of our constitution, was dictated by an emissary from Rome, and was floated through the Canadian Parliament in company with a large increase of sessional indemnities and a number of pensions, and a salary for the leader of the Opposition.

# LAST CHANCE GULCH TO-DAY

## BY JACOB A. RIIS

THE sun was setting on an autumn day in the closing year of the Civil War, when two weary miners came out of the foothills of the Big Rockies and halted on the brink of a small stream, where the mountain gorge opened into the wide plain. They had come far and were tired. All summer they had roamed through the hills with a party of prospectors who were now scattered over many miles, searching for the gold that was known to be there, but without luck.' It was getting late; the winter snows were not far away, grub all gone. It was high time to strike for the trading posts on the Missouri, or the settlements in the Bitter Root Valley, unless to the privations of the trail were to be added the risk of being snowed in and starvation. Their eyes swept the prairie at their feet moodily, following the course of the brook.

"Here," said the older of the two, throwing down his pack—"here is water; let us try our luck. It is our last chance."

The name thus unconsciously bestowed became famous forever in the history of placer mining. That of the miner is long forgotten. No one knows what became of him or his comrade. But Last Chance Gulch became synonymous with vast, delirious wealth. Forty million dollars in shining gold was dug out of the bed of that mountain stream. From east and west greedy hordes poured in. Before the winter's snows melted, flour in the camp that had shot up in a night, as it were, was a hundred dollars a sack, in gold. Greenbacks by the fistful could not buy a square meal. It was gold, gold, and for a while the supply seemed unlimited. Every foot of the gulch was turned over; every pan of the black sand down under the pebbles and loose rock came up heavy with the yellow metal. Only the other day a contractor digging a cellar in Helena came upon a square yard that seemed never to have been disturbed—the gold-diggers had strangely overlooked that—

and took it home in his cart to wash it over. That cartload, that might have been tossed up on the dump with the rest but for his prying eyes, panned out thirty-five dollars. But the end was reached with the gulch. The source of all the wealth, which men sought with straining eyes that never saw the blush on the mountain brier or the glory of the autumn woods, was never found. At least so they say in Last Chance Gulch. It may be that they are wrong and that they have found all there was to find. A mining engineer with whom I traveled east told me of another explanation than the one of which the gold-seekers dream—a vast bulk of pure gold from which the drift in the brook had been chipped. Water, he said, under very heavy pressure does not turn to steam, but remains as it is, superheated, and in this condition has the power to dissolve and carry minerals, which, upon issuing into the open, it at once gives up, depositing gold or silver or other metal that it has picked up on its way. And so it may be that the brook itself was the mine, the repository through ages and ages of the slow distillation of those steep hillsides. And men need seek no further. Who can tell?

The city of Helena, the capital city of Montana, stands squarely over the golden gulch to-day. The main street follows its course, the Gold Block marking the spot where the two miners of the sixties threw down their packs and started in to try their luck. Just below it the tiny stream mumbles yet on its way in the bed the mines gave it back. Public-spirited citizens are urging the city to make a little park on its banks, so that Last Chance Gulch may not become a mere memory to the generation that is growing up. Of the rough camp the last traces vanished long since, but of the early pioneers a few remain, grown old, but with the fires of the dauntless frontiersman burning yet under their bushy eyebrows. I spent the most interesting hour I can remember with Judge Cornelius Hedges, the same who, in the seventies, with a company of soldiers, led a party of explorers into the unknown region a hundred miles to the south, whence reports of burning springs had been brought for years by Indians, and found the Yellowstone wonders; then, when his companions proposed to exploit them for private gain, had the courage and the patriotism to insist upon the Government taking the region in hand and making of it a National park forever. The old Judge chuckled long and silently when I asked him about his practice as a lawyer in those days. And then he told me of the first lawsuit in Last Chance Gulch.

The council of miners had adopted an ordinance making it law that a couple of logs laid across a lot would hold it for ten days. Within that time the squatter must make good his claim. A man's logs had been moved and the claim taken up by another. The first comer sued him for trespass.

The trial aroused great interest. The entire camp took a holiday and crowded into the shanty where the " Squire " held court. Over night another lawyer had come in on the stage, and Hedges and he strove mightily over the evidence, each doing his best for his client, till the Squire got hungry and adjourned the trial for supper. The crowd betook itself to the saloon across the way to discuss the case. But the miners had grown tired of the new sensation. They were busy making money and could not afford the loss of another day, yet they felt that they must see the case through. Various propositions were made to settle the case, and when a motion was jumped to put the lot up at auction and divide the proceeds between the lawyers, who had both done well, it was carried with a shout, as just and fair. The lot was sold on the spot, and brought seventy-five dollars.

" We were satisfied," said the Judge with a wink, " but the Squire got mad for being left out, and wanted to have both the parties to the suit up and fine them for contempt. But I told him he could hardly do that. You see, he didn't know much law."

Sterner days followed, before an ordered and orderly community grew out of the wild camp, when respect for law had to be taught at any cost, and leaders came from among the people to shoulder that task, and its responsibility too. The calm statement, when the authorities had let three crooks go for a bribe, " We will try these men in a miners' court," was notice that the days of lawlessness were over, and, as the event proved, they were. But now and again the logic of the rope had to be employed. It was after Montana had a Governor, an Irishman, that a notorious evil-doer was sent to jail. He had been a Fenian, and his friends got at the Governor when he was in a jovial mood and made him pardon him out. The fellow took the stage for Helena; but runners had gone ahead with the news, and the vigilantes met the stage on the way, took the man out, and hanged him with the Governor's pardon in his pocket, taking first the precaution to indorse the document : ".If he [the Governor] does it again, we will hang him."

" And the Governor ?" I asked.

The Judge nodded : " He thought it over for a while, fumed some, but decided to let it go at that. Those were hair-trigger days."

In company with Randall J. Condon, a New Englander who, as Superintendent of Instruction in Helena, has left his stamp on the community to its lasting good—Judge Hedges is another old Yankee—I drove up the gulch, miles and miles, almost to its beginning in the very heart of the Rockies. Only a little way ahead of us rose the continental divide between East and West. Once well out of town, the gulch lay just as the gold-diggers had left it, all its soil turned over in regular heaps that looked like nothing so much as rows of graves. And graves they were, of dead hopes and ambitions ; for though many grew rich here, more found their hopes turned to ashes. And I am not so sure that they were the only ones, that there are not other things buried here by those even who found pay dirt and made it pan out. For there is that about gold-digging that blots out all else and makes of life a mere gambling game against fate, eating the soul out of the man and narrowing his horizon to the crooked gorge and its rocks and gnarled trees. So it seemed to me as we drove up and up, passing gaunt and silent shapes toiling away at their drifts in the gathering twilight. They did not speak as we passed, and when spoken to answered in monosyllables, with a nod and a wistful look, that the "dirt" in the shaft was "looking up." They did not seem ever to be looking up, out of the gulch.

These are the successors of the early gold-seekers, who drive shafts, trying to wrest their secrets from the hills. Of the placer miners' tribe but a single representative is left:—Old Jerry, who, despite his seventy years, yet pulls his windlass and twirls his pan as deftly as the most skillful in days gone by. The whole story of Last Chance Gulch is in the old man's face, and his faith is yet unshaken that some day he will strike it rich. One day last summer he walked into the office of his friend Mr. Condon and announced that he had come to make him an offer. He guessed the office of School Superintendent was more bother than it was worth, and, as he had sized Mr. Condon up as a likely chap, he would give him half of his claim if he would chuck up his job and join him in the hills. The Superintendent has the offer under advisement yet.

But the sun has set upon the day of the Jerries and their kind, and it will never come back. Capital has entered the gorge, expecting no such dazzling returns as the prospectors of old, but making a business of gold-mining and getting a fair return. Steam-engines puff and shriek among the hills; above Jerry's claim hydraulic rams are battering down the rocks in a giant "wash" the like of which not even his wildest dreams could have conceived; and the Missouri has been dammed twelve miles away that power might be brought in to run a stamping-mill with its big mechanical "pans" in which the gold is caught by quicksilver and held until the chemist's wand sets it free. Man's mind has followed the cruder method of the hand, and with it much of the human interest, the individuality, has gone out of things. Yet Last Chance Gulch is better off to-

day than forty years ago when the world went wild over it. Better even with its graves, over which the brier rose creeps once more, trying to hide with caressing touch what is buried there.

It was clear when we left Helena, with only our light-weight overcoats and a single bear-skin robe, in the open buggy. We had been so absorbed in the gulch that we hardly noticed the twilight coming on and turning to dusk. A light snow had begun to fall, that made the darkness less obtrusive. Now, of a sudden, we woke up to the fact that we were far in the mountains, fifteen hundred or two thousand feet above Helena, and in the heart of a chilling cloud that settled about us like a cold, wet blanket. We turned, but the snow, that fell in great white sheets by this time, had blotted out road, brook, graves, and all, making a white blur of the landscape. Happily, the gorge was narrow and our horse knew the way. It was well, for the cold grew sharper fast, and the snow stung our faces like needles. I was chilled through, and as I sat waiting to be tumbled into the brook any moment, it occurred to me that my old wish to die like a wounded animal, on a rock in the woods, when my time came, was not all I had thought, sitting by the warm fireside. It was the difference between profession and practice again. I rubbed my spectacles and glanced at Mr. Condon. To my utter surprise, I found myself riding beside a snow-man that seemed to have been standing out in a sleet-storm all night. Great snowballs depended from his mustache; his fingers were frozen to the lines. But when I shouted "Santa Claus," he yelled back that I was another. And so I was. Just then we came, at an abrupt turn, into the shelter of a hospitable hill, and the temperature went up with a bound. The horse was racing down the steep, and soon, to our great relief, the first electric light of the town made a blur in the storm that had followed us down.

So ended what had proved a real adventure in Last Chance Gulch. Its old luck had once more come uppermost, and been ours. But I think it would have taken a hammer to break the ice on our coats when we got out of the buggy. It was like armor. I know now how the knights of old felt who had to carry it around, and my fervor for the old days went down several pegs, with my preference for tℏ backwoods as the place to lay my bones.

# LESSONS IN CRIME FIFTY CENTS PER MONTH

## BY A NEWSPAPER READER

IT is safe to say that no newspaper proprietor out of Bedlam would set the above announcement at the head of his paper; but if the law compelling goods to be accurately labeled goes into effect, some variant of it will probably have to be used, not only on the so-called "yellow" papers, but on all the daily and weekly publications served by the Associated Press. Attention is asked to the following extracts, clipped during one month from one newspaper—one of the best in its State, claiming to be the best in six States—and comprising only those items of news that gave specific directions for committing the crimes reported. There was ten times as much educative material for would-be lawbreakers, that any one not feeble-minded or insane would interpret by the very act of understanding what was done or attempted; but in these several cases the lesson in crime was patiently and lovingly unfolded and explained, so that any one so caring to do could add it to his or her repertory.

### STRANGER'S VISIT PROVES COSTLY
[September 18]

This begins: "Stephen A. B——, of — Broadway, has told the police of a new dodge, by which he was relieved of fifty dollars late yesterday afternoon." Here follow minute directions for "relieving" unsuspecting citizens of their spare cash.

### STORY OF A FREE RIDE
[September 16]

This is a short story, or "storiette," in the Sunday edition. It is given a very honorable place, and evidently is offered in good faith as an amusing and interesting account of an exploit that would reflect honor on and secure instant sympathy for the doer thereof. An irresponsible scoundrel of the cheerful, good-natured sort thinks up a scheme that beats the railways out of a transcontinental fare, and it is so ingenious, admits of so many possible adaptations, that the whole fraternity of beats and bounders must be extremely grateful for having it explained. It is subtly done; so subtly that even the trained reader will unconsciously take sides with "Billy," and feel rather glad that he got to the Pacific coast, on nothing, successfully, until he harks back to the principles that Mother used to insist upon as the only possible moral baggage for a gentleman. The ninety and nine will naturally go by the instinctive feeling so recklessly aroused and subtly appealed to, and file the scheme away for possible usefulness.

### POLICE ROUND UP IDLE PERSONS; HIT UPON NEW TRICK
#### PATROLMAN TELLS HOW THE UNWARY ARE ROBBED OF MONEY AND WATCHES BY SLY PICKPOCKET
[September 19]

We quote: "'Tis a new dodge the rounders have up their sleeve,' said one of the patrolmen concerned in the general ingathering. 'It's this way the trick is turned.'" Step by step, with the painstaking accuracy of a Fagin, the great newspaper proceeds to explain the criminal problem, set forth in letters an inch tall and very black at the head of the article, so that a little child could perfectly understand both the principle worked on and the method of doing the work.

### ALLEGED CARD SHARP CAUGHT IN PITTSBURG
[September 19]

"Member of Leading Political Club Detected with—" The cheating device is clearly indicated in the heading, which is that for specially important news, about three inches of column space ; following which is a third of a column of text illustrating and driving the lesson home.

### INFERNAL MACHINE FOR JACOB SCHIFF

CUNNINGLY CONTRIVED DEATH DEVICE PREPARED FOR THE MAIL. AD-DRESSED TO FINANCIER

[September 24]

This is announced in exactly the same type, and the heading is spaced in exactly the same way, as the item about the card-cheating affair, which, under wholesome conditions, would never have been heard of outside the limited circle concerned. Both despatches are equally important, therefore, according to the makers of newspapers ; and the only responsibility created by being the custodian, temporarily, of either fact, apparently, is to inform every one who can spell out a line of English print just how to cheat at cards so as to " win a fortune " before being found out, and exactly the way to construct an infernal machine that will pass through the mails without detection. The knowledge of the largest number of persons must be enriched by those two pieces of information in the quickest possible time. Half-grown boys, brain-boozy with dime novels and detective stories ; unbalanced, embittered out-of-works ; professional agitators, in dread of not being able to keep from dropping back into useful obscurity ; and ¦all the reckless, irresponsible, discontented elements in the population, are in need of nothing at the hands of the only educators any of them have the least respect for but to be told exactly how to cheat at cards and how to construct " practicable " infernal machines. If all the college professors in the country, and all the ministers as well, had set aside the 24th of last September for giving lessons in those two arts and crafts to their classes and congregations, we should probably have roared our disapproval to high heaven. But all of them, professors and classes, ministers and congregations, would not be a patch on the sleeve of the mighty host that goes to school in perfect good faith to the newspapers, which are disseminating that kind of culture every day of every year instead of once in a lifetime.

Probably as perfect an example of this deliberate education in crime as any among my clippings is the following under date of October 20, which is the last I need quote. I have skipped many reports, necessarily, because of the space a full list would have required, aiming to give only such typical ones as would illustrate the work which is being prosecuted so indefatigably ; viz., the education of all the people in practical crime.

### CLERKS GUILTY OF BIG THEFTS IN PITTSBURG BANK

TELLER DESCRIBES HOW, WITH ASSIST-ANCE OF BOOKKEEPER, AS MUCH AS $10,000 A DAY WAS TAKEN

After explaining what led him and his associate to begin stealing from the bank, " Wray, acting as spokesman, told the story of how they obtained the money." It is all there, as frankly explanatory and exhaustive as a legitimate lesson in a commercial course. The problem is, " How to rob a bank of half a million dollars before anybody misses anything?" After reading the papers on this evening, it is safe to say that every intelligent person knew one successful way in which it could be done. And no man resented the dumping of such information into the mind of his boy.

That newspapers have some sort of working agreement by which news of a kind that is objectionable to them is pocketed and squelched, by what amounts to a conspiracy of silence, recent events abundantly prove. The Supreme Court lately rendered a far-reaching decision, accompanying which is an important adverse opinion. In the ordinary course of news distribution this decision and this dissenting opinion should receive as much space as the initial series of events that led up to them received ; but few newspapers have uttered a word in regard to this phase of the subject. And if it is thus proven that they can act as a unit in suppressing some important news, may they not as readily agree not to publish a continuous course in crime ?

# MR. PERRY'S "WHITMAN"[1]

THIS biographical study of Whitman comes like a breath of fresh air after the overheated accounts of the poet which have been put forth by some of his friends and disciples of late years. Each of these books contains some record and impression which has value, and the student of Whitman cannot afford to leave them unread; but when Mr. Carpenter, for instance, permits himself to use about Whitman the language generally used about Christ, the student who wants to know the real Whitman, and cares no more for the legendary Whitman than for the legendary horseman who threw his head at Ichabod Crane on the Pocantico Bridge, cries out for fresh air and a little sanity. Whitman was in many ways an extraordinary person; he was capable of great nobility, as his heroic work in the hospitals in and about Washington showed; he looked at American life from a new point of view and interpreted it with original insight and power; it is not too much to say of him, as Mr. Burroughs has said, that his work gives us a new kind of climate; but he did not abrogate the moral law, he did not create new literary forms, he did not dethrone the old sovereigns in the world of letters, he did not substitute life for art, and he is not the ultimate and final poet of democracy.

Mr. Perry brought the methods of the scholar to his task, and for the first time the world has an adequate and candid account of Whitman's antecedents and conditions, and of the outward happenings of his life. This record is not only more complete but it is more intelligent than any that has come from the Whitman cult; it shows that faculty for preserving the significant and rejecting the unimportant fact which idolaters rarely possess; and this exercise of the genius of selection, which was denied Whitman, brings out the vital relations of the man and his work as they have never been brought out before. This is one of the distinctive notes of Mr. Perry's biography,

and in many respects its most important contribution to the understanding of Whitman. All true writing is autobiographic in a very real sense; but Whitman's work was more deeply charged with his personality than that of any of his contemporaries; there are, indeed, few poets of his rank whose expression was so much a part of themselves, and the form and shape of whose lives are so distinctly reflected in their work. Here is the source of Whitman's strength, the secret of his originality. He began and ended with himself; but he was, fortunately, a man of very unusual type, and in "celebrating" himself he "celebrated" a very considerable section of humanity. Here also is to be found the secret of his limitation; luminous and plastic as his imagination was, he never could see beyond the limits of his own horizons. What lay beyond of knowledge, character, achievement, or art was, in his judgment, of slight value. So firmly was he convinced of the representative authority of his own nature that he rarely took the trouble to find out whether there were other persons of importance in the world. Hence the colossal egotism which often mars his work and the ridiculous inadequacy of his judgments of men who had been audacious enough to write poetry. It must be added that he sometimes showed striking insight into the character and quality of the literature which he did not produce; but he generally spoke as if Camden were the center of the world, and when he was through with the other poets who pass in long array in various reports of his talks and in his letters, they look very like mutilated figures on a Greek frieze.

In pointing out the identity of Whitman's work with the man rather than with the accidents of his conditions and history Mr. Perry has given the world an example of the best interpretative criticism; it is clear, cogent, convincing, and full of illumination. Commenting on "Leaves of Grass," he writes: "To interpret as formal song what was intended for rhapsodical speech is to mis-

[1] *Walt Whitman.* By Bliss Perry. Houghton, Mifflin & Co., Boston.

read Walt Whitman. Here was no born maker of poetry, like Shelley, transforming his thought and emotions into a new medium and scarcely conscious of the miracle he is achieving; but rather a man burdened with sensations, wrestling with language, and forcing it into accents that are like the beating of his own tumultuous heart. Both Shelley and Whitman 'communicate' passion; but in one case we are listening to a pure aria that might conceivably issue from a violin or a skylark, while in the other we are listening to a declaimer with 'Tears in his eyes, distraction in 's aspect.' Not to apprehend 'Leaves of Grass' as a *man speaking* is to miss its purport."

The language of the "man speaking" and the forms in which his thought ran were not, however, the spontaneous improvisations of a poet who had escaped from art to nature and found a wholly original method of expression. The effects in Whitman's verse were as carefully calculated as those in Pope's verse. When his powerful imagination was deeply moved, as in "When Lilacs Last in the Dooryard Bloom'd," and "Out of the Cradle Endlessly Rocking," he was borne by great tides out of the waste of professional Bardism in which he often posed, and the reach of his inspiration is high-water mark in American poetry; when he worked at the bench and turned out the average Whitman poem, he was cumbersome, awkward, and ineffective; "the tangible matter often chokes the imaginative flood; there are too many logs in the stream; the observer and describer are too much for the poet. The trouble with Whitman's agglutinative or catalogue method is not that he makes catalogues, but that the enumerated objects remain inert objects merely. He is often like a yard-man coupling parlor-cars whose names are rich in individual associations—Malvolio, Manitoba, Mazzini, Manchuria, Maria. But however excitedly those musical names are ejaculated, this does not start the train."

Mr. Perry's study of the verse forms in "Leaves of Grass" is also a very valuable contribution to the understanding of Whitman; indeed, his analysis and interpretation of the book are singularly lucid, thorough, and convincing. The background of the volume, its indebtedness to contemporary thought, the typical character of its egotism and the significance of its sexual imagery, are treated with insight, firmness, and that saving grace of humor in which Whitman and his idolaters have been conspicuously deficient. The verse of this unique volume has intimate affiliations with such prose as Ruskin often wrote, and, in its worst estate, with the forgotten work of Mr. Tupper and other early Victorian verse writers. Mr. Perry quotes at length a poem by the once popular author of "Ten Thousand a Year" on "The Lily and the Bee," in which appear all the familiar Whitman devices—"catalogue, ejaculation, apostrophe, epithet, and high astounding term:"

"NAPOLEON! NELSON!
—Behold, my son, quoth the Royal Mother, this ancient wondrous country—destined scene of mighty doings—perchance of conflict, deadly, tremendous, such as the world has never seen, nor warrior dreamed of.
Even now the attracting center of world-wide anxieties.
On this spot see settled the eyes of sleepless Statesmen—
Lo! a British engineer, even while I speak, connects the Red Sea with the Mediterranean: Alexandria and Cairo made as one."

Still more striking is the parallelism with this passage from the same poem:

" Poor Bee! Dost thou see ME?
And note my speculations,
Thinking so curiously, all so confident!
Of thee, thy Being, Doings!
—MYSELF! the While!
Unconsciously contemplated by Intelligence, unseen!
Transcending mortal man
Yet far himself from the Supreme
As finite from the Infinite!
This moment loftily scanning ME,
Suspending for awhile his cares sublime,
And gazing down on ME,
On all MY Fellows clustering round
In this our Hive,
Of fancied splendour! vastness!"

Whitman drew his material from many sources, and his characteristic verse was akin to some of the oldest literature. He was intensely modern, but he was also intensely antique; he owed as much to the work of other men and the thoughts of other times as Longfellow or Lowell. Emerson, who had a shrewd eye and a luminous wit, said, that "Leaves of Grass" was a combination of the Bhagavad-Gita and the New York Herald !

What Mr. Perry has done is to throw a beam of clear light upon Whitman's genius and career, and bring the real man into view; and no greater service could have been rendered the author of "O Captain, My Captain" than to rescue him from the merciless idealization of a cult and set him squarely within the region of sane criticism. Whitman was a colossal *poseur;* he would smilingly confess as much if he could be interrogat:d. Philosopher, sage, and poet as he became at Camden, calmly accepting the faith of ardent youth who interpreted his most dubious passages as entirely dramatic, he had been the father of several illegitimate children, and had written anonymous reviews of his own books of such an extraordinary character that one knows not which to rate highest, his audacity or his obtuseness to even average standards of modesty. Of the physiological and sexual elements in his verse, Mr. Perry says, with admirable discrimination, that while certain passages are highly offensive, they bear the mark not so much of his imaginative energy as of his automatic describing-machine, and are for the most part as innocent of poetry as a physiological chart. "To a healthy-minded person these lines are like accidentally opening the door of the wrong dressing-room: one is amused, embarrassed, disenchanted, or disgusted, according to one's temperament and training."

Whitman was not the poet he thought himself to be; he was neither a man of the first order of creative genius, nor is he the ultimate poet of democracy; but he was a striking and impressive personality and a poet endowed with breadth of sympathy, feeling for brotherhood, the sense of human comradeship, an imagination of tidal flow and vitality; he is a distinct force in our literature, an original and native voice, and a powerful interpreter of one great phase or aspect of democracy. "He will survive," writes Mr. Perry, "not so much by the absolute perfection of single lyrical passages, as by the amplitude of his imagination, his magical though intermittent power of phrase, and the majesty with which he confronts the eternal realities. . . . Of the totality of his work one may well say, 'The sky o'erarches here.' Here is the wide horizon, the waters rolling in from the great deep, the fields and cities where men toil and laugh and conquer. Here are the gorgeous processionals of night and day, of lilac-time and harvest. The endless mystery of childhood, the pride of manhood, the calm of old age are here; and here, too, at last is the

'Dark mother always gliding near with soft feet,'

the hush and whisper of the Infinite Presence."

# Comment on Current Books

*Brunetière on Balzac*

The general impression, critical as well as popular, that the late Ferdinand Brunetière, the eminent French critic, was entirely out of sympathy with the later movements in French literature; that he was heart and soul a classicist, and that his mind was closed against the beauty of the Romantic writers, can hardly survive a careful reading of this strong piece of literary criticism. Balzac was in many ways offensive to M. Brunetière, and the critic makes no concealment of that fact. The faults of the novelist—his exuberance, his passionate interest in money, a certain grossness that runs through his work, a touch of vulgarity, sometimes in the work and almost always in the man—these and other qualities offend M. Brunetière, and he does not fail to characterize them with the utmost frankness and definiteness. On the other hand, the book is almost iconoclastic in its assertion of Balzac's claims to the position of the first novelist in the literature of the world, and in its analysis and definition of his style. Not even Taine's study of Balzac, which was immensely influential in affecting literary opinion in France and elsewhere, was so radical and thoroughgoing in its affirmation of Balzac's greatness and permanent influence as this compact volume. As a piece of writing it lacks grace and ease; but as a piece of literary analysis nothing so exhaustive, so penetrating, and so decisive has been written about the author of "Père Goriot." (Honoré de Balzac. By Ferdinand Brunetière. J. B. Lippincott Company, Philadelphia. $1.50.)

*Christ in Civic Life*

Among many recent works on the social teachings of Jesus this is of unsurpassed value. It grew out of a series of Sunday morning talks to students in Cornell University. These utterances of a Christian teacher thoroughly versed not only in the New Testament, but also in his department of political and economic science, cover a wide range in thought and practice, and are put into a form at once compact and clear. The subject is distributed into twelve sections, and each of these into seven topics, the whole thus forming a course for daily study through a three months' period. It is thus admirably serviceable for class instruction as well as for private use. Each daily topic, illustrated by appropriate references to the New Testament and modern authors, receives an exposition, terse and discriminating, of the principles involved and of the ideal to be pursued. Thus the whole work may be regarded as the *Principia* of the Christian life in its social relations. For all pastors and other teachers in this field, too often neglected in the churches, it is an eminently desirable help. (The Political and Social Significance of the Life and Teachings of Jesus. By Jeremiah W. Jenks, Ph.D., LL.D. The International Committee of Young Men's Christian Associations, New York. 75 cents.)

*The Fourth Gospel*

This is a fresh work of the first rank among the many on its subject. Assuming and passing by the results of the critical discussion of the authorship of the Gospel, as held by the majority of European scholars, it is wholly concerned with the literary form, the purpose, and the theology of "John," whom it identifies with no definitely determined individual. Under his simplicity of style it finds an elaborate design, and "a complex work of art." A twofold purpose is seen in it; primarily, the expression of a profound personal religion, and at the same time the adjustment of it intellectually to a new age and environment, in the reconciliation of Hebraic with Hellenic ideas. "It is John more than any other teacher who has imparted the secret of that living fellowship with Christ which is the central message of Christianity." The then current philosophical doctrine of the Eternal *Logos* presented a convenient metaphysical expression of the divine worth of the person of Christ, and John availed himself of it. It served the need of that

time, but belonged to that time only. The essence of John's thought must be distinguished from its transient form. "More life and fuller" is the world's comprehensive need, and John's teaching that this is found supremely in Christ gives the highest conception of Christ's supreme worth to the world, and the principle of continual religious development. This principle is seen working in the Gospel itself, whose writer blends with the words of his Master his own words as equally with those the utterance of his Master's spirit. The Fourth Gospel is shown as reflecting the conditions and needs of the third generation of Christian disciples. The young church was building itself up on a basis of doctrine with sacramental seals and symbols. It was engaged in controversy with the older religion in which it had been cradled, and was itself cradling incipient speculations which, when further developed, it expelled—the fantasies of Gnosticism. The relation of John's work to these various exigencies of a period of crystallization are amply and critically treated. Discrimination is constantly made between the spiritual substance of the Evangelist's conceptions and the theological or metaphysical forms investing them. One cannot accept all the interpretations here put upon the record. The "mother," whom Jesus commended from his cross to the beloved disciple, could hardly have been "the ancient faith" of his mother church. But the merit of the volume is in the primacy it gives to the vital heart of the Gospel, its "magnificent conception of God himself eternally present in the believer, through Christ, who unites us with himself, as he is united with God." (The Fourth Gospel, Its Purpose and Theology. By Ernest F. Scott. Charles Scribner's Sons, New York.)

*Ibsen's Collected Works*

Four volumes of the new edition of the collected works of Ibsen which have long been in preparation have now been issued, to be followed in the course of time by seven more, the eleven volumes to include Ibsen's work in its entirety. Two of the plays, "The Feast at Solhaug" and "Love's Comedy," are now put into English for the first time. No statement is made in regard to the character and extent of the revision; that some revision has been made is, however, evident, and where it appears it has been done with good judgment. Mr. William Archer, who has long been the English interpreter of Ibsen, has done his work with sufficient, though not with final, thoroughness and skill. Mr. Archer sometimes fails to get, in the judgment of students of Ibsen in the original, the directness, simplicity, and dramatic strength of a writer who, whatever the limitations of his view of life, was pre-eminently a playwright who rarely used a superfluous word, and who never sacrificed a situation for the sake of fine writing. Each volume is supplied with an introduction which differs from many other introductions because it is illuminating. Mr. Archer knows his Ibsen from beginning to end, and he is able to put behind each play the background against which it was written; the introductions, taken together, presenting about all there is to know about Ibsen's life, and, in connection with his letters, putting into the hands of the serious student practically all the information he needs to form an intelligent judgment of the dramatist's work. These introductions are bibliographical as well as biographical, and are full of interesting personal reminiscences. (The Collected Works of Henrik Ibsen. Copyright Edition. Brand. Charles Scribner's Sons, New York. $1 per volume.)

*The Modern View of the Bible*    Since Dr. R. Heber Newton, many years ago, wrote upon "Right and Wrong Uses of the Bible," many books have appeared upon this subject, and there is still need, not so much of more books, but of more readers, for the wrong use of the Bible is still distressingly common. Dr. Selleck, whose volume on "The Spiritual Outlook" we warmly commended a few years since, treats his present subject with tenderness and reverence toward honest fears of Biblical criticism, but with a firm exposure of their mistake, and demonstrates the gain to spiritual interests which accrues from the modern view of the Bible, its inspiration, and its authority. After briefly popularizing the conclusions of Biblical scholars, Dr. Selleck presents a view of the value and use of the Bible thus understood, and lays emphasis on its educational influence as the great instrument for the awakening of moral and spiritual life, especially in the school and the home. The book is an excellent combination of the conservative spirit with a radical method in a constructive treatment of its subject. (The New Appreciation of the Bible. By Willard Chamberlain Selleck, D.D. The University of Chicago Press, Chicago. $1.50.)

*Tent and Testament*    This record of a camping tour in Palestine is from the hand of a scholarly and critical traveler, well read in the observations made by men of his kind, and capable of testing their correctness. Throughout a route which lay in part aside from the common track of tourists his interest in verifying Biblical sites and Biblical allusions fully justifies the title of his record. The narrative is sufficiently enlivened with incident and anecdote to give it continuous interest, and is amply illustrated. The prolonged discussions required by controverted questions as to Nazareth, Bethlehem, Capernaum, and other localities are set off into appendices, and the whole is conveniently indexed. (Tent and Testament. By Herbert Rix, B.A. Charles Scribner's Sons, New York. $2.50, net.)

## Letters to The Outlook

### JOHN BROWN, JASON BROWN, AND GENERAL LEE

Your readers may be interested, apropos of the hundredth anniversary of General Lee's birth, and the articles about General Lee published in The Outlook for December 22, in an experience which Jason Brown, the oldest surviving son of John Brown, related to me in October, 1906, when he spent some days at my home in Concord.

Returning from California some years ago, Jason Brown fell in with General Longstreet, then living in Atlanta, and asked the General how the negro question is to be settled. Longstreet replied, "If people would let it alone, it would settle itself in time;" adding that the negroes were getting education, were becoming landowners, etc., and would gradually come to their true position. Going on to New Orleans, Jason had a day or two to wait, and went out to the Soldiers' Home of the "Louisiana Tigers," Longstreet's best soldiers at Gettysburg. He was warned by some one to conceal his name, but said he wished to be known for what he was; he registered himself in the Home's office by his true name, and, seeing a portrait of General Lee in the office, he remarked that one of the last things Lee did in the Union service was "to arrest my father at Harper's Ferry." "Are you a son of John Brown?" "Certainly." And by that name he was made known to the Confederate veterans, who received him most heartily. Indeed, he would be kindly received anywhere that simple goodness and copious knowledge on all practical subjects are respected.

You may be interested further in some particulars about Jason Brown, as one of the few remaining personal links connecting our time with that of his father.

For the first time in nearly sixty years he revisited Boston last fall. His errand in New England will appear singular to those who do not know his earnest and unusual character. For half a century—he is now eighty-four years old—he has been interested in the navigation of the air, and nearly forty years ago he and his brother Owen, then living in Pennsylvania, got the famous aeronaut Wise to build a balloon for them. But he became satisfied that the balloon is not the proper air-ship, and has for many years favored heavier constructions, with an independent motor, making the flight depend on momentum rather than buoyancy. Knabenshue, the Ohio experimenter in air-ships, found Mr. Brown so well informed and helpful that last year he engaged him, at the age of eighty-three, to assist in his ascensions at Columbus in the State Fair of Ohio. He engaged him again at Trenton, New Jersey, and at the Brockton Fair in Massachusetts, where he spent a week, and aided in the successful ascensions and flights there. His home lately has been at Akron, Ohio, where he lived before going to Kansas in 1855; but for some twenty years he lived in California, at first in Pasadena with his brother Owen (who is buried on a mountain top near Pasadena), and then in the redwood forest of Santa Cruz County, where he cleared land and planted a vineyard and orchard, which he still owns. He intends to join the family of his brother John at Put-in-Bay Island in Lake Erie and devote himself, as of old, to fruit culture. He is one of the few survivors of the fight in Osawatomie fifty years ago; he marched and shot beside his father in that resistance of fifty men against five hundred, in which the Missouri raiders got the worst of it, although they sacked and burned part of the little town. It was this battle which Vice-President Fairbanks and many thousand persons celebrated at Osawatomie last summer. In the Kansas troubles of 1855-6 Jason Brown's cabin was burned, his cattle stolen, and he was himself captured and threatened with death; but his life was saved by an honorable Kentuckian named Jacobs. His character remains, after forty-seven years, much what his father described it in a letter to Mrs. Marcus Spring, written from his Charlestown prison eight days before his execution. John Brown wrote:

I have a son Jason at Akron, a very laborious, ingenious, temperate, honest, and truthful man. He is very expert as a gardener, vine-dresser, and manager of fruit trees, but does not pride himself on account of his skill in anything: always has underrated himself; is bashful and retiring in his habits; is not (like his

father) too much inclined to assume and dictate; is too conscientious in his dealings and too tender of people's feelings to get from them his just deserts, and is very poor. He suffered almost everything but death on the way to and while in Kansas, and returned to Ohio not a spoiled but next to a ruined man. He never quarrels, and yet I know that he is both morally and physically brave. He will not deny his principles to save his life; and he "turned not back in the day of battle." At Osawatomie he fought by my side. He is a most tender, loving, and steadfast friend, and on the right side of things in general, a practical Samaritan (if not Christian).

One of your correspondents has spoken of the magnanimity shown in The Outlook's articles about General Lee, the military leader of the Confederacy. May I quote part of a letter from a Confederate soldier which shows equal magnanimity respecting John Brown and his work, a magnanimity which it is pleasant to recognize as manifested toward a man who at one time evoked the bitterest feelings in the South:

*To John Brown, Jr., Put-in-Bay, Ohio.*

Dear Sir: Duty took me to Harper's Ferry at the time of the Raid in 1859 (I was then connected with the Baltimore press), and by chance was brought into close personal contact with both your father and your brother Watson. After the assault I assisted your father to rise, as he stumbled forward out of the historic engine-house, and was able to administer to your brother, just before he died, some physical comfort which won for me his thanks. I gave him a cup of water to quench his thirst (this was about 7:30 on the morning of the capture), and improvised a couch for him out of a bench, with a pair of overalls for a pillow. I remember how he looked—singularly handsome, even through the grime of his all-day struggles and the intense suffering he must have endured. He was very calm, and of a tone and look very gentle. The look with which he searched my heart I can never forget. I asked him, "What brought you here?" He replied, very patiently, "Duty, sir." After a pause I again asked, "Is it, then, your idea of duty to shoot down men upon their own hearthstones for defending their rights?" He answered, "I am dying; I cannot discuss the question; I did my duty as I saw it." . . . I write you with deep earnestness, and with respect. The war, in which I took part on the Southern side, eradicated many errors of political opinion, and gave growth to many established truths not then recognized. I have for my own part no regrets for my humble share in the revolt; but I have now to say that I firmly believe the war was ordained of God for the extermination of slavery; and that your father was an elected instrument for the commencement of that good work.

I am, sir, with respect, yours truly,
       C. W. TAYLEURE.

The entire letter will be found in my "Life and Letters of John Brown."

       F. B. SANBORN.
Concord, Massachusetts.

### A SOLDIER'S VIEW

Unless it can be demonstrated that the discharge without honor of the entire battalion of the Twenty-fifth United States Infantry was lawful, was right, and was necessary, that battalion has invented a mode by which the enlisted men of such a battalion can successfully defy law and discipline, and the morale and effectiveness of our army be seriously impaired.

Will you allow an old soldier briefly to state in your columns why and how this is so?

The post was at Brownsville, Texas; so close to the dwelling-houses of the people that the shots fired on that night were distinctly audible at the post and headquarters of the battalion guard on duty. This guard had an officer of the day, an officer of the guard, non-commissioned officers, and private sentries. All sentries on post, and several officers and non-commissioned officers, had to remain awake, alert, observant of every noise or indication of disorder. They all heard, or were in duty bound to hear, all the shots fired in Brownsville that night. The first shots made it the duty of said officers, sergeants, and corporals forthwith to see that all sentries were on the alert; to arouse their guard; to direct the arrest of every soldier or person who entered or attempted to enter the post; to cause immediate inspection of quarters, and to note the name and company of every absentee; inspection of arms racks, and to note whose guns were missing. Experienced soldiers know that if all did their duty the commander of the battalion would know, at least as early as morning guard mounting, the name of every man who was out of the post that night, and the offenders would be in arrest. If duty was done, it was impossible for any soldier who was out of the post when the shooting began to re-enter the post without the knowledge of the guard. The inspections made necessary by the firing necessarily made many men in quarters aware of the absentees.

It was the duty of officers, sergeants, and corporals to question each soldier under their respective charge; it was the duty of every soldier so questioned to answer truly and tell every fact known to him that was material to the inquiry.

Nothing but concert and agreement practically embracing the enlisted men of the battalion could possibly prevent the battalion commander from learning, within twenty-four hours after the shooting, the name of every soldier who had been out of quarters and post that night.

The fact that not only weeks but months have passed and none of those names are known proves, beyond all reasonable doubt, that there was a concerted agreement and conspiracy, practically embracing the battalion, to protect the guilty and prevent their punishment.

Before President Roosevelt acted, every effort had been made by both civil and military authorities to find evidence sufficient to establish who did the shooting—and such

evidence could not be found. Therefore no punishment by a court, either martial or civil, could be made.

The question before the President was simply this: Shall a battalion whose enlisted men have by combination and conspiracy refused to do their duty of making true answers to rightful questions, and thereby demonstrated their ability to defy law and authority, be continued in our army?

The men can never forget their success in that defiance. If no punishment shall follow, other regiments also will know how successfully to defy law and authority. As an officer I would be unwilling ever to have that battalion near any troops under my command. Other officers of experience and judgment cannot help thinking and feeling as I do. The statute cited by Senator Foraker does not apply to such a case. The courts hold that the "letter" of a statute is controlled by the object and purpose of its enactment. Justice to Congress requires that no court shall hold that Senators and Representatives intended that act to apply to the facts above stated.

To preserve the morale of the army, to enable officers to maintain discipline, it was absolutely necessary that the battalion of the Twenty-fifth Infantry should cease to be in the army. They were not discharged as a punishment for the shooting in Brownsville. The discharge was because of the conspiracy to refuse, and the actual refusal, to perform the military duty of making true answers to the rightful questions put by their officers, and by Inspector Major Blocksom. The discharge could not be with honor. It was necessary to state that it was without honor because that was the fact. The order of the Secretary of War to re-enlist any man who can establish that he was not guilty either of the shooting or of the refusal to do duty gives to the few possibly innocent men all the protection that, under the facts and for " the good of the service," can be given them.

THE OLD SIXTH CORPS.

## *" THOSE LOST GARMENTS "*

Your correspondent " Y." writes in a very womanly and appealing way in regard to the common representations of the infant Jesus in pictures of the Nativity. She adds: " From the old masters down to their present very far removed successors, the greatly swathed Madonna holds a little naked Jesus and seems to be satisfied."

I venture to call her attention to one very notable exception. In the famous picture of Correggio in the Royal Gallery in Dresden, " La Notte " (the Nativity), the infant is tenderly "wrapped in swaddling-clothes," so that only his face and head, from which stream the light that irradiates the scene, are uncovered. E. N. W.

## "FRIEND" AND "BROTHER"

As a member of a Quaker family for several generations, residing in Philadelphia, the very stronghold of Quakerdom in the United States, I cannot forbear a slight criticism on an article in The Outlook of December 22 or 29 on the Mormons, in which the writer states that the Mormons, "like the Quakers," address each other as "brother" and "sister." What manner of Quakers, I wonder, could your correspondent have in mind! Quakers address one another as "Friend," but, oh! *never* as "brother" and "sister," in Philadelphia at least.

Ardmore, Pennsylvania. QUAKER.

## "THE GENTLE ART OF KILLING FISH"

The prime question is not whether it hurts the fish; it is whether it hurts or helps the man. And this question, as Professor Bailey suggests, cannot be disposed of by a general rule. Each man can decide only for himself. Thus I can speak for one who kills fish (occasionally, when they don't get away) and partridges (still more rarely), and who, on the whole, justifies himself in his own heart.

It was my fortune to pass my boyhood on the plains in pioneer days, where one or two guns were as much a part of the household equipment as the coffee-pot or the photograph album. The shotgun was expected to make substantial contribution to the support of the family, and the rifle behind the door gave a real sense of protection. During many a long, glorious boyhood day I tramped the prairies with my gun, and if I brought home a jack-rabbit or a fat mallard at night it was as if my tired feet trod on air. I was a boy then, and a perfect savage of course, and the killing was a lust in itself without ever a qualifying qualm; but the visions of those days walk with me yet, and the training I received in that school was worth more than all I ever got from Ray's Arithmetic and Reed and Kellogg's Grammar.

So much being told, it hardly needs to be added that now, in middle life, I find two hours in the field with my gun worth more by way of renewing my youth than a trip to Paris or weeks of reading Thoreau. It is possible, of course, to go to the woods unarmed, or carrying nothing more deadly than a camera. There are large satisfactions to be found in the fields by any one who has any points of contact with the world of nature. But there is a zest to catching black bass which no one can claim for the mild and sanctimonious study of maple-trees, and the excitement of an occasional shot at a flying duck will do more to bring back the animal spirits to a tired, anæmic office drudge than twenty weeks of rapt contemplation of the beautiful mountain peaks.

To be perfectly honest, I must allow that advancing years have brought some change of heart, and that I now experience some unpleasant twinges when the beautiful trout finally lies gasping on the grass. But—but! I also feel those same twinges when I meet a poor woman suffering for clothing and remember that my moonstone shirt-studs (which I never wear) would buy her a warm dress, or even when I think that the money which enables a hired choir to entertain me for a few minutes on Sunday morning might be the entire support of a missionary in a far dark land where men need light worse than I need entertainment. The fact about these little stabs of sentiment is that, however creditable they may be to us, we are obliged to let them pass without much tangible effect. I am glad I have a conscience, and I try not to abuse it, but I understand it must not be overworked. F. A. WAUGH.

Amherst, Massachusetts.

## SCIENTIFIC CRUELTY

In a recent Sunday edition of the Sun there appeared a report of the meeting of the American Association for the Advancement of Science held in New York City the last week in December, at which Professor John B. Watson read a paper describing experiments made by him to show that rats have a sixth sense. He placed a rat in a covered box from the center of which a maze led to escape and food.

After the rat had learned to traverse the path with all of his senses present, Dr. Watson then eliminated them one by one. First he removed the eyes from the rat. Still the animal went through the maze without any difficulty. Then he removed the olfactory nerves, and the same thing happened. Thinking the animal had done it possibly by the sense of touch, he froze the feet of the rat, but the rat still went through the maze. Then, to make the test final, he completely covered the head of the rat with collodion, and yet it managed to escape. This, said Dr. Watson, seemed to point to the fact that rats might have a sense which might be called one of direction, which may or may not be possessed by other animals.

The report says that the paper aroused comment. It is probable that it aroused indignation and horror in two-thirds of the readers of the Sun. Comment would hardly seem to be necessary, but I will quote a few statements from an article by Bishop

Lawrence favoring vivisection [within limits] which appeared in The Outlook of April 9, 1904:

Now, if there is any case where an animal is cruelly operated on, if it is put to unnecessary pain, it is time for those who have the evidence to call in the police. Our people will not tolerate cruelty. . . . Granted even that some pain and suffering are necessary, we must remember that these experiments are carried on with the sole purpose of so advancing science as to relieve men and women from far more suffering and agony than animals endure.

Will the Professor or any of his fellow-vivisectionists kindly tell us of what suffering and agony men and women will be relieved by this discovery that rats have a sense of direction? It is a curious bit of information, but does it tend to prolong human life? It certainly does not add to the sum of human happiness to know that animals are being subjected to such torture. Some one may say that it was "only a rat," but is it not quite probable that the professor will now proceed to find out whether this sense of direction "may or may not be possessed by other animals"?

It would be interesting if we could know whether or not the Society for the Prevention of Cruelty to Animals consider the rat an animal, also whether the treatment above described constitutes cruelty as they define the term.       JOSEPHINE C. LARKIN.
Concord, New Hampshire.

### ANOTHER CHINESE HERO

Reading in The Outlook Mr. McCormick's article, "Two Chinese Heroes," I am reminded of an incident related to me a few years since during a voyage from Brisbane, Queensland, to Batavia, Java, which shows devotion and heroism on the part of a poor Chinese servant rarely if ever equaled. On a small island inside the "Great Barrier Reef," North Queensland, an Englishman was engaged in gathering and curing the *bêche de mer*, a delicacy greatly prized by the Chinese. One day this man was obliged to visit a distant town for supplies, leaving his wife and infant child with the one Chinese servant at their home. During his absence the servant came to the house in great alarm, saying that the natives had come from the mainland and were proceeding down the island towards their house. It was known that the natives were cannibals, exceedingly cruel and ferocious. The proprietor having taken the only boat, the Chinaman hastily placed a jug of water and a little food in a large copper vessel used for cooking the marine snails, assisted the woman and child into this singular bark, and paddled away to an uninhabited island three or four miles distant, where the woman and child were made as comfortable as possible. The natives reached and destroyed the little home.

So long as she lived the woman kept a diary of events, among other things writing that the Chinaman would not share in the least their scanty store of food and water, and finally, after days of denial, he went off by himself, where later he was found dead, starved to death, in the brush, wrapped in his old ragged quilt.

Both woman and child succumbed after days and nights of privation, and all were later found, with the diary history of the little tragedy.

When I have heard or known in our own favored land of abuse of the Chinese, I have loved to tell of this instance of heroic self-denial of "one of the least of these."

GREENLEAF A. GOODALE.
Colorado Springs, Colorado.

### THE CONGO REFORM ASSOCIATION

The situation in the Congo Free State has been stigmatized as "the open sore of the world." For the facts see The Outlook of January 5. The Congo Reform Association, organized by men of National repute in this country, is carrying on a campaign of public enlightenment, to the end that our Government may be led to exert the influence of the United States in relieving the Congo natives from their wretchedness under King Leopold's atrocious rubber-getting régime. This Association is now in immediate need of funds. Inquiries may be addressed to John Carr, Treasurer (Chairman of the Board of Directors of the First National Bank of Boston), 723 Tremont Temple, Boston, Massachusetts.

### NOISELESS BRIDGES

*In re* your editorial paragraph of January 12 on "A Noiseless Bridge," an American railway engineer who has been studying overhead structures abroad tells us that the elevated in Berlin is noiseless through use of ballast. The Boston elevated experimented with ballast on a stretch of track along Atlantic Avenue, and it is stated by engineers who studied the experiment that it was so successful that the company had the ballast removed lest the public discover the improvement and demand its adoption throughout the system.

A. CHAMBERLAIN.
Winchester, Massachusetts.

# Libby's Pure Extract of Beef

## The True Food Test is Purity

The highest praise that can be given to any food product is to say that it is absolutely pure. Conscientious cleanliness throughout the Libby establishment insures positive purity.

Appetizing flavor, extra strength and absolute purity are the result of the perfected Libby methods, the model Libby kitchens and the use of choice lean beef in the making of

## Libby's (Natural Flavor) Extract of Beef

The new 84-page book, "How to Make Good Things to Eat", gives many delightful recipes for luncheons, dinners, and evening spreads, that every housewife will appreciate. It will be sent free on request.

### Libby, McNeill & Libby, Chicago

# Ham

Ham is a food that builds healthy bodies—because it contains the vital elements needed to make bone and muscle. Ham furnishes both heat and energy—stimulates every function of the body.

And Ham is delicious! The very smell of it sizzling in the pan makes your mouth water. But to have the sweet, juicy, tender kind, you must remember the Brand—Swift's "Premium."

Yes, "Premium" in fact as well as name. There's a "Premium" on the best Ham—Swift's "Premium." And its Premium in quality and flavor as it steams on the platter at Breakfast time.

Be insistent—when you ask for Ham be sure you get

**For February Breakfasts**

Everything depends on how you begin the day. A wholesome, easily digested breakfast helps to make a day successful. Try—

Fruit
Hot Biscuits
Swift's Premium Ham
Browned Potatoes
Coffee

# Swift's "Premium"

There is a Premium on every good ham or piece of bacon—"Swift's Premium." It is burned into the rind and no matter where the ham or bacon is bought, these words "Swift's Premium, U.S. Inspected and Passed" appear as a guarantee—a testimony of quality — an assurance that Swift's Premium Hams and Bacon are uniformly sweet, tender and juicy—wholesome. When you buy ham or bacon ask for "Swift's Premium."

**SWIFT'S PREMIUM**
U.S.INS.P.S.D. EST.3

Swift & Company, U. S. A.

# The Outlook

## Saturday, February 9, 1907

# Ship Subsidies

### A Study of Comparative Conditions

# Railway Overcapitalization

### By William L. Snyder

# The City of the Dinner Pail

### By Jonathan T. Lincoln

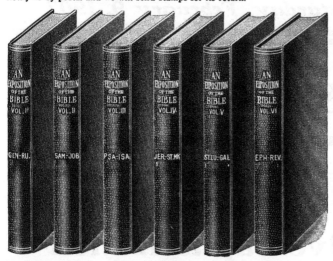

# The Outlook

SATURDAY, FEBRUARY 9, 1907

**To Prevent Land Monopoly**

With a view to the correction of existing land frauds, three interesting measures introduced by three Northwestern members are before the United States Senate. It was appropriate that Senator Hansbrough, of North Dakota, as Chairman of the Committee on Public Lands, should introduce a bill providing that the Government shall not hereafter part with the title to any coal, lignite, petroleum, or natural gas deposits on the public domain, the measure being largely in accord with the recommendation made in the President's recent Message. The bill further provides, however, that all of the public lands now withdrawn from settlement as containing coal be thrown open to settlement, subject to the above provision. The bill introduced by Senator La Follette, of Wisconsin, also reserves the title to underlying supplies of coal, gas, or other fuel and lighting materials, and proposes to lease on royalties such lands as private enterprises may desire to control for mining purposes ; the measure specifies minimum sums which shall be charged lessees as royalty. Finally, Senator Nelson, of Minnesota, introduced last week a measure which, like the others, would reserve to the Government the title to the hundred million acres of coal, oil, and mineral lands which have hitherto been open to entry. Under the provisions of this bill all of this land may be leased at a price to be fixed by the Secretary of the Interior, who will thus be able to regulate the supply of these necessities and to control the price. Mr. Nelson would impose the following conditions on the lessee of Government land :

First—That such lessee should sell his product to all persons without discrimination and at a just and reasonable price.
Second—That no lessee should enter into any combination in restraint of trade.
Third—That no lessee should by any means attempt to effect or promote a monopoly of the commodity in which he dealt. Violation of any of these provisions will entail forfeiture of the lease.

It is not necessary for us to estimate the relative value of these measures. We welcome them all because they recognize what we believe to be a fundamentally sound economic principle, that common wealth stored in the soil belongs to the Nation and ought not to be put up as prizes in a *quasi* lottery to be seized upon by the most shrewd, energetic, and grasping. The Senate bills and the courageous course of Mr. Hitchcock, Secretary of the Interior, are a welcome indication of a permanent and justified change in our public land policy.

**The Postal Commission**

Under an act of Congress approved January 26, 1906, there was appointed a Commission of six members of Congress, with Senator Boise Penrose at its head, to consider the postal service with reference to second-class matter—that is, the newspapers and periodicals of the country, which under the present law are transported and delivered, and have been for many years, at the rate of one cent a pound. Several hearings were held and voluminous testimony was gathered. The report of the Commission has now been made public. It is a document of sixty-three pages, of which fifty pages are devoted to a review of the facts gathered and the conclusions reached by the Commission, and thirteen pages are devoted to the draft of a bill which it is understood will be immediately introduced in Congress. It is intimated—but we cannot say with how much of truth—that an effort will be made to attach the bill as a rider to the Appropriations Bill, with the apparent purpose of crowding it through with little or no discussion before the close of the present session, which

287

terminates on the 4th of March. The provisions of the bill are certainly peculiar. It is scarcely of popular interest to recite them in detail, for no one who is not a publisher or a postal expert would understand them. The leading provision is a change in the postal rate on periodicals, which in the case of The Outlook, for instance, would increase its annual postage account to the Government from the sum of $19,500 for one hundred thousand copies to $45,000—two and one-quarter times as much as at present. There are a dozen or more provisions of the most revolutionary sort. One of them provides that "an issue of a newspaper or other periodical may be composed of parts or sections, but all such parts or sections shall be made of the same size, form, and weight of paper." This means—if it means anything—that no magazine shall longer present its fine illustrations on coated paper, unless the entire issue be printed on the same kind of paper, and that no finely illustrated newspaper supplements shall go through the mails. Another provision forbids the advertising pages to occupy "more than fifty per centum of the superficial area of any issue of the publication." Still another requires the printing conspicuously in every issue of a statement of its regular subscription price "for single subscriptions and for subscriptions taken by clubbing arrangements, or otherwise, for two or more subscriptions," and requires that "the full subscription price according to the statement thus printed shall be charged in all cases, without reduction by rebate, premium, gift, or otherwise." If the law is passed in its present form, it will immediately kill a large number of periodicals—some good and useful, others mischievous or useless—and will inflict grave hardship on all periodicals and newspapers except the local country weeklies, which are magnanimously, or shrewdly, left untouched.

❀

**The Ideal Postal Law** We cannot believe that the Congress of the United States will enact into law, within the space of a single month, a bill whose consequences to the public

press—and therefore to the public itself —will be so serious. The only logical, and we may say the only honorable, course will be to let the whole matter go over to the next Congress, and until a law can be arranged which will meet the situation with less disturbance to business interests, and with a clear recognition of the equity involved as regards both publishers and the reading public—who in the long run must pay for any increase in the cost of their periodical literature. The whole postal system rests upon the idea of rendering, under governmental supervision, the most convenient service to the whole people at the lowest possible cost. It is undoubtedly true that there are now inequalities in postal rates and postal service that need correcting, and it is certain that the Government has long paid to the railways a price for transporting mails which is far in excess of the rates at which other similar service by the railways has been rendered. There is need of careful study of the whole subject, and in our judgment there is need of readjustment among the various classes of mail matter. The Outlook has urged upon its readers from time to time during several years its conviction that the ideal classification of mail would be one that should enable any postmaster or postmaster's clerk, at any cross-roads post-office within the United States, to determine instantly the rate which any piece of mail matter should pay. This could be accomplished by a law that might be printed in clear type on a piece of paper half as large as a man's hand, and be understood in five minutes by any school-boy. Let the mail be divided into three classes, with no subdivisions whatever : First, all letters ; second, all printed matter of every kind ; third, everything else—and the thing is done. There is no doubt that postage should be paid on all mail carried, including that of Congressmen and Department officials, and also including local country newspapers. It should be entirely possible to find a rate for each of these three classes of matter that would be fair to the whole people—letter-writers, publishers, readers, manufacturers, and consumers—and the total elimination of the irrational censorship that has grown up around the publication of newspapers and periodicals, which is as un-American as the Russian practice of blacking out that which is unacceptable to the Government, would be forthwith accomplished.

❀

**Monopoly Methods** The report rendered to Congress last week by the Inter-State Commerce Commission declares that " the ruin of its competitors has been a distinct part of the policy of the Standard Oil in the past, systematically and persistently pursued," and as to the present that " it may become necessary to the uprooting of established wrongs and the prevention of others that the Government shall fix in the first instance the rates and regulations for the transportation of this traffic." These utterances from a high official source go far to sustain the widespread distrust of the Standard Oil, felt not because its business is enormous in its proportions, but because its methods are secretive and complicated, because it has avoided publicity of accounting and hence does not allow its stock to be listed, and because its dealings with competitors have, it is alleged, been tricky and unfair. Of late years, the report says, the Standard has not received rebates, but " it has nevertheless enjoyed secret rates possessing all the elements of illegal rates." It has had a system of espionage over the shipments of its competitors. It has reduced prices in localities where competitors have erected storage tanks, while maintaining prices in other localities. It has induced railway companies to buy all their lubricating oil from the Standard at double the price they could get elsewhere—a source of profit as good as a rebate. It buys advertising space in newspapers to fill with reading matter, not appearing to be paid matter, which " furnishes many of the ideas of great benefits conferred upon the public by the Standard Oil Company." It has deluded the public into believing that companies purchased by the Standard were independent and competing. It has paid employees of independent companies for information about their business. It has " sold different grades of oil at different prices

from the same barrel." " One independent testified that seventy-five per cent. of his product went abroad, and said that he could compete with the Standard in Germany, where its methods as followed in this country would not be tolerated, but that he could not compete with it here." The great advantage possessed by the Standard Oil Company, the Commission points out, is not its legitimate economies but the possession of great pipe lines. An act to regulate commerce makes these pipe lines nominally public carriers subject to certain limitations, and the owners of the pipe lines must publicly file tariffs for their use, but so far the independent operators have benefited not at all by this act, to enforce which the Commission finds an intricate and difficult task. The Commission, in view of the fact that in no other important traffic is there an approach to the monopoly of the Standard Oil Company, and in view of its fears that new discriminations may arise more frequently than old ones can be routed out, looks for a remedy to the drastic rate-fixing plan suggested in the sentence quoted at the beginning of this paragraph—a method already adopted by the Legislature of one State. The report includes much of the analysis of facts contained in the report on the distribution of oil made public some time ago by the Bureau of Corporations and then summarized in The Outlook. The Outlook has never been able to see why the Standard Oil Company should not follow the example of the next largest industrial corporation, the United Steel Corporation, as regards publicity, open accounting and open methods of competition, and the placing of its affairs under a single group of responsible officers known to the public. This report shows that to do so would help remove the hostility that now exists on the part of the people at large towards the Standard Oil Company.

❀

**The Panama Contract** It must be a very ill-informed or ill-disposed critic who should find in the proposed agreement with contractors to carry on the construction work of the Panama Canal evidence that the Government has found the work beyond its strength. In fact, the Government is not giving over to others the building of the Canal; it is simply adopting a recognized method of getting the work done quickly and economically, while retaining the supreme power in its own hands. As a man about to build a house may choose to engage individual mechanics to do "day's work," or may put the entire work at a "lump sum" in a contractor's hands with a supervising architect to check and inspect, or may hire a contractor to do the actual construction out of material furnished by the owner, the contractor to receive a percentage on the cost, so the Government has its choice between similar methods, and chooses that corresponding to the last described—a not uncommon system in building work. The reason for this decision has been admirably stated by Mr. Shonts as follows:

The question may be asked, Why does not the Commission gather together experts in each branch of the work, and with them as heads create its own organizations and do the work by day's labor? If the elements of time and cost did not enter so vitally into the undertaking, the Commission might do this; but because of the unprecedented and greatly extended industrial activity of the time, and the consequent violent competition for all classes of superintendents, foremen, subcontractors, skilled mechanics, and even ordinary laborers, it would take the Commission years to secure men and build up departmental construction organizations which would equal in efficiency those now controlled by the leading contractors of the United States. If, therefore, the Commission, by associating with it the best-trained construction men available, can receive the immediate benefit of the existing organizations which these men control, and which they have spent years in perfecting, and can by reason of their assistance complete the Canal in shorter time and for less money, is it not the part of wisdom and sound business judgment to do so?

But, some one may say, if the contractors are to be paid by a percentage on the cost, their financial interest would be to make the cost as high as possible. The United States Government is hardly so simple as not to protect itself as to this point and many others. Thus, the specifications provide that as soon as the contract is signed a committee of five engineers, consisting of three Govern-

ment engineers and two who represent the contractors, and with Chief Engineer Stevens at its head, shall, from data in existence or to be gathered on the Isthmus, fix a fair estimate of the total cost of the specified work and of the length of time the work ought to take, and then establish a system of special rewards or premiums on the one hand, and of deductions from the total pay on the other, according as the contractors do better or worse than the estimates call for. Moreover, the great departments of engineering and sanitation are to be kept entirely in the Government's hands; so also are the housing and subsistence of employees, the police, municipal, and governmental functions, the operation of the Panama Railway, and the auditing of all accounts. And the contractors, under heavy penalties, must carry out the Chief Engineer's requirements, and must do nothing contrary to the Government's demands as to the health, comfort, and living of the laborers. Briefly stated, the Government is to furnish machinery, material, and tools (except hand tools); the contractors are to find and pay the laborers, and see that they do the actual work. The specifications clearly and minutely show precisely what is to be done and how and where, exactly what the division of responsibility shall be, and in scores of ways guard the Government's interest at every point. A few illustrations are: the agreements that the contractors shall take over all skilled employees now on the Commission's pay-roll; that they shall carry out existing contracts; that they shall comply with the laws both of Congress and the Canal Zone as to the hours and character of labor; that they shall work night shifts if the Chief Engineer requires; that they shall be financially responsible to the Commission for injuries to the Canal by neglect. In other words, except for the engaging of labor and superintending the actual work, the Canal Commission and its Chief Engineer reserve to themselves the fullest powers both at large and in detail. No one can possibly read the form of contract submitted to bidders without seeing that not the contractors but the United States is to build the Canal, and that it is adopting this method because it believes it to be the quickest and best.

❀

**A Victory of Peace**  Among the evils of war are the feuds which endure long after the conflicts that engendered them. Rare is it in the history of the world when the survivors of contending armies forty-two years after a bloody battle meet together on the anniversary of the event to form an association made up of the survivors on both sides for the purpose, not of mourning over a defeat or exulting in a victory, but of strengthening the sentiments of friendship and brotherhood under a common flag. The battle of Fort Fisher occurred on January 15, 1865. It was one of the hardest-fought battles of the war. It was a struggle for the key to General Lee's position. With the capture of this stronghold his communication with the outside world would be cut off. Officers and men on both sides realized the immense importance of the battle, which soon became a close hand-to-hand conflict. The Confederate force of about 2,500 men was commanded by Colonel William Lamb, and the defenders were mainly North Carolinians, who fought with a desperation worthy of the noblest cause. The Union forces from first to last numbered about 5,000. Brigadier-General Newton M. Curtis led every assault, and, picking up a soldier's musket, was the first to mount the parapet, and continued the fierce fight with bayonet and clubbed musket. Wounded in several places and finally rendered unconscious by a fragment of shell which destroyed his left eye, General Curtis was dragged off the field. Four hours after, the defenders having exhausted their ammunition, the Union forces entered the fort with little opposition. Both of the wounded commanders were borne to the same hospital, and when, after weeks of suffering, General Curtis was able to rise from his bed, his first act was to go, supported by two of his soldiers, to the bedside of Colonel Lamb, extend his hand, and express his admiration for the magnificent defense he had made. "God does not mean," he added, "that this land of ours shall be divided between rival nations; one or the other of us must win." The friendship thus formed was cemented during convalescence. Years after, a Northern university first conferred upon the Confederate commander and afterwards upon "the fighting Quaker," General Curtis, an honorary doctor's degree. Colonel Lamb was made, too, an honorary member of one of the Union posts. On January 15 of this year, the forty-second anniversary of the battle, a reunion was held at Wilmington, North Carolina, called by the Confederate survivors of the battle, supported by the citizens of Wilmington and the Governor of the State. Generous and fraternal greetings were exchanged. The next day the fort was visited, and the exchange of courtesies and reminiscences lasted until ten o'clock at night. The following day a meeting was held in the Court-House and an association was formed of the Fort Fisher survivors. Membership is confined to those who engaged in the battle on either side. About one hundred men from the North participated in this reunion, and from beginning to end there was not a word or act or indication of anything that was not cordial, sympathetic, and harmonious.

❀

**France : A Possible Compromise**  Any indication of an approach to a working basis between the French Government and the Roman Catholic Church is very welcome. The text of the declaration drawn up at the recent plenary Council of the French Bishops, published last week, contains a definite statement by the bishops of their fidelity to their previous declarations and protests, a demand for recognition of the hierarchy of the Church, for inviolability of its property, and for freedom for worship; with the statement, which may afford a basis of joint action, that the bishops will consent to make trial of the organization of public worship under certain conditions—among them, the making of an administrative contract between bishops, prefects, mayors, and curés, giving to the latter the use of places of worship with necessary guarantees for permanence and moral security of religious service, and the safeguarding of the hierarchical principle. The bishops agree to work together to have this contract accepted everywhere, but if they fail to secure that end, in order to avoid arbitrary decisions by magistrates, the whole plan will fall to the ground. A draft of the proposed contract is appended to the declaration, and contains a formal stipulation that the priest enters into it by virtue of powers conferred on him by his bishop; that its validity will fall to the ground if the bishop does not maintain the power of the priest; that the mayor must renounce all interference in the religious administration of the parish, except when public order is disturbed, and that the contract will be invalid unless signed by the bishop of the diocese. Under this contract the authority of the hierarchy is safeguarded by the recognition of the subordination of individual priests to the bishop; and a degree of permanence is provided for by the demand that the contracts shall be for a period of eighteen years, and that they shall be accepted unanimously throughout France. The fact that this contract is submitted with the approval of the Pope adds to its significance. There are about thirty-six thousand communes in France, and it would seem to be impossible to secure unanimous adoption of this arrangement unless strong pressure is brought to bear by the Government. The sudden flurry in the Cabinet last week, which took the form of an apparently sharp disagreement between Premier Clemenceau and Minister Briand, was terminated by the explanations of the Premier, and apparently indicates that the Government is quite as ready to meet the bishops as the bishops are to meet the Government on a basis that will save the dignity of both parties.

⊛

*A Setback to Socialists*  The movement in Europe and England towards radical Socialism, which for some time past has seemed to be gaining great headway, has received at least a temporary setback in several countries. In the German Reichstag it has sustained a substantial loss in number of representatives; yet it cast the largest vote in its history. The results of the primary elections for the Russian Duma which

have been in progress have not been fully reported, but apparently the extremists have not made the progress they expected. Workingmen, who stayed away from the polls at the former election, have shown great interest in the present election, and have voted with the Social Democrats rather than with the Socialists of the extreme type, favoring a programme that looks toward constitutional changes rather than immediate revolution. At the three days' session of the Labor Congress held at Belfast, Ireland, the most notable issue was the struggle for control between the Socialists and the trade-unionists. A motion offered by a Socialist that the party declare as its ultimate object the overthrow of the present competitive system of capitalization and the establishment of a system of public ownership and control of all means of livelihood was defeated by votes representing 835,000 as against 98,000 members. It was formally agreed that it was not necessary for the Socialists to become trade-unionists, or for the trades-unionists to become Socialists. Mr. Keir Hardie, who led the advanced Socialists, was overwhelmingly defeated in the convention. The political policy of organized labor as defined by the Congress involves freedom from affiliation with the extreme Socialistic propaganda, and the endeavor to secure legislation by holding a balance of power between the two main parties. Considerable opposition against public ownership and collectivism was manifested at the Congress.

⊛

*Storage Reservoirs in the Adirondacks*  One of the most precious possessions, not only of New York State, but of the whole country, is the Adirondack Mountain region. It is wild and beautiful; it is also varied, for on its upper peaks traces of arctic vegetation and bird life may be found, while to its southern foothills come bird visitors from warmer zones. As a health restorer the dry air of these uplands has an international reputation. Despite the improvements made in the Adirondack region from the æsthetic, the recreative, and the hygienic points of view, frequenters of that favored region believe that the region has not nearly reached its full development as a summer and winter resort. On the other hand, however, economists and utilitarians declare that its water-power possibilities have scarcely been touched. If these resources could be exploited without jeopardizing other and more valuable features, every one would rejoice. Unfortunately, however, the economic history of the Adirondacks, as seen in the wholesale and scandalous cutting of timber there, long ago convinced the public that such exploitation of mountain values means a loss to the people in general and an illegitimate gain to a few private interests. To prevent this loss a law was passed, the spirit of which is now incorporated in the State Constitution:

The lands of the State, now owned or hereafter acquired, constituting the Forest Reserve, as now fixed by law, shall be forever kept as wild forest lands. They shall not be leased, sold, or exchanged, or be taken by any corporation, public or private, nor shall the timber thereon be sold, removed, or destroyed.

Despite this, some of the State lands have been illegally lumbered, and too many acres have been worked into private possession, though latterly, of course, not so freely as the despoilers wished. Owing to the passing of spruce, hemlock, pine, and balsam, logging has apparently reached its climax. Hence the question of water-power now engages the attention of the despoilers. There are five watersheds in the Adirondacks—the Mohawk, Upper Hudson, Lake Champlain, Black River, and St. Lawrence. The possible development of this region is believed to be nearly six hundred thousand horsepower, worth, of course, many million dollars a year. To develop this power, storage reservoirs must be constructed along the various streams to equalize the flow. Much of the land which would be overflowed by the stored water is owned by the State. The Constitution forbids the overflowing of these lands because they are a part of the State Forest Reserve. The construction of the proposed storage reservoirs to occupy most of the Adirondack lakes cannot, therefore, be accomplished without State aid. In the closing days of 1906, after certain manufacturers and promoters had failed

to obtain the State Water Storage Commission's consent, they did succeed in obtaining the passage through the Legislature of a concurrent resolution proposing a Constitutional amendment which should grant the use of such State forest lands as might be needed in constructing storage reservoirs. This resolution was passed after a public hearing had been denied, and without time or opportunity for public protest. The amendment must be voted upon by the Legislature of 1907, and then, if approved, handed to the voters at the next general election for final action. Such an amendment would patently subject the State Forest Reserve to the control of individuals and corporations which seek to exploit it for individual profit and not for the State's larger benefit, certainly not for the benefit of all our people.

*The Sanitary versus the Utilitarian* What would these storage reservoirs in the Adirondacks mean to the future of that region? When the existing reservoirs there are drawn down in the dry summer months, the dangerous odor from the exposed muck invariably spoils the neighboring territory for summer camping or for homes. For instance, when, to float the logs of a lumber company, the water was drawn from North Lake, about which many small camps had been built, the residents were unable to remain. The same was true when Lake Placid's level was changed to meet the exigencies of a sawmill; but Lake Placid is happily no longer an instance, since cottage-builders and hotel men have purchased the water rights in order to protect their health by keeping the water on a level. A change in the level of most of the lakes—their overflow at one season and the withdrawal of their water at another—would produce epidemics of diphtheria and similar diseases in places which instead should minister to sanitation. The Adirondack region can hardly be developed as a healthful playground and as a power-source at the same time. Yet the State is asked to furnish more than half the necessary land in the heart of the mountains, ruining them as a playground for the public. If that region is to be kept clear from miasmic vapors and the streams maintained free and pure—the fit home of the brook trout—the present reservoir scheme will have to be killed. If the mountain country is to remain largely a natural wilderness, where men may hunt and fish, camp, tramp, and find recreation, it must be undisturbed by this kind of utilitarian force. The parting of the ways as regards the future of the Adirondacks would seem to have been reached. At all events, this was the opinion freely expressed at a meeting just held in New York City by the Association for the Protection of the Adirondacks, of which Judge Henry E. Howland is President, and the New York Board of Trade and Transportation, of which Mr. William McCarroll is President.

❦

**The Beam and the Mote :
Applied to Automobiles**

The best way to disarm criticism is to remove its object. This is the method adopted by the Automobile Club of America in dealing with the spirit of hostility to automobiles. As was recorded last week in The Outlook, certain officers of the Club have qualified as special policemen for the purpose of calling to account those users of automobiles who drive their vehicles in violation of the law. Now the Committee on Public Safety of the Club has issued a circular outlining the principles which should govern the driver of an automobile. The spirit of this circular is so admirable that we wish a copy might be fastened to the door-post of every garage and that its precepts might be graven on the heart of every chauffeur. The Committee reminds the automobilist that the machine, unlike the horse, is completely under the driver's will. " Being thus under perfect control," says the Committee, " it is entirely the operator's fault, barring accidents to the mechanism, if it is controlled in such a way as to bring disaster to others." The Committee recognizes the fact that pedestrians are often guilty of " contributory, even criminal, negligence ;" nevertheless, it puts the burden of caution squarely on the automobile driver :

The best interests of automobilism require that automobilists, wherever there is possibility of damage to others, shall drive with the greatest self-restraint and always well within the limits of safety to all users of the highway ; and while it is true that there are many examples of carelessness on the part of the general public, yet our carefulness must provide against their carelessness, our consideration against their heedlessness, our intelligence against their lack of intelligence in the use of the highway. This is the burden that is laid upon us by the fact that we are driving the newest and most powerful vehicle. The best interests of the sport demand this ; every instinct of courtesy and decent behavior demands this, as well ar the common dictates of humanity.

The Committee cautions the automobilist to exercise special care in meeting or passing street-cars, in making way through crowded city traffic, in passing intersecting streets and rounding corners and curves. It urges strict observance of traffic regulations and the spirit of the laws, the wisdom of avoiding the use of searchlights on ferryboats and well-lighted streets, care not to cause offensive odors or noises, and the reduction of speed " at grade crossings and in passing teams." " We b- lieve," concludes the Committee, " that if these few plain, practical suggestions were taken to heart by automobilists everywhere this coming year, it would be the means of avoiding many accidents, and would do much to remove prejudice now in the minds of the public." We may add that the immediate effect of this circular will be to remove much prejudice. People who have, reasonably or unreasonably, been hostile to automobiles will, after reading these words, be inclined to say, " Automobilists, after all, have their rights ; it is probable that pedestrians and drivers of horses do not get all the blame they deserve. We had all better be more careful." The issuing of such a circular is the part of highest wisdom. We commend this spirit in the face of criticism and correction to railway managers, politicians, churches, and—ourselves.

❦

**" Salome "**

The withdrawal of Richard Strauss's " Salome " from the stage of the Metropolitan Opera-House in New York, in response to the demand of the directors of the Metropolitan Opera and Real Estate Company, including many of the foremost men in New York, is significant because the action was in a certain sense compelled, not by the puritanical or strait-laced element in New York, but by men who represent the broadest artistic taste and a catholic knowledge of the world. When any work of art is criticised from the moral point of view, there is an immediate outcry of "Puritanism," "prudery," and "provincialism." There is quite as much cant, however, among people who profess to follow art for art's sake as among those who look at art primarily from the ethical point of view. The revival of interest in Oscar Wilde's work is simply the fashion of an hour ; the man's story cannot be told in any public print, and "Salome" belongs to his degenerate period. Its principal motive is one which can hardly be made a subject even of conversation between self-respecting men. It does not belong to the region of wholesome passion ; it belongs to the region of erotic pathology. The play includes a dance which cannot be characterized with accuracy in any decent print, the physical motive of which ought to make it impossible for any Occidental woman to look at it. There is very good reason to believe that the composer seized upon the play as a setting for his music simply because · it had secured a sensational success. It has not been seen in London ; it has been very severely criticised in France ; it has been popular in Germany. If it had been popular in all parts of Europe, nothing would have been settled for Americans. Many things that are neither decent nor artistic are popular abroad among certain classes of people. The fact that an older society applauds settles nothing for a younger society. Vice, disease, and bad taste are not redeemed because they afflict or are practiced by elderly people. Corruption is more offensive in an old nation than in a young one, as it is more offensive in old than in young people. One can forgive much to the overflowing impulses of youth, but one shrinks with abhorrence from the diseased imagination of old age. It may not be wise to put George Sand's "Indiana" into the hands of children, but that free-spoken study of early passion is wholesome reading compared with Balzac's "Cousin Bette," with its pathological study of the diseased desires of old men. It is to the credit of New York that the usual cant has not been heard in this case, and that an instinct sound alike in morals and in art has expressed itself, not only promptly, but efficiently.

❂

**A Profitable Sanatorium**　The materialistic side of a great city like New York— the gigantic office buildings, the palatial private residences, the hundreds of automobiles, each costing as much as a good-sized country house, the lavish display of jewels and costumes nightly at the scores of theaters and restaurants, the millions of dollars appropriated for building great railway terminals, tunnels, and subways under our streets and rivers—this materialistic phase is so much in evidence that it sometimes assumes an importance in the mind of the observer which is out of proportion to its relative influence upon the life of the city. There is underneath this money-making and money-spending surface of New York a great current of self-sacrificing helpfulness for others that not only flows steadily, but flows with increasing volume as the days go on. One is conscious of the work of the churches, hospitals, and schools because of the visible evidence of their existence in architectural form, but there are numerous private societies, too little known by the public, of men and women who are trying to help their less fortunate fellow-men. The Outlook has lately had occasion to mention the Grenfell Association and the Association for the Blind as examples of the altruistic work carried on in New York. The recent annual meeting of the Stony Wold Sanatorium calls attention to another one of the admirable private societies that are doing a real service to the public. This organization has built and maintains a sanatorium in the Adirondacks for the treatment of incipient tuberculosis in working women and children. It began in a very simple and modest way six or seven years ago in the effort of the wife of a New York physician to interest women who have every advantage of social position and material comfort

in the terrible sufferings that are endured by working women and children
of this city when their homes are invaded
by the dread specter of tuberculosis.
The society thus beginning in a small
way has now grown to important proportions and has enlisted the approval
and co-operation of some of the most
distinguished physicians and scientific
experts. It is taking an important and
influential part in the concerted attempt
which has been made in this country to
stamp out the plague of tuberculosis. A
characteristic feature of the organization
is found in the auxiliaries that are allied
with it in the support of the main institution. There are about twenty of these
associated circles, each having its own
officers and each carrying on its own
individual work in support of the parent
institution. Mr. Joseph Choate, at the
annual meeting of Stony Wold, made the
address of the occasion. He said that
he, in common with hundreds of other
citizens of New York, was overwhelmed
with appeals for support of all kinds of
good works, but that none seemed to be
more worthy of the attention of New York
women than the Stony Wold Sanatorium.
His advice to the ladies of the society
was to give money themselves only as a
last resort, since they give themselves
personally to the work, but to see to it
that their husbands and fathers and sons
and grandfathers and grandsons give
liberally to its maintenance. There is
every reason why the successful men of
New York should give Stony Wold a
generous support. There is a great economic as well as altruistic value in the
work that it is carrying on. It is not
only saving individuals from death and
suffering, but it is teaching every patient
who comes under its ministrations what
hygienic precautions to take against the
germs of tuberculosis and the conditions
under which they exist. No man who
contributes to the support of Stony Wold
knows but that he may be thus actually
contributing to the saving of the life of
his wife or children. It is well known
that tuberculosis is spread through the
garment trade, for example, more than
through any other one agency in this
city. The sweat-shop has been a hothouse for the propagation of the tuber-

cular bacillus. Every working-girl who
is taken out of such surroundings and
put into the sunshine, the sanitary associations, the cheerfulness, the orderliness,
the happiness, and the mental uplifting of
Stony Wold may thus become the very
protector of those who believed themselves to be the sole benefactors in the
case.

❀

**The Telharmonium :**
**Its Musical Basis**

The remarkable
musical instrument
called the Telhar-
monium, the invention of Dr. Thaddeus
Cahill, is now on public exhibition in
New York. Last May, before the instrument was publicly exhibited, The
Outlook described it. Inasmuch, however, as one of its features, to which we
were not then at liberty to refer, has
since become publicly known, we give
some further account of it. As a ray of
ordinary white light, appearing to our
eyes a simple thing, is in reality a product of seven different kinds of rays—
violet, blue, green, etc.—so an ordinary
musical tone, simple as it seems to our
ears, is in reality a product of many
different "partial tones," as they are
called, which, like the rays of light
in the spectrum, can be separated by
means of the proper apparatus. When
one strikes middle C, for example, on
the piano, the string vibrates as a
whole at one rate of speed, say 256
times a second ; it also divides into
halves, which vibrate twice as fast, 512
times a second; it also divides into thirds,
which vibrate three times as fast, 768
times a second ; and so on indefinitely.
Each of these different systems of vibration gives a different "partial tone," so
that in the ordinary piano tone we hear
perhaps seven or eight partial tones,
which merge for our ears in a single
impression. The elastic bodies used in
musical instruments differ to such a
degree, however, that some instruments,
*e. g.* violins, have more partial tones than
others, *e. g.* flutes, and in some, such as
the clarinet, certain partial tones are more
prominent than others. To this difference in the number and relative strength
of their partial tones are due, as Helm-
holtz has shown, the differences in tone-
quality, or *timbre*, of the various instru-

ments, the general rule being that the greater the number of the partials the more brilliant is the quality, and that the fewer the partials the more "cool," "pure," or "flutey " is the quality.

❀

**The Telharmonium :**
**Its Method of**
**Operation**

Now, the peculiarity of the telharmonium is that it produces each partial tone separately, and mixes them in any number and relative strength desired. Specially constructed dynamos generate electric currents having each a definite number of "alternations" or electrical impulses per second ; an arrangement of keyboards and stops something like that of an organ enables a player to switch on any current or currents desired ; these currents pass into an apparatus like a telephone transmitter and cause its diaphragm to vibrate, or, in other words, become transformed from electrical currents into sound waves. Suppose, for example, we pass into the transmitter a current alternating 256 times per second ; the diaphragm emits the tone middle C, in a remarkably pure, flute-like quality. Still keeping this current on, we now add another of three times the alternation of the first, or 768 a second, and another of four times the first, or 1,024 per second ; we thus add the third and fourth "partials," and our middle C takes on a clarinet-like quality (the tone of the clarinet is mainly first, third, and fourth partials). In this manner we can proceed, building up any quality of tone we desire. The instrument as at present exhibited has two manuals or keyboards. Each keyboard is provided with eight "stops" which serve to bring into play the first eight partial tones of any compound tone. Thus one performer can play on the first keyboard a melody with clarinet tone (by pulling out stops 1, 3, and 4), while another performer plays an accompaniment on the other with flute tone (stop 1 alone). The electric currents controlled by the players can be conveyed, like other currents, almost any distance and to any number of receivers. The performers may thus play for many widely scattered audiences simultaneously. To a musi-

cian not the least interesting feature of the telharmonium is that to which we have referred as having been only recently made public. As is now generally known, the system of tuning in "equal temperament" introduced in Bach's day, and since then universally employed, gained certain capital advantages to the musician at the cost of other minor disadvantages, the most serious of which was that the interval of the major third, so important in harmony, had to be made slightly flat and impure. In the telharmonium, by a system of several banks of keys for each manual, separated in pitch by a very minute interval, it becomes possible, by playing the "third" in a triad or common chord on a different bank from the other two tones, to obtain a perfectly tuned major third. This introduces a purity of harmony unfamiliar to musical ears since the days of Palestrina, while not sacrificing the all-important innovations of Bach. May we not hope that the telharmonium will, through this peculiarity, become an influence toward rendering more subtle our sense of consonance and dissonance, and thus aid in the future development of musical art? Though many details still remain to be worked out, it will at once be seen what vistas of new possibilities, both for musical effects and for acoustical research, are opened out by this remarkable invention.

❀

**The Telharmonium :**
**Its Musical Effect**

What, at the present time, are the most striking impressions of a musician or musical layman on hearing the telharmonium? In the first place, the purity of its "intonation " is extraordinary and delightful. It is absolutely, mechanically, "in tune," and can never get out of tune. Since the dynamo shafts revolve at a fixed rate of speed, and are geared one to another with unchangeable accuracy, and since each current is produced by a wheel with a special unchanging number of teeth, the relations of the different vibration rates remain perfectly uniform. On no other instrument in ordinary use is this the case. Pianos and organs get out of tune, the intonation of instruments of the violin family depends on the placing of perverse human fingers on the strings, and that of the wood-wind and brass instruments depends on human lips and lungs. The mere matter of being absolutely in tune is no small part of the curious fascination of Dr. Cahill's invention. In the second place, the possibility of giving a perfectly pure tone, such as is obtained by using only one or two partials, and at the same time getting a strength of vibration and uniformity of quality through wide ranges of pitch, such as are impossible to instruments of the flute order, gives a unique charm to familiar music. To listen to even an ordinary waltz tune played in this suave, full, even tone is to get a new sensation. The very purity might of course become monotonous if continued too long, but for a while it is, as one enthusiastic hearer remarked, " like stroking velvet and eating ice-cream at the same time." The string tones, it must be confessed, are not yet satisfactory. This is probably in part due to the presence in the violin quality of certain high upper partials, above the eighth, not yet provided for in the mechanism, and in part to other peculiarities in the most brilliant of musical tone-colors that may not depend on partial tones at all. This absence of brilliancy, mordancy, incisiveness, makes the telharmonium but a sorry substitute for an orchestra—even a small one— and, in view of it, one hopes that the promoters of the instrument will not hurt its prospects by claiming too much for it. It is not a substitute for an orchestra ; but it is something better, a unique instrument, a new musical species.

❀

**America's Example**　In connection with the radical legislation now being enforced in France, it is interesting to note that our State statutes provide a method by which religious societies may become incorporated by a process similar to that provided for the incorporation of civil corporations. The management and the control of the property and of all temporal affairs are placed in the hands of particular persons, generally called trustees, whose duties are similar to those of the directors of business corporations. On the religious side, however, the trustees and all the members of the corporation are subject to the discipline, rules, and customs of the particular religion to which the incorporated body belongs. Take the State of New York, for instance. The provisions of its General Corporation Law apply to all corporations of every kind. There are municipal corporations, stock corporations, non-stock corporations, and mixed corporations, each with its own subdivisions. A business corporation is one form of stock corporation and has its own particular laws, and a religious corporation is one form of a non-stock corporation and has its own particular laws. But with regard to religious corporations we have special provisions for the Roman Catholic, Greek, Episcopal, Presbyterian, and other churches. Our statutes are not so sweeping as is the new French law. The New York statute says :

The trustees of every religious corporation shall have the custody and control of all the temporalities, and the property, real or personal, belonging to the corporation, and of the revenues therefrom, and shall administer the same, in accordance with the discipline, rules, and usages of the corporation, and of the ecclesiastical governing body, if any, to which the corporation is subject. . . . But this section does not give to the trustees of an incorporated church any control over the calling, settlement, dismissal, or removal of its minister, or the fixing of his salary, *or any power to fix or change the times, nature, or order of the public or social worship of such church.*

On the other hand, by the new French law the associations " formed to provide for the cost, maintenance, and *public worship* " of a religion may arrogate to themselves powers which ought to belong solely to those in purely religious control. In New York the law recognizes the right of the bishops to share in the administration of the property of their dioceses :

The Archbishop or Bishop, and the Vicar-General of the diocese to which any incorporated Roman Catholic church belongs, the rector of such church, and their successors in office, shall, by virtue of their offices, be trustees of such church. Two laymen, members of such incorporated church, selected by such officers, or by a majority of them, shall also be trustees of such incorporated church, and such officers and such laymen-trustees shall together constitute the Board of Trustees thereof.

This is the crucial point in the change of ecclesiastical administration in France. The separation law there disregards the final authority of the bishop—in other words, that of Rome. This is a severer blow at the Vatican than any possible loss of property, and it is this which ultimately moved the Pope to his apparently stiff-necked position. While conditions in France are different from those in America, due to the suspicion that the Roman Catholic Church there has been a hindrance in the direction of political integrity, the Government could hardly go as far as does our law. But it might modify its chief offending provision by providing at least for the representation, in every association and in every declaration, of the bishop of the diocese or the parish priest. Lovers of liberty, both of Church and State, will hope that America's example may aid France.

❦

**John Gibson Paton** The recent death of the Rev. John G. Paton at Melbourne, Australia, closed one of the most remarkable careers of modern times. In the forty-third year of his apostolate to the New Hebrides, at the Ecumenical Missionary Conference of 1900 in New York, the presence of his good gray head was one of its major attractions. He had found in that group of Pacific islands, northeast of Australia, a race of as debased savages as any on earth. On one island, now for years a Christian island, five missionaries had been murdered by these cannibals. He, the last one left, continued to labor on in constant peril of his life. "Very often," said he at the Conference, "I would seize a rifle that was presented to me, and hold it off." His heroic patience at length saw fruit. Though cannibalism is not yet extinct, the major part of the New Hebrideans have been won from it. Shipwrecked mariners need no longer dread that once dark and bloody

ground. Christianity has been firmly rooted. Thousands of converts lead Christian lives. The Bible has been translated into twenty-two dialects. Great churches measuring 100 x 40 feet have been built and filled. Hundreds of native preachers and teachers, the survivors of many who sealed their faith by martyr deaths, are prosecuting the work of enlightenment and evangelization. Dr. Paton's "Autobiography" is largely a fascinating recital of his victorious struggle with barbarism. Dr. Paton was a native of Scotland, born at Dumfries in 1824, appointed to his island mission in 1858. His achievement gives him rank among the illustrious pioneers of Christianity in the dark regions of the world. Those who proclaim that Christianity needs to be superseded by a scientific programme for the humanization of mankind have an equal opportunity with his to put belief to the test of trial.

❦

**The Congregational Home Missionary Society** The Congregational Home Missionary Society, which for eighty years has been very influential in building up Christian civilization throughout the great West, completed, at a meeting of its Directors held recently at New York, the reorganization that was begun a year and a half ago at the annual meeting in Springfield, Massachusetts. There were present, besides the Directors, the Secretaries of the fourteen State Home Missionary Societies, the Superintendents of the Missionary States, and the members of the Executive Committee. The Rev. Charles S. Mills, D.D., of St. Louis, President of the Society, conducted the protracted four days' sessions, and a spirit of harmony and enthusiasm prevailed throughout. The most important single item of business was the election of the Rev. H. C. Herring, D.D., of Omaha, to the position of General Secretary, in which he becomes the chief executive of the reorganized society. Dr. Herring is widely known in the West as an eloquent speaker, a strong organizer, and a man of power in the denomination. The two senior Secretaries, the Rev. J. B. Clark, D.D., and the Rev. Washington Choate, D.D., are retained in the service of the Society, the one as Editorial Secretary, which position he has filled for three years, and the other as Treasurer. The Society under its new constitution is practically a federation of the State Societies—its governing body being a board of twenty-one directors, of which the majority are nominated, one each by the fourteen State Societies. This change will, it is believed, do away with the friction that has existed for some time between the National Society and the State Societies, and it is hoped that the revenues of the Society and its consequent efficiency will be greatly increased thereby.

## Ship Subsidies and Special Privilege

The President has sent Congress a special Message in favor of ship subsidies. While the Message is specifically a recommendation of the bill now before Congress providing for subsidized steamship lines between the United States and South America and between the United States and the Philippines, China, and Japan, it is an argument in general support of the subsidy method of developing foreign commerce. The statistics quoted by the President and the arguments put forth by him are just as applicable and just as effective in the case of those who wish to see our commerce with Russia, Scandinavia, Denmark, Germany, Holland, France, and England increased. The President states the case as follows :

Our shipping to South American ports is almost a negligible quantity ; two years ago during a period of twelve months over three thousand steamers and sailing vessels from Europe entered the port of Rio de Janeiro, while in the same period there entered that port no American-owned steamers and only seven American sailing vessels, two of which were in distress ; our commercial competitors in Europe pay in the aggregate some twenty-five millions a year to their steamship lines ; American ships not only have to compete against this subsidization, but against the lower wages and cheaper cost

of maintenance of foreign ship-owners ; subsidies will encourage our ship-yards, which are necessary to the National defense ; the benefit of subsidies will be conferred not merely upon seaports and merchants in foreign commerce, but upon the whole country, because the cargoes will be supplied by the producers of the whole country ; and, finally, the prime reason for the deplorable state of American shipping, and for reviving and strengthening it by subsidy legislation, is that " those who now do business on the sea do business in a world not of natural competition but of subsidized competition."

The President has put the case for ship subsidies as strongly, we think, as it can be put, but he has not convinced The Outlook, and we hope he will not convince Congress. We believe the theory of ship subsidies to be a fallacious one in economics, and the application of it to be specially injudicious and reactionary at the present juncture of the industrial history of the United States.

It must be admitted without question and with regret that the present condition of American ships and shipping is deplorable. It may even be fairly called disgraceful to a country possessing the most extensive seacoasts, the finest harbors, and the ablest sailors in the world. But is the granting of subsidies the only method of developing our shipping industry ? We think not. Let us remove some of the artificial obstructions placed by law in the way of American ships before we attempt to force them over those obstructions by misapplying Federal power.

The Hamburg-American Line of Germany, which is the greatest commercial shipping line in the world, is just building the largest steamship that has yet been constructed. She will be of 44,000 tons, 750 feet over all, and 80 feet beam. Her size may perhaps be realized more easily when it is stated that her crew will number five hundred, that she will carry over three thousand passengers, and that for the benefit of her first-cabin passengers she will be provided with a swimming-tank 75 feet long and 25 feet wide and with tennis courts. Is she being built in Germany, the most systematically protected country in the world, in order to protect German ship-builders? Not at all. She is being built in Great Britain, Germany's most effective competitor in the foreign commerce of the world. But when she is launched and finished she will fly the German flag and be navigated by German sailors, and owned and managed by German merchants. American merchants, American sailors, and American shippers are forbidden by law to enjoy the benefits of free ships which have enabled Germany, with about the worst seacoast in the world, to build up the second greatest mercantile marine of the world. Let the United States try the effect of free ships, free raw material for its ship-yards, and a simplification of its complicated shipping laws before it decides that it is necessary to add ship subsidies to its already top-heavy and perplexing protective system.

The Outlook has collected some statistics concerning ship subsidies which appear on another page. We think it may be demonstrated from these statistics that subsidies do not foster a sound, a profitable, or a permanent merchant marine. We do not agree with the President that, living in a ship subsidy age, we must do as the ship subsidizers do. We are not convinced that it is necessary to become subsidizers in order to get first-rate American ships handled by first-rate American sailors. But if it were, we should still oppose ship subsidies and should regret the President's position, for a reason which appears to us to be conclusive. This country, under the President's leadership, has entered upon a campaign against special privilege which is having, and which will continue for a long time to have, a profound effect upon our political and industrial system. That we are living in an age of special privileges is a reason for attacking them, not for increasing them. Some of the best railway men have said, as the President says of sea commerce, We are living in a time of railway rebates; we are not free to do as we like; we must do as the other railway rebaters do. The street railway managers have said, and said to President Roosevelt himself when he was Governor of the State of New York, We are living in a time of perpetual, non-taxable franchises; living in a land and in a time of franchise-grabbing; we cannot handle street transportation unless we do as the other franchise-grabbers do. But he did not think this a reason for railway rebates and non-taxable franchises.

As our readers know, The Outlook believes that Secretary Root's visit to South America was an event of historical importance. It ardently believes in cultivating intimate and friendly relations between the United States and the South American States, but in its opinion it will be better for the future welfare of this country, its institutions and its people, to let South American relations grow slowly, to even stand by and see Japan carrying cargoes in English-built ships which our protective system forbids us to buy, rather than to add the special privilege of ship subsidies to our industrial system, which the country is making superhuman efforts to free from the taint of special privilege.

⊕

## A False Alarm

We advise our readers not to take too seriously the warnings of certain Washington correspondents of impending war with Japan over the school question. When correspondents cannot find news, it becomes necessary to make it; when discovery fails, invention is called into exercise. There is no danger of war with Japan on the school question. The only danger, and that we do not think is serious, certainly not imminent, is that sensational journalists in America and Japan, unconsciously co-operating, may fan race prejudices into a wholly irrational race passion. That Japan should declare war against the United States because California does not make the kind of school provision for Japanese children that Japan desires is a preposterous notion. It is no business of any other nation what provision America makes for the education of children residing within her territory. People who migrate to America must take the school provisions which they find here. A law prohibit ing resident Japanese from educating their own children at their own expense Japan might resent. But what school taxes our Nation shall levy and how we shall expend them when they are collected is no concern of any other Nation. We may provide only for the education of white children, as some of the Southern States formerly did; or for education in the religion of the Episcopal Church, as England practically does; or in that of the Roman Catholic Church, as most Latin countries formerly did; or in no religion at all, as the United States does; and no other nation would have any right to complain. It is true that Japan showed great courage in her war with Russia; but no less did she show great wisdom in her diplomacy in the peace negotiations; and to attribute to her a policy of attempting to dictate to a sovereign nation how it shall conduct its public school system is to do her a dishonor that she has done nothing to deserve.

❀

# An American Poetic Play

Special interest attaches and special recognition ought to be given to every endeavor by an American writer who has a literary conscience to put on the stage in this country plays which have quality, wholesomeness, and atmosphere; for the theater, for reasons which The Outlook has many times pointed out, exercises a great influence on a great number of people who are not in any serious way readers of books and to whom thoughtful men speaking on subjects' of prime importance do not have access. The love of the story, instinctive in every rational human being, and just as normal as the love of truth and the love of right action, has evoked a great and noble literature of fiction. It has also made possible a great and ignoble body of shallow, pretentious, vulgar, or demoralizing stories. It is impossible to endow men with power without exposing society to its misuse. That does not, however, in the judgment of any sane person, constitute a reason for withholding that power. What is needed in all cases is such a

general standard of morality, of good taste, and of workmanship as will put the bad under condemnation and recognize the good.

For this reason special interest attaches to Mr. Percy Mackaye's "Jeanne d'Arc," now being presented in one of the theaters in New York City. Mr. Mackaye was graduated from Harvard ten years ago; studied at the University of Leipsic; has spent a good deal of time in Rome, London, and other foreign cities, and is now living in New York. He has published several plays of ambitious scope and of very considerable poetic and dramatic interest. His very sympathetic prose rendering of the prologue and ten of the "Canterbury Tales" was a by-product of the study of Chaucer and his time which bore fruit in "The Canterbury Pilgrims;" a play of rich humor, of picturesque diction, and of many delightful touches of lyric joy and grace; there are passages in the play which only a poet could have written. "Fenris the Wolf" was in a different key; more powerful, of broader sweep and deeper maturity, but not quite convincing, because the central idea was not worked out through subordination of the accidental and immaterial and clear definition of the dramatic movement. Mr. Mackaye attempted a work of extraordinary difficulty in writing this play, and the abundance and complexity of his materials were too great for his skill, and, while the play was full of suggestion of his talent, it was not a wholly successful piece of work.

In "Jeanne d'Arc" Mr. Mackaye returns to his early manner and deals with a much more manageable situation. There is clearness, definiteness, deft handling of the familiar story as a whole, and there are passages which belong to pure poetry by reason of beauty of imagery or diction. The central figure stands out distinctly and is touched throughout with the delicate illumination of pure thought and reverence for a singularly beautiful and lonely spirit encompassed with doubt, sinister ambition, dull puerility, and crude brutality. The happy phrase that waited on Mr. Mackaye in "The Canterbury Pilgrims" does not forsake him here. It comes at his bidding most easily in the charming first act, with its rustic Domremy background:

" Smell, boy ! Smell this day ! and mark what myth
Still lurks i' the nostril: 'tis a charmèd grotto
Where sleeps a nymph, to whom a thousand flowers
Make odorous minstrelsy ; and for her love
The tender lyric of the fleur-de-lys,
The blue-bell's clear *chanson*, the daisy's ballad,
Yea, and the languorous rondel of the rose—
Are all respired.—*Encore la poesie !*"

Jeanne's account of her visions conveys a sense of her purity, her *naïveté*, her faith ; that combination of maidenly sensitiveness and resolute bearing which astonished and puzzled her followers in after days. Looking at Domremy as the night falls on the hamlet, her heart yearns for its peace even while her spirit rises to the height of her mission :

"How happily doth all the world go home !
The bee hath left the shutting marguerite
To dust his wings at Pierrot's garden-door
And hum all night to drowsy chanticleer ;
The rooks are whirling to the nested eaves.—
Thou little darling town of Domremy,
Good night ! Thou winkest with thy lids of vines,
And layest down within the golden stream
Thy yellow thatches and thy poplars pale ;
And thou, too, art upgathered in home-fields ;
But thy Jeannette must pass away from thee.
For He who once disdairèd not to stay
His wandering star o'er tiny Bethlehem
Hath, in His love of France, sent unto thee
His shining messengers to fetch thy Maid.
O little town, hush still thy breath and hark !
Amid thy narrow streets are angels arming,
And o'er thy stepping-stones immortal feet
Are bearing light the undying fleur-de-lys ;
And from thy roofs clear horns-of-Paradise
Are blowing wide unto the zenith."

Months later, at the point in her lonely path where the parting of the ways gave her the choice of life or death, and the message comes, " Thy mother !—waiteth for thee," borne onward against her heart by the doom of her work, she answers :

" Show her this,
And tell her I would rather spin at home,
But for a web begun God sendeth thread
And I must spin for France."

And through the thunder of the cathedral chimes and the shouts of " Noël " she hears the tinkling bells and sees the sheep grazing in the quiet fields of Domremy.

The poetic and dramatic possibilities of the story of " Jeanne d'Arc," than

which there is no more striking and beautiful in history, have produced a literature of considerable size, and have tempted the skill of poets and dramatists as well as of mere makers of plays for immediate popularity. In Mr. Mackaye's play the incidents in the career of Jeanne d'Arc which are commonly regarded as historical are reproduced with essential fidelity to what is accepted as fact. From the opening of the play at the village festival in Domremy to the fall of the curtain on Jeanne awaiting the arrival of her executioner, her lover at her feet, her spirit lifted to a great height, the voice of Saint Michael confirming her heroic resolve, the story is told with insight, feeling, and dramatic skill. It is not a great drama, but it has a fine tone throughout ; it has charm, literary quality, and many of the elements that ought to make it a success on the stage. Mr. Mackaye has given us a drama of genuine feeling and poetic insight ; if he disciplines his imagination to the point where it becomes order and light as well as opulence and variety, he will go far ; there are lyric touches in his work that awaken great hopes for his future.

❋

# Can We Pray to Our Own Instincts?

A correspondent writes us as follows :

There is no evidence that prayer is a means of communion and fellowship with God. Prayer is private, and what a man feels and what are his experiences in prayer are known to himself alone, except as he chooses to tell his fellow-men. So far, however, as the evidence is accessible, it shows that the communion and fellowship merely mean that a man who is accustomed to examine into his own life and on his examination to acknowledge his own sins, to repent of them and be sorry for them, to determine to lead a better life, to uproot the evil and build up the good in his own nature, and who carries out these determinations, becomes from the process a better man, a stronger man, a more contented man, a more spiritual man. This result—a better man, etc.—does not prove communion with God, but that the course of self-examination pursued has brought the person into closer touch with the highest instincts of his own nature. It does not prove that he has seen God or heard him talk, or that God has in any way communicated to him any thought or feeling, but shows that his spiritual nature will grow, as does his body, if he gives it proper food and exercise.

"Food and exercise." What is food? It is something outside the man which he takes into himself and incorporates in his body. It is this something outside of himself but by him incorporated in himself which makes the growth possible. But if there be nothing spiritual outside of man which he can thus take into himself and incorporate in himself, there is no food for the spirit. The man is left to feed upon himself, as the fabled serpent that began at its tail and finally devoured its whole body. "Food and exercise." But if there is no spiritual reality on which man can feed, he grows not by food and exercise, but by exercise alone.

How long must a man saw wood while he is fasting, in order to grow strong? For a prayer that is coming into fellowship with God our correspondent substitutes a prayer that is "coming into closer touch with the highest instincts of his own nature." Man is to pray; but he is to address his prayers to his own highest instincts. Then he is not one, but two; for an object cannot come into closer contact with itself. In order to get rid of the conception of a personal God who inspires, educates, uplifts, develops his children, it is necessary to split man into separate personalities, one of which is inspiring, educating, uplifting, developing the other. And this process must go on indefinitely. For the "higher instincts" of a boy are not the highest instincts of a developed man, and they can grow to the highest instincts of a developed man only as they are fed by some other higher instincts, and then in turn by other still higher instincts, *ad infinitum.*

Whether God gives things to his children in answer to their requests is a question on which good men may differ. There is always room to question whether the thing received was a result of the request or not. But that the spirit of man can hold communion with the invisible Spirit of God, and from such communion receive comfort, counsel, strength, peace, joy, is attested by so many and so various witnesses of different temperaments, in different epochs, trained in different religions, that it can be doubted only by doubting the veracity of human consciousness, which is the basis of all knowledge. The experience of inspiration derived from communion with God is more universal than the experience of inspiration derived from either art or music. The testimony to the reality of friendship with God is probably as nearly universal as the testimony to the reality and value of human friendship. Matthew Arnold has summed up the argument very briefly:

"If, on the other hand, they ask, 'How are we to verify that there rules an enduring Power, not ourselves, which makes for righteousness?' we may answer at once: How? Why, as you verify that fire burns—*by experience!* It *is* so; try it; every case of conduct, of that which is more than three-fourths of your own life and of the life of all mankind, will prove it to you."[1]

Our correspondent has unconsciously added to this world-wide testimony to the reality and efficiency of prayer. For he has made it clear that to growth some fellowship with a higher power is necessary; that this necessity is as evident in the spiritual as in the intellectual or the physical man; and that this truth is so wrought into his consciousness that he who denies prayer to God is obliged to substitute prayer to his own highest instincts. If one tells us not to eat meat but to eat vegetables, we may accept his counsel; if he tells us not to eat vegetables but to eat meat, we may comply. But not if he tells us never to eat at all. He may tell us we cannot pray to God but may pray to the Virgin, and we may comply; he may tell us that we may not pray to the Virgin but we should pray to God, and we may comply. But if he tells us not to pray at all, our starved souls rebel, and we pray to our own instincts. And not in vain: for doubtless the All-Father, who has answered innumerable prayers that were offered to Jove, Buddha, or the Virgin Mary, answers thousands of prayers that are, in the mind of the worshipers, only an aspiration.

[1] Matthew Arnold, "Literature and Dogma," p. 267.

# The Spectator

Washington is a peculiar city. The Spectator is convinced of this. While no longer a "wilderness," it is still in many respects a village. Continuing to boast "magnificent distances," it has refused to admit the exigency of haste. The first impression the stranger receives after leaving the railway station is that the municipal machinery has for some reason run down. The streets are so wide that they looked deserted, and the pedestrians on the sidewalks strolled along as though none was in a hurry. No wonder, he thought, that the little Washington boy clutched his father's hand excitedly and cried, "Daddy, where's the fire?" when he was first taken to New York. Even on the street-cars the usual order is reversed, and instead of the "Step lively there," the continual effort is to prevent persons from alighting while the car is in motion. But then the conductors of the street-cars in Washington count their regular passengers as their personal friends. Did not the Spectator see one touch his hat to an old lady, who had taken an adjacent seat, and, while collecting her fare, exchange with her pleasantries on the weather? And did not she, noting the Spectator's ill-concealed surprise, explain to him that the conductors on that line were always so considerate of her comfort and safety that she liked to show her appreciation by friendliness? And so it goes. On every side there is noticeable informality. Every one seems to know every one else, and none's affairs, it is whispered, remain long in privacy. A paradox: a city at the same time cosmopolitan and provincial.

❦

But a change is coming over it. Sophistry is creeping in, conventions are being set up, old standards abolished. The Spectator remembers, and it is not so many years ago, when a woman of gentle breeding and true culture could go to any social gathering in Washington in a muslin gown, or a plain silk frock, and be appropriately dressed—when it was not necessary to be rich to go into official society; but it is not so now. In those days "Stewart Castle" was thought to be a great house, but to-day, were it still standing, it would seem but a modest dwelling in comparison to its immediate neighbors. Around Dupont Circle since then have been erected half a dozen private residences that are truly palatial, and along the intersecting avenues many more of similar type have recently been built. Washington is fast, apparently, becoming a winter capital—a social retreat for the leisure rich. And these people—these modern mound-builders—have brought and are bringing new ways and customs to the old city, once so genuinely hospitable, so indolently content. They are not only erecting their roof-trees, but setting up their standards of morality and wealth. Social entertainments have become more lavish and burdensome, dress more costly and remarked.

❦

It is easy to wag one's head wisely and declare that "it was not so in my day," but the Spectator does not mean to croak. He is willing to admit that Washington has improved—that as the Nation's capital it is more imposing. Good sense will, he believes, in time prevail, and there is sufficient of this commodity still in the market to hold the "balance of power." Indeed, he is told upon good authority that Washington is still not a bad place in which to live if one is comparatively poor, and from personal observation he is inclined to credit the statement. At least, one with a slim purse will find plenty of excellent company there; for the scientists employed in the several departments of the Government have but modest stipends, and the professional men, army and navy officers, and old inhabitants are not, as a rule, overburdened with wealth. There is in fact, he has found, a coterie of workers who, finding congenial interests, have made up a circle of their own, to which accomplishment, rather than worldly possessions, gives the password.

❦

Lack of enterprise is proverbial in Washington. Unquestionably, it is easier to spend fortunes there than to make them. Even the storekeepers content themselves with small returns and enter very little into competition. Going to a large furniture establishment where the Spectator was a total stranger, and making a small purchase, he was asked if he did not wish to have it charged, much to his surprise, and, replying in the negative, was urged to do so because it would save him a walk to the cashier's desk. Every one will trust you, from the street vender to the hotel clerk. " Never mind, boss," said a little urchin selling papers; "if you ain't got the change ter-day you kin give it to me termorrow." Almost everywhere credit is given, with the result that the majority of those who depend upon small salaries live beyond their means, and the money-lenders flourish.

⊕

Curiously enough, nothing seems very far away in Washington, and nothing very great. After the Spectator had been there a few days, he began to feel as if California were his next-door neighbor, and Russia but across the way. He heard a trip to the Philippines discussed as commonly as an excursion to Mount Vernon; and meeting at dinner a Senator from the far West, a member of Congress from the South, and a diplomat returned from a foreign country, all of whom he had known as boys and found not infrequent visitors, he felt closely in touch with the several sections of the globe that they individually represented. No resident of the District of Columbia can vote, hence no one is partisan, and the whole country is each man's possession. The citizen at the National Capital is concerned chiefly, it seems, with National affairs. He has no State to claim his allegiance, and therefore he gives it to the whole land—the land which, living at the seat of government, he covertly thinks that he owns.

⊕

Knocking (figuratively) at the door of one of the great Government Departments, desiring some information, the Spectator found it quickly opened and easy of access. Within, the same informality existed as without; the same leisurely ways and friendliness. The austerity and convention which he had

expected to encounter were entirely absent, and while he believes that he saw some imposing spools of traditional red tape, none was unwound for his entanglement. To be sure, he was sent to a great many wrong people before he found the right one—the one who could give him the specific information that he desired—but all were courteous, willing to engage in conversation, and willing to lay their own work aside, if need be, to further his.

⊕

And what is more, the Spectator found Washington a beautiful city. It is not strange that the people saunter on the streets, when the prospect is so pleasing. On every side there is a picture. No single section pre-empts all the beauty. At any turn you may run across a little park, and all the streets are blessed by ample sky-lines. It is not the Government buildings alone that make it what it is, nor the imposing private residences, nor even the wide avenues and extensive parking; but all these together, with its setting. Simultaneously the city has grown over a wide area; as the suburbs are reached, the houses are set farther apart, until suddenly city is lost in country. No one can tell when the boundary line is crossed; no one knows when the city dweller becomes a suburbanite.

⊕

The Spectator bought some picture-postals to send to his friends, but he finally decided not to send them, for they did not seem to give his version of the story. They were true as far as they went, but they left out the best part. They did not show the Capitol in its real majesty, with its beautiful dome hanging above it like a great brooding bubble in the pale morning light; nor the Monument in its simple dignity silhouetted against a mass of gray clouds; nor the wet streets at night with their merry reflections and myriad fairy lights; no, nor even the restful charm of the dimly lit avenues, with their broad vistas, at early twilight on a winter evening. These are Washington as the Spectator saw it, and as the reader must see it if he would know it and realize its charm.

# SHIP SUBSIDIES[1]

THREE ostensible objects have been sought by the promoters of ship subsidy bills in Congress: (1) to encourage commerce, (2) to establish mail lines, (3) to strengthen the National defense. With most promoters it is believed that the real object lying behind these ostensible reasons has been the use of public money by a favored few in two departments of trade—ship-building and ship-owning.

The bills before the present Congress offer a great change from their predecessors, the real object of which unblushingly appeared in the proposed payment of the lion's share of the subsidy to one or two concerns.

The bill passed by the Senate provided for more moderate expenditure ; it eliminated speed limits ; it provided for more mail contracts; it required the many vessels entitled to cargo subsidies to maintain a certain proportion of naval reserves in their crews ; finally, vessels receiving subsidy would, in the event of war, be put at the Government's disposal for military purposes.

The Mail Subsidy Bill now before the House changes cargo subsidy to mail subsidy, benefiting freight facilities thus indirectly and not directly. Instead of the number of mail contracts provided for by the Senate bill, the House bill would authorize but five; namely, between one of our Atlantic coast ports and Rio de Janeiro, between an Atlantic port and Buenos Aires, between a Gulf port and Colon, and between certain specified Pacific ports and Valparaiso, Australia, the Philippines, China, and Japan. This particular bill's provision for a naval reserve, approved by the Navy Department, consists in the voluntary enrollment of any officer or man in the merchant service ; furthermore, it is optional with each ship to carry or not these naval reserve men, thus removing the fear of conscription suggested by the sailors' unions. Steam-

ships to perform this postal and strategic service must be built in the United States from plans approved by the Navy Department, with a view to their use as auxiliary cruisers or transports, and to be held at the Government's disposal in time of war. Finally, there must be maintained among the crews of these ships an increasing proportion of American citizens, reaching one-half in five years, and a certain number of American boys as cadets.

Even in its commendably amended form the House bill is open to criticism: (1) because it provides for a service to Rio and one to Buenos Aires, when the latter should and could include the former. Why should six hundred thousand dollars be annually paid out to a line which for five thousand miles of its total distance coincides with another, the call at Rio detaining the mails for Argentina insignificantly ? The fact that no American steamship of any kind now runs in the South American trade constitutes no reason for such depletion of the people's money as would be involved in this double taxation. Present sailings between New York and South America average about one every other day, and by steamers of a thousand to ten thousand tons. According to a statement emanating from the New York Chamber of Commerce, " there is no lack at present in regular opportunities for the transportation of freight between the United States and the countries of South America, at rates which competition has reduced to a very low level."

The present measure may be criticised (2) because on the Pacific routes it simply builds up existing and well-established lines—the Spreckels line to Australia, the Harriman (Pacific Mail) and the Hill lines to the Philippines and China. Messrs. Spreckels, Harriman, and Hill are amply able to build their own ships without Government aid, as may be seen from the fact that some of the largest steamers in the world have been added to these trans-Pacific routes.

[1] An editorial on this subject appears on another page.—THE EDITORS.

There are now afloat on the Pacific about half as many American steamers as would be required to undertake the above-mentioned contracts. Nor can the mail subsidy be justified as a mail proposition alone. The proposed service would fall short of the present system so far as frequency of service is concerned.

Most men agree that we should pay well for the swift carriage of our mails, and that we should pay well for the naval strengthening of our National defense. But even in the Mail Subsidy Bill before the House these three provisions may hide another purpose—the use of public funds to stimulate ship-building and ship-owning.

A principal reason why ship-building does not flourish more in the United States is because there is not sufficiently great inducement to construct vessels to transport an over-protected trade. Instead of devising a subsidy bill to aid shipping, we would better remove the Dingley tariff. That is the way to equal-ize conditions. It has not been adopted because our Government has been con-trolled by over-protected manufacturers. The Government may now well be con-trolled by those who realize that trans-portation charges are a tax on the prod-uct. If the foreigner transports more cheaply than we can, he lowers the tax.

Another factor in the cost of manu-facture is the cost of labor. American high wages are due, first, to our ability to produce greater value, proportionately to labor expenditure, than is the case abroad. But the cost of labor is also due to the artificially high prices occasioned by the restriction of distribution through tariffs and monopolies. The laborer would lose nothing by a reduction in his wages if artificially high prices of living were reduced in like measure, which would be the case if the restriction of distribution due to our labor tariff were removed.

Subsidy bills are based on wrong premises, if by them their supporters expect greatly to increase our commerce. The true method for increasing that com-merce is to enact a law to give to our people a chance under American regis-try to build or buy ships where they choose.

That policy is criticised by a gentle-man who for a long time has been the able Secretary of the Merchant Marine Commission:

*To the Editors of The Outlook:*

In your comment upon Secretary Root's argument at Kansas City for the upbuilding of the American merchant marine you fall into a serious error—indeed, into several errors—in matters of fact.

Taking issue with Mr. Root over the propo-sition that subsidized mail liners—not cargo or "tramp" ships, but mail liners—must be built in the United States, you declare that that is not the policy of Germany. But it is exactly the policy of Germany. Her subsidy law and her contracts absolutely require that the subsidized mail ships shall be built in German yards, by German workmen, and, as far as possible, of German materials.

This is not only the policy of Germany—it is the policy of maritime nations in general. You will find very few postal steamers under any flag, except perhaps the Russian or Asiatic, which are not native-built. Great Britain, though professing a free-trade pol-icy, stipulates in so many words in her latest contract with the Cunard Company that subsidized ships must be "built in the United Kingdom."

This prudence is natural enough. The great mail liners of all countries are regarded as national vessels—first cousins, as it were, to regular men-of-war. Our own ocean mail law requires that these ships shall be built under rigid official inspection on designs approved by the Navy Department, and all four of the steamers for the Ward Line—one of the few of our subsidized companies—lately launched at Philadelphia have their decks strengthened ready for the mounting of batteries of several long-range guns. Not only this, but our law, like the law of other nations, recognizes the especial national character of these mail ships by requiring that an increasing proportion—finally one-half—of their crews shall be citizens of the United States. The cooks, the servants, and the rude, unskilled labor may be foreign-ers, but the responsible force, the skilled, navi-gating, seafaring men, must be Americans.

If you will refer to the lucid and able report on German shipping transmitted in 1900 by Mr. Frank H. Mason, then our Consul-General at Berlin and now at Paris, you will realize that the whole truth as to Imperial aid to the German merchant marine is not told in the familiar assertion of Herr Ballin, of the Hamburg-American Line, that, with two trifling excep-tions, his company has never had a subsidy. This is a part of the elaborate propaganda carried on in this country against national encouragement to the American merchant marine. It takes no account whatever of the hauling, at nominal cost, on German State railways of materials for ship-building, of the discriminating railroad rates on goods exported in German vessels, and of many other expedients possible in the empire but not to be invoked in the republic. As Consul-General Mason says:

Not only has the German merchant marine been thus liberally and consistently supported by subsidies of money from the public treasury, but it has been encouraged, applauded, and honored by the entire influence of the Imperial Government, which in a country like this, where royal favor is so potent and eagerly sought for, is an important element of success.

One word further: Your editorial suggests that American merchants have a 'smarting sense of deprivation and injury under the law which prohibits the hoisting of the Stars and Stripes above a foreign-built ship. This is a point to which the Merchant Marine Commission gave particular attention in its year and a half of inquiry all over the United States. Everywhere the question was put to merchants and ship-owners whether they believed in a " free ship" policy and desired it, and believed that it would upbuild our ocean commerce. The general reply everywhere from these men, these experts, who not only know all about their daily business but would have been the beneficiaries of a " free ship " policy if there were any benefit in it, was such that, while several, probably nearly half, of the members of the Commission leaned toward " free ships " when the inquiry began, the matter was not so much as mentioned in the final recommendations.

Moreover, when the pending shipping bill was framed, it was specifically approved by the National Board of Trade, the National Association of Manufacturers, the American Bankers' Association, and similar authoritative bodies in every section and in almost every commercial city in the Union. This bill passed the Senate promptly by a good majority, and the opposition which it has encountered in the House is very largely from the far-inland element which doubts whether it is worth while for us to have anything to do with "abroad," or to make any systematic effort to extend our foreign commerce.

I happened to be called from Boston—being of our seafaring Yankee race—to serve as Secretary of the Merchant Marine Commission. That is why I am writing you, and I am aware that this letter goes too much into detail, and is too long, for publication. It is for your own eyes, and it is sent with a hope that your opposition to National encouragement of mail lines—based on a manifest misunderstanding of important facts—is not irrevocable. This is one matter, and another and a different matter is the subsidizing of cargo ships, which you have not touched and I have not mentioned.

You are, I should judge, rather opposed to the protective policy in general, but surely not more so than the English free-traders, who from 1850 to the present time have found it not inconsistent with their economic faith to vote $250,000,000 in subsidies to mail steamship lines on terms and conditions substantially like those of the ocean mail sections of the bill now pending in Congress.

WINTHROP L. MARVIN.

Washington, D. C.

The Outlook's correspondent refers to the subsidy policy of the maritime nations in general. But has this policy given a merchant marine to England? Or to the more highly protected France and Italy? Or even to Germany, latterly so triumphant in ocean commerce? A sandy, low-lying North Sea coast line of less than three hundred miles is broken by two well-known harbors, Hamburg and Bremen, and by a small port, Emden. Hamburg and Bremen lie far back on the Elbe and Weser Rivers respectively, the mouths of which are not easily kept clear of sand-bars and are not deep enough anyway to admit the entrance of the largest ships. Transatlantic travelers must disembark at Bremerhaven or Cuxhaven, and even there disembarkation means the use of tenders in most cases. Kiel, Lübeck, and the other harbors on Germany's Baltic Sea coast line, less than five hundred miles long, are of practically no use in the development of her deep-sea trade, owing to the long voyage which must be taken around Denmark. Contrast these conditions with our own coast line, comprising more than half of the twenty-one thousand miles of distance from Hudson's Bay around Panama to and around Alaska, a stretch which includes at least a dozen of the world's best harbors. With this wealth of resource we are asked to revivify our merchant marine by granting subsidies, when, despite poverty of resource, Hamburg has become the largest port on the European continent and Bremen its most important emporium for cotton, tobacco, and petroleum, and with these two ports as a base, Germany has been able during recent years to develop a merchant marine second only to England's, and, in particular, has now the largest ocean-carrying steamship line, whose enormous commerce in every part of the world has been built up without a cent of subsidy, save an insignificant amount for a year or two on two of the boats in the China service.

But Mr. Marvin thinks that this state-

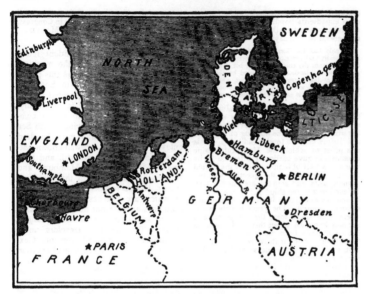

GERMANY'S SEACOAST

Compare this and the two poor natural harbors of Hamburg and Bremen
with the splendid coast line of the United States and its numerous harbors

ment as to the Hamburg line does not tell the whole truth. He reminds us, for instance, of "the hauling at nominal cost on German State railways of materials for ship-building." Now, how can transportation at reduced cost be construed into a subsidy given to a steamship line? If any one derives a benefit from this it is the ship-builder.

The correspondent then cites the "discriminating railroad rates on goods exported on German vessels." But it is not true that the largest line in the world enjoys any advantage of discriminating railway rates on goods exported by its vessels over the vessels of any other nationality.

Moreover, the correspondent may be reminded that this particular line has nothing whatever to do with shipments from the interior. It accepts goods at the port only. If reduced rates exist, the German exporter (and why not the American importer?) would enjoy them. But surely not the steamship line, except

that it might get freight which otherwise would go to another country.

The correspondent may also be reminded that, while the German mail is carried to America by a company subsidized by the German Government, it is also carried by a company not subsidized, the rate being a dollar for an amount slightly over two pounds. The company is paid at the same rate for mail carried from America to Europe, while mail carried by the American Line obtains a far higher compensation under the subsidy contract which the American Line enjoys by favor of our Government.

Again, the rate received by the Hamburg Company is paid whether the ship was built in Germany or not. The prices to be paid for the construction of its ships are determined by competition, estimates from English as well as German builders being always invited. In this competition nearly thirty English and Scotch firms have been successful, and have built ships for the Germans.

The triumphant competition of the Germans in the ocean carrying trade, not only in the number and tonnage of boats, but also in their speed and comfort, has now forced the British Government, jealous of the transatlantic record, into a contract with the Cunard Company, by which the Government not only pays for the conveyance of mails, but actually lends its money for the construction of two new mail steamers. Of course the Government, with justified pride, inserts in the contract the words quoted by Mr. Marvin, that the subsidized ships " must be built in the United Kingdom." Why should they be built anywhere else? It would cost more. The instance which Mr. Marvin cites proves nothing. Let him take his example from England's neighbor, France, where the law is similar, if more stringent. What is the result? One of our consuls in France reports that the shipowners there, at first disposed to give orders to domestic builders, found the latter constantly increasing their prices, until the point was reached where the builders were accused of calculating the amount of premium which proposed construction would command and adding that amount to their own cost price, thus absorbing the premium for navigation and the one for construction.

In saying that during the past half-century England has voted two hundred and fifty million dollars in subsidies to mail steamships, Mr. Marvin implies that this has largely built up the merchant marine of that country. There are no English subsidies, however, aside from the contracts at reasonable prices to carry mails. Most English lines have no mail contracts, and of course get no subsidies. It has been repeatedly stated without contradiction that not one English ship in fifty receives any subsidy. The English merchant marine derives its greatness from its ninety-eight per cent. of unsubsidized vessels, not from its two per cent. of ships supported by subsidies.

This fact, and the fact that the largest line in the world has been built up without subsidy, are sufficient proof that the English and German merchant marines are not dependent upon subsidies. Nor does either nation pay a subsidy in the sense contemplated by the Senate bill. Should the House bill pass, conferees would be appointed. Will not the final result be their agreement on a measure resembling the Senate rather than the House bill? There is the danger.

# LINCOLN

*Born February 12, 1809*

*BY J. L. H.*

Fate struck the hour!
A crisis hour of Time.
The tocsin of a people clanging forth
Thro' the wild South and thro' the startled North
Called for a leader, master of his kind,
Fearless and firm, with clear foreseeing mind;
Who should not flinch from calumny or scorn,
Who in the depth of night could ken the morn;
Wielding a giant power
Humbly, with faith sublime.
God knew the man His sovereign grace had sealed;
God touched the man, and Lincoln stood revealed!

# RAILWAY OVERCAPITALIZATION

## BY WILLIAM L. SNYDER

THE legal proceedings instituted by the Attorney-General of Minnesota to restrain the Great Northern Railroad Company from issuing new stock aggregating $60,000,000, in addition to the $150,000,000, the amount of its present issue, presents a question not only as to the power of the State of Minnesota to deal with the matter, but the broader question as to the power of the Federal Government to institute similar proceedings. The enormous overcapitalization of corporations engaged as inter-State carriers operates as a direct tax on inter-State commerce. It is important to inquire whether State control is relaxed; whether a sovereign State maintains laws which promote and foster such injurious practices. The greater question is, Can the country, in such cases, seek relief which will be adequate, through the action of the Federal Government, which is, after all, the only power having jurisdiction to regulate inter-State commerce?

The facts, as disclosed by the bill of complaint filed by the Attorney-General of Minnesota in the case of the Great Northern, would seem to present a case requiring the action of the Federal authorities. In such a controversy the Federal courts would have jurisdiction. An amendment to the Constitution of the United States conferring additional power upon Congress, and further diminishing the power of the sovereign States, is not necessary, because the commerce clause of the Constitution is ample to cover all cases of overcapitalization by carriers engaged in inter-State commerce, where such overcapitalization is a direct burden on such commerce. The fact that the carriers are private corporations, created under State laws, is not material. Their charters, and the laws of the State which granted them, will afford no protection for the unlawful acts of the carriers, if it appears that such acts directly affect commerce among the States by imposing unlawful burdens thereon. A brief review of the facts and authorities will demonstrate the correctness of this contention.

The Great Northern Railroad Company was authorized by its charter to issue capital stock to the extent of $30,000,000. It is a transportation corporation engaged in inter-State commerce, and received its charter from the State of Minnesota. The conduct of this corporation is typical of the conduct of nearly all of the great transportation corporations in the United States in this, that, since the day it was organized, it has habitually ignored the law under which it came into being, and has violated the statutes of Minnesota, apparently without let or hindrance. Primarily it owes allegiance to the Commonwealth of Minnesota. But it exercises its powers in relation to inter-State commerce subject to the exclusive supervision and control of the Federal Government. The Minnesota Legislature has seen fit to prohibit carrying corporations organized under its laws to issue capital stock in excess of the amount authorized by their respective charters, without the consent of its Railroad and Warehouse Commission. The law is clear, and provides that such corporations, in case they desire to increase their capital stock, shall make written application to the Commission and procure its written consent to the issue of additional stock.

The law has been entirely ignored by the Great Northern, which, in connection with the Northern Pacific and the Chicago, Burlington, and Quincy, operates a system embracing the commerce carried on within the vast territory, north of the Union Pacific, lying between the Great Lakes and the Pacific Ocean. As the country grew in wealth and prosperity, as the population of this fertile region increased, as its mineral and agricultural resources have been gradually developed, the earning capacity of the Great North-em has increased five hundred per cent. It formerly earned and paid to its stockholders, over and above all fixed charges and expenses, $2,100,000 annually, or seven per cent. on its $30,000,000 of capital stock. Its earnings gradually increased to $4,200,000 annually. Instead of paying fourteen per cent. on the $33,000,000 of original stock, it issued $30,000,000 additional, without legal authority and in direct violation of the laws of Minnesota, and paid seven per cent. on the $60,000,000. Its net earnings increased to $6,300,000 per year, and its stock was again increased to $90,000,000. The earnings grew to $8,400,000 annually, and the stock was increased accordingly to $120,000,000. The net earnings soon exceeded $10,-500,000 annually, and another increase of $30,000,000 of stock was issued, making the aggregate value of the stock at the present time $150,000,000, on which it pays the handsome sum of $10,500,-000 annually, or seven per cent. on this entire issue. But so great has been the growth and development of the country that this company now seems to be earning net every year $14,700,000, which will justify an additional increase of $60,000,000 of stock, as the increased earnings will enable it to pay seven per cent. on $210,000,000, instead of on $150,000,000, the amount of its present issue.

The commercial history of the world affords nothing to equal this wonderful exhibition of economic achievement, which has been duplicated in like manner by the other great transportation corporations of the United States.

The figures are startling when we consider that these vast sums are not earned in ordinary business transactions, by the employment of private capital in ordinary commercial pursuits, where success among competing rivals is the result of superior skill and business ability. If this money, levied upon and taken from the public by a private corporation engaged in inter-State commerce, were used to build new railways and to increase equipment, trackage, and terminal facilities to an extent which would enable every traveler and every shipper to use

the highways with convenience and comfort, so that no such thing as a car famine would ever be heard of, perhaps no complaints would arise and no remedies be invoked.

The enormous increase in the revenues of the carrier has been absorbed by the stockholders who subscribed for the stock and who receive the dividends. But the money paid to the carrier for the stock apparently has not been used to increase carrying facilities. How has it been used?. Increased facilities have been furnished. from time to time, but such as have been provided are grossly inadequate. The carrier has failed absolutely to increase its facilities so as to provide adequate public service or anything that approaches it. In failing to do so it has failed to perform the duties for which it was chartered, and has failed to fulfill the ends and purposes for which it was created. And this lamentable failure is not a private matter, but is essentially a matter of public concern.

The carrier has failed to keep abreast with the increase of population and the enormous increase of business, which is now six times . greater than when it earned seven per cent. on its original capital. It has failed to furnish sufficient trackage, equipment, or adequate terminal facilities. Statistics show that railway mileage has increased only twenty per cent. in ten years, while the earnings . have increased one hundred and ten per cent. Trackage as distinguished from mileage is also miserably inadequate. As a consequence, the increased traffic has so far outgrown the facilities furnished by the carrier that the inhabitants of the territory who are compelled to rely on this particular railway to carry on their business cannot, with ordinary celerity, move their crops or the products of their mines or their factories. The investigation of the fuel famine, and car shortage in the Northwest, held in December last, revealed the fact that fifty million bushels of grain, as nearly as could be estimated, remained on the farms or in the country elevators of North Dakota. It was further shown that in some localities no freight trains passed the depots at times for periods ranging from three to four weeks. It is clear that one railway cannot do the business which requires the services of at least three. Consequently many have been ruined, thousands have been injured pecuniarily, and the growth in population and general business prosperity must also suffer.

The perennial increase of wealth above referred to, which may be said to be the direct result of increased population, should inure to the benefit of the State. It is the unearned increment appropriated by the carrier to his private use, but which the carrier should have used to increase facilities for traffic and transportation. This unearned increment, doubtless, is what the President refers to in his recent message to Congress, in which he says that the people, while they do not wish confiscation, and desire those who invest in railway securities to receive a fair return upon their investments, "will not tolerate efforts to make the railway pay dividends on watered stock. They are justly indignant at manipulations of securities and tricks of organization by which the effort is made to secure a monopolistic grip upon a community, and then capitalize the value of the control as a basis for unreasonable exactions. They are willing to see legitimate business pay legitimate profit, but they insist upon being well served and fairly and impartially served." In other words, the unearned increment which should be used by the carrier to increase its facilities so as to prevent congested traffic and car famine, and to enable it to perform its duties faithfully, is capitalized "as a basis for unreasonable exactions" and used to pay dividends on watered stock.

The protest which has arisen has increased in volume and intensity, until, goaded by incessant complaints and the general discontent of the people, the officials of the State of Minnesota have finally been driven by the sheer force of public opinion to take some action to enforce the laws of the State, which have been ignored for years. Whether the enforcement of these laws will furnish an adequate remedy for the evils complained of is not material to the

present inquiry, which concerns more efficient and far-reaching action by the Federal Government in the premises.

It would be impossible for the directors of a private corporation to create wealth to the extent of $14,700,000 annually unless they were permitted to exercise the power of taxation, which power resides exclusively in the sovereign. In other words, a corporation which operates a public highway exercises the powers of the sovereign. Permission to fix rates and charges for transportation of persons and property is permission to exercise an attribute of sovereignty. The public highways of the country are constructed for public use, to accommodate public travel and secure public convenience. They are absolutely essential to the Government. The sovereign cannot surrender its power over its highways, because the entire community has an interest in preserving the power undiminished. The impairment of the power in the least degree would render the carrier supreme and make the State subordinate. The sovereign cannot surrender it any more than it can surrender the taxing power which is essential to support the Government. Yet private corporations, in operating the public highways of the country, incidentally exercise the power of taxation ; but, unlike the sovereign, they exercise this power, as their business is now conducted, largely for private gain and emolument. The power to tax can be legitimately exercised only for the benefit of all the people. It must be exercised by the sovereign to maintain the integrity of the Government. The people pay the tax into the public treasury for the benefit of the commonwealth, to operate the machinery necessary for its administration. The public highways of the country are its avenues of commerce, and are essential to the existence of the State, for without commerce there can be no civilization.

When, therefore, the Government conferred upon a private corporation the privilege of operating a public highway, it permitted it to exercise a high special privilege and to perform the powers of the sovereign. Under our system it was deemed better wisdom to allow the duty , of operating these highways, which are also military and post roads, to be performed by private corporations, upon the assumption that they would discharge that duty faithfully and well. When the carrier assumed the duty thus imposed, it entered into an obligation to carry for all, upon equal terms and conditions, and to operate the highways it was permitted to construct, primarily for the benefit, use, and convenience of the public, and to live up to all the duties imposed by law upon common carriers. To this end these corporations were created, and to accomplish this purpose they were permitted to be called into being. They received their charters and franchises as trustees, not for syndicated wealth, but for the people who compose the government which conferred these high special privileges. The President has said in this connection, in his recent message to Congress in discussing the delinquencies of public service corporations, " In special privilege they live, and move, and have their being."

When public transportation corporations fail to fulfill their mission, and fail to achieve the ends and purposes of their creation, they have violated their charters, and the trusts and obligations imposed upon them. The indictment against them is that they do not carry for all upon equal terms and conditions. They do not move traffic with ordinary celerity. They do not transport persons in comfort, nor at times suited to public convenience. They do not furnish adequate equipment, trackage, or terminal facilities to keep pace with the increasing population and the expanding volume of business. They have failed to confine themselves to their duties as carriers, but have assumed to become miners, shippers, and manufacturers.

In so doing they have acquired private interests, the retention of which is repugnant to their public duties. As carriers, exercising special privileges and sovereign power, they have allied themselves with commercial enterprises. They have acquired extensive holdings in corporations engaged in mining coal, producing and refining oil, in the manufacture and sale of iron, steel, sugar, and ice; as dealers in cattle and live stock, in dressed

meats, and in all the necessaries of life. By giving special rates for the carriage of these articles over the public highways to corporations in which they, as directors of the carrying corporations, are interested—because they own stock of the trusts and participate in their dividends—they practically choose who shall use these highways, to the exclusion of shippers not thus favored, and thereby make them no longer public but private. The result is a gigantic conspiracy against trade and commerce, the conspirators being the public carriers and the great trusts with which they are partners and allies. The carriers and the industrial combines have practically secured a monopoly of trade and commerce in the necessaries of life.

This result, so far as the carriers are concerned, could never have been accomplished without the exercise of the sovereign power which the carriers exercise exclusively in operating the public highways of the country. In other words, the creature has become, in one sense, a separate branch of the Government, coordinate with the creator in the exercise of the sovereignty conferred.

The State of Minnesota has a right to complain, but the law limits its activities to commerce within the borders of the State. Its courts have the power to enjoin the corporation which it created, and compel its creature to give the State officials a bill of particulars before permitting it to issue more stock. But it is obvious, from the facts above referred to, that the issue of this stock will affect directly commerce extending far beyond the confines of Minnesota. This aspect of the question gives the Federal Government supreme control of the situation, and the jurisdiction of the Federal courts attaches in a controversy which affects inter-State commerce.

The Supreme Court of the United States, in the De Cuir case, ten years before the Inter-State Commerce Act was passed, set aside as null and void a statute of Louisiana which attempted to regulate the conditions of travel on steamboats plying the Mississippi River along the borders of several States, upon the ground that Congress alone could legislate with regard to inter-State commerce. The Chief Justice used this pertinent language: "State legislation which seeks to impose a direct burden upon inter-State commerce, or to interfere directly with its freedom, does encroach upon the exclusive power of Congress." It is clear that if the State of Minnesota should pass a law which imposed a burden on inter-State commerce, or which would interfere directly with its freedom, the law would be void. The Great Northern Railroad Company is a creature of the State of Minnesota, having been created by its laws. The creature is not greater than the creator. If the State could not impose a burden on inter-State commerce, neither can the corporation which is its creature. But the corporation has levied the tax and imposed the burden, and seeks to levy more tax and increase the burden. If the Circuit Court of the United States, in the absence of any Federal legislation, could enjoin the enforcement of the Louisiana statute, as it did in the De Cuir case, because the statute created a burden upon or interfered with the freedom of inter-State commerce, why can it not enjoin the acts of a transportation corporation for doing precisely the same thing in a different manner?

The rule is that any act of a State which directly affects inter-State commerce is void, and can be enjoined and forbidden by a proper suit in a Federal court. It follows, therefore, that any act of a corporation created by a State which directly affects and imposes a burden upon inter-State commerce may, in like manner, be enjoined and forbidden by a proper suit in a Federal court.

No amendment to the Constitution is necessary. No additional legislation is necessary. The De Cuir case was decided when there was no Inter-State Commerce Act in existence.

Reference in this connection might be made to the recent decision written by Mr. Justice White, and concurred in by every member of the Supreme Court, in the Chesapeake and Ohio case, in which the Court decided that to permit a common carrier to engage in business other than a carrier in commodities carried by it was contrary to public policy, and that contracts made in the conduct of such a commercial transaction were null and void, and could not be enforced by the carrier. The Court observed that "if a carrier may become a dealer, buy property for transportation to a market and eliminate the cost of transportation to such market, a faculty possessed by no other owner of the commodity, it must result that the carrier would be in a position where no other person could ship the commodity on equal terms with the carrier, in its capacity as dealer. No other person owning the commodity being thus able to ship on equal terms, it would result that the owners of such commodity would not be able to ship, but would be compelled to sell to the carrier." It is true that the Court said that the act of the carrier was also in violation of the provisions of the Inter-State Commerce Act with regard to the publication of tariff rates, but the Court directly held that the conduct of the carrier in engaging in business other than that of carrier was condemned by public policy. This prohibition against carriers engaging in business as merchants and miners is now incorporated in the statute by an amendment to the Inter-State Commerce Act.

# THE CITY OF THE DINNER-PAIL

## BY JONATHAN THAYER LINCOLN

THERE are cities in America nearly if not quite as cosmopolitan in population as Fall River—the City of the Dinner-Pail, I like to call it —but none in which the people of many lands are so intimately associated in their daily lives; for the industry of this manufacturing community is not diversified, there is no opportunity for the people of different ancestry to follow this or that occupation—they must all make cotton cloth or perish; and so it is that the children of Shem, Ham, and Japhet live and toil side by side. There are nearly one hundred cotton factories in the City of the Dinner-Pail, operated by half as many corporations. Over three million spindles and nearly one hundred thousand looms whir and clatter within the granite walls of the factories, and from daylight until dark nearly thirty thousand men and women earn their daily bread making cotton cloth.

Years ago thrifty New England folk built mills along the wooded banks of the river which furnished power for the machinery, and less successful New England folk operated the spinning-frames and looms. The factories were small, and the city then was nothing more than a little manufacturing town. As the cotton industry developed the village grew; newer and larger factories were built; English and Irish workers came, then French Canadians, and finally Portuguese and Italians, Armenians and Russians, Polanders, Swedes, Norwegians—the people of every race and language. The city now numbers one hundred and twenty thousand souls, and is the center of one of the greatest industries in the country. There are those who shun the City of the Dinner-Pail as if it were the City of Dreadful Night; they gather their skirts about them and pass it by, little knowing the vastness of its human interest, little dreaming of the poetry that lies beneath the smoke pouring from the factory chimneys.

Fortune has never been kinder to me than on the Sunday morning when I first went to service at St. John's Church, in the City of the Dinner-Pail. I was a very young man then, but one year out of college, and just commencing business. At the university I had formed many friendships, and had become, by some kindly chance, one of a little company of men, slightly older than myself, living in Boston—an interesting literary group; all clever men, and some of undoubted though untried genius. Since then one of the number has written some of the sweetest verses in our language; one has made his name familiar to every lover of Gothic architecture; one has written essays which to me at least are as sweet and fanciful as those of the gentle Elia; and one has painted pictures of rare beauty. Some have failed, poor chaps, their genius turning out to be mere talent; and one whose mind was keenest and whose soul was sweetest died before his days of apprenticeship were done. We used to meet in an attic over a paint shop in the heart of the busy city, and discuss with youthful enthusiasm the absorbing problems of the day. We were all idealists, despising Mr. Howells and the writers of his school, while our enthusiasm for George Meredith knew no bounds. We were devout followers of the Pre-Raphaelite brotherhood, and worshiped the name of William Morris; we hated the rush and hurry of a commercial age, and railed at "progress" when understood to mean electric cars and telephones—in a word, we believed that mankind had been brutalized by machinery, and our mission was to preach the gospel of John Ruskin and save America from the hands of the Philistines.

Returning to the City of the Dinner-Pail, I found myself in a different atmosphere. Rossetti's name was next to unknown; Morris may have been thought of as the inventor of a comfortable easy-chair, but not a single Kelmscott book was owned in the city. And as for George Meredith, if one of his novels strayed from its shelf in the Public Library, it was because some immature young person believed him to be the author of "Lucile." The City of the Dinner-Pail was then, as it is now, the busiest of New England manufacturing towns, a workaday city where no vice was so disgraceful as idleness; where thousands of men and women, yes, and children too, toiled from early morning until nightfall in the factories earning their daily bread; where the manufacturers themselves worked early and late at their desks, and where the talk of the home even centered on business.

One day, as I was busy at my desk over a particularly elusive trial balance, a man older than myself by about four years entered the office. He was an athletic young fellow, whose face indicated a cheerful, energetic disposition, and his dress marked him as an Episcopal clergyman. His errand was quickly explained. He had remembered me as a member of his college society. His parish was composed of English operatives, and as the winter had been unusually severe, many of his parishioners were in need. One case particularly interested him, and he asked me to help him find employment for the man. There was a peculiar charm of manner, a mingling of sincerity and good humor, of common sense and enthusiasm, about the rector of St. John's which at once attracted me to him, and led me the next Sunday to accept his cordial invitation to attend service at his church. I found St. John's an unpretentious Gothic structure of native granite, situated a mile or more from the center of the city. There were good lines enough in the building to suggest, in a crude way, some little English parish church, and, entering it, the suggestion became complete. I felt myself for a moment in the "old country," and, listening to the responses, heard the dialect of Lancashire. The illusion was, however, only for the moment; with the voices speaking the dialect of a country beyond sea were mingled the nasal tones of New England; for in St. John's parish Yankee sons are begotten of English fathers.

The Protestant Episcopal Church is the one heirloom left to us by England, when she officially departed from our shores, which time has altered least. To thousands in our generation it proclaims the message that the splendid history of England is our history too—that all her glorious traditions are ours by right of inheritance; and as I sat in St. John's church that Sunday morning listening to the responses in which were mingled the dialects of Lancashire and New England, I was alive, as never before, to the grandeur of this heritage. And what hearty responses these were! Listening, I understood that the people of St. John's worshiped God with whole hearts. It was hard to realize that these people, devout, single-hearted, enthusiastic in their quest for truth, were the same men and women who, working at the spinning-frame and loom, had so often seemed to me merely the vital part of the machinery. That moment I determined to know them better, and I here record with love and gratitude that many of the happiest hours of my life have been spent in their companionship. When I left St. John's that Sunday morning, I realized that the life about me was not the dismal, sordid thing that fancy had painted it, but, instead, possessed an interest passing the imagination, and with an unwonted enthusiasm I sought to find my own place in it.

At half-past five each morning in the City of the Dinner-Pail the factory bells ring out in merry chorus; only the older factories keep up the custom, but they are so numerous that the bells are heard from one end of the city to the other. On many a dark winter morning the sound of the bells has awakened me to reflect for a moment on the lot of those who "get up by night and dress by yellow candle-light," and I have returned to my dreams while already the streets were beginning to be thronged with the army of the dinner-pail. And what a motley army it is which, in the early morning, hurries through the streets to the day's work in the many factories! It is composed of men and women of every race and language—the greatest numbers, however, being of French, Irish, and English parentage.

The French Canadian population, numbering about thirty-five thousand, is centralized in the eastern part of the city. Walking the streets, one hears French spoken quite as often as English; boarding-houses bear the sign of " Maison de Pension," while other signs over the shop doors set forth in French the dealer's wares. High on a hill overlooking the beautiful lakes which skirt the city to the eastward stands Notre Dame College, in which are enrolled over twelve hundred students, and near the college buildings towers the great church of Notre Dame. In the adjoining streets are the parochial residence, the convent, and the schools. Not far away is the office of L'Indépendant, a daily paper of no mean circulation, printed in French. In its columns may be found recorded the meetings of such societies as the Ligue des Patriotes, the Garde Napoleon, the Société de St. Jean Baptiste, and such clubs as the Laurier and La Boucane, the Cercle Montcalm, and a score of others.

As one walks the streets of the French quarter it is hard to believe one's self in a New England city. If one were to enter the houses, this belief would be even more difficult; here he would find customs very foreign to the soil in which they flourish; he would hear the affairs of the home discussed in a foreign tongue; he would find no trace of the Puritan traditions deep-rooted in another section of the city among the few thousand of New England descent who dwell there, but, instead, the traditions of a Latin race. While he would find so much that was foreign in suggestion, he would, however, discover, if he looked beneath the surface, a deep-rooted Americanism; for these people are loyal citizens of the United States. The French voters who go to the polls take a keen interest in politics; they influence new immigrants to become naturalized, and, when their papers are received, to exercise the right of suffrage. Here, as in their Northern homes, the French Canadians run slight risk of extinction through race suicide, for their families are large. I have heard of instances where the children of the same parents numbered more than twenty, and

families of twelve and fourteen occasion no comment among them. Large families beget either shiftlessness or thrift, and in the present instance it is the latter which obtains, for thrift is the predominant characteristic in the homes of the French quarter. The French Canadian loves the dollar; he dreads nothing more than a strike, because a strike enforces idleness and idleness entails loss of wages. There are no French Canadian labor leaders.

The Irishman who makes his home in the city is the same Irishman who makes his home everywhere in the land—as he himself might state it. There are twenty-five thousand Irish-Americans in the City of the Dinner-Pail ; the ancestors of some came before the first factory was built; and many an Irish family can claim to be among the oldest in the community. From these families come many of the foremost citizens, conspicuous in every profession as well as in every trade and craft. Most of the twenty-five thousand, however, came in recent years; some came yesterday, fresh from the old sod, as green as their emerald isle, clad in homespun, and speaking an unintelligible dialect; but before a decade has passed all will have become enthusiastic citizens of the great Republic.

The English operatives, some of whom we have seen at their devotions in St. John's Church, bring with them the customs and traditions of the old country. They give tea-parties at which the guests sing unending ballads to monotonous music; Shrove Tuesday brings the inevitable pancake, Christmas its plum pudding and the Yule log. Perhaps at Christmas time transplanted traditions are most in evidence, for at this season of the year the hearts of men go out to all mankind, and in the cosmopolitan community each speaks his message in his own tongue, and, as in the day of Pentecost, each hears the message of the others in his own language. The English trim their churches with their own hands—it is no meaningless ceremony with them; they gather the greens and wreathe the holly to welcome the coming of the Christ child. On Christmas Eve the candles are lighted in many homes, and shine a welcome through the windows to the wayfarer; and, best of all, after the midnight service in the church, the waits go about the sleeping city—no whir of spindles or clatter of loom is then heard—singing carols. The voices of the singers ring out on the winter air:

"It came upon the midnight clear,
 Ihat glorious song of old,
From angels bending near the earth
 To touch their harps of gold:
Peace on the earth, good will to men
 From Heaven's all-gracious King.
The world in solemn stillness lay
 To hear the angels sing."

And those who sing this carol are the same men and women who throughout the year stand beside the spinning-frame and loom in the noisy factories.

A description even of the Christmas customs of the folk of the many nations who work side by side in the mills would fill many pages; and a volume which should include also a description of the Old World traditions which survive in the family life would be of vital interest to the student of sociology; for the City of the Dinner-Pail strikingly illustrates the wonderful process of assimilation which is going on throughout our country. Each year immigrants from every nation under heaven come to our shores and are transformed into loyal citizens. It is, happily, not true that the traditions of the old home vanish in a moment as by a miracle; they remain, slightly modified, perhaps, for generations; but they survive in the home, not in the civic life; and the survival of these customs lends a peculiar charm to the study of life among the toilers.

Some one has facetiously said that "American" was spoken at the building of the tower of Babel. Underlying this saying is a truth which one can easily understand by walking, some Saturday evening, through the main street of the City of the Dinner-Pail. Years ago, when the great city was an insignificant factory town, and all the spindles in operation would not equip the smallest of its many mills to-day; when these spindles were tended by the sons and daughters of farmer folk, whose grandchildren now look pityingly at the operatives returning from the day's work, dinner-pail in hand; when the

sight of any of the foreigners who crowd the streets to-day (the Italian woman, her head surmounted by a huge bundle tied up in a bright shawl; the pretty French girl, dressed stylishly, if cheaply; the Portuguese laborer smoking his cigarette; the long-bearded rabbi; the Dominican monk in the garb of his order) would have created a stir of excitement to be talked of for days in the community—years ago it was the custom of the village folk, after their Saturday supper of baked beans and cold corned beef, to go "down street," as the saying was. The shops were open, and thither went the village folk to make the week's purchases, pay the past week's bills, and, if the night were pleasant, leisurely to walk up and down the street. Besides this the village offered meager pastime for its people. Nor was there great need for amusement, save on Saturday nights; for work began at sunrise and ended at sunset, and it was only on the evening before the Sabbath that the good people of the town were inclined to sit up o' nights. When the mills multiplied and the foreigners came, they, too, took up the custom of going "down street," and this custom has survived until to-day. On other evenings Main Street presents no unusual appearance, but on Saturday night the sidewalks for a distance of half a mile north and south of City Hall—the limits of the village street as it was in the old days—is crowded with good-natured, laughing men and women. Nowhere in the world, not even on Broadway or Piccadilly, could we find a crowd more dense. It is interesting to note that this unusually crowded condition is limited to a single mile of sidewalk in the very center of the city; that the crowding begins at about seven in the evening and ceases at nine, as abruptly as it begins; that the greatest numbers promenade on one side of the street, which must have been the "proper side" in the old days; and that the vast throng congested within these narrow limits seem bent on no business. The shops are open and are well patronized, but the number of shoppers is insignificant compared with the thousands who walk aimlessly along, an irresistible current of humanity. What multitudes of events in every land under heaven have contributed to gather here these men and women of so diverse heritage! Here are united the strength and vigor of the North, the gentle, careless spirit of the South; here East meets West, and all are welded in a mighty whole. What meaning has their presence here to us who seek to understand the " Social Question," who seek to solve the " Labor Problem "?

The first fact—so evident that a specific statement of it seems unnecessary— is this : every man and woman making up this throng is a human being, an individual, distinct and different from every other individual that God has created. Evident as is the fact, there is a tendency in our time to neglect its meaning. Our very phraseology when we refer to these working men and women indicates the trend; we speak of the labor element, the labor vote, the demands of labor, when we mean the workers—the individuals who toil in the factories, the votes of these individual workers, and the demands for better conditions of life which these individuals, acting with a common impulse, make upon their employers. In the old days "help" was the word used to designate the workers, and this difference in language has a deeper significance than at first appears. It means that men and women who in the early days of the factory system helped their employers—that is, were associated with them in the manufacture of cotton cloth— now sell their labor as they might sell coal and cotton were they dealers in these commodities, and that somehow, in the complicated development of the factory system, the individuality of these workers has been so merged with the great machine of which they are the parts that in our common speech we fail to make the proper distinction between labor and the laborer, between the commodity and the man who sells the commodity.

If we were to follow these men and women to the thousand homes to which they will return, we should find these homes far more attractive than the average citizen is prone to think. We should also come to know the workers as individuals, and in our minds separate the commodity from the man who sells the

commodity; and, becoming acquainted with these persons in their homes, we should learn to use discrimination in accepting as truth much that is written about them in sensational magazine articles, much that is printed in the authoritative-looking volumes of the doctors of philosophy. The library shelves groan with the weight of books catalogued under the head of sociology, dealing with what is loosely called "The Social Question," or, what amounts to the same thing, "The Labor Problem." Many of these volumes are written by scholars who have thought deeply along economic lines ; some are the work of sensational writers who cry that the rich are growing richer and the poor are growing poorer, and nothing but a revolution can restore the balance; while other authors are apologists for the present system and tell us that, all things considered, the worker has no reason to be discontented; yet discontent exists, and the fact must be explained. In the face of this vast literature we are still in need of an adequate criticism of our workaday world.

In the last generation the factory day began at dawn and ended at nightfall. Then, as now, some workers were contented and some rebellious; by turns the ten-hour and the eight-hour day were heralded as the dawn of the workingman's hope; but still some are satisfied and some discontented. In our vain efforts to solve the labor problem we rush from one ineffectual remedy to another, because we are unable to view the problem in its true perspective. If we could follow the men and women who crowd the main street of the City of the Dinner-Pail each Saturday evening, go to their homes and become acquainted with the worker as an individual, many errors that now distort our vision would be corrected.

At half-past five each morning in the City of the Dinner-Pail the factory bells ring out in merry chorus, and half an hour later the streets are thronged with the army of the dinner-pail, hurrying to the day's work in the factories. Twenty-seven thousand men and women make up this host of labor—men and women, that is the fact to be remembered. Once in the factory, they will become the vital part of the great machine which annually turns out so many million yards of cotton cloth ; but now, as they hurry to the day's work, we recognize in each an individual human soul, separate and distinct from every other. Fearful injustice has been done these men and women by persons with the best intentions—persons who write books about them—slandering their manhood and their womanhood. This army lives on frugal rations, fights hard, sleeps well, every year advances, never retreats. The social unrest that so many talk about and fear is a healthy unrest—it is the sign of social progress.

Less than a century ago, when the factory bells rang out upon the morning air, what manner of men and women responded to the call? New England folk, men and women, boys and girls from the neighboring farms. To-day their children own these factories, and the Yankee operative has all but disappeared. The English followed, then the French, not to starve and fail, but to follow the law of human progress. In every generation of these factory folk men and women appear in whom is embodied the aspiration of the class, the aspiration which underlies the social unrest. The immediate cause of that unrest may be some condition incident to the factory system, but these immediate causes are not primal causes ; the fundamental cause is inherent in that impulse of the race that compels it to rise from worse to better, from better to best.

The case of an elderly slasher-tender with whom I am acquainted is an instance of this impulse working in the individual. This man was a Lancashire operative of the class that supplanted the Yankee worker when, in the process of social evolution, the New Englander ceased to tend the machinery in the factories. He and his wife took equal chances with the other operatives in the mills, they worked under the same conditions with equal opportunities, yet they were able to send their children to high school and normal school, and thus the latter became teachers instead of weavers; their grandchildren will go to college, and, alas! will forget the link that unites them with the toilers. The case of the slasher-tender is not peculiar;

there are many hundred such cases in the City of the Dinner-Pail. He is not some meteor-like exception of a man who rises from rail-splitter to President and is used by the preacher as an example with which to exhort listless boys ; he is typical of a phase of the industrial question that the reformers have overlooked.

We see evidences of the working of the law of human progress in classes of toilers, here in the City of the Dinner-Pail, as well as in individuals. Matthew Arnold suggested culture as the antidote for anarchy. Mr. Frederic Harrison and the reformers laughed at him. "Do something," they cried ; "do something; no good can come of dreaming ; culture cannot put food into infants' mouths." Reformers then, as now, were in a hurry. But the poet was wiser than the reformers knew. Here, in the City of the Dinner-Pail, the English replaced the Yankee workers, and French Canadians are replacing the English. The Yankees did not starve, and the English are not starving. The Yankees became manufacturers, they became clerks and merchants and doctors and lawyers and teachers ; and the English are following in the footsteps of the Yankee. Every individual did not rise ; thousands failed hopelessly —that is the law—individuals perished, but the type survived, and in surviving advanced. The English replaced the Yankee, and the French are replacing the English, and in the life of the French Canadian operative I see an evidence of the law of progress working in a way that suggests Matthew Arnold's remedy. I have already referred to the great church of Notre Dame, which, surrounded by the college building, the convent, and the schools, stands high on the hill overlooking the city. You may say that minster, the spires of which may be seen for miles about, stands for the power of the Roman Church, and so it does. But it stands for a power mightier still than the ecclesiastical dominion of the Bishop of Rome ; it stands for the aspiration of the race ; and, in a particular sense, it stands for the law of human progress at work among the French Canadian operatives. Who built that great church high on the hill overlooking the city? It was built by French

Canadian operatives—thousands of them —each giving his mite from the meager wages earned day in and day out, standing beside the spinning-frame and loom. Many hundred thousand dollars in wages is the measure of their sacrifice. The church is built in mighty proportions; the aspiration which built it is a mighty aspiration. But if you come to study the building with the eye of an architect, forgetting its real meaning, you will see recorded in its stones the fact that the aspiration, mighty though it be, is at the same time crude and uneducated. Had Ruskin seen that building, he would have had another argument to show the brutalizing effect of machinery. The church is neither classical, nor Gothic, nor Byzantine, nor Egyptian, but a very hodgepodge of every order of architecture in the history of that useful art. But who was the architect? From what class did he spring? From the same class to which belong the men and women who built the church by their sacrifice. And when the building in all its rawness, but in all its vast proportions too, was completed, these same operatives gave again, each his mite, and an Italian painter of great talent— some of us believe great genius—came to the City of the Dinner-Pail and gave four years of his life to decorating the walls of the church. He painted a series of pictures illustrating the human life of Christ, and in a mighty canvas depicted the last judgment in such a manner as to attract to Notre Dame students of art, who, as they study the picture, forget the crude walls that frame it, forget the noisy city with its whir of spindles and clatter of shuttles, finding here in such an unexpected corner of the world a work of art which raises their souls to the height of vision. In the great Church of Notre Dame I see an evidence of the law of progress operating in a class of working people seeking its end through culture. That the people themselves are unconscious of the law and of the means by which it operates does not lessen the force of the law nor deny the means.

We turn from the individual and the class to the whole community, and here in no less striking manner we see evidences of the law of progress seeking its end through culture. Given a city of one hundred and twenty thousand persons, seven-eighths of them of the operative class, and you would little expect to find that in all those things that make for the higher life of the community this city should have kept pace, nay, even have outstripped, its progress in material things. Yet such is the case. The first free public library in the world was established in Boston, and nine years later the City of the Dinner-Pail followed the example of the Modern Athens. We might look for the first free public library in a great intellectual center, but we should hardly expect to find the second in a workaday community. The impulse that prompted the establishment of the library in Boston came, without doubt, from those who knew the blessings of the intellectual life and desired to dedicate a great public institution to the advancement of learning. The impulse which led to the establishment of a similar institution in the City of the Dinner-Pail found its source, I believe, in an aspiration that looked beyond the factory walls—the fruit of the law of human progress at work among the toilers.

More natural than the establishment of a public library, perhaps, was the introduction of free text-books in the public schools years before free text-books were required by State law. In a community of wage-earners, where even a small sum spent for books would be a burden to the individual, it was natural that the municipality should be called upon to bear the burden; yet at the same time the fact that the community anticipated the law is an evidence of its faith in the value of education, its effort to combat anarchy with culture. More natural still, but nevertheless an evidence of the aspiration of its citizens, is the fact that before the law of the State required manual training to be taught in the high schools of all cities of twenty-five thousand inhabitants and over, such a course was made a part of the school curriculum in the City of the Dinner-Pail, while the same community was among the first to establish a free kindergarten and a public training-

5

school for teachers. It may be said that all these evidences of a community alive to the blessings of education were due, in the first place, to the sagacity of far-seeing individuals, public servants, themselves educated *men and actuated by philanthropic zeal, and in a measure this is so; but that such individuals should be developed in this workaday city, in the very heart of Philistia and daily touching elbows with the populace, is the best evidence of that aspiration to which I refer; and if this fact were not enough to prove the truth of the statement, then the enthusiasm with which the toilers take advantage of these many opportunities opened to them could be cited as conclusive evidence. Had there been no free normal school, the slasher-tender's daughters would not have become teachers; but it was not the training-school that enabled them to live their lives in the school-room instead of the factory, it was the law of progress dominating the mother's mind—that mother who for so many years tended eight looms in the noisy weave-room—the unconquerable desire in the mother's heart to give her children better things than she had known. And again turning from the individual to the working people as a whole, we find the final evidence. It is no small thing for three thousand operatives, after spending ten and one-half hours at work in the factories, to attend school from seven o'clock until nine in the evening. Yet so they do, not only in the textile school, seeking to increase their efficiency as operatives; not only in the primary and intermediate schools, seeking to fulfill the educational requirements of the State law; but in the evening high school, seeking that culture which is the fulfillment of the law of progress.

In the introduction to his " History of English Literature " Taine says: " Neither mythology nor language exist in themselves ; but only men who arrange words and imagery according to the necessities of their organs and the original bent of their intellects. A dogma is nothing in itself. Look at the people who have made it ; nothing exists except through some individual man ; it is this individual with whom we must become acquainted." In just this way, there is no labor problem separate from the men and women who create it. To understand the problem we must know the individuals, and know them as they really are—the worker at the loom and in his home, the employer at his desk and in the world of men.

The City of the Dinner-Pail offers a rich field for investigation to the student who desires thus to understand the labor problem.

# RELIGIOUS MEETINGS FOR WORK-INGMEN

## *ONE MINISTER'S EXPERIENCE*

THE Outlook asks for a brief account of my experience in attacking the problem of the Church and the workingman—or at least trying to find out what the nub of the problem is—by the direct method of going to the men. Leaving my country parish and coming to New York City with this specific aim, I first made the acquaintance of a body of from fifty to sixty workingmen in a Settlement club. By race and birth they were American, German, Irish, Austrian, and Jewish. By trade and occupation they were draymen, tailors, butchers, salesmen, machinists, students, street-cleaners, plumbers, janitors, firemen, policemen, minor city officials, street-car conductors, office clerks, blacksmiths, and so on. I found them an intelligent, clean, self-respecting, sound set of men, generally temperate, always considerate, unfailingly interesting. Several of the best and ablest were ward workers for Tammany.

From the point of view of my " problem " their most significant characteristic was complete openness and simplicity of nature, amounting indeed to boyishness. They were genuine, they said what they meant, they showed their feelings.

As I became more and more impressed with their genuineness and simplicity, they seemed to me more and more to offer the rarest of fields for religious cultivation—like soil waiting for seed, good soil where seed could not fail to bear. They seemed precisely such men as the Master sought and cultivated, and found ready to receive his message and become its conservators.

They were ready for the seed, but that seed plainly must be a message freed from every shred of conventional, doctrinal, or ordinary " religious " phraseology, else to them it would be Greek; and it must be the simplest, essential elements of the truth of God for man and man for God if it were to find its way home. This thorough simplification and reduction of the Christian message to its essential elements is precisely what has resulted from the modern changes in religious thought. The field seemed ready and the seed ready, but not the sowers; and even were the sowers at hand, how were they to gain entrance to the field? Not as yet through settlements, for the special aim of these seems to preclude religious planting; nor through the churches, for the gates and lanes of the church do not lead to this field.

In order to see what could be done in · the way of reaching this class of men with a simple, direct, wholly religious message, I left the settlement, and first made a study of what was being done with the workingman in view by the churches and missions of the East and West Sides, for more than one church is trying to grapple with the problem. In the meetings of these churches I found women, but not workingmen; I found workingmen in church clubs, gymnasiums, and classes, but not in the church. In the church which, considering its size, location, and what it stands for, I supposed had done much towards a successful solution I found not one workingman. The statements of pastors making the most direct efforts were uniformly discouraging. St. George's Church (Dr. Rainsford's) constituted the

only break I discovered in this uniformity.

Meanwhile I was trying to find a way to get to these men myself with the message. Would street preaching do it? or talking in the saloons? Was there a settlement that wanted to experiment with preaching or with recognized religious work? Could I get into factories, as Dr. Hillis was going into the Navy-Yard? or could I gather groups here and there in the homes, and sow the seed that way? I then found that the New York Young Men's Christian Association was holding weekly noon meetings in several shops. It was ready to accept my services. The first thing for me to do was to gain admission to more factories. The Young Men's Christian Association name I found to be a good introduction to the employers, though once it elicited vehement expressions and the request that I " go do my missionary work among those Young Men's Christian Association men; they needed it." In the extension of the work during the winter, I visited, I suppose, sixty or seventy factories, machine shops, and foundries, made inquiries, and if they employed only men, to the number of fifty or more, I laid my proposition before the superintendent or some member of the firm. The proposition was that representatives of the Young Men's Christian Association be allowed, as an experiment, to come into the factory at the noon hour on a given day in two successive weeks to hold a fifteen-minute " meeting." If the experiment " took " with the men, and proved no interference with the work and no detriment to the firm, meetings should go on. Otherwise they should cease. Frequently the courteous but decided reply was that inflexible regulations forbade admitting any one to the floors. Sometimes by urging the fact that I talked the religion of work and faithfulness, helped to make thoughtful and conscientious employees, and had never failed to gain the hearty approval of the firm after trial, I could discover a loophole in the regulations. Once a big, pugnacious superintendent, bringing his fist down on the office counter, broke in before I could finish my sentence: " We don't have that sort of thing here. . . . No, I say, nothing of that sort *here*." Which I quite enjoyed. And once a suave member of the firm was "full of sympathy for the work," "believed in and regularly supported the Young Men's Christian Association," was "active in the church," but it "was against their principles to interfere in any way with the religious convictions of the employees—as with their politics." "Quite out of the question, I assure you, quite out of the question." Which left a bad taste in my mouth. Now and then the plan was immediately and cordially welcomed. As a rule, there was half-hearted consent to the experiment, with manifest skepticism as to the men's approval—an attitude that underwent a marked change after a few weeks' trial.

The supply of speakers has been sufficient only to start meetings in the larger shops, employing from about two hundred to six hundred men. The meeting consists of five minutes of cornet or other music of a popular character to call the men together on some central floor right amidst the machinery, then a straight, simple talk ten minutes long, more or less, according to the length of the "nooning"—usually half an hour—and, if there is time, a musical selection, frequently religious, to close. The men will come the first few times from curiosity. Thereafter the meeting turns on the speaker's power to send home in practical fashion the truths of men's relation to God. At the second meeting the men vote on the question as to whether we shall keep on coming. They have never yet turned us down. An expression of shop opinion before the meetings began would invariably show scant respect for the proposition. When they find out the sort of religion we talk—practical, elemental, universal—about work and manliness, self-mastery, and good will, things they had not thought of as being religious, their hearty and responsive attitude is immediate and significant, coming from Protestants, Catholics, and Jews alike.

My talk invariably starts from God; it aims to make God real—not at all to proselytize; it takes its shape avowedly from some word or incident in the life of Christ; it is enforced with illustrations, and it is applied to the things men are thinking about and living through. Their attitude is often shown by a word as they pass—"That's all right;" "You told the truth to-day;" or by a grip of the hand as an older man says, "Just keep on, you'll wake us up yet!" One man, saying good-by as he was about to begin work in another place, remarked, "Do you know, I like to hear you talk; I never heard any one talk the way you do. You make religion a part of what we are doing every day." Another, in a committee meeting at the Young Men's Christian Association, told how the influence of the meetings had led him to break off a slavish dependence on tobacco, and said, "I want you men to know that your meetings are doing good, more good than you think."

Following the talk, I aim to have a few words with one or two, trying to bring God home to their thought individually. Unless the time is up, a group of listeners will ordinarily form about us. I find the men, as a rule, willing to talk. A man who is ready with a clear-cut religious opinion will prove to be one of the few "good" Roman Catholics.

Occasionally, in place of a meeting some circumstance leads me to start informal conversation with a chance group. It is then that I get points and learn things. Sometimes the talk is about God or religion, sometimes about trades unions or Socialism. A Jew is the readiest for discussion. And he holds to a religious topic—never Judaism versus Christianity, but something to do with the nature of religion itself.

A committee has been appointed from each shop where the meetings have been going on for some time. These committees represent the men at the Young Men's Christian Association, serve us as an advisory board, and constitute a general organization that arranges for an occasional entertainment for shop men and their families in the Association Hall.

My experience has made the general problem seem bigger than ever—nothing less than a reformation of the Church; first in its theology, to bring about a tremendous simplification of its message, and—far more vital, of course—in its spirit, to give it so much of the Christly spirit that it cannot but be by nature the workingman's social home, and cease being what it really though unintentionally is, a class institution.

As for "tangible results," I do not get over a feeling of surprise when I hear the question. It is not the sort of work that shows its results in a year, or two years. "Tangible" results may come and may not come. From such soil an early harvest in a definite religious quickening and deep seeking after God, with a turning to the Church, is possible. Or

perhaps, since the thought of the Church is so far from their thought and her ways from their ways, a Church of their own might spring up, the spontaneous outgrowth of their need for true, united religious expression—a need as sure to make itself felt and to shape its own fit and adequate utterance as it is sure that God dwells in men. I do my work and I shape my message on the lines my Master chose and followed. I know that hungry men are fed and torpid men made hungry. I know that no work is more fundamental or more lasting than that. Its issue is with God.

# A SPRAY OF ROSEMARY FOR "POOR GOLDIE"

### BY ROSE CHURCHILL

IN marked contrast to all the long announcements of the gorgeous pageantry of "Lord Mayor's Day" is the simple invitation to join in the celebration of Goldsmith's birthday which follows, as it were, in the wake of all the merrymaking on London's 9th of November. At the bottom of the small notice was this modest appeal, "Sympathizers welcome." Having learned that the company of "sympathizers" who gather each year to recall the memory of "Poor Goldie" is composed of but a scattering few, we ventured to swell the numbers, and turned our footsteps that dull November afternoon down Chancery Lane and through a low gateway under a picturesque, half-timber building. Beside that barren slab, marked with the brief inscription "Oliver Goldsmith," a wiry, energetic little man was bravely beginning his oratorical efforts before an audience of three or four. This gradually increased to a dozen or more, and at the height of its popularity may have boasted twenty-five persons. Shut in between the ancient Temple Church, where rest in peace those early crusaders of dauntless England, and a high office building (that is, high as our conservative cousins would count buildings) was a heterogeneous

company of wayfarers. Here was a sharp-featured woman in rusty black garments with an anxious expression. Beside her stood a tall, well-groomed gentleman of ruddy and phlegmatic countenance. Leaning against the iron rail beside the church was a forlorn individual from the ranks of the "unemployed," who apparently preferred loafing inside this quiet haven to being constantly "moved on" in the crowded thoroughfare outside. A young office-boy had evidently prolonged his lunch hour to see what was going on in the old Temple Churchyard. So the little company ran. Some who had apparently happened upon the celebration lingered just long enough to satisfy their curiosity and went their way. The "wreath," which was to be laid at three o'clock, consisted of a bunch of green reposing on the top of the slab, and of several tiny sprays of violets such as street venders offer one for a few pence.

After our orator of the day had exhausted his praise of the immortal Goldie, he called upon an old gentleman of gentle mien and old-world dignity to recite the "Deserted Village." Every year, for a longer period than they can calculate, this same old captain has stood by the lonely grave in the bleak November breezes and recited, entirely from memory, the whole of this long poem. Here is a picture that would be worthy of the cleverest pen or brush. Tall and erect in spite of his eighty-two years, he spoke with a fire and enthusiasm that might well be a model for the modern school-boy declaimer. Overcast skies and chilling breezes had developed into a gentle shower by this time. A little gust blew around the gray church, fluttering the captain's white beard and depriving him of his long, picturesque black cape. All unheeding, he proceeded, quite unconscious of wind, weather, and dwindling audience. Once or twice his voice almost broke, and once in the passage about the " parson " he almost lost his place, but he recovered himself quickly and went on. No village parson could have beamed with more benignant smile than he, and there was something quite touching in his rendering of the " broken soldier."

Unfortunately, it was fast being brought home to us that if we remained much longer upon the damp churchyard stones our place would very shortly be under them. So, in cowardly fashion, we slipped out, leaving the captain to reach his climax without us. As we started down towards Fleet Street we could still see the old orator continuing his long recitation. The gray, smoke-stained buildings towered above him, and from the back windows of some of the offices leaned lazy clerks with cynical smiles. The ceaseless roar of the vans in the great thoroughfare without seemed to form a thundering orchestral accompaniment to this plaintive song. We turned away wondering if that voice would haunt us forever, going on endlessly with its pathetic strain. The evening shadows were settling down early on this dark wintry day. Our old captain had done this for many years, but what can one look forward to at eighty-two? Oh! who will do homage to poor Goldie by the time another November wind has come again? We turned into the street, and were soon lost among the countless thousands who pass unheeding where a few tender-hearted " cranks," as the world would call them, were trying to keep one memory green with a spray of rosemary for " Poor Goldie."

# *A NEW DRAMATIST.*

M RS. DARGAN'S volume of plays published last autumn will receive serious attention from all who care for the drama as a form of literature and for poetry for its own sake. It is not, however, a first book; and while Mrs. Dargan is not many years out of college, she has not come suddenly to her extraordinary power of characterization and her extraordinary freshness of imagery and diction. Many who read " Semiramis and Other Plays," which appeared two years ago, recognized her rare gifts of dramatic construction and poetic expression and were confident that her strength and charm would come into more vital unity through work and time. There are abundant signs of immaturity in the first book of plays, and only a very young writer would have attempted the dramati-

[^1] *Lords and Lovers and Other Dramas.* By Olive Tilford Dargan. Charles Scribner's Sons, New York.

zation of such a character and experience as Poe's; but there are also indisputable marks of original force of mind and imagination; the quality of promise which comes from strength and vitality rather than from facility and sensibility.

In the four plays—two of them connected—which make up the volume happily entitled " Lords and Lovers " there is much to give the lover of poetry that keen joy which comes from hearing a clear, rich, strongly sustained song from a new singer; the deep satisfaction of recognizing a fresh piece of that kind of work which exhilarates, vitalizes, and widens the vision; a work, in a word, of that art whose chief function is to deepen and heighten the sense of life. The first two plays center about the young Henry III.; the second is a prose drama of contemporary Russia, vivid in description and original in dénouement; the third is laid in Syracuse in the time of Dionysius the Younger. The three poetic plays are constructed along well-established lines and show the influence of the older dramas; the prose play is not untouched by the spirit of contemporary play-writing. Mrs. Dargan is in no sense an imitator, and her work is in no sense an echo of other and familiar things said long ago; but she has traveled along the great highway rather than taken the by-paths which have tempted and claimed so many contemporary dramatists. Her view of life, in a word, is that of Shakespeare rather than that of Ibsen or Südermann. It has breadth, balance, the relief of humor. It is a broad and generous outlook and interpretation rather than a lime-light revelation and protest. The recent journalistic exploits in this direction are really local and specialized applications illustrative of that use of the muck-rake over the whole surface of human life which has given the later dramatic literature of the Continent its vividness, intensity, and repulsiveness. It is a great relief to get back to the highway after so many and such prolonged visitations to madhouses, hospitals, and sewers. There are ruffians on the highway; there are deeds of violence and scenes of shame; but there are also the serenity of the sky to touch mean things with poetry, and the breath of the fields to counteract evil odors; and there are generous and noble souls, who have affections rather than lusts, and who are free and spontaneous without becoming lawbreakers and scoundrels. In view of what Mrs. Dargan has achieved and of her great promise, her sanity is of immense importance to her art and to the permanence and representative value of her work.

She has, largely as a result of her breadth of view, that kind of Shakespearean catholicity which makes room not only for all sorts and conditions of men, but for sentiment and humor as well as for tragedy. Her plays are peopled by men and women of the sort that make up the world—the mean, the vicious, the cruel, and the generous, the clean, the loyal, the merciful. There is, therefore, in these plays the variety and contrast that give a drama not only richness and range, but the vividness of effective

shading and modulation of tone. The plays are unmistakably the work of a woman, which is only saying that they reveal individuality and the special quality of temperament. This is notably clear and captivating in passages of pure sentiment:

" It was not you, my heart. But say it were,
Should I pull down my heaven because a bird
Makes flying blot against it? 'Tis the doubts
That darkly flitting show love's constant sky
Forever radiant.

　　　·　　·　　·
　　　　　　　　Dearer than life, good-night.
I leave my prayers like candles set about you,
And as they fail think of me on my knees
Renewing them from Heaven."

The humor of the plays runs free from a fresh spring and has a clear, full flow. It is not easily quotable, because, being humor and not wit, it lies in the conception and management of episodes rather than in detachable lines. The play of speech between Orson and Eldra in the second part of " Lords and Lovers " is not only clever but full of character; and the peasant or servant talk throughout the dramas has a robust flavor which is hardly to be found in recent writings outside the pages of Mr. Hardy's novels. The freshness of imagery and of diction which give joy to a jaded reader are found on almost every page, and make it quite certain that Mrs. Dargan is first of all a poet. The vigor of her speech gives fire to such a passage as this:

" Methinks were I the king,
Or Pembroke with his power in my mouth,
Each English road should be ablaze to-night
With swift flint-striking hoofs. Now to our shore
Puffs up the wave may prove oblivion's maw,
And drink these Dover cliffs as they were sands,
Yet England sleeps, with one lone heart at watch."

The freshness of her handling of familiar emotions and similes, the poetic quality of her diction, touch many lines with something very like finality:

" Her princess feet like well the solid earth.
She is a flower that sips of sun and dew,
But feedeth most from root-cups firm in ground;
While you are made of music, love, and air,—
A being of the sky—a lover's star,
Although he be a king. The grace of heaven
About your beauty plays, and drops as soft
Upon my eyes as light from the lark's wing."

Here is a fresh handling of a familiar illustration :

"They know 'tis death—they know 'tis death.
                    And what
Is that? We are all guests in God's great
    house,
The Universe, and Death is but his page
To show us to the chamber where we sleep.
What though the bed be dust, to wake is sure;
Not birds but angels flutter at the eaves
And call us, singing."

Mrs. Dargan has evidently read her Shakespeare wisely and well, and her work bears testimony to the inspiring influence of a companionship which stimulates and invigorates rather than subdues and masters. Occasionally the Shakespearean manner is caught and curiously combined with a distinctly feminine note :

"But there's a world not this,
O'er-roofed and fretted by ambition's arch,
Whose sun is power and whose rains are
    blood,
Whose iris bow is *the small golden hoop
That rims the forehead of a king.*"

The two parts of "Lords and Lovers" form a contribution to dramatic literature of real importance. They are not without faults of construction and infelicities of diction. Mrs. Dargan, it must be remembered, is still a young writer, and her work has the opulence of imagery and diction and the occasional awk-wardness of youth. Her touch is at times as firm and decisive as that of a master; at other times it is uncertain and amateurish. One finds in these plays such pure poetry as this :

.            "For I love to say
Good-by to my dear stars ; they seem so wan
And loath to go away, as though they know
The fickle world is thinking of the sun,
And all their gentle service of the night
Is quite forgot ;"

such strength and dignity of expression as this :

        "I'll not fear to dare
The darkest shadow of defeat that broods
O'er scepters and unfriended kings ;"

and such fallings away from grace of diction and dignity of speech as these :

"Who can keep mum when death
Turns the last screw ?
    .    .    .    .    .    .
        I've but that youth,
Brief youth that held its morning roses up
And fled, and this bare, aged now that drops
But aching moments till I've found my son."

It seems ungracious to point out defects of taste, infelicities of diction, affectations of style, when so much beauty of a fresh and noble kind is poured out as from a full mind; but Mrs. Dargan has created her own standards and is her own judge when she falls short of the final touch of energy and charm.

## Comment on Current Books

**The American Ten Years' War**
This, as its title would lead one to suspect, is another contribution to the already voluminous literature dealing with the Civil War. But it is a distinctly original contribution—is, in fact, unlike any other account of the struggle we have yet read. It represents, to put the matter briefly, an attempt to narrate the varying phases of the conflict in the form of a prose epic. "A new Ten Years' War we witness on our Western Continent," explains the author, "not altogether unlike the far-famed Trojan one ending in the destruction of Ilium and the restoration of Helen. Again every community will muster its contingent of soldiers and send them forth to the war under its leading man or hero, to fight for the great cause, which meant in the olden time that Hellas and not Troy was to determine the civilization of the future. But now a restoration is to take place far deeper than the Grecian or that of Helen; the mighty struggle is not now for the ideal of beauty, but for the ideal of freedom." From this lofty view-point, then, and in the language of sublimity, would Mr. Snider unfold the drama, dating its beginning, not from the firing on Fort Sumter, but from the first invasion of Kansas by the Missourians in 1855. Opinions will differ as to the success attending his effort. For ourselves, despite the obvious fact that his insight and imagination far outstrip his artistic power, and despite the singular circumstance that he bestows the scantiest attention on the campaigns and battles that vindicated the ideal of which he sings, we strongly incline to the belief that his book could be read to advantage by all who would approach more detailed, if more prosaic, studies of the conflict with an appreciation of the significance underlying its external aspects. It is

quite evident that Mr. Snider has thought profoundly and as a rule clearly of the momentous events of which he writes, and if too frequently he leaves the impression of straining after effect, he undoubtedly contrives to set the essentials forth in bold relief. (The American Ten Years' War. By Denton J. Snider. Sigma Publishing Company, St. Louis.)

*European Diplomacy* In this, the second volume of his history of European diplomacy, Dr. David Jayne Hill continues and completes his survey of the foundation period which antedated the emergence of diplomacy as a definite system of international intercourse. Having shown how the struggle between the Empire and the Papacy gave room and occasion for the rise of national monarchies, Dr. Hill now proceeds to trace the evolution of the modern state through the warring efforts of these monarchies to attain, if not supremacy, as conceived in the earlier ideal of universal dominion, at least primacy ; and their subsequent adjustment to a system of balanced and co-ordinate power based upon the principle of territorial sovereignty. " It is in this transition," he explains, " that the permanent traditions of Europe really have their origin." Such being his view, it is no surprise to find the emphasis placed, not on the Thirty Years' War with its epoch-marking Peace of Westphalia, but on the earlier conflicts leading to that war and arising from the relations between France, Spain, Germany, England, Italy, and the Papacy, and on the growth of the Reformation during the rivalry of Charles V. and Francis I. As before, Dr. Hill's tone is admirably impartial and his treatment scholarly ; so that in these important respects we find no reason to modify the opinions expressed in our October 7, 1905, review of his first volume. But the promise of that volume is hardly so well fulfilled in the matter of narrative, which is somewhat lacking in the ease and freshness exhibited in the account of the crude diplomacy of the earlier centuries, and is, it seems to us, overburdened with detail. At the same time, of course, criticism must take into account the increasing complexity of the subject and the manifold difficulties besetting any writer who would make plain the tortuous diplomacy of such monarchs as Ferdinand II., Francis I., Charles V., and Philip II. And certainly, if in not quite so interesting a way as before, Dr. Hill succeeds in setting forth clearly the essentials which it is his main business to develop. (A History of Diplomacy in the International Development of Europe. By David Jayne Hill. Vol. II. The Establishment of Territorial Sovereignty. Longmans, Green & Co., New York. $5, net.)

*The Great American Plateau* Dr. Prudden is well known to many readers as a popular but accurate writer on scientific topics. Here he gives the reader " glimpses of the rugged southwest country, with its quaint aborigines and the ruins of an older folk." Dr. Prudden has long been acquainted with that interesting country in which the cliff dwellers once lived, and which is filled historically with the romance of early Spanish exploration. Of prehistoric remains, of the life and work of primitive house-builders, and of the present conditions of Indian life on the great plateau he tells us much, while the natural wonders of the locality are graphically described. (On the Great American Plateau. By T. Mitchell Prudden. G. P. Putnam's Sons, New York. $1.50, net.)

*Jamaica* It is hardly necessary to point out the exceeding timeliness of this volume on Jamaica. Public interest is now and will continue to be for some time specially directed toward the country which has suffered from earthquake, fire, and distress ; and nothing could more aptly and satisfactorily answer the questions aroused by that interest than the present book. It is written in a notably sprightly style of description and is very far removed either from dull historical writing or from guide-book minuteness. The author brings out vividly the character and human side of the natives, the commercial needs and difficulties of the Jamaican situation, and makes for the reader scores of little pen-pictures of queer and out-of-the-way features of the life in the island. There are twenty-four full-page illustrations in color painting by Mr. A. S. Forrest, and these add very considerably to the interest of the volume. The book may be commended to the attention of those who have already visited Jamaica or to those who are likely to do so. (Jamaica. By John Henderson. The Macmillan Company, New York. $2, net.)

*Life in Ancient Athens* Much as has been written about the political and social sides of life in Athens in the ancient days, nothing can be found covering so satisfactorily and completely the subject here treated as does this book. The author's aim is to depict the life of a typical Athenian in classical times from day to day in all its social and political aspects. This he has done most clearly with complete avoidance of anything like dry-as-dust or even didactic methods. We have, accordingly, chapters on the house and its furniture, on woman's life and the fashions, on the training of boys, on festivals and the theater, on military and naval matters, on the mutual relations of citizens, foreigners, slaves, and women, and on perhaps a dozen other topics of equal importance and of equal human interest. In a different way and with a different scope, Professor Mahaffy's "Social Life in Greece" is perhaps the most popular and readable book in the class to which the present work belongs, but by confining his treatment to Athens Professor Tucker has, it seems to us, increased the interest and made possible a fullness of description which Professor Mahaffy's book did not undertake. The illustrations have been carefully selected and are really interpretative. (Life in Ancient Athens. By T. G. Tucker. The Macmillan Company, New York. $1.25, net.)

*On the Eve of the War* After reading the preceding volumes of the "American Nation" serial history of the United States, it is somewhat surprising to find Admiral Chadwick's contribution entitled "Causes of the Civil War." He would be dull indeed who could not grasp that mighty conflict's causes from the exhaustive survey afforded by the pages of Professors Hart, Garrison, and Smith. Fortunately, although four chapters are devoted to a restatement of earlier conditions, movements, and events, Admiral Chadwick's volume is misnamed, being in reality a narrative of the happenings of the two years immediately preceding the resort to arms in the effort to preserve the Union. As a narrative it is easy, compact, and lucid. The Admiral, it seems to us, is inclined to take an over-roseate view of Southern slavery, and a rather narrow one of the motives and conduct of those who lent comfort and aid to John Brown. On the other hand, the student cannot but feel grateful to him for his careful and informing analysis of the last attempts at compromise and of the course pursued by President Buchanan, and for his spirited account of the crucial occurrences at Fort Sumter pending the assault and surrender. With the fall of Sumter his volume closes, and the way is thus finally and definitely prepared for the story of the great war, to be told by Dr. Hosmer. (The American Nation. Vol. XIX. Causes of the Civil War. By Admiral French Ensor Chadwick, U. S. N. Harper & Brothers, New York. $2, net.)

*Progressive Orthodoxy* The author of this little book is already known widely and favorably by his recent Yale lectures on "The Message of the Modern Pulpit." His present work puts before thoughtful laymen the main points of evangelical doctrine as now held by what twenty years ago began to be known as "progressive orthodoxy." It is for those who desire a statement of fundamental Christian truths more accordant with modern thought and experience than what they find in the historic creeds. It is a luminous help to the clear thinking that grasps essential reality. It is also sane in stopping at the line where it is more reasonable to wait for more light before exploring further. This quality, however, is not so manifest in its discussion of the divinity of Christ—a truth which requires the fullest appreciation, on the one hand, of the immanence of God in man, and, on the other hand, of the God-consciousness which is possible to man. (The Main Points. By Charles Reynolds Brown. The Pilgrim Press, Boston. $1.25, net. Postage, 15 cents.)

*Sidney Herbert* It is distinctly surprising to find Lord Herbert of Lea the subject, at this late day, of two bulky volumes of biography. More than forty-five years have elapsed since his death, and in his lifetime, although more than once a member of the British Cabinet, his career was hardly such as to place him among the distinguished men of his generation, and certainly was not such as to warrant his biographer's assertion that had he lived longer he would have been Prime Minister of England. His chief claims to remembrance rest on his charming personality and on his connection with the little group of Parliamentarians who banded themselves together to keep alive Sir Robert Peel's principles and policies. Indeed, it is as a history of the Peelites that this biography is chiefly interesting, and especially for the fresh light it throws, not on Herbert, but on Gladstone, the most distinguished and the most able of the Peelites. For the rest, we must admit that we have found the work formidable and rather dreary reading, cumbered with detail and correspondence of little consequence to any save the special student of the administration of the British War Office, in which Herbert served first in the now extinct post of Secretary at War, and later as Secretary of State for War. To this, however there is one noteworthy exception—Lord Stanmore publishing, in the course of his elaborate and unnecessary defense of Herbert's part in the mismanaged Crimean War, a series of letters which develop phases of Miss Florence Nightingale's character that will astonish and grieve all admirers of the famous heroine of Scutari. (Sidney Herbert: A Memoir. By Lord Stanmore. E. P. Dutton & Co., New York. Two volumes. $7.50, net, per set.)

# Letters to The Outlook

## THE RELIGION OF THE AGNOSTIC

Your editorial on "The Agnosticism of Abraham Lincoln" (The Outlook, November 17, 1906), emphasizes in a way which should be welcome to every earnest-minded man, whatever his philosophy or his faith, the fact that there is, between followers of the agnostic method on the one hand, and professors of religious faith on the other, not merely a possible *modus vivendi*, but an actual and substantial basis for concord and mutual understanding. This common ground is the recognition of righteousness, of justice, as foremost and supreme among the conditions essential to human welfare.

In reply to the question, "What is an agnostic?" you say that Huxley "more specifically defines the basis of his no-theory of the universe" in the letter to Kingsley from which you quote a passage. This passage is illustrative, indeed, of Huxley's position, but it can hardly be said to define it. In the course of his controversy with Dr. Wace concerning Agnosticism and Christianity, Huxley did explicitly define in a few words what he, the inventor of the term, meant by agnosticism. He says: "Agnosticism, in fact, is not a creed, but a method, the essence of which lies in the rigorous application of a single principle. . . . Positively the principle may be expressed: In matters of the intellect, follow your reason as far as it will take you, without regard to any other consideration. And negatively: In matters of the intellect do not pretend that conclusions are certain which are not demonstrated or demonstrable." (Collected Essays, Vol. V., pp. 245–246.)

To many men of the generation now past middle age the memory of Huxley is dear, because he, above all other teachers of his time, gave them the light and the leading without which the intellectual ferment of their youth, and the ardor of their revolt against theological tyranny, might have resulted in loss of hold on that ethical ideal, love and reverence for which constituted, in Huxley's view, the essence of religion. Will you allow me to adduce another brief quotation illustrative of the attitude toward religion of this typical and pre-eminent "agnostic"? In one of his essays on "Science and Hebrew Tradition" Huxley writes:

In the eighth century B.C., in the heart of a world of idolatrous polytheists, the Hebrew prophets put forth a conception of religion which appears to me to be as wonderful an inspiration of genius as the art of Pheidias or the science of Aristotle. "And what doth the Lord require of thee, but to do justly, and to love mercy, and to walk humbly with thy God?" If any so-called religion takes away from this great saying of Micah, I think it wantonly mutilates, while if it adds thereto I think it obscures, the perfect ideal of religion. But what extent of knowledge, what acuteness of scientific criticism, can touch this, if any one possessed of knowledge or acuteness could be absurd enough to make the attempt? Will the progress of research prove that justice is worthless and mercy hateful; will it ever soften the bitter contrast between our actions and our aspirations; or show us the bounds of the universe, and bid us say, Go to, now we comprehend the infinite? (Essays, Vol. IV., p. 161-162.)

As you have well said, "religion is always a kind of poetry;" and in so far as neither religion nor poetry is concerned solely or primarily with matters of the intellect, it follows that the method or principle of agnosticism is as little applicable to the one as to the other. If this restriction, so earnestly insisted on by Huxley, were borne in mind in current usage, there would be less of the all too common tendency to set up agnosticism in antithesis to religion, as if agnostics constituted a sort of anti-religious sect; and of the prevalent idea that the agnostic method can be hostile to that love of justice and mercy and humility which is the core of religious life.             W. T. Van Dyck.

Beirut, Syria.

## THE GENTLE ART OF KILLING FISH

May I suggest, in reply to Mr. L. H. Bailey's two questions in your number for January 12, that a profitable discussion of this subject is rendered difficult on the one hand by the disinclination of the sportsman to admit any weak point in his case, and on the other by the refusal of his critic to abandon the weakly subjective standpoint of pure sentimentalism? The sentimentalist, not usually made of very stern stuff, conjures up a picture of the agony of some dumb creature, and firmly shuts his eyes and mind to any and all palliative circumstances. The sportsman is too apt to retort with a denial that the game really suffers, and that the balance of nature, having been disturbed by so-called civilization, must be restored, etc.

Now, for the genuine sportsmen, men like Charles Kingsley, Theodore Roosevelt, H. P. Wells, Charles Hallock, Dr. van Dyke, Dr. Rainsford, and Caspar Whitney, the whole question, put honestly, is one of compromise, but with the salutary advantages so over-

333

whelmingly in favor of hunting and fishing that their answer to Mr. Bailey's first question would undoubtedly be, "Yes, it *is* worthy a man and worth the while—a thousand times yes."

Their critic is commonly a man who is not himself interested in sport. He forgets that angling and the chase have a venerable history, beginning with the first efforts of man to provide food for his family, and that their development has been steadily along the line of march of civilization, until at the present time the American sportsman, who abhors the slaughtering game drives of imperial huntsmen and British pheasant and partridge shooters, stands as a model of the humane woodsman, who kills as little as possible and always with the minimum of suffering to the quarry. The critic cannot possibly appreciate the love and interest of the sportsman for the implements of his art, their development, intrinsic beauty, and delicacy of workmanship; the engrossing interest inspired by observing the working of new rods, guns, etc., the incomparable fascination of the study of the habits of fish and animals, which must be mastered before success can be hoped for in the chase; the pleasure of watching the intelligent working of his canine friends; the cumulative joys offered by an expedition to good trout waters, with its delicious anticipation, the delight of the preparation of and addition to the tackle and outfit, the crescendo of interest caused by the approach to the grounds, the choice of implements, and at last the supreme joy of the actual practice of an art every detail of which has been, perhaps for years, a well of study and delight. But, alas! the layman cannot feel a tithe of the fascination, the compelling witchery, of all those things so beautifully set forth in Kipling's "calling of the red gods." He forgets that woodland sport takes its devotees to the pure bosom of nature, whose every phase is replete with beauty, with the spirit of human heroism and wholesome bodily effort, of good fellowship, of love for nature and forgetfulness of the unspeakably disgusting vulgarities of the "civilized" battle for life. He refuses to believe that some men crave the strenuous, and that for these photography or pedestrianism alone will not suffice to allow the working off of energy or the proper storing up of health for the unnatural tasks which our artificial life demands of all save an infinitesi-

mal few. He cannot see the charm of self-discipline in nerve-racking moments when the sudden pulling-himself-together for a cool and supreme action regulates a man's mental poise for perhaps a lifetime.

The sportsman would have many other things to say in his defense. He would adduce the beauty of the trophies, the delicacy of game food eaten in the woods, but very particularly the fact that he never kills an animal or a fish the body of which he cannot use legitimately, that he limits his bag strictly, and that he kills, in the great majority of cases, quickly and without pain.

And now, having enumerated a few of the advantages of these pastimes which make healthier bodies, purer hearts, and better citizens, the sportsman, if he is really frank, will confess that the one poisoned swamp in his paradise lies in the act of killing. But, while admitting that this is a sad and regrettable necessity, he sincerely and undoubtingly believes that it cannot for a moment outweigh the benefits and delights of legitimate hunting and fishing.

In regard to the question of "fair play," if that were strictly and logically admitted, what would become of the slavery of domestic animals? One must admit that man tyrannizes over them, and also that wild animals are no match for modern weapons. If, however, fair play means more than even chances for the game to escape, then indeed all hunting and fishing, when legitimately practiced, are fair, since the quarry actually does escape far more often than it is brought to bag. If this were not so, half the joy of the chase would vanish. *Res severa verum gaudium.*

Possibly the sportsman's justification may be found in the above, but will a people accustomed for ages to magnify the more (not to say sentimental) at the expense of the æsthetic be able to render it justice?

EDWARD BR...

Annapolis, Nova Scotia.

## "THOSE LOST GARMENTS"

It is evident that "Y." (see The Outlook for January 5) forgot that an artist paints Art's sake only, not for History's, that an artist might possibly consider baby curves of the nude, or partly figure of the infant Jesus more beautiful than the little rigid form incased in swaddling-clothes.

85, NO. 7

287 Fourth Avenue, New York City
1436 Marquette Building, Chicago

PRICE TEN CENT

# The
# Outlook

*Saturday, February 16, 1907*

❦

**The Government and Niagara Falls**

In an editorial paragraph in The Outlook of two weeks ago an injustice was done to the Niagara Falls Power Company. As Mr. Francis Lynde Stetson, the counsel who appeared before Secretary Taft on behalf of that company, states in a letter on another page, the disgraceful conditions which Secretary Taft seeks to remove are not in any degree chargeable to the Niagara Falls Power Company. The Niagara Falls Hydraulic Power and Manufacturing Company, an entirely distinct concern, is solely responsible for the defacement of the beauty of the gorge at the point in question. The Niagara Falls Power Company has made commendable and successful efforts to erect its buildings and maintain its grounds in a form attractive to the eye and appropriate to their situation. It is fair that this effort of the Niagara Falls Power Company to preserve as far as possible the æsthetic beauty of Niagara should be recognized. It must also be admitted that there are those, like Mr. H. G. Wells, the English Socialist, who believe that Niagara Falls harnessed to the industrial service of all the people is a nobler spectacle than the splendid untouched waterfall of the days of the French explorers. It is also true, as Mr. Stetson intimates, that æsthetic, moral, or social reformers ought scrupulously to refrain from employing subterfuges or evasion. But there is left the main issue, as The Outlook sees it, of the Niagara contest, an issue which is much broader and more fundamental than the question of the industrial development of Niagara Falls. Are the statutory rights in private property superior to the right of the people through the State to regulate the uses of that private property so that it shall not infringe upon the public welfare? If Niagara Falls is to become primarily a source of industrial power, the public has a right, both moral and legal, to regulate that development in the interest of the whole people. When public rights and private rights come into collision, the inevitable limitations of the latter cannot be called spoliations.

❦

**America and the Sixth Commandment**

Is life reasonably safe in the United States? In an address at Nashville, Tennessee, last week Judge Thomas, of Alabama, gave many figures which are far from reassuring. He compared the homicides in this country with the homicides in other civilized lands in proportion to population. Taking the figures for 1905, in Australia there were 20 homicides per million inhabitants; in England and Wales, 8.4 per million; in Japan, 14 per million; in the Dominion of Canada, our neighbor, 12.4 per million. In Germany, in 1899, the number was 4.6. It is shameful to discover, in the light of these figures, that in the United States the number of homicides per million inhabitants was, in 1905, 115, and in 1906, 118. Only Italy among European nations has a worse record, and we have to go back several years to find it. Moreover, while in Italy the proportion of homicides has been decreasing, in the United States it has been increasing, until it now surpasses that of Italy. The United States seems to be approaching the standard of Mexico, where people kill one another at the rate of 142.1 per million. Even there vast improvement has been made. The United States seems to be the only civilized country (with the exception of the Dominion of Canada) where homicides are actually increasing, as it is the country with the worst record in homicides among the nations of first rank. What is the cause? Judge Thomas convincingly eliminates climate, national traits, racial characteristics, forms of government, illiteracy, density of population. Two obvious explanations rise to almost every American's mind. One is the vast number of foreign-born people in this land. It is easy to lay homicides to the door of the immigrant. Judge Thomas presents figures which seem to acquit the alien element. Some of the facts bearing on this point are stated by Judge Thomas as follows:

The South is not affected by it. In New England, Vermont and New Hampshire, with the lowest rate of homicides, have most immigrant and emigrant classes; Connecticut, with twice the rate of homicide as Massachusetts, has about the same rate of mixed population; and Rhode Island, with about three times the rate of homicide of Connecticut, does not exceed it by ten per cent. of immigrant and emigrant people, and has less of this element than Vermont and New Hampshire, yet has eleven times their rate of homicides. Nevada with the highest and Vermont the lowest rate of homicide have emigrant and immigrant populations within ten per cent. of each other. In the Pacific States the proportion of homicides and immigrant and emigrant people seem to have little relation. Nevada, with four times the rate of homicides of Wyoming, has the same rate of mixed population. Colorado, with more than twice as many homicides as Washington, has the same rate of mixed people.

The other obvious retort is that the negro is responsible. It is true that the negro population is more guilty than the white; but Judge Thomas makes this rejoinder:

If one should charge to the negro five-sixths and to the whites one-sixth of the homicides committed, as stated by Lombroso, there would be 1,976 homicides annually that he admits were committed by the whites; and if then we deduct the negro population from the total population, it would still give the whites a rate per million of more than Austria or Belgium, five times as much as Germany, three times that of England, and twice that of France or Japan. However, the fact is that there were 4,425 white homicidal prisoners, at the time given above, to a white population of 66,990,000, or sixty-six white homicidal prisoners per million white population, which is three times (or more) as bad as that of most European countries except Italy and Spain, and exceeds that of Spain by thirty-two per cent.

Judge Thomas thus refutes the arguments of those who ascribe the preva-

lence of homicide in the United States to the immigrant and the negro.

@

*The Reasons for America's Bad Record*　In a single phrase may be stated the real cause, as Judge Thomas finds it, for the unenviable eminence of the United States in homicides. It is "excessive individualism." Where the people are sensitive to their duties to society, homicides are few; where the people are unrestrained by what may be called social conscience, and are swayed by personal considerations, homicides are numerous. This excessive individualism is exhibited in many forms. It shows itself in those courts that emphasize technicalities for the defense of accused individuals at a great cost to society; it shows itself in those juries that are swayed by sentimentality in seeing, for instance, the grief or suffering of a guilty prisoner's wife and are heedless of the danger to society involved in the freeing of the prisoner; it shows itself in the "pistol habit" of the West and the South, and of communities in other sections; it shows itself in the pardons granted by Governors in response to pathetic appeals or as a result of fear that the convict's guilt may not have been mathematically demonstrated. Judge Thomas recalls the escape of criminals on such grounds as these: because of "an old soldier father;" because the prisoner's mother had become insane; because the prisoner's little son had pleaded for him; because the prisoner was a woman. Have not low standards of honor and duty toward society, Judge Thomas inquires, "taken shape in organic and statute law, now directing, now restraining, the enforcement?" Judge Thomas looks over the "bird's-eye view of American life as given by the Chicago Daily Tribune," and notes the vast increase in manufactures, in trade, and in products of the soil, the concomitant "large increase in robberies, larcenies, and embezzlements, homicides and suicides of alarming number," and "no proportionate general increase in the last twenty-six years in the number of legal hangings;" and he comments: "We can but be impressed that when the individual is pursuing self-ish ends he has been very active, and where doing for the general good or supposed general good he has been pas-sive." No more serious criticism of the American people has ever been delivered than this. Unhappily, it seems to be only too easily corroborated. The easy good nature of Americans with regard to all public matters is daily demon-strated. It has encouraged the political boss, it has permitted the growth of cor-rupting corporations, it has allowed the vile tenements to exist, it has compla-cently watched the despoiling of forests, it has ignored menaces to life on our railways, and, as Judge Thomas convinc-ingly shows, this deadly good nature, this soft-hearted, soft-headed willingness to let public matters wait on private pref-erences, is more than anything else re-sponsible for crimes of violence. The sermon that Judge Thomas preaches is not of the sort that smug congrega-tions call "enjoyable." We wish that many might hear it, and of those who hear that many might heed.

❦

*The Chicago Epidemic* The most serious epidemic of disease that has af-flicted Chicago and its suburbs within the last fifteen years seems now to be subsiding after a con-tinuance of three weeks. Scarlet fever has been most prevalent, the number of cases of that ailment approximating six thousand in the city, according to phy-sicians' reports to the Department of Health. Of diphtheria cases the num-ber has been somewhat less than twenty-five hundred in the same three weeks. In a minor degree, measles has been epidemic. One bright spot in the record for a city that has boasted for years of its freedom from contagion and prevent-able disease is the fact that the type of disease has been "light." Since the first of January to the middle of last week the total number of deaths from scarlet fever has been 149; from diph-theria, 98. Health officials point to the fact, by way of contrast, that during the first month of the year 592 persons died of pneumonia and 326 of consump-tion. More, they say, died of cancer

than of diphtheria. Nevertheless the alarm has been a real one. Many families have taken their children out of town; thousands have kept their children out of schools; a few church services have been stopped; many social gatherings have been abandoned; and in some of the parks even skating has been discour-aged because the congregating of the young was deemed unadvisable. The seriousness of the epidemic was no sooner realized by the people than there fell upon the Chicago Health Commis-sioner and his staff an avalanche of crit-icism and complaint. It fell to the lot of the health authorities of two suburbs—Evanston and Oak Park—to grasp the situation before Chicago officials awoke to it. In Evanston it was found that nearly all of one hundred and forty cases of scarlet fever were in a restricted area, in houses supplied with milk by one large concern from one receiving station. The Evanston officers quickly cut off the milk supply, while the Chicago and State health authorities were con-tending that there was no danger of con-tagion from this source. Subsequently both of the latter sent inspectors to the dairy under suspicion, and stopped the shipping of milk from that point.

❦

*Causes and Lessons* But it has not been dem-onstrated that milk was the ruling cause of the epidemic generally; physicians say it is but one of many avenues of infection. In the suburbs all of the schools and churches were closed for a time, but it was thought unwise to take this step in the city. The authorities considered that the children were under better public health control while in school. And just here is one of the chief points of criticism as to Chicago's health methods. Since the schools opened in September there had been but fourteen health inspectors at work guarding more than three hundred and fifty public school buildings! Once the gravity of the situation was partly comprehended, the Health Commissioner called on the Council Finance Com-mittee for authority to hire one hun-dred inspectors temporarily. Under the stress of popular clamor this appeal was instantly granted. A few days later the Commissioner asked for two hundred and fifty more emergency doctors, and the authority this time was speedily given. Had one hundred inspectors been working in the schools since autumn, it is believed that the epidemic would have been averted. In the height of the panic it was found that the afflicted houses were not all placarded, the Health Commissioner having concluded that this ordinance was unwise, inasmuch as it led some doctors to hide their cases. The City Council then peremptorily ordered that every house be placarded. Then, when the health officials had been urged into that activity which people thought commensurate with the needs of the hour, they were able to throw a large share of the blame on the Council Health Committee—which is made up of the less efficient Aldermen—by quoting the health bulletins issued in October and again in December. These bulletins appealed for more school inspectors and warned directly against threatened scarlet fever epidemic, but the Aldermen paid no heed and so matters drifted on until the crisis. Then came abundant, if late, activity. It is believed that the best guard against a recurrence of the trouble is efficient school inspection, and this is Chicago's first lesson out of the passing situation. The second lesson, which will be learned unless the scare abates too rapidly, is the need of an adequate hospital for contagious diseases. This might have been Chicago's for the asking for the last four or five years, but the Aldermen, under pressure from citizens, have practically barred such an institution out of the city by setting up impossible conditions in the way of frontage consents. Mr. and Mrs. Harold McCormick have been ready to expend practically a million dollars on building and endowment whenever they should be allowed to purchase a site where a license might be secured; but the Council—and the citizens—have stood in the way. Had such a hospital existed in Chicago this winter, much suffering and hardship, spread of disease, and probably many deaths would have been averted. The Council just now is in the temper to modify its hospital ordi-nance. Will it do so before the impulse is gone? Physicians like Dr. Frank Billings, President of the State Board of Charities, pointing out that the cause of scarlet fever is unknown, say that one great hope in such a hospital is that its laboratory advantages may lead to the discovery of the germ—if it is a germ—and thence to a serum.

❦

*A King's Ransom for American Education*

"The largest sum ever given by a man in the history of the race for any social or philanthropic purpose." Thus the General Education Board characterizes the latest benefaction of John D. Rockefeller. Thirty-two million dollars will be placed by him before April 1 in the care of the General Education Board. The size of the gift is, however, but incidental to its real importance. If it were not so large, it would be, of course, less effectual; but its real greatness lies in the object to which it is devoted and the means selected for the accomplishment of its purpose. The object is really the directing of educational development in the United States; the means is an independent board of men who have long had this object in view as an ideal. The General Education Board holds its corporate rights by virtue of the Federal Congress. It is permitted by its charter to do "any valuable educational work" within this country. The Board is self-perpetuating. It is made up of men who have for years been studying the conditions of education in the United States. Its Chairman, Mr. Frederick T. Gates, has had the imagination and executive ability to work for the formulation of an educational policy that would include not one institution or one State, but the whole Nation. Dr. Wallace Buttrick, the Secretary of the Board, by traveling and observation has become an expert on the condition of American educational institutions; and his imaginative foresight enables him to use his knowledge in directing a large policy. All the members of the Board, every one of them well known as a leader either in business or in education, have regarded the problem before them as one calling for educational statesmanship. In 1902 Mr. Rockefeller intrusted to the Board one million dollars for the promotion of education in the South ; later he gave into the keeping of the Board ten million dollars for the promotion of collegiate (as distinct from academic) education throughout the United States. With these funds, and others that have been intrusted to it, the Board has been able to act as a gardener, pruning here, fertilizing there ; planting in barren places, and, if not actually destroying, yet at least neglecting, growths that were unhealthy or unneeded. Its power, however, has heretofore been limited because the money at its disposal has been designated for special ends. In this latest gift Mr. Rockefeller practically says that he trusts the Board's wisdom and the wisdom of future generations more confidently than his own. One-third of the new gift he gives unconditionally to the general endowment fund of the Board. The income from that may be used as the Board directs. As to the rest, he reserves to himself and his son the right to decide later if it is to be devoted to special objects. With this financial power in its control, the General Education Board is in position to do what no other body in this country can, at present, even attempt. It can determine largely what institutions shall grow, and, in some measure, what shall stand still or decay. It can look over the territory of the Nation, note the places where there is a famine of learning, and start new educational plants of any species it chooses, or revive old ones. It can do in many ways what the Government does for education in France or Germany. Its power will be enormous ; it seems as if it might be able really to determine the character of American education. The funds it holds represent only a fraction of the amounts which it will really control ; by giving a sum to an institution on condition that the institution raise an equal or a greater amount, it will be able to direct much larger amounts than it possesses. More than that, it will become increasingly an adviser of philanthropists. Even now its counsel is sought and its judgment determines the course of philanthropists

who, without expert knowledge, desire to aid education. Moreover, it can administer any gift intrusted to it without cost, as its administrative expenses are already provided for ; so that the person who wishes to give a hundred dollars for education may put that sum into its hands with the knowledge that the money will be used exclusively for an educational purpose. In these ways it is estimated that the Board will be the means, within the next decade, of controlling from one to two hundred millions of dollars.

❦

*The New Jersey Senatorship* The withdrawal of Senator John F. Dryden, of New Jersey, from the contest for the Republican nomination for the United States Senate, and the election of Mr. Frank O. Briggs, the present Treasurer of the State of New Jersey, ended a contest in which the whole country was interested. The defeat of Senator Dryden in the campaign for re-election was a decided though not a decisive and final victory for the reform element among the Republicans of the State. The agitation against Senator Dryden's re-election was directed, not at his personal character, but at his affiliations ; he is a type of public man against whose appearance in political life in this country there is a growing antagonism, deep-seated and far-reaching, which aims at the entire separation of money-making from politics and politics from money-making. New Jersey has still much to do in the way of dealing with public affairs in a rational way. This fact was shown, first, by what appears to have been the dominant feeling that the nomination must go, not to the best man in the State, but to some one from the southern section. It went, therefore, to Mr. Frank O. Briggs, who now holds the position of Treasurer of the State and Chairman of the Republican State Committee, and who was Mr. Dryden's legatee. He is in the prime of life ; was born in New Hampshire ; graduated from the Phillips Exeter Academy ; entered West Point, from which he was graduated in 1872 ; served five years in the United States Infantry ; went to Trenton and became associated with the Roebling Company, of which he is now the assistant treasurer; he was Mayor of Trenton from 1899 to 1902, and was appointed State Treasurer in the latter year; he has been twice sent to the Legislature, and three years ago he was put at the head of the Republican State Committee, conducting the campaign which resulted in the election of Governor Stokes; he has also been for a number of years a member of the State Board of Education. There is nothing against the new Senator except the fact that he is regarded as a machine man, and that he was the choice of Senator Dryden as his successor. The fact that he has been connected with large corporations does not disqualify him from dealing with public affairs from the standpoint of public interest. Indeed, his attitude on the taxation of corporations justifies the hope that he may treat public questions as a statesman and not as a representative of special interests or political factions. Senator Knox, of Pennsylvania, is a conspicuous example of the ability of a man who has served great corporations and who is equally capable of serving great public interests. The doubt in the case of Senator-elect Briggs concerns his conception of politics. If he belongs to the old order of politicians who represent business rather than public interests, the people of the State will have to face the fact that they must remain practically unrepresented in the United States Senate until a new election takes place. Mr. Kean, the other Senator, is, unfortunately, a negligible quantity. The people under the leadership of Mr. Colby have scored a victory, but they are only at the beginning of the campaign for the redemption of the State from machine control.

❦

*Labor Successes in the New Parliament* The fifty-three Labor members who are now in the House of Commons have influenced in a remarkable degree both the legislative and the administrative policy of the Campbell-Bannerman Government. Their most striking legislative success is the Trades Disputes Act, which protects trade union funds from judgments in the law courts like that in the memorable Taff Vale case, and makes a more satisfactory settlement from the trade union point of view of the law as to picketing at strikes. Prior to the Taff Vale decision, which was a disastrous one for the Amalgamated Society of Railway Servants, it had never been supposed that trade union funds could be assailed. This act relieves trades unions from financial responsibility for acts for which other organizations are liable, and is a piece of special legislation of a kind that labor organizations, if they were far-sighted, would fight. It is said in defense of this rank class legislation that the older English trade unions accumulate funds for benevolent purposes as well as for defense or aggression; that they pay their members out-of-work, sick, and superannuation allowances, and make grants for funerals; that it would have needed a complete reorganization of the financial arrangements of the unions to have put these benevolent funds beyond the reach of the sheriff's officer. They have always constituted much of the cohesive strength of the unions. Nevertheless, in claiming for themselves an exemption denied by law to other organizations, the trades unions have, in the judgment of The Outlook, violated a principle which they ought to uphold, and made a serious blunder in tactics which may bring confusion to them in the future. Next in importance to the Trades Disputes Act is the amendment and extension of the employers' liability code—an extension which brings seamen and domestic servants within the provisions of the Workmen's Compensation Act, and which is designed to reduce the occasions for lawsuits in the administration of the act. The permissive act under which local school authorities can provide meals for needy children is a Socialistic rather than a Labor measure. But the Labor men were responsible for its introduction. They all supported it; and the Labor and Radical members from Scotland were especially affronted when, chiefly at the instigation of Sir Henry Craik, who represents the Scotch universities in the House of Commons, the House of Lords carried the amendment by Lord Balfour of Burleigh excluding

Scotland from the scope of the act. Sir Henry Craik was the only Scotch member in the Commons who opposed the bill. His opposition there was quite futile; but his attitude on the measure has added strength to the growing movement for ending university representation—English or Scotch—in the House of Commons.

❖

*Administrative Concessions to Labor*

The question of a compulsory eight-hour day for miners again came before the House of Commons in the unusually prolonged session of 1906. There is some lack of agreement on this question. The miners of Lancashire and Yorkshire, of the Midlands and South Wales, as well as the miners of Scotland, are in favor of legislation. The miners of Durham and Northumberland, led by veteran members of the House of Commons of such high standing as the Rt. Hon. Thomas Burt and Mr. Charles Fenwick, Deputy Chairman of Committees (both miners by trade and both miners' trade union officials) oppose the Eight Hours Day Bill; and as a result of this division of opirion among the men most concerned, the Government has referred the question to a Royal Commission. Many administrative changes in favor of labor were announced during the session. Recognition was given by Mr. Sydney Buxton, Postmaster-General, to the paid officials of the postal and telegraph clerks' associations, a recognition persistently refused to trade-unionism in the Post-Office during the Tory régime; and by a departmental order issued at the instance of Mr. Lloyd George, President of the Board of Trade, seamen's union secretaries or other trade union officials may now appear on behalf of seamen in disputes as to wages or conditions of service between seamen and ship captains which come before the local marine boards at the ports. During the session Mr. Henry Broadhurst retired from the representation of Leicester; and to the seat he had occupied Mr. Franklin Thomasson, the proprietor of the Tribune, the new London Liberal morning newspaper, was elected. Mr. Broadhurst

was the third trade union representative in the House of Commons, having been elected for Stoke as far back as 1880. The trade-unionists who preceded him were the late Mr. Alexander Macdonald (1874–1881) and Mr. Burt, who was elected in the same year as Mr. Macdonald, and who has ever since represented Morpeth. Mr. Broadhurst, when he retired, was grouped neither with the trade union members nor the Independent Labor party. He was of the third group—the Labor-Liberals. Of the Labor men who came prominently to the front in the new Parliament—besides Mr. Burns, who is now of Cabinet rank, and by his work on the Local Government Board has amply justified his inclusion in the Campbell-Bannerman Administration—Mr. David Shackleton, secretary of a Lancashire textile union, and of the Independent Labor group, achieved most distinction by his work in committee on the Trades Disputes Bill and on the bill extending the Workmen's Compensation Act of 1897. The Independent Labor group, with Mr. Keir Hardie as leader, still sit on the Opposition side of the House, with the Irish Nationalists as neighbors; and, like the Nationalists, they hold the Government at arm's length. They nominated two candidates against Liberals at by-elections—at Workington and at Leeds. They did not capture either seat; but at Workington their persistence lost the seat to the Tories. For a vacancy in Derbyshire, which now exists, the Liberal whips have adopted a miners' trade union official. The seat is safely Liberal; so that in the session of 1907 the number of Labor men will be the same as it was in the session of 1906, before the retirement of Mr. Broadhurst.

❖

*The Mexican Railway Merger*

The entrance of the Mexican Government into the railway business is a significant event in the world of transportation. On the discovery of oil-fields in Mexico several years ago, parties identified with the interests of the Standard Oil Company secured control of the Mexican Central Railway, and there seemed reason to believe that they were also aiming to acquire the Mexican National Railway. Fearing that the country's entire transportation service might ultimately fall under the oil monopoly's domination, the Mexican Government secured control not only of the National but also of the International and the Interoceanic Railways. These have since been operated under one management as "The National Lines of Mexico." The merger just completed adds to these lines the Mexican Central and the Hidalgo and Northeastern. While the Government also controls the Vera Cruz and Pacific and the Tehuantepec Railways, these will for the present be operated independently. The Tehuantepec Railway was the other day opened to the public by President Diaz. The only lines of much size left in private control are the Mexican Railway, between the capital and Vera Cruz ; the Pan-American, reaching to the Guatemalan frontier ; the Sonora extension of the Southern Pacific, and that portion of the Kansas City, Mexico, and Orient Railway which is under construction across northern Mexico. The most notable feature of the Government's action seems to us hardly so much its magnitude as its negotiation without any cash outlay—the Government simply lending its credit to guarantee the interest and principal of the second mortgage bonds, these being preceded by an issue of prior lien bonds and by three classes of stock. Since the present earnings of the property seem sufficient to meet all charges, the Government deems the risk of burdening its treasury worth taking. On the other hand, Government indorsement is a sufficiently valuable consideration to make it worth while. for those recently in control to transfer their control to the nation. All of the concessions stipulate that at the end of ninety-nine years the property shall revert to the Government. The corporation to be organized to take over the merged companies will have a capitalization exceeding a hundred million dollars in our money. Of a board of twenty-one directors, with headquarters in Mexico, twelve members will reside in the capital of that country and nine in this country. The accomplishment of Government control is due chiefly to the efforts of Señor Limantour, Mexico's Minister of Finance, to whose ability the increasingly gratifying monetary position of his country is also due. If one of Señor Limantour's motives has been to prevent the great trusts from getting a foothold in Mexico, others have been to eliminate unnecessary competition, to improve operation, and to bring harmony by means of combination. In his success we see a reconciliation of the principles of government ownership and those of private corporations, a union of the management by the government in the interests of the public with the flexibility of private operation. We shall follow the development of the Mexican plan with interest.

❀

**Dry Farming**    An unusual convention in which representatives of sixteen States took part lately adjourned at Denver—the Dry Farming Congress. Its object was to encourage settlement on the high plains, the "semi-arid" section of the West, by spreading the teachings of the newest theory in agriculture. This theory is that, by proper tillage and scientific methods of conserving the moisture, profitable crops can be raised where the rainfall is less than twenty inches annually, in a territory heretofore looked upon as fitted only for pasture and such crop-raising as could be accomplished by irrigation. The enthusiasts of the new idea declare that farming can be carried on to the very foothills of the Rockies, thus bringing into the productive area of the West a territory four hundred miles north and south, and over a hundred miles wide, not to mention other portions of the interior where rainfall is below the usual requirements for successful agriculture. No particular secrecy attends the plans. First place seems to be given to a thorough pulverizing of the surface by frequent cultivation, securing thereby a "dust blanket" whose function is to absorb all the moisture that falls, and to retain it after it has fallen. If all the rainfall can be kept on the land, instead of allowing it to rush to the streams, and so seaward, and if evaporation can be arrested, these scientific farmers claim, one full crop can be raised every two years at least—in years of generous rainfall every year. They point to successful experiment farms as proof of their accomplishments. We may make discount on the more buoyant statements. It is somewhat suspicious that the most enthusiastic advocates are connected with real estate companies and are seeking buyers for land; it should be remembered, also, that the past three years, during which the new agricultural cult has risen, have been seasons of excessive rainfall for the high plains country. But even with these allowances the dry farming idea has much merit. It is based on better methods of tillage and the adaptation of means to conditions in a businesslike and intelligent manner. The Government is about to establish experiment stations in the semi-arid belt to determine what crops and what tillage are best—a distinct concession to the dry farming theory, for a few years ago such an undertaking would have been ridiculed as a waste of effort. Much has been done for irrigation and the territory that can be reached by ditches and laterals. If now the upland plains beyond the reach of running streams can be brought to reasonably profitable cultivation, this country will be utilizing its soil to the utmost. Dry farming may not accomplish all claimed for it, especially when drought comes—and the Government weather service declares that the climate of the high plains is not permanently changed—but it is encouraging intelligent agriculture. If settlers and investors will consider it as a promising experiment rather than as an accomplished fact, when applied to the territory of least rainfall east of the Rockies, it will do the West much good.

❦

*National Union of Farmers* An organization with seven hundred thousand farmers as members, designed to control the marketing of grain, has, it is stated, established in Chicago headquarters from which it will direct the producers of the Middle West. It aims not alone at raising the price of wheat and cotton, but aims to eliminate the middleman's profit in selling the output of Western farms and ranches. Many attempts at accomplishing this, ranging from the social Grange to the political Farmers' Alliance, have been made, and all have failed. A looseness of organization when dealing with farmers widely separated and unwilling to undertake co-operative effort on a large scale has been the inevitable result of these unions. This modern undertaking evidently is not free from such dangers, for it is reported that the cotton-raisers of western Texas, to the number of one hundred thousand or more, have seceded from the central organization and will manage their own affairs. Lectures by itinerant organizers and conventions for the display of oratory will not hold a nation-wide organization together, much less one composed of farmers, and this new union must have behind it a direct, simple plan for betterment of the agricultural communities if it is to win permanently. The farmer almost alone of the toilers of the world has kept his independent way; he has no walking delegate, no union scale, no system of licensed apprenticeship. Neither has he indulged in high finance nor in the formation of powerful trusts. Yet upon his labors is based much of the prosperity that makes possible the trust magnate's development. It is possible that the new union has seven hundred thousand members, but unless they are held with unyielding force and obey the directorate as one man. it will have little effect in realizing the dream of "dollar wheat," which seems to be the Western farmer's ideal of material bliss. If the farmers of the Nation succeed in raising materially the price of their crops at initial points, the consumer must prepare to pay more for the finished product when delivered at his door—unless the rise to the farmer shall come, not from the consumer, but in lessened expense of getting the product to market. Some day this may be accomplished, but reports concerning the present undertaking do not indicate that it is to succeed permanently in changing the American farmer's condition—which, by the way, is not one of great suffering. It may, however, prove helpful in showing the advantage of co-operation, and some localities may derive benefit. It will be interesting to see if there are secured the benefits to which a membership as large as that claimed should entitle the new union.

❋

**A New York Problem**  It is very easy to point out the overcrowding of all means of conveyance in the city of New York, but it is not so easy to indicate the ways in which this overcrowding may be obviated or lessened. The editorial on "The Discomforts of New York" which appeared in these columns a few weeks ago has prompted a correspondent to call attention to one very interesting element in the problem—the direct relation between the height of buildings and the congestion of the means of travel to and from the localities in which these great buildings are erected. The population of a large office building during business hours is equal to that which fills a theater or a church covering the same area of ground-space. It would be easy to imagine the condition of half a mile of highway if it were lined with buildings of this capacity. The Outlook's correspondent is over-moderate in his statement. Some of the great buildings in the city contain as many persons as live in good-sized country or suburban towns. To transfer the population of a good-sized town or of a large theater and put it on a very small area of ground by means of a tall building, and then multiply these buildings within a small area, is to create the situation in which New York finds itself. The metropolis, as this correspondent points out, adds one or two stories to its height every year, and the condition produced may be brought before the mind by imagining one building of vast size on Manhattan Island with a limited number of exits in the form of ferries, railways, and bridges. This building contained enough people, years ago, to use every exit almost to its full capacity. It has gone on year by year adding to its height without adding proportionately to its number of exits, with the result that at certain hours in the morning and eve-ning these exits are crowded to the point of suffocation. In the meantime people are pouring into the city in great tides, not only for business but for pleasure purposes; and every new hotel, no matter what its capacity, is no sooner opened than it is filled. Unless the city is to be honeycombed by subterranean tunnels or penetrated by railways built on cause-ways, there seems to be no prospect of permanent relief until some form of aerial navigation is discovered.

❋

**A Safety Devices Exhibition**  The First International Exposition of Safety Devices and Industrial Hygiene has just been held in New York City, under the auspices of the American Institute of Social Service. Public attention was fittingly called to it on its opening by a dinner at which Governor Hughes made a significant address. "We shudder," said Mr. Hughes, "at the carnage of war, but we give little attention to the perils of our industrial army, and to the useless sacrifice of life and productive efficiency which is the result of preventable accidents in industry. . . . From the experience of other countries the conclusion is forced upon us that a very large proportion of the injuries which annually occur in this country are wholly unnecessary." It was the purpose of this exposition to demonstrate the improved methods which would prevent this annual sacrifice. Not only were there a large number of photographs showing these methods as adopted in foreign countries, but many of the safe-guarded machines themselves were shown in actual operation. Many foreign cities have permanent exhibitions of this kind, and they have proved of great public utility. America has up to this time been extremely negligent in the matter of accident prevention, and the Exposition of Safety Devices comes at an opportune moment. It is hoped that a permanent Museum of Safety Devices may be established as a result of the interest aroused. No more important agent for the promotion of social welfare than a bureau of accident prevention can be instituted in our great manufacturing centers. It is an encouraging sign of the times that Governor Hughes has given the movement his indorsement. Governors and legislators in other States would do well to follow his example. On another page the Spectator speaks more particularly of some phases of this highly important exhibition.

●

*Fluvial Eloquence*    Rivers have always appealed to the poetic nature of the sensitive. It may be that the motion of the water, by subtle suggestion, sets in operation the flow of language. A large collection of verse might be made dealing with the Oxus, the Indus, the Euphrates, the Nile, the Tiber, the Rhine, the Danube, the Loire, the Charles, the Hudson, the Mississippi; but the latest river to liberate the imagination and inflame the poetic sense is the long-neglected Tombigbee, a stream which has suffered somewhat by the unfortunate suggestiveness of its name. The House of Representatives, long the nursery, not to say the hotbed, of fervid and flamboyant eloquence, has produced another great orator in the person of one of the Representatives from Mississippi. Poetry flows, sometimes, on unexpected occasions and receives its initial impulse from very prosaic incidents; one would hardly have expected the debate on the River and Harbor Bill, long associated with plans of far-seeing lobbyists, to evoke a lyrical flow of speech only paralleled by a certain famous account of a ball at the palace in Athens, sent home by an American Minister who, after describing the great privilege of dancing the opening measure with the Queen, gave an account of his walk home through the silent streets once trodden by Sophocles and Demosthenes, and recalled the fact that the same moon shone on the American Minister that shone on Pericles. This time, however, it was not ancient Athens, nor any foreign river, but the domestic stream called the Tombigbee, the glories of which were recounted with a lavish tongue:

"I love the Mississippi," declared the orator, "oh, that beautiful name that we treasure, which we love, and to which we cling; little ones around the fireside at home are taught to sing its praises and to speak forth in reverence to its virtues. But the Missis-

sippi, my friends, sinks into insignificance in its grandeur and its beauty when it comes in comparison to the Tombigbee. . . . I am sure it is prompted by the interest in this great river about which I am talking, because we all know it appeals to the heart of every American citizen throughout this broad land, and the regret that they have to-day, and they have expressed that regret to me often, is that it has been so long neglected. I have heard its murmuring waves as they went singing their beautiful song toward the Gulf since early childhood, and they have continued to sing along the path of my life and have given me inspiration to love the beauties of nature and admire those grandeurs and those glories that come alone from the great creative hand of God above."

●

# The Longfellow Centennial

Of general interest in literature, in the sense in which interest in literature is felt in Italy, Germany, and France, there is as yet very little in this country. Of readers there is an army, of students of good writing there are more perhaps than in any other country; but of the degree and quality of interest which puts a new book on a level with a political issue in the talk of average men there is very little in America. One may pass many days on the piazza of a summer hotel among active and able men of affairs and never hear the title of a book on the stream of talk. In Italy, France, and Germany, on the other hand, the appearance of certain books is a public event, an incident in the national life that divides interest with the policies of the government and the state of trade. Literature has not yet, in this sense, become a National institution among Americans. They have great respect for it as a resource, a charming diversion, an evidence of culture; they do not feel its necessity or recognize it as an integral part of the life of the Nation, as significant as the question of the limitation of governmental authority or the regulation of the railways.

Longfellow, as nearly as any other American writer, has won recognition as a figure of National significance and relations. Lacking the grasp and insight, the genuinely representative quality, of

Emerson; the penetration, the rich and dusky imagination of Hawthorne, the individuality of invention and art of Poe, the humor and opulence of thought of Lowell, the deep and full movement of imagination of Whitman, he is, nevertheless, the best known of them all. It is not too much to say that he is nearer the heart of his country than any other of its poets; that his verse is more a matter of popular knowledge; that the celebration of the one hundredth anniversary of the day of his birth on the 27th day of this month will assume the proportions of a National event, while at the same time it will be marked by many private commemorations.

The reasons for this popular regard are not far to seek; and the fact that they lie on the surface is itself an explanation. Longfellow walked on the highway and kept company with his fellows in the manifold experiences of life. There was nothing occult or esoteric about his thought or his art; he always lived in the open. One of the most cultivated men of his time, and a pioneer of the riper and richer knowledge of the languages and literature which he did much to commend by his own charm, his work in prose and verse was singularly free from purely literary associations, from the tone and temper of the professional man of letters. He never went into out-of-the-way places for unusual emotions or courted strange experiences along the byways of experience; he kept to the main road, with an instinctive sense of finding what he wanted there, and a conviction that he belonged there.

He walked with men with no sense of lowering the aims of his life or the standards of his art. In his quiet way he had the courage and clear judgment of a born poet, who believes that the impulsion of native gift or of vital interest is a better guide than professional maxims or the conventional attitude of the expert and schoolman. He was a scholar in a real if not in the highest sense, but he was refreshingly free from the pose of scholarship and the limitations of its purely professional point of view. Where his poetry is thin, as it sometimes is, the lack of rootage is due

not to his themes or his sympathies, but to the limitations of his nature.

He had also, as part of his capital as a poet of National significance, great simplicity of manner. He rarely used the literary dialect; he used habitually the universal language. It has been his happy fortune, in consequence, to be the companion of children in every generation since he began to write; and one of the most significant features of the commemoration of his birth will be the remembrance of the poet in schools from the Atlantic to the Pacific. The new writer of the serious temper, who approaches life by a private road and speaks with the authority of individual impression and experience, almost invariably finds his audience among enthusiastic young men and women, and his fame grows as they carry his work to the front. A generation or two ago the books of Emerson and Carlyle were found in the room of every aspiring and open-minded student, and it was in the colleges that the writers of "Nature" and of "Sartor Resartus" secured their most ardent advocates. Longfellow made his appeal still earlier in time, as Sir Mortimer Durand has pointed out on another page, and touched the heart of childhood with the divination of simplicity, purity, tender human affection, and the happy phrase of those who practice the art of being young until they become masters of its secrets.

Domestic and local, in the sense of finding their interest in near and familiar things, as Longfellow's poems often are, it is significant that they touch those simple and beautiful things that belong everywhere to the happy years when the home is the world and the locality the universe. No American poet has been so widely translated, none has been domesticated in so many foreign countries. There is a peculiar fitness in the adoption of this Laureate of childhood, home, and love by so many alien peoples, for he was one of the first to knit again the ties that had been severed by the separation of the New from the Old World. During the seventeenth and eighteenth centuries New England was an isolated community, developing by force of its own inward impulse rather than by contact with the ideas of the world at large. With the advent of the nineteenth century there came a change that affected the whole country, but that was most radical and far-reaching in New England. The Middle States and Virginia and the Old South were absorbed in other interests; the New England mind was eagerly searching for material with which to satisfy its craving for a larger experience of life, a deeper and richer culture. There were evidences of reaction against the rigid repression, the sharp limitations of thought, the somber surroundings, of the old order of life. The New England mind—eager, restless, and serious—demanded the range of the whole field of knowledge, and its imagination craved color, warmth, sentiment, and beauty. There was a vast disparity between the culture of the Old World and that of the New; the New World was unconsciously craving the richer life of the older races. Work enough had been done on the new continent to make men aware that some things were not to be gotten out of the soil. There was a growing sense of isolation and detachment, a deepening consciousness of separation from the organic life of the race. In a word, the time was ripe for rapid assimilation of the culture of the older races by the new people, which had, so far as thought, scholarship, and taste were concerned, suffered an arrest of development and fallen behind Europe in the evolution of the higher civilization.

At this opportune hour New England found access to the modern languages, to modern literature, and to the study of other religions. Men like Everett and Ticknor became the forerunners of the long line of American students who have drunk deep at the fountains of knowledge in Germany. The inexperienced mind of the young race flung itself with ardor on the rich art of the older races. The names. of Dante, Montaigne, Goethe, Molière, Cervantes, became familiar to American students, and the cultural power of the great poets was eagerly appropriated.

Among the men to whom this fresh contact with the ripe resources of an old civilization came with something like inspirational effect was Longfellow. Like all his contemporaries in the field of poetry save Whittier and Whitman, he shared the best traditions of New England training; he was the son of a professional man; he was college-bred; he had three years of foreign residence, filled not only with ardent study of French, German, Spanish, and Italian, but with a wealth of impressions from that rich Old World which, to the sensitive imagination of a young American from a world too new to have history, associations, art, beauty, or atmosphere, must have been a true wonderland of romance and achievement; he held professorships first at Bowdoin and later at Harvard. These facts are significant alike of Longfellow's unusual opportunities and of his good fortune.

He was not a man of original poetic force; his imagination was sensitive rather than creative, his poetic gift graceful and tender rather than virile and self-directed. He was largely dependent on the suggestions of legendary or historical associations; his imagination was responsive rather than originative. He was a translator, not only in the specific but in the more inclusive sense of the word. He was sensitive to beautiful, romantic, significant incidents, events, associations, and his musical faculty made his hand as responsive as his imagination. His work includes many renderings of beautiful thoughts from the poets of other races, domestic legends, stories drawn from many sources. In all this he was not a borrower, as Poe unjustly and ignorantly charged, but a translator. He interpreted the Old World to the New, as did Irving; he helped to equalize intellectual conditions; he brought into our literature a gentleness of sentiment, a simple but genuine beauty, a grace of feeling, and a joy in history and art that have enriched it for all time. A scholar by instinct, training, and profession, he kept a heart so tender and a nature so unaffected and simple that children understand him and love him as they understand and love no other American poet. He had none of the Puritan intensity of conscience, but all the Puritan purity of heart, and this has made him pre-eminently the poet of the domestic affections. The notes of great poetry are rarely heard in Longfellow's verse, but his charming faculty of transcription has given us the idyllic music of " Evangeline," which, with " Hiawatha," is to be counted among the few American legends.

After his death Longfellow paid the penalty of great contemporaneous popularity ; a shadow passed over his reputation, and it became the fashion to speak of his work as of slight importance. Depreciation of the author of " Evangeline " was, for some people, a sign of the higher culture. Of late years a sounder critical judgment has gained ground, and to-day the freshness of feeling, vigor of imagination, quiet energy, which characterize some of the poet's mature work, find adequate recognition. This is not the occasion for a critical estimate ; it is the moment for generous recognition of Longfellow's service to American literature in its initial stage, of the soundness of his methods, the elevation and dignity that he gave to the profession of letters, the impulse that he imparted to generous minds eager for a larger share of the common fund of knowledge, beauty, and greatness of achievement stored up in the vast treasury of the past. More convincing than any comment on the true poetic quality of his verse at its best is the evidence of such examples as the sonnets that precede the translation of Dante's "Inferno:"

" Oft have I seen, at some cathedral door,
A laborer, pausing in the dust and heat,
Lay down his burden, and with reverent feet
Enter, and cross himself, and on the floor
Kneel to repeat his paternoster o'er ;
Far off the noises of the world retreat ;
The loud vociferations of the street
Become an undistinguishable roar.
So, as I enter here from day to day,
And leave my burden at this minster gate,
Kneeling in prayer, and not ashamed to pray,
The tumult of the time disconsolate
To inarticulate murmurs dies away,
While the eternal ages watch and wait.

How strange the sculptures that adorn these towers !
This crowd of statues, in whose folded sleeves
Birds build their nests ; while canopied with leaves
Parvis and portal bloom like trellised bowers,

And the vast minster seems a cross of flowers !
But fiends and dragons on the gargoyled eaves
Watch the dead Christ between the living thieves,
And, underneath, the traitor Judas lowers !
Ah ! from what agonies of heart and brain,
What exultations trampling on despair,
What tenderness, what tears, what hate of wrong,
What passionate outcry of a soul in pain,
Uprose this poem of the earth and air,
This mediæval miracle of song !"

●

# A Theological Battle

It is difficult for an American to understand how a single English preacher should cause such a ferment as has been caused in England by the recent utterances of the Rev. R. J. Campbell, of the City Temple. England is a small country, and London is its center. If an earthquake visited London, all England would be shaken by it ; but an earthquake destroyed San Francisco, and Chicago, New Orleans, and New York went on their way undisturbed. A not very serious theological upheaval in the City Temple has sent a tremor throughout England from Cornwall to the Scottish border.

Like his predecessor, Dr. Parker, Mr. Campbell is a preacher of great personal power—warm-hearted, sympathetic, magnetic, and a master of epigrammatic style ; and, like his predecessor, deficient in power of connected thinking. There are not many preachers in England better fitted to inspire a congregation to higher and holier living ; and there are probably not many less fitted to frame a system of philosophy. Whether he has attempted this difficult task, or whether others, taking his epigrammatic sentences, have attempted out of them to frame a system for him, we are not quite sure. In either case it is the impossible that has been attempted. System-makers habitually fail when they endeavor to make a system out of the isolated utterances of a spiritual preacher. Paul is a much more systematic teacher than Mr. Campbell, but it would be hardly fair, from Paul's statement that " all the law is fulfilled in this one word, Thou shalt love thy neighbor as thyself," to conclude that Paul discarded the law, "Thou shalt love the Lord thy God with all thy heart, and with all thy soul, and with all thy mind." It is equally unfair for a critic of Mr. Campbell to conclude from his reported statement, "Whatever can be said about the love of Christ may be said about the love of John Smith," that to Mr. Campbell "Christ's love and the love of John Smith may be expressed in terms of the same value." At least two-thirds of the curious turmoil which has been produced in England is due to the fact that system-makers have taken Mr. Campbell's rhetoric as though it were the exposition of a new philosophy. Possibly he has taken it so himself.

Added impulse to the discussion has been given by the formation of a New Theology League "for the encouragement of progressive religious thought." Started as an alliance for aggressive propaganda, it has apparently been converted into an alliance for defense. Its organization has created a sensation and provoked additional hostility. All men, including theologians, love a fight. And the public, by aid of the press, is forming a ring to witness the encounter between the theological athletes, and occasionally a bystander takes a hand. But if the following statement issued by three members of the League as an expression of "our own personal opinion" is a reflection of the views of the League, there is nothing in them which to American theologians would appear new, though to some of the conservative school in America they might appear alarming:

The ultimate reality and the one hope for man is the Holy Love of God, who, though transcendent, is immanent in nature and humanity, but supremely in Jesus Christ.

God is the Father of all men, and all men are implicitly his children, made in his image and at unrest till they live for him alone. The germ of divine life is in every soul. The story of the Fall is, in Dr. Dale's words, "an inspired myth," conveying a vital religious truth. By man's sin he has strayed from God, but even the prodigal is still God's child. His very remorse is " the sign of the inextinguishable divinity within his soul."

The Bible is the record of God's progressive revelation, but it has a human element, and all its parts have not equal spiritual significance.

Jesus Christ was God incarnate in the flesh. The question of the Virgin Birth does not touch the fundamental position of Evangelical Theology. Our theory of the process cannot affect the fact of the Incarnation. Seeing Christ we see the Father. The whole life of Christ was a divine self-sacrifice to awaken and develop the latent divinity of man.

The Atonement is an eternal process, and is set forth in all its fullness in the life and death of our Lord. All who love and suffer so as to lift men to God are helping " to fill up that which is lacking in the sufferings of Christ."

If this is the New Theology of Mr. Campbell, he might have learned it all from Horace Bushnell.

There are many affirmations in the old theology, as popularly defined, which no longer appear thinkable to men of the new school of thought. Such are the doctrines that the Bible is verbally inspired and in all its parts equally authoritative; that man was made perfect, committed four thousand years ago an act of disobedience in the Garden of Eden, and all the sin and misery of human life have followed in consequence; that God's wrath burns with an unquenchable flame against the human race because of that first sin and the hereditary sinfulness which has resulted; that the just punishment for sins, large and small, is an eternity of torment; that it is just to transfer the punishment of sin from the guilty to the innocent; that this has been done, and that thus and only thus can a way of escape from torment be found by guilty man. But though to the men of the new school of thought this philosophy is unthinkable, it presents in mediæval forms of thought an experience of faith which is eternally true. Only theologians are concerned when theology is attacked, but when this experience of faith is thought to be attacked all those into whose life it has entered resent the attack as one upon their spiritual life: the faith that the Bible is a unique fountain of cheer, comfort, guidance, and inspiration; that sin is a terrible reality, and that every yielding to temptation and indulgence in sin is a fall from our higher life and a separation from our God; that a pure and loving Being does and must abhor sensuality and greed, however refined the form in which they present themselves; that sin carries its own punishment with it, and that "whatsoever a man soweth, that shall he also reap;" that we are members one of another and are blessed in one another's virtue and suffer in one another's wrong-doing ; that not only do the innocent suffer with the guilty, but that innocence chooses to take upon itself the shame and sin of the guilty in willing self-sacrifice; that this divine spirit of self-sacrifice finds its highest revelation in Jesus Christ, who in this, as in all his life and character, is the supreme ideal for humanity and the supreme revelation of the invisible God ; and that in this spirit of self-sacrifice by the innocent for the guilty is the hope of the human race.

The preacher may attack this faith, or so preach that he is thought to be attacking it, in which case he will arouse the resentment of all those to whom it is a sacred treasure. He may interpret this faith in the terms of the old theology, in which case he will satisfy and help a decreasing number in the Church and alienate an increasing number outside the Church. He may speak to this faith directly without intellectually interpreting it, in which case he will give help to that large number of persons who feel religious truth without attempting to formulate it in philosophical forms. Finally, he may interpret this faith in intellectual forms which show it to be at least not inconsistent with reason, nor with that evolutionary conception of life which in our time underlies all scientific and philosophic thinking, in which case he may do something to win back to Christian fellowship those who have been driven from it because they have been taught to confound religious faith with theological formularies which they cannot honestly accept and will not accept perfunctorily.

It is because Mr. Campbell is thought to have attacked this faith that he is himself so vigorously attacked. We do not believe that he has really done so. His past ministry and his spiritual character make it far more probable that his new interpretation of faith has been mistaken for an attack upon it. But whether he is an assailant or a defender of faith, he has done good. For the world should gladly welcome anything, whatever it may be, that turns laymen aside from a discussion of State politics, commercial speculations, and social fashions, to a discussion of the spiritual problems of sin, forgiveness, and practical righteousness.

❀

# A Pregnant Silence

There is nothing in the Old Testament more sublime than the gradual unveiling of the truth of immortality, disclosing itself in human consciousness like the breaking of the day over the earth. The central fact in the New Testament which sent the disciples, eager, tireless, and dauntless, to men and women burdened with the sorrows and mysteries of life in many countries, was the rising from the dead of One who said, " I am the resurrection and the life," who had brought others back from the Gate of Death and himself returned to demonstrate to living men the survival and victorious life of the spirit beyond the grave. The gospels and epistles find their culmination of interest, their supreme value, in the witness they bear to the fact that one rose from the dead. This was the message which the Apostle Paul carried from Jerusalem to Rome, and this was the great truth which armed him invincibly against the whole world organized against him. There is, however, almost no disclosure in the Book of Life of the form and manner of the world to come ; there is nowhere any recognition of curiosity about these matters or any attempt to satisfy it. The supreme concern of prophet, apostle, and of the Master himself was to make men understand the spiritual meaning and quality of life, and to so clear their vision and reinforce their wills that they might live as the children of God. For us all the one vital matter is to live every day in the light of immortality, not to frame theories as to our occupations and resources in other stages of that life.

There is, however, a deeper and more compelling reason for this significant silence : our inability to understand, if a revelation were made to us. The conditions and the occupations of the spirit, the peace and splendor of a life which gives full play to all the noblest possibilities of human nature and evokes all its highest powers without hindrance of any kind, are so entirely beyond our present capacity to receive and comprehend that nothing could be put into language that would penetrate our intelligence. If we could look through the Gate of Heaven with the eyes that look out upon the earth, we should see nothing; if we could stand at that Gate, we should hear nothing. We forget that language can take us only a little way beyond our experience, and when it does pass beyond, if it is to be intelligible to us, it must draw its images from familiar things. This is true not only of spiritual but of material things. If the men of the stone age had been told of the pictures, statues, churches of the Middle Ages, they would not have understood what was told them, and would have remained not so much incredulous as absolutely uncomprehending; for one must have the capacity for believing before one can have the capacity for incredulity. If our ancestors of two hundred years ago had been told of many of the uses of light and air to-day, they would not have scoffed, because they would have received no idea definite enough to be the object of derision. To-day the great mass of men and women do not understand and cannot explain how musical sounds are produced by waves of light from an electrical lamp; but they accept and enjoy the result because the magical development is made from forces and processes which, in their elementary applications, they do understand.

For this reason, if there were no other, what is called spiritism could say nothing of real importance to us if communication with spirits in the next stage were really established. The demonstration of immortality on a physical basis might be a comfort to those who think it is possible to establish spiritual facts by physical proof; but beyond the bare fact of continued existence we should learn nothing. The only so-called "communications" concerning the next stage of life that have risen above mere personal gossip or feverish attempts to satisfy curiosity by projecting present conditions into the future have taken the form of assurances of perfect content, coupled with the declaration that nothing could be told about the occupations and resources of the spirit world because no statement could be understood. There is nothing in our present experience that could interpret to us the form and manner of that larger and freer life. We are as incapable of understanding how they who have gone on bear themselves and in what manner they find the peace and joy of heaven and rise in ever-widening circles of knowledge, as our children are of understanding the abstract ideas that are matters of familiar thought to us.

If our curiosity were wholesome, it could not be gratified; if God spoke to us directly of those matters, we should not understand. But our desire for that knowledge, although often passionate in its intensity, and springing from the depth and fervor of our love for those who yesterday were light and life to us and to-day are silent in the appalling silence of death, is not wholesome. It is not our business to study the life to come when we know so little of the life that now is; to become absorbed in the contemplation of escape from burdens, and rest from labor, and freedom from sorrow, when burdens, labor, and sorrow are teachers sent from God to prepare us for the larger and freer life. Many a school-boy would like to be done with school and have the freedom and authority of a man. Many a school-boy has imagined that he could be a man if he could rid himself of school and masters, and does not know that the only path to the kind of manhood that summons him from afar is the manhood that is shaped by schools, lessons, discipline, self-denial. Heaven is not simply or primarily a place of rest, where no duty calls and no work waits; it is pre-eminently a place of growth. It is a joy to be won, not a felicity to be simply waited for. There are many classes in this great school in which we are learning the lessons of life, and heaven will not be the same to all who pass from that school. When the gate opens, the vision that breaks on the view of those that enter, by that law of growth that runs through all worlds, will get its measure from the eyes that look at it. Rest, peace, purity, will come to all who carry the possibilities of those things with them. But heaven will be greater to those who have gone far in the education of the spirit than to those who have only begun to learn the deep things of God. Our concern now is not with the form and manner of life beyond, but with such a shaping of life here that when the gate opens we shall take with us that purified vision which shall see God.

It is, in a word, the radiant beauty of the fuller life, its sublime occupations, its inexhaustible interests, its deep-seated happiness, that arrest us on the threshold and leave our curiosity or our passionate desire unsatisfied. We could not understand if we were told, because the heavenly so transcends our mortal experience. The measure of its divine fullness, the compass of its happiness, are the very things which keep us in suspense and ignorance. It would be a very meager heaven that we could understand ; a very limited fulfillment of the possibilities of our nature that we could comprehend. That we cannot know what the absent ones do and how they move and have their being in the world in which care and pain and sorrow and death have no place ought to be to us a deep spring of comfort and faith.

❦

## The Spectator

The Spectator feels indignant. He has been accused of taking a rose-colored view of things, of being a dilettante, of writing in the vein of the "woman's page," whatever that may be. The Spectator denies the too soft impeachment. He knows that he has convictions, that he is sometimes almost too serious, and that his soul can stir with righteous indignation. And while he cannot escape from his predestined habit of observing, he feels that his readers will on this occasion permit him to redeem himself from the charge of frivolousness by turning to a somber subject. He hopes that nothing " triflin'," as our Southern friends say, may escape him at this particular time, whatever his previous failings may have been.

❦

And surely even an incorrigible humorist would feel like stopping his out-

put of jokes if he could have been with the Spectator on a · recent afternoon. For the Spectator was learning about accidents to life and limb and how they occur ; and, better still, how they can be prevented. His interest had been awakened in this subject by hearing a member of the Peace Society say that the work of preventing industrial accidents was of greater moment even than the prevention of war ; and the statistics quoted seemed to justify the opinion. The assertion was made that in · the United States alone we kill and wound every year in our industrial army more men than fell in all the battles in any year of our bloody Civil War ; and, still more astounding, that the casualties of the greatest war of modern times, that between the Russians and the Japanese, were fewer than those that occur every year in peaceful America through railway collisions and the ceaseless sacrifice exacted in factories and workshops by the Moloch of machinery.

❦

" You will not believe me, perhaps," said the Spectator's informant, " but there is one great manufacturing concern in the United States that either kills or maims one workman every day in the year. And do you realize that on every single day of the year the railways of this country kill twenty-six persons and wound two hundred and thirty ? You do not realize this, because ours is a big country, and only the big accidents are reported in the newspapers, and the industrial ones are not always recorded even locally. But all over this land men, women, and children are killed or injured in large numbers every day by accident, and the total for a year makes a casualty list greater than that of any battle that ever was fought. Waterloo, Gravelotte, Gettysburg, Mukden—these scenes of bloodshed are not so fearful as the annual carnage that reddens our American towns and cities in the struggle that is led by our captains of industry. The regiments of labor are the ones that suffer the most appalling losses ; and their losses are worse than those of battle, because men go into battle expecting to be killed, and because a vast number of these industrial accidents are preventable. Men do not go to their daily work expecting to be killed or hurt, but to go home again to their happy families ; and the accidents that send them home dead or mutilated must be prevented."

❀

That was the word the Spectator was waiting for. He is more interested in prevention for the future than in the horrors of the past or the present, and he thinks his readers are too. The afternoon referred to was spent by the Spectator at the First International Exposition of Safety Devices and Industrial Hygiene, conducted under the auspices of the American Institute of Social Service in New York. Several large rooms were devoted to exhibiting moving machinery with accident preventers, models of safety appliances of all kinds, and photographs and other illustrations of what foreign countries are doing in this direction. The Spectator stopped before a large machine, looked and listened. "One of the most dangerous machines that is used in factories," said the demonstrator who was showing the mechanism to a group of visitors, "is this punching machine. It doesn't kill people, but very frequently it takes their fingers off and leaves them maimed for life. And here, by this simple device," pointing to a circular piece of steel that surrounded the descending punch, "the finger is saved. This, by the way, was invented by a boy. You remember it was a boy who invented an important part of the steam-engine. He did that to save work. This boy invented the punch guard to save his fingers. At any rate, it will save many fingers that he never saw." The Spectator turned from the punching machine to see a young man showing how the machinery of a factory could be stopped almost immediately when a worker got caught in cogs or belting. The simple pressing of a button stopped the adjacent machinery within five seconds, while allowing the machinery on other floors to continue in operation. The Spectator remembered once seeing a poor girl at a college settlement reception who wore a red skull-cap all through the evening. She was a factory girl who had been scalped by getting her hair caught in a whirling belt. If this safety device had been used in that factory, she might have been saved from this terrible experience.

❀

"Many American workmen," the Spectator was told by an intelligent mechanic who was explaining a piece of woodworking machinery, "hate the trouble of using safety devices. This 'jointer' is a very dangerous machine. The man runs the board over these rapidly revolving knives. If the knives strike a knot, the board may be thrown one side, and the man's hands go down on the knives. Many a time I have seen this happen. A man was in here yesterday who had lost two fingers in this way. He said it made him shiver to run this board through, though his fingers were perfectly protected by this device. I took one of these guards to a planing-mill not long ago to put it on a machine. The workman said, 'You can put it on, but I won't use it.' I put it on, and a few weeks after went to see it. I found the man was using it and glad to have it. He said, 'When you first came, I thought you had one of those clumsy things that would interfere with my work. This is all right.'" Americans, employers and workers alike, require simplicity in safety appliances. And very simple things often most effectively prevent accidents. For instance, many accidents occur through the workers slipping on smooth floors in front of machines on which they are working, and falling into the machinery. The simple device of a rubber mat on which they may stand is an almost certain preventive of this. Here in two large photographs were seen an interesting illustration of this accident preventer.

❀

"Yesterday," said the man who was showing a safety device for a freight elevator, "a boy was seated during the noon hour on the platform of a freight elevator in a New York factory. His legs were dangling over the edge. Somebody on the floor above started the elevator by pulling the rope. Before the boy could get up he was caught and his legs were cut off. If this device had been in use, this accident could not have happened." The device was a wooden plug which had to be stepped on before the elevator could start. No unauthorized person could start the elevator from a floor above or below. Near by this was a safety device which prevented a freight elevator starting till the gate was shut. It brought to mind an accident of which the Spectator was personally cognizant. A workman had stepped back to an elevator which he had left a moment before. The elevator had gone upward, and the man fell through the shaft eleven stories and was killed.

❀

Few of us have seen the effect of bursting fly-wheels, or know why they explode. Photographs of wrecked mills, the result of these accidents, were shown to the Spectator. The governor of an engine is supposed to regulate the speed of a fly-wheel. Sometimes the governor gets out of order, or a belt is broken, and the machinery begins to run at a frightful speed. It may be only a matter of a few seconds when the centrifugal force sends the enormous wheel flying in pieces, scattering death and destruction about. Here was a device which automatically prevented this " racing." Then, again, a great many accidents occur through the flying apart of small emery wheels. This also can easily be obviated through devices here shown.

❀

Four hundred and thirty men were accidentally killed in one recent year in the anthracite mining regions of Pennsylvania. Many of these accidents occur through the falling of shaft buckets. Here was a safety device 'o prevent this, exhibited by its inventor, a poor miner who could not pay his exhibition fee. Here also were electric miners' lamps, which would prevent fire-damp explosions. And, in another field, that of domestic work, an ingenious lamp was shown which automatically extinguished itself when upset or partly turned over. " Four people yesterday met their death from escaping illuminating gas," the Spectator was told as he paused before another exhibit. This was a device which immediately turned off the flow of gas when the Spectator, taking the part of a rural " Rube," blew out the flame. Here also were inclosed cog wheels, and protectors for band-saws, and shock-preventers, and devices to close automatically the open railway switch that slays its hundreds every year, and improved clamps to keep rails from spreading, and efficient trolley fenders, and scores of other safety appliances, most of them simple and practicable.

❀

And why are they not used? Why does the sacrifice of human beings go on? The pity of it! Because, for one reason, the cheapest thing in the world—or in America at least—seems to be human life. These appliances all cost money, and it is cheaper not to use them. In some way, the Spectator believes, we must make it more expensive to kill and maim men and women than to safeguard machinery. The Spectator heard with the greatest interest how Germany has worked out the problem. Germany needs men for her army. Therefore she tries to save them. Germany helps to insure her workmen against accident. Therefore she is interested financially in preventing accidents. Thus the State has a vital interest in requiring the safeguarding of machinery, the caring for injured workmen, and instruction in avoiding accident. In the German factory dangerous places and parts of machinery are painted red—the danger signal! Workmen are not allowed, through bravado or indolence, to disregard the use of protecting appliances. Hospitals and convalescent homes are maintained. Nothing is left to benevolence alone, but law, and rigidly enforced law, requires that work shall be conducted in a humane way. And the Spectator, while applauding vigorously the many liberal and kindhearted employers who conduct model workshops, some of which were illustrated in the Safety Appliance Exposition, solemnly believes that Americans must devise some system that shall, with the sanction and the penalties of law, make human life, in factory and workshop and on the railway, the most sacred thing in the world. Till then we shall not be entitled to call ourselves really civilized.

# LONGFELLOW'S CONQUEST OF ENGLAND

## BY SIR HENRY MORTIMER DURAND

THREE years ago, at a dinner given to me by the Lotos Club of New York, I used the following words:

"And now, before I sit down, will you let a wanderer who comes from the land of the lotos lay one white flower of gratitude on the grave of an American poet? I owe much of the pleasure of my life to American writers of every shade of thought, from Holmes and Hawthorne to that candid friend of my country, the Editor of Life, whose paper has given me many a happy half-hour in India and Persia and other distant lands. But I owe to one American writer much more than pleasure. Tastes differ and fashions change, and I am told that the poetry of Longfellow is not read as it used to be. Men in my own country have asked me whether the rivers of Damascus were not better than all the waters of Israel, whether Shakespeare and Milton and Shelley and Keats were not enough for me, that I need go to Longfellow. And Americans have seemed surprised that I did not speak rather of Lowell and Bryant and others. Far be it from me to say a word against any of them. I have loved them all from my youth up, every one of them in his own way, and Shakespeare as the master and compendium of them all. No one, I suppose, would place Longfellow as a poet quite on the same level with some of them. But the fact remains that, for one reason or another, perhaps in part from early association, Longfellow has always spoken to my heart. Many a time, in lands very far away from the land he loved so well, I have sought for sympathy in happiness and in sorrow—

'Not from the grand old masters,
    Not from the bards sublime,
Whose distant footsteps echo
    Through the corridors of time,'

but from that pure and gentle and untroubled spirit."

What I feel about Longfellow many English men and women also feel, and I sometimes doubt whether Americans have at all realized how completely Longfellow has won his way into the hearts of my countrymen. He has gained a hold upon the people of England which no other American poet has ever gained. Students of poetry, of course, read, and occasionally prefer, other American poets, and no educated Englishman is wholly ignorant of their works. But as regards Longfellow it is not too much to say that his poems have become thoroughly incorporated with the great body of English verse. Many of them are taught to every English child. I do not believe that the majority of our children are even aware of the fact that the man who wrote the "Wreck of the Hesperus," "The Reaper," "Excelsior," and other well-known pieces was not an Englishman. In my boyhood, though I was aware of the fact, I yet never thought of Longfellow as being in any way distinct from the English poets. He took his place quite naturally with his English fellows, with Wordsworth and Shelley and Tennyson and the rest. One of my earliest recollections in connection with literature is of my father sitting by the drawing-room fire reading "Coplas de Manrique." Longfellow was at least as well known in our house as any English poet of the day, better perhaps than any except Tennyson. It was, I think, the same in most English houses of that time—nearly fifty years ago. The community of language, and the English habit of mind with reference to Americans, who are not regarded in England as foreigners, may have had something to do with this, but there must have been other reasons, for, as I have said, other American poets have not gained the same hold upon the English people. When their works are essentially of the soil, like the delightful verses of Bret

Harte, this is natural enough, but even when they are not they somehow remain to the mass of our people distinct and comparatively unfamiliar. Longfellow is to be found as an honored guest, or rather as a welcome friend, in every English household. Perhaps the American poet who comes nearest to him in this respect, though a very long way behind, is a poet of a totally different order, Edgar Allan Poe. Bryant, whom Longfellow called his "maestro," was never really well known to the English people, nor was Emerson, nor Lowell, nor Whitman, nor any of the others.

Many of Longfellow's shorter pieces have become familiar to every Englishman in the form of songs, which is in itself a notable proof of his great popularity.

He was, and I believe still is, popular in the truest sense—known to and loved by all classes of the people. Hawthorne writes to Longfellow in 1855, from Liverpool:

I am very sorry you are not coming over at present, both on my own account and yours. You ought to be in England to gather your fame, which is greater, I think, than you are likely to estimate. No other poet has anything like your vogue. Did you hear how the Harrow school-boys, a few months ago, decided by a formal vote (as I understand) that you are the first poet of the age? I make great play at dinner-tables by means of you. Every lady—especially the younger ones—enters on the topic with enthusiasm, and my personal knowledge of you sheds a luster on myself. Do come over and see these people!

In the following year Hawthorne writes again:

In London, a few evenings ago, I happened to be at Evans's supper rooms, to which I was introduced by Mr. Albert Smith. The proprietor introduced himself to me, and expressed a high sense of the honor which my presence did him. He further said that it had been "the dream and romance of his life" to see Emerson, Channing, Longfellow—and he was kind enough to add, me—sitting together at a table in his rooms! I could not but smile to think of such a party of roysterers drinking at one of his tables, smoking and listening to a Bacchanalian catch from his vocalists! The band played "Hail Columbia" and "Yankee Doodle" in my honor, and several of your songs were sung! The proprietor entreated me to lay this "edition de luxe," as he called it, of his programme "at your feet." You must certainly go there when you come to London.

"Evans's" was a supper room in Covent Garden, much frequented when I was young. It was famous for its "Welsh rabbits" and other delicacies. Small tables were dotted about the room, and there was a stage at the end from which the "vocalists"—all men or boys —entertained the audience. The singing was good, and the proprietor a very well known character. It was the fashion to go to Evans's on the night of the University boat race, when the fun used to get fast and furious, and occasionally ended in a free fight. It was not exactly the place where I should have expected to see Longfellow—but he was fond of his pipe and his bottle of Rhine wine—and Evans's was quite respectable.

Hawthorne goes on: "I have been in all sorts of parties within the last few weeks, and in every single one of them your name is spoken with the highest interest and admiration. Your fame is in its fullest blow; the flower cannot open wider. If there is any bliss at all in literary reputation, you ought to feel it at this moment. I am not quite sure that it is a very enjoyable draught; but if you drink it at all, it is best to take it hot and sweet and spiced to the utmost. So do come over to England this summer."

Longfellow's biographer tells how, when Longfellow did go to London in 1868, "out of a group of people upon the sidewalk a laboring man came forward, and, asking if he were the poet, begged to be allowed to shake hands with him," and then put the poet to flight by reciting a verse of "Excelsior;" how he took his doctor's degree at Cambridge and was cheered by the undergraduates; how he was welcomed by poets and statesmen and all the most distinguished men in the country; how he was received "cordially and without ceremony" by Queen Victoria, and also by the Prince of Wales, now King Edward; and how, after his death, "the gratitude of many of England's best and noblest has placed his marble image among her own honored dead, in the shadowy seclusion of Westminster's Poet's Corner."

Longfellow's conquest of England was the more remarkable because, at the time that he began writing, the attitude of English critics toward American literature was, to say the least, extremely cold. In 1844 Longfellow animadverted strongly upon it. " I dislike as much as any one can," he writes, " the tone of English criticism in reference to our literature." It is a proof of his great qualities that he was able to overcome so entirely and so rapidly the prejudice which existed. It is perhaps creditable also to the open-mindedness and to the judgment of the English people that they were able to break away so thoroughly from their literary traditions. " Who ever reads an American book ?" the critics asked ; and the answer of the people was, " We all do—and love it."

To many Americans it seems strange that Longfellow should have met with so much more success in England than other American poets, and it is not altogether easy to explain, or understand, what the reasons were. In 1868 an English newspaper wrote of him in the following words :

" He is the familiar friend, who has sung to every household, and set to music their aspirations and their affections. He is the poet of our sober English nature, with its deep undercurrent of earnestness and enthusiasm, yet with its dislike of extravagance, and its joy in the tender relations of life. He shows us the poetic side of ordinary events."

There is much truth in these words, but it is not perhaps the whole truth. The travel and wide reading necessitated by Longfellow's work as Professor of Modern Languages at Harvard gave him a certain detachment of mind, a breadth of knowledge and sympathy, which fitted him to write for others besides his own nation. Some of his poems, too, though not many, were on purely English themes. For instance, " King Witlaf's Drinking Horn," " The Norman Baron," " The Luck of Eden Hall," " The Warden of the Cinque Ports." Then his poems on slavery, though open to criticism in some respects, appealed strongly to the English feeling of the day. Above all perhaps is the fact that with the English people character has always counted for more than anything else, and whatever may have been Long-

fellow's faults of execution, there could never be the slightest doubt as to the purity and loftiness of his aims. Finally, his extreme simplicity of language, if it sometimes verged on the commonplace, made him readily understood by many to whom more ornate poetry would have been incomprehensible. He was understood by the people and he was understood by the young, and what one understands and loves when one is young retains through life the charm of association. A recent number of an English magazine, commenting upon the poetry read by English girls of the present day, states that Tennyson is the poet most read, Longfellow the next.

As to the rank accorded to Longfellow by the English people, I think any attempt to determine that accurately would be unprofitable. It would be unprofitable in the case of almost any poet. Tastes differ, and there is rarely a consensus of opinion on such a point. All that can be safely said is that, on the one hand, Longfellow is not regarded in England as a poet of the very first rank, and that, on the other, he is regarded as a genuine poet, whose best work will live as long as the English language lives.

I have indeed heard him decried and ridiculed by some people. I have heard it said that his verse is feeble stuff, " not poetry " at all. But he is in good company—Wordsworth used to be decried and ridiculed.

Longfellow of course has his limitations. No one would ascribe to him the majesty of Milton. Wordsworth, whose manner is at times like Longfellow's, is, I think, both stronger and in his simple passages more perfect.

" The gentleness of heaven broods o'er the sea ;
Listen ! the mighty Being is awake,
And doth with his eternal motion make
A sound like thunder—everlastingly."

" Thy soul was like a Star, and dwelt apart :
Thou hadst a voice whose sound was like the sea ;
Pure as the naked heavens, majestic, free."

" A violet by a mossy stone
Half hidden from the eye !
Fair as a star, when only one
Is shining in the sky."

" Will no one tell me what she sings ?
Perhaps the plaintive numbers flow

For old, unhappy, far-off things,
And battles long ago."

Those passages are after Longfellow's heart—but they have a quality to which Longfellow rarely, if ever, attains. Further, he has not the dreamy grace of Coleridge, or the fire and compass of Byron, or the wonderful felicity of language which distinguishes Keats. He does not take us into Shelley's fairyland. He could not have written "The Cloud" or "The Skylark,"

"That orbèd maiden with white fire laden
Whom mortals call the moon
Glides glimmering o'er my fleece-like floor
By the midnight breezes strewn;
And wherever the beat of her unseen feet,
Which only the angels hear,
May have broken the woof of my tent's thin roof,
The stars peep behind her and peer."

There is a music in that which is not Longfellow's. By his contemporaries, too, he is excelled in certain particulars. He had not the finish nor perhaps the depth of Tennyson. He has given us nothing like "In Memoriam." You cannot imagine him writing with almost superexquisite alliteration of

"The moan of doves in immemorial elms,
The murmur of innumerable bees."

He has the same idea, but it is not worked out with the same patience and care :

" And the reader droned from the pulpit
Like the murmur of many bees."

In wealth of language and classical feeling and beauty of cadence he cannot compare with Swinburne :

"When the hounds of spring are on winter's traces,
The Mother of months in meadow or plain
Fills the shadows and windy places
With lisp of leaves and ripple of rain;
And the brown bright nightingale amorous
Is half assuaged for Itylus,
For the Thracian ships and the foreign faces,
The tongueless vigil and all the pain."

—

"When a Goddess the pulse of thy passion
Smote kings as they reveled in Rome,
And they hailed thee risen, O Thalassian,
Foam white from the foam."

The fact is, I think, that Longfellow was apt to be a little hasty and careless in his work. It was his natural tendency, and the rapidity of his success perhaps increased it. His father writes to him in 1825 : " I think you publish your productions too soon after they are written, . . . without allowing time for reflection and examination. If you re-examine them, you will find some defects which would have been corrected if you had adopted the course I recommend." And Longfellow answers : " Your opinion upon the subject of my writing coincides in a great measure with that of Mr. Parsons, the editor of the Gazette, who says that I must use more care—or that it will be for my own advantage to use more care than my communications generally exhibit." But the habit stuck to him. In 1845 he writes in his journal, " Before church wrote ' The Arrow and the Song,' which came into my mind as I stood with my back to the fire, and glanced on to the paper with arrowy speed—literally an improvisation." In 1848 I find another entry : " Wound up with ' King Witlaf's Drinking Horn,' which I painted with a sweep of the pencil just before dinner." Of course it is true that some of a writer's happiest things come to him in this way. And it must be remembered also that Longfellow was a college professor whose days were not his own. He could hardly afford the time to finish and refinish his literary work after the manner of Tennyson, whose poetry was elaborated with the minute patience and care bestowed on the carvings of a Hindu temple. Still, it would have been better if he could have done so. In poetry form must count for much. As Ben Jonson said, when praising Shakespeare's art, " A good poet's made as well as born."

But, granting all this, it may be said, in the first place, that if Byron and others wrote some things which Longfellow could not have written, they certainly wrote some things which he would not have written. He always remained on the higher level from which they too often descended. His critics will answer, " Oh, yes. Nobody denies that he was an eminently respectable person. The question is whether he wrote poetry." But that is not a complete answer. As was said when Longfellow took his degree at Cambridge, it is the function of poetry " to solace the ills of life and draw men from its low cares *ad excelsiora*." That is just what Longfellow does, and in spite of any want of finish or imagination, or poetical rush and swing, the purity and high aim of his verse give it a dignity and power which cannot be ignored. Take, for example, the poem called "The Light of Stars." It is one of his early poems, and it is full, more full than most, of the defects for which his detractors ridicule him. Yet who can read it without being the better for it?

> " And thou too, whosoe'er thou art,
>     That readest this brief psalm,
> As one by one thy hopes depart,
>     Be resolute and calm.
>
> O fear not in a world like this,
>     And thou shalt know erelong,
> Know how sublime a thing it is
>     To suffer and be strong."

Poetry must be judged by the power it exercises, the feeling it arouses, not solely by its form; and Longfellow does arouse deep feeling in the great majority of men, though he may have no message for the dilettante, delicate-handed priest of an æsthetic cult. "Beauty is truth, truth beauty," Keats said. We must not omit the latter part of the saying. Macaulay, another writer whose verse is decried, as "not poetry," is, I think, to be justified on the same grounds.

> " But hark! the cry is Astur!
>     And lo! the ranks divide,
> And the great Lord of Luna
>     Comes with his stately stride.
> Upon his ample shoulders
>     Clangs loud the fourfold shield,
> And in his hand he shakes the brand
>     Which none but he can wield.
> He smiled on those bold Romans,
>     A smile serene and high;
> He eyed the flinching Tuscans,
>     And scorn was in his eye.
> Quoth he, ' The she-wolf's litter
>     Stand savagely at bay;
> But will ye dare to follow,
>     If Astur clears the way?'"

That is rough, perhaps, but—not poetry? why, it stirs your blood like a trumpet-call! Poetry is for all the world, not for the critic only.

And surely there is much beauty of form in Longfellow as well as beauty of spirit and purpose. The English Spectator, which, according to his biographer, wrote satirically of the earlier poems, such as the "Psalm of Life" and "Excelsior," also wrote of "the sweet and limpid purity, the shy and graceful humor, the cool and perfectly natural colors and forms" of his later poems—especially "Hiawatha." At times he is not without the spirit and fire which he is accused of lacking. Only a short time ago I heard one of the most distinguished of living Englishmen make that remark, and then proceed to recite from memory verse after verse of the "Slave's Dream:"

> " Before him, like a blood-red flag,
>     The bright flamingoes flew;
> From morn till night he followed their flight,
>     O'er plains where the tamarind grew,
> Till he saw the roofs of Caffre huts,
>     And the ocean rose to view.
>
> At night he heard the lion roar,
>     And the hyena scream,
> And the river-horse, as he crushed the reeds
>     Beside some hidden stream;
> And it passed, like a glorious roll of drums,
>     Through the triumph of his dream."

"That is really fine," he said. "I suppose Longfellow has contributed more to the stock of pieces one knows by heart than almost any other poet."

The fact is that different poets appeal, not only to different tastes, but to different moods. It is possible to enjoy with an intense enjoyment the delicate fancy and form of Shelley, or the rush and cadence of Swinburne, and yet to find at other times comfort and inspiration from the simple language and noble thought of the American poet. The one thing does not exclude the other, any more than listening with thorough enjoyment to a finished orator prevents one from being moved to the depths by a few earnest words spoken straight from the heart.

That is Longfellow's real strength; he speaks straight from the heart. And so he is loved by a great number of my countrymen. Possibly he is loved rather than admired. If so, I feel sure that he rejoices to know it.

# THE EVIL OF CHILD LABOR

## WHY THE SOUTH SHOULD FAVOR A NATIONAL LAW

### BY A. J. McKELWAY

THE Beveridge-Parsons Bill, which has attracted the attention of the whole country and is now being debated in Congress, provides, in brief, that no common carrier shall transport from one State to another the products of any mine or factory where children under fourteen years are employed. The common carrier protects itself against violation of the law by requiring that the mine or factory shall deposit with the railway agent every six months a certificate to the effect that no children under fourteen years of age are employed or have been employed during the preceding six months. The mine or factory protects itself from the violation of the law by the simple expedient of not employing children under fourteen years of age.

Of course the bill has been drawn with reference to the clause of the Constitution which gives to Congress exclusively the right to regulate commerce between the States, with foreign countries, and with the Indian tribes. The power to regulate commerce involves the power of prohibiting the transportation of articles of commerce. The States had that power before yielding it to the Congress. The transfer of that power was absolute. Therefore the question of States' rights is not involved. The issue is rather one of expediency, whether the regulation of this evil should be left to the local authorities alone, either of State or city, or should be also undertaken by the National Government.

It should be said that the proposed bill necessarily concedes the necessity of State laws on the subject. It touches the evil in its two sorest spots, the employment of children in mines and in factories. It leaves to the States, or to the localities involved, the correction of the evil in stores, in the street trades, perhaps in the sweat-shops, unless they can

be brought under the definition of a factory. But it is believed that the proposed National law will cut the heart out of the evil throughout the Nation. And it is also held, by those who have had considerable experience with the failures of present laws without an elaborate and expensive machinery of enforcement and inspection, that it will be almost automatic in its operations.

For the corporations engaged in mining and in the various manufactures are growing to have a wholesome respect for Federal law. The Department of Justice at Washington has been displaying an activity that has excited the keenest appreciation of the people at large, and they will never suffer again what has been endured through its inactivity. The factories are small and few that will sell their products in the State of their manufacture only and thus be protected by the operation of the States' rights principle. And the mines and factories are few that will run the risk not only of prosecution but of an embargo on their goods.

To quote freely from Senator Beveridge's masterly Constitutional argument on this question, it has already been decided in the lottery case that the power of Congress to regulate inter-State commerce extends to the prohibition of the transportation of lottery tickets. The police power of all the States might have abolished the evil. But the simple and effective remedy, supplementing State laws, was the prohibition of the transportation of lottery tickets, as by the express companies. That has abolished the lottery in the Union. Again, the power of Congress over inter-State commerce and over foreign commerce is exactly the same. Congress has already prohibited in the McKinley and Dingley tariff laws the importation of goods made by convict labor. Congress has the power, it it sees fit, to prohibit the transportation from one State to another of goods made by convict labor. It would seem to follow as the night the day that it has the power to prohibit the transportation from one State to another of child-made goods.

And now, why should the South favor this law? First, because it is in general sympathy with the recent applications of this power for the protection of the people of the States, such as the pure food law, the meat inspection law, the railway rate law. It has learned, through long and sometimes bitter experience, that one State is no match for the oppressive corporations when they want to do business in that State from the bulwark of the State that charters them. They have actually found the Federal courts the protectors of the corporations doing an inter-State business until Congress passed the laws that the Federal courts could act upon. It may be argued, from the lawyer's point of view, that the pure food and meat inspection laws are for the protection of the consumer and not for the correction of evils incident to their manufacture. The people have forced many such distinctions into the background to get at an evil. But there is also a rapidly growing conviction in the social conscience that people have a right to be protected against the purchase of child-made goods, that they have a right to know whether the goods were made at the cost of the lives and health of little children. Probably the Lottery Bill would have been declared unconstitutional fifty years ago, because the conscience of the people had not been educated to the enormity of the lottery evil. Yet the people have ever been impatient with fine-spun distinctions when they were determined to abolish a great and cruel wrong.

Now, just as the Louisiana Lottery wrung tribute from the whole country, so a State cannot protect itself against all the consequences of child labor in a bordering State. Tennessee, for example, has an age limit of fourteen, with a fair factory inspection. South Carolina, just beyond its borders, has an age limit of twelve, with the legal permission that children of any age who are orphans or the children of dependent parents may work in the mills, and has no factory inspection. Tennessee manufacturers have tried to get the Tennessee age limit lowered. They say that they are being punished, from the business point of view, by the fact that they have to observe a better law than that of South Carolina. Moreover, Tennessee is losing her citizens to South Carolina. I have seen a company of fifty people from East Tennessee on the train, in charge of an agent, bound for the South Carolina cotton-mills, and the agent told me that he had "shipped" five hundred recently, and that there were other agents besides himself. If Tennessee had been one of the original thirteen colonies, she would have had the right, as a State, before entering the Union, to prohibit the importation of cotton goods from South Carolina. But the States gave the right to regulate commerce to the Nation. And there are National rights as well as States' rights—and duties—belonging both to the States and the Nation. Again, the child labor evil in the South to-day is greater than it is in any other part of the country, perhaps than in any other part of the civilized world. The South, as a whole, is not responsible. The evil is almost confined to one industry, which has always been cursed with it, and is too much cursed with it now in other sections. But the South has suffered in this regard through the enormous expansion of the cotton-mill industry and the necessarily slow progress of remedial legislation; and it takes a long time for humanity to win against the power of money. Surely the South should be unwilling to bear the odium of oppressing her little children when one industry is almost entirely responsible for it and that is mainly confined to four States. And she should not put herself in the position of perpetuating this infamy through opposition to the only effective means, in my humble judgment, that has ever been proposed to end it.

The cotton manufacturers have grown sensitive about this singling out of their business, and some of them affect to believe that the agitation which is now Nation-wide is all the result of their competition with the New England mills. Of course the idea is absurd on the face of it. There is practically no competition between the two sections in the labor market. New England capitalists are largely interested in one way or another in many of the Southern mills, and in the main the Southern mills, partly because of the unskilled labor that they employ, are engaged in making coarse goods, while the New England mills are making the finer goods with their skilled labor. It has even been demonstrated that the same class and quality of goods made in the South and in the East bring a considerably lower price when made in the South, through the bad reputation the Southern mills have won for the indifferent product of unskilled, that is child, labor.

But the census bulletin just issued, Number 69, analyzing the statistics of the Census of 1900, furnishes startling and absolute proof of the bad eminence the South has attained as the employer of child labor.

Without going into the statistics, let the census bulletin state the following conclusions :

To a greater extent than any other manufacturing or mechanical industry, the cotton-mill furnishes employment for children. . . . Almost two-thirds of the total number of cotton-mill operatives, ten to fifteen years of age, were in the Southern States . . . due not so much to the concentration of this industry in the South as to the greater tendency in the South to employ children. . . . In the North about one cotton-mill operative out of every ten was ten to fifteen years of age, while in the South the corresponding figures were about three in every ten. Of the total number of child cotton-mill operatives . . . North Carolina, South Carolina, and Georgia contained forty-nine per cent. . . . Not only do the cotton-mills of the South employ more children in proportion to the total number of operatives than their competitors in the North, but they employ a relatively larger number of young children. . . . The effect of child labor laws is especially noticeable in the figures for child bread-winners under ten years of age. In the selected area three hundred and seventy-five such children were reported as breadwinners under ten years of age, and of these five were in the North, where the employment of children is restricted by law, and three hundred and seventy were in the South, where no such law was in force in 1900. These figures, however, represent only a minimum of the child cotton-mill operatives under ten, for the enu-

merators were not required to report the occupation of such children, and thus it is probable that many were employed who were not so reported. This probability is indicated by a comparison of the figures for children nine years of age with those for children of ten. Between those ages the number at home decreases and the number employed increases, and the increment in both cases is marked. . . . The probable explanation is that many under ten are employed, but are not reported as having a gainful occupation, and so are not classified as being at home. . . . An estimate gives the following numbers [for children under 10]: For Massachusetts, 5 ; for Rhode Island, 8 ; for North Carolina, 394 ; for South Carolina, 419. The actual minimum for Georgia was 184, which makes a total for the three leading Southern States of 997. Of the total number of children [the bulletin is still speaking of the children of cotton-mill communities] five to nine years old, one out of every two in the North goes to school, as contrasted with one out of every five in the South ; and of those ten to fourteen, the figures are, for the North, four out of ten, and for the South, one out of thirteen. In marked contrast with the figures for the employed children ten to fourteen years of age are those for the general white population, ten to fourteen. The figures for the South . . . indicate that illiteracy is almost three times as common among the employed children included in this study as among the children in the general white population.

So much for the conclusions from the census statistics made by Dr. Joseph A. Hill, chief of the department of Revision and Results.

These census figures for 1900 cut the ground from under the feet of those who are apologists for the system of child labor. They have but lately shifted their ground. They used to say that child labor of course prevailed, but that it was a good thing, that it gave an industrial education along with a livelihood. But the growing horror of the evil among all humane people has changed this ground to the other, that child labor is a bad thing, but that there is very little of it, and that about to pass away entirely. Recently two cotton-mill manufacturers came from one of the Carolinas to New York, to the meeting of the Civic Federation, to contradict the exaggerated accounts of the evil, and to commend the manufacturers, especially, for what they were doing for the cause of education. Three statements made in an advertisement of the National Child Labor Committee, published in The

Outlook, have been made points of attack: that there were sixty thousand children under fourteen in the Southern cotton-mills, that little girls eight years of age worked a twelve-hour night in the cotton-mills, and that a President of the American Cotton Manufacturers' Association stated that seventy-five per cent. of the spinners of North Carolina were fourteen years of age and under. The fact is that the evil is minimized · by manufacturers when an appeal is made to public opinion, and the number of children employed is magnified when the appeal is to the commercial instincts of a Southern Legislature.

Mr. R. M. Miller, Jr., of Charlotte, North Carolina, formerly President of the Southern Spinners' Association, afterwards President of the American Cotton Manufacturers' Association, in an interview in the Raleigh Post, January 31, 1905, was reported as saying "that the McKelway Bill would work incalculable injury to the milling interests of the State. Nearly seventy-five per cent. of the spinners of this State are between the ages of twelve and fourteen." Mr. Miller afterwards corrected this statement to the one quoted in The Outlook, that "seventy-five per cent. of the spinners were fourteen years old and under." As to the working of girls of eight years a twelve-hour night, there are sixty-six mills in North Carolina that work at night, and the hours are sixty-six a week, which, with the half-holiday given on Saturday, amount to twelve hours a day or night, for five days of the week. The census figures for 1900 in the selected areas of Charlotte, Asheville, Greensboro, Raleigh, and Winston-Salem show in the partial reports of the enumerators, who were not required to report children at work under ten, the following facts: Employed, 1 child of five, 1 of six, 2 of seven, 11 of eight, and 23 of nine, and from this the minimum estimate is made of 394 children from five to nine years of age in the cotton-mills of North Carolina.

In Spartanburg and Greenville Counties, South Carolina, the corresponding figures are, for the children at work in the cotton-mills: 1 child of five, none of six, 14 of seven, 34 of eight, 98 of nine—

the same minimum estimate being 419 child workers under ten in South Carolina. Is it an exaggeration to say that little girls of eight toil at night in the cotton-mills?

The bulletin gives for 1900, 96,467 cotton-mill operatives in the Southern States. This does not include the operatives of knitting-mills, which also manufacture cotton and are popularly called cotton-mills, where children also are freely employed. Of course the industry in the South has grown by leaps and bounds since 1900, the amount of capital invested being about doubled. The Blue Book for 1906–7 reports by fair calculation 209,000 operatives in Southern cotton and knitting mills. Thirty per cent. ten to fifteen would make a total of 62,700 of children employed. To which we may add, say 3,000 children under ten, making 65,700. But this is on the theory that there has been no increase in the percentage of children employed in the Southern mills since 1900. My opinion is that there has been an increase, and for the following reason. The building of new mills has made a pressing demand for labor lest the spindles should be idle. The high price of cotton has tended to draw the operatives back to the farms, the real competition in the labor market being between the mill and the farm that is dependent upon tenant labor. Now in this process the smaller families have been going back to the farm, where the man can make a living for his wife and children, and the larger families have been drifting to the mills. I have before me a copy of an agreement between a cotton-mill association and the people sought for the mill, in which transportation is agreed to be furnished for families with "three or more workers." Suppose, under this demand for any labor that will do the work, there has been an increase to thirty-five per cent. of children in the cotton-mills. That would make 78,150 for children under sixteen, so that the estimate of 60,000 under fourteen does not seem to have been such an exaggeration.

But there has been the beginning of restrictive legislation in the Southern States. North Carolina, South Carolina, and A'abama passed child labor laws in 1903 and Georgia in 1906, effective 1907 and in other provisions in 1908. The age limit of twelve, with exceptions, was reached by a gradual process in South Carolina in 1906. The natural question is, Has not this legislation restricted the abuse of childhood that did obtain in 1900?

In answer, I would say that the arousal of public sentiment has possibly taken the children of six and seven out of the mills, unless these were inconspicuously located. But there is no factory inspection, no compulsory education laws, and there has not been a single prosecution for the violation of the child labor law in these States that I have ever heard of. Every now and then a child of seven or eight will be injured in a mill, and then there is a temporary cleaning out of the children. The better class of mills do undoubtedly try to observe the law, but it is easy for the family that wishes to hire the child of eight or nine or ten to move to a conscienceless factory. It is a matter of common knowledge that the laws are violated. Of course factory inspection by the States will help to enforce the laws when we can get it. But the age limit is two years lower, and in some exceptional cases four years lower, in the South than in the rest of the civilized world, and the double task of reaching a proper age limit and a good standard of law enforcement will scarcely be reached in the South in our generation.

So that, with these appalling facts in view, the South must face, not the question of States' rights, but the vital question, before the very bar of civilization itself, whether her people really want to rescue these little children from the known consequences of premature toil. Shall the South proclaim to the world that she cares less about her own children, of purest Anglo-Saxon strain, than the North has cared for the children of the foreigner? The illiteracy of the South can be excused partly on the ground of the poverty that followed war. But indif-ference to this problem and hostility to an effective solution of it can only be explained by the fact that we have put our new-found prosperity above the sacredness of human life, even the life of sacred childhood itself.

And if that should be the attitude of the South as represented in the political sphere, then we of the South who want to save the children of this generation must make our appeal to the Nation for help. The story that a half-dozen innocent negro men are held in peonage excites the Nation, and the criminals are punished. Cannot the Nation find a way to save 60,000 little white children, also held, willingly or unwillingly, to labor?

I am one of those who believe that the Nation has already heard this cry of the children, of the North as well as of the South, for the numbers are greater in the North, while the proportion is greater in the South. There is no appeal more powerful than that which helpless childhood makes. There is no vengeance like that of the lioness robbed of her whelps. Woe betide those who would stand in the way of the Nation as she rushes to the defense of her children!

And it seems to me that the great corporations, the manufacturers, the coal barons, the "interests," as they are sometimes called, should be slow to array themselves against the rights of childhood. There is to be a tariff controversy in this country at no distant day. With the revelations that have been and will be increasingly made about the oppression of the children, will the protected interests be in good position to ask the continuance of the favor of the American people, especially if the defeat of remedial legislation in the interests of the children can be laid to their charge? Can they ask for the protection of infant industries when proved guilty of the exploitation of infant industry? And would it not be well to stop the agitation and the revelations by the speedy passage of a National law? Remember the meat-packers!

# MY LADY OF THE ROCKY MOUN-
# TAINS

## BY KATHARINE F. ELLIS

THERE is no denying the fact that I was decidedly sleepy and fast growing stupid and cross as the moving train bore me onward to my destination and I realized the fact, more and more, that I must sit there all through the night—*there* in the ordinary day coach without so much as a pillow to save my poor neck from dislocation. Every berth in the Pullman was taken, and I was face to face with my first experience of sitting up all night—a prospect far from pleasing.

It was on a train of the Oregon Short Line, going from Butte, Montana, to Salt Lake City; my companions, two widows of middle age, whose best days had been spent on Montana ranches. I had early in the evening drained them dry, so to speak, of all interesting information. They had told me of coming West at a time when the swiftest mode of transportation to Montana was by steamer on the Missouri River as far as Fort Benton, thence by stage to Helena. I was duly interested in all they had to tell: their trip of seventy-five days from St. Louis to Fort Benton; their journeyings to different valleys, not stopping until they found the one best adapted for their business of stock-raising; their lack of neighbors and consequent loneliness; but all this had happened years ago, and they were now sitting beside me as comfortable and placid as if life had been for them a flowery bed of ease, and happy as children at their prospect of a winter in California. They had ceased to hold my attention; I cared no more for their past with all its hardships than I cared for their future with its easy life and pleasures. They were negative sort of women, who could never hold my interest, unless perhaps at meal-time, when I might be at their mercy. I could not forget my own discomfiture and the prospect of a sleepless night, and looked about me for something or somebody to occupy my thoughts. Since that night I have tried to put myself back into the same condition of mind that I was then enjoying, and have vainly wondered how I could have survived the night had not My Lady of the Rocky Mountains come to my rescue. She gave me food for thought and field for action—but I must introduce you to her in the proper fashion.

It was at Dillon, Montana, that she came on board—a pale, sweet-faced woman of thirty, carrying in her arms a very tiny baby, and followed by a procession of boys of varying sizes and ages. Kind friends accompanied her, bringing lunch-basket, telescope bag, and roll of blankets, and with a hurried good-by left her alone with her small army of boys. My sleepiness vanished, and I was alert in an instant. What right had I to complain of the lack of a night's sleep when that woman would not catch so much as a nap? How *could* she sleep with the care of that family on her mind? And, besides, I heard her say as her friends left, "Yes, I must change cars at Pocatello." "What time?" "Oh, about two o'clock in the morning."

Impulsively I rose from my seat and soon found myself standing beside her, offering my assistance, expressing my interest in her family, and giving assurances of my ability to deal with children from a month old up to any age. While thus advertising myself, I was taking inventory of the children, noting ages, size, and personal appearance. The oldest was a curly-headed, manly little fellow of eleven; the next in the descending scale was like his mother in looks, and he was about eight; then came a space of five years before we came down to the fat, rollicking boy of three; next to him was the last year's baby of fourteen months, and finally the wee new baby boy in his mother's arms. The seat which was turned facing the mother held the three smallest youngsters, while the oldest boy was beside her. Did they cry and fuss and tumble over one another as they sat there? Not a bit of it; each one acted as if he were a duly appointed body-guard to the mother, besides taking the part of a wise elder brother to the one just below him in the scale.

She moved slightly towards the boy, as if expressing a desire that I should sit beside her, and I, nothing loth, was soon wedged into the third of a seat, not even thinking that I generally required a good two-thirds of any seat. In such manner began my acquaintance with My Lady of the Rocky Mountains, which acquaintance, to be exact, lasted from nine in the evening until two in the morning—five hours, yet hours replete with enjoyment and rich in information. So interested did I become in My Lady's fortunes, both past, present, and future, that I speedily forgot all my own troubles, and was sleepy no longer.

"Could I hold the baby, and give her a little rest?" "Certainly," was the answer, for I knew that with that baby in my arms it would be much easier for me to get nearer to her life's history. I learned that her husband was then on the train—at that moment looking after the baggage—but he would leave at the next station, and return to their ranch alone, while she kept on to her mother's home in Kansas. When he came to say good-by, I complimented him on his fine family of boys, to which he replied, " I am very proud of them," and the little faces turned up to his for a last good-by kiss evinced *their* fondness for him.

"Will he drive home to-night?" I asked. "Oh, no," she replied, "he will stay over night here at Dell, which is the nearest railroad station to the ranch, and drive home to-morrow," and there came into her face an expression as if she realized for the first time the growing divergence of their paths.

"But if Dell is the nearest point to the ranch, how did it happen that you all took the train at Dillon, some fifty miles further off?" And then, with a fond look at the baby in her arms, and at the same time adjusting the bottle to the second baby's convenience, she explained in this fashion: "We all came down to Dillon two months ago, as I could not have the services of a doctor and nurse at the ranch, and just as we were ready to go home again I decided to go to Kansas to see my mother; as I only decided yesterday noon that I would go, you can imagine that we had some hustling to do to get ready."

"How old is the baby?" I asked, assuming it to be at least six weeks old, for it had been so enveloped in cloak and bonnet that I had not had a good look at it. She replied, "Three weeks," with a placid air as if there was nothing strange in the whole proceeding. "Three weeks!" I gasped, looking closely at her to make sure that I was not mistaken. "Yes," she said, "three weeks old to-day, but I am so much better and stronger than I was last year when that one came"—pointing to the last year's baby—"that I call myself well." "And did you go to Dillon *last* year?" I asked. "Oh, yes," she said, "there is nothing else to do; I could have no attention at Dell—where my husband left the train— so we go on to Dillon, take a furnished house or some rooms, put the older children in school, and wait—" "For the stork to come your way?" I interrupted. Smiling in a gentle sort of a way, she said, "Yes, that's just it."

I looked across at the last year's baby, who had now fallen asleep on his three-year-old brother, and had a feeling of pity for him that he should so soon have his place usurped; but my pity was evidently uncalled for, as at that moment he opened his eyes and looked at me as if he wanted to say, "It's all right, for I was glad of the chance to go to Dillon, and but for the new baby's coming I might never have seen the world—and Dillon." He shut up his eyes and went to sleep again, and for a few moments I was busy thinking what My Lady's life had been. I noticed the new shoes and the white collars and neckties worn by the boys, the handsome overcoat on the three-year-old, the white cloak and dainty lace bonnet on the new baby, and said to myself: "She is taking them home well dressed, but how she has worked to do it!" The mother was neatly and suitably dressed for traveling, and there was nothing in the appearance of any one of them to indicate that they were from a Montana ranch high up in the Rocky Mountains—I beg your pardon, ranchers of the great Northwest; I have modified my opinions, and should have said that they were not like the dwellers of ranches as I had supposed them to be. I was therefore all the more surprised when I learned of their isolated life, their lack of school privileges and society of any kind, and then and there I felt that my previous conception of ranch families must go to the four winds if this family was a type of all. As if in answer to my thoughts, she told me of her life from the time she married twelve years ago and came with her husband to Beaverhead County in Montana, settling within a mile or two of the summit of the Rockies. They bought nine hundred and sixty acres of "improved" land, the improvement consisting of a one-room cabin only, which the original owner had been obliged to put up in order to maintain his claim to the property. The dimensions of this room were sixteen by twenty feet, and in that room they lived until after their fourth child was born. A year ago they built a log cabin of five rooms, the husband doing all the heavy work and the wife the papering. "For," she added, "we must do it all ourselves, even to the cutting and hauling of the logs, or else do without our new home."

"And do you mean to say that you all lived in that one room—slept, cooked, and ate there—your husband and yourself and the four children?"

"I do mean just that," she said, laughing at my evident consternation; "it's only a matter of planning. You see," she went on to explain, "I put the two beds together at one end of the room, leaving space enough between them for a trunk in which we kept most of our clothing. Then for a table I had a large dry-goods box, opened at one side, in which were shelves and hooks for pots and kettles and similar kitchen utensils. But now," she added, proudly, "we have three chambers, a parlor, and a kitchen, but I don't know that I am any happier than I was in the one-room home. My husband and I worked together; I always helped him outdoors when the babies

were asleep, and we saved our washing for rainy days when he could help me indoors."

Their capital in the beginning was three hundred dollars, with one pair of horses, and at the present time their horses and cattle range the mountains, and each year bring them in a good living income. I confess I was not as deeply interested in the details of stock-raising, the number of head they owned, and the market price, as I was in her domestic life and work, and her ability to accept as a natural, every-day existence one that seemed to me exceptional in its hardships and lack of enjoyment.

I was able to draw my own conclusions, however, that they had prospered financially, or they could not present the well-fed and well-clothed appearance now so apparent.

"But have you no one for neighbors?" I asked.

"No one but a few bachelors who live on neighboring ranches and occasionally give us a call."

I thought of all that it must mean to a man who "baches," as they say out in Montana, to go into that well-kept home where children were sweet and well-mannered, and the bread did not taste of too much soda. How those men live alone, year after year, as they do, is a conundrum, but, as Kipling says, "that's another story." My mind was running on those bachelors as My Lady was going on with her talk; I brought myself back and listened.

"We have to go twenty-five miles for our mail and for all our supplies, except what we send to a mail-order store for. My husband goes to town several times in the fall until the grub-stake is all in for the winter."

"The what?" I asked. "What is it that you put in for the winter?"

"Grub-stake," she replied, as if everybody ought to know what that is; but as my face maintained its blank expression, she was kind enough to explain that all ranchers buy their winter's supply of food in the fall months, and this supply is called, in miners' parlance, "grub-stake." She said, "We always buy—" and then came an enumeration of varying amounts of food products which made my head whirl, and I begged her to stop until I found pencil and paper, for I knew that even if I had been able to remember the quantities stated no one would have believed me unless I was able to verify my statement. With pencil in hand I said, "Now you may begin," and here is the list just as she gave it to me: 1,000 pounds of flour, 400 pounds of sugar, 50 pounds of lard, 50 pounds of coffee, 1,500 pounds of "spuds" (which being interpreted to an Eastern farmer meaneth potatoes), 300 pounds of cabbages, 350 pounds of carrots, 250 pounds of beans—and here she interpolated that they all just loved baked beans. "And there are the dried fruits," she added, "the canned goods, and lots of other things I can't remember."

"And has your grub-stake been put in for the winter?" I asked.

"No; my husband will go home now, and after driving in the forty calves to their winter quarters—for the cows with their calves are not allowed to range in the winter—he will take his big wagon and drive to town, buy our grub-stake, and carry it back to the ranch. We made out the list together before I left, but he knows just as well as I do what is needed for the family. When all that is done, he will come for us—perhaps in a month or so—and we shall all come home together."

"I should almost have thought you would have left the oldest boy at home as company for his father," I remarked.

"Yes, his father would have kept him except that he knew I needed his assistance." I had noticed his willingness to do everything his mother asked of him, from taking off the second baby's cloak to the picking up of its bottle, and not once did he act in any way that did not show that it was his business to play the part of a family helper, so I christened him "little father." During our conversation the "little father" had slipped out into another seat, where he had stretched himself-out and fallen asleep, without so much as loosening his necktie. And she told me of what that boy could do—get a breakfast for the family when she was sick; take care of the fires; wait on the younger children, and"—but she

did not enumerate further, breaking off with—" My children must help me, or I could never get along as I do."

But I could not get away from the thought of that grub-stake, and kept referring to it again and again, inquiring "how they could ever eat so much." "Why, my husband," she said, "thinks nothing of eating a whole mince pie in the evening, with a big piece of pork cake thrown in"—but before she could continue that evening bill of fare I was asking about the pork cake—what was it like, how did she make it?"

"As you have your pencil and paper," she said, "you may as well put that down with the rest of your information, for I have the rule right in my head, I've made it so much." So, for the benefit of other ranchers who may have husbands and children with big appetites, I'll give it in full:

One pint of salt pork, chopped; one pint of cold coffee; two pounds of sugar; one teaspoonful of soda, and flour enough to make it good and stiff; plenty of raisins and currants.

"This rule makes a large quantity," she added, "and I always bake it in a milk-pan. When I have that and a dozen mince pies on hand, I think I am provided for, at least for a few days."

As we were talking I noticed the fine quality of the baby's dress, with its hemstitching and drawn-work, and asked if it was possible that she put all that work into her baby clothes. "Oh, that is only a common dress," she said; "I have three others much handsomer, with finer work," and in a somewhat exultant fashion—as much as to say, "I am not so commonplace as you may think I am"—she said, "And all my sheets and pillowcases are finished in the same way, with hemstitching and drawn-work." And when I asked how on earth she found time to do such fancy work, she said that after the children were in bed she worked and her husband whittled. "So," she added, "we have our little home full of all sorts of pretty things he has made." Of course I tried to convince her that she was a very foolish woman to do that unnecessary work—while in my heart I was admiring her ability to do it—but her defense was that she had no club to attend, no neighbors to visit, no church work to take her time, so she had a right to do the things it pleased her best to do.

Hemstitching and drawn-work in a log cabin twenty-five miles from a post-office, and in the wilds of the Rocky Mountains! What *would* she tell me next? "And I take eight magazines, and read them all, too." I was now prepared to have her tell me that she had established a public library in her neighborhood, that it had been endowed by Mr. Carnegie, and so on; but at this point the subject changed to shopping—how did she manage to buy the clothes for herself and family?

"Well," she said, "I can't go shopping like other women. So when my catalogue comes from a mail-order store, I say to my husband, 'Let's go to Chicago to-night and buy all our winter clothes.' So we sit down together and make out a list from that catalogue of all sorts of wearing apparel, from the baby's stockings to overalls for the boys; and we haven't paid a single cent for car-fare, either. We frequently order a hundred dollars' worth at a time, as there is economy in buying all we can in that way rather than paying twice as much for the same things in the near-by stores."

The children by this time were beginning to wake up. The wee baby squirmed a little, as if he didn't like his bonnet; the fourteen-months infant sat upright with a smile and his mouth put up for a kiss, while the older boys were putting on coats and straightening out neckties— and there it was nearly two o'clock in the morning, and not a murmur or a whimper out of one of them. "I am glad," she said, "that they have waked up, as it will be so much easier changing cars while they are awake than to take them up from a sound sleep."

"But how can you manage, with all your bags, to get these children out from one train into another?"

"Oh, I'll get along some way," she said, and while I helped with the putting on of coats and hats, she was giving to each child his special part of the programme. As the train moved more and more slowly, the children were getting into line, and when at last the cars came to a standstill, all were ready to move, and it was in this fashion that they passed from my vision: My Lady, with the new baby in arms, carried the telescope bag with the other hand; the oldest boy carried in his arms the last year's baby of fourteen months; the eight-year-old boy led by the hand the one who was three years; and that three-year-old—nothing but a baby himself—actually tugged off the bundle of pillows and blankets, being encouraged by his mother, who said, "He thinks he's a little man." I followed in the rear with the lunch-basket, and saw them handed down the steps, one by one, and they went out into the darkness which enveloped them.

I returned to my seat in the car, which now seemed so lonely, and the sleep that had been kept in abeyance for so many hours now came in broken naps. With every turn in the seat and with every twist of my neck to make myself more comfortable, I had visions of a procession of children—but the children of my dreams had been transformed into angels whose wings were spread. And often have I seen them since in my day-dreams—My Lady of the Rocky Mountains and her little army of boys.

# SOME LIBRARY STORIES

## BY A LIBRARIAN

THE changes from old to new in the matter of library administration and the distribution of books have been so rapid as to seem like the growth of a night. The day when libraries guarded their treasures in what Mr. Koopman has called "book jails" and prided themselves on never buying two copies of a volume, and the modern era when wonderful buildings and duplicates to the number of hundreds are available make one dizzy with contrast. The great city library was often a reference library only. The country library was opened for half a day each week, or, as in one village, Thursday night after prayer-meeting one could "draw books." This premium upon church-going one youthful lover of Mayne Reid and Oliver Optic remembers availing herself of gladly. And old ideas die hard. Even now the arduous duties of the librarian are considered by the thoughtless properly fulfilled by any one with feet to carry him to the shelves and hands to give out books. In a New England State, and not long ago, lived a little lady who combined the occupations of librarian and sempstress and who complained that it "took so much" of her time to cut the edges of the ragged books the publishers were careless enough to leave."

The humble class of people who in these days come to a library and the queer things they do are naturally little known outside, but the librarian's sense of humor is often tickled and his sympathies awakened. Some of the actual experiences of one worker within a short space of time may be of interest and indicate the necessity for education, sympathy, tact, and skill in this profession.

It is always astonishing to find that people know so little of authors, even as to names, and in our library, where the books are open to all, we used to congratulate ourselves that such safe and readable writers as Mrs. Alexander and Mrs. Barr stand on the front shelves. And somehow one never gets used to the old sailor who will read nothing but the quietest home love story, and the motherly personage known in our country districts as a "monthly nurse," who dotes upon the detective story.

To be sure, there are those who know a little of certain novelists. One reader is a great admirer of Crockett, but surprised us by saying that she wanted the "Stickit Minister's Wooing," as she supposed it was a sequel to the "Minister's Wooing." An old lady slammed down one of George Meredith's brilliant volumes with the exclamation, "There ain't one word of sense in that from cover to cover!" Old Garrity is well named, for a most garrulous soul is he, expecting to talk by the half-hour about what he has brought back to the desk and what he wants to take away. He is perpetually begging for something about Ireland, and we had exhausted our slender store. He had been highly pleased with Walter Besant's "Fifty Years Ago," because, as he truculently remarked, "Daniel O'Connell was the greatest man that ever lived, and Mr. Walter Bee-sant gives him high praise." Finally, I was driven to tell Garrity that I had no more distinctively Irish history, but that much of Ireland appears in English history, and as a happy compromise I offered him the "History of Our Own Times," by his countryman, Mr. Justin McCarthy. What was my disappointment to have this happy suggestion received with an indignant sniff. "Huh!" replied the old man, "I never did think much of thim McCarthys. They're about the meanest set of folks ever I came acrost." Whereupon, all too late, it flashed upon me that there is almost a blood-feud in that part of our town known as Dublin between the race of Garrity and McCarthy.

A young woman came mincing in one day, and, with that peculiar note we all recognize as the silly voice, proceeded to put me through an examination. "Got any books by Charlotte Braeme?" "No." "Laura Jean Libbey?" "No," somewhat stiffly. "Georgie Sheldon?" "No," with marked stiffness by this time. "Oh, dear, ain't you? Well, I s'pose you got some o' Mr. Shakespeare's works. I think they're elegant. I've read 'em three times."

Happening to meet a distinguished college professor whose specialty is literature, I told him this story, whereupon he commented that it illustrated the universality of Shakespeare. This had not struck me. I had thought it illustrated the universality of the father of lies. It never occurred to me that the girl was telling the truth, but perhaps this is the difference between the outlook of the college professor and of the librarian.

To me appeared one morning a little old woman with white hair, cut very short, and a bonnet of the sort which closely resembles an inverted tin pan. Shabby black ribbons held this under her chin. Her calico dress was clean but faded, and on her arm hung a big brown covered basket of the antiquated shape that we associate with the belongings of our grandmothers. She had kept a book over time, and had been notified by card. She approached the desk with a manner nicely compounded of grievance and bravado, as she advanced, saying, "I couldn't help it; I was sick—I couldn't help it—I finished it soon's I could."

I replied gently that I was sorry, but the fine was only four cents, whereupon the statement was reiterated with this addition, "I can't hear, I'm very deef." I tried again, much louder, but it was no use. I then had recourse to paper and pencil, writing the words I had just spoken. The woman's eyes fell upon the screed for a second, when she hastily remarked, "I can't read it. My eyes are weak. Can't I please have another book? Please, can't I? I finished it soon's I could."

I meekly assented, and the borrower turned, with great deliberation and apparently perfect eyesight, to the shelves to select her book. Meanwhile I had written, "We will let the fine go this time, but please be more careful in

5

future." Madam Innocent read this promptly and shamelessly, with no explanation of her suddenly recovered eyesight, and trotted out with "Elsie Dinsmore" safely reposing in her brown basket.

A pretty young widow, who asked with such manifest embarrassment for some sort of book that should tell how to write a letter, I longed to direct to Samivel Weller, or, better yet, to answer in a friendly way, "Tell me all about him; I'll help you write the letter."

Fortunately for our young assistants, who really cannot read everything, there seems to be a sort of second sense developed which makes them discover the sort of book that will please certain classes of people. For sooner or later almost everybody comes to the desk for advice.

The librarian in a small city or a country town may be a person of importance, and then, besides being considered responsible for everything that goes on in the library, and every book that is or is not there, he is often considered responsible for a good deal that goes on outside of it.

A shabby man met the president of our library, and fervently remarked: "You don't know how much good the library is doing; why, it is better than the police."

I have spoken of having once considered Mrs. Barr, as a writer, "safe." But my faith in this regard was shaken. An elderly woman, an entire stranger to me till she came to the library, seemed lonely, and I had taken especial pains to serve her. One day I received the following penciled letter from her: "You have almost broken my heart by sending such a dreadful book for my husband to read aloud. Not one word in it is really applicable to me, but you must have intended it so or you would not have sent it"—and so on for several pages. Imagine my consternation till I found the book to be the apparently innocent "Paul and Christina." After such an experience one can picture the poor librarian being held responsible by a wild mother because her son had become a gambler from reading Bulwer's "Money," or a skeptic from reading

"Robert Elsmere," and so on through the gamut of brother-keeping.

And then there is always with us the burning question as to the morality of the books chosen. Once I was soundly berated for the wickedness of a certain volume, and then asked, without a quiver, for another story by the same author.

To the breathless school-boy who demanded the "Fool's Dictionary," I was tempted to reply that I had often longed for such a compilation; but by patient questioning I found that he wanted "Poole's Index."

A young fellow innocently inquired for "Pilgrim's Progress" that he might learn something about the Pilgrim Fathers. You may say that this shows the folly of a little learning; but this was an Italian, and it was something that he should know that there are such historical characters as the Pilgrim Fathers, and that there is such a book as "Pilgrim's Progress."

Indeed, one may well feel that the generation now growing up, and accustomed to the use of books in our libraries, will show a marked difference in education from past generations. The boys and girls develop a readiness to assimilate the sort of knowledge they find there which is often surprising, and their air of pride and ownership is interesting and amusing.

# TWO ENGLISH POETS[1]

POETRY, like the Bible, has been officially declared extinct so many times that many people have been hypnotized into the belief that the race has really lost its soul in exchange for various tangible commodities, and that the appearance of Mephistopheles to claim the forfeit under the bond is only a matter of time. Meanwhile volumes of verse appear from time to time which seem to indicate that the imagination has not entirely gone into trade, and that the children of song still play in the great modern workshop. Two poets have recently appeared in England whose work is highly encouraging to those who believe that men still keep the gift of song in spite of this preoccupation.

The slender volume of "Poems" by Mr. Noyes has those qualities which promise fresh contact with the materials of which poetry is made, and not a vain repetition of old moods and a skillful resetting of well-worn motives. He is, to begin with, a singer and not a thinly disguised philosopher or a reformer who has possessed himself of a musical instrument. He has a voice of compass and sweetness, and his tones flow clear and sweet, with the courage of a real talent and the richness of a full nature. It is less than a decade since Mr. Noyes was rowing in the Exeter eight at Oxford, and he has just passed his twenty-sixth birthday. He has, therefore, the great gift of youth, and he has not wasted it. He was a contributor to several English periodicals of high rank—the Spectator, the Bookman, the London Outlook, the Speaker—before his name appeared on the title-page of a book; five small volumes now stand to his credit—"The Loom of Years," "The Flower of Old Japan," "Poems," "The Forest of Wild Thyme," and "Drake, an English Epic;" the present volume contains representative selections from this work, with a number of pieces that now appear for the first time.

Mr. Noyes shows thorough knowledge of verse forms and captivating ease in their use. He has both the spontaneity and the opulence of imagery and diction of the poet in whose making nature has had a liberal share. "The Passing of Summer," upon which the reader comes as soon as he opens this volume, brings that sense of richness which still awaits one when he takes down Keats and lets the book fall open at random. Such verses as these stand in no need of gloss or comment:

" Tell us no more of Autumn, the slow gold
      Of fruitage ripening in a world's decay,

[1] *Poems.* By Alfred Noyes. The Macmillan Company, New York.
*The Worker and Other Poems.* By Coningsby William Dawson. The Macmillan Company, New York.

The falling leaves, the moist rich breath
Of woodlands crumbling through a gorgeous
   death
     To glut the cancerous mould !
Give us the flash and scent of keen-edged
   may
Where wastes that bear no harvest yield
   their bloom,
Rude crofts of flowering nettle, bents of
   yellow broom.

The wild thyme on the mountain's knees
Unrolls its purple market to the bees !
   Unharvested of men
   The Traveler's Joy can only smile and die !
Joy, joy alone the throbbing white-throats
   bring,
Joy to themselves and heaven ; they were but
   born to sing.

What though the throstle pours his heart
   away,
A happy spendthrift of uncounted gold,
Swinging upon the blossomed briar
With soft throat lifted in a wild desire
   To make the world his may,
   E'er the pageant through the Gates is rolled
Further away ; in vain the rich notes throng
Flooding the mellow noon with rapturous
   waves of song.

The feathery meadows, like a lilac sea,
Knee-deep, with honeyed clover red and
   white,
Roll billowing ; the crisp clouds pass,
Trailing their soft blue shadows o'er the
   grass ;
   The sky-lark, mad with glee,
Quivers, up, up, to lose himself in light ;
And, through the forest, like a fairy dream
Through some dark mind, the ferns in branch-
   ing beauty stream."

The *abandon*, flowing music, and rich
color of these lines attest the signature
of a true poet with the great gift of joy
in his keeping. It is as a singer that
Mr. Noyes is presented in this selection,
and his lyric quality and charm pervade
the volume and harmonize with such lines
as these from " Haunted in Old Japan :"

" *All along the purple creek lit with silver*
   *foam,*
*Silent, silent voices, cry no more of home ;*
*Soft beyond the cherry-trees o'er the dim*
   *lagoon*
*Dawns the crimson lantern of the large,*
   *low moon.*

We that loved in April, we that turned away
Laughing, ere the wood-dove crooned across
   the May,
Watch the withered rose-leaves drift along
   the shore,
Wind among the roses, blow no more.

Lonely starry faces, wonderful and white,
Yearning with a cry across the dim sweet
   night,

All our dreams are blown adrift as flowers
   before a fan,
All our hearts are haunted in the heart of
   old Japan.".

Mr. Noyes has the heart of a child in
his free, spontaneous, joyous acceptance
of life and possession of the world ; but,
like every man of the childlike spirit,
so akin to genius and so often its companion, he has looked into the abysses
and. bears the burden of the mystery.
Such pieces as " A Night at St. Helena,"
" Christ Crucified," " De Profundis,"
" The Song of Re-Birth," must be read
in connection with his songs if his
compass is to be understood and the
measure of his talent taken. These
longer poems will not bear mutilation ;
they must be read in their entirety.
That Mr. Noyes is not afraid to touch
the old themes and that he touches them
with a firm and resourceful hand is evidenced by this " Song :"

" I came to the doors of the House of Love
   And knocked as the starry night went by ;
And my true love cried, ' Who knocks ?' and
   I said,
   ' It is I.'

And Love looked down from a lattice above
   Where the roses were dry as the lips of the
   dead ;
' There is not room in the House of Love
   For you both,' he said.

I plucked a leaf from the porch and crept
   Away through a desert of scoffs and scorns
To a lonely place where I prayed and wept
   And wove me a crown of thorns.

I came once more to the House of Love
   And knocked, ah softly and wistfully,
And my true love cried, ' Who knocks ?' and
   I said,
   ' None now but thee.'

And the great doors opened wide apart
   And a voice rang out from a glory of light,
' Make room, make room for a faithful heart
   In the House of Love, to-night.' "

Mr. Dawson comes out of Oxford also,
but with a very different instrument in
his hand. He, too, is a lyric poet, but
his manner has more abruptness and
energy of phrase and his themes more
insistence. He sings as one under compulsion of present conditions, and his
song is more likely to arrest immediate
attention than Mr. Noyes's, though it is
doubtful if it will live so long in the
hearts of those who hear it. If the lines
entitled " Being a Poet " have any note

of autobiography, it is evident that Mr. Dawson takes his vocation seriously and will not stand with the " idle singers of an empty day."

In the initial poem which gives its title to the volume, " The Worker," Mr. Dawson sounds the distinctive notes of his verse: passionate sympathy with contemporaneous experiences and conditions, ardent feeling, and a forcible though sometimes unmusical expression. The picture of the workman in his soiled clothes, with grimed hands, bending over the body of the dead child and speaking out of the skepticism of a despairing moment, reveals the strength and the weakness of Mr. Dawson's work. His poetry is, so to speak, too close to the age in which it is written. For that reason it is likely to be heard, for it is the voice of the moment; for the same reason it is not likely to endure. It would be unjust to Mr. Dawson, however, to give the impression that he is simply a journalist in verse. He has moods of pure poetry, as the reader of " Anchored Wings," " The Orchard of Song," and " Singing to Flo " speedily discovers. The little volume, taken as a whole, is moving rather than convincing. It contains many things which, if read with insight and sympathy, would deeply stir the emotions of those who care for the sorrowful, the outcast, and the disinherited in our time; for Mr. Dawson, while in no sense an advocate, vividly personifies and experiences the sorrow of the world of to-day. A single selection, chosen as much for its brevity as for its quality, will bring out the characteristics of this interesting and significant volume of verse :

### AN OLD DESIRE

O to be as Christ was in happy Galilee,
To walk the world with healing and hands
     of charity,
To suffer with each cripple till our love
     should make him straight,
O to be as Christ was, and die without the
     gate.

If we had His compassion, what comfort we
     could make
For those in dread of dying upon some
     storm-tossed lake,
To walk, in spite of tempests, in the valleys
     of the sea,
And spend our strength for sinners in deeds
     of sympathy.

O to be as Christ was, to die upon a Cross
In some obscurest country, nor count our
     dying loss,
If only by our dangering one bondsman
     might be free,
And turn again from sighing to fields of
     Galilee.

## Comment on Current Books

**Besant's Mediæval London**    The great work long planned by Sir Walter Besant has been carried on since his death with intelligence and with thoroughness. The present volume is uniform with three previously published dealing respectively with London in the time of the Tudors, of the Stuarts, and in the eighteenth century, while it is the second of the two volumes in which mediæval London is described, the first having to do with the historical and social aspects of London in the Middle Ages. As we understand it, the text had been prepared by Sir Walter as it stands shortly before his death. Physically the volumes of this series are worthy and beautiful. The format is that of a quarto, the cover design is rich but not over-ornate in its red ground and gilt type, and the illustrations, which are numerous, have been gathered from ancient sources and early books with assiduity and fullness of knowledge. Everything pertaining to old London was a subject of delight and one may say of living interest to Sir Walter Besant. The importance of the special subject here treated, that of the ecclesiastical and religious life of London in the thirteenth and fourteenth centuries, can hardly be exaggerated, for through this side of life we reach directly and intimately the human traits, the impelling motives, and the degree of social cultivation that characterized Englishmen in the English capital at this time. As the author says: " If churches and religious houses make up religion, then London in the thirteenth and fourteenth centuries surely attained the highest point ever reached in religion." Here we see not only the abbeys, priories, nunneries, friaries, and churches themselves pictorially reproduced, but we have picturesque glimpses of the life of the " vast army of ecclesiastics from archbishop to Franciscan friar; hermits, anchorites, pardoners, limitours, somnours," and other church officers  We select a single passage for quotation, not only because it is significant in itself, but because it gives, we think, a fair idea of the broad and readable way in which this work treats what many might expect to prove a dry-as-dust, antiquarian record—words which precisely describe the exact contrary of the present volume:

No street but reminded the citizens, by the sight of a spire or a wall, that the Church was with him always, to rule his life and to shorten his period of purgatory, on the simple condition of his obedience. Religion endeavored to rule the whole of society; religion claimed to control the whole conduct of politics and practical economy; but the power of religion has never been equal to her ambition; religion could not put a stop to war, or to the violences and outrages of war. Had she been able to do so, the world would now be held and bound in chains and slavery. Yet it was well that there should be the Church to restrain men in some degree. She kept in her own hands, so far, all learning, all science, all the arts, all the professions. The forms, duties, and rules of the Church attended all men from infancy to the grave. At the bidding of the Church the whole nation, from the King downwards, renounced meat for a fourth part of the whole year. This fact alone marks the enormous power of the Church. For hundreds of years the Church preached respect for human life and self-restraint with more or less vigor, and with more or less success. Sometimes the Church has fallen upon evil times; her ecclesiastics have been ambitious, worldly, licentious, avaricious; but they have always been, as a whole, superior to the world around them. Thus it may be said that the Church might always have been better, but that the world was always worse.

(Mediæval London.  Vol. II. Ecclesiastical. By Sir Walter Besant.  The Macmillan Company, New York.  $7.50.)

*The Christian Ideal*  The central reality in the life of Jesus was his saturation with the thought of God, his God-filled consciousness, his entire subjection to the Spirit of God.  "The heart of Christianity" exhibited in this volume is just this heart of Jesus Christ.  The author writes in deep conviction of this, as one who aspires to realize it daily and fully.  Much of his work is a plain and simple argument with nominally Christian people who have no such aspiration, and are content with a low ideal of the life proposed in the Gospel to the follower of Christ.  It is just a heart-to-heart talk with such, as sane as it is simple, and convincing to the open mind that is conscious of obligation to a closer discipleship.  (The Heart of Christianity.  By Rev. T. S. Linscott, D.D., F.R.C.I.  The Bradley-Garretson Company, Philadelphia.  $1.50.)

*A Clergyman's Helpmeet*  In this "story of a pioneer in temperance work" many an American worker in the same line will greet a congenial spirit.  In 1858 Mrs. Wightman, then the young wife of the vicar of Shrewsbury, England, was moved by the wretchedness of drunkards in the parish to begin a movement for total abstinence.  Despite criticism and difficulty, she persevered with voice and pen, devoting the profits of her books to the enlargement of her work.  One of these, "Haste to the Rescue," brought many Anglican clergymen to adopt total abstinence, and promoted the organization of the Church of England Total Abstinence Society.  The Bishop of Shrewsbury in 1904 compared its influence in England to the influence of "Uncle Tom's Cabin" in America.  The distinctive trait of Mrs. Wightman's work till her death in 1898 was the deep and fervent religious spirit which was from first to last its spring and soul.  (Mrs. Wightman of Shrewsbury.  By the Rev. J. M. Fletcher, M.A.  Longmans, Green & Co., New York.  $1.50.)

*The Divine Reconciliation*  A new line of approach to a familiar theme, and a broader conception of the theme than the word usually conveys, give this book both freshness and interest.  "Atonement" (*at-one-ment*) is more than expiation, more than forgiveness; it is full reconciliation to the sovereignty of the Eternal Goodness, with faith in its quelling and quenching of all evil.  The testimony of the world's best literature from Homer to Tennyson is presented to show "that both poets and theologians have expressed—the former in the beauty of art, and the latter in the clear-cut statements of dogma—the same elemental principles," however crudely or imperfectly in various instances.  The usual conception of the divine atonement stops with the case of the individual sinner: it does not touch the larger problem of the evil he has wrought in others; complete atonement must ·somehow provide for this also.  "Not merely the eradication of personal sin, but the cure of cosmical evil, is included in a gospel of reconciliation."  And this is the actual Gospel, the actual atonement which "this indwelling God, whom, because most fully manifested to us by Jesus of Nazareth, we call the living Christ, is making . . . cleansing what has been stained, and making whole what has been severed," until all evil is overcome.  This gospel of reconciliation, witnessed to by the world's noblest literature, as well as by the Christian Scriptures, is also taught by the profoundest philosophy, as Professor Royce has shown (see "The World and the Individual," Volume II.).  At the basis of it is the fact that our life is not external to the life of God.  The distinction drawn between the historical work of Jesus and the eternal work of the immanent Spirit in the reconciling process is incidentally helpful, by its exhibition of identity and difference, toward the harmonizing of Trinitarian and Unitarian modes of thought, which other recent writers are helping on. The author of this fruitful improvement of current theology is minister of the First Congregational Church in Waterbury, Connecticut. (Atonement in Literature and Life. By Charles Allen Dinsmore. Houghton, Mifflin & Co., Boston. $1.50, net.)

*Faith and Freedom*    A large and difficult task is attempted in this volume of the Kerr Lectures, given last year in the Glasgow United Free College. It is a critical review of two centuries of debate upon the problem of Faith and Freedom, which arose in the Protestant Reformation. Luther built upon the postulated freedom of the Christian man. The Reformation, which emphasized the relation of this freedom to God, raised questions of its relation to society, civil and religious. Subsequent controversy tended to make it clear that freedom is the fundamental spiritual idea, and faith its necessary correlate. The progress of debate toward this conclusion, as it runs along in the works of more or less influential thinkers critically reviewed by the lecturer, forms the body of the volume. Jesuitism and Pascal's "Pensées," English Deism and Butler's Analogy, Rationalism and Kant on Pure Reason, Romanticism and Schleiermacher's Discourses on Religion, the French Revolution and Newman's "Apologia," the Development Theory and Baur's Church History, the Theory of Experience and Ritschlianism—each subject including the contribution of various parties to the debate—make up a conspectus of a highly diversified field. The main difficulty, as Dr. Oman remarks, is to fix upon the right point of view for an estimate of the net result, and to this Ritschl, so far as he follows Kant, is helpful. It is Kant whose fixing of the seat of authority within effected, as has been said, a Copernican revolution in philosophy, though he left a dualism between God and the world for his successes to eliminate—a dualism to which Dr. Oman seems needlessly reconciled. In summing up the controversy he finds its issue to be a vindication of the absoluteness both of faith and of freedom. The ideals and purposes of individuals have an absolute worth which societies and institutions cannot transcend. Only as we are free can absolute conviction come into any life. (The Problem of Faith and Freedom in the Last Two Centuries. By John Oman, M.A., B.D., D.Phil. A. C. Armstrong & Son, New York.)

*Historical Reprints*    This is the third volume in the valuable series of reprints now being issued under the general editorial supervision of Dr. J. Franklin Jameson, director of the department of historical research in the Carnegie Institution, the purpose being, in Dr. Jameson's words, to provide "a comprehensive and well-rounded collection of those classical narratives on which the early history of the United States is founded." The editor of the present volume, Rev. Dr. Burrage, has for the most part gathered his material from Hakluyt, the collection embracing, in addition to accounts of the voyages of Cartier and Drake, the Hore, Hawkins, Gilbert, Barlowe, Lane, Grenville, White, Brereton, Pring, and Popham relations. Thus the student is afforded an intelligent view of the first discovery and settlement of the Atlantic coast from Florida to Newfoundland, and will find his understanding of the quaint, old-time narratives greatly forwarded by the notes and introductions provided by Dr. Burrage. It seems a pity, however, that room was not found for the Ribaut, Laudonnière, and Le Moyne narratives, having to do with the early and ill-fated French settlements in Florida and South Carolina. Even though it is necessary to exercise the greatest critical caution in perusing these, they are undoubtedly valuable as well as exceedingly interesting, and are particularly valuable for the information they give with respect to the customs and manners of the Indians. (Original Narratives of Early American History: Early English and French Voyages. Edited by Henry S. Burrage, D.D. Charles Scribner's Sons, New York. $3, net.)

*The Journal of American History*    We have been attracted to the first number of the first volume of the new quarterly with this title, first, by its extremely pleasing and one may almost say sumptuous appearance, and, secondly, by the fact that a public service is rendered through such an undertaking. Its form has certain unusual features which are both interesting and ingenious. For instance, in this number there are printed in color reproductions of the first flag to float over American soil (the red cross of St. George, planted at Labrador by Cabot in 1497), the first flag to float over permanent settlements in America (the flag of the Mayflower in 1620), the flag of Cromwell and Charles Second, the first flag of Colonial Secession, the first flag of the American Republic, and the first flag of American Expansion (that to which two new stars were added in 1795 for the first new States). The flag as it is to-day is furnished also separately, very prettily made in silk, with instructions as to where it should be placed in the book. The magazine contains a large number of articles; too large, in fact, to make mention of the individual articles desirable further than to say that, besides strictly historical subjects and portraits, there are included papers relating to the Lee centenary and the Longfellow centenary, and pictures and poems about pioneer life in America, country life in America, and old-time book-lovers. The quarterly comes to us from the Associated Publishers of American Records, and is printed at New Haven, Connecticut.

*The Lamp of Sacrifice*   The author of this volume of discourses on special occasions is widely known as the editor of a great religious journal, the British Weekly. He has acquired distinction in literary work and as an expositor of the Scriptures. The pen of a ready and vigorous writer is easily recognizable in his pages. Equally so is an intensely evangelical spirit. Dr. Nicoll is more strongly attached to older modes of theological thought than literary men in general. He is indisputably right, however, in holding that many representatives of Christianity fail to measure up to the Old Testament type of religion found in the Psalms. It is an aggressive, militant religion that he stands for, declaring that it is "the first duty of many Christians to make their homes among the poor, and until this duty is more generally fulfilled progress will lag." Such utterances give significance to the title of this volume. (The Lamp of Sacrifice. By W. Robertson Nicoll. A. C. Armstrong & Son, New York.)

*A Mediæval Saint*   One of the earliest and closest companions of St. Francis of Assisi, who used to call him "The Knight of our Round Table," was Brother Aegidius, better known to English readers by his Anglicized name, Giles. An uncultured man, but full of shrewd common sense, touched both with humor and imagination, he was pre-eminently an embodiment of the genuine Franciscan spirit of piety and humanity. The present volume treasures his "Golden Sayings," held in highest esteem by the Roman Catholic Church, and introduces them by a brief sketch of his life. It is well worth reading and reflection by Protestant Christians, often too content with discarding the ascetic form of mediæval saintliness, and too neglectful to replace it by a form of piety as impressive on the present age as that was on the past. (The Golden Sayings of the Blessed Brother Giles of Assisi. By Rev. Fr. Paschal Robinson. The Dolphin Press, Philadelphia. $1. Postage, 6c.)

*Science and Theology*   In this volume an eminent German divine, recently a Court chaplain, addresses persons reared in Christian faith, whom the exaggerated pretensions of certain scientists have on one side drawn to suspect Christianity, and on the other side to suspect science. He reasons with them to show that they are alike mistaken; that the alleged warfare of science on religion does not occur within the proper domain of science, but only in the field of philosophy—which is certainly true. Taking up successively the subjects of Creation, Providence, Prayer, Miracles, and the Person of Jesus Christ, he argues that science and religion nowhere collide, and that the Christian view is entirely compatible with all proper claims of science, to which he makes large concessions. His theology is generally of a liberal evangelical type, though his brief reference to the heavenly "intercession" of Christ is cast in the archaic form. Philosophically he views "monists" as all of them Haeckelites—a strange misrepresentation. On the whole, it is a useful book to credit to a country which has sent us too much of the contrary kind. (The Scientific Creed of a Theologian. By Rudolf Schmid, D.D. Translated by J. W. Stoughton, B.A. A. C. Armstrong & Son, New York. $1.50, net.)

*Stories of Plot and Adventure*   No man in our generation has written of adventure in a wider and truer sense than Mr. Stewart Edward White; for, as distinctly and powerfully as any other writer, he has made readers feel the terror and mystery of the Far North. For his best work Mr. White needs a big background of forest or of open country. In his latest story, "The Mystery" (McClure, Phillips & Co., New York, $1.50), written in collaboration with Mr. Samuel H. Adams, he takes to the sea and carries his readers through adventures which, for novelty, breathless suspense, and blood-curdling audacity, must be ranked with the most astonishing tales of the kind. The story of the professor who ships on a beautiful schooner from San Francisco in search of a far island where he can carry on experiments with the most powerful destructives is told from beginning to end without stopping for breath, so to speak. Adventure succeeds adventure; climax follows on the heels of climax; catastrophe overtops catastrophe. In a certain way it is very well done; but it is a tour-de-force, not a piece of real writing; much better than most books of its kind, but not so good by any means as Mr. White can do when he writes of the things he knows under the compulsion of genuine and vital interest. "The Malefactor" is a frankly sensational story with little pretense to literary art but constructed with all that skill in development of plot and exciting interest of which the author, Mr. E. Phillips Oppenheim, is an acknowledged master. In its way this story is a modern variant of the Monte Cristo motive. The hero, if he may be so called, emerges from prison with a secret which enables him to make millions and with a firm intent to avenge himself on those whose wickedness has exposed him to unjust suffering for ten years. He trains himself not to exhibit the slightest emotion, sentiment, or kindliness. How he deals with his enemies and what part he takes in life itself are questions worked out very cleverly and in such a way that it would be quite unfair to the prospective reader to forestall the author's narrative. (Little, Brown & Co., Boston. $1.50.) Still a third book of this general class is Mr. H. Marriott Watson's "The Privateers" (Doubleday, Page & Co., New York, $1.50). This is a crude piece of preposterous sensationalism, quite unworthy the author of "Galloping Dick." It has action in excess, but no real imagination, while the supposed American speculators (their war to gain the hand of an English girl, who is, unknown to herself, an heiress, furnishes the object of plot and counterplot) are like nothing in nature.

# Letters to The Outlook

## PRIVATE RIGHTS IN NIAGARA FALLS

With your kind permission I would like to correct a misapprehension on the part of the writer of the considerate summary of Secretary Taft's Niagara Falls decision in your issue of this date.

With some apparent reason the writer has assumed that the Committee of Experts named by the Secretary is "to advise him what changes can be made by the Niagara Falls Power Company" to relieve the lower Niagara gorge of certain offensive aspects on the American side. This is not so. The Niagara Falls Power Company is not in any way responsible for the objectionable conditions, nor is it held to be so by Secretary Taft. This will be seen upon a more careful reading of his decision.

On the contrary, it has been recognized and acknowledged by all familiar with the facts, notably at the public hearing, by Professor John M. Clarke, State Geologist, speaking for the preservation of the Falls (and also by Secretary Taft in his decision), that the Niagara Falls Power Company was and is entitled to credit for the character and the conduct of its works and their setting. This pioneer company has spared neither pains nor expense to give to its works a noble and dignified aspect, which has been the subject of general recognition and commendation.

At all times since its organization in 1886 this company has been equally anxious to avoid impairment of the scenic grandeur of the Falls. At the hearings, and everywhere, without dissent, it has been conceded that neither the operations of this company nor of its subsidiary, the Canadian Niagara Company, would have appreciable effect upon the flow either of the American Falls or of the Canadian Falls. Any detrimental effect would be due to installations and operations begun after, and independently of, those of the Niagara Falls Power Company.

Whether your writer is justified in his conclusion that the work has been stopped without "doing injustice to the power companies" is matter for discussion if not for denial.

In the *uncompensated* destruction of the riparian and statutory rights of the Niagara Falls Power Company, the Congressional action has inflicted a tremendous injury, which between private persons would be deemed an injustice. Perhaps it is to be included as the latest of what were called by Ouida "the immoralities of the law"—spoliations which estimable citizens would justify for the public, though never for themselves. Doesn't that seem like an insinuation that, in support of supposed public interests, ardent advocates are in danger, as sometimes corporate agents are supposed to be, of failing to regard the rights of others?

In this particular case the only Constitutional warrant for Congressional action must be sought in the grant "to regulate commerce with foreign nations and among the several States." Therefore the Burton Act has been made to rest upon the pretended purpose that it is to preserve the navigability of Niagara Falls, and the quality of the Niagara River as a boundary! Of course this pretended purpose is a sham, as much so as any of the shifty devices sometimes imputed to the trust-makers. Naturally enough, the promoters of the Burton Bill felt no confidence in the power of the Congress to enact a law which, if entitled truthfully, would have been exclusively "An Act to preserve the scenic grandeur of Niagara Falls." This title would have expressed every purpose really intended or desired by the framers of the bill; it would have been also the epitaph of the bill, for the Federal Congress cannot legislate merely to protect scenery within the boundaries of a State.

Thus it results that a sham, perhaps too opaque for judicial scrutiny, but nevertheless a sham, is the sole authority for this attempted impairment of rights of the Niagara Falls Power Company. However, it does not also result that the company must acquiesce in the conclusion expressed by your writer that no injustice has been done to the company. Its devastated rights rest upon foundations which can be shaken only by a force which may shatter also the upper and nether millstones of countless owners of mill rights throughout the country. It would be a mistake to assume that the property of the Niagara Falls Power Company was received by gift from the State of New York, or that it lacks the guarantees of ownership attaching to water rights generally. The water rights of the Niagara Falls Power Company were and are those belonging to it as owner of twelve hundred acres of upland and nearly three miles of water front of the Niagara River. These rights and this property were acquired, not from the State, but from private owners, and were paid for and are held like any other private property. The State of New York by statute recognized and limited these rights of the company, but granted to it no property whatever.

The mere fact of Federal legislation has detracted seriously from the value of these rights; but that they can be impaired without compensation either by Federal legislation or Federal treaty is denied by constitutional lawyers of high repute.

I would not be understood as disputing the right of the United States to limit the importation of power from Canada, or the right to take the power plants on the American side for public use, upon making compensation therefor, just as is usual whenever private property is taken for a public park. The expense would be considerable, but this should not be avoided by spoliation. Indeed, I am not certain that in the promising development of storage batteries the accumulation of power during the hours of darkness would not repay the Government for its cost of expropriation.

                FRANCIS LYNDE STETSON.

[See editorial comment on another page.— THE EDITORS.]

## CENTRALIZED DEMOCRACY

It may or may not be true that what The Outlook of January 26 calls a " Centralized Democracy " is the true way out of our present difficulties regarding some great social problems. It is possible that there is no danger of a monarchy in our present tendencies, though both of these points are open at least to argument. But a grave question underlies the discussion. Granting that the end may be a good one, and conceding that the motive for seeking it is the best, we still must ask ourselves, What of the means by which we are reaching out towards the end? Are these thoroughly good and just?

This, the second in the trinity of the elements of all moral questions, and one of the greatest importance, The Outlook does not seem to consider. The implication in the minds of many readers who do not stop to think on the subject will probably be that the means used to reach the end are entirely justifiable.

But suppose we are to be made into a " Centralized Democracy." How shall it be done? Shall we reconstruct our Constitution in the prescribed way, by formal amendment? Or shall we make it over by successive acts of Congress, the decisions of the Judiciary, and the action of the Executive? That, to many, seems to be the real political question before us.

But if we take this latter method, what will be the moral effect of it? Can we treat our Constitution, which we have held to be radically unlike the British Constitution, as that is treated, and amend it from time to time by a simple act of Congress? Or can we do it by straining its language so as to make it mean anything that will suit our purpose, without undermining the foundations of intellectual and moral honesty? It may be that our system of government, resting on the provisions of what Mr. Bryce call a rigid as opposed to what he calls a flexible constitution, is all a mistake. But even then we must, as an honest people, get back to the flexible in an honest and safe way. If we gain mere political efficiency at the cost of intellectual and moral integrity, we all see, or should see, that in the end we have lost our soul. In short, is there not a moral issue underneath the whole question that we must face in the clearest manner? And are we not in great danger of obscuring this moral issue in our eagerness to attain a desirable object? This seems, to at least one of your readers, the most important of all the questions to be asked and answered in our discussions of the way out of present difficulties. Mark Twain and the North American Review apparently fear that the moral conditions created by the attainment of a Centralized Democracy are the very ones which make a monarchy possible.

On the political question of the centralization of our democracy a great deal, of course, can and should be said. The proper

adjustment of the powers of the municipality, the State, and the National Government to the best advantage, forms a living issue at all times in a society that is growing, as all societies must grow while they live. Let us not ignore that problem by any means. But let us, above all other things, keep in mind the need of so doing our political work as to keep true to the great underlying regard for the fundamentals of political and social morality.    SAMUEL W. DIKE.
Auburndale, Massachusetts.

[The changes now going on under a liberal construction of the Constitution are not greater than those accomplished under Chief Justice Marshall in the last century.—THE EDITORS.]

## THE CORPORATIONS AND THE PEOPLE

In your issue of January 12 Judge Grosscup seeks a remedy for the evils resulting from the corporation form of proprietorship in the business world. A remedy presupposes a disease. It seems to me that the Judge follows rather closely those who assert, or imply in their assertions, that there is something *per se* vicious in a corporation, or, at any rate, that because some corporations are viciously conducted all corporations are vicious. It is a mere commonplace to say that the difference between a corporation and a partnership is not nearly so great as Mr. Bryan, for example, would have the voter believe. In view of what follows I may be pardoned for illustrating: A, B, C, and D own respectively one-half, one-fourth, one-fifth, and one-twentieth interests in a manufacturing concern. So long as they conduct their business as a partnership the interest of each member of the firm cannot be transferred without much inconvenience. They form a corporation with capital stock of, say, $20,000, and the partners receive, respectively, certificates for $10,000, $5,000, $4,000, and $1,000. Now a single signature will transfer an interest. Of course I do not wish to be understood as stating that this is the only advantage which can be gained by the individuals in the transaction. Furthermore, I would emphasize the fact that because the State has been asked to step in and create a new legal body, it has the undoubted right—and it is its duty—to prescribe and enforce the conditions under which it will grant our partners the privilege of becoming a corporation.

I am not, therefore, differing with Judge Grosscup in so far as he suggests the adoption in the United States of certain principles which have accomplished satisfactory results

in restricting the formation of corporations in Germany. I simply raise this question: Has not the distinguished Judge diagnosed the disease as more prevalent and more virulent than it is?

He says, " The clerk in the mercantile establishment no longer looks forward to an individual career—he is the employee of a great corporation." Individual careers in business and labor have become almost obsolete. " The salesman looking forward to ownership is no more." " There are now no proprietor artisans, no expectant apprentices." These are astounding statements. If the Judge has correctly gauged the breadth of his premises in reaching such tremendous conclusions, then we are certainly mortally sick as a nation, too far gone for any medicines to do good. What are the facts? Certain immense combinations have been formed which are grouped under the unmeaning term " trusts." In a very few lines of manufacture such combinations have been able largely to influence, possibly even control, both the price of the raw material which they use and the price of that which they produce. It is to be noted, however, that such combinations operate, *i. e.*, *manufacture*, in only a very limited number of cities. At such points the conditions mentioned by Judge Grosscup obtain in large measure. Enormous department stores have sprung up which, because of their large capital, economies in operation, and able management, undersell and often drive out of business the small merchant. But such establishments can operate only in the largest cities, and even there by no manner of means monopolize retail business. What about the thousands of smaller American cities, country towns, and villages? I live in a city of 35,000 population. There are many corporations there, but they are all such as I have described above, owned locally—with the exception of the public utility corporations—and certainly they are innocent. There is not a contracting carpenter who employs more than twenty-five or thirty men. There is no blacksmith shop where more than half a dozen men are at work—in every case the proprietor being one of these. Of the several machine and repair shops, one is owned locally by a corporation in which the superintendent, who has risen from the ranks, is a stockholder, the others by firms or individuals, and so on through the whole list of business enterprises. Any carpenter, blacksmith, bricklayer, machinist, who has the worth to rise above his fellows may establish an independent business to-day with no more limitations upon him than there were forty years ago. WHY NOT? The mere fact that a butcher in a smaller city—or any other—buys his beef, the blacksmith his steel, the implement dealer his harvesters, from the several trusts which are popularly supposed to control the manufacture of such products does not limit the opportunity of these men to enter upon individual careers. Until some one can point out to me some method by which the steel trust or any other trust can and does paralyze individual thrift, restrain ambition among men outside of its immediate sphere of action and not in its employ, I must believe that Judge Grosscup has not only overstated facts in the larger cities, which probably gave him the basis for his generalizations, but has almost entirely misunderstood conditions in the business world—by far the larger business world—elsewhere.

I simply do not understand how the statement can be gravely made that "in the new industrial life, though the savings have largely increased, the people invest *for themselves* little if any of their savings." Such may be the case to a limited degree in trust-controlled cities (if any such there are), but if there is anything these terrible trusts or Chicago department stores can do to prevent a man in the city where I live, or in any like city, from investing his savings, or discourage him from so investing, in the stocks of a considerable number of trading corporations, in a shop of any sort which suits his fancy, in a home, in anything that his father invested in, then I can only say that to discover this condition is far beyond the power of the average mind.

HENRY N. MORRIS.

### AN IMPRESSIVE LESSON

During the past week there has been on trial in St. Louis a young man who was, until recently, receiving teller in the United States Sub-Treasury. He was accused of embezzling $61,500, and was acquitted of the charge. Of that charge and acquittal this communication has nothing to say, only to call attention to several interesting and significant facts developed during the trial. First, the peculiar manner of handling Government funds. Employees of the Sub-Treasury had made a practice of taking out Government funds when in need of money, and giving a memorandum slip, called a "yellow," to balance the account. The Sub-Treasurer drew money against his salary "time and time again." There was no lock on the door of the teller's cage and no guard on the window outside. Other employees often went into the teller's cage, even when the teller himself was not there. Upon a recent occasion he had paid out $20,000 too much in a single

transaction with one of the city banks—that of redeeming mutilated currency. He had paid $10,000 too little to another bank, and $18,000 too much to the third teller in the Sub-Treasury. These errors were discovered and rectified later.

Second, the conduct of the defendant after he "discovered" his shortage. He deliberately undertook to conceal the shortage for an indefinite period, his excuse being that he thought the money would turn up somehow or somewhere ; he did not tell his superiors about it or notify the banks, as he had done at once in previous cases of shortage ; he covered up the shortage by a false entry in the gold certificate account, because the money would not be so easily missed among bills of large denomination ; he got the money from his friend, the paying teller, when he found that the chief clerk was going to check him up, and returned it to the latter's cage when he was absent. This return of the money was noted by the chief clerk, who checked him up again, and thus discovered the shortage. Although it would seem that every man who is in a position of trust is bound to give a reasonable accounting of the funds intrusted to him, the defendant only said, " I do not know ; I cannot say where it went." Inasmuch as he has been acquitted, the loss falls upon the Sub-Treasurer ; therefore a bill will be introduced in Congress asking for the relief of him and his bondsmen. If this passes, the public will foot the bill.

Third, the private life of the defendant and some of his associates. After investigating the defendant's habits, the chief of the secret service reported that he had been for a long time in the custom of visiting certain resorts, buying wine and spending more money than his annual salary of $1,800 justified. The defendant replied, " I didn't spend more than I got. I am one of those fellows who can make more noise with a five-dollar bill than others do with twenty dollars. We fellows in the Sub-Treasury always appear to have lots of money, and I'll tell you how it is. When I wanted money, I took it from my cash and put in a 'yellow' which I could take up when I returned the money or when pay-day came. I am pretty well known around town, and you know how it goes. Some one says, 'Come, let's have a drink,' and then it's all off." It developed that he and the paying teller, who so kindly loaned him the $61,500 when he was to be checked up, were in the habit of " having a lunch together, then drinks at several places, then hiring a carriage and 'going down the line,'" not being able to remember the particular houses they visited, however. The judge remarked at this point, " I don't think this evidence of the defendant going down the line, as you call it, is competent unless the Government shows extravagant expenditure. *Hundreds of men do the same thing every day.*"

The above facts are simply a few bald statements from a mass of similar evidence, and the sole purpose of presenting them here is to afford your readers a brief glance, though a most unpleasant one, of the loose business principles and lax morals of " hundreds of men," of their total failure to realize the obligation every man owes to his fellows, the obligation to be honest, decent, and manly. These facts might well provide the text to a thousand preachers, teachers, and parents for a practical sermon on clean living.

SAMUEL M. COULTER,
(Professor of Botany, Washington University.)

St. Louis, Missouri.

### ANOTHER CAUSE OF ' RAILWAY WRECKS

The American Juggernaut rolls on, the pall of news of awful railway wrecks continues, the trail of gore both widens and lengthens, no adequate excuse or reason is given for the grievous wrong, and the gruesome surfeit grows rather than lessens. As a railway traveler I have crossed the continent from ocean to ocean, and from the Assiniboine in the north to the Gulf and the Rio Grande in the south. I have been in wrecks, and helped carry away the dead and care for the injured. I am " kid " enough to want to jump off at every stop and see things, and know pretty well what is going on in railroading. I am pleased to count among my warmest friends railway superintendents, managers, and train-despatchers; I am not unfamiliar with the heroes of the cab and the caboose, and I know many of the trials of the section boss and his men, and have a large sympathy for all.

My profession and work are those of a physician and pharmacist, and have been so for a third of a century. Travel is my enjoyment and diversion, my recreation. I can endure the mal-odor of the smoker, but I prefer the purer air of the platform if need be. I am not prejudiced against the habitual smoker, and recognize his right. From what I know of the infirmities of humanity and have observed of their deviations from norm, I am persuaded that if tobacco was eliminated by those who manage railways and trains, greater precision and safety would be attained, the human factor of error and frailty would

cease to a great extent, and **fewer wrecks** result and fewer lives and limbs **be sacrifi** Every treatise on chemistry **and thera** tics, every botany and every **dictionary** well as every standard authority on the ject, classes tobacco among **narcotics** narcotic is a substance that puts **partl** wholly to sleep, that stupefies, **lessens** sense of responsibility, lures the **sub** ease, and makes him or her **indiff** duty. Let readers look up the words *t* and *narcotic;* see if an individual **under** influence of such a substance can be as apt, as responsive, as one who is free from its bane.

Science has measured the speed of transmission of nervous impulses in the normal individual, and their responses are known: what they are in the tobacco-stupefied has not been experimented on; but if railway managers will make this test among themselves and their employees as carefully as they do those for impaired vision and hearing, they will find that the tobacco habitue's quick responses are not at all comparable with those of the normal man.

The crowded mile-a-minute schedules of competing roads and of these hurry times demand that every man's faculties be at normal at least, and not depressed or debased by any drug habit; when this is so, man will be found superior to any block signal or any automaton.

The train-despatcher's office at the division end is usually as full of tobacco smoke as is the prairie grade crossing or switching station or the mountain hamlet's five by nine office, where the weary and lonesome occupant dwells amid a Stygian atmosphere of soft-coal smoke, kerosene oil, and oil of tobacco; the engineer takes the throttle while his system is saturated with his morning pipe or cigar; the conductor tosses his stub away ere he dons his blue and gold and takes his final order, his mind dazed with nicotine. The triumph of mechanical skill in the engine, the reliability of the roadbed, are not to blame; perfection here has attained its acme, it is believed. But man, their creator, benumbs himself, and as such is no longer master of time, space, or substance; stupefied with tobacco, he can conceive no initiative, has no resources in the presence of impending danger, is too slow to act in emergency, he cannot arouse his nicotine-paralyzed nerves quick enough to act in response to electric click or the rushing speed of a mile-a-minute " flyer," and pain and death and ruin follow, and the Associated Press again palls.          D. LICHTY,

Rockford, Illinois.

**Public Lands and Private Monopoly**

The President's special Message urging legislation for the preservation of mineral (including coal and oil), lumber, and grazing lands still belonging to the Government emphasizes the value of a plan for the distribution of public documents which The Outlook has often urged. If this Message could be obtained at any post-office by the payment of an insignificant sum, say five cents, for the cost of paper, presswork, and mailing, it would be read by thousands of American citizens who will now be dependent for their knowledge of it upon fragmentary reports in the daily papers, and it is reasonable to expect that those daily papers which are under capitalistic influence will give very fragmentary reports of this Message, or none at all. The President urges that the Government should retain ownership of all coal lands, with a system of leasing for the purposes of mine operation. There is nothing novel in this suggestion. "In all the great coal-producing European countries except Great Britain, coal is mined under government leases." There are special reasons why fuel resources should be kept under government control, but the principle involved applies to other land values.

Mineral fuels, like the forests and navigable streams, should be treated as public utilities. This is generally recognized abroad. In some foreign countries practical control of a large portion of the fuel resources was allowed years ago to pass into private hands, but the existing governments are endeavoring to regain this control in order that the diminishing fuel supply may be safeguarded for the common good instead of being disposed of for the benefit of the few—though the mistake of the preceding generation in disposing of these fuels for a nominal return cannot always be corrected by the present generation, as the cost may be so enormous as to be prohibitive.

The President states very fairly the objections to the policy which he proposes and effectively replies to them, and he summarizes the advantages of the policy in a compact paragraph. These include the preservation of fuels especially suitable for special industries, facilitating coal-mining for local markets by miners without large capital, prevention of monopolistic control, and protection of the people against unreasonable and discriminating charges for fuel supplies. These arguments apply equally to lumber and grazing lands. Perhaps, however, the strongest argument for his policy is that furnished by the fact that out of 2,300 cases of public land entries in four specified districts, in over half of them no compliance with the law was found, and in many cases deliberate fraud. The policy of giving away public land in small sections to bona-fide settlers for agricultural purposes has proved profitable to the Nation, but if the people could get an opportunity to vote on the question whether they would give away mineral lands, forest lands, and grazing lands to great corporations to be operated for private profit, the vote in favor of that policy would be so small that it would count as "scattering."

**The Japanese Question**

The conferences held last week between the President and representatives of Californian sentiment, and also doubtless between the Administration and leaders of Congress, resulted in what the press despatches called "a complete solution of the Japanese problem." The thing most desired by those Californians who have been disturbed on the subject is the prevention of the immigration into this country of Japanese coolies. Apparently these Californians are willing, if this end can be brought about, to deal with the school question in such a way that, while proper and desirable limitations may be placed on the control of the schools, these limitations shall not be based on purely racial ground nor be of a kind to give offense to Japanese national pride. The method determined upon to keep out Japanese coolie labor is not by means of treaty, but by legislation. The general immigration bill which has been long held back in conference in Congress has been pressed forward, with an amendment which authorizes the President to reject the passports issued by any foreign nation to its citizens to go to the insular possessions of the United States, or to the Panama Canal Zone, when, in the judgment of the President, such passports are being used by the holders to gain entrance to the United States proper to the detriment of labor conditions. The Senate on Saturday passed the bill as amended. It will be noted that this provision does not refer by name to the Japanese or to any other nation, and thus there is no discrimination which could be offensive to Japan. It is understood, also, that the Japanese Government is itself opposed to the emigration of its subjects to the United States, and has refused, and desires to continue to refuse, passports to its lower class of laborers to come to this continent, although it easily grants passports to Hawaii and to the Philippines. It is believed that under the amendment the President can entirely stop the practice now in effect under which Japanese laborers obtain passports to Hawaii, and, having thus gained access to American territory, come unchallenged to what may be called the continental territory of the United States. The question at once arises whether sufficient consideration has been given to the fact that Hawaii differs from the Philippines in that it is not merely an insular possession, but a Territory of the United States. This distinction has been positively laid down by the Supreme Court, and on the face of it there seems to be no difference between the passing of an alien subject from Hawaii to California, and the passing of an alien subject from the Indian Territory to Kansas, It would, of course,

be unconstitutional for the United States to prevent the passing of any of its own subjects from one part of American territory to another; but the decision of the United States Supreme Court that Congress has a right to exclude or expel absolutely all aliens or any class of aliens from the United States would seem necessarily to include a right to exclude them from any one part of the United States although admitting them to another part.

❋

*The Congo and the Senate*    On Friday of last week the Senate passed, in a modified form, the resolution concerning the Congo State introduced by Senator Lodge. The resolution in its final form is as follows:

*Whereas,* It is alleged that the native inhabitants of the basin of the Congo have been subjected to inhuman treatment of a character that should claim the attention and excite the compassion of the people of the United States; therefore, be it

*Resolved,* That the President is respectfully advised that, in case he shall find such allegations are established by proof, he will receive the cordial support of the Senate in any steps, not inconsistent with treaty or other international obligations or with the traditional American foreign policy which forbids participation by the United States in the settlement of political questions which are entirely European in their scope, he may deem it wise to take in co-operation with or in aid of any of the powers signatory of the Treaty of Berlin for the amelioration of the condition of such inhabitants.

Extreme caution is an obvious characteristic of this resolution. The inhuman treatment, which the Senate is not willing to accept as an established fact,' qualifying it by the phrase "it is alleged," has been thoroughly proven by a commission appointed by the King-Sovereign of the Congo himself. There is no need for further investigation. Though the worst has not been officially revealed, what has been officially revealed is sufficiently atrocious to warrant vigorous interference on the part of responsible Powers. Nevertheless, discreet understatement in a matter of this kind is much more weighty than violence of language, however closely corresponding to the facts. We hope that this resolution, pledging the Senate to the support of the President in any action not inconsistent with international obligations or with the policy of avoiding purely European disputes, will lead England and the other nations which created the Independent State of the Congo to take vigorous action. We hope that these Powers will not permit the remedy to leave their hands by letting the Congo State pass into the control of Belgium—at least not without definite action on their part. There appears to be no reason why the United States should not invite the Powers to a conference, exactly as President Roosevelt invited Japan and Russia to a conference in which the United States was not a participant. Whatever action is taken ought to be taken at once.

❀

**Shall the Tariff be Revised?** Last week Massachusetts spoke with no uncertain sound on the tariff. A petition was forwarded to President Roosevelt bearing the signatures of Governor Guild and of 222 out of the 280 members of the Legislature. The petition urges the immediate revision of the tariff. It indorses the principle recently approved by the Foreign Commerce Convention in Washington to create maximum and minimum tariff schedules to be applied without the intervention of treaties but otherwise following the general precedent of the reciprocity clause in the McKinley tariff in favor of such countries as will make concessions to us. It favors the establishment, as urged by that Convention, of a tariff commission, which shall impartially investigate and from time to time report to Congress when schedules appear to need modification. Should the limitation of time make immediate action impossible at this session of Congress, the President is begged to use the powers placed in his hands for the consideration of this subject *without further delay*. That would mean a summons to Congress to treat the subject in special session, and this course, we have good reason to believe, would be favored by the Massachusetts Senators and all but possibly one or two of that State's Representatives. The Massachusetts petition declares that "in all cases of tariff revision the test should be, not, ' Is such

a duty demanded ?' but, ' Is such a duty needed ?' " Duties will always be demanded so long as powerful manufacturers can control Congress. But Massachusetts manufacturers at least have discovered that they have been overprotected. They are increasingly restive under the prohibition of free raw materials, especially of free coal from neighboring Canada. It is highly significant that the ultimate source of the Massachusetts petition was the manufacturers, not the consumers.

❀

**"Not Cheapness but Equal Rights :" Criticised** A correspondent, replying to a paragraph in The Outlook of the 26th of January, takes exception to our denial of the statement in the New York Sun, "On all sides there is an insistent clamor for lower rates for all classes of transportation," and of the analogous though somewhat exaggerated statement by Mr. W. W. Finley, the new President of the Southern Railway, that there is at present a "proposition almost universally made to decrease rates by legislative action." In reply to these statements The Outlook affirmed that the demand of the American people is not for "goods carried at lower cost," but "that goods shall be carried on terms equally open to all." In support of the propositions of the Sun and Mr. Finley, our correspondent affirms that "there are pending in Congress several propositions to reduce railway earnings by direct legislative action." One of these is the proposition to make a general reduction in railway mail pay ; another, a series of bills the general purpose of which is to reduce inter-State passenger rates to a maximum of two cents a mile, which would necessitate the abolition of reduced rates for commutation tickets, excursion tickets, etc., and "the discontinuance of special rates to clergymen, of special charity rates, and of low rates to conventions and gatherings of all kinds." He also puts emphasis on measures pending in State Legislatures to reduce rates. These last are, so far as we have observed, generally bills to fix passenger rates at two cents a mile. This latter movement, we may add, has attained such proportions that the Washington correspondent of the New York Times affirms that certain of the railways are applying to the President to exert his influence against such legislation.

❦

*"Not Cheapness but Equal Rights:" Reaffirmed*

We do not see in the facts which our correspondent states any reason to modify materially the paragraph which he criticises. The proposition to make a general reduction in railway mail pay is not new. For at least ten years experts have been demanding that the Government shall not pay the railways for carrying the mails any more than the express companies pay the railways for carrying similar matter on trains traveling at a similar rate of speed. The bills before Congress and before the State Legislatures to reduce passenger rates to two cents a mile are only indirectly connected with the Federal legislation to regulate charges for freight transportation. Nor is there any indication that in the bills before the Inter-State Commerce Committee of the House such a reduction is the result of any "insistent clamor" or that they interpret "a proposition almost universally made." Legislation reducing passenger rates to two cents a mile even in the well-settled portions of the country ought not to be passed by either Congress or State Legislatures without careful inquiry into the cost of transporting passengers and careful consideration of what is a reasonable profit to pay the railway company. It does not appear to us, however, that railway companies ought to be allowed to charge more than the cost and a reasonable profit on the general passenger traffic in order to enable them to give special rates to commuters, suburban residents, travelers to conferences, and clergymen. If it is a fact that the railway companies, or any of them, are seeking the influence of the President against State action reducing passenger rates, the fact furnishes a very significant support to the principle laid down by the President at least two years ago, that railway rates should be regulated by Federal, not by State, action. This principle, which he invoked on behalf of the traveling public, is equally necessary for the protection of the railway corporations. If all railways engaged in inter-State commerce were to be chartered by the Federal Government, as the National banks are, this fact would bring them under both Federal protection and Federal regulation. Whether the State could regulate freight and passenger rates on such a railway within the State lines we are not prepared to affirm ; but it is safe to say that if adequate regulation was furnished by the Federal Government there would be very little attempt to interfere with such regulation by State action. The Outlook still persists in its opinion that the "insistent clamor" and the "proposition almost universally made" by the public is "not cheapness but equal rights."

❦

*Overcapitalization and the Great Northern Railway*

The large number of letters which have been received by The Outlook commenting upon the article on Railway Overcapitalization by Mr. William L. Snyder in the issue of the 9th of February indicates that the subject is one of very wide interest. Many of our correspondents fly to the defense of the Great Northern Railway Company, under the mistaken impression that the author of the article was attacking that corporation. It seems to us that an intelligent reading of the article gives no ground for this impression. A New York banker sends a table indicating that the increase of stock from $25,000,000 to $150,000,-000 has been largely in return for cash payment on the part of subscribers to this stock. This correspondent says: "In all cases I think you will find that the money received was spent either to increase the facilities of the road or to apply toward new trackage." Mr. Snyder in his article did not conceal or deny the fact that this increase in capital stock was properly and legally subscribed for by the public. He simply asserted his opinion that an inadequate proportion of both capital and revenue had been spent upon increasing traffic facilities, and too large a proportion has been divided among the stockholders in the form of dividends. In other words, Mr. Snyder's contention is that the taxing power of the railways, as illustrated in the case of the Great Northern Railway Company, has taken from the shippers and travelers more than it ought to have taken for the benefit of the stockholders. This seems to us to be a debatable matter of opinion, which is to be supported or controverted by facts and figures and a judgment of experts, and not by general statements. The fundamental question is whether this taxing power may be or is now limited by the Government. The Outlook expressly disavows any desire to make an attack on the Great Northern Railway. It considers that road, from the point of view of engineering, financial management, and facilities afforded the public, one of the very best railway systems of the country. Mr. James J. Hill is an acknowledged genius of high abilities and ideals in the field of railway construction and management. It is for this very reason that his road and his views of railway management form significant and pertinent object-lessons in the discussion of railway regulation. The Outlook has in the past devoted a large amount of space and attention to the discussion of the relation of the public—that is to say, the Government—to the regulation of railway rates, operation, dividends, and capital. It will continue to do so in future, with as keen a desire to protect the interests of the investor as it has to promote those of the shipper and traveler. So far as the Great Northern Railway Company is concerned, we leave that phase of the subject here, with a quotation from the letter of a Chicago reader:

The Great Northern Railway was incorporated in 1889 with a capital of $20,000,000 to take over the St. Paul, Minneapolis, and Manitoba Railway and several other minor lines. Its first annual statement, in June, 1890, and its last annual statement, in June, 1906, show as follows:

| | Capital Stock. | Net earnings. | Mileage. | Engines. | Cars. |
|---|---|---|---|---|---|
| 1890 | $20,000,000 | $2,274,000 | 3,000 | 259 | 8,299 |
| 1906 | 150,000,000 | 19,464,000 | 6,358 | 785 | 35,054 |

From these figures it would appear that the Great Northern Railway *has* spent *some* money in increasing its trackage more than double, its engines three times, and its freight cars more than four times in the past sixteen years. It extended its line across the conti-

nent through country that is enormously expensive for construction, and built the two huge trans-Pacific steamers at a cost of two millions apiece. Mr. Hill was the first man to point out that the railways of the country were not keeping pace with the growth of the country in trackage; that additional equipment would not greatly aid in solving the present congestion, as there were not tracks enough on which to move the business offered. Mr. Hill desires to issue $60,000,000 more stock, not for the purpose of concealing the earnings of the Great Northern Railway, but to build more tracks and equipment.

No one has denied, certainly neither Mr. Snyder nor The Outlook, that the best-managed railways in this country have increased their equipment in the last twenty years. The whole question is one concerning the just proportion of increased equipment to increased dividends. Our correspondent's own figures show that in the case of the Great Northern Railway the capital stock has increased fivefold and the net earnings eightfold, while the mileage has only been doubled, the engines increased only threefold, and the cars only fourfold. This discrepancy between the increase of capital and net earnings and the increase of equipment must be apparent to the most casual observer. Are such discrepancies just and proper, or should they be regulated by some statutory or charter provision, as in the notable case of the Boston and Albany Railroad?

❦

*Ex-Governor Higgins*

Frank W. Higgins, who died last week, was the successor of Benjamin B. Odell, Jr., and the predecessor of Charles E. Hughes as Governor of the State of New York. It was not his least service that he made possible the transition from the one to the other. When he came into office he was known as an unostentatious and scrupulously honest man. He had demonstrated his ability as a business man, and his faithfulness as a public servant in the Legislature. His predecessor, Mr. Odell, had not only bequeathed to him a State government accustomed to boss dictation, but, even after ceasing to be Governor, assumed to be the real power in the administration. Governor Higgins made no parade of his own virtue, but he quietly and effectually eliminated Mr. Odell and his machine from the administration, and, with the co-operation of others, eventually from the Republican State organization. During Mr. Higgins's term of office the insurance scandals arose. At first Governor Higgins, conservative by nature, did not favor an investigation. He feared that if it were begun people would expect it to be a prosecution, and, finding it in fact an investigation and not a prosecution, would fail to give it the support it required. There was at the time very good reason for such caution. When, however, he saw that public opinion was set, not upon a prosecution, but upon an investigation, he recommended to the Legislature the appointment of a joint investigating committee. The laws which were framed as the result of the investigation were passed during his administration and were approved by him. It was to no small degree because of his influence, moreover, that the Legislature during his term of office succeeded in producing a body of statutes which were of extraordinary importance and merit. During the latter part of his term Governor Higgins was a very sick man; he was suffering from the disease which within a few weeks after his retirement brought him to his death. At the same time he was made the target of acrid and unscrupulous criticism. He was called inconstant, timid, and inactive. Yet, except for his withdrawal from the candidacy for re-election on the ground of his health, he kept his physical condition to himself. With reticent heroism he kept at his task till the end. Contrary to his physician's orders, he even went to the inauguration of Governor Hughes, to welcome into office the man whose nomination he had taken part in securing. Mr. Higgins will not be remembered as a great statesman; he nevertheless rendered great service to his State. His career is worthy of record because it illustrates the fact that the citizen of high character who devotes his best energies to the public service, even if he has but moderate ability, can make himself invaluable. Democracy does not require men of genius, though it can use them; but the very existence of democracy depends upon men of integrity and public spirit.

**Niagara**
**A Mischievous Bill**

Eternal vigilance is evidently going to be the price of preserving the scenic glory of Niagara—if, indeed, commercialism does not finally triumph. On February 8 Colonel Alexander, of Buffalo, introduced in the House of Representatives a bill which reads as follows:

That the provisions of the Act approved June 29, 1906, entitled "An Act for the Control and Regulation of the Waters of Niagara River, for the Preservation of Niagara Falls, and for Other Purposes," shall not be held to prevent the diversion of water from Niagara River below the falls under a franchise granted by the State of New York to the Lower Niagara River Power and Water Supply Company, provided that this privilege shall only extend to the diversion of water from points a distance not less than one mile below the Falls; provided, further, that the total amount of such diversion shall at no time exceed 40,000 cubic feet per second.

The Burton Bill, which it is sought thus to amend, wisely included the Rapids in its preservative intention, and Section 4 requests the President to open negotiations with Great Britain "for the purpose of effectually providing by suitable treaty with said Government for such regulation and control of the waters of Niagara River and its tributaries as will preserve the scenic grandeur of Niagara Falls and of the rapids in said river." The statement of the counsel of the Lower Niagara River Power and Water Supply Company, made last April before the House Committee on Rivers and Harbors, showed its intention of proceeding under its charter to construct a tunnel under the city of Niagara Falls, beginning just under the steel-arched bridge (the main bridge from which the Falls are viewed), and proceeding about a mile and a half to the "Devil's Hole." The quantity of water which this new bill would authorize the withdrawal of is equivalent to almost twenty per cent. of the flow of the river at this point, and is completely equal to the total authorized diversion above. All the agitation which has stirred the country for a year and a half on this subject has been for the preservation of Niagara Falls as a whole. More than eighty per cent. of the mass of letters from influential persons now on file in Secretary Taft's office urge the retention of all the glory of Niagara. This assault, therefore, on the Whirlpool Rapids—which are only less inspiring and majestic than the Falls themselves—is in direct defiance of the expressed will of the people, and if it should prevail the previous work would be largely nullified. The only safety is in keeping definitely all the ground that has been gained by the enactment of the Burton Bill, and in continuing the agitation until such international action is taken as shall settle it permanently that no industrial use shall be made of Niagara which will destroy or deface its beauty as one of the scenic wonders of this continent.

❦

*The House of Lords* The British Parliament was opened by the King and Queen in person with great state on Tuesday of last week, and the Speech from the Throne was listened to with profound attention, and promises to be one of the few royal speeches that become memorable. The King took occasion to acknowledge in a characteristically gracious and adequate way the sympathy for and the service rendered to the sufferers from the Jamaica earthquake by Americans, but the striking feature of the address was a definite though necessarily vague statement that the Government was considering the question of putting an end to the veto power of the House of Lords. The Liberals hold that they have the warrant of the people of England for the Education Bill and the Plural Voting Bill, and that the House of Lords is not only pursuing a systematic course of defeating the measures brought forward by the Liberal party, but that it has now set itself against the will of the people of England; a position inconsistent with the essentially democratic character of the government of Great Britain. The House of Lords has taken this position before, and has always, after a vigorous fight, been brought around, either through overcoming the opposition by increasing the number of peers, or through its perception that it had touched the danger-point and must recede. When the Upper House set itself obstinately against the passage of

the Reform Bill of 1832, it was brought to terms by the threat of the wholesale creation of new peers by the King. That had been done before and had been regarded as a lowering of the prestige—a kind of adulteration—of the English nobility. What makes the situation more offensive is the fact that the House of Lords now practically belongs to the Conservative party; that it automatically records the decrees of that party and opposes those of the Liberal party. When the second Home Rule Bill was thrown out of the House, Mr. Gladstone gave expression to the growing sentiment of a large section of the English people that a way must be found which should prevent the obstruction by the hereditary house of legislators of legislation proposed by the elective house. The Liberal Premier, Sir Henry Campbell-Bannerman, is in a position, by reason of the enormous majority behind him, to deal strongly and decisively with the situation. What the programme of the Government will be it is impossible to forecast, as it is not probable that recourse will be had to the creation of a large number of new peers. That is only a temporary expedient; and some gentlemen who are transferred to the House of Lords have a fashion of becoming more conservative than the Conservatives. There are some Liberals as well as some Conservatives who would welcome a dissolution and an appeal to the country, but this would not be decisive. A more radical change is likely to be proposed, though not such a change as will involve either the end of the Upper House or reducing it to a mere consultation body. Very likely nothing will be done, for the very good reason that, if the House of Lords follows its own precedents, it is likely to yield at the last moment.

❦

*Revolution by Hysteria* A midwinter madness seems to have settled upon the Suffragettes in England, and they are throwing away whatever moral support they may have secured, by the insane attempt to cast to the winds all fundamental English ideas of the manner in which political and social changes should be brought about. On Wednesday of last week, the day after the assembling of Parliament, a desperate attack was made by a small army of women on the House of Commons, and, after six hours of vigorous skirmishing, the assailants were finally dispersed, sustaining slight injuries to their persons and serious injury to their costumes. The battle-ground was strewn with hair-pins, hat-pins, ribbons, sections of head-dress. Fifty-seven of the attacking party were captured. The police suffered no greater loss than that of a few helmets and a few painful but not dangerous scratches. The attacking party was urged on by the fiery speeches delivered in the afternoon, one of the speakers giving the keynote of the situation in the declaration: " The time for words is passing away, and the time for action has come." A crowd to the number of two hundred organized themselves and marched to Westminster Hall, singing " John Brown's Body." They were warned by the police that, while the procession would not be interfered with, they would not be permitted to enter the Houses of Parliament. When the Parliament buildings were reached, an attempt was made by the police to break up the demonstration. The assailants stood firm, some of them organizing into small parties and dashing at the doors of the House, from which they were repulsed by the police. It may be suspected that if a cartoonist from Punch was present he selected as the most striking incident the attack made by a woman on a policeman with a muff. The police appear to have been good-natured and to have avoided violence so far as possible during the first attack. When the second attack came, however, their patience was exhausted, and there was something very like a riot in Parliament Square. Another picturesque incident at this stage of the struggle was the seizing of a member of the House of Commons by his coat-tails, his angry assailant shouting, " If you go into the House, I go too." The member escaped with his life, but not with his coat. Revolutions in England do not begin by beating the helmets of policemen with muffs, or tearing the tails from the coats of members of the national legislature. The movement is too violent to

last, but it is likely to have a very unfortunate effect on the prospects of suffrage in a country which is not only conservative by instinct, but which has also great respect for manners. Revolution by hysteria will not command the support of rational suffragists among English women ; it will only furnish subjects for cartoonists.

❦

**A Veteran Correspondent**    It does not often fall to the lot of a newspaper correspondent to overturn an English Ministry, nor to be knighted in recognition of his professional work. Sir William Howard Russell, who died last week at the age of eighty-six, began his services as war correspondent for the London Times in the Crimean War, and with his letters there arose really a new era of journalism as regards special correspondence. He did not merely tell of battles and maneuvers in condensed despatches, as had been the custom before his day, but in well-written, carefully prepared articles discussed large questions as they appeared from the field, while his scorching denunciations of military incompetency and failure to care for the soldiers' health roused public feeling in England so hotly that one Cabinet was replaced by another. In this country the name " Bull Run Russell " clung to him because of his over-vivid description of a battle which his detractors claim he never saw. If he erred in his estimate of the meaning of the Civil War and of the future of America, his mistake was one not altogether unnatural in view of the disastrous rout of Bull Run, and one, moreover, which many Englishmen unfortunately shared. Time, the great softener, had doubtless removed much of the asperity long felt toward Russell here. Sir William, as he became in 1895, had also served the Times, the Telegraph, and perhaps other English papers in the Indian Mutiny (he was at the taking of Lucknow), in the Prusso-Austrian campaign of 1866, in the Franco-Prussian War, in the Zulu troubles, and in the military operations at Alexandria and Tel-el-Kebir, while his letters of travel—cheerful, gossipy, and shrewd—were mailed from a long list of strange and distant countries and cities. Few men saw more of the events of the latter half of the nineteenth century than he, and few newspaper writers have interested and informed so large an audience.

❀

**The Strange Case of George Edalji**    By applying to an actual case the principles of detection which he has formulated in his famous "Sherlock Holmes" stories, Sir Arthur Conan Doyle has discovered what he believes to be a remarkable miscarriage of justice in an English court. George Edalji, a young lawyer, was, in 1903, arrested and convicted as being the principal in a series of outrageous maimings and killings of domestic animals. Sir Conan heard of the case, made an investigation, and proved to his own satisfaction, and to thousands who have read his narrative, Edalji's innocence. The story he tells, as printed in the New York Times, is briefly as follows: Thirty-one years ago the Rev. S. Edalji, a clergyman of the Church of England, became vicar of Great Wyrley. He was of Parsee origin, but was married to an English woman. Of his three children George was the oldest. When George was about twelve years old, Mr. Edalji had occasion to have a maid-servant arrested for sending him anonymous letters and writing ribald sentences about him on outhouses and buildings. Though she was bound over to keep the peace, the letters continued; among them were letters abusing George Edalji and even threatening his life. These letters also contained vulgar expressions of admiration for the local police. In some the name of the clergyman was forged. There was a document that even pretended to be a confession by George Edalji and another person that they were the authors. Hoaxes of various sorts were practiced. In one case the chief of the constabulary expressed himself as convinced that George was the offender. In 1903 there broke out an epidemic of crime. Month after month horses, cattle, and sheep were found ripped open. Anonymous letters were sent to the police accusing George of the crimes. Some of these the police believed George

wrote himself. One night the Edalji house was guarded. The next evening, while several constables and detectives were on watch, George Edalji, who by this time had become a lawyer, reached home about half-past six; after a while he put on a blue serge coat, walked to a bootmaker's in the village, and then walked about till supper-time; he returned to the vicarage at 9:25. After supper he went to bed. The next morning a pony was found ripped open. A sergeant had seen the pony apparently well at eleven. At midnight a heavy storm arose; at 6:20 the pony was discovered to be injured; at 8:30 a veterinary surgeon, after examination, stated that the injury had been done within six hours. The police raided the vicarage. They found a coat (not the blue one which George had worn during his evening walk); it was old, worn, and stained; according to the police, it was damp, though this is denied by the family. Some whitish stains on it proved to be starch stains; some brown and reddish stains, not shown to be fresh, were examined and found to be of mammalian blood—possibly meat gravy. The police declared also that there were horse-hairs on the coat; but this the family denied. The coat was taken away by the police. There was also taken by the police a piece of the pony's hide. That was in the morning; over twelve hours later (when there had been plenty of chance for hairs to be transferred from the hide to the coat) the police surgeon picked twenty-nine undoubted horse-hairs from the coat. The hairs, moreover, corresponded to those on the piece of hide. The crime was committed either before or after half-past nine. If before, which seemed impossible from the veterinary surgeon's statement, what had this old coat, which Edalji did not then wear, have to do with it? If after, how could the alibi, apparently established by the police themselves while on guard, be explained?

❀

**Was it an Injustice?**    In spite of the questionable character of the evidence, George Edalji was found guilty and sentenced to seven years' imprisonment. In accordance with English practice, he had no chance to appeal.

While he was in jail awaiting trial, and after he began to serve his term, the outrages and the anonymous letters continued. Did the police regard this fact as a cause for reasonable doubt of their theory? Not at all; rather as a confirmation of it. They argued that the other members of the gang to which they alleged Edalji belonged were perpetrating the crimes in order to create the impression that Edalji could not have perpetrated the preceding ones. At last a man was convicted of committing an outrage of the same character as the others, and was sentenced to prison for three years. Another man—or rather boy—confessed to disemboweling his own horse, but later contradicted his own confession and fled the country. This brief outline necessarily omits some of the evidence—such as footprints, muddy shoes, and the like, which Sir Conan Doyle very effectually shows to be worthless. Two facts, however, which he cites as indicating the inherent improbability of the guilt of Edalji should be mentioned: first, that Edalji was very studious, altogether unlikely to be a companion of ruffians; second, that he was afflicted with extraordinary astigmatism, so that he could distinguish objects a few inches away only with difficulty, and was not capable of performing in the dark the feats necessary for the commission of the outrages of which he was accused. His staring, bulging eyes, however, which were evidence of his innocence, together with his dark skin, due to his Parsee origin, made him seem queer to English villagers and therefore helped to fasten suspicion upon him. The tribunal in which Edalji was tried was the lesser court of Quarter Sessions; and a Knight without legal training presided. A memorial on behalf of Edalji, signed by ten thousand people, including hundreds of lawyers, was addressed to the Home Office; but it had no effect. Apparently the complaint was referred to the police whose prosecution convicted the prisoner. After three years of imprisonment Edalji was released—apparently on the ground that the other man convicted was sentenced to but three years. There was, however, no pardon, no acknowledgment of injustice.

The case of Edalji affords an illustration of a defect in English legal procedure quite the opposite of that which has been a scandal in American criminal cases. In England a convicted prisoner has no right of appeal. The consequence is that it is only by the interference of the Government that errors in procedure which work injustice can be corrected. The Outlook has urged a revision of American criminal codes in order to prevent criminals from escaping punishment by taking advantage of technical errors. Though the English practice avoids this evil, it is not the only remedy. A convicted prisoner ought not to be allowed to go free because a judge made an erroneous decision on a minor matter; that we should learn from American experience. But from English experience we should also learn that a convicted prisoner ought to have the right to show that, by an error in the conduct of a case, he has been denied the chance to refute the charges against him.

❦

*Giosue Carducci and Queen Margherita*

Last November the Nobel prize for literature was awarded to Giosue Carducci, the greatest of the Italian poets of our time. In comparison with the poverty against which for seventy years he had struggled, the money was a fortune. But it came only three months before his death. He passed away last week, and the occasion is one for national mourning. For Carducci was emphatically Italy's national poet. His early poems not only disclosed his poetical and political radicalism, but did as much as anything to fan the flame of Italian unity; they kept alive the national spirit during the long struggle for Italian unification. Though most of Carducci's poems celebrate revolution and republicanism, his glowing patriotism, his appreciation of the power of love, and his sensitiveness to beauty, whether in nature or in man, made him the literary idol of republicans and monarchists as well, and chief among the latter the present Queen Dowager, the beautiful, benevolent, and intelligent Margherita, a modern Vittoria Colonna. For her Carducci cherished a chivalric devotion which has found expression in one of his finest odes. Some years ago he was troubled by the thought that at his death his large library would be dispersed and sold piecemeal; he wanted it preserved for the stimulation of scholars and poets. The Queen came to his mental and material rescue. She not only purchased the library, but she also purchased the poet's house, leaving both for his use during his lifetime. The Queen may now offer the library to the University of Bologna, where for nearly half a century Carducci was Professor of Italian Literature. It seems strange that the foremost Italian poet should be comparatively little known abroad. This is because his style and versification practically baffle translation.

❦

*The Religious Education Association*   The fourth General Convention of the Religious Education Association, held at Rochester, New York, February 5 to 7, proves the effectiveness and vitality of an organization whose formative period has been watched with many hopes and some misgivings. That this Association does not duplicate or interfere with the specific work of other organizations is now evident beyond a doubt; that it has a definite field and mission of its own is still more plain. "The purpose of the Religious Education Association is: To inspire the educational forces of our country with the religious ideal; to inspire the religious forces of our country with the educational ideal; and to keep before the public mind the ideal of Religious Education, and the sense of its need and value." Printed on the cover of the programme, and voiced again and again through the Convention, this inspirational purpose ruled the thought of the whole gathering and made of one spirit many men of many minds. The annual address of the President, Dr. Faunce, of Brown University, voiced this spirit of the Association in at least five respects—open-mindedness, loyalty to the character and method of Jesus Christ, demand for contact between theory and experience, conviction that religion and education concern the whole of human nature and not detached parts

of it, and, finally, the sense of the Association's service to the Nation. The most outstanding feature of the Convention was thus its breadth of vision and temper. Made up of widely divergent ideas and callings, gathering its three hundred and fifty delegates from twenty-two States and three foreign countries, it yet showed no discord and no controversy. This was a second noteworthy feature of the Convention, that its unity of spirit gathered in the single exaltation of Jesus Christ, not doctrinally, but as the most vital fact of personal life. This was expressed in the address of Professor Coe, of Northwestern University. A third characteristic of the Convention found its most striking expression in an address by Dean Hodges, of Cambridge, on " Philanthropy and Theology "—" the heart makes the theologian," and only intimate living contact with the world of man can hold the ideal forces of religion and culture to a practical working unity of service—and was in evidence in all the sessions of its seventeen departments. The message of the Religious Education Association was finely summed up by its new President, Dr. King, of Oberlin College, on the last night of the Convention—a great moral ideal that shall inspire the whole of life and fortify against the great National dangers springing to-day from our lack of thought, passion for material comfort, and lack of a sense of law.

❦

*A New Missionary Movement*   At the Laymen's Missionary Dinner in New York City last week the Rev. Henry Sloane Coffin put the object of the Laymen's Missionary Movement effectively by recalling the text, " Let not your left hand know what your right hand doeth." Both hands, he said, should be busy at work, not one hand working and the other hand watching the work. To get the men of the churches heartily enlisted in that missionary work which now is so largely carried on by ministers and women, a general committee has been organized of prominent men in the different denominations, to constitute, not a new missionary board, but an interdenominational organization to work through existing boards. It will particularly have in mind two specific purposes—one, a campaign of education in the churches at home, aimed through parlor and dining-room conferences to reach and influence the more influential men of the churches; the other, the appointment of a commission of laymen, fifty or more in number, to visit, at their own expense, the foreign missionary fields, and report the results of their investigation to the churches at home. It is expected that the first of these visiting delegations will sail from the Pacific coast early in August, visiting Japan, China, Korea, the Philippines, India, Arabia, Africa, and Turkey.

❁

**The Promise in This Movement**  The character and promise of this movement are indicated by the type of men interested in it—such men as Mr. William J. Schieffelin, of New York, Mr. Joshua Levering, of Baltimore, the Hon. John W. Foster, of Washington, and Senator Crane, of Massachusetts. This movement seems to The Outlook admirable in its spirit and purpose. If the men identified with it can and will take an active part in it, and be responsible for it, and if under their guidance a lay delegation of efficient business men can and will visit the foreign missionary fields for the purpose of making an honest investigation followed by a perfectly fearless report of conditions, it is certain that if the criticisms which have been leveled against missions and missionaries are true, the defects will be exposed and corrected, and if they are false, the falsehoods will be exposed and the missionaries and their work justified. The only criticism The Outlook has to make upon this movement is that the suggestions offered in the pamphlet before us for the guidance of the visiting delegation are not adequate. We need not merely to know what are the missionary forces at work on the field, what the number and character of individual conversions, whether the work is carried on economically, what the native churches are doing and

whether they can do more, and what can be done to promote comity and union between the churches. These are important; but of equal and perhaps greater importance is it to know what the missions are doing to promote the spirit of Christianity, and so the development of a Christian civilization, among those who are not professed converts. Since the establishment of Christian missions modern schools have been established in Turkey under Mohammedan control; the burning of widows has ceased in India, and the condition of child widows has been improved; the school system of China has been revolutionized, and China has begun to recognize the value of progress; Japan has been revolutionized, and from being a feudal has become a democratic country. One of the questions, and not the least of those on which this visiting commission should throw light, is, How far have these and kindred changes been due to the influence of Christian missions upon the non-professedly Christian population in the various countries?

❁

**A Retreat for Social Workers**  It was a felicitous thought which Union Theological Seminary embodied in devoting the birthday of that great servant of humanity, President Lincoln, to a sort of retreat for social workers. Morning and afternoon were occupied with addresses on the general subject of Religion in Social Service. "The Religious Basis of the Social Movement" was described by Professor William Adams Brown, as consisting in recognition of the moral imperative immanent in history, the definite goal of its purpose, and a place and a value for every man therein. "There is no surer test of a man's religion," said he, "than his view of history." Of "The Fundamental Religious Fact in the Light of Modern Thought" Professor Knox said that religion itself is an elemental fact in nature, independent of intellectual explanations of its environment. The old "evidences" of Christianity and arguments to prove the existence of God from the world as it now is are obsolete. Religion is the trust in a divine ideal which strives to make it real. Concerning "Ethical Religion" as emphasizing conduct Professor McGiffert referred to "dangerous arguments" for it, based on future reward or punishment, and on the will of God rather than ideal good. It is ethical conduct with faith in the growth of good through social service, recognizing a higher Power as at the back of our work. Professor Frame spoke of "The Social Message of Jesus." He was the Prophet of ideal humanity, intent on the ethicizing of religion. His other-worldliness was the better-worldliness of the future which is here in its beginning. The question for us is our accord with his social attitude as outlined in three great utterances—"Love your enemies;" "The Last Judgment," with its ethical tests; the prayer to "Our Father." Of "The Ultimate Aim of Social Reform" Professor Fagnani said: "It is the removal of conditions which make for misery. This is not a happy world. Happiness is the feeling which results from the normal functioning of the human organism. But the church has been too shy of happiness. It should champion the things that ought to be. Nothing is too good for a son of God. The motto of social reform is, 'God and the People.' Its ideal is given in Daniel's vision of governments of brutes superseded by the government of humanity." Professor Hall defined "Our Common Service" by saying that the Church is a society for righteousness. In this time of social stress and unrest the Church is in danger of caring more for its organization than for the realization of its design by working for the redemption of collective humanity. Its true bond of union is not in ideas, but in ideals; not in symbols and creeds, but in the service of humanity which reveals the Father in righteousness incarnate. Dr. Coffin, of the Madison Avenue Presbyterian Church, closed the day with an inspiring address on "Inspiration."

❦

**A Great Teacher**   The death of Professor Charles E. Garman, of Amherst College, last week will make little impression outside the circle of his pupils. For his whole life was devoted with singleness of purpose to them. He knew no public outside of his class-room. Happily for him, he was not without appreciation in his chosen kingdom. Their appreciation was characteristically testified to in the volume published last summer, dedicated to him by thirteen of his former pupils who are now occupying prominent positions as educators, most of them in colleges or universities, each of whom contributed to the volume an essay on some phase of philosophy. For nearly a quarter of a century Mr. Garman had been Professor of Moral Philosophy in Amherst College, and the fact that thirteen of his pupils have attained in early life eminent positions as philosophical teachers bears testimony to the excellence of his work. Fifty years ago philosophy was taught as a perfected system; that is, the teacher had a certain definite philosophy which he communicated to his pupils, as the teacher of physical science instructs his pupils that the earth is round and revolves about the sun. The extreme of this method was well illustrated in a school in which less than half a century ago the pupils were expected to commit Butler's Analogy to memory and recite it verbatim, unless, as the teacher sarcastically told them, they could phrase the passage better than did Dr. Butler. In reaction against this method came what we may perhaps call the laboratory method, in which the problems of life are thrown out at the students and they are left to wrestle with the problems and reach their own conclusions, with little or no help from the teacher. The avowed object of this method is to train the pupils to philosophical thinking, not to conduct them to sound conclusions. The difficulty with this method is that it is too much to expect that a boy of eighteen will reach, unaided, sound conclusions on subjects upon which philosophers from Plato to Hegel have been putting their best endeavors. A good many students, given metaphysical nuts to crack, only crack their own teeth. Professor Garman combined the first and the second methods; he put the problems in philosophy before his students with absolute candor; he evaded no difficulties, stifled no inquiry, assumed as proved no dogmas. But he guided the thinking of his students toward what he believed to be sound conclusions. They worked in the laboratory, but under his direction. Some of them did not reach his conclusions; more of them forgot the conclusions which they did reach; but practically all of them were inspired by the spirit of free inquiry, and with the conviction that free inquiry conducted with reverence for the truth can be trusted eventually to reach trustworthy conclusions. The affectionate respect with which the graduates from his class-room look back upon him can be compared only to that with which Thomas Arnold has been regarded by the graduates of Rugby. Professor Garman's death will be keenly felt by a large circle of devoted friends whose friendship has in many cases survived the separation of years.

●

*The Sinking of the Larchmont* Among the many calamities by sea and on land the past year, none can compare in heartrending suffering with that near Block Island on Monday night of last week. The steamboat Larchmont, of the Joy Line, on its way from Providence to New York, was struck amidships by the three-masted schooner Harry Knowlton. The night was clear though intensely cold, and to the non-nautical mind there seems no excuse apparent for near approach between the vessels. While it would be neither fair nor wise to attempt to anticipate the results of official inquiry, it may be noted that a sailing vessel has, under ordinary circumstances, the right of way as against a steamboat, and that the schooner's officers declare that they had not varied their course for twenty minutes before the collision. It would seem on the face of it that the burden of defense lies with the steamboat's officers, and that they should give a convincing reason for not sooner varying their course so as to give the schooner a wide berth. Every one who has been a frequent passenger on steamboats and even on ferryboats knows that the practice of passing altogether too close is a common one.

Another matter which the commission of inquiry will have to consider thoroughly is the conduct of the officers and crew of the steamboat. Nothing could be more unjust than to base an adverse opinion as to this on the statements of one or two surviving passengers who after the collision were terrified and half frozen. The captain admits that his boat was probably the first to be got into the water, but claims that he had done all in his power to urge forward the launching of the other boats before getting into his own, and that it was only because of the quicker work and greater skill of his crew that their boat reached the water first. At least one passenger, on the other hand, impeaches the conduct of the captain toward the passengers, and others quote the " unwritten law " that a captain should be the last to leave his ship. So far as is known at this writing, the number of the dead will be not far from one hundred and forty; only nineteen persons escaped alive, two of whom were women, and all suffered severely, some dangerously, from the effects of the cold; two deaths have since occurred among the nineteen survivors of the night. The horrors of the exposure are indicated by the fact that the physicians who saw the bodies recovered say that all died not from drowning but from freezing, that one boat came ashore with only one of ten alive, the others having succumbed to the cold, and that one man committed suicide in the boat because he could not endure the suffering. The Larchmont was an old boat, its hull of wood; it had compartment divisions of wood, but, if the doors were closed, it is evident that the divisions were quite inadequate to keep the boat up even for a moderate space of time when struck amidships. While the primary blunder in this disaster appears to have been made in the pilot-house, there are facts that warrant the question as to how far this frightful loss of life may be ascribed to lack of rigid restriction as to build, age, and safety appliances of coastwise passenger boats. National steamboat investigation should be extended and State investigation radically reformed.

# Lenten Meditations
## Thy Will

"Thy will be done" is more than a prayer of submission: it is a prayer of consecration. Submission may be the subjection of a weaker will to a power that is dreaded; consecration is the dedication of a quickened and inspired will to a Person who is loved and honored. The slave submits to the master whom he fears, and says, "I obey." The bride, when she promises to obey, consecrates her life to the husband whom she loves. The conscript and the volunteer both say, "Thy will be done;" one submits himself, the other consecrates himself. When Christ in Gethsemane says, "Thy will, not mine, be done," he does not merely submit to the inevitable. In the same breath in which he confesses to his Father his dread of the morrow, he implores him not to let that dread stand for a moment athwart the Father's purpose. When he bids his disciples begin their prayer with the petition, "Thy kingdom come, thy will be done, on earth as it is in heaven," it is as if he said to them, All other desires are conditioned on this, all other petitions are subordinate to this. Desire bread, but if by hunger you can better serve your Father's will, prefer hunger. Desire to be kept out of temptation; but desire trial and temptation if through them you can build up your Father's kingdom. You rightly ask to be delivered from the Evil One; but do not fear to encounter him if by the encounter you can win a victory for your Father's cause. Ask to be forgiven as you forgive, for it is only by forgiving as you are forgiven that you can do your Father's work.

This, too, is the meaning, or should be, of that, alas! too often meaningless phrase, "For Christ's sake," with which we are wont to close our prayers. All prayers for ourselves and others should have this as their consummation, that we and they may better promote the kingdom of God on the earth, as all requisitions of a soldier in camp should be that he may do loyal campaigning more efficiently.

What is God's will? The Psalmist has described it in describing God's work:

He forgiveth all thine iniquities;
He healeth all thy diseases;
He redeemeth thy life from destruction;
He crowneth thee with loving-kindness and tender mercies.

This is the history of the world: Man sinning, God forgiving; man sick, God healing; man destroying himself, God rescuing him from his self-destruction; man raking in the muck-heap, God proffering him coronation. To pray, "Thy will be done," is to pray that we may have some share in this work of forgiving, healing, saving, crowning. For this we ask for food and forgiveness and guidance and deliverance, that so God's kingdom may the quicker come and his will be the better done.

To realize that there is a divine will at work in the world, that some men are thwarting it, and some are ignorant of it, and some are identifying themselves with it; to desire to be in the latter class, to pray with our lives as well as with our lips, "Thy will be done"—this is consecration. It gives moderation to triumph in our victory, because it is God's victory, not ours; it gives joyful resignation in our defeats and disasters, because so we can make our defeats and disasters God's victory; and it gives always a courage which nothing can daunt, and a hope which nothing can quench.

"Not in dumb resignation
  We lift our hands on high;
Not like the nerveless fatalist,
  Content to do and die.
Our faith springs like the eagle's
  Who soars to meet the sun,
And cries exulting unto Thee,
  'O Lord, Thy will be done.'"

❂

# Starving Russia

In all probability destined to be one of the greatest and most powerful nations of the civilized world, Russia is passing through a disciplinary and formative period of almost incredible suffering. Harassed, thwarted, and oppressed through decades of internal dissensions, discouraged, impoverished, and wounded by a great foreign war, she is now stricken with a terrible famine. A recent visitor to the suffering district, Mr. Leroy Scott, gives elsewhere in this issue of The Outlook a vivid account of the effects of the famine. According to conservative estimates, more than twenty millions of men, women, and children are directly and physically suffering for the lack of food. These people face not merely the pains of hunger, but the terror of those diseases which follow in the footsteps of famine. In this extremity Russia is turning to America for help; and when her cry is once heard and realized, we cannot doubt that the help will be forthcoming.

Mr. Nicolas Shishkoff, a recent member of the Russian Duma, has just arrived in New York to present the cause of starving Russia to the people of this country. Although he has been an influential figure in Russian political affairs, he is neither a revolutionist nor a representative of the Government; he comes as a private philanthropist, pure and simple, asking for much-needed help for his fellow-men and ours. Mr. Shishkoff belongs to the hereditary nobility of Russia, his mother being a princess. He has been a large landholder, and most of his life has been spent as an agricultural and estate proprietor in the province of Samara. He has for more than twenty years been a member of various local and provincial bodies which have had charge of the welfare and improvement of the peasant class. During the great famine of a dozen years ago he was prominent and active in the work of relief, and was appointed to conduct an investigation of the economic condition of the peasants throughout the central provinces of Russia. He belongs to that remarkable body of men of modern Russia who, while of aristocratic lineage and possessing liberal education and accomplishments, have sacrificed rank and property in their active sympathy with the struggles of the common people for political freedom and constitutional rights. Mr. Shishkoff is hoping to organize a National Relief Committee in this country which shall work in co-operation with the United Zemstvo Famine Relief Association of Russia, the national organization of which he is the accredited representative.

Two possible objections may be made in this country to giving money to the famine-stricken peasants of Russia. One will come from conservatives, the other from radicals. The conservative may say, "These peasants have brought all this suffering on themselves by rebelling against governmental authority, by burning estates, by refusing to pay taxes, by sulking in their villages, and declining to till the soil under the direction of Government officials; I am opposed to revolution, and I think the only way to suppress a famine is first to suppress a revolution." The radical may say, "There would have been no famine if it had not been for the unjust and cruel oppressions of a despotic government— a government which, for its own selfish purposes, has denied the peasants education and a knowledge of how to apply the simplest modern scientific ideas to their agriculture, has taxed them so outrageously that they have had no money to buy tools and seed and fertilizer and cattle and horses, has taken all the able-bodied farmers and farm laborers away from the fields and plunged them into the destruction and misery of an unnatural foreign war; the way to suppress famines is to suppress such a despotic and destructive despotism."

But these arguments in the face of human wretchedness and misery become mere theories, and the American people are not in the habit of stopping to discuss theories when the question is one of life-saving. When a passenger steamer goes down on a freezing winter night in the waters of Long Island Sound, those who are rescued by the exercise of self-sacrificing heroism are at once warmed, fed, and clothed. When this first duty is accomplished, we then discuss the question whether such accidents are not preventable by building steamers with water-tight compartments, by a more rigorous inspection of lifeboats, by a modification of the shipping laws to provide for better discipline and a higher state of efficiency among steamboat officers and sailors.

Let us by all means support, on the one hand, the proper enforcement of national authority, and on the other the proper demands for popular rights and political liberty. But when we can do anything effective to mitigate the sufferings and prevent the deaths, not merely of individuals here and there, but of whole villages of men, women, and children, we may perfectly safely drop for a moment the discussion of political principles, and unite with hearty accord in feeding the starving.

❀

# A Popular Essayist

Very few writers of the serious temper, using chiefly the essay form, have attained popularity so suddenly as Mr. Arthur Christopher Benson; and readers in all parts of the country are interested in the personality of a man whose work, while it is in a certain degree reticent, is at the same time so intimate both on the intellectual and spiritual side. Mr. Benson has had a very fortunate education for his work. His father, the late Archbishop of Canterbury, was a man of great charm of nature and sweetness of spirit. No one who ever saw him will forget the mingled refinement and strength of his face—one of those faces, like Stanley's, Church's, and Keble's, which reveal the latent sweetness and spiritual fineness of the best English character. Mr. Arthur Christopher Benson, his son, was born in 1862, received his early education at Eton, perhaps the richest in historical associations of the great English public schools, certainly the most beautiful in situation—the school in which Prime Ministers have been bred for many generations, and from the playgrounds of which Windsor Castle looms in majesty like a symbol of English state. From Eton Mr. Benson went to King's College, Cambridge, affiliated in origin with Eton, as New College, Oxford, is with Winchester. He had several years' experience as a teacher at Eton, and is now a Fellow of Magdalene College at Cambridge, a college which Americans will remember as beyond the long line of colleges on the river.

Mr. Benson's reputation as a writer in this country is a matter of the last few months, but he has served a long apprenticeship, and the list of his acknowledged books, as it appears in "The Memoirs of Arthur Hamilton," just reprinted in this country, includes sixteen titles. Other volumes with which he is credited do not appear in this list, and are omitted probably because the author desires to allow them to pass into oblivion. "The Upton Letters," which appeared about two years ago, attracted the attention of thoughtful people; but it was not until the publication of the volume of delightful essays with the attractive title "From a College Window" that Mr. Benson became what may be called a popular writer, if the adjective "popular" can be used in connection with an essayist of Mr. Benson's meditative mood. A glance at his earlier books brings out the fact that he is the author of five biographies. Of these, the Lives of Rossetti, FitzGerald, and Walter Pater, in the English Men of Letters Series, have been widely read by students of literature; and the study of Pater has taken its place as the most intelligent and well-balanced account of Pater which has appeared. There are five volumes of poems the authorship of which Mr. Benson acknowledges; and two books of prose essays, "The Thread of Gold" and "The House of Quiet," which appeared anonymously some time ago, attracted a great many readers by reason of the vein of reflection on the serious aspects of life which ran through them, and found expression in a very attractive style, suggestive, sympathetic, and sound in form. These books are in no sense original contributions to English writing of the time; but they have something of the charm of the English rivers. They flow through a ripe and peaceful country, with a gentle motion which carries the reader on, but not so rapidly as to blur the images of overhanging trees and quiet places which fall into its depths.

Concerning the authorship of "At the Gate of Death," which appeared anonymously with the imprint of Messrs. G. P. Putnam's Sons, there was not the slightest question among those who had read "The Upton Letters;" and "The Memoirs of Arthur Hamilton," which appeared in London in 1886, and has been recently reprinted by the Messrs. Putnam, bears the stamp of the same.

meditative temper, the same refined and thoughtful style. If the title of the new book of Mr. Benson's, recently announced, "By Quiet Waters," defines either its content or its manner, it will take its place in the group with "The Thread of Gold" and "The House of Quiet." So far as their spirit and style are concerned, these books come naturally from the atmosphere of Cambridge, with its wealth of old associations, the dignity and beauty of its ancient halls and gardens, and the inimitable charm of its river, whose brief half-mile, as it runs between the colleges, is a kind of vital and gracious summary of all that is ripest and most distinctive in older England. So far as their matter and the interests with which they deal are concerned, however, it would seem at the first glance as if, like some flowers which bloom sporadically on an alien soil, they had come to expression in an unfriendly atmosphere. Oxford has been described as the University of Movements, and Cambridge as the University of Men. It is one of the peculiarities of Cambridge that, although its pre-eminence in mathematics has been conceded for many decades, it has been pre-eminently the mother of poets. Almost every college is associated with some gracious singer; and one looks up at the windows of the oldest buildings and associates them definitely with some of the greatest English poets.

But if Cambridge has been mathematical in the emphasis of its instruction, and the home of late years of a good deal of religious indifferentism and of a critical spirit, it must not be forgotten that it was also one of the homes of Puritanism; and that from time to time men of religious genius have appeared among its teachers or students. As one recalls, in its quiet streets or lovely gardens, the uproar of London, the staccato cries of Paris, the roar of New York, he feels that he is in "The House of Quiet," and is glad of a chance in that tranquil atmosphere to read a book which deals, not with action or achievement or adventure, but with the calmer joys of living, the finer exaltations of the spirit, the deeper peace; in a word, with the rich and often neglected resources of the

meditative life. "The Upton Letters" are in a somewhat different vein, and happily combine suggestive comments on boys with charming descriptions of landscape and quiet meditations on human relations and the deeper experiences of life. The essays in the volume "From a College Window" have been so widely read that a knowledge of their quality and their themes may be taken for granted. It is enough to say that no more delightful book of the quiet life has appeared for many a day, nor one that lends itself to reading aloud more graciously.

Mr. Benson has set at naught two theories very widely held. Forty years ago, when Carlyle, Emerson, and Matthew Arnold were in the hands of thoughtful men, it was still good form for a man of letters to take an interest in religious questions and to deal with the religious issues as if they were matters of vital importance and universal interest. Of late years it has been the fashion to charge every writer who touched these themes with didacticism, and with endeavoring to become a preacher. The difference between the preacher and the artist lies in the manner. One may deal in the most serious way with the most serious things and remain pre-eminently an artist, or one may deal with the most trifling things and be pre-eminently a preacher. The deeper religious experiences, which lie below the region of debate and theological discussion, belong pre-eminently to the man of letters, because they are pre-eminently the issues of life. Mr. Benson is, first of all, a religious writer; but he is not a preacher, he is essentially an artist. He lets the truth enforce itself. His endeavor is to set it forth with perfect sincerity and with vivid charm. He is reverent of the traditions of the past, but not in any sense a slave to their authority. He endeavors to translate with freedom the religious experiences of men to-day in terms of twentieth-century speech. "At the Gate of Death," for instance, is a kind of prose "In Memoriam," recording all the various phases and aspects which death takes on in all the moods through which mortal man passes. It is a register of doubts, the alternate passage of shadow and light, shot through by the fundamental hope that illuminates and that finally conquers.

Mr. Benson has happily disproved also the theory that, in order to secure attention in this day of much writing and publishing, one must shout like an auctioneer, or scream like a victim of hysteria, or deal with forbidden things, or paint with a flamboyant brush all manner of morbid, abnormal, and unwholesome experiences. No books could be further removed from the world of noise, confusion, appeal to popular prejudices, cheap and smug interpretations of religion or philanthropy, than Mr. Benson's books. They contain the work, not only of a thinker, but of a man of academic taste and surroundings. "From a College Window" happily characterizes the point of view of the writer, though without the limitations that sometimes mar the prospect and blur the vision from the college outlook. Writing from an environment almost as quiet to-day as it was in the time of Gray, the author of "The Upton Letters" and "At the Gate of Death" sees life sanely and with warm human sympathies, and envelops his readers in an atmosphere of rest and thoughtfulness, in a style at once fluent, accurate, and beautiful without over-emphasis or exaggeration.

❀

# The Evidences of Christianity

The evidences of Christianity, to be effective, must be looked for in present experiences, not in past history, for the simple reason that past history itself must first be proved before it can become proof to the present generation. If the miracles of Jesus Christ are relied upon to prove the truth of Christianity, the miracles must first be proved; if his resurrection is relied upon, the resurrection must first be demonstrated. But generally he who is skeptical about Christianity is still more skeptical about the miracles and the resurrection. The witness to Christianity must be a living witness, whose testimony can be heard and who can be cross-examined. This

truth, which it were well if the defenders of the faith more generally recognized, was very clearly put before his congregation by Dr. Mason W. Clarke, of Brooklyn, New York, in a recent unpublished sermon, from which we make a few extracts:

I do not personally know whether Christ turned water into wine or not; but whether he did or not, he did change Saul of Tarsus into Paul the apostle—that was the greater miracle; and this is the kind of miracle that has been the constant accompaniment of Christ's presence in history.

When the question comes to us to-day, What shall we do with this Jesus who is called the Christ? it is of the Christ of this present hour concerning whom it is asked. Whether he was born of a virgin or not is not the issue; whether he rose from the dead or not, as a tangible form, is not the issue; whether he worked miracles of power is not the issue. The issue is concerning this deathless Person whom multitudes are loving and serving now, who is the inspiration of countless lives to-day, who is the comfort and joy of unnumbered throngs of human souls, the Christ who is every day we live changing poor lost men into new creations, and who is giving hope and courage and redemption to the world. What shall we do with him? We must read the story of Jesus of old in the light of what Christ now is.

If you were to bring from the grave some old inhabitant of Pompeii and show him the dark side of New York, he would look wearily up into your face and tell you that they did all these things in his day, only perhaps a little more heartily and vivaciously than we do now. If you were to call up some ancient Babylonian and lead him through these scenes of vice and shame, he would assure you that it is old to him, and not half so interesting as it was in the open life of Babylon.

But suppose you were to call up an old Pompeian sinner and a debauched citizen of ancient Babylon and show them the Christian side of our modern life, take them to one of our hospitals, for instance. How their eyes would brighten. "We never saw this in Pompeii or in Babylon. This is truly interesting. Who ever heard of such a thing as this?" Take them to St. Christopher's, and imagine their amazement. "Why, do you care for sick children like this? We used to let them die, or throw them out into the woods to perish of exposure. This is really interesting." Take them to the Society for the Prevention of Cruelty to Children. How they would pinch themselves to see if they were awake! Take them to our Christian houses for the poor and afflicted and despairing, and watch their expressions. "Why, this is something new! We never had these things in our day."

When the Chinese Commissioners were in this country, they were taken about by a delegation of citizens to see the sights of Chicago—the railway stations, the stock-yards, the great factories, the great department stores, the sky-scrapers. Asked what interested him the most, one of the chiefs of the Commission replied, "The Hospital, Hull House, and the Young Men's Christian Association work." These interested them most because they were the most unlike what they had in China. They had railways, though not so great; slaughter-houses and factories and shops, though not on so large a scale; houses, though not so many stories high. But hospitals for the care of the sick without charge, social settlements for the benefit of the poor who can pay nothing but gratitude and do not always pay that, and a Young Men's Christian Association where young men of culture and social position are devoting their lives to fraternal service of the lonely, the unsocial, and the tempted —these were to the Chinese Commissioners absolutely new. No wonder these commonplaces of a Christian civilization interested them more than our social pomps and our commercial equipments.

Jesus Christ made certain definite promises to the world, at the same time giving the warning that it would take a long time and require victory over many obstacles before they could be perfectly fulfilled. Here is one of these promises:

The Spirit of the Lord is upon me, because he hath anointed me to preach glad tidings to the poor; he hath sent me to heal the broken-hearted, to preach deliverance to the captives, and recovering of sight to them that are blind, to set at liberty them that are bruised, to proclaim the acceptable year of the Lord.

If he has done this or is doing it, then he is to be believed. If he has not done this or is not doing it, then he is not to be believed. What are the facts? Has Christianity been glad tidings to the poor or not? Are they better off in Christian America than they were in pagan Rome, where half the population were slaves, and of the other half a large proportion lived on the edge of starvation, from which they were preserved only by gifts of food from the rich? Not yet does every man sit under his own vine and fig-tree, but nearly half the families in America own the land they occupy. How about the broken-hearted? The scholars tell us that the ancient pagan tombs contain no inscriptions of hope. At the Christian funeral we sing Mrs. Browning's "He giveth his beloved sleep," or Edward H. Bickersteth's

" Peace, perfect peace, death shadowing us
    and ours;
Jesus has vanquished death and all its
    powers."

And flowers, emblem of life springing out of death, cover the coffin and the newly closed grave. How about the captives? The only remnant of slavery in Christendom is in the Congo country, and there it is ill concealed under forms of law which we have good reason to believe will not long sustain it. The blind? In every Christian land schools, asylums, and industries for. the blind. with a written language invented for their especial use. The bruised by oppression? In Russia the imperialism of the Cæsars is fighting a losing battle for its life, and everywhere west of Russia the recognition in theory, and largely in practice, that governments exist for the benefit of the governed. The acceptable year of the Lord? Everywhere hope beckoning men on from the dull despair that is miscalled content; everywhere in Christendom increasing numbers of men and women hoping and struggling toward better days for their children, if not for themselves. There is still "the man with the hoe." There are still the slums. But these are the relics of a paganism under which the great majority of the population were doomed to a life of drudgery and housed rarely better and often worse than the beasts of the field.

The evidences of Christianity are to be found, not in facts which occurred in the first century, but in facts which are occurring all about us in the twentieth; as the evidence that there is an irrigating plant.in the mountains of Arizona is to be found, not in an engineer's report that he has built one, but in the verdure which clothes the once desert plain which irrigation has converted into a garden.

# The Spectator in Mediaeval Rothenburg

HE Spectator had a fixed idea (derived from exactly where he cannot say) that Nuremberg was a delightfully ancient, sleepy spot, where one stepped into the atmosphere of five hundred years ago, and walked as in a dream of mediæval days. It was a shock, therefore, to land there one evening in a big modern station, amid the largest and most rushing crowd he had encountered in all Germany. It was a far worse shock to look out of the window next morning and see, in front of the hotel, the same large and glaring vehicle that infests our American cities, guard, mega-phone, and all, with the legend " Seeing Nuremberg " placarded upon it. Shock number three came with the discovery that Nuremberg, as one of the most progressive commercial cities of the Em-pire, was holding a big exposition, and very much more interested in it than in the historic past. The Spectator enjoyed Nuremberg; nobody could help

it; but he felt dazed all the time he was there from the violent upset his mind had received.

❀

It was not until he had reached the seclusion of Rothenburg on the Tauber that he "met up" with the reality of what he had expected. Very few people who go to Nuremberg go to Rothenburg on the Tauber. The Spectator was among the fortunate few because a friend, who hadn't time to go himself, urged him not to miss it. It takes time to go to Rothenburg, because it is on a branch road, whose time-tables are too much even for the man at Cook's. The traveler starts in the early afternoon for a junction remembered by the Spectator as " Dumb-bell," that being the nearest he could get to the German word by simplified spelling. "Dumb-bell " being reached an hour behind time, the Rothenburg train makes up leisurely. Then it starts, goes half-way, remembers that it has forgotten something, comes back for miles, changes its mind again and makes a fresh detour, and finally, in the twilight, lands its passengers far down by one of the gates of the Red City on the Tauber. Here is no big station, no hurrying modern crowd. When it comes to " seeing Rothenburg," travelers need expect no megaphonic communications. A blessed sense of peace and hope came into the Spectator's heart as he left his luggage with a sturdy youth with a handbarrow, and loitered up the road, past the spot where Gustavus Adolphus of Sweden camped in 1632 (a mere yesterday to Rothenburg, which was founded in 420 by the Franks) and through the famous Röderthor gate, with its little red-tiled, flower-crowded square turrets hanging over the green moat. Here, at last, were the Middle Ages waiting for their admirers.

❋

Not that Rothenburg has not a hotel omnibus—indeed, it possesses two, as the Spectator afterward found out. Not that it has not electric light in its streets and hotels, and can accommodate automobiles. Not that, outside its gates, at the foot of the hill, where its famous Wildbad Springs lie, it has not a celebrated modern sanitarium, overflowing with science and clients. But the real

Rothenburg is untouched by these things. It is jealous of old ways, proud of memorial custom. New houses are built outside its gates in any desired. But inside the town the burger whose mediæval dwelling is about his ears cannot rebuild it in twentieth-century style—nor does he want to. He rebuilds it exactly as it stood for centuries, and he paints afresh the old house-motto on it that has greeted the passer-by for perhaps four hundred years. On every street these quaint rhymes flourish upon gable and façade. The shoemaker's house, where generations of his trade before him have waxed thread and driven peg, bears the stanza :

> Im Hause meiner Väter
> Klopf' ich allhier das Leder
> Und mache meinen Reim dazu
> Ich sorge nicht wer's nach mir thu'.

A little higher up the Rödergasse shines out this patriotic distich, between two elaborately painted baskets of roses :

> Deutsches Haus—Deutsches Land
> Schirm dich Gott mit starker Hand.

And a thoroughly German sentiment, which has suited the dwellers behind it

A STREET NEAR THE RATHHAUS

THE KOBOLD TOWER

for centuries, is to be read on the Herrenstrasse:

> Gott lieben macht selig
> Wein trinken macht frölich
> Drum liebet Gott und trinket Wein
> So werdet ihr selig und fröhlich sein.

The Spectator's hotel had its motto, too. It was a delightful combination of two old houses of the noble family of the Winterbachs, nearly opposite the Rathhaus itself, and its rhyme was:

> Im Kaiserstuhl sass Wenzeslaus,
> Die Stadt bezahlt' ihm Wein und Schmaus.
> Verhüll Dein Haupt, mein Lieber,
> Die Zeiten sind vorüber.

All up and down the street near it were the old patrician houses of Rothenburg. Here, on one house-front of the Jagstheimers, was proudly inscribed the fact that the Emperor Maximilian had been twice a guest within the walls. In another, "The Child of Rothenburg," the imperial Frederick, nephew of Barbarossa, was born. In another still Charles the Fifth stayed for over a week in 1546. His stay was not entirely voluntary, however, as he had meant to pay only a short visit to the Red City. But the Rothenburgers entertained him so royally in the Rathhaus that a nine days' fit of the gout followed, during which time the high and mighty sufferer probably cursed the day in which he entered the gates.

❀

The Rathhaus, built originally in 1240, is one of those complete delights that leave nothing to sigh for. Rothenburg centers round it. Its Renaissance façade is decorated with masses of flowers and trailing vines in the most overflowing bloom. Up to its high, square tower-top, by winding stair and ladder, climb, three times a week, at half-past eleven in the morning, the choir of St. Jakob's, armed with cornet, dulcimer, shawm, psaltery, sackbut, and all the rest of it. On the stroke of the half-hour, to the north, the east, the south, the west, sound out the trumpets, followed by a verse of an old chorale. The Spectator, standing on the street corner in delighted attention amidst a group of Rothenburgers, noted with an added joy the ceremonious offering of snuff-boxes by one sturdy burgher to another. and

THE STRAFT TOWER

the sneezes of good-fellowship that ensued. No matter if an automobile did chug by in the middle of it all; even gasoline could not spoil the atmosphere of the past.

❀

The Rathhaus, naturally, is the home of legend and story. The staircase which the choir climb is comparatively new, and thereby hangs a tale. Once, in 1501, a pair of storks built in the top of the tower, and the town watchman, being as much without reverence for them as a modern flat-house janitor, threw down their nest with the young in it. The parent storks thereupon came with lighted straws in their bills and set fire to the tower. The watchman was burned, the stairway fell, the great bell tumbled, and only the four bare walls of the tower remained. The beautiful old doorway at the foot was, however, uninjured, and eventually the tower was restored and the bell rehung. The storks, in the meantime, left Rothenburg in a body, and did not return for many years. Nowadays it is a high crime in Rothenburg to interfere with them. But they have never tried to raise another family in the Rathhaus.

❀

All the towers in Rothenburg are pretty well filled, anyway, and have little room for birds' nests. The old town uses them for its poor, renting their queer little watch-tower rooms to little old women or very aged men. The visitor is thus always sure of an eager welcome

A BIT OF THE OUTER WALL AND MOAT

and a minute and garrulous history of every inch and corner, while a modest fee is highly appreciated. It is rather a good charitable idea, and helps to account, perhaps, for the fact that not a beggar is to be found in the Red City, in all the round of its walls and towers. And such walls and towers! The Spectator spent his days in wandering around and finding new towers all the while, and new views of the old ones. Young German artists of the Munich school were forever setting up their easels in the best places in this happy hunting-ground. The artist and the American have found out Rothenburg, and the former live in dread lest the latter should spoil it. So the painters are distinctly not genial. The Spectator did not blame them, for he remembered the automobiles.

❀

Which tower it was that he reached by the spiral staircase from the little old church, and the secret passage into the walls, the Spectator does not remember. But never did any boy dream of a more romantic scramble. From the tiny gallery of the old frescoed church a secret door in the paneling, left inadvertently open, led into a dark winding passage, with creaking boards underfoot. The Spectator had left the old custodian waiting in the church porch; he had not the faintest idea whether he was allowed to go on, or where the passage led, but how forego so beckoning a chance? A turn, a rude loophole, and, lo! he was in a gallery within the wall, with a lookout far over the vine-clad slopes of the valley of the Tauber. Bean-poles and kindling-wood were comfortably stored along the gallery walls, where ammunition and stores used to be heaped during those sieges of which Rothenburg stood so many in its stirring history. On and on the Spectator went, the wall turning and winding and fresh views opening, from loophole and buttress here and there, up and down unexpected steps, till a little flight of them at last brought him into another tower, and so out again into the mediæval streets. Fearing his left-behind cicerone might be worried over a lost tourist, the Spectator hurried back through a picturesque arch to the old church, only to find the wrinkled old dame knitting placidly in the sunny doorway, quite ready to wait thus for hours on end. As she had no English and the Spectator little German, their explanation was by gestures. The Spectator swept his arm round and round, in imitation of the spiral staircase, and then round the circuit of the walls. She raised both hands in astonishment, then, receiving her fee with an indulgent smile, hurried into the church to fasten the secret door. The Spectator shrewdly suspects, nevertheless, that it was meant to be left open—at any rate, he is very glad it was.

❀

Wall and tower from outside are, after all, more satisfying. Did the armies that besieged Rothenburg off and on during dozens of mediæval wars, small and great, enjoy its beauty as they camped in grain-field and vineyard, and looked up at its

PORTAL OF THE OLD RATHHAUS

ruddy circumvallations? Mediæval Germans must have loved beauty, for they created so much of it; and the Red City, rising from stream and valley, turn after turn, tower after tower, belfry and spire and red-huddled roofs rising behind the walls and between the towers, must have pleased the eye of the roughest warrior. From below the curious old double bridge Tilly and Piccolomini and Turenne have looked up at this city on a hill, this "German Jerusalem" as it used to be called, and laid their plans for its conquest. Every arched gateway has its story and its tragedy, and the inscription on the Spital Gate, "To those that enter, welcome; peace to those that depart," was often a mockery to the hapless ones dragged in or out to their doom. The Spital Thor, with its deep moat and mighty fortifications, was called the "Nightcap Tassel" by all Rothenburg when the Emperor Albrecht the First gave reluctant permission to build it. "Your town looks already like a nightcap," he said, angrily, to the persistent burghers, alluding to its rambling shape; "well, put the tassel on;" and the name clung to the huge tower, with its quadruple pepper-box turrets, ever after.

❦

One thing, however, the Spectator was forced to miss in the Red City—its Festival Play, given twice a year in the Rathaus to commemorate the "Meister-Trunk" or "Master-Drink," by which Nusch, the ex-burgomaster, saved his town in the day of Tilly's triumph in 1631. Rothenburg had resisted the great captain too well to please him. When the town surrendered at last, Tilly and his staff, followed by a horde of mercenaries, made their entry into the Rathaus, called before them Senate and Burgomaster, and condemned them all incontinently to death. The executioner was sent for, and meanwhile the victors refreshed themselves with Rothenburg wine—pure, clear, and famous to this day for its excellence.

The cellarer's daughter, trembling, brought in the mighty Pokal, or stirrup-cup, of glass, holding three quarts. The whole staff drank from it in turn, and did not exhaust it. Tilly, struck with its size, and enjoying the generous wine, cried out in ferocious pleasantry, "I will show mercy to all, on condition that one of you empties this full cup at one draught!" No one answered at first. Then Nusch stepped forward, and lifted the brimming Pokal. All watched incredulously, for all believed it impossible to drink the glass dry. Higher and higher the valorous burgher tilted the mighty cup, and hope began to dawn in the Rothenburgers. The last drop of the draught was watched breathlessly by friends and foes alike. "Thy promise?" gasped Nusch, as he actually accomplished the impossible. "It shall be honorably kept!" cried Tilly. On the words, Nusch sank insensible to the floor. For three days he lay between life and death, and his first remark as he recovered was, "I could never save another town!" However, he received a patent of nobility and a pension, and lived to the average pensioner's age—eighty. At Whit-

PARSONAGE OF THE TOWN CHURCH

suntide every gate and tower is manned in his honor by halberdiers in costume, while Tilly and his men march through the Spital Thor to the Rathhaus, and the "Meister-Trunk" is enacted over again. The real Pokal is too precious to be used on these occasions. It is preserved at the house where the descendants of Nusch live. The Spectator can testify that it is a most interesting piece of old painted glass, with the Emperor, the seven Electors, and the seven Princes on it, and a lid with the arms of Nusch, and that it holds more than any one man could possibly drink to-day.

The Spectator had missed the Festival Play by two good weeks. That was not to be helped. But he got some idea of it, nevertheless. One day, coming out of St. Jakob's—the quaintest of old churches, with its picturesque sexton's house, its archaic statues of saints, its pews for men on the one side and women on the other, with a silver name-plate marking each person's exact place in every pew—he saw a crowd of infantile Rothenburgers besieging a shop window opposite the Rathhaus. There, in the corner, was a pfennig-in-the-slot machine with the festival play in it. The Spectator dropped in the pfennigs, and Tilly and his men, in jointed cardboard, marched across the foreground, gathered in the Rathhaus, drank from the Pokal, and so on. Nusch next appeared and drained the cup, and each small Rothenburger, edging to get a closer view, was loyally enthusiastic. It was not a perfect machine; it joggled and balked at times, and had to be thumped by the oldest small boy; but the Spectator never had more fun out of a few pfennigs in his life, and was only sorry that, for want of more change, he had to leave brave Nusch at last, with the Pokal half drained and the supreme moment suspended in the air, so to speak. May the next good Americans who go to Rothenburg get there at Whitsuntide, and see the real thing !

ANCIENT BRIDGE OVER THE TAUBER

# IN THE LAND OF
# THE GREAT HUNGER

### BY LEROY SCOTT
#### ILLUSTRATED BY THE AUTHOR

HE Great Hunger that lurks always at Russia's door has entered; and thirty millions of people are gripped in its consuming fangs. And by the time the harvest of 1907 shall have vanquished its gaunt figure, God alone can guess how many hundreds of thousands of new wooden crosses will widen the peasant graveyards.

We had heard in St. Petersburg and Moscow many stories of the hunger that spreads over a third of European Russia —the worst famine in Russia's history, one of the worst of modern history; and we (Mrs. Scott and I) decided to look upon these stories in the original. Moscow friends advised us to go into Samara, one of the easternmost provinces. Famine was much nearer, but for the advice there was good reason. At this time, in late November, the Government was using every legal and illegal trick, every power of police, church, army, prison, Siberia, to prevent the election of a liberal second Duma; and among the mildest of these methods was the attempt to quarantine the peasant voters against the overwhelming anti-Government feeling of the cities. We were assured that in many provinces we would be strictly

barred from entering the country, and if we did manage to elude authority and enter it we would very likely be arrested and held for days in some verminous jail. But in far-off Samara there were people that would see to our safety and guidance.

After two days and nights of wind-mad, snow-buried steppes, we left the crawling train at Buzuluk, a little town sitting close beside the Asiatic border. Here all was done for us that had been promised; and the next morning, at the first duskiness, we made our start. Our sleigh was a rough-axed affair, with body of woven reeds, and was drawn by three shaggy little post-horses, their brown fur fluffy with frost, their tails and manes great frost plumes. We ourselves were so deeply wrapped in fur on fur that the searching wind could not find us. And so we glided swiftly away—the inner horse trotting, the two outer galloping, the bell in the yoke jangling musically— away through the lifting night, across vast reaches of treeless, unfenced plain, into the region of the Great Hunger.

Not till the sun was burning on the white horizon did the horses stop. We had gained a typical village of the steppes. Along the wide streets straggled thatched huts, built of sun-baked, straw-knit brick, their outside plastered with clay. Beside each hut was a little farm-yard, inclosed by a rectangle of outbuild-

RUSSIAN PEASANT MOTHER AND CHILD

ngs, their roofs all of straw, their walls either of clay or a wickerwork of twigs. In all the village there were but three wooden houses; timber was to be secured only by laborious dragging from far-placed forests.

At the largest of these wooden houses we had stopped, for before it huddled a crowd of men, women, and children, shrinking deeply into their sheepskin coats, on their faces a gray, hopeless patience. Within was a relief station, conducted jointly by the local Zemstvo and the Red Cross Society, and the crowd were awaiting the daily distribution of food. That took place at twelve; it was now but half-past eight.

We passed through the gate into the farmyard, empty of all life, and thence, halving our height, through a low door into the house. Its wooden walls, its floor of wood instead of clay, its two rooms instead of one, all repeated what had been told us—that it was the house of the richest man of the village. The owner, gray, shaggy, red-bloused, led us through the first room, which a great soup-caldron packed with a blinding steam, into the second room, and seated us on a rough bench in a corner beneath a cheap brass ikon. And as many of the crowd as could enter pressed about us. We asked our host the blackest of

questions: How had the harvest been? From the two little square windows we could see the white land over which we had galloped; and out toward this the old man swept a gnarled hand.

"Out there lie our fields. We have little land, and much of our small crops goes for taxes. Even when God blesses with harvests, we barely live from one year to the next.

"Two summers ago our fields gave us almost nothing. We thought last winter would end us—that we should never see the spring. The winter took all that we had saved—all! When spring came, we put in our seed, though the earth was dry. We thought, ' Surely this year God will give us a rich harvest!' But no rain fell. In some places the grain came up, thin, yellow. In most places it came not up at all.

"We saw ahead another black year. We prayed for rain to save the little that had sprouted, for that little would help keep us alive. Week after week we prayed, but no rain came. All that fell from Easter till the end of harvest, one man could have drunken it! We saw our few sprouts wither. Only here and there did a stalk come into head—and that head was empty. We turned our starving cattle into these best fields to get from them what they could. For the

PEASANT GIRLS AND WOMEN

rest, our fields were black, dusty. They were like the road. From all our land we took nothing—nothing !"

This was not one man telling the story of the fields of one village. In him thirty millions of people were speaking, and were telling the story of a third of European Russia.

These people were living solely on that which is given them, and this comes from two main sources—from the Government, and from the Red Cross and Zemstvo funds. The Government grants monthly to each person under eighteen and over fifty-nine, forty pounds of flour. All between these ages, and infants under one, get nothing. Other rules bar many families from receiving the Government allowance, and to aid these families is the chief effort of the Red Cross and Zemstvo relief. Daily, in such villages as have Red Cross kitchens, there are given to each child and each old person of these families a pound of black bread and a small portion of soup, made of cabbage and potatoes, strengthened with shreds of meat or a little oil. Again nothing for the adults.

But the adults are not utterly without

414

food, for the portion of childhood and old age is divided among the workers of the family, and the pound of bread to each becomes half a pound or even less. Now the adult Russian peasant, who lives almost wholly on grain, is accustomed to eating daily five pounds of black bread. Divide your own daily ration by ten and see! And they that have this tenth are the fortunate ones.

I knew that a man could keep alive a short time on half a pound of bread, but how a man—yes, a fifth of a nation—could live from harvest to harvest on no more, that I could not imagine. I put the brutal question to the crowd : " And how will you live till summer ?"

Their faces tightened. They did not look at one another—they dared not. And they did not answer—for there was no answer.

The old man raised his eyes to the brass-sheeted Mary of the ikon. He crossed himself.

"God have pity on us!" he whispered.

And then the crowd broke loose and told us each his own details of the story the old man had told us as a whole.

And the details were all the same—no bread, a wasting, agonizing hunger. One old woman there was among them, almost shrunken down to mere bone, who cried silently all the while; and at length we gained her story. There were four in her family, herself and her three grown sons, and upon her pound a day the four were living. Only, she did not divide it into fourths; she divided it into thirds, and for weeks she had eaten only crumbs.

In this village there were but two words, "hunger" and "bread," the one a moan, the other a prayer; and in the next village also there were but the same two words. In the third village the priest—his unshorn hair falling about his shoulders, on his breast the three-barred crucifix—led us among the houses of his people. Before entering the first, I looked about the barnyard and the little wicker farm buildings. There was not a head of grain, not a living creature. Beside the cow-shed was a heap of dry weeds, weighted against the wind by a harrow; nothing else could I see to suggest the harvest.

The house was on the plan of all peasants' houses: a little outer room, used for stores, and an inner room, twelve or fifteen feet square, the ceiling head-high, lighted by two foot-square windows, and a quarter filled by a great brick oven. This, the living-room, was furnished with a bed, a table, two benches, all home-made, and the never-missing ikon in the chief corner, the "red corner," as the peasants call it. On the clean earthen floor was one child, on top of the oven was another, on the bed lay the father, and at the bare table sat the mother and a second woman, the mother's sister—all with the listlessness of exhaustion.

We questioned as to the cause of the man's illness, and were told, "He's just weak." We did not need to be told the cause of his weakness.

"What have you to eat in the house?" we asked the mother.

"Nothing," she said, her listlessness almost seeming indifference.

"Not a single piece of bread?"

"Not a crumb," she said.

"But you have eaten to-day?"

"Yes. We have had part of theirs." She nodded at the two children.

**415**

We asked about the weeds beside the cow-shed, and she told us that when the too-late rain had come, weeds had sprung up over their fields; and these they had carefully gathered, as all the village had done. That heap of weeds was all that their land had yielded them. They had thought these weeds would keep their cow through the winter, but long ago they had sold her, and sold all else. And now they had left only the weeds.

We had heard in Moscow of a strange—strange to us—use the peasants of the hungry villages were making of weeds; and we questioned her further.

"Yes, we have done that," she said. "But the bread we got from the seed of the weeds. it made us all sick."

We went from the dusky room out into the street's blinding light, and our eyes were blinded not only by the sun. In the street had gathered a great crowd, in coats of sheepskin and of patched and repatched homespun; and since we were obviously from that vague, beyond-their-village world to which their voices could not reach, from which alone could come help, they followed us about all the while we were in their village and begged us to send them bread.

In the next home conditions were much as in the first—and in the next, and the next, and the next. Nowhere was there as much as a pound of bread for a person. And then we came into a house where lived a family of five—a father and mother in the forties, two sons, one nineteen and the other twenty-two, and a daughter of thirteen. Of these five the Government's regulations gave aid to but one—the girl. But her monthly portion, given on the first, had long ago been eaten. We asked on what they were now living; and they told us that each day the girl went forth to beg from their neighbors—such fortunate neighbors as out of a family of five received aid for three, or for six out of ten.

"And they give to you?" I marveled.

They did. Some a bite of bread, some a bit of potato from their Red Cross soup. And these little fragments she carried home.

That a famishing people could divide with those not of their kin the little on which they starved—this we could hardly believe. It was the first time we had met the fact. But the priest told us that several families in his village were living on this charity of starvation—and afterward we met the fact over and over again. Sympathy and generosity, these are at the foundation of the Russian peasant.

A TYPICAL CLAY HOUSE IN A PEASANT VILLAGE

THE EXTENT OF THE FAMINE

The darker shading shows the area of most complete destitution. In the lighter area conditions are not quite so bad, but still serious. There have also been crop failures and great hardships outside the indicated regions

Out in the street again, we paused amid the attending crowd. Surely these idle hands could do something to feed this awful hunger! "Why don't you go to the cities and seek work in the factories?" we asked of the men. "Earn money there, send it home, and save yourselves and your people!"

"Many of us have already tried to do that," they replied. "But at the factories there was no work. Every one said to us 'No.'"

"But try again!" we insisted.

"Yes, but where shall we find factories that will have us?"

Where indeed! Factories are com-

PART OF A CROWD GATHERED BEFORE A RED CROSS KITCHEN FOR THEIR DAILY ALLOWANCE OF BLACK BREAD AND CABBAGE SOUP

paratively few in Russia, and those few were in other parts, distant long journeys on the railway—and the nearest railway was forty versts away from this village. And other starving villages, as I knew, had no railway within a hundred or five hundred versts.

"And the money for the trains?" they continued. "And for our food on the journey, and while we search? Here in the village we have barely anything to eat, but when we leave the village we shall have nothing at all. Tell us—where shall we get the money?"

"Can't you sell something?" we cried in desperation.

And they said, "Already we have sold all."

Yes, they had sold all! There was not another word left us, and we turned away. They were right; for them there was nothing but to remain in their village—to starve, and see their people starve.

We went through barnyard after barnyard. All were utterly empty—save in one here and there we found the barely vital framework of a dwarfish horse or cow. And through house after house; and if for the contents of most houses I had paid a dollar, I should have been giving charity. Yes, they had sold all! Their horses they had sold, some to neighboring Tartars, also starving, who ate horseflesh, but most to hide dealers, who bought merely for the skins. Three dollars apiece was the price. Their fleshless cattle they had sold at a similar rate. Their sheep had gone for fifty cents and a dollar, and some had been exchanged for half their weight in flour. The peasants had sold this meat instead of eating it, because they are almost wholly vegetarians. Black bread—that is the only food. And they sold not only because there was nothing on which they could live, but because there was nothing on which the stock could live. It had to be sold, or lost entirely.

And they had sold not only the present. They were selling the future—offering any bargain that would gain them bread. Many had sold to landlords and a few richer peasants, for immediate cash, their labor for the next summer at a third the usual rate. Some were renting their

land, cash down of course, for the next year at a tenth and a fifteenth of its regular rental. And some were selling their next year's crop from their land : bargaining to plow their fields, sow them with their own seed, tend, harvest, and deliver the crop to the buyer, all for a dollar an acre. These men did not think of what monstrous usury they were begging to pay ; they did not think of how, horseless and without a kopek toward a horse's price, they could plow their fields, nor of the new crisis they would face in the autumn, even if the harvest were good. They thought only of how they might get through the day and get through the morrow.

As it was in this village, so was it in thousands of others. And in one, a Tartar village in the neighboring province of Kazan, the stripped people had been driven into yet another variety of despair-bargain. An enterprising buyer of women for the brothels of Constantinople came into the village, selected what pleased him and made his offer. The peasants had nothing else ; they were hunger-mad—and when the dealer went away he took with him the eight most beautiful girls of the village. For them he had paid from fifty to seventy-five dollars apiece—prices that Constantinople would richly multiply. Very likely this dealer, or his brethren, have been buying for their market in other villages, for the opportunity is too rare a one for their business acumen to miss. But this I do not know.

Yes, the village we saw has sold its all—all but its daughters. As we clambered into our sleigh to leave, the crowd pressed about us—men, women, children—famine-eaten, blackly despairing, yet newly hopeful. To them, as I have said, we represented the far-off outside world from which might come help. All God's blessing upon us !—would we not have pity and send them bread? The men stood with bared heads; some of the women were crying, some even kneeling in the snow. And as we drove away their voices went up, sobbing frantically, prayerful, in a last appeal.

"Do not forget us !" they cried. "Do not forget the hungry ones !"

Our galloping horses swept us over a

A VILLAGE PATRIARCH

vast stretch of land, treeless to the end of the eye's reach, and as flat as a frozen lake. Here and there were weeds, richly plumed with snow, that had escaped the peasants' gleaning; these alone relieved the flat whiteness that went on and on till it entered the grayish blue of the horizon. As we glided along, my mind ran back to questions I had asked about the quality of the Government's flour and the answer that had been given me. The flour was most infamously adulterated—with earth, with every costless alloy known to commissarial thieves. It often had no more than fifty per cent. of the proper nutritive value. So the half-pound of bread was really but a quarter.

This we had been told elsewhere again and again. It is notorious throughout Russia that the famine fund is a rich source of "graft" to those who have control of its expenditure. Officials, contractors, sub-contractors, all dip in their hands, and dip deeply. The officials get their share by awarding contracts to the highest briber, the briber his by delivering rotten flour. Or the two establish an underground partnership, which is usually conducted on this plan: The official arranges with the contractor to deliver to a certain district, say, a million poods of flour (a pood is forty pounds) for a million and a half of rubles. The contractor sends half a million poods of flour, and mixed with it half a million poods of some adulterant, and there is a matter of several hundred thousand rubles to be divided between the partners—of which the smaller share goes not to the official. And the show-girls and champagne dealers of Paris are the happier, even if the peasants are not.

The Government, until the last few weeks, has done nothing to stop this robbery of famine bread—not charity bread, if you please, for it is the peasants' own, paid for by their taxes. But recently the frauds have roused so tremendous a scandal that the Government could no longer refrain from taking notice. A commission was appointed to investigate. The guilty, with indignant virtue, threw blame upon others; the systemless business methods of an irresponsible bureaucracy made proof and conviction impos-

sible, and the situation remains practically what it was before. The Government has no time for such matters—has no time to govern; has time and energy only to try to crush, by every manner of relentless violence, the growing spirit of liberty.

The Government's favorite method of remedying an evil condition is to deny the condition's existence. What is cheaper and easier?—and what better calculated to keep Russia's borrowing power strong among the nations? During the terrible famine of 1891, much less terrible than this year's, one means the Government took to relieve the situation was to forbid the use of the word "hunger." A heavy penalty was attached to its use, being in the case of newspapers suspension on the third occurrence of the word. Close your eyes, and there is no evil! This year the Government has recognized the existence of the famine by its grant to the starving districts of sixty-five million dollars—far, far too little—and even admits that greater hunger Russia never knew. But, after all, says officialdom, no one is suffering; everybody will pull through nicely. And the peasants' daily half pound continues to be half earth.

The latter part of the journey to the next village was lighted only by the moon, in a double halo of incandescent gold and pink. In this village also the priest led us among his people, and here also there was nothing. The first house sheltered sixteen people—twelve adults and four children. In the "red" corner, the light of a tiny hanging lamp in her wasted face, sat a young mother with a baby in her arms. The baby, as were the other children, was thin, white; and was weakly suckling at a shriveled breast. We asked the mother how much food the house received. It seemed an effort for her even to raise her eyes, and her voice was a meager whisper. "For three," she said.

Three pounds for sixteen people—a fifth of a pound apiece. No wonder the empty breast!

In the next house we found an old mother, her unmarried daughter, a daughter-in-law, and the latter's child. The young husband had set forth into the unknown two months before to seek work, and no word had come from him—for a postage stamp is the price of a pound of bread. In the autumn the father, who was seventy, had begun to go to other villages to beg. There had been a horse then, and the old man had ridden, but it had long since been sold. Three weeks before, he had set out for a region in which rumor said there had been a harvest. When he came back he would bring them the pieces of bread—if any there were—that he had not eaten on the way. That would not be before a month or six weeks—for the journey was long, and the weather was cold and snowy, and he was old.

In the next house also the father had gone away to beg and the son to look for work. From the low ceiling of the little room hung a cradle, over which leaned a shrunken grandmother and a young woman who may have been fresh and pretty before the hunger had eaten her away. The poor child was burning with fever, and its face was almost hidden beneath scrofulous scabs. We asked the two watchers if it had had any medical attention. It had, and the grandmother, her wrinkles running with silent tears, told us how the aid had been gained. A week before, frightened at the child's condition, she and her daughter had bundled it up and set out in their sledge for the nearest doctor, fifty versts away. Their horse was so weak that it was constantly falling. The daughter had to get out and lead it; but it still fell, and the grandmother had to take the other bit. A fierce snow-storm came on, then darkness; they could hardly stand for weakness; they were almost frozen; but fear for the child would not let them stop. And so these two starved women, holding up a starved horse, tramped on and on through the bitter, snow-blinding night.

The old woman stopped and covered her face, and her thin body shook. After a moment we asked, "And you finally got there?"

"Yes."

We gazed at their wasted figures. "How?" we marveled.

"We got there on our tears," she said.

And thus the stories of the village went on. Out of the seven hundred families, the priest told us, only nine had a thing of their own to eat.

That night we slept in the priest's house. We were to have made another before-day start, but our sleigh was late in coming. When we were bundled in and on the way, we asked our driver the reason for the lateness. He told us that, hours before, he had begun to look for new horses (our three of the day before had been sent back to their post station), and not till a few minutes since had he been able to collect two that could do more than merely stand upon their feet. And this in a village which

THEY MAY NOT LOOK HUNGRY, BUT THEY ARE

THE BEST HORSES IN THE VILLAGE

ordinarily had a thousand horses! This best pair of the place that we had were merely bonework and skin, with lassitude for energy. As they tottered across the steppe, rarely venturing into a trot, I felt that we, too, should be at their heads supporting them along their journey.

At the next village we got a slightly better pair, and drove on through the swirling snow. Presently we saw coming toward us along the faintly marked road two black figures, which the decreasing distance developed into little girls, apparently about nine and eleven. Both wore sheepskin coats, shawls over their heads, and on their feet a kind of slipper made of loose-woven flags. Over her shoulder the elder of the two carried a coarse linen bag.

We stopped and questioned them. They were of a type that the chronic hunger has made common, and to which it has given a name—"crumb-collectors," or, more literally, "crumbers." They lived in the village in which we had passed the night, and their home was as all other homes. Two days before they had gone out to beg pieces of bread, and they were now homeward bound with their charity. At our request the older girl opened her bag, and we saw a score or more of scraps of bread, none larger than two fingers—all the alms of starving people. Most were bits of the common peasant bread, but among them were

many pieces that looked never to have grown on stalk of wheat or rye. I picked up one of these pieces. It was hard and black and gritty; looked like a piece of asphalt picked from a broken pavement. I knew its material, for I had met such bread before. It was made from the seed of wild grasses and weeds. The chief weed is called *agrostemma gilhago :* I give its name for the sake of the scientific.

"But how can you eat such bread?" we asked.

"We soak it in water. Then it's good," the older girl answered.

We told them good-by, these two little "crumbers," and they plodded off in their flag shoes, bending low against the cold wind. And here let me say that weed bread is not the only substitute for bread in the starving regions. The screenings of the threshed wheat and rye, composed of shriveled grains, chaff, seed of weeds, and dirt, usually the portion of chickens and cattle, is being eaten where it can be had. In parts where the oak grows, acorns are ground into flour, and from this is made a bitter bread, the loaves as solid and heavy as bricks. Straw is ground into flour, and bark, particularly of the oak, is powdered, and these are mixed with rye flour in the proportion of half and half; and thereby the stomach is distended, even if it is not fed.

423

We drove through village after village, and in all we heard from starving lips the same breadless story. Nowhere did more than two per cent. have any food save what was given them. At length we came into a village where the women gazed covertly at us from behind veils, and where, instead of a cross on the church steeple, there was a crescent, and we knew we were in a village of the Tartars. Here the old mullah, in a dark-green, priestly robe and white turban, led us about, half the males of the village at our heels. He took us first to his church, which, after leaving our shoes at the door, we entered in our stocking feet. Half a dozen turbaned old men were squatting on the floor in evening prayer, but otherwise this house of Allah was absolutely empty; a dollar would have covered its contents. Next the mullah took us into the little school-house, cold, and also utterly bare. No school was for the children this winter, for this village of two thousand souls had not the fifteen dollars for the teacher's yearly salary. And then the mullah took us into the clay houses of his people.

As we entered the first—its one living-room was about eight feet square, and was half filled by a raised wooden platform, which is the sole furnishing of the houses of most Tartar peasants—a woman seized something in her arms and dashed by us out into the snowy cold. The priest called to her reassuringly, and, face covered, she slipped back among us. That which was in her arms was a year-old child, as bare as at birth. We asked what food she had, and she answered by setting her all before us—an iron dish holding a single clean bone and a thin layer of grease.

In the next house lived seven, of whom three received the Government grant. When their portions for this month had come, a family that received no aid had borrowed half the grant on promise of its early repayment. But the family had not been able to repay, and now the seven had not one grain of flour, nor chance of any for two weeks to come. They seemed too worn away to feel either hope or despair.

We passed one house, larger and better-looking than those about it, from whose two windows four dark-skinned, black-haired, beautiful children were watching us. I thought, "Here is something different—a relief from this awful blackness." And so we entered. In the house were bare boards and bare earth. Of the four children, two boys squatted on their dusky bare legs in Oriental fashion, in nothing but the last rags of shirts that ended at the waist; and two girls, of seven and ten, huddled, bare-legged, in a corner, the younger in a dress of slitted rags, the older in rags that fortunately held together. These tatters of calico were their best clothes, their father told us; for two empty years he had been able to buy them nothing. Yes, they were going to eat to-day—their first food since two days before, when they had divided a few bites of bread. We asked to see what the coming meal might be. The father called into the second room, which custom forbade my entering, for the wife was there. We gazed through the door and waited. After a moment a dusky hand pushed into view, along the clay floor, an earthen pot. We looked into it, and quickly turned away. In it were the entrails of a horse.

We asked, when we were again in the street, if there was no one in the village who had food of his own. Yes, one. Allah had been good to this man. His land had given him back a third of the seed he had put into it. With this and what the Government allowed him he had enough. The mullah pointed him out to us amid the following crowd. He seemed the marked man of the village. His fortune had rechristened him; they referred to him as "The man that is not hungry."

House after house was as those described. As we walked on down the street the mullah motioned to either row of bordering huts. "All—all are so!" he said. And the tears dripped down his wrinkled face to the snow.

If they were so now, what would they be like by spring? I put the question to the mullah.

He hid his face in his hands. All his body quivered. When his hands fell, his face was streaming.

" Ah! I don't dare think of it," he whispered. "Only Allah knows!"

Yes, only Allah knows. But man can make a near guess. And when I think upon what is before this village and the other villages we visited, and the thousands of villages we did not see, I can scarcely write. The Government fund, even if put in honest flour, is not enough to carry them all through, even as live specters. Reliable private relief societies state that five dollars will save a life, but they cannot get five dollars in sufficient quantities; for all Russia is poverty-stricken, tax-stricken, government-stricken. There is not enough—not half enough!

The people now have still a little of the strength of summer, a little of the strength given by the sale of their cattle. But this strength is fast fading. Scurvy and spotted typhus have already appeared, and, as the peasants' physical resistance lessens, will spread as plagues; and with them will come every other disease that attends an exhausted body. A man at the front of the relief work in the province of Samara, where conditions are at the very worst, said to me, "In 1891, in this province, the famine carried away sixty thousand persons. This year the famine is much worse and the aid is much less. We shall be fortunate if of our three million we lose no more than two hundred thousand." And there is famine in twenty-six other provinces. No wonder the mullah dared not think!

We had no words to brighten those things the mullah dared not think upon, so we gave him a silent good-by. At the next village we got stout post-horses again—three of them. Forty versts, galloped through blackness and a stabbing snow—over vast silent plains—through sleeping villages whose dogs yelped after us like wolf-packs; then two days on a creeping train; then Moscow again, where I write this—and our cross-section of the Russian famine was over.

But it was not over—never can be over; for I have witnessed scenes that can never be forgotten. As I write these last lines the scenes flash back upon my mind as lantern pictures on a screen: breadless houses, and silent, empty barnyards; the weeping old mullah, daring not to look upon the spring of his people; babies suckling vainly at shriveled breasts, inexorably dry; little "crumbers" in shoes of braided flags, bending away against the wind with their poisonous bread; two wasted women holding up a staggering horse throughout an agonizing night; half a village, despairing, hopeful, many sobbing, some prayerfully bowed in the snow, crying out:

"Do not forget us! Do not forget the hungry ones!"

# "AND A LITTLE CHILD SHALL LEAD THEM"

### BY LAURA MARQUAND WALKER

O childish heart, awake to sudden pain
To find that human which seemed all divine,
Yet steadfast looking from thy loving eyes
And folding in your little hands to mine:
I, who was given thee, with great behest,
To lift and guide thy feet through night and day,
Find thee, instead, helping to bear my load,
Yet singing and rejoicing all the way.

Thus childhood with its fearlessness and faith,
Filled full of Heaven whence it lately came,
Takes note that we are mortal, but speeds on
Bearing a torch topped with Celestial Flame.

ETHAN ALLEN HITCHCOCK
Secretary of the Interior

# PUNISHING THE LAND-LOOTERS

## BY HENRY S. BROWN

IT has seldom fallen to the lot of a man who has reached the age allotted by the Psalmist, of threescore years and ten, to accomplish the work that Ethan Allen Hitchcock will have to his credit when he relinquishes the portfolio of the Interior Department on March 4, 1907. He has exposed a class of offenses against the Government and the people of the United States which in magnitude dwarfs all of the infamous operations of "rings" that have periodically startled the country. In the number of persons involved the frauds against the Public Domain exceed those in the Post-Office scandals, the Star Route frauds, the Whisky Ring abominations, and the Crédit Mobilier affair combined. Including timber depredations, the indictments number 1,021, and the convictions 126. In the value of money concerned, the size of the stake for which the land operators were planning surpasses anything except that of the flotation of a billion-dollar corporation in Wall Street. An estimate has been made by Senator La Follette, of Wisconsin, that the Secretary of the Interior and the Commissioner of Indian Affairs, Mr. Francis E. Leupp, in safeguarding the oil and coal lands of the Indians of the Five Civilized Tribes, were protecting property on which were coal measures worth at least one billion of dollars. In urging the withdrawal from entry of 64,000,000 acres of coal and other mineral lands he has protected, for the public, fuel and other valuable commodities the value of which cannot be estimated, but which will certainly equal the wealth of any one of the highly cultivated States of the Middle West. In exposing the theft, under color of the law, of timber, agricultural, and grazing lands, he has succeeded in setting under way suits for the restoration of property valued at many millions.

When Secretary Hitchcock started on this work, he was already sixty-eight years old. He is now in his seventy-second year. A clever system of collusion, espionage, influence, forgery, bribery, and falsification of records had concealed from him the true facts for several years, just as it had deceived several of his predecessors. This system had extended to the very Department itself. The head of the Land Office in Washington, the man upon whom the Secretary had to rely for all matters of administration, was himself in the conspiracy. Scores of local agents of the Department were in collusion. Senators and Representatives were in sympathy with the system. Governors, judges, prosecuting officers, bank presidents, lawyers, and in fact representative men of every class, were favorable to the most liberal interpretation of the land laws. Viewed in the light of three years' disclosures, such interpretations meant that the laws should be evaded; that hundreds of thousands of acres intended for homesteaders should be turned over to speculators; that the superb forests of the Pacific coast should go, not to the men whom the law recognized as having a claim, but to lumber companies; that the mineral lands should pass into the control of corporations and railways.

The "lid" began to come off the General Land Office in Washington in the very last days of December, 1902. One morning, with some correspondence before him, the Secretary telephoned across F Street to the old Post-Office

FRANCIS E. LEUPP
Commissioner of Indian Affairs

building, in which the General Land Office is situated, and requested Mr. Binger Hermann, the Commissioner, to favor him with the report made on land frauds by J. S. Holsinger, a special agent of the Department, located at the time in Phœnix, Arizona. It is easily conceivable that this order created consternation in the mind of Mr. Hermann. The request meant that there had been a leak in the system, and that the Secretary knew of the gigantic steal of public lands which Mr. Hermann had been industriously covering. Mr. Hermann appeared in a few minutes with the report. The Secretary glanced at it. It bore the date of Phœnix, Arizona, November 12, 1902. On the back was the stamp of the General Land Office, showing that it had been received November 18. 1902. It was now very near the end of December. The report had, therefore, been in the hands of the Commissioner for nearly six weeks.

The Secretary looked over the report. It showed that very prominent and wealthy men had been engaged in frauds against the Government which involved hundreds of thousands, perhaps millions, of its choicest lands.

"Mr. Hermann," said the Secretary, a few days later, "can you give me any explanation as to why you have never called my attention to this important matter?"

Mr. Hermann hemmed and hawed and stammered, but he did not give a satisfactory explanation.

"Well, Mr. Hermann, by the direction of the President, I must ask you for your resignation."

Mr. Hermann was visibly agitated. He refused to believe the Secretary was in earnest. He blustered, and demanded to know why he was required to resign. The Secretary merely tapped the Holsinger report—the reason was there. Now, Mr. Hermann was a very powerful man in the Republican party in the public lands States. He had been a member of both branches of the Oregon Legislature, a deputy collector of internal revenue, a receiver of public moneys at a land office, Judge Advocate of the Oregon militia, and a member of Congress for six terms. He also had been

the head of the Land Office for six years. Naturally, political influences rushed to the protection of Mr. Hermann. Senators and Representatives sought to have the Secretary change his mind. It was the Secretary's first tussle with the political power of the men interested in the grand scheme of pirating the public domain. If he had weakened then, this article would not have been written. But, with the hearty support of the President, he "stood off" the friends of the dismissed Commissioner of the Land Office; and, vowing revenge and demanding a vindication, Mr. Hermann left office February 1, 1903. Here what appears to have been a mistake in tactics was made. If Mr. Hermann had been summarily ejected from the office the very day the Secretary became convinced that he was disloyal to the Government, the Secretary's task might have been simpler. Appeals were made to let him remain a month, and granted. During the month, it is charged, he ordered destroyed thirty-four letter-press books containing thousands of letters and documents relating to these very land frauds that were yet to be uncovered.

To Oregon Mr. Hermann went for his vindication. Thomas H. Tongue, a member of Congress, had just died. Mr. Hermann became a candidate for election to the place. During the campaign his political opponents appealed to the President and to the Secretary of the Interior for a statement as to the offenses for which Mr. Hermann had been dismissed. This was refused. Had it been given, it would have resulted in many persons escaping punishment, and in serious damage to others of the Government's criminal prosecutions. So while Mr. Hermann was seeking his vindication, which came when he was elected by 2,271 plurality, agents of the Interior Department were also in Oregon preparing evidence for the indictment of Mr. Hermann and many of his associates, some of them more prominent and influential than he.

The Secretary was now fairly started on a work that was to try him as few men have been tried. He knew that his fair-weather days were over, and that until he finished his task or laid it down he would know nothing but stress and storm. With the removal of Mr. Hermann interests with influence reaching from the Atlantic to the Pacific flew to arms. They sought to drag the Secretary down. Stories were spread that he was about to be removed from office for incompetency; that he was making a "bluff" about the land frauds in order to impress his chief, the President, and hold on a little longer. Human ingenuity was taxed at invention of vexatious reports and misleading attacks. But the Secretary merely bided his time, used every recourse of which he could avail himself to get at the bottom of the frauds, and scoured the country for information and evidence. He even remained silent under the reports that he was soon to leave the Cabinet, and when it became necessary to throw some frightened culprit off his guard he caused to be published reports minimizing the extent of the alleged depredations. But the time was coming when he would strike, and strike hard.

The land frauds were all based upon an apparent compliance with the law, and those who engineered them were familiar with the intricacies of the various statutes. A very brief statement of the working of these laws will enable the reader more easily to grasp what happened when the Secretary began to act. There are three important acts of Congress relating to lands which enter into the question—the Homestead Act, the Desert Land Act, and the Timber and Stone Act.

The Homestead Act allows a prospective settler to take up a quarter-section, 160 acres of land, and perfect his title to it by five years' actual residence, when the land is given to him and the title perfected. There is a commutation clause which permits the settler to purchase the land after fourteen months' residence. This commutation clause was adopted because it was claimed that it would enable the settler in need of money for improvements to borrow on his land. It really enables speculators and others to use innumerable human tools to concentrate many holdings in the hands of one owner.

The Desert Land Act permitted, until 1891, any settler to take up 640 acres of semi-arid land which might be susceptible of irrigation, and purchase it for $1.25 an acre. This amount was cut to 320 acres in 1891, but the law permitted the assignment of the original entries, and the working of the law was much the same as the Homestead Act.

The Timber and Stone Act provided that application should be made by a citizen to the nearest land office for 160 acres of valuable timber and stone land. After an advertisement had been made for sixty days, proof that the land was really what it was represented to be was offered, and title followed upon the payment of $2.50 an acre—a small fraction of the actual value of such land. This also worked to concentrate holdings.

In addition to these were one or two other laws that figured in the work of despoiling the public domain. One was a provision that any person who had land within a forest reserve of the United States might, on furnishing proof, exchange this land for agricultural or other valuable land owned by the United States outside the limits of the forest reserve. Another was what was known as the Kinkaid Law of 1904, under which persons in western and northwestern Nebraska might take up, instead of 320 acres under the Desert Land Act or 160 acres under the Homestead Act, a full section of 640 acres. Of both of these laws we shall hear more as we proceed with the narrative.

The point from which Mr. Hitchcock started was that indicated in the Holsinger report. The report dealt with matters which had come to the attention of the special agent of the Department through the dissatisfaction of one of the men who had been employed by the most important of the land sharks. It showed that John A. Benson, Frederick A. Hyde, and Henry P. Dimond, of San Francisco, had been engaged in a scheme by which they had been regularly getting possession of fraudulent titles of school lands in the States of California and Oregon, which had been included in the forest reserve of the United States, and were exchanging these fraudulent and worthless titles for desirable public lands elsewhere. These frauds, beginning on

BINGER HERMANN

the Pacific coast, extended to most of the public land States in the West. The Government had already been despoiled of some 40,000 acres, but the plans of the syndicate then under way included millions of acres.

There were numerous signs of great activity in the entire West for the absorption of public lands in an illegal way. Emboldened by past successes, many other syndicates and combinations than that of Benson and Hyde were engaged in raiding the public domain. Secretary Hitchcock dropped practically everything to cope with this pressing emergency. The work of parceling out the public land and perfecting titles came virtually to a standstill. The general charge of the correspondence in preparing cases for recovering stolen lands was in the hands of Judge James I. Parker, Chief of the Division of Lands and Railroads. A. B. Pugh, as Special Assistant United States Attorney, was sent into the field, and was one of the active prosecutors. It became necessary to call in Secret Service operators, to employ outside experts, and to remove various officials in widely scattered land offices, while surveying parties and special agents took the field and invaded the enemy's country.

But Secretary Hitchcock also found it necessary to look closer home. When Senators and others were making daily pilgrimages to the White House and to the newspaper offices in an effort to discredit him, he learned that the dismissal of Mr. Hermann had not ended treachery in the General Land Office. One of the men in the investigation struck a new trail of John A. Benson, and it ran directly into the Special Service Division at Washington. Benson had been an old offender away back in the eighties, and knew all the ropes. He had been concerned in extensive frauds in California through fictitious surveys, and he escaped

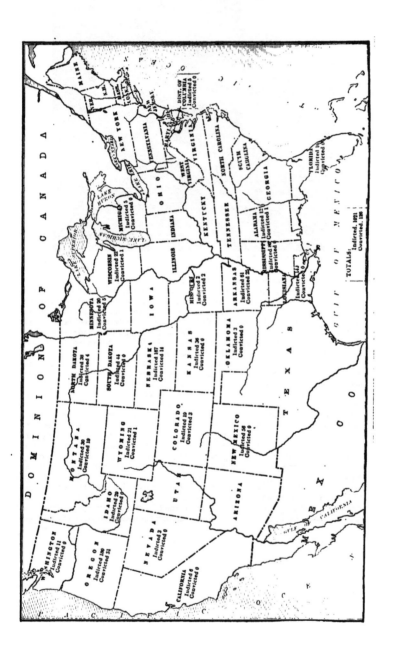

punishment by leaving the country. The Government recovered only a small portion of the land filched from it by means of the "Benson Surveys," as they were called. Benson had men in the Special Service Division in his pay. They were detected, and a trap was laid for the men suspected. One of the agents of Benson in the Department wrote a letter, under directions, telling him to come to Washington. He did not come, for the reason that the man who wrote this letter sent another secretly to Benson telling him of his danger. But finally he was decoyed and came to the seat of government. He went to the Willard Hotel and telephoned W. D. Harlan, Chief of the Special Service Division, to join him at his room. Harlan, cowed, acted under the orders of John E. Wilkie, Chief of the Secret Service, and W. J. Burns, who had been specially engaged for these Oregon and California frauds. He was searched before he went to see Benson. He was searched when he came out, and he had a $100 bill. Benson before dismissing him had sent him to the washroom, where he found the money. The next day William E. Valk, also an employee of the Land Office, was sent for by Benson. The same programme was observed, and Valk came out with two $100 bills.

Secretary Hitchcock was now ready to deliver the first blow. The methods of Benson, and the action of Hermann in destroying the records, had warned him that it was to be a game of diamond cut diamond. He had already made the case against Benson, Hyde, and their associates, and indictments had been found against them; but no inkling of this had leaked. Benson was arrested in Washington immediately after he had this interview with Valk, and the others were apprehended on telegraphic orders. The arrests, and Benson's sensational apprehension while practically bribing officials of the Department of the Interior, startled the country. The land thieves for the first time began to realize that they were in grave danger.

Other agents of the Department were working in Oregon. Some revelations began to come from that State which made persons think that the whole State must be honeycombed with fraud, and that the most prominent men in it were involved in the frauds over ears and eyes. The very finest timber of these splendid Oregon forests was falling into the hands of the despoilers. The very choicest grazing and agricultural lands were going into the possession of grazing or speculative land companies. Homesteaders were being shut out. This was done, not merely by means of "dummies" who were paid so much to take up homesteads or timber land and transfer the titles, but by means of forged applications and forged entries. As was subsequently shown by the conviction of Surveyor-General of Oregon, the men whose duties required them to protect the public interest on the scene were in league with the movement. Applications and entries were turned up for lands that were located 250 miles from the land office where they were on file. The Secretary of the Interior, with one stroke of the pen, stopped the operation of all the entering of land in Oregon, and ordered prosecution of every one involved, high or low. The next attack delivered by the Interior Department was even more dramatic than that concerning the Benson and Hyde ring. The Federal Grand Jury at Portland began to turn out indictments, and it was reported that Senators and Representatives in Congress would be implicated. One sensational incident followed another. The President, acting after interviews with Secretary Hitchcock and Attorney-General Knox, appointed Francis J. Heney as special land fraud prosecutor at Portland. This was done over the heads of the Oregon delegation in Congress. He next removed District Attorney Hall, who had obstructed Heney, and Hall was later himself indicted. The President also rejected the recommendations of the Oregon Senators in the matter of the successor of Mr. Hall.

One of the first of the Oregon cases will serve to show how high the arm of justice was reaching. The Butte Creek Land, Lumber, and Live Stock Company had obtained possession of the greater part of Wheeler County. For conspiracy and violation of the various land laws

JUDGE JAMES I. PARKER
Chief of Division Land and Railroads, Interior Department. One of Secretary Hitchcock's most active aids

there were indicted Binger Hermann, whom we last saw getting a vindication at the hands of the voters of the State; John H. Hall, ex-District Attorney; Edwin Mays, ex-District Attorney; F. P. Mays, State Senator; Hamilton H. Hendricks, Secretary and Treasurer of the Butte Creek Company; and C. E. Loomis and E. D. Stratford, special agent of the Land Office.

But higher and higher the hand of justice was reaching. It soon became apparent that United States Senator John H. Mitchell would be caught in the toils. Representative J. H. Williamson had already been indicted. Much evidence indicated that Senator Mitchell was in league with the conspirators; that he had formed a law partnership with Judge A. H. Tanner; that while he was drawing a salary of five thousand dollars as Senator he was practicing before the department and accepting fees as a lawyer, thus selling his influence as Senator. This was an offense against the

434

statutes of the United States, and Senator John R. Burton, of Kansas, had already been convicted of violating it. Senator Mitchell was a man of great influence, and had had a remarkably romantic history. Reared in western Pennsylvania as John Hipple, he had gone West because of some trouble and had changed his name to John Hipple Mitchell. The first time he returned East was as a United States Senator from Oregon, and as a wealthy man. He had been defeated for the Senate several times, and had been returned twice, and it was reported that he had made and lost several fortunes.

At the first definite sign of danger Senator Mitchell hurried to Washington to assure the Administration that he had done nothing improper. He claimed to have made a contract with Judge Tanner years before, in which it was specifically stated that no fees should be paid to him as a result of anything he did before the departments in the interest of the clients of the firm of Mitchell and Tanner. The danger became more threatening to Mitchell each day. The Grand Jury was in session at Portland. Mitchell's friends urged him to return. Instead, he despatched his private secretary, Harry Robinson, to Oregon with a sealed letter to Judge Tanner, in which he made the statement that it was always understood that no fees for department practice should be paid him, and asked that all books of the firm be shipped to Washington. The Secret Service knew of the sending of this letter. When

between himself and Mitchell bearing date of 1901, in which it was agreed that Mitchell should have his salary, get one-half of the proceeds of law cases, but that he would accept no fees for appearing before the Departments in legitimate matters affecting his constituents. The watermark on the paper on which this contract was written was " Edinample." The Government showed that no sample of this paper had appeared on the Pacific Coast until 1903. It also showed by the color of the ribbon of the typewriter on which it had been

FRANCIS J. HENEY
Special Prosecutor of Land Frauds in Oregon

Robinson was within about fifty miles of Portland, he was joined by William J. Burns, of the Secret Service, who accompanied him to Portland and took him as a witness directly before the Grand Jury. He was questioned about the letter, gave it to the Grand Jury, and it proved to be very damaging to Senator Mitchell. The Senator was indicted. He defended himself in a dramatic speech on the floor of the Senate, and tears poured down his withered cheeks as he asserted his innocence.

Senator Mitchell's conviction was accomplished only after one of the finest chains of circumstantial evidence was forged about him. Judge Tanner, in Mitchell's defense, produced a contract

written that it was not in existence before 1903. The contract had three words misspelled—" legitimate," " salary," and " constituents." When Tanner's son was asked to write a sentence containing these words, he made the same mistakes. Then he broke down and admitted that he had " faked " the contract of 1903, and said that Department fees, instead of being the property of his father, were the property of Senator Mitchell. Mitchell was convicted and sentenced; he got a stay of execution, and died suddenly. Judge Tanner was convicted of perjury, but was pardoned by the President. But for the statute of limitations United States Senator Fulton would also in all probability have

7

been indicted in connection with Oregon land matters.

One of the most daring of the Oregon thieves was S. A. D. Puter. He was a giant in stature and a man of iron nerve. At Mitchell's trial he swore to paying the Senator $1,000 to perfect a title in Washington. He was associated in the land frauds with men and women. In his fight for liberty one of his women confederates was of great assistance to him, and later his undoing. He became a fugitive, and Operator William J. Burns was assigned to run him down. Burns was warned that Puter was a desperate man, and that he carried a revolver in a specially made pocket in front instead of behind. Burns arrested Puter in the corridor of the Boston branch post-office in Back Bay late one afternoon while he was getting his mail at the general delivery window. After telephoning for an officer to take charge of Puter, Burns started with his prisoner out of the post-office, supposing the officer was close at his heels. The officer was not there. It was just twilight, and the street was densely crowded. Burns kept his eye on Puter's right hand, watching for a move toward the pocket which he had been told about. Instead Puter reached into the inside breast pocket of his raincoat, drew forth a handkerchief, and wiped his forehead with it. When the hand was withdrawn from putting the handkerchief away it held a revolver, which, quick as a flash, was pointed full at Burns's stomach. Burns has arrested more counterfeiters than any other officer in the Secret Service, but here he found

ARTHUR B. PUGH
Special Assistant United States Attorney in the land fraud prosecutions

that he was completely out-maneuvered. Without a word, keeping his pistol pointed directly at the detective's abdomen, Puter backed slowly away through the crowd, then, turning, ran like a deer and escaped. He was subsequently captured and convicted, and is now serving a sentence of two years in prison in Oregon.

The drag-net of Secretary Hitchcock was now drawn around every public land State. There seemed to be no limit to the rapacity of the land sharks. Attention soon became centered on the illegal fencing of the public lands in Nebraska, Kansas, Montana, Colorado, and other States. Horse and cattle companies largely absorbed the public lands in those sections that are ·semi-arid. The law says that there shall be no fences erected upon or around public lands. The fencing had become more general in the neighborhood of the land-grant railways. In these land grants the lands had been divided into quarter-sections, the Government retaining each alternate quarter-section. The object, of course, was to encourage the settlement of the country, and to avoid the concentration of these homesteads in the control of grazing companies. The Northern Pacfic has a grant of almost twenty miles on each side. The Central Pacific land grant is ten to thirty miles across. The method that was followed by the grazing companies was that they would get possession of the railway land and fence that and the public land in one compact inclosure. In a square comprising thirty-six quarter-sections of 55,706 acres,· or nine square miles, a cattle company would have eighteen quarter-sections that it had purchased from the railway and eighteen quarter-sections owned by the Government, but would assume control over the entire tract. While the land would be theoretically open to home settlement, it was actually beyond the reach of the homesteader. · He who entered upon one of these illegally fenced quarter-sections usually took his life into his own hands.

A few instances will serve to show how these lands were held by the cattlemen under " border law." The records of the Interior Department show that near St. Francis, Kansas, the Dewey Cattle Company had erected fences inclosing 51,040 acres, or a little less than eight square miles. John Berry and his four sons took up land under the Homestead Law, and the fences of the cattle company interfered with his passage to the outer world. He was completely cut off. The cowboys of the Dewey ranch threatened to kill the entire family if the fences were interfered with. John Berry and his four sons, on returning home from the nearest town, found it necessary to cut a fence of the cattle company. Just as they rode through, a band of cowboys swooped down upon them and opened fire. The elder Berry was hit, but was able to keep the saddle, and he and his sons were soon beyond reach of the cowboys, who pursued, firing as they rode. Twenty cowboys followed the men to their homes, took them by surprise, and killed two of them instantly. Three others got to the house and defended themselves, killing three of the cowboys. The house was fired, and, as the three endeavored to make their escape, they were shot to death. This was in June, 1905.

A widow named Mrs. Howell had taken up a homestead in Oregon in the neighborhood of the Ayres Cattle Company. The cattle company apparently determined that she must be driven out. The fences of this company were up in defiance of law. One night a gang of armed and masked men, some of whom were identified as the employees of the company, visited the house and made a . demonstration for the purpose of driving her out of the country. This was in March, 1905.

When one of the special agents of the Department in Kansas was brought to book for not being active in regard to fencing in a Western State, he made a report to the Department in which he said that the fencing law was always treated as a joke. The Senator who appointed him told him to do nothing. The other Senator was attorney for the cattlemen. This special agent is not now in the service.

It is estimated that at least 5,000,000 acres of land are inclosed by illegal fences. This would be an area of 7,812 square miles, nearly equal to the area of Massachusetts, larger than New Jersey, and only thirty-two square miles less than the area of Delaware, Connecticut, and Rhode Island combined. In Nebraska alone suits concerning an area of 1,349,319 acres are pending. But it is estimated that the illegal inclosures in that State equal 2,698,-638 acres.

In many instances these companies claimed to own the land that they had fenced. To test the working of the Homestead Act and the Desert · Land Act it was found. in one instance, that out of thirteen homesteads purchased by a company after fourteen months' alleged occupancy by the homesteader, twelve had really been acquired by persons working in collusion with the cattle companies. In Nebraska the Kinkaid Law, which enabled a single person to take 640 acres, was discovered to have been a great aid to fraud. Persons in the employ of the grazing companies would take up sections and turn them over to ·their employer.

It was difficult to make headway against these cattle companies. They were composed for the most part of wealthy stockholders who had entered into the business under the motto "Might makes right." One surveying party, accompanied by Secret Service men, made a survey of 280,000 acres. The companies explained that the fences had been put up under a misapprehension and had been taken down. A second expedition was sent out and made photographs of the fences still up. In many instances the cattle companies claimed that the fences were on their own land. This is an old excuse. How they manage this is shown in a diagram accompanying this article. It is taken from a Supreme Court decision against fences

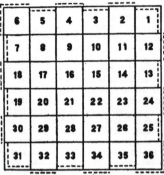

| 6 | 5 | 4 | 3 | 2 | 1 |
| 7 | 8 | 9 | 10 | 11 | 12 |
| 18 | 17 | 16 | 15 | 14 | 13 |
| 19 | 20 | 21 | 22 | 23 | 24 |
| 30 | 29 | 28 | 27 | 26 | 25 |
| 31 | 32 | 33 | 34 | 35 | 36 |

HOW THE CATTLE COMPANIES ATTEMPTED TO EVADE THE LAW

The cattlemen obtained by purchase from the railways the alternate quarter-sections, 1, 3, 5, 7, etc., and the corresponding quarter-sections in the adjacent squares of equal size. By putting their fences in the positions shown by the dotted lines they could claim that the fences were entirely on their own land. At the same time they inclosed not only their own quarter-sections, but the quarter-sections 2, 4, 6, 8, etc., owned by the Government.

surrounding public land in the case of Camfield vs. the United States.

The greatest battle with the fencers was that waged against the Nebraska Land and Feeding Company. which controlled the "Spade Ranch" and had 400,000 acres under fence. Bartlett Richards is President of this company; Will G. Comstock, Vice-President; C. C. Jameson, Treasurer, and Aquilla Triplitt, Agent. The fences inclosed the public lands, and the offense was a particularly flagrant one. After much difficulty the officers of the company were brought to trial on the charge of illegal fencing. The company had no defense to offer. To the astonishment of the Department and the Administration, when these men pleaded guilty they were sentenced to pay a fine of $300 and to be imprisoned for six hours. These six hours were passed in the custody of the United States Marshal in the Omaha Club. The President ordered the removal from office of the United States Marshal and of United States District Attorney Baxter, and orders were issued to press other prosecutions against the "Spade Ranch." This time it was a much more serious affair. New indictments were found charging in thirty-six counts conspiracy to defraud the Government of its lands. At the trial it was shown that under the Kinkaid Law the company had solicited scores of persons to take up sections of land and on getting title turn it over to the company. The company promised to pay each person from $300 to $1,000 per claim. All of the officers of the company were convicted on December 19, and other persons who were in collusion with them will be placed on trial later. This is one of the greatest victories achieved by Secretary Hitchcock in his long campaign against the land-looters. There are other cases of similar character pending all over the West against timber, cattle, and land companies.

Within a few weeks there have been further sensational developments in different lines from those detailed above. The Inter-State Commerce Commission, acting as the prober, but in conjunction with the Interior Department and the Department of Justice, has uncovered an apparent collusion between capitalists and applicants for mineral lands, by which, for a nominal figure, large tracts of coal lands in the Rocky Mountain region have passed into the hands of the Union Pacific Coal Company and other concerns. These disclosures are held to be sufficient to justify (if any justification were necessary) the action of the Interior Department in having withdrawn from entry 64,000,000 acres of coal and mineral lands in North Dakota, South Dakota, Montana, Wyoming, Colorado, New Mexico, Utah, Oregon, and Washington. This is an area almost equal to that of New York, Pennsylvania, and New Jersey combined.

More recent still have been the disclosures, only hinted at officially as yet, regarding the disposal of town sites and the allotment of other lands in Indian Territory. So unsatisfactory has been the state of affairs regarding the Five Civilized Tribes, and so serious and contradictory have been the stories regarding oil and coal leases, that Mr. William Dudley Foulke was sent to the Territory by the Government, and has made his report. Only recently a Senate committee took Secretary Hitchcock to task for

WILLIAM J. BURNS
United States Secret Service

withdrawing about 5,000,000 acres of land from allotment because he felt that the terms under which the lands were to be disposed of were bad for the Indians. One thing which caused this action was a scheme to purchase 200,000 acres for a game preserve.

From the above imperfect sketch it will be seen that the task of protecting the public domain is one of extreme difficulty as well as of supreme importance, and sometimes it is very exciting. At the beginning of the Government the public lands amounted to 2,295,000,000 acres. The quantity of land that has passed in the last twenty-four years from the Government to States, individuals, and corporations is equal to a strip of territory across the continent, including all of New England, New York, New Jersey, Pennsylvania, Ohio, Michigan, Indiana, Illinois, Iowa, Minnesota, Wisconsin, Nebraska, North Dakota, South Dakota, Montana, Idaho, Wyoming, Washington, and Oregon. There have been since 1862 one hundred million acres taken up in homesteading. Where has the remainder of the public lands gone? To railways, lumber companies, cattle companies, and speculators, and large portions have been allotted to the States.

It is generally admitted that if the depredations upon the public lands had not been checked in 1903 by Ethan Allen Hitchcock, backed by a courageous President, the end of the present administration would have seen the Nation despoiled of all of its remaining agricultural lands that are susceptible of irrigation, and of its richest remaining treasures in the forest and in the mines.

## THE RETURN TO THE FARM

### BY CONSTANT TROYON

Reproduced by courtesy of the American Art Association

# A FAMOUS TROYON

 F Constant Troyon could have been present in New York on January 25, at the sale of the thirty pictures known as the Henry collection, a remarkable representation of the Barbizon school, his astonishment would have known no bounds. In 1840 and '50, when he was one of that famous group of French painters composed of Millet, Corot, Dupré, Rousseau, Daubigny, and Diaz, who studied and painted round about the little village of Barbizon, he was glad enough to get five hundred francs, that is to say, one hundred dollars, for a picture. When the display of his cattle paintings at the Exposition of 1855 had made him famous and had brought his work into great popular favor, he thought himself, and was thought by his colleagues and the public, to have achieved great financial success because his canvases then brought as much as six thousand francs, or twelve hundred dollars. The picture reproduced on the opposite page brought $65,000 at the Henry sale—the highest price ever paid in the United States for a single picture at a public sale. Those who have never attended one of the sales in Mendelssohn Hall conducted by the American Art Association can hardly appreciate their dramatic character. Of the large gathering, of course only a small percentage are buyers; the rest go from motives of partly artistic and partly dramatic interest. Mr. Kirby, the veteran expert and auctioneer, stands in a sort of little pulpit at one side of the stage. When a famous and desirable picture is put up, the bidding rapidly mounts by thousands and then more slowly by hundreds of dollars until it is knocked down to the successful purchaser. In the case of the Troyon the bidding was started at $25,000 by Senator Clark, the mining multi-millionaire of Montana. The bidding was briskly carried on against him, and the picture was finally sold to a well-known dealer in this city at a price which sets the judicious observer to thinking that there may be some basis after all for President Roosevelt's warning against over-swollen fortunes. Troyon is one of the greatest modern masters of cattle painting. In technique, in the treatment of light and shade, and in beauty and truthfulness of finish he is probably unsurpassed in his particular field. His light and shadow effects are characteristically displayed in " The Return to the Farm." But in the estimation of artists he lacks the poetic, the imaginative, and the spiritual feeling which lie underneath the works of some of the others of his Barbizon colleagues. Troyon was born in 1810, in Sèvres in France, his father being connected with the famous porcelain works of that place. Through the influence of his father and mother he received his earliest artistic impressions, and he began his artistic career as a decorator. He might possibly have developed into a highly successful workman in the field of industrial art, but the impulse for painting was too strong to resist, and he began, somewhat as Millet did, to wander about the country painting landscapes, and when his funds gave out supported himself by china decoration. When he was about thirty years old he fell in with the little group of men at Barbizon, and it was from this time that his real artistic career began. His essential genius is indicated by his instant appreciation of the heroic attempt of the Barbizon men to rescue the art of France from the stilted and artificial influences of the classic and studio schools, and to take the painters "back to nature" for their inspiration.

POPE PIUS X.

# THE MEN AROUND THE POPE

## BY SAMUEL J. BARROWS

THE American visitor at Rome finds on the Alban Hills two objects of interest, one the Papal Villa, the Castel Gondalfo, where the Holy Father spends his summers, and the other the villa of the American College. On these historic hills eighteen college boys are engaged in an athletic game. From the way they "get under the ball," from the way they drive it at the bat, take a high fly or a low grounder, it is perfectly evident that they are American boys. No others can handle a ball like that. How much better this than to be fighting beasts in the Coliseum! Among the spectators are some from the Papal Villa, one of them wearing the Cardinal's hat. He watches the game with intense interest. The players, too, watch this tall, spare man when their eyes are not on the ball; they are proud of his applause. He knows all the points of the game. He might serve as umpire.

But this alert, keen man has another and a vaster field. He is, if not the umpire, one of the principal actors in an international contest which the whole world has watched with eager interest. The "diamond" stretches from the Alban Hills to the Seine. It is not a conflict of arms, but a conflict of diplomacy.

Next to the Pope no one stands out so conspicuously to-day on the Roman side of the political arena as this man, Cardinal Raphael Merry del Val, the Papal Secretary of State. The official documents which have gone to the French Government, and to all the Governments with which the Holy See has official relations, bear his signature. To borrow a phrase from the game he admires, it was he who set the ball in motion from the Roman side by sending a missive to the courts of Europe. This letter was written April 2, 1904, from the chambers of the Vatican. It stated that "the coming to Rome in an official form of M. Loubet, President of the French Republic, to pay a visit to Victor Emanuel III. was an event of such exceptional gravity that the Holy See could not permit it to pass without calling to it the most serious attention of the Government which your Excellency represents." It pointed out in courteous but positive language the offensive character of the visit rendered to the Italian Government, intentionally brought about by that Government to enfeeble the rights and to wound the dignity of the Holy See. It stated that if the other Catholic powers had done the same thing, the recall of the Papal Nuncio would have immediately followed.

The result of this letter was the recall of the French Ambassador at the Vatican. The open war between France and the Vatican began.

Who is this man called to such unexpected prominence? But a few years ago he would not have dreamed of occupying the place he holds. His early ambition was to be a simple Jesuit father; but his education and his ability deflected him from the work of a humble missionary and led to his unusual elevation.

Raphael Merry del Val was born in London, October 10, 1865. His father was Secretary of the Spanish Embassy to Great Britain, his mother an English woman of Spanish origin. His name Merry is an indication of the Irish blood in his veins, for he gets it from a grandparent coming from Dublin. His father, having aided Alfonso when that Prince was sojourning in England, was gratefully remembered when Alfonso ascended the throne; he advanced him to the position of Minister Plenipotentiary to the Court of Belgium.

The education of the son, beginning at his father's home in London, was continued at St. Michael's College at Brussels, under the care of the Jesuit Fathers. Here he felt distinctly drawn toward a clerical life. In Belgium his knowledge of the French language was also perfected. He studied philosophy in the Seminary of St. Cuthbert, England. His father afterwards being accredited by Spain to the Vatican, the son went to Rome. Pope Leo took a fancy to the

Passing through the diaconate, he was ordained a priest in Rome, January 1, 1889. Within a year after his ordination he was appointed President of the College of Noble Ecclesiastics, where he had studied when first coming to Rome. His knowledge of languages led to his appointment as consultor of the Congregation of the Index, which decides as to

CARDINAL OREGLIA
President of the Congregation on Extraordinary Ecclesiastical Affairs

genial and handsome young man, and it was by his express wish that the student entered the Academy of Noble Ecclesiastics, continuing his studies also at the Gregorian University in philosophy, theology, and canon law. The favor of the Pope was shown by bringing the young man into the Vatican as one of his secret chamberlains. His degree of doctor in philosophy and theology was received from the Gregorian University.

prohibited books. His knowledge of English well fitted him for a mission to Canada with reference to the question of schools. He received from the University of Ottawa, Canada, his doctorate in canon law. At the age of thirty-five he was created by Pope Leo an archbishop *in partibus*, that is, an archbishop without a see. This honor is often conferred on those who are retiring from service, but in the case of young Merry del Val it was a prelude to further activity and distinction.

When Leo was dying, three years ago last July, it became necessary to appoint the Secretary of the Conclave of Cardinals. The Secretary is the only one present in the council in the Sistine Chapel who is not a Cardinal. Monsignor Volpini, a friend of the Pope, was appointed

after his election he was appointed Pro-Secretary of State. In the month of November following he was raised to the dignity of the cardinalate and confirmed in his office as Secretary of State. He was the first Cardinal created by Pius X.

While there are strong points of sympathy and affinity between Pius X. and Cardinal Merry del Val, they are con-

CARDINAL RAMPOLLA

Secretary of State under Leo XIII. ; still one of the most influential counselors at the Vatican

to this office. At that time Leo was at the point of death, and Volpini apparently in the best of health. Without warning, the Secretary suddenly passed away. Leo was never told of his death, and it fell to Cardinal Oreglia, the dean of the College of Cardinals, who is the head of the Church in an interregnum, to appoint a successor. Merry del Val became thus the Secretary of the Conclave which elected Pius X. Within a few weeks

trasted in age and training. Joseph Sarto, the Pope, was born in Treviso in Italy, in 1835, and is consequently thirty years older than his Secretary of State. The Holy Father passed through every ecclesiastical grade of the Church to the very highest; he was a young seminarian, a sub-deacon, deacon, priest, curate, professor of seminary, rector of seminary, vicar-general of diocese, bishop, archbishop, patriarch, cardinal, and Pope.

CARDINAL MERRY DEL VAL
Papal Secretary of State

Nothing has been left out of his training except diplomacy, and the knowledge of languages and politics that goes along with it. Merry del Val, on the contrary, has never had actual parochial work, but has had that cosmopolitan life which is so good a training for diplomatic service. English is his native tongue; he speaks it with a broad English accent, with a smooth and apt diction. He has a perfect command of Italian and French, and can preach in any of these languages. Spanish he naturally learned from his parents; and has, too, the thorough command of Latin which is a part of the traditional education of Rome. With all his cosmopolitan training and his experience of life on two hemispheres, he has, however, the instincts of the priest and the educator. A hard and brilliant student, he takes a great interest in boys' clubs in Rome and brings them out to the Papal Villa for recreation and

games. A Catholic friend who has stood very close to him describes him as " an intense and pious believer, with supreme faith in the supernatural, in the Church, in the divinity of Christ, and in the absolute unshakableness of his commission to the Church." Here, too, these men of different mold and make and training come into close accord; for Pius X., though not a man of scientific education, has that same intense faith in the Church and the supernatural and in Christ that makes him defy the world. " No one, for instance, would order his bishops in France to take an attitude which turns them out of church and house and home—no one would do that who was not a believer."

In his capacity as Secretary of State, Cardinal Merry del Val carries on diplomatic relations with countries having representatives at Rome. The main European countries represented are

Austria-Hungary, Bavaria, Belgium, Luxembourg. Prussia, Portugal. Spain, and Russia: and there are representatives from several South American republics. In addition to his title as Secretary of State. Cardinal Merry del Val is Grand Knight of Malta, President of the Commission of Cardinals for the administration of property of the Holy See, member of the Congregation of the Inquisition, of the Council of Rites, of Extraordinary Ecclesiastical Affairs, and is also a member of the Pontifical Commission for the Unification and Codification of Canon Law.

How far is Merry del Val responsible for the diplomatic policy of the Vatican? Officially he holds the same relation to the Pope that Secretary Root does to the President. He has charge of the department of foreign affairs, but he is also a member of a cabinet of counselors. On this subject a high Catholic dignitary said to the writer: "I believe that the Holy Father holds Merry del Val in the highest esteem and has great regard for his opinions, but to ascribe to him the entire responsibility for the policy of the Vatican, as the public apparently does, is fanciful and legendary; that policy is the outcome of the deliberate action of the body of Cardinals."

To understand the action of the Vatican, one must know how it is organized. There are thirty-five Cardinals always living in Rome; they are Cardinals *in curia*. These Cardinals carry on the executive interests of the Church. They are subdivided into committees, numbering from seven to twenty Cardinals, and the same Cardinal may be a member of several committees or congregations. The most important of these committees are the Congregation of the Propaganda, which has to do with missionary affairs and ecclesiastical administration; the Congregation of the Index; and the Congregation of Extraordinary Ecclesiastical Affairs. There are many other committees and organizations relating to ritual, discipline, dogma, and education—among them the Inquisition. Questions coming up in regard to France are probably discussed in the Congregation on Extraordinary Ecclesiastical Affairs. The prefect or president of this Congregation

is the venerable Cardinal Oreglia, who heads the list of Cardinals, next to the Pope, in the hierarchy of the Roman Catholic Church. He is now in his seventy-ninth year, and is the only Cardinal living who was created by Pius IX. He was elevated to this office December 22, 1873, and is the *Camerlengo* or Chancellor of the Pope. Of the fifty-one Cardinals of the Church, Cardinal Richard, of Paris, is the oldest, being in his eighty-eighth year. Cardinal Coullie, of Lyons, is in his seventy-eighth year, and Gruscha, of Vienna, is in his eighty-sixth. Merry del Val, on the other hand, is but forty-one, the youngest in the number, being fourteen years younger than the Cardinal nearest to him in age.

The other Cardinals on the Congregation on Extraordinary Ecclesiastical Affairs, besides Oreglia and Merry del Val, are the two Cardinals Vannutelli and Agliardi, Satolli, Rampolla, di Pietro, Gotti, Ferrata, Mathieu, Taliani, Steinhuber, Segna, Vives y Tuto, and Cavagnis.

Of this group of men who stand nearest to the Pope in this emergency, Cardinal Rampolla's name is familiar, as the Secretary of State of Leo XIII. He is sixty-four years of age, and one of the most influential counselors at the Vatican, a member of several of the most important committees. Serafino Vannutelli has had an extensive diplomatic career as a representative of the Vatican at foreign courts. His brother, Vincenzo Vannutelli, is a noble figure, standing about six feet six in height and well proportioned. Satolli was at one time Papal Legate to the United States. He is considered one of the great Catholic theologians of our time, and is especially distinguished as a Thomist, or follower of Thomas Aquinas. Steinhuber is a German Jesuit, eighty-two years of age, and also distinguished as a theologian. Gotti is the head of the Congregation of the Propaganda, one of the most important of all the departments. Ferrata has had diplomatic experience as Papal Nuncio at Paris, and may be presumed to know well the French situation. Mathieu is of French birth. Segna is prefect of the archives of the Vatican. Vives y Tuto is a Spaniard, a Capuchin, a theologian, and in age next to the youngest Cardinal.

These sixteen men are in the eyes of the world the most important men who stand around the Pope in the Franco-Roman conflict. They constitute, as it were, the cabinet of the Pope in this emergency. Extraordinary questions are considered by them, and recommendations or conclusions reported to the Pope. Deliberations are held in secret. Catholics are all agreed that in matters of temporal sovereignty or welfare the Holy Father is not assumed to be infallible. He is therefore at liberty to avail himself of the experience, wisdom, and training of his personal and constituted counselors. And that is what is meant by "The Vatican."

In the conflict between France and the Vatican great questions of principle are involved. These principles have been set forth with lucidity and fairness, as it seems to me, in the columns of The Outlook. But the movements of history are also interpreted through personality. We cannot understand the religious situation in France to-day without knowing something of Charles VII., Francis I., Louis XIV., Bossuet, Napoleon I., Briand, and Clemenceau. Nor can we understand the spirit and tradition of the Roman Catholic Church in this matter except as we know the personality and character of Gregory VII., Boniface, Pius VI., Pius IX., Leo XIII., and their devout successor, Pius X., and his council of cardinals.

# CREATIVE AMERICANS

## *WILLIAM JAMES*
### *LEADER IN PHILOSOPHICAL THOUGHT*
### *BY GEORGE HODGES*
*Dean of the Episcopal Theological School, Cambridge, Massachusetts*

OUGHT perhaps to begin this sketch of Professor James with a list of my disqualifications for writing it. But that would take too long. It may suffice to say that I have but a halting knowledge of his philosophy, and that I am far from assenting to some of the articles of his theological belief. A few months ago, at a Harvard dinner at which Mr. James was guest of honor, one of the speakers recited as best he could the argument of Mr. James's Ingersoll Lecture on Human Immortality. The guest of honor listened with great patience. When it was ended, he said that if the recitation had been made in his class-room he would have marked the speaker *B minus*,

I cannot hope for even so modest a valuation as that.

I remember, however, that Mr. James said of the students at Stanford University, "They believe everything I tell them." It surprised him, it was so different from the attitude of mind to which he was accustomed at home. He did not altogether like it. He has no place in his philosophy for dogmatism. He does not believe that many things are definitely settled yet. He rather resented the unquestioning acceptance which seemed to imply that things must be everlastingly so because he had come so far to say them. I am further encouraged by the terms in which he replied to an invitation to subscribe to a fund for a new golf links. He said, with his generous subscription, that he hated the game but liked the people who play it. I confess that I find philosophy—even

Mr. James's philosophy—hard reading; but I like the philosophers, Mr. James best of all.

Mr. James's work is pervaded by a quality which is, unhappily, rare among metaphysicians—he is always interesting. This is largely because he deals so frankly and constantly with the concrete. He sails out boldly into the deep, with the sea beneath and the sky above, but he keeps out of the fog. If the shores are not in sight, the stars are. He is never separate from reality, never remote from common sense, and never forgetful of the common man. He is assisted by a lively sense of humor. When he is tempted to follow his argument into regions where logic takes the place of life, " I hear," he says, " that inward monitor of which W. R. Clifford once wrote, whispering the word ' bosh !' "

Accordingly, Mr. James is a consistent empiricist. His materials are facts. He deals with actual experience. To this he came not only by the natural disposition of his mind, but by the processes of his education. His first degree was not in arts, but in medicine. He was studying bodies when his contemporaries were studying books. He was getting at truth by way of the tangible fact. There it was before him, visible and unmistakable, a mighty serious matter profoundly affecting human happiness ; and he was to find out the meaning of it, and the effect of it, and how to master it. It was only by slow degrees that he became a psychologist, and in his psychology he never lost sight of the physical conditions. One of his distinctive contributions to science is his insistence on the determining influence of the body. We are sad because we cry, we are afraid because we run away. A merry countenance maketh a cheerful heart.

Mr. James changed over from medicine to psychology, from physics to metaphysics, but he carried with him all that he had learned. Better still, he carried with him the quality of mind which had at the beginning made medicine attractive to him. He continued to care immensely for the concrete and to be suspicious of any affirmation which was but remotely related to verifiable fact. He greatly

enlarged his range of facts ; he perceived that an emotion, a habit, even an eccentricity or a prejudice, is a fact of which we are to take account as seriously as any phenomenon which may be stated in terms of weight or dimension ; but it was in facts that he was interested. It is characteristic of him that when the University of Edinburgh asked him to give twenty lectures on Natural Religion, he determined to give two courses of ten lectures each, one on " Man's Religious Appetites " and the other on " Their Satisfaction through Philosophy," but the first course presently took such possession of his mind that he postponed the second and gave his twenty lectures on the " Varieties of Religious Experience."

I am maintaining the proposition, which nobody, I suppose, will dispute, that Professor James is not only the most eminent but also the most interesting of all our contemporary philosophers. I am trying to make out the quality of his interest. I find it to consist in the perpetual presence of the concrete. That, after all, is what we care for. That is what commands our middle-class attention. The abstract may be profound, it may be a necessary form of philosophical expression, it may be true, but it is a foreign language. Whoever uses it begins to speak in the Hebrew tongue. The concrete is the vernacular. Whenever we hear it in a lecture, in a sermon, in a printed book, we sit up and listen. Professor James thinks in it and speaks in it. This is a great part of the secret of the singular charm of his style, in which he unites the dialect of psychology with the idioms of common speech. " The God whom science recognizes must be," he says, " a God of universal laws exclusively ;" to which philosophical statement he adds an immediate translation, " a God who does a wholesale, not a retail, business." It is like the collocation of Latin and Saxon words in the Book of Common Prayer.

It is perhaps Mr. James's respect for concrete human experience which imparts to his mind a notable disposition of intellectual hospitality. All facts, all actual situations, are encountered by him with frank cordiality. All philosophers aspire to divest themselves of prejudice, but Mr. James succeeds in this endeavor without any evident effort. He is never worried or nervous about his possible prejudices. To some philosophers a prejudice is like a contagious disease. At the sight of it they run away in terror of catching it. ·I know several eminent philosophers who never go to church, for fear of catching a prejudice. They instruct their pupils that churches are perilous places for philosophers. But Professor James goes to church every day in the week—except Sunday. He sometimes stays away from church on Sunday, but every week-day finds him at prayers in the Harvard chapel. And he has no scruples against church-going on Sunday, though he finds the service a bit long, he says. He braves all the menaces of prejudice, and behaves himself, even in religion, like a normal human being, following the ancient and universal instincts, and thus entering intimately into common life. I do not see that it does him any harm. One might fairly characterize his intellectual position, echoing with a little change a phrase of his own, as the Philosophy of Open-Mindedness.

This serene possession of an open mind is notably apparent in his treatment of several forms of thought at which most philosophers have looked with contempt. He was the first eminent person to deal seriously with the phenomena of Christian Science. He pointed out its universal qualities, and showed its place in the history of human thought. He found that Mrs. Eddy is related to Martin Luther and Walt Whitman and the Roman Catholic Alvarez de Paz, who wrote a book on " Contemplation." He found an open road between the shrine at Lourdes and the shrine at Concord, New Hampshire. He gave Christian Science a dignified past, and brought the mental healers into the fraternity of the philosophers. He founded it all on human nature, and ascribed even its vagaries to the imperfection of our knowledge. Man is still a mystery. Nobody knows that better than the psychologist whose business it is to study him. Mr. James has a hand of welcome for anybody who has found out anything about man. And he is of

the opinion that Mr. Dresser and Mr. Wood and Mr. Trine have visited dim regions of our subliminal self into which few physicians have ventured.

So also with spiritualism. Human beings have now been dreaming dreams and seeing visions and dreading ghosts for innumerable centuries. It is a queer world, and all manner of queer things are continually coming to pass in it. For the most part, these strange incidents have been thrown by philosophers upon the rubbish-heap. They are so much slag and cinder. The normal intellectual processes go on like the output of a mill, made by reason and logic as by machines, and serving the daily and essential purposes of life ; but behind the mill, lumbering up the back yard, red with rust and green with weeds, are piles of odd, misshapen, rejected stuff, old superstitions, panics, and lunacies.

Mr. James has poked about a good deal in this back yard, looking for by-products. He is of the opinion that there is something to be found in these places of waste and disorder. He belongs to the Society for Psychical Research, and has greatly interested himself in the singular sayings of Mrs. Piper and other unusual persons. The unusual, which shocks the conventional philosopher, invites him. He is of one mind with the patriarch in the desert who said, " I will now turn aside to see this great sight, why the bush is not burnt." The varieties of Religious Experience which are examined in his book are abnormal varieties.

The fact of sub consciousness is perhaps the most important discovery which has been made as yet in the back yard of the mind. Telepathy has been found there. The researchers have also been encouraged to say of spiritualism and other occult doctrines that there may be something in them. Just what it is, they do not know. Mr. James says of Mrs. Piper that most of her utterances are hopelessly incoherent, but that now and then there is a single note of something real and strange. He does not pretend to understand it. His position is that the unexplained is the proper field of philosophic adventure and discovery.

He hopes that somebody will sometime find something in the cinders, or learn how to make something out of the cinders.

This large intellectual hospitality distinguishes Professor James from most of his contemporaries, and imparts to his thought an originality which proceeds naturally from the unusual materials with which he deals. He is concerned with man in the concrete, with the individual just as he is, proper or improper. It might perhaps be said that he is interested in men rather than in man. Least of all is he desirous to conform the individual to the type. He is not endeavoring to prove a theory. He is trying to see things as they are. His open-mindedness proceeds, not only from his keen interest in facts, but from a certain modesty of disposition. His mind keeps open house, and welcomes all who come, whether on foot or on horseback. He does not consider himself too good to converse with them, and he is always more ready to learn than he is to teach. He hates to make speeches. Once, he says, when he had to speak after dinner on some significant occasion, he wrote out his remarks two weeks before, and committed the thing to memory, and recited it to himself three times a day—forty-two times; and then, when the moment came, his courage failed him, and he took the paper out of his pocket and read it. But in his lecture-room he is wholly at ease, speaking with unfailing freedom and felicity of phrase; yet always informally, by way of conversation, and with no assertiveness of manner. We are all students together, he seems to say, none of us knowing very much about these vast and immeasurable matters; let me tell you what I think and you shall tell me what you think.

This modesty of Mr. James's mind inclines him to give his philosophy a didactic, even a homiletical, turn. He believes that a philosopher ought to be a useful citizen, and that the true aim of the study of human nature is to learn lessons which when they are taught shall help people to be better. His chapter on Habit applies the truths of psychology, as a sermon applies the truths of religion, to common conduct. It has helped hundreds of people out of darkness into light. It has contributed to the making of character. "Keep the faculty of effort alive in you by a little gratuitous exercise every day." A great number of people have these words in mind as if they were a text of Scripture, and are made different by them.

Professor James is one of the most religious of professional philosophers. They all deal with the high matters with which religion is concerned, but some of them maintain with much care an exterior and impersonal attitude towards them. I remember a sermon which was preached by President Faunce, of Brown University, on the text, "O God, thou art my God." It is one thing, he said, to cry, "O God," in recognition or even in admiration, but quite another thing to cry, "Thou art my God." It is the difference, indeed, between philosophy and religion. Professor James perceives that the being of God makes an inevitable difference with the individual. "That no concrete particular of experience should alter its complexion in consequence of a God being there, seems to me," he says, "an incredible proposition." He classes himself, accordingly, with the supernaturalists, and is not content with the easy doctrine which finds in the supernatural only nature under another name. "We and God," he says, "have business with each other; and in opening ourselves to his influence our deepest destiny is fulfilled. The universe, at those parts of it which our personal being constitutes, takes a turn genuinely for the worse or for the better in proportion as each of us fulfills or evades God's demands." It is true that he goes on to remark that something might perhaps be said in favor of polytheism. But this is only Mr. James's way of assuring us, after his excellent sermon, that he has no intention of entering the ministry.

# THE FOUNDER OF AN AMERICAN SCHOOL OF ART

## BY JESSIE TRIMBLE

SINCE it is generally admitted that American illustration at present ranks higher than that of any other nation, and since it is increasingly admirable, there is interest in the question, "Chiefly to whom is the credit due for raising our standards until illustration has become the basis for a National school of art?"

Even among those who differ with him on many points. it would be hard to find a great number of people taking exception to the statement that the man who has done most to revolutionize American illustration is Howard Pyle.

If the development of American illustration does actually amount to the birth of an American school of art, in the sense that we know certain French, Italian. Spanish, or Dutch painting, the logical deduction seems to be that Mr. Pyle will be looked upon as its originator. And an "American school of art" means something far more than is represented by the colony of artists now for six years gathered around Mr. Pyle at his home in Wilmington, Delaware.

The genius of Howard Pyle is so diverse that in any way to describe it is extremely difficult. The nearest thing to definition is to call it American. When analyzed. the inspiration of his paintings, his illustrations, and his teaching appears to lie in one or another trait of character typically American.

For example, Mr. Pyle is a worker of such untiring persistence, and in so splendid an array of ways, that he seems like an American business man. He preaches a doctrine of work. consequently of democracy, and finds time in between painting, illustrating, teaching, and lecturing to write books so good as to give a great many people more inter-

ested in literature than art the plausible misconception that Mr. Pyle is a writer before he is an artist. They are fortified in this idea by their happy recollection of those charming stories such as "Pepper and Salt," "The Wonder Clock," "Twilight Land," "The Garden Behind the Moon," "The Rose of Paradise," "The Merry Adventures of Robin Hood;" of more recent novels, "Jack Ballister's Fortunes" and "Rejected of Men;" and of Mr. Pyle's distinctive treatment of the stories of the Round Table.

Yet, although a third volume of the books about King Arthur and his Knights will be issued this winter as another evidence of Mr. Pyle's literary activity, several new paintings are to be added to his already notable work in full color; and his efforts to help the young American illustrator seem constantly and in surprisingly new ways to widen. Distinguished though his long literary career has made him, Mr. Pyle's enduring distinction is more likely to come through the influence he has had on American art.

For twelve or fourteen years variously occupied as a teacher at Drexel Institute, the Art Students' League, and at Wilmington in his own school, Mr. Pyle has in the thirty years of his art life worked out for himself a theory of artistic expression that must almost of necessity affect permanently the trend of American art.

While his American capacity for work seems a part of the quality of his genius, his American type of mind shows itself in that strongest characteristic of his art—its practical value. This, in combination with his classic taste as a lover of the beautiful, continually demonstrates his belief in truth and use as the sound basis for art.

Mr. Pyle's belief in America, his willingness to trust the development of his own talent to it, have been proved sincere. Not only has he never studied abroad, but he has never been abroad! He does not urge his pupils to go abroad. And in the purest American environment he has changed for the better the illustrating of scores of young men and women in the United States. Certainly one-half of the notably successful illustrators of America have stud-

ied with Howard Pyle. And he has helped them through the application of methods universal in their profoundly simple teaching that life—one's own conception of life—must be the inspiration of all work. That conception the artist carries ever with him, having no need to go abroad to find it.

Mr. Pyle is an American educator. He educates the view-point. He helps

HOWARD PYLE

his pupils to find themselves, to "see straight." It is this passion for seeing straight, for honest art, no affectation, no sham, that makes different from so much instruction the whole spirit of Mr. Pyle's teaching. It is no wonder that modern illustration, including such strictly commercial work as advertisement drawing, useful certainly, and capable of the finest treatment, appeals to Mr. Pyle as the unassuming foundation on which may be erected a "school" of American art.

There is, however, an important qualification. Illustration, in Mr. Pyle's opinion, deserves this high place only when it aims to approach the merit of the finished painting. If Mr. Pyle has revolutionized our drawing, he has done so by holding out constantly this ideal, not only in his teaching but in his own work. Magazine readers will remember the attention given his pen-and-ink drawings some twenty years ago when he was illustrating those delightful stories he used to write for young people. His simple, decorative pen-and-ink sketches were for a while almost without imitators, the crowd clinging to the fussy, careful drawings now scarcely ever seen. Those illustrations were indeed as perfect in their way as are Mr. Pyle's paintings.

Now, quite aside from the unconscious influence Mr. Pyle has had on American illustration, he has exerted a conscious influence. He has wished to help. His desire to teach young illustrators, his earnestness in their behalf, his prodigality in assisting them, single him out from those who hoard their talents and keep back of their gifts. It is well known that Mr. Pyle never refuses to see an art student who asks his help, while the Wilmington school is without a parallel. People study there free of charge. Money cannot buy entrance. The only pupils are those invited by Mr. Pyle, and they are invited because he has seen in their work possibilities that he may help to bring to reality.

It is in Wilmington, the town of Mr. Pyle's ancestors and his birth, that there is seen a specific embodiment of his long efforts for the upbuilding of an American school of art. His pupils there have proved the nucleus for a colony of painters doubtless permanent.

The several groups of which Mr. Pyle is the center work with him in ways variously intimate. The first group includes the newcomers, who are in the school studio and receive daily instruction. Also, for reasons perhaps of personal friendship with Mr. Pyle, there are in this close association several men long since established as illustrators, N. C. Wyeth, for example, Stanley M. Arthurs, and Frank Schoonover.

The building in Franklin Street occupied by these young men adjoins Mr. Pyle's own studio—low-thatched, low-toned structures fast gathering an additional covering of vines and climbing roses. Wilmington as a town is unusually green and shady, and Mr. Pyle's studios, with their foreground of flower gardens and heavy lawn, are a picturesque addition to the natural beauty of the place. Those studios are workshops, plain as they are attractive. The old-world touch about them—the great knockers on the old-fashioned half-doors, the high windows, high mantels, valuable desks and chairs taken from former-day houses in the vicinity of Wilmington—reminds the visitor that Mr. Pyle is not only an authority on matters colonial, but a collector of antiques and the possessor of many fine specimens in bric-à-brac, furniture, and woodwork.

Pupils who have had their share of Franklin Street are, many of them, found in the Bancroft and Orange Street studios. These work less directly under Mr. Pyle, but attend morning criticism and the Saturday afternoon lecture. Over twenty artists are considered regular members of the school. Eight or ten of these are young women. It is said, however, that although some of Mr. Pyle's best-known pupils are women, he has no very strong faith in the permanent artistic ambitions of the feminine sex, and rarely encourages women to study with him. He is merely another man who believes that the average woman with ambitions loses them when she marries.

There are artists in Wilmington who have come because Mr. Pyle is there, but who are not studying with him.

They have a distinct affiliation with the school, however, through that important part of it, the Saturday afternoon lecture open to the public. It takes a long time to grasp the significance of all that Mr. Pyle is giving away to so many people, in his efforts to save the artist's time, to teach him quickly some of the things Mr. Pyle himself spent years in mastering.

The Saturday afternoon lecture attracts people from far and near. Philadelphians frequently go down, and New York art editors take the trip occasionally as a sort of " bracer." The occasion is nothing less to the man or woman looking for renewed enthusiasm. It is a tribute to Mr. Pyle's success in his effort to be practical that the lectures are distinctly popular. The audience always includes some who are not artists.

So strongly does illustration as example and motive for work affect the pupils of Howard Pyle that his school might almost be called one of illustration. But its significance is far wider. Illustration is merely the outlet. Painting is the ambition of every pupil, and the ambition of Mr. Pyle for every pupil. It no longer necessarily follows that because a man is an illustrator he may not some day be an " old master."

Having the ambition to make the best possible illustration practically compels the illustrator to be a painter. Mr. Pyle's pupils are themselves a demonstration of the soundness of his theory. Many of them are painters who have come to devote themselves solely to painting only after long service in illustration.

Miss Violet Oakley's rise to distinction as an artist in stained glass and mural paintings was preceded by the study of illustration with Mr. Pyle. There are few murals in this country more lovely than Miss Oakley's work in the Church of All Souls, New York, and she has the honor of having her paintings in company with those of Mr. Abbey on the walls of the State Capitol at Harrisburg, Pennsylvania.

Certainly the illustrations of Miss Jessie Willcox Smith, Miss Elizabeth Shippen Green, Miss Charlotte Harding, and Miss Sarah Stillwell, pupils of Mr. Pyle, do more than approach the finished painting, are truly that. W. J. Aylward

A CORNER OF MR. PYLE'S STUDIO

MR. PYLE AT WORK ON A HISTORICAL COMPOSITION

a man of whom Mr. Pyle is justly proud, makes pictures of subjects connected with the sea that are paintings no less than illustrations. Mr. Aylward went to Manila last spring on the Dry Dock Dewey. Through Mr. Pyle's influence with President Roosevelt, he thus secured a unique opportunity of studying the scenes he most enjoys painting.

The outsider, familiar only with Mr. Pyle's remarkable capacity for work, with his fundamental belief that artistic expression to be valuable must be the outpouring of deep beliefs and strong purposes, in short, that character is the basis of art as of other things great, might perhaps wonder just what type of "artistic atmosphere" would be produced by the types of "artistic temperament" approved by Mr. Pyle.

457

An Example of Mr. Pyle's Later Work.

The artistic temperament with which the Wilmington school overflows does not come up to that cynical definition of the term as synonymous with laziness. But it does come up to the meaning of artistic temperament in the light of modern America. Keenly appreciative of the beautiful, deeply devoted to its ultimate expression, conscious of talent, the young men and women at Wilmington differ from such a school abroad, perhaps, only in the practical, the somewhat conscious acceptance of truth and use as a working basis for art. Mr. Pyle's view-point has been characterized as a little like that of the steam-engine. There is no easy doctrine in the Wilmington school about working when you feel like it, but rather, "Work and you *will* feel like it!"

Mr. Pyle's work of all sorts is intellectual, "literary," if an art that teems with the emotional can be so. He preaches that the basis for a good picture is a clear intellectual conception of the thing to be expressed. The clearer the mental conception, the more convincing its expression upon the canvas. It is said that Mr. Pyle began to draw and paint because there were so many things he could make clearer in writing by making them first clear in drawing.

On the same principle, he urges his pupils to write stories and illustrate them, not only to stimulate the imagination, but to make more vivid the subject for actual drawing. It is his constant reminder that art is not merely the decoration of a canvas with color, but the objectification of thought and feeling.

Mr. Pyle's love for truth in art has of itself gone far towards making American illustration excellent. He has fought exaggeration, in direct opposition to the technicians who develop their technique primarily to play tricks with it, to get "effects." While Mr. Pyle teaches his pupils how to draw, he teaches them first to have something to draw. His watchword, "Put yourself in the picture!" is very different from the shallower teaching, "Watch *how* you put yourself in!"

The school at Wilmington differs in many ways from other art schools. It is made continually interesting. Drudgery seems to have been omitted. The day-in-day-out copying from casts, a feature of the usual training almost invariably hateful to the pupil, is not known in Wilmington. Models are used only as reference. Mere transference has no place in the curriculum of this informal school. The culture of the imagination is a vital part of Mr. Pyle's theory. And he sees no particular benefit to the imagination in eternal copying. There is no work from the nude excepting as the student is taught to draw the nude figure from imagination, afterwards to be paralleled with nature.

Costume models are used in the morning to teach the use of color and brushes, the details of light and shade. But in the afternoon even they are banished. Compositions wholly creative occupy the last half of the day.

Indeed, Mr. Pyle's use of the model is so important as, understood, to make intelligible the whole plan of his instruction. He demands that every effect shown on the canvas be the creation of the artist's own mind. An idea back of the model must be the inspiration of the picture. While many painters scour the country for the right model, one who looks perhaps like their vague conception of the picture they wish to paint, Mr. Pyle's pupils are taught to wait for the clear mental vision, to use the model only on general points as a refreshment to the memory.

Practicing what he preaches, Mr. Pyle uses the same model for nearly everything. And that one, John Weller by name, is a feature of Wilmington art life. Weller has been Mr. Pyle's factotum for twenty years, and has posed for nearly every kind of picture. He is a man of talent on his own account. As a restorer of old furniture he is unequaled in Wilmington, and he is responsible for the admirable renovation of many of Mr. Pyle's antiques. Weller also has charge of the beautiful Venetian costume chest and the valuable collection of costumes in it. These are loaned on occasion to the pupils, and one of them, referring to the fact, said:

"We have to go to Weller when we want to borrow anything. We may get mixed on our periods, but Weller won't. We may want to dress a Colonial in an 1825 or a 1625 or something of that sort, but you won't catch Weller letting the wrong thing out of the box."

With the sanity of his American ideas, Mr. Pyle is no blind enthusiast about the superiority of art and artists in time past. Although strongly influenced in his earlier days by Dürer and Holbein, although constantly pointing to such of his favorites as the Sistine Madonna, to Segantini's country scenes in the Alps, and other pictures alike only in that all are great, the names of some Americans are as constantly upon his lips—Winslow Homer, Inness, George De Forest Brush, St. Gaudens, and Daniel Chester French.

If the development of Mr. Pyle's pupils is proof of his theory that the highest ideals for illustration push the idealist onward into the purest artistic expression, his own art is an even more apparent vindication. It is no idle comment to say that he is to-day painting better than he has ever painted. Many people believe that he is entering upon the period in which his creative power will display itself as never before. While that beautiful imaginative work, "The Travels of the Soul," is known widely, while every study Mr. Pyle has made of colonial life is remembered for its accuracy and vigor, thus far he has undertaken nothing so important as the murals now being done in the Wilmington studio. One of these, "The Battle of Nashville," is about completed for the St. Paul Capitol. The second, "The Landing of Carteret," will eventually be placed in the new Essex County Court House at Newark, New Jersey. This large panel is six by sixteen feet, and even in its beginning is an imposing piece of work. Of previous murals, perhaps none by Mr. Pyle are better known than a large decorative design in four panels representing "The Genius of Art," which has been placed in a private home.

If a "school of art," in the broad sense, be correctly defined as a distinct group of artists working by similar methods to express diverse conceptions of truth, Mr. Pyle is the leader of such a school. Certainly no other American artist has a following so large or distinguished.

MR. PYLE'S STUDIO AT WILMINGTON

# THE PERMANENT ASSISTANT SECRETARY OF STATE

## BY GAILLARD HUNT

SOME years ago a certain under-official in the State Department went to the Secretary of State, James G. Blaine, and asked him to appoint him to a vacancy among the Assistant Secretaries. "Why," said Mr. Blaine, "it would not be doing you a kindness; you would lose the place when the administration changed."

"Why so?" said the applicant. "Look at Adee."

"Well," said Mr. Blaine, slowly, "Adee is—Adee."

Volumes could not have said more. He stands in a class by himself, without prototype or understudy, and when he shall pass off the stage a search will have to be made for some one now unknown to play his rôle. What Mr. Blaine himself thought of him was shown in a remark he once made to a visitor who happened to enter his room as Mr. Adee was leaving it. "There goes a great man," said he.

I have said that Mr. Adee has no prototype; but he had a precursor. This was William Hunter, of Rhode Island, who was appointed a clerk in the State Department in 1829, became a chief of bureau in 1833, and chief clerk in 1852, when Daniel Webster was Secretary of State. There was then no Assistant Secretary, so Mr. Hunter frequently acted as Secretary. The office of Assistant Secretary was established in 1853, but it was not then (and has not become since) an office of permanent tenure, and Mr. Hunter often filled it during the frequent interregnums, until in 1866 the office of Second Assistant Secretary was created by Congress expressly in order that he might be appointed to fill it, which he did for twenty years, until he died in 1886. His continuous service in the Department covered a period of fifty-seven years, and for over forty years of that time he was the fixed center about which the conduct of our international affairs revolved. Upon his death, Alvey Augustus Adee, then Third Assistant Secretary, was promptly promoted to his chair, which he has occupied ever since. Thus only two men have served as Second Assistant Secretaries of State, and their combined service covers forty years; but counting from the time that Mr. Hunter had in charge the duties which he continued to perform as an Assistant Secretary, and which Mr. Adee has performed since his death, there have been more than sixty years of the combined service of Mr. Hunter and Mr. Adee, from the administration of Millard Fillmore to that of Theodore Roosevelt, and from Edward Everett to Elihu Root. Thirteen Presidents and thirty-two Secretaries of State have come and gone in that time. Two wars have been fought, and Mr. Adee could doubtless tell how several wars have been narrowly averted.

Mr. Adee succeeded to Mr. Hunter's chair, and the word is used advisedly, for he sat upon the same seat that Mr. Hunter had used, and upon the same old leather cushion that had been flattened and worn smooth in long service for Mr. Hunter. But one of Mr. Adee's first conclusions on taking his new seat was that the old cushion was undesirable, so he rose and with his own hands lifted it from the chair. As he did so, there fluttered to the floor a number of large sheets of paper closely written in his predecessor's well-known hand. They were the draft of a treaty which had been negotiated many years before, and in this safe hiding-place Mr. Hunter had put and forgotten them, and sat upon them. Mr. Adee remembered how, when the draft was lost, Mr. Hunter had been enraged and had ordered the

be made to his accomplishments as a Shakespearean scholar, and no one will dispute his title to high rank in this branch of learning who has ever read his erudite and exhaustive introduction to King Lear in " The Bankside " collection and collation of first folio and quarto texts of Shakespeare. A lifetime spent at the Government desk has not dried up his imagination, and in the old copies of some magazines may be found excellent stories of his, while his knowledge of poetry· and poetical construction is greater than that of most poets. He had a much-loved brother, David Graham Adee, a poet of no mean attainments, and the two often worked together.

A few years after the Spanish War was over, the Boxer uprising in China occurred, and the members of our Legation were prisoners in Peking in hourly danger of death. In the midst of the preparations to save them Secretary Hay was obliged to leave Washington, and, the Assistant Secretary being away, Mr. Adee stepped into the breach and managed without a single blunder a situation so delicate that even a small mistake might have brought a great disaster.

These are only a very few of the many notable things Mr. Adee has done ; but perhaps his greatest service to his country has been, not in the things he has done, but in the things he has prevented others less experienced than himself from doing.

There is no office after the Presidency which ranks higher than the office of Secretary of State, and seldom has there been a man chosen to fill it who did not measure up to its standards ; but the instances have been few where the Secretary of State has had experience in dipiomatic usage and world politics, and the international questions with which he has to deal are nearly always old questions with a long line of previous positions taken by the Government, sometimes stretching back for a hundred years. To act without observing the rules which international practice has prescribed, or to act without knowledge of previous action taken by the Government, would often prove ruinous to the interests of the United States ; and it is because this fact has always been recognized that the State Department is the most stable of all the Government Departments, and the one in which fewest changes are made in the personnel. Mr. Adee is the personification of this stability. He represents tradition and conservatism, evolution rather than revolution, steady advance rather than hasty action and retreat. The continuous strength of the management of the foreign policy of the United States has commanded the admiration of intelligent foreigners and the pride of patriotic Americans, and the credit for it in our day is due to no one more than to Alvey A. Adee.

JAMES LANE ALLEN

# *KING SOLOMON OF KENTUCKY* [1]

## *BY JAMES LANE ALLEN*

### *WITH AN INTRODUCTION BY HAMILTON W. MABIE*

"THE middle of a fragrant afternoon of May in the green wilderness of Kentucky;" these words, at the beginning of the first chapter of "The Choir Invisible," mark the hour and place which put a background of rare and opulent beauty behind the work of a writer whose imagination, insight, and humor are always touched with a certain distinction. As Anthony Van Dyck was pre-eminently the painter of gentlemen, Mr. Allen is pre-eminently the recorder in fiction of men and women of sensitive honor, refinement of feeling and habit, detachment from buying and selling, gay courage and gallant devotion. These gentlefolk are sometimes emigrants and often country people ; but the charm of inborn and inbred personal dignity, and that delicacy of manner which is the subtle language of the soul of civilization, are the more conspicuous because they are brought out against the simple furnishings of a primitive life. The insight, the feeling for fineness of

[1] Reprinted from "Flute and Violin," by the permission of the Macmillan Company, New York.

nature, the beautiful regard for the sanctity of personality which inspires the best manners, put Mr. Allen's short stories in a place by themselves, gain a certain heightened charm from the fragrant stretches of wood and meadow upon which his readers always look, and give him pre-eminence as a reporter of American idealism. The special and characteristic fact about idealism in this country is its association with the simplest social conditions and the plainest circumstances of life. Abroad one finds it sometimes in palaces, oftener in universities, studios, ancient homes; it lives with the fortunate and finds expression in the arts. In this country, from the beginning, it has subtly taken on the guise of democracy, chosen humble homes, and thriven like a wild flower on the edge of the wilderness. Those who know America through the newspapers have not found it; they have not found and they will not find the country which produced Emerson, Lincoln, Lee, Lanier; the country which hides its idealism behind a thousand practical tasks and cherishes indestructible hopes in quiet places, and translates them into character and life.

The author of " King Solomon of Kentucky "—the third of the twelve stories of permanent value which The Outlook is reprinting in its Magazine Numbers—is an idealist whose work is grounded in reality and is the fruit of the historical method. In the Introduction to the revised edition of " A Kentucky Cardinal " and " Aftermath " one finds these significant words: " In so far as literature is concerned, the same experiences have taught me, and have always compelled me, to see human life as set in Nature; finding its explanation in soil and sky and season: merely one of the wild growths that spring up on the surface of the earth amid ten thousand others. I hold this to be the only true way in which to write of Man in fiction, as it is in science. I further hold that if a writer is ever to have that knowledge of a country which reappears in his work as local color, he must have gathered it in his childhood." The gaining of that knowledge in childhood, when the imagination is as active as the faculty of observation, is a cardinal point in his creed: " Wring out of the heart of a man the last essence of his knowledge of a country, and it will be the scenes of boyhood pleasures." If one were dealing with the fundamental aspects of Mr. Allen's work, he would perhaps say that artistic feeling and scientific temper are very subtly blended in it, and that beneath its extraordinary beauty there lies a philosophy wholly and intensely modern: the vital relation of art to soil and race which Herder divined and which Taine applied with such searching and illuminating power. The title of two of Mr. Allen's later and longer stories reveal his point of view and the very definite tendency of his thinking—" The Reign of Law " and " The Mettle of the Pasture."

Readers of Mr. Allen's short stories come at once under the spell of a style which, in diction, construction, and suggestion, is as individual as it is musical, and are often so captivated by the pleasure of cadenced and enchanting speech that they overlook the significance of these stories in American literature. They are striking in the combination of the selective genius of an idealist with the accuracy and thoroughness of method of a realist; for the man of scientific interests is always something of a realist. In the stories which make up " Flute and Violin," in " A Kentucky Cardinal " and " Aftermath," in " A Summer in Arcady " and in " The Reign of Law," the background is sketched with an accuracy based on the most thorough observation and filled in with the most sensitive feeling for truth. That background, fortunately, is one of the most opulent in richness of vegetation and splendor of sky. The stories are not set accidentally and arbitrarily in the Blue Grass region of Kentucky; they are rooted in its soil and penetrated with its radiant influences.

In like manner the realist has, from careers monotonous, obscure, or even repulsive in outward appearance, chosen traits, qualities, and experiences which are of no condition but belong everywhere to the finer soul of humanity. Here, too, there is a touch of realism; but it is a realism of truth to the higher as well as the lower facts of life. "King Solomon of Kentucky" wears his crown late; but, on the court-house steps, to be sold to the highest bidder, the instinct of a gentleman was in the vagrant, and Mr. Allen has touched his unpromising hero with that divining hand of human sympathy that is the open sesame to the nobilities of the human spirit however hidden in dress and place. The humor and pathos of the story convey an impression so definite and faithful that its publication led to a search for the grave of "King Solomon," its identification, and the placing of a monument over it in the Lexington Cemetery.                    H. W. M.

## I.

IT had been a year of strange disturbances—a desolating drought, a hurly-burly of destructive tempests, killing frosts in the tender valleys, mortal fevers in the tender homes. Now came tidings that all day the wail of myriads of locusts was heard in the green woods of Virginia and Tennessee; now that Lake Erie was blocked with ice on the very verge of summer, so that in the Niagara new rocks and islands showed their startling faces. In the Blue-grass Region of Kentucky countless caterpillars were crawling over the ripening apple orchards and leaving the trees as stark as when tossed in the thin air of bitter February days.

Then, flying low and heavily through drought and tempest and frost and plague, like the royal presence of disaster, that had been but heralded by its mournful train, came nearer and nearer the dark angel of the pestilence.

M. Xaupi had given a great ball only the night before in the dancing-rooms over the confectionery of M. Giron— that M. Giron who made the tall pyramids of méringues and macaroons for wedding suppers, and spun around them a cloud of candied webbing as white and misty as the veil of the bride. It was the opening cotillion party of the summer. The men came in blue cloth coats with brass buttons, buff waistcoats, and laced and ruffled shirts; the ladies came in white satins with ethereal silk overdresses, embroidered in the figure of a gold beetle or an oak leaf of green. The walls of the ball-room were painted to represent landscapes of blooming orange-trees, set here and there in clustering tubs; and the chandeliers and sconces were lighted with innumerable wax candles, yellow and green and rose.

Only the day before, also, Clatterbuck had opened for the summer a new villa-house, six miles out in the country, with a dancing-pavilion in a grove of maples and oaks, a pleasure-boat on a sheet of crystal water, and a cellar stocked with old sherry, Sauterne, and Château Margaux wines, with anisette, "Perfect Love," and Guigholet cordials.

Down on Water Street, near where now stands a railway station, Hugh Lonney, urging that the fear of cholera was not the only incentive to cleanliness, had just fitted up a sumptuous bath-house, where cold and shower baths might be had at twelve and a half cents each, or hot ones at three for half a dollar.

Yes, the summer of 1833 was at hand, and there must be new pleasures, new luxuries; for Lexington was the Athens of the West and the Kentucky Birmingham.

Old Peter Leuba felt the truth of this, as he stepped smiling out of his little music-store on Main Street, and, rubbing his hands briskly together, surveyed once more his newly arranged windows, in which were displayed gold and silver epaulets, bottles of Jamaica rum, garden seeds from Philadelphia, drums and guitars and harps. Dewees & Grant felt it in their drug-store on Cheapside, as they sent off a large order for calomel and superior Maccoboy, rappee, and Lancaster snuff. Bluff little Daukins Tegway felt it, as he hurried on the morning of that day to the office of the Observer and Reporter, and advertised that he would willingly exchange his beautiful assortment of painted muslins and Dunstable bonnets for flax and feathers. On the threshold he met a florid farmer, who had just offered ten dollars' reward for a likely runaway boy with a long fresh scar across his face ; and to-morrow the paper would contain one more of those tragical little cuts, representing an African slave scampering away at the top of his speed, with a stick swung across his shoulder and a bundle dangling down his back. In front of Postlethwaite's Tavern, where now stands the Phœnix Hotel, a company of idlers, leaning back in Windsor chairs and planting their feet against the opposite wall on a level with their heads, smoked and chewed and yawned, as they discussed the administration of Jackson and arranged for the coming of Daniel Webster in June, when they would give him a great barbecue, and roast in his honor a buffalo bull taken from the herd emparked near Ashland. They hailed a passing merchant, who, however, would hear nothing of the bull, but fell to praising his Rocky Mountain beaver and Goose Creek salt ; and another, who turned a deaf ear to Daniel Webster, and invited them to drop in and examine his choice essences of peppermint, bergamot, and lavender.

But of all the scenes that might have been observed in Lexington on that day, the most remarkable occurred in front of the old court-house at the hour of high noon. On the mellow stroke of the clock in the steeple above the sheriff stepped briskly forth, closely followed by a man of powerful frame, whom he commanded to station himself on the pavement several feet off. A crowd of men and boys had already collected in anticipation, and others came quickly up as the clear voice of the sheriff was heard across the open public square and old market-place.

He stood on the topmost of the court-house steps, and for a moment looked down on the crowd with the usual air of official severity.

"Gentlemen," he then cried out sharply, "by an ordah of the cou't I now offah this man at public sale to the highes' biddah. He is able-bodied but lazy, without visible property or means of suppoht, an' of dissolute habits. He is therefoh adjudged guilty of high misdemeanahs, an' is to be sole into labah foh a twelvemonth. How much, then, am I offahed foh the vagrant? How much am I offahed foh ole King Sol'mon?"

Nothing was offered for old King Solomon. The spectators formed themselves into a ring around the big vagrant and settled down to enjoy the performance.

"Staht 'im, somebody."

Somebody started a laugh, which rippled around the circle.

The sheriff looked on with an expression of unrelaxed severity, but, catching the eye of an acquaintance on the outskirts, he exchanged a lightning wink of secret appreciation. Then he lifted off his tight beaver hat, wiped out of his eyes a little shower of perspiration which rolled suddenly down from above, and warmed a degree to his theme.

"Come, gentlemen," he said, more suasively, "it's too hot to stan' heah all day. Make me an offah! You all know ole King Sol'mon; don't wait to be interduced. How much, then, to staht 'im? Say fifty dollahs! Twenty-five! Fifteen! Ten! Why, gentlemen! Not *ten* dollahs? Remembah this is the Blue-grass Region of Kentucky—the land of Boone an' Kenton, the home of Henry Clay!" he added, in an oratorical *crescendo*.

"He ain't wuth his victuals," said an oily little tavern-keeper, folding his arms restfully over his own stomach and cocking up one piggish eye into his neighbor's face. "He ain't wuth his 'taters."

"Buy 'im foh 'is rags!" cried a young law student, with a Blackstone under his arm, to the town rag-picker opposite, who was unconsciously ogling the vagrant's apparel.

"I *might* buy 'im foh his *scalp*," drawled a farmer, who had taken part in all kinds of scalp contests and was now known to be busily engaged in collecting crow scalps for a match soon to come off between two rival counties.

"I think I'll buy 'im foh a hat sign," said a manufacturer of ten-dollar Castor and Rhorum hats. This sally drew merry attention to the vagrant's hat, and the merchant felt rewarded.

"You'd bettah say the town ought to buy 'im an' put 'im up on top of the cou't-house as a scarecrow for the cholera," said some one else.

"What news of the cholera did the stage-coach bring this mohning?" quickly inquired his neighbor in his ear; and the two immediately fell into low, grave talk, forgot the auction, and turned away.

"Stop, gentlemen, stop!" cried the sheriff, who had watched the rising tide of good humor, and now saw his chance to float in on it with spreading sails. "You're runnin' the price in the wrong direction—down, not up. The law requires that he be sole to the highes' biddah, not the lowes'. As loyal citizens, uphole the constitution of the commonwealth of Kentucky an' make me an offah; the man is really a great bargain. In the first place, he would cos' his ownah little or nothin', because, as you see, he keeps himself in cigahs an' clo'es; then, his main article of diet is whisky—a supply of which he always has on han'. He don't even need a bed, foh you know he sleeps jus' as well on any doohstep; noh a chair, foh he prefers to sit roun' on the curbstones. Remembah, too, gentlemen, that ole King Sol'mon is a Virginian—from the same neighborhood as Mr. Clay. Remembah that he is well educated, that he is an *awful* Whig, an' that he has smoked mo' of the stumps of Mr. Clay's cigahs than any other man in existence. If you don't b'lieve *me*, gentlemen, yondah goes Mr. Clay now; call *him* ovah an' ask 'im foh yo'se'ves."

He paused, and pointed with his right forefinger towards Main Street, along which the spectators, with a sudden craning of necks, beheld the familiar figure of the passing statesman.

"But you don't need *any*body to tell you these fac's, gentlemen," he continued. "You merely need to be reminded that ole King Sol'mon is no ohdinary man. Mo'ovah, he has a kine heaht; he nevah spoke a rough wohd to anybody in this worl', an' he is as proud as Tecumseh of his good name an' charactah. An', gentlemen," he added, bridling with an air of mock gallantry and laying a hand on his heart, "if anythin' fu'thah is required in the way of a puffect encomium, we all know that there isn't anothah man among us who cuts as wide a swath among the ladies. The'foh, if you have any appreciation of virtue, any magnanimity of heaht; if you set a propah valuation upon the descendants of Virginia, that mothah of Presidents; if you believe in the pure laws of Kentucky as the pioneer bride of the Union; if you love America an' love the worl'—make me a gen'rous, high-toned offah foh ole King Sol'mon!"

He ended his peroration amid a shout of laughter and applause, and, feeling satisfied that it was a good time for returning to a more practical treatment of his subject, proceeded in a sincere tone:

"He can easily earn from one to two dollahs a day, an' from three to six hundred a yeah. There's not anothah white man in town capable of doin' as much work. There's not a niggah han' in the hemp factories with such muscles an' such a chest. *Look* at 'em! An', if you don't b'lieve-me, step fo'wahd and *feel* 'em. How much, then, is bid foh 'im?"

"One dollah!" said the owner of a hemp factory, who had walked forward and felt the vagrant's arm, laughing, but coloring up also as the eyes of all were quickly turned upon him. In those days it was not an unheard-of thing for the muscles of a human being to be thus examined when being sold into servitude to a new master.

"Thank you!" cried the sheriff, cheerily. "One precinc' heard from! One dollah! I am offahed one dollah foh ole King Sol'mon. One dollah foh the king! Make it a half. One dollar an' a half. Make it a half. One dol-dol-dol-dollah!"

Two medical students, returning from lectures at the old Medical Hall, now joined the group, and the sheriff explained :

" One dollah is bid foh the vagrant ole King Sol'mon, who is to be sole into labah foh a twelvemonth. Is there any othah bid? Are you all done? One dollah, once—"

" Dollah and a half," said one of the students, and remarked half jestingly under his breath to his companion, " I'll buy him on a chance of his dying. We'll dissect him."

" Would you own his body if he *should* die ?"

" If he dies while bound to me, I'll arrange *that*."

" One dollah an' a half," resumed the sheriff ; and falling into the tone of a facile auctioneer he rattled on :

" One dollah an' a half foh ole Sol'-mon—sol, sol, sol—do, re, mi, fa, sol— do, re, mi, fa, sol ! Why, gentlemen, you can set the king to music !"

All this time the vagrant had stood in the center of that close ring of jeering and humorous bystanders—a baffling text from which to have preached a sermon on the infirmities of our imperfect humanity. Some years before, perhaps as a master-stroke of derision, there had been given to him that title which could but heighten the contrast of his personality and estate with every suggestion of the ancient sacred magnificence ; and never had the mockery seemed so fine as at this moment, when he was led forth into the streets to receive the lowest sentence of the law upon his poverty and dissolute idleness. He was apparently in the very prime of life—a striking figure, for nature at least had truly done some royal work on him. Over six feet in height, erect, with limbs well shaped and sinewy, with chest and neck full of the lines of great power, a large head thickly covered with long reddish hair, eyes blue, face beardless, complexion fair but discolored by low passions and excesses—such was old King Solomon. He wore a stiff, high, black Castor hat of the period, with the crown smashed in and the torn rim hanging down over one ear ; a black cloth coat in the old style, ragged and buttonless ; a white cotton shirt, with the broad collar crumpled, wide open at the neck and down his sunburnt bosom ; blue jeans pantaloons, patched at the seat and the knees ; and ragged cotton socks that fell down over the tops of his dusty shoes, which were open at the heels.

In one corner of his sensual mouth rested the stump of a cigar. Once during the proceedings he had produced another, lighted it, and continued quietly smoking. If he took to himself any shame as the central figure of this ignoble performance, no one knew it. There was something almost royal in his unconcern. The humor, the badinage, the open contempt, of which he was the public target, fell thick and fast upon him, but as harmlessly as would balls of pith upon a coat of mail. In truth, there was that in his great, lazy, gentle, good-humored bulk and bearing which made the gibes seem all but despicable. He shuffled from one foot to the other as though he found it a trial to stand up so long, but all the while looking the spectators full in the eyes without the least impatience. He suffered the man of the factory to walk round him and push and pinch his muscles as calmly as though he had been the show bull at a country fair. Once only, when the sheriff had pointed across the street at the figure of Mr. Clay, he had looked quickly in that direction with a kindling light in his eye and a passing flush on his face. For the rest, he seemed like a man who has drained his cup of human life and has nothing left him but to fill again and drink without the least surprise or eagerness.

The bidding between the man of the factory and the student had gone slowly on. The price had reached ten dollars. The heat was intense, the sheriff tired. Then something occurred to revivify the scene. Across the market-place and towards the steps of the court-house there suddenly came trundling along in breathless haste a huge old negress, carrying on one arm a large shallow basket containing apple crab-lanterns and fresh gingerbread. With a series of half-articulate grunts and snorts, she approached the edge of the crowd and tried to force her way through. She coaxed, she begged, she elbowed and pushed and scolded, now laughing, and now with the passion of tears in her thick, excited voice. All at once, catching sight of the sheriff, she lifted one ponderous brown arm, naked to the elbow, and waved her hand to him above the heads of those in front.

" Hole on, marseter ! Hole on !" she cried, in a tone of humorous entreaty. " Don' knock 'im off till I come ! Gim *me* a bid at 'im !"

The sheriff paused and smiled. The crowd made way tumultuously, with broad laughter and comment.

. " Stan' aside theah an' let Aun' Charlotte in !"

" *Now* you'll see biddin' !"

" Get out of the way foh Aun' Charlotte !"

" Up, my free niggah ! Hurrah foh Kentucky !"

A moment more and she stood inside the ring of spectators, her basket on the pavement at her feet, her hands plumped akimbo into her fathomless sides, her head up, and her soft, motherly eyes turned eagerly upon the sheriff. Of the crowd she seemed unconscious, and on the vagrant before her she had not cast a single glance.

She was dressed with perfect neatness. A red and yellow Madras kerchief was bound about her head in a high coil, and another was crossed over the bosom of her stiffly starched and smoothly ironed blue cottonade dress. Rivulets of perspiration ran down over her nose, her temples, and around her ears, and disappeared mysteriously in the creases of her brown neck. A single drop accidentally hung glistening like a diamond on the circlet of one of her large brass earrings.

The sheriff looked at her a moment, smiling, but a little disconcerted. The spectacle was unprecedented.

" What do you want heah, Aun' Charlotte ?" he asked, kindly. " You can't sell yo' pies an' gingerbread heah."

" I don' *wan'* sell no pies en gingerbread," she replied, contemptuously. " I wan' bid on *him*," and she nodded sidewise at the vagrant.

" White folks allers sellin' niggahs to wuk fuh *dem ;* I gwine buy a white man to wuk fuh *me*. En he gwine t' get a mighty hard mistiss, you heah *me !*"

The eyes of the sheriff twinkled with delight.

" Ten dollahs is offahed foh ole King Sol'mon. Is theah any othah bid ? Are you all done !"

" 'Leben," she said.

Two young ragamuffins crawled among the legs of the crowd up to her basket and filched pies and cake beneath her very nose.

" Twelve !" cried the student, laughing.

" Thirteen !" she laughed too, but her eyes flashed.

" *You are bidding against a niggah*," whispered the student's companion in his ear.

" So I am ; let's be off," answered the other, with a hot flush on his proud face.

Thus the sale was ended, and the crowd variously dispersed. In a distant corner of the courtyard the ragged urchins were devouring their unexpected booty. The old negress drew a red handkerchief out of her bosom, untied a knot in a corner of it, and counted out the money to the sheriff. Only she and the vagrant were now left on the spot.

" You have bought me. What do you want me to do ?" he asked, quietly.

" Lohd, honey !" she answered, in a low tone of affectionate chiding, " I don' wan' you to do *nothin'* ! I wuzn' gwine t' 'low dem white folks to buy you. Dey'd wuk you till you dropped dead. You go 'long en do ez you please."

She gave a cunning chuckle of triumph in thus setting at naught the ends of justice, and, in a voice rich and musical with affection, she said, as she gave him a little push :

" You bettah be gittin' out o' dis blazin sun. G' on home ! I be 'long by-en-by."

He turned and moved slowly away in the direction of Water Street, where she lived ; and she, taking up her basket, shuffled across the market-place towards Cheapside, muttering to herself the while :

" I come mighty nigh gittin' dah too late, foolin' 'long wid dese pies. Sellin' *him* 'ca'se he don't wuk ! Umph ! If all de men in dis town dat don' wuk wuz to be tuk up en sole, d' wouldn' be 'nough money in de town to buy 'em I Don' I see 'em settin' 'roun' dese taverns f'om mohnin' till night?"

She snorted out her indignation and disgust, and, sitting down on the sidewalk under a Lombardy poplar, uncovered her wares and kept the flies away with a locust bough, not discovering, in her alternating good and ill humor, that half of them had been filched by her old tormentors.

This was the memórable scene enacted in Lexington on that memorable day of the year 1833—a day that passed so briskly. For whoever met and spoke together asked the one question: Will the cholera come to Lexington? And the answer always gave a nervous haste to business—a keener thrill to pleasure. It was of the cholera that the negro woman heard two sweet passing ladies speak as she spread her wares on the sidewalk. They were on their way to a little picture gallery just opened opposite M. Giron's ball-room, and in one breath she heard them discussing their toilets for the evening and in the next several portraits by Jouett.

So the day passed, the night came on, and M. Xaupi gave his brilliant ball. Poor old Xaupi—poor little Frenchman I whirled as a gamin of Paris through the mazes of the Revolution, and lately come all the way to Lexington to teach the people how to dance. Hop about blithely on thy dry legs, basking this night in the waxen radiance of manners and melodies and graces I Where will be thy tunes and airs to-morrow? Ay, smile and prompt away I On and on I Swing corners, ladies and gentlemen I Form the basket I Hands all around I

While the bows were still darting across the strings, out of the low, red east there shot a long, tremulous bow of light up towards the zenith. And then, could human sight have beheld the invisible, it might have seen hovering over the town, over the ball-room, over M. Xaupi, the awful presence of the plague.

But, knowing nothing of this, the heated revelers went merrily home in the chill air of the red and saffron dawn. And, knowing nothing of it also, a man awakened on the doorstep of a house

opposite the ball-room, where he had long since fallen asleep. His limbs were cramped, and a shiver ran through his frame. Staggering to his feet, he made his way down to the house of Free Charlotte, mounted to his room by means of a stairway opening on the street, threw off his outer garments, kicked off his shoes, and, taking a bottle from a closet, pressed it several times to his lips with long outward breaths of satisfaction. Then, casting his great white bulk upon the bed, in a minute more he had sunk into a heavy sleep—the usual drunken sleep of old King Solomon.

He, too, had attended M. Xaupi's ball, in his own way and in his proper character, being drawn to the place for the pleasure of seeing the fine ladies arrive and float in, like large white moths of the summer night; of looking in through the open windows at the many-colored waxen lights and the snowy arms and shoulders; of having blown out to him the perfume and the music; not worthy to go in, being the lowest of the low, but attending from a doorstep of the street opposite—with a certain rich passion in his nature for splendor and revelry and sensuous beauty.

II.

About ten o'clock the sunlight entered through the shutters and awoke him. He threw one arm up over his eyes to intercept the burning rays. As he lay outstretched and stripped of grotesque rags, it could be better seen in what a mold nature had cast his figure. His breast, bare and tanned, was barred by full, arching ribs and knotted by crossing muscles; and his shirt-sleeve, falling away to the shoulder from his bent arm, revealed its crowded muscles in the high relief of heroic bronze. For, although he had been sold as a vagrant, old King Solomon had in earlier years followed the trade of a digger of cellars, and the strenuous use of mattock and spade had developed every sinew to the utmost. His whole person, now half naked and in repose, was full of the suggestions of unspent power. Only his face, swollen and red, only his eyes, bloodshot and dull, bore the impress of wasted vitality. There, all too plainly stamped, were the passions long since raging and still on fire.

The sunlight had stirred him to but a low degree of consciousness, and some minutes passed before he realized that a stifling, resinous fume impregnated the air. He sniffed it quickly; through the window seemed to come the smell of burning tar. He sat up on the edge of the bed and vainly tried to clear his thoughts.

The room was a clean but poor habitation—uncarpeted, whitewashed, with a piece or two of the cheapest furniture, and a row of pegs on one wall, where usually hung those tattered coats and pantaloons, miscellaneously collected, that were his purple and fine linen. He turned his eyes in this direction now and noticed that his clothes were missing. The old shoes had disappeared from their corner; the cigar-stumps, picked up here and there in the streets according to his wont, were gone from the mantelpiece. Near the door was a large bundle tied up in a sheet. In a state of bewilderment, he asked himself what it all meant. Then a sense of the silence in the street below possessed him. At this hour he was used to hearing noises enough—from Hugh Lonney's new bath-house on one side, from Harry Sikes's barber-shop on the other.

A mysterious feeling of terror crept over and helped to sober him. How long had he lain asleep? By degrees he seemed to remember that two or three times he had awakened far enough to drink from the bottle under his pillow, only to sink again into heavier stupefaction. By degrees, too, he seemed to remember that other things had happened—a driving of vehicles this way and that, a hurrying of people along the street. He had thought it the breaking-up of M. Xaupi's ball. More than once had not some one shaken and tried to arouse him? Through the wall of Harry Sikes's barber-shop had he not heard cries of pain—sobs of distress?

He staggered to the window, threw open the shutters, and, kneeling at the sill, looked out. The street was deserted. The houses opposite were closed. Cats were sleeping in the silent doorways. But as he looked up and down he caught sight of people hurrying along cross-streets. From a distant lumber-yard came the muffled sound of rapid hammerings. On the air was the faint roll of vehicles—the hush and the vague noises of a general terrifying commotion.

In the middle of the street below him a keg was burning, and, as he looked, the hoops gave way, the tar spread out like a stream of black lava, and a cloud of inky smoke and deep-red furious flame burst upward through the sagging air. Just beneath the window a common cart had been backed close up to the door of the house. In it had been thrown a few small articles of furniture, and on the bottom bedclothes had been spread out as if for a pallet. While he looked, old Charlotte hurried out with a pillow.

He called down to her in a strange, unsteady voice:

"What is the matter? What are you doing, Aunt Charlotte?"

She uttered a cry, dropped the pillow, and stared up at him. Her face looked dry and wrinkled.

"My God! De chol'ra's in town! I'm waitin' on you! Dress, en come down en fetch de bun'le by de dooh." And she hurried back into the house.

But he continued leaning on his folded arms, his brain stunned by the shock of the intelligence. Suddenly he leaned far out and looked down at the closed shutters of the barber-shop. Old Charlotte reappeared.

"Where is Harry Sikes?" he asked.

"Dead en buried."

"When did he die?"

"Yestidd'y evenin'."

"What day is this?"

"Sadd'y."

M. Xaupi's ball had been on Thursday evening. That night the cholera had broken out. He had lain in his drunken stupor ever since. Their talk had lasted but a minute, but she looked up anxiously and urged him,

"D' ain' no time to was'e, honey! D' ain' no time to was'e. I done got dis cyart to tek you 'way in, en I be ready to start in a minute. Put yo' clo'es on en bring de bun'le wid all yo' ysdder things in it."

With incredible activity she climbed

into the cart and began to roll up the bedclothes. In reality she had made up her mind to put him into the cart, and the pallet had been made for him to lie and finish his drunken sleep on, while she drove him away to a place of safety.

Still he did not move from the window-sill. He was thinking of Harry Sikes, who had shaved him many a time for nothing. Then he suddenly called down to her :

"Have many died of the cholera? Are there many cases in town?"

She went on with her preparations and took no notice of him. He repeated the question. She got down quickly from the cart and began to mount the staircase. He went back to bed, pulled the sheet up over him, and propped himself up among the pillows. Her soft, heavy footsteps slurred on the stairway as though her strength were failing, and as soon as she entered the room she sank into a chair, overcome with terror. He looked at her with a sudden sense of pity.

"Don't be frightened," he said, kindly. "It might only make it the worse for you."

"I can' he'p it, honey," she answered, wringing her hands and rocking herself to and fro; "de ole niggah can' he'p it. If de Lohd jes spah me to git out'n dis town wid you! Honey, ain' you able to put on yo' clo'es?"

"You've tied them all up in the sheet."

"De Lohd he'p de crazy ole niggah!"

She started up and tugged at the bundle, and laid out a suit of his clothes, if things so incongruous could be called a suit.

"Have many people died of the cholera?"

"Dey been dyin' like sheep ev' since yestidd'y mohnin'!—all day, en all las' night, en dis mohnin'! De man he done lock up de huss, an dey been buryin' em in cyarts. En de grave-diggah he done run away, en hit look like d' ain nobody to dig de graves."

She bent over the bundle, tying again the four corners of the sheet. Through the window came the sound of the quick hammers driving nails. She threw up her arms into the air, and then, seizing the bundle, dragged it rapidly to the door.

"You heah dat? Dey nailin' up cawfins in de lumbah-yahd! Put on yo' clo'es, honey, en come on."

A resolution had suddenly taken shape in his mind.

"Go on away and save your life. Don't wait for me; I'm not going. And good-by, Aunt Charlotte, in case I don't see you any more. You've been very kind to me—kinder than I deserved. Where have you put my mattock and spade?"

He said this very quietly, and sat up on the edge of the bed, his feet hanging down, and his hand stretched out towards her.

"Honey," she explained, coaxingly, from where she stood, "can't you sobah up a little en put on yo' clo'es? I gwine to tek you 'way to de country. You don' wan' no tools. You can' dig no cellahs now. De chol'ra's in town en de people's dyin' like sheep."

"I expect they will need me," he answered.

She perceived now that he was sober. For an instant her own fear was forgotten in an outburst of resentment and indignation.

"Dig graves fuh 'em, when dey put you up on the block en sell you same ez you was a niggah! Dig graves fuh 'em, when dey allers callin' you names on de street en makin' fun o' you!"

"They are not to blame. I have brought it on myself."

"But we can' stay heah en die o' de chol'ra!"

"You musn't stay. You must go away at once."

"But if I go, who gwine tek cyah o' you?"

"Nobody."

She came quickly across the room to the bed, fell on her knees, clasped his feet to her breast, and looked up into his face with an expression of imploring tenderness. Then, with incoherent cries and with sobs and tears, she pleaded with him—pleaded for dear life; his and her own.

It was a strange scene. What historian of the heart will ever be able to do justice to those peculiar ties which bound the heart of the negro in years gone by to a race of not always worthy masters? This old Virginia nurse had known King Solomon when he was a boy playing with her young master, till that young master died on the way to Kentucky.

At the death of her mistress she had become free with a little property. By thrift and industry she had greatly enlarged this. Years passed, and she became the only surviving member of the Virginian household, which had emigrated early in the century to the Blue-grass Region. The same wave of emigration had brought in old King Solomon from the same neighborhood. As she had risen in life, he had sunk. She sat on the sidewalks selling her fruits and cakes; he sat on the sidewalks more idle, more ragged and dissolute. On no other basis than these facts she began to assume a sort of maternal pitying care of him, patching his rags, letting him have money for his vices, and when, a year or two before, he had ceased working almost entirely, giving him a room in her house and taking in payment what he chose to pay.

He brushed his hand quickly across his eyes as she knelt before him now, clasping his feet to her bosom. From coaxing him as an intractable child she had, in the old servile fashion, fallen to imploring him, with touching forgetfulness of their real relations:

"O my marseter! O my marseter Solomon! Go 'way en save yo' life, en tek yo' po' ole niggah wid you!"

But his resolution was formed, and he refused to go. A hurried footstep paused beneath the window and a loud voice called up. The old nurse got up and went to the window. A man was standing by the cart at her door.

"For God's sake let me have this cart to take my wife and little children away to the country! There is not a vehicle to be had in town. I will pay you—" He stopped, seeing the distress on her face.

"Is he dead?" he asked, for he knew of her care of old King Solomon.

"He *will* die!" she sobbed. "Tilt de t'ings out on de pavement. I gwine t' stay wid 'im en tek cyah o' 'im."

## III.

A little later, dressed once more in grotesque rags and carrying on his shoulder a rusty mattock and a rusty spade, old King Solomon appeared in the street below and stood looking up and down it with an air of anxious indecision. Then shuffling along rapidly to the corner of Mill Street, he turned up towards Main.

Here a full sense of the terror came to him. A man, hurrying along with his head down, ran full against him and cursed him for the delay.

"Get out of my way, you old beast!" he cried. "If the cholera would carry you off, it would be a blessing to the town."

Two or three little children, already orphaned and hungry, wandered past, crying and wringing their hands. A crowd of negro men with the muscles of athletes, some with naked arms, some naked to the waist, their eyes dilated, their mouths hanging open, sped along in tumultuous disorder. The plague had broken out in the hemp factory and scattered them beyond control.

He grew suddenly faint and sick. His senses swam, his heart seemed to cease beating, his tongue burned, his throat was dry, his spine like ice. For a moment the contagion of deadly fear overcame him, and, unable to stand, he reeled to the edge of the sidewalk and sat down.

Before him along the street passed the flying people—men on horseback with their wives behind and children in front, families in carts and wagons, merchants in two-wheeled gigs and sulkies. A huge red and yellow stage-coach rolled ponderously by, filled within, on top, in front, and behind with a company of riotous students of law and of medicine. A rapid chorus of voices shouted to him as they passed:

"Good-by, Solomon!"

"The cholera 'll have you befoah sunset!"

"Better be diggin' yoah grave, Solomon! That'll be yoah last cellah."

"Dig us a big wine cellah undah the Medical Hall while we are away."

"And leave yo' body there! We want yo' skeleton."

"Good-by, old Solomon!"

A wretched carryall passed with a household of more wretched women, their tawdry and gay attire, their haggard and painted and ghastly faces, looking horrible in the blaze of the pitiless sunlight. They, too, simpered and hailed him and spent upon him their hardened and degraded badinage. Then there rolled by a high-swung carriage, with the most luxurious of cushions, upholstered with morocco, with a coat-of-arms, a driver and a footman in livery, and drawn by sparkling, prancing horses. Lying back on the satin cushions a fine gentleman; at the window of the carriage two rosy children, who pointed their fingers at the vagrant and turned and looked into their father's face, so that he leaned forward, smiled, leaned back again, and was whirled away to a place of safety.

Thus they passed him, as he sat down on the sidewalk—even physicians from their patients, pastors from their stricken flocks. Why should not he flee? He had no ties, except the faithful affection of an old negress. Should he not at least save her life by going away, seeing that she would not leave him?

The orphaned children wandered past again, sobbing more wearily. He called them to him.

"Why do you not go home? Where is your mother?" he asked.

"She is dead in the house," they answered; "and no one has come to bury her."

Slowly down the street was coming a short funeral train. It passed—a rude cortège: a common cart, in the bottom of which rested a box of plain boards containing the body of the old French dancing-master; walking behind it, with a cambric handkerchief to his eyes, the old French confectioner; at his side, wearing the robes of his office and carrying an umbrella to ward off the burning sun, the beloved Bishop Smith; and behind them, two by two and with linked arms, perhaps a dozen men, most of whom had been at the ball.

No head was lifted or eye turned to notice the vagrant seated on the sidewalk. But when the train had passed he rose, laid his mattock and spade across his shoulder, and, stepping out into the street, fell into line at the end of the procession.

They moved down Short Street to the old burying-ground, where the Baptist churchyard is to-day. As they entered it, two grave-diggers passed out and hurried away. Those before them had fled. They had been at work but a few hours. Overcome with horror at the sight of the dead arriving more and more rapidly, they, too, deserted that post of peril. No one was left. Here and there in the churchyard could be seen bodies awaiting interment. Old King Solomon stepped quietly forward and, getting down into one of the half-finished graves, began to dig.

The vagrant had happened upon an avocation.

### IV.

All summer long, Clatterbuck's dancing-pavilion was as silent in its grove of oaks as a temple of the Druids, and his pleasure-boat nestled in its moorings, with no hand to feather an oar in the little lake. All summer long, no athletic young Kentuckians came to bathe their white bodies in Hugh Lonney's new bath-house for twelve and a half cents, and no one read Daukins Tegway's advertisement that he was willing to exchange his Dunstable bonnets for flax and feathers. The likely runaway boy, with a long fresh scar across his face, was never found, nor the buffalo bull roasted for Daniel Webster, and Peter Leuba's guitars were never thrummed on any moonlit verandas. Only Dewees & Grant were busy, dispensing, not snuff, but calomel.

Grass grew in the deserted streets. Gardens became little wildernesses of rank weeds and riotous creepers. Around shut window-lattices roses clambered and shed their perfume into the poisoned air, or dropped their faded petals to strew the echoless thresholds. In darkened rooms family portraits gazed on sad vacancy or looked helplessly down on rigid sheeted forms.

In the trees of poplar and locust along the streets the unmolested birds built and brooded. The oriole swung its hempen nest from a bough over the door of the spider-tenanted factory, and in front of the old Medical Hall the blue jay shot up his angry crest and screamed harshly down at the passing bier. In a cage hung against the wall of a house in a retired street a mocking-bird sung, beat its breast against the bars, sung more passionately, grew silent, and dropped dead from its perch, never knowing that its mistress had long since become a clod to its full-throated requiem.

Famine lurked in the wake of the pestilence. Markets were closed. A few shops were kept open to furnish necessary supplies. Now and then some old negro might have been seen driving a meat-wagon in from the country, his nostrils stuffed with white cotton saturated with camphor. Oftener the only visible figure in the streets was that of a faithful priest going about among his perishing fold, or that of the bishop moving hither and thither on his ceaseless ministrations.

But over all the ravages of that terrible time there towered highest the solitary figure of that powerful grave-digger, who, nerved by the spectacle of the common misfortune, by one heroic effort rose for the time above the wrecks of his own nature. In the thick of the plague, in the very garden spot of the pestilence, he ruled like an unterrified king. Through days unnaturally chill with gray cloud and drizzling rain, or unnaturally hot with the fierce sun and suffocating damps that appeared to steam forth from subterranean caldrons, he worked unfaltering, sometimes with a helper, sometimes with none. There were times when, exhausted, he would lie down in the half-dug graves and there sleep until able to go on; and many a midnight found him under the spectral moon, all but hidden by the rank nightshade as he bent over to mark out the lines of one of those narrow mortal cellars.

### V.

Nature soon smiles upon her own ravages and strews our graves with flowers, not as memories, but for other flowers when the spring returns.

It was one cool, brilliant morning late in that autumn. The air blew fresh and invigorating, as though on the earth there were no corruption, no death. Far southward had flown the plague. A spectator in the open court-square might have seen many signs of life returning to the town. Students hurried along, talking eagerly. Merchants met for the first time and spoke of the winter trade. An old negress, gayly and neatly dressed, came into the market-place, and, sitting down on a sidewalk, displayed her yellow and red apples and fragrant gingerbread. She hummed to herself an old cradle-song, and in her soft, motherly black eyes shone a mild, happy radiance. A group of young ragamuffins eyed her longingly from a distance. Court was to open for the first time since the spring. The hour was early, and one by one the lawyers passed slowly in. On the steps of the court-house three men were standing: Thomas Brown, the sheriff; old Peter Leuba, who had just walked over from his music-store on Main Street; and little M. Giron, the French confectioner. Each wore mourning on his hat, and their voices were low and grave.

"Gentlemen," the sheriff was saying, "it was on this very spot the day befoah the cholera broke out that I sole 'im as a vagrant. An' I did the meanes' thing a man can evah do. I hel' 'im up to public ridicule foh his weaknesses an' made spoht of 'is infirmities. I laughed at 'is povahty an' 'is ole clo'es. I delivahed on 'im as complete an oration of sarcastic detraction as I could prepare on the spot, out of my own meanness an' with the vulgah sympathies of the crowd. Gentlemen, if I only had that crowd heah now, an' ole King Sol'mon standin' in the midst of it, that I might ask 'im to accept a humble public apology, offahed from the heaht of one who feels himself unworthy to shake 'is han'! But, gentlemen, that crowd will nevah reassemble. Neahly ev'ry man of them is dead, an' ole King Sol'mon buried them."

"He buried my friend Adolphe Xaupi," said François Giron, touching his eyes with his handkerchief.

"There is a case of my best Jamaica rum for him whenever he comes for it," said old Leuba, clearing his throat.

"But, gentlemen, while we are speakin' of ole King Solomon we ought not to fohget who it is that has suppohted 'im,

Yondah she sits on the sidewalk, sellin' 'er apples and gingerbread."

The three men looked in the direction indicated.

"Heah comes ole King Sol'mon now," exclaimed the sheriff.

Across the open square the vagrant was seen walking slowly along with his habitual air of quiet, unobtrusive preoccupation. A minute more and he had come over and passed into the court-house by a side door.

"Is Mr. Clay to be in court to-day?"

"He is expected, I think."

"Then let's go in; there will be a crowd."

"I don't know; so many are dead."

They turned and entered and found seats as quietly as possible; for a strange and sorrowful hush brooded over the court-room. Until the bar assembled, it had not been realized how many were gone. The silence was that of a common overwhelming disaster. No one spoke with his neighbor, no one observed the vagrant as he entered and made his way to a seat on one of the meanest benches, a little apart from the others. He had not sat there since the day of his indictment for vagrancy. The judge took his seat and, making a great effort to control himself, passed his eyes slowly over the court-room. All at once he caught sight of old King Solomon sitting against the wall in an obscure corner; and before any one could know what he was doing, he

hurried down and walked up to the vagrant and grasped his hand. He tried to speak, but could not. Old King Solomon had buried his wife and daughter—buried them one clouded midnight, with no one present but himself.

Then the oldest member of the bar started up and followed the example; and then the other members, rising by a common impulse, filed slowly back and one by one wrung that hard and powerful hand. After them came the other persons in the court-room. The vagrant, the grave-digger, had risen and stood against the wall, at first with a white face and a dazed expression, not knowing what it meant; afterwards, when he understood it, his head dropped suddenly forward and his tears fell thick and hot upon the hands that he could not see. And his were not the only tears. Not a man in the long file but paid his tribute of emotion as he stepped forward to honor that image of sadly eclipsed but still effulgent humanity. It was not grief, it was not gratitude, nor any sense of making reparation for the past. It was the softening influence of an act of heroism, which makes every man feel himself a brother hand in hand with every other—such power has a single act of moral greatness to reverse the relations of men, lifting up one, and bringing all others to do him homage.

It was the coronation scene in the life of old King Solomon of Kentucky.

# BLAME

## A MEMORY OF EISLEBEN, THE PLACE OF LUTHER'S BIRTH AND DEATH

### BY R. W. GILDER

In a far, lonely land at last I came
Unto a town made great by one great fame.
Born here, here died the noblest of his time,
Whose memory makes his century sublime.
But, O my God, I was not happy there,
For down below in dark and caverned air,
Outstretched and cramped, the pallid miners lay.
Their shortened lives, their absence from the day,
Burdened my spirit with a sense of blame.
Now you, and you—I see you flush with shame.

# Comment on Current Books

**Among the Novels** Few novels of late publication have more of dignity of purpose than "The Far Horizon," by Lucas Malet (Mrs. St. Leger Harrison). One notes first that it has the negative merit of being entirely devoid of any passages of questionable taste such as marred this author's "Sir Richard Calmady," or of morbid occultism such as may be found in her earlier work. Affirmatively speaking, its highest merit is in the distinction and quiet nobility of its chief figure, Dominic Iglesias. He is of Spanish descent but has lived his whole life in England, and that life has been spent, on the personal side, in devotion and sacrifice for his mother, on the business side as a capable, modest, unappreciated clerk in a great banking house. In later middle-age, turned away from his daily work by his ignorantly condescending employer, he faces the problem of making a social place for himself and of occupying his idle hours. He finds himself among commonplace, narrow people. Mrs. Harrison proves all too abundantly that they are bores, and spares not the reader in doing so. But into his life comes by chance his very antipodes in temperament, a woman who has been sinned against and has sinned; who is generous, lively, and witty; who is as undignified as our Spanish friend is sober. One cannot say that this sprightly person is as well drawn as Iglesias, but the contrast is essentially a capital one. How the friendship works itself out, how the quiet man who has been facing the problem of old age and unhappiness deals with that of passion and self-restraint, must not be told here. The book has an undercurrent of religious intention (Mrs. Harrison, report says, is a recent convert to Roman Catholicism), but it is in the main to be looked at as a study of one finely conceived character, and as incidentally a gently pleasing picture of London suburban atmosphere and locale. (Dodd, Mead & Co., New York. $1.50.)

Mrs. Henry de la Pasture gained the affection of many readers two years ago by her "Peter's Mother." A second novel, "The Man from America," was hardly so pleasing—ineffective but inoffensive. Now in "The Lovely Lady of Grosvenor Square" she renews the charm of the first book. Of plot there is little, and that quite artless; the construction is, technically speaking, clumsy enough; but in a simple, gentle, ingratiating way we are shown a true-hearted and sweet country girl thrown alone, or practically so, into a big London house, and acting like a womanly, sincere sort of person in all her perplexities and troubles. Like most of Trollope's heroines, she is rewarded in the end with a nobleman and a fortune, but she deserves them. The book would be nothing if it were not for its genuine humor, which is none the less welcome because it is not boisterous. (E. P. Dutton & Co., New York. $1.50.) Mrs. Alfred Sidgwick's "The Kinsman," on the other hand, is rather rampant in its fun, but is in that way decidedly amusing. Like Mr. Thurston's "The Masqueraders," it turns on the exact resemblance of two men, and strains credulity a bit. But once granted, the adventures of the two cousins (one a lazy and morally irresponsible clerk, the other a cultivated gentleman) are ingeniously worked out with odd surprises and with constantly new situations. (The Macmillan Company, New York. $1.50.)

Mr. David Graham Phillips's "The Second Generation," as its name foreshadows, is a study of the curse of inherited wealth. Old Hiram, the miller who cares for his children so much that he will not spoil them by making them rich, but dies paralyzed in agony (as we understand the narrative) because his instinctive love makes him wish to reverse his action, is a fine character, worthy of any book. His children, however, as soon as they begin to learn their lesson, are a bit priggish, and the whole book, although sober-minded and excellent in many ways, is too long-drawn-out and somewhat stolid. (D. Appleton & Co., New York. $1.50.) It is far more artistic, however, than the next story the reviewer picks up—"Frost and Friendship," by George Frederic Turner, a queer combination of the "Prisoner of Zenda" type of tale with political conspiracy in an imaginary European country and of a record of winter sports, such as curling, tobogganing, and ski-ing. There are exciting incidents, but improbabilities end by becoming absurdities. (Little, Brown & Co., Boston. $1.50.) Disappointing in another way is Eleanor Hoyt Brainerd's "Bettina." We remember with joy Miss Brainerd's Nancy and her sprightly misdemeanors, but her Bettina is but a shadow, and the story too slight to make into a book. (Doubleday, Page & Co, New York.)

There is an effect of carefully wrought, delicate embroidery about the new novel by Mrs. Freeman (Mary E. Wilkins), called "By the Light of the Soul" (Harper & Brothers, New York. $1.50). The characters stand out clearly against a background of marvelously minute, analytic detail. Tiny stitches are set in graceful patterns, repeated again and again to make the smooth, perfect effect. Maria Edgham, born with tremendous emc tional possibilities and a highly spiritualized love of beauty, was caught in a cobweb of slight yet sufficient strength to fetter her whole life. The plot of the story, while it seems to develop naturally—until the morbid ending—is not one that carries with it convincing power. Yet it is certainly novel, and admirably managed. Apart from that, the exquisite skill, the art that deceives by its very simplicity, which we associate with all Mrs. Freeman's work, is as evident in this story of plain folk as in all other tales by the same author. She is able to impress us with the absolute necessity of life being lived as she portrays it.

*American Problems*　In this volume of addresses— ethical, sociological, educational —by the President of Colorado College, the main emphasis is laid on moral ideals, and on moral culture as " the cornerstone of all culture." The outlook is hopeful, the tone animating, the responsibility of the individual for social progress is strongly pressed. That the Golden Rule, truly understood, " is the chief unwritten law of the Nation; if not always applied in the first and second person, abstractly it is the universally acknowledged social principle," one would like to believe. But it is not—as the writer's context takes it to be—a rule of mere justice, for equal rights and "a square deal." It is the rule of benevolence, taking the lead of others in doing good; it enjoins competition in giving benefits rather than in getting, and bids one set the example of it to others. This is as yet neither the common practice nor the common theory. (American Problems: Essays and Addresses. By James H. Baker, M.A., LL.D. Longmans, Green & Co., New York. $1.20, net.)

*The Art of Living*　This little book of a hundred pages might be described as a silhouette portrait of Jesus Christ. It is intended as an aid to Bible students, and as such is valuable. It would have an independent value to readers if the latter half were worked out with the same artistic unity as the first half. The book is non-theological, human, full of Christ's spirit, and not archaic but fresh in its mode of treatment. (The Art of Living. By Glenn Clark. Published by the Author, Des Moines, Iowa.)

*Certain Court Ladies*　To his " Youth of La Grande Mademoiselle " and his " Louis XIV. and La Grande Mademoiselle " M. Arvède Barine now adds

a volume on certain " Princesses and Court Ladies," among them Marie Mancini, Christina of Sweden, the Duchess of Maine, and the Margravine of Baireuth. As in the previous volumes, the text is vivacious and sprightly, and is heightened by many interesting pictures. (Princesses and Court Ladies. By Arvède Barine. Authorized English Version. G. P. Putnam's Sons, New York. $3, net.)

*Evelyn's Diary*　The appearance of two new and very handsome editions of " Evelyn's Diary," with only a brief interval of time between their publication, is good evidence of the interest in the human story as it is told in biography and autobiography, which has brought forth such a great number of " Lives " of people of quality, individuality, and distinction during the past few years. Among various editions of Evelyn none surpasses in convenience, editorial thoroughness, and beauty of form this edition, in three volumes, presented with a combination of simplicity and elegance that mark only the best book-making. Paper, type, size of page, are all that could be desired; the portraits in photogravure and the various illustrations in half-tone are well selected and extremely well printed; and the books are meant not only for ornament but for use. Mr. Dobson's qualifications as the editor of this edition need no exposition. He is perfectly familiar with the period in which Evelyn lived, and with the whole body of literature and social and political custom and habit to which he was related. He furnishes a long introduction which presents all known facts in regard to the diarist's career. One may not agree with him when he says that the Diary is not " a psychological document, making intimate revelation, conscious or unconscious, of its writer's personality." A great many readers will feel that the very simple personality of Evelyn is clearly conveyed by his reports of the happenings and doings with which he was associated or in which he was interested. That he was less individual and piquant than Pepys goes without saying; but the fact that he tells us so little as compared with Pepys does not mean necessarily that he was more restrained or reticent; it may mean that he had less to say. There are passages which unpleasantly bring out the thinness of the man's nature and the vein of selfishness that ran through his intellectual life. On the other hand, he deals with many subjects with a gravity, a sincerity, and a depth of feeling which convey an impression of a strong and deep nature. However this may be, the position of the Diary in English literature and among books of its class was long ago settled. It is one of the classics of autobiography. And these three beautiful volumes fitly dress a work which must find its place on the shelves of any collection of English writing that makes pretense to completeness. (The Diary of John Evelyn. With an Introduction and Notes by Austin Dobson. 3 vols. The Macmillan Company, New York. $8 per set.)

***Ideal Buddhism Expounded***  As there are Christians and Christians, so there are Buddhists and Buddhists. The Sicilian brigand, who worships the Virgin with offerings of his spoils, and the missionary who Christianizes cannibal islands, are poles apart. So is this " Lord Abbot " of Japanese Buddhists from the Buddhism of the populace often met with in the East. He himself insists on the difference between a higher and a lower type of Buddhism. The higher, as expounded in these addresses to American audiences, has remarkable affinities with the sublime mysticism of the Fourth Gospel. Higher Buddhism claims as its own the God-consciousness expressed in Jesus' saying, " I am in the Father, and the Father in me." Its moral precepts may be summed up in Christian terms. Of course the test of superiority in any comparison of religions is in their efficiency for the purification and uplifting of personal and social life; and here Christianity is content to rest its case as against Buddhism. The essential defect of the Buddhism exhibited so attractively in this volume is its overemphasis upon a subtle intellectuality, and, with that, its undervaluation of the volitional element, the will, as compared with the reason. Its denial of immortality, its assertion that there is no permanent unity of consciousness capable of surviving death, proceeds from a defective psychology which has adherents among us, but is repudiated by masters in that science. (Sermons of a Buddhist Abbot. By the Rt. Rev. Soyen Shaku. Translated from the Japanese by Daisetz Teitaro Suzuki. The Open Court Publishing Company, Chicago.)

***Jowett's Essays***  Named in the title of the volume, the first in this collection is of historical importance as well as of intrinsic value. When it appeared in 1860 in the famous volume of " Essays and Reviews " by seven English scholars, its dictum, " Interpret the Scripture like any other book," excited great indignation throughout the Anglican Church, which for the time that volume plunged into bitter controversy. The present essays are nearly all on Biblical and theological topics. The essay on "Casuistry," the branch of ethics which is concerned with conflicting duties, strangely recognizes only the perverted form in which Jesuits have gained for it the bad name that Jowett gives it. Not so did his great countryman, Richard Baxter, regard it in his work on cases of conscience. These essays reveal the keenness and force as well as the limitations of the great Master of Balliol, a character sketch of whom by Sir Leslie Stephen appropriately introduces them. (The Interpretation of Scripture and Other Essays. By Benjamin Jowett. E. P. Dutton & Co., New York. $1, net.)

***Lutheran Theology***  These volumes, left all but finished by the author at his death, present the system of theology as taught in the Lutheran churches, in whose Seminary at Gettysburg he was for many years Professor of Systematic Theology. They are, as one would expect, strongly marked by the close adherence to the confessional orthodoxy of the sixteenth century which characterizes American Lutherans. It appears that belief in the salvation of all infants dying in infancy is gaining ground among them, and Dr. Valentine argues for it, while acknowledging that " the majority of our Lutheran dogmaticians " have their doubts as to the unbaptized infants of non-Christians. These volumes give, even for those who dissent from their teaching, an interesting presentation of the most that can be said for views of the relation of God to the world with which modern science and philosophy have decisively broken. The point of divergence appears to be at the sources of theology. If these are found only in the Old and the New Testament, the theology of the sixteenth century is, as theology, secure, whatever science and philosophy may say against it. But it is from outside the Bible that modern learning brings to the interpretation of the Bible resources not available in Luther's time. The physical sciences, the science of mind, or psychology, historical criticism, comparative religion, all are sources of theology, all contribute to the revelation of God as in his world. Dr. Valentine correctly holds that it is the office of reason " to judge and decide upon the claims of a given revelation to be of divine origin and authority." The veriest "rationalist" would agree to this. But the view that " the claims " thus submitted to reason are contained only in ancient parchments as anciently understood, without revision by comparison with other and later revelations of fact and truth, leads to the most untenable conclusions. Theological systems of the traditional type are vitiated throughout by their initial fallacy of thus arbitrarily limiting theological material and the credentials of its sufficiency for reason. (Christian Theology. By Milton Valentine,

D.D., LL.D. In 2 vols. Lutheran Publication Society, Philadelphia. $5.)

**Mosby's Men**　This is the second, possibly the third, book recently published telling through the narrative of a Confederate soldier who served in Mosby's irregular cavalry, popularly known as guerrillas, the extremely romantic and stirring adventures of that command. A better subject for furnishing exciting incident and wartime anecdote could hardly be imagined. This book has less of real dramatic quality and less of humor than that by Mr. Munson of which we recently spoke, but is still a readable true story. It is illustrated by many portraits. (Mosby's Men. By John H. Alexander. The Neale Publishing Company, New York. $2.)

**Naturalism and Religion**　It is proper to protest against the identification of a false conception with the name of Nature that the term "Naturalism" has effected. The falsity of reducing Nature to a series of material things and changes has been so thoroughly exposed by writers adept both in science and philosophy that it is now nearing the level of a vulgar error. Such errors linger in the popular mind after they have been dislodged from philosophic thought. The present volume by a Göttingen professor gives in a compact form to the general reader the main points in the great controversy that now seems to have been fought almost through. The gist of the argument in more elaborate works, such as Dr. James Ward's lectures on "Naturalism and Agnosticism," some ten years ago, is presented here in eleven chapters by a discriminating thinker, as hostile to exaggerated assertions in a religious as in a scientific interest. He points out that it is not in the proper domain of science, but "in the teacup of logic and epistemology that the storm in regard to the theories of the universe has arisen." And he acutely concludes that the theory of naturalism, that there is no such thing as free creative mind, is refuted by its own existence as the actual progeny of such a mind. (Naturalism and Religion. By Dr. Rudolf Otto. Translated by J. Arthur Thomson and Margaret R. Thomson. G. P. Putnam's Sons, New York. $1.50.)

**Queen and Cardinal**　This is the story of the life of Anne of Austria, chiefly dealing with the events of that life during the period when she was Queen Regent. Naturally, it is largely concerned with the relations between the Queen Mother and Cardinal Mazarin. The question as to whether a private ceremony of marriage ever took place has never been authoritatively settled, although the opinion of most students of that period is that there actually was such a marriage. No real light is thrown on the question by this book, which is in its nature rather a popular narrative than a historical search into new material. Marriage or no marriage, the author records his belief that "into Anne's sad and lonely existence a great romance entered at a time when her youth and beauty had waned and she had already attained middle age, and it lasted until the end of her days." Letters and memoirs quoted seem to establish this fact, although it will surprise those readers, not inconsiderable in number, who derive most of their ideas about the period from Dumas's novels. Altogether the book is readable, though it is not important, and might well have been published in less pretentious guise. (Queen and Cardinal: A Memoir of Anne of Austria. By Mrs. Colquhoun Grant. E. P. Dutton & Co., New York. $2, net.)

**Shakespeare and the Modern Stage**　A collection of essays dealing with such subjects as "Shakespeare and the Elizabethan Playgoers," "Shakespeare in Oral Tradition," "Pepys and Shakespeare," "Aspects of Shakespeare's Philosophy," "Shakespeare in France," and similar, though not always related, topics from the hand of one of the first living authorities on Shakespearean text. These essays may be regarded as a by-product of Mr. Lee's indefatigable industry in Shakespearean investigation and research; an incidental gleaning in a field which he has already thoroughly harvested. "The Commemoration of Shakespeare in London," "The Municipal Theater," "Shakespeare and the Modern Stage," and "Mr. Benson and Shakespeare," show that Mr. Lee has an open mind, and that his ample scholarship is used in a modern spirit. He is not blind to the defects of the dramatists of whom Shakespeare was the leader; nor, as a critic, is he hedged about by undue reverence for their ways of doing things, their point of view, and their method of stage management. One of his strongest claims to attention is the fact that he has rigorously held the speculative impulse in check, and has brought to the study of the dramatist, not only as much knowledge as any man of his time, but robust common sense. He is also, it may be added, a very interesting writer. (Shakespeare and the Modern Stage, with Other Essays. By Sidney Lee. Charles Scribner's Sons, New York. $2, net.)

# T̲ͪ̊ͤ Outlook

**The New Immigration Law** After a year of incubation a new immigration law has been hatched by Congress. It makes no great change in the policy of the United States in its dealings with incoming aliens. For the most part it merely either revises the phraseology of existing law or modifies existing methods of regulation. Some of its provisions, however, are important. The head tax on every immigrant is increased from two to four dollars. The "Immigrant Fund," which is the permanent appropriation out of which the expenses of the immigration service are paid, will thus be increased. Incidentally, too, some undesirable immigrants, in view of the increased cost, may be discouraged from applying for admission, though it seems to us doubtful whether this provision will prove a restrictive measure of any special value. The new law adds certain classes to those ineligible for admission, such as imbeciles and feeble-minded persons (who are not now legally included under the terms "idiots" and "insane persons"), persons afflicted with tuberculosis (which has not been construed as a loathsome or dangerous contagious disease), those who are mentally and physically defective so as to be incapable of earning a living, and girls and women entering the United States for immoral purposes. The new law also puts greater restrictions and responsibility upon the transportation companies; it requires of them a more detailed accounting for the passengers, and places upon them the cost of transporting not only those aliens suffering from physical disabilities which existed before emigration, but also all aliens entering the United States in violation of law and such as become public charges from causes which existed prior to landing. What is more important still, it requires the companies, by explicit directions, to provide more ample accommodations for steerage passengers than they are now forced to supply. In this respect the law not only protects America, but also humanely regards the comfort of aliens. That the law is not oppressive is shown by the fact that of the one hundred and seventy-five steamships that brought steerage passengers to New York during the last fiscal year, one hundred carried no more on any voyage than the new law permits. The only provisions which add any new feature to existing law are three. One is that which enables the President in his discretion to refuse to allow aliens to enter the continental territory of the United States from foreign countries (to which they have passports) or from the insular possessions of the United States or from the Canal Zone. As we indicated last week, this has special bearing on the Japanese immigration question, though it does not mention the Japanese by name. Another of these provisions is that which establishes a bureau of information for incoming aliens, in order to facilitate their proper distribution. This has long been needed; it has been urged by the Commissioner-General of Immigration, and, it is hoped, will do much to prevent the congestion of aliens in a few great centers, especially New York. It is in accordance also with the effort to direct immigration to the South, where it is especially needed. The third provision, which is potentially the most valuable of all, is that which creates a Commission to investigate the subject of immigration and to report its findings and recommendations to Congress. The Commission is to be composed of three Senators, three Representatives, and three persons to be appointed by the President. This provision also authorizes the President to call an international conference on immigration to secure the co-operation of the nations in dealing with the movement of people into the United States. This undertaking to treat the question of migration scientifically and comprehensively is more significant than any regulation in the law. If the investigating commission is well chosen and the international conference is wisely directed, they may lead to action of great moment to the whole civilized world.

❀

*The Case of Senator Smoot* — The Senate, on Wednesday of last week, by a vote of 43 to 27, defeated a resolution to declare vacant the seat of Senator Reed Smoot, of Utah, having previously declared by a still larger majority that a two-thirds vote was necessary to accomplish the object sought. In an editorial elsewhere are discussed the principles involved in this case. As the evidence taken before the Senate's committee many months ago was at the time rather fully reported in The Outlook, it seems right to summarize briefly here also Senator Smoot's speech of last week in his own defense. In it he declared that he was not and never had been a polygamist; that the doctrine of polygamy had never been obligatory, but only permissive; that only a small percentage of Mormons had ever been polygamists; and that the Church's manifesto discontinuing polygamy had been more widely circulated than the original revelation on marriage. When this manifesto was adopted, he said, there were 2,451 polygamous households in the Church, now there are not over 500; then among the Church's higher officials there were twenty-three polygamists and three monogamists, while of fourteen such officials chosen since only two were polygamists, and of seven apostles chosen since Mr. Smoot was made an apostle only one was a polygamist. As to those Mormons who had polygamous families before the manifesto, a general policy of forbearance, it was asserted, was avowedly accepted as desirable by prosecuting attorneys, and toleration was exercised by most people in Utah, Mormon and non-Mormon alike. Coming to the important question of polygamous marriages since the manifesto, Mr. Smoot

admitted that some have taken place (usually in Mexico or Canada), but said that they were rare and had not received sanction or encouragement from the Church, and put himself on record personally in these words:

I have no hesitation in declaring to the Senate and to the American people that, in my opinion, any man who has married a polygamous wife since the manifesto should be prosecuted, and, if convicted, should suffer the penalties of the law, and I care not who the man might be, or what position he might hold in the Church; he should receive the punishment pronounced by the law against his crime.

Referring to treasonable obligations alleged to form a part of the Mormon endowment ceremonies, Senator Smoot said: "There does not exist in the endowment ceremonies of the Mormon Church the remotest suggestion of hostility or of antagonism to the United States or to any other nation." He pointed to the loyalty of Mormon soldiers who had taken these endowment oaths in the Mexican War, the Civil War, the Spanish-American War, and that in the Philippines; and, for himself, solemnly declared that " in every vote and action as United States Senator I shall be governed in the future, as I have been in the past, only by my convictions of what is best for the whole people of the United States, under my oath to support the Constitution and laws of this Nation. . . . I owe no allegiance to any church, or other organization, which in any way interferes with my supreme allegiance in civil affairs to my country—an allegiance which I freely, fully, and gladly give."

❀

*A Palpable Injustice* — On February 16 the House passed a bill (H. R. 24,987) to authorize the sale of about one million acres of the Rosebud Indian Reservation in Tripp County, South Dakota; and its sponsors are endeavoring to get it rushed through the Senate. The bill stipulates that $6 per acre shall be paid for any of the land filed upon within three months after the tract is opened for settlement, $4.50 per acre during the succeeding three months, and thereafter at the rate of $2.50 per acre. Readers of The Outlook may recall that three years ago, when it was proposed to open the Gregory County section of the Rosebud Reservation at the rate of $2.50 an acre, it was clearly shown in an article by Mr. George Kennan (February 27, 1904) that the land in question was worth at least double that amount. The agitation resulted in a compromise price of $4 per acre. Most of that land is now valued at from $15 to $20 per acre and upwards. Tripp County immediately adjoins Gregory County, and, in addition to the fertile quality of the soil, its value has not been lessened by the extension of railways to the borders of the reservation. Manifestly, the Government, as guardian, is under obligation to see that its wards get full market value for their property—a conception of the obligation of Congress successfully urged by Commissioner Leupp in framing a law authorizing the sale of 505,000 acres of Kiowa lands in Oklahoma during the past year. In the sale of Indian tribal property the same principles of justice should be observed as are applied in the management of wards' estates in courts of probate. The Hon. M. E. Clapp, Chairman of the Senate Committee on Indian Affairs, in a letter recently sent to the Indian Rights Association, says on this point:

My own theory of opening these reservations is that the land should be sold to the highest bidder and the proceeds paid to the Indians. . . . I quite agree with you that the lands should be sold, and whatever they are worth—whatever they bring in the market— should go to the Indians, and I have favored this upon the opening of reservations since I have been a member of this Committee.

It is true that the report (No 7,613) on the bill submits an agreement signed by 705 of the 1,368 adult male Indians of the tribe—a few more than one-half. But under the treaty of 1868 any cession of lands to be valid must be agreed to by *three-fourths* of the adult members of the tribe ; and Section 2,116 of the United States Revised Statutes also provides that no purchase or other conveyance of lands from any tribe shall be of any validity unless made by *treaty* or *convention* of the tribe. Consequently, as the necessary three-fourths of the male adults of the tribe have not agreed to the proposition,

and as the names of many of those on the so-called agreement were secured under threats that if they did not sign it a bill would be passed that they might not like so well, the responsibility, whatever action is taken, rests with Congress. The Senate ought not to pass the present bill in its present form ; it should either postpone action on the bill, or amend it so that an appraisement of the lands will be provided for prior to its disposal. Friends of justice and fair play would do well to send at once a protest against this bill either to the Hon. M. E. Clapp, Chairman of the Senate Committee on Indian Affairs, whose letter quoted above shows that he is opposed to the bill, or to the President, who must assent to the bill if it is to become a law.

❋

*Penny Wise Pound Foolish* The extraordinary spectacle is presented of the present session of the House of Representatives about to go out of existence, after voting eighty million dollars to provide for river and harbor exigencies, but refusing to vote three million dollars to provide for a proper continuous waterflow into those rivers and harbors. The water now comes in a flood or in scant supply. These phenomena have been caused by the wholesale cutting of trees without reforesting on the rivers' upper channels. The inevitable consequence is the loss of the spongy ground which would hold back the water, the denudation of mountain slopes, and the consequent erosion of the soil. The end is a land barren for all time. During the past fifteen years in New Hampshire, for instance, about ninety thousand acres have been completely denuded. The channels of the Merrimac and Connecticut are already affected, and the harbors are filling. The rivers are either flooded or comparatively dry. In either case there is damage. In the first case both crops and factories suffer—a single flood cost one Merrimac company a million dollars. In the second case navigation is impeded, for the sailing of boats is impracticable when the mills upstream close their dams and so withhold the water supply. But the State of

New Hampshire is too poor to provide for a great State forest reserve. So is each of the Appalachian Mountain States where like conditions prevail. These two regions, North and South, are of wonderful beauty and should be preserved for their scenery alone; they are of equal value as health resorts, and fortunately are very accessible; and their timber resources are of singular worth, the White Mountains offering the last remaining vestiges of our primeval forests and the Appalachians containing a stand of hard woods unparalleled for variety. The waterflow over a great section is involved. This makes the question a National and not a State affair. Waterfalls and rapids are capable of producing large electric power. The disappearance of these forests will check the water supply of the five principal rivers of New England, on which her manufacturing interests depend, and of all the largest rivers south of the Ohio and east of the Mississippi. Fourteen States are thus directly interested. These facts have commended themselves to the Governors of every one of these States and have caused them strenuously to support the bill before Congress to establish forest reserves in the White and Appalachian Mountains. The Senate, to its lasting credit, unanimously passed the bill. It has also been unanimously recommended for passage by the House Committee on Agriculture, one of the largest committees. Finally, the bill enjoys in advance the President's approval. Why does it not come to a vote? Because the Speaker indicates that he will not vote for it in the Committee on Rules. He says: "To buy up half the Southern States is 'too big.'" He may be reminded that the floods in one year, 1902, caused a loss in the Southern States of $18,000,000, sweeping away cotton and saw mills and distributing silt over the farms. One wonders how the former "watch-dog of the Treasury" can take this position, especially on a measure likely to lessen the swollen River and Harbor Bill by much more than the $3,000,000 asked to purchase lands suited to National forest reserve purposes, to maintain the forests, and reforest the clearings. Only a few days

are left of this session. If the bill does not now pass the House, it will again have to come before the Senate. But that is a small matter compared with the denudation, which will have rapidly extended, with irreparable damage to the water power and also to timber and agricultural interests. Moreover, the prices of land and timber are rapidly advancing, and the Government can never again act as advantageously as now. To awaken the appreciation of these facts in the Speaker's mind there is evidently needed all the power of public opinion.

❦

*Justice for the Filipinos*

The fact that the Filipinos will for the first time this year choose representatives for a legislature naturally suggests inquiry into the extent of their progress towards free institutions and the exercise of self-government. What the United States has done since peace and order were established is in a large way well known: it has, to quote a recent address by ex-Governor Ide, devoted itself "to the establishment of schools throughout the islands; to the introduction of over a thousand American teachers for the purpose of teaching the English language, and teaching the Filipinos how to teach; to the building of school-houses; to the organization of a civil service more rigid and more thorough than prevails in the United States or any State thereof; to the promotion of sanitation, bringing about a reduction of nearly one-half in the death rate of the city of Manila; to the thorough investigation of the methods of extermination of diseases of animals; to scientific work tending to the industrial prosperity of the people; to a reform in the currency; to a reorganization of the judiciary and legal procedure, such that justice is administered as promptly, honestly, and economically as in any State in our Union; to the building of roads and bridges; to the settlement of land titles; to ending long-standing agrarian difficulties by the purchase of land belonging to the religious bodies and the sale or lease thereof to the tenants or occupants; to reforms in taxation, whereby a multitude of petty taxes which fell upon the poor and the weak have been removed and the burden transferred largely to tobacco and alcoholic products; to the introduction of new railroads and the improvement of inter-island transportation by water ; to the organization of municipal, provincial, and central governments, such that the element of local autonomy forms the best of schools for training in the arts of government ; to diffusing a common language, with which to unite all parts of the archipelago together ; to teaching the people how to maintain good order ; to keeping the government solvent and able to pay its own expenses." It is equally true that the Filipinos have in some ways shown themselves glad to profit by these opportunities, and have been especially eager to send their children to our schools. They have also increasingly recognized the good faith and unselfish purpose of the American occupation. So that Judge Ide sees reason to feel confident that in the Philippines at least may be disproved Mr. Benjamin Kidd's assertion that " there never has been and there never will be, within any time with which we are practically concerned, such a thing as good government, in the European sense, in the tropics, by the natives of those regions."

❦

**What Remains to be Done** But our task is very far from completion. For instance, Judge Ide points out that school provision can be made for only half a million children, while a million and a half are clamoring for admission to the schools. At present, he holds, the great lack of the Filipino people is a middle class. "There is a small, very small, body of highly educated people, some of them educated abroad, a mere handful, and then there is the great mass of untrained, uneducated, and ignorant people, and between the two classes there is a tremendous chasm yet to be filled." To meet fully such problems as this of education is impossible for the simple reason that the Philippine Government is poor. And it is poor because Congress refuses to do justice to the Philippines in the matter of the tariff. There is still an opportunity for this session of Con-

gress to take the action urged upon it again and again by the President and by all friends of a right policy in the islands. The export tax on hemp, Judge Ide declares, has taken between one and two million dollars from the poverty-stricken insular treasury and employed it for the benefit of the cordage trust ; the coastwise shipping law has extended a doctrine wise in itself and for our own coastwise trade to a situation where it can work only hardship and injustice ; the prohibitive tariff on sugar and tobacco is not only " a monstrous injustice," but gives the Filipino " the feeling that the American colonies had when subjected to discriminating and ruinous trade regulations by Great Britain." These are the words of an administrator and organizer of recognized ability and of six and a half years' experience in the Philippines. If the views they express are not just and sound, Congress should have the courage to state that fact and refuse to act upon them ; if the views are right, then Congress should be ashamed of reasonless inaction.

❦

**Business Principles in Public Business** Governor Hughes, of New York, has given another striking example of the straightforward, businesslike methods which he is employing in his administration. He requested the resignation of Otto Kelsey, the State Superintendent of Insurance. Mr. Kelsey declined to resign saying that he had faithfully performed the duties of his office, and that his department was prepared to give the Governor the most cordial, disinterested, and effective cooperation. Under the law he could be removed from office only by the Senate, upon the recommendation of the Governor. Before making this recommendation Mr. Hughes called the Superintendent before him for a hearing, held the hearing in the audience-room of the executive suite, which was open to the public, and, before a large audience, subjected the Superintendent to a searching cross-examination which revealed that Mr. Kelsey had not even read in full, much less mastered, the report of the

Armstrong Committee on the conditions in the insurance companies, and had kept in office two subordinates who had been shown by the report to have been grossly derelict in duty. He protested that he had not had time to "clean house," although he had been in office eight months. The hearing showed not only incompetency on the part of Mr. Kelsey, but utter inability to appreciate his shortcomings. This condition of mind was further emphasized by his supplementary statement sent to the Governor after the hearing. After giving him ample opportunity to defend his administration of the department, Governor Hughes sent a message to the Senate asking for his removal, and there appears to be very little reason to doubt that the Senate will approve the Governor's course, as it has been already approved by the press and people of the State. Mr. Kelsey has had an excellent political record; there is no question of his personal integrity; he took with reluctance the office to which he was appointed by Governor Higgins. But the appointment was a political, not a business, appointment. He had honesty, business ability, and party loyalty; but there was no reason to suppose that he had either the special training or the peculiar talent which sometimes serves in lieu of training, to reorganize the Insurance Department of the State and institute a new policy of insurance management. The incident emphasizes the inadequacy of political appointments for business positions in an era in which the State is undertaking the conduct of great business operations. Governor Hughes has practically recognized the new era by applying to the public service the principles which any good business man would observe in his private business, and making ability to discharge the duties of a business office the primary and indispensable qualification.

❀

*Ferryboat Whistling*　　The law and rules of 1897 concerning steamboat whistling in our Atlantic and Pacific harbors are being increasingly and gratifyingly observed. This is specially evident in New York harbor. Across it

travel 199,000,000 out of the 261,000,000 passengers transported in the harbors from our northern boundary to the Delaware Capes. In a comparatively few years the able and efficient Supervising Inspector at New York, Captain Ira Harris, has evolved order out of former chaos and has induced compliance with the laws and rules from all but one of the companies operating ferryboats in New York harbor. The Delaware, Lackawanna, and Western Company persists in using a system of its own, not only defying the regulations which are a part of the law of the land under Act of Congress, but disarranging the service of other and law-abiding companies, the Erie, for instance, whose president has properly protested to the Inspection Bureau against allowing such defiance. It is not surprising that the Lackawanna boats have met with more collisions than have any others. One of them occurred last summer, the other vessel being an excursion steamer. The Inspector ordered the suspension from service for a hundred days of the pilot of the ferryboat. On his return from an inspection of the New England harbors, Captain Harris found that the Lackawanna Company was evading the suspension. The pilot was still practically acting, though the reports of trips were not signed by him. Thereupon Captain Harris definitely suspended the pilot, who had been performing duty without a license. Furthermore, the Bureau of Steamboat Inspectors charged the superintendent of the Lackawanna ferries, the company's counsel, and a third person with attempting to nullify the Supervising Inspector's order. At the ensuing hearing Captain Harris discovered that the company's counsel was taking an active part in the investigation in which that counsel was to be a witness. The counsel claimed that the company could employ any lawyer it desired. Captain Harris promptly adjourned the case to obtain a ruling on this point from the Department of Commerce. The whole matter has now been referred to the Attorney-General of the United States. The case illustrates the cynical defiance, not only of law and order, but also of neighborliness, by a great corporation, whose president's only defense is that his pilots are not members of the American Association of Masters, Mates, and Pilots I This same railway president, Mr. Truesdale, has been deprecating what he considers to be the popular hostility to railways. If he seeks for a reason for such hostility, he need not look for it on other railways' premises. The fact is, there is no animosity toward railways as such; but there is a growing impatience with those railways which appeal to the Government for protection but ignore or resist Governmental restraint.

❦

**The Philadelphia Election**

The Mayoralty election in Philadelphia has been concluded by the victory of Congressman John E. Reyburn, the Republican candidate, by a majority of 33,000 over William Potter, the City Party candidate, who received 97,000 votes. The successful candidate has had a long public career, although he has never served in municipal office. He was formerly a member of the State Senate at Harrisburg, and latterly has served as Congressman at Washington. He is a man of large personal means and of excellent personal character, but the fact that he was backed by McNichol and Vare, two of the largest city contractors in Philadelphia, led to his being called "the contractors' candidate." He has asserted, however, both before and since his election, in the most unequivocal terms, that he is not under any obligations to any leader, and that he intends to give Philadelphia a business administration of its affairs. The City Party nominee, the Hon. William Potter, was formerly Minister to Italy under President Harrison, and has been actively identified with the City Party and with the various movements that clustered around the independent fight in Philadelphia since Mayor Weaver's break with the Republican organization in May, 1905. The success of the Republican candidate has been variously explained and interpreted, but one fact stands out prominently, and that is the tremendous influence of an effective organization. The machinery of the Republican party has been maintained intact and has been kept at a high point of efficiency, and its effectiveness has been demonstrated, first, in securing a large registration of its voters, and, secondly, in having its voters marshaled at the primaries; at the primaries 98,000 votes were polled for the various Republican candidates, and again on the day of election 130,000 men recorded their preference for Mr. Reyburn. While the City Party has maintained an admirable organization, it had to depend in most instances upon the voluntary efforts of men who had other business than politics. The consequence was that it suffered from its inability to reach the voters ·and bring them out. Another factor which seems· to have contributed to the success of the Republican candidate lay in the defection and inaction of the Democrats. While they nominated Mr. Potter on their ticket, no effort was made by them to bring out their voters, and this inactivity had its natural effect in diminishing the support accorded to the City Party candidates. The election, like that of last fall, was generally conceded to be honestly conducted, owing to the effectiveness with which the Personal Registration Law has been enforced. The Mayoralty primary on January 26 was the first held under the new Uniform Primaries Act passed a year ago by the special session of the Pennsylvania Legislature. The result was the largest vote ever polled at a primary election, but the candidates nominated were those favored by the leaders of the respective party organizations. The City Party made a considerable gain in both branches of Council, electing a number of first-class men. Among those elected to the Common Council was George Burnham, Jr., of the Baldwin ·Locomotive Works, and for many years Treasurer of the National Municipal League. A number of other men of good character were chosen at the same time, thus insuring a more careful consideration of municipal questions in the municipal legislature.

❦

**The House of Lords an Elective Body?**

In· the House of Lords last week· Lord Newton introduced a bill proposing the reconstitution of the House on a partly elective basis.

He seeks to remove the excessive preponderance of hereditary peers by stipulating qualification through service to the State *or previous election*, and provides for a certain number of elected peers and for the nomination by the Crown of life peers, these not to exceed one hundred in number. Thus the Lords might cleverly forestall the expected reform of their House to be proposed in the Commons. Actual conditions, from the Liberal standpoint, were recently described by the Attorney-General of the present Cabinet when he declared that the House of Lords was entirely out of harmony with modern democratic institutions and must go down. Whether anything of it would be left, and, if so, in what form, could not yet be determined. If the House of Lords set itself against the national will, it would be like a heap of sand setting itself against the rising water. The Government would endeavor to give effect to the will of the people, he said, by means of bills, which the Peers would promptly throw out, and that would lead to a combination between the Crown and the people to defeat the aristocracy. It would mean a rearrangement of constitutional and political forces and a struggle of no slight difficulty. In the meantime there would be pressing and urgent legislation that would not brook delay, and the Government would undertake such legislation with a determination to carry it through in spite of all opposition. All this is very well, but what if the House of Lords reforms itself into a semblance, for instance, of the Upper Houses of Italy or Prussia, where the hereditary element is comparatively small? We hope that such a change will take place; indeed, that the House of Lords will ultimately resemble our own Senate. But it must be trying to the Liberals to see their thunder stolen by Lord Newton's clever bill.

⊛

**Why the New Duma is Radical**  The Duma is the lower house of the Russian Parliament organized last year under the Emperor's Freedom Decree of 1905. The first Duma was summarily dissolved by the Emperor and elections ordered for a new Duma to meet in March, 1907. The elections are not yet completed. So far, more than four hundred members have been elected, leaving about a hundred still to be chosen. The extreme Radicals are to form the largest force which may be counted upon to act as one body. Their strength already exceeds two hundred members. They are divided into Revolutionist, Labor, Socialist, and Nationalist groups, the first two being ably represented by Mr. Tschaykcnsky and Mr. Aladyin, now in this country. The Cadets, or Constitutional Democrats, who are moderate Radicals, have, by Government abuse of power, been reduced to seventy-odd members of those already chosen, but it is expected that their total will reach about a hundred. They stand sturdily, not for the chaos into which extremists would plunge the country, but for the grant of a liberal Constitution and for universal suffrage; in general skillful parliamentarians, they represent the most intelligent public opinion committed to a clear programme. The Moderates now poll about sixty members; these include the "Decembrists," who take their name from the martyrs for political liberty in the December, 1825, outbreak. The Conservatives so far number seventy-five. If this proves to be their full parliamentary strength, as their rivals claim, it will be seen how overwhelmingly the new Duma is to oppose the present Government. The first Duma was anti-bureaucratic; the second Duma is apparently anti-dynastic. Despite the Government's success in preventing the nomination of many men who had perhaps unwittingly laid themselves open to suspicion, the second Duma is more radical than the first. It was a tragic error to dissolve the first Duma. The Government has now a doubly difficult task, for if it could not deal with the demands of the first, how will it deal with those of the second? So grim is this exigency that there are already suggestions of possible rioting fomented by the reactionaries and of connivance by the authorities. This has received color through an outbreak at Odessa, where the notorious General Kaulbars is in charge. There are perhaps many reactionaries, driven to the wall, capable of organizing "pogroms," or massacres, like those which have already disgraced Russian civilization and made the name a byword among the nations. But few will believe that Premier Stolypin or the Emperor would connive at this. If they were held back by nothing else, they would be by the fact that the enormous radical gain has as its cause not only political tyranny, but also the famine which has prostrated twenty to thirty millions of muzhiks or peasants. The accounts of the famine have aroused widespread sympathy. Last week The Outlook referred to the mission to this country of Mr. Nicolas Shishkoff on behalf of the Russian famine sufferers. Through his efforts a Russian Famine Relief Committee has been formed for the collection and forwarding of funds. Of this committee the treasurer is the Morton Trust Company, whose standing as American bankers insures the very best management of the finances; the chairman is Bishop Potter; the secretary is the Rev. S. J. Barrows, 135 East Fifteenth Street, New York City. In order to make the records exact it is requested that all communications and contributions be made through the secretary.

*War in Central America*

One of the exasperating little wars between the southern republics of this continent has broken out between Nicaragua and Honduras. We use the word exasperating because it is both annoying and, to a certain extent, disheartening to the great nations of America to find that the ·smaller republics, such as those now engaged in controversy, disregard the counsel and admonition of those who may be called their elder brothers, who point out to them that such a dispute as the present is precisely the kind of thing that ought to be settled by arbitration. It is understood that only a week ago despatches were received in Washington indicating that peace between the two quarrelsome countries was assured, and that the urgent advice of the United States, Mexico, Guatemala, and other countries that the difference between Honduras and Nicaragua should be adjusted by arbitration had been accepted and that only a few details were

left to be arranged. Soon, however, both sides began to accuse the other of violating the truce existing, and war was soon formally declared. The dispute between the two countries is essentially one of disagreement as to encroachments on disputed territory by one or the other country. President Zelaya, of Nicaragua, has personally cabled to the American papers that he was obliged to go to war because his small garrison on the frontier had been attacked by the force of Honduras, which looted, burned, and killed, and that, arbitration having been agreed upon, President Bonilla, of Honduras, had dissolved the court by withdrawing the Honduran arbitrator. From the capital of each of the two countries comes the assertion that its troops are marching on the capital of the other and will surely be victorious. It may be pointed out that when such ill-tempered and fiery countries as these two indulge in what seems to us at this distance a causeless war, we are apt to consider them as typical of Central and South American character and political life, forgetting for the moment that turbulent nations like Nicaragua, Honduras, and Venezuela might well be contrasted greatly to their disadvantage with such fine, progressive, and strong nations as Argentina, Brazil, and Chile.

*The Election of Dr. Judson*

The selection of Dr. Harry Pratt Judson to succeed Dr. Harper as President of the University of Chicago was in reality a confirmation by the Board of Trustees of the choice of the faculties and students of the institution. It was also a promotion for services of great importance and a recognition of unusual equipment of ability and experience for the position. A graduate of Williams College, which has bred many university and college presidents, Dr. Judson began his professional career as a teacher in a school in Troy, New York, whence he was called, in 1885, to a professorship in the University of Minnesota. When the present University of Chicago was organized, in 1892, he accepted the chair of political science in the institution, with the rank and duties of Dean. He was at Dr. Harper's right hand during the years when the lines of a great university were being marked out, and an organization novel in many of its features and unique in its freedom from mere academic tradition was elaborated and perfected. Dr. Judson has been familiar with every stage of the evolution of the University and with all the details of its administration. The University of Chicago has entered on the second stage of its extraordinary career, and Dr. Judson is specially well equipped to give its organization solidity and its educational work thoroughness and efficiency. His wide interest and study in the fields of history, politics, and international law have preserved him from the narrowness that is the danger of the specialist; while his duties as Dean have kept him in vital touch with the life as well as with the work of the University.

❋

**A New Liquor Law for South Carolina** The State Dispensary system by which South Carolina has for fourteen years regulated the liquor traffic has been abolished by the State Legislature. The result was anticipated when the policy of the State Government was determined by the State primaries last fall. Senator Tillman, who had instituted the State dispensary, argued for it vigorously during the campaign. He attacked the opponents of the system without mercy, and, it may be added, without much regard for ordinary good manners. His candidates, however, were defeated; and many believe that, if he had been confronted with a strong opposing candidate for his seat in the Senate, he would not have been himself re-elected. By means of the dispensary, the State itself, with the exception of a few manufacturers, was the sole dealer in liquors within its own borders. Officials of the State, with headquarters at Columbia, bought all the liquors that could be legally sold in the State, and from there disposed of them to the various local branches. These branches retailed the liquor; they were open during the daytime only. They were not drinking-places, as no liquor bought

of them could be drunk on the premises. The large profit to private concerns, which is a stimulus to the sale and therefore to the consumption of liquor, was thus eliminated. Open saloons were as strictly contrary to law as in a prohibition State, and in practice were at least quite as rare. Whatever profits the State reaped were devoted to education. The profits of the retail dispensaries were divided between the county and the town in which the dispensary was placed. The opportunity for graft, however, was enormous. Whisky dealers could not be expected to neglect the chance to secure sales by offering valuable commissions to State employees. The people of the State became convinced that the State dispensary was a fountain of corruption, and they have now brought it to an end. This does not mean that there will be no more dispensaries in South Carolina. The twenty-five counties (out of forty-one in the whole State) which now have State dispensaries, and hereafter those counties which vote for the sale of liquor, will maintain dispensaries of their own; the counties which vote against the sale of liquor will have neither public dispensaries nor legalized private saloons. In other words, South Carolina has become a strictly local option State, though it differs from such local option States as New York and Vermont in limiting the option to that between sale by the county and no sale. The believers in State prohibition in South Carolina are very numerous; they will no doubt watch very critically the working of the new system. That it is more wholesome than the one it has superseded is hardly doubtful.

❋

**The President on Academic Criticism** In an address before the members of the Harvard Union at Cambridge on Saturday of last week President Roosevelt drew the contrast between the healthful spirit of the well-trained man and the unwholesome temper of the academic mind. He found a common basis with his audience by taking the first illustration of his subject from college athletics. He contrasted the idle criticism of athletic abuses with healthful participation in vigorous sports as a means for the development of the democratic spirit and of the virtue of courage. He emphasized still more strongly the necessity of scholarship, contrasting routine with creative work. He then exhorted college men to take their part in the work of government:

> Above all, you college men, remember that if your education, the pleasant lives you lead, make you too fastidious, too sensitive to take part in the rough hurlyburly of the actual work of the world, if you become so over-cultivated, so over-refined that you cannot do the hard work of practical politics, then you had better never have been educated at all. . . . I want you to feel that it is not merely your right to take part in politics, not merely your duty to the State, but that it is demanded by your own self-respect, unless you are content to acknowledge that you are unfit to govern yourself and have to submit to the rule of somebody else as a master—and this is what it means if you do not do your own part in government.

With the theorists who "gather in parlors to discuss wrong conditions which they do not understand and to advocate remedies which have the prime defect of being unworkable," Mr. Roosevelt made it plain that he had little patience. The trouble with them was, he pointed out, that they met no one but themselves, refused to mingle with their fellows, and cultivated "a curiously impotent spirit of fancied superiority."

> In popular government results worth having can only be achieved by men who combine worthy ideals with practical good sense. . . . It is a very bad thing to be morally callous, for moral callousness is disease. But inflammation of the conscience may be just as unhealthy so far as the public is concerned. . . .

That he was speaking out of experience Mr. Roosevelt made clear by his concluding remarks. He illustrated his point by reference to the critics of the Philippine policy of the Government; and with regard to much of the opposition to the policy of Federal control of corporations he had these things to say:

> There has been a curious revival of the doctrine of State rights in connection with these questions, by the people who know that the States cannot with justice to both sides practically control the corporations, and who therefore advocate such control because they do not venture to express their real wish, which is that there shall be no control at all. . . .
>
> Honest and fair-dealing railway corporations will gain and not lose by adequate Federal control; most emphatically it is both the duty and the interest of our people to deal fairly with such corporations, and to see that a premium is put upon the honest management of them, and that those who invest in them are amply protected. . . .
>
> Our present warfare is against special privilege. The men—many of them, I am sorry to say, college men—who are prompt to speak against every practical means which can be devised for achieving the object we have in view—the proper and adequate supervision by the Federal Government of the great corporations doing an inter-State business—are, nevertheless, themselves powerless to so much as outline any plan of constructive statesmanship which shall give relief. I have watched for six years these men, both those in public and those in private life, and though they are prompt to criticise every affirmative step taken, I have yet to see one of them lift a finger to remedy the wrongs that exist. So it is in every field of public activity. States' rights should be preserved when they mean the people's rights, but not when they mean the people's wrongs; not, for instance, when they are invoked to prevent the abolition of child labor, or to break the force of the laws which prohibit the importation of contract labor to this country; in short, not when they stand for wrong or oppression of any kind or for national weakness or impotence.

This address is a capital illustration of the President's method of reporting not only his acts but also his principles of action to the American people, and thereby clarifying and solidifying the public opinion on which as President he depends.

# Lenten Meditations
## Daily Bread

"Give us this day our daily bread" is first of all a recognition of the divine origin of our normal human cravings. Self-denial for its own sake is not Christian. There is no virtue in treating such human cravings as of themselves evil. It is God who has placed within us what psychologists call the food instinct; and it is God who has filled the world with those things that will feed his children. Instead of lashing the appetite, we are bidden by Christ to ask God that the appetite be rightly satisfied. And if this is true of hunger for food, it is also true of the desire for other material things.

The Lord's Prayer is not a piece of hardened ritual; it is a suggestive collection of typical petitions. As we are bidden to pray for our daily bread, so ought we to pray for all that can sustain and strengthen us. Our clothes, our lands, our books, our money, all are of God; and from him we should be ready to ask for such as our daily needs require.

But this petition is not one of self-indulgence. The request that we have made, "Thy will be done on earth," is to interpret and direct our petition for the satisfaction of all our desires. When we pray, "Give us our daily bread," we really ask God but for what is needful that we may be enabled to do his will on earth. The Douay version translates this petition, "Give us this day our supersubstantial bread," and the Roman Catholic Church interprets this as a plea for the sacramental grace that is bestowed in the Eucharist. Can we not say that it is a plea for that spiritual strength which God is ready to bestow by means of all his gifts? There is no material thing which, if we use it rightly, may not have for us a "supersubstantial," a spiritual, value. This for us is the test by which to determine whether the good things of life are for us really good or not. This is the test which Christ himself applied. He neither condemned nor approved bread or clothing or shelter, houses or books or riches, as such. He used them or disregarded them as they were instruments or obstacles in his doing of his Father's will. He who made wine for a wedding feast, himself rejected, when feverish on the cross, the proffered wine and myrrh. He who sent away the young man who would not renounce all his possessions, himself wore a fine garment, and made friends and disciples of the rich. He who refused to make food to satisfy his own hunger in the wilderness, himself fed the faint multitude and taught his disciples to pray for bread. By his life he has shown in what spirit we should pray that our own desires be fulfilled.

Art which corrupts and corrodes is not food that we can ask of God; but art which liberates the imagination and invigorates the spirit is of that daily bread for which we may pray. Wealth which becomes an end in itself is no more food than a banquet is to a gourmand; but wealth which remains a means for human service is of that daily bread for which we may pray. Ritual and observances which leave the human spirit more faint-hearted in the midst of human misery that must be fought and human imperfections that must be corrected are not food from the Father of men, even though they be accompanied by fasting; but every ancient collect and every churchly celebration which imparts energy to us in the bearing of our own and others' burdens is daily bread that we may seek with prayer. If we have not the spirit of him whose meat it was to do his Father's will, we shall find little sustenance in the most ample of possessions or the most pious of practices; but if we have his spirit, we may find in all our experiences an answer to the prayer, "Give us this day our daily bread."

"Be not anxious for your life, what ye shall eat; nor yet for your body, what ye shall put on. . . Seek ye his kingdom, and these things shall be added unto you."

●

# The Smoot Case

Mr. Smoot has been retained in the Senate of the United States by the decisive vote of 43 to 27. Disregarding the purely political questions and the purely sentimental influences involved in this case—and both ought to be disregarded—the issues involved are four in number.

I. The Constitution provides that "no person shall be a Senator who shall not have attained to the age of thirty years, and been nine years a citizen of the United States, and who shall not, when elected, be an inhabitant of that State for which he shall be chosen." It has been contended that the Senate has no right to add to these qualifications; that it cannot exclude any one who possesses these three qualifications. In our judgment, there is no good ground for such contention. The Senate is not bound to admit to its membership a confessed or convicted criminal, or a man of flagrantly immoral character, or a man afflicted with a chronic loathsome and contagious disease, like some forms of leprosy. The larger right and duty of the Senate appear to us clearly expressed in the clause of the Constitution that " each House shall be the judge of the elections, returns, and qualifications of its own members." It cannot admit any one who does not possess the specified Constitutional qualifications, but it may exclude any one for any reason which in its judgment constitutes a proper and adequate disqualification for membership in the Senate.

II. Membership in a religious organization does not constitute a proper and adequate disqualification, whatever the religious organization may be. To exclude a man from the Senate merely because he is a Brahman, or a Mohammedan, or a Spiritualist, or a Mormon, would be clearly inconsistent with American principles and with the spirit of Article I. of the Amendments to the Constitution of the United States : "Congress shall make no law respecting an establishment of religion, or prohibiting the free exercise thereof." Refusing to admit a Mormon as a member of the Senate would not be technically prohibiting the free exercise of the Mormon religion, but it would be palpably in violation of the spirit of this provision.

III. There is no charge of immoral conduct or character against Mr. Smoot. He is not a polygamist. He cannot, therefore, be excluded on the ground upon which Mr. Roberts was excluded in 1900 from the House. He is not violating any law of the land or any fundamental moral principle. On the contrary, he appears to be a man of unquestioned purity and integrity of character.

IV. The formal charge preferred against Mr. Smoot by the majority of the Senate Committee was that he comes to the Senate, " not as the accredited representative of the State of Utah, . . . but as the choice of the hierarchy which controls the Church and usurps the functions of the State." In fact, Mr. Smoot is " the accredited representative of the State of Utah ;" if he is also "the choice of the hierarchy," that is no reason why he should be refused his seat,

That he belongs to a powerful religious organization which is also a powerful political organization constitutes no adequate reason for his exclusion. If it did, the same reason might be cited to exclude a Senator who belonged to any other religious organization which was accused of exerting a political influence. It might equally be cited for the exclusion of a Senator who belonged to a trades union or to a trust or to a political machine, and who was under suspicion of expecting to use his Senatorial power to aid the organization which had given him his election. A society might be avowedly organized for the purpose of destroying the Nation, and a representative of such a society should be refused a seat in either House ; but there is no pretense that the Mormon Church is organized for any such treasonable purpose. Evidence that Mr. Smoot had taken an oath or made a pledge of hostility to the American Nation or of supreme allegiance to the Mormon Church, putting it above his allegiance to the Nation, would be good ground for excluding him from the Senate. But the vote of the Senate we take to be equivalent to its declaration that he has taken no such oath and made no such pledge.

We have not read all the evidence in this case : life is too short. But we have read with care the protest against Mr. Smoot's election signed by representatives of the " League of Woman's National Organizations " and presented to the Senate by Senator Dubois, of Idaho, and we find in it no reason stated that justifies their demand for Mr. Smoot's exclusion. They have not expressed and they cannot express too strongly the importance of protecting the purity of the home and the sanctity of the family. But this cannot be done by asking Congress to violate both the spirit of the Constitution and the principles of political justice. To refuse a seat in the Senate to a man of irreproachable moral character because he entertains a religious faith and is a member of a religious organization which are oppugnant to the judgment and conscience of a vast majority of the people of the United States does violate the spirit of the Constitution. To admit to all the rights and privileges of Statehood a Territory known to be dominated by an organization which is both ecclesiastical and political, and then refuse to allow such State to elect its own Senatorial representative as other States are allowed to elect theirs, does violate the principles of political justice. It was a mistake to admit Utah to Statehood; but that mistake cannot be rectified by refusing to her the prerogatives of Statehood now that she has been admitted. The way to counteract the evil influences of the Mormon Church is by educative and religious influences, and these can be effective only as they are accompanied by the most scrupulous regard for her Constitutional and legal rights.

· ⬡

# Better than an Income Tax

The exceedingly well balanced and comprehensive article on "The Income Tax" on another page is based on the tacit assumption that a tax is an enforced contribution from the members of the community and is necessary to pay the expenses of maintaining the government. Mr. Henry George and Mr. Thomas G. Shearman have maintained that if the State were put in possession of the property which properly belongs to the people, but which has now been taken possession of by individuals, no such contribution would be necessary; the income from this property would pay all the expenses of government. Whether this is true or not, it is certain that the burden of taxation would be greatly lessened if the people were allowed to receive a fair rental on property which is clearly theirs, but which private persons are very vigorously striving to get for their own use.

Mr. Brown's interesting and instructive article on "Punishing the Land-Looters," published in The Outlook of last week, stated that an acreage nearly equal to the whole area of Delaware, Connecticut, and Rhode Island combined had been *illegally* fenced in by private parties. Other mineral, forest, and grazing lands have been thrown open *legally* to settlement; that is, Congress

has passed laws under which they are to be given away; and the President is urging that they be not given away, but be leased, and the rental paid into the United States Treasury, and bills to effect this result have been introduced into the Senate. We have no means of giving even an approximate estimate of the value of these lands. But the eager opposition of certain Congressmen to their retention by and for the people indicates that the value is very considerable.

There was reason for giving away small holdings to actual settlers who would use them for farms and build up populous communities; there is no reason for giving away millions of acres of mining, forest, and grazing lands to great corporations to exploit them for their stockholders and leave the lands unpopulated. These lands belong to the people of the Nation. If the Nation keeps them, the rentals would sensibly reduce · National taxation.

. Add to this property of the people which some Congressmen are so eager to give away, the railway franchises. The tracks, cars, engines, and terminals of the railway corporations are private property. But the strip of land over which the road runs is, or ought to be, the property of the people. The Interborough Railway Company pays the city of New York a rental for the use of the subway. That is inherently just and right. If the great inter-State commerce railways paid the Nation or the several States a rental for the strip of land which they have taken for their roadbed, this again would sensibly reduce the necessity for taxation. And this rental can be collected in the form of a tax on the railway—not on its track, its cars, its engines, and its terminals, but on its right of way.

If the people can keep the mineral, forest, and grazing lands which belong to them and can get a landlord's rent for them, and if they can recover from the railway corporations in the form of a franchise tax a fair rental for the right of way which the State has given them, there would be no need of an income tax. If the workers in the community can come by their own, they will not need to levy a contribution on their own industry in order to secure protection for their persons and property.

❀

# A Double Lesson

In one week two notable railway disasters have occurred, both apparently due to the same cause—excessive speed in rounding a curve. They disgraced, not impecunious, single-track roads in sparsely settled regions, but the two wealthiest and most prominent of American railways, running through thickly settled districts.

The first accident took place on the Harlem division of the New York Central; the second on the main division of the Pennsylvania. In the first, twenty-three persons were ground to death, and over a hundred were injured; in the second no passengers were killed but many were injured. The Harlem train was an electric local; the Pennsylvania train was the famous eighteen-hour Chicago special, the regular running time of which is nearly a mile a minute. The Harlem train was six minutes late, the Pennsylvania train was between half an hour and an hour late. Both engineers naturally wanted to make up time, and both trains were running at excessive speed, if we may believe the testimony of those traveling on them; the Harlem train was thought by passengers to be going at the rate of seventy miles an hour, and some passengers had already become alarmed; the Pennsylvania train was probably running at equal or greater speed. When both trains reached the sharp curves, the one just beyond Woodlawn Cemetery, the other following the bank of the Conemaugh River, near Johnstown, the speed, it is alleged, caused the last cars to leave the track, dragging the others off.

This is the probable explanation. The railway companies claim, however, in the one case, that a bolt may have been dropped from the preceding train, in the other that the brake rigging may have broken under a forward car, and in both cases that a rail was found out of alignment. The last claim is justified, but the cause was probably the pressure of the train itself upon the rail at the sharp curve. If speed and weight are greater than they can bear, rails will spread. The Harlem train was drawn by two motors. Each weighed nearly a hundred tons. While the two were hardly longer than a large locomotive, the total weight was about a third more. Again, the two motors were not only heavier but were capable of higher speed than the ordinary locomotive. The passenger cars were not steel, as they might well have been, but were old-fashioned light wooden cars such as could easily be thrown from the tracks and take fire as they did; the Pennsylvania cars were fortunately heavy, solid Pullmans, and to this is due the almost miraculous saving of life.

The New York Central had just established its electric service on the Harlem Branch; indeed, the wrecked train was making its second trip. But did newness of service insure caution? According to the testimony in the coroner's investigation, the engineer in charge had been employed by the company as a motorman only since February 1; the first day he ever ran an electric motor on a passenger train was a week before the accident; he had no speedometer; he was ignorant of the distance in which he could stop a train; he had never been informed by his superior as to the possible maximum speed of his engine and its exact power; finally, the Assistant Superintendent of the road did not reprimand him for speed, though with him at the time in the cab! According to the testimony at the State Railway Commission's investigation, no trains had been operated to test the line, barring one night, before the public service was begun; the motormen were instructed in their duties solely on a short run of track where there were no curves; there was no way by which motormen could know just how fast they were going; lastly, the engineers confessed that they did not know precisely what effect the use of the two motors would have, or what would be the precise pressure on the rails with an increase of weight and speed!

Why did not the New York Central company send its engineers to Schenectady, where the motors were made, to have the benefit of a fortnight's work on the test track there? Why did not the company, following the New York City Subway's example, operate its line for a month before opening it to the public ? Why did not the company, if it had to begin public service at once, at least employ experienced men ? The ignorance which the men showed in the investigations is enough to make one afraid to travel on any railway, if such conditions must characterize our best roads. Indignation mingles with grief at the revelations of the past week.

To this must be added the sense of shame that we do not enjoy the advantage of the Government supervision which for many years has prevailed in England. That supervision affords remarkable immunity from such disasters as compared with any immunity enjoyed here. The past year's record of railway accidents has been the most dreadful in our history. Had there existed the supervision and authority of a Bureau of Railways similar to the English, the Harlem horror and many another would probably not have occurred. The English Bureau forms a department of the Government Board of Trade. When an accident takes place, the mute but reliable witnesses afforded by the wreck are not allowed to be immediately cleared away, as they are here : their testimony may be of vital importance in the Government investigation at once instituted. The Bureau not only fixes the responsibility for the disaster and prescribes remedies against a repetition, such recommendations having the force of law, but it also supervises every introduction of a new system of service. When the Birkenhead tunnel tramway under the Mersey River at Liverpool was electrified, the company's long experimental trial of the motive power was supervised by officials of the Bureau ; nor was the railway allowed to be opened to the public until authorized as safe by the Government. Thus the English Bureau's success has been not only in investigating the comparatively rare railway accidents in England as contrasted with our record, but even more in *preventing* them. The Bureau stimulates the English railways, as by a moral tonic, to provide for more intelligent and effective service than exists here.

How long shall America lag behind England ? Shall we not inaugurate such a system ? Coroners' investigations do something ; State Railway Commissions' investigations do more. But every State has not a Railway Commission. Besides, there is needed the exclusive service of trained men more expert than any coroner or any State Railway Commissioner could be. Will not Congress duplicate the English Bureau by a Bureau in our Department of Commerce, or by a distinct service in our Inter-State Commerce Commission, paying ample salaries to secure the best experts ? Congress has distinguished itself in the domain of railway legislation—it has provided for proper freight rates. But must there be another railway massacre to convince it that it has failed in a more elemental duty—to provide for the preservation of human life ? Only a few days are left of its own life. Will it heed, as by a death-bed repentance and resolution ?

⊛

# *The Spectator*

As the Spectator opens his daily mail and reads in letters and newspapers of the severe weather experienced in the East, he is thankful that kind Providence has made him of late a resident of Riverside, that beautiful and thriving little city in the orange belt of California. Though the California climate may not always be all that he expected, he compares existing conditions as he finds them here with weather reports from other localities, and can appreciate his blessings and minimize his discomforts. If his ardor has been dampened by days and even weeks of rain, his spirits have been brighter and his enthusiasm greater when, by contrast, the days of sunshine and balmy air have been given him. He had been led by excessive optimists to believe that cloudless skies and perpetual sunshine would be his portion so long as he might choose to remain within the enchanted State. Other spectators, however, had mentioned in an incidental way, between bursts of enthusiasm, that California was subject to all sorts of weather, barring, of course, snow-storms and blizzards, and that one must expect rain even out of the rainy season, as well as frost and ice in the early morning when the thermometer may register from fifty to sixty at noon of the same day. *This* Spectator was, therefore, in a measure prepared for the varieties of California weather that he has now experienced for himself.

❀

The Spectator has been told that the excessive rainfall of the present season is unusual; that not for fifteen years has the amount been in any one winter what it has been up to the first of February of 1907. The Spectator's object, therefore, of knowing what the climate of California is like during the winter season is defeated, and if he would really know it as it is in all its varying aspects he must come several winters in succession and thereby strike a happy average, as well as be a better judge of its mingled virtues and defects. As the Spectator has sometimes been wicked enough to exult over some slight fault or frailty in a friend whose superiority has been somewhat galling though praiseworthy, he is at the present time glad to see this wonderful and rightly praised country when not on its best behavior. It teaches him that nothing is perfect, not even the climate of California, and that the greatest blessings to mankind oft come in disguise; for as a result of this unusual season of rain the grain crop of the State will be enormous. To the ranchman there has been no disguise in this blessing of the rain.

❀

There have been days—and many of them in succession—when rain or gray skies have been largely in evidence. No driving through the orange district; no exploring of the neighboring foothills for those who can take long walks; no opportunity for the kodak operator to take his " snap-shot " picture—*nothing* in the way of outdoor pursuits and pleasures. But when the sun does shine, and the sky is blue, and the well-oiled roads permit the Spectator again to pursue his wanderings, he forgets all about those other days with their all-pervasive chill and dampness, and agrees with the

" oldest inhabitant " that there can be no place on the face of the earth where one may find more enjoyment and less that is undesirable than right here in Southern California. If he growled a little because his plans were interfered with, or made ironical remarks about his overcoat left in an Eastern closet, he has been forgiven because of his willingness to praise all the beauties and virtues of the country disclosed to him " between the acts," or, more correctly speaking, between the drops.

❀

And even under gloomy skies or through the glass of a rain-spattered window, the Spectator was willing to admit that Riverside is very beautiful. Her orange-trees are close at hand, in front door-yard and in back, on the sides of a house or surrounding it, and, in truth, the green, glossy leaves form a large part of the city's foliage. The graceful pepper-trees, with alternate palms, bordering so many of the streets, make the Spectator feel that he has indeed entered a garden of Eden, but in *this* garden the serpent is not in evidence.

❀

The Spectator has been much interested in a contrivance built into the roofs of houses here called a solar heater. Its object is to furnish hot water through the house on demand, said water to be heated by the rays of the sun. The Spectator has no knowledge of the mechanical part of the device—if there be any other than the legitimate rays of the sun—but he only knows—no, he has been told—that it is the simple working of the law of cause and effect: cause, sun; effect, hot water. Or, in reverse order; no sun, no hot water. The Spectator long failed to find a house in which this solar heater is placed where hot water has come on demand at such times as he demanded it, but he doesn't for one minute think of blaming the occupants of the houses, for that law of cause and effect is ever in his mind, and, knowing that there had been no sun, how could there be hot water? The only mystery to the Spectator has been why people continued to place solar heaters in their homes and consider them valuable as a means of furnishing hot water. He has gazed upon them from all sides, their skylights revealing their location in the roofs, and he has tried to see something ornamental about them which, aside from their utility, would justify their existence. But no artistic point is revealed to the Spectator, try as hard as he may to find it, and he is forced to fall back upon the original theory that the solar heater is a necessity, and if it fails in wet and cloudy weather, its virtue is none the less unimpaired.

❀

The Spectator, for the first time in his life, was away from his own table on Christmas Day. He prophesied a lonely time among strangers, the width of the continent between himself and his family, but to his great joy he was remembered by a family living twenty miles from Riverside, and invited to join them at their orange ranch. What cared the Spectator now for misty-moisty weather—some one had remembered his existence and called him from his solitary meal to the heart of a family on whom he had no claim except a friendship with relatives in the East. While traveling in the cars to the valley where the ranch is located, the Spectator recalled those words of a recent poem:

" Old friends are best, we lightly say,
  But as they fall upon the way,
  Keep full the ranks with newer friends,
  Till time the adjective amends."

❀

A modern house in the midst of orange groves, superb views, congenial family, a Japanese cook in the kitchen, surely ought to fill one's soul with thankfulness; but when the Spectator felt the warmth of furnace heat and saw the blazing fire upon the hearth, he knew that he had what his body longed for, and his soul could wait for a warmer day to feed upon views of snow-topped peaks. He was told that the dinner hour was six-thirty, and as that time approached and he realized that he did not possess the appetite which would give zest to the meal that he was sure would be presented, he took himself out for a walk in order that the proper vacuum might be created. As he passed down the steps and by the rose-bushes, he stopped to pick some pink buds, as exquisite as would be found in June, and with these in hand he walked up the avenue of palms to the foothills lying back of the house. Here he wandered among the rocks, looking in vain for some slight sign of vegetation—a wild flower, a blade of grass, anything to relieve the bleak and barren aspect and make him believe he was on California soil. The sage stalks were dry and brown; the thistles were nearly all blown away; no grass was revealed, if ever there had been any, and but for the glimpse of the orange-trees, palms, and pepper-trees down at the ranch, he might have been walking this Christmas Day on the hills of his own New England town. But he looked at the rosebuds in his hand; surely he could not find those in his own home yard in the month of December. His gaze rested on the distant mountain ranges where the snow was catching a few passing gleams of sunlight, and, turning so that he could look further up the valley, he beheld a most perfect rainbow—so beautiful that that portion of the valley was bathed in its colors. The Spectator forgot the dinner awaiting him and cared for nothing but the beauty of the scene. Then came the other thought—how could this peculiar climate be described, with its rosebuds and early morning icicles, its snow-covered ranges and rainbows, its orange groves and furnace heat? " A paradoxical country," was all he could say.

❀

The dinner was all that a Christmas dinner should be, the pickled figs, ripe olives, and manzanita jelly giving new varieties of relish to the Spectator; but the one thing that made real to him the fact that he was eating a Christmas dinner at a California ranch was an act of his host that revealed the true instincts of a ranchman. The gentleman of the house had appeared at the table in full dress. His manner of serving had been irreproachable, but something else besides his guests and his dinner was on his mind. Excusing himself from the table as dessert was coming on, he stepped to the window, and there upon the lawn a small moving object caught his eye. In a second he was out of the room, and before his sudden disappearance could be questioned, the report of a gun told the story; he had shot a rabbit. The Spectator sighed for his kodak as he imagined the picture there presented—this immaculate Gibson gentleman poising his gun by moonlight for a shot at a rabbit.

❀

The Spectator has returned to Riverside and is now enjoying the fulfillment of prophecies set forth in guide-books. The sun shines, and the solar heater is no longer a misnomer, for it is living up to its reputation as a heater of water; violets scent the air from their low hiding-places; roses are beginning to bloom; oranges can be seen on all sides; the clouds have rolled by and the distant mountains are revealed in all their beauty; the foothills are putting on their spring dress of delicate green. All Nature smiles here in California, and the Spectator smiles, too, as he reads of snow and ice at the East; he has a sense of pity for those less fortunate mortals who did not hie away to this golden State of California early in the season.

# MONTE CAVO

## BY GIOSUÈ CARDUCCI

### TRANSLATED BY ROBERT HAVEN SCHAUFFLER

In recording last week the death of the poet Carducci The Outlook said: " It seems strange that the foremost modern Italian poet should be comparatively little known abroad. This is because his style and versification practically baffle translation." Since those words were printed the following admirable English rendering of one of Carducci's most beautiful poems has been translated for The Outlook. Monte Cavo, anciently known as Mount Albanus, rises in the center of the Alban Mountains not far from Rome. On its crest is the ruined sanctuary of the Latin League, where in very early times a great sacrificial festival was annually celebrated. An ancient basalt-paved way, the *Via Triumphalis*, leads to the summit. Up this roadway wound the triumphal processions of those generals to whom the Senate refused a triumphal recognition at Rome. The view from Carducci's beech-tree embraces the Alban, Volscian, and Sabine Mountains, the sweeping shore-line of the blue Mediterranean, the Roman Campagna with its shimmering lines of ruined aqueduct, and, faintly silhouetted against the distant horizon, the dome of St. Peter's. Few modern poems express more beautifully the immortality of life and time in contrast to the evanescence of mortal things.—THE EDITORS.

Hail! king of beech-trees on this mountain crest,
  Raising aloft thy rugged bole and thick,
  And, like a many-branching candlestick,
Reaching thy gracious arms above the rest.

The young trees murmur and gleam in the sun, and toss,
  Breeze-fondled. Vibrant harmony they sing,
  Stung with desire; and every fibrous thing
Takes, in the sun and the wind, a rarer gloss.

The undulating lines of the foothills join
  The little towns vivaciously together,
  Saluting each by each; and from the nether
Soft sliding shadows seek their vantage-coign.

Good-morrow, Frascati! whose buoyant, teeming air
  Is impregnate with young creativeness.
  When the good autumn comes, your peasants press
Grand liquor from your vineyards everywhere.

Good-morrow, Rocca di Papa I high, so high
  You cling upon your crag precipitous,
  Like flocks of mountain goats the impetuous
Assault of wolves has come to terrify.

Good-morrow, Marino I and Castel Gandolfo, good-day I
  Who offer your lips for the hearty breeze to kiss,
  Respecting your ancient, rustic beauty—this
That holds in crescent-wise arms the emerald bay.

Behold Albano, Genzano, and, near the tall bridge,
  Arriccia, comrade of Nemi which ruled the towns neighboring
  What time the feudal Orsini, mightily laboring,
Piled them a massive stronghold high on the ridge.

Closed in the whorls of the hills as in whorls of a shell,
  There the sad waves of the two lakes curl evermore,
  Mournfully washing on desolate reaches of shore
Rich on a time with forests no iron dared fell.

Wide the campagna extends, in silence furled—
  In silence profound and in its potent peace.
  And far beyond the pallid fields one sees
The sacred place which once contained the world.

Lies the City, wrapped in a vaporous shroud,
  Like to a person by deep sleep oppressed.
  Never an echo carries to this crest
Aught of the mighty clangor of its crowd.

Here it is sweet to lie and quite forget
  All of the tumults and annoys of life.
  All of the tumult here, the murmurous strife
Of young leaves that upon the green twigs fret.

By every plant that sheds a murmur dim
  Upon the· air; by every nimble stem;
  By every stone and tree,—by all of them
Is raised a solemn, an imperious hymn:

" I hymn the candid praises of eternal
  Life which is in the flame and in the spring,—
  In insect, ocean, planet, everything,—
In the rude clod and in the Judge supernal;

Of life which knows to whizz and hum and boom.
  Eternally it murders and creates.
  In action and in thought it radiates,
And glows within the cradle and the tomb."

Stretch over me, O beech, thy mighty arms,
  Who viewest from thine height the plains and skies.
  This hour is mine, though countless unborn eyes
Shall know in coming centuries thy charms.

# THE INCOME TAX

## A Study of its Advantages and Disadvantages as a Form of Federal Taxation

### BY PHILIP S. POST

This is the fourth and last of a series of articles dealing with four of the most important subjects discussed in President Roosevelt's Message at the opening of this session of Congress. Mr. Post's article on "The Inheritance Tax" appeared in The Outlook of January 5; Judge Grosscup's article on "The Corporations and the People" in The Outlook of January 12; while two articles on "Lynching and Race Riots" will be found in The Outlook of February 2.—THE EDITORS.

THE Income Tax: Is it the fairest and most equitable tax ever devised, or is it the most odious and generally condemned mode of taxation resorted to by any nation?

Twice Congress has enacted an income tax, the first in 1862, and again in 1894. The act of 1862 was a war measure, passed at a time when Congress was seeking to drain every available spring of National revenue. With the public mind engrossed with the fate of armies, the tax was adopted without any widespread discussion. Its constitutionality was upheld, the Supreme Court perhaps unconsciously feeling the imperious demand of the war that in no wise should the arm of the Government be weakened. The rates varied from three to ten per cent. The law was repealed in 1871.

On August 18, 1894, Congress again enacted an income tax. Before it had become generally operative, the Supreme Court, by a vote of five Justices to four, declared the law unconstitutional. It is noteworthy that its enactment had not been preceded by any general debate among the voters. The income tax was not an issue in the campaign of 1892, and the country had no serious reason for anticipating that the Congress then being elected would enact such a statute. The public interest awakened by its passage soon died away, the adverse decision of the Supreme Court having apparently removed the question from the realm of National politics. To this place it has been reinstated by the recommendations contained in President Roosevelt's annual Message.

If the United States is again to adopt the income tax, it is most desirable that Congressional action should be preceded by a full and thorough popular debate as to its merits. This is desirable with respect to all important enactments. It is peculiarly true as to this proposed tax, which, more than any other tax known to governments, requires for its success and efficiency the support of a well-informed and thoroughly convinced public opinion.

It has seemed fitting, therefore, to present a study of the advantages and disadvantages incident to this form of taxation.

*The Advantages.* The income tax, say its advocates, is "the fairest and most equitable tax ever devised." In the earliest times taxation lacked equality. A tax was either a gift regulated by the generosity and loyalty of the members of the clan, or an extortion limited only by the power and rapacity of the ruler. Through the rude equity of the poll tax, falling alike upon every male subject, by successive stages more equitable standards have been reached, until there is now a general acceptance of the maxim that income is the most equitable test by which to measure the amount that the citizen ought to contribute to the support of the Government that shelters him. "To arrange a system

503

of taxation which shall correspond as closely as possible to the net revenue of individuals and social classes, and which shall take into account the variations in taxpaying ability, has thus become the demand of modern civilization."

In the light of the historical development of taxation, it is argued that income should appear to the lawmakers of progressive States a sound basis for the imposition of public burdens. There is an evident equity in this standard. Clearly it is the duty of the citizen to support the Government in proportion to his capacity to support himself. The test may not be absolute; but in what truer scales can be measured the distribution of these burdens? It is confidently asked, What can be fairer than that each citizen should annually contribute a just portion of his net income for the support of the Government or State under which he has elected to live, and in default of which he would not be likely to have either gain, income, or property? Cumulative testimony supports the allegation that the income is one of the most equitable, productive, and least objectionable forms of taxation, and that it accords in the highest degree with those canons or maxims which are regarded by nearly all economists and jurists as the highest embodiment of human wisdom on the subject.

Thus the broad claim is made that the income tax is the fairest of all taxes; that it tends to relieve the poorer classes and places the load upon the shoulders of those best able to bear it; that even for persons of large means it is advantageous; that the private revenue of an individual, by reason of trade conditions, varies greatly—in some years he may make much, in other years, without any appreciable change in the amount of his property, his income may be trifling; that whereas the general property tax mercilessly demands its due regardless of the year's profits or losses, the income tax accommodates itself to the varying condition of the taxpayer, bears lightly upon the business man who is struggling to keep his head above water, and postpones its heaviest call until the year of plenty.

The tax is in this regard the protector of legitimate business. The prediction has been ventured that its substitution for the usual property taxes would save many a man from bankruptcy. Unlike license taxes, it does not make it difficult for the man of small capital to begin business; unlike the personal tax, it does not levy toll upon a stock of merchandise from which, because of financial depression, the owner is perhaps deriving no profits; unlike the real estate tax, it does not increase the rent charge of every store and factory, whether succeeding or failing. The tax on incomes wisely and mercifully regards the present ability of the taxpayer, relieving him in adversity and participating in his prosperity.

The income tax has the further claim of reaching certain professional classes who under existing laws largely escape taxation. Their gains are great; they live comfortably and even luxuriously; they provide for their families by life insurance or other untaxed investments; yet they contribute not to the State under whose protection they thrive. This, it is said, is a financial injustice to the other classes who do pay; and, more, it is harmful to the Commonwealth itself. It creates a group of persons—often well educated, with opportunities for information and leisure for public service—who, because they pay nothing to the State, become indifferent to the duties of citizenship. They feel no direct monetary concern in the business of the State. They disdainfully disavow any interest in politics. Whatever contribution they make is the result of indirect taxation, and this is paid unconsciously. The exact amount contributed by any citizen because of the internal revenue and customs duties is unknown and unascertainable. There would be a social and political value to the country in a Federal tax under which every citizen would consciously pay a definite sum. Such payment would induce a more careful scrutiny into civic affairs, and would tend to awaken that direct and universal interest in public administration which is the safeguard of democratic government. This would be followed by more orderly methods of business on the part of individuals. Men would keep stricter accounts. They would know how they stand themselves, and financial failures due to ignorance and lack of method would be lessened.

A general tax levied upon the net income of individuals has this great recommendation: it has no tendency to disturb prices. In this it differs from certain other taxes, which, being laid on consumption, influence prices and affect markets and values. It is contended that all such taxes fall most heavily upon the poor; that whenever the levy is made, not on the basis of the amount received, but on the basis of the amount consumed, by the taxpayer and his family, it is a scheme of taxation which, of necessity, rests with disproportionate weight upon the masses of the people; and that "this flagrant injustice to the poorer class of contributors" can be compensated for only by an income tax in which small incomes shall be entirely exempt.

In this view the tax ceases to be merely a mode of raising revenue, and becomes an instrument of tremendous social and economic importance. Equality of taxation should be the first purpose of every well-ordered body politic; and it is confidently claimed that equality of taxation is impossible in any community without the income tax; that it is a measure by which to prevent certain kinds of property from obtaining "a position of favoritism and advantage inconsistent with the fundamental principles of our social organization;" that it is the only protection that the American people have against "the dominion of aggregated wealth;" that the great problem before the statesman is not how to obtain money for official expenses, but how to employ the taxing power so as to curtail riches and produce a more equal level of private possessions; that conditions in the United States call for the application of what is termed the Jeffersonian doctrine, that an equality of wealth must be preserved among the people "by taxing large wealth heavily, smaller wealth lightly, and least wealth not at all;" that this can be accomplished by a tax on gains and profits so framed that it will not touch the smaller incomes, but will lay a vigorous hand upon the annual receipts of the rich. It

is proclaimed that the income tax is alone capable of producing these equalizing results; that justice and wisdom demand its adoption; and that it will prove not a burden but a benefit to the Republic.

Considerations such as these have developed a strong tendency all over the world to employ this tax as a means of raising a portion of the public moneys. Its sponsors point with assurance to the fact that it has proved a satisfactory source of revenue in the countries where it has been adopted; that when once placed on the statute-books it has generally been continued and extended; that the difficulties of collection have been found to be exaggerated; and they contend that the experience of nations like England and Germany, and the increasing use of the tax by civilized States, form the best and most conclusive evidence in favor of its wisdom and efficiency.

*The Disadvantages.* The critics of the income tax—with a positiveness equaling that of their opponents—hurl back the assertion that it is "the most odious and universally condemned mode of taxation resorted to by any nation;" that, in spite of its theoretical justice, it has generally failed in its actual operation; that, however fair and alluring its principles, in practice it has been found to be unequal and unjust, undemocratic in spirit, inquisitorial in method, debauching to the public morals, the parent of perjury, the burden on the back of industry, an assault upon property, and a step toward communism.

There can be no denial that the income tax is unpopular. It is immediate, undisguised, personal taxation; and against this human nature always has, and probably always will, rebel. It meets violent opposition where indirect taxes are cheerfully borne.

A salient cause for this repugnance lies in the fact that the tax invades the right of privacy. If it is to be efficiently enforced, every person must lay bare the details of his property and business. Every item of his private transactions, whether entirely personal or in connection with others in situations of the most sacred trust, is subject to exposure. His financial strength becomes the object of envy; his weakness is told to his competitors, and becomes the sweet morsel of a gossiping public. The tax engrafts the spy system on the arm of the government, and in its train come a horde of impertinent revenue officers. In its administrative features it answers Samuel Johnson's choleric definition of the word excise as "a hateful tax."

A tax which is offensive to the citizen and which he regards as unreasonably oppressive is necessarily difficult of collection. Evasion is its legitimate child, and evasion must be followed with methods of collection constantly increasing in harshness and stringency. As the Roman tax-gatherer found in torture a frequent aid in discovering concealed property, so agencies in their nature arbitrary and inquisitorial must be used in the collection of this impost.

These methods and agencies find scant welcome in democratic countries. They belong essentially to despotic governments, and are peculiarly unsuited to republican institutions. This revenue cannot be collected unless the tax-gatherers have the power to compel the production of the private books and papers of the citizen upon which to base the assessment. This is a power which the legislature will hesitate to confer, and which, if given, will prove of doubtful efficiency. "It may suit the purposes of despotic power, but it cannot abide the pure atmosphere of political liberty and personal freedom."

The taxation of incomes invites fraud, deception, and dishonesty. Mr. Gladstone said that an income tax made "a nation of liars," and that nothing does more "to demoralize and corrupt the people." Practically, it is not an equitable tax on incomes, but rather a tax on "ignorance and honesty;" only those pay their full proportion who have not learned the methods of evasion, or, knowing the means, are too honorable to use them. It allows a man in failing condition to report a fictitious income, and thereby impose upon the business world; while the actual recipient of large gains conceals them to avoid the tax.

Before adding to its fiscal system this tax which demands either universal honesty or universal espionage, the country should listen to the overwhelming testimony against the personal property tax as now attempted to be enforced by the various States. Tax commissions have declared that the system is "debauching to the conscience and subversive of the public morals," that "it puts a premium on perjury and a penalty on integrity," and that "the attempt to enforce these laws is utterly idle." If the assessment of personal property is subject to such difficulties and evils, what will be the extent of the perjuries and public demoralization under an attempt to enforce an income tax? The statistics of revenue collected during the Civil War tell a graphic story. In 1869, with all incomes in excess of $1,000 subject to the tax, only 259,388 persons out of 37,000,000 acknowledged the receipt of any taxable incomes. It has been stated that only officials connected with the Treasury Department can form any adequate idea of the amount of perjury and fraud which pervaded the country from 1867 to 1872, and that American ingenuity was never more strikingly illustrated than in devising methods for evading taxes.

The impositions of the State should interfere as little as possible with industrial activity. No needless check should be laid upon the hands engaged in the beneficial work of adding to the aggregate of the National wealth. This principle the income tax ignores and violates. It is a tax on brains, enterprise, and industry; on mind and energy. It is an encouragement to shiftlessness and idleness. It punishes the active and frees the indolent. It exacts a contribution from the worker at the time when every dollar of capital may be most vitally needed in the building of his business. As was recently said by Andrew Carnegie: "This Nation will never regret anything so much as attempting to collect a tax from men engaged in business —bees making honey for the National hive."

For a century constructive statesmen have sought to add to the Nation's progress by encouraging manufactures and inviting the investment of capital. It is worth while to consider the effect which an income tax would have in nullifying these efforts. The modern movability of capital must be taken into account. As water seeks its level, so capital seeks those fields where it is least hampered by exactions. Would not ¬ progressive income tax—even though moderate and managed with the utmost circumspection—lead to an enormous transfer of American capital to other lands?

The tendency of income tax legislation to enlarge the class of exempt persons is noticeable. The law of 1862 at first relieved incomes under $600, then under $1,000, and later under $2,000, while the law of 1894 freed all incomes under $4,000. The exemption of all save the larger incomes seems now to be an inherent attribute of the tax. It is surely its most popular and attractive feature. This, it is submitted, is essentially class legislation. It differs not in real character from the English statute of 1691, which taxed Protestants at a certain rate, Catholics at double the rate of Protestants, and Jews at another and separate rate. All such discriminations, as a logical outcome, lead to oppression and abuses, and general unrest and disturbance in society. The plain duty is before every citizen to contribute his proportion, however small the sum, to the support of the government. It is no kindness to urge him to escape from this obligation. In giving his mite he will have a greater regard for the government and greater respect for himself. The humblest subject should not be put in the conscious position of a pauper of his government.

It is startling to consider the effect which an exemption of $4,000 has in transferring the burden of this tax upon an infinitesimal portion of the population. In democratic countries, where every citizen has a vote regardless of property, there is naturally a strong temptation to shift the load of governmental revenue upon the shoulders of the wealthy few. There is a sinister significance in the extent to which Congress yielded to this temptation in 1894. An income of $4,000 at five per cent. represents a fixed capital of $80,000. Thus this law rejected as objects of taxation every citizen whose taxpaying ability represented $80,000 or less. It compelled less than two per cent. of the taxable inhabitants

to contribute ninety-five per cent. of the entire tax. Commenting on these figures, Senator Edmunds, with fine scorn, exclaimed: "And this we call' a free government—a government of equal protection of the laws!"

It is protested that the philosophical considerations of men who love liberty and wish it to be perpetuated are all arrayed against such a scheme of government. It is so evidently unequal, discriminating, and partial that it is a misnomer to call it taxation. It is unmasked confiscation. Surely such legislation should not find shelter beneath the Constitution. It defies not only the principles of that great document, but it sweeps away personal and property rights which the Supreme Court has declared to be beyond and above the Constitution:

> It must be conceded that there are such rights in every free government beyond the control of the State. A government which recognized no such rights, which held the lives, the liberty, and the property of its citizens subject at all times to the absolute disposition and unlimited control of even the most democratic depository of power, is after all but a despotism. It is true it is a despotism of the many—of the majority, if you choose to call it so—but it is none the less a despotism.[1]

With solemn earnestness it is affirmed that the violation of this doctrine of elemental rights will be followed by further invasions, and that, as one vice follows another, we will soon have possibly one per cent. of the people paying the taxes, and finally a provision that only the twenty persons having the greatest estates shall bear the whole taxation— "and after that communism, anarchy, and then the ever following despotism."

. . . . . .

The foregoing statement of the reasons and arguments which have been presented for and against the taxation of incomes discloses how intense and fundamental the difference of opinion upon this question is. While extreme and somewhat violent utterances are not unexpected when coming from the stump or legislative halls, there is a profound significance in some of the statements contained in the divergent opinions filed by the Supreme Bench in the Income

[1] Loan Association vs. Topeka, 20 Wall, 655.

Tax Cases,[1] where one learned Justice denounced the tax then proposed not only as unconstitutional, but as an assault on wealth and a usurpation of power, while another expressed his deep conviction that the denial of the power of Congress to levy the tax approached the proportion of "a national calamity" and might prove the "first step toward the submergence of the people in a sordid despotism of wealth."

Amid these antagonistic opinions, what is the true course? A trustworthy chart has been prepared by President Roosevelt in his declaration that in this kind of taxation, where the men who vote the tax pay but little of it, there should be a clear recognition of the danger of inaugurating any such system save in a spirit of entire justice and moderation; and that it must be made clear beyond peradventure that the aim is to distribute burdens equitably, and to treat rich men and poor men on a basis of absolute equality.[2] But will the country steer faithfully by that chart? In 1894 Congress drifted upon the dangerous reefs of discriminating taxation.

If the mirage of its impractical fairness shall again lure Congress to enact an income tax, it should at least be so framed as to fall upon a reasonable percentage of the population. It should not by its narrow scope nullify the uniformity mandate of the Constitution, for, as has been said, when that occurs, "it will mark the hour when the sure decadence of our present government will commence." And it is further submitted that, before any income tax legislation whatever is undertaken, Congress may wisely act upon the President's recommendation for a progressive inheritance tax. Such a measure will accomplish many of the good results and avoid most of the evils attendant upon the income tax. Let Congress, therefore, impose a reasonable tax on inheritances, and test its possibilities of revenue and its equalizing powers, before resorting to a tax of doubtful constitutionality, which in practice is unequal, discriminating, obnoxious, and inefficient, the foe of industry, the shroud of personal honesty, and a stranger to the true spirit of our laws and institutions.

# IS WORKMEN'S COMPENSATION PRACTICABLE?

## BY ARTHUR B. REEVE

WHO takes care of the thousands of men, women, and children who are caught in the wheels of our record-breaking prosperity and turned out cripples? Who takes care of the many more thousands of widows and orphans who are cast adrift by the loss of the wage-earner of the family?

Half a million workers, it is estimated, are doomed every year to be killed or injured. Few have savings that will tide them over a long rainy day; fewer still will receive any compensation for their wasted lives or limbs. Many will become a burden to their friends and families—families, perhaps, which under

normal circumstances they supported; others will ultimately become a burden on public and private charity.

Poor-relief statistics show that the cost of maintaining a pauper throughout his natural life is about $6,000. If only one in ten of these victims is totally incapacitated, it means that private and public charities are called on every year to contract to pay out some three hundred million dollars in the future.

The economic loss, also, can only be estimated, for who shall calculate flesh and blood in dollars and cents? The statistician of the greatest industrial insurance company in America is inclined to place the net annual economic gain of an average worker at $400. At the prime of life that would make his esti-

---

[1] Pollock vs. Farmers' Loan and Trust Co., 157 U. S., 429; 158 U. S., 601.
[2] Annual Message, December, 1906.

mated future economic value something like $10,395. Statistics gathered in several States indicate that from two to four per cent. of industrial accidents are fatal. That would mean that productive power with upwards of $100,000,000 is annually lost, in the face of the demand all over the country for more labor. What is the economic loss through injuries cannot even be estimated.

How many widows and orphans and other dependents are left cannot be accurately estimated. Charitable workers tell us that a large proportion of those they meet with were rendered dependent in this way. In a special study in 1899 of 1,386 persons injured in the factories of New York State there were found to be 1,629 dependent wives, children, or others, a ratio of 1.18 dependents to one injured person. By the 1,123 killed in coal-mining in Pennsylvania 604 widows and 1,419 orphans were left, a total of 2,023—nearly two for each man killed. If only one dependent were affected by each of the half-million annually killed and injured, it means that another half-million are temporarily or permanently suffering with the wage-earner himself.

It is unfortunate, one may say, but it has always been that way and always will be. The reformer who would more equitably distribute this burden is called a visionary. Perhaps, however, it can be demonstrated that it need not always be that way. As for the reformer, perhaps he is not so visionary as he seems; perhaps the machinery which he would set in motion to better things is already constructed and needs only modification and an initial impulse to go a long way toward solving the question. Let us see.

First of all comes the theory on which rests the compensation of the working-man for all accidents suffered in the course of his trade. Stated brutally, it is that he is at least on a par with the machinery he runs. The employer does not ask the charity of the State or the savings of his employees to repair or replace the wear and tear on his machinery; it is charged in in the price of the commodity manufactured, and the consumer pays it as a legitimate cost of production. How about the wasted lives and the twisted limbs of the work-

men? Is not the "risk of a trade" as legitimate cost of production as the wear and tear on machinery? If human life goes into the mining of coal or the manufacturing of steel, why should not I, the consumer of coal, the user of steel, pay the cost? Why should the charity of the State of Pennsylvania or the savings of relatives of the unfortunate victim pay the price?

But, one objects, perhaps it was the negligence or the ignorance of the victim himself. Perhaps, I retort, it was the greed of an employer who had so many paying contracts that he couldn't shut down a furnace that threatened every day to explode and shower the "careless" and "ignorant" workers with a molten rain of white-hot iron. Let us call it quits. Is the misery any the less whether the fault inclines to the one side or the other?

Perhaps the subject seems now to be hopelessly involved—the idea of negligence has gone out of it altogether. "But that is the workman's compensation of Social Democratic Germany and of Great Britain," it is objected by the manufacturer. Exactly. "We cannot afford to take up that; competition is so keen that these rivals will distance us." Perhaps we cannot afford *not* to take it up. That is a dangerous argument—a sort of heads-I-win-tails-you-lose. We will be distanced if we take it up; yet other nations creep up on us though they have taken it up. In this aspect the case is not sentimental, or one of social reform; it is a matter of good business and pure patriotism.

What should be the programme? Modern philanthropy is being more and more seeking the causes that underlie the effect, poverty. It is becoming preventive without ceasing to be palliative. So with this programme; first of all it must deal with prevention, but concurrently it must deal with palliation.

Prevention of accidents is being more talked of now than ever before in this country. The American Institute of Social Service has been holding an exposition of safety devices for machinery and industrial hygiene in New York City, and endeavoring to establish a "museum of security" like those in Amsterdam,

Berlin, Munich, Vienna, Paris, and other European cities. Preventive legislation is more common on our statute-books than ever before. State and Nation are gradually taking up the questions of industrial accidents and industrial diseases.

Palliation is being taken up actively also in a rather different way than it ever was before. Within a year New York and Chicago have established "bureaus for the handicapped," where the wrecks of dangerous trades are, as far as possible, given chances to obtain work in lines that do not require the use of their lost limbs. Cleveland has followed suit. Now President Roosevelt adds the weight of his approval to a Federal employers' liability law as far as it is possible to go. Illinois and Massachusetts are vying with each other in investigating the subject. The Governor of Connecticut has recommended a new law as to employers' liability.

What is to be the end of this activity? Scarcely a well-informed insurance man in the casualty and employers' liability companies can be found who does not see the end clearly. It is simply and solely workmen's compensation for all accidents in the course of their trades. It will mean, we are told, a readjustment and reclassification of rates—ultimately a tremendous expansion of the business of insurance—but whatever it means, it is slowly coming, and the sooner it is recognized, and the system by which it is to come evolved, the better it will be for both capital and labor in the end.

This suggests a parenthetical thought of some interest. Both organized capital and organized labor seem to be peculiarly unprepared to meet it. Organized capital has little defense to point to except a few scattered "pension" systems and a movement for "social betterment" that excites suspicion in the recipients. On the other hand, of one hundred letters addressed to the international organizations of as many unions in the most dangerous occupations, not one came back with any statistics of the extent of industrial accidents other than that the situation was graded from "horrible" to "good."

As for workingmen's insurance against accident and the employers' liability for compensation for all accidents, they are not the impossibility they seem on the face of the statement. For they are already being practiced voluntarily by thousands of employers in the United States.

Insurance companies are writing a form of insurance called "workman's collective" insurance. Sometimes it is paid for by the employer, sometimes it is paid for by the employee as a condition precedent to his employment. In either case it tends toward meeting the growing demand for indemnification of the employee for injury regardless of his negligence or of the criminal liability of the employer. It is nothing more nor less than collective accident insurance.

One standard company writes a policy, which is generally followed by the others, covering the time a workman is engaged in his work, while for about fifteen per cent. additional premium it will give him accident insurance to cover every hour of the day, working or not. In case of death it pays one year's wages up to $1,500, the same sum for the loss of two limbs or two eyes, for one limb one-third the sum, for one eye one-eighth, not exceeding $200. In the event of temporary disability it pays one-half the weekly wages for a period not exceeding twenty-six weeks, or a sum not exceeding $500.

As a "transition" form of insurance between the time when few workmen are compensated and the time when all will be, this is the best that exists. Where the employer pays the premium, it keeps him in good touch with the employee. The premium seldom rises over ten dollars per employee a year, and is more often below that sum. It is like an addition to his salary. In the more selfish cases the employer, acting as trustee, deducts from each man's wages a pro-rata payment. The premium each employer must pay is based on the relative danger of the trade and the estimated pay-roll at the beginning of the year, together with the actual pay-roll at the end.

Several instances where large employers of labor take advantage of such insurance show that workmen's compensation is not an idea wholly alien to them. A large grain elevator company in the Middle West, employing hundreds of men, has for years taken out such insurance for a pay-roll of upwards of $300,-000. An iron company (not in the trust) in Pennsylvania does the same thing.

Many employers follow the method of a large lumber company in Michigan, which makes it a rule that every one who comes into its employ shall pay his proportionate share of the premium. This is a condition on which he is employed, and a matter of discipline.

Here, then, is a means ready to hand for the evolution of workmen's compensation. The law should be carefully prepared in such a way as not to permit of the employer's shifting the burden of the premium to his workmen rather than of passing it on as a cost of production. The strengthening of employers' liability laws is badly needed, while insurance would distribute the burden equitably as a risk of trade. Insurance companies, fearful of losses, would supplement State inspectors in enforcing laws regarding safety devices and hygienic conditions.

Along with benefits to employers and employees come the benefits to the State itself. The lightening of the heavy burden of public charity, as a result of the reckless waste of life and limb, would be considerable.

Quite important as a consideration for the employee is the fact that such insurance does not bar recovery by suit in a court of law in case of criminal negligence of the employer. It probably mitigates proportionally the amount recoverable, since a sum of damages has already been received by the injured party. In that respect the employer is benefited. But the benefit to the employee is greater.

In a recent case an employee sued and recovered damages from a street railway company in New York. He secured a verdict of $2,000—of which $1,500 promptly went to the lawyer and $100 in witness fees, leaving $400 as the price for nearly all that made life worth living to that man. Insurance would have given this man more than the sum recovered, outright, and still he would have had as good a cause of action. He would not have coined his limbs wholly into dividends for the railway, nor his suffering into " contingent fees " for the lawyer who exploited him.

The German system of insurance includes a small contribution from the State. Possibly, in view of the benefits to the State and to employees, something like the German system could be evolved here, in which the employer would bear the greater share of the cost of insurance; the State contributing a small percentage and the workman paying the additional percentage that would secure for him straight accident insurance.

At any rate, many insurance men, social reformers, labor leaders, and some large employers of labor, concur in the idea that workmen's compensation is as inevitable as it is equitable. The problem must, if possible, be worked out so that in the transition stage it entails the least possible hardship on all parties concerned in the reorganization ; but it must be worked out in such a way that it shall accomplish the purpose for which it is designed.

# THE JAPANESE FROM A WOMAN'S POINT OF VIEW

It was at the special request of the editors of The Outlook that this unconventional, conversational, and in our judgment exceedingly entertaining account of Japanese life and character was written. Obviously, the article makes no attempt to deal with Japan in a scientific or learned way. The author had rather unusual opportunities to see the domestic and social sides of the Japanese—their homes, habits, prejudices, ways of thinking and acting, and especially their attitude toward foreigners and views upon foreign customs and manners. Just as Mrs. Hugh Fraser ten years ago or so gave us in her book "An Englishwoman in Japan" a more realizing sense of how the Japanese feel and act than had been gained from any ethnologist or other solemn professor, so the present writer, an American woman, brings us very close, as it seems to us, to the true Japanese man and woman of the present day. Just at this time, when the discussion as to the admission of Japanese children into American schools and of Japanese labor into American markets is filling the newspapers, it is peculiarly interesting to get this direct and lively narrative of Japanese home life.—THE EDITORS.

YOU ask me, "What do I think of the Japanese?" Perhaps you think you are asking a simple question and will get a simple reply, but you will not. I could say concisely and literally, I think *everything* of them, but you would have no idea of the field of likes and dislikes that my everything would cover. I simply adore them—in spots—and often, metaphorically speaking, have sat at their feet in my profound admiration and respect. On the other hand, no other people in the world, high or low class, have ever exasperated me to such a degree. There have been moments when it seemed as if nothing less than a Russian knout in my hand would ever relieve my mind. I have asked myself again and again, Why is it, when I admire and appreciate these people as I do, that I do not like them better than I do?

If one runs through Japan taking in the cherry-blossom-fairyland-time, one is simply in love with everything; but if one stays longer, and begins to feel a desire to come near to the people, to understand them and be one of them, one is lost in misunderstandings. A thousand years would be no better than a day in which to learn the ins and outs of the Japanese character, for, paradoxical as it may seem, the better you know them the less you know them.

Without exaggeration, one can say of Japan's people as well as of her climate everything that is good and everything that is bad, and substantiate this contradictory statement by more than a hundred illustrations each way. The good is very, *very* good and the bad is horrid—that is, if we judge them by our own infallible standards of conduct. When the Japanese considers us from his point of view, he no doubt considers us commercially and materially very, *very* good and useful, but morally and artistically horrid.

If I give you examples in the contrasts between our customs and habits of thought and theirs, you will better understand the complexities in drawing any sweeping conclusions for or against them.

The American, with his pre-natal consciousness of being "IT," has no sympathy for any other point of view in life or thought than his own. We simply cannot believe that a Japanese thinks the fine fresh color in the cheeks of American girlhood coarse and common; that our erect carriage of the body with chins up is an unbecoming flaunting of, to him, inelegant independence; that our method of dress, with the small waist, which so plainly emphasizes the distinctions in sex, is immodest; that the charm, vivacity, and responsiveness of our women are unwomanly and undesirable; and that in our Sunday-go-to-meeting garments we are the most ludicrous sights in the world. This, though, is what every Japanese thinks, unless he has fallen under imperial, diplomatic, or coast town influences. Then compare the codes of polite conduct. Ours is not national but a go-as-you-please, individual affair, elastic, spontaneous, and responsive, depending largely upon environment, sometimes upon birth and good breeding; while the Japanese is a cut-and-dried, non-changeable, national affair, a code of etiquette with an elaborate ritual that is functional in act, mode of speech, and phraseology. Bows are of a prescribed lowness and length of time in posture according to rank. There is a language for the coolie, o..e for the upper classes, and one to acquire if you are presented at court; even the inevitable smile is an etiquettical form.

Whatever the tides may do in Japan, *time* waits, while all men, women, and children perform the rite of good manners. The high-class woman in the first-class railway compartment, after her don-a-san has exercised his lordly prerogative and gone out ahead of her, arises with quiet ease, makes low waist bows to her fellow-travelers of different lengths in time according to the high or low degree of those she is bowing to, and leaves the train with a calm that rises superior to all consideration of the brief stops of a flyer.

The maid whom you invite to return to her home is the subject of polite consideration from the moment it is known that she is going until the last moment when her belongings are piled on to a man-cart and she takes her departure. All the rest of the serving household stop their individual occupations to honor her by doing nothing. She dons the kimono appropriate to the occasion, drinks tea and eats sweetmeats separately with each companion, smokes several small pipes of good will, makes profound obeisance to don-a-san, och-san, cook-san, boy-san, and all the other sans, and departs in the full glory of a functional farewell. The other servants may all have been strangers; she may not be of their class, nor good, nor honest, nor comfortable to live with, but farewell courtesies are her hereditary right. Our method of

speeding the going of an unworthy servant and only showing consideration for a worthy one, whom we have liked and respected, a Japanese would be unable to understand as being more sincerely polite than his own.

The rickisha man will converse indefinitely with another servant, while you wait, with no idea that you think he is unmannerly.

The man in the train with a heavy bronchial cold will expectorate before your face and eyes, because he is performing a necessary act and it would be more polite to perform it than not to.

The servant who always cheerfully replies, " Yes, madam," when he should emphatically say, " No, madam," does so with polite intent and not at all meaning to annoy or deceive you. He would willingly have said, " No, madam," had he only understood that the truth would have been more convenient than his idea of politeness. If you unexpectedly run into some one in a state of half-dress, you ignore each other as entirely as if you both were invisible bodies; you do the same if you meet under the circumstances of performing some occupation that is considered beneath your dignity. The friend who dries his naked body in the sun on the beach after a sea bath may be looked at, but is never greeted or recognized.

The Japanese have a code of ethics that applies from birth to death and on through all eternity, which provides a rule for customs in dress, habits, religion, morals, and manners. Each season has its own flower for decoration, its own religious observances, duties, and games. Twice a year you fly kites! Twice a year you play battledore and shuttlecock with gayly colored feather cocks and battledores done up in silken raiment. Once a year little girls play with the ancestral dolls brought out from the godowns (or storehouses), and little boys play with huge fish. Once a year you set your house in order and prepare food for the annual visitation of the spirits of your dead. Once you clean house, and no unkind authority interferes with your putting all your worldly possessions into the middle of the street, while you sweep all the bad out and make ready to gather in the good of the new year; and one glorious *once*, every man Jack in the Empire may drink saki to his heart's delight, regardless of results. A year between drinks makes for a sobriety that might recommend itself to temperance organizations.

In the early spring the women put on blue and white cotton kimonos, and the shops are filled with such artistic fabrics that one longs to buy everything in sight—but then that is one's chronic state of mind when in Japan! The babies wear for two weeks after birth solferino pink; from that time on a gorgeous riot of pinks, yellows, blues, and reds are worn until eighteen; then, as you are getting on in years, you wear softer, delicate shades in kimono and obi. When you are married, as you should be by the time you are twenty-two, you wear sober colors and wonderful silvery moonlight-gray obis, and always on ceremonial occasions a black kimono. When you reach the feebleness of sixty years, you are free and independent, honorable, and can cut your hair short, wear scarlet, and do anything you will in the few remaining days of your life. The arrangement of the hair indicates maidenhood or marriage, and in life you fold your kimono together in front one way, and in death you fold it over the other. It is a source of great disturbance to your maid if you make the mistake of not knowing just when you are alive or dead, and it is the more confusing because you seem to come down one morning dead and another living. You will perceive that the only time the Japanese has no rule of three to guide him is when he runs off his hereditary etiquettical track into the complication of foreign relations.

It is generally conceded that the human character is formed on certain logical lines; it is either positive or negative in its tendencies to weakness or strength. If you are a lazy person, you cannot be a supremely industrious one; if you are honest, you are not dishonest; if selfish, you are not generous. But each Japanese character is a special study in the combination of contradictions. The Japanese is both quick and slow, exact and inexact, selfish and generous, honest and dishonest. Characteristics common to the na-

tion are untiring patience, perfect control, and dogged persistence and indomitable determination to do each his own way. I trust you will pardon slang if I remark that for pigheadedness the Japanese takes the cake of the world. He has plenty of hard common sense, and enjoys a good story as well as we. He says that he is full of sentiment, but I don't think he is; he thinks *hard*, and he can hold his tongue, which we can't. At least, in Japan the official class are close-mouthed and the common people talk, while with us the officials talk and the common people don't.

When a Japanese thinks any subject out and decides a certain course to be just and right, he performs it uninfluenced by circumstance, feeling, or sentiment. The occasional American who beats his wife does so in heat of passion and momentary excitement; the occasional Japanese who beats his wife beats her without heat of passion and with thoughtful intention, because she has done some wrong act. He may love her well, but she deserves punishment and he proceeds to give it without temper, and throughout the performance he speaks gently to her and smiles according to the rules of national etiquette.

He thinks that to drown or chloroform a cat or dog is inhuman and cruel, but he will drop an animal into a deep, dry well and let it die a slow but natural death of starvation without the slightest compunction or any intention to be cruel. Indeed, he will do it to save the animal from the foreigner who would inhumanly use chloroform.

In his own interest he is as selfish as any human being can be, but in his care for his parents, for the children of dead relatives or friends, and in sharing with them in some misfortune, he is not only generous but he looks upon the additional burden as a duty to be cheerfully undertaken.

Some characteristics the same as our own he puts to a different use and with such a different method in reasoning that we would not recognize them as our own. He lets "the other fellow do the worrying" as often as we, but in a different way. If you are cheated in business relations, it's your lookout. He really has no intention to be dishonest in selling you a cracked cup or vase, a leaking jar, or a spotted yard or yards of silk. It's your affair. His ability to sell you cracked cups and leaking jars is purely and simply an evidence of his business acumen. If you discover the imperfection, he willingly and smilingly replaces it, and cannot understand your annoyance at having to retrace your four-mile rickisha steps to have the wrong made right, especially when you were too stupid to attend to the matter at the proper time—when you bought the article. No Scotchman or Jew ever more keenly loves or enjoys his close bargain in which there is a chance that he may get the best of you ; but in other ways his integrity is unimpeachable. In all the time I was there I never had a thing stolen in hotels or my own house. One continually hears of great business contracts carried on with absolute square dealing. Foreigners will say that they would rather deal with Japanese banks than foreign ones. The Scotchman who built one of the electric roads in Tokyo said that he had been in Japan seven times, and had had enormous deals in which the most scrupulous honesty was observed in every transaction. Japanese boys who look to be not more than eight or ten years old are employed in banks and shops, and are intrusted with thousands of dollars for deposit. The rickisha boy will run his legs nearly off to return a package accidentally left in the " ricky." Your house-boy's accounts are always straight. The poorest dealer in the street fairs invariably makes the right change. And, on the whole, I fancy, as a nation they are as honest as we used to be.

Every Japanese feels that he is as surely born with certain inalienable rights as that he is born with two arms and two legs ; and he is so engrossed in his own rights that he has not much time to study the rights of his employer. One of these rights is respecting his special perquisites ; every working person has them. The cook who makes a per cent. on all food bought has no idea of being dishonest either in the money taken or in the wasting of his employer's time in spending all between whiles in bargaining. Your lordly boy has a per cent.

from every bill paid, and does not scorn to walk out and demand his largess from the poor little coolie woman who grubs up weeds from the grass at fifteen cents a day. If you try to slide out, unknown to your guardian-angel boy-san, and slip a gift into little coolie's hand, it is always a failure, for boy-san, who is never far off, appears in time to discover what is going on. Graft in Japan, as here, is not paid much attention to until it grows to unreasonable proportions in the households of the wealthy.

In the Japanese way, servants are devotion itself ; they have separate quarters which they regard as their own, where you are not expected to investigate, and which are gradually filled to repletion with an accumulation of relatives in assorted sizes—parents, grandparents, children, wife, a few aunts, uncles, and cousins, perhaps a stray friend, and sometimes a servant for the servant's family.

Your servants expect and wish to perform every possible service for you. I have seen a Japanese mother holding her little child while one maid fed it from a bowl held by another maid, and a third would be fanning them all. They are always on duty, night and day, and they jealously guard all your belongings, feel a pride in your position, look into all your boxes and drawers to know what you have, and show a childish delight in all your purchases ; but no wages, nor love, nor training would ever induce one to do what he was told to do, in the way he was told to do it. That an American employer, paying higher wages than any Japanese ever would, has the right to have things done the way he orders them done would never enter the Japanese mind, and he is truly quite unconscious that in this he is simply horrid. You say to your boy, " Zuki, I much hurry ; take rickisha and come back quick ;" you know he can do the errand within an hour, but you wait three, and Zuki gravely tells you, " Shop he very slow," but you know that Zuki-san put the "ricky" money in his pocket and walked. He doesn't think it dishonest, because he reasons that " you were willing to pay and he was willing to walk and save the money." If you try to explain and expostulate, boy-san will smile, bow low, and say, "Very sorry I make mistake," but "mistakes" go on happening until the days heap up into years. There was once a day when there had been so many mistakes that I was cold with exasperation, and bethought me of trying Japanese calm myself, and I really believed that I scored a point. I took a long breath and then said in gentle, most beguiling tones, "Toku Taro, you very smart boy." Toku Taro bridled with pride, bowed low, and said, " Yes ! yes ! madam." " You like American money ?" " Yes ! yes ! madam," Toku Taro murmurs; then in oily tones I went on to say, " Yes, you very smart boy—if you stupid boy I forgive mistakes, but you very smart; and now, to help you remember not to make mistakes, I will pay American money when you do American way, but when you do Japanese way I pay Japanese money," and this time we both smiled and bowed as the audience was over. Another inalienable prerogative is that you must give boy-san your entire confidence, turn yourself inside out as to motives for orders, reasons for your acts; the wheres, whens, and whys of every move must be elaborately explained. You are not to act independently of him; and when you do, you are made to suffer various disagreeable consequences. He cannot understand the American way of acting without talk, or that he isn't in your mind at all, or that you supposed he knew things from having heard them talked of in the family. If you turn one away for reasons good to yourself but not to him, he will, by various ingeniously skillful methods, prevent you from getting any one else; but if he leaves of his own desire, he will do all he can to fill his place.

You often hear the Japanese speak of each other as lazy, but I do not think them lazy, rather that they are wasteful of time. The maid or boy who has a morning caller stops all work, which it is impolite to go on with, and will smoke and talk for hours, but will sit up late into the night to do the work neglected in the morning. The Japanese worker may sleep in the day, but he makes his time good in the long run, and there is no street in Japan where you will not find men and women at work up to midnight; and in all the large manufacturing plants they work ten hours the same as many of our men do, with even a shorter noon hour for lunch.

All sense of exact time has been left out of the Japanese composition, and you must plan for a sliding scale in all appointments. If a man keeps you waiting two hours, he is serenely unconscious of anything being out of the way; or a he, or a she, will as serenely appear two hours ahead of time; the man due at nine A.M. turns up at seven A.M., and the lady who is to make calls with you at four arrives at two. The workman due Saturday morning to fit in outside windows turns up Sunday evening at seven, and even though it is snowing and blowing he cannot understand why you are not willing to have him stay and work until midnight. The packer, after many conferences, will set his own day and faithfully promise to arrive with his men at nine A.M., but at eleven he will saunter in alone to see what is to be done. The interpreter-secretary would say, " Please don't say four o'clock so quick; say between three and five o'clock." When he was late and I not on hand, he would cheerfully go without his dinner, sleep on his cushion, and wait all hours until my return. If he were willing to wait for me, why should not I as willingly wait for him ?

On the other hand, they hold the foreigner to strict account in various ways. If it happened that I did not have as many pieces of clothing in the laundry as I was wont to, the noble-faced Tsura would promptly appear, bow her dusky head to the floor, ask for my honorable condition, of don-a-san's honorable old age, and, after taking an hour of time and more of my honorable temper, she would indicate that my laundry had not as many pieces as it should have; it might even up another week, or I might pay the same at the end of the month, but that would not do—there must be the same weekly number, whether I had them or not. If don-a-san sent his duck suits to a man laundry, Tsura heard of it through the Japanese friend's wireless before the day was over, and would promptly appear to ask the meaning of such a base act. Having a certified number of garments each Monday to ward off a week-end visit from Tsura finally got on my nerves, and my temper became so dishonorable that we separated, I paying the bill with a comforting margin and Tsura-san paying a farewell visit and presenting me with a delicious American cake. The laundryman would kindly expect laundry whenever he happened in; he'd wait, but that a definite day was more convenient to me was incomprehensible. Equally incomprehensible is the idea that your laundry is to be done to suit you, and not on the general principle that, although flannels are not to be starched, everything else is; that it's impossible to wear all your undergarments stiff as boards isn't an issue in the question of laundry. You may spend a fortune in the exquisite embroideries, but they are returned from the first washing ruined by starch and having been ironed flat on the top side; and a colored fabric never survives the first onslaught of Japanese washing fluid. You can well imagine that one is in a state of righteous rage most of the time, and what a moral support a Russian knout would have been; but one does not even have the satisfaction of showing disapproval. It does no good. The Japanese regards exhibition of temper as a huge joke, and treats you as if you were a sick baby—tries to smooth you down, or, happy thought! makes you a present. The present is the trump to play in every game, and when in doubt in Japan to give a present is a saving grace. Although you *are* made to mind your p's and q's, if you can make up your mind to put one side all independence and the pet little individual ways dear to your heart and let things be Japanese, you get excellent service; and not only that, but all your serving-sans announce their intention of returning to America with you. Persistence like that of the Japanese is not to be overcome except by the most exhausting strenuosity in fighting against it; and in all my experiences I was haunted by the story that Mr. William Jennings Bryan tells of the Japanese boy who wrote to him that he'd "read his sixteen-to-one speeches with so much interest that he wanted to go over to America to live with him." Mr. Bryan

replied immediately that his household was complete, and that it would be entirely impossible for him to arrange to have the boy come. Return mail brought word that the boy "had decided to come; that he knew he could make himself useful; and he would sail on such a steamer." Mr. Bryan then cabled a large-sized "No," not to come. But another three weeks saw boy-san at the Bryan front door. Persistence gained the day, and he was taken in, and still remains after many years. I had visions that I might not be able to withstand this persistence, and that some day I would be returning to the land of the blessed with a comet-like tail of kuramya-sans, Tsura-sans, and boy-sans who would insist upon following me.

The Japanese do not show feeling when we expect them to, and do show it when we do not. It fairly made my blood boil to see the wounded brought into Tokyo day after day, stretcher after stretcher carrying hundreds of pale-faced, maimed men slowly through the streets to the hospitals, with never a cheer or sound of approval from the solid lines of lookers-on. The foreign man who carried his hat in his hand and the foreign woman with tears running down her cheeks were such objects of curiosity that the helpless ones would turn their heads to stare at them. The Japanese populace would walk miles and flood the streets with banners and lanterns at the hours the wounded were expected, and then, when they arrived, the crowd did not do one blessed thing but stand and giggle.

They send their men off with the blare of trumpets and vociferous banzais, but when they return after having fought the good fight, their compatriots receive them with inane giggles.

There never was, to our minds, anything more pathetic than the war funerals. The solemn dirge, the slow-pacing horse of the dead officer, the son walking beside the small box on the gun-carriage that held the shattered particles of a father's body, and the war-widow in her soft white mourning garb and uncovered head, aroused one's deepest sympathy; but the long procession would slowly wend its way between compact masses of smiling faces and cheerful talk.

In many ways they show great respect for their dead, and pay calls at the last resting-place for years, leaving visiting-cards in small boxes which are placed in the cemetery lots for the purpose, and also leaving huge upright pickets of wood with names put on in black; some of the graves of the dead fairly bristled with these ten or twelve feet high pickets which stand upright in the ground. But when they come to tell you of a death in the family, they do so with smiling cheerfulness; when you show any natural concern, they become more giggly, and, thinking of your foreign ideas, will say, "Yes, yes, very sad." The giggle often gets on one's nerves as much as Tsura-san's week-end visits, and it is difficult to keep one's mind concentrated upon the fact that these people are feeling when they laugh in grief as we do when we cry, the more so because they also laugh for fun as we do; but when you settle down to thinking of it, it's pure custom whether you laugh or cry, and the Japanese really feels the same kind of sorrow with his laughter that we do with our tears.

He looks upon his physical body and its needs as just natural, a part of nature, like a tree or any growing thing that he is not responsible for: if it is more comfortable to be covered, all right, be covered; but if it is more comfortable to be *un*covered, all right, be *un*covered; he does not think of it either way—it's unimportant. On the other hand, the emotions that are controlled by the mind he hides behind a defensive cast-iron stoicism, and thinks it as indecent to uncover his feelings as we do to uncover our bodies. If he is suffering mentally or physically, he bears it unmoved; and he never makes any demonstration of affection in public. The characteristics of courage and fortitude are so common that to be without them would be shameful. The wounded men in the hospitals would drag themselves up to perform the rites of politeness, and then quite cheerfully show one the place where the ball had gone in; and the men who were returned to Tokyo because of illness and without a wound were so ashamed that they did not let their families know that they were in the hospitals. The laws

for keeping the body covered are of course obeyed as far as possible, but without an understanding of their meaning. The policeman who was discovered in the altogether on the sea-beach declared that he had obeyed the law, as he "had worn his trunks into the sea; that now he was only drying himself."

The Japanese has none of the Anglo-Saxon instinct which with us often takes the place of exact knowledge; he does not "catch on" with our readiness, and he thinks with arduous round-about-ness and cannot approach a subject squarely and at once. Our way of plumping into the middle of things is most disconcerting; he likes to be able to get ready by degrees. He says that our houses crowded with furniture, pictures, and good and bad junk are confusing to the eye and demoralizing to all concentration in thought. He depends upon the soft light, the perfect proportion, and the simpleness in his homes and temples to promote contemplation. He desires to ruminate and to chew his cud of thought over and over. One beautiful object in art absorbs him, and when his mind is filled to satisfaction with the color, outline, or story, he removes the precious object to his godown and brings out another to brood over.

The child is taught early in life to reverence all things in art, and to obey. He is literally to do his duty in that state of life to which he is called, and if happiness comes his way it is to be enjoyed as a God-given day in June, not as a right, but as an incidental ray of light amid the shadows of life. Everything that is taught in schools, manufactories, or in the field is taught slowly, with patient reiteration—there are no short cuts to knowledge. The officer who drilled raw recruits hours and days in our great garden or in the adjoining street never raised his voice in command, but he evidently went over the same ground of instruction hour after hour, day after day. In a long winded talk he would explain what he wanted done, then he would go through the movements himself, then with each man separately, and finally all together. The practice of running in companies over the great Military Reservation was kept at continually, but with an informality impossible to our ideas of military training. A man who was quickly winded sat down where he fell out of ranks and fell in when he recovered, and no one howled at him or jumped on him. The eminent surgeon who lectured Fridays in the Red Cross would gently reiterate the same thing for an hour—something we would have learned in a few moments. He wrote the proceeding on the blackboard, then he talked it, then he would pick up a piece of cloth, cut a bandage or whatever he needed, and again painstakingly go over the same ground demonstrating the act. No detail was omitted—"you must not talk, laugh, cough, or sneeze upon these rolls." The audience of princesses, duchesses, countesses, and lesser titles patiently listened and afterwards practiced folding and refolding emergency packets, each one of thousands and thousands to be folded exactly the same way. I asked why there would be any hurt if once in a while the right side flap was under side instead of top side, but the surgeon said, "No, the exact uniformity must be maintained;" and I wished that that surgeon had had the training of Japanese shoemakers and tailors. A shoemaker might make you a hundred pairs of shoes, but he would take your measure carefully for each pair, and each pair would be a little larger than the other; when you rose in wrath and objected, the next pair would be too small. The tailor also takes a new measure for each article made, and gradually pares edges down until the garment is always a little too small or a little too large. That you prefer your shirt-waist to fit your individual size is quite too unreasonable for consideration. All shirt-waists look alike to him, whether in sizes thirty-two or forty.

No Japanese has learned a thing until he understands it; he cannot learn by rote, nor study with his eyes without use of his mind; and he has the infinite patience to teach, and to learn, until understanding is complete. There is nothing that is mechanical that he cannot learn to understand and to do to perfection. No mechanism is so intricate or delicate that he cannot reproduce it.

He will follow any design if you have the patience to explain it slowly, over and over again and then again, until he says "he knows;" after that he will work with a skill and deftness that are unsurpassed. A body of workmen will accomplish by hand and physical power alone the laying of huge stone walls and foundations, with a skill, rapidity, and quiet impossible to us, with the most modern mechanical appliances.

I doubt if any Japanese convert to Christianity ever understands his new belief any better than the policeman understood the law for bathing-clothes. He may become a good Japanese Christian, but not a British or an American Christian; he cannot regard Sunday as a church day and not one set apart for the doing of odd jobs, nor can he replace his hereditary ideas of politeness with plain truthfulness. Sad to relate, none of us wished to take our servants from the ranks of converts. A maid came to me one day when I was making a change in my household and brought me excellent recommendations; she also said that she could cook, had lived in the family of an American physician two years, and had learned English. She stood by my side and in beguiling confidence murmured, "Beef-steaky, oysters, onions, potatoes, hot biscuits, pancakes, and apple pie." Pancakes and apple pie carried the day, and I engaged her, even though I had to wait a while for her. The first morning after her arrival, when coffee did not appear, I went down to investigate, and found my one treasure, the dear little Samurai maid, in a splendid fit of giggles, but there was no cook and no coffee. Towards noon cook-san trotted in with a beaming smile and a prayer-book in her hand, and said, in a tone that showed that she expected to meet with heartfelt sympathy, "I Christian, I go church." My heart sank into my boots—to have waited two whole weeks for a Christian cook-san! Time quickly developed the fact that she could not recognize "beef-steaky" or any other of the delectable eatables she had mentioned by sight, that she had no idea of cooking, and that she did not speak or understand more than a few words of English. She dusted my books with soap and water, went to church, and obligingly stood by learning English while I did the cooking, and when I told her to go she said that she did not want to, that she thought we got on very well, and I could keep on teaching her to speak English and to cook. When I declined both to teach and to pay the wages of "an excellent cook who spoke good English," to my relief she declined to stay. I can assure you that a background of time makes this episode far more amusing than it seemed when it happened. The day after, when on my way to hunt up a native heathen cook-san, I fell in with another Christian. A little Japanese woman shoved herself over on the car seat until she was near me and looked up at me with a smile. When I had smiled in return, she ventured to open conversation by saying, " You American ?" " Yes." " You live Yokohama ?" " No, Tokyo." " You missionary ?" " No." Then with pride she announced, " I Christian—Bible very nice book ;" to both of these remarks I smiled a response. She then said, " Every one in your country very good." With surprise in my tone, I replied, " Oh, no, not every one." This evidently surprised her, for she insisted, " Every one very happy in your country ;" again I replied, " No, not every one." But once more she tried, " Every one going to be married in your country very happy," and with joy I replied " Yes," which unfortunately encouraged her to say, " Every one in your country very good, very happy, and very what you say very rich," and my inconvenient sense of truth made me reply again, " No, not every one." At this she looked at me with wonder and said, " You Christian ?" While I was wondering what in the world I was, anyhow, the train stopped and the little woman got off. The general idea seems to be that Christianity has made America a perfect paradise. A bright young student said to me one day, " You seem to be very good in your country ; you haven't any one left who needs religious instruction, or you would not send so many missionaries over here."

The serious bar sinister in our relations with the Japanese is their lack of warm-hearted responsiveness ; they are never really companionable, and never by hook or crook let you find out what they are really thinking. They smile and smile, but with the mouth alone, once in a while perhaps with the eyes, but never with the heart or soul. If a man wore goggles and peeked over a high stone wall at you, you'd know about as much of how he really looked as you do of the mind of a Japanese after you have talked to him a month. He keeps his feelings in cold storage, and they don't thaw out except on the edges of polite society talk of wind and weather. It's the more exasperating because you know he has heaps of interesting ideas and thoughts—and then he's often good-looking, and in such immaculate attire, and gives such an impression generally of being a man of the world that one expects him to be simply delightful ; but it is a bore continually to bump your head against the stone wall of his reserve.

The only particularly free speech of these people is in their criticism of the acts of the Diet or the acts of the Government. Through the press the common people have their frank say upon every subject.

When you add Japanese dogged persistence and patience together, you have a strong combination for good and evil acts, and I have not decided yet that we do wish to make an American citizen of him. He can take our merchandise and missionaries and welcome as long as he does not want t come and investigate Christian principles on their own soil. We'll be glad to help him progress as long as he progresses over into Korea and Manchuria ; and we do want him to keep an open door for us in his beautiful park-like country where we all love to play.

Not understanding underlying cause and effect in each other's character-formation will be another stumbling-block in the way of sympathetic relations, and whatever our friendship for Japan may become, it will have to be a friendship based upon mutual misunderstanding and an amiable agreement to disagree.

As Zuki-san writes, " Please you pardon my disrectful long letter," and believe me     Regardfully yours,

          AN OBSERVER.

# FRÉDÉRIC MISTRAL'S MEMORIES
## OF HIS EARLY LIFE[1]

**M**ISTRAL begins his memoirs by describing his native village and the home of his fathers: "As far back as I can remember, I had before my eyes, over yonder to the southward, a mountainous barrier whose crests, slopes, cliffs, and valleys wore from matins to vespers shifting, undulating hues of blue, now dark, now light, now dark again—the chain of the Alpilles girdled with olive-trees like the clustering rocks of Greece, a veritable belvedere of glorious legends. . . . My village, Maillane, occupies the middle of a large and rich plain, which, in memory, perhaps, of the consul Caius Marius, is still called Le Caieou. The old homestead in which I was born, fronting the Alpilles and touching the Clos-Crema, was called the *Mas du Juge*. It was a holding which required for its proper maintenance four yoke of oxen, a head driver, several plowmen, a shepherd, a domestic (whom we called 'the aunt'), a few workers hired by the month, and, in the busy seasons, many day-workers, male and female, for the care of the silkworms, the weeding, the haying, the harvesting, the vintage, the seed-sowing, or the olive-gathering."

Mistral's father, for whom he has such unbounded admiration that he usually refers to him as "the master" or "*mon seigneur père*," "was the last," to use Mistral's own language, "of the patriarchs of Provence." Though bluff and gruff to a degree, after the manner of the old-time paterfamilias of Provence, he was profoundly religious, and so hospitable and charitable withal that the poor added to their prayers at his funeral this petition: "May as many angels accompany him to heaven as he gave us loaves of bread!"

Mistral's account of his father's first meeting with his mother is almost Biblical in its beautiful simplicity, of which a translation can give but a vague idea:

One year, on the day of Saint John, Master François Mistral was in the midst of his wheat-fields, in which a band of reapers were mowing with sickles. A swarm of gleaners were following the rakers gathering up the ears which had escaped the rakes. Suddenly my *seigneur père* remarked a beautiful girl who stood aloof hesitating, as if she were afraid to glean like the others. He went towards her and said:

"Mignonne, who is your father? What is your name?"

The maiden answered:

"I am the daughter of Étienne Poulinet, the mayor of Maillane. My name is Délaide."

"What!" exclaimed my father, "the daughter of Poulinet, who is the mayor of Maillane, goes gleaning?"

"Master," she replied, "we are a large family, six girls and two boys, and our father, although he is well off, when we ask him for money to deck ourselves out with, says to us, 'My dears, if you want finery, earn it.' And that is why I have come to glean."

Six months after this meeting, which recalls the ancient scene of Ruth and Boaz, the gallant yeoman solicited the hand of Délaïde from Master Poulinet, and I was born of this marriage.

The parents named the baby Frédéric in memory of a poor little fellow who had done their love-errands cleverly for them while they were "keeping company," and who had died of sunstroke shortly after their marriage.

When the mother took this baby out in her arms to the houses of the relatives and neighbors (in accordance with an old Provençal custom), two eggs, a hunch of bread, a pinch of salt, and a match were ceremoniously offered to him, with the following sacramental words: "Mignon, be plump as an egg, be good as bread, be wholesome as salt, be straight as a match." At six months of age, on St. Joseph's Day (in accordance with another old Provençal custom), this same baby was delivered from his swaddling-clothes, and, supported by leading-strings, was made to take his first steps upon the altar of St. Joseph in the village church, while his godmother chanted, "Avene, avene, avene!" ("Come, come, come!")

The two chief delights of Frédéric as a small boy were sharing the tasks of the farm-hands and listening to the

[1] *Mes Origines: Mémoires et Récits de Frédéric Mistral.* Plon-Nourrit et Cie, Paris.

marvelous Provençal legends, religious and secular, which his good mother told him while she held him on her knees and spun.

The day before Christmas the little Frédéric did his little part in bringing in the Yule log, assisted at its benediction, and listened spellbound to the stories that were told before its blaze while the family were sitting up waiting for the midnight mass. On New Year's Day he aided in the distribution of bread to the poor which his father never failed to make. On the eve of Epiphany he set forth on the highroad with other toddlers in the hope of meeting "*Les Rois Mages*" (as the "Wise Men of the East" are called in France), who came annually to Maillane to worship the child Jesus; and in this quest he trudged up hill and down dale until he fancied he saw them in the fleeting pageantry of the sunset.

After a year or so in the village school, in which he distinguished himself chiefly by his truancies, Frédéric was sent to a boarding-school in a ruined abbey perched high among the mountains, where he and his companions led a half-savage existence, to the great profit of their constitutions and imaginations if not of their book-learning. "After a little," Mistral says of his sojourn at this school, "we became wild, *ma foi* as a litter of game rabbits. . . . The heights round about were covered with thyme, with rosemary, with asphodel, with box, and with lavender. . . . The odor which rose from them under the sun's rays intoxicated us. . . . The

study hour over, we fluttered away like partridges up the hills and across the valleys."

From his next boarding-school, in the city of Avignon, Frédéric ran away home because his yearning for the open became more than he could bear.

In his last boarding-school (likewise at Avignon), one of his teachers was Roumanille, a Provençal poet who encouraged the poetic ambition the boy was beginning to feel stirring within him, and inspired him with a mighty yearning to restore the lost prestige of the language of Provence. Thereafter he took more kindly to study, and when he had finished his education at the Law School of Aix he deliberately returned for good and all to Maillane, firmly resolved to consecrate himself exclusively to the rejuvenation and exaltation of Provence. It seemed to him that his love of nature and of simple, unspoiled human nature could nowhere be gratified so fully as in the primitive atmosphere of his native village, where he could witness, and play a part in, "the majestic movements of agriculture, eternally hard, but eternally independent and calm."

Mistral offers the rare and edifying spectacle of a life in perfect harmony with his creative work. Indifferent to the allurements of the French capital, he has remained faithful to his mission as he has conceived it, and by this loyalty to an ideal he has become not only the pride and the glory of Provence, but one of the first men of France.

# *Comment on Current Books*

*Actual Russia*

What is a verst? Who are isvoschiks? We look in vain for a glossary to explain the interesting text in this well printed, illustrated, and mapped book, brimful of little-known facts about Russian towns. For example, as showing German influence, the author instances the town of Yaroslav, which boasts of possessing more millionaire tradesmen than any other town in Russia; all of its best posts of the intellectual kind are filled without exception by Germans. As to Kishinev, a name always to be associated with a frightful massacre, the author says: "It is as untrue

that the atrocities which horrified the world were sanctioned by the Russians as a nation, as it is untrue that the American nation lynched and burned its negroes at the stake. . . . But Russia must not drive her Jews away, nor must she try to stop their advance or turn them into Nihilists. *They are a necessary element of her own prosperity* [the italics are our own]. They are like the sharp tool indispensable to the skilled workman, but ready to cut like a razor if not handled properly." The author's description of persons is not so prominent as her description of places, but there are occasional piquant anecdotes; for instance, that about the vases in the Hermitage at St. Petersburg. The vases were once sent by Emperor Alexander I. as a present to the Tycoon of Japan, but returned by the latter with the announcement that "it is impossible for the Tycoon to accept a present from an inferior." As is appropriate, the author of that clever sketch of the Trans-Siberian Railway, "A Ribbon of Iron," dedicates her present volume to Prince Khilhov, who is regrettably enough now only the *ex* Minister of Ways and Communications in Russia. (Russia: Travels and Studies. By Annette M. B. Meakin. The J. B. Lippincott Company, Philadelphia. $4, net.)

*Advice to Investors*　On this subject an abundance of good counsel is here given to a class of people the majority of whom need it. The book is packed with information concerning rates of interest, stocks and bonds, cycles of prosperity and depression, signs of fair weather and foul, critical points, when to buy and when to sell. Mr. Hall desires to safeguard the interests of honest investors exposed to "operators" who go gunning for them, and he warns the reader as to certain pirates who infest Wall Street, several of whom he names. It is a good service to chart and light the navigable waters of a legitimate business endangered by buccaneers as well as by hidden reefs and shoals. The point open to serious criticism is likely to occur to any conscience that is both reflective and scrupulous. The title-page, "A Fortune at Fifty-five," points toward it. The second chapter brings it to the front, showing how a young man with $1,000 in hand may make it $1,000,-000 at middle age by buying good securities cheap and selling them dear. To buy for less and sell for more is perfectly legitimate in a market in normal conditions. But to buy cheap and sell dear in a market whose normal conditions are disturbed, *regardless of the causes* of cheapness and dearness, no scrupulous conscience will approve. And Mr. Hall states that the security market is "not left to itself," but is unscrupulously interfered with by "manipulators." He has apparently not reflected that his recommendation to investors to avail themselves of the gainful opportunities so created is simply advice to profit by other men's dishonorable methods. (How Money is Made in Security Investments. By Henry Hall. Address Orders to Author, 52 Broadway, New York. $1.50.)

*Balboa*　The capital series of "Heroes of American History" already comprises accounts of Columbus, Cortés, Pizarro, and Ferdinand de Soto. Vasco Nuñez de Balboa is the appropriate subject of a new volume, for Balboa was perhaps the most high-minded and generous of all the Spanish-American soldiers of fortune. It is strange that less seems to have been written about him than about any other explorer in his class except Ponce de Leon. As Mr. Ober says, both these names are familiar to every student of history, both are well known even to the casual reader, but both have been neglected by the biographer. Young and old readers alike should be interested in the present volume, especially in its chief dramatic episode, the discovery of the Pacific. (Vasco Nuñez de Balboa. By Frederick A. Ober. Harper & Brothers, New York. $1.50, net.)

*The Coming of the Saints*　The beginnings of Christianity in western Europe no historian has recorded. The silences of history are in the present volume filled in with the voices and echoes of tradition. Of these, skillful use has been made in this volume, in which the kernel of truth is critically sought for under the husk of legend. The book of Acts testifies (viii. 4) to a missionary dispersion of Christians resulting from their persecution in Judea. Paul arriving at Rome found a church already there. Among the pioneers in France tradition includes the sisters of Bethany and their brother Lazarus. What is of special interest to us, the tradition which attributes to the Joseph in whose tomb Jesus was laid the planting of Christianity where Glastonbury Abbey stands, is as strongly supported as any. As to this, the author sees significance in the names of Hebrew origin which are prominent in the stories of the Arthurian knights localized in that part of England, and in the "marked and undeniable" traces of Jews in Cornwall. When he takes into account the fame which for centuries has attracted toilsome pilgrimages to spots associated with the names of reputed Christian path-breakers into heathendom, it is difficult to deny that historical fact lies somewhere between utter rejection of the traditions and entire acceptance of them. These "studies in early Christian history and tradition" are marked by ample learning and good judgment, and afford ground enough for the religious imagination to indulge in some reconstruction of the unrecorded past. (The Coming of the Saints. By John W. Taylor. E. P. Dutton & Co., New York. $3, net.)

*Comparative Ethics*　This substantial work by a former tutor and fellow of Oxford exhibits as the basis of a theory of moral evolution the rules of conduct and ideals of life that have obtained in the successive stages of moral development. The first volume reviews forms of social organization, ideals and practices in the fields of law and justice, of relations between the sexes, communities, and classes, and finally of property and poverty—thus presenting a history of advancing conceptions of good in a comparative point of view. The second volume is devoted to a history of the growth of ideas concerning the grounds of morality, and of the religious, scientific, and other elements affecting them. These historical facts being common property, one is not concerned with them here, however interesting, but with the generalizations based upon them. The reality they reveal is regarded "neither as a providentially ruled order, nor as a process of fortuitous combinations and dissolutions, but as the movement towards self-realization of a mind appearing under rigidly limited conditions of physical organization in countless organisms, and arriving for the first time at a partial unity in the consciousness of a common humanity with a common aim." Furthermore, " in this conception of a self-directing humanity lies the basis of scientific ethics." And this humanity is not merely the totality of human beings, not an aggregation, but an organism and its animating spirit, " a spirit subject to conditions, and achieving its full growth only by mastering them." But whence is this spirit of humanity does not appear. What it is is apparent only in its synonym "mind." Evidently it has only in modern times come to self-consciousness, and is still an infant crying for the light. In the long historic development no ultimate purposiveness is recognized; on the contrary, "the disorders and reactions of history are fatal to a purely teleological view of the world process." Thus the immanent mind which so slowly comes to self-consciousness in humanity is left, like Melchizedek, without a progenitor. The apparently non-theistic philosophy of moral evolution which ends thus is a torso, all complete but the head. (Morals in Evolution. By L. T. Hobhouse. Part I. and II. Henry Holt & Co., New York. $2.50, net.)

**Complete Works of Abraham Lincoln**　The publication of Volumes XI. and XII. complete this very important and satisfactory work, which bears the name of The Gettysburg Edition. Volume XI. includes a speech of General Garfield on "Lincoln and Emancipation," a collection of letters and telegrams, the draft of a message which was never made public, and an indexed bibliography compiled by Mr. Daniel Fish, occupying nearly 240 pages, and of great value to students of Lincoln. Volume XII. presents an anthology of Lincoln's sayings, a chronological index, and a general index of all the volumes. These two volumes bring to an end a publication of permanent value, not only in American political history, but to American literature. (Complete Works of Abraham Lincoln. Edited by John G. Nicolay and John Hay. New and Enlarged Edition. Vols. XI. and XII. Francis D. Tandy Company, New York.)

**Dr. John**　Mr. Wardlaw Thompson tells us in his interesting volume some remarkable facts concerning that veteran missionary in China, Dr. Griffith John. It is notable that Dr. John has been able to overcome what might seem to normalists a possible handicap, namely, a very precocious religious life. At the tender age of eight he felt a conviction of sin. While a mere lad he became a Sunday-school teacher, and at fourteen a preacher. It is almost a relief to us to know that Dr. John himself acknowledges preaching at the age of fourteen to have been a failure. Nothing daunted, however, he began again at the age of sixteen, and now with apparent success. When he was twenty-two years old, he went to China, and has labored there ever since. While the book affords a glimpse of an interesting personality, its chief value to many may be found in its account of actual conditions in China, with special reference to the opium traffic, to the power of Confucianism, and to linguistic difficulties. Dr. John can certainly speak with authority as to all of these subjects, especially the last named, since his most important occupation has been in translating the Bible. In this, as in other tasks, we are given to understand that he has attempted a middle course between classical Chinese and the colloquial language, and that the result has justified that course. (Griffith John: The Story of Fifty Years in China. By R. Wardlaw Thompson. A. C. Armstrong & Son, New York. $1.50, net.)

**The Eastern Church**　Whether Greek, Russian, Balkan, or Syro-Arabian, the Eastern Church is of increasing interest to us. On the historical side this is evident in the greater attention paid by students of Church history to that curious quarrel which finally, in 1054, severed the Orthodox or Eastern Catholics from all Trinitarians, especially from the Roman or Western Catholics. On the practical side the interest is heightened by the presence in America of startlingly augmented numbers of Greeks, Russians, Rumanians, Bulgarians, Montenegrins, Serbs, and Syrians. The children of these immigrants are, as a rule, reared in our public schools, and it is often difficult to teach them the services of their Church in the languages of their parents, and still more so in old Slavonic or old Greek. The adoption of the English language in those services seems the sole solution of the problem of ministering to the wants of parishes whose members represent many Slav tongues and dialects, and where the children are being educated in the language of their parents' adopted country. Indeed, the policy of the Russian Church—now a thousand years old, and numbering nine-tenths of the hundred million members of the Eastern Church—has been to have its services celebrated in the tongues spoken in the lands inhabited by its members. Hence it is desired eventually to make English the language, in this country, of the many adherents of that Church. Under these circumstances the appearance of the Service Book, translated and compiled by Isabel Florence Hapgood and collated by her with the Service Books of the Greek Church, is timely. Her well printed and bound volume, a model of its kind, emphasizes the interesting and impressive features of the Eastern Church, whether one attends its services in Russia or Greece, Rumania or Servia or Syria. Following the Jewish pattern, the Eastern Church reckons its day from sunset. Hence worship begins with the Evening Service. This typifies Old Testament times as foreshadowing Christ, and precedes the liturgy of the morning, wherein Christ's life is symbolized. The present volume contains the order of services as prescribed for vespers, compline, matins, the communion, the great feasts, ordination, marriage, unction, "the Office at the Parting of the Soul from the Body," the burial of the dead, requiem offices, services for the founding and consecration of churches, thanksgivings, and various special prayers. The language of the prayers and in the liturgies is generally inspiring and often sublime; the translation is evidently vigorous. For the Scripture lessons, as translated into English, the King James's Version is used, and for the "Psalms and Verses" the Prayer-Book version of the Psalter. The Psalms should thus become more impressive than ever, chanted as they are by male voices only and without any instrumental music. The present volume affords a welcome survey of the events of the Russian Church year, of which the great feasts include Christmas and Easter, of course, and Epiphany, Transfiguration, Palm Sunday, Ascension, Pentecost, the Birth, Presentation, Annunciation, Purification, and Assumption of Mary, "the Birth-giver of God," and finally "the Exaltation of the Precious and Life-giving Cross." There are many lesser feasts. The uninitiated will appreciate Miss Hapgood's interesting prefatory chapter and various helpful notes on Eastern ecclesiastical symbolism; for instance, a single domed temple is a symbol of the Great Head of the Church; three domes typify the three Persons of the Trinity, and five symbolize Christ and the four Evangelists. Again, the lights always used in the Eastern Church, even if the service be performed in full sunlight, are "to show that the Lord, who dwells in light ineffable, illumines the world with spiritual radiance; to denote that the hearts of faithful believers are warmed by a flame of love toward God and his Saints; and also to show forth the spiritual joy and the triumph of the Church." Thus this laudable volume should be of value, not only to American ecclesiastics and their congregations, but also to students of liturgies and to sojourners in the various lands where the Eastern Church exists, and to all who would become better acquainted with its undeniable majesty, impressiveness, and exquisite symbolism of ritual. (Service Book of the Holy Orthodox-Catholic Apostolic (Greco-Russian) Church. Compiled, Translated, and Arranged by Isabel Florence Hapgood. Houghton, Mifflin & Co., Boston. $4, net.)

**German Religious Life** In his admirable "History of American Christianity" Dr. L. W. Bacon has done justice to the early life of the Lutheran and Reformed Churches planted here by colonists from Germany. With their colonial history, here given in somewhat larger detail, this volume gives an ample account of the earlier coming of the sects which had separated from the State Churches of Germany, as the Mayflower Pilgrims had separated from the Church of England. Of these the Mennonites, formerly known as Anabaptists, planted Germantown in 1683, and somewhat later came the first congregation of Dunkers (signifying, in German, immersionists). To the Mennonites is due the distinction of being the first protestants against American slavery. From the Dunker press came in 1745 the first Bible printed in this country in a European tongue. Sympathetically is the story of these "picturesque, mystical, pious folk" related, but with an expression of relief at ending the account of "ignorant and narrow-minded disputants, of pathetic or wrong-headed saints or solitaries." These, says Dr. Bacon, "furnished the material for that curious 'Pennsylvania Dutch' population which for more than two centuries has lain encysted, so to speak, in the body politic and ecclesiastic." The Moravians, the Methodists, and the German Churches during the Revolution are worthily commemorated in the concluding chapters of this interesting narrative. (German Religious Life in Colonial Times. By Lucy Forney Bittinger. J. B. Lippincott Company, Philadelphia.)

**The Heart of a Woman** A recent magazine article called attention to the nude in autobiography. The soul that yearns to expose its innermost recesses to our gaze is ever with us—filling the discreet with amazement. While there is nothing in the least objectionable in the Heart disclosing itself in these verses, there is also nothing of special value. The lines are of easy, rippling quality, and the sentiment is perhaps as perfectly exemplified in the poem called Prayer as in any one of the collection. Real passion never babbles. (The Heart of a Woman. By Almon Hensley. G. P. Putnam's Sons, New York.)

**A New Hampshire Politician** The biography of the late Senator Rollins involves the political history of New Hampshire for the eventful period of nearly thirty years subsequent to the birth of the Republican party. In that party he was a standard-bearer, and earned its rewards in preferment to public trusts, three times as a member of the House and once as Senator at Washington. A man of high probity, energy, and capacity, his Senatorial career would doubtless have been longer, as it deserved to be, but in New Hampshire the predilection for rotation in office, and certain personal ambitions, prevented. This memorial of his life is well deserved. In general, as presenting the political story of a generation that has just passed off the stage, it exhibits in the predominance of local and personal above National interests the adolescent stage of politics, from which more graduates into statesmanship are needed for the country's welfare. In the sketch given of Ruel Durkee readers of "Coniston" will recognize the prototype of Jethro Bass. (Life of Edward H. Rollins: A Political Biography. By James O. Lyford. Dana Estes & Co., Boston.)

**Pioneer Promoters** In the many volumes composing his "Historic Highways of America" Mr. Archer Butler Hulbert has deserved well of students of American geography and history. In the present single volume he again lays them under tribute. His province is still largely the same, a description of the doings of our early pioneer-promoters, but in this particular book he confines himself to the Middle West. The graphic quality of his text is heightened by a number of effective illustrations, mostly portraits, as is appropriate in a volume the consecutive chapters of which consider Washington, the promoter of Western investment; Richard Henderson, the founder of Transylvania; Rufus Putnam, the father of Ohio; George Rogers Clark, the founder of Louisville; Henry Clay, the promoter of the first American highway; Morris and Clinton, the fathers of the Erie Canal; Thomas and Mercer, rival promoters of canals and railways; Lewis and Clark, leaders of the expedition to the Far West, and also explorers of Louisiana; John Jacob Astor, the promoter of Astoria; and, finally, Marcus Whitman, the hero of Oregon. The book is a direct and forceful contribution to American history, and is well printed, as its text merits. (Pilots of the Republic. By Archer Butler Hulbert. A. C. McClurg & Co., Chicago.)

**Principles of English Verse** Professor Lewis announces in his preface that his little book is designed chiefly for "general readers." It ought to be in the hands of lovers of poetry who are not entirely familiar with the technical forms of the different kinds of verse which give them pleasure. English meters are in certain respects extremely complicated; but, as Professor Lewis says, their fundamental principles are simple; and in this compact and easily read volume, in untechnical language, the various kinds of meter are described with sufficient fullness and illustration to give the intelligent lover of poetry all the information he needs and to furnish also an excellent text-book. (The Principles of English Verse. By Charlton M. Lewis. Henry Holt & Co., New York.)

**A Prophet Abroad** The first impression one receives from Mr. Wells's book upon America is that our only hope is the speedy coming of "The Day of the Comet" (Mr. Wells's Comet) to change us in every particular. Upon second thought, however, the modest disclaimers of the author, his realization that in three months he cannot know all about our land and people, and his keenness in pointing out undoubted defects, call for serious attention. While longer acquaintance would undoubtedly alter Mr. Wells's sense of proportion and emphasis, yet in many ways he shows himself a sympathetic if often a severe critic. He came here to search for realities. He failed to find men, with one or two exceptions, who were willing to discuss the future of America except in a rhetorical or facetiously disgusted way. He found that the typical American had a distrust of lucid theories and logic, talking unwillingly of ideas— but thinking. He is extremely acute and often witty in describing the different social atmospheres of our cities. Boston especially attracts his pungent pen—and New York is not neglected. "Boston," he says, "presents a terrible, terrifying unanimity of æsthetic discriminations." The question in Mr. Wells's mind remains, "Is America a giant childhood, or a gigantic futility?" On the whole, he is inclined to believe that, by sheer virtue of size, free traditions, and the habit of initiative, the leadership of progress must ultimately rest in America. The book is full of quotable sentences, and nothing could prove the actual maturity of the American people better than the interest and good nature we feel in just such inadequate representations of our country as this is. (The Future in America. By H. G. Wells. Harper & Brothers, New York. $2, net.)

*St. Catherine of Siena* Few figures of the fourteenth century stand out so clearly as does the heroic figure of St. Catherine of Siena. The author of "Mademoiselle Mori" makes us realize this, though, in general, it must be owned that none too picturesque phrase is used to this end. In successive chapters we are informed about Catherine as peacemaker, as politician, and as ambassadress, about her life in Siena, Avignon, Florence, and Rome. Sometimes there is a fine bit of characterization; for instance, "Although Dante praises Dominic, he clearly prefers Francis. But Catherine was a woman, and the robuster character of the Spanish monk (Dominic) appealed to her." The interesting illustrations are taken from portraits and pictures by Sienese and other painters. (Saint Catherine of Siena and Her Times. By the Author of "Mademoiselle Mori." G. P. Putnam's Sons, New York. $2.75.)

*Souls of Cities* Rome, Venice, Seville—do not these names evoke visions of cities that are something more than cities? They have personalities, they have souls and temperaments. We love to be in them and breathe their atmosphere and their rich, varied, individual life. They give themselves to us if we but sojourn in them long enough and submit to their charm. Mr. Symons journeys from city to city; he sees those above mentioned; he also sees and sojourns in Naples, Prague, Moscow, Budapest, Belgrade, Sofia, Constantinople. Some of these he loves; some he hates. In both cases he tells us why and with frank thoroughness. His very moods and his emotional bursts of confidence, his visions and ideals, sink gratefully into the reader's mind, for the reader is very apt to have formed something of the same opinion. Whether or not Mr. Symons evokes personal memories in the reader's mind of the cities described,

his book is one of the few which one dares to put alongside Hawthorne's note-books on England, France, and Italy, Lafcadio Hearn's books on Japan, Mrs Wharton's "Italian Backgrounds," and Vernon Lee's "Spirit of Rome"—books that are hardly for the tourist, unless the tourist becomes a sojourner. (Cities. By Arthur Symons. E. P. Dutton & Co., New York. $2.50, net.)

*Tibet* The long despatch from Dr. Sven Hedin in Tibet, printed in recent newspapers and recounting his latest discoveries there, lends added interest to a reperusal of the important books already published describing that part of the world; for instance, Reid's "Through Unexplored Asia," Dr. Landsdell's "Chinese Eastern Asia," Dr. Hedin's "Central Asia and Tibet," Crosby's "Turkestan and Tibet," Deasy's "In Tibet and Chinese Turkestan," and Colonel Waddell's "Lhasa." Mr. Holdich's volume is the latest addition to the list. "Tibet the Mysterious" has little to do with Lhasa. Instead it interestingly describes the exploration of the great wilderness of stony and inhospitable altitudes which lie far beyond the capital in a hitherto practically unknown region. (Tibet the Mysterious. By Colonel Sir Thomas H. Holdich, K.C.M.G. Frederick A. Stokes Company, New York. $3, net. Postage 20 cents.)

*William Blake* Ideas about art, literature, politics, religion, and life are generally expressed in familiar correspondence with a simplicity, clearness, and personal atmosphere hardly to be found in more formal writing. Take the letters of Stevenson or of John Richard Green as examples. If any man's work in art and literature needs the illumination of his personality, it is William Blake's. His pictures and poems seem to us generally strange, often occult, sometimes incoherent, yet ever and anon evincing a vein of sound reason and of inspiring ideal. Blake's ideal was sublime. It was nothing less than the union of the Divine through Art and Love. But Blake's methods were eccentric. To understand them we should regard him as a Celt rather than as an Englishman. If so, we can better appreciate his works, explained as they are by the spontaneous, unreflective, impetuous letters now published in connection with Blake's biography by Frederick Tatham. Tatham was Blake's most intimate friend, seeing him continually and enjoying unique opportunities for gathering reliable material for a biography. That biography, written long ago (Blake died in 1827), is now published in full for the first time as printed from the original manuscripts. The account lacks both scholarship and grace, but these are supplied by Mr. Archibald Russell's valuable introduction and notes. From them we gain a juster perspective than Tatham gives, perhaps even than the late Dr. Garnett gave in his valuable monograph, and possibly a more comprehensive view than Mr. Swinburne gives. A new edition of the long critical essay on Blake by Mr. Swinburne is published coincidently with the Tatham life, a criticism of course specially stimulating in its treatment of Blake's poems rather than of his pictures. Blake and Rossetti were the only two English artists equally distinguished in poetry and painting. (The Letters of William Blake: Together with a Life by Frederick Tatham. Edited by Archibald G. B. Russell. Charles Scribner's Sons, New York. $2, net.—William Blake. By Algernon Charles Swinburne. A New Edition. E. P. Dutton & Co., New York. $2, net.)

# Letters to The Outlook

## A DISTINCTION AND A DIFFERENCE

The Cleveland street railway situation received a large measure of attention in The Outlook of February 2. But if I may claim the privilege of a rejoinder, I should like to point to a misconception which accounts for an apparent disagreement between the author of the article entitled "Private Rights in Street Railways" and the writer of the editorial comment entitled "Public Rights in Street Railways."

The editorial is an admirable statement of an issue of first importance. The Outlook's advocacy of the proposition that the streets of a municipality and the traffic thereon must be controlled by the people of the municipality has my entire support, though we might not agree as to how this control should be exercised. But this is not the question I was discussing in the article referred to. The Cleveland controversy is undoubtedly a phase of the conflict to which The Outlook refers. But it no more follows that the work Mr. Johnson is doing is for the best interests of the citizens of Cleveland or the larger public because he says it is, than that Mr. Hearst labored for the best interests of the citizens of New York and for the cause of municipal ownership because he echoed a popular cry and claimed to stand on the side of the people. My main argument is not, as stated in the editorial, that I believe the people of Cleveland ought to trust their interests in the streets to Mr. Andrews and his colleagues rather than to Mr. Johnson and his associates, because Mr. Johnson's record is open to suspicion and Mr. Andrews is a man of probity. Such a conclusion is, of course, clearly illogical. I do not know where one will find in my article any justification for such an interpretation. My contention is simply that Mayor Johnson's financial interest in one of the competing companies, and the kind of thing he has done, reveal his real purpose better than anything he said, just as Mr. Hearst's financial interest in his newspapers and the kind of thing he has done are better evidence of his interest in the public's welfare than his words. What Mayor Johnson has done is contrary to clearly established principles governing the conduct of public officials, and to condone the offense because the result may be beneficial to the material interests of the city tends to weaken the public conscience by encouraging the belief that the end justifies the means. Of course I know that The Outlook advocates this teaching no more than I advocate control of the streets by private interests. H. A. GARFIELD.
Princeton University.

[The contest in Cleveland was not a theoretical one; it was one between the Mayor representing the people and a private company which had in certain periods of its history corruptly procured control of the streets. To lay emphasis, in this very definite struggle, on an alleged technical irregularity of the Mayor, and to ignore the corrupt and perhaps extortionate foundation upon which the rights of the private company rested, was, in our judgment, inconsistent with the general public policy of which Mr. Garfield has always been an effective advocate.—THE EDITORS.]

## WALT WHITMAN

### I.

I have read with interest your review of Mr. Perry's "Whitman." It is the first really sane and critical article on Whitman that I have seen for a long time. My father lived next door to Walt Whitman in Camden for many years, and part of the time I was at home and knew the poet very well.

You are quite right in describing him as a *poseur*. The style of his dress, his open, wide-collared shirt, his attitude toward the public, were all, in my opinion, poses. His moral character was as you state it, and my family say that he morally injured some young men that they knew.

Whitman had a kindly disposition, and used to give mittens in the winter to the ferry hands and car drivers and conductors. One of his favorite amusements was to ride back and forth on the ferryboats, where he presented a very picturesque appearance. He lived very carelessly, and in one corner of his room was an immense heap of newspapers and magazines reaching almost to the ceiling.

In my opinion, much of his poetry was not thought to be inspired even by himself, but was written to eke out an existence, as there was a demand, especially in England, for something believed to be character-istically American, and so he wrote it to suit. I also knew several of his admirers who have written about him. One of them has attained, as nearly as any one in recent times, to the rank of a "Boswell." But the democracy about whom he wrote and for whom he wrote cared nothing for his poetry, and this, to my mind, shows the complete failure to strike the keynote of democratic feeling.

I think that your article will do much good in counteracting the strange worship of Whitman.     W. E. BUTTON.
Frankford, Philadelphia.

II.

I am ashamed of The Outlook and ashamed of Bliss Perry, whom I have known for years, to so slur over the foulness of that brute beast, Walter Whitman. Too idle and helpless to earn his own living, consorting with the toughs and bums of this city and Camden, spending all his last days with a "buxom widow" as housekeeper, the father of six illegitimate children, the destroyer of two homes at least, not one honorable act or sentiment to his credit, it gives one a moral nausea to hear reputable periodicals and decent people mention his name with the least degree of allowance. He should have been shoveled into the earth without cere-mony, and all his belongings, personal, house-hold, and literary, burned over him to clear the earth as far as possible of his malodorous name. How long, O Lord, before we can hear one word of sanity and decency from our leading periodicals respecting such brute beasts who happen to have some little smart-ness in trick literature!
Philadelphia.     JAMES H. ECOB.

### NOISELESS BRIDGES

In regard to the "Noiseless Bridges" communication of A. Chamberlain, Winchester, Massachusetts, in The Outlook of Feb-

ruary 2, I beg to say that General Bancroft (the President of the Boston Elevated Railroad Company), in an address last year to the students of the Massachusetts Institute of Technology, said, in effect, that an elevated railway could be made noiseless by the use of ballast, as is shown conclusively by the Berlin Elevated, but that it was not practi-cable to use ballast in the northern part of the United States because it would afford lodgment for the snow that now sifts through.
     A. R. H.
Abington, Massachusetts.

### A SUCCESSFUL NEGRO SCHOOL

Your donation of $10 means $80 to the Slater Industrial School for colored people at Winston-Salem, North Carolina. This school is perhaps yielding better results than any similar institution in the entire South. Its influence has totally and absolutely eliminated all race spirit in its vicinity. The school buildings and grounds are worth $50,000. The white people raised $10,000 cash for a hospital for the negroes, and they did the labor free; thus they have an up-to-date hospital for their sick, in which colored girls are also graduated as trained nurses.

The harmonizing effect of the school and hospital is certainly beyond description, which is proof positive that this is the true solution of the great race problem. The entire institution is under the able manage-ment of the People's National Bank, one of the largest banks in the State. The State and county contribute $5,500 yearly, and the Slater Peabody Funds $1,200 yearly, to the maintenance of the institution.

Owing to the marvelous effect of the school and hospital upon the colored race, the State now offers $12,000 in addition to the yearly grant if the trustees will raise the same amount. With $24,000 cash in hand for material, the colored people will do the labor free, as they did in building the hospi-tal, thus increasing the value of the plant to $48,000. A New York City philanthropist will give half of the $12,000 when the other half is raised, hence the raising of $6,000 means $48,000 to the institution.

Seldom do we see an altruistic donation multiply eight times when it becomes bricks and mortar, as in this case.

The race question is a National problem and a serious one, too, which every true American citizen is keenly interested in help-ing to solve. This school and hospital are doing a great work along these lines, and it is very imperative that the capacity be in-creased.

If every one who reads this letter will send a contribution to the treasurer, Colonel

W. A. Blair, President of the People's National Bank, Winston-Salem, North Carolina, we assure them it will be of large service.

57 Broadway, New York.     J. P. R.

## MORMONISM IN IDAHO

I quote a paragraph from an article which appeared in your valuable magazine under date of December 29, 1906:

In Idaho, where of course there was no church influence, the results tell an interesting story. It must be understood that the northern counties are Gentile while the southern counties are Mormon. The great battle was as to whether Senator Dubois, Democrat, who has been very active in combating the political schemes of the Mormons in Idaho, should succeed himself in the United States Senate. Now the northern counties of Idaho went Democratic by small majorities, while the southern and Mormon counties went Republican by immense majorities. A clear line of cleavage runs across Idaho. On one side of that line the people vote one way, on the other side another way. There is only one thing to explain this fact. On one side of this line the Mormon Church dictates how its adherents vote; on the other side the Mormon hierarchy does not control, and American methods and results obtain.

The above does a great injustice to a State. Should a condition of affairs exist such as indicated above, it would be deplorable in the extreme. I have no right to assume that the writer of this article willfully sought to misrepresent the facts, and yet it is difficult to understand how one could assume to inform the public upon a subject about which he was so woefully ignorant. He does not seem to know even the geography of the State, much less its politics, and a most casual investigation of the results of the last campaign will disclose the utter falsity of the facts above set forth.

It is true that the Northern counties are Gentile, but it is not true that the Southern counties are Mormon counties. At least six of the Southern counties are exclusively Gentile counties.

It is true that one of the principal questions of the campaign was whether Senator Dubois should be returned to the United States Senate, but it is absolutely false that, as we are given to understand from this article, he carried the Northern counties or the Gentile counties. And it is equally false that a line of cleavage runs through Idaho, upon one side of which was found the vote for Senator Dubois and upon the other side against him by reason of Mormon dictation.

Senator Dubois did not carry a single Gentile county in the north. He carried one member in one county and three in out of a total membership of twen the Legislature. The county in carried the three members has al a Democratic county, with one and that was the Presidential year in Roosevelt was a candidate.

Coming to the Southern counties, ried but one Gentile county in the which county has very generally been cratic in off years. For illustration, in County, where the Mormon question been more thoroughly discussed than in other county in the State, and which i clusively Gentile, the Republican candi for. Governor lost the county by some hundred, while the Republican l ticket was elected by from twenty-one hundred to twenty-five hundred. If the issue of Mormonism prevailed at all in the State, it was upon the Senatorial matter. Elmore County, a Gentile county and also a Democratic county, nevertheless returned one member out of two, Republican. Owyhee County, a Gentile county and also a Democratic county generally speaking, returned one member out of two, Republican. In other words, in the exclusively Gentile counties the Republicans elected thirty-two members and the Democrats eighteen. If there is a line of cleavage in Idaho, the question arises, Where is the line located? There is one thing that is positively certain, and that is that it is not between the Gentile and Mormon counties; and the writer of the above-mentioned article could have known that had he desired to have been informed before he communicated his exceptionally valuable article to the public.

Had it not been for some factional difficulties in the Republican party which arose entirely outside of the Mormon question and which were due entirely to local conditions, the Democrats would not have had to ex five members of the Legislature. The only counties in which we lost Republican members of the Legislature where we should have elected were those counties in which local factional troubles prevailed. I believe that every well-informed man, regardless of politics, will admit, should he speak candidly, that there were not five hundred votes changed in North Idaho by reason of the Mormon question.     W. E. BOROH.

Boise, Idaho.

# *Libby's*

## (Natural Flavor)
# Food Products

Goodness, wholesomeness and purity are qualities that make the name Libby the standard for excellence in appetizing food products.

# Libby's Baked Beans

are prepared in the spotless Libby kitchens by the famous Libby method that retains all of the nutritious food value of the choicest beans, while giving them the most delicious flavor.

You can depend upon Libby's Baked Beans always being the same, as appetizing in appearance as they are delicious to the taste.

**Ask your grocer for Libby's, and insist upon getting Libby's**

The new 84-page booklet, "How to Make Good Things to Eat," gives many delightful recipes for luncheons, dinners and evening spreads, that every housewife will appreciate. It is sent free on request.

**Libby, McNeill & Libby, Chicago.**

I am authorized to say to you that this A
ministration has made and will contin
to make the Federal stamp upon meats a
meat-food products stand for somethii
—*Extract from address before the New York State Breeders' Associati*
*Syracuse, N. Y., December 18, 1906, by*

### Hon. George P. McCabe
**Solicitor for United States Department of Agriculture**
*[See "U. S. Agricultural Dept. Bureau of Animal Industry Circular No. 10.*

# All Swift's Products ar
# "U.S. Inspecte(
# U.S.and passe(

**"Under the Act of Congress of June 30, 1906."**

It means pure, wholesome products if the name "Swift" is back of the
Ask your dealer for these Specialties :

| | |
|---|---|
| Swift's Premium Ham | Swift's Silver Leaf Lard |
| Swift's Premium Bacon | Jewel Lard Compound |
| Swift's Premium Sliced Bacon | Swift's Cotosuet |
| Swift's Premium Lard | Swift's Jersey Butterine |
| Swift's Premium Milk-Fed Chickens | Swift's Beef Extract |
| Swift's Premium Butterine | Swift's Beef Fluid |

Brookfield Pork Sausage

## Swift & Company, U.S.A.

e
# Outl👁️ok

*Saturday, March 9, 1907*

# THE RENASCENCE
# OF THE
# COUNTRY HOME

## BY SYLVESTER BAXTER

❋

**The Fifty-ninth Congress**

The Congress which came to an end on Monday of this week was, in point of achievement, one of great distinction. Its principal task was that of making more efficient the control of the Federal Government over great commercial powers. Such acts as the Railway Rate Law, the Pure Food and Meat Inspection Laws, and the so-called Immunity Law, were significant not only because of what they actually accomplished, but also because of the policy of extending Federal activity which they expressed. Besides, this Congress determined the method of constructing the Panama Canal, extended the resources of the country by making alcohol commercially useful, improved the consular service, made naturalization uniform, and in other matters provided important legislation. At the close of the first session last summer, The Outlook described and explained its principal achievements. The second session, which began last December, was much shorter than the first, and much less prolific of important measures. A great deal of time was consumed in the Senate by the case of Senator Smoot, who was finally freed from liability to expulsion, and, vainly, by the discussion of the case of the discharged negro soldiers. Nevertheless, the impression that this session has been ineffective is not well founded. In the first place, our lawmakers have been busy directing how the money of the Government should be spent. During the three short months of this session they have been shopping to the extent of almost a thousand millions of dollars. That is an enormous sum. We do not believe it has been spent heedlessly, though it may not have been spent altogether wisely. Some of it has gone to the very much needed and highly justified object of higher salaries for certain public services. Some of it has gone for increasing the efficiency of the army and navy ; and as these branches of the public service become more and more constructive instruments, money spent upon them becomes more and more remunerative. Some of that money has gone into pensions, and public opinion approves of generosity in that direction. The expenditure of this vast amount is alone a big task.

❋

**The Second Session Its Achievements and Failures**

That the general impression concerning the ineffectiveness of the second session is not well founded may be seen from a brief survey of its acts. Of all the subjects about which Congress passed measures during this session four called forth independent legislation of importance. By independent legislation we mean legislation not merely supplementary to other acts of the same Congress. The subject of immigration was long under consideration ; the bill which was finally passed, as summarized in The Outlook last week, made some valuable improvements in the present immigration policy of the country, helped to adjust the strained relations between this country and Japan, and, by providing for a thorough investigation of the immigration problem and for an international conference on the subject, is likely to lead to a more thorough and scientific control of immigration than could have been secured by any of the devices, such as educational tests or arbitrary limitation of the numbers of immigrants, which have heretofore been proposed in Congress. The subject of protection to workingmen was dealt with in two important bills : one penalized " shanghaiing "—the kidnapping of men for the purpose of shipping them as sailors ;

the other, introduced by Senator La Follette, but greatly amended, limited the hours of labor of railway employees. The former of these measures was urged by labor organizations; it cannot, however, be regarded in any sense as class legislation, as it was urged also by considerations of common humanity; it became law. The latter was subject to searching criticism, and aroused opposition from some railway interests; it was urged, on the other hand, by railway telegraphers, who sent thousands of messages to Congress on its behalf, and by others; like the other bill, however, it is not a class measure, for it is in the interest of every traveler by rail, and, we believe, of the railway companies as well as their employees. This bill occupied a great deal of the time and energy of Congress. It was, fortunately, passed on the very last day of the session. A third subject was the economic development of the Philippines. This will be greatly promoted by the passage of a bill establishing in the islands a bank which is authorized to grant loans "to those engaged in agriculture for the sole purpose of assisting agriculture in the Philippine Islands "—a bill strongly urged by Secretary Taft. The remaining subject was the corruption of elections by contributions to candidates and parties by corporations; Congress at this session prohibited all such contributions which were within the scope of its legislative powers.

❧

*Other Acts and Omissions*　　The Fifty-ninth Congress also was occupied during the session in supplementing legislation passed earlier in its existence; such as, amendments to the Meat Inspection Law and the Denatured Alcohol Law; an expatriation law defining what constitutes the lapse of citizenship and thus filling out a lack of the naturalization and other laws; a law (approximating what the President had asked for) extending to the Federal Government the right of appeal in criminal cases, and thus reinforcing the anti-immunity measure passed at the last session and making easier proceedings against individuals indicted in corporation cases.

The acceptance by the Senate of the Santo Domingo treaty, though tardy, deserves commendation. In addition, Congress carefully considered but declined to enact a bill granting ship subsidies. Although we cannot approve the methods by which the bill was both promoted and opposed, we consider the result a distinct victory for sound principles of government. So also we welcome the failure to make more cumbersome the procedure against people who make fraudulent use of the mails. Other omissions, however, of Congress ought to be condemned. Chief of these is the omission to do justice to our island wards. To the end of the session the Senate declined even to discuss the question of relieving the Philippines of our tariff burdens; and Congress failed to give citizenship to Porto Ricans, who are now people without a country. Almost as deserving of censure was the killing of the bill to provide a forest reserve in the Appalachian and White Mountains. This bill, though passed unanimously by the Senate and urged repeatedly in Presidential messages, was stifled practically by a single man—the Speaker of the House. This seems to us to be a most flagrant instance of autocratic "usurpation." We are sorry, too, that Congress saw fit to let child labor legislation, the liberal modification of the Chinese exclusion act, and the provision for permanent housing of legations and embassies fail; but these failures are slight in comparison with the refusal to do justice to our island wards, and the arbitrary interference with the attempt to preserve the inestimable treasures of forest and water in the Eastern mountain ranges. These serious failures of a Congress which, in view of its constructive work, really deserves to be called great, we hope will be corrected soon after the next Congress assembles.

❧

*A National Loss*　　The resignation of Senator Spooner, of Wisconsin, is a public calamity; the cause which necessitates it comes near being a public disgrace. After sixteen years of service in the United States Senate, he retires at the age of sixty-four to resume private practice because the Senatorial salary is not sufficient to pay the necessary living expenses of an economical Senator in Washington and leave any margin for his family or his own old age. Senator Spooner has been too devoted to the public interests to divide his time and energies between the service of his country and his private practice, and he is unwilling to draw further upon his moderate reserve. Thus one of the ablest debaters in the Senate, unexcelled by any of his associates in his knowledge of Constitutional law, his reputation for integrity unblurred by even a whispered suspicion, a strong party man but one who regards party organization as a means for the promotion of political principles, a vigorous fighter but always a fair one, is lost from the counsels of the Nation in a Senate which the parsimonious policy of an extravagant Nation is gradually converting into a club of millionaires. Mr. Spooner's resignation emphasizes the truth that the people must either provide a " living wage " for their public servants, or expect the public offices to be filled by men who accept them in order to promote private interests.

⊛

**The Panama Canal Situation**

Tne failure of Mr. Oliver (the contractor whose bid was the lowest under the elaborate requirements laid down by the Government) to offer, after the ten days given him in which to revise his original bid, such an arrangement as regards the financial backing and co-operation in actual construction as was in all respects satisfactory to the Canal Commission and the President, has led, in connection with the resignation of Mr. Stevens, the Chief Engineer, to the determination on the part of the Government to place an army engineer in charge of the work. The officer chosen for this important post is Major George W. Goethals, of the Engineer Corps, and he will have as assistant engineers Major Gaillard and Major Siebert, who will be expected to be so familiar with the responsible part of the work that in case of necessity

either might succeed Major Goethals. The new Chief Engineer of the Panama Canal is at present a member of the General Staff of the army, and has been active as a member of the Fortifications Board. Major Goethals has been connected with the engineer branch of the army for about twenty-five years, and has had large experience in important engineering work, and especially in the improvement of rivers and in the building of canals—experience which precisely fits him for the nature of the work to be carried on at Panama. There are certain unquestioned advantages to our Government, in carrying out its great task on the Isthmus, to have its Chief Engineer in the work of construction a military officer, directly subject to the orders of the War Department, assigned to this particular task in the same way that every military officer is ordered to specific duty, and not free to resign for personal reasons, nor because he prefers some other form of employment, nor in any way able to question the authority of the Government to keep him at this task until it shall see good reason to supersede him or promote him. And this use of army organization, discipline, and trained skill is only one more illustration that our regular military force is far more than a body of fighters waiting for a possible war, and that it may effectively be used as a means of constructive civilization. The plan which has been under consideration for placing a very large part of the actual work of construction under a general contractor was taken up by the Government, as has been already pointed out by The Outlook, not with any intention of giving over the responsibility of building the Canal to others, but because it seemed at least possible that, with the retention by the Government of large powers of supervision and of many governmental functions, the work might best and quickest be done in that way. At present, at least, it now seems that such arrangement is not advisable, but the failure of the recent proposed offer to contractors does not in the least prevent the United States from taking up later on the question of the desirability of having part or even all of the work offered assigned to general contractors after proper competition by them.

❦

**Mr. Stevens's Resignation** The resignation of Mr. Stevens as Chief Engineer, while it makes it possible for the Government to use its army organization for the direct control of the work of construction, was received with genuine regret. There never has been any question that Mr. Stevens was doing efficient work on the Canal, and he has been praised cordially and repeatedly by the President and by all of the press correspondents who have studied conditions on the Canal. The form of contract which was recently submitted for bids was drawn up by Mr. Stevens, and that fact was acknowledged publicly and fully by the President. Both Mr. Stevens and Mr. Shonts had favored the experiment of asking for contractors' bids. The letter in which Mr. Stevens offered his resignation has not been made public, but various surmises have been published as to his reason. It is understood that he was extremely opposed to the acceptance of the bid made by Mr. Oliver and his associates. The Government followed his judgment as well as its own in rejecting that bid, and there seems to have been no reason why he should have supposed that the revised proposition by Mr. Oliver would be accepted, and in point of fact it was not accepted. It is thought, however, that Mr. Stevens was uneasy as to this, and that he practically threatened the Government with his resignation if his wishes on this point were not carried out. At all events, his letter seems to have been couched in such terms that there was really no alternative other than prompt acceptance of his threatened or conditional resignation. Other reasons assigned as probable causes for the resignation are Mr. Stevens's preference for private rather than Government employment, and his feeling that the work had now advanced to a point that did not make the future task of the Chief Engineer as important as it had been heretofore. It has also been said, upon what authority we do not know, that Mr. Stevens did not sympathize with the general policy of the Administration in regard to Government control of railways, and that this may have affected his action.

❦

**Loyalty to Party** Inexperience in political transactions need not imply any lack of political wisdom. This fact was illustrated by a speech which Governor Hughes, of New York, made last week. It required discernment to understand that the Republican organization at Albany might profit by some instruction on party loyalty; Governor Hughes had that discernment, and the assembled Republicans received the instruction. Party loyalty, however, as the Governor described it, might not be recognized as such by some politicians. According to him, it is practically equivalent to sound public service. This is what he said :

I have been a Republican from the time I came of age. . . . I do not condone any public wrong because it is committed by a Republican any more than I should were it committed by a Democrat. Nor do I think that loyalty to party requires support of anything wrong either in policy or in administration which we should feel free to condemn if the wrongdoing could be charged to those of a different political faith. . . . I count it the highest loyalty to the party to insist that the work done under Republican auspices shall be honestly done and well done, and that our record of administration shall not be smirched by either corruption or inefficiency. Organization is essential to successful effort, and no sane man would expect any political undertaking to be successful which is not skillfully organized and wisely managed. But the success of political organization will depend upon its ideals. . . . Give the people the idea that the main purpose of organization is to secure control for personal advantage or for favored interests, and sooner or later they will bring to grief the best-laid plans of the most astute leaders. But, on the other hand, convince them that organization is directed to the purpose of maintaining an honorable party policy and of promoting an administration of government in the interest of the people, and they will rally to its support.

Governor Hughes then rehearsed the figures recording the results of the elections in the State since 1894 ; and declared that these figures showed that on State issues the Republican party would be doomed to defeat unless it should give " new assurances to the people of

its capacity to govern in their interest."
The Governor, before closing, uttered a
warning; we suggest that the leaders of
his party have it framed and hung up in
party club rooms. It is this: "No man
is a friend of the Republican party who
asks me or any one in authority to appoint
a man cr to retain a man who is not equal
to his job." This plain reference to the
principle on which he acted in recommending to the State Senate the removal of
Mr. Kelsey, State Superintendent of Insurance, indicates how seriously Governor
Hughes regards the case as a test of the
competence of his party. The Outlook
agrees with the Governor. Mr. Barnes,
the leader of the Albany organization,
who in the minds of many has attained
the rank of boss, took occasion to give
Mr. Hughes some practical counsel. He
scouted the notion of valuing any public
opinion except that declared by ballots.
If Mr. Barnes had heeded Mr. Hughes's
figures, he would have learned that they
were all gathered from the ballot-boxes.
From Governor Hughes's figures we
select the following for example:

While Governor Odell received 111,000 in
1900, his plurality in 1902 was short of 9,000.
While Governor Higgins was elected by
80,000 in 1904, in the last election all the Republican candidates for State officers save
one were defeated.

It will probably take some time for it to
sink into the heads of many party leaders that this is really an argument for
honesty and efficiency.

❦

**Political Contributions by Corporations** There have been
two criminal pros-
ecutions against
Mr. George W. Perkins, of the firm of
J. P. Morgan & Co., arising out of
transactions with the New York Life
Insurance Company. One of these is
still pending. The other prosecution was
for larceny in paying money out of the
funds of the life insurance company
to the National campaign fund of the
Republican party. Mr. Perkins paid
the money out of his own funds in the
first instance, but on account of the
New York Life Insurance Company, and
was afterwards reimbursed on the order
of President McCall. According to the
definition of the penal code of New York

State, any officer in possession of money
who appropriates the same to his own
use or to that of any other person than
the true owner is guilty of larceny. The
charge against Mr. Perkins was that his
act in contributing funds of the New
York Life Insurance Company to the
support of the Republican campaign
came within this definition. The Court
of Appeals, by a vote of four to three,
holds that it does not come within this
definition. Essential to the crime is the
intent to despoil the owner of his property. "That is necessary to complete
the offense, and if a man, under the
honest impression that he has a right to
the property, takes it, it is not larceny,
if there be a colorable title. The charge
of stealing property is only substantiated
by establishing the felonious intent."
Because this felonious intent is lacking,
Mr. Perkins is adjudged not guilty by
the court. Incidentally it is worthy of
note that the evident reluctance of Mr.
Jerome to institute these criminal proceedings against Mr. Perkins is justified
by the decision of the Court of Appeals.
There is no pretense that he obtained
or expected to obtain any personal advantage by the contribution of the corporate
funds to the Republican Campaign
Committee, and, in the judgment of The
Outlook, he is morally as well as legally
acquitted of the charge brought against
him. The law did not at the time prohibit contributions by corporations to
the campaign funds. The contribution
in this particular case was a misjudgment, and to that extent a misuse of
funds, but a misuse of funds owing to a
misjudgment by an officer is neither
morally nor legally a larceny if it is
honestly made for the benefit of the corporation.

❦

**The Harriman Investigation** The testimony taken before the Inter-State Com-
merce Commission in
New York last week, especially Mr.
Harriman's own admissions, has set the
whole thinking public seriously considering the right and wrong uses of railway
capital. Whatever may be said of the
definition and proper limitation of overcapitalization, it is plainly injurious that

the controlling power of a great railway system should raise enormous sums on the credit of its present prosperity and future prospects, and apply those funds, not to improve or extend the road, not to secure stockholders by increasing the surplus, not to benefit shippers and patrons by lower rates, but to gain financial control of other railways through buying up their stock in Wall Street and juggling their finances with exorbitant profits to intermediate syndicates, individuals, and banking firms. Commissioner Lane put his finger on a vital point when he asked Mr. Harriman if he did not think that the law should intervene somewhere and should restrict him in his power to use money raised for railway purposes for the acquisition of other railways. But Mr. Harriman would not admit that the amount of the issue of a railway's securities should be regulated by law, and promptly acquiesced in the supposition that, if he could market enough securities, he would gladly absorb the Santa Fé, the Northern Pacific, the Great Northern, and in the end spread not only over the Pacific but the Atlantic coast. This sort of thing has been acutely characterized as changing railway corporations from enterprises in transportation to a vast means of gambling in securities. What is objected to is not legitimate expansion, but the use of credit and capital to obtain new control of outside property, that in turn to be exploited to get something else, and so on indefinitely to build up a house of cards which would ill stand adversity; and in doing it to trample remorselessly over the interests of minority stockholders and of the public, to loot the new acquisitions, and perhaps to impair even the railway system for which the series of deals is made. In six months last year the Union Pacific bought over a hundred million dollars' worth of outside railway shares. What kind of attitude such operations lead to was shown in Mr. Harriman's cool reply to the question if he considered it right to put on the public $19,000,000 of common stock that would never pay a dividend. His "Did we ever say to the public that a dividend would be paid?" unpleasantly recalls the remark attributed to another railway financier, "The public be damned."

●

*What the Evidence Showed* The transactions which a general policy of absorption by purchase may involve are such as the famous Chicago and Alton "reorganization"—a term, assuredly, which may cover a multitude of sins. This has been extremely succinctly and, we judge, accurately described in the New York Sun's headlines as follows : "They [that is, Mr. Harriman and three associates, acting as a private syndicate] buy the road, issue $32,000,000 of new bonds, buy them themselves at 65, pay themselves a 30 per cent. dividend on their stock out of the proceeds, sell the bonds all the way up to 96, the price to the New York Life, increase the capital stock, and let Union Pacific have the preferred at 86½." And the Wall Street Journal thus ironically points out "a way to make money :"

First, buy control of a railroad.
Second, look over the books and discover the sums paid out of income for improvements, but which are charged to operation.
Third, capitalize these sums.
Fourth, pay yourself a dividend from the proceeds, in violation of law.
Fifth, sell the road to a rival company after the cream has been skimmed.

How large personal profit the members of the Chicago and Alton syndicate made was not shown in evidence, for Mr. Harriman refused to admit the authority of the Inter-State Commission to ask this question and similar ones, and it is not yet certain whether the Commission will attempt by mandamus to compel him to reply. But even his wonderful clear-headedness must have sometimes left him in doubt in this deal whether he was acting for the interest of the Chicago and Alton, the Union Pacific, or E. H. Harriman. At all events, when the field was cleared the Chicago and Alton was " capitalized " at about three times the original amount, and its former eight per cent. dividend-paying power had practically disappeared off the face of the earth. Illinois courts may still have a chance to decide whether the bond issue (largely used to pay the syndicate members a thirty per cent. stock dividend) was valid, for the Constitution of that State has this provision:

No railroad corporation shall issue any stock or bonds except for money, labor, or property actually received and applied to the purpose for which such corporation was created; and all stock dividends and other fictitious increases of the capital stock or indebtedness of any such corporation shall be void.

❀

*Possible Future Results*

Other testimony bore on the methods of acquisition by the Union Pacific of Illinois Central stock and Southern Pacific stock, and, apart from the methods of these transactions, the Commission is considering the bearing upon Union Pacific expansion of the provisions of the law which forbid mergers between competing railways. Mr. Harriman seemed to hold that the Commission was going beyond its powers in taking up the matter of general stock-buying by a railway (other than as it might constitute a merger with a parallel or competing line), and that it ought to confine itself to the question of rates. But the Commission clearly held that the relation between the fixing of rates and the capitalization and conduct of railways is intimate and interdependent; and if this view is sustained, the door is wide open for broad dealing with great public questions. Thus it is asserted that rates are relatively higher on the Union Pacific and Southern Pacific than on other roads, and that the reason is that money must be had to pay dividends on excessive capitalization put forth to buy up stock of other roads in the market. Such an allegation also as that the Union Pacific transferred three hundred thousand shares of Southern Pacific to Mr. William Rockefeller with a purpose to depress the price of the latter stock might fairly call for an explanation, because (if true, and as to this we have no knowledge) the deal might have had a serious effect on rates. All in all, out of a mass of testimony involved and contradictory, it seems probable that the Inter-State Commission has gathered material upon which it may very probably base legal action, and which certainly may afford material for one of the most important reports it has ever rendered, and this report may well include suggestions for general legislation by Congress relating to overcapitalization and the limitations of railway deals.

❀

*Settling Chicago's Traction Question*

Mayor Dunne, of Chicago, who was elected two years ago on the issue of immediate municipal ownership of street railways, has not been able to carry out what he promised. Instead, in the closing months of his administration, a settlement ordinance is passed over his veto, but it will not become effective unless ratified by a referendum vote April 2. The advocates of the settlement plan profess great confidence that it will meet with popular approval on a referendum vote. It was due to the activity of the Mayor and his friends in getting up a very large petition, however, that the people are to be afforded an opportunity of voting on the ordinance. There are really two ordinances, one running to each company, but they are so dovetailed as to make one comprehensive plan of settlement. The existing properties of the companies have been valued by experts, and an agreed price has been fixed of fifty million dollars. The companies are to put in such new money as may be necessary to rehabilitate the plants, estimated at forty million dollars. The city is to have the right to take over the property for municipal operation at any time on six months' notice by paying the agreed present valuation of fifty million dollars, plus the new money put in for rehabilitation, with an addition to the new money of ten per cent. for construction profit and five per cent. brokerage charge. The city also reserves the right to authorize another corporation to take over the property on specified conditions. Until the city does terminate the grant in one of these two ways, the companies are to remain in possession, give unified operation, and practically universal transfers. They are to receive upon their recognized investment an annual return of five per cent., after paying operating expenses, taxes, repairs, maintenance, renewals, and depreciation. Of the remaining earnings, fifty five per cent. are to go to the city and forty-five to the companies. Provision is made for a board of supervising engineers to pass upon construction and management. This board mu:t approve all contracts and may fix salaries. One of these engineers is to be selected by the city, one by the companies, and the third, Mr. Bion J. Arnold, is named in the ordinance. Mr. Arnold has been the city's expert adviser for several years past.. Under the new arrangement he will also be the engineer in charge of construction, representing jointly the city and the companies. There are provisions for public accounting designed to enable the city to understand all the operations. The agreed valuation of fifty million dollars contains an item of nine million dollars for unexpired franchise rights. It is liberal to the companies also in that it allows them full value for some cable equipment that must be at once discarded. Five or six years ago the two systems now valued at fifty million dollars were represented by outstanding securities having both a par value and a market value in excess of one hundred million dollars. Mayor Dunne, who went into office as the champion of municipal ownership, has undoubtedly been the cause of weakening the municipal ownership sentiment in Chicago, not so much because of the extravagance of his pre-election pledges as on account of the weakness and incompetency of his administration generally. The work of Mr. Walter L. Fisher as special traction counsel is the single brilliant achievement of the Dunne administration, but that achievement the Mayor himself has now repudiated by practically forcing the resignation of Mr. Fisher. There is a striking difference between Mayor Dunne, of Chicago, and Mayor Johnson, of Cleveland, for the latter, with all his radicalism, is possessed of administrative ability of the highest order.

❋

*High Speed on Railways*
Last week another railway accident occurred, due to high speed, and resulting in a wreck similar to that of the Pennsylvania "flyer" the week previous. A Baltimore and Ohio train, running to make up lost time, left the rails near Connellsville, Pennsylvania, and, after bumping two hundred feet along the ties, was thrown into a ditch. The passengers broke the windows of the cars, and escaped just as the cars became ignited from the engine and began to burn fiercely. Vain efforts were made to save the engineer, who had been caught under his wrecked engine; he was burned to death before the passengers' eyes, and the fireman was fatally injured. About thirty passengers were cut and bruised. They were saved from a worse fate, for had the train happened to take a slightly different course after leaving the rails, it would have gone over a fifty-foot embankment. The accident may be of more use than most railway disasters have been, in impressing on the minds of the operators in ultimate authority the perilous condition under which fast trains in America are run. For the train fortunately included the private car of the Superintendent of the Pittsburg Division of that line, in which was a party of officials on a tour of inspection. Their opinion may be unanimous as to the thoroughness of their inspection ! Of the one hundred -and sixty-odd serious railway accidents during November, December, and January, most were not directly attributable to high speed, but a far greater prrtion were so directly attributable in the February list. Thus during the past fortnight popular attention has been graphically directed to this particular cause, and the effect has been realized, as not before, of lateral hammering against the outer rail, especially when single-spiked on ties of comparatively low elevation, whether the whole train be unexpectedly heavy, or whether the locomotive's center of gravity be lowered, as in the change from steam to electricity. Most laymen, too, learned with surprise that so important a company as the New York Central does not provide speedometers to the engineers of its fast trains. But not all companies err in this respect. For instance, on the Burlington the locomotive cab of every fast passenger train is so provided ; furthermore, engineers are ordered not to exceed a certain speed-limit which varies on the

various divisions ; for example, where the road is well ballasted, double-tracked, and has heavy rails, the limit is sixty miles an hour; in other divisions it does not exceed fifty miles; nor are engineers allowed to run beyond these limits, no matter how far they may be behind time. Most railway operators would welcome the general introduction of such rules. But they will hardly be so introduced and enforced except by a power, not the railway, "which makes for righteousness." The Inter-State Commerce Commission has investigated one notable recent accident. We wish that it would investigate more, and answer, as the railways do not always, when men ask, "Were both track and train strong enough ? Was the track clear ? Were the signals apparent despite the weather ? Were bridges and turnouts interlocked with the signals? finally, Was there obedience to orders among employees ? If the Commission is too overburdened to undertake such investigation, fixing responsibility and prescribing remedies, then let us demand the institution of a Bureau of Railway Accidents in the Department of Commerce. In England a similar Bureau, conducted by eminent experts with mandatory powers, has induced such a spirit of confidence on the part of the railways that they practically invariably accede without criticism to the Government's recommendations.

❁

*The Transvaal Election* The recently held first general election to the Transvaal Parliament— the Parliament created by the Constitution which was granted by letters patent in September, 1906—was to some degree like the Presidential elections in this country during the reconstruction period. The issues of the war of 1899–1902 were fought over again, and the campaign was further embittered by the fact that at the time the poll was taken there were between two and three thousand unemployed white men on the Rand ; and this in spite of the fact that for months past there has been a large exodus from Johannesburg owing to stagnation in development work at mines where stamps are not yet at work. Excluding Socialists and labor

men, there were three parties to the contest. The Progressives are the party of the great mining houses on the Rand ; the Nationalist party is composed of British electors opposed to the enormous political influence which the mining houses have hitherto exercised ; while the Boers at Johannesburg and Pretoria and in the rural constituencies are organized in Het Volk. There was a coalition between the Nationalists and Het Volk. These two parties united against the Progressives, and adopted as the chief plank in their platform a declaration that the one question on which the election must turn was, "Who shall control the Transvaal—the people or the mining houses ?" The Progressives on their part insisted that the question was, "Shall the Transvaal be governed by the people of the Transvaal, or from Downing Street?" They were aggrieved by the action of the British Government in making legislation concerning non-European labor subject to review in London, and in the campaign they made no attempt to conceal their hostility to the Campbell-Bannerman Government. In this way the question of Chinese labor was forced to the front. The Nationalist and Het Volk coalition was successful, and General Botha, one of the foremost generals on the Boer side in the late war, will be the Prime Minister of the Transvaal. His victory is a striking illustration of the admirable spirit in which the British Imperial Government maintains liberty of thought and freedom of elections in its colonies.

❁

*The Policy of the New Premier* Now that it has fallen to General Botha to constitute the Transvaal Ministry, much significance attaches to an interview which General Botha gave to Reuter's correspondent at Johannesburg for transmission to London on February 13. "British supremacy," Botha then said, "will be safer in the hands of the Boers than in those of cosmopolitan capitalists. We have fought and suffered grievously more than anybody else in this country. That is past, and no one is so foolish as to want it over again. The question of the flag and of supremacy have been settled for all time. They are both now outside politics. We are now concerned with our domestic affairs. Having got free government, our natural desire is, and our sole endeavor will be, so to govern that the country shall prosper and the two races be drawn together. At Vereeniging I signed the treaty of peace. I then solemnly accepted what is so dear to you—your King and your flag. They are now our King and our flag." General Botha further declared in this interview that Het Volk had no hostility to the mining interests on the Rand. He was equally emphatic, however, in his statement that Het Volk did object to the men who control the mines also controlling the political destinies of the Transvaal. He recalled the fact that when he was at Johannesburg with his commandoes in the early days of the war, it would have been possible for him to have done irreparable damage to all the mines along the Rand. " I recognized then, as I recognize now," he said, " that my people must look to the mines for help, and I protected the mines then ; so shall I see that they are not injured now." This was preliminary to a further important statement—a statement that has much significance now that General Botha is Premier—regarding his attitude on the Chinese question. "This talk of wholesale Chinese repatriation regardless of consequences," he said, " is nonsense. I say emphatically that nothing shall be done to embarrass the mines so far as unskilled labor is concerned. We want to restore confidence in the country. Could we do that by crippling or hampering the mines ?" As to the language and education questions, both of which have been the subject of much controversy and some apprehension in England as well as in the Transvaal, General Botha was equally explicit. "We want," he said, " to pursue a just and liberal policy. It is an accepted principle that English shall be the compulsory language." The statement about Chinese labor is perhaps the most important that General Botha made in this interview, for the question of Chinese contract labor has been and is likely to be again an acute one in the Transvaal. One of the first duties of the new Premier will be to attend the Colonial Conference which is to meet in London in April. The Premiers of all the self-governing colonies are to be at this third conference of the Empire ; and General Botha will sit side by side with the Premiers who organized the colonial contingents to fight the Boers in the war of 1899–1902.

❦

**Fruits of Christian Enterprise** There are now at least ten schools for girls in Peking. The leaders in this new work are " the sisters of princes, the wives and daughters of dukes, the families of some of the highest officials. A year ago there was not one such school as these outside of missionary circles." This fact speaks significantly for the intellectual enlightenment now advancing in China. It is just a hundred years since Robert Morrison, of Scotland, landed at Canton, the pioneer Protestant missionary. The inertia to be overcome was immense, but it has been overcome. This year it is proposed to erect, as the " Robert Morrison Memorial," a Young Men's Christian Association building costing $100,000. In the Peking schools some distinguished women are daily teaching daughters of the rich and poor together. Courses of lectures somewhat of a university extension sort have been given in the Christian churches at Peking, and largely attended by progressive men and women. A nephew of the Empress Dowager, Duke Te, regularly attended, and, of his own proposition, gave one lecture. Princesses came to the mission compound to lecture to women of all classes there, and social entertainments for the company by the ladies of the mission followed. This will be news to those who have been babbling about Chinese hostility to missionaries from America. The national spirit of Japan, and the growing strength of Christianity there, are both evinced by the recent action of the Japanese Missionary Society in taking upon itself the support of thirty native churches aided until now by the American Board. Thus declining further dependence, the Japanese church leaders ask the missionaries to work on in a ministry at large as associate evangelists. The need of such is curiously attested by an advertisement in a daily newspaper soliciting some Christian preacher to visit a certain town. The Japan Times lately remarked: " Among the thinking classes the need of a religion is beginning to be felt." Japanese laymen have organized the Okayama Missionary Society for evangelistic work in that prefecture.

❀

*Christian Leadership in the Orient* It is noteworthy that American churches are repeating in the Orient the policy which nourished Christian institutions when first planted here. Harvard was founded to secure a supply of cultured leaders for a generation reared amidst the unfavorable conditions of a colony in the wilderness. Likewise, the purpose of the later founding of Yale was to train men for the service of Church and State. The type of Christianity which created the early American college is now establishing in many non-Christian lands colleges for the fertilization of the minds into which the seeds of spiritual life have been dropped, thus to raise up men and women capable of religious and social leadership among their countrymen. This has proved remarkably effective in Japan. Large sums have thus been productively invested in other lands also. What was done for the emancipation of Bulgaria by men who had studied in Robert College is a well-known instance. In China there has just been opened at Changsha, the capital of conservative Hunan, a province of twenty million people, an infant Yale, sustained by the Yale Foreign Missionary Society, broadly unsectarian, its officers mostly graduates of Yale. This is hoped ultimately to grow into a university which may do for China what Yale has done for America. Its faculty of seven enjoy the favor of the Viceroy and other eminent men disappointed with the results of sending students to Japan. These Christian colleges, in which the awakening touch of modern thought is felt amidst the combined influences of science and religion, set a standard for progress, and enjoy increasing respect. Evident as it is that edu-

cation must go hand in hand with evangelization, it is certain that educational work must, for the present at least, be the main task of the missionary, while evangelistic work must be chiefly put upon the native graduates of the missionary schools, trained there for Christian leadership. And it becomes increasingly evident that under such leaders Oriental Christianity is not to be a close reproduction of its Western type, but to draw a distinctive quality from the soil in which it grows. Conservative observers like President Hall think it possible that Oriental Christianity " may ultimately advance beyond the West in spiritual interpretation of the doctrine of Christ." Givers to educational work should compare the varying productivity of a dollar in different fields. The sum required for one professorship in some American institutions would defray the entire charge of one of the ten colleges sustained by the American Board of Missions. These colleges are at the center of the educational system of every country they serve, and largely shape it, their graduates ranking with the best educated there. From the seminaries of the Board come the pastors and preachers needed by six hundred churches, besides the evangelists and missionaries of the native societies. Yet these seminaries cost the Board each an average of only $2,500 a year. It may be questioned if any institutions in our country exert so wide an immediate influence upon races, religions, and nations as these missionary colleges and seminaries.

❀

*The Treatment of the Insane in France* Several humanitarian measures have been under consideration in the French Parliament in the present year. One of the most important relates to the treatment of the insane. The old law concerning the judicial and medical disposition of the insane goes back to the government of Louis Philippe, dating from June 30, 1838. It has been in existence, therefore, for sixty-eight years. It was a great improvement over previous statutes and was a crystallization of doctrines of the French Revolution developed under the influence of Pinel. It took the insane out of the category of animals dangerous to society and regarded them as human beings. Nevertheless, though the law was good for 1838, it has long been surpassed by the laws of other nations which have revised their system of treating the insane. It did not organize public relief in a manner sufficiently complete to promote the patient's cure, and it failed also to safeguard individual liberty sufficiently. Asylums were still too much places of restraint instead of hospitals for cure. The new law is not merely an amendment of the old. It is a synthesis of the progress that has been made with reference to the insane in these last seventy years. For the protection of the individual new formalities are imposed before commitment to asylums. The mere certificate of a physician does not, as formerly, suffice; but a detailed medical report is required, which is prepared with the knowledge of the Magistrate, the Mayor, the Justice of the Peace, or the Commissioner of Police. The report must be definite and precise, and must be sent to the director of the establishment and also to the Procureur of the Republic. Within fifteen days after the commitment there must be a new certificate, and the commitment to the asylum becomes definite only when the president of the tribunal has pronounced it. In case of opposition to such an order of the court, another expert medical examination is ordered. It is thus the doctors who decide whether a person is insane, but the commitment must be always a judicial process. There is provision also for surveillance of the insane who are committed to private institutions or homes. The new law, however, is not merely a safeguard for liberty; it is above all a curative measure. Provision is made in the same law for epileptics, idiots, cretins, and dipsomaniacs. The departments are obliged to establish within ten years asylums for the insane and special quarters or institutions for the other classes above named; and to provide for the organization' of family colonies. The fundamental idea is that the conditions of life of the insane should conform as much as possible to the conditions of normal life and should thus exercise an improving influence.

❦

**A Veteran Journalist**   For the lifetime of a generation Marshal Huntington Bright, who died at Tarrytown, New York, last week, had been the editor of Christian Work; having as his special charge the editorial pages of the paper and largely writing them with his own hand. His devotion to his work and its variety and freshness were a constant source of surprise to his friends who knew how heavy was the tax on his vitality. His father was a man of literary tastes and poetic feeling, and the son was born with fine instincts, a high sense of honor, independence of judgment, and that quality of loyalty which binds a man's friends to him with bands of steel. He had a New England academy education, supplemented by special courses in Harvard College. He entered the army during the war, served with credit, and received the rank of major. Later he had very interesting experiences in the Far West. His best work and his ripest years were given to Christian Work, to which he brought the fruits of wide reading, a quick and versatile mind, interest in many sides of life, and a ready and effective style. He was progressive in thought, though never radical; he kept pace with investigation in science and scholarship, but always had his own point of view; he was a lover of literature, and especially of poetry; and he found immense delight in Nature, with whom he was on terms of intimacy. In the historic village of Tarrytown no one was better known or counted more friends; nor was any man a truer custodian of its traditions and literary associations. His talk, abounding in wit and full of suggestion, was the delight of his friends. He was one of the most gifted and active members of a literary club in the community which recently celebrated its thirty-ninth anniversary, and he was the first president of the Quill Club in this city. At a time when so much greed and vulgarity are coming to light it is a pleasure to recall the long and useful life of this high-minded gentleman of the old school, punctilious in all duties, honorable in all relations, full of unworldly charm of character.

❦

## Lenten Meditations
### As We Forgive

" Forgive us our trespasses, as we forgive those who trespass against us :" this prayer has been to some a stumbling-block. What! it is asked, shall we set a standard of forgiveness to the Almighty? Are we to go to God with boasting in our mouths, bid him note how merciful we are, and call upon him to be equally merciful? On the contrary, if we did not limit our petition for forgiveness by our own willingness to forgive, we should be guilty of effrontery. No request is worthy to be called a prayer which expresses a desire for that which we ourselves are unwilling to grant. The debtor who, while pressing those who owed him, asked his lord to remit his own debt, was guilty of a double offense ; he was guilty of the debt and he was guilty of arrogance. A prayer for forgiveness uttered in an unforgiving spirit is a piece of brazen impiety. The petition, " Forgive us as we forgive others," is not only a prayer for pardon ; it is also a prayer for a spirit of decent reverence.

There is, however, another reason why the petition for forgiveness is qualified by the degree of the forgiveness we extend to others. It lies in the fact that it is impossible for God to forgive us otherwise. The limitation is not in God, it is in ourselves. We can be forgiven only according to our capacity to receive forgiveness ; and our capacity to receive forgiveness is measured by our ability to forgive. What is forgiveness? If it were remission of penalty, this would not be true. But forgiveness is something much more fundamental than that ; it is the establishment, or rather the re-establishment, of friendly and intimate relations between persons. As it takes two to make a quarrel, so it takes two to achieve reconciliation. To be forgiven by God means to be once more in agreement with him, to have a spirit compatible with his spirit, to have a will like his will. An attitude of animosity toward

our fellows, however, is inconsistent with agreement with God ; it is the product of a spirit incompatible with his spirit, of a will unlike his will. He who does not love his fellow-men cannot be on friendly terms with the Source of all love. We must choose. If we wish to cherish our grudges, let us do so knowing what price we pay. If we really desire forgiveness, that is, really desire to be in right relation with our Ruler and Father, we shall hate the very notion of holding a grudge. There is no way by which we may walk humbly with God, unless we do justly and love mercy.

❦

## Railway Overcapitalization

Elsewhere in this issue of The Outlook Mr. A. B. Stickney, President of the Chicago Great Western Railway, and Mr. W. L. Snyder, of the New York Bar and an authority on inter-State commerce legislation, discuss the question whether the Great Northern Railway Company is overcapitalized. The Great Northern Railway is undoubtedly one of the most skillfully planned and best-managed railway systems of the United States. Mr. J. J. Hill, who may fairly be called its creator and, under the present system of railway finance and operation, may also fairly be called its sole proprietor and manager, is a man of great force of character and possesses constructive genius of a very high order. His primary and laudable ambition has been to establish and administer a great industrial corporation which, by developing the commerce of the Northwest and the Pacific Coast, shall add to the prestige, prosperity, and the power of his country. Work of this kind is as truly patriotic and public-spirited as the work of the statesman who frames laws and policies for his country.

It is because of this very pre-eminence of the Great Northern Railway that we think it forms an appropriate and significant object-lesson in one of the great political controversies of the time—the controversy as to what shall be the relation of the railways to the Government.

The debate as to whether the Great Northern Railway is overcapitalized or not is merely incidental to the main question. Some of the officers of the State of Minnesota—and Mr. Snyder agrees with them—think that the Great Northern is overcapitalized ; that to protect itself against "cut-throat competition " it has bought the controlling interest in other railways at an excessive price; that in carrying on this competitive warfare it has been forced to neglect the needs of its own community ; that to pay interest on capital issued to buy out competitors it has been compelled to discriminate and rebate in making rates to shippers. On the other hand, Mr. Stickney expresses the opinion, supported by tabulated figures, that the Great Northern's physical property could not be reproduced to-day for the bond and stock capitalization of the road ; that a very slight reduction of the freight rates of the railways of the country would bring upon us a condition of disastrous bankruptcy ; that the railways know best how to manage their own business; that they have been interfered with too much by legislation and by public agitation ; and that if the people of the country push any further their attempt to find a new basis of relations between the Government and the railways, they will only bring disaster. We propose in this article to state four general propositions suggested by these two opposing views of a typical American railway system.

1. The importance to the whole American people of the continued prosperity and efficiency of the railways can hardly be exaggerated. The oldest man and the youngest infant in the land depend upon the railways for the necessities of life; rapid, safe, constant, and widespread transportation of goods and passengers is absolutely essential to all the interplay of modern civilization; the hardworking, thrifty, and industrious have contributed several billions of dollars to the construction, equipment, and maintenance of the railways. These investors need protection as well as the travelers and shippers. There is no such thing as legislation "against" railways that is not also legislation "against" the peo-

ple. A farmer who supports a bill framed as an attack upon railway managers because he considers them to be his enemies is really making an attack upon himself. The interests of the railways are the interests of the whole people.

2. The railway builders and managers of this country have, as a whole, been public-spirited men who have contributed by their skill, their courage, and their energy enormously to the welfare of the whole country. They have, however, as a general rule, been allowed to carry on their work in accordance with the dictates of their own judgment. They have been supported generously by the people, not merely from private investments, but from the funds of general taxation. As a class they have grown to regard the railway business as a private business carried on under the laws which govern private business. Twenty years ago the average railway man re garded transportation as a commodity to be sold like any other commodity at a price fixed by the seller. If the customer does not like the price, let him leave it and go to some other establishment. Let the customer, the seller, and competition settle all questions of price; let the stockholders who are skillful enough to buy control of stock settle all questions of financial management ; and let the Government keep its hands off.

3. Little by little the people of the separate States began to realize the financial, industrial, and political power of the railways. In a blind and groping way they attempted to protect themselves against the dangerous exercise of this power. They frequently passed laws that were unintelligent and unjust to railway managers and stockholders. Partly from instinct and partly educated by the railway leaders, the people of the country slowly but surely turned to free competition as the one great relief from the real and fancied evils of railway despotism. The whole tendency of State and Federal legislation was to protect, encourage, and revive competition, and to prohibit the railways from combining to destroy it. With keener insight and clearer foresight the railway managers of the country saw the destructive

and weakening tendencies of free competition. They thereupon began to take protective steps by pooling—this was forbidden by law; by mergers and holding companies—this was forbidden by law; and now the railway financiers are endeavoring to control destructive competition by creating great systems under the ownership and management of one corporation. Mr. Stickney stands for the great system, but he wants it controlled by its president and board of directors solely. Mr. Snyder stands for free competition maintained by law.

4. The Outlook differs from both these experts. In our opinion, free competition in railway administration is an antiquated and useless method of transacting the railway business of the country. It is destructive alike to the interests of the people and of the railway. Natural law is against it, and statute-books full of legislative acts cannot maintain it. Combination and unification of management is the only method by which the rights and interests of shippers, travelers, investors, and managers of railways can be protected and preserved with justice to all. But these combinations, these railway empires, as the Wall Street Journal happily calls them, must be governed, not by their own independent sovereigns, but by the sovereign power of the United States, to use the phraseology of President Roosevelt.

Concentration of power and ownership is bound to come. It rests almost entirely with the railway managers of the country to determine whether that concentration of power shall be left in their hands subject to rigorous Federal regulation, or whether their opposition to Federal control shall result in the more drastic, and in our judgment more undesirable, form of Government ownership. How may Federal supervision of railways be exercised so as to control the evils of overcapitalization, stock-jobbing of securities, and irregularity and favoritism in rates, yet preserve all the advantages of private initiative, private management, and legitimate private profit? These questions and possible answers to them we shall consider hereafter.

# Is Mrs. Eddy Sane?

Proceedings have been commenced in equity by Mrs. Eddy's next of kin to have a receiver appointed for her property on the ground that she is mentally incapacitated. These proceedings lend additional interest to the life of Mrs. Eddy that is being serially published in McClure's Magazine and to the volume recently published on Christian Science by Mark Twain. Neither of these publications can be regarded as exactly unprejudiced. Yet both seem to be written in a spirit of fairness, or at least with an endeavor to be fair. Georgine Milmine, in McClure's, gives full quotations to support all her statements; in truth, the quotations are so full as somewhat to impair the sustained interest of the narrative. And if Mark Twain mercilessly ridicules certain pretensions of Mrs. Eddy and her disciples, he ridicules only what is ridiculous, and treats the fundamental faith of the cult with entire respect.

There is some real ground for Mark Twain's ironical suggestion, "Let us consider that we are all partially insane." The doctors generally agree that a perfectly healthy body is a rare exception to the general rule; and we believe that the expert alienists do not think that a perfectly sound mind is much more common. But not every mental unsoundness constitutes an insanity of which the law can take cognizance. The question in the Thaw trial is not, Is Mr. Thaw's mind perfectly sound? Few persons would believe that it is so. The question is, "Was the unsoundness at the time of the homicide such as to render him morally irresponsible for his actions?" So the question in this case is not, Is Mrs. Eddy's mind perfectly sound? Few persons outside of her cult would doubt that she is "queer." The question for the court is, Has she the kind and degree of unsoundness which unfits her for the care of her property? Two quotations from Mark Twain's book will seem to illustrate very clearly this distinction:

Here fame-honored Hickory rears his bold form,
And bears [bares?] a brave breast to the lightning and storm,

While Palm, Bay, and Laurel, in classical
     glee,
Chase Tulip, Magnolia, and fragrant Fringe-
     tree.
Vivid? You can fairly see these trees gal
loping around. That she could still treasure
up, and print, and manifestly admire these
Poems, indicates that the most daring and
masterful woman that has
appeared on the earth in centuries has the
same soft, girly-girly places in her that the
rest of us have.

But that is all that it indicates. It
does not indicate that she is incompetent
to look after her own interests in business transactions. On the contrary, the
facts as stated by Mark Twain indicate
that she is rather more worldly-wise in
managing property interests than is altogether consistent with either her philosophy that matter is not real, or with that
disinterested spirit which we ordinarily
expect of a great religious leader. For
Mark Twain analyzes the constitution of
the Christian Science Church and the
Metaphysical College and shows that
the whole organization in all its parts
and functions is subject to the absolute
and unlimited will of Mrs. Eddy. President, Board of Directors, Treasurer,
Clerk, Readers, Healers, all are her creatures, dependent for appointment on
her approval, and some of them directly
and all of them practically subject to
removal at her pleasure.

The magnificance of it, the daring of it!
Thus far she is
     The Massachusetts Metaphysical College;
     Pastor Emeritus;
     President;
     Board of Directors;                    -
     Treasurer;
     Clerk; and future
     Board of Trustees,
and is still moving onward, ever onward.
When I contemplate her from a commercial
point of view, there are no words that can
convey my admiration of her.

We do not attempt to anticipate the
decision of the court before which Mrs.
Eddy is to be brought by proceedings
which have been instituted to determine
her mental capacity. We only define
the issue, that our readers may clearly
understand it. The question before the
court is not, Is the Christian Science
philosophy rational or erratic? nor, Is
Mrs. Eddy well balanced or ill balanced?
but, Is she competent to take care of
her interests in the ordinary business

transactions of life? So far as either
Georgine Milmine's Life of Mrs. Eddy
or Mark Twain's portrait of Mrs. Eddy
throws any light on this question, they
both indicate that she is a woman of
extraordinary shrewdness, who has managed her financial interests with a skill
which might be the envy of a Lawson or
a Harriman.

# The Russian Revolution

There are two movements in this country for the relief of the Russian people.
One, represented by Mr. Shishkoff, seeks
to succor the famine-stricken Russian.
The Outlook expressed its sympathy with
that movement in its issue of February
23. Funds in support of it can be sent
to the Rev. S. J. Barrows, 135 East Fifteenth Street, New York. The other
movement is on behalf of the Russian
revolutionists, and is represented in this
country by Mr. Tchaykovsky and Mr.
Aladin. A public meeting on behalf
of this movement was held in Carnegie
Hall on March 4, at which addresses
were made by Tchaykovsky, Aladin,
William Jay Schieffelin, Felix Adler, and
George Kennan. The editor-in-chief of
The Outlook presided at this meeting
and made the opening address, which
we here publish as an expression of the
sympathy of The Outlook with the fundamental aim of the Russian revolutionists
and its belief that Americans should
give to them both moral and material
support.

When an American invites his fellow-
citizens to give their moral and material
aid to revolutionists who are endeavoring to overthrow the government
of a country with which his own country is at peace, it behooves him to
state clearly and concisely the reasons
for such action. The presumptions are
always against war; they are always
against revolution; they are always
against interference in the affairs of one
nation by the people of another nation.
This threefold presumption must be
overcome in order to justify the extension of moral and material aid to the

evolutionary party in Russia. The reasons for extending such aid must indeed be very compelling. Before introducing to you the speakers whom you have come to listen to, I may be permitted to state very briefly the considerations which, in my own mind, have overcome this threefold presumption against the cause with which we are asked to identify ourselves.

The primary object of government is the protection of persons and property. We differ among ourselves widely as to other functions. Some of us are socialists and some individualists. We differ widely among ourselves as to the best form of government, and some of us believe, as I do, that there is no one best form, that different political organizations are needed for different communities and different epochs, and that a the best government which best fulfills its appointed ends. But monarchists, aristocrats, democrats, individualists, socialists, all agree in this, that the primary function of government is to protect persons and property. If it fails to do this, whatever its form, whatever other functions it may pretend to fulfill, it fails in that which is primary and fundamental and which justifies its existence. We may differ on the question whether governments derive their just powers from the consent of the governed, but no American questions that governments are instituted and should be administered for the benefit of the governed and primarily for the protection of their persons and their property, and few Americans will question the affirmation of our Declaration of Independence " that whenever any form of government becomes destructive of these ends, it is the right of the people to alter or to abolish it, and to institute a new government . . . and provide new guards for their future security." Because the Russian Government signally fails to protect persons and property; because it has become destructive of those ends for which governments are instituted among men; because the last vestige of hope that it can be so modified as to become an instrument for the preservation of life, liberty, and the pursuit of happiness has disappeared, we on this platform believe

that it is the right and duty of the Russian people to overthrow their present government and to provide some new guards for their future security.

We are not here to protest against autocracy because it is autocracy, nor against bureaucracy because it is bureaucracy; nor to demand that the Russian people adopt our form of government or use our methods for the protection of fundamental rights; nor to insist that it shall extend its functions and become more socialistic or limit its functions and become less socialistic; nor even to demand that it shall adopt what we are accustomed to regard as fundamental guarantees of liberty, such as the separation of Church and State, a representative assembly, the responsibility of the ministry to that assembly, and the responsibility of both to the people through some form of popular suffrage. All these ideas we believe in, but we have no wish to impose them upon another people. We are here because we believe that the people of Russia have the right to have their persons and property protected by their government; that this is a fundamental right; and that it is palpably, flagrantly, and continuously violated by the Russian Government.

The indictment which our fathers presented against George the Third is insignificant in comparison with the indictment which the history of our times presents against the Czar of Russia. He has caused or permitted thousands of his Jewish subjects to be massacred in cold blood, and other thousands to be pillaged and driven poverty-stricken into exile. In a single year he has caused over thirty thousand persons to be fined, imprisoned, or exiled without semblance of trial. He has habitually allowed both men and women to be tortured within fortresses, and this when no definite accusation by any responsible accuser had been brought against them. He has allowed scores of villages to be pillaged, hundreds of homes to be burned, and unnumbered girls and young women to be given over to shameful violation. He has allowed massacres, planned or carried into effect by governmental authorities, civil and military, for the purpose of terrorizing the population. He has contemptuously disregarded the

Constitution of Finland, openly and flagrantly broken his solemn pledges to the
Finnish people, and made of what was
once the most loyal and happy part of his
Empire a disloyal and wretched province.
He has plunged his country into an un-
justifiable war of aggression, for which it
was wholly unprepared; and has driven
at the point of the bayonet thousands of
Russian peasants to fight in a distant
land for no other purpose than to gratify
the greed or the ambition of court favorites. This war has been conducted without competence and without mercy—the
Red Cross not respected, non-combatants
frequently killed, the wounded often put
to death, hospitals deliberately fired
upon. He has allowed both in the civil
and military administration a corruption
unparalleled in modern times: soldiers
furnished with shoddy clothing and insufficient and unfit food, a navy sent to
sea so ill prepared as to fall an easy
victim to the first effective assault upon
it, and even bread sent into famine districts made of rotten flour and infamously
adulterated with earth. When his people have marched to the palace appealing for relief, he has permitted them to
be shot or sabered in the public square.
When public clamor grew too loud to be
disregarded, he has promised freedom of
the press, freedom of assembly, and freedom of worship, only to disregard each
promise whenever the exercise of such
freedom appeared inconvenient to any
subordinate official of the bureaucracy.
He has called upon provincial governors
to report on the conditions of their
provinces, promising them that their
reports should receive careful consideration, and then has punished by dismissal
from office or with exile governors whose
reports were distasteful to him. He has
convened an assembly of the people,
promising them freedom of deliberation,
and then has dissolved the assembly as
soon as the debates became perilous to
his autocratic power. He has proved
himself equally unable to protect from
the assassin the lives of his ministers and
the lives of his peasant population. His
policy has been as vacillating as that of
Louis XVI., his promises as futile as
those of Charles the First, his despotic
exercise of authority immeasurably more

intolerable than that of George the Tl
The civilized world justly holds
Czar responsible for these high cn
for they are perpetrated in his name
under his authority. If the R
Government authorizes them, it is in
ably despotic; if it is unable to prev
them, it is intolerably incompetent.
either case it is intolerable; and it
the right, it is the duty, of the R
people to throw off such gove
and provide new guards for their fu
security. A political organization un
which such crimes are perpetrated is
worthy to be called a government; ii
organized anarchy.
Is it said that the Slav is unfitted
freedom? I reply that no people
fitted for despotism except they
supinely submit to it. Whether R
is ripe for a republic is not the questi
the question before us is whether
Russian is to hold his life and his p
erty as a tenant at will of an unscn
lous bureaucracy. So far as I can ju
if I were living in Russia to-day, I shou
be a Constitutional Democrat. Ang
Saxon temperament and tradition combine to incline us to take one step at a
time; that one step for Russia would be
the organization of an assembly containing in some form representatives of all
classes and able to speak for them with
untrammeled liberty of speech. But I
am not here to express sympathy for any
particular reform or any particular group
of reformers, but for the Russian people,
and for their common endeavor to throw
off the yoke of their bondage and to secure
for themselves, their homes, their wives,
and their children the right to live in peace
and security. Is it said that the evils in
our own country are such that we cannot cast the first stone against another
country? But this is no reason why we
should not protest on behalf of those
who in other countries are being stoned
to death. Is it said that conditions in
Russia are no concern of ours? Whatever concerns our fellow-men concerns
us. Human brotherhood is not confined
within the limits of church creeds, political boundaries, or race lines. Are
precedents desired for that expression
of popular sympathy which this meeting
is convened to afford? They are abun-

dant : in the sympathy of France for America in our Revolutionary War; in the sympathy of England, moved by the eloquence of Gladstone, for the Italians suffering under the oppression of King Ferdinand II.; in the sympathy of America for the Greeks in 1824, and for the Hungarians under the leadership of Kossuth in 1849; and in the act of Russia herself intervening in 1877 in the name of humanity to rescue the inhabitants of Bulgaria from the unspeakable Turk.

It is true that the criminal classes have taken advantage of the general disorder to pillage and murder; it is true that individuals aroused to a frenzy of despair by cruel oppression have employed assassination in private revenge; it is also true that some of the methods resorted to by secret revolutionary tribunals do not commend themselves to the American judgment and the American conscience. But we do not judge a revolution by the sporadic acts of violence which sometimes accompany it, nor even by the methods which the revolutionists sometimes employ; we judge a revolution by the causes which have led to it, and by the ends which it has in view. If revolution is ever justified, the revolution in Russia is justified by the causes which have provoked it; and the end that the revolutionists have in view—the substitution of a representative for an autocratic government—must commend itself to all who believe in justice and liberty.

Thus far I have spoken to you, my fellow-Americans, on behalf of the Russian people. In closing, I turn to these representatives of the Russian people and speak to them on your behalf and on behalf of the American people whom you here gathered represent. Gentlemen, we Americans do not identify ourselves with any particular group of Russian reformers; we do not stand as sponsor for any particular methods which any group may adopt; but we assure you and your compatriots of our sincere sympathy in your endeavor to overthrow the Russian bureaucracy and to establish in its place a government which will secure protection for the lives, the liberties, and the properties of the Russian people.

# The Spectator

The Spectator's experience warrants him now in embarking on a street-car trip with a wonderful expectation. Not that his hope does not sometimes fail. An adventure would not be an adventure if it came every day. But all the elements of adventure are present in a street-car, and frequently they combine. There are human nature, uncertainty, an independent relationship, and, above all things, that transiency which gives such a zest to all undertaking, keeping the mind alert.

❀

The Spectator boarded a cross-town car at the ferry-house end of Twenty-third Street. There was the usual crowded wait while the outgoing passengers swarmed to the ground; then the incoming scrambled up. It will probably never be known what had happened in that mysterious car; whether some old-fashioned gentleman had been taking snuff, whether some housekeeper had spilt red pepper, what tickling sprite was abroad. But no sooner were all the passengers squeezed compactly into the seats and suspended from the straps than they began to sneeze.

❀

The performance was not obtrusive at first; anybody may sneeze in our climate. A young girl gave delicate utterance, her face in her handkerchief; a stout old man echoed her with resounding emphasis; a baby startled itself, interjecting; and two or three elegant ladies suffered distressing, abrupt perturbation in the midst of their dignified calm. Then gradually it became apparent to the vaguely awakening car that good sport was abroad. A perceptible wave of attention swept through the crowded company, working a genial relaxation. There was probably no event in the world which could so easily have reduced that assembly of technical strangers to their natural basis of friendliness as just this so human, so vulgar besetment, this ridiculous malady. So vulgar—that was the exquisite point. It appears that the searching tests of good humor are not elaborate situations in which one may stand on his dignity, but the commonest accidents of daily life. Perhaps it is better, in the long run, to grade one's dignity to the common level ; then one can walk, not stand, on it. One can even safely fall down.

❁

The Spectator took an absorbing interest in watching the different occupants of the car serve their turns with the malicious plague. Some of them were quite frankly pleased; they contributed their ejaculations to the sum of the general humor with a laughing good will. Several were shyly embarrassed, deploring the public attention. But one or two were superbly scornful, and of course they furnished the best fun of all. One magnificent gentleman, in a high hat and a fur-lined coat, held himself grandly aloof in his manner, expressing a high disdain. " Well, of all the vulgar, disgusting proceedings !" his profile said quite explicitly, as he hung on his strap and gazed out of the window. The hopeful Spectator would not for the world have taken his eyes from him. Presently tiny tremors began to agitate the majestic calm of the classic countenance. The Spectator received an ecstatic poke from the market-woman who neighbored him. " He's a goner !" she chuckled, in audible tones. The proud lips tightened convulsively, the fine eyes blinked very fast; he had heard that chuckle, he tried his best, he would not, he would not— no use ! Away went the gold-bowed eye-glasses on the spring of the most emphatic sneeze that the car had yet brought forth. Laughter ? The people in the street turned to look, smiling vaguely in sympathy. " A Sunday-school picnic ?" they asked one another. But the gentleman in the fur-lined coat pulled the bell-strap and dismounted, purple with indignation.

❁

The most of the passengers were now chatting amiably together. The eagerness of their intercourse had a pathetic significance, considering the stolidity with which they usually travel. So repressed are they by convention, poor things ! The social atmosphere of the car was presently that of an afternoon tea—a very democratic afternoon tea, including all classes and ages. The Spectator remembers that he received excellent advice from his neighbor, the market-woman, as to the care of hens in winter.

❁

The initial impulse to friendliness meantime held on its teasing way. The charter members of the trip—if one may call them that—ceased to deride one another for their involuntary ejaculations; but they banded together to watch newcomers with a delighted expectation. The car stopped, and a young woman got on. She was very pretty. The Spectator rose, urged by a sudden protective desire to save her from her fate. It would surely be going too far to laugh at this fair young gentle thing. But she took his seat with an inclination of her graceful head, and presently, to his grief, he saw her face begin to quiver. Alas ! He would have implored the people, if there had been time and means. But she sneezed in her film of a handkerchief, and all the people shouted. The Spectator will not soon forget the startled look of those blue eyes up into his face. What was the matter ? What had she done ? Then an inspiration seized him. He took off his glasses and sneezed five times with deliberation, punching a young man on the next strap with his elbow the while. " Sneeze, you fool !" he exhorted. The young man sneezed, and the whole car sneezed as well as it could for its laughter. As for the young woman, it is not known how much, if anything, she understood of the peculiar circumstance; but it is known that she had a frank and generous heart in which no pride or resentment lurked, for she joined in the general laughter until the tears stood in her eyes.

❁

Ah, well, that was a famous trip ! The Spectator looks back on it wistfully, and almost resolves to carry a pepper-pot in his pocket to sprinkle all street-car aisles withal. It seems a pity, when so very little is needed to break down polite barriers, that that little should not be supplied. We have set ourselves a curious task of strangeness and silence. The Spectator supposes we might ride in a street-car to the Promised Land of Brotherhood—if we only would.

# THE RENASCENCE OF THE COUNTRY HOME

## BY SYLVESTER BAXTER

IN recent years our American civilization has gained a new regard for country life. The present esteem for it, the hold which it exerts upon men to-day, the delight now taken by the many where once all but few found dreariness—these are recent phenomena. Among the more fortunately circumstanced classes, who up to within half a generation were distinctively city dwellers, it is becoming the rule to make their country residences their true homes. In the older parts of the United States, the sections where the greatest cities lie and where in general the urban population is largest, the trend of families to the country is the strongest. Massachusetts, for instance, is the most urban of all the great States. An enormous preponderance of the population lives ·in cities and in the urban-like townships that range all the way from six or eight thousand to ten or fifteen thousand inhabitants. It is precisely here, as well as throughout New England in general, that the tendency to return to the land is the strongest. It is also marked in the Middle States, in the pleasant Wisconsin and northern Illinois regions tributary to Chicago, and in various parts of California. Then in the country itself the wealth derived from the soil is universally developing the gentleman farmer—" nature's gentleman " in good earnest—with his college-trained sons and daughters ; farming scientifically, fertilizing the land with brains, achieving the genuine refinements and the sensible luxuries at the command of the well-to-do ; giving a National scale to the enviable traditions of the landed family that always have given a distinctive character to the Southern States. In all parts we find that now, as in England it always

has been, the true home of a family is becoming more and more the country abode that with us originally was intended for only a few weeks' sojourn in the summer.

The character of the country house has therefore changed from that of a more or less provisional dwelling-place, however elaborate or elegant it may have been, to that where the home associations are the strongest and where the lares and penates of the household are permanently installed. The family turns to the country earlier in the spring, perhaps with the first faint unfoldings of the leaves. It lingers late in the fall, often through the pageant of the woodlands, until the trees stand bare, until the Thanksgiving feast is celebrated where most fittingly it should be, at a board spread where spreads the open landscape.

In turn the city house now becomes the temporary abode. Indeed, so indifferent to city life do many become that they content themselves with a well-furnished flat through the months of ice and snow. In this they find a dwelling sufficient to their needs while they enjoy the customary round of the theaters, concerts, and other social pleasurings, which, after the wholesome currents of country activity that normally have been flowing about them, leave them easily satiated with more artificial conditions of enjoyment.

It is not only the very wealthy who are thus turning to country life. The more moderately circumstanced are responding to the same influences. Their response would be even more general were it not that the problem of the schools impels a reluctant return to town at the very time when the soft September dusk imparts its snug coziness to the countryside, enhancing the sense of its intimate domesticity. The wealthy are little bound by such limitations; the older children go away to boarding-schools, the younger are governess-taught at home or wherever else the family may be tarrying. But with the great majority home must be where the school is. With the larger number it is happily the public school, the school where the sound lessons of democracy are imparted by daily experience. Even for the merely well-to-do the growing tendency in rural parts towards public school improvement is making the country home more and more possible. The little cross-roads school-house stands abandoned. Large and thoroughly equipped public schools are established at central points, with free transportation from the remotest sections by special omnibus or by trolley when available.

American country life, as originally it was even with us and has always and traditionally been in England, is becoming the normal and the essentially home life for those elements in the population that are not bound to the city by necessity or need. Even in midwinter the country home is not entirely forsaken. Not infrequently the young people, if not the entire household, open up the house and fill the rooms with domestic cheer, while for a week or so, perhaps, they enjoy the invigorating outdoor sports and indoor festivities of the season.

In the elaborate great establishments that in many parts, as in the Massachusetts Berkshires, are rivaling the homes of the British aristocracy, there is too often a life that in house-parties and with week-ends goes the pace that characterizes the same people everywhere—the unenviable life of which Mrs. Wharton has given us veracious pictures in her "House of Mirth." This elegant vulgarity of the excessively rich who fundamentally are too ignorant to know how to use their possessions intelligently, or otherwise than in costly feeding, luxurious dress, or extravagant display, is not the true country life that is growing up among us. Nevertheless, even this has saner aspects in the country than elsewhere. But our true country life gains its favor because of its naturalness, its

freedom from and the various conventional restraints that are imposed by life in town. It should also be said that in many of our great country houses the family life, however leisurely, is wholesome, unconventional, democratic, and characteristically American.

The country home as a popular institution is made possible by reason of its increased accessibility. Fifty years ago even the immediate suburbs of our great cities were, in effect, more remote, more inaccessible, than the distant country is to-day. In Boston, for instance, street-cars had only just begun to replace the "hourlies"—the omnibuses that, plying at sixty-minute intervals between the urban center and places like Roxbury and Cambridge, were then deemed sufficient for the public needs. Even thirty years ago the more remote suburbs were served by trains that ran infrequently; "theater trains" only once, or at most twice, a week; no trains at all on Sundays. Now late trains run nightly to places twenty, thirty, and forty miles away; theater-goers reach their homes at the ultimate points as early as they used to get to the immediate suburbs in the old "hourly" days.

The electric trolley-car and the automobile, the bicycle, the good roads that are becoming the rule in many sections, are doing wonders to suppress the isolation that once made country life intolerably dull—a daily routine of vegetative monotony. The good-roads movement has spread to all sections of the country since Colonel Pope began his enlightened propaganda of twenty years ago. While, in this respect, some parts still remain literally in the Slough of Despond, in other sections there are now practically nothing but good roads. Massachusetts and New Jersey possess vast networks of perfect highways. The new South is awaking in this respect as in so many others. The improved highway, indeed, has become one of the great factors in the renascence of the countryside. It makes for sociability as well as for convenience and economy. It has given us the bicycle for errands as well as for most wholesome exercise; moreover, the whole family thinks nothing nowadays of jumping into an automobile to "go neighboring" for the day, announcing themselves by telephone and visiting friends not only in the next county, or the next but one, but even in the next State! It is now no more trouble to do this than it lately was to take the family buggy and jog along three or four miles to the next village, going at a walk, or at most a slow trot, to favor poor old Dobbin. Not only with the man of affluence, but with every well-to-do farmer, will it soon be the regulation thing to possess an automobile—in the latter case not the luxurious touring-car, to be sure, but at least a good runabout or some other motor-car equivalent of the buggy or the "carryall."

One great reason why country life has grown in favor so remarkably is because it has appropriated to itself so much that formerly was exclusively of the city. In recent years much of the best of the country has been brought to the newly enlightened city—frequent open spaces, abundant playground facilities, great public parks where the charms of the natural landscape are presented in their most ideal aspects. But there is a return wave, a reflux of corresponding energy. Thus the best of the city is likewise imparting itself to the country. Hence we have a "rapproachement" between the urban and the rustic. We are achieving the urbanization of the countryside. Indeed, do not certain modern tendencies suggest the total elimination of the city from the ideal civilization that we are growing towards? The age of the sky-scraper, to be sure, may not jibe with this idea. But the sky-scraper may be only a provisional institution after all. On the other side of the Atlantic it is not at all a metropolitan concomitant. While it means congestion of population, the great forces of quick transit are, on the whole, making for diffusion. Hence it seems reasonable to expect that the ·processes now at work will gradually transform all the inhabitable parts of the country into what in effect will be one vast and interminable suburban region—if "suburban" be not a misnomer where there is no urban.

Suburban life, in its best estate, as found in the aggregations of tasteful and prosperous homes fringing off into the country about some of our great cities, comes very near being the ideal life, the prototype for the Utopian conditions that the future should hold for us. We find it in the pleasant New Jersey regions, beyond the Harlem in Westchester County, or out on Long Island; in the famous cluster of Greater Boston communities, like the Newtons, Milton, Belmont, Arlington, Lexington, Winchester; and in the delightful rural margins of Philadelphia. Here are plenty of air and sunlight; tranquil surroundings; ample lawn and garden space, with trees, turf, and shrubbery; sociable relations with good neighbors, but not near enough to hear the dinner-table clatter next door or to receive involuntarily through open windows confidences as to family affairs.

The sort of suburb where the houses elbow one another and one has the undesired freedom of his neighbor's phonograph or mechanical piano-player—instruments which there generally play nothing but ragtime—affords homes worse in many respects than are made by city blocks, or even flats, where non-conducting walls and floors at least preserve the peace between dwellings. In the suburb as it should be, there are charming scenery and rural pleasuring all about, with attractive drives and delightful walks; a river or a lake, or an arm of the sea, for boating and bathing. Quick and frequent transit brings business within convenient reach, also the amusements and social pleasures of the city. Such life is wholesome; even when comfortable to the degree of luxury, as it may be, it remains unostentatious, more or less unconventional, and inherently democratic in its standards.

The extent to which the differences between the country and the city are diminishing is indicated by the fact that the yokel, the traditional rustic agape in the town, "Reuben," the "jay," is becoming rare. While the type is by no means extinct, it is now more familiar on the stage than in reality. In fact, the city, except in the matter of mere bigness, offers comparatively little in the way of absolute novelty wherewith to impress the average rustic mind of to-day. Abundant books, the same monthly and weekly periodicals, the same daily newspapers, cheap excursions, electricity for lighting and transit, have acquainted the countryman with the most essential things that the city has to offer. Like the American who visits London and for the first time sees St. Paul's and the Parliament Houses, he finds it all so familiar in pictures that it seems as if he had always known it. We have all heard the story of the country child returned from his first visit to New York. The most novel thing he had to tell about was the most out-of-date, back-number thing he saw—the ridiculous little horse-cars dragged by poky old nags! Many a country youth of twenty years cannot remember the time when trolley-cars did not run past his door or at least through his village. Likewise many a country-man in town to-day is disposed to sniff contemptuously at the prevalent and unhygienic gaslight. At home the neighboring waterfall not only illuminates his house for him cheaply; he even milks his cows by electric light! Many a village is ahead of the city in posses-sion of up-to-date modern conveniences. Think of sojourners in the country dreading to return to town on that account! Times have changed since the days when the average country dweller had to break the ice in the toilet-pitcher mornings through the winter. Health in the country is better now-adays, also, as a rule, for cold air was by no means synonymous with pure air under those conditions.

The country-seat is an old institution in New England. Far back in the Colonial days the country residence reflected the life of "home," as England then was called by everybody this side the ocean. Such country-seats dotted the more immediate environs of pre-Revolutionary Boston. Not a few of them to-day stand like verdurous islands of fair and widespread acres amidst the sea of houses that metropolitan expan-sion has spread around. One such noble estate has remained in the hands of the same family for more than two centuries, its broad pastures still resist-ing the pressure exerted by waxing taxes to bring them on to the market at square-foot prices. All through eastern Massa-chusetts the same tendency is filling the idyllic landscape with stately country homes—twentieth-century heritage of the days when Sir Harry Frankland and Agnes Surriage lived so much of their romance at the Hopkinton estate. So we see dozens of out-of-the-way towns, their very names strange to the Boston ear until very recently, becoming all of them what Brookline was not so long ago—the seats of a rich and elegant life, the permanent homes of many an affluent household, families whose names stand with the choicest in the Blue Book. Not only Bostonians or the wealthy families of other centers of trade through New England have their country homes in these places. Neighbors on every hand are families from all over the United States, mainly from the West, but many of them hailing from the South and the Pacific slope. Altogether, this movement is converting New England into the great summer pleasure-garden for the Nation. The joy of living has to-day become a char-acteristic note of summer in the land of the Puritans. With the children of these summer residents from the West and elsewhere their country and seaside homes hold the deepest place in their affections. Every year they are impa-tiently eager to come back into the land of rocky hills, rolling pastures, pleasant bays, and the marvelous clear water of brooks and streams. They are as loth to depart. So they seize their first opportunity to make their homes where the soil claims their hearts. Conse-quently the numbers of the Western-born whose business holds them in the East are a subject for astonishment.

But our talk is properly of the move-ment countryward from the town, rather than from one section of our great land to another. The latter phase was merely instanced as a notable aspect of the general influence of the country's charms upon those who have been made receptive to them. The city-born boy finds in the country a wonderland, full of joyful surprises, inexhaustible in delight-making powers. The country lad first knows the town with a strange exhilaration, a quickening of his whole being. The rush and the whirl of move-ment, the roar of traffic, the human rivers in the streets, the ever-changing spectacle of the passing show, even the curious odors which arise from numerous activities in this quarter and that and blend into something indescribable that strikes his young nostrils with an unwonted appeal, not unlike that which the more grateful scent from the land has for the inward-bound sailor—all these intoxicate his soul. For years and years the country-born man may live submerged in the powerful currents of urban being. Their fascination is strong upon him from the first; it holds him for years in its thrall. But there surely comes a time when, sooner or later, the city's life palls upon him; the rush and the roar become intolerable; the din in his ears grows maddening, as of hammer and anvil in endless reiteration; the signs and the placards conspire to insult his eyes with frantic visual yells; the general coming and going are purposeless; it all seems a weariness of the soul, a vanity of vanities. Then suddenly he recalls with ardent longing the almost forgotten scenes of his childhood, the dull existence that once he turned his boyish back upon, as he hoped, forever.

Nevertheless he may from time to time have revisited the old scenes. Old ties could not so easily be severed. Family obligations called him back. Perhaps a sister married, an aunt died, an estate was to be settled. The intervals may have been infrequent, years lying between. Each time he noted the changes; occasionally when the local weekly fell into his hands he remarked with a faint curiosity the little doings of the neighborhood, the recurrence of the well-known family names that eventually came so largely to mean the children and perhaps the grandchildren of his old schoolmates.

At last it all rises up before him again—a tidal wave of emotion rolling in upon the shore of his soul and bearing him back upon its crest. The old recollections, the beloved old scenes, every remembered feature of them graven upon his heart: the dear old house so long forsaken, its unlighted windows gazing into his soul as in mute reproach; his mother's grave, and his father's—he went years before—in the quiet village cemetery! There is a tug at his heart-strings; the lure of the land has grown irresistible.

> "Upon all the hills broodeth rest,
> In the tree-tops the breeze maketh quest
>   With scarcely a breath;
> The birds in the woodland are sleeping.
> Only wait! Soon wilt thou be keeping
>   The long rest of death."

The perfect lines here imperfectly echoed in English were written by Goethe on the summit of the Gückelhahn in Thuringia. When the writer once stood there in his youth, gazing over the hushed Whitsuntide landscape at sunset, deep in the valley below a mill-wheel slowly casting its wreath of musical pearls, he felt how the ineffable peace of the scene must have drawn the poem from the master's soul, as now he feels how the same bond with nature must draw back to the Earth-mother her country-born child.

The return of the native to spend his remaining years amid childhood scenes brings a serene joy. Had he come prematurely, the absences, the vacancies left by old friends and companions, might have tinged the familiar scenes with melancholy. But now the vanished past lives again in his mind, together with the new-made present, that he readily grows into as he readapts himself to his native environment. It is indeed another village, another world, that has grown up meanwhile. But the old is also still there for him, just as the boy that once he was persists in his consciousness, as young as ever beneath the accrued layers of his elderly manhood. Indeed, a complex company of his former selves makes of his being a multitudinous composite. This induces in him a fraternal though unreciprocated recognition of comrades and playmates in the children and children's children of the Charlies and Hals and Willies and Susies and Mollies of yore.

He takes the old homestead in hand and makes it livable and comfortable, even luxurious, though respecting in the truest sense of the word the primal homeliness of it. Maybe there are additions meet for the prosperous state of the returned son—rambling annexes, verandas, bay windows, dormers. The beloved old-fashioned flower-garden is expanded and glorified. The touch of art soothes away from the place the austerity of old. Smooth driveways, paths pleasant to the feet, wind through gracious shrubberies. A friendly foreground honors the noble spreading landscape before the house. Indoors the sense of domesticity is enhanced. The fine old fireplaces have been unmasked and restored; their immediate successors, the gloomily ferocious stoves, are banished in favor of a kindly tempered heater in the enlarged cellar. The sense of domesticity is enhanced by the exposure of the sturdy ax-hewn timbers of oak, the ceiling plastered between—timbers that make the stout house good for another century or two.

The village and its life have changed correspondingly. In place of the dull monotony, relieved only by petty gossip and the meager interests confined within a narrow horizon, there is now a tranquil movement in touch with the great world outside. There is a tastefully housed public library, given by some world-prospered and grateful son of the place. The magazines and the best weeklies are generally taken in the village homes. The people find time to read, to think over and intelligently discuss the literature of the day as well as the great thoughts of the past. Few city folk have such time to give from their business and their distractions. Local activities are now of more account than they were.

Village improvement constantly gives new work, makes new duties, as its scope enlarges. The modern arts and crafts movement, reviving good old handicrafts and introducing new ones—weaving, basketry, wood-carving, metal-work, lace-making, cabinet-work—has made life more worth the living and given profitable occupation for many a village. In various New England villages colonies of artists have given themselves as leaders in the work with unselfish enthusiasm, and thus have enhanced the general charm of the scenes whose beauty first attracted them.

As to amusement, how the opportunities have increased! Everything that country life can yield in the way of pleasure has been availed of and developed.

Old and young share in the benefits. Ball games in the old days were primitive compared with those of to-day. Then there is croquet, the first game to call whole families out of doors, and still held in deserved honor. Tennis, of course. And golf, the passion of old people as well as of the young. Every village of any account has its golf links, every town with urban pretensions and of proper quality its country club. Aquatic sports add themselves thereto— boating, canoeing with paddle or with sail, knockabouts, sailing dories, power-boats, and larger craft of all types. Every lake or decent stream is a paradise for amphibious youth and for men who thereby prolong their youth. Then the delights of the open road. The bicycle, pleasurable and immensely useful, is with us to stay, though the "craze" has departed. It has revolutionized country life in important aspects, and has made possible its legitimate successor, the motor-car. Who knows how soon human flight, only just now achieved with the motor-driven aeroplane, may not introduce a wonderful new element of recreation and of utility into country life, annihilating space for transit almost as effectively as the telephone has done it for speech? The latter, indeed, has become one of the greatest boons for the country, bringing whole neighborhoods into immediate contact, the lone farmstead into the village world, and promoting human solidarity as few other things have done since the railway movement began.

It is not only the affluent to whom the blessings of country life are possible. The instance of a mechanic known to the writer is typical of many. He married a wife from a Cape Cod town. His wages amounted to about $1,200 a year. The wife inherited the old home. The very day that school closes she leaves for the Cape with the children, and they stay till the end of vacation, to the joy and health of all. Some day the place will be the permanent home of the elders; the children will have gone out into the world themselves, returning perhaps after many years to the dear old spot, as so many are doing in these days.

# Railway Overcapitalization

In its issue of February 9 The Outlook published an article entitled " Railway Over-capitalization," by Mr. W. L. Snyder, of the New York Bar, which has attracted more than usual attention from its readers and its newspaper contemporaries. A large number of correspondents regarded it as an attack upon Mr. J. J. Hill and the Great Northern Railway Company. A savage editorial in the New York Sun and a more courteous but not less intense editorial in the able Wall Street Journal expressed the opinion that Mr. Snyder was writing in general ignorance of his subject. The fact is, as will be seen from his article printed herewith, that Mr. Snyder had made a careful and expert study of the facts from a legal standpoint. In its issue for February 23 The Outlook disavowed, both for Mr. Snyder and for itself, any intention of throwing aspersion on Mr. Hill's honor, good faith, public spirit, and genius as a constructive railway man. We are, therefore, glad to give Mr. Stickney's account of the material prosperity of the Great Northern Railway a prominent place in our pages. The sensational examination of Mr. E. H. Harriman by the Inter-State Commerce Commission directs public attention to the whole subject of railway operation and finance with new force at this time, and we ask those who desire to know what The Outlook's attitude on the subject actually is to read the following papers by Mr. Stickney, Mr. Snyder, and Professor Fisher, and the full expression of our own editorial opinion which will be found on another page.—THE EDITORS.

## I.—A DEFENSE OF THE GREAT NORTHERN

### BY A. B. STICKNEY

#### President of the Chicago Great Western Railway Company

BACK in the sixties of the last century, when Jay Cooke undertook the construction of the Northern Pacific Railway, northern Minnesota and North Dakota, including the Red River Valley, were generally considered almost worthless for agricultural settlement. To correct this impression, Mr. Cooke organized a party of correspondents of many important Eastern newspapers and sent them on an exploration trip to see for themselves and write up the country as they saw it.

The party rendezvoused at Minneapolis, and made a sort of " royal progress," with carriages, saddle-horses, and camping outfits.

All the correspondents except one made notes of the characteristics of the country from day to day. When the party had reached the fertile valley of the Red River, the leader called aside the correspondent who did not make notes, and, with considerable anxiety, said : " I see you are taking no notes. I hope you are not ' going back ' on this country when you get home." " Going back on this glorious country !" says the

correspondent ; "not by any means. I am taking no notes because when I get home and start to write I don't want to be ' trammeled by facts.' "

It would appear that many, and perhaps most, of the newspaper and magazine writers on the problem of railway rates and the capitalization of railways have the same feeling. They do not investigate facts because when they begin to write they don't wish to be " trammeled by facts."

A conspicuous illustration may be found in The Outlook of February 9, 1907, in an article entitled " Railway Overcapitalization." Speaking of the Great Northern Railway Company, it says, as a premise of fact upon which to base the general argument :

It formerly earned and paid to its stockholders, over and above all fixed charges and expenses, $2,100,000 annually, or seven per cent. on its $30,000,000 of capital stock. Its earnings gradually increased to $4,200,000 annually. Instead of paying fourteen per cent. on the $30,000,000 of original stock, it issued $30,000,000 additional, without legal authority and in direct violation of the laws of Minnesota, and paid seven per cent. on the $60,000,000. Its net earnings increased to $6,300,000 per year, and its stock was again increased to $90,000,000. The earnings grew to $8,400,000 annually, and the stock was increased accordingly to $120,000,000. The net earnings soon exceeded $10,500,000 annually, and another increase of $30,000,000 of stock was issued, making the aggregate value of the stock at the present time $150,000,000, on which it pays the handsome sum of $10,500,000 annually, or seven per cent. on this entire issue. But so great has been the growth and development of the country that this company now seems to be earning net every year $14,700,000, which will justify an additional increase of $60,000,000 of stock, as the increased earnings will enable it to pay seven per cent. on $210,000,000, instead of on $150,000,000, the amount of its present issue.

The commercial history of the world affords nothing to equal this wonderful exhibition of economic achievement, which has been duplicated in like manner by the other great transportation corporations of the United States.

The quotation conveys the impression that the present property of the Great Northern, with $150,000,000 of stock outstanding, is the identical property, and no more, which it possessed at the time when the writer says it had $30,000,000 of stock outstanding, and that the sole purpose of issuing the additional $120,000,000 of stock was to enable the company to distribute its earnings to the stockholders without appearing to pay more than seven per cent. dividends.

The statement is so obviously untrue that the writer must be regarded as belonging to that class of sensational scribblers who never allow their pens to be " trammeled by facts."

The following tabulated statement, compiled from Poor's Manual, shows the number of miles and the stock and bonds outstanding on the 30th day of June of each year; also the dividends paid during each year:

| | Miles. | Bonds. | Stock. | Dividend Paid. |
|---|---|---|---|---|
| 1890 .... | 3,006 | $65,735,000.00 | $20,000,000.00 | None |
| 1891 .... | 3,292 | 67,966,000.00 | 20,000,000.00 | 3½% |
| 1892 .... | 3,417 | 69,149,200.00 | 20,000,000.00 | 5 " |
| 1893 .... | 4,257 | 103,435,754.54 | 20,000,000.00 | 5 " |
| 1894 .... | 4,328 | 105,080,454.54 | 25,000,000.00 | 5 " |
| 1895 .... | 4,496 | 105,279,354.54 | 25,000,000.00 | 5 " |
| 1896 .... | 4,498 | 105,433,254.54 | 25,000,000.00 | 5 " |
| 1897 .... | 4,559 | 106,141,854.54 | 25,000,000.00 | 5 " |
| 1898 .... | 4,698 | 112,669,454.54 | 25,000,000.00 | 6 " |
| 1899 .... | 4,996 | 97,239,454.54 | 89,226,610.00 | 6¼" |
| 1900 .... | 5,418 | 96,577,454.54 | 98,413,500.00 | 7 " |
| 1901 .... | 5,451 | 96,683,454.54 | 98,711,750.00 | 7 " |
| 1902 .... | 5,849 | 97,975,454.54 | 123,853,000.00 | 7 " |
| 1903 .... | 5,888 | 97,190,454.54 | 123,996,750.00 | 7 " |
| 1904 .... | 5,951 | 96,648,454.54 | 124,129,250.00 | 7 " |
| 1905 .... | 6,110 | 100,753,939.39 | 124,365,625.00 | 7 " |

The statistics for 1906 are not yet published in the Manual.

In 1890 there was outstanding, in addition to the $20,000,000 Great Northern Railway stock, $20,000,000 stock of the St. Paul, Minneapolis, and Manitoba Railway Company, all of which except $359,500 has been acquired by the Great Northern Railway Company.

In 1890, therefore, the total bond and stock capitalization was $105,735,000; in 1905 the total capitalization was $224,725,126, making an increase in sixteen years of $119,490,126.

In 1890, when the total bond and stock capitalization of the Company was $105,735,000, its 3,006 miles of railway were prairie lines in Minnesota and North Dakota. During the sixteen years between 1890 and 1905, in which its total capitalization increased $119,490,126, it has constructed 3,104 miles, including the expensive lines over the Rocky and Coast ranges of mountains to the Pacific coast, and expensive lines in the mountains, and has expended large sums of money in improving its former prairie lines and in the purchase of equipment, and in enlarging and improving its terminals.

It has built steamships which sail on the Great Lakes and on the Pacific Ocean.

Its terminals at Minneapolis-St. Paul, at Duluth-Superior, and at Seattle are superior to all others. At Duluth-Superior, in my judgment, its facilities for handling grain, including its elevators, are superior to the facilities of all the railways in the cities of Baltimore, New York, and Boston combined.

That Mr. Hill had the genius to build a line across the unsettled plains and the mountains to the Pacific in 1890-93, without a land grant or other Government aid—a feat never before accomplished—and to build in sixteen years over three thousand miles, and made the improvements specified by only doubling the capitalization, seems to the people of the West a " wonderful exhibition of economic achievement."

The facts in respect to the capitalization and property of the Great Northern afford no evidence of overcapitalization.

The writer has not always agreed with Mr. Hill upon railway problems, but fair play is fair play, and fair argument in the discussion of economic problems is always "trammeled with facts."

The public seem to demand "untrammeled" sensation. Perhaps the writers might be able to make equally sensational articles showing how the people are being robbed, by the railways' collecting too high rates, based upon the following facts:

(1) The 215,506 miles of railway in the United States carried in 1905, 28,-706,734,960 cwt. of freight. A reduction in rates of 6¾ mills per cwt., regardless of the distance hauled, would have reduced the net income of the railway companies $14,566.98 more than the aggregate amount of their dividends.

(2) A further reduction of 9.06 mills per cwt. would have reduced their net income $10,000 more than the aggregate amount of interest, which the railways paid on their bonds and other indebtedness.

It is altogether probable that if these insignificant reductions were made by legislation, and the majority of the roads were thus forced into bankruptcy, a tremendous sensation would be created.

## II.—THE CASE AGAINST THE GREAT NORTHERN

### BY WILLIAM L. SNYDER

*Of the New York Bar, and author of "Snyder's Annotated Inter-State Commerce Act" (Baker, Voorhis & Co., New York, 1906)*

An article which I contributed to The Outlook of February 9 on "Railway Overcapitalization" has been widely criticised by financiers and misreported by the newspapers as an attack upon the Great Northern Railway. It was not an attack, but a simple statement of the present tendency towards railway overcapitalization as illustrated by the history of the Great Northern. There is nothing in my first article to justify the assumption that the additions to the capital stock of the road were not made for cash received. On the contrary, my assertion was and is that the cash so received from the stockholders was used for buying up competing lines at a high price instead of for properly developing the main lines of the Great Northern itself.

Two suits have been instituted recently in Minnesota which throw more light upon modern methods of railway capitalization than has yet been brought out by legislative investigation.

The first of the recent Minnesota actions referred to was brought by the Attorney-General of the State to enjoin the issue of $60,000,000 new stock by the Great Northern Railway, a Minnesota corporation, until the company had secured the consent of the State Railroad and Warehouse Commission.

The second suit grew out of the first, and was brought to forfeit the charter of the St. Paul, Minneapolis, and Manitoba Railroad, which it is claimed has been absorbed by the Great Northern, upon the ground that in permitting itself to be swallowed up by a rival company "it has ceased to perform the functions for which it was created, and has, therefore, forfeited its right to exist as a railroad company under the laws of Minnesota."

The facts made public in these suits would seem to justify the conclusion that stock has been issued from time to time by the Great Northern Railroad which has been used to absorb rival competing lines in order to establish a monopoly in transportation, by perfecting a trans-Canadian system to be operated in connection with the American lines north of the Union Pacific from the Great Lakes to the Pacific Ocean. The American system includes the Northern Pacific, the Great Northern, and the Chicago, Burlington, and Quincy, which latter has been absorbed by the two companies first named. The Canadian lines operate from Winnipeg westward across the continent to Vancouver. The combined systems would, if the transaction is carried out, embrace a monopoly in the transcontinental railway system west of the Mississippi, including the greater portion of the continent of North America. It appears also that these important operations are being carried forward at the expense of the American commerce which is dependent on the Great Northern and its branches. These have been neglected to such an extent that they are entirely inadequate to meet the demands of the increasing population, and thousands have been ruined and sustained direct financial loss by reason of the lack of railway facilities, which it was the duty of the Great Northern, as a public carrier, to furnish.

In the first suit to enjoin the issue of $60,000,000 Great Northern stock, all that was required of the defendant in order to end the litigation was to file a written application with the Railroad and Warehouse Commission of Minnesota requesting permission to issue the stock, show the necessity for it and the purpose for which the proceeds were to be used. Instead of complying with the law, the Great Northern filed a statement with the Minnesota authorities in which it was set forth that the proceeds of the new stock were to be used to take up the bonds and stock of its subsidiary separate or leased lines. It was said that part of the funds were to be used (*sic*) to build new lines to form a nucleus for a new trans-Canadian railway, projected westward from Winnipeg to Vancouver. The subsidiary companies whose stock and bonds were to be absorbed were the Dakota and Great Northern, the Montana and Great Northern, the Billings and Northern, the Washington and Great Northern, the Portland and Seattle ; the Vancouver, Victoria, and Eastern Railway and Navigation Company ; the Brandon, Saskatchewan, and Hudson's Bay Railway Company, and the Midland Railway Company of Manitoba.

Of these the Dakota and Great Northern is one hundred and forty-three miles in length and is leased and operated by the Great Northern. The Montana and Great Northern has about the same mileage, and is also leased and operated by the Great Northern. It is claimed that the latter company now owns the stock of the Washington and Great Northern. These various lines are all embraced in the comprehensive trans-Canadian project.

In view of the fact that the Great Northern has failed to furnish proper and adequate facilities to meet the necessities occasioned by the vast increase of population along its own route, which dereliction of duty has resulted in financial loss and ruin to thousands, the Great Northern now promises, with a portion of the proceeds of the sale of the new stock, to increase its mileage, trackage, and terminal facilities, by building a good second main track, acquiring new terminals, and reducing grades along the line.

The Governor of Minnesota took it upon himself to ask the President of the Great Northern the cause of the failure of his corporation to discharge the public duties for which it was chartered. Mr. Hill's explanation is significant. He says :

The discrepancy between the growth of traffic and the additions to railroad mileage and the extension of terminals, shown by new mileage of less than one and one-half per cent. a year since 1904 to take care of a traffic increase averaging eleven per cent. a year for ten years past, presents and explains the real problem.

Does it ? In view of the fact that Mr. Hill's corporation since its original issue of $30,000,000 has sold new stock to the extent of $120,000,000, and now has stock outstanding to the extent of $150,-000,000 which yields a net income of seven per cent. or $10,500,000 annually to its stockholders, the inquiry which presents itself is, What has been done with this capital ? How is it that the Great Northern, with its millions of new capital and increased earnings, has increased its mileage less than one and one-half per cent. a year, in view of the fact that its business was increasing tenfold that amount annually ?

The answer may be found in the developments growing out of the second suit brought to annul the charter of the St. Paul, Minneapolis, and Manitoba Railroad Company on the ground that it is merged in the Great Northern. On January 25, 1907, two days after Judge Hallam granted an injunction to restrain the new issue of Great Northern stock, Chief Justice Start, of the Supreme Court of Minnesota, issued a writ of *quo warranto* to compel the St. Paul, Minneapolis, and Manitoba Railroad Company to show cause why its charter should not be forfeited, because it was absorbed by the Great Northern, which now claims to operate the road under a lease. The Attorney-General claims that on February 1, 1890, the stockholders in both companies were identical; that the Manitoba Company transferred to the Great Northern all of its property at a price largely in excess of its true value. In other words, that the Great Northern paid a premium of $5,000,000 in the purchase of the stock of the Manitoba Company. It is claimed that the Manitoba property was purchased with stock of the Great Northern Company, which latter stock, it is alleged, was unlawfully issued and is what is familiarly known as watered stock and upon which dividends are being paid,

For these reasons the Attorney-General claims that when the Manitoba Company, on February 1, 1890, assigned its property to the Great Northern, "it ceased to perform the functions for which it was created, and has, therefore, forfeited its right to exist as a railroad company under the laws of Minnesota." The charter of the Manitoba road was originally granted May 22, 1857, by the Territory of Minnesota to the Minnesota and Pacific Company, which became bankrupt in 1879; and the Manitoba Company, with the approval of the Legislature, purchased its road and franchises. The Territorial charter contained a provision that the road should never pay in taxes more than three per cent. on its gross earnings, and it was claimed that the Manitoba Company acquired the same right. In 1905 the tax on railways in Minnesota was raised from three to four per cent. on gross earnings, which the Great Northern was called upon to pay. As the Manitoba road was practically merged in the Great Northern, the latter claimed, in order to escape the increased tax, that, notwithstanding the merger, the Manitoba Company was still in existence. The Attorney-General assumed to test this question in *quo warranto* proceedings against the Manitoba.

The Great Northern claims also that there are outstanding 3,400 shares of Manitoba stock held in England, France, Spain, and Holland, by parties who re-fused to assent to the merger with the Great Northern, to whom the latter guarantees and pays six per cent. dividends.

But the claim of the Attorney-General is that the Great Northern, which was chartered originally in 1856 as the Minneapolis and St. Cloud Railway, and rechartered September 18. 1889, under its present charter, is nothing but a holding company, owning directly no mileage, but, through its ownership of a number of subsidiary companies and the control of their stock, and controlling also the Manitoba, the Eastern Railway of Minnesota, and a number of other lines by virtue of perpetual leases, has secured a monopoly of the carrying trade in the vast territory extending from the Great Lakes to the Pacific Ocean, both in Canada and in the United States.

It is obvious that the Great Northern, as far back as 1890, used part of its illegal stock, as well as the proceeds thereof, to secure control of the St. Paul, Minneapolis, and Manitoba Company. It is clear also that the proceeds of stock issues were used to acquire control of a number of subsidiary lines above referred to, which form part of the trans-Canadian system. Here, then, we have an answer to the question put by the Governor of Minnesota to the President of the Great Northern—an answer which discloses the reason why "additions to railroad mileage and the extension of terminals, shown by new mileage" has increased less than one and a half per cent. a year since 1904. The population in the United States along the route of the Great Northern and its branches—Minnesota, the Dakotas, Montana, Wyoming, Idaho, Oregon, and Washington—has increased over one hundred and ten per cent. since 1897. The capital of the company which was originally represented by a stock issue of $30,000,000 is now represented by stock aggregating $150,000,000. Instead of this capital being used to increase mileage, trackage, and terminal facilities, as public duty required, in order to accommodate communities which have grown up and settled along the line of the road, and which are entirely dependent upon it for their individual welfare and commercial success, the capital has been used apparently to absorb rival lines, destroy competition, and build up a railway monopoly affecting a territory embracing nearly half the continent. Communities which have established themselves relying on the good faith of the carrier to discharge its public duties are permitted to suffer because, as there is no other rival competing line and no other railway, they cannot get to market. Their grain is in the fields or in elevators being eaten up with storage charges, the products of the factories are not promptly transported, the product of the mine is not promptly shipped for want of adequate facilities. In many localities the community is practically stranded for lack of carrying facilities, because the carrier has failed to live up to the obligations imposed upon it by law. Commerce, instead of having free play, as the result of competing lines of communication, is subjected to unlawful restraints and monopolies which are forbidden by the express terms of the statute.

## III.—STOCK WATERING

From " The Nature of Capital and Income," by Irving Fisher, Professor of Political Economy in Yale University ( The Macmillan Company, New York, 1906 )

We have considered two ways through which the book-value of capital, surplus, and divided profits may exaggerate the true condition of the stockholders' property ; namely, through misfortune or the unforeseen shrinkage of the assets, and through misappropriation of stockholders' funds, even when stock had at the outset been issued at par. There remains to be considered a third way, namely, through the issue of stock below par, or for services, patents, etc., at unduly high prices.

To illustrate this way of overvaluing capital, or " stock-watering," suppose a company to be capitalized at $200,000, and that this company issues at the beginning 1,000 certificates of the par value of $100,000, but sells them for only $60 per share actually paid into the treasury. Here is $60,000 paid-in capital, represented by $100,000 face value of stock certificates, leaving a margin of $40,000 "water." Suppose, further, that another block of $100,000 of the stock is given to an inventor for his patent, the real value of which is only $10,000. Finally, suppose that bonds are issued to the extent of $300,000, and are floated at par. Then the company has received in actual cash only $360,000. Of this sum only $60,000 has been received from the stockholders. The patent, which has also been contributed in return for $100,000 of stock, and which is worth only one-tenth of that sum, makes the total balance due the stockholders $70,-000. But, the company is capitalized at $200,000. Consequently it will be necessary for the bookkeeper to exaggerate the assets to the extent of $130,-000.

He may do this as follows :

ASSETS

| | |
|---|---|
| Plant [cost $360,000]............: | $400,000 |
| Patent [worth $10,000]........... | 100,000 |
| | $500,000 |

LIABILITIES

| | |
|---|---|
| Bonds.......................: | $300,000 |
| Capital ........................ | 200,000 |
| | $500,000 |

Here $90,000 of the exaggeration is put under patent and the remainder in an overvaluation of the plant. Many other methods of stock-watering are possible. A common one is to allow the plant to run down ; i.e., to fail to make proper repairs, while retaining its old book value in the balance sheet. A railway may be " skinned " in this way, by diverting to dividends what should be paid to a depreciation account. This operation, however, is not commonly called stock-watering, but mismanagement.

It is sometimes said that stock-watering is not wrong, as long as all the terms and conditions are known. This is much like saying that lying is not wrong, provided everybody knows that it is lying ; for a false balance sheet is only one form of a false statement, and, ordinarily, a false statement is made with intent to deceive. The object may be, for instance, to mislead intending bond-holders by making them believe that there is a larger security for their loans than actually exists. We see here one reason why honest men often *under*value their assets. They prefer, if there is any error in their valuations, that the error shall be against themselves rather than in their favor; in other words, that their representations as to financial strength shall be well within the truth. Yet it not infrequently happens that undervaluations of assets may, like over-valuations, serve the purposes of dishonesty—to " bear " the speculative market, for instance.

Many attempts have been made to prevent the frauds which result from stock-watering. For instance, the State or National Governments compel publicity of accounts in the case of insurance companies, National banks, and inter-State railways. The stock exchanges require similar publicity in regard to "listed" securities. Any company whose securities are listed on the New York Stock Exchange must publish its assets and liabilities at stated intervals. But this rule is too general to be very effect-ive. In some cases the law requires the entire nominal capital to be paid into the company, in cash or securities at their market value, as in the case of National banks.[1]

[1] Revised Statutes, § 5140 (Act June 3, 1864, § 13).

# THE FRIENDSHIP OF THE GOOD

## BY WILLIAM DE WITT HYDE

The friendship of the good, and of those who have the same virtues, is perfect friendship; good people being both good absolutely and good to one another. Such friendship, therefore, endures so long as each retains his character; and virtue is a lasting thing.—*Aristotle, Nichomachean Ethics, viii., 111, 6.*

The title to our new-found wealth, Dear Friend,
　Runs with the power to make our hearts more free,
More generous, more gentle; to the end
　That all may share God's gift to you and me.

I see thy features in each human face;
　I hear thy mandate in each civic call;
I own thy kindred in the lowliest race;
　I love thy likeness in the souls of all.

Thou shalt seek me where noble duty draws;
　Thou shalt find me where kindly mercy leads;
Thou shalt serve me in serving the just cause;
　Thou shalt love me in doing lovely deeds.

Our friendship for each other lasts so long
As both shall love the right and hate the wrong.

# HOW IS IT WITH THE RUSSIAN REVOLUTION?

## BY WILLIAM ENGLISH WALLING

Why is it that Americans do not definitely take the side of the Revolution against the Czar? Americans have always been in full sympathy with every people struggling for freedom, they have always expressed that sympathy and they have often succeeded in making it felt abroad—we need go back no further for an example than the war with Spain. Why does not our sympathy definitely take the side of the people in their struggle against the Czar? Why are we remaining more or less neutral at such a moment? Americans are suspending their judgment about the Revolution because they have not yet received a satisfactory answer to three great questions: First, Are the Russian people united and do they know what they want? Second, Are they making every effort to wage an organized warfare against the Czar, after the manner of the recognized revolutions of history? Third, What is there that Americans can do about it? The following article by Mr. William English Walling is written in reply to these three questions.—THE EDITORS.

FIRST, the Russian people are united and they know what they want. No people, in fact, was ever more united during a revolutionary period than the Russians are to-day. The scope of the struggle is immense; so large that probably no human mind has yet grasped its full significance, or is likely to do so for many years to come. There is only one issue, and at the same time there are an infinite number of issues. Czarism has suppressed in the Russian people everything that a civilized people holds dear. In struggling together against Czarism the people are struggling for the right of development, not in any one single direction, but in almost every direction that can be named. The professors are struggling for academic freedom; the peasants for land; the workingmen for the right to organize; citizens for the right to govern themselves; publicists for the right to speak and write; and the people at large for every elementary human right, for not one is safe at the present time.

As a result, there are as many parties as there are groups of people which emphasize one or another aspect of the struggle. But it by no means follows that these parties are struggling against one another. In fact, there is no possibility of fundamental confusion. The objective of every liberal, radical, and revolutionary organization is to take *all* the power away from the incompetent,

564

immoral, and murderous régime that is at present in control. All oppositional parties are agreed that the Government has never listened to any argument except that of violence, that the past warfare of the people against the Government, whether the best possible or not, has been entirely natural and justifiable, that no one but the Russian people itself should be consulted in the regeneration of Russia, that the Duma or the constituent assembly should have absolute and supreme power, and that a system of universal suffrage should be established, by which the common people should control the destiny of the nation.

This is the situation. Unity is its necessary and inevitable consequence. But this unity also exists in fact. Various revolutionary and oppositional organizations sometimes feel bitterly against one another for what they consider to be a misinterpretation of the main purpose of the revolution, or a dangerous error in the method of the fight. Nevertheless, they remain generally united, and the practical result is simply that there has been an unconscious and unwilling but nevertheless a perfectly definite division of labor between the parties. The Liberals or Constitutional Democrats have provided the parliamentary organization and the leading parliamentary ideas; the Peasants' Union and the Labor Group have directed the peasantry into politics ; the Social Democrats have organized the general strikes ; the Social Revolutionists have organized such guerrilla fighting as is already going on, and are most actively occupied with the immediate preparations for insurrection.

The unity is a matter of fact. Perhaps the half-dozen most noted of the moderate liberals in Russia are Gutchkov, Shipov, Heyden, Trubetzkoi, Lwow, and Stachowich. These men are the most moderate of Russian public men, and within the past year all have taken a very prominent part either in the Duma or in governmental functions. All are opposed both to the Government and to open revolution. None are ready to go as far as the Constitutional Democrats, who in many indirect ways have aided and are aiding the active insurrectionists. Yet at the present moment five of the six are willing to co-operate with the revolutionary parties against the Government in the elections. Gutchkov alone remains in the conservative party—that of the 17th of October—and wishes to *put down the revolution first.* The others, members of the Party of Peaceful Renovation, all see the absolute necessity of *putting down the Government first.* Alone among men of public reputation, Gutchkov stands in favor of the Government.

The leader and organizer of a group a little more progressive than these, but still rather more moderate than the Constitutional Democrats, is Maxim Kovalevsky, well known as a professor and publicist to the people of England, America, and France. Mr. Kovalevsky is the editor of the second most important liberal paper in Russia, The Strana, of St. Petersburg. In a recent number, speaking of the necessity of co-operation with the Social Democrats, he said : " There is only one question in Russia to-day. That is, whether Russia is to be a European or an Asiatic nation ; whether the people are going to continue to be slaughtered like cattle or not."

In the coming elections all the liberal and revolutionary parties will act together. There will be many different combinations and a great many different names, but the common action will nevertheless be effective and united on the great charter of Russian freedom.

For the Russian people have already got their Magna Charta, and the outside world does not seem to know. We must recall the remarkable unity of the last Duma. The address to the throne, it will be remembered, was signed by all but an insignificant minority of its members. In the voting on every important question proposed in that address the majorities were overwhelming—sometimes the vote was unanimous, sometimes the majorities were four hundred to one, to three, five, or six. This unity was secured not only by the powerful pressure and intelligence of the Constitutional Democrats who occupied the center, but by the full recognition of the necessity of unity by both of the extremes. After the Duma had dissolved, both the most active and the most peaceful extremes were more than ever impressed with the necessity of making the great fight on the basis of the address to the throne. Whatever agitation and discussion of other revolutionary objects may be in the air, all the wise leaders of every oppositional and revolutionary party are at one in the necessity of concentration for the Russian Magna Charta, the address of the Duma to the throne.

Second, the Russian people are doing everything in human power to wage an organized war against the Government. It could hardly be possible that a nation as united as Russia in its general objects, and even in the methods of their attainment, should fail to appreciate the importance of organizing physical effort.

The revolutionists know that in the bloody crisis which must inevitably come a larger part of the army can be relied on to remain neutral and that a certain portion will even come over to the revolution. They hope, therefore, that it will be perfectly possible to wage with growing success a guerrilla warfare against the Government. In the Baltic Provinces, in the Caucasus, and to a certain extent in Poland, this warfare has already begun, and the Russian people are wholly in sympathy with these rebels of a foreign race. There is no disagreement on the advisability and necessity of bringing the guerrilla war over into Russia as soon as the Government has finally refused to deal with the coming Duma.

This organized warfare is, like the national unity, not only a necessity of the situation, but it is a fact. There is already a high degree of organization in the guerrilla war in the Caucasus, the Baltic Provinces, and Poland, to say nothing of the splendid success of Finland, which won its temporary and partial freedom precisely because the people were drilled and armed. Arms are being landed now in Finland, the Caucasus, and the Baltic Provinces in shiploads of several thousand rifles each. Arms are being imported into Poland from every part of the Austrian border, even to a new species of dismounted machine gun. Already there are hundreds of thousands of automatic revolvers in the people's hands. At the present rate of organization there will soon be as many rifles, and the time will have come for the guerrilla warfare to spread from the outlying provinces into Russia proper. When it does so, it will find ready to aid it a peasantry that has already broken out in rebellion in a thousand different places during the last year, and a splendidly organized railway union, ready not only to strike at the proper moment, but to do what is an absolute military necessity of the situation—that is, effectively to destroy the lines.

But we must remember that this organization is necessarily slow. The Government is executing several hundred revolutionists a month, sending tens of thousands to Siberia every month, and every month locking other tens of thousands in the Russian jails. With its system of hundreds of thousands of police, Cossacks and spies, well paid by money the Czar has borrowed from abroad, the Government is able to throw almost inconceivable obstacles in the way of the movement.

Third, Russia is united and waging the most intelligent and practicable form of warfare possible under the circumstances. But what can aroused and sympathetic Americans do? This question also will soon be answered.

There are at the present moment in America, or will be within a few days, prominent representatives of every one of the most important political parties of Russia. For some months the news-papers have been full of the speeches of Levine, the representative of the moderate Jewish party, and of Lieber, the representative of the more revolutionary element. Leading representatives of the Social Revolutionary party, which has done the most effective work among the peasantry, Tchaikowsky and Gerschunin, have been in the country for several weeks. Aladyin, the leader of the Labor group and one of the most prominent men in the Duma, an excellent speaker in English, will soon be here. Within a few days there will arrive a typical and representative Constitutional Democrat, a member of the central committee of the Zemstvos and a member of the Supreme Council of the Empire, who resigned, however, as soon as the Czar refused to deal honorably with the Duma, Mr. N. A. Shishkoff. Mr. Shishkoff also speaks excellent English.

Each of these men has been telling or will tell the American people what they can do for the Russian cause. Mr. Shishkoff, and of course all the others as well, is most anxious to get financial aid for the pauperized and bleeding Russian people. Mr. Shishkoff has made an appeal for relief which has already appeared in The Outlook. Contributions may be sent to Mr. S. J. Barrows, 135 East Fifteenth Street, N. Y. City.

But all will stand together in favor of the latest movement for the support of the Russian people abroad—namely, the national protest that is now being prepared against the horrible manner in which the Czar is waging the internal war, slaughtering, torturing, robbing, and violating the people. This protest will not settle the revolution, but it will have a tremendously useful effect. Mr. Kennan's book on Siberia, for instance, is appreciated by every educated Russian. Its influence, they all agree, cannot easily be expressed in words. Every organized foreign protest against Russian conditions has had its immediate effect inside of Russia. So sensitive is the Government to foreign opinion that, with one or two exceptions, every foreign writer or correspondent going into Russia has been treated with courtesy by the officials in spite of the fact that a large majority have been clearly and fearlessly hostile to the Government. There is no question that the Government is most sensitive to foreign opinion.

Let everybody who is moved by the terrific and tremendous conflict that is going on in Russia express himself freely and openly on all occasions against Czarism. Let every one read the illumi-nating speeches and statements made by the accredited representatives of the Russian people now in the United States, and attend, if possible, the meetings that are being held in this country. Then let every one join in the coming protest of all the enlightened peoples against the unspeakable atrocities of the Czar!

# WHEN THE FEVER WAS AT UIST

## BY EDITH RICKERT

### Author of " The Reaper," " Folly," etc., etc.

IT was when the fever was at Uist that Father Murphy came to the island ; and he knew no more of the state of affairs than did the Pope himself. The secret had been kept well. There were only the steamboat-men to carry the news abroad ; and they, knowing that it is unlucky to spread the news of disaster, were as mute as haddock. So throughout the summer they were fighting the sickness all over the island, and some won through, but more were buried ; and with the turn of autumn Father Murphy came.

Very young he was, empty of experience, and full of good intentions. So when Father Tulloch developed a bad lung and had to be sent southward, there was an interregnum long enough for the fever to creep in from—God knows where—before the Powers-that-be decided which young priest should be sent to cut his wisdom-teeth on the savages of the West.

So the Bracadaile had a first-class passenger as she plowed up The Minch ; and although the sailors looked at him crossways for a while, as being an Irishman and no apparent lover of the sea, they granted him a degree of admiration when, obviously seasick, he hung out on deck and would not yield. But so much of his fortitude was used up in the conflict that he did not venture upon conversation until the ship turned into smooth water, and the captain himself came to the wheel for putting into the harbor.

" You know this place well ?"—the Irishman lisped a little.

The big brown Norseman looked at him, drew his conclusions, and said, laconically : " Born here."

" Looks—a good sort of place." Conscience would not permit more praise, as the young man turned his blue nose and spectacles towards the clump of huts among the heather.

" Ay."

" Good land ?"

" No bad."

" And the people ?"

" Why, they're just like other people whatever," says the captain, with a touch of scorn.

" You see, I've come to take Father Tulloch's place."

The captain's eyes, bent upon the ecclesiastical garments, seemed to say : " Do you take me for a fool ?" But aloud he was more polite : " Dear, dear ! . . . I'm a Free Kirk man myself." He was silent but for giving orders, until the engine was stopped and his part was over. Then said he :

" You'll know about the fever ?"

" What fever ? I had not heard. . . . Is it bad ? Do they die of it ?"

" Ay, that do they." The captain watched him, then twisted his mouth into a grim smile : " It'll no be safe to land, ye ken. If ye like, I'll take you on to Dunvegan. . . ."

But he was left in the middle of his sentence. The new priest was ashore with a glossy fat bag in each hand.

He was met by a shuffling old man whose eyes did not meet his glance.

" Sir, it was Ian MacPherson was asking me to meet you, the day—"

5

"Is it the fever?" interrupted the priest.

"Nobody will be seeing him since the Sabbath," said the other, unabashed by the previous lie that he had told.

"And you are afraid to go to his house?" asked the priest again.

"Afraid, is it? Na, na. It's just the judgment of God, I'm thinkin', and them that has it must abide."

"Look ye," said Father Murphy, and although he was still blue from the sea, his face had authority. "I don't know what kind of doctor ye have in this God-forsaken hole, but it's clear to me that something needs doing to change this state of affairs. And ye can tell him or not as ye like."

And in this rashness he justified the wisdom of the Powers that-be, in sending him where he could do as little damage as possible.

That night, while he sat by his study fire and listened to the roll of the sea, he questioned and cross-questioned his housekeeper; and at the same time they of the post-office questioned and cross-questioned the old man who had fetched him from the boat. And on both sides it was pretty well decided that there was no love to be lost.

When Father Murphy came down to his breakfast the next morning, he found the doctor waiting in his dining-room. He seemed to the priest like a wind-blown furze-bush with two gleams of the sea through the tangle. And if the doctor had sought for an image in his own mind to describe how the cleric looked to him, he might have used that of a bluebottle fly in spectacles.

"I'm told," began the doctor, abruptly, "that ye've been making me pretty compliments; and I've just looked in to give ye my thanks."

It was no wonder that the young man stammered and failed to explain himself, thus taken by surprise.

The doctor listened, with the glimmer of sarcastic laughing in his beard: "And now that ye've come, ye'll give an Irish *whisht*, and the fever will just take wings and fly away to Skye, or maybe to Strome Ferry, where the doctors are as wise as the priests."

But Father Murphy hung on to his poirt, somewhat as he had clung to the ship's rail, in the teeth of the wind, the day before.

"How many cases are there?" he got out.

"Huh!" said the doctor. "Nine or ten among the Catholics."

"But altogether?" persisted the priest.

"Maybe thirty-seven—unless there's fresh ones this morning."

"Then I repeat that's it's a pretty state of affairs," said Murphy, with heat.

"And I agree with ye," retorted the doctor, still more hotly. "And I say it's none o' my doing!"

"But you pretend to care for them all!" was the challenge.

"No pretense about it. I do what I can."

"And they die on your hands!"

"Am I their Maker? They are born and they die. I go my rounds the day. What more?"

"What more?" said Murphy, stumbling over his words. "What more? I'll tell ye. Ye should have sent word to the proper authorities and had the thing taken out of your hands. . . ."

He stopped for breath, and the doctor took up the word, beginning with portentous slowness: "Ye callow loon—" Wrath conquered him: "Damnation! I'll not take it from ye!"

But the priest would not retract a word. "Ye should have got help from Glasgow—"

"Glasgie, is it?" He broke into a roar of laughter that shook the room. "And now, since ye've come here to teach me my business, I'll just go straight and get help from Glasgie—oh, ay, ay!"

His laughter rumbled down the passage, and he himself was gone before the priest could find another word.

This was the first encounter between them; but they had many another while the fever was at Uist.

Father Murphy spent most of the time before the next mail-steamer touched in gathering the facts and presenting them, as best he might, in a letter to the authorities. This despatched, he began to consider how he might help his people. At first, indeed, he tried services and sermons; but the church continuing almost empty, he hired a pony, loaded her to the best of his judgment, and began to make a sort of round, with food for the convalescent, oil for the dying, prayers for the dead.

Frequently he met the doctor, likewise burdened, with saddle-bags full of food and medicine. They exchanged curt greetings, but never a word more.

"Opinionated young fool!" mumbled the doctor in his beard.

"Cross-grained old idiot!" was the unpriestly phrase for which Father Murphy had sometimes to do penance.

One day, at the post-office, he heard it said that the Widow McCaskill, who lived seven miles along the seaward hills, had not come as usual for her pension letter. Of this, it was agreed, there could be but one explanation. Sick at heart for expectations of his own that had not been fulfilled, Father Murphy set out on foot, his pony having sprained her knee.

It was a wonderful hot day for October, the air as thick and close as in August; and by the time that he had covered little more than half the distance the priest was clean exhausted, and sat down in the shade of a rock among the heather. There he fell into a despondent muse, whence he was aroused by the padding of a horse on the sandy road below.

Dr. Campbell pulled up, and looked at him with a sarcastic smile. "Ah," said he, politely, "I've been meaning to ask ye this long while—heard from Glasgie yet?"

The priest went red with anger. "If the postmaster told ye the one thing, he might have told ye the other," said he, not without spirit.

Campbell gave a nod that might mean anything, and rode on, with a reluctant spark of appreciation in his eye.

But the priest was thoroughly sick of himself, and of the mess he had made of his first appointment. He sat on among the dying heather, wondering if he ought to give up and ask for some other sort of work. As a student he had had a pretty taste in illuminating missals; but this had not helped him much in his dealings with men. When it came to a contention with barbarians like this savage doctor, he felt that his strength was like that of a spent swimmer in rock-surf.

He was stirred by a drop of rain on his forehead. One of the strong sudden showers of the Hebrides had gathered in the tension of the atmosphere.

As he rose and looked about for shelter, he was aware of a woman, bent under a great load of peat, standing in the road below him. He had a feeling then that she had been there some time, perfectly quiet under her burden, looking up at him with gray eyes as luminous as agates in the dull brown of her face. He judged her young, chiefly because she bore no marks of age. She was barefooted and bareheaded, and the new-risen wind drove her coarse, straight black hair in long ribbons across her face.

"Fine day," said she, with the usual salutation, and added, "but it will be coming on to rain soon, and our house is just over the brae."

He thanked her and jumped down into the road; and then she added, shyly, looking at him out of the corners of her eyes: "The doctor was telling me there was a new priest come; but I will never be having time to go to the church."

At the door of the loosely piled stone hut, its thatch overgrown with grasses and wall-flowers, she would have *shooed* away the chickens fluttering in to take shelter from the storm; but the priest said, with feeble humor, that they should be allowed to stay, being of the same family with themselves.

He sat dreamily on a three-legged stool in the dark cottage, while his hostess knelt to blow into flame the peat embers of the round hearth in the center of the room, and hung the kettle, as the smoke poured out and filled the air.

"It is the storm makes it fall," said she, with an apologetic smile.

And he, coughing a little: "It is all like Ireland."

She took down from a peg a little baking-board, and got out flour and other things.

"What is this?" he asked.

"Some scones to your tea," she said, shyly; and before he could make any answer, the rain was upon them with a terrible beating and rush as of another Deluge.

For all the smoke, there was the cheer

of red fire-glow in the room; and the priest was content to be silent, but felt it his duty to make conversation:

"What is your nam_?"

"Ishbel."

"And your father?"

"He is a fisherman. He will be at sea the day."

"And your mother?"

She was dumb, and he hastened on to, "You have brothers and sisters?"

"Five, and all at school now. But it's thanks to the doctor that I have them still to bless myself with. It's no more than a month that three of them was down with the fever, and he took the others away to his own house, and sat up with the three at the worst . . . Oh, if ever blessings should be poured on any man's head . . ."

By this time the scones were browning in the ashes, and the tea was made in the brown pot on the hearth; and Ishbel had brought out cheese and heather-honey, and was' a little aggrieved that her guest would not listen to talk of an egg.

"It's the doctor that has always an egg," says she, "and he'll be coming now any minute on his way back from the Widow McCaskill's—poor thing!"

He stirred out of his dream: "But I am mad. It's myself must be getting on. I set out this afternoon for Borve. . . ."

The door burst in, followed by a drift of rain and the doctor in seaman's oil-skins.

"Hey, lass," he shouted through the smoke, as he brushed the rain from his eyes, "I've tied up Brown Bess in the cow-shed. What's this? A man?"

He compressed his lips as he recognized the priest, and in silence hung his dripping coat and hat upon a peg and took the other three-legged stool.

Ishbel looked nervously from one to the other as she began to give them their tea; and when she found that neither man would speak to the other, her anxiety grew into distress. She tried little piteous sentences that each answered in turn directly to herself; but she was too stupid, it seemed, to make them talk to each other.

At last, in despair, perceiving that the rain had ceased, she flung wide the door. Both looked at the vision that swept in

upon them of distant amethyst hills, of leaps of light upon the road, here sparkling with broken quartz, there overrun with a rush of amber burns that streaked the brae where no water had been before. Far away they could watch the retreating footsteps of the storm over the fallow sea.

"Can ye look at that," said Ishbel, coming back to them in a little glow of indignation, "and not speak to each other, and good men both, whatever?"

Then began Father Murphy: "I bear no grudge . . ."

The doctor's laugh interrupted him. "Nor I. But I must be off, or Brown Bess will catch cold."

When he led his beast round to the front of the cabin, the priest was ready with an awkward little speech of conciliation.

"Words—words—words—" exclaimed Campbell, rudely, and sprang into the saddle. "Cl-lk," he said to Brown Bess.

But even as she moved away he turned and listened again and looked sharply.

"Words?" said he. "It's sheer babble. Blest if he hasn't got it himself! Ishbel, if your five brothers and sisters can spare ye a bit, ye'll just follow after. Ye'll be needed, and the Widow McCaskill will do very well, for her daughter-in-law came last night. Now, my man, ye'll up here."

Quite how he managed it none of the three remembered; but the next moment he had the dizzy, swaying youth before him on the horse; and Brown Bess, a little surprised and a little cross, was nevertheless answering his cl-lk in her usual steady fashion.

That night the news was told at the post-office, and thence spread like thistle-down in the wind, that the new priest was taken bad, that his housekeeper was gone to her sister's at Borve. and that Ishbel was come over the hills to nurse him. And they said then that he seemed a good sort of young man whatever, though nothing to Father Tulloch, and that if he had not been an Irishman maybe . . . But there was none among them that did not wish him recovery.

However, it was little enough they knew of the struggle that went on in the sick-room between the three of them and the fierce disease, or how they came to understand one another in the fighting. . . .

It was all over the island one day that priest and doctor alike received important-looking letters. And it was Dr. Campbell himself that carried them up to the sick-room. "One for you," said he, gruffly, "and one for me. How many times did you write?"

"Three," said Father Murphy, when they had read the two documents together. "And you?"

"Two times three," said Campbell, "before you came and after. And now that two-thirds of the cases are nicely convalescent, including this last, the Glasgie grandees will be coming to stamp out the disease. They'll spread their nurses thick about the island, to teach the people all the things they don't want to know; and they'll sit drinking my whisky at my house while they prepare reports for medical journals on the mysterious nature of the disease, and that will be the end of the fever at Uist."

And yet it was not quite the end. For the old man and the young it meant a friendship that lasted until the wind-blown doctor with the sea-blue eyes passed away into the elements of his native isle. And even when the priest had lost his early zeal, and had grown fat and pursy in the oblivion from which the Powers-that-be had never seen fit to recall him, the memory of that time lingered with Ishbel, who had brought them together. When she was an old woman, with married daughters, and sons drowned at sea, she used to take out of her press sometimes two treasures wrapped in pure white linen. One was a battered leather whisky-flask, picked up long before in the tracks of Brown Bess, and the other was a beautifully illuminated missal with the name Ignatius Murphy in Gothic letters on the fly-leaf. And the Highland woman's agate eyes would grow misty and dim, but hardly with sorrow, as she remembered the days of the fever at Uist.

# THREE POETIC DRAMAS[1]

TWENTY years ago and more Mr. Stedman predicted the revival of the drama as a literary form of vital and contemporary quality and interest; and many times during the intervening years those who are sensitive to the unspoken thought of their time have been aware of an attitude of expectancy, an air of hope, toward the future among those who love literature for its own sake. The reaction toward excessive energy in the writing of novels, the persistent tendency of the tremendous putting forth of force in dealing with materials to find expression in ideas as well as in things, the deepening sense of that social solidarity which is the soul out of which dramatic situations constantly arise, have seemed to point to the revival of the drama as most vitally expressive of the life of an age which takes refuge in stories from its cares and

labors, and whose conscience, penetrating social and industrial conditions to the living tissue of humanity behind them, is beginning to turn to the drama with something of the zest and passion of the men who read or saw Shakespeare's plays as they came from his hand. On the Continent the dramatic movement has of late years overshadowed every other form of literary activity in its force and passion and in public interest. Ibsen, Sudermann, von Hauptmann, Maeterlinck, d'Annunzio, stand for a large group of powerful, original, daring, and variously gifted men who have made the drama what the novel was twenty years ago.

In England a novelist of such assured position and sustained success as Mr. Hardy has succumbed to the vital attraction of the drama, and in "The Dynasts" has shown how a man of genius can waste rich material in the endeavor to do that for which he is unfitted. Mr. Wilde has found a more audacious and lively successor in Mr. Shaw, who is amusing,

[1] *Nero*. By Stephen Phillips. The Macmillan Company, New York.
*The City: A Poem Drama, and Other Poems*. By Arthur Upson. The Macmillan Company, New York.
*Alcestis and Other Poems*. By Sara King Wiley. The Macmillan Company, New York.

irritating, and interesting even when he mocks himself and makes game of his audience. Mr. Pinero and Mr. Jones are expert playwrights rather than dramatists by the compulsion of genius ; but the publication of their plays in book form is significant of the general interest in the drama. Mr. Stephen Phillips has cast in his fortunes with the drama, and has given the world a few plays of poetic charm. His earlier work in this field gave promise of superior achievement, which his later work has not quite fulfilled. "Nero," although by no means lacking interest nor occasional lyric passages of great charm and melody, must be characterized as the least interesting of the group to which it belongs. It is not possible, however, to dismiss Mr. Phillips, as some American critics have been in the habit of doing, as a writer of small account. He belongs among the first contemporary English poets ; and although this does not give him very high rank measured by absolute standards, it entitles him to careful study. He is a thoughtful poet who takes his work seriously ; he is an accomplished craftsman who has made himself to a very considerable degree the master of the technique of one of the most difficult of the arts. His work has never failed to convey the impression of a zealous student of literature, associated in taste and interest with the best in his field, and bringing forth his own work not without the corrective touch of self-criticism. He is not a prolific writer. At the end of about fifteen years of publication only half a dozen thin volumes bear his name. In "Nero" he attempted to reconstruct, along lines effective for poetic purposes, the dilapidated character of Nero, and in this endeavor the play shows ample knowledge and abundant skill.

Nero, as interpreted in the play, is an æsthetic degenerate of a type with which the modern world is much too familiar. The defect in the drama lies in its failure to convince the reader that such a man existed. Those charming bits of diction which readers of "Ulysses" and of "Paolo and Francesca" remember are to be found also in "Nero," but by no means so abundantly. Mr. Phillips

has a dignity of diction which rarely fails him, and which sometimes covers, though it does not conceal, a very commonplace thought or a weak dramatic situation. The utmost that can be said of this play as a whole is that it will not detract from Mr. Phillips's reputation. But it must be added that, at his age and with his experience, every new drama ought to register distinct progress in his art.

Mr. Arthur Upson, whose "Octaves in an Oxford Garden" found many appreciative readers, has written a poetic drama of unusual beauty of motive in "The City ;" a play which differentiates itself sharply in theme and spirit from the plays of passion which have come of late in large numbers from the presses. The King of Edessa, in Mesopotamia, lies desperately ill of a disease beyond the healing skill of his physicians. The fame of the great Physician at Jerusalem has reached him, and a courtier has been despatched to invoke the ministry of the marvelous power at the command of the strange Healer of the bodies and souls of the afflicted. The search ends on an "olive-sprinkled hill" beyond the walls of Bethany. The urgent letter is placed in his hands, but before words have been spoken the Physician seems to understand, and hands the messenger a scroll on which a few words are written. Then comes the great tragedy before the eyes of the courtier, and he who had healed others dies at the hands of savage men. When the Queen hears these words she cries out in her anguish :

"Oh, let them never leave their quiet hills,
These prophets that dream well for all the
     world !
Let them remain in mountains far from man
Where nothing fiercer than the lion roams,
Communing with the kindly elements—
The earth that is their mother, and the winds
That are such spirits' brothers, and the fire
Of splendid storms that like their words
     breaks forth,
And waters that flow out like their great love !
They are of other worlds and strangers here:
Let them remain in mountains—or in gar-
     dens !"

When the scroll is unrolled, these words appear :

"As to the part of your epistle which
Concerns my going hence to visit you,
Know that I have a mission to fulfill
In mine own city, and must here remain
Till all its ends be satisfied. Yet you

Of your infirmity shall know full cure,
And those most dear to you have peace."

This vague message is interpreted by a sudden light that streams into the mind of the King; he faces a rebellion in their strength and in the illumination of a vision of the nobler city that is to be:

" Again the third time I was lifted up.
A mighty, living, beautiful walled town,
A-wave with trees, lay shining on the plain.
And underneath her walls a river glided,
Safe bearing her full many a peaceful sail.
And there lived folk who all day worked and sang,
And folk that to and fro sped silently;
And here and there some sat apart and thought.
From all whom throbbed a joy in unison
With the warm earth and her enfolding heavens;
Through all, the strong, perpetual streams of life
That through the universe unceasing flow.
And this dream ended not with cloud or mist,
But slow receded in its radiance
Till it grew small as towers and sails and stream
That whiten yonder to the rising moon.
And as it went I heard a voice that said:
'Thou, Abgar, art the King of cities three:
The Past, the Present, and the Yet-to-Come.
Out of the Past the Present by slow pain
And undiscerning upward agonies;
Out of the Present, by as many throes,
The city of Celestial Harmony.' "

The play ends in a climax nobly conceived in the spirit of the great Teacher, and its beauty lies largely in the play of light from a new order of life over the brutality and strife of the old order.

From " Octaves in an Oxford Garden," which are included in the volume, the two opening stanzas will suggest the fine vein of meditation and the delicate feeling for rich and beautiful association which run through the pain:

" The day is like a sabbath in a swoon.
   Slow in September's blue go fair cloud-things
   Poising aslant upon their charmèd wings,
Stilled to the last faint backward smiles of June.
Softly I tread, and with repentant shoon,
   Half fearfully in sweet imaginings,
   Where broods, like courtyard of departed kings,
The old Quadrangle paved with afternoon.

No footfall sounds within the empty hall;.
   No echoes people corridor and stair;
   The sunlight slumbers on the silent square,
Forgetful of slow shadows by the wall.
Yon is the passage where low lights do fall
   And linger longest (I have watched them there),

Beyond which you will find a spot most fair,
A comfortable and a holy spot withal."

Mrs. Drummond's " Alcestis " is a lyric treatment in dramatic form of one of the most appealing and beautiful Greek myths; a story which has modern interest and is more easily interpreted to modern feeling than most of the great tragedies in which Greek thought on the deep things of life found poetic expression. This latest rendering of the old story follows the lines of the Greek drama, but in sentiment, emotion, and richness of diction is the work of a woman bred in modern conceptions of love and marriage, and of the deep and holy instincts of modern womanhood. In free play of imagination, frankness of creation, passionate devotion, and exaltation of sacrifice, the play is fundamentally lyrical. This quality is strikingly shown in two passages spoken by Alcestis, which convey a clearer impression of Mrs. Drummond's spirit and manner than the most elaborate characterization:

" This breast stirs in the wind of love, soft blowing;
Forget the world, remember how I love thee,
And I will sing of love and night and spring.

Through clustered bloom of orchard trees
   Murmurs the evening breeze,
And rippling like a shallow stream
   Lulls to a drowsy dream.
In the pale sky the moon hangs pale,
   The apple petals sail
And sink in deep grass, gleaming green,
   Where darkening shadows lean.
The robbins twitter, settling slow;
   The nearing cattle low;
Their herders whistle as they come,
   And children scamper home.
All that went forth to toil and quest
   Gather to love and rest."

" A cold breath strikes upon my happiness
Like sudden fierce spring winds on early flowers.
I hear the heavy plashing of his oars
Who comes to take me to the realms of death.
Admetus, I have lost thee in the gloom,
I shall not ever feel thy clasping arms,
Nor the soft pressure of my children's lips,
Nor hear their bird-sweet callings at the dawn,
Nor watch them grow in beauty and in strength,
Nor guide and guard their tender steps from harm.
My heart grows faint, my body chills and fails;
Alas! I am too weak. Give courage, Zeus!"

# Comment on Current Books

**A Comprehensive View of Italy** The accomplished biographer of Lessing and Schopenhauer has produced an interesting and valuable book on Italy. Her aim is not so much to describe the Italy of the past as actual conditions in the peninsula. In that description she is thoroughgoing, she dips beneath the surface. She has interesting things to say about the court, artists, authors, archæologists, scientists, inventors, dramatists, and journalists. But, what is more striking, she seems equally at home whether putting such a poet as Ada Negri or such an archæologist as Giacomo Boni in their proper places, or in discussing agrarian and fiscal conditions. Her treatment of those conditions should commend it to students of economics. They may well read her chapter on agriculture, if for nothing else than because it shows how a high tariff may prostrate industry; for instance, the sugar duty is so heavy in Italy that the native fruit grower must export his fruit to be put into preserves elsewhere, while the salt tax, for example, is so rigidly enforced that the whole coast is patrolled lest people should take sea-water for evaporation. The income tax in Italy varies from ten to twenty per cent., the land tax from thirty to fifty per cent.; in consequence the land rarely yields over three per cent. (The Italy of the Italians. By Helen Zimmern. Charles Scribner's Sons, New York. $1.50, net.)

**The English Berkshire** No one who has journeyed or who would journey by river from Oxford to London should fail to read Mr. James Edmund Vincent's detailed and delightful description of the part therein of the Berkshire bank. For a hundred miles of the Thames borders Berkshire's upper boundary. Travel by river, indeed, is practically unavoidable unless the traveler omits much that is interesting, for, save at rare intervals, the roads do not follow the river's winding course. In the general description Windsor Castle is naturally the subject of a chapter, and a capital one. It is pleasantly gossipy, as compared with some other descriptions in this excellent series of "Highways and Byways." Indeed, in that series the talk about persons might be slightly more emphasized. We are always grateful, in the present volume, whenever its author comes to such places as Hendred House and its memories of Sir Thomas More, or to Sunningwell Church, the burial-place of Samuel Fell, D.D., Dean of Christ

Church, and who, alas! is to be remembered for all time as a disagreeable man, because of a familiar nursery jingle-rhyme. Mr. Vincent's text is immensely reinforced by Mr. Griggs's many and charming illustrations. (Highways and Byways in Berkshire. By James Edmund Vincent. The Macmillan Company, New York. $2.)

**Italian Travel** An extremely pleasant little book of Italian travel is that by Anne Hollingsworth Wharton. She travels from one end to the other of the peninsula and describes her adventures and those of her women companions. Her accounts of life in the various towns of Italy are as unhackneyed as they are simple and unaffected. (Italian Days and Ways. By Anne Hollingsworth Wharton. J. B. Lippincott Company, Philadelphia.)

**Men Who Made the Nation** A thoroughly well made reprint of Dr. Sparks's well-known book, presenting an outline of United States history from 1760 to 1865; one of the volumes in Macmillan's Standard School Library, which includes a long list of books that have proved entertaining and useful, or have, as in the case of Charles Kingsley's "Water Babies" and Lewis Carroll's "Through the Looking-Glass," taken their places with the classics. These books are substantially printed; in many cases they are well illustrated; in all cases they are well bound. Threescore and more volumes include books on American history, biography, classic legends, fiction, nature study, and poetry. (The Men Who Made the Nation. By Edwin Erle Sparks, Ph.D. The Macmillan Company, New York. 50 cents.)

**Modern Poets and Christian Teaching** Two volumes intended to analyze the relation indicated in the above title are devoted to the poetry of Tennyson and of Sidney Lanier. The single purpose of the author of the first, William E. Smyser, is to present the poems of Tennyson in which he has expressed his religious faith. Mr. Smyser judiciously restrains his personal views, and allows the poet and the circumstances of the time to speak. Tennyson's faith was never narrowed to a creed, but it was nevertheless clearly conceived and clearly enunciated in many beautiful and familiar poems. Restless, hostile to the sluggish church, disgusted by lifeless sermons "worse than the cawing of rooks," as Jane Carlyle said, the group of thinkers to

574

which Tennyson belonged found utterance for their discontent. "In Memoriam" is the wonderful record of spiritual struggle brought upon a strong soul through heavy sorrow. The author goes carefully through the stages of philosophic and religious thought expressed in the great poems up to the last volume of verse—"A slender sheaf from autumn field"—when Tennyson awaited death in serenity of hope and full confidence. The second volume, upon Sidney Lanier, is by Henry Nelson Snyder, who writes with keen appreciation of the peculiarly noble spiritual nature of the Southern poet, who came through stress of body and mind into a wide comprehension of the infinity of Love, and, feeling the burden of an unspoken message, burned to tell his fellow-men of their privilege. The climax of his faith is expressed in his poem "The Crystal Christ"—"the noblest chanting of his *credo*." The meaning of his message is found in the "purity of his soul, in the cheerful manliness and high nobility of his character, and in his knightly struggle against disease and conditions that tended to hold him back and retard his development." The book is a sympathetic appreciation of the poet. (Modern Poets and Christian Teaching: Tennyson. By W. E. Smyser. Sidney Lanier. By Henry Nelson Snyder. Eaton & Mains, New York. $1, net, each.)

***The "Moral Social" Ideal*** Our increasing intimacy with the Spanish-speaking countries to the south of us in commerce is being quickly followed, we are glad to say, by an appreciation of what is being done by them in the domain of education. One way to get a glimpse into that domain is to read some text-book prepared for use in Central and South American schools or colleges. A good example is Professor Eugenio de Hostos's "Moral Social." The author is the Director-General of the Normal School in the Dominican Republic, and the second edition of his "Moral Social" is now announced. It is a good book and should do good. It was prepared on broad lines, and clearly outlines the relations of the individual with society. (Moral Social. By Eugenio M. de Hostos. Segunda Edicion. Libreria Editorial de Bailly-Bailliere e Hijos, Madrid.)

***Patrollers of Palestine*** The experiences of a lively party of tourists, men and women, who journey through the Holy Land, their conversation carried on by various characters such as "The Enthusiast," "The Pessimist," etc., form the subject matter of a posthumous book by the late Rev. Haskett Smith. As the editor of "Murray's Handbook to Syria and Palestine" and the author of other books on the Holy Land, Mr. Smith resided long in Palestine, closely studying the idiosyncrasies of the natives, often wearing their costumes and speaking their language. The present volume therefore gives to all who are interested in present-day Palestine, as well as in its historical and religious significance, a certain intimate atmosphere hardly found in other works on that subject. (Patrollers of Palestine. By the Rev. Haskett Smith, M.A., F.R.G.S. Longmans, Green & Co., New York. $3, net.)

***The Practice of Prayer*** This is in its essentials an excellent little book. One who may dissent from some of the writer's theological conceptions can agree with his religious convictions. Only through prayer does God become to us a reality. "The dynamic of prayer is holiness." "Preparation for prayer is the life lived in harmony with the truth we profess to believe." "If we can but learn the true secret of preparation, we shall find that our whole life becomes a prayer." This is the idea within St. Paul's precept, "Pray without ceasing;" in this is the true definition of prayer as communion with God. Dr. Morgan seems to think of the transcendence and the immanence of God as spatial. They are rather to be thought of as dynamic; this is a spiritual, the other a physical, conception. In this view the common objection fails, that prayer can have only a subjective value, efficacious only on one's self. Prayer at least touches God immanent in the praying soul. (The Practice of Prayer. By G. Campbell Morgan, D.D. Fleming H. Revell Company, New York. 75 cents, net.)

***A Romance of Perugia*** Early fifteenth-century romances are again to the fore. Mr. Egerton R. Williams, Jr., has made a notable contribution to this class of books, illustrated with a few colored pictures by Mr. J. C. Leyendecker. Mr. Williams's hero is Ridolfo, of the famous Baglioni family, which for a century and a half held despotic sway over Perugia. The heroine is Gismonda, Ridolfo's wife, a pale, fair Florentine, a miracle of beauty, gentleness, and goodness. Ridolfo was of course a warrior, not to say a pillager. The story tells how Gismonda affected the warrior's tempestuous life and how she saved him from himself. The author of "The Hill Towns of Italy" well knows how to envelop his romance in a Renaissance atmosphere, against which his characters stand out picturesquely. They are not historic, save in being types closely resembling, now this, now that, historical character. Of course Ridolfo is a rather conventional type of an Italian despot, but Gismonda is hardly as conventional type of an Italian heroine. With Mr. Williams, one must admit that there is some necessity for so sharp a contrast, in that the early Renaissance seems to admit but few half-way natures; the people seemed, as a rule, utterly bad or actually divinely inspired. Among the latter, one character in the book, Fra Bernardo, is no mere type; he surely has a prototype in San Bernardino. The scene, as will be expected from the above, is laid in and about Perugia; and the geographical and historical illustrations should interest lovers both of Perugia and of that epoch which we know as the early Renaissance. (Ridolfo: The Coming of the Dawn. By Egerton R. Williams, Jr. A. C. McClurg & Co., Chicago. $1.50.)

*Through Scandinavia to Moscow* "We sat glumly together." "Our carriage was packed full up with men and women who looked dourly at us." One turns page after page of Mr. Edwards's entertaining volume content to find such phrases as these and to be in the company of an every-day, unpretentious traveler who has, withal, an uncommonly keen appreciation and a pithy way of "putting things." Mr. Edwards's is a simple, straightforward account, not so much of history, economics, art, and literature in Scandinavia and northern Russia as of the folk-life there. Some good books have already described that life in greater detail; for instance, Jessie Brockner's "Danish Life in Town and Country," Mr. Woods's "Norwegian Byways," Mr. Curtis's "Denmark, Norway, and Sweden," Dr. Newton's "A Run Through Russia," Miss Hapgood's "Russian Rambles," and Madame Blanc's "Promenades en Russie." But for a quick glance Mr. Edwards's, in its way, is as practical as any. The interest of the text is heightened by the many illustrations from the author's clever kodak snapshots. The book is well printed, and with almost never a typographical error such as "Bahnhoff," page 218, for instance. (Through Scandinavia to Moscow. By William Seymour Edwards. The Robert Clarke Company, Cincinnati. $1.50, net.)

*Village Sermons* To various memorials of Bishop Westcott's noble life and learning which have appeared since death bereft the Church of England of his voice, his son has added this volume. The forty sermons it contains were preached on various occasions from 1852 to 1881, while he was serving a rural parish, and are published in the hope of their helpfulness to "other country parsons." (Village Sermons. By the late Brooke Foss Westcott, D.D., D.C.L. The Macmillan Company, New York. $1.50.)

*The Virgin Birth* If there is a more thorough and scholarly defense of the virgin birth of Jesus Christ than this monograph of Mr. Sweet, we are not acquainted with it. It is a fine testimony to the thorough scholarship which we are persuaded characterizes many a country pastor who remains throughout his life unrecognized even in his own parish. It is not and does not pretend to be impartial; it is a defense of the orthodox doctrine. But it is fair-minded, erudite, thorough. It reports and criticises the various rationalistic theories which have been offered to explain the presence of the narratives of the Birth and Infancy of Jesus in the Gospels, and we think the author succeeds in showing that these rationalistic hypotheses are inconclusive and unsatisfactory. He presents also clearly and effectively the textual grounds for accepting the narratives. There is nothing in the condition of the early texts to throw doubt upon them, and in style and spirit they are unlike the apocryphal Gospels and like the canonical Gospels. We may add that their existence in Tatian's Diatessaron demonstrates that certainly as early as A.D. 160, and probably as early as A.D. 100, they were accepted by the Christian Church as of equal authority with the rest of the Gospel narratives. In dealing with the singular silence of the rest of the New Testament on the Virgin Birth the author is not equally successful. His attempt to interpret John i. 14, "The Word was made flesh," and Galatians iv. 4, "Made of a woman," as indications that John and Paul recognized the Virgin Birth comes perilously near special pleading. We may sum up the statement of the question in a sentence thus: There is nothing in the form or style of the narratives to indicate that they are of post-apostolic date; the history of the text makes it clear that they are of equal, or substantially equal, antiquity with the rest of the Gospel narratives; and all attempts to account for their introduction into the narratives, if they are not historical, are forced and unsatisfactory; but, on the other hand, there is no indication that the Apostolic Church placed great emphasis or attached special importance to the Virgin Birth, or that the doctrine occupied any important place in primitive Christian theology, since it is never referred to in Christ's reported teaching, nor in the apostolic sermons, nor in any of the Epistles. (The Birth and Infancy of Jesus Christ. By L. Matthews Sweet. The Presbyterian Board of Publication, Philadelphia. $1.50.)

# Letters to The Outlook

## "AMERICA AND THE SIXTH COMMANDMENT"

The publicity you give to Judge Thomas's speech is needed. That speech is a breath of fresh air blown in upon the stagnant atmosphere of self-complacency in which Americans have always lived. The unblushing assumption everywhere in our press that every clean thing in conduct, individual and national, is " American " and every unclean thing " un-American " is galling to many of us to meet almost everywhere self-righteously in print.

Judge Thomas's analysis is of patent facts that *saute aux yeux* and long have. It is undeniable that the most distinctively " American " section, Kentucky and the Southwest, where ancestry on this continent goes back a little further and not a little more purely American than in other parts, is where will be found the greatest incidence, not alone of homicide, but of cowardly murder.

The Italian, like his forbear the Roman legionary, enters *corps à corps* upon his *lutte* with his enemy, but what shall be said of the savages who hide in court-houses with Winchesters and open fire upon their well-marked man ?—type of thousands of murders from safe concealment that from the very first have meanly distinguished the most " American " of all our communities.     G. C. L.

Salem, New Jersey.

## CONDITIONAL GIFTS TO COLLEGES

Will you permit a subscriber who habitually looks to The Outlook for wisdom on public questions to ask for your views on a point briefly hinted at in your issue of February 16?

In referring to the magnificent gift of Mr. Rockefeller to the General Education Board you say: " The funds it holds represent only a fraction of the amounts which it will really control; by giving a sum to an institution on condition that the institution raise an equal amount, it will be able to direct much larger amounts than it possesses." This subject has repeatedly come before me in a very practical form. I am not a multi-millionaire; I am not even a millionaire ; but my income is more than I need for my family expenses, and I am consequently visited from time to time by college presidents and other educators who are in need of money to maintain their institutions. It has happened a number of times in the past that such a college president has appealed to me for a special contribution in addition to my customary subscription, on the ground that a certain Mr. Dives had promised to give him, say, $25,000, on condition that he would raise double the amount through other subscribers.

I have often felt a certain resentment at what seemed to me the exercise of a moral taxing power by a big philanthropist over the little ones, but from sympathy for the overworked and underpaid college president have yielded.

Not long ago, however, a college president came to me and said that Mr. Crœsus had offered to give his institution $25,000 for a building provided the college would raise the same amount for an endowment. At the same time Mr. Dives had offered $25,000 for an endowment provided the $25,000 offered by Mr. Crœsus could be increased to $75,-000. But neither the $25,000 of Mr. Dives nor the $25,000 of Mr. Crœsus could be counted in meeting the conditions imposed by the other. Thus the president was obliged either to undertake the arduous task of raising $75,000 or reject the tempting offers of $50,000.

It at once occurred to me to ask myself, Why cannot the system be pushed a little further? I might, for instance, offer one thousand dollars to establish a Lazarus fund of five thousand dollars on condition that four thousand should be raised by other persons, but that my one thousand should not be counted in making up the Crœsus or Dives funds. And if others impose the same conditions, we might keep the college president constantly traveling after a beautiful *fata morgana* of endowments which he would never reach. The system would thus die a natural death. But while it has not yet been pushed to its limits, may we not raise certain questions which naturally suggest themselves in connection with it.

(1) Is it for the best interests of education to lay this heavy burden upon college presidents, who are obliged, in order to meet the onerous conditions imposed by generous givers, to leave their regular work and for the time become mendicants? Some farmers are in the habit of hanging a beet just above the reach of their hens in order that the latter may get exercise by jumping after the luscious tidbit. But is it desirable to increase the activity of presidents of small colleges by applying the same method to them ?

(2) Does not this system impose an undue burden upon the small giver? I am, of

**577**

course, not referring to the case of a man who offers $25,000 towards a fund provided three others will each contribute an equal amount. The practical working out of the system which I have described above is that many people of very small means, often in the neighborhood, pledge sums which it takes them years to save from their small incomes to help meet the conditions imposed by the large donor, whose name is associated with, if not formally attached to, the fund which they have helped to build up.

(3) Does not this method import into philanthropy the spirit of sharp bargaining which is condemned both by law and by ethics in business? It is claimed that some very large shippers have offered to give their business to a railway on condition of receiving a discriminating rate, which, of course, is given at the expense of the small shipper. If a rich man offers to create a large fund on condition that other givers, mainly small ones, shall make up two-thirds of it, is there not a strong family resemblance between the methods, even though one may be called business and the other generosity?

I ask these questions not in a spirit of hostility to our multi-millionaires or of criticism of their motives. I assume that they wish to do the maximum of good with what money they give away, and I know that the success of the method described above in increasing the funds of colleges is thought by some to be its ample justification. But I cannot help wondering whether people fully realize at what cost and at whose cost this success is obtained.　　　　　LAZARUS.

## JUSTICE TO WHOM JUSTICE IS DUE

Having read the article in The Outlook's issue of January 26, " Justice for the Blind," I think a few words in justice to the State of Massachusetts for the efforts expended in behalf of the blind of the State are due. In Massachusetts, at least, the blind are not considered objects of charity. On the contrary, everything is being done to eradicate any such idea. Every sightless child in the Commonwealth, whether from the home of poverty or from the home of the millionaire, is entitled to a thorough education at the Perkins Institution. In fact, there is constant vigilance on the part of those interested in the blind to see that no child is overlooked who should be in school. And every effort is brought to bear upon the parents to induce them to send the child, where any reluctance is shown. Not only do the children have as

thorough an education as seeing children, but in addition many branches of manual labor are taught. There are competent teachers in all the departments. Sewing is taught in a thorough and most systematic manner, so that at the end of the course any girl is competent to cut and make her own garments and even to draft patterns—an art which the majority of seeing girls are incapable of doing. There is also a splendid course in knitting and crocheting. The boys learn piano-tuning, cane-seating, etc. Mattress-making is another branch which receives special attention. As for bead-making, it is entirely out of the question. It is of absolutely no value, and therefore not taken into consideration at the Perkins Institution. Nothing is made there that cannot be put to some practical use. Furthermore, any child who has completed the course at Perkins Institution, aside from the educational advantages and manual training, has been under a most refining influence, and cannot help but be benefited thereby. This portion of the work is no new departure, but has been in existence for years. Within the past seven years a new feature has developed—that of home teaching. There are four teachers employed by the State to teach the adult blind in their homes. Reading, writing, knitting, crocheting, hand sewing, machine stitching, and typewriting have all been successfully taught. There is a store at 383 Boylston Street, Boston, where work done by blind women of the State is sold. A high standard of work is required. The patrons of this store are among the wealthy who pay good prices and consequently demand correspondingly good work. Many of the ready-made articles bought at the various stores would not be accepted at this store, not being up to standard.

As a rule, the blind are very cheerful, and in almost all cases are grateful for any little help that will enable them even partly to support themselves. Generally they do not want charity nor pity. There are seeing people who claim " the world owes them a living." The blind are willing and anxious to be independent, and are only too happy to take up any work that will in any way aid in their support. The State of Massachusetts is doing all in its power to help the blind to help themselves, and to put them on a basis with seeing people. Not by any means does it treat them as inmates of asylums or objects of pity.　　　FLORENCE M. PUDDEFOOT.
South Framingham, Massachusetts.

# $21,300,523.40
## Is a Large Sum

It represents the amount of death claims paid by
this Company in a single year—1906. This was not
the result of investments made by care-free, well-to-do
people. It came very largely from men who went from
slight inconvenience to great self-denial to keep up the
policies that would when needed keep up the home. Of
such, largely, is the membership of

# The Mutual
# Life Insurance
# Company

Their confidence and their patronage have made and kept
it the largest and staunchest life insurance company in the
world. The vast sum saved and being saved by the new
management must benefit all policy holders, and cannot
but attract those who seek the greatest protection, and
therefore make its agents welcome everywhere.

## The Time to Act is NOW.

For the new forms of policies consult our
nearest agent, or write direct to

**The Mutual Life Insurance
Company of New York,
N. Y.**

# The Next President

TWO years of President Roosevelt's administration have just been completed, and the country is beginning to consider what kind of a man it desires to have take the President's place two years from now. Mr. John Callan O'Laughlin, the Washington correspondent of the Chicago Tribune, has prepared for The Outlook two articles on the Presidential Possibilities of 1908. Mr. O'Laughlin is one of the ablest of the newspaper correspondents at the National capital. Many of our readers will remember the commendation of his work which was made by ex-Secretary Long in his History of the American Navy. Mr. O'Laughlin has had unusual opportunities for getting and recording impressions of political leaders, and also for forming his own estimate of political personalities. The first of his articles discusses possible Republican candidates, the second the Democratic candidates. They are personal and frank and critical, without being prejudiced or intrusive upon the private rights of the public men described. We believe these articles will be read with very wide interest. The first will appear in our issue of March 30, and the second in the issue following.

❀

**International Peace**

What it is hoped and believed will be the most important congress of private citizens ever held in behalf of international peace and arbitration will assemble in New York City on April 14 for a three days' session. Its official title is "The National Arbitration and Peace Congress." Mr. Andrew Carnegie is the President, and the list of vice-presidents and members of the General Committee includes some of the most distinguished statesmen, lawyers, clergymen, educators, business men, labor leaders, and editors of the country. The Congress convenes in April for two reasons : first, in order that its deliberations and recommendations may be presented to the second Hague Congress, which is to meet in June ; and, second, because of the presence in this country at that time of a body of distinguished visitors from Great Britain, France, Germany, Belgium, and Holland, who have been invited by Mr. Carnegie to be his guests at the dedication of the Carnegie Institute in Pittsburg on April 11. The programme as so far arranged is a most interesting one. There will be nine morning, afternoon, and evening sessions, at which addresses will be made by Mr. Carnegie, Governor Hughes, Secretary Root, Ambassador Bryce, Mr. Bryan, and other men of distinguished international reputations. It is hoped that President Roosevelt, who is greatly interested in the object of the Congress, will be present and speak at the public dinner with which the sessions of the Congress will close. American public opinion, supporting the President and the Department of State, had very weighty influence in the organization and the successful work of the first Hague Conference, to be held next June, will undoubtedly, if its delegates receive the necessary support from their various countries, exercise a profound influence upon future international relations in the civilized world. Thus the New York Peace Congress has a most important function to perform, and ought to have the attention and co-operation of every American citizen who desires to see this country a leader in international comity. Further information concerning the Congress and its programme may be obtained by addressing Mr. Robert Erskine Ely, Secretary of the Executive Committee of the Congress, at 19 West Forty-fourth Street, New York City.

❀

**A Supplementary Note**

The reader will find Mr. Bonaparte's article on "Two Years of a Government that Does Things" entertaining; the student of current history will find it suggestive. What we add here is by way of a supplementary note, for the purpose of giving some details of a National development which Mr. Bonaparte has described so picturesquely in general terms. The process of nationalization has gone on in this country under the Constitution ever since the Union of States was formed. Two courses of decisions of the United States Supreme Court have in recent years accelerated this process. The first is that the United States is a Nation; that it has all the powers and prerogatives of nationality except as they are expressly or by necessary implication of the Constitution denied to it; that, for example, it may acquire territory by war or by purchase, and such territory is not a part of the United States and its residents are not citizens of the United States, and the provisions of the Constitution do not extend over such territory and cannot be taken advantage of by such subjects. This decision, or rather these decisions, constitute a recognition by the highest judicial authority that the United States is a Nation with all the characteristics necessary to enable it to take its place among other world powers. It may choose not to do so, but it is not prevented from doing so by its Constitution. The other decision, or series of decisions, has the effect to confer upon Congress power to deal with all inter-State commerce, and with all the instruments of such commerce, unhindered by any supposed conflicting rights of the States. These decisions may be summed up in the words of Justice Bradley, of the Supreme Court (1887): "In matters of foreign and inter-State commerce there are no States." Upon these decisions is based what the critics of the present Administration condemn as an unwarrantable and unconstitutional extension of Federal powers, but which is certainly warranted by a long and nearly unbroken course of judicial decisions interpreting the Constitution. Under the one or the other of these courses of decisions may be classified the following list of results accomplished, or initiated and put in the way of accomplishment, by the present Administration during the two years of its existence :

*Foreign.*—The initiation of the call for the second Hague Conference.

The Russo-Japanese peace.

The extension of the Monroe Doctrine making responsibility for and protectorate of American Republics commensurate.

The cultivation of a better understanding between South and North America.

The beginning of practical work on the Panama Canal.

Agricultural bank established and coastwise law postponed for Philippines.

*Domestic.*—Railway rate regulation.

Food inspection.

Quarantine nationalized.

Naturalization nationalized.

Public lands protected from spoliation.

Rights of labor protected on inter-State railways.

Prohibition of political contributions by corporations.

Prosecution of trusts.

Consular service reorganized.

Public opinion which approves and public opinion which disapproves unite in attributing much of the Congressional action of the past two years to the influence of the President. He shares with Congress both the credit and the blame—if blame there be. For he has been the recognized leader of his party, and has been not only the executor of the laws but also has served as a *quasi* prime minister in initiating and promoting their enactment. The Outlook believes in the soundness of the decisions under which these results have been accomplished, and in the main heartily approves the results themselves.

⊛

*President Roosevelt's New Cabinet*

March 4, 1907, marks the final readjustment of President Roosevelt's Cabinet. Let us speak of its members in their official order. The country is of course to be congratulated that Elihu Root, of New York, remains the Secretary of State. Leslie M. Shaw, of Iowa, the retiring Secretary of the Treasury, whose financial method has been marked by much ingenuity, gives place to George B. Cortelyou, of New York, late Postmaster-General ; he had previously been First Secretary of Commerce, and previous to that he had been private secretary to Presidents McKinley and Roosevelt. The marked attention to detail and high administrative qualities which have characterized Mr. Cortelyou's career are an earnest of what may be expected of him in his new position. If the country is to be congratulated on Mr. Root's retention of office, it is none the less to be congratulated that William H. Taft, of Ohio, whose diplomatic and administrative ability has been shown in the Philippines and in Cuba, remains in office as Secretary of War. William H. Moody, of Massachusetts, one of the most efficient of our Attorneys-General, takes a place on the Supreme Court bench ; the new Attorney-General is Charles J. Bonaparte, of Maryland, certainly a no less able man ; he has been Secretary of the Navy. The new Postmaster-General is George von Lengerke Meyer, of Massachusetts, recently Ambassador to Russia, previous to which he was Ambassador to Italy. The new Secretary of the Navy is Victor

H. Metcalf, of California, who has been Secretary of Commerce. The retirement of Ethan Allen Hitchcock, of Missouri, as Secretary of the Interior causes general regret. Mr. Hitchcock's unsparing prosecution of the land thieves has earned for him the lasting gratitude of his country. It is to be hoped and expected that his successor, James R. Garfield, of Ohio, will prove worthy of such a heritage; .certainly Mr. Garfield's investigations as Commissioner of Corporations, especially into the affairs of the Standard Oil Company, constitute an achievement worthy to rank with Mr. Hitchcock's. James Wilson, of Iowa, remains the Secretary of Agriculture, and has the distinction of being the only member of President McKinley's Cabinet now in office. Oscar S. Straus, of New York, succeeds Mr. Metcalf as Secretary of Commerce, and brings to his office a large knowledge of the subjects comprised in his department. Two changes in commissionerships also deserve mention. As Commissioner of Corporations Mr. Garfield is succeeded by Herbert Knox Smith, of Connecticut, his efficient Deputy Commissioner; and as Land Commissioner, William A. Richards, of Wyoming, gives place to Richard A. Ballinger, of Washington, ex-Mayor of Seattle. Mr. Ballinger is a graduate of Williams College (as are Secretary Garfield and Mr. Leupp, the Indian Commissioner), but he is a thoroughgoing representative of Western life. He will have a specially important work in carrying out the new policy of the Administration with regard to public lands. He was urged to take the Commissionership against his own personal inclinations, as a matter of public service in order that the West and the Pacific Coast might be represented in the new treatment of settlers, graziers, miners, and lumbermen in their relation to the Government.

❦

*Against Federal Child Labor Legislation* Mr. Edgar Gardner Murphy, in an article published in the New York Evening Post for March 9, puts forcibly the objections to Senator Beveridge's Child Labor Bill. The spirit of this article is admirable. No one will attribute to Mr. Murphy either sectional prejudice or indifference to the cruel injustice of child labor. His arguments against the bill deserve to be considered in the same spirit of fairness with which they are urged. Following his own order, they are briefly these : (1) We are the citizens of a democracy distributed under specific local governments to which are intrusted local police regulations. If, whenever the duties of these State governments are not performed, they are to be assumed by some external power, the sense of local responsibility will be seriously impaired. (2) We have no good reason for believing that Federal administration would be better than State administration. The Nation's care of the Indians does not indicate that it would be pre-eminently successful in undertaking to care for the children. (3) It cannot constitutionally care directly for the children. Senator Beveridge himself admits that Congress has no power to pass a law directly stopping child labor. The fact that Congress can accomplish the desired end only by indirection is not necessarily fatal, but is a serious disadvantage. (4) The bill is necessarily limited in its effect. It cannot prevent children from being employed in the manufacture of goods to be sold within the State, and Mr. Murphy believes that the provision for preventing the sale of child labor products outside the State can be easily evaded. (5) For these reasons it is not possible to depend on Federal legislation for the upbuilding of a permanent and comprehensive system for the eradication of the evils of child labor. "Such a system is possible only under the slower but freer processes of local State legislation." In the last analysis reformers must depend upon public opinion to protect the child, and local legislation and the agitation which must precede it furnish the best means of awakening this public opinion. (6) The proposed bill is unconstitutional. It differs from the Pure Food Law, the Lottery Law, and the like because those laws protect the people of one State from injury at the hands of people of another State, while the object of this bill is to protect the children of a State from injuries perpetrated by industries carried on within that State. It is not pretended that the transportation of child labor goods will injure the people of the States to which those goods are carried.

❀

**For Federal Child Labor Legislation** The distinction which Mr. Murphy makes between the Pure Food Law or the Lottery Law and the proposed Child Labor Law is a real one, and the question whether the Child Labor Law is Constitutional can be finally settled only by the Supreme Court of the United States. We believe, however, in view of the trend of the decisions of that Court, that it would be held Constitutional. The inter-State railways are the highways of the Nation, and we think a Nation has a right to prohibit the use of its highways when that use is promoting and strengthening a great injustice, even though the injustice is locally perpetrated and only the people of the locality directly suffer from it. The other objections of Mr. Murphy rest upon the assumption that the people must choose between Federal and State legislation, and that Federal legislation will tend to discourage State legislation. His argument that this will be the case is not to us convincing. We think, on the other hand, that agitation for local police regulations prohibiting child labor on sanitary grounds within the State will be aided by the passage of Federal legislation putting the stamp of National disapproval on such child labor, and putting what we may call a " taboo " on all goods into which child labor has entered. The sentiment of the State on behalf of justice to the child will, in our judgment, be strengthened, not weakened, by such an expression of the sentiment of justice on behalf of the child by all the States acting in co-operation. It will not only be easier to enforce child labor laws in Pennsylvania if the product of child labor cannot be sold outside of Pennsylvania, but it will also be easier to enact and maintain such laws if all the surrounding States have agreed in a public act of condemnation. If it were true that the defenders of the children had to choose between Federal action

and State action, we should be inclined to agree with Mr. Murphy and prefer the State action. In our judgment, there is no such alternative. We may have both, and each legislation will support the other. Readers who wish to make a further study of this subject are advised to write to Mr. Edgar Gardner Murphy, Post-office Box 347, Montgomery, Alabama, for his argument against the Beveridge bill, and either to Senator Albert J. Beveridge, United States Senate, Washington, D. C., or to Mr. S. M. Lindsay, Secretary of the National Child Labor Committee, 105 East Twenty-second Street, New York, for arguments in favor of the bill.

❀

**The Federal Investigation of Child Labor** Those who believe that the Federal Government must deal with the child labor question need not be at all discouraged by the failure of the Beveridge bill to receive consideration in the session of Congress just closed, or the ex-cathedra statement of the Senate Judiciary Committee that Federal legislation is unconstitutional. In spite of this hastily expressed opinion of the Committee, Congress has taken action which it appears to us will result in Federal legislation in the near future. A bill was passed and has been signed by the President authorizing and directing the Secretary of Commerce and Labor " to investigate and report on the industrial, social, moral, educational, and physical conditions of woman and child workers of the United States wherever employed, with special reference to their age, hours of labor, term of employment, health, illiteracy, sanitary and other conditions surrounding their occupation, and the means employed for the protection of their health, persons, and morals." For this investigation the sum of $150,000 has been appropriated. There are some interesting stories told in connection with the successful enactment of this legislation. Opponents of any investigation, supposedly those who are responsible for the abuses of child labor, at first endeavored to have the investigation nullified by cutting out the special appropriation. Public sentiment, however, was too strong to be resisted, and the necessary money was provided. Vigorous efforts were also made by the opponents of the measure to throw the investigation into the Census Department, in which case it would have been purely statistical and of very little human interest. The census authorities themselves pointed out the inadequacy of any such investigation as they could make. After some pretty sharp strategical fighting in Congress, the investigation was finally assigned, to the Department of Commerce and Labor, with the hearty approval of the National Child Labor Committee. The terms of the bill are so explicit and the provisions for the investigation so thorough that in due course of time the country will have the facts in an authoritative form. If, as some of the influential employers of child labor assert, there are no abuses, there will be no need for reformatory legislation. But if evils and suffering are disclosed upon a scale which the private societies and experts believe to exist, Federal legislation is sure to follow. The friends of child labor reform, whether they believe in National or State action, or, as The Outlook does, in both, will undoubtedly welcome this Federal investigation and aid it in every way that they can.

❀

*The Prevention of Railway Accidents*
In the case of the recent accident on the Harlem Division of the New York Central near Woodlawn Cemetery, New York City, by which twenty-four persons were killed and a hundred and fifty injured, the Coroner's jury found last week that the responsibility was "divided between the construction and operating departments." Dissatisfaction with this lack of specification caused the Coroner thereupon to hold the President and Directors of the company responsible, but he has now ruled that the corporation is responsible, as bringing the case more quickly before the Grand Jury. The corporation may be held for manslaughter in the second degree. Sufficient cause, it is claimed, is found in the testimony. This shows that the engineer took the fatal curve at excessive speed, which, together with the train's weight, sheared off the heads of the spikes holding down the rails ; that the train was already six minutes behind time on a stretch of road on which the schedule calls for a speed of nearly a mile a minute ; finally, that the train's engineer was new to his work and had no speedometer in his cab to show how fast he was going. We hope that the District Attorney and the Grand Jury will single out the particular persons really responsible, that they may be made to feel the weight of popular condemnation. If the Coroner's jury did not specifically fix responsibility, it made certain timely recommendations : that the railway company be compelled to reinforce the fastenings of the outer rails on all curves, constructed as the one in question was proved to have been, by adding spikes, rail-braces, or increased super-elevation ; that until this strengthening is completed the company be required to lower its speed on such curves to so-called equilibrium speed, or to a speed absolutely safe to protect the lives of passengers and employees ; finally, that the company be compelled to install such instruments or make such tests to determine speed under varying conditions as will enable motormen to know with reasonable exactness the speed at which trains are traveling. It is a satisfaction to add that the New York Central Company promptly accepted one of these recommendations, by issuing an order limiting the speed of trains in the electric zone to forty-five miles an hour on straight roads and thirty-five miles on curves. Last week's accident at Tivoli on the Hudson River, by which only the presence of a freight train on the outside track prevented the cars of a derailed passenger train from plunging into the river, has perhaps hastened the New York Central's institution of a new safety plan, which, if successful, may be commended to all railways. The system about to be installed will connect all the rails between New York and Buffalo by electric wires. These will be looped into the signal towers. If a rail breaks, or if any attempt is made to remove one, the electric connection will automatically not only notify the towerman but also set the signals at danger, warning an on-

coming train. According to the statistics compiled by New York Central engineers, broken rails and weakened roadbeds have caused more than three-fifths of American railway wrecks during the past five years. Hence there is special interest in the success of the system which the New York Central is praiseworthily introducing. We repeat, however, that all these questions of railway appliances would be most quickly and generally brought before the country by the institution of a governmental Bureau of Railway Accidents, similar to that which has for many years done effective service in England.

❀

**State Control of Public Utilities** An important and voluminous bill for the control of public utilities has been introduced into the Legislature of New York. It embodies the recommendations on the subject which Governor Hughes made in his first message. It deals with three general subjects—the creation of two State Commissions as instruments of State control, regulations as to rates and other matters of public service, and limitations as to the financial and other aspects of the organization of public service corporations. The present Railroad Commission has proved itself insufficient and irresponsible to the people. This the bill abolishes, as well as the State Gas Commission, the Inspector of Gas Meters, and the Board of Rapid Transit Commissioners, which had charge of the subways in New York City. In the place of these bodies the bill creates two Commissions, one to control all the public utilities of New York City, the other all those outside of the city. By a careful and definite division of powers, the two Commissions control those utilities operated partly within and partly without the city. Each Commission consists of five members, appointed and subject to dismissal by the Governor. Each Commissioner receives an annual salary of $10,000, and holds office for five years. The term of one Commissioner on each Commission expires every year. Each Commission has large powers within its jurisdiction. It can hold hearings, summon witnesses, and administer oaths. It has the power to sanction or prohibit the assignment, transfer, or lease of any franchise, and the issue of stocks and bonds (limiting the capitalized value of a franchise ɒ the amount which the corporation has actually paid to the State or municipality for it); to determine the form of accounts and reports of public service corporations; to require co-operation between two or more common carriers; to fix maximum rates; to investigate accidents; to order adequate service, alterations, safety devices, motive power, equipment, regulations as to the number and efficiency of employees, and the like; and to require of municipalities engaged in operating public utilities to report according to a designated form. Moreover, to the Commission of the district comprising the metropolis are given the powers of the present Board of Rapid Transit Commissioners. Every order of a Commission is to be in force until abrogated by itself or by a court declaring it illegal. As to rates and other matters of public service there are such conservative provisions as the prohibition of a higher rate for a shorter than for a longer haul "over the same line in the same direction," "under substantially similar circumstances and conditions," except by order of the Commission, the prohibition of discrimination in rates and service, the requirement that schedules be published, and the like. Indeed, the bill provides explicitly for co-operation between the State Commissions and the Inter-State Commerce Commission. As to financial transactions, the most important provisions not already mentioned are those prohibiting the capitalization of a merger beyond the amount of the capital stock of the constituent bodies, and prohibiting any stock company hereafter to acquire, except as security, more than ten per cent. of the stock of any railway, street railway, gas, or electric corporation organized or existing under the laws of the State. Opposition from certain public service corporations of the State was to be expected, but it is evident from a statement of Mr. Shonts, President of the company controlling the transit in New York City, that this opposition will not be unanimous. No more important measure has recently been introduced into any State Legislature, and none which appears to be in its general provisions more in accord with the healthful movement in the Federal Government toward control of corporations.

❀

**Our Masters the Police**

At the instance of Police Commissioner Bingham, of New York City, a bill has been introduced into the Legislature of the State and has passed the Lower House, which is designed to mitigate the present evils of the metropolitan police force. At present the force is practically an immovable body commanded by a very movable head. The laws and the courts have justified the policeman in regarding his office primarily, not as a post of responsibility, but as a piece of property. No matter how inefficient, undisciplined, and even corrupt he may be, he can keep his grip on his position unless he is convicted before a court of law. At present every member of the force reaches his grade by a prescribed method of promotion. Patrolman, roundsman, sergeant, detective, captain, inspector—from the bottom to the top—each member of the force has the right to resist his dismissal from his grade by his commanding officer on the ground that his place is a possession of his own, of which he cannot be deprived without due process of law. What Commissioner Bingham's bill does is to strike at this vicious system—not in its root, but in its highest branches. The bill abolishes the inspectorship as a distinct grade. Instead it provides that the Commissioner shall detail captains to act as inspectors. Nominally, these captains so detailed will be inspectors. They will have the duties, authority, and pay of inspectors. But they will no longer be in possession of the office of inspectorship as a piece of property. The Commissioner can end the detail at will. Similarly, membership in the detective force, instead of being a separate piece of property, is made an incident in the duty of those members of the uniformed force whom the Commissioner may select. Other less impor-

tant changes are made in the present law. If there is any defect in the bill, it is that of leniency. Probably, however, no more drastic bill could be passed. It is argued that a corrupt city government could subject to itself more completely the whole police force if this bill were to pass. Of course that is an argument based on distrust of municipal self-government. As it is at present, the city government is unable to control the police for good or ill except by corrupt collusion with lawbreakers. The police should be like an army, the responsive instrument of a leader. If then there were corruption, the people would know whom to blame; if efficiency, the people would know whom to trust.

❀

**Shall the City Cook Its Milk**
**The Affirmative**

A controversy not altogether free from acrimony has arisen in New York City over the milk question. The issue is between those who believe in pasteurizing practically the entire milk supply and those who advocate other methods. Upon the decision of this question depend the lives of hundreds of children next summer. To pasteurize milk, it perhaps should be explained, means to raise it to a temperature of 155° to 167° for thirty or twenty minutes respectively, in order to kill the disease germs in it, and then to cool it rapidly to a temperature of about 50°. This can be done roughly by allowing a kettle of water to come to a boil, removing it from the fire, putting a sealed bottle of milk into the water, allowing it to remain there for half an hour, when the temperature of the water will have been reduced and that of the milk greatly raised, and then putting the bottle of milk into nearly ice-cold water until it is to be used. This is not the most accurate way, but it will kill those germs which cause the intestinal disturbance that is so dangerous to infants and is responsible for a large part of the annual infant mortality. In an apparatus designed for the purpose the process can be made very accurate and effective for killing those minute organisms which cause scarlet fever, diphtheria, tuberculosis, and typhoid fever, and which are easily conveyed in milk. For several years Mr. Nathan Straus has philanthropically maintained in New York milk depots at which carefully pasteurized milk has been sold without profit. At these depots milk, not only pasteurized, but also properly modified for infants' use, has also been dispensed, and mothers have been instructed in the care of it and the proper ways of feeding it to their babies. The results obtained by means of these depots have led Mr. Straus to advocate very strongly the pasteurization of all the milk that comes into the city, except that small amount of high-priced milk which after bacterial test is "certified" as being free from danger. It has been proved by observations conducted by the Rockefeller Institute and the city Health Department that of children fed on milk purchased from grocery-stores, 44 per cent. did badly; of those fed on condensed milk, 40 per cent. did badly; of those fed on bottled milk, 39 per cent. did badly; and of those fed on milk from these milk depots only 19 per cent. did badly. The difference in death rate was still more striking, being nearly 2 per cent., exactly 2 per cent., nearly 1 per cent., and less than three-tenths of 1 per cent., respectively. It is also pointed out that if the milk supply of the city were pasteurized, contagion from tuberculous cattle and from infectious diseases in the households of dairymen would be eliminated. Moreover, the example of such European cities as Berlin and Copenhagen, which have adopted wholesale pasteurization, and the approval of eminent European scientists are cited. With arguments such as these, Mr. Straus, supported by many, if not most, of the New York newspapers, has urged upon the Board of Aldermen and the State Legislature measures which would make it impossible for any but the exceptionally well to-do to obtain raw milk in New York City. Notwithstanding these arguments, the great majority of those who have expert knowledge of the subject, in this country at least, regard the proposition to pasteurize practically the entire milk supply of a large city as not only unnecessary and unwise, but positively perilous.

**Shall the City Cook Its Milk**
**The Negative**

The case against wholesale pasteurization of milk may be stated in part as follows. There is a very material difference between such pasteurization as is done in milk depots or in a household and the sort of pasteurization that would have to be done by municipal authority. In the one case the milk, upon being pasteurized, is put into bottles which are immediately sealed, or is pasteurized in the sealed bottles themselves, and is not exposed until consumed; in the other case it is pasteurized in bulk—as, for instance, in pipes—and then is exposed necessarily to contamination. Now, as pasteurization not only destroys hurtful germs, but also the properties of the milk that resist the germs, pasteurized milk, if afterwards contaminated, is a more dangerous vehicle of disease than raw milk. If pasteurized milk were sold about the city as raw milk is at present, it would absorb more readily than it does now those minute organisms that render it a medium of disease, it could not be so fresh (for the process of pasteurization would delay its distribution), and it would not warn consumers by turning sour so soon (for pasteurization destroys the harmless bacteria that cause it to sour). Besides, since dealers would be saved from complaints about sour milk, they would be made less rather than more careful in handling it. So far, then, from rendering harmless any insufficiency of inspection, which the believers in wholesale pasteurization argue cannot for years be made adequate, wholesale pasteurization, while lulling consumers into a false sense of security, would vastly increase the burdens of milk inspectors and make their work more difficult if not entirely impossible of accomplishment. It is a mistake, moreover, to attribute to pasteurization only, or chiefly, the good results obtained by the Straus milk depots, the "Gouttes de Lait," as the French milk dispensaries are called, and similar institutions. These results are due not only to pasteurization, but also to the proper modification of milk for infants by the addition of cream, lime-water, and so on, and to the education of mothers in the care of the milk and in proper methods of feeding. Rochester, New York, tried the plan of pasteurizing its milk, but greatly reduced the death rate of the city by abandoning wholesale pasteurization and substituting for it the careful inspection of farms, dairies, creameries, processes of transportation, and milk shops, coupled with systematic education of producers and consumers. Following the most expert advice, a body of citizens called the New York Milk Committee, organized under the auspices of the New York Association for Improving the Condition of the Poor, is opposing the plan for general pasteurization, and is advocating instead an immediate increase in active and efficient State inspection of cattle and condemnation of tuberculous cows, an enlargement of the force of city milk inspectors to keep the farmers and dealers up to high standards, the establishment by the city, with the aid of private philanthropy, of milk depots like the Straus depots, where any mother can obtain, at no special cost, milk properly pasteurized and modified to suit the individual needs of her child, and can receive, what is even more important, advice and help. To such depots the mothers will come. That has been abundantly proved. If the Committee can persuade the State to enforce its present laws regarding cattle, and the city to add at once an adequate number to its force of inspectors, and to establish these milk depots, hundreds upon hundreds of babies who are otherwise doomed to die this summer will be saved.

⊛

*The Adirondack Forest Reserve in Danger*  On another page Professor Fernow, the eminent forestry expert, calls attention in a timely communication to the great lack of the Adirondack Forest Reserve. The State Constitution, adopted in 1894, reads :

The lands of the State now owned or hereafter acquired, constituting the forest reserve as now fixed by law, shall be forever kept as wild forest lands. They shall not be leased, sold, or exchanged, or taken by any corporation, public or private, nor shall the timber thereon be sold, removed, or destroyed.

This " let alone " policy has, of course, nothing to do with scientific forestry,

which means not only a setting apart of certain timber tracts, but a proper provision for their cutting and reforestation. New York State will undoubtedly modernize its Constitution at some future time. But it is much better to adhere to the present Constitutional provision than it would be to favor the Water Storage Bill now before the Legislature. This bill constitutes an amendment to the Constitution. It passed the Legislature of 1906, despite the fact that no public hearing was allowed on it. It will, if it passes the present Legislature, be submitted to the vote of the people. In his recent message Governor Hughes dealt with the subject of water-storage in the Adirondacks, saying that such power so acquired should be saved for the benefit of the entire people ; it should not be surrendered in whole or in part to any private interest. In the New York Board of Trade and Transportation's recently published memorial a similar position was taken ; the memorial called attention to the policy of Massachusetts, which has so conserved its water-power resources as to enable it to take front rank in the textile industries. The increase of the use of water-power in New York State has been due to the expansion of the paper and wood-pulp industry. This industry flourishes only at the expense of the forests. Even if its forests did not suffer, State lands in the Adirondacks should not be jeopardized by increasing the water-storage on practically all of the many lakes, so that public health would be in danger every time the water was drawn off. The history of water-storage in that region is a sufficient indication of what would be the result were it established on a large scale. The few large private holders of Adirondack forests would be injured, of course, but the great injury would come to the thousands who annually resort thither for sport, rest, and health. That mountain region has been a source of physical invigoration to many, not to a few, as Dr. Fernow seems to indicate. As to the " privileged rich men " who are " leagued together " in the Association for the Protection of the Adirondacks, there are, perhaps, half a dozen millionaires among the thousand or twelve hundred members. The vast majority is made up of people of modest means, who love the mountains and woods and streams and the living creatures in them. Nor is the sentiment which has rallied to the Association's action in protesting against the water-storage plan a millionaire sentiment. The Association's action has been supported by the leading papers of the State and by people everywhere in Boards of Trade, Civic Associations, and Adirondack Clubs; this sentiment represents not a class but the mass.

&#10070;

*The Significance of the Second Russian Duma*    Last week the second Russian Duma convened. It was called to order by the Vice-President of the Council of the Empire, the upper house of the Russian Parliament, the Duma constituting the lower house. The opening ceremony began with a Te Deum intoned by the Metropolitan of the Russian Church. Around him were grouped the clergy, Cabinet ministers and other officials, and the Conservative deputies. But the great mass of the Radicals looked on with indifference. The Metropolitan then addressed all the deputies, begging them to forget differences and work for the welfare of their country. After singing the national anthem, the Imperial Decree was read, and the balloting for the office of Presi-

dent of the Duma took place. The election of Feodor Golovin may be regarded as the most significant act of either the first or second Duma. For he received the unanimous vote of the Constitutional Democrats and the Radicals, and probably some votes from the more liberal of the Octobrists. The event shows that the half-dozen factions into which the opponents of the autocracy are divided are not so permanently opposed to one another as has been reported. Moreover, it indicates the failure of the reactionaries' efforts to foment strife among those factions. The solidarity displayed by them augurs well for the Duma's future. The new President is also the President of the Moscow Zemstvo or Provincial Council. He is a member of one of the oldest Russian families, is well-to-do and thus has a material stake in the country's prosperity, is a foremost Liberal, but is respected by men quite irrespective of party, having many friends both in the court circle and among the peasants.

&#10070;

*The Duma's "Right" and "Left"*    These sections into which the Duma is divided are of increasing interest. Until the first Duma met, they were comparatively vaguely defined. They are now seen to group themselves into Conservative, Liberal,

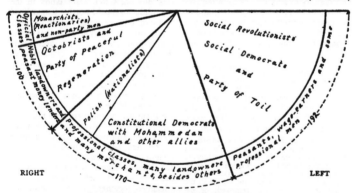

POLITICAL PARTIES IN THE DUMA

The parties sit in the order indicated, the Radicals on the left of the Speaker, the Conservatives on his right. The figures in the dotted lines indicate the number of members, according to the latest returns, sitting in the respective divisions. Outside the semicircle is described the character of the constituencies represented.

ınd Radical sections. In the Duma, as ın other Continental parliaments, in the ıemicircle of seats facing the President the Conservatives sit on his right and the Radicals on his left. Hence they are known by the expressive names " Right " ınd " Left." The Right comprises two groups, the Conservatives or reactionaries, standing for the official classes, and the Moderates or Octobrists, this name being taken from the Emperor's Freedom Manifesto of October, 1905; the Octobrists are composed largely of landowners and money-lenders, and, while opposed to autocracy, hardly allow their leanings towards liberalism to outrun the Manifesto's limits. The two sections together may exceed a hundred members. The Center of the House is composed of Liberals, namely, the Constitutional Democrats and their allies among the Nationalists, the latter being the Poles and other border subjects, who are aiming towards local self-government, and the Mohammedan representatives. In the previous Duma the Constitutional Democrats constituted the largest political party, and they would probably continue their preponderance in the present House, but for the Government's arbitrary change in the election laws and its prosecution of some of the best members of the former Duma. Had it not been for this, the Constitutional Democrats might have been returned in almost double their strength. As it is, they with their allies number about 170 members. The Left is composed of three groups—first, the Party of Toil, which may be thought to correspond to an industrial labor party, but is in reality much more of a farmers' union ; the Social Democrats, some of whose members are opposed to revolution ; and, finally, the Social Revolutionists, whose title sufficiently defines them. These Radical groups number almost two hundred members. The hope of the Duma is in a coalition. It is a reasonable hope, because for a generation both the French and German parliaments have been so governed. In this coalition the Constitutional Democrats will naturally form the rallying point; they will endeavor to frame such legislation as will attract to its support the

Octobrists of the right and the Party of Toil to the left. It is expected that any measure that is proposed by the opponents of the Government will be met by measures already drafted by the Government. Indeed, the Government may submit its measures immediately. The period of time since the first Duma's dissolution has been busily spent by the upholders of autocracy in framing legislative measures. If these provide for a constitution, universal suffrage, equality of citizens before the law, and radical agrarian reforms, they will mark a turning-point in Russian progress. If they do not, they will be met by a solidarity of opposition which, compared with the unwieldy and unworkable solidarity of the first Duma, has already shown its ability to strike as one man. In that fact lies the significance of the second Duma.

⬤

*Municipal Reaction in London* As the result of the County Council election, what may be described as the Tory party in London municipal affairs is again where it was in 1886. It then controlled not only the City of London—lying within the boundaries that now mark the limits of the ancient city—and the municipal affairs in what are now the twenty-eight boroughs outside the City of London, but also certain boards of the whole metropolis. By the Local Government Act of 1888 the old Metropolitan Board of Works, whose closing years were in disgrace owing to exposures of graft, was superseded by the County Council. Since the first election in 1889, although the elections for Councilors are held every three years, the Progressives were in control until March of this year. During these eighteen years, though the municipal Tory party never lost its hold on the City of London, the Progressives were responsible for the municipal policy of Greater London ; for all the works which are metropolitan rather than local in their character. It was under their auspices that the widening of the Strand and the construction of Kingsway—the great thoroughfare running north from the Strand and connecting this southern artery of London with Holborn—was constructed. All the parks and commons, not of the royal demesne, within the area of Greater London have been under the management of the County Council, which has added seventy parks to the forty then existing, and has increased the area of the parks and open spaces from 2,600 acres to 5,000. In the nearer parks the Council has provided for the recreation of the people. The London asylums for the care of the insane have also been under the management of the Council instead of under poor-law control as prior to 1889. In the later period of Progressive rule the Council took over and electrified the street-car system on the south side of the Thames; and also took over from a private company the street-car system in North London and electrified a part of this system—as much as was practicable until streets in the populous central borough of St. Pancras were widened and a number of dangerous curves eliminated. The Council had imposed on it by Parliament in 1904 all the work that from 1870 had been in the hands of the London School Board. In a word, between 1889 and 1907 it became the local Parliament for Greater London, controlling all London's affairs except the police, who, save within the confines of old London, are under the control of the Secretary of State for Home Affairs. Municipally London, in its larger aspects, was remade. The remaking was expensive. London enjoyed its five thousand acres of parks. Its working classes, in particular, benefited from the cheap street-car fares, and the all-night services of which there were none before the days of the County Council. They had the benefit also of full weight in coal supplies and of the strict administration of the Weights and Measures Act which the Council has enforced.

❦

*Why Reaction Has Come*
The remaking of London was needed; but it was expensive. Rates increased. Londoners generally began to feel the cost of this improved municipal housekeeping by the County Council and the twenty-eight borough Councils. Last November the Progressives suffered defeat in the borough elections—the worst defeat since municipal councils superseded the old vestries in 1899. Besides the growing burden of County Council government, the Progressives had come into conflict with many vested interests. The theater and music hall proprietors had no liking for the close oversight of their structural arrangements by the Council; and the proprietors of the music halls found the censorship exercised by the Council irritating. The brewing, liquor, and saloon interests are almost invariably Tory in municipal as well as in national politics. They threw their influence against the Progressives. So did the Anglican clergy and the supporters of those elementary schools in London which by the Education Act of 1903 are still largely under clerical control. So also did the promoters of electric light and power schemes which the Council had thwarted by undertaking to obtain authority from Parliament to establish a great municipal light and power station. In London, too, there is some reaction from the great wave of Liberalism of last year. The result of all these forces and of the most bitterly fought election in the municipal history of the metropolis is that for the next three years the Tories or Moderates—now calling themselves Reformers—will be in full control of the County Council. They start the new term with the support of 85 in a Council of 120 members. This strength will be augmented by the filling up of aldermanic vacancies; and, in brief, the municipal affairs of London—Greater London and the boroughs—are now under control of the Moderates. The first result will be that the County Council Electric Power Bill will be dropped. The promoters of public utilities companies will again have an opportunity to advance their plans for the supply of light and power to the metropolis; and it is probable that the Council will proceed no further with the electrification of street-car lines north of the Thames, even if the systems on both sides of the river are not leased to companies. This overturn has been hailed in some quarters in this country as a defeat for municipal ownership. Of course it is not.

It is rather a check to certain experiments in municipal operation—a very different matter. The election of the Tories also puts to rest one bugaboo—the control of elections by municipal employees. These employees did vote, we understand, pretty solidly for the Progressives, but their votes were cast ineffectually.

❀

**The End of a Sect-Maker**    John Alexander Dowie, who died in the city of his own creation in Illinois last week, was a foreigner who invaded America and created, out of Americans as subjects, a kingdom for himself. By persuading people that he had healed them by prayer, as thousands of quacks do by nostrums, he won their gratitude; by ordering them about, he won their allegiance; and by inducing them to invest in real estate and other ventures, he won their money. Having them, heart, soul, and pocketbook, he rewarded them with sensations. He instituted elaborate but obvious forms of ritual; he fought single-handed the viper press; he roared out epithets at his opponents; he drove about with a kind of little pomposity; he built a city—such as it was—founded a bank, a newspaper, a manufacturing enterprise; he assumed holy offices to which he attached Scriptural names. He lashed himself into a condition approximating insanity, brought upon himself a financial scandal, wearied the aforetime interested multitude, alienated most of his followers, and now is dead. His career indicates, as the New York Tribune has acutely commented, the fact that the American people are deficient in the power of critical judgment. Dowie could never have gained following among people steeped in tradition, nor among people who, disregarding tradition, examined, weighed, and studied with discrimination anything new. He found his little kingdom among a people who were restrained either by tradition or by critical powers. Until we either have acquired more traditions or more discrimination, we may expect to find continued successors to Joseph Smith and John Alexander Dowie.

# Lenten Meditations
## Not Into Temptation

"Lead us not into temptation:" many thoughtful minds have stumbled at this petition in the Lord's Prayer. How strange, they think, to ask our heavenly Father not to lead us into temptation! How is it possible to think of him as so doing? The common explanations do not quite content them. The real difficulty is not removed until the mistake of taking that petition by itself, apart from those next preceding, is corrected—a frequent mistake, indeed, among Bible readers, who isolate a text from its context, with consequent misunderstanding.

The petitions immediately preceding ask for daily bread—all things serviceable to earthly life—and for the forgiveness of sins. But experience and observation warn us that the gifts corresponding to these needs have often become temptations. A petition that they may not become such then naturally suggests itself. We may be tempted to use in a way that is sometimes selfish, sometimes immoderate, gifts which were intended for sustenance and efficiency in our Father's service. Not all who utter the Lord's Prayer are active in benevolent work, or temperate at their daily table. We may also be tempted to abuse our reliance on the Father's forgiveness by making it the nurse of a neglectful rather than of a conscientious regard to his will. Many who pray for it are making little or no effort to overcome their faults, and to become more scrupulously dutiful. The ancient sect of antinomians, who believed that the Christian was freed from the moral law, has always had a large non-professing but practical following.

Thus liable to be turned to evil as are these two great gifts—the one for the physical, the other for the moral, life—it is a deeply religious instinct which conjoins petitions for them with a petition that we may be delivered from so perverting them. In this natural connection this petition in close reference to the preceding two really means, "Lead us not *thereby* into temptation:" that is, in fuller terms, Let not the gifts we ask for the bodily and the spiritual life become temptations to evil uses.

Thus viewed, these petitions make the unity of the Lord's Prayer more apparent. In the midst of it is the heart of it, "Thy Will be done," the cry, not of passive self-resignation, but of active self-dedication to dutiful doing. To this as their goal the two preceding aspirations, "Hallowed be thy Name," "Thy Kingdom come," lead up. To this as their end look back the two outward requests for the means to it in outward sustenance and inward grace, and they are emphasized by asking finally for safeguarding in the use of these as means to it, for final victory over evil.

Too often has religion been divorced from morality in the two lines of human need which this petition covers. Too commonly is it permitted to cloak a ragged morality, hiding and forgetting its need of repair. Too often is it fancied to atone for lack of moral vigilance and vigor. It is to be delivered from that sort of religion that Christ in this petition bids us pray. When we beseech God not to lead us into temptation, we beg that no gift of his may dull, that every gift may sharpen, our conscience.

❀

## Equalization of Salaries

A movement of the women teachers of New York City to secure an equalization of salaries for men and women in the public schools is of more than local significance, since it brings to the fore for discussion a principle of universal application. That principle has been stated, "Equal pay for equal work." This popular phrase has, however, been repudiated as "unfortunate" by some of the advocates of the movement, who have substituted therefor "Pay the position." It is very clear from the figures presented by the advocates of this movement that some revision of salaries is called for. It does not appear to be reasonable that a principal of a school should be paid a lower salary than subordinate teachers working under

her because she is a woman and they are men.

But neither of the principles avowed by the advocates of this movement appears to us to be sound. It is not true that we should pay the position; we should pay for the service; and different services may very well be rendered by different persons occupying the same kind of position. The phrase "Equal pay for equal work" seems far more like an expression of absolute justice. The difficulty with it is that in the higher forms of service there is no standard for measuring the work so as to declare what is equal. Charles Dickens and Anthony Trollope did, so far as one can judge from reading their biographies, something like an equal amount of work in writing their novels, but they did not receive equal pay. Many a country minister on a salary of five or six hundred dollars a year is doing quite as much work and work perhaps of quite as good quality as that of other clergymen whose salaries are five or six thousand dollars. There are hundreds of physicians in our great cities who do their very best work in the hospitals and dispensaries for nothing, who perform without pay for the poor operations for which they would charge thousands of dollars when performed for persons who are able to pay for the service.

The advocates of equal pay in schools for equal work have suggested the following standard: "There is but one way in which to judge of the equality of work; and that is by results. The pupils of the woman teacher are graduated by exactly the same standards and tests as those of the man teacher. Does the Board of Education make any modification of its demands when a woman teacher is involved? Not in the least. The superintendents and principals fill out the same blanks and judge from identical standards in rating the work of either." But this standard, though as good a one as could be suggested, is inadequate. Intellectual results are not the only results of school work; they are not even the most important results. It is the general opinion of educational experts that in the higher schools more men teachers are needed his is not because the pupils of men achers pass better examinations than ie pupils of women teachers; it is ecause the masculine element is needed i the educational community; because, ir example, the average boy, if he is iught only by women, comes to regard :holarship as a purely feminine accomlishment and look upon it with someiing like contempt. He needs to underand that manliness and scholarship iay and often do go together, and he in learn this only by seeing them together i the teacher whom he respects both ir his manliness and for his scholarship. t is for this reason that in private :hools the wise principal often looks ir athletic qualities in a teacher who is nothing to do with athletics.

We repeat that, in our judgment, the hole question of salary adjustment eeds better adjustment. The fact that icrease of salaries will involve increase f cost to the community is not a serius objection. Most communities in merica can well afford to give their :achers better compensation. But the uestion of sex ought not to enter into ie problem at all. The school should btain such men teachers as are necesiry to secure the masculine element, ich women teachers as are necessary ) secure the feminine element, and in etermining the salaries should take ito account a number of elements—the hount of work performed, the price :cessary to be paid to secure the serv-e, the living expenses of the person :ndering the service, and to some ex-nt at least the indefinable quality of iaracter and capacity to impart char-:ter which cannot be measured by any ird and fast rules.

⊛

# 'nterpreting the Constitution

A correspondent, supporting the posi-in of the Rev. Samuel W. Dike (Outlook, pbruary 16, p. 379) that, if the Federal jwer is to be extended beyond the limits ended by its framers, the extension puld be made by amendments constitionally adopted, not by a process of judicial construction, sends us an address of ' Mr. Justice Brewer, of the United States Supreme Court, delivered before the Virginia Bar Association last summer, which sustains the same view. Judge Brewer says:

> We often hear the declaration that something more than a knowledge of the law is necessary for a successful judge; that he should be endowed with the spirit of constructive statesmanship. By this and other ways there is expressed the thought that the new conditions of life call upon the court to give a new and different meaning to the language of the Constitution, a meaning larger and broader than that which, according to the rule so clearly stated by Chief Justice Marshall, was the meaning of the framers of the Constitution and the founders of the Government.

> I know that there are changed conditions and a different social and business life from that which obtained when the Constitution was framed. It may be that new laws are necessary, possibly amendments to the Constitution, but it must always be remembered that this is a Government of and by the people, and if additions and changes are necessary, let them be made in the appointed way. Never let the courts attempt to change laws or Constitution to meet what they think present conditions require. When they do this, they clearly usurp powers belonging to the legislature and the people.

There are two conceptions of the United States Constitution: one, that the Constitution created the Nation and gave to it all its powers, and that it is to be strictly construed, like a power of attorney given to an agent to manage an estate; the other, that the Nation created the Constitution, and that it is to be construed liberally as a statement of fundamental principles designed to indicate how the powers of the newly formed Nation were to be distributed among its several departments. One regards the Nation as the agent of the States, the other regards the States as members of the Nation. Mr. Justice Brewer's address inclines to the former view, but, with characteristic candor, he makes it clear that the decisions of the United States Supreme Court are based upon the latter view. Thus he refers to Mr. Justice Bradley in the Legal Tender Cases:

> The United States is not only a government but it is a national government, and the only government in this country that has

the character of nationality. . . . Such being the character of the general government, it seems to be a self-evident proposition that it is invested with all those inherent and implied powers which at the time of the adoption of the Constitution were generally considered to belong to every government as such, and as being essential to the exercise of its functions.

So Mr. Justice Gray in the Chinese Exclusion Case:

The United States are a sovereign and independent Nation, and are vested by the Constitution with the entire control of international relations, and with all the powers of government necessary to maintain that control and to make it effective.

So Mr. Justice Brown in the Insular Cases:

We are also of the opinion that the power to acquire territory by treaty implies not only the power to govern such territory, but to prescribe upon what terms the United States will receive its inhabitants, and what their status shall be in what Chief Justice Marshall termed "the American Empire."

But perhaps the most striking illustration of this enlargement of Federal powers under the Constitution by judicial construction, quoted by Judge Brewer, is furnished by the decisions of the Court that the admiralty jurisdiction of the Federal courts does not stop at tide-water, but extends over all the navigable waters of the United States, including its canals.

We think from a careful reading of Mr. Justice Brewer's address that he both agrees with and fully sustains the statement in The Outlook that "the changes now going on under a liberal construction of the Constitution are not greater than those accomplished under Chief Justice Marshall in the last century." No recent decision of the Supreme Court has given such extension to the powers of the Federal Government as Chief Justice Marshall's decision that the Supreme Court can set aside as unconstitutional any act of any State Legislature—a decision contemptuously disregarded by President Jackson at the time, but now universally recognized as the supreme law of the land, and as much a part of the Constitution as any of the Amendments. Mr. Justice Brewer deprecates these changes wrought by judicial decisions, but in this he dissents

from a majority of the Supreme Court by whose authority the changes are being made. Whether this liberal construction of the Constitution as a document of political principles capable of adaptation to the changing conditions of a growing Nation, rather than of inflexible rules by which the power of the Nation is unalterably limited, imperils individual liberty, as Mr. Justice Brewer appears to think, or safeguards individual liberty, as The Outlook thinks, is a question which we do not here discuss.

❧

# The Spectator

If the great American weeklies are not careful, they will destroy a great American illusion. Does not hoary tradition countenance the belief that the only really ingenious and mechanically up-to-date people on earth foregather under the Stars and Stripes? Why, then, these recurring series of articles on "Things they do better in Europe"? The Spectator finds that these pernicious creeds insensibly affect his patriotic point of view. Not many days ago the exigencies of the Boston rapid transit system stranded him at a certain transfer station called Roxbury Crossing. The day was a wild one; the wind drove the dust in stinging particles into the Spectator's unfortunate eyes. Just before him two employees of the street railway company were engaged in sweeping out switches. At every stroke of their brooms a fresh cloud of germ-laden dust was consigned to the breeze, to be wafted to the eyes and throats of the transferees, to whom came neither cars nor rumors of cars. Over the Spectator's mind there flashed a vision of the way they do switch-clearing in Europe: how a man armed with a dirt-plow—a pointed steel implement shaped to fit the rails—walks the track, pushing his little rail-cleaner before him at the end of a broomstick; how the dust gathers in a pan behind the plow; how at intervals the man dumps it beside the track in neat piles; how another man with a cart follows and takes the dust away. At the thought there rose in the Spectator's mind a traitorous doubt whether after all we *are* the cleverest nation under the sun, as we have long fondly believed.

❀

Before the taste of the pavement was out of his mouth, the Spectator had recalled a number of foreign arrangements which he would like to see copied at home. He remembered the clatterless milk-cart of Hamburg—a thing like a hose-truck, with bright brass cans swinging silently from hooks along the sides. Then there was the sliding change-tray in the booking-office at Hanover—a tray with ribs like a washboard, on which the most obstinate coin could not contrive to stick. You put your money on it and slid it through to the ticket-seller, and he slid it back with the tickets and change. The Spectator bethought him of a morning in Copenhagen, when he watched the mail-collector making his round. The man jerked open his pouch, hung it on hooks in the bottom of the mail-box, and turned a crank. Presto! the letters plumped all together into his bag, and the collector was off in less time than it would have taken an American carrier to gather in his first handful. That post-box dumped like a dump-cart. Truly, a beautiful simplicity—one of the things one wonders at not having thought of before. But what was it doing in Scandinavia, so far from the resourceful Land of the Free?

❀

Yes, be it patriotic or not, the Spectator feels impelled to add his contribution to the list of things they do better in Europe. It's not inventions alone that he would like to import. He would like to see on the back of every American school-child a comfortable knapsack like those in which the little students of the Old World habitually carry their books. Why drag down the young shoulders and cramp the gait of our school-going boys and girls when they might wear their burden where Christian wore his and be as free as air? The Spectator would like to bring over, too, a certain kind of park bench which had the merit of being always empty for the accommodation of tired strangers.

❀

If the Spectator had his choice which of all the Old World institutions he would bring over to New York, he thinks he should choose that *omnium gatherum* of conveniences—the Danish telephone kiosk. Suppose that at the four corners of Union Square there stood neat summer-houses, each with a brisk and capable little woman inside it waiting to furnish the hurrying New Yorker with postage-stamps or postals (and the opportunity to write the same on the premises if it suited his turn), to send telegrams, reserve theater tickets, and give him the use of a pay 'phone! Think of the saving of time, the temper, and the legs! Kongens Nytorv, in Copenhagen, is fitted up like that. Indeed, it must be a shock to an imported Scandinavian, of whatever persuasion, when he finds that in New York he must either call a messenger or travel several city squares to send a telegram. In Christiania despatches are simply dropped into a box on the side of the first street-car that comes along, there being a telegraph office at every trolley station. And really, when one comes to think of it, why not?

❀

Consider the manifold internal advantages of a European street-car. The Spectator does not remember whether the convenience was common to all German towns, but he knows that in Hamburg there is a bright-faced clock in every car. This enables the passenger to fidget intelligently when bent on catching a train. The Spectator doubts whether the little brass detention-pens for lighted cigars that he saw on Danish street-cars could be with success attached to the back platforms of our own trolleys, for he does not believe that even the ocular demonstration of a number would satisfy an American that he had his own and not another's cigar. But in the Norwegian capital the cars had a beneficent and importable device for announcing the next stop. The Spectator has no notion how the thing worked except that it was a cylinder with a scroll running round it, and that periodically it flopped over with a loud premonitory click. Probably the motorman controlled it, since the Spectator could not detect the agency of the conductor. How the Spectator blessed it as it unrolled before him those queer Norwegian street names which appeal so frankly to the American eye, so obscurely to the American ear! Why not an arrangement like that on the electrics of Broadway?

❋

And the foreign conductors—if the Spectator could only import them! The thought moves him almost to the point of tears! Little would he care whether it was the blue, brass-bound kind of Germany, who say " Please, pretty," when they demand your fare, salute you if you ask a question, and dismount before you when the car stops, or the overawing, military kind of the far North. For all are courteous and all are clean. It hurts the Spectator's National pride to think what disgust must fill the soul of a European the first time he sets eyes upon the untidy uniform of the average American conductor. Ill-brushed, soiled and shiny about the change pockets, if not actually worn through, the livery would disgrace any business corporation except the American street railway companies.

❋

The Spectator realizes that life on an American trolley must be hard upon the clothes. Nattiness may be impossible. But is it also impossible that the hands of our conductors be kept within speaking distance of cleanliness? During a recent visit to Cambridge the Spectator one evening boarded the historic Memorial Hall Special which bears Cantabrigians to the concerts of the Symphony Orchestra. The aisle was packed with men in evening dress and young girls in gay party cloaks. Through the chattering crowd pushed an unusually strenuous conductor, laying hold unceremoniously of one shoulder after another, and the hands with which he touched the light fabrics of the ladies might have been those of a coal-heaver or a plumber! There flashed across the Spectator's inner eye a vision of his first Stockholm conductor—a Northern Adonis, tall and svelt, with drooping fair mustache, his personal magnificence enhanced by a perfectly fitted Prince Albert of light blue-gray, white gloves, and a natty military cap. This resplendent

creature never soiled his fingers nor yet his gloves by contact with dirty money. He carried what looked like a dark-lantern of glittering brass and plate glass, into a slot in which you dropped your fare yourself. Why not the dark-lantern and the decent white gloves for us?

❋

Ingenuity and even convenience may be carried too far, as the Spectator is painfully aware. He once crossed from Copenhagen to Lübeck on the delightfully appointed Swedish steamship Malmö, which boasted a patent seagoing table, balanced in the center so as to keep a perfect level no matter how the vessel pitched. It was, as Stevenson says, " a good idea, but failed to please." The Spectator wavered into the tiny saloon, and sat down to admire the table bearing its load of dishes so steadily that the water did not stir in the glasses. Unfortunately, the seats did not swing with the table. The Malmö listing suddenly to leeward, the Spectator beheld his plate sinking uncannily away from him, and the next moment the table rapped him smartly on the knees. The passengers—Swedes, Germans, and Americans alike—shrieked and clutched wildly at the cloth, then bethought them, and tried to pretend that they were quite used to this sort of acrobatic dinner. The table meanwhile self-righteously preserved its dignity and its dishes. The Spectator inwardly vowed that he would not be taken off his guard again. But when, presently, just as he was spearing a far-away morsel, his edge of the table rose up and almost smote him under the chin, it came over him with conviction that it was not dinner that he wanted at all, but something stationary to look at, something that did not tip and tilt and slide away after that unreliable fashion. That table was the cleverest invention he ever beheld. He will guarantee that not a dish is broken even when the Baltic is at its wildest—and also that nine-tenths of the passengers who contract for dinner upon its bearing board think better of it before a second course is out. Economically it is a great thing. But the Spectator hopes he may never meet its like again.

# Two Years of a Government That Does Things

## BY CHARLES J. BONAPARTE

Attorney-General of the United States

DURING the campaign of 1904 a distinguished lawyer of his own State advocated Judge Parker's election because the speaker wanted, and thought the people likewise wanted, a President who wouldn't "do things." Doubtless he knew his own wishes, but the result showed him woefully amiss as to those of the people. Seldom has there been shown more signal incapacity to interpret public opinion than was thus displayed. In truth, readiness and ability to "do things," in contrast to talking about doing things or finding good reasons not to do things, have been always or nearly always what the American people found and liked in our truly popular public men. From the days of Old Hickory (to go no further back) to the present, the men really close to the voters' hearts have been men of achievements, not men of promises, nor yet men of doubts and scruples; and President Roosevelt owed his overwhelming victory at the polls more clearly and surely to the widespread and well-founded belief that he unequivocally belonged to the first class, and yet more emphatically didn't belong to either of the others, than to any other of its various causes.

It may be worth a moment's pause to note the essential characteristics of the two kinds of politicians and public servants I have last mentioned—those, namely, who don't "do things." From our birth as a Nation until now we have had in public life men, some of them, men of conspicuous ability, whose conception of the art of government has been always to find insuperable objections to any imaginable course of action, and who perpetually discover in our Federal Constitution marvels of impotency.

The most fateful and tragic exhibition of the statesmanship taught in this school was undoubtedly President Buchanan's policy towards Secession; but a comparatively unimportant incident, happening some sixty years earlier, curiously illustrated its merits. We had been compelled to send a small squadron to the Mediterranean by reason of piratical depredations on our commerce on the part of the Barbary powers. The United States schooner Enterprise, forming part of this force, was attacked, without any provocation, by a Tripolitan "polacca" of somewhat superior strength, whose captain probably mistook her for a merchantman. After a sharp engagement and severe loss, the corsair surrendered; when, greatly to their own astonishment, the surviving Tripolitans and their vessel were released and sent home with a warning not to molest other American vessels! This edifying proceeding was strictly prescribed by the orders of President Jefferson; who held that, since the Congress had not yet formally declared war against these petty robber States, which were all the time impudently seizing our merchant ships, as well as enslaving and barbarously maltreating our sailors, he could use our navy only to repel actual aggression, could not take the offensive in any form, and, more particularly, could not make prizes. It may be that even to-day some may be found to applaud such scrupulous avoidance of "usurpation" and "centralization" on the part of the Executive.

The other class of public men to whom I have alluded differ from Mr. Lincoln in believing that you can "fool all the people all the time," or, at all events, enough of the people to get and keep

599

office through their votes. They guess at what the voters want, founding their guesses usually on the assumption that everybody wants to get what belongs to somebody else without paying for it, and then promise forthwith to bring about this hypothetical millennium, if given power, without the least regard to the possibility of doing this, or the consequences of trying to do it. If one such promise doesn't seem to "take," they try another even more extravagant. I have not yet heard a suggestion that the canals of Mars be acquired and exploited by our Government, but this suggestion would bear a close analogy to some which I have heard, especially if it be true that there are no canals in Mars. These statesmen have a touching faith in the people's bad memory; they hope to get power by promising the sun, moon, and stars, and, when the time for performance comes, to find that the voters have forgotten the promise.

Two years have now passed since his choice as President commissioned Theodore Roosevelt to " do things " for the American people. What things has he done? And how well or ill has he done them?

### ABROAD

The consent, we may almost say the instinct, of mankind has ever attached peculiar honor for a ruler to the title of ' Peace-maker;" no designation has been more coveted by chieftains who longed to live after death in the memory of men: *pacificus* [1] was the legend on coin or arch or statue which each holder of imperial sway saw most gladly coupled with his name. This title has been conferred on our President, not by himself nor by any flatterer, official or private, but by judges no less competent than impartial, foreigners to him and to us, and sustained in their verdict by the assent of the civilized world. The first "thing," or at least the first big "thing," he " did " after his inauguration was to run the risk of rebuff and failure and consequent blame, to forget the precepts

[1] I need hardly pause to point out that *pacificus*, as used in such inscriptions, means, not " peaceful," but *pacem faciens*, the maker (or restorer) of peace. It was applied to many sovereigns (*e.g.*, to Charlemagne) whose reigns were filled with warfare and all the best years of whose lives were spent in arms.

and the precedents of a policy which would shut out our country from international fellowship with nineteen-twentieths of the human race, and to employ all the legitimate influence of a great nation—a nation too strong to be flouted, and in this case too clearly disinterested to be suspected of guile—to restore the incalculable blessing of peace to Russia and Japan and the lands which were their battlefield. Beside this great achievement, his share in promoting the peace of Central America, in staying civil strife in Cuba, in discouraging rebellion in Santo Domingo, seem trifles; but these trifles have served to spare humanity no little bloodshed and misery, and to earn for his country and himself no little credit and respect.

A certain class of talkers and writers among us have been sorely puzzled, and, I am strongly tempted to suspect, just a little chagrined, by the honor he has thus earned and enjoys. For those who protest against drills in the public schools, against reviews at Jamestown, even against tin soldiers as toys, lest we and especially our children be infected with " militarism," it is an enigma and little less than a scandal to have a man with a military record, a friend to the army and to the navy, an advocate of ample provision for the National defense, in short, a true son of Belial, or rather of Moloch, receive the Nobel prize and be distinguished among contemporary rulers as the friend and promoter of peace. Doubtless all this accords well with Washington's admonition that " if we desire to secure peace, it must be known that we are at all times prepared for war;" but these good and wise people have far outgrown the antiquated views of Washington.

As a means to peace, and also as an end only less important than peace itself, this Administration has " done " some " things," and tried or begun to " do " more " things " in furtherance of the " harmony and liberal intercourse with all nations" which the Farewell Address declares to be " recommended by policy, humanity, and interest;" if it has not yet done or completed all it has thus commenced or tried to do, agencies beyond the control of the Executive, and in some cases even of the Federal Government, will, by the fair-minded, be blamed for the failure or delay. "Harmony" with a nation such as Japan is not fostered by incidents such as the exclusion of Japanese children from the San Francisco schools, nor yet by a discussion, in the press and elsewhere, such as that incident aroused; nevertheless we may now reasonably hope that among the "things done" by the Administration will be counted a settlement of this controversy as satisfactory as blind and narrow prejudice may permit. Moreover, when we seek "liberal intercourse" with foreign nations, it is well to remember that in such matters a one-sided "liberality" is seldom long-lived. Again in the words of the Farewell Address: "It is folly in one nation to look for disinterested favors from another:" *do ut des* is the accepted principle of all rational and successful diplomacy; and when a statesman is compelled to approach foreigners with empty hands, it is unjust and childish to complain if his hands remain empty. The justice and common sense of the American people ought to be, and I believe they will be, fully satisfied with what the Administration has done in this field of its labor; if during the next two years it shall, at last, obtain the really cordial and patriotic support from public opinion and other public servants for which it hopes with unwearied optimism and which is plainly needed to make fruitful for good its consistent policy in South America, in the Antilles, on the Isthmus, and in dealings with the Older Worlds, the four years ending March 4, 1909, will, I venture to predict, bear comparison in this respect with any like period of our National history.

## AT HOME

To judge fairly the "things" President Roosevelt has "done," we must have definite ideas as to what "things" the American people wished and chose him to "do." We were troubled then, as we are still, by evils incidental to prodigious National prosperity, and, as a result of this prosperity, phenomenally rapid increase in National and individual wealth. The immense masses of

capital controlled by some men or small groups of men enabled them, through the facilities for corporate organization afforded by our laws and the facilities for personal intercourse afforded by long-distance telephones, wireless telegraphy, ocean cables, and other fruits of modern enlightenment, to form aggregations of productive wealth so vast as to threaten the commercial liberties of our people. Directly, these combinations operated to destroy fair and healthy, by fostering unfair and unhealthy, competition; indirectly, they tended to debauch our politics, our press, the management of our corporations, our State and municipal authorities, and even our courts of justice. Enlightened public opinion had slowly and, on the whole, reluctantly reached the conclusions that these evils could not cure themselves (as many had hoped and said they would), that no general and permanent cure could be reasonably expected from the States, and that a remedy ought to be sought in vigorous, even, if need there were, in drastic, action on the part of the National Government.

To deal with this situation, two more or less definite policies of action and one of inaction competed, and may be said still to compete, for popular approval. The men who made up the things to be reformed were clear that no reform was needed. They said, and say yet (probably they believed, and perhaps they believe even yet), that without such combinations and their incidents the transaction of business on the scale of these days would be impossible and prosperity would disappear. On the other hand, certain speakers and writers advocated, and certain politicians professed to advocate, some avowedly, some with a large measure of self-deception as to their own meaning, and all with greater or less consistency and candor, the destruction, more or less rapid and complete, of the prosperity which had, incidentally and indirectly but undoubtedly, created or fostered the conditions to be cured. To effect this it was proposed, on the one hand, to unsettle practically all existing business relations in the country by a promise of sudden and sweeping but vaguely stated changes in the tariff; and, on the other, to drive capital out of the country or into hiding by socialistic and confiscatory legislation.

Our President had expressed himself often and emphatically in disapproval of both of these policies: he could not be made to see that our country must go to Mr. Mantalini's "demnition bow-wows" unless, to use an illustration furnished by facts, a monster corporation or trust was allowed to pay only six cents on the hundred pounds for its freight over railways it controlled when its humbler rivals had to pay eighteen cents; but neither could he see the good sense and good morals of a policy which, in last resort, would make everybody in the country poor because a few people in it were too rich for its good and their own, which would kill the goose that laid the golden eggs, not, as in the fable, to seek for them in her body, but to prevent her laying too many of them in a few favored nests. He believed that the Nation could and should regulate and control its productive wealth without destroying this wealth or making it unproductive; and, for his part, he was willing to try to do this; the people believed, as he did, that the thing could be done; the people also believed that he was the man to do it; and, by its votes, the people gave him the job.

I have contrasted "fair and healthy" with "unfair and unhealthy" competition; this contrast is often imperfectly understood, and from the fact arises no little confusion of thought. Every one in trade is supposed by economists, and also by the common law, to be ever striving to reduce the cost or increase the value of what he has to sell, so that he may undersell his rivals, while yet earning for himself a fair profit; this process is held wholesome and salutary by the wisdom and experience of mankind. But our great trusts are usually formed and maintained through competition of another kind altogether: they often, even habitually, crush out dealers who will not join them by underselling the latter without regard to profit or even cost—in short, by losing money themselves that others may likewise lose, and looking for their profits to their undisputed monopoly in the near future, when

they can charge the helpless public whatever may be needful to recoup their temporary loss. Competition such as this means, not a contest of business ability, industry, and thrift, but a contest of endurance, or, in other words, of resources; and it is no less wasteful materially than debasing morally to the community. Moreover, as each species of vermin has its peculiar parasite, the modern trust has bred the blackmailing "independent," the bogus enterprise existing only that it may sell out, whose struggle with the trust it would "bleed," so far as genuine, takes shape in the same cut-throat competition. In these contests of willingness and ability to lose money, the influence, often amounting to absolute control, of the trusts over our great transportation companies has been freely used and very effective; "rebates" and "differentials" and discriminating rates generally have been the most useful weapons of our huge monopolies.

The present Administration has sought to make competition fair and healthful, first, by trying, so far as its resources might permit, to enforce rigidly and impartially the laws which forbid and punish harmful combinations in restraint of trade; secondly, by obtaining and making effective, so far as it could, legislation to prevent any form of discrimination by any kind of common carrier or other public agency for transportation. In both fields of action it has done much hard work; and in both, but particularly in the second, it has accomplished results at least justifying their cost. In large measure "rebates" and their like now belong to the past, and discrimination, if not unknown, has become furtive and covert. Moreover, several of the trusts have been dissolved, in so far at least as agreements or decrees of courts of equity can effect their dissolution, and even those among them once inclined to say with Tweed, "Well! what are you going to do about it?" have been taught the unwisdom of open defiance to the law.

It is a "thing" worth "doing" to teach or remind citizens of any class and all classes that laws exist to be obeyed and not to be evaded; and there is likewise need to do this, for the fact now seems to be often forgotten by at least some citizens and with respect to some laws. Thus the statute forbidding laborers on public works of the United States to work more than eight hours in any one day, although obeyed by officers of the Government, had been practically a dead letter for contractors until President Roosevelt first ordered its effective enforcement some fourteen years after it became a law. So completely had the idea that to disobey this act was criminal faded from the minds of those habitually guilty of the offense that many of them protested, and still protest, with sincere indignation against their own prosecution before they should have completed the contracts for which they had made bids supposing they could disregard the law with impunity; they assert a vested right to commit crime![1]

It has been and is the aim of this Administration, an aim pursued with unswerving fidelity during the past two years, to show all Americans, whether rich or poor and of whatever class or condition in life, that the laws made for their common good demand the prompt and unquestioning obedience of all alike.

These laws, like all things human, may be faulty; if they are, it is the duty, no less than the right, of a good citizen to do what in him lies to make them all that they should be for the general good. But, such as they are, and whatever his judgment of their merits, he deserves the name of a good citizen only if he respects and not if he eludes them. Because, and in so far as, they believe this, and do as they believe, Americans have a government of laws, not of men; and most of all because it has steadfastly sought to foster such belief and assure such obedience, the Federal Administration of the past two years at home claims to have "done things" worthy to be praised for the doing, to have merited the people's trust and deserved well of the country.

[1] It should be said that the constitutionality of this statute has been recently questioned, and further prosecutions under it deprecated until after that question shall have been passed upon by the Supreme Court; no criticism of this suggestion is, of course, intended.

# EDUCATIONAL EFFICIENCY
## THE CARNEGIE FOUNDATION
### BY ROBERT W. BRUÈRE

THE Carnegie Foundation for the Advancement of Teaching is securing results that far exceed in value any that were foreseen by the general public, or probably, indeed, by Mr. Carnegie himself at the time when his gift was announced. When, in April, 1905, Mr. Carnegie determined to set aside ten million dollars for the establishment of a fund "from which to provide retiring pensions for the teachers of universities, colleges, and technical schools in our country, Canada, and Newfoundland," the opinion rapidly got abroad that the Carnegie Foundation, as the fund when first incorporated was called, constituted a monumental charity. From all parts of the continent letters addressed to Dr. Henry S. Pritchett, the President of the Foundation, by individuals who felt that their services had entitled them to relief from their lifelong cares, brought appeals for help. The writers apparently believed that the floodgates of prosperity had been opened to their profession, and that bounties were to be distributed indiscriminately to all who asked. Alas! experience has already made it clear that the financial problems of the Foundation are relatively unimportant. With a fair approach to accuracy, the financial limitations of the fund have already been defined. The pension roll will probably never include at any given time more than four hundred names, representing a probable maximum of one hundred and fifty institutions and three thousand professors. In a short time the pensions, having once been allotted, will distribute themselves all but automatically; but when that time arrives, the major work of the Foundation will still for the most part remain to be done.

Charity, as ordinarily conceived, has never been the inspiration of Mr. Carnegie's benefactions. The greatest gift which he and his fellow captains of industry have brought to the Nation is not represented by sums of money ; their lives have taught them the significance and uses of efficiency, and to lead the Nation along the roads of efficiency appears to be Mr. Carnegie's aspiration. Libraries were making a desultory progress through the country. They sprang up here and there in response to urgent local needs. Scattered communities were gradually learning what libraries might accomplish as instruments of enlightenment. But the Nation at large had no well defined sense of libraries as efficient servants of the democracy until Mr. Carnegie made their distribution almost universal. American inventors were the amazement of the world. In various parts of the country individual scientists were conducting researches of the highest practical and scientific importance. And yet the scientific spirit had not penetrated the Nation. In systematic application of science to industry we trudged like an undisciplined mob behind the well-marshaled forces of Germany. In co-ordinating the work of many investigators, and in concentrating their scattered light upon the fundamental riddle of life, we lagged behind both France and England. Science, though strong in its individual disciples, was not efficient in its service to the Nation at large. It needed organization and discipline ; and to this end Mr. Carnegie established, in 1902, the Carnegie Institution at Washington, with an endowment equal to those of the Royal Society of London, the Academies of Science at Paris, Berlin, Vienna, and Rome, the Royal Institution of London, and the Smithsonian Institution combined, with the largest freedom to perform for America the offices which these societies administered in Europe. It showed, therefore, a curious misapprehension of the spirit in which Mr. Carnegie is accustomed to disperse his wealth to suppose that the Carnegie Foundation was a charity fund. It might have been perceived at the beginning that the promotion of efficiency in our educational life was the principal end he had in view.

How, it may be said, is a fund of ten millions of dollars, the revenue from which has been specifically appropriated to "retiring pensions for the teachers of universities, colleges, and technical schools in our country, Canada, and Newfoundland," going to promote educational efficiency in America ? Let us answer question with question. How many people are there in the United States who know the number of colleges and universities supported by the people of the Nation ? How many of us know what the educational status of these institutions is ? To what extent are they co-operative in their effort to develop a national as well as a local and provincial intelligence ? In Germany, for example, there are twenty-one universities. All of these are under the general supervision of Ministers of Education. With a splendidly varied equipment, and representing through their professors every conceivable religious, social, political, and scientific point of view, they are all inspired by large considerations of national policy. They are united in their educational standard and in their aspiration to promote the welfare not only of Prussia, let us say, or Bavaria, but of Germany as a nation. Institutions of higher learning in Germany, though under the immediate jurisdiction of the several States in the Empire, are permeated by a national rather than by provincial ideals. In America there are some seven hundred institutions calling themselves universities, colleges, and technical schools. They represent no common aspiration whatever, no uniformity of standard, but "every possible grade of academic development and every possible degree of State and denominational control." Where there is so much incoherence, there must be great waste of power on the part of both professors and students. Where there is blind absorption in local and individual problems, there must be striking inefficiency from a larger, from a national, point of view.

What has the Carnegie Foundation done, what does it plan to do, to correct this evil, to co-ordinate the activities of hundreds of institutions and make them efficient instruments of education to the Nation?

In his letter to the twenty-five men to whom he intrusted the administration of the Foundation Mr. Carnegie limited in the following wise the application of his gift. "The fund," he wrote, "applies to universities, colleges, and technical schools, without regard to race, sex, creed, or color. We have, however, to recognize that State and Colonial governments which have established or mainly supported universities, colleges, or schools, may prefer that their relation shall remain exclusively with the State. I cannot, therefore, presume to include them. There is another class which States do not aid, their Constitution in some cases even forbidding it, viz., sectarian institutions. Many of these, established long ago, were truly sectarian, but to-day are free to all men of all creeds or of none— such are not to be considered sectarian now. Only such as are under the control of a sect, or require trustees (or a majority thereof), officers, faculty, or students to belong to any specified sect, or which impose any theological test, are to be excluded."

When President Pritchett and his administrative associates came to execute their trust, they found that there was no way of determining what institutions were, not only under denominational or State control, but, properly speaking, colleges, universities, or technical schools at all. These names in America, they found, represented anything from a grammar school or academy to institutions like Harvard and the Massachusetts Institute of Technology. Before they could proceed with their pensioning plan they needed to determine what, under the circumstances, these names did, or for practical purposes should, signify. This work of definition and the resultant work of classification, though incidental to Mr. Carnegie's plan, proved, as by-products so often do, to be of even greater value from the point of view of educational progress than the pensions themselves.

To begin with, a circular was sent out in the early part of last summer asking for information relative to (a) the educational standards of the institution, (b) the relation of each institution to the State, both in matters of control and support, and (c) the relation of each institution to religious denominations. This circular was addressed to six hundred and twenty-seven institutions in the United States and Canada. From four hundred and twenty-one of these replies had been received on November 11, 1906. But chaos had been brought only nearer home. Before these answers could be satisfactorily classified, Dr. Pritchett and his associates had to agree upon a definition of a college, in order that they might in turn be able to recognize an academy or high school when it called itself a college, and a college when it called itself a university.

If the definition was to be of any far-reaching value, it was important that it should be as little arbitrary as conditions would allow. A fairly good definition of a college already existed in the statutes of the State of New York. In the Revised Ordinances of the State of New York the following definition occurs: "An institution to be ranked as a college must have at least six professors giving their entire time to college and university work, a course of four full years in liberal arts and sciences, and should require for admission not less than the usual four years of academic or high school preparation, or its equivalent, in addition to the pre-academic or grammar school studies."

Even here, however, it will be observed, some ambiguity still exists. What is meant by the "usual four years of academic or high school preparation," not only in New York, but in the country at large? Furthermore, how does this definition affect the status of technical schools, and what implication does it make with regard to the financial security of institutions designated as colleges?

To these questions the Foundation has made the following succinct and interesting answers: "The usual four years of high school preparation" is equivalent to fourteen courses in a given subject with recitations five times a week for one year, each course so defined being designated a "point." To be ranked as a college, an institution must have a productive endowment of not less than two hundred thousand dollars. And a technical school to be ranked as a college " must have entrance and graduation requirements equivalent to those of the college, and must offer courses in pure and applied sciences of an equivalent grade."

When the eagerness of educational institutions to be admitted to the benefits of the Foundation is taken into consideration, it will be seen what an important instrument of standardization these definitions are destined to become. Associations of colleges and universities both in the West and the East have attempted to accomplish the result aimed at by the Foundation; but they have never possessed similar financial resources to alleviate the pains which always attend educational growth.

The term college having been defined, it was necessary to make a more accurate description of a denominational institution than Mr. Carnegie's letter of gift provided. In addition to the institutions comprehended in the scope of Mr. Carnegie's sentence cited above, it was determined by the Foundation that a clause should be added requiring the trustees of all institutions in any way associated with religious sects, and applying for admission to the benefits of the fund, to certify by resolution to the trustees of the Foundation not only that no denominational test is imposed in the choice of trustees, officers, or teachers, or in the admission of students, but that no denominational tenets or doctrines are taught to the students.

On the basis of this classification, and omitting State institutions, toward which the attitude of the Foundation has not yet been definitely fixed, only fifty-two universities, colleges, and technical schools have been admitted to the benefits of the Foundation and placed upon the " accepted list." Of these, twenty-two are in New England and New York alone, whereas only one, Tulane University, of New Orleans, is in the South ; and even Tulane has been admitted on the ground of entrance requirements to be adopted in 1907. Vanderbilt University and the Randolph-Macon Woman's College, excluded from the " list " for denominational reasons, are

the only two other institutions of higher learning south of Mason and Dixon's line whose entrance requirements are up to the standard adopted by the Foundation. The discrepancy between the admission and graduation requirements revealed by these figures can hardly be accounted for by considerations of local needs. Provincialism, and reluctance or inability to keep astride of the times, seem to be responsible for much of it. Some outside power is needed to bring the standards together.

How the work of standardization will proceed may be observed in the results which the Foundation hopes to accomplish in the South. Dr. Pritchett and his associates have made a careful examination of the educational conditions in that section. They have found that the status of education in Virginia is in many respects typical, and that the relation of the University of Virginia to the secondary schools is characteristic. They believe that if the University of Virginia could be persuaded to assume an attitude of leadership, it might render services of the highest value to the educational and consequently to the social and economic life of the South. The situation is approximately this : The University of Virginia is justly proud of its splendid history. Many distinguished men have been enrolled, not only on its faculty, but among its graduates. It boasts of its large annual enrollment, of the severity of its examinations, and of the abnormal number of students who annually fail in the examinations and are consequently dismissed from its halls. This last point is noteworthy ; it has been especially emphasized and has secured special consideration. Upon investigation, it has been learned that while Harvard, for example, requires sixteen " points " for admission, the University of Virginia requires not more than six and a half. Many scores of boys are annually admitted to the University who should, therefore, be at the beginning of their third year in the high school. At mid-years, or in their sophomore year, owing primarily to their inadequate preparation for college work, great numbers of them are " flunked." Now, a college " man " will not endure the humiliation of returning to the preparatory school. The system consequently results in the demoralization of the educational careers of many students. This is its first and most flagrant evil. But the result of the system upon secondary education in Virginia, and therefore in great measure upon that of the South, is possibly more far-reaching and more pernicious in its influence. In discussing the effect of the low standard of the University's entrance requirements upon secondary education, the principal of one of the high schools of Virginia said: "We cannot keep our students if the University is willing to accept them when they ought to be beginning the third year of their high school work. It is unreasonable to suppose that any boy is going to remain a 'prep' when he can become a college 'man.' If the colleges would stiffen their entrance requirements, we should be able to develop the high school curriculum. The high schools are ready to do their duty if the colleges will do theirs, and the time has come when carelessness in this matter is sure to retard the entire educational life of the South."

In commenting upon this situation, President Pritchett observed that he and the Trustees of the Foundation had no desire to interfere in any way with the free and wise development of education in accordance with the needs of varying environments, or to force up colleges which ought to be junior colleges or academies into a position in advance of the requirements of education. But they do believe, he declared, that any hope for advance in either higher or secondary institutions of learning depends very largely upon the willingness of the men in charge of them to come to some fair agreement as to the line which should separate the college from the academy or the high school. The University of Virginia, as well as other colleges of the South, has been urgently invited to adopt a standard which will make it eligible to the benefits of the Foundation. And as an earnest of the spirit in which the appeal has been made, the Trustees of the Foundation have voted generous retiring allowances to five distinguished men " who have served conspicuously

the cause of education in Virginia." At the head of these stands the name of Professor Noah K. Davis, of the University of Virginia.

I have emphasized the significance of the Foundation's work of standardization, because its far-reaching effects were hardly foreseen by the Trustees of the Foundation themselves, and because it illustrates, more perfectly than the pension system projected in Mr. Carnegie's letter of gift, the founder's eagerness to promote efficiency in every department of public life, and more particularly in every branch of public education. But great good has already been accomplished by the distribution of retiring allowances, and much injustice has been corrected. Up to October 1, 1906, eighty-eight pensions had been granted —forty-five to professors in "accepted" institutions, thirty-five to individual professors, and eight to the widows of professors. The total amount expended has been $122,130, an average of $1,387 a person per annum. The average allowance to professors in "accepted" institutions is $1,552; to individual professors, $1,302; and to widows, $833. Dr. Pritchett's assertion to the effect that pensions have been granted in each case, not as a charity, but as a right, is substantiated by the presence upon the list of pensioners of such names as those of Professor Noah K. Davis, of the University of Virginia, already referred to; Professor Francis A. March, of Lafayette College; Professor Hiram Corson, of Cornell, and Professor Henry P. Bowditch, of Harvard.

It is undoubtedly pleasant to contemplate the poetic justice which these benefactions consummate; but even here Mr. Carnegie's major intention must be borne in mind. I have already stated that the revenues of the Foundation will at most suffice to provide retiring allowances to some four hundred persons, representing not more than one hundred and fifty institutions and a probable maximum of three thousand professors. Clearly, the value of the Fund will lie as much in its limitations as in its application. It will establish an important precedent for the pension system among educational institutions. In his letter of gift Mr. Carnegie wrote: "I have reached the conclusion that the least rewarded of all professions is that of the teacher in our higher educational institutions. New York City generously and very wisely provides retiring pensions for teachers in her public schools." The implication is that the pension system for teachers is a just system, and should be established as widely as possible. And the reason why Mr. Carnegie considers the system both just and wise he also states: "Very few indeed of our colleges are able to provide retiring pensions for their teachers. The consequences are grievous. Able men hesitate to adopt teaching as a career, and many old professors whose places should be occupied by younger men cannot be retired. . . . I hope this fund may do much for the cause of higher education"—by removing a source of deep and constant anxiety to the poorest-paid yet one of the highest of all professions. Release from anxiety will of course mean greater freedom of action on the part both of the administrative and professorial bodies, and, consequently, greater educational efficiency.

It was in view of the National bearing which the work of the Foundation had assumed that it was decided in the early part of 1906 to exchange the charter which had been granted to the " Carnegie Foundation " by the State of New York for a charter to be obtained from Congress, and to change the name of the institution. Moreover, by the term of the act of Congress by which the "Carnegie Foundation " was enabled to transfer its property to the "Carnegie Foundation for the Advancement of Teaching," the principal offices of the Foundation are to be maintained at Washington.

At present the Foundation shares the offices, in the capital, of the Carnegie Institution of Washington, and its work is chiefly conducted from New York City. Sooner or later, however, the transfer to the National capital will be made, and there are already signs of close co-operation between the Foundation and the Federal Bureau of Education.

In history the achievement of the Foundation will probably rank high as pioneer work. Mr. Pritchett and his associates are performing a valuable public service by carrying the principle of pensioning teachers, already applied in some cities like New York, into the Nation at large, by familiarizing the public with the actual status of higher education in the country, by bringing educational institutions into co-operative relations with one another, and by establishing standards which, when generally adopted, will do much to promote efficiency both in the administrative and instructorial departments of American schools and colleges. When the Foundation has taught the country what its duty towards the teachers of its children is, its work will be fully accomplished.

To find the guardian of a vast industry that was fostered in its infancy by the Nation, fostering in turn the growth of infant National institutions, is not only curiously engaging, but of the best omen. Think what the result to the American democracy would be if all public trusts were administered with the conscientious and far seeing wisdom that has marked Mr. Carnegie's private enterprises! Consider what a powerful influence the Carnegie libraries, the Carnegie Institution of Washington, and the Carnegie Foundation for the Advancement of Teaching are exerting towards this end!

# THE HUMOR OF THE NATIONS

## BY ARTHUR BARTLETT MAURICE

THE end of Émile Augier's most admirable comedy finds the conventional grouping, rascality put to flight, the Duke and Antoinette thoroughly reconciled and looking forward to a happy and united life, but the incorrigible Poirier himself still secretly nursing his ambition for social and political advancement. " We are in 'forty-six," he says, in a final aside; " I shall be Député from Presles in 'forty-seven, and a Peer of France in 'forty-eight." Now at first sight there is in this nothing intrinsically funny. Yet not only when " Le Gendre de M. Poirier " was first presented in 1855 did the line move Parisian audiences to howls of merriment, but it is still regarded and referred to as one of the most admirable specimens of wit to be found in French comedy. The whole point lies in the fact that the audiences of 1855 still remembered keenly what the boastful Poirier, in 1846, could not foresee : that the revolution of 1848, which overthrew the Government of Louis Phillipe and established the Second Republic, had entirely abolished all titles in France. It is an admirable illustration of a rare form of wit. It is not only essentially French, but it turns on the events of a brief two years of French history; yet the political explanation makes it of immediate appeal to the cultivated man or woman of any nation. Regarding it simply as a stage stroke, it was irresistible at the time of its presentation; to-day, even in France, in a new play it would have little effect; elsewhere it would be lost entirely.

Fundamentally the wit of all nations rests much on the same bases—it is drawn from the same common stock. The differences lie in the form of presentation, the stamp. A nation's wit may be compared to a nation's money. A French twenty-franc piece in a shop in Bond Street or Piccadilly, an English sovereign in the Rue de la Paix—provided each rings true and is of full weight—both are likely to be accepted without the slightest hesitation, just as among cultivated people of any nation the gold pieces of wit will be appraised at their just value. Yet in Cornwall or Gascony the napoleon or the sovereign will be scanned suspiciously, while the two-franc piece or the half-crown, in the wrong place, will be found utterly useless. It is the baser metal. The whimsical analogy of wit and money may be carried further. As there is a close relation between the currencies of the Latin peoples, so is there in their wit. As the currency of Spain, for example, has depreciated to such a point that in some parts of that country the bankers' signs read, "English, French, German, and American Money Exchanged," and then beneath, as an afterthought, " Also Spanish Gold ;" so the Spanish wit of to-day is an ironic reflection on the period of national grandeur and the splendid traditions of Cervantes.

There are certain situations, relations, and institutions which have always stood as objects of the common laughter. Wit everywhere has always interpreted them in much the same way, and to them no one nation may be said to have brought any really distinctive note. Take the most hackneyed and familiar of all butts. Quite at random, one may choose from five or six different languages four and twenty hits at the expense of the mother-in-law, and no one will be able to say that this concerned a French household, that an Italian, or that a Swiss. The young or the old dandy who resorts to stratagem, takes to his heels, or avoids certain streets in order to evade the importunities of the long-suffering tailor or bootmaker; the lawyer discomfited by the witness whom he is trying to bully— these and twenty others are the stock comic situations which belong not only to all countries but to all times, which were quite familiar in ancient Athens and Rome, and which have come down to us through the centuries without material change. It is not by any means that the wit founded on the comedy of

609

manners has not had strong and marked national characteristics always. But for the sharpest lines of contrast one must turn to the fields of national dislike, jealousy, and prejudice.

Since the time of Hogarth, and probably long before, national prejudice has been one of the sturdiest bulwarks and the most vigorous inspirations of British humor. What a glaring gap there would be in the comic literature of England if one could take away everything based on the parsimony of the Scotch, the liking for drink and the Donnybrook Fair proclivities of the Irish, the blustering pretense of the Yankees, and the general ineptitude and all-round shortcomings of the French! As we turn over the old pages and glance at the old pictures of the men whose names stand for the British wit and humor of the Victorian Era, what a fine contempt for the foreigner is evident! The shafts of wit aimed at the foibles and frivolities at home are pointed enough, but we realize that it is all strictly *en famille*. Thackeray castigates the snobs of England, laying on the lash with an unsparing hand; but suppose some German or American critic of the time had written slightingly of the Barnes Newcomes, the Lord Farintoshes, the Steynes, of British society? Would not the great satirist have been the first to be outraged in his feelings, and the loudest in his cry of " hands off "? What frank dislike underlies his portraits of the ridiculous Alcide of " Pendennis," of M. de Castillommes of " The Newcomes," of Frenchmen in general! When Dickens gave us a thoroughgoing British scoundrel or hypocrite, he hastened to atone for the deed by introducing half a dozen personages of benevolent mien and amiable disposition; but where, Americans may well ask, are the redeeming countrymen of Colonel Diver and General Choke? What a fierce and intolerant patriotism was that of George Cruikshank and John Leech! How valiantly they expended the heritage of hatred that had come down to them from Rowlandson and Gillray! You cannot follow Leech through any single month of Punch jokes and pictures without perceiving how deep-rooted was his conviction of the complete superiority of everything

British. Had he been otherwise, his hold on the affections of the English fun-loving public would have been far different. Every man whose business it has been to amuse the British readers has felt this influence. Du Maurier, half Frenchman that he was, could never wholly break away from it. There have been long periods in the latter half of the nineteenth century when it was as necessary, in order to conform with the national ideas of humor, to depict a Frenchman as insecure in his saddle and ill at ease in the hunting field as it was in 1800 to present him with pigtail and curl-papers, his shoulders always higher than his ears, and invariably saying, " By gar! aha! vat you tell me, sare!"

The parsimony of the Scotch may be exaggerated, and it may not be; but certainly Scotsmen have not been responsible for perpetuating the legend. The Scotch humor is too canny. The reason that the world at large regards parsimony as a national characteristic is wholly due to the cumulative effect of the jokes on this score that have found expression south of the Tweed. Ask the average American for an example of Scotch humor and he will probably offer the story of the disconsolate Highlander bemoaning the exactions of London : " A turrible place, Sandy; I hadna' been here twa hours when bang went saxpence!"

It would be as absurd to attempt to analyze the comic genius of the English as it would be to offer that specious but perfectly preposterous saying that the English have humor but no wit, and the French wit but no humor. One can draw definite conclusions about nations like Germany and Italy; but in countries which have been so rich in comic expression as England and France, all that one can do is to indicate certain subtle lines of distinction. For example, the well-dressed inebriate is a valuable asset to the English fun-maker ; he is seldom a factor in the Continental joke. It is not that he does not exist, he simply does not amuse. But in English humor there have been thousands of precursors to the pictorial skit of a few weeks ago which shows a happy but helpless gentleman who has mistaken a drinking fountain, and, with the tin cup pressed to his ear, is mumbling, " 2747 Girard, please, Misb." There is not space here for more than brief mention of the stock butts of the British joke—the coster and the cockney, the irascible army officer on half-pay, the over-zealous subaltern, the countryman with his burr, and the various ridiculous figures of the hunting-field. As an example of the English comic spirit, which is perhaps wit, and perhaps humor, and perhaps a combination of both, let us take a scene from an almost forgotten play by Richard Steele. The play is "The Funeral," and the undertaker Sable is talking to his employees about their duties:

*Sable.* Ha, you! A little more upon the dismal (forming their countenances); this fellow has a good mortal look—place him near the corpse; that wainscot face must be o' top of the stairs ; that fellow's almost in a fright (that looks as if he were full of some strange misery) at the end of the hall. So— but I'll fix you all myself. Let's have no laughing now on any provocation. Look yonder, that hale, well-looking puppy ! You ungrateful scoundrel, did I not pity you, take you out of a great man's service, and show you the pleasure of receiving wages? *Did I not give you ten, then fifteen, and twenty shillings a week to be sorrowful—and the more I give you I think the gladder you are !*

The French have not only been conscious of their own wit, but at times they have been conscious of it to the blind exclusion of the wit of other nations. Some of the greatest French humorists have been utterly unable to appreciate or even to understand the humor of other peoples. When the work of Mark Twain was shown to the late Alphonse Daudet, the creator of Tartarin was quite honest in saying that he could see nothing amusing in Tom Sawyer or Huckleberry Finn. Renan believed so implicitly in the supremacy of the French comic genius that he maintained that, whatever their speech, all nations should be taught to laugh in French. Chamfort said of the old régime that it was "an absolute monarchy tempered by good sayings." Even in adversity the French have never forgotten to laugh and have always demanded that they be amused. In the days of the Revolution, in one column of the paper would appear the lists of the victims of the guillotine and in another

the evening's entertainments. If you will look through the Parisian press during the terrible months of the siege and the Commune, you will find no diminution in the amount of jokes printed.

The ignorance of the French in matters outside of their own country is not merely an impression of foreigners. It is frequently a butt for the boulevard jokemakers. When Thackeray, in "Vanity Fair," represented a certain French duchess receiving from Miss Crawley a letter denouncing the former Becky Sharp, and being unable to read a word of it because she had been only twenty years in England and consequently had no knowledge of the language, he was sounding a note that has had constant repetition in French jests. In one of his best jokes the inimitable Cham played upon it at the time of the Exposition of 1867. There were a great number of eminent strangers in Paris, and Cham, with delicious irony, drew up a code of ceremonial for the use of the Parisians : "When you are presented to a foreign sovereign, the most polite thing to do is to leap through the ring in his nose. Otherwise," he adds, with a superb gravity that is worthy of Swift, " he might think that you had come merely for your amusement."

A figure which belongs essentially and entirely to French jest is that of Joseph Prudhomme. The type itself is as old as Molière; but the name—which is diagnostic—and the particular character was the invention (in 1857) of Henri Monnier. Prudhomme is the incarnation of the pompous, purse-proud, bourgeois spirit which has been so hated and so unsparingly pursued by French artists and men of letters. He is a compound of vanity, greed, and cunning prudence ; an oracle of the smug commonplace. His morality is a pretense and a sham. He delights in red tape and the assumption of petty official authority, and in certain moments likes to play at being a soldier in service in the National Guard. In this last respect Balzac anticipated Monnier by his portrait of Crevel in " Les Parens Pauvres."

In England two phases of the artistic life in especial have been subjected to satire. One has to do with the proverbial—in all times and countries—indigence of the author, the painter, and the actor; the other with the various ephemeral literary fads and the postures of the exquisites and the eccentrics in whom Du Maurier found suca huge delight. In France the artistic life is held up to laughter under twenty different aspects. You see the poet not only in his garret, but also rejoicing in his favored haunts. You become acquainted with his affectations, his jealousies, his loves, and his hyberboles. Another phase of French, and in fact Continental, jest will not be discussed at any great length here. Brilliant as some of the wit that has played about it has been, it is not *virginibus puerisque.* The spirit is the same in the complications of Molière's "George Dandin" and in the farce of "Labiche," which shows the wife chalking the hours of appointment on her husband's back for the information of her lover.

The distinctive contribution of Italy to humor has been the pasquinade. Some four hundred years ago Pasquino was a fashionable tailor in Rome. His shop was the place where many eminent Romans met to exchange the gossip and scandal of the day. Pasquino was a wit himself, and his epigrams upon conspicuous persons were so much repeated that in time he was credited with every bit of witty malice, and those who started a bitter jest attributed the satire to the tailor as a matter of safety. Here is a typical political pasquinade which appeared at a time when Italians were wishing for the death of Ferdinand II. of Naples, called King Bomba. Pasquino imagines a traveler just arrived from Naples, and asks him for the latest news:

"I have seen a tumor" (*tumore*). "A tumor? But what is a tumor?" "For answer take away the t." "Ah! a humor" (*umore*). "But is this humor dangerous?" "Take away the u." "He dies! what a pity! But when? Shortly?" "Take away the m." "Hours! In a few hours! But who, then, has this humor?" "Take away the o." "King! The king! I am delighted. But, then, where will he go?" "Take away the r." "E-e-eh!"

As an indication of the strange contradictions of simplicity and complexity which go to make up the Italian character, the following story is essentially

Italian. Fasolacci is a young man about town who has been spending right and left, and one day finds himself unable to pay his hotel bill. Owing to the avarice of his father, he appeals to his uncle:

*Dear Uncle:*
If you could see my shame while I write, you would pity me. Do you know why? Because I have to write for one hundred francs and know not how to express my humble gratitude.
No, it is impossible to tell you; I prefer to die.
I send you this by a messenger who awaits an answer.
Believe me, dear uncle, to be your most obedient and affectionate nephew,
FASOLACCI.
P. S.—Overcome with shame for what I have written, I have been running after the messenger, in order to take the letter, but I could not catch up. Heaven grant that something may happen to stop him, or that this letter may get lost!

The uncle is touched, considers, and replies:

*My beloved Nephew:*
Console yourself, and blush no longer. Providence heard your prayer. The messenger lost your letter.
Good-by. Your affectionate uncle,
ARISTIPPO.

Despite the comparatively high order of excellence of such comic papers as Fliegende Blätter, Simplicissimus, and Der Wahre Jacob, the contention that German humor shows no sense of measure and no instinctive tact is by no means unsound. Germany, it must be remembered, has never produced a great comic dramatist or a great satirist. Another thing to be remembered in studying the German humor of the past fifty years is that much of that nation's comic talent has come to the United States and found its expression amid new surroundings. As in France one of the most popular subjects for jest is the soldier (the *piou piou*), so in Germany the comic writers find a rich field in the awkwardness of the new recruit and the arrogant authority of the drill-sergeant. A beautiful illustration of the cumbersome spirit of the national humor is found in the German version of Punch's advice to people about to marry. Instead of the brief and illuminating "Don't" of English wit we have, "If you are going to be married, my son, I will give you some good advice." "And what is it?" "You had better not."

Thirty years ago the infantile simplicity and tameness of the average German joke impressed James Parton, who, from the comic press of that period, selected the following as typical:

Two young girls, about twelve, are sitting upon a bench in a public garden. Two dandies walk past, who are dressed alike and resemble one another. "Tell me, Fannie," says one of the girls, "are not those two gentlemen brothers?" This is the reply: "One of them is, I know for certain; but I am not quite sure about the other."

A strapping woman, sooty, wearing a man's hat, and carrying a ladder and brushes, is striding along the street. The explanation vouchsafed is the following: "The very eminent magistrate has determined to permit the widow of the meritorious chimney-sweep, Spazzicammino, to continue the business."

A silly-looking gentleman is seen conversing with a lady upon whom he has called, while a number of cats are playing about the room. "Why have you so many cats?" he asks. The lady replies: "Well, you see, my cook kept giving warning because I locked up the milk and meat, so I got the cats as a pretext."

Two noble ladies chatting over their tea: "Only think, my dear, we are obliged to discharge our man." "Why?" "Oh, he begins to be too familiar. What do you think? I saw him cleaning the boots, and I discovered, to my horror, that he had my husband's boots, my son's, and *his own*, all mixed together!"

Yet, despite the absolute absence of any sort of tradition, Germany to-day has a certain conceded place in the wit of the nations, and this is entirely due to the individual achievement and the influence of Wilhelm Busch. The distinctive contribution of Germany to pictorial humor has been the series of pictures without words or with very few words. Perhaps in this line Busch has never quite attained the comic effects of Caran d'Ache, but the breadth of his humor and its heart appeal have won him an audience vastly larger than that of the brilliant Frenchman. Some of his creations, like Max und Moritz, Hans Huckebein, and Plisch und Plum, have become universal possessions; it is not Goethe or Schiller that in the Fatherland one hears often quoted, but the homely lines of Busch, whose drawings are published in editions as large as those of the American popular novel.

# THE SPIRIT OF THE GAME

## BY LUTHER HALSEY GULICK

WE cannot imagine a man writing a great poem just because he thought he ought to—that it was his duty. He might do a creditable piece of work, correct in every particular, and one that would pass muster with the critics; but it would not be great. Great achievements are not brought about in that way. Something else enters into them. Kipling did not write the "Barrack Room Ballads," with their wonderful swing and force, because he had to. When Lincoln was composing his superb Gettysburg Oration, he was not sacrificing himself to a necessity, or trying to do merely what he thought was right—he was moved by a great and exalting desire, the desire to give expression to his deepest feelings of reverence and affection and patriotism. It was without doubt an obligation for him to pay his tribute; but it was something more than a sense of duty that called forth immortal words like those.

And so of every man who makes himself count largely in the world's affairs: the explorer who penetrates into the inaccessible ice-fields of the North, the artist who paints his soul into a picture, the financier who causes idle capital to become richly productive, the teacher who calls forth the best possibilities in his students, the scientist who gives up his life to patient research in the laboratory—these men are not actuated merely by a sense of duty.

I have had the fortune to know personally a number of successful inventors and to watch them at work. What has struck me most is that the inventor himself does not seem to be *working* at all. There is no compulsion, so far as he is concerned. Without any direction on his part, some force has laid hold of his mind, has harnessed him complete, drives him day and night, during meal times and during rest times, and will not let him go until it has been embodied in visible form. This is a creative idea. It is not duty. The man surrenders himself to it gladly, indifferent to the cost, indifferent, almost, to the consequences, feeling only the powerful and exhilarating joy of realizing concretely the idea that has been born in his brain.

It is in this spirit that most men who have made great contributions to humanity have done their work. Think of Charles Darwin. He had hit upon a tremendous hypothesis—organic evolution through natural selection. It was revolutionary; to follow it would make him enemies everywhere; he would be called an opponent of religion, a traitor to humanity. Darwin did not think twice; he could not; there was only one way for him. An idea had taken possession of his whole being—and it was he who made the greatest contribution to human thought in the last century. There was a " must " here, perhaps: but it was not the " must " of duty: it was the " must " of passionate surrender to an ideal.

In fighting for their homes and for the preservation of their rights, the Continental Army were doing their duty; but how different was their attitude from that of the Hessians! I am perfectly well aware that the word " duty " has many shades of meaning, and that I have deliberately selected one. But is not this perhaps as profound a meaning as any?

When a boy has rigged up a little paddle-wheel in the stream in the meadow, and has devised a way by which a thread may be attached to the axle and a small block of wood hauled up against the current, he has been doing *essentially* the same thing as Edison when he has been evolving a new elec-

trical attachment. In the absorption of the occupation he has forgotten all about his needs everything else has become of no consequence; the enthusiasm and joy of a certain ideal have taken possession of him. That is play. It is the spontaneous enlistment of the entire personality in the pursuit of some coveted end. We do not *have* to pursue this goal we wish to: it is our main desire. In the light of it all other things—dinners, or punishments, or the world's opinion—become inconsequential. We have not taken possession of the idea, the idea has taken possession of us.

In play the whole personality is absorbed. There is nothing perfunctory, nothing done by routine, nothing mechanical. This is the spirit in which the greatest discoveries are made, the greatest fortunes built up, the greatest poems written.

What is it that keeps the financier still engaged in great commercial transactions long after he has accumulated enough to meet all his needs and those of his family? It is because he likes the game: it absorbs him; it is not merely his business—it is his greatest satisfaction, his " play."

Walt Whitman wrote his poems on that sort of an impulse; it was in them that his powerful and astonishing personality found its fitting expression. You feel in every line of " Leaves of Grass " the wonderful vitality of the man, his enthusiasm, his passion for humanity. Never a line was written in response to a sense of duty. Whitman was conscious, perhaps, of a message to give; but he gave it because he simply could not keep it to himself, not because his conscience forced him.

The little girl who spends the whole afternoon quietly in the corner attending to every need of her sick doll, refusing to surrender her responsibility to another—she is the same person who later on in life keeps watch day and night beside the bed of her sick baby, aware even in sleep of every motion that the little sufferer makes. The attitude of the mother to the baby is identical with the attitude of the little girl to her doll.

Well, what reason is there for the little

girl's being so concerned about the welfare of her doll? Psychologically that would not be easy to explain. But it is clear that there is no sense of compulsion there; the care is given spontaneously, eagerly, in response to an idea. And the mother-spirit, thus expressing itself in so many of life's relations, is one of the most precious and most dynamic influences in the whole world. Which is the same thing as saying that the spirit in which "play" is the motive force is the most dynamic, the most effective spirit for the solution of any vital problem.

It is the way in which we take the responsibilities and problems of life that makes it either a deadly bore—a mere dull round of routine and drudgery—or the most interesting and absorbing game, capable of enlisting all the energy and enthusiasm we have to put into it. The people who accomplish things are the people who play the game. They let themselves go; they are not afraid.

There is a good reason at the basis of all this. The fact is that a higher state of personality is involved in play than in "work." Under the stimulus and enthusiasm of play, muscles contract more powerfully and longer than under other conditions. Blood-pressure is higher in play. The man who eats because he is hungry, and enjoys every mouthful of food, has a far better chance of having a good digestion than the man who simply eats because he thinks he ought to—because his doctor has directed it.

We accomplish really great things only when we can bring to bear all the forces of our personality. This cannot be done by sheer will-power. There must be love and enthusiasm and joy, an interest that will absorb and dominate us. Effort will not produce this. It is a matter of attitude.

The mother who loves her child will do for it much the same sort of thing as the nursery-maid who is merely doing her duty; but there will be a difference in the quality of the influence exerted, and in the result.

It is far more interesting to play the game than to work at it. When you work, you are being driven. When you

6

play, you do the driving yourself. To be your own master is pleasanter than being mastered. And there is more satisfaction in doing one's best, in doing a thing artistically and right, than in doing what is after all a merely creditable job. Some of the old violin-makers could hardly bear to part with the instruments they had made; it was like giving up a part of themselves. They loved their violins. They were conscious of having done fine work; they had made an art out of their business. It was their play. So it is with every piece of work to which we have given the best that is in us. It satisfies us profoundly.

We play, not by jumping the traces of life's responsibilities, but by going so far beyond life's compulsions as to lose all sight of the compulsion element.

Two small sisters I know of had been cross and out of sorts.

"Let's play being sisters," said Emmeline. So they played, and had a lovely time together.

What was the difference between playing sisters and being sisters? Merely a matter of idealization.

I like that stirring poem of Henry Newbolt's, where the "spirit of the game" saves the day for the British regiment—makes a hero of every man:

"There's a breathless hush in the Close to-night—
　Ten to make and the match to win—
A bumping pitch and a blinding light,
　An hour to play and the last man in.
And it is not for the sake of a ribboned coat
　Or the selfish hope of a season's fame,
But his Captain's hand on his shoulder smote—
　'Play up! play up! and play the game!'

The sand of the desert is sodden red,—
　Red with the wreck of the square that broke;—
The Gatling's jammed and the Colonel dead,
　And the regiment blind with dust and smoke.
The river of death has brimmed his banks,
　And England's far and Honor a name,
But the voice of a schoolboy rallies the ranks:
　'Play up! play up! and play the game!'

This is the word that year by year,
　While in her place the School is set,
Every one of her sons must hear,
　And none that hears it dare forget,
This they all with a joyful mind
　Bear through life like a torch in flame,

And falling fling to the host behind—
  ' Play up ! play up ! and play the game !' "

*There* was a transformation certainly, yet as simple and logical as any of the others. A regiment exhausted and disorganized, facing nothing but utter defeat. The sharp, ringing call of the old cricket-field : " Play up ! Play the game !" It was an injection of new energy.

Translated it meant : Fix your mind on the thing to be done ; forget everything else—your own feelings, your fear, your discouragement. Throw your whole personality into this thing, and carry it through to a finish. Play the game !

This motive or conception, which is caught by the spirit of the day in the phrase, " Play the game !" is the deepest motive in the life of many people, particularly men. Deeply analyzed, it looks back to faithfulness to one's comrades, the being true to the life one is living—to living on an ideal level.

# THE HOHENLOHE MEMOIRS[1]

WHEN the German edition of Prince Hohenlohe's Memoirs appeared, there was a great sensation. For the first time the story of Prince Bismarck's resignation was apparently told in full. For the first time, too, some secret motives which had dictated recent German policy were laid bare. It was no wonder that the papers were full of telegraphed excerpts from the work. The handsomely published German original has now been received in this country. It is interesting to compare with it the well-printed and remarkably good English translation which closely follows.

The Memoirs are valuable, first of all, as throwing new light on the development of political Germany during Prince Hohenlohe's life of over fourscore years. This light is notably clear, because we are informed by one who, as narrator, possessed five striking advantages.

First, he was a truthful person. His notes form a surprisingly comprehensive and open presentment of personal and political conditions. Bismarck was called brutally frank. But Hohenlohe was never brutal, if franker than any German chronicler has been.

Secondly, Prince Hohenlohe was a South German. His was the atmospheric Southern geniality, not so characteristic of the North Germans. Men were everywhere won by that warmth and humanity, and they confided in Hohenlohe, who speedily became an envied repository of knowledge.

Thirdly, the Prince enjoyed an advantage impossible to a Prussian, whose country had for two centuries been preponderant in German politics. It would be surprising if any Prussian narrator of events in Germany were not prejudiced. But Hohenlohe was a Bavarian. He thus had the detachment which every historian should seek. Doubtless, too, one reason for writing his memoirs was that they should be not only a record of past events, but also a warning against a repetition of Bismarckian Prussianized particularism.

Next, this truthful, winsome, judicial observer was a man of action. If birth and residence gave to him a certain detachment, his career did not detach him from the great events which he describes. In them he was not only an actor ; he was often one of the chief actors, whether as parliamentarian, as ambassador, as delegate to congresses, as Cabinet Minister, as provincial governor, or, finally, as Imperial Chancellor.

Lastly, a signal advantage lay in the fact that Prince Hohenlohe was a *liberal* Roman Catholic. " I could never bind myself," he says, " to render any assistance to that party [the party of Roman Catholic reaction] without repudiating my whole past inner life and all my most sacred convictions." This breadth of thought was not unnatural. for. though the sons of the elder Hohenlohe were

[1] *Denkwürdigkeiten des Fürsten Chlodwig zu Hohenlohe-Schillingsfürst*. Im Auftrage des Prinzen Alexander zu Hohenlohe-Schillingsfürst. Herausgegeben von Friedrich Curtius. In zwei Bände. Deutsche Verlags-Anstalt, Stuttgart und Leipzig. *Memoirs of Prince Chlodwig of Hohenlohe-Schillingsfürst*. Authorized by Prince Alexander ot Hohenlohe-Schillingsfürst. Edited by Friedrich Curtius. English Edition. Supervised by George W. Chrystal, B.A. In 2 vols. The Macmillan Company, New York. $6, net.

brought up as Roman Catholics, the daughters were trained in the faith of their Protestant mother. Religious toleration was thus for them the indispensable condition of domestic happiness.

Thus notably equipped for his work as observer, chronicler, and commentator, we have in these volumes a summary of the results of Prince Hohenlohe's statesmanship and that of others. We hardly know whether we are more interested in the movements themselves or in the men who planned them. To the special student and to the future historian the description of the movements may be the more valuable. But to the general reader the volumes' value lies largely in their anecdotal and reminiscential features. Is it not generally true, indeed, that we learn to know men first, movements second?

Our interest is first of all awakened in the writer of these pages. He was the antithesis of the stolid, stupid type which we see in cartoons and caricatures. His was a courtly refinement, a keen intelligence, which matched that of such Germans as the Bunsens of his day or the Sternburgs of ours. His spiritual nature is shown in a letter to his sister just as he was beginning his political career:

It does one good in the wild tumult of political life to plunge back now and again into better days. It gives one the same feeling to go from time to time into a church, as I love more especially to do now that the beautiful offices for May are being sung in the twilight. For in political work, which is a thing of great utility and most congenial to me, the soul consumes itself."

On the relations of the Prince to his family his sister writes:

We all turned to him when in the slightest doubt or difficulty. His keen judgment and reassuring calm, and the brotherly love which was evident in all his counsels, gave them great weight. . . . At Schillingsfürst one used to go to his little study and sit down in a small armchair beside him at the writing-table, and he would look up from his work and instantly give his whole attention to whatever you had to say. Words cannot describe it; I can still feel his penetrating gaze. . . . I can never cease to admire Chlodwig, and how calm, unselfish, and patient he is in all his actions. Let them say what they will about masculine energy, firmness, and proper self-assertion—that is all very well in its way; but a delicate, noble

mind is an infinitely higher thing. Better to have that alone, without those qualities, than the other way round. To-day he was speaking again of sacred things. I cannot describe the extraordinary impression it makes on me, how it moves me to hear him pronounce the name of Christ; it seems to come from the depths of his heart.

The Prince's sister-in-law says:

We had many a delightful time together in the Austrian Alps, where my husband had rented one of the finest chamois shootings in the country. My sister-in-law threw herself passionately into this noble sport. Her husb nd fulfilled his duties as a hunter most corre tl , but with far less enthusiasm. He took Latin classics with him when out stalking, filling my boys, who were still at the gymnasium in those days, with amazement. I remember being out with him once in his last years. We had a long wait, and to pass the time he recited from memory and without one stumble whole poems of great beauty. In our fine enthusiasm, of course he missed the chamois which were being driven to him.

The character of my brother-in-law always seemed to me to bridge the gulf between two periods. His mind, though deep-rooted in the feudal traditions of his caste, had yet a lively and intuitive sympathy for all the liberal views which have only come to the fore in our modern days. To his benignant philosophy it was given to smooth rough edges, to mediate between conflicting forces. Whether the conflicting elements in his own breast did not bring him frequent suffering none can say; he veiled it in impenetrable silence. His imperturbable calm seemed to me simply the peace after a hard-won victory over self.

Prince Hohenlohe was one of the earliest to realize that evolution into unity must needs come, whether or no. Said he, " Deep in the hearts of all Germans lives an inspiring belief in a unified, free, and powerful German Fatherland." He could not bear to think that Germany was broken up into fragments, and weak fragments at that.

No one will deny that it is hard on a thinking, energetic man to be unable to say abroad, " I am a German !" . . . and not to have to explain, " I am a Hessian, a Darm-städter, a Buckeburger; my Fatherland was once a great and mighty nation, now it is shattered into eight and thirty splinters."

He grasped at the idea of the 1848 Constituent Assembly, convoked from all Germany, and when that Parliament appointed the Archduke John as " Imperial Administrator " for Germany and Austria, when the Archduke appointed an Imperial Ministry, and the Ministry intrusted Prince Hohenlohe to notify the courts of Athens, Rome, and Florence of the Archduke's accession, the young envoy gladly fulfilled the commission. Alas that this hope of Imperial unity (like the Frankfort Congress of 1862, to which the Prince was a member) was to last but a few months, and reduce Prince Hohenlohe's activities to those of the Bavarian Upper Chamber !

This, however, did not prevent visits to other countries. In 1850, at Paris, Prince Hohenlohe met Guizot, who, " as you can see at once, has a striking personality. He is the only man I have seen so far in this Parisian society who does not appear to be thinking of something else all the time one talks to him."

Prince Hohenlohe also paid a visit to the English Court. After one of the dinners, he says,

I went to sit near Prince Albert. In his whole attitude of mind there is something distinctly doctrinaire, and I thought how unfortunate it was for the Prince that he should come straight from a German university to his present position, without having had the corners rubbed off by contact with the practical world. . . . After dinner . . . the Queen spoke in a very sympathetic, unaffected, and natural way to me (quite unlike the apathetic chatter of Continental sovereigns). At eight o'clock I again dined at Court, where I met the Prince of Wales, who had just returned from his Continental travels. He . . . is a very well-bred young man, rather in awe of his father. It is a pity he is not taller for his age.

Hohenlohe's relations to the English Court were far more cordial than were Bismarck's. The Queen had always known the Prince well, as his aunt was her sister. But now Prince Hohenlohe appealed to her even more than before. The Prince Consort was dead, and Prince Hohenlohe was his old friend. Moreover, since Prince Albert's death the Queen's connection with Germany had been somewhat severed, and, as chance would have it, at that very time German influence in England was watched with suspicion—the time of the Schleswig-Holstein affair. The account of it given by Hohenlohe to the Queen must be regarded as a peculiarly trustworthy narrative.

During the later sixties the Austro-German war was the all-absorbing event, and its consequences were specially felt in Bavaria, which had sided with Austria.

Hohenlohe was disgusted with the whole affair, and wrote : " When once Germans get to loggerheads, they can't stop."

But the Prince's personal triumph was at hand. With the close of the war Bavaria's political power was forever lessened. The particularist King and people now turned to the broad-gauge man who was a German first and a Bavarian second, and begged him to take the helm of the ship of State. He remarked dryly : " Seventeen years ago I spoke on the reorganization of Germany, expressly recognizing that I was at variance with the opinion of the Bavarian people. I bowed then to the opinion of the majority." The majority was now with him.

As Bavarian Premier Prince Hohenlohe lent his best efforts in the South, as did Bismarck in the North, toward union. Their proposal that the South German States associate themselves in establishing a league with the North German Confederation was finally successful.

But all events paled before those of 1870. With that fire of war the Prince had little to do directly, but much with its outcome—the unification of Germany under the King of Prussia as Emperor, and popular representation in an Imperial Reichstag. The King of Bavaria was induced to put himself at the head of German Princes in the offer of the Imperial Crown, and Prince Hohenlohe became First Vice-President of the youthful Reichstag. He was now brought into closer connection than ever with Bismarck, who had been further ennobled.

In the evening I went to Bismarck's house ; I was placed upon the sofa in front of a table covered with teacups and bottles of beer, and also with herrings and oysters. His new Highness speedily arrived, and sat down by me. He began by consuming innumerable oysters, herrings, and ham, and drank beer with soda-water: He said that the Reichstag made the same impression upon him as a story told him by his parents of his youth. It appeared that he had had a garden, and used to pull up the radishes every day to see how thick the roots were, and thus the Reichstag was treating itself.

Again :

At eleven o'clock Bismarck arrived. We smoked and drank beer and Maitrank. By and by Bismarck reached the stage of anecdotes. He treats every one with a certain arrogance. This gives him a great ascendency over the timid exponents of the old European diplomacy. His successes stand him in good stead, so that he is the terror of all diplomatists.

Notwithstanding, Bismarck could appreciate Hohenlohe:

You are the only grand seigneur in Bavaria who is faithful to the Empire, and at the same time has the confidence of the King of Bavaria.

During this time many interesting people came to Berlin. For instance:

A great fuss has been made with Stanley, Dean of Westminster, who has arrived here from St. Petersburg. Last night he and his wife were at Bismarck's, till the smoke of our cigars drove him away from the supper-table. He is a polished gentleman, who has great influence at Court. He wears the clergyman's habit habillé, and a sort of black petticoat reaching to his knees. It looks exactly as if he had put on one of his ten-year-old daughter's black twill petticoats over his waistcoat by mistake.

Then came the Prince's long ambassadorship at Paris, the highest post in German diplomacy. During it we have comment on all sorts of men and manners, especially concerning Thiers, Gambetta, and Grévy:

Thiers came to me yesterday and asked me if I would come to him to-day to speak to Gambetta. I naturally accepted. Gambetta was already there when I entered M. Thiers's beautiful study. . . . I have never seen the present and the past so incarnated as in these men. . . . Gambetta makes a good impression. He is courteous and friendly, and, at the same time, you can see in him the confident, vigorous statesman.

Gambetta's opinion of the Jesuits is interesting in view of the events of the past two years in France; he thought "stronger measures required," as, for example, the closing of all establishments of non-authorized orders. As early as 1876, too, Thiers foreshadowed the Franco-Russian alliance. He asserted, said Hohenlohe, "that Russia will be isolated and assailed by England and Germany. His [Thiers's] aim is probably to win over the Russians to France, and to represent France as the deliverer who will help Russia." As to President Grévy's idiosyncrasies we read:

Visited Grévy to-day. He received me with his usual pleasant cordiality. He must have just finished breakfast, for he cleaned his back teeth with his first finger, which made him put half his hand into his mouth.

He then stuck his first finger into his nostrils, and rubbed various parts of his face with his fingers. . . . But he set forth the necessity of the republican form of government in France in weighty language, and was not a little impressive, thanks to his clear exposition.

In 1885 Hohenlohe resigned the Paris ambassadorship to become Governor of Alsace-Lorraine. In 1888 William I. and Frederick III. died. The lovable character of the first appears in Hohenlohe's observations:

It is one of the Emperor's greatest merits that, by his tactful amiability, he always succeeds in keeping these two [Bismarck and Moltke] in their proper places. The fact cannot be too strongly emphasized that the gracious personality of the Emperor has been of the utmost service in all the great successes which have been achieved in the past year [1870]. It requires self-abnegation to look on, without envy, at the ovations which Bismarck and Moltke receive. My respect for the old man has greatly increased on that account.

Again:

At four to Babelsberg, where I dined with the Emperor. . . . Old age seems to have come upon him quite suddenly. . . . After dinner the Emperor thanked me for all that I had done. . . . " I know," he said, " that whatever you have a hand in will go well." I parted reluctantly from the old man, whom I may never see again.

Of Frederick the Noble's last days we read:

I found the Emperor with the Empress. . . . One notices the suffering expression of his eyes. The Empress excused her presence through the necessity of supporting the Emperor in conversation. . . . When the Empress remarked that I looked very well, I replied that this was due to hard work, which was an excellent thing for the health, and that I also thought that the Emperor would benefit by the amount of work he had, at which he nodded approvingly. . . . The Emperor then wrote some words of sympathy. . . . When I took my leave and expressed my sincere wishes for his recovery, the Emperor placed his hand on my shoulder and smiled sadly, so that I could hardly restrain my tears. He gave me the impression of a martyr; and indeed no martyrdom in the world is comparable with this slow death. Every one who comes near him is full of admiration for his courageous and quiet resignation to a fate which is inevitable and which he fully realizes. No doubt I saw him yesterday for the last time.

And now two remarkable events happened: a new Kaiser began to reign and the old Chancellor ere long resigned. Of William II. we read that, so late as

1888, he was "not popular in Germany and will have to be very careful to turn popular opinion in his favor." But the (then) Crown Prince was delivering himself of those keen judgments of men which have since become famous :

We referred to Russia, and he praised the Emperor as a good and honorable man, but said that he was rushing upon the fate of Louis XVI.

Later :

The Emperor William II. gives me the impression of a wise, conscientious man. When I speak with him, I am always reminded of Prince Albert (Queen Victoria's consort). He resembles him in voice, and has the same earnest manner.

Suddenly Bismarck resigned (1890). When Hohenlohe said to him that this was a very unexpected event to him, Bismarck observed :

"To me also," for three weeks ago he had had no idea that the affair would end in this way. "Anyhow," he added, " it was only to be expected, for the Emperor now wishes to reign alone." He then mentioned the individual points of difference between himself and the Emperor: the Workman's Compensation Law, which the Emperor wanted, though it was really nothing more than a Workman's Compulsion Law. This brought him to the question of the Presidency of the Ministry, and he said that it was an impossible state of affairs if any Minister were allowed to do business with the Emperor on his own responsibility without consulting the Cabinet Council or its President (Bismarck).

The venerated Grand Duke of Baden, who was a good friend to both sides, asserted, as quoted, that—

The main cause of the breach between the Emperor and Bismarck was . . . the question of the Cabinet Order of the year 1852, which Bismarck wished to impose upon the Ministers without the Emperor's knowledge, thus making it impossible for them to report directly to his Majesty. . . . Bismarck is said to have got so angry in the course of his discussion with the Emperor that the Emperor afterwards said " it was all he could do to refrain from throwing the ink-pot at my head." To these differences were added the Emperor's mistrust of the Prince's foreign policy. He suspected Bismarck of attempting to guide the policy of the country upon secret plans of his own, and of acting

with the object of abandoning Austria and the Triple Alliance and of securing an understanding with Russia.

A month later the Kaiser gave his now well-known version to Prince Hohenlohe : the question at issue was whether the Hohenzollern dynasty or the Bismarck dynasty was to reign.

As far back as 1870, Windthorst, that sharpest of politicians, declared that Bismarck would retire and Hohenlohe take his place. In 1877 Bismarck's daughter told Hohenlohe that he was the only man on whom her father could rely. " She also mentioned the fact that her father had often thought of me when he was tired of vexations and wanted to resign." But Caprivi succeeded Bismarck, and it was not until 1894 that Hohenlohe was called to the helm, which he held with great distinction until 1901. He was seventy-five years old when he became Chancellor.. But, as William II. said of one year's work of that Chancellorship, " No Chancellor has ever been distinguished by the passing of two measures [the Civil Code and the Naval Estimates] so important to the domestic and foreign development of the country." Friendship between the old and young man had waxed strong ; it was already strong in 1890, when " the Emperor pressed my hand so that my fingers cracked."

Nearly eighty-two years old, Prince Hohenlohe laid down the burden of the Chancellorship. A few months later his sister wrote :

God gave us the most beautiful summer weather during those days, and we were surrounded by an abundance of roses. . . . We walked about the rooms where our childhood had been spent together. . . . From the castle a pleasant path leads through trees . . . and thence can be seen the wooded hills of the Solling. It was so solemn when my brother slowly walked along this path and said : " It is sixty years now since our father died." In the vault he laid two wreaths of white carnations . . . and was glad when I quoted the text, " It is sown in corruption, it is raised in incorruption." . . . Exactly three weeks afterwards my brother was laid with his parents in Schillingsfürst.

# Comment on Current Books

**Biological Philosophy**

The author has undertaken the difficult task of solving the fundamental questions of philosophy with the aid of biology alone. For its light he regards a valid epistemology, a valid ontology, as yet waiting. It is unusual to-day to revert, as he does, from the conception of energy to the conception of substance as the prime problem of philosophy. It is true, indeed, that "some kind of substantial and permanent Being as the source of the perpetual flux of things" must be postulated; though our knowledge of it can be only of its qualities and energies, not of its inscrutable substance. But this permanent Being Mr. Montgomery discovers in our familiar acquaintance, "living substance . . . the only genuine substantial existent in nature. For it alone maintains its identity, though continually undergoing changes." Of course this identity cannot be attributed to the changing molecules which from time to time constitute the living substance. "Some steadfastly organizing power is here evidently at work." True enough; but what is it? We are told that this apparently causative power is not really a cause, but an effect—"the direct result of the interaction of the organic substance with its environment." Life, says our biologist, is merely "the result from moment to moment of . . . a definite cycle of chemical activity." But why chemical activity in the interaction of organic substance with environment is essentially different in a living and a dead body does not appear. There is a "creative stress" in living organisms, a recognizable purposiveness, a "genuine teleology," a working toward an end, but somehow it sets itself a-going; it is pronounced "arbitrary and fantastic" to refer it to a transcendent "Reason," or "Intelligence," or "Spirit." Is not this something like the obsolete theological notion of "creation out of nothing"? Futile as is all such philosophizing, there are valuable practical applications of biology in ethics, education, and sociology, and these Mr. Montgomery has instructively presented, though disadvantaged by a heavy and otherwise somewhat defective literary style. (Philosophical Problems in the Light of Vital Organization. By Edmund Montgomery. G. P. Putnam's Sons, New York. $2.50.)

**Eternal Life**

This little book is based on several positions fundamental in modern religious thought, in that "natural" and "spiritual" are not mutually exclusive terms, but the natural is a manifestation of the spiritual; that there is a close analogy between natural law and spiritual law; that death in order to life—a dropping of the lower to possess the higher—is essential to normal development, "die to live" is the law of spiritual advance. The line of thought here followed upon these principles is deeply religious in spirit, but uncritical in form. "All forms of life, natural, social, business," can hardly be granted to be "manifestations of eternal life;" nor can it be admitted that truth and love are contrasted as "the positive or active" and "negative or sympathetic" elements of eternal life. This flavor of idiosyncrasy is widely apparent. A Tolstoyan attitude of non-resistance to social evils is deemed essential to a spiritual church. The writer's thought is saturated with the Bible to a most commendable degree, but uses it too largely in the allegorizing mode peculiar to the Gospel of Matthew and the Epistle to the Hebrews. (Eternal Life. By William Parker. Murdoch, Kerr & Co., Pittsburg, Pa.)

**The Essentials of Aesthetics**

An admirable handbook is this for teachers, and for the general reader also, in its compendious presentation of a subject that branches into many lines of specialization. It is treated analytically, in exhibiting the sources of the highest arts, and the methods of their development in their entire field. Synthetically, the relations of difference and identity which obtain between art and science on one side, and art and religion on the other side, are defined with a distinctness at present highly desirable, and the true use of the arts for culture and humanity is discriminatingly evinced. The products of many artists at present greatly praised—men who stigmatize moral objections to their work with pen or brush as due to lack of æsthetic culture—Professor Raymond pronounces untrue "to the first principles of æsthetics still more than of ethics." The reader is conducted through a richly diversified field of the sights and sounds of nature, and of the products of the human voice and hand, including even the gestures of the orator. The conclusion reached is that "the mere fact that effects are 'true to nature' by no means justifies their use in art of high quality." Art, as Professor Raymond justly contends, can justify itself only so far as it promotes wholesome thought and conduct. It is impracticable here to comment on special features of this many-sided work, enriched with many apposite illustrations of its treatment of details in architecture, music, painting, poetry, and sculpture. But it can be said that its superior in an effective, all-round discussion of its subject is not in sight. By his series of seven volumes of comparative æsthetics Professor Raymond has obtained an international reputation. (The Essentials of Æsthetics in Music, Poetry, Sculpture, and Architecture. By George Lansing Raymond, L.H.D. G. P. Putnam's Sons, New York. $2.50, net.)

**Jewish Messianism**  For Christian as well as Jewish readers this is an instructive book. "The hope of Israel," for which Paul declared he was a prisoner at Rome, still, as ever, distinguishes the Hebrew race from every other, and through many centuries it has been both the cause and the consolation of sufferings. An outline of the development and history of this unique hope through Biblical and subsequent times to the present, the conditions which influenced it, and its influence upon the Jewish people, is succinctly given in the present volume. No prophetic word of Jesus appears to have been more amply fulfilled than that many false Messiahs should spring up. The expectations of a second coming of Christ that have deluded portions of the Church afford a parallel—a faint one. Most Jews still cherish expectation of a personal Messiah, and Zionism is regarded as an advance toward the greater ideal of the Messianic era. (The Messiah Idea in Jewish History. By Julius H. Greenstone, Ph.D. The Jewish Publication Society of America, Philadelphia.)

**A Man Without a Country**  The contrast between the papers making up the volume of "English Hours" and those in "The American Scene," by Henry James, gives one food for reflection. The former, while having a characteristic detachment, are often so vivid, so refreshing, that the reader is left in a delicious glow. The latter, in even greater detachment, and with their overwhelming and bewildering convolutions of phrase, make one thankful that the writer of "The Upton Letters" has described this author's style so perfectly that nothing can be added. He says that when he reads Henry James he never is sure "who has got the ball." Sometimes, in the vagueness, a doubt arises whether there *is* any ball. No one can read this volume all through without at intervals coming up to breathe. One misses, to a depressing extent, the charming felicities we expect from Mr. James. Yet one reads with interest, never losing the hope that he will say something. That hope, of course, is occasionally fulfilled. Mr. J "likes" Grant's tomb. He almost "like several other objects in America—the H vard Union, the White House, the Capi and Florida. He favors us with such d cious combinations as "momentary greg ous emphasis," which, we gather from context, refers to the applause at a foo game on Soldiers' Field. He ruminates i semi-sadness over the departing glories of Washington Square, and deplores the lack of memorial tablets upon New York houses, recalling the fact, however, that it is useless to label a house that invariably makes way for a sky-scraping "apartment." He writes with exquisite grace and delicate color of the Hudson and New England and the South. Then, turning to more prosaic observations, he is justly impressed by the well-shod Americans, and their striking advantages in dentistry. The other side of that observation, the ugly side, always impresses Americans in England. We see there the "strange irregularities, protrusions, deficiencies, fangs and tusks and cavities" enumerated by Mr. James. He wonders that our men who pay so much attention to their footgear are so careless about their hats. Perhaps we cannot attend to both, and in that are like our English neighbors. Of Charleston and Richmond Mr. James writes in querying mood. He wonders whether "the *only* focus of life in the South had been slavery," and with that has disappeared everything. He regards the only Southern book of distinction published in many a year to be Professor Du Bois's "The Souls of Black Folk," and he wonders at the fact. It is far from Mr. James's practice to focus anything himself, and so we are left in mid-air at the end of the book, wondering, as he wondered, and as far from a definite idea of his actual impressions of "The American Scene" as was he, the detached observer, himself. (The American Scene. By Henry James. Harper & Brothers, New York. $3, net.)

**Pluralistic Theism**  In this acutely and cautiously reasoned work a constructive philosophy undertakes to vindicate the judgment of common sense upon the validity of religion and religious knowledge. By religion is understood "simply the recognition that life has spiritual values, and the demand that the world shall be so conceived as to give a basis and guarantee for those values." It is pointed out that science, simply as science, is concerned only with facts, not with their values; with obvious methods, not with their hidden meanings; with the *what* and *how*, not with the *why*, of things. What science thus leaves out religion and philosophy take up—the former in an emotional, the latter in an intellectual, attitude, but with a final interest fundamentally the same, to justify the demands both of human feeling and of human reason. The treatment given to skeptical objections to theistic beliefs is elaborate and candidly appreciative. It is addressed to earnest thinkers, it presumes patient consideration, and may weary those who are disinclined to intellectual exercise. As a persuasive to see things whole it is in general a good antidote to the skepticism that grows out of partial and fragmentary views. Yet it is doubtful whether the type of theistic belief to which the argument conducts is the least difficult to adopt. Pluralism, the type here adopted, regards the ultimate reality as "a confederacy of free beings," whose center is God, but whose consciousness lies in part outside of God's consciousness. This, indeed, avoids some difficulty found in an all including ethical monism, but only, as it seems, at the cost of greater difficulty. No part or element of life can be really external to the life of God. The contrary view is maintained in twenty pages (153–173), to which it is enough here to refer. Pluralism has been elaborately argued for in Professor Howison's "Limits of Evolution." The representative exposition of monism is Professor Royce's "The World and the Individual." (The Religious Conception of the World. By Arthur Kenyon Rogers, Ph.D. The Macmillan Company, New York. $1.50, net.)

*Pro Fide* Many will find this volume a serviceable help in solving doubts concerning religion. The author, a lecturer on theology in an Anglican Church college, tells us he has tested the strength of many of his positions in debates with secularists. He assumes a frankly critical attitude toward the Scriptures, and draws largely on teachings of modern science. Whether as a text-book of apologetics it is adequate to slay the doubt of any skeptical inquirer on whom it may be tried will depend on the completeness of the skeptic's armor. It undertakes to prove the existence of God by the concept of a "first cause," which, as Professor Royce says, "has been responsible for some of the most fatal of the misfortunes of religion and humanity." The design-argument for the existence of God is of the now antiquated type, based on particulars of apparent contrivance rather than on the general evidence of a gradually developing purpose. The same may be said of the argument for immortality; it is old, *minus* the necessary modern improvement. The transcendence of God is affirmed, but not his active immanence;

and we are told that God "permits" sin to exist—a perilous concession, and, in view of the scourges with which he is working to abolish sin, not true. The use made of Scripture cannot be commended as always judicious with skeptics, *e.g.*, to prove that "Jesus claimed the divine attributes of omnipotence and omnipresence." Such are the serious defects of a work in which gold is mixed with stubble. On the other hand, the author's sympathies are with the philosophy of "personal idealism," and he rightly conceives of personality as the ultimate reality. (Pro Fide. By Charles Harris, B.D. E. P. Dutton & Co., New York. $2, net.)

*Tolstoy's Gospel Harmony* Although the eccentric philanthropist whose Gospel studies are here presented is a light shining in a dark place—the baptized paganism of the Holy Orthodox Church of Russia—it is but comparatively that he is a light. The interest attaching to his person imparts to this volume whatever interest it possesses for us. Vehement recoil from the unreason of a Christianity distorted and caricatured carries him far past the center of reasonable judgment. Of the evolution of religion to be seen in the Old Testament he is ignorant, and thinks its Hebrew type as foreign to Christianity as the Hindu. His ethical and religious impulse is pure, though not always enlightened. His great interest is how to live in the right way, and this he has found in the teachings of Jesus, whom he regards as simply "a great man," his mother's illegitimate child. The Four Gospels contain it all, and much else which he rejects—especially all miracles. He has read them in the Greek, and reproduces here in parallel columns the original, the English Authorized Version, and his own, in which last some strange readings appear—the strangest of them in John i. 1: "The comprehension of life became the beginning of all" is presented as alternative to "In the beginning was the Word." The text is regularly followed by commentary, and each chapter concludes with a free paraphrase of the teaching contained. The unique principle of this Gospel Harmony is its adherence to the sense of the teaching regardless of the historical order, though this is not altogether thrown aside. Its chief merit is the moral earnestness which predominates amidst intellectual limitations. Two volumes of an expensive edition of the author's works are here bound in one at a reduced price. (The Four Gospels Harmonized and Translated. By Count Leo N. Tolstoy. Translated by Leo Wiener. Marshall Jones Company, Boston. $3.50.)

From one dam to another there should be either strips of cultivated land or forest left between, these not to be more than a hundred feet or even less in width, which could be cleared of underbrush, and if necessary burned to check forest fire, or in places ditches could be led along from the face of the dam and water allowed to flow and saturate the soil between them.

A swamp, except in autumn, is not a particularly beautiful object, and after a severe drought it is a menace to all the surrounding woodland. Fire will get in, smolder, eat down to the roots, then a high wind comes, and particles of burning leaf-mold and twigs are carried long distances. While a swamp is on fire nothing can be done except to watch and back-fire when necessary, and this last is always a dangerous, if not desperate, expedient.

The only way to save the Adirondack forests is to save them from fire first—everything else is secondary; and to save them from fire is to localize forest fires when they do occur, as occur they will; to do that I can think of no better way than to flood all the swamps possible and connect the ponds and lakes with fire-breaks wherever it is possible to do so.

(Rev.) SAMUEL F. ADAM.
Franklin, New York.

## NATIONAL MUSIC

Mr. Henry T. Finck's musicological writings have so far had no more ardent admirer than I am, and I gladly subscribe to every word he said in praise of our unfortunate MacDowell's work. [The Outlook for December 22, 1906.] But when he spoke of the probabilities of a National music in this country, and rejected the folk-song as a root and the negro as its soil, he must—as great men are wont to do at times—have "nodded." The longed-for American composer, to Mr. Finck's mind, must have "individuality." He might as well have said that the American composer must breathe and be a biped.

Poetic individualities are born of the *people*, of the *masses;* not of the classes. Goethe and Mendelssohn were no exceptions, though they seemed to be. For their time coincides with the period of Germany's lowest political depression, and such periods, through the commonness of misery, bring all social strata into close touch with one another. Neither does a musical individuality drop ready made from the sky. It must form itself here upon earth, and if it is to be of an ethnical type, it must grow up amid the musical colloquialisms of its nation. No root, no plant—the proposition does not seem occult. How Mr. Finck could refer to Grieg, Chopin, *et al.* (though wisely omitting Beethoven), for *his* side of the argument passes the powers of my logic.

That the negro melody is African Mr. Finck will not be able to prove. What can be conjectured about it is that it is Portuguese, dating from the time when Gouvea captured fifty Moors of high caste, who were exchanged by Henry the Navigator for a thousand negro slaves—a hundred negroes for each Moor. *These negroes had no songs,* for it happens that the tribe from which they came, having no articulate scale, employed only crude instruments of percussion. It was in the third or fourth generation of the original five thousand, plus the numerical growth of nearly a century and minus the last vestige of race-memory and original language, when they were shipped to the rising colony of Brazil, which is Portuguese to this day in every respect except politically. When the New England colonies were founded, their slave trade was a coast trade; not with Africa, but with Brazil. Piracy has hardly contributed more than five per cent to this trade.

Thus the negro had learned the white man's song, and he kept it. He imparted the plaintive note of suffering to it, and gradually, as he learned to talk in English, he adapted the rhythms of his songs to the cadence of English speech. As to suffering, as an art-generating force and source it is no longer open to dispute; and it is equally indisputable that the negro melody has acquired a National significance in America. Stephen Foster wrote only one song that has become really a folk-song, and that is the one in which he speaks the American negro's musical idiom, "Way down upon the Suwanee River."

As to the Indian, he may be interesting to the historian, anthropologist, and ethnographer; but since the racial superiority over the negro, absurdly enough claimed for him, has only served to keep him aloof from our civilization, he is to us a mere curiosity.

That Dvořák has "abandoned" his belief in the negro melody as a fount of our National music, courtesy compels me to accept as true after Mr. Finck's assertion. A belief, however, that can generate such a master work as the Symphony "From the New World" must have amounted to a conviction, and of its abandonment we had a right to expect some slight expression, which Dvořák's facile pen could have easily given it—but it didn't. Could Mr. Finck misconstrued the courteous acquiescence that fine, but word-poor, soul as a change of faith? CONSTANTIN VON STERNBERG.

| | |
|---|---|
| CAPITAL . . . . . | $1,000,000 |
| SURPLUS . . . . . | 500,000 |
| UNDIVIDED PROFITS . . . | 777,673 |
| RESOURCES . . . . | 28,166,637 |

---

E XECUTOR AND TRUSTEE OF ESTATES— This Company acts as executor and trustee under wills, and administers the estates of clients who desire to benefit from the experience, as to investments, possessed by this Company and its Directors.  Depositors are always able to command freely the facilities of this Company.  Interest is paid upon deposits, which are subject to withdrawal upon notice or demand.

---

For April

# THE GLORY OF THE CITIES

## 1— WASHINGTON

### BY J. HORACE McFARLAND

The Cake in the Hand is worth two in the store

If it isn't **PEARS'** leave it in the store

OF ALL SCENTED SOAPS PEARS' OTTO OF ROSE IS THE BEST.

❀

*State Railway Legislation: Bad*

In a majority of the States laws have been passed or are pending covering four subjects in the domain of railway transportation: (1) the endowment of State railway commissions with arbitrary powers; (2) demurrage, or charges for the detention of cars; (3) passenger rates; and (4) franchise and stock transactions. Some of these measures are unreasonable. State measures regulating railways and other public service corporations may be divided into three classes. One class consists of those laws or proposed laws of which the sole purpose is repression. They are the natural product of popular resentment engendered by the alleged arrogant or blundering actions of railway managers and popular impatience with artificially perverted commercial conditions. They have been framed in a spirit of battle, and without any very intelligent knowledge of the facts. A second class consists of those laws, or proposed laws, of which the purpose is to extend unearned privileges to the railways. They may have been introduced in response to a popular demand, but they have been framed in a spirit of partisan friendliness to special interests. The third class, as yet small, consists of those laws, or proposed laws, of which the purpose is the maintenance of the sovereignty of the people and even-handed justice to the railways. To the first of these categories seem to belong many of the State measures which have recently been passed or are pending. These are evidently the product of inadequate knowledge. Concerning the powers given to commissions, for instance, the Texas Commission annulled the Sunset Limited train of the Southern Pacific Railway last week, so it is announced, because it was fifty minutes late, the annulment being due to the Commission's recent order requiring passenger trains to run within thirty minutes of their schedules; as the Sunset Limited is an inter-State train, the case shows how unreasonably the interests of through passengers may be affected by State legislation. As to the subject of demurrage, the bill which has been rushed through the New York State Senate is a good example of possibly well-meant but unwise action. Under the guise of reciprocity in inducing railways to supply cars with reasonable promptness and in sufficient numbers for shippers, also for inducing shippers to load and unload cars with equal promptness, and not to use them for storage, the bill enables the shipper to order from the railways any number of cars, whether needed or not, and to require railways to furnish them within four days, under a forfeiture of a dollar a day for each car for failure to meet the demand. So far from reducing the evils aimed at, such a law might be used as a means of evading the prohibition of rebates, for a shipper might order many cars, use what he really needed, and collect demurrage for what he did not get and *did not want*. But the great majority of the acts of State Legislatures have to do with passenger rates, and the States which have passed legislation fixing the maximum that railways may charge for transportation of passengers are West Virginia, Maryland, Ohio, Indiana, Illinois, Missouri, Iowa, Nebraska, North and South Dakota, Wisconsin, Alabama, and North Carolina. It is interesting to note that the railway companies operating in Wisconsin have agreed to the rate decreed in that State. We believe that Wisconsin is the only State in which such a settlement has been made, and it reflects credit upon the system instituted some years ago by Governor, now Senator, La Follette. The railways operating in the "revolutionary " States can (1) refuse to obey the law and stand suits for penalty as well as damages to passengers, or (2) establish new tariffs, complying with the law, and test the law's constitutionality in the courts on the ground of confiscation. Of course the latter method has been chosen. The new railway tariffs include a withdrawal of excursion and other special rates and a discontinuance or marked increase in commutation rates. The Outlook refuses to believe, however, that the railways seriously contemplate so short-sighted a revenge as to inaugurate a petty system of rechecking baggage on crossing the frontier of certain States. The most serious feature of all unreasonable State legislation is its hampering of railways engaged in inter-State commerce. This commerce is under the exclusive regulation of the Federal authority. While State laws operate only within their boundaries, they inevitably produce an effect far beyond them. In this connection we note that the Chicago Great Western Railway Company has started a suit in the United States Circuit Court at St. Paul, Minnesota, to enjoin the enforcement of freight schedules adopted by the State Commission of Minnesota. If necessary, the case will be carried to the United States Supreme Court. The company takes the ground that the schedules fixed by the Minnesota State Commission, though they apply only to commerce within the State, constitute an interference with inter-State commerce, inasmuch as they are unreasonably low and tend to detract from the capacity of the road to do its business as a common carrier among the States.

❁

**State Railway Legislation : Good** To the comparatively small class of measures hostile to neither the railways nor the people, but designed to maintain both popular sovereignty and railway prosperity, belongs the railway law of Wisconsin. At the time that law was passed, in 1905, The Outlook reported in outline its main provisions, but it is of interest to note this law now with reference to the present situation. By that law Wisconsin created a Commission of three, appointed by the Gov-

ernor ; the Commission has power, not to draw up schedules indiscriminately, but to fix rates, for passenger as well as freight traffic, upon the complaint, not merely of shippers, but also of any person, concern, or municipality. The Commission has authority to examine, of its own initiative, any rate or charge ; in this way complaint may be brought by the whole State rather than by any element within it. The Commission is free to adjust rates to local conditions ; and of course leaves the railways free to do so as well, so long as they do not make unjust discriminations. Its discretion is thus not strictly limited. By a very skillfully drawn provision, dilatory processes in the courts are avoided. There is no appeal to the courts ; but of course any railway may bring action in the courts if it claims that the decision of the Commission is confiscatory. In that case, however, the burden of proof, which, until a rate is deemed unjust, rests upon the complainant or the Commission, is shifted to the railway. Moreover, the railway cannot bring any evidence before the court which it has not already laid before the Commission in order to give the Commission a chance to rescind or modify its order. The Commission has also powers regarding free passes, value of physical properties, indebtedness, hou.s and wages of labor, accidents, and the like. It is in accordance with this law that the Wisconsin Commission, as noted above, has fixed a two-and-a-half-cent passenger rate. In contrast with many other State measures, this law is an attempt to apply intelligent thought and foresight to a careful study of conditions. Of the same character with the Wisconsin law is the Public Service Commissions Bill now before the New York Legislature. The New York bill, however, is more inclusive. Its general provisions, which we reported last week, are in brief résumé as follows : The State is divided into two districts, one containing New York City, the other the rest of the State ; over each district a Public Service Commission has jurisdiction; the two Commissions have practically the same powers; they fix rates, on complaint; they summon witnesses; they must act in harmony with the Inter-State Commerce

Commission ; they pass upon the acquirement of franchise rights and upon the transfer of franchises and of stocks ; they can examine into the franchises, capitalization, and management of railways ; they may recommend legislation ; require co-operation between two or more public service corporations ; prescribe forms of reports ; examine into accidents ; prescribe remedies, such as appliances, standards of skill in employees, and so forth ; set standards of light ; supervise gas and electric meters ; institute summary proceedings. In addition there are provisions regarding passes, restrictions upon stockholding companies, regulations as to rates for long and short hauls, publication of tariff schedules, and the like. It is in such measures as the law of Wisconsin and the bill before the Legislature of New York that the salvation of the railways as well as the people from reckless State legislation very largely lies. So far as State laws are concerned, the issue now lies between such measures as these and the slap-dash making of rates by Legislatures. We believe that the time is approaching when the majority of railway presidents will not only not oppose such a bill as the Public Service Commissions Bill of New York, but will be glad to see a comprehensive law of the same character find a place among the Federal statutes.

❦

*Plans for Increasing Railway Freight Capacity* Railway freight facilities must be brought up to present commercial demands upon them. Mr. Hill, President of the Great Northern Railway, has stated that the necessary increase in trackage, terminals, locomotives, and cars would cost a billion dollars a year for five years. But this is not all. When that money is spent, it would only even up freight facilities to actual demands. There would be no provision for an inevitable future and increased demand. That future may be provided for in two ways—first, by enlarging the present standard track gauge of four feet eight and a half inches to six feet, together with a proportionate increase of rolling stock, thus affording room for greatly augmented traffic ; secondly, by a general electrification of all our railways. The first plan is practically impossible, not only because of its enormous cost under any circumstances, but also because of the necessity to operate the roads coincidently with their reconstruction. Moreover, even if the gauge were increased, there would have to be a corresponding increase in locomotive strength. On the other hand, a general electrification of American railways would need but half the sum necessary to increase the gauge and rolling stock. Furthermore, it could be instituted without interrupting traffic. Again, electrification provides both increased speed and cheaper motive power. Finally, the freight trains of the future may be at least a mile long. Such a train could be profitably operated only by electricity and under the multiple unit system, by which the breaking in two of a train, now occurring with too great frequency, would be largely prevented. The number of engines would depend on the grades, as now, but would of course be several times the present number, and, distributed throughout the train, would be unified and managed by the operator at the head of the train. Naturally, such trains would demand a rearrangement of termini—a rearrangement bound to come in any event. Thus every indication is that the congestion of the railways and all the attending difficulties of operation are likely to be greatly relieved by the rapidly widening application of electric power.

❦

*Forest Reserves* On the eve of the adjournment of Congress President Roosevelt issued a proclamation adding some seventeen million acres of forest lands to the National Forest Reserves already established. This was just before he signed an act of Congress abridging his authority to create reserves in the States of Colorado, Wyoming, Montana, Idaho, Oregon, and Washington. The President showed characteristic wisdom, courage, and determination in opposing this wish of Congress. That wish had been largely the expression of those seeking to divert to private ownership as great a share as possible of the remaining forests. In other words, private interests would satisfy the appetite of the present generation by sacrificing a great future inheritance. Fortunately, there was no question of the President's power under the statute of 1891. In addition, the surveys for particular reserves had long been under way; in many cases the preparation of the necessary papers had been ordered two years ago. As the President said, the utmost care and deliberation had been exercised in deciding upon the boundaries of the proposed reserve; if he did not act, reserves which he considers very important for the interests of the United States would be wholly or in part dissipated before Congress again had an opportunity to consider the matter, while under the action which he has taken they will be preserved. If the next Congress chooses to review and reverse the President's action, it can do so by action taken with fuller opportunity for considering the subject on its own merits. The President adds that if by any chance land more valuable for other purposes than for forest reserves is shown to have been included, he will forthwith restore it to entry. The creation of the reserves means that our timber is to be kept in tne interest of the home-maker, rather than in that of great private owners and lumber syndicates. This is the object, not merely of our forest policy, but of our whole public land policy.

❀

*Porto Rico*    Mr. Beekman Winthrop, the Governor of Porto Rico, has been appointed an Assistant Secretary of the Treasury under Mr. Cortelyou. This appointment must be regarded in the light of promotion. We are not surprised at the demonstrations of regret which come from the people of the island. Mr. Winthrop's tact in political administration, and no less the tact of his wife in social administration, have done a great deal to commend Americanism to the people of the island, and to counteract the evil influences of some Congressional neglect. It is a noteworthy testimony to the wisdom of his administration that the Council, which is composed partly of natives and partly of Americans, has rarely (we believe never) divided on racial lines. It may be hoped that incidentally Mr. Winthrop, having his home in Washington, may be able to impress upon Congressmen the importance of some of those needed reforms which he has urged upon our Government in his annual messages. The most important of these, in our judgment, are an act making Porto Ricans citizens of the United States and an act imposing a slight tariff on foreign coffees as a means of stimulating coffee growth in Porto Rico. Mr. Regis H. Post, who takes Governor Winthrop's place, has been his Secretary of State, and is thoroughly familiar, therefore, with Porto Rican conditions. He is one of that class of young men, happily increasing, who have gone into public service in order that they may serve the public. When Mr. Roosevelt was Governor of the State, Mr. Post was in the Assembly, where as an independent Republican he gave Mr. Roosevelt's reform policies efficient support. Mr. Winthrop's administration has been so admirable that Mr. Post will find some difficulty in following him; but we expect to see the same good spirit maintained and the same wise policy pursued under the new Governor as under the old.

❀

*Archbishop Ireland on the French Church*    The New Cathedral Bulletin of St. Paul has published a very interesting sermon by Archbishop Ireland on "The Church and the State in France." While this sermon was preached before the final legislation was effected, it may be accepted as the view of liberal American Roman Catholics. In this and the following paragraphs we give our readers a résumé of the sermon. The Archbishop declares that, while the situation at the moment is undoubtedly serious, there will come at the end a clearer understanding of mutual interests. He affirms his love both for the Church and for France. Since 1801 the relations of the two have been regulated by a Concordat under which the Catholic religion was recognized as that of the great majority of the French people; its free exercise guaranteed; annual stipends assured to bishops and priests; churches and other buildings for religious use, confiscated during the Revolution and not afterwards alienated by acts of the Government, placed at the disposal of the bishops; the Pope, in return, conceding the right of nomination of archbishops and bishops to the State, canonical institution to be given by the Pope, and that only such priests be appointed to chief parishes as should be acceptable to the Government. The Church property was placed at the disposal of the bishops, thus restoring the *status quo* existing before the Revolution. The Church has always held that the ownership of ecclesiastical edifices was fully restored to it, and has supported its contention by the fact that the Concordat invokes the authority of the Pope " to quiet title as to such ecclesiastical properties as had been alienated by the Government," and on the similarity of language between the act of the Constituent Assembly which placed the properties of the Church " at the disposition of the nation," and the language of the Concordat, which places what remained of the properties " at the disposition of the bishops." Annual stipends were to be paid to bishops and priests, not as a gratuity, but as a restitution of values taken by the State from the Church.

❀

**The Amendment of the Concordat** The Concordat, with all its provisions, has now been annulled. Americans, the Archbishop says, must not be misled by the phrase " separation of Church and State." In this country this means liberty and justice; " in France it means servitude and oppression." "We are ready," said the Pope to the Cardinals, " to submit to the separation of the Church from the State, but it must be a fair separation—such as obtains in the United States, in Brazil, in Great Britain, in Holland;" and the Archbishop declares, " No Catholic in the United States makes objection to separation; for here separation means exactly what it purports to mean." The law of separation in France has its good points. It restores to the Church the liberty of naming her bishops and priests. It has also its evil points; the

3-4

control of houses of worship, residences of priests and bishops, seminaries for the education of clergy, is vital to the Church, and the proposed " associations of worship " do not secure sufficient control of these properties. In the United States " the discipline of the Church is recognized in the organization and working of those corporations; the bishop of the diocese is *de jure* member and president; should a controversy bring the corporation before the civil courts, the issues involved in the controversy are discussed and judged with due regard to the Church's own spirit and laws. In other words, religious corporations are so organized and so regulated that in forming them, while she complies, as she must, with the laws of the land, the Church retains full control of her properties and guards them against all use contrary to her own laws." The Catholic Church is ruled, first by the Pope at Rome, next by the bishop of the diocese; its whole organization is hierarchical. In the " associations of worship " this principle is not only not recognized, but " explicitly excluded ;" and an association of worship, if it wishes, can "put aside priests, bishops, and popes, and conduct and regulate public worship, subject in final appeal only to the Council of State." The Catholic Church will never agree " to lodge the possession of her temporalities or the regulation of her worship in associations independent of the control of her hierarchy." The " associations of worship " are so limited in authority and so circumscribed that they offer the Church no guarantee of stability, no permanency of possession of her properties. If services in a house of worship are suspended for six months, or if repairs are not duly made as the agent of the Government might judge, the Church loses the property. The income of the associations is limited to the barest necessities of public worship. They can neither receive nor hold funds for works of private or public charity. The allowances for priests, which were not gifts but payments for properties confiscated, have been withdrawn. It would not be difficult to obtain from the Church a renunciation of those allowances, but some sort of compensation ought to have been offered her. The State now becomes the absolute owner of all properties confiscated in 1789 and afterwards placed at the disposal of the bishops in 1801. Cathedrals and other churches may be used by the Church as a tenant-at-will ; episcopal and parochial residences and seminary buildings are within two, or at the most five, years to be vacated by their present occupants and returned unreservedly to the State. This, the Archbishop declares, is confiscation of the blackest dye.

❀

*The Attitude of the Church* Under advice from the Pope, the bishops of France refused the associations offered by the law of separation. Her religious orders have been suppressed, the members scattered ; French citizens are not allowed to live in religious communities ; they cannot consecrate themselves to the solitude of the cloister, or even to works of charity in asylums, hospitals, or school-rooms. It became illegal for a priest to celebrate mass, " for Catholics to gather around the altar, for bishops to reside in their palaces, for students of theology to greet their teachers in the class-room." The Archbishop interprets this state of affairs as due largely to the hatred of religion in the minds of men who are governing France, and to the theory of the omnipotence of the State. The Catholic Church represents religion to France. The Archbishop quotes M. Jaurès, the Socialist leader, as saying, " If God himself appeared before the multitude in palpable form, the first duty of men would be to refuse him obedience, to consider him, not a master to whom all should submit, but as an equal, with whom men may argue." Another member of the majority said, " The triumph of the Galilean has lasted twenty centuries, and it is now his turn to die." The Archbishop declares that the clergy are somewhat to blame. : Too many of them have retained the spirit of passive obedience inherited from the old régime. They have never learned the virtues of public life; "saints before the altar, they are cowards before an electoral urn." The French Catholics, moreover, have been unfortunate

in many of their leaders, who have been partisans of " buried political régimes." Monarchists are still numerous among the old nobility, and too many of the clergy still read their politics in Bossuet and Massillon. This is the weakness of French Catholics. No one understood France better than did Leo XIII., and he bade all Catholics seek the welfare of the country and of the Church, as loyal adherents of the Republic. Had he been listened' to, " in all probability the religious persecution of the present day would not have come. Monarchical ideas and plottings have done dreadful injury to the Church in France."

❀

*Madame Blanc* By the death of Thérèse de Solms Blanc, better known by her pen-name " Th. Bentzon," France is the poorer. But, fortunately, her rare personality remains crystallized in all that her pen has left—novels, essays, books on education, books of criticism and travel. Her novels are too little known. They have singular strength, sweetness, and charm. " Tony," " Constance," and " Un Remords " are far beyond the average and were deservedly " crowned " by the French Academy, the highest honor to which a French writer can aspire. In Madame Blanc's essays we come in closer touch with her personality. Here we find a point of view, womanly in the best sense of the word, combined with convincing breadth and force. Most of her essays were published in the Revue des Deux Mondes. She owed the position which she held for many years on that foremost of French reviews to Comte d'Aure, her stepfather and equerry to Napoleon III. The Comte d'Aure . introduced the young writer to George Sand, who in turn tried to interest Buloz, editor of the Revue, in her. Fortunately, Buloz saw one of the aspirant's stories in the Journal des Débats, and gave her the coveted place on the review. From it came the aid given to French education, sociology, and life by a series of papers which drew their inspiration quite as much from this country as from France. Madame Blanc's attention had always been drawn towards England and America. She was accustomed to say, " At the bottom of what I have done I find first of all my mother's influence, but this was combined with the influence which dear Miss Robertson, my English governess, gave me in inspiring simplicity and love of truth." She would add, " My interest in America dates from the day when Miss Robertson gave me one of Washington Irving's books to read." Perhaps her early marriage, the long absences of her husband, and the melting away of her fortune drew her attention more than it would otherwise have been drawn to the conditions of women's existence in France as compared with those in America. She early turned her attentior. to American authors, becoming especially interested in the stories of Sara Orne Jewett—and what stories are more peculiarly American ? Her criticism of them drew from Miss Jewett a note of acknowledgment to the unknown " Th. Bentzon," a pseudonym taken by Madame Blanc from the family name of her grandmother. Thérèse Blanc visited America repeatedly. More than any American woman she studied, appreciated, and portrayed our country and its ideals, as any one may see who consults her " Choses et Gens d'Amérique," " Récits Américains," " Questions Américaines," " Femmes d'Amérique," and " Nouvelle France et Nouvelle Angleterre." The motive in all these books seems to be to show to French men and women the advantages of certain American social and educational customs and ideals. These volumes constitute quite as impressive a tribute in their way to our civilization as does Mr. Bryce's " American Commonwealth." Madame Blanc was a progressive in her religious as well as in her social opinions, and in the recent religious crises in France her broad-gauge views were especially evident. Herself a sincere Roman Catholic, she had long desired the separation of Church and State, so that the Church might attain its true spiritual strength. Thus in her every activity we have the example, first of all, of a great gentlewoman who had a genius for making friends and keeping them, of a philanthropist whose energies were bounded by no creed, and of a writer whose influence was constructive and elevating.

**The Sage Foundation**

One of the most notable of recent events is the establishment by Mrs. Russell Sage of the Sage Foundation for the improvement of social and living conditions throughout the country. The generous endowment of ten million dollars, which puts this Foundation on a level in magnitude with the great educational foundations established by Mr. Carnegie and Mr. Rockefeller, aims at the improvement of social and living conditions by means of research, publication, educational support and maintenance of charitable and beneficial activities, agencies, and institutions, and the giving of substantial aid to activities, agencies, and institutions already established. It is proposed by Mrs. Sage to investigate causes of evil social conditions and to suggest remedies and put into operation practical means of overcoming these evils. The Sage Foundation may establish new agencies or contribute to existing agencies, as the General Education Board creates its own agencies or aids existing educational institutions. It will aim to take up the larger and more difficult problems in such a way as will secure co-operation and aid in their solution. The Board of Trustees includes a group of men and women who combine in an unusual degree disinterestedness of spirit with practical knowledge of the problems with which this Foundation proposes to deal : Mr. Robert W. de Forest, Miss Helen Gould, Mr. Cleveland H. Dodge, Miss Louisa L. Schuyler, Mrs. W. B. Rice, all of New York City, and Mr. John M. Glenn and Dr. Daniel C. Gilman, of Baltimore. Mrs. Sage, who is in vigorous health and intensely interested, will take part in the work which she has initiated. Mr. de Forest is reported as saying that there is no present intention of establishing new forms of charity ; the income, which will be at least half a million a year, will be given to a great extent to existing charities, which will also be used as the work of investigation. It is too early to announce a definite programme, but the magnitude of the Foundation encourages the hope that it will not only reinforce existing methods of bettering social and vital conditions, but, by co-ordination and leadership, make possible a great advance in the field of practical altruism.

❀

**The Lee Memorial**

At a meeting held recently in the Chamber of Commerce at Richmond, Virginia, the preliminary organization of the Lee Memorial Association was effected, and the form of the permanent memorial to General Lee was announced. The suggestion of President Roosevelt, embodied in his letter to the committee having charge of the Lee memorial meeting in Washington, had already been anticipated by Mrs. Minor, of Richmond, whose work in behalf of the memorial has been tireless. She proposed that the memorial should take the form of an endowment of a Chair of American History in Washington and Lee University. This suggestion was adopted by the University, and at the meeting in Richmond, President Denny, after a brief report of the preliminary steps, announced that it was proposed to raise the sum of $100,000, of which $25,000 is to be used in enlarging and beautifying the College Chapel, in a recess of which, behind the desk, the remains of General Lee repose under the strikingly beautiful reclining statue by Mr. Valentine, of Richmond; and $75,000 is to be set apart as the endowment of a Chair of American History, to be forever associated with General Lee's name and memory. It was pointed out that the part played by General Lee in some of the greatest events in American history, his noble service to education and to the young men of the South in the closing years of his life, and the inspiring quality of his nature and spirit, made this form of commemoration peculiarly fitting. The evident appropriateness of establishing the chair in the University which bears General Lee's name, and in which he served as President, was recognized from the beginning. It is a question whether a larger sum of money ought not to be raised. If the Chapel is to be made a permanent memorial of General Lee, in which articles of every kind associated with his personality and his career are to be gathered, the work ought to be done with monumental dignity and beauty, and in the endowment of professorships the increasing cost of living which is likely to come in the future must be taken into account. Addresses were made by the Governor of Virginia, by Dr. Denny, President of Washington and Lee University, by Mrs. Minor, from whom came the suggestion of a professorship of history, and by Mr. Mabie.

❀

**Everett D. Burr**

The Outlook in the past few months has several times brought to the attention of its readers the admirable work of the Congo Reform Association. For accurate information upon the terrible conditions of slavery existing in the Congo and the movement in both Europe and the United States to remedy those conditions the public was greatly indebted to the painstaking labor and intelligent investigations of one of the most active representatives of the Association, the Rev. Everett D. Burr. Dr. Burr's recent accidental and violent death, which occurred mysteriously during a railway journey, has produced in the minds of his friends a shock from which it is hard to recover. The last three months of his life he made New York his center, throwing himself with characteristic ardor into the task of arousing and enlisting the intelligent sympathy of the American people on behalf of the oppressed natives of the Congo. Through pulpit, platform, press, correspondence, and personal visits, he engendered a popular agitation which at last made itself felt with telling effect in Washington. This is the way he occupied his vacation after an arduous pastorate of seven years at Newton Center. He began his career as pastor of the Memorial Baptist Church in Chicago. It was at Ruggles Street in Boston, however, that he first achieved distinction, not only as a preacher and pastor, but as philanthropist, in friendliest relation with Mr. D. S. Ford, the editor of the Youth's Companion, who made the Ruggles Street Church under Dr. Burr's charge a channel through which he expended approximately $40,000 a year in institutional work. Upon the death of Mr. Ford, he became pastor of the Baptist Church in Newton Center, a place of refined homes—a most attractive suburb of Boston. Here the Baptists have their oldest and best-equipped divinity school. The atmosphere of the town is saturated with intellectualism as· well as a richly matured Christian consciousness. His purpose seemed to be to bring the want of the great adjacent city face to face with the material, mental, and moral wealth of this prosperous suburb. Social enthusiasm formed the very staple of his character.. A strikingly handsome person, a genial disposition, a vibrant and well-trained voice both in singing and speaking, brilliant conversational powers, Christlike sympathy with every kind of suffering and oppression, considerable first-hand acquaintance with the science of sociology, a spirit essentially modern and perfectly attuned to the social compunction and compassion which constitute the tone of our time—all these combined to effect an equipment for social service which gave him peculiar distinction in his profession. While to the last he did not deviate from the essential faiths of the communion to which he belonged, the ethical and social side of Christianity appealed to him more profoundly than its doctrinal and ecclesiastical aspects. If public opinion in this country succeeds in stirring the Belgian authorities to creating any real and permanent reforms in the Congo, the result will be due in no small measure to Dr. Burr's own personal and arduous labors.

❀

*Milk for the City*
The crusade for pure milk which two or three of the New York newspapers seem to have undertaken has not been altogether enlightened ; but it has done some good in directing public attention to a matter literally of life and death. The notion that the city should guard its milk supply is of comparatively recent origin. At a public meeting conducted by the Section on Public Health of the New York Academy of Medicine last week Dr. L. Emmett Holt, one of the foremost American authorities on the hygienic care of children, reminded his hearers that thirty years ago milk was sold in bulk, ladled by drivers with dirty hands out of open cans in milk-wagons into receptacles left over night beside kitchen doors and exposed to dust and filth and germs ; that till 1873 there was no inspection of milk in New York City, and that it was not till 1896 (scarcely more than ten years ago) that general inspection was established. Now milk is very generally sold in tightly closed bottles ; city inspectors test the milk to discover and prevent adulteration, and examine railway stations and cars to see that the milk is kept not only clean, but, what is equally important, cold while it is in transit. Indeed, these inspectors invade counties outside the city, not only in the State, but in the four other States from which the milk supply of New York comes. These inspectors from the Health Department of the city of New York of course have no authority outside of the municipality ; but their commands are obeyed "up the State," i New Jersey and Pennsylvania, and even in Canada, for the dairyman knows that if he does not comply the city will shut his milk out from its market. So in a generation there has been a great advance in this department of preventive medicine. But more remains to be done. In the case of New York, which reaches out four hundred miles to get its milk, and receives it twenty-four to forty hours old and distributes it, not only to well-regulated households, but also to overheated, closely crowded, ill-ventilated tenements, the problem is a vast one. In cannot be solved in the cavalier fashion advocated by zealous newspapers, which would have the city save itself from germs by cooking practically its whole milk supply. Dr. Holt remarked that most of the milk used by children in the city was apparently either pasteurized or boiled ; for when he and Dr. William H. Park desired to observe a number of children fed on raw milk they had great difficulty in finding them ; the tenement-house mothers had been educated largely to boil or pasteurize the milk they feed to infants. The newspapers have emphasized much the danger of conveying tuberculosis, scarlet fever, typhoid, diphtheria, and even measles in milk. At that meeting it was made plain that measles is practically never thus conveyed,

diphtheria very rarely, and the other three diseases to a very small degree. As Dr. Park, Director of the Research Laboratories of the New York City Department of Health, pointed out, the danger of conveying contagious diseases by milk has been grossly exaggerated by the press. The chief danger from milk is shown in the number of infants who die from those intestinal diseases grouped together under the common name of cholera infantum. And the mortality is due not only to polluted milk but also to ignorance in methods of feeding. Rochester (a small city compared to New York) has greatly reduced its death rate simply by securing a supply of fresh, pure milk and educating mothers in methods of feeding. New York can never get so fresh a supply. There the milk to be fed to infants, as distinguished from milk for general consumption, had better, perhaps, be pasteurized; but, more important still, there, as everywhere, it should be properly modified by the addition of cream, sugar of milk, lime-water, and so forth. For this purpose milk depots should be established where mothers could get the milk properly prepared in sealed nursing-bottles and receive instructions in caring for it and feeding it to their children. Instruction, too, in the utmost importance of breast feeding (for which there is no nearly adequate substitute) could be given at these various centers. Anything the city can do to promote the establishment of such depots it should do at once; for, as Dr. Goler, the health officer of Rochester, has said, if it is not the business of a city to protect the lives of its own people, it has no business at all.

&#9673;

*Insanity and Criminal Trials*    The much-advertised proceedings in the Thaw case give popular interest to a paper recently read at Bridgeport, Connecticut, by Dr. George Franklin Shiels, which we find in the Evening Transcript reprinted from the Medical Record. Dr. Shiels brings out clearly the difference between the medical and the legal definition of insanity; they are essentially different. He defines legal insanity in the following terms: " A man or woman is insane who

does not know the difference between right and wrong in regard to any specific particular act, and who further does not know the consequences of committing such act." The insanity may be temporary, but it must be such as to render the person morally irresponsible for the act done. When a person is accused of a criminal act and is defended on the ground of his insanity, how is the law to determine whether he was morally responsible for his act or not ? The present method appears to us, as it does to Dr. Shiels, very imperfect. The physician cannot apply the tests which he is accustomed to apply in dealing with questions of insanity, for the medical and legal definitions are not the same. Moreover, he is employed by the accused on the one hand, or by the State on the other, and is not likely to be impartial. "There are few men," says Dr. Shiels. " who, when employed in the interests of an individual or a corporation, can resist the tendency toward bias, and I have actually seen cases where such witnesses have sworn to opinions to which in their calmer moments, when free from bias, they could not have given their support." He naturally adds, " Were I a jury which had to consider such evidence, I should give it little or no weight." As a substitute for the present method, which allows the State to call one set of experts, the defense another set of experts, and the jury to decide between them, he proposes as an alternative method that, either each side select two experts, the four a fifth, and the five present their report, or that the matter be left entirely in the hands of the court to select the experts whose testimony shall be presented to the jury.

&#9673;

*An Honorable Action*    The Outlook two weeks ago reported the decision of the Court of Appeals in the case against Mr. George W. Perkins in which his act in contributing money of the New York Life Insurance Company to a Republican campaign fund was charged as larceny. The court held that the act did not come within this definition, as it lacked the element of felonious intent. Notwithstanding this decision, Mr. Perkins has repaid the amount involved, with interest (about $54,000), to the insurance company. In his letter accompanying the payment (after stating that the political contribution was made at the request of the President of the company and that the company later on reimbursed Mr. Perkins) he says:

The payment was made without any thought on the part of the President or myself of personal advantage, but solely in the belief that it was for the best and broadest interests of the policy-holders, both at home and abroad. In dismissing the criminal proceedings instituted against me for accepting reimbursement, the courts have intimated that the payment, and therefore the reimbursement, was not for a proper corporate purpose.

It need not be pointed out that this repayment was voluntary and spontaneous, and that it was an act of scrupulous honor.

❦

**Weighing the Soul** The report that certain physicians in Boston have discovered that the human soul weighs from half an ounce to an ounce has been received with incredulity in Europe, and has been spoken of with disrespect by certain American scientific authorities. The attempt to weigh the soul has been tried many times, but this is the first time, so far as we are aware, that definite results have been secured and the figure at which it turns the scale accurately registered. It will be impossible to settle this question by experiment in any single locality. The weight of a soul in Chicago, for instance, may be very much greater than the weight of a soul in Boston; in Paris, on the other hand, the opinion seems to prevail that the soul has no weight whatever. The Outlook suggests the endowment of a society for determining the weight of the soul in different parts of the world; first securing by scientific tests exact results, then providing for comparative studies, and finally for publication of theses. It may not be without significance that at the very time when Mrs. Eddy's reputation as a prophetess is suffering serious collapse, and long and oft-repeated exposures of spiritism have brought discredit on that ancient cult, Boston, which has been long one of the largest importing ports in the world in the matter of religions, has come to the rescue and put a

solid foundation for all the various creeds, cults, and superstitions, which, as a leading Boston clergyman once declared, "flourished more abundantly and grew to ranker proportions on Columbus Avenue than in any other part of the world."

❦

# Lenten Meditations
## Deliver Us

After the acknowledgment of God's Kingdom, its preparation, coming, and perfection, after man has made profession of loyalty and confession of sin, he asks his Liege for strength greater than human, that there may be deliverance from evil.

This is the climax of the Lord's Prayer. If hunger for God is expressed in begging for forgiveness, it is more evident in the petition for deliverance. We pray not only for absolution from the past, but for exemption from the future. "O keep my soul and deliver me: let me not be ashamed; for I put my trust in Thee." As David prayed, so we pray. How is the apparently infinite power of evil environment to be overcome save by a really infinite power of good? For, in the daily, hourly struggle with seemingly overmastering evil environment, a time comes when man's will and resource fail, when human science can do no more. Then men pray, and their prayer is no sign of weakness; it simply recognizes the existence of superhuman protection against evil.

"There is a power, not ourselves, which makes for righteousness." It delivers us, not always from evils that may affect the body, but from all ill that may hurt the soul. It delivers us not from complexity or perplexity or discomfort or hardship. It delivers us from *the* evil—from the thing that is not Divine Character. It delivers us, pulls us out, draws us out, from *that* evil—sin. As an ancient liturgy has it, "Deliver us from the Evil One and his works, and from all his insults and contrivances, for the sake of Thy Holy Name, which we call upon to supply our insufficiency." Only God can deliver from sin. That is the clear vision of these Lenten days—

" His own self bare our sins in his own body on the tree "—the Christ "delivered for our offenses " on the cross. " Truly this was the Son of God." With this conviction comes the coincident conviction of His perfection and of our imperfection. And then comes the " God be merciful to me a sinner."

Not only in life but in death, God delivers us. A father walks at night through a deep wood with his little son. Suddenly the lad fancies that he sees a dread Shape ready to spring upon him. " O save me, father !" he cries, and the man holds the boy close, thrilled by the sense of fatherhood, as the other is by the sense of dependence and sonship. God will hold us close in that supreme moment which we call Death. God longs for the acknowledgment of man's dependence. And the man longs to cry to the Eternal Father, at least in that moment, even though there be " no language but a cry."

God delivers us at all times. Not only because we need deliverance, but because we bind ourselves anew to him every time we pray. And he to us, for deliverance comes *as* we pray. It may be the boy-cry of implicit trust, the arms stretched out▪as if to clasp a Shadow-God ; it may be the man's deep, hoarse cry out of a life's heartaches, as " Out of the depths have I cried unto Thee, O Lord." With such a prayer the heart empties itself. It can no more. There is silence. Now comes communion with God. Not our petition, but his answer. It binds us to him. A Voice speaks in the soul, whether we pray for deliverance from environment or from sin or from death : " I will deliver thee, and thou shalt glorify me." " I will : be thou clean." " I will that they also, whom thou hast given me, be with me where I am."

When we reach the other life, and turn round to regard our course in this life, shall we not see ourselves perplexed, disheartened, tempted, affrighted beyond mere human endurance ? But shall we not also see that a Deliverer was ever at our side ?

Why do we not oftener cry, " Deliver us " ? Only thus is there real communion with God.

# The Railway Problem

We have received the following letter from Judge Potter, of the Supreme Court of Pennsylvania. Our readers will find on another page of this issue a report of the railway legislation of the various States to which he refers in his opening sentence.

Supreme Court of Pennsylvania,
Judges' Chambers.
Philadelphia, March 13, 1907.

*To the Editors of The Outlook :*

I inclose clipping to show that the fact that the States have waked up to the duty of correcting corporate abuses within their borders is being pretty thoroughly appreciated. The Outlook did not seem to be very strong in the faith that the States were able to cope with the situation. It has rather sided with the President in his desire for Federal control. But the giant is now awake. The people everywhere are realizing that the way to exercise effective control is through their own State officials, who know the needs of the localities in which they dwell. The present experience ought to put an end to all talk about the inability of the States to regulate abuses.

The only fear now is that the regulation may be too severe.

The situation does call for great wisdom and moderation. But the people have learned the lesson that the power is within their own hands. No need exists to call upon the Federal Government to do that which the people in every State can do for themselves.

Very truly,
W. P. POTTER.

The recent railway legislation in the various States appears to us to confirm the necessity for Federal regulation. For what the country needs is a uniform and harmonious system of railway regulation, and we cannot think that this will be given by unsystematic and inharmonious legislation by the different States. We do not, however, propose here to reply to Judge Potter's letter, but only to use it as a text for a restatement of the positions of The Outlook on this subject.

When the President first proposed, over five years ago, a Federal supervision and regulation of railways, two objections were interposed : one, that the railway traffic should be left to be regulated by free competition, and that the enforcement of existing laws against combinations in restraint of trade was all that was necessary ; second, that if any further ıegulation was necessary, it should be left to be effected by the States—for the Federal Government to undertake it was a usurpation of power. The answer to the first objection was that free competition might lower, rates, but it could not equalize them; the answer to the second objection was that State action might correct specific wrongs, but it could never secure that uniformity which is essential to justice and equal rights.

Events have justified both answers. The action of the Federal Government in enforcing the law against combinations in restraint of trade has elicited from railwaymen a stronger expression of their always dormant conviction that unrestricted competition in railway traffic is injurious alike to railway and to shipper, that combination is essential alike to secure economical administration and rates that are just and equal. And the independent action within one year of thirteen States, attempting to deal with the railway problem and to regulate passenger fares, as reported on another page, appears from current newspaper reports to be leading them to the conviction that State regulation is far and away more disastrous to railway interests than Federal regulation would be. What the country wants, and has all along wanted, is not lower rates but equal rights. The railways also need equal rights. Neither free competition nor State regulation can secure these rights to either the railways or the public. We hope that the promised but delayed visit of certain of the leading railway presidents to the President of the United States may yet be realized; it would be a first and a very important step toward a recognition of the principle that the interests of the railways and the interests of the people are not antagonistic, and that the way to secure both is not by battle, nor yet compromise, but by mutual understanding and agreement.

Two principles must underlie any such agreement:

I. What is needed is not unregulated competition but regulated combination.

II. This cannot be secured by the States; it must be secured by the Federal Government.

The Constitution of the United States

and the decisions of the Supreme Court thereon make the way perfectly clear for building up a new and harmonious railway policy based on these two principles. The Constitution gives to the Federal Government jurisdiction over inter-State commerce. This is an exclusive jurisdiction. All questions directly affecting inter-State commerce are taken out of the power of the States and given over to the Federal Government. In the words of Judge Bradley, of the Supreme Court, "In the matters of foreign and inter-State commerce there are no States." The Federal Government can charter corporations to carry on this commerce. It can determine the conditions in which and the instruments by which inter-State commerce may be carried on. Thus much the Supreme Court has decided to be the law of the land. And this furnishes a basis on which the railway presidents acting for investors and Congress acting for the general public can co-operate in securing equal rights both for the public and the investors. We venture here to outline such a system.

Let Congress charter the railway corporations engaged in inter-State commerce. The law might forbid any corporation not chartered by the Federal Government from engaging in such commerce, exactly as it forbids any foreign-built ship from engaging in coastwise commerce. But this would probably not be necessary. The great trunk lines would probably welcome Federal incorporation. The smaller lines would then be compelled by self-interest to follow suit. These National corporations, like the National banks, would be subject to Federal inspection. Such inspection would put an end to such stock-jobbing operations as Mr. Harriman recently described in his testimony before the Inter-State Commerce Commission. What injury such operations inflict on the general public is illustrated by the recent fall in stocks of all descriptions. Such National corporations, created and empowered by the Federal Government to carry on a work placed by the Constitution under the exclusive jurisdiction of the Federal Government, would be exempt, from vexatious legislation by the States. The great trunk lines would have one government, not forty-seven governments, to deal with. Local and suburban travel might still be subject to local regulation, but to none inconsistent with Federal authority and the power which Federal authority had conferred. The railways, being thus under one governmental authority and subject to one governmental supervision, should be not forbidden but encouraged to combine. Pooling should be not prohibited but promoted. The railways should be invited to co-operate in determining rates as they now co-operate in determining time-tables. And the public would be adequately protected by having all rates agreed upon by such combinations subject to supervision and revision by the Federal Government acting through some bureau or department organized for that purpose.

Fifty years ago the currency of the country was furnished by private banks, chartered by the State and subject only to State supervision and regulation. As a consequence, no man knew what the bills in his pocket were worth unless he also carried in his pocket a Bank Note Detective, published monthly for the purpose of giving the information. Then the Federal Government undertook to charter National banks. They remained State banks in this, that each bank was administered by and served the interests of the citizens of the State in which it was located ; but, being subject to National inspection, supervision, and control, a National security was furnished, not only for the currency which they issued, but for their depositors and stockholders as well. What the wit of man devised for our banking interests the wit of man ought to be able to devise for our transportation interests.

What the Nation wants is a railway system which will combine the energy and capital of private enterprise with the harmony and stability of a National organization. No change in the Constitution of the United States and none in the course and tendency of the decisions of the Supreme Court of the United States is needed for that purpose. The history of our National banking system indicates how such a combination can be secured

under the Constitution as it is interpreted by the Supreme Court. All that is necessary is, first, a frank recognition of the truth that America needs, not unregulated competition, but regulated combination, and that the Federal Government is the organization to secure it; and, second, an intelligent and sincere co-operation between the representatives of the railways and the representatives of the Government. Such co-operation, if it could be secured, would afford a welcome augury of a future railway system which would give security to the investor, safety to the traveling public, and just and equal rates to all shippers, large and small.

●

# Art and Democracy

Mr. Ernest Poole's description of the educational work carried on by the Chicago Art Institute under the direction of Mr. French, which appears on another page, is significant of the broadening of the influence of collections of pictures and schools of art, and of the hunger and thirst of hosts of people who have been denied the opportunities of art education in any form, but are eager for access to great works of art. Formerly a collection of pictures or statues, in this country at least, was regarded as the luxury of a few rich or cultivated people, and as having very slight connection with popular life. Art was appreciated by many ; but its significance as an expression of racial character or national aims or as a resource in the daily life of the people was not understood. Mr. Poole's article records a radical change of attitude. It is one of inspiration and of pathos. It shows at once how great is the longing for beauty among hosts of uneducated Americans, and how unconscious of its appeal and ignorant of its language are those other Americans who think that the end of living and of its activities is covered by the one word business.

In the rushing life of Chicago, the typical city of American energy and audacious activity, the Art Institute stands at a strategic point, and testifies, in the face of the most impressive material achievements, to the richness of life and to the reality of the higher aspirations. One who approaches the city from the Lake finds this low but stately building in a place where the Custom-house usually stands, while behind it rise great commercial structures which overtop it by twenty stories. If the new-comer judges by appearance, he will promptly rush to the conclusion that the business buildings stand for Chicago, and that the Institute is an exotic; but if he applies a spiritual instead of a material scale of values, he will understand that the symmetry, dignity, and detachment of the Institute embody the higher possibilities of the city, and meet the cravings of the American spirit as the great business structures behind it do not and cannot. Men never have lived by bread alone and never will, however they may endeavor at times to content themselves with the substance of the fields instead of with the Word of God, which is the soul, not only of all righteousness, but of all beauty, and is the inspiration of the higher interests of mankind.

It is the tendency of all professions involving skill to emphasize the technical elements over the vital, and to regard a special form of expression of the human spirit as more important than the life which it interprets. Art is often spoken of and widely regarded as the possession of a cult, the interest of a few, the practice of a little group of trained men and women. As a matter of fact, great art has never been produced except as the expression of a vital need and a vital love. In this sense art is fundamentally democratic. Its fertility depends, not on the appearance of a few men of gift, but on the penetration of the people at large with the passion for beauty. When Michelangelo declared that the best judgment of a statue was the judgment of the public square, he was speaking of a people who knew by instinct, by the cravings of their natures, trained and developed by familiarity with the best examples, the difference between good and bad work in marble. Art on a great scale has come everywhere only as it came in Athens, and later in Florence, and still later in Holland, because of the vitality, searching energy, and

passion for life which made those communities powerful in dealing with practical affairs. The Greek was not only an artist, but he was the shrewdest trader of antiquity; the Venetian not only expressed his civic life in the noblest terms of beauty, dressed it more magnificently than the life of any court, but he was also master of the trade of the East and anchored his ships in front of his palaces; the Dutch not only painted the most masterly portraits and conveyed the charm of atmosphere and light with unsurpassed power, but built their country out of the sea, made themselves the foremost merchants of their time, and battled for freedom with a dogged persistence and a heroic patience which put the little country in the center of the stage of human action for a century. Great art does not begin in the genius of a few gifted men; it begins at the very roots of the consciousness of great populations.

It is when the love of the beautiful and the passion for its expression are diffused through a people that men of genius are stimulated and inspired, their imaginations liberated, and their power evoked by the warmth of the atmosphere about them. The Japanese are the most artistic people of the day, not because a few men of genius are painting great pictures, but because the whole life of Japan is touched with beauty and penetrated by the artistic sense. If one wishes to understand why Japanese art has attained so marvelously delicate and subtle a touch, he will find it revealed in the Japanese collections in the Boston Museum of Art, where the domestic utensils in common use in the kitchen display a feeling for beauty, a freshness of invention and form, an individuality of taste, which betray the presence of a well-nigh universal love of the beautiful. The cathedrals which register one of the most magnificent movements of the artistic spirit were not built because a few great architects appeared, but because deep in the heart of the age were the passion of devotion and the passion for beauty of structure and form; so that these noble structures are imperishable records of a great popular movement.

Mr. Poole's story of the Art Institute

of Chicago does not attempt to describe the breadth of the work of technical instruction which is being carried on under its roof; but it does describe the broader work of education which makes it, in certain respects, the foremost institution in one of the greatest of American cities—a popular school for the whole Central West, a perpetual protest against absorption in material affairs, a visible registry of the spiritual scale of values, and, above all, a potent and eloquent teacher of the higher things of life to a struggling, working, and eager democracy.

❀

# The Future Life
## Some Misconceptions

If the silence concerning the form and manner, the occupations and conditions, of the heavenly life which the New Testament maintains had been preserved, or if the symbolism which it occasionally uses as suggestion had never been misunderstood as description, it would have been easier to think of the world to come naturally and simply. A vast amount of irrational and misleading imagery, an artificial and arbitrary projection of the order and method of this present life into the future, obstruct the thought which ought to lie within the vision of faith, not definite and formal, but beautiful as the mountains that rise against a remote horizon; substantial as the earth, but covered as with a veil.

The Bible has suffered far more from the literalists who read its sublimest imagery without a touch of imagination and interpret its parables and idyls as if they were bare records of fact, than from those who have tried to destroy its authority by attacking its accuracy of statement. St. Paul, who was a poet in an age of dialectical skill, has been the victim of a great injustice at the hands of those who have endeavored to run his free, rich, imaginative thought into the molds of formal logic; but St. John, the beloved disciple, to whom the heaven within interpreted the heaven above, has suffered most from those who have essayed to explain a book compact of imagination as if it were a kind of celes-

tial Baedeker. To read the Book of Revelation as description is to build up in the mind an ideal of heaven constructed of the most brilliant, hard, dead substances of earth; to visualize the most free, creative, vital, growing life of the spirit in gold, silver, precious stones, buttressed by walls and behind gates. The tired man or woman, longing for rest and quiet and eager with desire for the silence and sweetness of God's woods and fields, for the great sweep of his sky and the music of running waters which sing his praises in the quiet places of the meadows, instinctively turns away from the picture of the great, splendid city into which St. John's symbolism has been transmuted by unimaginative commentators. The heaven that rose before St. John could not be described; he could convey the glory of it only by symbols; and the inspiring and consoling revelation made to him has, by the transformation wrought by honest but uncomprehending students, hardened into the picture of a city as far removed from the longings and needs of the human soul in its hours of trial and loneliness as are gold and precious stones from those who cry out for food and drink.

Still more misleading and mischievous has been the conception of heaven as the court of the King of kings, ruling in the isolation and surrounded by the pageantry of an absolute monarch. For many decades theology has been gradually emancipating itself from the conception of God which took shape in a society organized into empires and governed by irresponsible rulers removed by a deep chasm from their highest subjects. It was natural that men who were accustomed to think of all political and social order in terms of absolute monarchy should think of the Almighty in the same terms immeasurably heightened. In their experience the king obeyed no law but his own will, and was surrounded by courts whose chief function was to make abject service splendid with form and ceremony, and to symbolize and glorify authority by surrounding it with pomp and magnificence. Nothing could be more artificial, arbitrary, unnatural, than life in attendance on rulers in whose breath were life and death, whose smile was fortune and whose frown was exile. The projection of the order of early society into the life of the world to come intensified the stateliness, rigidity, and frigid magnificence of Oriental courts, and made heaven a place of ranks and orders and crushing formalism of worship. Nothing could have been further removed from the vitality, reality, simplicity, radiant and penetrating love of the New Testament conception of life in the presence of a Father, the immovable foundations of whose power were set in the depths of fathomless love, than this strange transfer to the freedom of heaven of the forms and symbols of the servitude of earth. No one can approach the true idea of heaven until he has put away all the ideas and imagery of irresponsible power and Oriental courts.

Quite as misleading and much more widely diffused is the conception of heaven in terms of ecclesiastical habit, manner, dress, and occupation. These forms and fashions of the external ordering of religion are the stamp of its limitation in time and place, its conformity to the taste or craving of localities or groups of people, its adaptations to circumstance and condition. They are the signs and symbols of religion as a profession; heaven is the consummation of religion as a life. We are so accustomed to our various forms of worship, to the language of our theologies, to the imagery of many of our hymns, to the architecture of our churches, to the dress of our ministers, to all the externalities of religion as a vocation, that these passing things take on permanence, and shape and tinge our thoughts of the heavenly life. A great preacher said not many years ago that the popular idea of God seemed to be that of a gigantic clergyman. Many a boy has struggled for years to rid himself, when he thought of the Father in heaven, of a great, solemn, remote figure, utterly unlike the love in his mother's heart or the tender companionship of his father.

We have come also to identify the highest types of spiritual attainment with certain fixed types of character and vocation, and to think of sainthood as a kind of unnatural goodness. Mr. C. E. Benson, who has written of religion with insight and in a natural tone, says:

I think it is a misfortune of our mundane religious system that we grow to imagine that persons of an ecclesiastical type of sanctity, of a certain definite species of piety, are dearer and nearer to God than secular persons. It is, indeed, sometimes so; the virtues of generosity, ardor, sympathy, loving-kindness, do, indeed, often blossom and bear fruit in ecclesiastical persons; but such persons have no monopoly of these qualities. And there are also faults of the ecclesiastical temperament, such as spiritual complacency, narrowness of judgment, a tendency to condemn all whose beliefs deviate from their own—such faults, indeed, as are patently displayed in the lives of typical priests, men of great personal purity combined with a really appalling uncharitableness, faults which one cannot help feeling, if one reads the Gospel candidly, are far more repugnant, if one may use the words, to the spirit of Christ than even more gross sins. A man of base animal appetites may be converted, may grow to be ashamed of his sensuality, but a self-satisfied man, who is perfectly assured that he can interpret correctly the mind of God, can hardly be converted by any agency whatever.

To get comfort and inspiration from the thought of the life to come we must rid it of all these misleading preconceptions, these inadequate material images, these signs and symbols of our attempts to give the "life of God in the soul of man" expression in the dialect of localities or the *patois* of sects. No projection of the conditions of the life that now is into that which is to come can do any more than confuse and mislead us. Our highest vision of love, our deepest insight into purity, our widest conception of life and growth, our divinest passion for perfection, our most joyful sense of freedom, our keenest delight in the play of thought, imagination, humor, our sweetest affections and most ardent service—it is these that lead the way to heaven and suggest its radiant happiness, its inexhaustible interest, its limitless growth, its perfect content in His presence who gave His children the gift of beauty as well as of righteousness; of variety, freedom, and gayety, as well as of purity, service, sacrifice; who gives them at last the liberty of a home, not the rigid order and repression of a court.

# ANOTHER WOMAN'S VIEW OF THE JAPANESE

## BY ALICE M. BACON

We take pleasure in printing the following article, called out by " The Japanese from a Woman's Point of View" (The Outlook for March 2). Few recent articles in The Outlook have more thoroughly interested its readers, as has been shown in many ways. Miss Bacon, who differs here courteously in some points from " Observer," is widely known as the author of " Japanese Girls and Women," which has been generally recognized as the best popular book on this subject.—THE EDITORS.

IF an understanding of the Japanese were not just at this moment a matter of almost vital importance to us in America, it would not seem quite gracious to so modest and entertaining a writer as " Observer " to meet her effort with even the best-intentioned criticism. If it did not contain so many natural and therefore popular misconceptions of Japanese character, which have spread from the treaty ports to San Francisco, from San Francisco along the Pacific Slope, and which now threaten to infect the whole Union and our future relations with our nearest trans-Pacific neighbor, I should be inclined to leave the truth to make its own way sometime in the "eternal years of God." But inasmuch as the impressions set down by your "Observer" and indorsed by your editorial note will go into a large proportion of the intelligent Christian homes of our land, I cannot but be moved to follow them, and try to interpret from another point of view, closer and more intimate, the hieroglyphics which present so insurmountable an obstacle to many Americans in Japan.

Much of the article is devoted to describing the irritation of the American over the Japanese disregard of time. The rush of American life, governed by the clang of trolley-cars, the hoot of locomotives, the click of typewriters and telegraph instruments, the tinkle of telephones, the buying and selling of choice bits of time by the day, the hour, the minute even, has got on to the nerves of the American woman. She is continually on the jump, rushing from one engagement to another, important or unimportant as the case may be, unhappy unless she is in a hurry, worried if ever

644

so small a fragment of her precious time is left unoccupied. Take her across the Pacific, set her down in the heart of Tokyo, and unless she stays long enough to get the rush and hustle of America out of her nerves she will be irritated beyond endurance.

No Japanese has any idea of buying and selling time. No Japanese can be made to feel that some one else's apparently unreasonable haste should affect his nerves. When you hire your servants, you do not hire their time. You hire their service. What you want done they will do to the best of their ability, and many things that are not " so nominated in the bond " will be done from a conscientious regard for the duty that such service involves ; but their time is their own, and unless some convincing reason for hurry is given, no hurry can be had by the employer. This is especially the case in the relations of Japanese servants with foreign employers, for the Japanese, of whatever grade in life, marking the foreigner's display of emotion without apparent provocation, is apt to discount it. He regards his employer as a child, lacking in wisdom as in self-control, and pays little attention to his moods.

In Japanese service the servant is the humble friend of the family. He knows the family affairs, and interests himself in them. His advice is often asked and taken. He doesn't have to be told to hurry. Of course he hurries when there is need. But his hurry, like his service in all respects, is his own choice and for the seen good of his employer. He is not a horse to be driven, now faster by a stroke of the whip, now slower by a pull on the rein ; his service is more like that of the dog, who knows and loves and follows, watches over and defends his master, and hurries when he hurries. This is the ideal. How far it is from the reality we, who sometimes fail to reach our own ideals, may know; but perhaps it will help to explain the anomalies which strike the foreigner in his Japanese servants.

Perhaps the average resident in Japan has never discovered that blind, unreasoning obedience is not regarded as a virtue by the Japanese. It is in no way related to the ideal of service. No man puts his will and conscience in another's keeping. Each man must obey his reason, not his superior; and the superior can maintain his authority only by convincing those beneath him of his superior reason. In Japanese schools, unless a teacher can keep the obedience and respect of his students by his own personality, he cannot hold his place. Any appeal to higher authority for support in discipline would lower the teacher in the eyes of all. If he cannot convince the boys of the wisdom of good behavior, he is not the man for the place.

I asked one of the Japanese Admirals not long ago why it was that Japanese respected the authority of their own countrymen but were so difficult for foreigners to manage. He smiled pleasantly—he had lived much in foreign countries—as he answered, " We always try to let our men understand that what we want is just. If they feel that, they will do it." This seems to be the limit of authority throughout the country, but within this limit has been evolved not only a population as quiet, as orderly, and as well governed as there is on the earth to-day, but a fighting machine the most efficient in every detail that the world has ever seen.

Two charges are brought against Japanese servants that it is worth while to investigate a little. " The servant who always cheerfully replies ' Yes, madam,' when he ought to say ' No, madam,' does so with polite intent and not at all meaning to annoy or deceive you." This sentence cannot fail to bring to the mind of any one who has employed Japanese service hundreds of times when, stammering and confused, your servant has answered Yes to some question and then quickly changed it to No, and so back and forth with bewildering changes of base, until you made up your mind that the truth was not in him. It is only a difference in the idiom of the two languages that has done so much to defame the character of Japanese servants. The foreign employer seldom knows that assent to a negative question confirms the negative—really a more logical idiom than our own, in which an assent means not, " Yes, I didn't," but " Yes, I did." You come home some day and ask your boy, " Didn't you shake my rugs this morning ?" He blandly replies, " Yes, madam," and half an hour after you see him shaking them. He would willingly have said, " No, madam," had he understood that No meant Yes in that connection.

If you want to get answers that you can understand, ask no negative questions of your Japanese servants. No matter how well versed they may be in English, that particular idiom remains confusing to the end.

" The cook who makes a per cent. on all food bought has no idea of being dishonest, either in the money taken or in wasting his employer's time in spending all between-whiles in bargaining."

There are two important errors in this sentence. One is in the supposition that the cook's time belongs to his employer. As I have already shown, the servant sells his service, not his time. Any time taken for that service is not his employer's but his own, and if he performs the service satisfactorily it is no one's business but his own how much or how little time he takes about it.

But the more important error lies in the supposition that the cook's percentage is his employer's loss, and therefore dishonest. For generations the trade of Japan has been upon its own peculiar basis—a basis mediæval and feudal in its character. Prices have been set, not in accordance with the economic law of supply and demand, but in accordance with the rank or wealth of the purchaser. The merchant did not feel that it was honest to charge the same price to poor and rich alike. The foreigner (presumably rich beyond the dreams of avarice), like the Japanese noble, can make no purchases at shops run on the old Japanese plan without paying a price that will more than cover his cook's percentage. No well-to-do Japanese lady would think of going to market herself. She knows that she would be expected to pay much more than the cook would ask her for the same thing. It would be an expensive economy for any house-keeper to do her own marketing for the sake of saving the cook's percentage.

Buying in quantity never reduces prices. The more you want of anything, especially of such luxuries as are necessities to the extravagant foreigner, the more certain it is that you are rich and can afford to pay well for it. This is, possibly, unjust to the rich, but the Japanese argument that our way is unjust to the poor also has its merits. When you think of our own tenement-house population paying for coal and ice and groceries twenty to thirty per cent. more than our millionaires, there seems a shade of reason and justice and humanity in the Japanese system of distribution. Your cook's percentage merely splits the difference between what he would have to pay were he buying for himself and what you would have to pay if you did your own buying, and you and he are both the gainers. Yon may even be certain that the old lady who grubs up weeds is getting better pay from you, even with the boy's fee taken out, than she could get elsewhere with no fees to pay.

Did your " Observer " know, when she asked the surgeon if she might " once in a while " change the folding of the bandages on which she was working, that they were to be used on the battlefield, by the wounded soldiers themselves? When a man is bleeding to death, working, perhaps, with one hand, blinded, possibly, by a bullet, he has no time to explore for the flap and see whether it is " top-side or under-side." Every soldier was shown exactly how to open and use his first-aid bandage, and many lives were saved by that knowledge and by the " exact uniformity " which seemed so unnecessary to the questioning foreigner.

Of the Japanese understanding of Christianity, your writer was wiser in saying, " He may become a good Japanese Christian, but not a British or Amer-

ican one," than in her previous sweeping skepticism as to whether " any Japanese convert to Christianity ever understands his new belief any better than the policeman understood the law for bathing-clothes." The examples she cites of Japanese who have tried to follow the customs of American Christians without understanding the spirit are hardly sufficient to use as a basis for so wide a generalization. That the Japanese seldom understand or are successful in imitating the Christianity of America and England is possibly true. Now, as in St. Paul's time, " the letter killeth." But they are yearly growing into a more complete understanding of the Christianity of Christ. Even thus, from St. Paul's time on, " the spirit quickeneth." That they may some day be able to give us a new and better understanding of Christ's life and teaching, I, personally, see every reason to hope.

Does it seem strange to any one that the Japanese gentlemen and ladies whom one meets in the diplomatic society of Tokyo do not at once proceed to confidences with the foreigners next to whom they sit at dinner? Can " warm-hearted responsiveness " be expected from men who know that those to whom they are speaking will never go even half-way to meet them? When Japanese come to America, they try to do as Americans do. They learn the language, study the customs and history, eat the food and wear the clothing of the country in which they live. When foreigners go to Japan, they measure all things by their own habits and customs. They find fault with the Japanese who do not learn English as " stupid," and patronize those who do because they do not speak it like their mother tongue. They make no study of the history or thoughts or customs of the people, and secure no basis for conversation other than the merest society talk, and then complain that the Japanese lack " warm-hearted responsiveness." If we had taken one-quarter of the pains to understand the Japanese that they have taken to understand us, we should to-day be friends, not simply in a diplomatic sense, but in mutual confidence brought about by sympathy and good feeling.

# THE GLORY of the CITIES
## BY J. HORACE McFARLAND
## I—WASHINGTON

*THAT the 91,243 trees which line the broad highways of the Nation's capital city provide for it an unusual glory of greenery in summer and of symmetrical twig tracery in winter is due to the intelligent method which, under municipal and not individual control, has adorned one wide avenue with spreading elms, another with sturdy oaks or with rounded lindens, while sugar maples, Japanese gingkos, or European sycamores, each alone in beauty, possess the narrower streets.*

"IT is sometimes called the City of Magnificent Distances, but it might with greater propriety be termed the City of Magnificent Intentions. . . . Spacious avenues that begin in nothing, and lead nowhere; streets, mile-long, that only want houses, roads, and inhabitants; public buildings that need but a public to be complete; and ornaments of great thoroughfares, which only lack great thoroughfares to ornament—are its leading features. . . . Such as it is, it is likely to remain. . . . Few people would live in Washington, I take it, who were not obliged to reside there."

Thus pessimistically wrote Charles Dickens in 1842. He saw no glory in Washington, surely!

Now, however, with the Magnificent Intentions so considerably realized; with the spacious avenues beginning at points of architectural grandeur and leading along lines of beauty to other points of grandeur; with the mile-long streets stretched to four or five times his minimum, and lined with houses along smoothly paved roads, shaded by a very forest of trees; with public buildings of majestic size for housing the 25,000 persons who here do service for 80,000,000 of the public; with monumental ornaments ornamenting monumental thoroughfares, the great Englishman, could he write another series of " American Notes," would see in Washington these same leading features, but glorified, and in process of making the new world's capital the most beautiful abode of government in all civilization.

But what is the glory of Washington?

A MAJESTIC ENGLISH ELM EMPHASIZES THE GRACEFUL DIGNITY OF THE CAPITOL DOME

or, rather, what are its glories? For no candid study of the city will leave the inquirer in condition easily to focus his impressions upon any one of its many interesting features as supremely best.

If there is a chief glory of the city Washington, it must be the memory of the man Washington who conceived it, and whose prophetic vision could not only plan a dignified and adequate seat of government for the Nation that he had fathered, but could, with the practical eye of the trained engineer and the rare skill of the landscape architect, so locate and outline that capital city that, a hundred years later, the best talent of the Nation, when called in consultation, could only confirm his plans, and recommend their restoration where intervening carelessness had permitted departures.

For, be it known, it was President Washington who planned the city. Major Peter Charles L'Enfant was his intelligent assistant, and the capable working out, by this French engineer and Andrew Ellicott, his associate, of the great American's ideas has given to both deserved fame. Yet it was Washington who conceived for his new-born country the first plan ever drawn for a capital city of a great nation; who provided then for the governmental needs of a hundred millions of people while yet the United States could muster barely four and a half millions, dwelling in a mere fringe along the Atlantic. It was Washington's genius which, "with the spiritual vision of the seer and the scientific skill of the surveyor, fixed upon the most strategic and beautiful site in all the hundred-mile stretch of the Potomac where he was to choose," as Commissioner Macfarland puts it.

Other great capitals have grown into beauty more or less incidentally, and there is extant an impression that the plan of Paris, then a city of 600,000 inhabitants, gave the keynote for the plan of the new city upon the Potomac. Yet Paris owes its present beauty and its present city plan largely to the work done under Louis Napoleon, nearly fifty years after the death of Washington, who had not only thus early settled the unique plan of what he called "The Federal City," but had secured for it the land of the District of Columbia (mostly free of cost, by his personal influence and solicitation), and built the old Capitol, the President's House, and other structures.

Indeed, Paris may well have profited in 1850–59 by Washington's prescience, but, as well stated by Glenn Brown, it is an incontrovertible fact that "the unique and distinctive feature of Washington, its numerous focal points of interest and beauty from which radiate the principal streets and avenues, was not suggested by any city of Europe."

As Thomas Jefferson was intensely interested in founding the federal city, rendering to his great associate invaluable aid, and as James Madison also devoted his great influence and ability to the same work, it will be seen that the capital city wears a chaplet of glory in the names of its founders and supporters. Small wonder is it that, after visiting and critically considering the great civic works of Europe, as found in London, Paris, Rome, Venice, Vienna, Budapest, Frankfort, and Berlin, the eminent Commission appointed in 1901, including Daniel H. Burnham, Frederick Law Olmsted, Jr., Charles F. McKim, and Augustus St. Gaudens, should seek only to restore and develop the original designs of President Washington and Major L'Enfant! This able Commission, serving in an admirable spirit of high National pride, without compensation, had before them the best city plan ever devised, a model for all the world, and indeed a glory of Washington.

With all this advantage of its incomparable plan, Washington did· not—indeed, could not—rapidly develop into beauty. The Nation was weak; not all its statesmen saw beyond the moment, and the capital city, ravaged by fire during the War of 1812 (when the President's house first became the "White House" by reason of the white paint applied to cover the marks of the conflagration), fully deserved the sarcastic comments made by Dickens in 1842. The original plan was forgotten, the great Mall was invaded by business buildings and by a railway, and only the superb Capitol itself, hemmed in by disgraceful conditions, gave hope and promise. Then came the beginning of the revulsion, under President Grant, when Alexander R. Shepherd, a man with determination and imagination, began to work toward the execution of the first President's plans. Checked he was ; yet there was progress, until now, with the pride of the Nation in its capital city, increasing as each man becomes a better citizen by seeing the physical home of his Government, the way seems almost clear for the completion of the city beautiful, the city that must have been to Washington a dream of faith and hope when he fought through its place on the map.

No intelligent American walks the streets or gazes at the buildings of the Nation's capital without a swelling of National pride, and a better realization of the value of his citizenship. For Washington alone, of all the cities on the earth, belongs to all the people of a great Nation, and not merely to its inhabitants or to a ruler. Through his chosen representatives in Congress each American voter has an equal share in the actual detail of its government ; for, again, Washington alone of American cities is governed, not by its residents, but by the National Legislature.

Its residents do not have the franchise, though they are taxed five millions a year, which covers half the cost of maintaining the city, the other five millions being the share assumed by the General Government. As "Uncle Sam" owns more than half the land in the District of Columbia, upon which he pays no taxes directly, and as he controls all the expenditures and appropriates the whole ten millions as he—the Congress—sees fit, it will be noted that he—that is, "we the people"—has a good thing of the partnership which has prevailed since 1878. In addition the Government gets the water it uses distributed by the city free.

Now some one will exclaim, as I did promptly, that "taxation without representation is tyranny," and that it is a shame and not a glory that citizens of Washington do not vote. But *they* do not think so !

When I asked the able head of the District Commission, the Hon. Henry B. F. Macfarland, what he considered a

LIKE ARBOREAL CANDELABRA ARE THE HORSE-CHESTNUT TREES WHEN IN BLOOM

glory of the city he loves and for which he labors unceasingly, his reply was illuminating—and surprising :

" Washington, without the suffrage, is proud of its active civic spirit, constantly manifested through more than a score of actively maintained citizens' organizations, as well as through letters and public hearings. With no partisan politics, it has no graft in its administration, and real government by public opinion. Having no specific civil service law, it is nevertheless under the merit system.

" Washington is proud of its people—its law-abiding, Sunday-keeping people, of an unusual degree of intelligence. Office-holders ? Yes, we have twenty-five thousand of them in service, making, with their families, less than one-fourth of our population. They are a welcome addition to our wholesome society, for they are inevitably selected people, and make good citizens.

" Don't sympathize with Washington for lacking the voting franchise. Your vote gives you a restricted expression once or twice a year, but our active citi-zens express themselves continually, to the Congressional committees on the District of Columbia, and to the Commissioners. And they are heeded, too !

" A few days ago a public hearing was arranged upon the question of obtaining 75-cent illuminating gas. More than a hundred citizens were there, and they freely expressed themselves, pro and con. Do you do better than that in your partisan-governed, suffrage-using cities?"

I began to think less of my boasted privilege of voting, often without real civic expression, for candidates selected under a plan which might often be called the demerit system ! But the Commissioner went on :

" Washington is proud, too, of her society, of the opportunities for mental, moral, and social uplift open to any respectable person who becomes resident here. Not very long since, at a dinner, but one of several on the same evening, I met six gentlemen who had seen Daniel Webster, two of them having heard him speak. I do not name these gentlemen, but their presence together upon any occasion in the city of

THE AMERICAN LINDEN GRACES MASSACHUSETTS AVENUE
In the distance Thomas Circle is seen

New York would have been a matter of special note. Here it was merely incidental. In our halls great men from all the world are constantly addressing the public ; in our churches eminent divines are constantly heard. All nations send but its importance is less, its influence smaller, than anywhere else, for the reasons I have given."

And then the Commissioner's eye kindled again as he returned to that attribute of Washington of which he had

POPLAR TREES ON T STREET, N. W.

here their learned men, their scientists, their inventors—we have more scientists at work here than are in any other city. The inevitable association, the opportunities for the mentally alert, are stimulating and uplifting.

" The smart set ? Certainly, it is here, as it is in New York, Boston, Chicago ; written and spoken so often and so well : " I used to hope that Washington would become the most beautiful city in the world, but I now believe it is already so. I have seen Paris, and I no longer yield to it superiority. And as we proceed with the execution of Washington's marvelous conception we will inspire all the world with the harmony and beauty, the convenience and comfort, as well as the laws and customs, of the capital city planned by a great prophet, who could look a hundred years ahead at a time when the Federation of the States

and the majestic shaft of the Washington Monument dominating the view as twin radial centers; as the already striking outlines of the Mall became evident, and the notable "circles" and intersections served to locate the immense and digni-

THE NOTABLE JAPANESE GINGKO OR MAIDENHAIR TREE LINES THIS APPROACH TO THE AGRICULTURAL DEPARTMENT

was loose, and when many of his compatriots could see no need for such a national capital."

As we traversed Massachusetts Avenue and then the Sixteenth Street boulevard to Meridian Hill, where much of this great and singular city lay spread out at our feet, the noble dome of the Capitol

fied structures that house the Government's vast business, I could but share in the enthusiasm of my friend, and believe that Washington is even now a glory of and to the United States.

But there were flaws in the crystal, and the Commissioner's face clouded as he pointed out the unharmonious and jarring effect of several sky-scraping, matchbox-on-end apartment-houses. We live in America, and man's "sacred" right to flaunt discordant architecture—and hideous billboards—from his private property upon his defenseless neighbors has not yet been successfully traversed. Yet here in Washington there is hope; for there is no State constitution to protect the man who would say, in effect, "Am I my brother's keeper?" as he injures his neighbor through greed or through ignorance. A recently passed enactment prohibits the erection on any street or avenue of a structure higher than the width of the street. If a localized earthquake or a beneficent conflagration should remove from the view in Washington certain exclamation points of architecture that cry aloud in obtrusive disharmony to the great plan, I fancy the authorities could restrain their tears!

Note this "cornice law," ye cañon-making American cities, in this your proper model: no structure to be higher than the width of the street upon which it fronts. I think this law is a real glory of Washington.

Have I said anything about the trees of Washington? Of them I may only speak in restraint, for truly they would too greatly engage my tree-loving pen! No such trees adorn a city anywhere else in America, I believe. Each avenue planted with one variety only, not with the hit-or-miss result of individual preferences, these highways are ripening into a very great glory. "Unter den Linden" in America is on Massachusetts Avenue, and the oaks of East Capitol Street are superb. When the horse-chestnuts bloom on Thirteenth Street, one lingers long to enjoy the vista of flower and leaf. The gingko avenue giving approach to the Agricultural Department has taught the country the value of this sturdy but delicately beautiful tree. The superb European sycamores that shade the broad western approach to the Capitol, and those punctuating the White House sidewalk, show how intelligent care will produce the utmost tree luxuriance, despite sheet asphalt and granolithic paving. The shrubs, the evergreens, the great magnolias of the South, the symmetrical lawn trees that are profusely used to adorn the circles, the small parks or "squares," the triangular street and avenue intersections, the grounds about the public buildings—all these are admirable and an invaluable means of education to the whole country, twelve months in the year.

Only since 1872 has Washington been systematically planting and controlling trees under municipal authority. The $560,000 that has been spent in the work has in a generation added far more to the beauty and comfort of Washington than could twenty times as much have added, spent in any other way. The conditions previous to 1870, when as yet swine rooted in the streets of the capital city, did not foster tree-planting. But what a great tree means to a great building is seen in viewing the Capitol from the foreground of the superb elm (said to have been planted by President Washington) near its eastern front. And when it is noted that the planting of the Capitol grounds is a memorial of the genius of the elder Olmsted, increasing beauty of tree and shrub, in relation to the building and its approaches, is assured.

Again, American cities, note the glory of a city in its trees that has arisen in only thirty years, through intelligent public planting and control!

It may be said that I have spoken of the civic advantages of Washington only as seen through officially favorable eyes. I sought other views, and the ideas of a private citizen, a physician who has been a resident of the Federal city for thirty years, came to me:

"Washington is a moral and law-abiding city, with little disorder and less drunkenness. My practice takes me out at all hours of the night, and I am sure my wife would be as safe on the streets as I am at any time.

"Our churches are particularly alive in missionary work, and Washington is helping to evangelize the world by sustained and liberal contributions, and by an especial interest in benighted lands, of which we have unusual opportunities to hear.

"Our social opportunities are great, and they are used freely—more freely because of the higher tone given to our populace through the demands of the civil service examinations upon those aspiring to Government work.

"Vote? I don't want to vote, or to bother with partisan politics. Why should I? The Commissioners and the Congressional Committees hear us about our troubles, when we have them, and they heed us, too. I think we do better than you do, with your 'boss' fights and your foolish political methods of city government. We have full expression through our Board of Trade and our Business Men's Leagues; and we get more for our money than most cities

THE BEAUTY OF THE CAPITOL IS ENHANCED
BY THE WELL-PLACED TREES ON EVERY SIDE

IN MAY THE NOTABLE "EMPRESS TREE," OR PAULOWNIA, IS COV-
ERED WITH FLOWERS OF HELIOTROPE COLOR AND FRAGRANCE

do, even though we pay more than a proper share of the Federal Government's local expenses. Compare our tax rate, our parks, our clean streets, our schools, with those of cities of equal size, paying much higher taxes under partisan rule, and you will understand why we are satisfied to be 'disfranchised,' as you call it."

As I walked away from the doctor's comfortable home on a broad avenue shaded by four rows of well-kept red-oaks, pondering on what he had said, I noticed another glory of Washington. I saw no poles or wires on her great main thoroughfares. Electric cars there are,

in plenty—and I bought six tickets for a quarter, good on the lines of either of the two traction companies, with free transfers as needed. The underground trolley drives the cars, and underground cables carry other wires, in most of the city, and every year decreases the number of the few remaining poles, soon to be only a hateful memory.

Take notice again, ye voting and be-wired American cities: Washington has six-for-a-quarter fares, free transfers, underground trolleys, and yet her traction companies pay four per cent. yearly on their gross receipts to the city, while making decent profits for their stockholders. Naturally, the municipal owner-ship problem does not worry this non-partisan city—which is perhaps another glory.

As Washington has been blamed with being a city of Government clerks only—how correctly may be known when one compares the 25,000 Federal employees with the 326,435 inhabitants of the District on May 22, 1906—it seemed well to ascertain how these public servants look upon the city of their residence.

An official in the Forest Service was somewhat discouraging when he said that Washington is primarily an official city; that the Government employees are of mediocre average and without ambition; that "society" was too ex-pensive for the worker; and that the really capable officials come here at a sacrifice.

He added, however, that "conditions are constantly improving ;" and when I pursued my inquiries a trifle forcefully, he admitted that he lived in a suburb, outside the District entirely, had made no attempt—having had no opportunity

—to come into social relations in the city, and that "society," in his view, was the "smart set " of lavish expendi-ture. Am I to blame for feeling that he was not a fair witness, and that his state-ment plucked no leaf from Washington's garland of city glories ?

The next man, an investigator in the wonderful Plant Industry division of the more wonderful Agricultural Department, had a different view. He said :

" I like Washington as a place of resi-dence because it is a pleasant place in which to live, and especially because of the great opportunities it affords for study at first hand. We get the big men from all the world here, both in science, in practice, and in true society. I find the social life of the city, in which I have lived a dozen years, not only pleasant but profitable, for I constantly meet new people of great attainments.

" In my division, for instance, are two lawyers and a physician, doing good work for the Government, but here pri-marily for use of the unequaled oppor-tunities they find for special study—

GREAT ELMS DIGNIFY DUPONT CIRCLE, THE CENTER OF
THE OFFICIAL AND DIPLOMATIC RESIDENCE DISTRICT

opportunities freely available here, and nowhere else in the world.

"The Government employees? They are above the average, and, while some are unambitious, I believe they are superior in intelligence, in interest in their work, and in ambition to the employees of any great railroad. They are well paid for the most part ; and their shorter hours give them opportunities for study and for relaxation." ·

As I looked at the rosy-cheeked boys who called my cheery friend "Papa," I could see that Washington had a full share of one of America's chief glories— the American family !

To the expressions of the District official, the plain citizen, the Government employee, it seemed very desirable to add a Congressional view. This was supplied by Senator Gallinger, of New Hampshire, Chairman of the Senate Committee on the District of Columbia, in which position he succeeded the late Senator McMillan, himself long an enthusiastic friend of the Federal city. That Senator Gallinger, who had been intimately associated in the work of governing the District for sixteen years, has continued and even increased the interest which led Senator McMillan to foster the revival of the great Washington plan, needed no telling. As he sat in the beautiful Senate District Committee-room, made historically interesting by reason of the preservation in it of the marvelous cut-glass chandeliers under which Nellie Grant was married, and which the Senator rescued from the junk pile to which a White House refurnishing had consigned them, it was easy to see that he believed fully in the glory of Washington, present and to come, and that his belief colored his efforts.

"We work continually with the idea of making Washington the most beautiful city in all the world," said the Senator. "We believe that all American citizens who are, indeed, potential citizens of this, their capital city, would have it so if they could see Washington even as it is now.

"Do you comprehend the educational value of a great and beautiful capital? Nothing so increases patriotism as a visit to Washington, where many for the first time realize the immensity of the Nation, its wealth, its importance, and its world relations, as they see the Capitol, the Library of Congress, the White House, the Washington Monument, and the great governmental buildings. A better sense of averages and of proportion is established in their minds, and the influence of the city itself, in its broad avenues, its noble structures, its many groups of statuary, and its wonderful city plan, is wholesome, educative, and inspiring.

"Washington should, and does, and will, serve as a model to all America for municipal development. It is fitting that here should be worked out, by the Nation's representatives, the intimate problems of city government, and especially the making of a model city, the city beautiful.

"Several hundred girl graduates in New Hampshire educational institutions gave up class jewelry and graduating dresses last year to provide for a visit to Washington. To these young women that visit was memorable and of immense educational value. Washington should be visited, and studied, and enjoyed by all the people, for their own benefit and that of the United States."

I spoke to the Senator of the absence of the franchise among the citizens of Washington. He smiled as he replied:

"I don't think they miss the franchise any ! They express themselves continually, and with entire freedom. This Committee is practically the city council of Washington, and we are constantly giving hearings on various subjects.

"There are twenty or more Citizens' Associations in the city, and I think a week seldom passes in which they do not all memorialize this Committee, or obtain a public hearing, on some matter of city affairs.

"Sometimes the suggestions are impracticable. For instance, when we required, by Congressional enactment, the traction companies to change their routes so as to deliver traffic according to our plans at the new Union Station, the requisition meant the expenditure of nearly a million dollars for new construction. Yet here is a proposition, submitted as an amendment to that bill, that we shall ask Congress to increase the tax on their gross receipts from four per cent. to twelve per cent. annually, which is obviously unfair.

"We are always working on city problems. We must keep down black smoke, shut out, so far as possible, smoke-making locomotives from the new Union Station, look after educational and sanitary matters, and do countless things to make and to maintain Washington as a model city."

When I thought of the Boards of Aldermen and the City Councils that are the governing bodies of our American cities, and of their average composition under partisan conditions, I could not but feel that now, at least, Washington does vastly better under its interested Congressional committees, having absolutely no partisan relation to the city's affairs, treating its work from a National standpoint, and acting through an able Commission.

Charles Dickens intimated that no one would wish to live in Washington who could avoid it. He would be astonished to see the many superb residences now to be found there, in which live people of culture, eminence, and wealth who are in no way connected with governmental affairs. Why are they there?

Because they find the capital a most beautiful place in which to dwell, its climate suggesting summer absence only as does that of New York or St. Louis, and its opportunities for social intercourse being unparalleled. Any worthy person may secure admittance to the unique Wednesday evening salon of Alexander Graham Bell; any one may see and meet the great and the "near great." The entire vicinity, from Mount Vernon's sacred shrine to Arlington's hardly less memorable location, is rich in association with history, with action, and with present beauty. Why not, then, live in Washington if one can?

Have I shown some glories of our National capital? It is not perfect—for it is not finished, and we are not *quite* a perfect people!—but it shows to America many of the attributes that make for such perfection as is possible to fallible though aspiring humanity. And it is *our* Federal City, the tangible evidence in stone and metal and trees of the great dream of the Father of *our* country. It is as we have made it, and it will be glorious as we glory in it, and assist in completing its glories. Thus, after all, the glory of Washington is the United States, and Washington is the glory of the United States!

# TO A CHILD

### (WITH A COPY OF HANS ANDERSEN'S FAIRY TALES)

### BY HAROLD TROWBRIDGE PULSIFER

When the garden-gate closes behind you
　　With a click that is certain and sure,
And its bars seem to harshly remind you,
　　You have lost what you once thought secure;
When the lock on the gateway is guarded
　　By the hard-knotted growth of the vine,
While your feet in the path are retarded
　　By the weeds which your footsteps entwine;
When the bottle-crowned wall of the garden
　　Seems to frown at your plodding below;
When the strings of your heart seem to harden,
　　As though turning to ice and to snow,—
Let the leaves of this book be your key then,
　　Be your path and your postern-gate too,
That its deep tangled haunts you may see then
　　In a glass that is clearer than dew!

THOMAS MOTT OSBORNE

# AN "HONOR DEMOCRAT"

For many years The Outlook has maintained its belief that the merchants, manufacturers, bankers, and railway managers of this country are not all materialists. Generally speaking, their success in promoting and managing great affairs of business is in proportion to their idealism. Believing this, The Outlook has not been surprised at the influence, political and social, which has been exerted in the State of New York in a very quiet but very effective way by Mr. Thomas M. Osborne, one time Mayor of the city of Auburn. In the crucial political campaign last autumn between Mr. Hughes and Mr. Hearst, Mr. Osborne was one of the distinct figures. He is typical of that growing body of American young men who are carrying the enthusiasm for ideals into business affairs as well as into the arts and so-called "learned professions." The work which such men are doing in the community ought to be known to the public, and therefore we have asked one of his personal friends, without the knowledge of Mr. Osborne, to give our readers some account of the man and his work.—THE EDITORS.

"THE great vice of our people," says Phillips Brooks, "in their relation to the politics of the land, is cowardice. . . . It is the disposition of one part of our people to fall in with current ways of working, to run with the mass ; and of another part to rush headlong into this or that new scheme or policy of opposition merely to escape the stigma of conservatism. Neither timidity nor recklessness is really brave. No man on any side is truly brave in thought who is listening for other people's voices either to assent to or to contradict them."

As the people discover the quality of the new Governor of New York, they begin to understand how much the State and the Nation are indebted to certain members of the Democratic party who exerted themselves to bring about the election of Mr. Hughes and the defeat of Mr. Hearst. The success of the Democratic ticket, with the exception of its head, confirms the accuracy of the saying that "any decent Democrat could have been elected Governor of New York last November." We need to remember that the salvation of the State from the domination of the Hearst element of the Democratic party was due to the independent vigor and disinterested public spirit of some twenty thousand Democratic voters who marked their ballots for Mr. Hughes and then for the rest of their own party ticket. The acknowl-edged leader of these "Honor Democrats" was and is Thomas M. Osborne, of Auburn.

Mr. Osborne comes from an abolitionist stock and is of Quaker descent. His forbears were people not afraid of being in a minority. He belongs in the company of educated young Americans who make it a part of their ordinary duty to take some active part in public affairs. To name only the untimely dead, he belongs with such efficient promoters of the public good as Governors Russell and Wolcott, of Massachusetts, and the cousins Congressmen Sherman Hoar and Rockwood Hoar, men who inherited traditions of family honor and the power to see clearly, to think independently, and to will nobly.

The careers of such men refute the vulgar sneers about the incompetency of educated men and their inability to deal with practical politics. Mr. Osborne was at Harvard at the same time with Theodore Roosevelt, Robert Bacon, Curtis Guild, Sherman Hoar, William H. Baldwin, Jr., and many other young men who have proved in successful public careers that good blood and a sound education are not obstacles to political influence in a democracy. Some of these men are Republicans and some are Democrats, but they are all men who love their country, and believe in the good sense of their fellow-citizens and in the principles on which the Republic is founded. They are men who hate "boss rule," the spoils system, demagoguism, and all the evils of "special privilege." They are men who can be relied upon to stand firm for what they think is right, and to "keep the rudder true," whether the wind of popular prejudice be adverse or favorable.

Mr. Osborne was born and brought up in Auburn, the town where the great Republican William H. Seward lived and ruled in the minds and hearts of his fellow-citizens, and whose present member of Congress is the Republican leader on the floor of the House of Representatives. Osborne's father, David M. Osborne, by integrity and intelligent industry, built up the great shops of the Osborne Harvester Company, and was the honored Mayor of the city which his business enterprise had helped to develop. The son was sent to Adams Academy in Quincy, Massachusetts, and then to Harvard, where he spent four happy and successful years. There he got a good grip on the ideals of life that are transmitted from generation to generation in the Harvard atmosphere to those who are alert to use the opportunities of their college life. There he got hold of the idea that opportunity creates obligation, and that college-bred men have a duty to promote civic righteousness and good government. A generous disposition, a kindly humor, a large fund of information derived from reading and travel, a reasonable success in athletics, an exceptional musical taste and ability, combined with a manliness that everybody respected to make him popular in the best sense of the word, and these qualities have stood him in good stead in later life.

After graduation he plunged into business, and the death of his father almost immediately threw upon him great responsibilities. It seemed as if the business of D. M. Osborne & Co. could not go on without its directing head. A meeting of the stockholders declared in favor of closing the shops and mills, and taking down the sign over the office door. But young Osborne said, "No, I will not take down that sign. This business is going on." He assumed the presidency of the company, and for sixteen years conducted it with ability and success.

Mr. Osborne came back to his native city just when the Blaine-Cleveland campaign was absorbing public attention. Though of the strongest Republican inheritances, bred in the best anti-slavery traditions, he could not bring himself to support Mr. Blaine, and so cast for Mr. Cleveland his first vote at a Presidential election. Finding himself more and more allied by conviction and principle to the Democratic party, he became increasingly active and influential in its counsels. Auburn chose him to be President of its Board of Education, and he rendered valuable service in that capacity. But Auburn, like every community in which one party has had long and undisputed control, was "ring-ruled;" the city charter was antiquated, and the prevailing methods of administration were shiftless if not corrupt. Osborne assailed these intrenched traditions and customs with good humor, with keen sarcasm, with candid truth-telling, with unanswerable argument. Three years ago, after an exciting campaign, he was elected Mayor on a non-partisan ticket—the first Democrat ever elected to that office in the banner Republican stronghold. He proved an unexpectedly good campaigner. His success was due to his personal popularity, and the confidence of the people, who had known him from boyhood, in his ability and sincerity. He is democratic by temperament and conviction. To the boys at the George Junior Republic, where he is the President of the Trustees, he is "Uncle Tom." Among his friends he is the appreciative lover of good books and fine scenery, of music and drama. At his office desk he is the alert, resourceful man of affairs. On the stump he is no orator, but a plain-speaking man, attractive in bearing and appearance, big and good-tempered, lucid in argument, going straight to his point, taking everybody into his confidence, trustful of the good sense and right purpose of the people. He hits hard, but never unfairly. He never poses and never trims. Everybody knows that there is no envy or malice in his attack upon the "machine," and that he has nothing personal to gain in seeking public office.

As Mayor, though in his first term he had to deal with a hostile Council, he accomplished most of the reforms he had at heart. Though manifestly an idealist, he proved thoroughly practical. Though a reformer, he did not keep making futile expositions of the defects in men and things. Though critical, he was also constructive. He secured the new city charter which was so sorely needed, reorganized the different executive departments on a sound business basis, put through the public improvements that had been tied up with red tape or held up by people anxious for a share of the possible spoils, and generally managed the city affairs as he had managed his own shops. His messages and public addresses were absolutely candid. They taunted no one, they sneered at nothing, and there were no perversions or distortions of fact; but they stated plain truths and argued openly and fairly. If he discovered incompetency or rascality in any city department, he made sure of the facts, placed the responsibility just where it belonged, and then calmly and conscientiously told his fellow-citizens all about it. He recognized in them the real and responsible rulers. He guided his official course by certain rules, which by the time of his third Annual Message he had boiled down to five:

1. Allow nothing to be everybody's business.

2. Make everything some one's business.

3. Let no one interfere with or share another's responsibility.

4. Put in force a clear and simple system, but

5. Avoid red tape.

For himself he had but one ambition—to make the city administration thoroughly efficient, and to lift the civic life of the community to a higher level. He wanted to add to the comfort and well-being of all honest folk.

Such achievements, both political and practical, have made him a man marked for higher office and responsibility. His party recognized his ability and promise of usefulness. He was "available" in a political sense; and if he had only consented to "keep still" there would have been no question about his securing whatever promotion his party could command for him. But he has never been able to put party loyalty ahead of principle. And when Mr. Hearst and his followers and allies attempted to seize the leadership in the State, it was Osborne who organized the opposition, called the Albany Conference, fought the nomination, and swung the independent element of his party into line for Mr. Hughes, believing that he was thus rendering the best service not only to the State but also to the Democratic party itself. Patriotic Americans delight to honor such men. Mr. Osborne may bide his time. His executive ability is proved; he is not afraid of hard work, his honesty is unassailable, his courage has been thoroughly tested. He is sure of an increasing influence in public life, and it is to be hoped that some day he will be in the service of the State or Natiion.

Let another quotation from Phillips Brooks describe Osborne's political disposition: "The thoroughgoing partisan and the captious cynic are both cowards. The loud and indiscriminate applause of one, the other's miserable sneer, both are contemptible beside the open, sympathetic thoughtfulness of the man who believes in his country but thinks for himself, and so is always bringing an intelligent disagreement or an intelligent assent as a real contribution to his country's life."

MOTHER AND CHILDREN
By Elizabeth Nourse

# ART AND DEMOCRACY[1]

## FIRST PAPER

## HOW THE CHICAGO ART INSTITUTE REACHES THE PEOPLE

### BY ERNEST POOLE

BRONZE LION BY EDWARD KINNEYS AT MAIN ENTRANCE

"OF course we are still in our infancy," said the president. The Chicago Art Institute has been open nearly every day for twenty-seven years; its library of forty-five hundred volumes and prints of all the great pictures in Europe is visited yearly by over fifty thousand people; its almost daily lectures have an annual attendance of forty-five thousand; its constant succession of picture exhibits draw from four to ten thousand people in one free day—over six hundred thousand last year; its schools of drawing and painting, architecture, designing, sculpture, illustration, and normal instruction train yearly over twenty-four hundred; it employs sixty teachers, and always keeps some of them studying abroad; it has sent thousands of graduates back North and West and South to teach art in schools scattered all the way from Alabama to Oregon; and of its alumni, sixteen had pictures in the Paris Salons of 1904 and 1905. "We are still in our infancy," said the president.

It is a free day, a Sunday afternoon; a great modern exhibit is here, and the galleries, antique and modern, are thronged by ten thousand men and women and children come out of the forty

[1] This article will be followed by two others: one describing the successful effort in an Indiana town to interest the whole community in art; the other, the well-known arts and crafts movement in Deerfield, Massachusetts.

million in the West. Like the Louvre or the Vatican? No. The same rich lights and repose and a few of the same serene old works of the Masters. But the people! There is something grotesque and pathetic, and something deeply impressive too, in these ten thousand come from the millions beginning to see. Loudly critical, pretending, or humbly silent, dazed; shrewd, kindly, curious, amused, or just quietly happy; many languages are here, for Chicago is a mixing-bowl for the nations of the earth; many American dialects are here, for men and women are come from North and West and South; all kinds of attire are here, for here are rich people and poor, from city, village, farm, and ranch. Eyes understanding, eyes art-hungry, eyes hopelessly blind—all are here. Young people are here, trying to see and feel, and beginning, with a long life of health and power and widening vision ahead. America is here.

"Why, yes, young feller, I'd be glad to." The speaker was a short, stout, middle-aged man with sandy hair and shrewd, kindly blue eyes. "Though I don't suppose I know much more about pictures than you do. You see, I can't get here often. I run a grocery store down the State, and a two hundred and twenty acre farm besides. Just built a new barn. So I'm kept busy. Here, we'll go down this gallery.

"What makes me hot," he went on, "is that I didn't find this place sooner. I struck it, just happened in, about a year ago, and since then I've been here every time I'm in town. And I'm just beginning to get the hang of the pictures. Except this!" He stopped and pointed scornfully to a fantastic creation—probably a landscape.

"Now this," he said, "is what the catalogue calls 'By the Impressionist School.' Are you impressed? I ain't—not a bit—only downright annoyed. I can't make head nor tail to the thing! I've figured an' figured, but the closer I get to it, the worse it looks. The man either painted in his sleep, in a regular rip-roarin' nightmare, or else he struck work before it was done. Seems a pity, don't it, if this American business rush has to go into painting too!

"An hour ago I saw an old farmer contemplatin' at it, and he looked so long and hard and curious that I got close to listen. He was one of those 'blessed are the meek' kind of old ones, and so was his wife. They looked a long time, sort of dazed. 'Well, Jenny,' he said at last, with a quiet touch of a smile, 'there is plenty of paint here. Nice rich paint—ain't it it?' And they went on.

"Funny what queer things you can hear people say, if you listen," he remarked as we moved down the gallery. "Maybe you don't know how to use your eyes and ears without apparent effort, but if you'd run a country store for sixteen years—you would. Now look here." He stopped before a weird, fascinating night scene—"Arabs on the Desert."

"Here's something you can make head or tail to. It's what I call interesting. In the first place, it's the real thing; I don't know beans about Arabs, but I could swear they look just like this. And, second, look at the way he puts on his colors. *He* don't paint as if he was reelin' drunk! No, sir, he's got some self-respect. And there's nothing cheap about it either, like a circus poster. Look at that blurrish white moon! Look at them heavy-hangin' black clouds, and the dark mysterious face of that there camel. Look at this Arab chief's face under his turban, with eyes sunk 'way in, kind of ghostly. It makes you feel things, don't it? Well, that's Art. Give me scenes to make me think and feel, and then rich colors to give 'em a tone. That's it." He paused a moment, and added simply: "There ain't many colors in my town."

For the next half-hour he showed me, one by one, his favorites, which all supplied the color that was lacking in his town. An ancient German castle just before a storm, an altar scene in St. Mark's in Venice, dark rocking ships in harbor on a windy night, Sicilian flower-girls, "Alice," two lovers in a boat—not fishing—"Darius at the feet of Alexander," a gay studio scene in the Latin Quarter, "Bringing Home the New-born Calf." At last we stopped before "The Trial of Catherine of Aragon," and here

ALICE
By William M. Chase

for a long time we feasted our eyes on Abbey's soft rich reds and golds and blues.

"The wonder to me," he murmured at last, "is how the English people ever let that old villain of a Henry rule over 'em." More admiring and wondering. Some twenty minutes passed. Then he started

vise you to come here often. It's good for any young man. Good luck to you! Good-by!"

"See that measly little picture?" It was another free day. An indignant, practical-faced Chicagoan with glinting gray eyes grasped his solemn thin friend

PORTRAIT OF A GIRL—REMBRANDT

and jerked out his watch. "Train time! Yes, and more too! I'll have to hurry. Well, young feller," he turned, smiling, and held out his hand, "I hope I've shown you a little. I don't know much, except that I want all kinds of interesting scenes, because I can't afford a trip to Europe. And I want color, plenty of it, like this. My town is mighty bare in that way, and somehow this place has made me sort of picture hungry. I ad-

by the arm, pointed to Van Ostade's "Jubilee," and then to his catalogue. "Thirty—thousand—dollars! That's what they claim it's worth. Now look at it!" Two long looks of withering scorn. He turned with a knowing wink.

"A little touch of graft in the air— eh?" The two citizens turned and gazed at each other, the light of Reform rising and flashing in their eyes.

"Say, Jim," whispered the solemn thin

one, " do we taxpayers get stuck for all this ?"

" Not yet," Jim admitted. " It's run by a syndicate of about three thousand people with a few big wise ones on top. But sooner or later, mark my words, they'll get us all in ! And then the price of this blamed thing will be raised from thirty thousand to sixty ! Oh, I see their game," he murmured. " Plain as day. Watered stock." Again he turned a last indignant look on the meek, unoffending, world-famous little picture. " Two feet square. Not an inch more, an' shopworn at that. Thirty—thousand—dollars ! Come on !"

A Polish laborer turned and looked after them, his long, big-boned face breaking into a smile. Then he drew a deep, contented breath and looked back at a dark-brown Van Dyke, and at once forgot all the crowd. He was a giant, but his threadbare clothes hung loose and his hands were thin ; he drooped slightly as he stood there, resting his weight heavily on one foot, which had a big hole in the instep of the dusty shoe. One hand slowly tugged on his soft yellow mustache, and his big deep-blue eyes shone. Now and then he smiled and nodded slowly to himself.

" That big Pole ?" said the guard. "Oh, yes. He comes every Sunday. He don't say anything to me or anybody else. Only once long ago at closing time he asked me to mark out on some paper how to walk back to the Stock-yards. That's a good two hours' walk, but from the look of him I guess he walks both ways. He never misses a Sunday, though, not even in blizzards, and he always stays till closing time at five o'clock. I've seen him spend two whole hours in front of that one Van Dyke, without hardly moving. And Rembrandt's " Portrait of a Girl " is another old chum of his. Once he brought a little girl dressed up nicely in American clothes ; but she was like a good many Americans, she couldn't see what he saw. She fidgeted and giggled at him, called him ' a silly.' And the big chap looked kind of sad that day. Since then he comes alone."

" Right dis way, boys," said a tall, delighted negro preacher He wore a shiny old frock suit, and by the looks of his " boys " they had all come straight from his church. He led them through to the end of the modern galleries, stopped before "The Two Disciples at the Tomb," and stretched out his hand. All looked in admiring silence.

" Boys," he said simply, " dis yeah pictah took de first prize of all de hundreds of pictahs by all de American artists. An' de man who did it was a niggah." Instinctively the little group drew closer, and the voice grew intense and low ; from outside the circle you could barely hear it. " Why could he do it ? Because he got de beauty of God an' Jesus 'way deep down in his heart. Why do I keep bringin' all you boys, dozens and dozens, heah to see ? Because, boys, I know sometimes it ain't any fun to be cullud. An' sometimes in dis yeah big city it ain't easy to keep sobah an' steady an' pure in heart, an' good to youah wives an' little chilluns. Sometimes, even wid Jesus to help us, things don't look bright fo' us niggahs. It looks mighty like as if we was all left out, an' de only thing to do is jest to die, like de Indians did." Lower and lower : " We don't say nothin' to white folks, but we all feel like dat—sometimes, when we's blue. But, boys "—the voice rose slightly, and thrilled. " Heah— right heah—is what one niggah did by tryin' ! Just look at it good. An' den go out an' bring youah friends to see it. Because dis pictah will do you mo' good dan a whole dozen of sermons !"

A tall, silent, anxious-looking man walked slowly along the side of a gallery nearly empty of people. At each picture he stopped and drew close as though for a better view ; but each time he glanced furtively down at the artist's name. Once he bent suddenly very low, and his face brightened, but then grew disappointed.

" Can I help you, sir ?" asked the guard. The man straightened up and flushed.

" No, nothing at all, thank you," he said, hurriedly. " Much obliged all the same." But then, as the guard turned to go—" Oh, by the way."

" Yes ?"

" This painter." He pointed down at

the signature, "Millet. Is he a student—in the school?"

"No, sir."

"Well," the man hesitated. "Do you have many pictures here—by the students?"

"No, sir. Not yet."

"Oh." The man's face relaxed in deep relief. "I have a boy there myself," he said. "I was just wondering."

In the school studios, twenty-four hundred a year. They come in largest numbers from Illinois, Michigan, Indiana, Iowa, Kentucky, Kansas, the Dakotas, California; and many besides from Wisconsin, Minnesota, Florida, Alabama, Texas, Oklahoma, Utah, and Oregon. Excluding the juvenile school of six hundred, the average age is twenty. Ten years ago the proportion of women to men was seven to one; now it is not quite two to one. They are of all stations in life, for the fees are very low: twenty-five dollars for twelve weeks in the all-day classes; six dollars for thirty-six evenings. Out of every fifteen students, fourteen hope to make some branch of art a life-work.

There was one youngster who came from the pines. Born in a rude lumber village, his boyhood was spent under the dark, silent old trees, and there he seemed to see and feel things that his brothers and sisters missed. His parents could not make him out. They were devout Catholics, and perhaps it was this that gave him his deep religious feeling—or perhaps it was the pines. He went often
670

to the rough-hewn little church and studied the altar paintings; these he began trying to copy; and in time he did so well that the priest took one of his Madonnas. As he grew older and kept on painting, and refused to prepare for practical breadwinning work, his parents grew impatient. But he kept on. At last he left home and came here.

He had no money. One of the teachers liked the crude sketches that he showed, and a position as janitor was given to him. Like scores of others in the last few years, he paid his tuition by dusting casts and cleaning floors. At night he slept in a little cubby in a corner of a sculpture gallery. All morning and all afternoon he worked at pad or easel.

Then he got a position as waiter in a restaurant, and at this upward step in life he went to lodge with three other youngsters in an attic room. The four had two "double-decker" bunks. He had an upper berth. They had a battered stove, and wood gathered from alleys, and crackers, a little meat, plenty of strong coffee and a few more delicacies—all of which they divided, for often one would be wealthy and lavish with a dollar, when the other three were penniless. All winter, from daybreak until nine in the morning, from twelve to two, and from six to eight or nine at night, he worked in the restaurant. And all morning and all afternoon he worked at pad or easel.

He had already gone through the "Elementary," the "Intermediate," and the "Antique" classes. Down in the library, studying hundreds of photograph prints of the great pictures in the world, he spent hours and hours. He rarely missed·an art lecture.

Once he had pneumonia and lost his restaurant position, but in three weeks he came out of the hospital, got another job, and went on. His vitality was deep, on account of the pines. And in the attic they made light of all troubles and had some glorious good times— being very young.

All morning and all afternoon he worked at pad or easel. He worked up through the "Gallery," "Life," and "Advanced Life" classes. His pictures in exhibits took medals many times.

He is somewhere in Europe now—still working.

But, as in the Latin Quarter, so here there is another common story, that of the boy or girl who labors and starves to create beauty, and whose work is barren from the start.

In an ugly little town of Iowa a girl of eighteen saw the photographs of great paintings that appeared all one year in a popular magazine. She read the accompanying essays on art. She

began trying to copy the photographs' Then she saved money to buy water colors, and painted her drawings. Her proud old grandmother thought her a genius; her widowed father thought her a fool. When the grandmother died, the next year, the home and the town became unbearable. A well-to-do farmer asked her to marry him and she refused, and this made her father more bitter. She kept on painting. At last she ran away and came here, with some forty dollars to live on.

She found a position at last as chambermaid in a hotel. Only three evenings a week conld she come to the school; but by cutting down sleep she worked three or four hours a night at an easel in her tiny, narrow bedroom. She shivered in winter, in summer clothes— and bought more paints.

And all her work was wretched. Her teacher did his best; for her gentle personality, the eager look in her eyes when he came to her easel, the strained attention, caught his interest. After each severe criticism he tried to speak hopefully. And so for two years she worked steadily on.

Slowly her personality changed. She looked prematurely old and weazened;

JUNIOR CLASS SKETCHING FROM LIFE

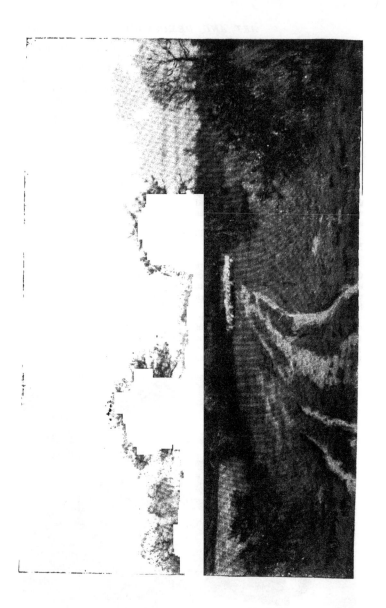

her gentle rounded face grew sallow and harsh ; her eyes grew bright, absorbed, and fiercely jealous—as all around her she saw other girls who worked no harder and whose work improved. She tried to deceive herself, she even bitterly accused the teacher of favoritism. And then she began to realize the truth, but worked on. As she worked, almost hopeless now, her passion for beauty gave place to an all-absorbing passion of jealousy, and this slowly centered on one girl student who had twice taken honors.

At last, just before a big competition, late one night, when the students had gone, she stole this girl's drawing, took it to her hotel bedroom, sat up all night staring at it, and finally tore it to shreds. And then she disappeared.

Others have the genius, but not the vitality. Some time ago a student discovered "a future Raphael," a wee ragged silent youngster, the son of a Greek fruit vender. The generous students grew excited over the urchin's powerful charcoal sketches, and took up a purse, and put him at an easel. And now the young Greek father was delighted, but the little son was silent, too happy to speak. He grew more and more absorbed, and his big black eyes grew doubly bright. Something seemed to be burning him up. A year later, all at once, his mind gave way. He is now in an asylum.

Then there is the practical genius. Not many years ago one wise, shrewd, but impoverished disciple of Rembrandt hit on an idea so inspiring that he lost not a day, but began. In a public library he searched the newspaper files of two Western States for the names of the newly elected State Senators. That summer, having scraped together some fifty dollars, he journeyed, armed with easel and huge rolls of canvas and quantities of bright rich paints, to the small town homes of these Senators. He saw their wives and daughters, and in a speech (carefully prepared in Chicago, and solemnly rehearsed in studios before his delighted chums) he told how Senator Joggs was now "a man in the

public eye "—."a man, simple, rugged, honest "—and yet—" one whose career as a statesman many of us are watching." For how plain it was that the Nation was again plunging into a terrible crisis ; how often was heard now the question, "Where is an Abraham Lincoln ?" How rugged and simple was Lincoln at the start ! What a pity that the Nation has so few portraits of Lincoln the young man ! What a pity if Senator Joggs should not now be painted ! And what wife, what daughters, had a better right to start an ancestral gallery for future generations ? What wife would refuse when the price was only fifty dollars, including the frame ? . . . And so shrewdly did he adapt this speech to each and every Joggs, and so swiftly did he paint Joggses into ancestors, and so hard did he travel, that all the next winter this wise, smiling student lived in affluence, and grew portly—on six hundred and forty dollars ! But, O ye shades of Rembrandt, what ancestors !

There are others who are practical in less irreverent ways. In the night classes are some seven hundred men and women, most of whom are busy all day in regular vocations, and come here to learn what will supplement the life-work they have chosen. For such, besides drawing and painting and sculpture, there are classes in architecture, · mural decoration, illustration, cartoons, and the designing of wall paper, laces, jewelry, book covers, rugs.

There is one of these night workers who five years ago was a clerk in the rug rooms of the best department store in the city. He came here night after night to study the designing of rugs. Now he himself draws each month dozens of designs for Oriental rugs; these are sent to Persia, and there the proud descendants of Cyrus the Great carry out the designs of Chicago !

These are but a few types from hundreds of stories—or rather beginnings of stories. The stories go on. Many of the former students are already widely known in the world's art centers. As painters : Myron Barlow, H. S. Hubbell, Frederick Marsh, F. C. Friescke,

Lawton Parker, Alson Clark. As sculptors: Bessie Potter Vonnoh, George Barnard, Charles Mulligan, Evelyn Longman. As illustrators: Orson Lowell, William Stevens, Albert Sterner, J. C. Leyendecker, Jules Guérin. These are a few of the many.

The influence of this center reaches far, for its normal school has already sent out hundreds of teachers. Some years back a young negro came up from the South and entered the studios here. He worked in both day and night classes and took honors, and then went back to his town in Texas to teach art for humanity's sake, in a lonely little school for colored children. He believes that in the deep, emotional, beauty-loving nature of the negro lie great possibilities for music and art. So he teaches. And so hundreds of other young men and women teach, in outposts large and small springing up all over the North and South and West. And of their thousands

of pupils, hundreds, it may be said, develop talent and come here.

They must come here, and keep coming in ever-swelling thousands, for Chicago is the inevitable center of the forty millions in the West. Strange foster-place of Art! Crude, gigantic, melodramatic city—its clouds of black and brown and bluish smoke whirling from trains and ships and factory chimneys, its vivid flames pouring all night from the flumes of its mills; its long cañon-like street vistas blackened with ever-hurrying crowds of people; its incessant babel—here muffled and nervous and low-throbbing, here clanging, clattering, crashing; its quickening race to make or buy or sell; its endless searching after things, things, things! Prodigious beginnings! Impenetrable future!

And out of all this grows a new home of art, with the same endless searching —after ideals. "We are still in our infancy," said the president.

BRINGING HOME THE NEW-BORN CALF
By J. F. Millet

# CREATIVE AMERICANS

## EDWARD C. PICKERING AND WILLIAM H. PICKERING

### ASTRONOMERS

#### BY RALPH BERGENGREN

READERS of the daily newspapers may remember about two years ago some passing mention of a scheme proposed by Director Edward Charles Pickering, of the Harvard Astronomical Observatory, whereby astronomy should be endowed on an international basis—the organization, in short, of a great astronomical trust "whose objects should be increased production, reduced cost to the public, and no profit to those forming it." The project, like so many others of lesser importance, went its way through the columns of the daily press, and then disappeared from public cognizance, shouldered out of sight by the next day's marching army of news items. Some months later, readers of the newspapers may have also noted the journey of Professor William Henry Pickering, of the same observatory, to Hawaii, there to examine the craters of Mauna Loa, Mauna Kea, Kilakea, and Haleakala, and compare their characteristics with those more distant craters, Eratosthenes and Plato, which his personal researches have done so much to make visible to us on the moon's surface.

These two items may well serve to typify the life and work of the two astronomers. In its broadest aspect their influence may be further summarized by a brief statement of the development of the Harvard Astronomical Observatory during their connection with it. To the wise sympathy of Director Pickering, both for the infinite minutiæ of routine investigations and for the broadest possible application of their results, to his ability to select and develop individual experts in the study of specific subdivisions of the work of the Observatory, and to his administrative skill in directing the investigations of a constantly widening sphere of astronomical study, may be fairly ascribed the present world-wide importance of his observatory for its studies of the physical and chemical properties of the heavenly bodies. The actual reduction of millions of visible stars to less than two dozen distinct types, touching each other in their essential characteristics and constituting an almost complete chain of evolution from a nova, or "new" star, to those whose redness may or may not mean (according to choice between opposing theories) that they are cooling off to a point at which they will cease to be visible, is but one among many of the interesting results of these investigations. At the same time, the Harvard Observatory has become unique among similar institutions in the possession of a photographic history of the entire heavens during the last twenty years, and also noteworthy in that it has already inaugurated the system of administrating funds for the benefit of smaller observatories the world over, which its director is so splendidly anxious to see extended to its furthest limits by the establishment of a large endowment. Concerning this large endowment, it is an interesting side-light on the man and his work that Director Pickering does not necessarily seek the honor of administrating it for his own observatory, university, or even

675

Nation, but sees instead the possibility of an administrative board representative of all the great observatories without question of location or nationality. Professor W. H. Pickering, on the other hand, has brought fame to the Observatory by his individual investigations of the nearer heavenly bodies, notably of the moon, and has thus materially widened the scope of an institution primarily devoted to knowing the stars rather than the planets, and to investigating the characteristics of thousands of these awfully distant bodies, in the true sense of that misused word, rather than those peculiar and significant markings that the rest of us know from childhood as the Man in the Moon.

Both men were born in Boston. The elder has stayed consistently at home, patiently building up the massive library of photographic star records, enumerating and studying thousands and thousands of these countless pinpoints of brightness in the great pincushion of the heavens, and at the same time developing in every direction the resources of his observatory and working out in detail a noble plan for uniting all astronomical study in one great institution. The younger has traveled, selecting sites for special astronomical investigations and at the same time constantly adding to the world's knowledge of the nearer, and therefore apparently larger, bodies. Their collaboration, springing naturally from divergent tastes united by a common ambition for the advancement of science, has given the Observatory the remarkably wide range of interests that make it the natural starting-point for new and even broader projects—such, for example, aside from the scheme for an international astronomical fund, as the establishment of an international observatory in the heart of Africa at a point already selected because it is probably the best possible location for the very delicate work of astronomical photography. In the public mind, indeed, their names have been more or less interchangeable, despite the fact that the work they stand for has been essentially different. To Director E. C. Pickering the world of astronomy owes the administrative development of a splendid institution equally prominent for specific scientific achievement and for the elaboration of a remarkable ideal of international helpfulness. To Professor W. H. Pickering it owes a widened sphere of astronomical knowledge investigated under conditions almost romantically separate from the routine work of the Observatory with which the results are inseparably connected.

Director Pickering's entrance into astronomy came in 1877, after ten years as a teacher of physics at the Massachusetts Institute of Technology, following two years as teacher of mathematics at the Lawrence Scientific School, from which he had graduated in 1865. His earlier life had shown no astronomical tendency except an aptitude for mathematics and an equal disinclination toward the classical studies that were then inseparable from a college education. The change from Latin and Greek, promptly enough abandoned for mathematics and chemistry as soon as the possibility of becoming a mathematician or scientist drew his attention to the then youthful scientific department of Harvard University, was, in fact, so delightful to the future astronomer that he promptly threw himself into brain fever by overwork. Details, computation, verification, were matters of direct, immediate fascination. To be an acknowledged master of them may be fairly stated as the ideal of the student—an ideal, however, that began to be modified and enlarged, immediately the young man had assumed a responsible teaching position, by the characteristic breadth of outlook that has since marked his administration of the Harvard Observatory. Where ordinarily a man would have been content with conditions as he found them, Professor Pickering has from the beginning looked forward from the concrete to the universal; and where another man might have paused by the way to grasp the commercial possibilities of a scientific discovery, he has gone forward to apply it to purely scholastic uses. Elimination, so often said to be the final test of art, has here done equal service in an equally important phase of human endeavor. Every important scientist has his occasional opportunity for money-making, and the age is not without its examples of men of science whose broadest usefulness has been sadly crippled by yielding to this incidental temptation.

These characteristics, the vital human elements that underlie his entire service to astronomy, both investigative and administrative, are well illustrated by two important achievements during his period as a teacher of physics at the Institute of Technology. When he entered the Institute, instruction, even in the now almost wholly experimental science of physics, was entirely by lectures and text-books. The student laboratory, which has become the most essential factor in scientific education wherever such education is now carried on, was absolutely unknown. Professor Pickering, in organizing and putting in successful operation the first physical laboratory for students, began a transformation that has since literally revolutionized scientific teaching. And in this laboratory, moreover, six years before Mr. Bell invented the telephone, Professor Pickering had evolved what was in many respects the receiving apparatus of the instrument, and was using it as an illustration in his lectures on sound. Although this apparatus was capable of receiving articulate speech from an appreciable distance, no effort was made to patent it. It was his belief then, as it still remains his belief, despite the fact that no man stands more firmly for the application of business methods to scientific administration, that the work of the scientist is apart from commerce, belonging to the world at large, without question of patents and royalties.

Astronomy at the Harvard Observatory was at this period in a state of transition. The first stellar photograph had been taken in 1850 by Professor Bond; and Professor Draper, although photography was still handicapped by the necessity of using wet plates, had made the earliest photographs of star spectra and so laid a foundation for the important departments of astrophysics that have since been so highly developed at the Cambridge Observatory. To those who could see far enough into the future it was evident that astronomy must enter new fields of observation, that the visual seeing, the infinite recording and comparison of visually observed phenomena that had given its best results in the past, must make way for newer and more intimately scientific methods; that the possibility of dividing the light of a star into a spectrum revealing the component elements of that distant incandescent body had brought new sciences to bear on astronomical investigation; and that the astronomer of the immediate future, so far as the Harvard Observatory was concerned, must be also a chemist and physicist. This was perhaps clearer to the far-seeing mind of President Eliot than to any other observer. At all events, when the death of Professor Winlock left the Harvard Observatory without a head, Professor Pickering was called to the directorship. Despite the advice of leading physicists who strenuously insisted that he was throwing away a dozen years of advance in one direction to start afresh in another, he promptly accepted the position, becoming at once an astronomer and an astrophysicist. At about the same time his younger brother, now Professor W. H. Pickering, had just graduated from the Institute and returned to it as an instructor in photography, remaining there until, in 1887, he joined forces with the elder Pickering at the Harvard Observatory. It was during the latter part of his time at the Institute that the photographs of the stars, taken with a small camera by Professor W. H. Pickering, first indicated the possibilities of widely extending stellar photography. These photographs, it so happened, were taken at his brother's observatory in Cambridge, and may therefore be fairly considered as the beginning of the movement that a few years later was including the photographing of the entire firmament.

Professor W. H. Pickering, therefore, brought to the Observatory, at a time when Director E. C. Pickering was turning serious attention to the possibility of a complete development of photography as applied to stellar observation, an expert knowledge of this new science of photography, then, by the discovery of dry plates, just entering its present wide field of utility. Both men, so far as individual human nature permits, were scientists in the spirit that Director Pickering describes as superior to any demand except the increase of human knowledge. The true aim, he has said, of the student of science is "the advancement of human knowledge and the determination of the laws regulating the universe. His sole object should be to obtain the best possible results, and he must be ready to make any sacrifice of his personal wishes for this end. Astronomy thus becomes international and wholly impersonal. To how many of us is this the one and only aim, regardless of all selfish considerations? We must not expect too much of poor human nature, and yet it can do no harm to make our ideal a high one. No man is likely to surpass his ideal, and even if it is so high that he cannot hope to reach it, he may go further than if he tries only for money or fame. The aims of the astronomer thus become the aims of astronomy, and there is no subject to which he can better give careful attention."

The fact remains, however, that a man must do his work after his own fashion, and in the collaboration of Director Pickering and his brother each cheerfully admits that the other has accomplished a kind of work which his colleague would under any circumstances have done less successfully. If Director Pickering has been responsible for the finding of new stars—and of the new stars discovered in the last two decades nine out of twelve have been located by either Mrs. W. P. Fleming or Miss H. A. Leavitt by examination of the photographic plates at Harvard—Professor Pickering has been responsible for new locations for astronomical observation. Always fond of outdoor exercise, especially walking and mountain-climbing, and equally attracted by travel and change of scene, Professor W. H. Pickering has to his credit the selection of a long list of astronomical stations, some of them chosen for temporary researches by Harvard astronomers and later utilized as permanent locations for other observatories, while others have become permanent stations of the Harvard Observatory. For Professor Percival Lowell he erected the observatory and telescope at Flagstaff, Arizona, which has since become famous through the work of its Director in studying the Martian canals. For the Harvard Observatory he established in 1891 its permanent southern station at Arequipa, Peru, where the Harvard instruments were able to include the stars of the southern heavens and so complete the work of the northern observatory by making its photographic record embrace the entire firmament. In 1900 he established the Harvard Astronomical Station in Mandeville, Jamaica, for the special purpose of a closer study of the moon's surface. Naturally, too, he has been the leader of various expeditions sent out from Harvard for the study of special phases of astronomy depending on special conditions. He has thus observed eclipses of the sun in Colorado, Grenada, California, Chile, and Georgia —all of which means more than astronomical knowledge, for it includes knowledge of men, diplomacy, and often the resource and quick decision of the explorer. And incidentally, sometimes without regard to the main issues of astronomy, sometimes in the quest of a good location for an observatory, he has ascended something more than a hundred mountain peaks, including Half Dome in the Yosemite and El Misti in the Andes.

Although Professor W. H. Pickering's name is to-day most closely associated with lunar investigation, his actual astronomical work is by no means confined to that planet. His discoveries include the Great Spiral Nebula in Orion; the rotation of Swift's Comet in 1892; the ellipticity and rotation period of the satellites of Jupiter; the ninth and tenth satellites of Saturn; and a long list of lesser miscellaneous discoveries almost any one of which would give his name a permanent place in the annals of astronomy. As an inventor he has done much to improve and perfect the mechanism of both photographic and visual astronomy—and this, it may be added, with no effort to turn his inventive faculty to commercial purposes. It would be entirely safe to say that no other astronomer has ever supervised the examination, both visually and in the permanence of the photographic negative, of so many stars as the Director of the Harvard Observatory. Few men, if there have been any at all, have looked at the heavens from more observatories where climatic conditions are especially well suited to delicate observation, than Professor W. H. Pickering. As a natural result of such conditions, the work of the older astronomer, permanently located in the midst of his constantly increasing library of star photographs and spending night after night studying the heavens for data as to the physical properties, magnitude, and movements of every visible star, has expressed itself in the accumulation of facts more or less common to the countless shining atoms of the celestial universe; while the work of the younger, traveling from station to station and visiting in turn so many places where conditions for "seeing" are especially in favor of the astronomer, has naturally devoted itself to the nearer bodies—to the moon particularly, to Mars in a lesser degree, and to the other planets whose neighborly relation to the own earth has always given them, incidentally, a marked popular interest. The Harvard Observatory in its studies of the solar system has thus developed a sphere of interest widely separated from the science of astrophysics as applied to the endless army of the stars.

Yet, after all, the living spirit that breathes in this wider field of sympathy and understanding must be very largely attributed to the personality of Director Pickering himself. As a great and important research institution, in which capacity it is the only one in the world that is part of an educational center and at the same time on a par with the famous government-supported observatories of America, England, or Germany, the Harvard Observatory has profited by the whole-hearted co-operation of a remarkably efficient staff of astronomers whose individual achievements cannot, unfortunately, find space in this article. But this staff has been largely of Director Pickering's making; the big outlines of the work of the Observatory as a whole have been his outlines; the direction of the two observatories, one at Cambridge and the other at Arequipa, has been his

7

direction, obviously impossible without the highly specialized skill of his assistants, but equally so without the fundamental ability to find and develop them. The Cambridge institution, moreover, has often loaned its instruments for investigations not conducted under its own auspices; its director, on more than one occasion, has surprised a capitalist by seeking financial assistance for outside astronomical research that could by no stretch of the imagination add to the fame or equipment of his own observatory; and the administration of funds bequeathed to the Harvard Observatory for astronomical purposes has been often interpreted with sufficient broadness to include any sincere worker who needed financial assistance to complete an important study.

To have captured photographically the first spectrum of a shooting star, the first spectrum of the aurora borealis, or the first spectrum of a flash of lightning; to have revealed definitely and conclusively certain characteristics common to our own earth and a neighboring planet; to have added thousands of new stars to our catalogue of the heavens, or to have increased by ever so little our human knowledge of a single one of these innumerable children of infinity—these are only a few of the interests of modern astronomy, and to the astronomer of pretty nearly the same importance. The making of men, both by personal influence and by adding to the world as a whole tangible examples of high living and thinking and of consistent devotion to any given form of usefulness, is not always taken into consideration in summing up an individual record. In the case of these men such separation is out of the question, for the personal equation has been, as for that matter it invariably is, a vital factor in producing successful work. Nor can the individual characteristics be separated in summing up the ideals and practical record of the institution that the one has made, as it now stands, by force of his own administrative faculty and scientific breadth of vision, and that the other has recently established even more prominently than before in the public mind by his specific investigations.

"The creature slid into the water so quietly as to cause scarcely a ripple"

# A HUNT FOR BABY ALLIGATORS

### BY · JULIAN A. DIMOCK

#### ILLUSTRATED BY THE AUTHOR

WITH weary minds and aching legs the boys returned at night. They had crossed marshes, waded prairie pools, and walked through pine forests and palmetto scrub the day long looking for little 'gators. Johnson wanted a young saurian. He was a biologist, likewise a tenderestfoot. There are degrees of tenderfoots. I am a tenderfoot myself, but not of the superlative degree. Johnson—well, he was superlative.

When the boys went out the next morning, Johnson and I went too. We started twice. The first time my friend stepped on the gunwale of the skiff in getting aboard. He failed to get aboard, but he did get a ducking! He could reel off Latin scientific names by the yard, but he never could learn the difference between the cat-head and the bight of a rope, on the boat in which we were cruising along the Gulf coast of Florida.

At first we had a scramble through a mangrove swamp which lined the shore. The mangrove's tangled mass of roots is above the ground, while nearly reaching down to them from above are the spreading, interlocking branches. Connecting the two are long, straight shoots called aerial rootlets. These, coming from the limbs above, take root in the soil beneath, serving at once to anchor the tree and make nearly impassable the swamp. A well-developed mangrove swamp is about as easy to cross as a jungle of barbed-wire fences, the trees being as obstructive as the wires, and the mosquitoes quite as sharp-toothed as the barbs and much more frequent. We got through without the use of any bad language. The perspiration was streaming down Johnson's face. He looked about twice as hot as I felt, and that was not exactly cool—but then Johnson was a superlative kind of man. For an hour we tramped through a marsh, the boys leading the way and breaking a path through the tall grass. A shrill whir sounded in front. Although it was my first rattlesnake, I intuitively knew the sound. The next instant there was the bang of the gun, and that danger was over. Mine was the face to blanch that time, for I am more afraid of snakes than I am of the devil. Half an hour later I nearly jumped over the man behind me, as I suddenly discovered a discarded snakeskin under my feet. The jump came first, and the inquiry into the age of the thing afterwards.

By the time that the rays of old Sol had neared the vertical, and had become correspondingly hot, we reached the pine woods. Now, there may be places hotter than Florida pine-land, even in this world, but I doubt it. Johnson wilted after the first hundred yards. He sat down and viciously swatted the mosquitoes. Then he wanted to know if we had any idea where we were going, or where we were, or how we could get back. The guides came to the rescue and cheerfully assured him that Bear Lake was less than a quarter of a mile away. I knew enough of that region to know what kind of a quarter that was, but it didn't seem necessary to enlighten my friend. We reached it two hours later. Johnson said that he was dead, but he wasn't that lucky, for he continued to fight the mosquitoes.

On the shore of the lake we found a boat made from dry-goods boxes. This was the trail of some 'gator hunter. The sun had opened the seams until the whole thing looked like a chicken coop. The boys were boat-builders enough to be able to calk the craft, while I sup-

" Harry waded into the pool and began grunting where one of
the midgets had gone down, hands outstretched to grab him "

" There was a quick lunge forward, and he held up to view a captive that squirmed and grunted "

" The pool was not waist deep, and the boys walked around without signs of effort "

plied the calking material from a wardrobe already scanty. We paddled around Bear Lake, but could find no little saurians. Even grown ones were few. It is a waste of time to follow on the trail of a skin-hunter.

"Evidently I must do without a specimen of the Mississippi alligator. I wish that it were possible to do without that walk, too, between here and the boat," said Johnson.

"I don't know nothin' about the Mississippi, no more 'n a rabbit, but I kin find you a little 'gator, and mighty near here too, if you'll let me go look," said Harry.

"You and William go ahead and look, while Mr. Johnson and I wait for you here; only don't get lost, for we never could find our way back," said I.

Around and near Bear Lake are a series of pools, or really mud-holes; these the boys began to explore, walking around the edge of the pools to look for the trails of the comings and the goings of the saurians, or for their sun-baths. Alligators are experienced travelers over land, especially during the dry season, when small pools dry up and they are forced to seek other quarters. Hunters become expert trailers and can follow the creatures with ease and certainty. In walking the 'gator rarely lifts his tail clear of the ground, and in soft mud it leaves a continuous line; while the belly, barely clearing, mashes down the grass. The size of the feet vary according to the size of the critter, and a hunter will tell you the approximate length of the maker of the footprints, always carefully adding, "If he ain't a stub-tail." Lest the argot of the region be to you as Sanscrit is to me, I will explain that a "stub-tail " is a 'gator who has lost part of his tail, probably in a fight with a larger relative.

Before long Harry returned and reported success, asking if we didn't want to see him catch the youngsters which he had located in a pool not very far away.

No 'gator, large or small, can resist a peculiar call that resembles the grunt of a pig. Let a hunter grunt a few times at the side of a pond, and if there is an alligator in it, he will slowly raise his head above the surface and gaze curiously around. An old and very shy one can sometimes resist, for sad experience has taught him that bullets are liable to greet his appearance above the water.

As we approached the pool a number of little heads dotted the surface, only to disappear when we reached the bank. Harry had spotted the location of each with the exactness of hunter-craft. He waded into the pool and began grunting where one of the midgets had gone down, hand outstretched to grab the youngster before he discovered his danger. In a minute the water began to quiver, the boy's muscles stiffened, he made a quick lunge forward, and held up to view a captive that squirmed and grunted and opened and shut his jaws with vicious snaps.

Johnson viewed the victim with eyes biologic, but to me only the fun of the thing appealed. I knew that I could do it too. I tried. The mud was not waist-deep, and the boys walked around without sign of effort, so I plunged in. It was mere pride that kept me from scrambling back after the first step. The mud was soft and sticky, and slowly I sank. The more I floundered the lower I sank. My past life passed in mental review. I thought good-bys and wondered how long it took to smother. I looked down expecting to see the water at my armpits, but it had not reached my waist, and the sinking had stopped! To go back was to face certain laughter, while to go forward might only be death. I went forward.

"Take it easier," said William; "don't struggle, and don't put your feet down so hard."

Excellent advice. Tell a drowning man not to sink, that you will reach him in a few minutes. It will be as easy for him to wait for you as it would have been for me to walk and not "put my feet down so hard." I reached the disappearing place of a 'gator and began to grunt. Probably I didn't speak his dialect, for he didn't come up. William came out and spoke 'gator talk, and the water shivered. I grabbed—and squalled! Now Harry had caught his animal just behind the fore legs, but I thought that he had grabbed promiscuous like, the

"Sometimes the youngsters would refuse to rise even after the most realistic of grunts.  Harry would feel around in the soft ooze—"

"Slowly the recalcitrant creature was lifted to the surface of the water on the toe of his boot—"

"And grabbed"

which I had done. I caught my youngster around the hind legs. He turned and caught me around the thumb, sinking his needle teeth to their full length. After that I let the boys do the catching, for I had learned how.

Sometimes the youngsters would refuse to rise even after the most realistic of grunts. This did not always save them, as Harry would feel around in the soft ooze with his foot until the little cub was located. Then slowly the recalcitrant creature was lifted to the surface of the water on the toe of his boot, and grabbed.

We tied the babies' jaws together with pieces of string, and began distributing them around in our pockets for the return trip. I had left my pockets in the calking of the boat, and so carried my share in a shirt-waist front. This was all right while they kept quiet.

"The old one is around here somewheres," suggested Harry.

"Go ahead and find her, then," said I.

There were a number of trails leading from this pool to adjacent ones. Selecting the most traveled-looking one, Harry followed it to a small pond. Stealthily approaching, he discovered Madame 'Gator and one of her babies asleep on their sun-bath. It may here be in order to say that Monsieur and the baby would lie down in peace and harmony only when the one was comfortably inside of the other. At the lubberly approach of Johnson and myself the creatures awoke and slid into the water so quietly as to cause scarcely a ripple. Instead of grunting for the lost 'gators, Harry took one of the youngsters from his pocket, and by a little judicious squeezing caused it to call for its mammy. Mammy answered at once. Right here Harry discreetly stopped, for alligators do sometimes attack people, and will come out on land to do it too.

On the homeward tramp Harry told us tales of his encounters with Big John and Mose, both saurians of local celebrity. The chance to get Big John came to him one night when he and his brother were out fire-hunting. For some unaccountable reason the creature allowed the boys to get very near to him. When Harry's brother saw the size of

" The mangrove's tangled mass of roots is above the ground, while nearly reaching down to them from above are the spreading, interlocking branches "

"John," he yelled at Harry not to shoot. The reptile, taking fright at the sound of the voice, sank out of sight, thus having perhaps the narrowest escape of its life, for if Harry had been alone he would have got him.

From a safe distance of time I considered the brother's conduct to be quite reprehensible and evincing much cowardice. My own behavior on a similar occasion is forgotten beneath an avalanche of mortification. A big saurian—and he really was mighty big—took the bow of my skiff in his jaws. His tooth broke, his hold loosened, and I shouted to my boatman, not, "Don't shoot," but, "Put me ashore quick!" Then I climbed a tree.

The homeward journey was like the morning's trip, only more so. Before we reached the mangroves the sun had gone down and it was as black as a hat. The additional crop of mosquitoes quite compensated for the lesser heat of the sun. The finding of the way will always rank among miracles with me. Johnson quickly got beyond comments, while only the determination to impress him kept me going. We reached the boat much too tired to eat. The weather was warm, and we were sleeping on deck. As the one that still had flutterings of life, I brought Johnson's mattress and bedding on deck. I even rigged his bar. Johnson fell asleep as I tucked it around him. My bluff was over; not for all the mosquitoes on Cape Sable would I have rigged another bar. I dropped to the deck and to sleep, for I too am a tenderfoot.

"He discovered Madame 'Gator and one of her babies asleep on their sun-bath"

# THE LEADERS OF THE RED HOST

## BY O. D. SKELTON

 FEW months ago the Kaiser was making a royal progress through a Prussian city. The vigilant secret police who were clearing the way before him came on an old applewoman sitting by the curb under the shade of an ample red umbrella. Immediately the old woman, apple-cart, umbrella, and all, were hustled away to a side street, lest perchance in the midst of the pomp and glitter and glory the Imperial eye should fall on the hated color and the Imperial temper be ruffled. The German police know the Hohenzollern way too well to follow the grim Egyptian plan of thrusting forward the skeleton at the feast.

With us in America, Socialism and the Socialist movement are as yet chiefly a problem of the future, though it may be the immediate future. But in Europe Socialism is a very present reality. It fills the political horizon as no other movement for a century past. Where it is not the dominant party, it is the party which the dominant party opposes—it provides the issues. The character and personality of the leaders of this red host may prove of momentous consequence. Nearly all are men of outstanding individuality, men who might be filling the seats of the mighty in officialdom, were they not dedicated to perpetual opposition. It is true, the orthodox Marxian Socialist would insist that Socialism is not the outcome of any individual's brain or any party leader's energy and magnetism, but the inevitable and irresistible sequence of the present organization of capitalist society. Yet it seems undeniable that much of the success of German Socialism, for example, may be set down to the astute and able guidance of its great leaders, just as much of the failure of American Socialism as yet to secure any definite permanent standing in the political field is due to the lack of strong personalities to attract and hold a great following, to give concreteness and concentration to the movement. Narrow doctrinaires, dilettante literary men, are not the stuff that popular leaders are made of.

Germany calls first for attention—the land where scientific Socialism had its birth and has to-day its greatest development both in theory and in popular support. For in spite of the check received in the recent khaki elections, the Social Democrats still poll twice as many votes as any other party in Germany. The check, too, was more seeming than real; though the party lost nearly half its seats, it gained a quarter-million votes. The causes of this paradoxical situation are various. The gerrymandering and hiving which have always handicapped the party—one agrarian vote outweighs four Socialist—operated with especial force on this occasion to nullify the gains made. The conservative forces succeeded in sinking their differences better than usual in face of the common red peril, and redeemed many seats with which their dissension had presented the Socialists. But chiefly the stay-at-home vote, middle class and peasant, rallied to the Chancellor's appeal to their German national spirit and overwhelmed the anti-Imperial and anti-Colonial Reds—a result which incidentally is bringing the con-

687

servative leaders to see the virtues of compulsory voting proposals. The vote indicates, on the whole, not so much that Socialism is losing its grip on the working classes as that it is further from the goal of complete conquest than its leaders imagined.

Of the men who have marshaled this host, built it strong in persecution, and held it firm in prosperity, August Bebel is easily the chief. For forty years this spare, wiry, keen-featured man has been in the forefront of the fight, until now his ascendency over the party, despite occasional rumblings and differences on questions of tactics, is so complete that, as von Vollmar charged in a recent Congress debate, not Wilhelm II. himself is so autocratic. He is the one great figure of the past still on the stage where once Marx and Lassalle, Engels and Liebknecht, played their parts. But he is not an old man yet, Bebel the ever young as his followers call him. When debate runs high in the Reichstag, there is no more agile or tireless figure than this white-haired and white-bearded man of sixty-six. His political career began early. Working as a turner in Leipzig in the sixties, he had his thoughts turned to social questions by contact with the misery and poverty of the workingmen around him. Curiously, it was not until after he had himself emerged · from the proletariat, and as a master turner was exploiting other wage-earners, that he became a Socialist—perhaps not so curiously either, since most leaders of Socialism have been recruited from the ranks of the Haves rather than the Have-nots. Under Liebknecht's inspirations, he helped organize the Social Democratic party at Eisenach in 1869. The same year he was elected to the Diet, and has been in Parliament or in prison ever since. His openly avowed sympathy with the French Socialists in the early seventies, and his fearless criticis.n of the powers that were at home, led to his conviction on charges of treason and lèse-majesté and imprisonment for three years altogether. After this recommendation from the Imperial authorities, his prestige became irresistible. On the local hustings, in the annual congress of the faithful, in the ever-growing ranks of the party in the Reichstag, he has been ever since the most persuasive and commanding figure. No fear of lèse-majesté blunts the fierce rapier-thrusts of his criticism of the policy of a Hohenlohe or a von Bülow or whatever other mask the Kaiser wears, his denunciations of all other isms than Socialism—Imperialism and Colonialism, Militarism and Marinism and Protectionism. He is easily the most eloquent orator and hardest-hitting debater in the Reichstag. He is not of imposing figure, but is gifted with a voice of rare mellow quality and a countenance of magnetic attraction when passion has banished the expression of weary melancholy habitual in repose. His speech is terse and vigorous, driven home with tremendous earnestness—one-sided and intemperate, it may be, compelling assent rather than persuading it.

Then there is Paul Singer, pre-eminently the strategist of the party, and a millionaire manufacturer before he became a convert to collectivism. He has for years been chairman of the standing orders committee of the Reichstag, this arch-revolutionary, charged with maintaining a strict observance of the traditional forms and ceremonies of Parliament. In South Germany the striking figure is von Vollmar, a Bavarian army officer who served in 1866 and 1870, was wounded in the latter war in a daring exploit which brought him the Iron Cross and a long convalescence, luring which he became interested in social questions and finally in Socialism. As a Catholic he has resisted and succeeded largely in repressing the earlier hostility of his party towards the Church, and as a South German has urged the necessity of adopting an agrarian policy which will appeal to the small peasant farmer of the South. On the literary side the leading men are Karl Kautsky, editor of Die Neue Zeit and chief high priest of the esoteric Marxian doctrine, and · in the wing Edward Bernstein, leader of the revisionist movement, which is the higher criticism of the gospel according to Marx.

It is now eight years since Bernstein—like Marx of Jewish descent, and, like Marx, brought to see the light by long exile in England—set his party by the

PAUL SINGER
Germany

ENGELBERT PERNERSTORFER
Austria

JULES GUESDE
France

JOHN BURNS
England

ears through his attacks on the most cherished doctrines of "scientific Socialism." He impugned the economic analysis on which the whole theoretical system was built up. He pointed to the failure of the Marxian prophecies; he called in question the wisdom of the Marxian tactics in these changed times. To understand the full damnableness of this heresy, it is necessary to realize the almost superstitious reverence which had come to attach to Marx's writings. The essence of his doctrines is familiar, but may be briefly recalled in its historic setting. The political restlessness of Germany in the forties gave him a revolutionary, proletarian bias. England, then outdistancing the world in industrial progress, showed him the capitalistic form that production was taking, and an English banker-economist, Ricardo, gave him the labor theory of value, from which he drew the deduction that, while labor is the source of all wealth, in competitive society the laborer's wages are not the full product of his labor, but, thanks to the operation of the iron law of wages, merely the minimum necessary to keep body and soul together, the difference, under the name of surplus value, being appropriated by the wicked capitalist. From the Hegelians of the left Marx got his key to past history—the idea that the political and social and religious structure of every stage of human society is determined by the mode of economic production of the time; from the Hegelian dialectic, too, came his theory that future progress could take place only by class struggle. From these conceptions his system followed: the goal, the collective ownership of all the means of production, corresponding to the collective working of the modern era; the means, class war—the proletariat, sinking deeper and deeper in misery and joined therein by the great majority of the middle class, finally were to be stung to desperation by their wretchedness and wrest the power from the hands of the few capitalist millionaires in control; the tactics, to let the inevitable doom of present society work out its speedy end, the worse the better, and to organize the Socialist army to step into the breach after the collapse.

It was a remarkably well-jointed doctrine, irrefutable once its premises were granted, and admirably adapted to propaganda purposes. At once Socialism became identical with Marxism; the early theories of the Utopists were abandoned. But the world has moved since 1867, and now its most progressive adherents feel that Socialism must move with it or be cast on the scrap-heap of discarded theories. In every country in Europe the party is rent by the revisionist movement, but in none so deeply as in Germany. On the side of the orthodox creed stand Bebel and Kautsky and Singer; the revisionists are headed by Bernstein the thinker, Vollmar the politician, and Auer the organizer. Bernstein grants only a limited validity to the labor theory of value and the theory of surplus value, shows that Marx's prophecy of the general sinking of the middle class into the proletariat and the further degradation of the proletariat itself has been disproved by the facts of increasing welfare of the working class in all lands and the tenacious grip of the bourgeois on his accustomed place. The concentration of industry, he further objects, has not meant concentration of ownership, for the joint stock corporation, to whose rôle Marx was strangely blind, has resulted in a widening of the ownership of great industries, so that one great corporation may have over seventy thousand stockholders.

The dispute is no mere hairsplitting about words: the practical tactics of the party are involved. Accepting the Marxian forecast, the coming revolution would work itself out by the momentum of deep-seated, impersonal economic forces which no conscious political actions on the surface could greatly hinder or greatly help. All that the Socialist party could do was to rouse the class consciousness of the proletariat and prepare it to take the reins the morning after the downfall of capitalism. It followed that no good Marxian could ally himself with a bourgeois party or palter with partial reforms which would only tend to patch and bolster up the rotten bourgeois structure and by reconciling the proletariat to its lot prevent that final spasm of despair which was to usher in the

:w earth. It was, in their view of affairs,
1 or nothing.

But the proletariat is not philosophic.
: cannot be persuaded, once it has been
)used to its wrongs and to its power,
› sit with folded hands while the slow
volution of the ages works out the sal-
ation of the coming time. Gradually,
s the dawning of the kingdom of Social-
im on earth, which Marx had predicted,
ame not, a change came over the spirit
f German Socialistic thought compara-

mon advantage, and, in short, begin here
and now to secure Socialism on the installment plan.

The logic of the situation is with the
revisionists. That it is impossible to
hold the support of the working classes
without securing some tangible reforms
is obvious. But, further, Socialism is
paying the penalty of success—gaining
the whole German world by losing its
Marxian soul. Inevitably, as the party
widens, its doctrines spread out thinner;

H. M. HYNDMAN
England

AUGUST BEBEL
Germany

ble to the modification of early Christian theology by the delay of the second
advent. Lassalle once declared that
workingmen were no longer to be put
off with checks on the Bank of Heaven;
neither, it seems, are they content with
checks on the Bank of the Future Socialistic State.

Accordingly, the practical men of the
movement, as the revisionists term themselves, have been demanding that the
Social Democratic party no longer content itself with a waiting negative policy,
but go in for positive reform, make alliances when need be with other progressive parties, accept office if to the com-

it is coming to be a commonplace Radical opposition. Under its banner range
all the democratic forces that are weary
of the Hohenzollern-Junker rule. While
the registered membership of the party
is four hundred thousand, it cast over
three million votes at the last election,
a large percentage coming from the
middle classes. It is difficult, too, for
a Socialist leader always to remember
to be class-conscious when, as is most
often the case, he is a university professor or editor or doctor or lawyer or capitalist converted at the eleventh hour.
With both leaders and rank and file thus
changing, the platform must also change.

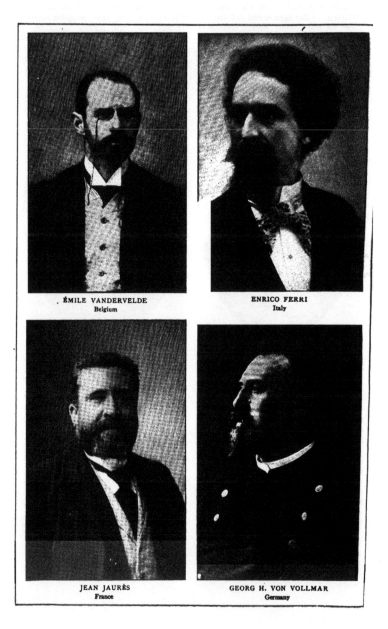

ÉMILE VANDERVELDE
Belgium

ENRICO FERRI
Italy

JEAN JAURÈS
France

GEORG H. VON VOLLMAR
Germany

So far as the minimum programme goes, the transition has already come; there is scarce a word in it to which the average voter in either party in the United States could not say Amen. Formally, the party congress has thus far refused, under Bebel's magnetic influence, to recognize the changed situation. But practically, through change of emphasis less mortifying to consistency than change of form, the new tactics are being accepted by the majority, and by none more than the greatest opportunist of them all, August Bebel.

Every country gets the Socialists it deserves. For all his cosmopolitanism, the Socialist is unable to escape the molding force of his national environment. It is no mere accident that while in German Socialism interest has centered about theories, and in English about measures, in French Socialism it has centered about men. Till a year or two ago the history of the French Socialist movement was a weary record of factional and personal strife between Broussists and Blanquists, Guesdists and Allemanists, and all the other fleeting, shifting fractions into which that unlucky fissiparous party was divided. But at last practically all have been gathered into a single party with two clearly marked wings—revolutionary and opportunist—and, though still at odds among themselves, present a fairly united front to the outer world.

In France as in Germany orthodox Marxian and heterodox revisionist stand face to face. The leader of the one wing is Jules Guesde, of the other Jean Jaurès. Look at the faces of the two men and see if politics is not largely a matter of temperament; one could almost read the political programme of each in his face. Look at Jaurès, the opportunist, at his square shoulders, his square jaws, his wide nostrils fairly snorting with the joy of life and the lust of battle, his restless, sparkling, good-humored eyes, the lips scarcely restraining the flood of speech that presses from within, a face that reveals full-blooded intensity, sympathy, imagination, yet essentially practical, even commonplace; in fact, a typical bourgeois face, but a bourgeois " touched with emotion." One is not surprised to learn that he has been a professor of philosophy, or that he is the most brilliant orator in France, or that he has made a fortune of late years as a clothing merchant. Contrast Jules Guesde, leader of the Implacable and Incorruptible Old Guard of Irreconcilables; a face that witnesses sincerity and narrowness in every line, eyes that have seen more evil than good in this weary world, and hate the evil more than they hope for the good; thin lips that will prophesy woe and send a shiver up bourgeois spines. It is the face of a man of one idea, spurning compromise as he would the devil, a man built of the stuff martyrs are made of, who would go to the stake rather than sacrifice one comma of his creed, who, had he been born a few centuries ago, would have founded a monastic order of unparalleled asceticism and proselytizing zeal.

Jaurès unites the politician and the academician in unusual degree. Twenty years or more ago, when but a stripling, he was a lecturer in philosophy in the University of Toulouse. He was elected in 1885 to the Chamber of Deputies as a Conservative Republican, and rapidly made his way to the front of that left center party. Defeat at the polls four years later sent him back to the University. While completing his studies for his doctorate there, he became more and more radical in his views, and when he re-entered the Chamber in 1893 it was under the Socialist banner. At once his breadth of view, his political adroitness, his ability as a leader of men, gave him high place in the ranks of his new associates, and every year since has strengthened his hold. It is perhaps as an orator that Jaurès has served his party best. As an orator of the impassioned, somewhat flamboyant type, France has not seen his equal since that other son of the South, Gambetta, whom he resembles in many points. He never speaks without raising the level of the debate above personalities to principles. His voice is rather harsh and metallic, and his quick gestures are of a monotonous sameness, but you forget that in a moment, captivated by the glow and fervor of the words that pour out in torrential eloquence. His speeches are one quick bioscopic succession of images ; he thinks in metaphors, reasons by visualizing his ideal. The flight of eloquence soars higher and higher as he is carried away by his own enthusiasm, or stirred to combat by taunts from the Right. Perhaps when it is all over, and the cheers and the counter-cheers have died away, if you boiled down its airy generalities and sonorous declamations, the solid residue would not be great. But who wants to boil down oratory like that of Jaurès?

Guesde has had a career more befitting the conventional Socialist leader. Like many another radical, he got his education setting type. At twenty he was writing against the pinchbeck Imperialism of Napoleon III., and was imprisoned six months in Montpellier for an article calling for a revolution. In the stirring times of 1870 he was a prominent Communard, and escaped sentence only by seeking refuge in Switzerland. Five years of exile hardened and embittered his revolutionarism, and turned it definitely into Socialistic channels. Permitted to return in 1876, he set about organizing a French Marxist party, and was so successful that two years later he was arrested again. He was largely responsible for the success of Socialism in gaining the ascendency in the industrial towns of the north—an ascendency which it was not able to maintain in the face of the banded opposition of all other parties. In the Chamber he gathered a small band of followers, but parliamentary Socialism did not amount to much until the accession of Jaurès and Millerand. With their coming, too, came the inevitable dispute about tactics.

In France this dispute has centered about two problems : Should Socialists form an alliance with other parties, and should a Socialist enter a non-Socialist ministry ? Guesde has steadily opposed both proposals, and for the moment at least, after a long struggle, has imposed his will on the party. He has urged that to adopt this opportunist policy means blunted ideals, the adherence of loaves and fishes politicians, the raising among the faithful of hopes of a dawning millennium doomed to disappointment so long as power is only partial. The revisionists, on the contrary, have dwelt

on the possibility of permeating the Government forces, of securing some instalment of reform to hearten the rank and file, and of guaranteeing the free nation against the attacks of its million ecclesiastical foes. To Jaurès the loaf of bourgeois republicanism is better than the no bread and less butter of servative reaction. To Guesde and republicanism and all other ideals developed before the year 1 of the Marxian era are anathema. For the present there seems no need of Socialist coöperation with the radicals ; Jaurès no longer is the unofficial leader of the House, the inconclusive Millerand experiment is not repeated. It is true that some of the ablest members of the Clemenceau Cabinet—M. Briand, who has had charge of the campaign for separation of Church and State, and M. Viviani, who holds the new post of Minister of Labor—are Socialists. But they are Republicans first and Socialists second, and it is clearly understood that they are fighting for their own hand, without any power to bind their former colleagues. The party, as a party, is contenting itself with setting the pace for the Government. With Clemenceau promising an eight-hour law, shorter military service, old-age pensions, increased income and inheritance taxes, and gradual purchase of railways by the State, the Socialists feel that their work has not been in vain.

Across the border in Belgium the outstanding figures in the Socialist world are Émile Vandervelde and Edouard Anseele. Professor Vandervelde, the author of a little book on " Collectivism " which is one of the ablest and most moderate statements of Socialistic theory in its later development, is perhaps better known in America by his work as leader of the Belgian attack on the Congo horrors. For Belgian Socialism, though active and well disciplined, has not been permitted to confine itself to a Socialistic programme pure and simple. Side issues, ecclesiastical and political, have been many and absorbing. First it was necessary to fight for the suffrage, a vantage ground from which their brethren in other countries started. Anti-clericalism provided another issue. The fight between the Black International and the

J. RAMSAY MACDONALD
England

J. KEIR HARDIE
England

THE COUNTESS OF WARWICK
England

EDWARD BERNSTEIN
Germany

Red knows no truce in Belgium, however it may slacken elsewhere on the Continent. The Jesuit, not the bourgeois, is the object of the Socialist's fiercest denunciation in Leopold's little kingdom. If recent election results may be relied on, neither side has of late gained much on the other. The Congo has been another red herring drawn across the trail. No little credit is due the Socialist deputies in the Chamber, under Vandervelde's dashing leadership, for their persistent and searching attacks on all King Leopold's get-rich-quick schemes on that Dark Continent which, it is believed, he has made darker.

But perhaps the chief interest in Belgian Socialism attaches to the co-operative experiments connected with the name of Anseele. Shoemaker, notary's clerk, painter, editor by turn, he found his outlet at last in founding the famous Vooruit in Ghent, a combination of club and co-operative store to which only adherents of the Socialistic Labor party are eligible. The movement spread rapidly until it now includes societies in all the large cities, and counts its members by the score of thousands. Each center furnishes its members with a library and club-house, sells them groceries, coal, clothing, insurance, medical attendance, at co-operative prices, and usually maintains a party organ. Thus the faithful are bound together by ties of material interest, and out of the profits funds are secured for further propaganda. This commercial bond, coupled with the party's preoccupation with current political issues, has saved Belgian Socialism from theoretical mistiness.

In Austria, as in Belgium, the fight for the suffrage has been the preliminary task of Socialism. For twenty years Victor Adler and Engelbert Pernerstorfer, leaders of the Austrian Socialist party, have agitated against the cumbersome and antiquated electoral system, based on the mediæval plan of class representation. The inequalities which marked this system may be briefly indicated by the following inscriptions from banners carried in a monster Socialist demonstration in Vienna recently:

" Nine aristocratic loafers elect one deputy to the Reichsrath."

"Twenty capitalistic freebooters elect one deputy to the Reichsrath."

" 4,200 city inhabitants elect one deputy to the Reichsrath."

" 12,300 peasants elect one deputy to the Reichsrath."

" 500,000 workmen elect one deputy to the Reichsrath."

It is true, Hungarian example, racial deadlock, and dynastic policy had much to do with the recent action of the Government in sweeping away this system at a stroke in favor of universal and equal suffrage. But no small share of the result is due to the able and incessant championing of the cause by Adler, the writer, and Pernerstorfer, the orator, of the party. The two leaders, although fellow-students at the University of Vienna, and now seeing eye to eye in policy, are men of very different antecedents. Adler, the son of a very wealthy Viennese manufacturer, had his first introduction to social problems through the second-hand medium of books. His conversion to Socialism was sudden, and, as usual with millionaire converts, thorough. He practiced his profession of medicine a few years, but gave it up to enter political journalism with such revolutionary zeal that his father practically disinherited him and the Government confined him to prison a year and a half. Mellowing with time and experience, he now wields wide influence as editor of the leading Socialist organ, the Arbeiter Zeitung, and by his treatises has won a place as one of the chief theorists of the party. Engelbert Pernerstorfer, born in poverty and orphaned at an early age, had a concrete, first-hand introduction to the same problem of social ill and social reform. He was too busy earning a living and putting himself through the University of Vienna to theorize about it for some time. Like Jaurès, whom he resembles in many respects, though lacking the Frenchman's brilliancy and magnetism, he first entered Parliament as a left center member, representing a bourgeois curia; there took up the cudgels for the working classes, lost his seat, and came back later as a Socialist. His powers of debate, his moderation, and his firm opposition to the obstructive tactics which have so often turned the Reichsrath into a bears' garden, mark him as worthy of the wide respect he enjoys in Vienna. Both Pernerstorfer and Adler are firm adherents of the revision movement, and favor an opportunist policy of social reform and alliance with other progressive parties. "The old cries," Adler writes, "about the proletariat being the slaves of the capitalist, about the increasing misery of the poor, about the uselessness of social legislation, are worn-out phrases."

They are not worn-out phrases in Italy. There Socialism still retains much of the ultra-revolutionary tinge which has characterized it from the beginning in all three of Europe's southern peninsulas. The revisionist movement, which is led by Signor Turati, has met with bitter and persistent opposition. The most interesting personality in Italian Socialism is undoubtedly the leader of the revolutionary wing, Enrico Ferri, a unique combination of careful scientist and fiery politician. Not many men have the honor of founding a new science, but Professor Ferri may justly be said to have achieved this distinction by his work in criminal sociology. Italy's restoration to a place of honor in the scientific world is largely due to the work her sons have done these two decades past in investigating the nature and genesis of crime and the criminal, studies which are revolutionizing penal treatment the world over. In this work Ferri shares first honors with Cesare Lombroso. The memorial which was presented to him last year on the twenty-fifth anniversary of his beginning university work—he has taught in Turin, Bologna, Siena, Brussels, Pisa, and now in the University of Rome—gave striking witness to the esteem in which his scientific brethren in all countries hold him. The connection between Ferri's science and his politics is clear. The distinguishing feature of his work has been to insist that crime cannot be cured by skillfully constructed codes of law or humane treatment of offenders, but only by bettering the adverse social conditions of which the criminal is the finished product. In Socialism he believes he has found the social regeneration needed, and, with an impatience strange in a man who has spent so many laborious days and years delving in endless musty statistics, demands its immediate and wholesale adoption.

At the opposite pole from Latin Socialism is the Anglo-Saxon variety. England has been an insoluble puzzle to Continental Socialists. All the materials for a Socialistic combustion, they have often pointed out, are found there in greatest abundance—the land monopolized by a few great families, the old yeomanry wiped out of existence, industrial capital concentrated, a proletariat massed in a few great towns where misery contrasts most appallingly with magnificence. If Englishmen were logical as Marxists spell logic, the social democracy should years ago have been in full swing in that little island. But sheer logic has never been one of the vices of the Englishman, and the revolution still hangs fire. Even now, when, at last, Socialism seems to be getting some grip on the British public, it is Socialism of a characteristically compromising, tentative, denatured type, Socialism "with the stamp of the vestry so congenial to the British mind, following the sordid, slow, reluctant, cowardly path to justice, grudgingly muddling and groping towards paltry installments of betterment," as Bernard Shaw wrote a few years ago trying to quiet the reproaches of his conscience for falling away from his own earlier and more fiery ideals by a few final epigrammatic flings at the humdrum policy he was adopting.

Of the three main currents in English Socialism, the Social Democratic Federation is nearest orthodox Marxism. Head and front of the "S. D. F.," as it is popularly known, is one of the most interesting personalities in British politics—Henry M. Hyndman. Few men have devoted themselves to a new cause with more persistence and ability, and with less visible reward. He had an unusual equipment for political life—good abilities, constructive as well as critical, a Cambridge training, the experience born of wide travel and much mingling with men of affairs, and, not least, an independent fortune. He has used that equipment at highest pressure. For a quarter-century he has been indefatigable as writer, speaker, organizer, preaching his message of Socialism so incessantly and so tellingly that the revised creed of individualism has been said to be, " Every man for himself and the devil take the Hyndman." And yet the Social Democratic Federation is at a standstill. Only one candidate for Parliament was returned at the last election, and Mr. Hyndman himself was defeated in a close contest at Burnley. After spending his life and fortune in the cause, he has to stand aside and see eleventh-hour laborers, men with not a tithe of his wide experience or keen ability, sweep past him into Parliament on the crest of the labor wave. His career is a standing lesson on what's in a name. Practically, his programme differs but little from that of the Fabians or the Labor Socialists. But the label of Marxian Socialism queered it. The Englishman prefers to swallow his dose of collectivism without knowing it. The Social Democratic Federation, it may be noted, has recently gained in the Countess of Warwick a recruit of thoroughgoing sincerity, who will make Socialism fashionable, if she does not first make it ridiculous.

Of the Fabians less is heard to-day than a decade ago. Perhaps, as a French critic put it, they gorged themselves with statistics and went to sleep ; or perhaps it is that they have brought the public up to their level and no longer stand forth in splendid isolation. Certainly it would be difficult to find a more able or more successful campaign of education than that instituted by this band of brilliant young men, which includes Sidney Webb, Bernard Shaw, William Clark, Hubert Bland, H. W. Macrosty. All men of middle-class origin and university training, their Socialism lacked the revolutionary tinge of the millionaire or proletarian varieties. Theory and goal were put into the background. Permeation, not proselytizing, was aimed at. Practical proposals of municipal reform were given stress. In some share the wave of municipal Socialism—now seemingly checked, for a time at least—which has swept over Great Britain for a dozen years must be set down to their skillful and moderated advocacy.

But to-day most interest and vitality attach to the third branch of Socialist activity—the Independent Labor party. The story of how this Socialist organization captured the trades unions, stirred out of their conservatism by the House of Lords decision on the Taff Vale question, and made an alliance whereby the International Labor party furnish the platform and leaders, and the unions the voters and the funds, is fresh in memory. The twenty-nine members who were returned to the present Parliament under this arrangement are not all Socialists, but the most active ones are, and of the rest Keir Hardie says : " Those, of my labor colleagues who are trade-unionists simply and not Socialists are prepared to go the length of nationalizing the railways, the coal mines, and the lands, and if they accomplish that in their lifetime may trust their sons to go further." Their immediate programme, though advanced, is not startling. Three demands, the protection of trades union funds from suit, the extension of the Workmen's Compensation Act to practically all trades, and provision for feeding breakfastless school-children at public expense, have already been carried. Secular education, a fourth plank, may possibly, though not probably, result from the present educational muddle. Old-age pensions must wait on financial reform. As for the nationalization proposals, they are not yet seriously pressed.

Two men stand out as leaders of this movement—Keir Hardie and Ramsay Macdonald. There was once a third, and, oddly, the third was also a Scot, claiming descent from the poet. But John Burns is too good a Liberal now to suit his labor friends. Years ago, when the London press was full of denunciation of this arch-agitator, he told his fellow-workmen at Battersea, "When the Liberal press begins to praise me, you will know I have betrayed you." To-day there is no politician in England more fulsomely lauded by official Liberal papers, and his straiter brethren do not hesitate to point the moral and wax sarcastic on the consistency of the man who once termed Albert Edward " the prince of outdoor relief paupers " now attending royal functions in full court paraphernalia, or accepting a government position worth £2,000 a year, when he of yore declared that no man alive was honestly worth more than £500 a year. But the impartial public, while recognizing one source of his conversion in his egotism and susceptibility to flattery, commend his level-headedness in recognizing the limits of possibility and trying in his post at the Local Government Board to accomplish something tangible in improving social conditions without weakening individual stamina.

The youngest man of the trio, Ramsay Macdonald, is whip and secretary of the party. By turn teacher, clerk, and journalist, he found his niche in organizing the party for the recent electoral struggle. His remarkable success stamps him as a leader of the type in which English Socialism has hitherto been lacking—hard-headed, practically efficient, not likely himself to care greatly for a point of dogma, and as the more able to restrain the centrifugal tendencies of those who do care. In a recent tour through Canada and the United States he commented severely on the futile revolutionarism of American Socialism. "Darwinism," he declared, "has made it as necessary to revise Marxism as Genesis."

Keir Hardie is a man of a different type. As his kindly eye might witness, there is more sympathy in his Socialism than in Macdonald's, more of the old flush of enthusiasm for humanity. To Macdonald the Socialist programme is a cold business proposition, to be put through as efficiently as skillful organization and bringing out the vote may accomplish; to Hardie it is a faith to be fulfilled, a vision to dream over and then to act, to bring the dreaming true. The external details of his career are of interest—he was a miner till twenty-four, secretary of the Lanarkshire miners' union for a few years, organizer next of the Scotch miners, his Radicalism slowly turning to Socialism; then in 1892 was elected to the Commons, which might have tolerated his proposals to upset the whole industrial organization of the country, but could not forgive his daring to enter that gentlemen's club without the time-honored silk hat. Note also his work in organizing the Independent Labor party, and his persistence last session in securing from the Cabinet the full price of Labor support. But perhaps the inner man is best revealed in an incident from his early life. After he had taught himself the alphabet down in the dark of the pit by scratching on a blackened stone, the first book he tackled was "Sartor Resartus." "How well I remember," he recalled recently, "sitting up o' nights in my little attic, staring at that wonderful book by the light of my pit-lamp. I could see there was something great in it, but it was far away, beyond my grasp. I longed to understand it. I grasped for the meaning among words of which I had never heard. It was a fearful struggle. Still I went on, and that was how I learned to read." And all through Keir Hardie's after life, however intemperate might be his policy, we see, shining through, the idealism and the doggedness here shadowed forth.

A PICTURESQUE BIT OF OLD MEXICO

# MODERN MEXICO

## BY COUNT MAURICE DE PÉRIGNY.

The establishment of more intimate and cordial relations between the United States and the nations of South America must be accompanied by a similar increase of intimacy between Mexico and the United States. Mexico is our first neighbor on the south, and while proximity ought to ally her to us, her Spanish origin brings her into a closer touch with South American peoples. Future citizens of this country who may travel to Argentina and Brazil by the Pan-American Railway of that day must first pass over Mexican soil on leaving their own country. Thus Mexico, by reason of both her national spirit and her geographical position, becomes an indispensable link with South America. In our judgment, the people of the United States are woefully provincial in their ignorance of the political, educational, and industrial achievements of Mexico. In publishing the following article The Outlook hopes to do something towards turning the attention of its readers in the direction of Mexico at this particular time, when the southern part of our hemisphere is receiving unusual consideration from the whole civilized world. The author is a member of various geographical societies and has been an extensive traveler. This particular paper is the result of four months of exploration and study in Mexico on his part. A French view of Mexico is valuable for the reasons which the author states in a letter to The Outlook: " To a Frenchman Mexico makes a strong appeal. It is a Latin country, and France, moreover, has exerted an important influence on its history. Napoleon III. wanted to build in the New World a Latin empire. The scheme was beautiful, but the United States Government was too powerful to permit its accomplishment. France was obliged to retire; she did not conquer the soil of Mexico for the Emperor of her choice; but she did peacefully conquer the Mexicans. In their ideas, their tastes, their literature, their art, French influence is strongly felt. In the schools the books of science, law, and medicine are French. Every Mexican of good birth speaks French fluently. Mexico calls France its intellectual mother and loves and admires her." It is to be hoped that some time she may regard the United States as an elder sister.—THE EDITORS.

AFTER a long period of discord and anarchy, after a series of revolutions and civil wars, Mexico had at last in 1857 obtained for itself a federal constitution. In 1861 the nomination to the Republic's presidency of the patriot Juarez seemed to give to this unhappy country a solid government and the hope of entering an era of peace. Unfortunately, the finances were in an awful state ; the interest on the loans, nearly all made at usurious rates, could not be paid. The Congress stopped the payment of the domestic national debt, after having done the same with the foreign debt and thereby caused the French Expedition into Mexico. But, the empire fallen, Maximilian dead, Juarez was re-elected as President, and at his death in 1872 he was succeeded by his Prime Minister, Lerdo de Tejada. Soon, however, the unfortunate country was troubled by a new revolution. General Porfirio Diaz was its leader, and the struggle began between the Lerdists and the Porfirists. Lerdo lost his control, ran off to Acapulco, and left the country in 1876. Diaz entered Mexico the 24th of November, was elected President, began an era of peace unknown before him, and at the end of his term, in 1880, retired in favor of his intimate friend, General Manuel Gonzalez. He retired to his native place, Oaxaca, as Governor, made a trip through the United States, and returned in 1884 to be elected President nearly unanimously. Since that time he has always been re-elected, and two years ago an amendment to the Constitution made the Presidential term six years instead of four.

Unweary worker, firm and energetic chief, able and honest administrator, sure of the army's support, Diaz has entirely reorganized Mexico, has made it a real country. Out of a most disturbed and revolutionary state he has made a peaceful and happy land. A distinguished soldier, he has shown himself a first-rate statesman, with an iron will, great practical sense, a clear knowledge of men and things. Before all, he sees the interest of his country; his ambition is to make Mexico a powerful and prosperous country, the Mexicans a great nation. In order to reach this end he has grouped about him a large number

these men have taken their country out of chaos, assured its tranquillity, consolidated its credit. They have made it a State rich and prosperous, a State recognized and respected by all.

How little it is known, this modern Mexico, even in the United States! People imagine a country hardly born to civilization, half-barbarous, inhabited by a multitude of Indian savages, always in revolution, where it is dangerous to travel

THE PATÍO OF A MEXICAN COUNTRY HOUSE

of faithful friends, like him devoted to the interests of the country: Corral, the Vice-President; Mariseal, Mena, and especially Limantour, the Minister of Finances. Diaz has secured peace for Mexico, has given it a firm government, but Limantour has furnished the resources which have allowed it to develop. In the creation of Mexico, in its organization as a modern State, these two names are associated, as they will ever remain, in the public gratitude. By their able and prudent administration

and much more so to stay. It was so of forty years ago, but under the strong direction of General Diaz's genius the order of things has been transformed. Mexico is now strongly constituted, regularly organized. Little by little the people, composed of heterogeneous elements too long divided by class prejudices, are beginning to understand the benefit of the constitution, and are willing to follow it to its full extent.

The first occupation of the Government under President Diaz was to pacify

the country, to clear the land and the city from bands of brigands, remains of the civil wars, who spread terror through the whole country. The organization of the rural guard, that of the city police in the federal district, and the energy of the President made this scourge disappear, and now, aside from a few regions where the last rebel Indians, Yaquis and Mayas, are placed, one can go everywhere through Mexico without any danger.

So established on a solid basis, with a strong financial credit, the Government tried to protect the country, to make the national flag respected, and therefore to create a good military organization. In peace, excepting the choice corps, the army is maintained by voluntary enlistments of men without work. Many individuals who as vagabonds would be dangerous for society are also enlisted, more or less voluntarily, and the influence of a strong discipline, with the certainty of the daily subsistence, improves naturally the morale of these soldiers.

One of the most important factors of this rapid and wonderful development of Mexico was, as for all young countries, the creation of a perfect network of railways. The railways are especially important in Mexico, where nature has erected tremendous obstacles to commercial traffic and to political unity. For that reason, since General Diaz has been in power, the construction of railways has been urged in all directions with an unwearied activity. Foreign capital, especially that of the United States, has answered eagerly the President's call. In 1876 Mexico had 578 kilometers of railways being worked; the 31st of December, 1901, it had 18,432 (about 11,000 miles). Three lines enter the United States and two connect Mexico with Vera Cruz. Others connect the capital with the Pacific, with the south, with the Isthmus of Tehuantepec, from which prolongations towards Guatemala and the State of Yucatan are planned. On all sides, in the different States, new local lines are building, developing the resources of every region. As a help to the railways, the Government has spent immense sums for the improvement of the harbors and the lighting of the coasts. Great works are in progress at Coatzacoalcos on the Atlantic and Salina Cruz on the Pacific. These are the two terminal points of the

PLACE MAJOR, CITY OF MEXICO

MODERN STEEL WORKS AT MONTEREY

MODERN SUGAR MILL

railway across the Isthmus of Tehuantepec, which will be one great commercial way between the Orient and the Occident. Other harbors on the Pacific are also improved—Acapulco, Manzanillo, Mazatlan. These harbors, unfortunately, are not connected with the capital. On each of the principal lines the engineers stopped at the Sierra Mountains, rebuffed by the difficulties of the passage ; but the connection of these harbors with the interior is of too vital an interest for the country not to have the Government make every effort possible to complete the proposed railways.[1] Thanks to these numerous railways and also an excellent system of posts and telegraphs, the relations between the different parts of the Republic have become more intimate and

[1] The line between Manzanillo and Guadalajara, on the main line, will be finished by the end of 1907.

more cordial. The particularist spirit of the provinces, a source of perpetual anarchy, has weakened little by little and has given place to a fine feeling of solidarity. There are no more Spaniards and Indians, there are only Mexicans. The action of the central power is sure and rapid, making easier the education of the peasantry and of the peons. And so, little by little, but slowly, alas ! the Indians are giving up their dialects to speak Spanish, and are learning how to read and to write ; and, thanks to the vivifying flood of primary instruction, progress is penetrating the smallest villages.

But what is needed in Mexico is hand labor. The land as a whole is thinly settled, and this is a serious obstacle to the rapid development of the country. To remedy this, the Government has encouraged the increase of foreign immigration, though it has not yet obtained great success, the immigrants being naturally attracted towards the United States by the prospect of easy work and large pay. Ignoring the true situation of Mexico, they fear the hardships of the climate, the difficulties of living, the dangers of a new country. What is needed most are workmen, tillers of the soil; most of the foreigners are tradespeople or engineers. The Spanish and American colonists are naturally the most important: the first, taking advantage of the sameness of language, of customs, and of religion, have prospered considerably and control the retail business, especially groceries. The Americans have brought in large capital, and hold enormous interests in mines, banks, and railways. The English prefer the management of mines, while the Germans go in for hardware. As for the French colony, very much liked and respected, it has the monopoly of the sale of stuffs and fashions. The Chinese, quite a large number of them, furnish the hand labor; they work in the mines, in railways, do the menial work, while the Japanese, the Mormons, and especially the Italians, are interested in agriculture. And yet, where could one find a wider field for laborious and intelligent energies than this country where there is every climate, a luxuriant growth, a rich and fertile earth, a propitious temperature, where there are millions of acres which give two harvests a year? The country is divided into large plantations which belong either to the State, to private individuals, or to corporations. The management of these " haciendas " demands a very large number of workers, overseers, and directors. The servants of all sorts have quarters of their own in small houses or cabins; the master lives in a special building, generally very large, and often beautiful. All around are grouped shops, stables, schools, a church, and the " tienda," which is a store where are sold the foodstuffs and the clothing necessary to the working population. In certain plantations the household may consist of three thou-

THE NEW POST-OFFICE IN THE CITY OF MEXICO

sand persons. These workers almost all belong to the soil, and receive, besides their salary, the privilege of cultivating a few acres for themselves. The foreigners are beginning to interest themselves in agriculture; formerly they paid more attention to mining, which constitutes the greater part of the wealth of Mexico. And the Government has taken all necessary measures to facilitate these enterprises and to give to capital two advantages essential for success—freedom and security.

Many pessimists believe that General Diaz is the indispensable pivot of the Mexican Republic, and that if he should die the Government would go to pieces. Everything seems, on the contrary, to show that Mexico has a great future before it. The excellence of the present institutions has been proved, the country has become more wise, perfectly quiet; every guarantee is given to investors. Revolutions are no longer to be feared; they would be too dangerous for the country, and would necessitate American intervention. But the Americans have no interest in wishing for this revolution.

Too great an empire always tends towards decadence, and it is preferable to have as a neighbor a peaceful and happy country than to dominate over a discontened and turbulent one.

# MY PICTURES

### BY MERIBAH ABBOTT

Some one gave me a picture—
A little glimpse of the sea,
Cliff and surf and a gull a-wing,—
I smell the salt and I feel the swing:
    How it comes back to me!
Rhythm of wave, and gleam of sand,
And a white sail rounding the point of land.

Some one gave me a picture—
A bit of a country lane,
Tangle of flower and fern and vines
Under the shade of the purple pines:
    Oh, to be there again!
There, where the ground-thrush hides her nest,
And the wild red strawberries ripen best.

So, pain-bound and helpless,
I lie and dream all day;
God is good, and the world is wide,
Sun and sea and the dancing tide,
    And a fair ship in the bay!
These are mine, and the skies of June
Sing, my heart, to the thrush's tune!

EDGAR ALLAN POE

# THE PIT AND THE PENDULUM

## BY EDGAR ALLAN POE

### WITH AN INTRODUCTION BY HAMILTON W. MABIE

N his short stories of mystery and terror Poe stands almost unrivaled; for while it is easy to indicate his affiliations with Hoffmann, it remains true that in "The Fall of the House of Usher," "Ligeia," and "The Mask of the Red Death," Poe's power of invention and exquisite sensitiveness to the descriptive value of words to convey the shadowy but definite and terrifying spell which he intends to cast over his reader are unique in the subtle use which he makes of them to detach the mind from actual surroundings and to convey it, as worshipers were led in the Egyptian temples, through long passages until the outer world had become a dim memory. It is in this power of banishing all other impressions from the mind and putting it into the possession of impossible figures and incredible situations that Poe shows his masterly artistic skill. These stories are all essentially unreal. The Lady Madeline and Ligeia are phantoms who never for a moment deceive us by any breath of the living soul. Nevertheless, we are so skillfully taken into their presence, and we live with them in an atmosphere so compounded of the things that deceive, enthrall, and impress, that even in our skepticism we shudder and feel ourselves bound by the same mysterious and awful fate that binds them. "The Pit and the Pendulum" lacks the beauty of diction and the spell of imagination which characterize the stories of Usher and Ligeia ; but in its cumulative energy of imagination and its analysis of the sensations of terror passing into torture it is a masterpiece, and fully deserves a place in this series of twelve short stories selected for their permanent value.

With a passion for beauty which, next to his love for his wife, was the deepest devotion of Poe, he united an interest in morbid temperaments and situations of mystery and terror that sometimes led him into grave artistic blunders. He has in more than one instance brought vividly before the mind situations or incidents· that cannot be described without creating a feeling of revulsion ; and this writer, who never sinned in any word or line against purity, sinned at times against sound feeling by touching too closely and handling too freely what is essentially repulsive. "The Pit and the Pendulum" lacks the richness of style of the stories of "Usher" and "Ligeia," the splendor of color of "The Cask of Amontillado" and "The Assignation;" but in the skill with which the materials are used so as steadily to increase the sense of horror, and in the vividness with which the entire scene is realized, it deserves a very high place among Poe's stories. In this story, as in many others, he masters the art of the short story as he himself has defined it, by securing "a certain unique or single effect," toward which every incident and word makes a definite contribution. A marvelous craftsman, who suffered from his lack of deep human insight and sympathy with his kind, Poe remains a magician in his ability to evoke scenes of terror and pictures of despair. Crime, insanity, disordered fantasy, lay always within the empire of his magical pencil. His work stands, as Mr. Bliss Perry has admirably said, "like some lightning-blasted tree, charred and blanched, lifting itself in slender, scornful strength above the undergrowth. No bird rests there save the hawk, restless-eyed ; there is peace for no man in its shadow. But it is fine-grained to the very heart of it, and ax and fire may sweep the hillside again and again, yet it will not fall." H. W. M.

Impia tortorum longas hic turba furores
Sanguinis innocui, non, satiata, aluit.
Sospite nunc patria, fracto nunc funeris antro,
Mors ubi dira fuit vita salusque patent.
*Quatrain composed for the gates of a market to be erected upon the site of the Jacobin Club House at Paris.*

I WAS sick—sick unto death with that long agony ; and when they at length unbound me, and I was permitted to sit, I felt that my senses were leaving me. The sentence—the dread sentence of death—was the last of distinct accentuation which reached my ears. After that, the sound of the inquisitorial voices seemed merged in one dreamy indeterminate hum. It conveyed to my soul the idea of *revolution*, perhaps from its association in fancy with the burr of a mill-wheel. This only for a brief period ; for presently I heard no more. Yet, for a while, I saw ; but with how terrible an exaggeration ! I saw the lips of the black-robed judges. They appeared to me white, whiter than the sheet upon which I trace these words, and thin even to grotesqueness ; thin with the intensity of their expression of firmness—of immovable resolution, of stern contempt of human torture. I saw that the decrees of what to me was Fate were still issuing from those lips. I saw them writhe with a deadly locution. I saw them fashion the syllables of my name ; and I shuddered because no sound succeeded. I saw, too, for a few' moments of delirious horror, the soft and nearly imperceptible waving of the sable draperies which enwrapped the walls of the apartment. And then my vision fell upon the seven tall candles upon the table. At first they wore the aspect of charity, and seemed white slender angels who would save me ; but then, all at once, there came a most deadly nausea over my spirit, and I felt every fiber in my frame thrill as if I had touched the wire of a galvanic battery, while the angel forms became meaningless specters, with heads of flame, and I saw that from them there would be no help. And then there stole into my fancy, like a rich musical note, the thought of 'what sweet rest there must be in the grave. The thought came gently and stealthily, and it seemed long before it attained full appreciation ; but just as my spirit came at length properly to feel and entertain it, the figures of the judges vanished, as if magically, from before me ; the tall candles sank into nothingness ; their flames went out utterly ; the blackness of darkness supervened ; all sensations appeared swallowed up in a mad rushing descent as of the soul into Hades. Then silence, and stillness, and night were the universe.          .

I had swooned ; but still will not say that all of consciousness was lost. What of it there remained I will not attempt to define, or even to describe ; yet all was not lost. In the deepest slumber—no ! In delirium—no ! In a swoon—no ! In death—no ! even in the grave all is not lost. Else there is no immortality for man. Arousing from"the most profound of slumbers, we break the gossamer web of *some* dream. Yet in a second afterward (so frail may that web have been) we remember not that we have dreamed. In the return to life from the swoon there are two stages : first, that of the sense of mental or spiritual, secondly, that of the sense of physical, existence. It seems probable that if, upon reaching the second stage, we could recall the impressions of the first, we should find these impressions eloquent in memories of the gulf beyond. And that gulf is—what ? How at least shall we distinguish its shadows from those of the tomb ? But if the impressions of what I have termed the first stage are not at will recalled, yet, after a long interval, do they not come unbidden, while we marvel whence they come ? He who has never swooned is not he who finds strange palaces and wildly familiar faces in coals that glow ; is not he who beholds floating in mid-

air the sad visions that the many may not view ; is not he who ponders over the perfume of some novel flower ; is not he whose brain grows bewildered with the meaning of some musical cadence which has never before arrested his attention.

Amid frequent and thoughtful endeavors to remember, amid earnest struggles to regather some token of the state of seeming nothingness into which my soul had lapsed, there have been moments when I have dreamed of success ; there have been brief, very brief periods when I have conjured up remembrances which the lucid reason of a later epoch assures me could have had reference only to that condition of seeming unconsciousness. These shadows of memory tell, indistinctly, of tall figures that lifted and bore me in silence down— down—still down—till a hideous dizziness oppressed me at the mere idea of the interminableness of the descent. They tell also of a vague horror at my heart, on account of that heart's unnatural stillness. Then comes a sense of sudden motionlessness throughout all things ; as if those who bore me (a ghastly train !) had outrun in their descent the limits of the limitless, and paused from the wearisomeness of their toil. After this I call to mind flatness and dampness ; and then all is *madness*—the madness of a memory which busies itself among forbidden things.

Very suddenly there came back to my soul motion and sound—the tumultuous motion of the heart, and, in my ears, the sound of its beating. Then a pause in which all is blank. Then again sound. and motion, and touch—a tingling sensation pervading my frame. Then the mere consciousness of existence without thought—a condition which lasted long. Then, very suddenly, *thought*, and shuddering terror, and earnest endeavor to comprehend my true state. Then a strong desire to lapse into insensibility. Then a rushing revival of soul and a successful effort to move. And now a full memory of the trial, of the judges, of the sable draperies, of the sentence, of the sickness, of the swoon. Then entire forgetfulness of all that followed ; of all that a later day and much earnestness of endeavor have enabled me vaguely to recall.

So far, I had not opened my eyes. I felt that I lay upon my back unbound. I reached out my hand, and it fell heavily upon something damp and hard. There I suffered it to remain for many minutes, while I strove to imagine where and *what* I could be. I longed yet dared not to employ my vision. I dreaded the first glance at objects around me. It was not that I feared to look upon things horrible, but that I grew aghast lest there should be *nothing* to see. At length, with a wild desperation at heart, I quickly unclosed my eyes. My worst thoughts, then, were confirmed. The blackness of eternal night encompassed me. I struggled for breath. The intensity of the darkness seemed to oppress and stifle me. The atmosphere was intolerably close. I still lay quietly, and made effort to exercise my reason. I brought to mind the inquisitorial proceedings, and attempted from that point to deduce my real condition. The sentence had passed; and it appeared to me that a very long interval of time had since elapsed. Yet not for a moment did I suppose myself actually dead. Such a supposition, notwithstanding what we read in fiction, is altogether inconsistent with real existence;—but where and in what state was I? The condemned to death, I knew, perished usually at the *autos-da-fé*, and one of these had been held on the very night of the day of my trial. Had I been remanded to my dungeon to await the next sacrifice, which would not take place for many months? This I at once saw could not be. Victims had been in immediate demand. Moreover, my dungeon, as well as all the condemned cells at Toledo, had stone floors, and light was not altogether excluded.

A fearful idea now suddenly drove the blood in torrents upon my heart, and for a brief period I once more relapsed into insensibility. Upon recovering, I at once started to my feet, trembling convulsively in every fiber. I thrust my arms wildly above and around me in all directions. I felt nothing; yet dreaded to move a step, lest I should be impeded by the walls of a *tomb*. Perspiration

burst from every pore, and stood in cold big beads upon my forehead. The agony of suspense grew at length intolerable, and I cautiously moved forward, with my arms extended and my eyes straining from their sockets, in the hope of catching some faint ray of light. I proceeded for many paces; but still all was blackness and vacancy. I breathed more freely. It seemed evident that mine was not, at least, the most hideous of fates.

And now, as I still continued to step cautiously onward, there came thronging upon my recollection a thousand vague rumors of the horrors of Toledo. Of the dungeons there had been strange things narrated—fables I had always deemed them—but yet strange, and too ghastly to repeat, save in a whisper. Was I left to perish of starvation in this subterranean world of darkness; or what fate, perhaps even more fearful, awaited me? That the result would be death, and a death of more than customary bitterness, I knew too well the character of my judges to doubt. The mode and the hour were all that occupied or distracted me.

My outstretched hands at length encountered some solid obstruction. It was a wall, seemingly of stone masonry—very smooth, slimy, and cold. I followed it up; stepping with all the careful distrust with which certain antique narratives had inspired me. This process, however, afforded me no means of ascertaining the dimensions of my dungeon; as I might make its circuit, and return to the point whence I set out, without being aware of the fact, so perfectly uniform seemed the wall. I therefore sought the knife which had been in my pocket when led into the inquisitorial chamber; but it was gone; my clothes had been exchanged for a wrapper of coarse serge. I had thought of forcing the blade in some minute crevice of the masonry, so as to identify my point of departure. The difficulty, nevertheless, was but trivial; although, in the disorder of my fancy, it seemed at first insuperable. I tore a part of the hem from the robe and placed the fragment at full length, and at right angles to the wall. In groping my way around the prison I could not fail to encounter this rag upon completing the circuit. So, at least, I thought; but I had not counted upon the extent of the dungeon, or upon my own weakness. The ground was moist and slippery. I staggered onward for some time, when I stumbled and fell. My excessive fatigue induced me to remain prostrate; and sleep soon overtook me as I lay.

Upon awaking, and stretching forth an arm, I found beside me a loaf and a pitcher with water. I was too much exhausted to reflect upon this circumstance, but ate and drank with avidity. Shortly afterward I resumed my tour around the prison, and with much toil came at last upon the fragment of the serge. Up to the period when I fell, I had counted fifty-two paces, and, upon resuming my walk, I had counted forty-eight more—when I arrived at the rag. There were in all, then, a hundred paces; and, admitting two paces to the yard, I presumed the dungeon to be fifty yards in circuit. I had met; however, with many angles in the wall, and thus I could form no guess at the shape of the vault; for vault I could not help supposing it to be.

I had little object—certainly no hope —in these researches; but a vague curiosity prompted me to continue them. Quitting the wall, I resolved to cross the area of the inclosure. At first I proceeded with extreme caution, for the floor, although seemingly of solid material, was treacherous with slime. At length, however, I took courage, and did not hesitate to step firmly—endeavoring to cross in as direct a line as possible. I had advanced some ten or twelve paces in this manner, when the remnant of the torn hem of my robe became entangled between my legs. I stepped on it and fell violently on my face.

In the confusion attending my fall I did not immediately apprehend a somewhat startling circumstance, which yet, in a few seconds afterward, and while I still lay prostrate, arrested my attention. It was this: my chin rested upon the floor of the prison, but my lips and the upper portion of my head, although seemingly at a less elevation than the chin, touched nothing. At the same time my forehead seemed bathed in a clammy

vapor, and the peculiar smell of decayed fungus arose to my nostrils. I put forward my arm, and shuddered to find that I had fallen at the very brink of a circular pit, whose extent, of course, I had no means of ascertaining at the moment. Groping about the masonry just below the margin, I succeeded in dislodging a small fragment, and let it fall into the abyss. For many seconds I hearkened to its reverberations as it dashed against the sides of the chasm in its descent; at length there was a sullen plunge into water, succeeded by loud echoes. At the same moment there came a sound resembling the quick opening and as rapid closing of a door overhead, while a faint gleam of light flashed suddenly through the gloom, and as suddenly faded away.

I saw clearly the doom which had been prepared for me, and congratulated myself upon the timely accident by which I had escaped. Another step before my fall, and the world had seen me no more. And the death just avoided was of that very character which I had regarded as fabulous and frivolous in the tales respecting the Inquisition. To the victims of its tyranny there was the choice of death with its direst physical agonies, or death with its most hideous moral horrors. I had been reserved for the latter. By long suffering my nerves had been unstrung, until I trembled at the sound of my own voice, and had become in every respect a fitting subject for the species of torture which awaited me.

Shaking in every limb, I groped my way back to the wall—resolving there to perish rather than risk the terrors of the wells, of which my imagination now pictured many in various positions about the dungeon. In other conditions of mind I might have had courage to end my misery at once, by a plunge into one of these abysses; but now I was the veriest of cowards. Neither could I forget what I had read of these pits—that the *sudden* extinction of life formed no part of their most horrible plan.

Agitation of spirit kept me awake for many long hours; but at length I again slumbered. Upon arousing, I found by my side, as before, a loaf and a pitcher of water. A burning thirst consumed me, and I emptied the vessel at a draught. It must have been drugged—for scarcely had I drunk before I became irresistibly drowsy. A deep sleep fell upon me—a sleep like that of death. How long it lasted, of course, I know not; but, when once again I unclosed my eyes, the objects around me were visible. By a wild, sulphurous luster, the origin of which I could not at first determine, I was enabled to see the extent and aspect of the prison.

In its size I had been greatly mistaken. The whole circuit of its walls did not exceed twenty-five yards. For some minutes this fact occasioned me a world of vain trouble; vain indeed—for what could be of less importance, under the terrible circumstances which environed me, than the mere dimensions of my dungeon? But my soul took a wild interest in trifles, and I busied myself in endeavors to account for the error I had committed in my measurement. The truth at length flashed upon me. In my first attempt at exploration I had counted fifty two paces, up to the period when I fell: I must then have been within a pace or two of the fragment of serge; in fact, I had nearly performed the circuit of the vault. I then slept—and, upon awaking, I must have returned upon my steps, thus supposing the circuit nearly double what it actually was. My confusion of mind prevented me from observing that I began my tour with the wall to the left, and ended it with the wall to the right.

I had been deceived, too, in respect to the shape of the enclosure. In feeling my way I had found many angles, and thus deduced an idea of great irregularity; so potent is the effect of total darkness upon one arousing from lethargy or sleep! The angles were simply those of a few slight depressions, or niches, at odd intervals. The general shape of the prison was square. What I had taken for masonry seemed now to be iron, or some other metal, in huge plates, whose sutures or joints occasioned the depressions. The entire surface of this metallic inclosure was rudely daubed in all the hideous and repulsive devices to which the charnel superstition of the monks has given rise. The figures of fiends in aspects of menace, with skeleton forms, and other more really fearful images, overspread and disfigured the walls. I observed that the outlines of these monstrosities were sufficiently distinct, but that the colors seemed faded and blurred, as if from the effects of a damp atmosphere. I now noticed the floor, too, which was of stone. In the center yawned the circular pit from whose jaws I had escaped; but it was the only one in the dungeon.

All this I saw distinctly and by much effort, for my personal condition had been greatly changed during slumber. I now lay upon my back, and at full length, on a species of low framework of wood. To this I was securely bound by a long strap resembling a surcingle. It passed in many convolutions about my limbs and body, leaving at liberty only my head, and my left arm to such extent that I could, by dint of much exertion, supply myself with food from an earthen dish which lay by my side on the floor. I saw, to my horror, that the pitcher had been removed. I say, to my horror—for I was consumed with intolerable thirst. This thirst it appeared to be the design of my persecutors to stimulate, for the food in the dish was meat pungently seasoned.

Looking upward, I surveyed the ceiling of my prison. It was some thirty or forty feet overhead, and constructed much as the side walls. In one of its panels a very singular figure riveted my whole attention. It was the painted figure of Time as he is commonly represented, save that, in lieu of a scythe, he held what, at a casual glance, I supposed to be the pictured image of a huge pendulum, such as we see on antique clocks. There was something, however, in the appearance of this machine which caused me to regard it more attentively. While I gazed directly upward at it (for its position was immediately over my own), I fancied that I saw it in motion. In an instant afterward the fancy was confirmed. Its sweep was brief, and of course slow. I watched it for some minutes, somewhat in fear, but more in wonder. Wearied at length with observing its dull movement, I turned my eyes upon the other objects in the cell.

A slight noise attracted my notice, and, looking to the floor, I saw several enormous rats traversing it. They had issued from the well, which lay just within view to my right. Even then, while I gazed, they came up in troops, hurriedly, with ravenous eyes, allured by the scent of the meat. From this it required much effort and attention to scare them away.

It might have been half an hour, perhaps even an hour (for I could take but imperfect note of time), before I again cast my eyes upward. What I then saw confounded and amazed me. The sweep of the pendulum had increased in extent by nearly a yard. As a natural consequence, its velocity was also much greater. But what mainly disturbed me was the idea that it had perceptibly *descended*. I now observed—with what horror it is needless to say—that its nether extremity was formed of a crescent of glittering steel, about a foot in length from horn to horn; the horns upward, and the under edge evidently as keen as that of a razor. Like a razor also, it seemed massy and heavy, tapering from the edge into a solid and broad structure. It was appended to a weighty rod of brass, and the whole *hissed* as it swung through the air.

I could no longer doubt the doom prepared for me by monkish ingenuity in torture. My cognizance of the pit had become known to the inquisitorial agents—*the pit*, whose horrors had been destined for so bold a recusant as myself—*the pit*, typical of hell, and regarded by rumor as the Ultima Thule of all their punishments. The plunge into this pit I had avoided by the merest of accidents, and I knew that surprise, or entrapment into torment, formed an important portion of all the grotesquerie of these dungeon deaths. Having failed to fall, it was no part of the demon plan to hurl me into the abyss; and thus (there being no alternative), a different and a milder destruction awaited me. Milder! I half smiled in my agony as I thought of such application of such a term.

What boots it to tell of the long, long hours of horror more than mortal, during which I counted the rushing oscillations of the steel! Inch by inch—line by line,

with a descent only appreciable at intervals that seemed ages—down and still down it came! Days passed—it might have been that many days passed—ere it swept so closely over me as to fan me with its acrid breath. The odor of the sharp steel forced itself into my nostrils. I prayed—I wearied heaven with my prayer for its more speedy descent. I grew frantically mad, and struggled to force myself upward against the sweep of the fearful cimeter. And then I fell suddenly calm, and lay smiling at the glittering death, as a child at some rare bauble.

There was another interval of utter insensibility; it was brief; for upon again lapsing into life there had been no perceptible descent in the pendulum. But it might have been long; for I knew there were demons who took note of my swoon, and who could have arrested the vibration at pleasure. Upon my recovery, too, I felt very—oh, inexpressibly—sick and weak as if through long inanition. Even amid the agonies of that period the human nature craved food. With painful effort, I outstretched my left arm as far as my bonds permitted, and took possession of the small remnant which had been spared me by the rats. As I put a portion of it within my lips, there rushed to my mind a half-formed thought of joy—of hope. Yet what business had *I* with hope? It was, as I say, a half-formed thought: man has many such which are never completed. I felt that it was of joy—of hope; but I felt also that it had perished in its formation. In vain I struggled to perfect—to regain it. Long suffering had nearly annihilated all my ordinary powers of mind. I was an imbecile—an idiot.

The vibration of the pendulum was at right angles to my length. I saw that the crescent was designed to cross the region of the heart. It would fray the serge of my robe—it would return and repeat its operations—again—and again. Notwithstanding its terrifically wide sweep (some thirty feet or more), and the hissing vigor of its descent, sufficient to sunder these very walls of iron, still the fraying of my robe would be all that, for several minutes, it would accomplish. And at this thought I paused. I dared not go further than this reflection. I dwelt upon it with a pertinacity of attention—as if in so dwelling I could arrest *here* the descent of the steel. I forced myself to ponder upon the sound of the crescent as it should pass across the garment—upon the peculiar thrilling sensation which the friction of cloth produces on the nerves. I pondered upon all this frivolity until my teeth were on edge.

Down—steadily down it crept. I took a frenzied pleasure in contrasting its downward with its lateral velocity. To the right—to the left—far and wide—with the shriek of a damned spirit! to my heart, with the stealthy pace of the tiger! I alternately laughed and howled as the one or the other idea grew predominant.

Down—certainly relentlessly down! It vibrated within three inches of my bosom! I struggled violently—furiously—to free my left arm. This was free only from the elbow to the hand. I could reach the latter from the platter beside me to my mouth, with great effort, but no farther. Could I have broken the fastenings above the elbow, I would have seized and attempted to arrest the pendulum. I might as well have attempted to arrest an avalanche!

Down—still unceasingly—still inevitably down! I gasped and struggled at each vibration. I shrunk convulsively at its every sweep. My eyes followed its outward or upward whirls with the eagerness of the most unmeaning despair; they closed themselves spasmodically at the descent, although death would have been a relief, oh, how unspeakable! Still I quivered in every nerve to think how slight a sinking of the machinery would precipitate that keen, glistening ax upon my bosom. It was *hope* that prompted the nerve to quiver—the frame to shrink. It was *hope*—the hope that triumphs on the rack—that whispers to the death-condemned even in the dungeons of the Inquisition.

I saw that some ten or twelve vibrations would bring the steel in actual contact with my robe; and with this observation there suddenly came over my spirit all the keen, collected calmness of despair. For the first time during many hours—or perhaps days—I *thought*. It now occurred to me that the bandage, or surcingle, which enveloped me was unique. I was tied by no separate cord. The first stroke of the razor-like crescent athwart any portion of the band would so detach it that it might be unwound from my person by means of my left hand. But how fearful, in that case, the proximity of the steel! The result of the slightest struggle, how deadly! Was it likely, moreover, that the minions of the torturer had not foreseen and provided for this possibility? Was it probable that the bandage crossed my bosom in the track of the pendulum? Dreading to find my faint and, as it seemed, my last hope frustrated, I so far elevated my head as to obtain a distinct view of my breast. The surcingle enveloped my limbs and body close in all directions—*save in the path of the destroying crescent.*

Scarcely had I dropped my head back into its original position, when there flashed upon my mind what I cannot better describe than as the unformed half of that idea of deliverance to which I have previously alluded, and of which a moiety only floated indeterminately through my brain when I raised food to my burning lips. The whole thought was now present—feeble, scarcely sane, scarcely definite—but still entire. I proceeded at once, with the nervous energy of despair, to attempt its execution.

For many hours the immediate vicinity of the low framework upon which I lay had been literally swarming with rats. They were wild, bold, ravenous—their red eyes glaring upon me as if they waited but for motionlessness on my part to make me their prey. "To what food," I thought, "have they been accustomed in the well?"

They had devoured, in spite of all my efforts to prevent them, all but a small remnant of the contents of the dish. I had fallen into an habitual seesaw, or wave of the hand about the platter; and, at length, the unconscious uniformity of the movement deprived it of effect. In their voracity the vermin frequently fastened their sharp fangs in my fingers. With the particles of the oily and spicy viand which now remained I thoroughly rubbed the bandage wherever I could reach it; then, raising my hand from the floor, I lay breathlessly still.

At first the ravenous animals were startled and terrified at the change—at the cessation of movement. They shrank alarmedly back; many sought the well. But this was only for a moment. I had not counted in vain upon their voracity. Observing that I remained without motion, one or two of the boldest leaped upon the framework, and smelt at the surcingle. This seemed the signal for a general rush. Forth from the well they hurried in fresh troops. They clung to the wood—they overran it, and leaped in hundreds upon my person. The measured movement of the pendulum disturbed them not at all. Avoiding its strokes, they busied themselves with the anointed bandage. They pressed—they swarmed upon me in ever accumulating heaps. They writhed upon my throat; their cold lips sought my own; I was half stifled by their thronging pressure; disgust, for which the world has no name, swelled my bosom, and chilled, with a heavy clamminess, my heart. Yet one minute, and I felt that the struggle would be over. Plainly I perceived the loosening of the bandage. I knew that in more than one place it must be already severed. With a more than human resolution I lay *still*.

Nor had I erred in my calculations—nor had I endured in vain. At length I felt that I was *free*. The surcingle hung in ribbons from my body. But the stroke of the pendulum already pressed upon my bosom. It had divided the serge of the robe. It had cut through the linen beneath. Twice again it swung, and a sharp sense of pain shot through every nerve. But the moment of escape had arrived. At a wave of my hand my deliverers hurried tumultuously away. With a steady movement—cautious, side-long, shrinking, and slow—I slid from the embrace of the bandage and beyond the reach of the cimeter. For the moment, at least, *I was free*.

Free!—and in the grasp of the Inquisition! I had scarcely stepped from my wooden bed of horror upon the stone floor of the prison, when the motion of the hellish machine ceased, and I beheld it drawn up, by some invisible force, through the ceiling. This was a lesson which I took desperately to heart. My every motion was undoubtedly watched. Free!—I had but escaped death in one form of agony to be delivered unto worse than death in some other. With that thought I rolled my eyes nervously around on the barriers of iron that hemmed me in. Something unusual—some change which at first I could not appreciate distinctly—it was obvious, had taken place in the apartment. For many minutes of a dreamy and trembling abstraction I busied myself in vain, unconnected conjecture. During this period I became aware, for the first time, of the origin of the sulphurous light which illumined the cell. It proceeded from a fissure, about half an inch in width, extending entirely around the prison at the base of the walls, which thus appeared and were completely separated from the floor. I endeavored, but of course in vain, to look through the aperture.

As I arose from the attempt the mystery of the alteration in the chamber broke at once upon my understanding. I have observed that, although the outlines of the figures upon the walls were sufficiently distinct, yet the colors seemed blurred and indefinite. These colors had now assumed, and were momentarily assuming, a startling and most intense brilliancy, that gave to the spectral and fiendish portraitures an aspect that might have thrilled even firmer nerves than my own. Demon eyes, of a wild and ghastly vivacity, glared upon me in a thousand directions, where none had been visible before, and gleamed with the lurid luster of a fire that I could not force my imagination to regard as unreal.

*Unreal!*—Even while I breathed there came to my nostrils the breath of the vapor of heated iron! A suffocating odor pervaded the prison. A deeper glow settled each moment in the eyes that glared at my agonies! A richer tint of crimson diffused itself over the pictured horrors of blood. I panted! I gasped for breath! There could be no doubt of the design of my tormentors—oh, most unrelenting! oh, most demoniac of men! I shrank from the glowing metal to the center of the cell. Amid the thought of the fiery destruction that impended, the idea of the coolness of the well came over my soul like balm. I rushed to its deadly brink. I threw my straining vision below. The glare from the enkindled roof illumined its inmost recesses. Yet, for a wild moment, did my spirit refuse to comprehend the meaning of what I saw. At length it forced—it wrestled its way into my soul —it burned itself in upon my shuddering reason. Oh, for a voice to speak! —oh, horror!—oh, any horror but this! With a shriek I rushed from the margin, and buried my face in my hands— weeping bitterly.

The heat rapidly increased, and once again I looked up, shuddering as with a fit of the ague. There had been a second change in the cell—and now the change was obviously in the *form*. As before, it was in vain that I at first endeavored to appreciate or understand what was taking place. But not long was I left in doubt. The Inquisitorial vengeance had been hurried by my twofold escape, and there was to be no more dallying with the King of Terrors. The room had been square. I saw that two of its iron angles were now acute—two, consequently, obtuse. The fearful difference quickly increased with a low rumbling or moaning sound. In an instant the apart-

ment had shifted its form into that of a lozenge. But the alteration stopped not here—I neither hoped nor desired it to stop. I could have clasped the red walls to my bosom as a garment of eternal peace. "Death," I said, "any death but that of the pit!" Fool! might I not have known that *into the pit* it was the object of the burning iron to urge me? Could I resist its glow? or, if even that, could I withstand its pressure? And now, flatter and flatter grew the lozenge, with a rapidity that left me no time for contemplation. Its center, and, of course, its greatest width, came just over the yawning gulf. I shrank back—but the closing walls pressed me resistlessly onward. At length for my seared and writhing body there was no longer an inch of foothold on the firm floor of the prison. I struggled no more, but the agony of my soul found vent in one loud, long, and final scream of despair. I felt that I tottered upon the brink—I averted my eyes—

There was a discordant hum of human voices! There was a loud blast as of many trumpets! There was a harsh grating as of a thousand thunders! The fiery walls rushed back! An outstretched arm caught my own as I fell, fainting, into the abyss. It was that of General Lasalle. The French army had entered Toledo. The Inquisition was in the hands of its enemies.

## *Comment on Current Books*

*Among the Novels* Many romance-writers have inventive facility, but comparatively few have the knack of sustaining a situation tensely and continuously. The late Hugh Scott (H. S. Merriman) had this faculty in a noteworthy degree; Sir Gilbert Parker has it; Mr. A. E. W. Mason has proved his possession of it in "Four Feathers" and "Miranda of the Balcony," to say nothing of his "Courtship of Morrice Buckley," the first, and some readers think the best, of his novels. Now, in "Running Water" (The Century Company, New York) one finds again that compelling story-interest which stirs and holds the attention without resort to ultra-sensationalism and without relaxing from sound and reasonably conservative literary form.

The several threads of the plot are singularly unlike—the passion for Alpine climbing, its hereditary transmission and its influence on a girl's character on the one hand, and on the other the murderous plots of swindlers who are luring a foolish young man to his death after heavily insuring his life. To bring the two elements into a well-balanced and reasonable story was not easy, and Mr. Mason, while he always interests his reader's mind, does not always convince him as to the plausibility of the incidents. Essentially it is as a tale rather than as a study of character that "Running Water" is entertaining.

Quite the contrary with Maarten Maartens's "The Woman's Victory" (D. Appleton & Co., New York). Here, in a dozen or so short stories, sometimes amusing, sometimes distressing or tragical, the author studies as many traits of feminine character—devotion, delicacy, resource, courage, love. There is a fineness and acuteness in these sketches, for they are little more, that few fiction-writers of our day could equal.

In "Prisoners of Fortune," by Ruth Perley Smith (L. C. Page & Co., Boston), an old man, sitting at ease in his quiet home, tells his life story, and recalls many perilous adventures. Pirates were common about American shores early in the eighteenth century, and their bloody deeds, and often their shameful end on the gallows, were recounted as warnings to venturous lads. Philip Campbell was caught in the fever of search for hidden treasure, and his hairbreadth escapes, his romantic love story, and his sufferings and successes are all put down in serious style, quite unrelieved by vivacity, but wholly consistent with the gravity of his day. A modern tale of sea adventure far more lively if not at bottom more probable is Mr. Louis Tracy's "The Captain of the Kansas" (E. J. Clode, New York). Mr. Tracy always writes of the sea, the shipwreck, and the distant dangers of far-off islands with verve and dash; and his men and women are all right so long as they act; but when they talk—alas! missish sentiment, mechanical vivacity, and swelling rhetoric first amuse and then bore. As a sea-story the book is capital, as a novel it is nothing.

While we are on the subject of sensational stories let us record our interest in "Seth Jones of New Hampshire," and especially in the historical introduction on the dime novel written by the veteran writer of novels, boys' stories and histories, Mr. Edward G. Ellis. About forty-eight years ago billboards the country over bore placards with the question, "Who is Seth Jones?" Later appeared in answer placards with that picture of a hunter beloved by all boy readers of the real, original, genuine, yellow-covered Beadle's Dime Novels, and the inscription, "I am Seth Jones." The book was Number Eight of the Beadle series, and it sold 400,000 copies. Now we have it reprinted as a curiosity of literature in a respectable cloth cover. We cheerfully testify that it is innocuous, simple, free from moral taint, and as little sensational as is humanly possible for a book with Indians, a kidnapped maiden, and a hunter with a coonskin cap to be. As Mr. Ellis must have been about nineteen years old when he wrote it, he will not be hurt if we say that "Seth Jones" is a very mild case of Fenimore Cooper and water. It is often said that many of the dollar and a half novels of our time are merely well-bound dime novels, but if this is a fair specimen of

the original dime novel our sensation-seekers would find it tame in comparison. Mr. Ellis makes out a very good case for the early dime novel, but, alas! Beadle was crowded out by Munro, "the pages became crimson," and "dime novel" became synonymous with vicious sensationalism. (G. W. Dillingham Company, New York.)

The foregoing remarks naturally lead us to consider Mr. Thomas W. Lawson's "Friday the 13th," which in cutting of throats and other suicidal exercises, in plotted villainy, ruin and blank despair, and most of all in ranting, roaring, heaven-shrieking rhetoric, was surely never surpassed by the yellowest of the yellow-backs. Not even Mr. Lawson can desire more than The Outlook to see the evils of stock-gambling abolished, and if this story will do any good in that way we give it our heartfelt benison; but we may also express our joy that the medicine, if potent, is administered in a small dose, and that after an hour's hectic tumult of soul we can dismiss the ills of tragic finance. (Doubleday, Page & Co., New York.) The very next book we take up is also a study in fiction of financial methods—happily, however, written more quietly. Mr. Edwin Lefevre's "Sampson Rock of Wall Street" (Harper & Brothers, New York) is minute and realistic in its pictures of speculators' methods and the tricks of manipulation. It has also good and sincere rendering of individual character both in the elder Rock and his son Sam. The first is a man who is in his large intention not a stock-gambler but a constructive man who means to be an industrial leader and developer of the country, but who works the market by every trick and deceit to get control of a railway he needs to carry out that purpose. His son, just home from college and Europe, loves the old man but hates his methods, and sets out to get the railway by fair purchase without incidental ruin of stockholders. The story is graphic and often exciting, but it has not quite the fascination of Mr. Lefevre's "The Golden Flood." It was a bold thing to base a novel so exclusively on financial battling—for the love story is extremely slight. One feels that the author has succeeded by sheer weight of ability, but that the experiment is one not to be easily repeated.

Jack London's "Before Adam" is a remarkable piece of imaginative work in that it pictures our primordial ancestors consistently and vividly. At least two other books of fiction had already dealt with this subject, but the charge that Mr. London has unfairly used them as material is absurd to any one who has read the books. In one respect

'Before Adam" is weak; it is too truth-oving as regards scientific records to leave nuch room for the emotional aspects of life. Mr. London's dog in "The Call of the Wild" und his wolf in "White Fang" are in a sense nore human than his tree-climbers or cave-dwellers or even fire-makers in this book. The story is a sort of literary *tour de force*, ubly done and curiously fascinating. (The Macmillan Company, New York.)

Mr. Edward Noble's "The Issue" is a distressful tale of the Thames and those who live by it, and of sea-life and sea-goers. It needs compression and it lacks brightness, but it is ambitious in its dissection of motives and character. One may hope that such undoubted ability as this writer possesses may in his next story be applied to entertain rather than to puzzle, and to give a clear picture of the joy as well as the misery of life. (Doubleday, Page & Co., New York.)

**American Legislatures** Mr. Reinsch has done far more than make a handbook relating to American legislatures and legislation. In accordance with the intention of the series of books to which this belongs, he describes comprehensively the manner in which the legislative bodies of the Nation and the States are organized and the scope and exercise of their respective functions. He also discusses from the standpoint of political philosophy and of practical dealings with public questions of importance the technical methods of legislatures and the trend of legislative bodies in directing their procedure to accomplish specific ends. The division of power between the executive and legislative branches and the interpretation of statutes by the courts have due attention. In every way the volume is not only informative but suggestive, and is eminently thorough in treatment. (American Legislatures and Legislative Methods. By Paul S. Reinsch. The Century Company, New York. $1.25, net.)

**Animals as Criminals** The author of this book has made a profound study of the extremely curious facts to be found in mediæval and even in modern penology relating to the prosecution and punishment of animals. One is surprised to find so much on this subject and so widespread prevalence of the extraordinary idea that evil-doing by animals was a subject for the law to deal with. Of course much of the judicial prosecution of animals had its origin in pure superstition, and came from the belief that they were bewitched or possessed of devils. The result accordingly was often formal excommunication by the Church; and, ludicrous as such a thing appears to us, it

was a very solemn affair in its time. But the idea extended far away from the idea of exorcism, and even to this day traces of the ancient beliefs on this subject may be found, as where, according to the author, the custom still survives, among superstitious and credulous persons in European countries and in some portions of the United States, of serving a sort of writ of judgment on rats or sending them a friendly letter of advice in order to induce them to quit any house in which their presence is undesirable. A case is quoted even as late as 1888 where such a letter was written in Maine, addressed in business style to "Messrs. Rats & Co.," and presumably, following the ancient custom, was rubbed with grease to attract the attention of the rats, rolled up and thrust into their holes. If such a thing can be done in our own time with serious intention, it is not hard to believe some of the extraordinary tales told by this author of the proceedings taken against snakes, cats, dogs, pigs, and horses. The author has succeeded in making an extremely readable and in a sense a learned volume, one which is a welcome addition to the curiosities of literature. (The Criminal Prosecution and Capital Punishment of Animals. By E. P. Evans. E. P. Dutton & Co., New York. $2.50, net.)

**How to be Happy** This tonic little book grew, the author tells us, from Wordsworth's remark that Coleridge could not fully understand his poems "because he was not happy enough." If any fail to appreciate the book, it will be because they lack the moral fiber for the climb which the way to happiness requires. The happiness it speaks of is found in the realization of the true self—the divine germ in humanity—through good work for a noble object and a high ideal. Such happiness, moreover, is affirmed to be, not a privilege of the few, but the duty of all; a short way of saying that it is realized through fidelity to what is best in us. Practical philosophy spiced with wit and humor, and blending with a broad and virile religion, characterizes the course of thought. "There are more homes the happiness and daily comfort of which are affected by their having ceased to pray than are conscious of the fact." The missing note, if any, in the book is of sympathy and encouragement for those that have lost heart and feel driven to the wall. (The Way to Happiness. By Thomas R. Slicer. The Macmillan Company, New York. $1.25, net.)

**The Law of Railroad Rate Regulation** This is a legal treatise of twelve hundred pages. It contains the full text of the Inter-State Commerce

Act and decisions both of the courts and of the Commission under this act, as well as a discussion of the general principles of public service law and the primary obligations of those in public employments, particularly of carriers. In brief, it covers comprehensively the whole law, both common and statutory, with respect to railway rate regulation. The range covered is illustrated by the fact that not merely railways but other public service corporations, as those dealing with cemeteries, water-works, gas-works, and the like, are included. The book appears to us a valuable addition to the editor's library, and, with its companion book of " Selected Cases " on the same general subject, to be well-nigh indispensable to the lawyer who has to deal with this subject. (The Law of Railroad Rate Regulation. By Joseph Henry Beale, Jr., and Bruce Wyman. William J. Nagel, Boston. $4, net.)

*A Library of Home Economics*  The extent of the field covered in this series of books and the practical character of the topics dealt with may be judged by the appended list of volumes. The editors and directors of the American School of Home Economics, by whom these books have been prepared, take as their motto the belief that "right living should be the fourth R in education " and that " home-making should be regarded as a profession." It is certainly true, as they declare. that there has been a great industrial evolution in the last two generations in the home as elsewhere, and it is equally true that the management of the home and the care of the family may now rightly be called both a business and a profession. Looking at the subject in this light, the volumes of this library may be regarded as the tools and formulæ for carrying on the work in a systematized and intelligent manner. It would be impossible to comment individually on each of these dozen text-books, but it may be said broadly that a wise discrimination has been exercised in the choice of the authors of the books, for these writers are recognized authorities and special students in the various fields with which they deal. In all cases, so far as we have observed, simplicity of statement and clarity in bringing essential points in due relation and proportion before the student's eye are qualities carefully sought for. The exposition of facts is helped by numerous drawings and diagrams, and brevity is equally sought for, but without sacrificing completeness in presenting the subject under discussion. (The Library of Home Economics: Vol. I., The House: Its Plan,

Decoration, and Care, by Isabel Bevier. II., Household Bacteriology, by S. Maria Elliott. III., Household Hygiene, by S. Maria Elliott. IV., Chemistry of the Household, by Margaret E. Dodd. V., Principles of Cookery, by Anna Barrows. VI., Food and Dietetics, by Alice Peloubet Norton. VII., Household Management, by Bertha M. Terrill. VIII., Personal Hygiene, by Maurice Le Bosquet. IX., Home Care of the Sick, by Amy Elizabeth Pope. X., Textiles and Clothing, by Kate Heintz Watson. XI., Study of Child Life, by Marion Foster Washburne. XII., Care of Children, by Alfred Cleveland Cotton. American School of Home Economics, Chicago.)

*A Normal Democratic Government*  " Newer Ideals of Peace " is not a felicitous title for Jane Addams's interesting and suggestive volume. It is interesting because it gives the reflections of a woman of extraordinary ability upon certain aspects of modern life which she has had extraordinary opportunities for observing. It is suggestive because she sees very clearly that the old conception of government as a mere keeper of the peace, a mere umpire to watch that the industrial game is played according to the traditional rules, is wholly inadequate to meet present conditions. It is imperfect because she has studied only one phase of our National life, and, in American fashion—we were tempted to write feminine fashion—she draws too large generalizations from her too specialized observations. We do not doubt, for example, that her graphic and dismal picture of the treatment of immigrants in America (pp. 44, 45) is true of *some* immigrants—chiefly those who are concentrated in certain of our cities. But Commissioner Watchorn, from his wider knowledge of the immigrant population, would give a very different report of the conditions and the sentiments of the immigrant population as a whole. But with the theme of this book The Outlook is in hearty sympathy, and that theme Miss Addams enforces by a great variety of valuable illustrations taken from real life in what is perhaps the most cosmopolitan city in the country. " Whereas representative government, from the nature of the case, has to do with the wicked, who are happily always in a minority in the community, a normal democratic government would naturally have to do with the great majority of the population in their normal relations to each other." Her book is larger, her theme more profound, than her title would indicate. (Newer Ideals of Peace. By Jane Addams. The Citizen's Library. The Macmillan Company, New York. $1.25, net.)

# Letters to The Outlook

## THE ENGLISH LABOR PARTY

In The Outlook of February 9, which has just reached me, you have a leader note entitled "A Setback to Socialists," in which you deal with recent happenings in Germany, Russia, and here in Great Britain. Whether you consider the elections in Germany and Russia "a setback to Socialism" in view of the votes is a matter of judgment, but when you proceed to make certain comments upon what happened at our Labor Conference last month in Belfast you depart from the sphere of opinion and come to that of fact. You make certain statements as follows: "The most notable issue was the struggle for control between the Socialists and the trade-unionists;" "Mr. Keir Hardie, who led the advanced Socialists, was overwhelmingly defeated in the convention;" "The political policy of organized labor, as defined by the Congress, involves freedom from affiliation with the extreme Socialist propaganda and the endeavor to secure legislation by holding a balance of power between the two main parties;" "Considerable opposition against public ownership in collectivism was manifested at the Congress."

As a matter of simple fact, not a single one of those statements is correct. The Socialist resolution to which you refer was moved, not by a Socialist society, but by a small trade union. The Socialist organizations present, instead of supporting it, opposed it on the ground that it was a breach of the understanding come to between the trade-unionists and the Socialists six years ago. Mr. Keir Hardie opposed the resolution, and, so far from being overwhelmingly defeated, helped to overwhelmingly defeat the other side. Moreover, the sentence stating that it was formally agreed that it was not necessary for the Socialists to become trade-unionists is one the import of which you do not seem to understand. If there was any big question involving policy before the Conference, this was it. Instead of being overwhelmingly defeated, Mr. Hardie and his Socialist friends overwhelmingly defeated the other side again. Nor is it true that considerable opposition was manifested against public ownership and collectivism. The Conference unanimously passed the collectivist resolution twelve months ago, and if it were asked to repeat the vote it would do so. The resolutions upon Land, Public Management of the Liquor Traffic, and so on, went through unanimously, and were all embodiments of the idea of public ownership and collectivism.

Finally, it is not true to say that the policy which the party laid down was that of securing legislation by holding the balance of power between the two main parties. That is exactly the opposite of what the party policy is. Our policy is to build up a party independent of the other political parties, and to get legislation through by the sheer force of the case that we can make out for it. It will be a very bad day for labor, not only in Great Britain but in America, when it comes to such a foolish resolution as you suggest we came to, namely, to get legislation passed by holding a balance of power between two unsympathetic political parties.

In view of the way in which your article has so grossly misrepresented what took place at Belfast, I would be much obliged if you would publish this letter in your next issue.       Yours faithfully,

J. RAMSAY MACDONALD,
Secretary of the Labor Party ; Member of Parliament for Leicester.

London, England.

[The paragraph to which this letter refers was based on cable reports. We are glad to present Mr. MacDonald's statement.—THE EDITORS.]

## RAILWAY RATE REGULATION

In The Outlook of January 5, under the head of "Railway Rate Regulation: The Next Step," you discussed the two theories of rate-making, the first of which you say is generally applied, and the second of which you think should be applied, in fixing the remuneration for service performed in the transportation of freight traffic.

The first theory is that transportation service is private property, and the railway sells it to the shipper for what the traffic will bear. The second theory is that transportation is not private property to be sold, but a public service to be rendered, and the price paid for this service " is not a price paid by a customer, but a toll paid by the purchaser."

In your opinion, " all that we have done so far is to give the Inter-State Commerce Commission power, on complaint that particular charges are unjust and unreasonable, to order them made just and reasonable;" and that what we next want is an official recognition by law of that second theory, and a conference by representatives of the people

inted by the Government and representa-
of the railways "in an endeavor to
e upon a certain general principle to be
ersally applied by the Government in
rmining what the tolls should be."
his would be a duplication of commis-
s, which of itself is of doubtful propriety ;
moreover, these two theories are, in fact,
e or less interwoven, and are of necessity
rally applied to-day in any fair adjust-
of rates. In our opinion, we should
long enough to determine just *what* we
already done before we begin an effort
lve this problem upon a new basis.

enerally speaking, there are two kinds of
imination—discrimination against indi-
als and discrimination against communi-

e present law has proved effective for
punishment of those who solicit and
who grant rebates, and consequently
feature depends upon the honesty and
essness of those to whom the enforce-
of the law is intrusted.

e question of the second form of dis-
ination, that against cities or communi-
demands not only the knowledge of the
points involved, but also an intimate
exact knowledge of the commercial con-
ns of the communities interested and the
irements thereof, and a fair adjustment
e rates involved as between the rival
s or communities, and also a fair and
consideration of the interest of the rail-
. Especially delicate is this feature,
use you are dealing not only with one or
zen rates, but with hundreds of rates ;
in readjusting these rates for one city or
nunity it will very likely involve the
justment of rates to and from numerous
r points.

e regulation of this is within the prov-
of the Commissioners, as is also the
lation of any inter-State rate that may be
plained of ; and the Commissioners are
engaged in various sections of the
try taking evidence on such complaints,
their decisions are promised at an early
. Thus certainly the powers of the Com-
ion are ample, I might say dangerous ;
n putting into the hands of the Commis-
the power to say what rates are un-
nable, and to readjust the transportation
ges of this country, we have given to the
mission, a body of not infallible men, a
er that is appalling to the capitalist,
cially when, in addition to bona-fide
plaints, every demagogue and red journal
ying for blood, and every complaint calls
readjustment, not by advances, but by
ctions, and out of decreasing revenue

must come the increased cost of operati
Thus it behooves the conservative journal
of the country, as a part of wisdom and fair
play, to stop this agitation until it can be
seen to what extent the Commission is equal
to the enormous task before it. If the present Commission prove incompetent, then
change the personnel of that body until we
secure an expert Commission, and have a full
demonstration of the effectiveness of the
present laws.         E. O. ALSTON.
Montclair, Colorado.

## MR. CAMPBELL AS A THEOLOGIAN

[A member of the City Temple sends The
Outlook the following protest against its
expressed judgment that the Rev. R. J.
Campbell, while a great preacher, "is not fit
to frame a system of philosophy." We gladly
give place to her eulogy of her pastor, while
it does not change our judgment. Mr. Campbell is a great preacher, but not a great theologian. The two terms are not synonymous.
In fact, it is very rare that the same man has
the abilities which fit him for both positions.—THE EDITORS.]

I have heard Mr. Campbell in his own
pulpit very many times during the past three
years, besides enjoying the honor of his personal friendship, and I should say that of
the many exceptional qualifications that go
towards his unique equipment as a preacher
none is more remarkable than his power of
sustained and connected thought. I never
heard Dr. Parker, but from all I have heard
of him I think it would be difficult to find
two men more dissimilar, excepting in the
possession of a magnetic personality. Mr.
Campbell preaches three times a week, twice
on Sunday, and on Thursday at noon for
city men and women. His sermons are delivered invariably without even the briefest
notes, being reported, *verbatim* for publication. They are characterized by beauty of
diction, simplicity and purity of style, and
lucidity of purport. The theme is never for
a moment lost sight of, and quotations and
references from the most varied sources
(besides the Bible, which Mr. Campbell
seems to have absorbed from cover to cover)
are ready in abundance to point a figure or
sustain an argument. That he is "a master
of epigrammatic style " *when he sees fit to
use it* I grant you; but I have wholly misunderstood the meaning of the term "epigrammatic " if it can be applied truthfully
in any general sense, to Mr. Campbell's
preaching.
    A MEMBER OF THE CITY TEMPLE.
Albany, New York.

Comfort, Luxury, Convenience, Health attend the
installation of

### "Standard" Porcelain Enameled Ware

in the home. For the sanitary equipment of the bathroom, bedroom,
kitchen, laundry "Standard" Ware is a constant guarantee of
satisfaction, and its life-long service distinctly increases the property
value of your home, while the china-like purity of its white enameled
surface is a constant source of pleasure and delight in usage.

Our Book, "MODERN BATHROOMS," tells you how to plan, buy and arrange your bathroom,
and illustrates many beautiful and inexpensive as well as luxurious rooms, showing the cost of
each fixture in detail, together with many hints on decoration, tiling, etc. It is the most complete
and beautiful booklet ever issued on the subject, and contains 100 pages. FREE for six cents postage and the name of your plumber and architect (if selected).

The ABOVE FIXTURES, Design P-38, can be purchased from any plumber at a cost approximating $70.00—not counting freight, labor or piping—and are described in detail among the others.

*CAUTION : Every piece of* **Standard** *Ware bears our* **Standard** *"GREEN and GOLD" guarantee
label, and has our trade-mark* **Standard** *cast on the outside. Unless the label and trade-mark are on the fixture it
is not* **Standard** *Ware. Refuse substitutes—they are all inferior and will cost you more in the end. The word
**Standard** is stamped on all our nickeled brass fittings; specify them and see that you get the genuine trimmings
with your bath and lavatory, etc.*

  Address **Standard Sanitary Mfg. Co** Dept. 22, Pittsburgh, U. S. A.

Pittsburgh Showroom, 949 Penn Avenue
Offices and Showrooms in New York: **Standard** Building, 35-37 West 31st Street
London, England, 22 Holborn Viaduct, E. C.
New Orleans, Cor. Baronne & St. Joseph Sts.
Louisville, 325-329 West Main Street          Cleveland, 208-210 Huron Street

## The Next President

The article "The Next President: Republican Possibilities" in t
week's Outlook will be followed next week by one on Democr:
Possibilities by the same author, Mr. John Callan O'Laughlin,
well-known newspaper correspondent.

## The Great Northwest

Mr. John Foster Carr, who went to Panama for The Outlook:
wrote an illuminating series of articles on the Canal, has been spe
ing several months in the Northwest under commission to write
The Outlook several papers on the remarkable industrial devel
ment of that section and some of its notable men, such as Mr. J.
Hill and Archbishop Ireland.

## The Idaho Murder Trial

No criminal prosecution of our time has had more important pub
interest than the trial of C. H. Moyer and W. D. Haywood, respe
ively President and Secretary of the Western Miners' Federatio
now going on in Idaho. They are charged with being concerned
a conspiracy to murder Governor Frank Steunenberg, of that Sta
Next week The Outlook will print a vivid account of the history
this case and of the labor war out of which it arose. The author
Mr. Luke Grant, of the Chicago Record-Herald, who will later
describe this trial in The Outlook.

## The Japanese in America

This subject has attracted and will attract lively public interes
Mr. John Foord, President of the American Asiatic Association, wi
have in the next Magazine Number of The Outlook an article tellin
who and what are the Japanese now here, with portraits of the
leaders in commerce, education, and art.

## The Gates of New York

Under this title Mr. Robert W. Bruère will discuss in The Outlook'
next Magazine Number the vast undertakings now going on t
handle the tide of traffic into, through, and out of New York City
Electric traction, the fourteen tubes now building beneath the tw
rivers, surface terminals, and the entire great work of constructio
now going on, are described graphically and with full illustration.

## A Practical Idealist

Next week Edward Everett Hale celebrates the eighty-fifth anniversary of his birth. In honor of the day The Outlook will print in its
next issue an article on Dr. Hale's personality, activities, and literary
methods from the pen of his son, Edward Everett Hale, Jr.

❀

*Bribery Prosecutions in San Francisco*
The Grand Jury at San Francisco last week returned sixty-five additional indictments for bribery against "Abe" Ruef, the boss who has held absolute rule in the city for several years. Bail was fixed by the judge at $10,000 on each count, making a total, with the hundred thousand dollars which Ruef has already put up, of three-quarters of a million dollars. In response to a request for telegraphic information, a trustworthy correspondent in San Francisco, and a man of high standing in the community, has sent to The Outlook the following statement of facts: The bribery charged in the indictments was in the matter of franchises for the United Railroads and the gas and telephone companies, and of permits for prize-fights. Each of the eighteen members of the Board of Supervisors has confessed separately to the Grand Jury, and the details of their stories tally exactly. In a typical case, that of the prize-fight permits, the prize-fight trust is said to have paid Ruef $20,000, of which amount Ruef paid $9,000 to Supervisor Gallagher, who distributed $475 to each member of the Board. In the case of the Gas Company the amount which each Supervisor is said to have received was $750. Mr. T. W. Halsey, manager of the Pacific States Telephone Company, who has also been indicted on ten counts for bribery, is charged with having paid $5,000 to each of fourteen Supervisors for his vote on a franchise for the company. Notwithstanding this, the Home Telephone Company, a rival concern, secured the services of Ruef, and, by paying through him, as the indictment alleges, $3,500 to each Supervisor, secured the passage of its own franchise and the defeat of its opponent's. These cases occurred before the earthquake and fire, but the opportunity for bribery in the case of the United Railroads was a direct result of the disaster. Four hundred thousand dollars is alleged to have been paid to Ruef for franchises permitting the United Railroads to electrify its lines and use overhead trolleys, which had been strongly opposed by public opinion; fifteen Supervisors are said to have received $4,000 each, one $10,000, and one $15,000. For a week, it is said, Ruef has been eager to confess, but Assistant District Attorney Heney, the special prosecutor for these cases, is unwilling to accept his confession unless he will plead guilty to a charge of felony, for which the penalty might be imprisonment for fourteen years. Ruef and Schmitz are mutually suspicious, each believing that the other is ready to confess. The chief interest now centers in the possibility of the prosecution of the original givers of the bribes, men in high position in the railway, telephone, and gas companies. The detection and punishment of these men are as vitally important as the conviction of the bribe-takers. The truth of the principle that the man who buys favors from a public official is at least as bad as, and in most cases probably worse than, the official who sells, is not always recognized. There is all the more reason why it should receive practical application in a case like this.

❀

*Oklahoma and Statehood*
The convention of delegates which has been at work all winter framing an organic law for the new State of Oklahoma has completed its labors. The Constitution, as provided by the enabling act, will be submitted to the President. If he approves its provisions, the citizens of the proposed commonwealth will vote on their acceptance—this election probably taking place next summer. The Convention had 112

delegates—100 Democrats and 12 Republicans. The Indian Territory end had 55, the Oklahoma end 55, and the Osage Nation 2. Naturally, the Osage delegates cast their lot with the Indian Territory contingent, giving it control of the Convention on matters affecting local interests. Many of the Indian politicians have been educated in Carlisle, Harvard, and Cornell, the leading families of the Five Civilized Tribes being wealthy. They manifested their ability and intelligence by blocking more than one project that seemed likely to injure their people. Most of the session was spent in an effort to abolish trusts and monopolies and rigidly to control railways and other public carriers. The provisions to this end are severe and mark a notable awakening to the dangers of unregulated corporation influence. To enjoy the right of eminent domain foreign railways must organize under the laws of Oklahoma, which, it is planned, will prevent common abuses of railway management. It is claimed by those opposed to the work of the Convention that capital will be slower than formerly to seek investment in the new State, and that railway building will stop for a time ; but these are remote contingencies, provided the first legislature uses reason in framing the statutes. Under the enabling act the Indian Territory end is to be " dry " for twenty-one years. The Indians and their allies thought that what was good for the redskin was likewise good for his white neighbor, so State-wide prohibition will be submitted to a vote separately from the Constitution, only a majority being necessary for its adoption. Naturally, the Indian Territory end will favor it, and, with the help of the prohibitionists of the Oklahoma end, it is likely to carry. Several provisions of which the delegates feared the President might disapprove were placed in the form of resolutions or instructions to the first legislature. Among these are the " Jim Crow " car regulations. Stringent laws on the negro question may be expected. The Indian himself is an ex-slaveholder, and while many colors and nationalities mingle in the citizenship of the new State, such votes as have been taken indicate that the racial traditions of the South are to be followed. Separate schools for negro children must be provided. In the creation of senatorial and legislative districts the State was gerrymandered beyond hope of Republican success unless a widespread political upheaval shall appear. The direct primary was not made mandatory ; the acceptance of free railway passes is forbidden ; the preamble invokes the guidance of " Almighty God," and the bill of rights is similar to that of other States. On the whole, with the experience of a century of State-making as a guide, Oklahoma has shown a variation chiefly in the regulation of corporations. This method of dealing with the corporation problem may be taken as the latest word in constitutions.

❦

*Rapid Settlement of the Southwest*   Oklahoma's rapid settlement has been responsible for the conditions under which its Constitution has been written. Only seventeen years from the sod, the new commonwealth already has 1,200,000 citizens, including about 80,000 Indians. A constant procession of settlers has poured across its borders, and its growth has been a marvel. Cities of 15,000 to 35,000 population have the luxuries and improvements of Eastern municipalities, and farms and ranches yield wonderful crops of corn and cotton, wheat and fruit. As many settlers have come from Texas and Missouri as from Kansas, more from Arkansas and Tennessee than from Iowa. It will take time for these variant elements to mingle and combine into a harmonious whole. The same influx of many sorts of people is taking place throughout the Southwest, which is just now receiving the largest immigration of any portion of the Nation. On homeseekers' days trains run from Chicago, St. Louis, and Kansas City in three or four sections, while excursions of land speculators are frequent in the older portions of the Middle West. Great areas of the Panhandle of Texas are being broken by steam plows ; crops are being planted this spring over whole counties where never before was grain produced. Land agents are advertising real estate at eight and ten dollars an acre, with promise of "forty bushels of wheat to the acre," an abundance of yield seldom reached even in the heart of the wheat region. Railways and land companies seem to have united in spreading these dreams of agricultural munificence, and have induced a vast amount of speculative buying of realty as well as a veritable exodus of ambitious farmers, the most considerable movement of settlers since the earlier days of Oklahoma's opening. New methods of tillage and crops adapted to a climate deficient in rainfall are the leading arguments in favor of permanent grain yields, but thousands of settlers will follow accustomed ways, and will be bitterly disappointed when dry years come. The high plains country of the Southwest, like other parts of the West, will have reverses, though perhaps not so serious in their results, because the dwellers have greater financial resources. The frontier is rapidly passing; soon the entire Mississippi Valley to the foothills of the Rockies will be cut into farms. Statehood for Oklahoma and the new tide of immigration mark the end of its pioneer era.

❀

*A Plain Duty for the New York Legislature*  To offend the farmers or to refuse to do its duty is the alternative that confronts the New York Legislature in the matter of race-track gambling. The issue was clearly presented at a hearing before the Codes Committees of the Senate and Assembly last week, on the bills prepared by District Attorney Jerome to abolish book-making on race-tracks. As was stated in The Outlook when the bills were introduced, the State Constitution expressly prohibits all forms of gambling everywhere in the State, and lays upon the Legislature the duty of enacting statutes to make this prohibition effective and to provide penalties for its violation. This duty the Legislature promptly performed, but in a curious manner. Gambling outside of a race-track was made a felony punishable by not less than one year's imprisonment; gambling inside a race-track was made

a crime for which the exclusive penalty was that the winner of a bet might be sued by the loser and required to pay to him twice the amount of his wager. The intent of such a provision is obvious. The methods by which it was enacted are indicated by a further provision that five per cent. of the gross receipts of the racing associations throughout the State shall go to the State for the encouragement of agriculture. The means by which agriculture is encouraged in this case consist in providing prizes for distribution at county fairs. This provision, so astutely inserted by the race-track attorneys who drew the bill, established a partnership in the profits from the racing between the racing association and the farmer. The influence of this partnership has been strong enough during eleven years to keep upon the statute-books this almost contemptuous evasion of the State Constitution. At the hearing last week the principal opposition to the Jerome bills came, as in years past, from the farmers. Mr. Jerome, in preparing his bills, had met the astuteness of the framers of the Percy-Gray Law by a provision that the sum of $210,000 should be appropriated from the general funds of the State for the county fairs. This amount would more than replace what the fairs would lose if the prevention of gambling should entirely drive the racing associations out of business. Mr. J. H. Durkee, President of the County Agricultural Associations, said that until this appropriation was made the farmers would oppose the anti-gambling measure; he made it clear that their only interest in the question of race-track gambling is a selfish one— how much can they make out of it? It is the conventional thing to look to the moral sense of the rural districts to overcome the vice of the cities; but in this case the effort for the enforcement of the Constitution has originated in the city and has met its most stubborn opposition from the country and even from some of the members of country churches. The moral issue before the members of the Legislature is plain: Shall they obey their oaths of office, in which they pledged themselves to uphold the Constitution, or shall they sacrifice duty to expediency?

Shall they put an end to the ridiculous condition of affairs which makes gambling on one side of a fence a felony, on the other side an offense only against the individual, not against the State; or shall they let their own selfish interests blind them to the requirements of justice and decency? Shall they refuse to permit to exist, under the protection of the law, a practice which the people of the State have solemnly decreed shall be abolished, or shall they exchange the right to violate the law for votes? For a decade the Legislature has chosen the latter alternative—a choice morally humiliating but politically safer. Will the present body rate its oath of office at a higher value?

❀

*Leaden-heeled Justice*

The difference between American and English jurisprudence, to which The Outlook has often called attention, is just now dramatically illustrated by the contrast between the Thaw trial in New York and the Rayner trial in London. In neither case was there any doubt about the killing; in both cases the defense interposed was the insanity of the accused. Horace George Rayner killed Mr. Whiteley, a well-known merchant of London, two months ago. He has been brought to trial, convicted, and sentenced, and, unless the sentence is commuted or he is pardoned by the Home Secretary, he will be executed within three months after the offense. The trial took one day. Harry Thaw killed Stanford White nine months ago. He has been brought to trial; the trial has already lasted about seven weeks, and unless all proceedings are stopped on the ground that he is now insane, it will probably last at least a week longer; and if he is convicted and the conviction is sustained on appeal, it will probably be three years at least before he can be made to suffer the penalty of his crime. Nor is delay the only fault in the American procedure. The only question in this case has been, Was Thaw so insane when he killed Stanford White that he is not morally responsible for the deed? The defense has insisted that he was so insane, the prosecution that he was not. Now the prosecution has become con-

vinced that Thaw, though sane when he killed White, is incurably insane now; while the defense is equally sure that though he was insane when he killed White, he is quite sane now. And now the Judge has been considering the wisdom of appointing a commission of experts to determine Thaw's present sanity. If he was insane when he committed the act, he ought not to be executed; if he is insane now, he ought not to be tried. Common sense would suggest that what the Judge is asked to do now, the law ought to authorize him to do in the beginning—appoint a commission of experts, but with power to pass on both questions, his insanity then and his insanity now. The decision of such a commission of experts ought to be conclusive. From it there should be no appeal to a body of non-experts, whether of judges or of jurors. The only appeal to the courts should be on the question whether the expert commission was properly constituted. The impartiality of the commission might be guarded by allowing both prosecution and defense a certain number of objections for cause, such as are now allowed in constituting the jury. There is something grimly grotesque in the method which the law now pursues. To determine whether Thaw *was* insane when he killed Stanford White we summon experts paid by the defense, who testify that he was insane; experts paid by the State, who testify that he was not insane; and a jury of non-experts to decide between the disagreeing doctors. But as soon as the question changes to *Is* Thaw insane now? it is proposed to dismiss both sets of experts and the non-expert jury, and constitute a non-partisan tribunal of experts to decide that question. Why not constitute such a tribunal at the outset to determine both questions?

❀

*The Consumers' League*

The National Consumers' League held its eighth annual meeting in Chicago on March 5. Of the five bills adopted the year before, as its programme of Federal legislation, three are already enacted and in force—namely, the bills providing for compulsory education in the District of Columbia, for pure food, and for an investigation of the conditions of work of women and children in industry. Thus two of the bills remain to be passed by the Sixtieth Congress, one creating a Children's Bureau in the Federal Government, and one regulating child labor in the District of Columbia. Besides these, promotion of the Beveridge Child Labor Bill was this year adopted as a part of the programme of the National Consumers' League. After the enactment of laws, Federal and State, comes the less .exciting task of enforcement. For this purpose the League has taken part in the effort to obtain a Federal appropriation adequate to the enforcement of the National Pure Food Law. For the coming year the League proposes to gather information on the standard of living of workingwomen as a basis for future intelligent action. Through its sixty-one leagues in twenty-one States it will co-operate with the kindred investigation by the Department of Labor and Commerce with all available agencies, official and unofficial. Live questions are the minimum wage and the hours of labor. Parasite industries consume young children, and pay to girls such wages that their families must contribute a share of maintenance. The extent of this parasitism has not been ascertained for any State or any industry. This is one main object of the present investigation. Another, of equal importance. is to discover the extent and result of unrestricted working hours. No progress has been made in the direction of a shorter working day for women. Teachers alone have a short day, and this is solely because their pupils cannot endure a longer one. In the trades the tendency is to get rid of all the slender protection hitherto afforded by State laws. Both the courts and the legislatures of various States have contributed to this movement. In Illinois the Supreme Court annulled the eight-hour law for women in 1895. The New Jersey Legislature of 1903 repealed the protecting statute in that State. This year in New York the highest court has been asked to destroy the law protecting women from work at night, and the Legislature is, at the date of writing, besieged by manufacturers seeking to make away also with limitation of hours. Meanwhile, the movement to protect men from overwork gains strength each year, and each year more legislation for this end is enacted. The miners in Arizona, Colorado, Missouri, Utah, and Montana have an eight-hour day established by statute. Men employed by contractors for the Federal Government work only eight hours a day, and the same limitation of hours is, in many States both East and West, imposed by law on contractors for State or municipal works. Indeed, so urgent has been the demand that the State, as a model employer, shall require no more than eight hours' labor from all men directly or indirectly employed on public works, that at the election of 1905 the Constitution of New York State was amended to provide for such a restriction. In addition, the army of letter-carriers (among whom there are only a handful of women) are protected by an eight-hour law, and at the recent session of Congress the unanimous demand of the railway telegraphers—all of them men—resulted in obtaining a restriction of their working hours to nine in twenty-four. Given a sufficiently urgent demand, the restriction of men's hours of labor is proved practically possible. The National Consumers' League holds, therefore, that concerted action is needed towards this end for working-women. Before legislation can be enacted and enforced public opinion must be informed, and it is to this task that the League addresses itself.

⊛

*The British Premier Outlines England's Policy*  The Speaker, the well-known organ of English Liberal political opinion, has become The Nation, and its initial number is marked by an editorial from the British Prime Minister, Sir Henry Campbell-Bannerman, on the attitude of his country at the forthcoming Hague Conference regarding disarmament. He holds as baseless those objections brought up both in Great Britain and in other countries against raising the question of the limitation of armaments, and contends that the original Peace Conference at The Hague was convened for the very purpose of discussing this question. Though the Conference failed to reach an agreement, Sir Henry declares that he never heard of any injurious consequence resulting from its discussion, and that it is the business of those opposing the renewal of the attempts to bring up this question to show that some special and essential change in the circumstances has arisen, to make another discussion inopportune. He then argues that if at the first Peace Congress it was desirable to attempt to limit the burden of armaments, it is still more desirable to-day, because this burden has enormously increased. He adds that the suspicion held eight years ago has grown to something like a certainty to-day, namely, that no limits could be set to the competitive struggle for sea power save by economic exhaustion. At the same time the points of divergence among the Powers have become not only less acute, but are confined to a far smaller field. Finally, general sentiment in favor of peace is now incomparably stronger than it was at the time of the first Hague Conference, and a peaceful adjustment of international disputes has attained both a practical potency and a moral authority undreamed of then. Turning from these general considerations to England's special position, Sir Henry says: " We have already given an earnest of our sincerity by considerable reductions in our naval and military expenditure, and we are prepared to go further if we find a similar disposition in other quarters. Our delegates, therefore, will not go to the Conference empty-handed." It has been suggested, however, that England's example will count for nothing, because her naval preponderance will remain unimpaired. To this Sir Henry well replies that throughout the world Great Britain's sea power is recognized as non-aggressive and innocent of designs against either the independence or the legitimate development of other nations : " Our known adhesion to two dominant principles, the independence of nationalities and the freedom of trade, entitles us to claim that, if our fleets are invulnerable, they carry with them no menace across the waters of the world, but a message of the most cordial good will." This message, coinciding with America's position, is based on an unalterable belief in the community of interests among nations.

❂

**Russia
The Government's
Programme**

Last week in the Duma, or Lower House of the Russian Parliament, Premier Stolypin laid down the Government's policy regarding certain reforms. They are as follows : Freedom of speech, of the press, of association and worship; habeas corpus on the same basis as other States; a single form of martial law ; local self-government ; reform of the zemstvos, or provincial councils ; responsibility of officials; agrarian reforms ; and popular education. This is substantially a restatement of the Emperor's manifesto of 1905, as follows :

We therefore direct our Government to carry out our inflexible will in the following manner:

First—To extend to the population the immutable foundations of civic liberty, based on the real inviolability of person, freedom of conscience, speech, union, and association.

Second—Without suspending the already ordered elections to the State Duma, to invite to participation in the Duma, so far as the limited time before the convocation of the Duma will permit, those classes of the population now completely deprived of electoral rights, leaving the ultimate development of the principle of electoral rights in general to the newly established legislative order of things.

Third—To establish as an unchangeable rule that no law shall be enforceable without the approbation of the State Duma, and that it shall be possible for the elected [representatives] of the people to exercise real participation in the supervision of the legality of the acts of the authorities appointed by us.

The Prime Minister's declaration of policy was courteous in tone, and was received in respectful silence. But the first speech, that of Prince Zereteli, of the Caucasus, on behalf of the Socialists, provoked vehement discussion. He moved for the rejection of the Premier's programme, and for a declaration of war against the Government. Very different was the speech of Prince Dolgoruki, which followed ; he is a distinguished member of the Russian nobility, is a philanthropist and statesman. He moved that the Duma, having heard the ministerial programme, should proceed with the order of the day. In this he was supported not only by the Constitutional Democrats, but by the Nationalists and the Group of Toil, which together formed a sufficient majority. This action is equivalent to saying: "We receive the programme of the Premier, but at the present moment we make no statement as to what our final attitude upon it shall be."

❀

**Russia: The Duma's Attitude**

The programme presented on behalf of the Czar by Premier Stolypin is in some of its aspects admirable. Freedom of speech, freedom of the press, freedom of worship, popular education, and the establishment of habeas corpus will appear to Americans to form a great advance towards general civil liberty. Unfortunately, however, the programme has been skillfully framed to present an appearance of advance without the reality. As Mr. Aladin has pointed out, how can a universal law of court martial and the right of habeas corpus—that is to say, absolute military authority and absolute civil authority—exist at the same time in the same State? How can the people feel assured that these laws, if passed or approved by the Duma, may not at any moment be suspended or annulled by the personal word of the Czar, as actually happened in the case of the manifesto of 1905? This situation explains the silence with which the Duma received a government programme so glittering with promises of freedom. Americans must be careful not to be misled by such promises in forming their judgment concerning the conflict in Russia. So long as the Russian monarch enjoys an absolute right of veto, so long will the Russian people continue to be held in political slavery. The encouraging feature of the situation is twofold: first, the Czar has begun to feel the latent power of the people—enough at least to ask their indorsement of laws framed and executed by himself; second, the popular and democratic wing of the Duma has exercised and displayed a remarkable power of organization and self-control. In our judgment, it would be a distinct

step backward for the Duma to accept the programme of Premier Stolypin. If internal peace is to come in Russia, the Duma must first establish beyond question its own legislative initiative and authority.

❀

**The Pope Confirms Archbishop Ireland**

Archbishop Ireland's statement regarding the attitude of some of the French clergy in the conflict between Church and State in France, reported in The Outlook last week as part of his admirable discussion of the whole subject, is apparently confirmed by a statement recently made by the Pope to Bishop Thomas O'Gorman, of Sioux Falls, South Dakota. In a telegraphic synopsis of the interview with Bishop O'Gorman the Pope is reported to have said that Archbishop Ireland's explanation was correct, and that the failure of many of the French clergy and of representative lay Roman Catholics to follow the advice given by Leo XIII. was responsible for recent troubles. The uncertainty in regard to the permanence of the republican form of government in France may be said to have been settled when M. Grévy became President. Unfortunately, many priests and members of the Roman Catholic party were unable or unwilling to read the signs of the times and to accept the Republic as finally established. Thereupon Leo XIII. put forth an encyclical, which attracted wide attention at the time, in which he called upon the bishops and clergy of the French Church cordially and sincerely to support the Republic; and he repeated this advice and restated this position several times afterwards, whenever a fitting opportunity arrived. Unfortunately, many of the clergy refused to follow the lead of the statesmanlike Pope. The French aristocracy as a class is strongly Catholic, and is entirely out of touch with modern France. Its members have been blind to the course of events since the Revolution. Many teachers in Roman Catholic schools were not only reactionary in their tendencies, but instilled into the minds of boys hatred of the Republic. This unfortunate attitude, as Archbishop

Ireland has pointed out, and as confirmed by Pope Pius X., has unquestionably been the occasion for the legislation in France which culminated in the annulment of the Concordat. Entirely aside from the question of the manner in which the separation of Church and State has been brought about, and recognizing the fact that in the agitation there has been much feeling which was not only anti-Catholic but anti-religious, it remains true that the great body of believers in the Republic in France, a majority of whom are Catholics, have felt that republican institutions were in peril unless the teaching was changed, and came reluctantly to the conclusion that the absolute separation of Church and State was essential if republican ideals are to be permanently established and universally accepted in France.

❦

*The Discoverer of Acetylene Gas and Smokeless Powder* — France follows Italy in national mourning. The Italian poet Carducci was not more eminent in literature than the French *savant* Pierre Berthelot in science. As was the case with his lifelong friends, Renan and Pasteur, the man in Berthelot transcended the technician. All three were types of generous manhood, uniting many engaging personal qualities which made them pre-eminently popular as professors. Therefore they were as beloved as they were eminent. Long a professor in the Collège de France, Berthelot's scientific work covered a particularly wide field. He had received his doctor's degree on presentation of a remarkable thesis giving an account of his artificial reproduction of natural fats. He was thus one of the pioneers of organic synthesis, and his labors in the determination of the carbon groups was perhaps the largest contribution to chemical progress made during the last half-century. His most celebrated discoveries were those of acetylene gas and smokeless powder. He thus made the whole world his debtor. The highest scientific honors were showered upon him, but he especially treasured the distinction of succeeding Pasteur as Permanent Secretary of the Academy of Sciences. When, a generation ago, Paris was threatened both by the Prussians and by the Communists, Berthelot was put at the head of the Scientific Committee of Defense, and his investigations in this connection led to his invention of smokeless powder and other important explosives. If his ideal of service to his fellow-men included, first of all, contributions from his own profession to the common weal, it also included energetic action in the political movements of his day. Accordingly he became a Deputy and then a Senator, contributing much of value to current legislation. He became Inspector-General of Higher Education, and did a work supplementary to that already accomplished by Jules Ferry. Finally, as Foreign Minister, he showed himself apparently as competent as he had in his laboratory. Berthelot's death was peculiarly pathetic, and again contradicts the opinion of some that there are but few happy and faithful wedded lives in France. Madame Berthelot, seventy years old, had been very ill. Her husband, eighty years old, insisted on keeping continual watch by her bedside. When, last week, her end came, his grief induced an attack of syncope, and he fell dead.

❦

*Quarrelsome Republics* — Apparently the petty war in Central America has practically ended in a complete victory for Nicaragua, and the troops of that country are about to occupy the capital of Honduras, Tegucigalpa. There appears to have been one battle of some fierceness fought, in which the Nicaraguans and their revolutionary allies were successful, and this was followed by the occupation of the most strongly fortified city in Honduras, Choluteca. This in turn was immediately followed by the flight of President Bonilla, of Honduras, who is supposed to be on the point of taking passage by steamship to some foreign port. Rumors of an attempt on the part of fiery Honduran generals and of equally fiery and ambitious soldiers and politicians from Salvador, the ally of Honduras, to renew the strife will, it may be profoundly hoped, prove without basis. This is the kind of a struggle which may be better characterized as a quarrel than as a war.

Now that the fight is over, it is to be hoped that we may in time learn its cause; certainly no reasonable and intelligible account of any adequate justification for war has reached this country. Disputes about incursions and trespasses by one side or another amount to little more than mutual recriminations, and nothing more regrettable in the history of the Central American republics has ever occurred than the fact that these three little nations found it necessary to break off a peaceful arbitration proceeding to which they had been persuaded by the great nations of both North and South America and hastily resort to arms. Among the many absurd tales which cloud the issues involved is one in which the initial dispute appears to have been about a mysterious mule. If this be true, the animal in question was certainly not the only obstinate and ungovernable party to the transaction.

❦

**Student Recruits** To put the claim of the Christian ministry before strong men and make it appeal to the modern man is the object of a new movement among students. In many respects it corresponds to the Student Volunteer Movement, which has for several years been influential in drawing vigorous, well-equipped young men and women into foreign missionary service. Last December a number of college students, among those assembled in a Conference of the Young Men's Christian Association at Pacific Grove, California, discovered that they were expecting to enter the ministry. The result was that they organized themselves as Student Recruits for the Christian Ministry, for the following purpose, as stated by themselves:

Our object is (1) to unite all students who purpose to enter the ministry, (2) to secure for the members organized fellowship in this purpose, and (3) to promote aggressively the consideration of the ministry as a vocation for Christian young men.

The two essential features of this movement are the signing of this declaration: "It is my purpose, if God will, to become a minister of Jesus Christ;" and the acceptance of the object. Originating in California, the movement has, of course, its existence principally in that State. The movement has the same general object as that of the conferences established by the students of Union Theological Seminary, New York, three years ago (and held annually since then)—for the purpose of commending to college students the opportunities and work of the ministry. Mr. John R. Mott, besides, has held conferences with college students on the same subject. It has often been maintained that both the numbers and the quality of men entering the ministry have in recent years been lowered. It is an encouraging fact to note that these movements undertaken to correct a downward tendency have originated, not among ill-trained men, but among those from whom the most effective ministers should be recruited.

❦

## Our Father
### An Easter Thought

The Lord's Prayer is contained in the two words with which it opens; and its various petitions are only amplifications of its devout and beautiful approach to God. In these words the whole movement of religious thought from the earliest Hebrew divinations of the Infinite is recorded; in them the soul of the religion of Christ is enshrined. The great First Cause, from whom the worlds proceeded and by whom the measureless forces of the universe were set in motion; the sublime Lawgiver, hidden by the clouds on Mount Sinai; the King of kings, set high above all the rulers of the alien races; the absolute Monarch whose will made right, and whose act stood justified because infinite power was behind it—all these lesser and partial conceptions became shadows of the night when the day broke on the world in the blessed word Father. Creator, lawgiver, ruler of rulers, sovereign over all men, he was and is; but these are not He; these are His functions; He is the Father. In the music of that word the discords of life begin to recede into the distance; in the unsounded depths of love in that word care and toil and sorrow and death take on a new meaning; in that sublime, word immortality rises like a star on the night of doubt and despair.

The first words of the New Testament set the Christ in the heart of the family and ally him with all the generations of his people from the days of the first patriarch. He lay in his mother's arms when the wise men brought the symbolic gifts; in a human home he learned the lessons set for all children born of woman; from that home he went up, a dutiful boy, to worship in the Temple as his fathers had done before him; in the shelter of that home he grew in strength and in that wisdom which begins with the fear of the Lord and ends with the joyful acceptance of His will; when he was lifted above the crowd of mockers and idlers and helpless disciples, in his hour of lonely agony, his prayer was, "Father, forgive them; they know not what they do;" and when the end came, he cried with a loud voice, "Father, into thy hands I commend my spirit."

In all the wonderful story of a life which grows more luminous with truth as time turns its penetrating lights upon it, the Christ is set always in the family; and the phrases which describe him ignore the division of time and eternity, the distinction between earth and heaven; he is always the son of God and the son of man. He never for an hour stands by himself; everywhere and at all times he is first and foremost a son, and his sonship is at once human and divine. A human mother suffers in his birth, broods over the manger in which he lies and watches over his infancy; a divine Father calls him out of his home, directs his life, clothes him with power, lays on him the awful privilege of self-sacrifice, speaks through his words, his nature, his life, puts death under his feet, lights for him the glorious morning of the resurrection, and receives him again unto Himself. On that wonderful morning of the first Easter, when the light that never was to go out in darkness broke on every grave, he said, "I ascend unto my Father and unto your Father;" and when, later, the doors were shut on the disciples trembling between great fear and great joy, he stood in the midst of them and said: "Peace be unto you:

as the Father hath sent me, even so send I you;" and he gave command that all men should be baptized "into the name of the Father, and of the Son, and of the Holy Ghost."

In the story which culminated in the resurrection, the Lord, although often lonely, solitary, and forsaken, is always the incarnation of the Father's love and purpose, of the son's obedience and self-sacrifice, of the immortality and unity of the family in heaven and on earth. In him the hidden relationship between God and man becomes visible; through him the love of the Father for his children streams like a great light; in his return from the sepulcher all the members of the family return victorious. From that sublime hour when he stepped forth serene and immortal from the tomb where they had laid him, the light shines back over the long road to the manger in Bethlehem and the figure of the wondering mother, and everywhere the mystery of the double parentage is revealed and explained. It is no longer a broken and defeated human life ending in a dishonored death; it is a human life transfigured by the divine. It is no longer the sad tale of a lonely man walking the way to the cross; it is the triumphant journey of the son of Mary and of God doing his Father's will on the earth and making all men aware that there is but one life here and there, one family on earth and in heaven, one Father alike in the homes built by the hands of men and the many mansions where the angels are.

Out of every home the dark and narrow gate of death opens in some hour of mystery and suffering, as it opened out of the little home in Galilee on the day of the crucifixion; and they that pass through come back no more, for they are with Him who held the gate ajar that the dream of Paradise might come true in the faith of men and the light of the Father's face might shine through the darkness. Son of man and son of God, the Christ stands between the invisible Father and the great household of his children; revealer of that love which is stronger than death, in which the family on earth and the family in heaven are bound together in immortal unity.

# Thomas Bailey Aldrich

"I wonder what day of the week,
  I wonder what week of the year,
Will it be the midnight or morning,
  And who will bend over my bier?

What a hideous fancy to come,
  As I wait at the foot of the stair,
While Eleanor gives the last touch
  To her robes or the rose in her hair!

'Do I like your new dress, pompadour?
  And do I like you?'—on my life,
You are eighteen and not a day more,
  And haven't been six years my wife!

Those two rosy boys upstairs,
  In the crib, are not ours! To be sure,
You're just a sweet bride in her bloom,
  All sunshine and snowy and pure!

As the carriage rolls down the dark street,
  The little wife laughs and makes cheer;
But I wonder what day of the week,
  I wonder what week of the year!"

It was impossible to associate age with Mr. Aldrich; there seemed to be nothing in common between his fresh feeling, his gayety of mood, the vivacity of his unforced and unfailing wit, the youth of his spirit, and any fading of imagination, any decline of vitality of mind. It is impossible to associate death with him unless one has wholly escaped the superstition which made the angel of the great emancipation the awful intruder of mediæval fancy. The simple wreath on the door of the home from which he had gone and on the purple pall that covered the mortal part of him when the last words were spoken was the symbol of his escape out of mortality, of the final freedom of the spirit, of the ultimate mastery. Fortune had long smiled on him, and did not turn from him at the end. Save one great sorrow, the years brought him gifts with generous hands. He had great happiness in the sanctuary of his life; he had troops of friends; he was surrounded by the books he loved; he had freedom from the cares of life, and leisure for travel, for work, for the art of friendship; he had the kind of recognition he valued; he not only finished his work, but he put on it the final touches of his fastidious art; and when all was done, he withdrew before any sadness of declining power came to him.

In its commemoration of his seventieth birthday last December, The Outlook, commenting on his power of self-criticism, said that he had so completed and sifted his work that his future editors will have little to do: "If one is compelled to choose between the nine or ten volumes of moderate compass which contain his prose and verse, one will take them all; for they fill small space on the shelf, and they bear the touch of a wonderfully sure hand. The wit of the poet is likely to preserve him from mutilation; he will escape the process which has rejected a large part of Wordsworth, Victor Hugo, and Whitman—to suggest the poets who lacked the salt of wit—in order to preserve the residuum from the impatience of later generations. He has, fortunately, taken himself seriously as an artist and not as a prophet, and has escaped the melancholy moments when the oracle speaks from habit rather than from imagination."

Mr. Aldrich was born in an old seaport, about whose wharves still linger the spicy odors of the days when the Far East paid tribute to New England. Unlike his contemporaries in the field of letters, he did not walk the well-trodden path through the university; his evolution was individual, and, like Mr. Howells, he nourished his imagination and formed his taste largely by familiarity with modern literature. The air of New Orleans, where he had the good fortune to spend a part of his childhood, may have aided in the development of his native aptitude for the romantic, the picturesque, the dramatic, conceived in lyrical mood. Whatever may be the reason, the strenuous temper was not in him.

Born in Portsmouth, he was loyal not only to the sea but to the old town so familiar to every reader of "The Story of a Bad Boy." Predestined as surely as was Dr. Holmes to live in Boston, and to take keen satisfaction in the fact, Mr. Aldrich was not, like the author of the "Autocrat," a product of New England in the forms of his thought; one must look deeper for the New England element in him. He wholly escaped the didacticism which sometimes blurred the art of his predecessors; he was born after the time which Lowell recalled when he said that all New England was a pulpit. He was not lacking in ethical convictions, nor did he hesitate to express them ; but he was a poet, not a reformer. He never questioned the wisdom of Providence in sending singers to refresh and cheer men, as well as preachers to arouse and stir them ; and he wisely chose to sing. It is in his lucidity, his keenness, his love of things good and pure, his deep-going refinement, his exacting conscientiousness, and in a certain clarity of vision and reticence, that one finds the evidences of his root-age in New England. He gains the ends of rich expression without a touch of sensuousness ; he is gay without being frivolous, and free without a suggestion of license. The atmosphere of his mind has the cool, clear breath of the New England climate ; the outlines of the world which lies in his imagination are soft without being hazy, and full of a beauty which has delicacy of fragrance and color rather than tropical warmth and richness.

In reading his verse one becomes aware of a certain reserve which is neither coldness nor caution, but an instinctive conviction that some things must be left to the imagination. He does not move one so quickly as many poets who sacrifice the finer qualities to immediate effect ; but what he writes preserves its charm, and, by its very restraint and moderation, gives an impression of finality. In the most popular of all his poems, " Baby Bell," there is this fine reticence which gives sorrow the poise and dignity of an experience that will hold its place and keep its significance long after the violence of the first emotion is spent.

So light is Mr. Aldrich's touch that the careless reader is in danger of missing its essential vigor ; for, with all his grace, Mr. Aldrich is a poet of masculine fiber. There is in his work none of the vagueness of aspiration which so often rests like a faint and rosy mist on contemporary poetry ; the outlines are distinct, the feeling is definite, the thought is sharply limned. The workmanship is delicate, sometimes dainty, but it is like the tracery on a Damascus blade, which embellishes the surface without weakening the fiber. The trained ear hears a note in this poetry which sometimes escapes those who have not studied it closely ; a note full of a quiet, gentle resonance and vibration, with a suggestion of carrying power. Such fragments of imagination as " Identity," " Destiny," " An Untimely Thought," haunt one with a sense of perfection, and carry in them the promise of haunting the memories of other generations. Indeed, this impression of longevity grows upon one as he reads Mr. Aldrich's verse with care : it is so portable ; it can be carried so easily ; so much of it has the aerial quality of those seventeenth-century songs which beguile and delight us as if they had floated into the world with last spring's flowers. There is good reason to believe that when much of the strenuous, didactic, emotional verse of the last thirty years has been forgotten, Mr. Aldrich will still be having his day.

The artists have a way of imposing upon their own times by the very harmony which evidences their power. They escape observation, as do perfect dress or manners, by freedom from excess, extravagance, or idiosyncrasy. Mr. Aldrich lived through the storm and stress of the last two decades of literary history without any apparent deflection from his orbit. He was familiar with what the younger poets have been doing in France, in England, and in this country ; but the lark in the field remotest from the highway could not be more free from any suggestion of agitation of spirit or uncertainty of artistic aim. It is possible that this aloofness was due in part to lack of quick sympathies with contemporary experience ; it is more probable that it was due to a very clear perception of artistic aims and a very keen appraisal of artistic resources. Mr. Aldrich appeared to know exactly what he wished to do. His instinct as an artist had the most careful training ; his intelligence as an artist is shown alike in the apparent ease of hand in some of his lines and the evident nicety of touch in others. He secured detachment of mood without loss of freshness and reality, and he has, consequently, written for the eye and ear of the future. He cared more for perfection than for praise ; and was content to speak a little less fervently to his own generation. So the finely trained orator often husbands his voice in order that its tones may fall, resonant and musical, on the ear of the farthest circle. The sonnet on " Sleep," for instance, has the quality of gathering feeling and disclosing thought in the exact degree in which one becomes familiar with it; the spell of the exquisite " Nocturne " steadily deepens as one yields to its delicate but ardent imagery; and where shall one turn for finer and freer description of the quality which goes home to the imagination than that which touches these lines with a skill quite beyond calculated craftsmanship:

"This is her Book of Verses—wren-like notes,
  Shy frankness, blind gropings, haunting fears;
At times across the chords abruptly floats
  A mist of passionate tears."

Those who confound restraint with coldness will also confuse art with skill, and emphasize Mr. Aldrich's fastidious craftsmanship at the expense of his spontaneity and force of imagination. Against this easy and superficial judgment the poet has protested in lines which constitute a confession of poetic faith, and which ought to be pondered in these days of easy writing and rapid printing:

"' Let art be all in all,' one time I said,
And straightway stirred the hypercritic gall.
I said not,' Let technique be all in all,'
  But art—a wider meaning. Worthless, dead—
The shell without its pearl, the corpse of things—
Mere words are, till the spirit lends them wings.
The poet who wakes no soul within his lute
Falls short of art: 'twere better he were mute.

The workmanship wherewith the gold is wrought
Adds yet a richness to the richest gold ;
Who lacks the art to shape his thought, I hold,
  Were little poorer if he lacked the thought.
The statue's slumber were unbroken still
In the dull marble, had the hand no skill.
Disparage not the magic touch that gives
The formless thought the grace whereby it lives."

Tennyson was not more exacting in the matter of workmanship than was Mr. Aldrich ; and the fastidiousness of both poets has its root in love of perfection, which is only another name for the artist's conviction that his work is done only when his thought takes such possession of a form that the two live henceforth immortal as one.

In reading the slender volumes of verse which record Mr. Aldrich's poetic activity, from " Baby Bell " to " Judith," one sometimes recalls Tennyson and sometimes Alfred de Musset; but Mr. Aldrich's quality and art were wholly his own. If he came under powerful influences, he escaped that subjugation of individuality which issues in imitation. His charm was individual, and can be explained only by reference to his own personality. Whatever his limitations of artistic perception and power, his field was his own, and he was master of it. His work is so significant, in its combination of purely poetic quality with a perfection of workmanship unique in American poetry, that it deserves wider attention than it has received. He belongs with the makers of pure song ; the Herricks and Lovelaces, in whom American poetry has not been rich.

❦

# The Don and the Athlete

It is more than a coincidence that in England, where university sport is clean, public life is comparatively free from corruption. The standards of fair play which the English youth imbibes in his public school and in his university remain with him as standards in political procedure and commercial transactions. The contrast between England and the United States in this respect is not to our credit. The criticism has been often made that we Americans take our sport too seriously. It is victory in sport that we take too seriously ; but sport as a species of conduct we have not yet taken seriously enough. Yale, it would probably be conceded by almost everyone, has achieved pre-eminence for athletic prowess. What, then, do Yale men take pride in ? and what do other college men envy Yale for ? Do Yale men, as they should, exhibit more disgust at unfairness in a Yale team than their opponents do, and more than they exhibit at a Yale defeat ? And are not other college men exactly like Yale men in this respect? These questions suggest what is chiefly wrong about American college sport. It is not its roughness; it is not chiefly its extravagance; it is its lack of wholesome standards of frankness and honesty.

Two college men, it is related in the Harvard Bulletin, were playing golf in an intercollegiate match. One man lost his ball, and, after the time allowed for search had elapsed, had to concede the hole to his opponent. Then his opponent, having accepted the score, pointed out the lost ball behind a bush, and explained that he could not have shown it before because he was playing for the honor of his college!

In the face of such a spirit as that, which is displayed in all forms of sport, the agitation about the abolition of football—or any other one game—is beside the point. What is needed is not the riddance of this game or the promulgation of that rule; it is rather the establishment and maintenance, from one college generation to another, of sound traditions.

The natural agents for the handing down of such traditions are those members of the university teaching force who have had athletic experience as undergraduates, and who are yet near enough to the undergraduate body to understand its common opinions and common feelings. It is by means of such men as these, whose interest in athletics has not lost its edge, and yet whose maturity and position enable them to be critical of the too eager love of winning, that wholesome traditions of sport in Oxford and Cambridge are transmitted. Such a man was Leslie Stephen when he was one of the two tutors at Trinity Hall, Cambridge. He was, as Lord Justice Sir Robert Romer says, a "great athlete." One of the men who was a student under him thus tells what Leslie Stephen did: "He *made* that boat of 1859, which was the pioneer of all Trinity Hall's rowing successes during these last fifty years. . . . He did all this for the ulterior purpose of making men of us and not loafers. . . . It was Leslie Stephen who did the 'making' of our and the next generation of undergraduates." Not every

tutor can be a genius like Leslie Stephen; but many men of less brilliance have done like service. It is by means of men of similar character and position that like traditions have been established and are now preserved in at least one American college.

The authorities at Harvard, it seems to us, have taken a step backward in reconstituting the Athletic Committee. They have decreed that the faculty representatives on that committee shall be selected, not by virtue of their interest in athletics and their intimacy with the undergraduate body, but by virtue of their administrative offices in the University. The qualities which have caused these men to be chosen to their offices are not the qualities which would assure their interest in athletics. Indeed, the very recommendation in accordance with which they were designated to act upon the Athletic Committee indicates that they will not be expected to take an active part in athletic management. If athletic sports are essentially bad, they ought to be abolished; but if they are essentially good, they ought to be under the direction of those who are greatly interested in athletic sports.

A professional trainer whose bad influence on college athletics has been notorious is reported to have remarked to a number of graduates who were considering the constitution of an athletic committee, "Don't put on any of them young profs who have been on the teams. Put on some of the old duffers; we can pull the wool over their eyes."

❋

# The Spectator

Certain places in the Spectator's experience realize—in the old Yankee phrase, "come up to"—their reputations, or the suggestion of their names. Land's End is one of these in its finality of rugged desolation, and so also is the North Cape. In a contrasted, antipodal sense, the same may be said of Chelsea, that section of London on the Thames, some four miles southwest of Trafalgar Square, associated with literary and artistic worthies. To any one who visits it, as did the Spectator last summer on a fine June afternoon, it has an atmosphere congenial to art and letters. Despite the complaint of an English friend, who as a small boy lived neighbor to Carlyle, that Chelsea "is spoiled by its very tiresome apartment-houses," the park-like effect and the river glimpses of Cheyne Walk on the embankment, the thick-foliaged trees that shade it and Cheyne Row out of it, in which Carlyle lived so long, and the old houses of gentle if not aristocratic origin, are still there to give an effect both quaint and picturesque. Thus Chelsea, at least near the Thames, is still a place where, as Dickens once said, "the city and country have met half-way to shake hands," the sort of place the devotee of art and letters might naturally choose for the last days, if not for working days. Curiously enough, three Chelsea houses, but a short distance apart, are noted, not as homes of the distinguished, but as the places where they died. It was to obscure lodgings here that Turner, the great colorist, fled from Cavendish Square when his powers began to fail—lodgings in which, when too feeble to walk, he was taken up into a little balcony on the top to bask in the sunlight that had been his life. Here returned Whistler, after closing his Paris home and studio following the death of his wife, to be buried shortly from the old Chelsea Church where he had often attended service with his mother. And here died George Eliot, in a house, like Whistler's, facing the Thames—of whose river views she made such frequent mention in her letters after her marriage to Mr. Cross—a house in which she was permitted to live but nineteen brief days.

❁

Of course the ostensible object in looking up Chelsea, the reason one gives to an unsympathetic friend who expects a reason for doing any particular thing on a trip, is to see the Carlyle house. In the Spectator's case this proved an object easier planned than executed, as his cabman had never heard of Carlyle or his house. This was a fact, as the cabman professed to have convoyed numerous Americans to various parts of London, to raise an unpleasant suspicion that all but a saving remnant of the Spec-

tator's compatriots were indifferent to the Sage. The house, as the guide-books state, is now a "museum," and is full of "relics," things which, the Spectator is obliged to confess, he is not enough of a hero-worshiper to appreciate himself, although he approves of them for others as officially indorsed stimuli to sympathy with literary celebrities. Among the "relics," the Spectator cared most for the letters to Mrs. Carlyle, which brought close home a realization of the writer's solicitous tenderness, something that appeals far more convincingly to the eye from the written than from the familiar printed page. Then, too, there was the typical English tub, which looked more absurdly small than ever as one imagined the great prophet compelled every morning to squat crampedly in it for his early ablutions. The bright bit of garden behind the house, where the Carlyles must have passed so many pleasant hours, meant far more to the Spectator, as suggesting the home life, than any number of household things conventionally arranged. Then the house itself fits the street and neighborhood as invitingly as it looks in the well-known pictures of it. For description of the interior one can do no better than Carlyle himself, who wrote to his wife in 1834, when thinking of taking it: "The house itself is eminent, antique, wainscoted to the very ceiling; broadish stair with massive balustrade (in the old style), corniced, and thick as one's thigh; floors thick as rock, and the wood of them here and there worm-eaten, yet capable of cleanness and still with thrice the strength of the modern floor. And then as to rooms, Goody! Three stories beside the sunk story, in every one of them three apartments, in depth something like forty feet in all."

❁

The house E. W. Godwin designed and built for Whistler is only a short walk away, in Tite Street. One would suppose, owing to the fame of the Whistler portrait of Carlyle, if for nothing else—a portrait painted when they were almost neighbors—that the good dame who has charge of the Carlyle house would be able to give inquirers exact directions for finding the Whistler house. This, the Spectator discovered, she was entirely unequal to, her directions having the indefiniteness characteristic of the person who, with one story to tell over and over, ventures from the daily round. Being of white brick, the house is easy to locate, which is all to be said of its exterior. Built on the street, with a plain, unrelieved squareness of outline, it is simply ugly, with nothing about it to suggest the specially designed house of the great artist. It is thus in painful contrast with Rossetti's home—one of the most attractive houses of the vicinity, with a pleasant garden in front, and an entrance through a fine iron gateway. Doubtless it pleased Whistler to heighten the effect of the interior by the uninviting, if not forbidding, character of the exterior. "By the irony of fate," as Whistler's friend Mr. Arthur Jerome Eddy tells in his "Reminiscences," "the 'White House' [it was so called from its bricks] was afterward occupied and much altered by the detested critic of the Times—detested, possibly, because he occupied and dared to alter the house —and Whistler asked, 'Shall the birthplace of art become the tomb of its parasite?'" This characteristic mot gives prophetic point to another, that when the "White House" was finally sold and Whistler moved out, he wrote: "'Except the Lord build the house, their labor is in vain that build it'—E. W. Godwin, R.S.A., built this one."

❦

In talking over Chelsea with his friend Mr. Ford Madox Hueffer—grandson of the Ford Madox Brown of the Pre-Raphaelite Circle— who as a small boy lived neighbor to Carlyle, the Spectator asked him whether he found in the Sage any of that gruffness traditionally associated with him. "On the contrary," was the reply, "the old man was exceptionally kind to youngsters. I remember," added Mr. Hueffer, "how I once got a rather bad tumble on Carlyle's doorstep, and he picked me up, set me on my feet, and assured me that 'it didn't hurt' in the most approved fatherly fashion." Trivial incident as this is, it is yet not without value as an

index of character. For the Spectator accepts a common saying that a good test of genuineness is a person's attitude toward children, who can always be trusted to detect a sham. Perhaps the same can be said of one's attitude to a genius, who is almost sure to be one of Lowell's "incurable children." At any rate, Carlyle and Whistler lived on very friendly terms as neighbors and as artist and subject, though, as Mr. Eddy says, "seemingly no two beings could be less sympathetic." Mr. Eddy adds: "Yet the philosopher, who had so few good words for any one, who was the implacable foe of sham and falsehood, who was intolerant of the society of others, who cared little for art and less for artists, freely gave his time and society to the most unpopular painter in England." Indeed, they had a common bond, "the attitude of the one towards literature and what his fellow-writers were saying, and the attitude of the other towards art and what his fellow-painters were doing."

❦

Apropos of portraits of Chelsea celebrities, there is one in Geneva of George Eliot, who can only, as already explained, be counted of Chelsea because of dying there—a portrait, in the Spectator's opinion, worth looking up by any of his friends visiting Geneva, it gives such a different impression from the prints by which she is generally known. This Geneva portrait hangs in the University gallery in an assemblage of uncompromising reformers, patriots, and other worthies, who accentuate its pleasant contrast. It is the portrait of an attractively gowned young woman—at the time George Eliot, it is said, was thirty, but the portrait looks younger than that— with auburn hair, fine blue eyes, and a pink and white smooth skin. The portrait is full face, which accounts, perhaps, for an apparently normal length of nose. There is in it nothing of the likeness to Savonarola which most people see in the common profile print, with its lines of care, doubtless due to delicate health, which likeness has perhaps unconsciously suggested a swarthy Italian complexion.

# THE NEXT PRESIDENT

## BY JOHN CALLAN O'LAUGHLIN

Correspondent of the Chicago Tribune

### FIRST PAPER

## REPUBLICAN POSSIBILITIES

THE Republican party has an embarrassment of riches in its Presidential possibilities. From their ranks it can draw a candidate associated in the public mind with any issue that may develop in the campaign of 1908. If it decide to "stand pat" on the tariff, there is Speaker Cannon. If it find revision necessary, there is Secretary Taft or Secretary Root. If radicalism become the central issue— and by radicalism is meant larger governmental control of corporations, including railways—there is Senator La Follette. If sound conservatism be considered desirable in order to offset the government ownership ideas of many Democrats, including William Jennings Bryan, there is Mr. Root again. If there should be wanted a happy mean between radicalism and conservatism—if, in other words, a man who will carry out President Roosevelt's policies be demanded—Secretary Taft once more forges to the front. If the party adopt a colorless platform, indorsing what has been done and repeating its indefinite pledge of 1904 with respect to tariff revision, there is the neutral Fairbanks.

Rarely is a tailor so happily situated that he can find a man to fit any coat he may decide to cut. The striking difference between an artist in such a situation and the Republican party is that the latter has many minds and does not know the kind of pattern to select or the back to fit it on when selected. Kansas, Massachusetts, and Wisconsin have declared for revision of the tariff. Other States also evince a leaning in that direction ; but the President insists that such action is not desirable until the next administration, and Speaker Cannon does not believe it should be attempted then. Indeed, the Speaker may be expected to go into the field in his shirt-sleeves and urge his friends to send to the Republican Convention delegates instructed to insist upon the principle of protection as embodied in the present tariff law. As a natural consequence it would follow that Mr. Cannon himself would be the nominee.

Here, then, will be the first spectacular skirmish of the Presidential campaign, and the sound of firing will be heard as soon as the forces now being organized appear in the open. Men of opposite temperament in the party, like the President and Senator Crane, of Massachusetts, for example, are united in advocating the adoption of a revision plank. Defeated by revisionists, ex-Congressman McCleary, of Minnesota, is urging the Speaker to hold fast to extreme protection. If revision must come, Speaker Cannon would want it up instead of down ; that is, he would favor a maximum and minimum tariff, with the Dingley Law the minimum. Mr. Dalzell, of Pennsylvania, returned to the House of Representatives by a reduced plurality, finds no warning in his humiliation. Nor, to hear them talk, do other advisers of Speaker Cannon heed the signs of the times. They have urged him to nail his colors to the mast, and he has done so. Speaker Cannon will rise or fall upon "stand-patism."

Now take Mr. Taft and Mr. Root, who have publicly assumed different ground from Cannon. "Speaking my individual opinion and for no one else," said Mr. Taft at Bath, Maine, during the campaign last September—"I believe since the passage of the Dingley Bill there has been a change in the business conditions of the country, making it wise and just to revise the schedules of the existing tariff." Here is a straight-from-the-shoulder declaration for revision, not three years hence, but immediately. Secretary Root, in a speech delivered in Washington January 14, referred to the necessity of reciprocal relations with foreign countries: "I do not think the subject of reciprocity can now be adequately considered or discussed without going into that broader subject, and that is the whole form of our tariff law. In my judgment, the United States must come to a maximum and minimum tariff." Everything the Secretary has said and done shows that he would like the Dingley Law made the maximum, with a lower scale for the minimum tariff. The difference between his attitude and that of Speaker Cannon is evident.

It is the purpose of the Republicans to make government ownership of public utilities a foremost issue of the campaign. Here they believe they will have the Democracy upon the hip. Mr. Bryan's withdrawal of his Government ownership declaration would seem to avert the possibility of this becoming a live issue. Not so if the Republicans can help it. They want to frighten the small investor as well as the large capitalist. They would like to range every man who holds or hopes to hold securities behind their candidate. They look back upon the campaign of 1896, and recall that it was these voters who sent President McKinley to the White House. Property-owners, big and little, feared the success of Mr. Bryan and his silver hobby. They felt that Mr. Bryan's election would disturb business and injure their interests.

I do not want to be a prophet of evil, but no one need be surprised should Wall Street bring home to property-holders in a most forceful way that not only must Government ownership be repudiated, but a safe man must be placed in the White House. Already the Street has demonstrated the effect of "Rooseveltism" by forcing down the values of securities, and greater depression is promised. In spite of the fact that the country is doing the largest import and export business in its history, that factories and mills cannot execute the orders given to them save under long delay, that the railways and other carriers are unable to handle expeditiously the freight placed in their charge, values are falling. Exposure is showing over-capitalization, which in part is responsible; but the real trouble lies in the desire of capital to compel general recognition of the evils of a progressive administration like that of Roosevelt, and the necessity of electing a man who may be depended upon to give what it terms a "square deal" to corporate interests. Apparently it is trying to drive public opinion uphill. Keen as are the individuals who control it, they fail to appreciate the force of the demand that all corporations serving the public, whether transportation, supply, or what not, shall do so, not for the profit of their stockholders, but for the benefit of the people.

It would be most unfortunate for any candidate to be nominated as the result of an agreement on the part of Wall Street financiers. But those interests that desire a "safe" candidate will point out that it is essential for Republican success that there should be a continuance of prosperous conditions. Prosperity was the slogan of 1904; it will be the battle-cry of 1908. "Let well enough alone" is a strong issue, and the people will be urged to leave the power in Republican hands because those hands have wrestled with and conquered huge governmental evils and will continue to deal with those yet unsettled and constantly arising. It will be pointed out that the President has recommended National supervision of corporations engaged in inter-State business; that he has recommended an income and inheritance tax; that he is paving the way to removing the evils of transportation, and that whenever and wherever it becomes necessary to protect the people from wrong and rapacity a remedy is devised and applied.

Which leads me to discuss what the President himself proposes to do—a matter of prime moment, as his conduct of the Government, his recommendations, and his vivid personality will be issues of the campaign. I think I may sum up his intentions by quoting a favorite expression he uses when referring to the Presidential campaign : " It is time for some one else to take his trick at the wheel." He says this with a finality that leaves no room for doubt. Hardly a day passes that the suggestion that he run is not made several times by men of political power, and it is repeated in hundreds of letters received from every section of the country, particularly the Middle and Far West. I have been in gatherings where the President declared himself opposed to a third term, and seen men rise up and shout emphatically : " No l No l You must run again ; the people are with you." And to those same men I have heard the President say back just as emphatically : " No l no l I *will not* run again." And he means it.

Under no combination of circumstances will the President be a candidate in 1908. The night of his election to the Presidency in November, 1904, when his plurality of 2,500,000 was larger than the total vote of Lincoln in 1860 or 1864, and almost four times larger than the plurality of Grant over Greeley, Mr. Roosevelt told the country : " The wise custom which limits the President to two terms regards the substance and not the form. Under no circumstances will I be a candidate for or accept another nomination." This statement was made with no thought that a possible condition might arise which would justify an effort to retain the office. It is hardly necessary to speak of the President's honesty, but I know that statement means to-day exactly what it said when prepared. I know further that the President never has swerved a hair's breadth from the position it describes. After the negotiations at Portsmouth which terminated the war between Russia and Japan, the President received letters of congratulation from all parts of the country commending the result of his mediation and declaring that he must consider another term in the White House. At that time the President believed his popularity was at the crest of the wave, and he looked for the recession as soon as the Treaty of Portsmouth was forgotten. But the American people have shown that they do not forget. His popularity forced the pas-

sage of the railway rate measure at the last session of Congress, and brought other reforms, all of which were grudgingly granted by the legislators at the Senate end of the Capitol.

Much of President Roosevelt's popularity is founded in the conviction of the people that in whatever he does he is actuated by the cleanest and highest motives. Many accuse the President of impulsiveness, an accusation more or less true, but I do not know of a big thing he has done that was not given, before action, the most careful and thoughtful consideration. Take, for instance, his decision in 1904 not to be a candidate for a third term, or what he considers a third term. He had reached this decision months before the election. It might have been a good card for him to let his decision reach the people before the votes were cast. He played no such politics. On the record of the three years and a half of his administration he was retained in the highest office of the land by a magnificent plurality. The landslide would have been a temptation to the ordinary man to withhold the declaration. The President knew that he could make the claim that his first administration really did not constitute a " term of office " in the sense in which the phrase had been employed by Washington and McKinley in their declarations against third terms. But he did not propose to be placed, during the four years he was to serve as President, in the position of a demagogue who was calculating the effect of every act upon another candidacy. He resolutely put behind him, and has kept behind him, all temptation in connection with a third term, in spite of the general knowledge, which he shares— and the President is a practical politician—that if he were to let it be known that he would run again all other aspirants in the Republican party would abandon their purpose to seek the nomination. But, to reiterate, the President will not run again. He once said that in the performance of his duties he necessarily had made many influential enemies who fought every measure he advocated, whether they were affected or not, because he favored it ; and he believed that another man should assume the Presidential office, a man with the same desire to make reforms and to advance the people's welfare, and with great strength of character, who would be able to achieve results because he had not yet made enemies.

With President Roosevelt out of the running, the Republicans of the country must make choice from the number of men who are willing and anxious to be their standard-bearer. " At this stage of the campaign of 1896," said a warm friend of the late President McKinley, " Hanna had so manipulated conditions in various States that it was McKinley and the field for the nomination. To-day, with Roosevelt determined not to be a candidate, it is the field." Nothing I have heard sums up the situation better. But the field is divided by a sharp line. Grouped on one side are the " Roosevelt Republicans," and on the other the " Conservative Republicans." The latter, of course, include all those who are opposed to the anti-trust and corporation regulation policies of the President. It is useless to suggest to them that the President really has done the Republican party a service ; that he has purged it of evils which were bringing about its undoing, and that he has brought it back to Lincolnian principles. And it is equally useless, so far as concerns any effect upon the President and his friends, for them to suggest that Mr. Roosevelt by his " attacks upon wealth " has fostered socialistic discontent which will destroy the country. Undoubtedly there is a wide difference between the President's supporters, on the one hand, and (for want of a better term) the Aldrich faction, on the other. It will not lead either to bolt the nominee of the Republican Convention, whoever he may be, especially as the Democratic candidate is certain to stand for more radical governmental measures, but it promises to provoke one of the most bitter and sensational fights in the history of the party.

This presupposes that the President will participate in the conflict. It is difficult to imagine him keeping out of a struggle fraught with such important consequences to the country and the party. I am satisfied that he will not seek to dic-

tate who the Convention shall name. But undoubtedly he will do as President what he would do if he were an ordinary citizen—make every effort to bring about the selection of a man who will serve the interests of the people, and not a particular class, and who will appeal to the voters. He has blazed a new way by the reforms he has inaugurated, and naturally he will want as his successor a man strong and qualified to pursue it despite opposition, able to finish off rough corners, and advance when the need shall develop. He will not support a man whose training and thought have been in a different direction, who believes in less regulation of corporate interests than he has advocated, who is willing to let the railways serve themselves rather than the people, who is opposed temperamentally to everything he has stood for, and thus will become his critic. The Panama Canal is one of the projects closest to Theodore Roosevelt's heart. He wants the next President to press it to completion as vigorously as he himself would do were he to continue in office.

There are a great many astute politicians in Washington who believe that Charles Warren Fairbanks, of Indiana, will be the Republican candidate for the Presidency. Ask what principles he stands for, and few will answer offhand. For years the White House has been his goal. It is his one passion, his mastering ambition, and it overshadows principles. He would accept any platform that may be framed.

The Vice-President is seeking to create a machine in every State in the Union. The trail of his agents extends from Florida to Wisconsin, from California to New Hampshire. If they find it impossible to secure his indorsement as the first choice of a State, they willingly put him aside for a favorite son, but insist that he shall be designated as the second choice.

Mr. Fairbanks does not rely solely upon agents by any means. He has missed few opportunities to meet the people. He has made more of a personal canvass than any other public man in the last six or eight years. Mr. Roosevelt engaged in a big speaking campaign during the campaign of 1900. McKinley the President could not descend to ask votes for McKinley the candidate. This was the task confided to the tail of the ticket. Nor could Mr. Roosevelt as President seek votes for election in 1904. Mr. Fairbanks made the speaking campaign of that year, and when he finished it was claimed that he had traveled a greater distance than even Mr. Bryan had in the famous campaign of '96·

The people like to get in touch with the men they place in office. It is unfortunate for the aspirations of Mr. Fairbanks that he lacks personal magnetism. He has the presence for the office he seeks. He is dignified, gracious, and engaging. He has many of the qualities of Mr. McKinley, but he cannot excite enthusiasm. He does not appeal to an audience any more than did President Harrison. His speeches fail to inspire those who hear them. But let the same men meet Fairbanks in his hotel, shake hands with him, and listen to his hearty voice and well-balanced compliments, and they will go away with a far more pleasant impression of him than they received from the platform.

Herein lies the value of the social functions the Fairbankses give. There is no other home in Washington that has been the scene of so many receptions and dinners. The latter usually are attended by men and women who can be of political service to the Vice-President, and few are deceived as to the purpose of an invitation. Mrs. Fairbanks makes a charming hostess. She was President of the Daughters of the American Revolution, and in that capacity, by tact and good judgment, kept out of controversies which among women cause everlasting enmities. She has a woman's machine, and cleverly manipulates it in the interest of her husband.

Mr. Fairbanks represents the conservative forces. He might be the choice of the Republican majority in the Senate if it could elect the President. He has made an admirable presiding officer. Certainly he has no active enemies in the Upper House. Mr. Fairbanks, it is generally believed, would be thoroughly acceptable to the big moneyed interests generally, and also to the politicians.

Time will tell whether he will be acceptable to the people.

Secretary Taft, against his own will, has been drawn into the maelstrom of Presidential politics. His ambition always had been to sit on the Supreme Bench. He is a lawyer. His decisions on patent law rendered when a Federal judge on the Ohio circuit have become principles of that branch of jurisprudence. He said to the President and to all his friends that he would rather wear the robe of a Justice of the Supreme Court than serve the people in the White House. Had it not been for the persistent pleading of the President and strong personal friends, he would have accepted the position of Associate Justice rendered vacant by the retirement of Justice Brown. "I am not a politician," the Secretary frequently has stated. "I have gone ahead and done my duty irrespective of politics, and I have not sought to make myself popular. Besides, I have been behind the scenes, and the office of President holds no attraction for me."

But the Secretary finally allowed himself to be placed in the list of possibilities, and indeed so announced in a statement he made publicly to "his friends among the Washington correspondents." The trouble with the Secretary for a long time—to quote one of his friends—was that he would not permit them to do what they think proper to advance his candidacy. He had an almost morbid fear of being placed in the attitude of struggling for the Presidency. Now, however, he has consented to leave his candidacy in the hands of his friends. It may seem that, as Secretary of War, and as the direct representative of the President in many matters outside of the War Department, he would be tempted to promote his candidacy. I do not believe the Secretary is influenced in the slightest degree by Presidential aspirations; he simply does not think of them. He loyally supported the President in connection with the dismissal of three battalions of the Twenty-fifth Colored Infantry, though he was well aware that in so doing he was perhaps cutting himself off from a large part of the negro vote. He knew nothing of the President's purpose in this matter before the order was issued. When he returned to Washington from Cuba, and later from the West, where he had gone to inspect army posts, the President was at Panama. The Secretary was impressed by the appeals of friends of the negro, and daringly suspended the order of his chief. He communicated with the President, and then, by direction of the latter, revoked the suspension. The memory of the negro is short-lived, however, and he will forget that Mr. Taft placed himself in an awkward position for his sake, and recall only that the Secretary has ably backed up the President's policy. Senator Foraker, of Ohio, stands out as the defender of the negro, and, by the way in which he handled the Brownsville incident, has "placed handcuffs" on the negro vote in his State. The President believed throughout the Brownsville discussion that Senator Foraker, as the representative of corporate interests, was using the incident for the purpose of assailing the Administration; it may be said further that Senator Foraker is too astute a politician not to understand the effect of the dismissal of negro soldiers upon the colored mind, and he employed it as a two-edged sword to cut both the President and Secretary Taft.

Senator Foraker and Secretary Taft are as dissimilar as two great public men can be. Mr. Foraker is an orator; Mr. Taft is not. Mr. Foraker has been associated always with great corporate interests; Mr. Taft has been rather the representative of the people in legal controversies. Mr. Foraker is rich; Mr. Taft is poor. Mr. Foraker is a politician and has been playing the game practically all his life; Mr. Taft is as straightforward as a child in politics. Senator Foraker is a veteran of the Civil War and can appeal to the old soldier vote; Secretary Taft was too young to enter the army of the Great Rebellion. Mr. Taft is inclined to act, and does act, without reference to his political future; Senator Foraker rarely loses a point in this connection. Both are men of courage. Senator Foraker consistently opposed the railway rate regulation bill and voted against it, though he knew it to be an immensely popular measure. Secretary Taft's decisions as a Circuit Judge ren-

dered government by injunction possible, and thus aroused the hostility of labor. Mr. Taft's speech in Ohio in 1905 disabled George Cox, the Republican boss of Cincinnati, prevented the election of a Republican Governor of the State, and brought him the open enmity of the Republican machine and Senator Dick, Foraker's colleague. Thus the two Senators and the Republican machine of Ohio are united in their determination to prevent Taft's indorsement as that State's Presidential candidate.

Indeed, Senator Foraker wants the indorsement himself. Fortunately for Secretary Taft's candidacy, the unit rule does not prevail in the Republican party. Senator Foraker will be able to secure in Ohio the four delegates at large, but he will be forced at least to divide the remainder of the delegation with his opponent. Although both men come from Cincinnati and it would seem that their fight should center in the southern part of the State, nevertheless it will be waged with the northern section as the battlefield.

Outside of Ohio Senator Foraker can look for nothing save perhaps in the Southern States, where the negro vote probably will be for him. Here he comes in conflict with Vice-President Fairbanks.

Mr. Taft's boom, which at first did not seem to take hold, is being vigorously nourished. President Roosevelt has made and is making opportunities for his Secretary of War. In the people's mind he is the right hand of his chief. He has executed Mr. Roosevelt's policies in the Philippines, Panama, and Cuba. He investigated the Bowen-Loomis controversy and other matters of political importance. He is recognized as the Administration's peacemaker. In the prosecution of the trusts and in railway regulation legislation he has been the adviser of the President equally with the Attorney-General. But in spite of his success in doing well everything intrusted to him, no lively enthusiasm has been manifested as yet for his candidacy. It may come with the activity of his friends. It would come if he were only active himself. But to-day he has no strength with politicians, and his labor decisions and waiting attitude give them hope that he will have none with the people.

There is not the slightest doubt that if Mr. Taft were to be the candidate, or if it were to appear that he has a good chance to secure the nomination, Mr. Root would energetically and faithfully support him. On the other hand, it is not to be doubted that if Secretary Taft believed that Mr. Root could get the nomination, he would aid him with equal energy and unselfishness. The President recently said that he would crawl on his hands and knees from the White House to the Capitol to bring about the election of Mr. Taft to be his successor. He would do as much for Mr. Root. Publicly and privately he has expressed the highest opinion of the intellectual and administrative capacity of his Secretary of State.

The Secretary's notable trip to South America tended to dissipate the suspicion of American motives entertained in that part of the world. Since his return he has made several speeches which have attracted wide attention, and in Kansas, for example, he created a disposition to overlook his past corporate connections. He has advocated ship subsidy as well as tariff revision. To the dismay of the Republican machine, he has revived the States' rights question by a speech in New York in which he pointed out the trend of the country toward centralization of government. According to a subsequent declaration, he merely intended to warn the country of the way in which it was moving. New York listened to his Utica address, in which he served as the mouthpiece of the President, and showed its confidence in his charges by refusing to elect William Randolph Hearst as Governor, though it put the remainder of the Democratic ticket into office. Nevertheless, Mr. Root is not what the politicians call popular even in his own State.

It is believed by the President that if the Secretary would consent to permit his name to be used, he could enter the Convention with the indorsement of New York. But there are other forces at work in that State, among them the Odell faction, which the President brought to its knees in the late gubernatorial campaign. Governor Hughes's message to the New York Legislature was promising, and made him Presidential timber in the rough. Will his performance justify the promise ? One candidate for the Presidency observed: "The people approve his words, but can he make good ? They will consider him if he stops the Bridge rush, improves traction transportation, provides cheaper gas, and brings about other much-needed reforms in New York City."

George B. Cortelyou, the new Secretary of the Treasury, is another New Yorker who is a Presidential possibility. Mr. Cortelyou could have been nominated Governor of New York, but declined to permit his name to be considered. When all the facts are known, he believes that his work as Chairman of the Republican National Committee will receive approval. At present, if he were forced to speak, he would be compelled to make statements which might prove embarrassing to the Republican party ; this is the sole reason he remains silent under criticism. Before the present wave of reform swept over the country it was considered an honor to hold the political "dough-bag." It is so no longer. The President's confidence in Mr. Cortelyou is shown by the fact that he has assigned him to more Cabinet positions than any other man in the Administration. As Postmaster-General, Cortelyou has extended rural free delivery and benefited the farmer. The latter knows to whom he is indebted. His recommendation brought better pay to employees of the postal service. He is a shrewd organizer, and his ability as a politician is not generally known.

Leslie M. Shaw, of Iowa, ex-Secretary of the Treasury, is the fourth member of the Cabinet willing to receive promotion from the people. Mr. Shaw has not the "ghost of a chance." He has made an excellent Secretary of the Treasury ; but in spite of numerous speeches and even undignified scrambling, he has aroused no enthusiasm among politicians or the people. If he could get Iowa, he might have his name mentioned in the Convention. But he cannot control his native State. Governor Cummins considers Mr. Shaw one of his worst political foes. He will fight him to the death. Mr. Shaw may get a few delegates, but if he does he will find the majority advocating the nomination of Governor Cummins.

There remains but one other man worthy of present consideration, and he looms large—Joseph G. Cannon, of Illinois, Speaker of the House of Representatives.

Were the Speaker fifteen years younger, his nomination would be one of the decided probabilities. But if nominated and elected, Mr. Cannon would be seventy-three years of age when inaugurated, and seventy-seven when his term of office expired. To-day he is as spry as a cricket. His brain is as active, his carriage as steady, as they were at fifty. He is a man of the people, plain and unassuming. He has the faculty of making friends and keeping them. He is a good speaker, blunt, coarse frequently, and has an inexhaustible fund of witty stories. His metaphors are the product of a sledge-hammer, but they drive home the point he wishes to make, and they please the common people.

Mr. Cannon does not appeal to radicals, nor is organized labor pleased with his attitude. President Gompers, of the American Federation of Labor, considered the advisability of attacking the Speaker in his Congressional district in Illinois, and thought better of it. Mr. Cannon has made no active, open canvass for indorsement for the Presidential nomination, but he will be named by Illinois and receive scattering support from all over the country. No doubt exists that, strongly as the Senate is for Mr. Fairbanks, the House is for Speaker Cannon. Two-thirds of the Republican Representatives would be glad to elevate him to the Presidency. They know of the movement started in 1904 to make him Roosevelt's running mate, and they appreciate his preference of the Speakership. They have ambled along the legislative way under his easy rein, though sometimes they have felt the spur of his decision. It is fair to presume that these men are the strongest politicians in their districts and can largely control the selection of district delegates. If "Uncle Joe" were to ask their support, which he has not yet done, and they agreed to give it, which, guided by interest in their own Congressional careers, they must do, he would be able to make a formidable showing in the Convention. In the late Congressional elections Mr. Cannon stumped contested districts vigorously, in part because he knew that without a Republican House he would cut a very small figure during the next two years and would not command the power to make or break men, which as Speaker he possesses. He has made enemies in the Senate because of his open attacks on that body, and because he has held up legislation in which Senators have been interested personally. These Senators for the most part are men of force in their respective States, and will be able, to some extent, to offset the work of the Congressmen.

What has been said will give an idea of the embarrassing situation of the Republican party. It has no lack of either principles or candidates. But exactly which principles to advocate and which candidate to select as its leader are problems that are taxing the brains of the wisest men in its fold.

# RUSSIAN DESPOTISM

## BY GEORGE KENNAN

TWENTY years ago last November, Mr. Edward J. Phelps, who was then our Minister to Great Britain, delivered an address before the Philosophical Institution of Edinburgh upon "The Law of the Land."

In the course of that address Mr. Phelps said:

The theory upon which our system of government rests is that mankind possesses certain natural rights, usually described as those of life, liberty, and property, indispensable to human freedom and happiness; that these rights are not derived from, but are antecedent to, government, which is instituted for their maintenance as its first and principal object; that government can never be allowed, therefore, to infringe or disregard these rights, nor to fail to offer redress for their invasion; and that when it ceases to respect and uphold them, the obligation of allegiance terminates and the right of revolution begins.

These constitutional principles are of perpetual duration and of perpetual authority; because the natural rights which they maintain are of perpetual obligation.

No change of time or circumstance, no new discovery of political science, no modification of the forms of government, can affect their validity or restrict their control.

If Mr. Phelps had been a subject of Russia instead of a citizen of the United States, and if he had spoken these words before the Juridical Society of Moscow instead of before the Philosophical Institution of Edinburgh, what, in all probability, would have happened to him?

He would have been arrested in less than twenty-four hours; would have spent three or four months in solitary confinement in one of the bomb-proof casemates of the fortress of Petropavlovsk, and would then have been sent to Siberia as a political criminal of the most dangerous type—a criminal who actually had the impudence and the audacity to assert that there is such a thing as the right of revolution.

But, as a matter of fact, would Mr. Phelps have *been* a criminal simply be-

cause he had stated a universal truth in Moscow instead of Edinburgh?

By no means. Crime is not a matter of geography.

If the speaker was a thinker, a patriot, and a statesman in Edinburgh, he would have been no less a thinker, a patriot, and a statesman in Moscow; and the real criminal would have been the Minister of the Interior who sent him to Siberia merely for stating a truth which is universal in its application, and which is the corner-stone of human prosperity and happiness. Leaving aside, however, this aspect of the case, let us apply Mr. Phelps's principles to the present Government of Russia and see whether it has any right to exist.

The late American Minister says that when a government "ceases to respect and uphold the natural rights of life, liberty, and property, the obligation of allegiance terminates and the right of revolution begins."

Has the present Russian Government afforded any protection to these natural rights?

Take, first, the right of property. A few years ago a Russian publisher of St. Petersburg caused a translation to be made of a well-known American book entitled "Dynamic Sociology," by Professor Lester F. Ward, of Washington. The manuscript was approved by the censor, who found nothing objectionable in it, and an edition of five thousand copies was printed and bound.

Just as the publisher, however, was preparing to put the book on the market, the Council of Ministers ordered the whole edition to be seized and burned, and the order was immediately carried into effect. Of course the publisher lost all the money that he had put into it, and was deprived of this property, not by due process of law, but by a mere executive order of confiscation.

Imagine what we should think and say in America if Secretary Hitchcock should send a force of Federal police to the publishing house of D. Appleton &

An address delivered by Mr. Kennan before the meeting in behalf of Russian freedom held in Carnegie Hall, New York, on March 4; stenographically reported for The Outlook and revised by the author. —THE EDITORS.

Co., in New York, and, without any process of law, seize and burn a whole edition of Herbert Spencer's "Social Statics." And yet this, or something like this, happens in Russia every week, and sometimes three or four times a week.

Between the 30th of October, 1905, and the 1st of June, 1906, the Russian police seized, confiscated, and destroyed, without process of law, no less than ninety-seven editions of books, pamphlets, and magazines, comprising more than five hundred thousand copies.

That which happens to the publishers of books happens in a still worse form to the publishers of periodicals.

I could name a score of Russian newspapers whose doors have recently been closed by the police and whose capital of from $20,000 to $100,000 has been absolutely wiped out without process of law by an order from the Minister of the Interior.

From these few examples it must be sufficiently clear, I think, that the present Russian Government not only gives no protection to property, but absolutely confiscates or destroys it when it is used in opposition to bureaucratic supremacy.

Mr. Phelps's second natural right is that of liberty, and this right the Russian Government has violated more flagrantly and cruelly, perhaps, than any other.

Under the so-called laws of reinforced and extraordinary defense it has arrested without warrant, and imprisoned or exiled without trial, not less than thirty thousand persons in the last twelve months. On the day when the first Duma assembled in St. Petersburg there were already eighteen thousand political offenders in prison, and four thousand more had passed through Moscow on their way to places of exile in Archangel, Vologda, and Siberia. Since that time the number of both prisoners and exiles has largely increased, so that now it certainly amounts to thirty thousand and may reach fifty thousand.

Probably two-thirds of these persons have been arrested without legal warrant and have been imprisoned or sent into exile without judicial trial.

The so-called law of reinforced defense, which authorizes such treatment of Rus-

sian subjects, and which is in force throughout five-sixths of the Empire, empowers Governors and Governors General (1) to prohibit public, social, or private meetings; (2) to close commercial and industrial establishments; (3) to suppress newspapers and magazines; (4) to make searches and seizures in public or private buildings; (5) to arrest and imprison citizens without accusation or warrant; (6) to send civil or political cases to military courts and try them there behind closed doors; (7) to banish political suspects to the remotest parts of the Empire; and (8) to issue imperative orders which shall have all the force of law and which shall cover cases not foreseen and specially provided for.

It would be hard to name any act of injustice which a bureaucratic official may not commit with impunity under the sweeping provisions of this Imperial ukase.

It is officially called "the law of reinforced defense;" but it ought to be entitled "a ukase authorizing officials to reinforce and defend themselves by violating the civil and criminal codes." In the face of the fact that thirty thousand Russian citizens have recently been imprisoned or exiled, two-thirds of them without trial, it is impossible to contend that the Russian Government throws any safeguards around liberty. In its dealings with property and persons it is as unscrupulous and ruthless as a highwayman or a brigand.

The third natural right referred to by Mr. Phelps is the right to life. Does the Russian Government pay any more respect to this than to property and liberty? The answer must again be in the negative. Finding it impossible to stop the rising tide of revolution by means of imprisonment and exile, the Government in 1906 resorted, for the first time, to terrorism in the shape of wholesale killing.

According to the Russian historical review, Builloe, the number of political offenders put to death in the first six months of last year was 970. Four-fifths of them were executed upon sentences of field courts martial, while the remainder were shot or hanged by executive order.

In the cases of those who were tried

by courts martial there was the form of regular judicial procedure, but it was nothing more than a form. The trial was held with closed doors; the law required that sentence should be pronounced inside of twenty-four hours and executed inside of forty-eight; the prisoner had no counsel, he had no time to summon his witnesses, and it was practically impossible for him to make any adequate defense.

Such a trial, judged by our standards of judicial procedure, is not due process of law—it is murder under cover of an Imperial ukase, and is no more legal than the assassinations of the terrorists.

This wholesale homicide is increasing rather than diminishing. In the first two weeks of last January 81 politicals were put to death, 63 of them by sentences of field courts martial.

If this rate of 81 executions in fourteen days be carried through the rest of the present year, 2,106 politicals will be shot or hanged before the first of next January.

In the same two weeks covered by this death record the number of politicals sentenced by military courts to imprisonment, exile, or penal servitude was 328.

This rate, if continued throughout the year, will bring the total number of political convicts up to 10,634.

These figures, of course, do not include the thousands of politicals imprisoned or exiled by administrative process, without any form of law whatever.

As a further illustration of Russian methods, take the history of the members of Russia's first representative assembly. Of the delegates to the first Duma, one—my personal friend Professor Herzenstein—has been murdered by Black Hundred assassins; one has gone insane; two have been cruelly beaten by the police; five have been exiled; ten are in hiding; thirty-three have been arrested and searched; twenty-four are in prison; and one hundred and eighty-two are under indictment on the charge of treason.

When it suits their purposes to do so, the Russian officials violate the laws without the slightest hesitation and apparently without the least shame.

Early in April last, while elections to the first Duma were in progress, Mr. Durnovo, who was then Minister of the Interior, sent to the Governors of all the provinces of European Russia the following telegram:

"Under the provisions of the law of reinforced defense, you are hereby instructed to arrest all students, Jews, and vagabond orators who make their appearance in the peasant villages, and keep them in prison, without regard to the judicial authorities."

A little later, in May, Representative Alikin, in behalf of the whole Kazan delegation in the Duma, went personally to Mr. Strizhevski, the Governor of Kazan, and asked him to release from the prisons of that province all politicals against whom no charges of any kind had been brought.

When the Governor refused to grant this reasonable request, Mr. Alikin ventured to say that the long imprisonment of persons not accused of any offense was having a very bad effect upon public opinion.

To this the Governor coolly and cynically replied, "We are not obliged to reckon with public opinion."

It would be easy to multiply proofs that the Russian bureaucracy does not respect nor uphold the natural rights of property, liberty, and life; but I have perhaps given facts enough to show that, in accordance with the principles laid down by Mr. Phelps in his Edinburgh address, the Russian Government has no right to exist, and it is the duty of the Russian people to overthrow it.

In his oration on "Harper's Ferry," delivered in Brooklyn on the first of November, 1859, Wendell Phillips said:

"Lawless, brutal force is no basis for a government, in the true sense of that word. No civil society, no government, can exist except on the basis of the willing submission of all its citizens, and by the performance of the duty of rendering equal justice between man and man. Whatever calls itself a government and refuses that duty, or lacks that assent, is not a government—it is only a pirate ship."

We all know what happens to pirate ships. They are chased off the face of the earth by the civilized powers; and such ought to be the fate of the Russian bureaucracy.

In the present state of international relations, and under the existing code of international law, it is impossible, perhaps, for one government to interfere with the domestic affairs of another; but it is not impossible for us, as free citizens, to extend a hand of sympathy and help, and to shout God-speed to those suffering millions who are struggling for freedom on the other side of the Atlantic.

With what sympathy and admiration they look to the United States of America as the realization and embodiment of all that they hope for in Russia may be shown by a pathetic incident in the history of the Russian revolutionary movement.

In the summer of 1876—the American Centennial summer—when there were confined in the great prison known as the House of Preliminary Detention in St. Petersburg more than three hundred political offenders—all of them in separate cells, but secretly in communication with one another by means of the "knock alphabet"—it was decided by them to have a general prison celebration of the American Centennial, Fourth of July.

As early as the first week in June the prisoners began to make preparations for the proposed celebration by requesting relatives, who were permitted to visit some of them once or twice a week, to bring or send to the prison, for their use, as many red and blue handkerchiefs, neckerchiefs, shirts, and pairs of red flannel drawers as could be brought or sent without exciting suspicion, and at the same time all of the prisoners who were permitted to have movable lights in their cells began to purchase and hoard cheap tallow candles. The colored garments were torn into strips; the candles were cut into inch-long bits; and both were distributed throughout the prison, either by attaching them to strings obtained by raveling out their stockings and swinging them, like pendulums, from one cell window to another, or by lowering them or pulling them up through the iron soil-pipes which connected the water-closet fixtures of the cells with the sewerage system of the city.

The prisoners had long before discovered that by scooping the water out of the closet traps they could open the pipes so as to make them speaking-tubes from cell to cell, and could even use them as a means of transferring little packages from one cell to another by tying such packages to long strings, throwing them into the pipes, and then pulling the strings up and down until they became entangled or twisted together. Out of the strips of colored cloth, obtained in this way, some of the women—who were permitted to have needles and thread and to do sewing in their cells—succeeded in making secretly small, rude American flags; and before the 1st of July almost every political offender in the prison had either a small American flag or a few red, white, and blue strips of cloth.

Day breaks, in the high northern latitude of St. Petersburg, in summer, very early; and on the morning of the 4th of July, 1876, hours before the first daylight cannon announced the beginning of the great national celebration in Philadelphia, hundreds of small, rude American flags or strips of red, white, and blue cloth fluttered from the grated windows of the politicals around the whole quadrangle of the great St. Petersburg prison, while the prisoners were faintly hurrahing, singing patriotic songs, or exchanging greetings with one another through the iron pipes which united their cells. The celebration, of course, was soon over. The prison guard, although they had never heard of the Declaration of Independence and did not understand the significance of this extraordinary demonstration, promptly seized and removed the flags and tricolored streamers. Some of the prisoners, however, had more material of the same kind in reserve, and at intervals throughout the whole day scraps and tatters of red, white, and blue were furtively hung out here and there from cell windows or tied around the bars of the gratings. Late in the evening, at a preconcerted hour, the politicals lighted their bits of tallow candles and placed them in their windows, and the celebration ended with a faint but perceptible illumination of the great prison quadrangle.

There seems to me to be something infinitely mournful and touching in this attempt of three hundred political offenders to celebrate together, in the loneliness and gloom of a Russian prison, the centennial birthday of a free people. Compared with the banners, the fireworks, the martial music, and all the glowing pageantry of triumphant liberty in Philadelphia, the rudely fashioned stars and stripes hung out from grated cell windows, the faint hurrahing and singing of patriotic songs through prison pipes, and the few bits of tallow candle, illuminating faintly at night the dark, silent quadrangle of the prison in St. Petersburg, may seem pitifully weak, ineffective, and insignificant; but judged by a spiritual standard, the celebration of the centennial Fourth of July in the House of Preliminary Detention, in the Russian capital, is an event almost as extraordinary—and to the heart and imagination of a freeman almost as impressive—as the great National celebration in Philadelphia. Human actions are not to be judged solely by the scenic effect that they produce, but are also to be regarded as manifestations of human emotion and purpose. When Mary anointed the feet of her Lord and Master as an expression of her devotion and love, it was a simple thing, almost a trivial thing; but Christ said, " She hath done what she could." When the Russian revolutionists hung out rude imitations of the star-spangled banner from their cell windows, and lighted, at night, their hoarded bits of tallow candle, as an expression of their devotion to liberty, it, too, was a simple thing, almost a trivial thing—but they did what they could. Some of them were weak from sickness and long solitary confinement; some of them had just come from the voiceless, bomb-proof casemates of the Petropavlovski fortress, where they had almost lost count of days and months; some of them were living in anticipation of the unknown hardships and privations of Siberia; and upon some of them was resting, already, the dark shadow of the scaffold; but in all their solitude, their loneliness, and their misery, they did not forget the American centennial Fourth of July. What little they *could* do to show their devotion to the cause of freedom, and their sympathy with a freedom-loving people on the centennial anniversary of that people's emancipation, that little they bravely did; and the spirit by which they were animated transfigured their pitiful celebration, with its tricolored rags and its paltry bits of candle, and made it infinitely more significant, in the world's history, than all the pomp and ceremony that attend the coronation of a Czar.

It seems to me that such people as these are deserving of our sympathy, pity, and help; and if I thought that sympathy, pity, and help would not be given to them, I should feel disposed to renounce my American citizenship and go to live in a country which is oppressed, down-trodden, famine-stricken, and wretched, but which contains men and women who have ideals and aspirations for which they are ready to die.

# CHINA'S GREAT FAMINE

## BY WILLIAM T. ELLIS

"WOLF! wolf!" has been cried so often concerning the failure of China's crops, and consequent famine, that when the gaunt wolf of starvation actually does appear at the door of three million people the world may be pardoned for appearing rather skeptical. This time, however, the alarm is real, as may be known by many signs—that shipload of cheap, flimsy coffins which I passed yesterday on the Grand Canal, for one, and the grimly bustling activity in every coffin-shop in Central China. Even so there are not coffins enough to go around, despite the existence of many benevolent societies expressly to furnish them, and despite the depth of the Chinese sentiment upon the importance of proper coffins, graves, funerals, and mourning. The children are being buried in a small square of matting, without any ceremony whatever; and the mother's only sign of mourning is a single white rag, the size of a lady's handkerchief, thrown over her head, or even a few strings of dried flax, so desperate is the poverty.

Possibly I am commencing my story wrong end foremost. The beginning of the famine should come before its result. That beginning was water—heavy rainfall during spring and summer, swollen streams and canals, overflowing banks, and submerged fields. Since the ancient canals are higher than the surrounding country, the farms remain submerged, many of them, to this day. The crops of this part of China are chiefly wheat, maize, buckwheat, beans, and peanuts; it is not a rice-growing or rice-eating section. The spring sowing was lost almost utterly over an area of over forty thousand square miles lying north of the Yangtze River, and mainly in the provinces of Kiangsu and Anhuei. The fall sowing of wheat is less than half the average, so it will be an entire year before full crops may be expected, although the famine will probably be broken in June and July.

So close do the Chinese live to their daily bread, in a poverty that is incredible to any Westerner who has not witnessed it, that the failure of the summer crops meant only one thing—famine for three or four million peasants. The entire ten million population of the flooded area is affected, to a greater or lesser degree. All prosperity in China, as elsewhere, rises and falls with that of the farmer. Soon the pinch of extraordinary poverty began to be felt all over the North River Country. Farms were mortgaged, live stock sold, personal possessions pawned, domestic pets eaten, the daily ration reduced, and stores of dried sweet potato leaves, ground willow bark, and roots and various weeds laid in.

Those whose mud houses had fallen down in the flood, and thousands of other families besides, piled their worldly goods and the babies on the family wheelbarrow and started toward the unflooded region south of the Yangtze River. Here they encamped outside the walls of several cities, where their very numbers, as a possible menace, inspired the officials to take some steps for their preservation. Many and various have been the temporary camps constructed by large bodies of people in various parts of the world at different times, congregated for one reason or another; but it is doubtful if any ever resembled these aggregations of hungry Chinese. The common coarse rush matting, about four feet by five in size, to be purchased for a few cash, was used for the construction of dwellings, sometimes only one piece sufficing, when the shelter would be only the size of a dog-house, and again three or four pieces being used, giving the hut the shape and almost the size of the top of a covered farm wagon. These shelters served to keep off a measure of wind and rain. Alongside of them, however, the meanest quarters in a great city's slums are paradise.

In this fashion were huddled together at the beginning of January hordes of refugees aggregating at least half a million persons—three hundred thousand at Tsinkiangpu, eighty thousand at Nanking, another eighty thousand at Yangchow, and thirty thousand at Chinkiang, to cite the principal centers. The Chinese official figures put the total number of these refugees at a million and a quarter. Compare these hosts with the " Coxey's Army " which fifteen years ago excited such an interest throughout America, remembering always that by far the greater number of famine victims remained in their homes.

Of the miseries of this multitude of men, women, and children, encamped on the bare ground in the middle of winter, and subsisting on a ration ranging from a bowl of rice to nothing at all, little needs to be said. All " ate bitterness," as the quaint Chinese phrase for mental suffering has it; many ate nothing else, and the deaths from actual starvation, and from disease superinduced by insufficient nutrition, mounted up into the thousands. The marvel is not that so many died, but that so few died. The low mortality rate—considering the circumstances—is due to the unrivaled endurance of the Chinese. Poverty is normal with them. Given food enough to enable them to " cross the day," as their expressive saying puts it, and they will undergo without complaint a degree of poverty that would incite "bread riots" anywhere in Christendom.

There again you have a Chinese characteristic; the Chinese are, with reason, said to be the quietest, most law-abiding and peaceful race of people on earth, despite the turbulences faithfully reported over seas. Imagine the city of Baltimore, its every man, woman, and child actually suffering from hunger, encamped on the outskirts of Richmond, and the latter city enabled to pursue its wonted way in peace, with all its grain warehouses and provision stores open to the street. That would be analogous to the situation at Tsinkiangpu, a city of considerably less than two hundred thousand inhabitants, which for a month has had three hundred thousand famine refugees miserably squatting beneath its walls. Tantalizingly, the heaps of grain and rice in front of the shops have increased in size rather than diminished, even as the price has increased two and three hundred fold. In the very refugee camps themselves, under the eyes of ravenous, starving people, grain merchants have safely displayed their wares, confident in the knowledge of the national orderliness and in the presence of several companies of China's new soldiery.

A supreme test of Chinese submission to authority, in the actual presence of that grim necessity which supposedly knows no law, was afforded by the breaking up of the immense refugee camps at Tsinkiangpu, towards the close of January. The officials saw several dangers threatening from the proximity of this multitude, destitute to desperation. The possibility of revolution haunted them as a specter. More certain was the danger of plague. The concreteness of the camps as a spectacle of woe would give the enemies of the Government a powerful argument. Moreover, so long as these tens of thousands remained, they could command a measure of help; dispersed, they could be safely ignored. Removed the camps must be.

Almost over night the deed was done. Payment for ten days' rations, at the rate of one cent and a half a day per person, was made in a lump, and assurance was given that the next payment would take place only at the homes

where the people are registered. There also the relief from the foreigners would be distributed; this last being a powerful consideration, for the Chinese have no confidence in the pledges of their own authorities to aid them, although the Government appears to be making sincere efforts in that direction. When promises failed to budge the refugees, their huts were burned or torn down over their heads.

The exodus from the camps back to the North Country was an anabasis for a Xenophon's pen. It was sunset when I first saw a long line of wheelbarrows, on the crest of the old bank of the Yellow River, silhouetted against the western sky. The dumb patience of a Millet painting was in the scene. The crude vehicles each held all of a family's earthly store, and two or three members of the family itself. Such pitifully poor possessions—a bowl-shaped iron cooking vessel, a few cheap rice-bowls, possibly a larger earthenware dish, a basket, a bundle of rushes for fuel, the mats that had lately served as a house, a ragged coverlet, maybe an extra pair of shoes too badly worn to pawn, and, in one case at least, a cheap straw hat. Sometimes the father would be pushing and the children pulling, with the smaller ones on top of the household goods, and a wee babe hidden inside the mother's coat, next to her breast, for warmth. Often the relationships were curiously assorted; the most typical specimen of starvation plus sickness that I saw was stretched out on a barrow, with a nephew trundling him. Again it was a big boy pushing the load and a grandmother with the babies. Sometimes it was a son pushing a mother.

Occasionally there would be no man at all in the group; some husbands and fathers have deserted their responsibilities. Others have thrown away the weak members of their households. I myself found a twenty-year-old boy, broken-backed and with only pitiful, useless little stumps for arms and legs, who had been lying for three days in a ditch, where his parents had cast him. Children, especially girls, are being sold for all sorts of purposes, mostly bad; one father sold his daughter for fourteen cents and two bowls of rice. Sixty cents is said to be a fair price for a girl just now, although I met a case to-day where a father was paid twenty dollars for his daughter and then robbed of all except one dollar by the go-between. The soulless traffickers in flesh and blood are reported already to have gone from Shanghai into the famine district. On the other hand, the patient, ox-like fidelity of these stolid men, trudging steadily on beneath the weight of wheelbarrow straps, is really noble ; there is romance in the patent fact that so many babies on the barrows are ruddy and healthy, while their parents wear the hollow, glassy eyes and dusty pallor of the starving.

While it is impossible not to treat of this whole calamity in ·bulk, yet an investigator is ever running across reminders that for each of the suffering millions the distress is as individual and personal and detached as the misfortunes of the hero of the latest novel. At Nanking the front wall of one of the yamens, several hundred feet long, is covered with the names of persons entitled to an allowance of rice from that one yamen ; these refugees are not a mere mass of misery; each has a proper name and all the hopes and fears and loves and sorrows that enter into a human personality.

Small wonder, then, that they cling so obstinately to life, even when life seems so little worth living. The barrenness of the lot of the peasant Chinese almost leads one to wonder whether so bare an existence is worth saving. Yet amazingly few take the way out of their troubles adopted by one man of whom I have heard, who spent his few last cash in the purchase of arsenic which he mixed with the family's one remaining meal of rice. The next day the household of eight was found dead. Braver is the attitude of these ragged peasants (and no one is entitled to use the adjective " ragged" until he has seen China's poor), who grimly, uncomplainingly turn their faces homeward, there to await, if strength serves them to travel so far, the starvation which seems inevitable. In the actual famine district itself, among the villages of mud houses, I found the people simply expecting and waiting death with a calm hopelessness ·that is horrible.

Let the world do its best, and thousands still must perish. Splendid efforts are under way t~ reach the sufferers with bread. An en getic, efficient, and representative Relief Committee, comprising consuls, high government officia's, Chinese and foreign, and leading merchants, missionaries, and professional men, has from Shanghai undertaken to arouse the world. By the middle of January thirty-five thousand bags of American flour, containing fifty pounds apiece, had been started into the famine district, to be sold at a low price. The Government has engaged to supply every sufferer with thirty cash (one and a half cents) a day, and is assuredly making great efforts to carry out this pledge, for the present at least. The actual distributers of the relief contributed through the Shanghai committee are the missionaries, who have been invested with full authority and responsibility, so that there may be no " squeezing " by the Chinese. The greater part of the affected area is occupied almost wholly by the Southern Presbyterian Church, with a few Roman Catholic missions and some stations of the China Inland Mission. This last, however, has declined to engage in relief work except for its own converts and adherents. The Southern Presbyterians have called to their aid a number of other representative missions, and are distributing aid without respect to any lines except those of want.

They are in for a long, hard pull. Famine conditions will prevail until late in June or early in July, when so much of a wheat crop as has been planted will be harvested. Various forms of relief work, as the cutting of canals to prevent a recurrence of this disaster, have been projected. Still, there will be need of all the relief that benevolence will furnish. Principle as well as interest is required in this big work of breaking the famine. The unsatisfactory part about feeding the hungry is that one's glow of self-complacency over a good deed has scarcely faded before the recipient is hungry again and asking for alms.

The first feeling of public pity over the terrible lot of these millions of suffering hinese will have passed away ere the eed of succor is ended. Even at the >w relief rate of one and a half cents day, vast sums will be needed to tide he famine victims over the period of absolute destitution. If the money is forthcoming, it will be an unrivaled tribute to the humanitarianism of twentieth-century civilization.

Central China, January 22, 1907.

# *THE SELF-REVELATIONS OF AN AGNOSTIC*[1]

THE interest in Mr. Maitland's biography of· Mr. Leslie Stephen is its autobiographical character. It is essentially a self-portraiture.. For American readers the book would have been better had the author, or editor—for he is more editor than author—given a little more historical background. Historically the letters need some interpretation. But if this be a defect, it is one which is due to an excess of virtue. In the Preface Mr. Maitland gives the key to his own self-repression: "In two or three words I will explain why I turn my hand to a work of a kind to which it is not accustomed, and then I will say no more of myself." When he does turn his hand to something more than mere incidental explanation, the result needs no apology. His portrait of Leslie Stephen in Chapter XX. is an admirable piece of miniature painting.

Leslie Stephen was born in 1832; in 1855 he was ordained a deacon in the Established Church; in 1859 he was ordained a priest; in 1862, to use his own phrase, he discovered, not that his creed was false, but that he had never really believed it. He could not, therefore, under the existing statutes, remain a tutor in Cambridge University, and so resigned his tutorship; ever after he was not merely a "come-outer," but a positive and somewhat aggressive opponent of the Christian Church. His philosophical position was that of agnosticism; his religious position that of an ethical culturist, and occasionally he spoke before a London Society of Ethical Culture. But his life was devoted to literature. After leaving Cambridge he lived in and about London, earning his living by his pen as a journalist, editor, author, and literary critic. During the later years of his life at St. Ives in Cornwall he was still in professional connection with London. His greatest work was his editing of the "Dictionary of National Biography." His most important distinct contribution to literature was, in our opinion, his "History of the English Utilitarians." Perhaps he is best known by his "Hours in a Library." He was twice married, both times very happily. He died February 22, 1904. The only adventures in his quiet life were those incident to his Alpine climbing, which was his favorite recreation.

The interest of such a story lies not in its incident. It might lie in the author's portraiture of other men, as does the life of the Duke of Argyll. In fact, however, Leslie Stephen lived largely the life of a recluse. He was a very companionable man, but only with a few companions. He was not a writer of gossip, not even in his letters to his most intimate friends. The interest of his life lies in the self-revelation afforded by his letters of a character possessed of great strength and some great weaknesses, who was honored by the degree of Doctor of Letters in 1892 by the University whose statutes did not allow him to remain in its teaching force as a tutor in 1862 because of his theological opinions. He was candid to a fault, modest to self-depreciation, as conscientious as a Puritan and as narrow, as aggressive in his disbeliefs as the most orthodox of his contemporories in his beliefs, an inveterate worker ·but without enthusiasm, a lover of his fellow-men and yet superficially a cynic,[1] with a heart as tender

[1] *The Life and Letters of Leslie Stephen.* By Frederic William Maitland. G. P. Putnam's Sons, New York.

[1] He writes to Charles Eliot Norton in 1893, "Remember that my cynicism does not get down into my heart."

as a woman's hidden under what was sometimes a very rough exterior. What he believed he believed with all his heart, what he disbelieved he disbelieved with all his heart, and his disbeliefs were as sacred to him as other men's creeds are to them. From his work you would say that everything was important; from his letters, that nothing was so.

His creed was of the shortest : " I now believe in nothing, to put it shortly; but I do not the less believe in morality, &c., &c. I mean to live and die like a gentleman if possible." This Confucian creed (written in 1865) served him for the rest of his life. He seemed incapable of understanding that any intelligent man could have a longer creed. Discovering, as he thought, that he had never believed, he jumped to the conclusion that no one else believed ; and, looking back with a sort of abhorrence on what he regarded as the sham beliefs of his own early life, he looked with equal abhorrence on what he regarded as the sham beliefs of all Christian believers. He can see nothing to respect in the intuitionalist. In 1876 he writes to Norton, " I despise most of your religious people," and affirms that " we are all agnostics, though some people choose to call their ignorance God or mystery." He dislikes George Herbert " because he seems to me always to be skulking behind the Thirty-Nine Articles instead of looking facts in the face ;" Balfour's " Foundations of Belief " are " about the very oddest foundations that any man ever tried to lay—being chiefly reasons for believing nothing ;" S. T. Coleridge's letters he characterizes as " amazing wrigglings and self-reproaches and astonishing pouring forth of unctuous twaddling ;" Maurice he believes to be " as honest a man as ever lived," but " of all the muddle-headed, intricate, futile persons I ever studied, he was about the most utterly bewildering ;" " the Psalmist takes his sorrow like a man . . . while the Apostle [Paul] is desperately trying to shirk the inevitable, and at best resembles the weak comforters who try to cover up the terrible reality under a veil of well-meant fiction." All this shows a curious inability to comprehend the position of the intuitionalist, or idealist, or mystic, who, differing in other respects, agree in this, that our knowledge of the invisible world is not a mere matter of rational deduction from observed phenomena, but that world is immediately and directly perceived by the spiritual sense, and that on this perception of the invisible all the most important acts of our life are based. Whether this be true or not is beside the question ; no man is equipped to argue with the believer who does not comprehend this fundamental basis of his belief and undertake to show that it is untenable. Leslie Stephen's letters afford no indication that he even knew that it was held.   •

If these letters illustrate, as we think they do, both the character and the cause of the illiberality of some liberals and the narrowness of some broad men, they equally illustrate the truth that a man who believes in nothing can yet have a splendidly courageous and self-sacrificing faith in morality and can live not only like a gentleman but like a hero. Though he does not wait upon the Lord and cannot mount up on wings like eagles, he can run and not be weary and he can walk and not faint. He can be asking all his life long, as apparently Leslie Stephen did, " What is the good of life on the whole ?" and confess to himself that he " can't quite make it out," and yet live a thoroughly good life—be honest, just, industrious, conscientious, kindly, generous ; but apparently he cannot be hopeful or enthusiastic. Certainly Leslie Stephen was all that these words connote and more, but we fail to find in these letters any sign of enthusiasm or any radiance of hope. About the most hopeful word we find is such as this : A journalist, " if he is an honest man (for all hypotheses are lawful) and speaks the truth with some vigor, may help things on a bit." But his general feeling respecting his work is not that it matters, but that it must be done : " You *might* know me better by this time, Milly ! Don't you know that I'm like a hoop ? When I'm not going at full speed, I drop." His most attractive work is not an inspiration ; his least attractive, the Dictionary, is confessedly a torment. And when great grief overtakes him, he has no refuge ; he is too honest to look for one in a faith which he has cast off, or even to use a phrase which might imply a remnant of that faith, and yet stumbles into what comes near to recognition of a Divine Goodness in One to whom he owes the great inspiration and joy of his life. Thus in a letter written after the death of his wife to James Russell Lowell: "I thank—something—that I loved her as heartily as I know how to love, that I would have died for her with pleasure, and that (still more) I scarcely ever saw a cloud upon her bright face."

We rise from reading this fascinating volume with a twofold conviction strengthened by its perusal : on the one hand, that an agnostic may live a life so true and so self-sacrificing as to deserve and to win the respect and the love of all who know him ; and, on the other hand, that his life will inevitably lack that enthusiasm of hope which cheers and inspires him that believes himself to be working under a Leader who sees the end from the beginning, under whose leadership no good work will fail to count in the final beneficent result.

# WISE AND OTHERWISE[1]

A CLEVER lady who had passed the limit of fourscore years turned from a book of reminiscences which she was reading and said, with a merry twinkle in her eye, "These old people are so garrulous !" She recognized and deplored the temptation that besets all writers of many experiences. There is a vast difference between being prolix and being discursive. In his record of a journey around the world Mr. Conway escapes being actually tedious, but is decidedly discursive, including, according to the dictionary, the elements of argumentativeness and "moving about." What value his book has lies in his ability to tell a story, certainly not in his estimate of conditions. More than the traditional grain of salt must be included by the wise reader as he amuses himself with Mr. Conway's opinions of either Oriental mysticism or Occidental theology. The wise men do not belong altogether to the East, and tilting at windmills or demolishing home-made men of straw will continue to occupy men to the end of the world.

Passing rapidly over his experiences in Australia and the islands of the sea, we come to Ceylon and a most interesting priest, Subhûti by name, who spoke English and was known as the author of a Pali grammar. When asked why he was borne by men in a sedan chair, instead of in a carriage drawn by horses,

he said that life was so sacred that he was afraid a horse might be vitally injured by carrying him. "But," said Mr. Conway, "might it not be the same with one of those men while he is carrying you ?" After a moment's silence he said, very sweetly, "But a man can tell me if he is suffering." Truly this was a gentle and a wise man, this Buddhist priest. Bishop Heber's hymn declaring that man "is vile" in Ceylon was particularly irritating to Mr. Conway. He returns to worry it again and again, much as a dog bites and shakes a harmless old shoe, even retailing an absurd story told him by a Moslem (whom he seemed to credit) as to Bishop Heber's animus in writing the line. By this time the reader who has any knowledge of Eastern men or lands from personal experience is vastly diverted.

Mr. Conway is ruthless in exposing what he calls "tricks" of all sorts, miraculous or legendary ; yet his credulous acceptance of the ordinary conversational inaccuracies current in the East is truly astonishing. He is the sort of traveler who fills the "griff" with unholy glee, because he is immensely flattered if a native addresses him as "Preserver of the Poor."

On Christmas Day Mr. Conway lectured in Colombo upon Christ and Buddha, pointing out the different aims of their respective birth-myths—"one, happiness in another world ; the other, happiness in this world."

Beside him sat the Primate of the

[1] *My Pilgrimage to the Wise Men of the East.* By Moncure D. Conway. Houghton, Mifflin & Co., Boston. $3, net.

Buddhist world, with whom he had a conversation upon Theosophists. The priest was troubled by the expositions of Buddhism given by the Theosophists. He declared the pretended Mahatmas to be non-existent, and quite without the circle of Buddhistic philosophy.

Mr. Conway's visit to Madame Blavatsky at her home in Adyar is described with great humor. He had known the lady in London. Her portrait is sufficient explanation of the fact that Mrs. Conway "was not attracted by her," though Mr. Conway found her entertaining because of her gossipy knowledge of contemporary persons and events. He felt it a duty, as he was a public teacher, to investigate Theosophy in India. He declares that his own idea was that "Madame Blavatsky had simply invented a new set of archangels and saints to supply that reverential fog amid which all impostures are possible." At the entrance of Madame Blavatsky's park stood a dilapidated blue pasteboard elephant which had been set up by a Madras believer. Upon being ushered into the house, "a lay chela" declined sweetly to shake hands with the visitor for fear his magnetism might be impaired, as he possessed the power of appearing at a distance in his "astral" body. "Colonel" Olcott was absent, but the "Countess" Blavatsky was graciously hospitable, and the visitor remained to dinner. He was eager to see some of the marvels of which he had heard, but was put off with stories of what had occurred or what would occur in the future. "I said that was just my luck in such matters; wherever a miracle occurs I was always too soon or too late to see it. My experience was that of Alice in the Looking-Glass—'Jam yesterday, jam to-morrow, but never jam to-day.'"

In a private audience Madame Blavatsky inquired the particular desire of her visitor. Mr. Conway said he wished to find out something about the strange performances attributed to the lady. What did it all mean? She said, with a serene smile, "I will tell you, because you are a public teacher, and you ought to know the truth: it is all glamour—people think they see what they do not see—that is the whole of it." So, Mr.

Conway continues, the clever woman spiked his guns.

She gossiped wittily about many things, but uttered no word of "Occultism" or any other "ism." At dinner there were several guests, among them a silent, unsmiling woman to whom Mr. Conway was not introduced. After dining he was ushered into the sacred room, and Madame Blavatsky looked on with an amused smile while two young Hindu neophytes prostrated themselves before the "shrine" or cabinet, within which were a small Buddha and pictures of two of the three Blavatsky Mahatmas. Upon leaving, Madame Blavatsky merrily suggested that she might make an "astral" visit to London and call upon Mr. Conway.

Mr. Conway found the leader of Theosophy a woman of the world and not a woman of imagination. Her impostures were not for the purpose of making money, but from a morbid desire to sway men. Her histrionic powers were taxed during his visit, because, as he learned afterward, the silent woman at the table was Madame Coulomb, who at that very moment was threatening the whole structure of Theosophy by her exposures. The publication of her disclosures in the public prints shattered entirely all the pretensions of Madame Blavatsky as a miracle-worker. Mr. Conway's lifelong interest in religion and religions added zest to his visit to India, and gained his admittance to many and varied groups of men. He met Mozoomdar, and with him discussed the character of Keshub Chunder Sen and the Brahmo-Somaj, reaching the conclusion that the movement differed but little from early Christian Unitarianism in America. The traveler's mind was open to every possible influence except that of Christianity. He found few traces of mission work in India, making among other statements an entirely erroneous one in regard to Ramabai and her work. It gratified him to note that "the literalism of Christian missionaries prevented their doing much harm." Perhaps after twenty years (his visit to India was twenty years ago) Mr. Conway has modified his opinion and is able to judge more fairly of actual facts.

# Comment on Current Books

**Birdcraft** A new edition of a recognized and valuable handbook about birds, in which about two hundred song, game, and water birds are carefully and systematically described, with many references to literary and personal associations, and with much else that will please as well as inform the student of bird-lore. The pictures are in black and white, and when one remembers some miscolored bird pictures in other books we are glad of it. (Birdcraft. By Mabel Osgood Wright. The Macmillan Company, New York. $2, net.)

**The Book of Psalms** The notice given to the first volume of this masterly work in The Outlook of October 13, 1906, is too recent for any repetition here. The present volume finishes the commentary. The special student and the ordinarily intelligent reader are both provided for; the former in full measure. The latter will find some strikingly new translations superseding the old. Dogmatic reasons will make it hard for many to give up the traditional reference of Psalm li. to David and his great sin. That this must be given up Professor Robertson Smith showed reluctant Scotland in 1880. It is not so hard now to agree with Dr. Briggs: "Psalm li. is a penitential prayer of the congregation in the time of Nehemiah." In Psalm cxix. he tells us that "all Christian translations err greatly" in misinterpreting the eight different Hebrew terms denoting the Law. In these two volumes Professor Briggs's special genius appears at its best. (A Critical and Exegetical Commentary on the Book of Psalms. By Charles Augustus Briggs, D.D., D.Litt., and Emilie Grace Briggs, B.D. Vol. II. Charles Scribner's Sons, New York. $3, net.)

**The Empress Eugénie** A large volume, written by Jane T. Stoddart, contains the life story of the latest if not the last Empress of the French. Born of mixed Spanish and Scotch parentage, brought up by a gay, rather daring mother, who, after acquiring the fortune of her deceased husband, the Count Téba, led an extravagant life in both Spain and France, Eugénie, a beautiful girl, attained her ambition and became an Empress. While scandal was not entirely unassociated with her unconventional progress, she showed such tact and generosity after she reached the pinnacle of power that much was forgotten and forgiven. Napoleon III. was for years devoted to her, and her ambitious plans centered in her only son. Her griefs and humiliations are known and excite pity everywhere. Her exile in England was relieved by the warm friendship of Queen Victoria and the royal family, but in spite of her almost fanatical devotion to religion, she is plunged in sadness and looks longingly forward to death. The author of this biography is gentle in judgment, and defends Eugénie from the accusations of personal ambition which were current at the time of the Franco-German War, when she came into prominence politically, during the physical and moral decrepitude of Napoleon III. Her deserted rooms in the Tuileries are said to have expressed her character, in its curious mingling of superstition and absolute worldliness. She vibrated between penances and wild gayety, a logical result of her birth, training, and circumstances, yet she won friends even in her most arrogant days, and as a lonely, aged, bereaved woman commands sympathy from all. (The Life of Empress Eugénie. By Jane T. Stoddart. Third Edition. E. P. Dutton & Co., New York. $3, net.)

**The First Two Tudors** Perhaps the most striking and certainly not the least pleasing feature of Mr. H. A. L. Fisher's contribution to the Hunt-Poole "Political History of England" is the emphasis he places on the reign of King Henry the Seventh. In his pages the first Tudor is no shadowy figure, paling in the brilliance of his more celebrated son; he is seen in clear relief, a living and masterful personality, the founder not in name only of his illustrious house. When, as Mr. Fisher makes very evident, the fortunes of war placed him on the throne, he found himself the ruler, not of a united and purposeful nation, but of a nation of malcontents embittered by long-continued internecine strife, and from the first he encountered revolt. Yet he did much more than merely maintain his kingship. With rare penetration and ability he raised himself above the aristocratic factions by which he was surrounded, brought peace and order out of war and chaos, and ere his death firmly established the beneficent absolutism of which his son was to be the unfaltering exponent. Of that son, of course, Mr. Fisher has much to say, and what he says is usually to the point, sane, and just. He recognizes that the whilom Defender of the Faith and later Maker of the English Reformation was gross, cruel, crafty, hypocritical, and avaricious, but he also recognizes that he was a great ruler of men, sagacious, penetrating, and a real statesman. Sometimes, indeed, and particularly in the important matter of the divorce, he inclines to an undue charity; but, on the whole, the portrait he paints is acceptable and convincing. It is painted, too, as is the entire period of which he treats, with a masterly hand, the hand of the historian who is writer as well as scholar. Perhaps an over-zealousness for detail is manifest here and there, as, for example, in the discussion of foreign relations, but even where detail is most abundant the sense of continuity and unity and interest is preserved. And, on occasion, Mr. Fisher shows himself capable of rising to heights of superb eloquence. (The Political History of England. Edited by William Hunt and Reginald Poole. Vol. V., 1485-1547. By H. A. L. Fisher. Longmans, Green & Co., New York. $2.60, net.)

*From Sumter to Gettysburg*   The story of the Civil War from the bombardment of Fort Sumter to the battle of Gettysburg is the subject of Dr. James K. Hosmer's "The Appeal to Arms," the twentieth volume of the "American Nation" serial history of the United States; and those acquainted with the scheme of this history need not be told that, in order to keep within the allotted limits, Dr. Hosmer has been obliged to condense his narrative rigorously. He has done this so ably, however, that, despite the multiplicity of movements and events, the reader is given much more than an outline sketch. By way of introduction Dr. Hosmer glances for a moment at the civil leaders on each side and describes briefly the geographical, racial, social, and economic factors which conditioned the great conflict. He then enters immediately upon what proves to be a most spirited, informing, and readable account of the successive campaigns and battles of the years under review. Necessarily there are occasional digressions to discuss concurrent political events, and in these the interest is similarly maintained at a high level. As may be imagined, scant space is devoted to the consideration of moot questions with which, as every student of Civil War history knows, the subject bristles; but there will be little inclination to dissent from the conclusions Dr. Hosmer voices, conclusions marked not merely by fairness but by shrewd common sense. His portraits of the great military captains are, if sometimes too compact, vivid and persuasive; and his exposition of the problems with which they were confronted, and the manner in which they attacked these problems, is clearness itself. So far as the strictly mili-

tary portion of the volume is concerned, perhaps the most striking feature is the account given of Jackson's Shenandoah Valley campaign in the spring of '62; while in non-military matters Dr. Hosmer is seen at his best in the chapter on emancipation. Altogether, we look forward with pleasure to the forthcoming volume in which he will conclude his story of the war. (The American Nation. Edited by Albert Bushnell Hart. Vol. XX., The Appeal to Arms. By James Kendall Hosmer. Harper & Brothers, New York. $2, net.)

*Liberal Education*   The papers presented in this volume have been read before important meetings of educational experts, and should be read by all college alumni who would keep pace with advancing change. The "Tutorial System in College," the "Changing Conception of 'the Faculty' in American Universities," "True and False Standards of Graduate Work," the "Present Peril to Liberal Education," the "Length of the College Course," and the "American College"—subjects of interest to all educated men—receive in these papers a searching and enlightening discussion. That the historic American college is the citadel of liberal knowledge, to be conserved as such in spirit if not in form, is their underlying conviction. How Princeton is doing this by its new tutorial system is attractively told. That there is great danger of subordinating true culture to the immediate efficiency in practical lines which technical education imparts is certainly true. Commercialism is an omnipresent foe to culture. More men of all-round ability are needed in American faculties. There is too much of the specialization which gains "intensive knowledge" at the price of "extensive ignorance." The main contention of Dean West is well sustained: whatever new paths of learning are opened, the old ideal of a truly liberalizing knowledge must be pursued. (Short Papers on American Liberal Education. By Andrew Fleming West. Charles Scribner's Sons, New York. 75c., net.)

*A Little Old World*   The Fogazzaro novels are good to read. In especial, the later ones stand for their author's ideals of life, religion, and work; first, a purification of the Roman Catholic Church, and then the active participation by Roman Catholics in the progressive religious, social, and political life of our day. In other words, men should be as broadly as they are intensely religious. But, aside from this, the Fogazzaro novels are good to read because of the characters therein depicted; these seem more like ourselves than do those of most novels of Italy, whether written by Italian romancers from Manzoni to Verga or by foreign novelists from Hawthorne to Marion Crawford. In "Piccolo Mondo Antico," for instance, the characters, especially the minor ones, have a humanness, pathos, whimsicality, and quiet humor which remind one now of Dickens, now of Fritz Reuter. "Piccolo Mondo Antico" has reached its forty-fourth edition in Italy—a sufficient comment concerning its popularity. Perhaps it comes the nearest to being a historical romance of any of Fogazzaro's novels. It represents "a little old world," for its scenes are practically confined to the lovely shores of the Lake of Lugano during the Austrian occupation half a century ago. Those humiliating days for Italy are well depicted, and, while the novel does not portray all the historical scenes which one might expect, it does throw a valued side-light on them. The hero, Don Franco, is none other than Signor Fogazzaro's father, and the heroine Luisa is his mother. Don Franco is hardly so much a "patriot"—to use the rather misleading title of the translation—as he is a religionist, a type of the Church in its conflict with unbelief; he prefigures "Il Santo," published in English as "The Saint," the third member of the trilogy of which "The Patriot" forms the first. A translation of the second, "Piccolo Mondo Moderno," is in press and is to be entitled "The Sinner." The trilogy is the more remarkable because it was unconsciously evolved rather than consciously planned. The "Antico" is not Signor Fogazzaro's greatest work. While it contains some striking descriptions of nature, recalling the author's "Idillii," and while in plot, character-drawing, and style it is superior to his "Malombra" and "Mistero del Poeta," it does not equal his "Daniele Cortis," which in these respects stands well-nigh unexcelled among novels dealing with present-day Italy. As to the English edition of the "Antico," though the vigorous translation may tally with the dictionary, it does not always preserve the novelist's originality of expression and atmosphere. (Piccolo Mondo Antico. Da Antonio Fogazzaro. Baldini, Castoldi e Cia., Milan. The Patriot [Piccolo Mondo Antico]. By Antonio Fogazzaro. Translated by M. Prichard-Agnetti. G. P. Putnam's Sons, New York. $1.50.)

*Professor Lanciani's Latest Volume* The literature which describes Rome has now been enriched by the publication of a notable and impressive-looking volume. It describes various happenings in the Eternal City during the Renaissance. Professor Lanciani is best known by his books on the archæology which illustrated the early republican and imperial eras—"The Ruins and Excavations of Ancient Rome" and "Ancient Rome in the Light of Recent Discoveries." But some of the matter in his "Destruction of Ancient Rome" and "New Tales of Old Rome" has to do with other than the Roman Imperial ages. In his present volume Signor Lanciani gives an account of the moral and material evolution of Rome from mediæval conditions. He describes the epoch beginning with the return of the Popes from Avignon, and emphasizes the later "Golden Days" as brought about by Paul III. and by the four personalities who, perhaps above all others, represented progress in finance, art, and morals, namely, Chigi, Raphael, and Michelangelo, and, possibly most interesting of all, Vittoria Colonna. In dealing with the lives of these illustrious persons the author has confined himself for the most part to little-known particulars, and his book thus awakens special interest. Of course, as an archæologist, his principal aim has been to illustrate the monuments of the Renaissance period in Rome, too many of which, alas! are concealed under modern superstructures. The text's value is doubled by the publication of about a hundred illustrations; a number of these are from subjects which have now been photographed for the first time. (The Golden Days of the Renaissance in Rome. By Rodolfo Lanciani. Houghton, Mifflin & Co., Boston. $5.)

*Religion in Japan* All intelligent Americans regard it as a matter of national interest to understand Japanese thought as well as that of any other modern people. Nor can the influence of religion upon the thought of a people be left out of account. This volume has interest, therefore, for the general reader. Its author is peculiarly qualified for appreciative treatment of his subject by his long residence in Japan, in whose Imperial University he served for years. Shintoism (the old nature-religion), Buddhism and Confucianism, imported from China—the former as worship of the Absolute, the latter as polity and ethics—coexist there, and in these three religions "the religion of Japan" finds various expression. Shintoism is religious patriotism; Buddhism is the faith of the unlettered and poor; Confucianism is "the religion of gentlemen." These three have been variously modified during the comparatively brief period of fourteen centuries covered by historical dates. The account of these changes constitutes a history of the development of that innate religious feeling in which all religions root. "Beneath the changing forms we seem to be able to trace an expansion and ennobling of the religious consciousness." The religion of Japan already finds a fourth expression in Christianity, as a part of the nation's new enlightenment. "Its influence already stirs Japan," says Dr. Knox, "and the future is with it." (The Development of Religion in Japan. By George William Knox, D.D., LL.D. American Lectures on the History of Religions, Vol. VI. G. P. Putnam's Sons, New York. $1.50.)

*Secretary Taft on Civic Duty*  The four lectures which Secretary Taft delivered at Yale last year have now been issued in book form under the title of "Four Aspects of Civic Duty." At the time of their delivery we editorially called attention to them, and we would merely remind our readers that, while addressed primarily to university undergraduates, they have a significance and value for every American, of whatever age or station, who would acquit himself creditably of his duty as a citizen. In the several lectures Secretary Taft spoke of civic duty from the respective standpoints of the college graduate, the judge, the colonial administrator, and the national executive, thus viewing it in each case from the vantage point of practical experience. In the first lecture he emphasized the responsibility that lies on the educated man of taking an active part in the political life of his city, State, and country; and incidentally gave a rapid but clear exposition of the views he entertains with regard to fundamental principles of economics and politics. In the second the emphasis was on the duty of the citizen in upholding the supremacy of the law, and on the necessity for certain reforms whereby the law may the better vindicate itself. The third was largely a review of the Philippine problem in the light of the experience obtained since the occupation of the islands, and with especial reference to the proper policy to be pursued by the American citizen who takes up his residence in the Philippines, the American citizen who stays at home, and the Filipino himself. The concluding lecture was occupied with a brief account of the structure and operation of the National administration, and of the attitude which in the speaker's opinion the citizen ought to adopt towards the administration. (Four Aspects of Civic Duty. By William Howard Taft. Charles Scribner's Sons, New York. $1, net.)

*Social Life in England*  A decidedly entertaining account of the growth of social institutions and modern customs in England. The absurdities of bygone fashion, the changes made by scientific inventions, domestic conveniences and inconveniences, old-time gambling, the abolition of dueling, the improvement of table manners, and a hundred other little landmarks of advancing civilization are discussed in an unconventional, amusing way. The result is a series of shifting society pictures not without significance and with a strong interest to all who like to delve into the quaint, queer, and curious. (A Short History of Social Life in England. By M. B. Synge, F. R. Hist. S. A. S. Barnes & Co., New York.)

*Songs for Schools*  Mr. Farnsworth has performed a much-needed service to public school music by collecting in one volume, well printed and bound and sold at a moderate price, the best of the traditional songs suitable for children's voices. One finds here the more important national tunes, the beautiful melodies of Stephen C. Foster, "The Old Folks at Home" and "My Old Kentucky Home," fine old English, Scottish, Irish, and Welsh folk songs, a few college songs, and a good selection of hymn tunes. Furthermore, one does not have to wade through the vast mass of trivial, dull, and insignificant tunes usually included in such collections, apparently on the hypothesis that anything is good enough for children to sing provided the words are interesting. This book is reassuringly free from such fatuities; indeed, it is hardly too much to say that every song in it is one that "no well-appointed child should be without." A special feature of the book is the placing of most of the complexities in the accompaniment, leaving the singers to sing the melody only. Mr. Farnsworth points out in his preface that the voices of good singers are often strained in the effort to sing in parts, and that part work by children's voices is often ineffective. This is undoubtedly true of the lower grades, and for them this book will be most useful, even if part work is attempted, as may by some be thought desirable, by the older boys and girls. Mr. Loomis's accompaniments show imagination and much technical skill, though in some instances one might question whether he has not elaborated his treatment more than is in keeping with the ruggedly simple nature of the melodies, and beyond the ability of most of those who will be called upon to play them. On the whole, this book is a long step in advance in the literature of school music. (Songs for Schools. Compiled by Charles Hubert Farnsworth, of Teachers College, Columbia University, with Accompaniments by Harvey Worthington Loomis and B. D. Allen. The Macmillan Company, New York. 60c., net.)

*Starting in Life*

Generally speaking, the boy who has parents or guardians, and opportunities for coming into personal contact with the best teachers, and means enough of support to relieve him of the anxiety of earning his own bread and butter during his boyhood, had better not attempt to determine too early in life his own future career. Nine times out of ten he cannot determine it even if he attempts to. There are, however, literally thousands of boys in this country whose first problem is how to feed and clothe themselves, and in addition perhaps how to be of material service to their families. Out of such boyhoods have grown some of the most useful men of the country. To boys of this type we should think Mr. Fowler's compendium would be not only interesting, but useful. It makes no pretense to literary merit, but gives the boy, in plain and homely language, descriptions, based often upon the experience of experts, concerning the opportunities and the demands of various professions and business callings. In view of the excellent purpose of the book and of the general success with which that purpose is carried out, it may be unimportant to point out the slight defects of arrangement which we find in it; but since Mr. Fowler is a recognized authority on "system," which he would apply to literature as rigorously as he would to business, we cannot understand why he sandwiches the architect between the department store and the manufacturer, or why he should flank his chapter on the steam railway with chapters on the stage and the artist. (Starting in Life. By Nathaniel C. Fowler, Jr. Little, Brown & Co., Boston. $1.50, net.)

*Success in Life*

The conditions of success in life being for the most part the same in all civilized nations, this volume, written apparently for Europeans, especially for Britons, may be read with profit by Americans. The author, a native of Hungary, has had large experience with Oxford undergraduates and other young Englishmen, and is a well-known author, gifted with a good literary style. He here discusses the constant factors of "energetics," or "the science of success," its variable factors, and success in special lines, as that of the journalist, the artist, etc. The many instances cited are mostly European. As to facts, although a shrewd observer, he is not always accurate, *e. g.*, affirming, in ignorance of the census, that "most white people in the United States are sons of a foreign father or grandfather." In undeveloped Hungary he sees "immense" openings for energetic Englishmen or Americans, whom he will be glad to inform about them. For the young man bent on success the best of all books is the Bible, and he strenuously commends it as such. A sagacious writer he is, though at times amusingly otherwise, as in predicting that the next great struggle will not be between an upper class and a lower, but "between the two sexes, both on the same plane." (Success in Life. By Emil Reich. Duffield & Co., New York. $1.50. Postage, 12c.)

*Trusts and Kartells*

Some upholders of the advantages of combination in trade claim that a scattered group of factories, managed by a board of experts, will, in the long run, prove more efficient than the older system, in which every factory had its own manager. The attraction of ownership, which has often made a newspaper owner of moderate intelligence a better editor than the brilliant man who has no capital or interest in the concern, may often outweigh the advantages claimed for the board of experts. So opines Mr. Hirst in his book on "Monopolies, Trusts, and Kartells," and pertinently adds: "Besides, who is to guarantee that the best men will be on the board?" He also pays his compliments to those who exaggerate the economic advantages of the trust, declaring that the achievements of the greater trusts at least show rather a restriction of output and an increase in price. Proper, regulated combination may be all very well. But that is not monopoly. How is a monopoly, a trust, evolved? Mr. Hirst seems to think that in England it is the child of English law, and that in America it is the child of our ultra tariff. While the German Kartell may have this double parentage, a more interesting feature of the Kartell lies in its difference in two important respects from our American trusts. First, it is not so apt to destroy individuality, though eliminating competitive war among the combining individual firms; secondly, it is more likely to succeed in "dumping" than our trusts do; from time to time the latter sell their surplus stock at low prices, and a high tariff makes it probable that the vast majority of these sales are made to foreigners. In Germany, however, the directors of the Kartell actually pay a subvention or bounty to exporting firms. Discussing particular American trusts, the author justly says of the Standard Oil that had there been an independent and impartial administration of Pennsylvania and Ohio railways, no oil monopoly could have been developed. He notes, nevertheless, that the Standard Oil Company forms one of the very few exceptions to the list given in Mr. W. R. Lawson's "United States Tariff for Trusts" (in the latter's " American Trust Problems "). In that list we find such pertinent facts as that our iron and steel manufacturers are protected by a forty-five per cent. duty on the manufacture of iron, steel, bronze, and copper; that the coal ring is protected by a duty of sixty-seven cents a ton on soft coal; that the meat trust is protected by a duty of two cents a pound on beef and lard and five cents a pound on hams and bacon; and that the sugar manufacturers are protected by nearly one cent a pound on sugar below a certain standard and two cents a pound on that above the standard. We are glad that these figures have been reprinted. They need to be frequently published, in order to remind our people of the aid given by the tariff to the trusts. While in the general discussion of the trust problem Mr. Hirst's book will be a helpful factor, it would have been still more helpful had it included some later information, especially concerning the results of governmental investigation of monopolies in this country. (Monopolies, Trusts, and Kartells. By Francis W. Hirst. E. P. Dutton & Co., New York. $1, net.)

*The World Machine* This is a valuable addition to the literature of popularized science. It shows how the modern conception of the Cosmos was worked out from the crude fancies of primitive men, through ages of observation and reflection, into the immense range and detail of accurately systemized knowledge. The chief contributors, ancient and modern, to the grand result receive due commemoration. The ancient astronomers are found not at all inferior to the modern, except in lack of modern instrumental and mathematical apparatus. The story is told, moreover, in good literary style, animated throughout, and at times picturesque, as in describing the zone of the asteroids as " the cinder-path of the solar system." The story, of course, is to be continued; the unsolved questions are named, and the fresh enigmas before which each new discovery halts. " Always at the end there will be a mystery; it will always be there." This ingenuous confession seems hardly congruous with the atheistical tone of the writer, with his affirmation that "reading any Reason or Intelligence into this strange wentletrap of a world . . . seems to the initiate eye . . . more unthinkable, more *unbelievable*, than ever." An apposite comment upon this conclusion is suggested by his later remark : " Sometimes among scientific workers one perceives a certain arrogance, as though the great problems of existence had been quite disposed

of." It does seem arrogant to set down the being who reads the secret of the stars as a mere mixture of " chemical ingredients . . . carbon, water, ammonia, and a few salts." Grant that all which science discovers is mechanism. To say therefore that mechanism is all is an amazing jump of false logic. Whence the mechanism? Here science ends, and here begins the philosophy which Mr. Snyder contemns. (The World Machine: The First Phase. The Cosmic Mechanism. By Carl Snyder. Longmans, Green & Co., New York. $2.50, net.)

*War Out of Date* Six centuries ago Dante's " De Monarchia " started men in thinking that the world's orderliness and lasting peace are not always or often secured by war. Three centuries afterwards Grotius's " De Jure Belli et Pacis " started men's thoughts anew in this direction. Seventy years later came William Penn's " Plan for the Peace of Europe." In the last century appeared Channing's " Discourses on War," Charles Sumner's " The True Grandeur of Nations," and, a few years before the Hague Peace Conference convened, Jean de Bloch's " Future of War." After these giants, the Rev. Walter Walsh's " Moral Damage of War " seems a pygmy. It is a rhetorical and aggressive, but it is also in its way a useful, arraignment of the war system. Mr. Walsh, an eloquent clergyman of Dundee, Scotland, was present at the Boston Peace Congress in 1904, where he made some fervent speeches. He now writes some fervent chapters, successively tracing the moral damage of war to the child, the soldier, the politician, the journalist, the preacher, the missionary, the trader, the citizen, the patriot, and the reformer. He supports his opinions with many references to specific events during the Boer War; indeed, in addressing himself primarily to a British public, Mr. Walsh's book is largely a presentation of the demoralization consequent upon some of the conditions which produced that war and which were characteristic of it. We could wish that the book contained an equal number of illustrations drawn from the Russo-Japanese War. Such volumes as Mr. Walsh's, Mr. Warner's " Ethics of Force," and Mr. Bridgman's " World Organization," published as they are at nominal prices in the interest of the Peace Movement, should attain a deservedly wide circulation. For, as a method of settling differences among nations, war is becoming recognized at last, we are glad to think, as unworthy of present-day civilization. (The Moral Damage of War. By Walter Walsh. Ginn & Co., Boston. 75 cents, net.)

# Letters to The Outlook

## CHILD LABOR IN THE SOUTH

I desire to make some reply to an article by the Rev. A. J. McKelway, of Atlanta, Georgia, who is employed by the National Child Labor Committee; the article appeared in your edition of February 16, 1907. The writer has been for twenty-six years engaged in cotton manufacturing in South Carolina.

Dr. McKelway states that "the child labor evil in the South to-day is greater than it is in any other part of the country, perhaps than in any other part of the civilized world." He quotes from Bulletin 69 of the Census Bureau, issued January 25, 1907, and also from the synopsis of the Census of 1900, but does not tell the whole story as told in Bulletin 69, and on page 42 you will find the following:

To a greater extent than any other manufacturing or mechanical industry, the cotton-mill furnishes employment to children. In 1900 the number of cotton-mill operatives ten to fifteen years of age was 44,427, and they formed eighteen per cent. of the total number of persons over ten years of age who reported that occupation. When compared with the number of children engaged in pursuits not of a manufacturing or mechanical nature, the figures for child cotton-mill operatives in 1900 are found to be smaller than those for three other groups—agricultural laborers, servants and waitresses, and laborers of a class not specified. The proportion of children at least ten years of age among the total number employed is greater in two occupations, namely, those of messengers and errand and office boys, and of agricultural laborers. Thus the occupation of the cotton-mill operatives ranks fourth among all occupations in the actual number of children employed and third in the proportion of children among the total number reporting.

It is a well-known fact that in the two occupations of messengers and office-boys the South employs comparatively few, and those young people are employed largely in the great cities of the North and not in the sparsely settled districts of the South.

Another error Dr. McKelway makes is in stating that it has been "demonstrated that the same class and quality of goods made in the South and in the East bring a considerably lower price when made in the South, through the bad reputation the Southern mills have won for the indifferent product of unskilled, that is, child, labor." Dr. McKelway would find great difficulty in establishing the truth of this statement, and, on the contrary, indisputable proof could be furnished that the statement is wide of the facts and grossly incorrect.

I am one of the several cotton manufacturers from Georgia, South Carolina, and North Carolina who are members of the Civic Federation, and attended the meeting in December last in New York City. I there made my protest against the misrepresentations made by the officials of the National Child Labor Committee in reference to Southern mill conditions.

I first alluded to the statement of Spargo in his book, "The Bitter Cry of the Children," on the authority of Dr. McKelway, that the spinning-frames in the Southern cotton-mills had adjustable legs, so as to be lowered to the floor for the convenience of the small children. I clearly demonstrated the absurdity of this statement, and the ignorance of conditions and the spirit of unfairness that prompted it. I also disputed the statement made by the officials of the National Child Labor Committee in their appeals for contributions that 60,000 children under fourteen are employed in Southern cotton-mills, and that little girls eight years of age worked a twelve-hour night in the cotton-mills. As a matter of fact, none of the weaving mills in South Carolina work at night, and to my knowledge only four of the yarn-mills do any night work, and I am informed only in the twister-room, where adults are employed. I was, and am, speaking for South Carolina, with whose conditions I am familiar, having access to the official records. There are about 9,000,000 spindles in the Southern States, and a low average would be 100 spindles to the side, and in the mills with which I am familiar the average number of sides attended by an operative is seven and one-half, which would indicate 12,000 people employed in all the Southern spinning-rooms. As a matter of fact, as far as my observation goes, in South Carolina about half the spinners are over sixteen years of age, and many of them women; but granting for the sake of argument that all the 12,000 are children, and that there are an equal number of young children employed as sweepers, doffers, band boys, drawing-in hands, and in the cloth-rooms, you would not find over 24,000 young people actually employed at any one time in the cotton-mills, and many of the sweepers and doffers and drawing-in hands are over sixteen years of age.

On page 47 of Bulletin No. 69 the comparative table is given of the total average number of wage-earners employed in the manufacture of cotton goods and small cotton wares, which, of course, includes the knitting-mills, as reported by the Census of Manufacturers. In 1905 the figures for the Southern States are 123,165. This is very

given eleven years of my life to this work, without compensation, and I now take pleasure in contributing to it the last piece of property in my possession. Having done this, I appeal for the help of my countrymen.

In the name of the Board of Directors who have given time and thought and money freely and repeatedly, and on behalf of the boys and girls who cannot plead for themselves, I appeal for contributions either large or small. Checks may be made payable to the Hon. Darwin R. James, Treasurer, and sent to 384 Washington Street, New York.

O. O. HOWARD.

Major-General, etc. (Retired), President Board Lincoln Memorial University.

[Since this letter was written a serious loss by fire renders the need of Lincoln Memorial University the more pressing.—THE EDITORS.]

### A WORTHY SUGGESTION

I live in a city of the Middle West. I am a member of the largest church in our city, the membership being over twelve hundred. I have belonged to this church thirteen years. When I first came into it, the pastor was a progressive Eastern man, and under him the church prospered. But his work was not, of course, wholly approved, and after a few years he resigned. Since that time the policy of the teaching has been most conservative. The membership has remained practically unchanged, but the attendance has greatly decreased. Yet that is not the most alarming feature. The attendance has *changed*. A large body of thinking people have either ceased attendance wholly, or attend, as they frankly admit, because, being members of the church, they feel under obligation.

This winter, feeling that something must be done, a two weeks' revival was held under a professional revivalist, the attendance at these meetings being about two hundred and fifty, not a few of whom were drawn from other churches; and of this small number many attended each *one* service.

There was added to the church, as a result of much individual work at this time, a small number, nearly all of whom were children under fourteen years of age. And there was another side to this. There was driven from the church a far greater number of grown and thinking people—not from actual membership, but, as it seems to me, a far more serious thing, from all feeling of sympathy and fellowship in the church life. Two questions now suggest themselves. Is the church as responsible for the ones driven out as it is for the ones drawn? Also, what is to become of those antagonized? These people are religious people, are in sympathy with all upward movement, but they are without a leader. And what I say of my church I may say of the score and more of other churches in this city. Now, what is to be done? May I claim the privilege of fools who rush in where angels fear to tread, and make a suggestion?

Could there not be a movement started by our colleges, something in the nature of University Extension work—a course of study laid out by our best thinkers on religious and kindred subjects, a regular study with text-books and suggestions of supplementary reading? Let the Old Testament be treated by Jews, the New by leaders in the churches, history by historians, and such science as bears on race development by scientists. I am conscious of the magnitude of the work, but I also feel the magnitude of the need. And I would have the course so simple and easy of access that all might have it. And I would have leaders available to organize, supervise, and occasionally lecture to the classes.                E. N.

### A LABOR OF LOVE

A biography of Mrs. Eliza E. Wheaton, a noble woman and the good angel of Wheaton Seminary, is soon to be published. It is a labor of love, prepared by Miss Harriet E. Paine under the direction of the alumnæ. The book is intended chiefly for those who knew and loved Mrs. Wheaton, and, above all, for those who have been associated with Wheaton Seminary. It is believed that the book will be a modest but valuable contribution to the history of the higher education of women in this country. The edition is to be a small one, and it is desired to call the attention of Wheaton's former pupils to the necessity of subscribing if they desire to secure copies of the biography. Addresses should be sent at once to Miss Clara M. Pike, 46 Chestnut Street, Boston, Massachusetts.                JULIA OSGOOD,

For the Committee of Publication.

5, NO. 14

287 Fourth Avenue, New York City
1436 Marquette Building, Chicago

PRICE TEN CE

# The Outlook

## Saturday, April 6, 1907

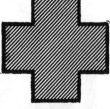

# The Outlook

SATURDAY, APRIL 6, 1907

**The Ohio Primary Campaign**

The issue joined in Ohio between Senator Foraker and the friends of Secretary Taft indicates that the country will have two opportunities to pass on the question whether the Federal Government shall exercise any supervision and control over the railways or not. Senator Foraker is a candidate in that State for re-election to the United States Senate. He is also a candidate for the Republican nomination to the Presidency. He is probably the ablest, he is certainly the most open and the most distinguished, of the anti-Roosevelt Republicans. In a published statement to the public he has offered a characteristic challenge to the Roosevelt Republicans of Ohio. It is said (how correct the report we do not know) that this challenge followed his proposal to support Secretary Taft's candidacy for the Presidency if Secretary Taft would support his candidacy for the Senate, and Secretary Taft refused to make any bargain or enter into any alliance. The report is reasonable, since refusal to make political bargains has always been characteristic of Secretary Taft. Senator Foraker's challenge is as follows:

I do not want any political honors from the Republicans of Ohio without their hearty approval. In order that there may be no doubt as to their preferences, I shall at the proper time request the Republican State Central Committee to issue a call for a Republican State convention, to be composed of delegates elected by the Republicans of the State at duly authorized primary elections, for the purpose not only of nominating candidates for State offices to be voted for at our next State election, but also to determine the preference of the Republicans of Ohio as to candidates for United States Senator and for President.

To this challenge Secretary Taft has made no reply. He has gone off to Cuba to attend to his duties and the Nation's interests there, leaving Ohio politics to Ohio politicians. But the challenge has been accepted by Secretary Taft's brother, an Ohio editor, in the following terms:

Senator Foraker's statement indicates that he is running for the Presidency and for the Senatorship. The friends of Secretary Taft are urging him for the Presidency. As the Senator has included the two offices in this primary contest, Secretary Taft's friends accept the proposition and will make it a distinct contest—Taft for the Presidency or Senatorship, or Foraker for the Presidency or Senatorship.

If the surmise of the New York Times correspondent is correct, and Senator Foraker expected to divide the forces opposed to him by offering himself as an alternative candidate for two offices, while his opponents would have Mr. Burton for their Senatorial candidate and Mr. Taft for their Presidential candidate, a condition which would give good opportunities for trading, he has been disappointed. Both men are put in the running for both offices, and trading is out of the question. And it is certain that such a primary election will crystallize the Roosevelt and anti-Roosevelt sentiment in all the States, with a great probability that Secretary Taft will be the leading candidate on the one side and Senator Foraker on the other.

**A Forecast of the National Issue**

The issue thus joined is not a merely personal one. It is a very clear issue between two conflicting policies. Secretary Taft is known to have been the President's constitutional adviser during the entire development of his railway policy, to believe in both the constitutionality and the expediency of railway rate regulation by the Federal Government, to have advised that under the decisions of the Supreme Court the Congress may not only regulate the rates, but, within certain defined limits, may delegate the power to determine whether any given rate is according to the standard which Congress has prescribed. He is known also to be a conservative rather than a radical advocate of that view, and to have favored providing in the bill for the possibility of a review by the courts of the Inter-State Commerce Commission's decisions. Senator Foraker, on the other hand, in his speech of last March took ground against the railway rate regulation bill in its entirety. He recognized the injustice of discriminations, whether between individuals or between localities, but maintained that the existing law afforded sufficient protection against such injustice. And he claimed that any attempt by Congress to regulate the rates charged by the railways was unconstitutional and would be held to be so by the United States Supreme Court. Of all the opponents of the railway policy of the President he is the most pronounced, and is therefore the logical candidate for all those who believe in leaving the railways without governmental supervision. Secretary Taft, on the other hand, is the most natural candidate of those who desire to see the Presidential policy maintained. Whichever of these candidates carries Ohio will stand a very good chance of carrying the National Convention, and failing in that will be morally sure to represent Ohio in the Senate. If Senator Foraker should secure the Republican nomination for the Presidency, the issue two years from now will be between governmental regulation and perhaps tariff revision, represented by some Democratic candidate, and a return to the old policy of *laissez faire* represented by Mr. Foraker. If Secretary Taft should be nominated, the question before the country would be, Into whose hands will the country intrust tariff revision and governmental regulation of railways? since Mr. Taft is known to believe in both, and represents those Republicans who believe in both. It is for these reasons that we say that the issue joined in Ohio between Senator Foraker and the friends of Secretary Taft indicates that the country will have two opportunities to pass on the question whether the Federal Government shall exercise any supervision and control over the railways or not: first, an opportunity within the Republican party, and then, should railway rate regulation be defeated there, a second opportunity in the general Presidential election upon the issue joined between the Republican and the Democratic parties.

❦

*The Moyer-Haywood Trial*

After numerous delays and legal skirmishes it appears probable that Moyer, Haywood, and Pettibone, officials of the Western Federation of Miners accused of complicity in the murder of former Governor Steunenberg, of Idaho, will be tried next month. The petition of the prisoners for a change of venue on the ground of prejudice was denied, and Boise was named as the city in which the trial will take place. Interest in this trial has been intensified recently, partly through the agitation of friends of the accused, and partly through the trial at Wallace, Idaho, a short time ago, of Steve Adams, supposed to be a member of the "inner circle" of the Western Federation of Miners. Adams was tried for the murder of Fred Tyler, a "claim jumper" in Shoshone County, in 1905. The trial, which resulted in a disagreement, was the result of a confession made by Adams while confined in a penitentiary at Boise with Harry Orchard. Orchard is the man who confessed to placing the bomb which killed Steunenberg, and in his confession implicated Adams, as well as Moyer, Haywood, and Pettibone. In another part of this issue of The Outlook is an article dealing with the assassination of Steunenberg, and giving an account of the arrest of the accused men and the subsequent efforts made by them to regain their liberty. The article was written before Adams was brought to trial. The general line of defense to be used in the coming trial was partly disclosed during the hearing of the Adams case. On the witness-stand Adams testified that the confession he made while in Boise penitentiary was obtained from him by detectives and State officials on the promise of immunity from punishment if he would only corroborate the confession of Orchard and help convict Moyer, Haywood, and Pettibone. He testified that Warden Whitney said to him, " You are a good fellow, and if you do right by the State the State will do right by you." He declared that when he was arrested by the sheriff of Shoshone County on orders from Governor Gooding, the sheriff said to him, " I have got inside information that if you tell what you know you will come out all right." Detective McParland, who obtained the confession from both Orchard and Adams, testified on the stand that he plied Adams with drinks and good cigars and that when he was " mellow " the confession was obtained. Adams on the witness-stand swore that the confession was untrue, and that he only partially knew the contents of the document when he signed it. The trial of Adams is interesting only because of its bearing on the more important trial. The defense tried to prove an alibi, and witnesses were produced who swore that Adams was distant from the scene of the murder on the date when the State alleged it was committed. After the defense had been heard the State asked permission to recall its chief witness to fix more definitely the date of the murder. The defense objected, and was sustained by the court, thus strengthening the alibi of Adams. The jury divided evenly, six standing for conviction and six for acquittal at the end of thirty-six hours' deliberation. The attorneys who defended Adams are the same retained in the other case, and they declare that the evidence in the Adams trial tended to prove their contention that a conspiracy exists on the part of the State officials and mine-owners to send Moyer, Haywood, and Pettibone to the gallows, guilty or innocent. The legal proceedings taken on behalf of the accused men since their arrest in February, 1906, have cost the Western Federation of Miners about $65,000, and the trial has not yet begun. The Legislature of Idaho appropriated $50,000 to bring to justice the murderers of Steunenberg. This action of the State makes it certain that a great legal battle will be fought to establish the guilt or innocence of the accused men.

*A Threatened Railway Strike* Labor conditions on railways west of Chicago became suddenly acute last week. The employees demanded an increase of wages and a decrease of hours; the companies felt themselves unable to grant the demands. The employees, through their organizations, then threatened a strike which would tie up at least fifty thousand miles of railway—an action which, at a time when transportation facilities are already glaringly inadequate, would bring disaster to the railways and to the public, and involve the wages of a great army of men. The railway managers asked the Federal Government that the arbitration law passed in 1898 be enforced to prevent the strike, if possible. This act provides means for settling disputes between common carriers and their employees on request of one of the parties. As applied to the present situation, the law provides that the railways may ask Mr. Knapp, Chairman of the Inter-State Commerce Commission, and Dr. Neill, Commissioner of Labor in the Department of Commerce and Labor, to " use their best efforts by mediation and conciliation " between the employers and the employees amicably to settle the dispute. If these officers fail in the task, then the act provides that the common carrier and the organization of strikers may each appoint an arbiter, and the two select a third; if they cannot agree on a third, Chairman Knapp and Dr. Neill shall select the third, and the decision of this commission so formed shall be " valid and binding," and shall have the effect of a bill of exceptions when filed in the United States Circuit Court in the district where the controversy arose or where the arbitration is entered into, and shall be final for both sides unless set aside for error of law apparent in the record. Both sides must faithfully execute the award; employees dissatisfied with it may not quit the service of their employer before three months after the award has been made without giving thirty days' notice of their intention; nor may the employer, dissatisfied with the award, dismiss employees before the expiration of three months without giving thirty days' notice. If not thus set aside, the awards continue in force for a year, and no new arbitration upon the same subject between " the same employer and the same class of employees " may be had until the expiration of a year. This law has been on the statute-books almost a decade. It was first invoked by the Southern Pacific Railway Company on the occasion of the Texas strike ; a few weeks ago it was again invoked by the same company when confronted with demands from telegraphers which threatened to tie up the entire system. The arbitrators are now in session in San Francisco, trying to settle the dispute. It is interesting to note that all the appeals which have been made invoking this law have come from the managers of the railways involved in the various controversies.

❋

**A Victory for the Great Northern Railway** An important decision favorably affecting the Great Northern Railway and unfavorably affecting the movement in several States to regulate railways by State commissions has just been unanimously made by the Supreme Court of Minnesota. As reported very fully a month ago in these pages, the Attorney-General of Minnesota sought to enjoin the Great Northern from issuing $60,-000,000 of additional stock, on the ground that the law explicitly directed that such an issue could be made only with the consent of the State Railroad and Warehouse Commission. Under the statute the railway was required to file its application with the Commission showing the necessity for the additional capital, and stating in detail the purposes for which the proceeds were to be used. The Great Northern declined to comply with these conditions, and the Commission refused its consent for the issuance of the stock. The County Court sustained the Attorney-General; the Supreme Court of the State has reversed that decision, and, all the judges concurring, declares that the statute giving the Railroad Commission the power thus to regulate the capitalization of railways is unconstitutional. The Legislature, says the Court,

may by statute impose the " terms, conditions, and limitations " under which new railway capital may be issued; it may create a commission to find the facts and to determine whether the new stock is issued in conformity to the statute; but it may not delegate to a commission what is really the legislative power of determining the " terms, limitations, and conditions." That is to say, the Legislature may enact in statute that no new capital may be issued by a railway corporation of the State for the purpose of buying the stock of another railway corporation, but it may not leave to the Commission the discretion of determining whether such a use of new capital is advantageous to the State and may be permitted, or disadvantageous and forbidden. Such a unanimous decision of such a court is not to be treated lightly, and is distinctly an important victory for the Great Northern Railway. We shall not, however, consider the principle settled that a legislature may not by statute make the approval of a specially created board of experts one of the constitutional " terms, conditions, and limitations " of the issuance of capital until the Minnesota decision has been reviewed and confirmed by other courts—possibly ultimately by the United States Supreme Court. Should this position of the Minnesota court be sustained in other States or by the United States Supreme Court, the growing and, we believe, on the whole the wholesome tendency to exercise government regulation of public utilities through small boards of experts would be definitely checked.

❋

**" The Kingdom "** Of the two oratorios which were performed by the Oratorio Society under the direction of the composer, Sir Edward Elgar, in New York, on the 19th and 26th of March, " The Apostles " had been heard before in that city, and had been conducted by the composer at Cincinnati. Some account of it was given in The Outlook on both occasions. It is enough here to recall that it deals with the calling of the Apostles, their association with their Master and their testing at the time of his death, that it is the presentation of the subject in a dramatic form, and that it not only utilizes a great chorus, solo voices, and full modern orchestra, but also adapts to the oratorio in many respects the form and devices which Wagner established for the opera or music-drama. "The Kingdom" is the second in what may be called a cycle of oratorios on the same subject. It begins where "The Apostles" ends. Its central event is Pentecost. The hearer who listens sympathetically will seem to be sharing the meditations and emotions of a devout Catholic who, divesting his mind of the externals of ecclesiasticism, is contemplating, in the light of ecclesiastical teaching and tradition, the origins of the Church. The words supply, as it were, the framework of thought. The music creates the atmosphere of feeling. At times the emotion is dramatic. In "The Apostles" this dramatic element is, so to speak, visualized. The voice of Judas, for instance, utters his remorse while the temple chorus is heard singing one of the imprecatory psalms; and as he thinks on what he has done, his despair is molded by the psalm he hears. In "The Kingdom," on the other hand, the dramatic element is, so to speak, more subjective. For example, when Peter, addressing the multitude, declares, "Let all the house of Israel know assuredly that God hath made him both Lord and Christ, this Jesus whom ye crucified," there is borne upon the voices of the chorus the sentence, "His blood be on us and on our children," and upon a solitary voice the words of Christ bidding the daughters of Jerusalem to weep not for themselves but for their children. It is as if the words of Peter had awakened in the multitude, or rather as if the devout contemplator of the scene would recall to the multitude, the bitter, reckless words of the mob and the warning of its victim. There is in this case no pictured external reality—as in the case of the temple choir; the voices are but a memory; the dramatic contrast is wholly within the mind. Another instance may be cited. When the Apostles in prison recall that Jesus had said that some of his disciples would be crucified, the orchestra sounds the chords associated with Peter, thus calling to mind the

Church tradition that Peter's death was by crucifixion. The music of "The Kingdom" is, as it should be, formed largely out of the same thematic material as that of its predecessor. It is, as is befitting the character of the oratorio, more contemplative. Yet contrasts abound. At times there is but a thread of sound, at times a veritable web of beauty. At the close of each performance Sir Edward was enthusiastically recalled three or four times. As at the performance of Pierné's great work, "The Children's Crusade," the audience was not as large as it ought to have been. The people accustomed to attend musical performances in New York have lately been engrossed in the relative merits of various orchestral conductors, and in the contest between rival opera impresarios and their cohorts of singers. It seems as if they were more concerned about the personality of performers than absorbed in the music produced. Nevertheless, both audiences were large.

❀

*Sir Edward Elgar's Music* This is the third time that Sir Edward Elgar has visited the United States. The first time he came to receive an honorary degree from Yale; the second time he came to conduct certain of his own compositions at the Cincinnati May Music Festival. It is Sir Edward Elgar's distinction that he has interested the musical public of all the world in English music. Now, beside d'Indy and Debussy of France, Strauss, Reger, and Mahler of Germany, Boito and Puccini of Italy, England can rightfully place Sir Edward Elgar. It has been said that Sir Edward is the first great composer that England has produced since Purcell, who lived in the latter half of the seventeenth century. Of his compositions Professor Edward Dickinson, in his admirable volume "The Study of the History of Music," writes that they "indicate a technical knowledge of the highest order in counterpoint and orchestration, as well as a prolific vein of melody." Yet instruction in the technique of composition Sir Edward practically never received. The son of the organist of St. George's Roman Catholic

Church in Worcester, he obtained his knowledge of the theory of music incidentally to its practice. There have been other composers who have, like him, owed their mastery of their medium less to books and teachers than to practical experience with instruments and voices. As to his vein of melody, there are critics who have not discovered it. One newspaper writer, for instance, describes his oratorio " The Apostles " as marked by "hopeless dullness" and "unutterable insipidity," and Sir Edward himself as near the front in the competition for " unmelodiousness." Each to his taste. There are hearers of Elgar's music, on the other hand, who find themselves haunted by his themes, and who feel in his music that indescribable something that marks it as his and no one else's—the expression, as it were, of a musical personality. In any case it is clear that the music of Sir Edward Elgar, though it elicits all sorts of comments, arouses anything but indifference.

❦

*Sir Edward Elgar's Personality* The man whose musical compositions have been the subject of world-wide discussion and even controversy is temperamentally at the farthest remove from the sensationalist. He has no love for publicity. One can well imagine his desire to work in retirement and offer the product of his pen to such as will hear. On the other hand, he is not beset by that form of vanity which drives some men from their fellows and makes them conspicuous by their seclusion. He is a man of very definite and decided views, whether they concern English politics or his own art. In spite of the apparently revolutionary character of some of his compositions, he is of conservative temper. He has no philosophy of music to expound, no musical prophecy to utter. In spite of his success in creating descriptive music, he does not belong among those apostles of the art who would make it representative like painting or sculpture. To him so-called programme music is a by-path in the musical highway. He is a man of many interests, and has the none too common gift of the sense of humor. A

sketch of Sir Edward, with portrait, was published in the Magazine Number of The Outlook for last October.

❦

*Pobiedonostzeff* The death of Constantine Pobiedonostzeff, ex-Procurator-General of the Holy Synod of the Russian Church, may have a material effect on the political fortunes of Russia. Dr. Andrew D. White, in his autobiography, gives a very interesting account of this man of extraordinary contradictions. Scholarly, with a mind interested in all theological and socialistic points of view, recognizing the shortcomings of his own Church, interested in American institutions and American literature, translator of Thomas à Kempis's " Imitation of Christ," especially fond of Ralph Waldo Emerson's writings, so that " for years there had always laid open upon his study table a volume of Emerson's writings," one volume of which he had also translated, sensitive to beauty in literature, art, and ceremonial, and kindly and gentle in his personal relations—such are the facts that present one side of his nature. Upon the other side he was a thoroughgoing mediævalist, considered all Western civilization a failure, anticipated an early collapse in the systems and institutions of western Europe, regarded Socialism and Anarchism as the natural fruits of democracy, and atheism and irreligion as the inevitable results of religious liberty ; he opposed, with a conscientious cruelty which won for him the title " the Torquemada of the nineteenth century," all that which we count progress in America ; abhorred the free school, the free church, the free press, freedom of assemblage and debate ; regarded the Established Church of the Empire as the only true form of Christianity ; and pursued, upon conviction, a repressive policy toward all other forms of religion, and especially toward the Jews, with a kind of holy vindictiveness. He was the chief religious if not also the chief political adviser of the Czar— certainly the imperial conscience, apparently also the imperial intelligence. His relation to the Czar appears to have been somewhat analogous to that of the cardinals of France to the kings of the seventeenth century. It may be hoped that with his death some counselor with a little more of the spirit of the twentieth century may get the ear of the Czar. But it is to be feared that the Czar has already been cast in the Pobiedonostzeff mold, and the breaking of the mold will not produce any change in the cast.

❦

**Agrarian Unrest in Russia** Individual inefficiency, landlord absenteeism, and oppressive taxation are responsible for much of the peasants' suffering in eastern Europe. The fact that the land does not produce what it ought is largely due to the system by which peasants have exhausted the fertility of the soil which they have tilled either for the commune or for some absentee landlord. The position of the peasant in eastern Europe is pitiable. If first of all he needs to know how to cultivate the land he has under his control, he also needs more land and better economic conditions. In Russia he sees millions of acres called Crown lands, Cabinet lands, Church lands; the income from the first going directly to the Emperor, that from the second supporting an enormously large Imperial family, that from the third supporting the too often indolent clergy. He also sees millions of acres of land owned by men whom he has never seen. The absentee owners of land are apt to live in great cities like Paris, thinking much of their own amusement and little of the distress of those who are working for them. These lands are farmed out to administrators; in some cases these administrators, supported by corrupt officials, demand excessive rents . and impose conditions of practical servitude. Under these conditions and excessive taxation the peasants live in rotten huts and are now on the verge of starvation. The exportation of rye, the principal crop, and also of wheat from Russia has been large, but the past twelvemonth shows an alarming decline. The Russians need all they have and more. The Emperor and the bureaucrats, who oppose an extension of the people's power in Parliament, may remember that revolution has

no surer friend than famine, and that, under any circumstances, the greatest of all questions in Russia is the agrarian.

❦

**Agrarian Unrest in Rumania** What may be expected in Russia is now happening in Rumania, until half a century ago controlled by Russia. Agrarian conditions are similar in both countries. The Rumanian peasants have risen against the exactions and tyranny of the administrators of great estates and against the new taxes recently voted by Parliament. Marauding bands have pillaged and murdered, have destroyed the telegraph and telephone lines, and have attempted to hold up trains. But the army, by stern repression, has now apparently the upper hand. The Jews have suffered more than other people, because many Jewish shopkeepers are also managers of farms of absentee owners. But the estates of the landlords, controlling a trust which has leased half the cultivable land in North Rumania, were the first to be sacked. The King, an able and conscientious ruler, has issued a proclamation announcing the immediate suppression of some of the heavier taxes, declaring that many lands will be leased directly to the peasants, that no syndicate will be allowed to hold more than eight thousand acres, that the Government will facilitate the raising of money to pay rents, and will revise the terms of the agricultural agreements which at present practically enslave the peasantry. All this has not been accomplished without a Cabinet crisis. Premier Sturdza, who again takes the helm, was at the head of the Government from 1901 to 1905, and by rigid economy established his country's finances on a sound basis. He was unable, however, to reduce the debt per capita as much as it should be reduced ; it is about twice the per capita debt of our own country. The Rumanian peasant is about as heavily taxed as the Russian peasant. It is not impossible that Russia may catch fire from Rumania. Such appears to be Premier Stolypin's opinion. He has ordered the governors of all the Russian provinces to prohibit the printing of any news concerning the Rumanian agrarian disorders. He well knows that absentee landlordism and oppressive taxation account for the Rumanian rising, and will account for any Russian rising that may take place.

⊛

*"Light Through, Work"* The title of this paragraph is the motto, chosen by its blind members, of the New York Association for the Blind. The attention of readers of The Outlook has already been called to the beneficent and efficient work of this Association, which is now issuing an appeal for contributions to enable it to complete an endowment fund of $100,-000. The work out of which the Association has grown was begun four years ago in a modest and unheralded way by two young ladies of this city in their own home, by distributing tickets for oratorios and other musical and dramatic performances. The idea was suggested, says the founder of the Association, by " seeing some small blind boys who were having a beautiful time at a concert in Italy." Over five thousand tickets have been distributed in this way from this private house. Through this personal friendliness for individual blind people these ladies became intimately acquainted with the deplorable condition of the adult blind in the State of New York. Out of these personal endeavors has grown the New York Association for the Blind, which is indorsed and directed by some of the most distinguished citizens of New York. Miss Helen Keller is an officer of the Association and actively interested in its success. At present the executive office of the Association is in the private house of the founders, who have veritably turned their home into a school for the blind. The primary object of the Association is not to amuse the blind, nor merely to train their capacity for communicating with their seeing fellowmen, but to train them to become self-supporting workers and producers. Classes are maintained in telephone switchboard operating, stenography and typewriting, lace-making, hand and machine manufacture of knitted and sewn garments for women and children, basket-weaving, artistic marketable bead-

work, etc., etc. Blind of both sexes have been put in commercial positions. Blind men and women have even been trained to become telephone switchboard operators, and the telephone company, at first skeptical, has volunteered the information that these graduates of the school compare most favorably for efficiency with seeing operators. The work of the Association has so grown that it is in great need of two houses—one for the men's workshop, to give employment to forty men in chair-caning, broom-making, mattress-making, and willow-weaving, and the other for offices, class-rooms, club and meeting rooms, and women's commercial industrial work. Even with the present limited facilities a number of blind men and women have been kept from beggary and the poorhouse, and in addition have discovered a source of happiness they never knew before. They have been given " light through work." Full information about the Association, its achievements, its plans, and its needs may be obtained of the Secretary, Miss Winifred Holt, 44 East Seventy-eighth Street, New York City.

⊛

*Hale and Hearty at Eighty-Five* Two qualities in Dr. Edward Everett Hale, who celebrates his eighty-fifth birthday on Wednesday of this week, account for the extraordinary fertility of his mind, the vitality of his interests and occupations and their variety. From his early manhood Dr. Hale has not only had all kinds of irons in the fire, but he has kept them glowing. He has practiced several professions in an age in which specialization has become a fad that sometimes passes the line of sanity, and has succeeded on high lines in them. This many-sidedness is explained by one of his favorite maxims, " To look out and not in ;" and it is this quality which has made it possible for the son who bears his name, and who shares generously in his ability, to write of him in perfect taste and with charming frankness and feeling in this week's issue of The Outlook. Dr. Hale has harmoniously combined the ethical passion of the religious teacher, the human feeling of the philanthropist, the quick sense of news-interest of the journalist, and the genius for expression of the man of letters. He belongs to a singularly interesting group of contemporaries. Among preachers he is to be counted with Dr. Robert Collyer and Theodore Cuyler, among writers with Mr. Charles Eliot Norton, Colonel Higginson, Mr. John Bigelow, and Mr. Trowbridge. Born in Boston, and a New Englander by all the ties of race and intellectual descent, Dr. Hale has been a man of National outlook and interests. Perhaps as much as any of his contemporaries he has embodied the American spirit, its regard for fine traditions of learning, character, and manners, its keen interest in its own time, its love for education, its passion for helpfulness, and its unshakable belief in the authority and the final triumph of right thinking, right speaking, and right living. As much as any American he has reverenced man, and that reverence is the root of his fine attitude of brotherliness. His distinctions have been many ; he has won success in different fields. Probably no living American is more highly regarded by the whole Nation ; but his chief distinction lies in his beautiful illustration of the democratic spirit at its highest, the spirit of universal helpfulness.

❀

# The Function of the President

The well-informed correspondent of the Chicago Tribune has told our readers something about the current gossip in Washington concerning Presidential possibilities. Our readers have been admitted into the secret but not sacred conclave of the Washington politicians. It may be a little early yet to be considering Presidential possibilities. But it is never too early to consider what kind of a man the people need for President. They must consider carefully the function of the office before they can judge wisely of the candidates for that office.

The first duty of the President is to preserve order and enforce law. He must therefore have the courage to prosecute all lawbreakers and prevent all lawbreaking—whether by the mob attacking the railways or by the multimillionaire misusing them.

His second duty is to conduct efficiently the business of the Government. He must have the wisdom and the force to do things : to ferret out and expel corrupt officials, to see that the money appropriated by Congress is honestly and economically expended, that the mails are promptly carried, the public funds justly administered, the coast well lighted, the great banking operations of the Treasury Department conducted in the public interest, the dredging of the rivers and harbors and the digging of the Panama Canal efficiently carried on. In short, he must be a capable business man.

But this is not all. The President of the United States is not only its Chief Executive, he is also its Prime Minister. He is an important part of the legislative department of the Government. The framers of the Constitution recognized this fact in providing that " he shall from time to time give to the Congress information of the state of the Union, and recommend to their consideration such measures as he shall judge necessary and expedient." History has abundantly confirmed their wisdom. This provision has been ample to confer on him an important function in the deliberations of the legislative body.

The Congress is composed of members each one of whom is elected by a local constituency to represent primarily local interests and express a local opinion. The Senator represents a State ; the Representative a District. He does this partly by deliberate choice, because if he fails to do so he will not be re-elected ; partly unconsciously, because he shares the opinions and the interests of his locality. To say that he does this is not to criticise him ; that is what he is sent to the Congress for. If he did not represent those opinions and interests, his constituents would do right in sending some one else to take his place. For the Congress is composed on the theory, not that these four or five hundred men are honest enough and wise enough to comprehend the interests of the entire Nation and to legislate for the Nation in disregard of local opinion and interests, but that the way to ascertain the opinions and interests of the Nation is to compare those of all its separate localities, and by the comparison, and in some cases the collision between them, seek a result that will be just to all.

In this legislative department there is one man and only one who represents the entire Nation. He represents no local constituency, no district, no State, no section. He is elected by the whole country, responsible to the whole country, and therefore equally accessible to the whole country. The opinion of Nebraska has no weight with a Senator from New York. In fact, the Senator from New York has almost no means of knowing what that opinion is. But with the President the opinion of New York and of Dakota, of New Jersey and of Louisiana, are equally weighty. The doors of the White House swing open to the citizen of one State as readily as to those of any other. Mr. McKinley in the House represented the State of Ohio; in the Presidential chair he represented the Nation.

For these reasons the President, whether he will or not, is the leader of his party. If he refuses to lead, it stands still. If he leads whither it will not follow, either party anarchy or party revolt follows. Neither the Speaker of the House nor the Chairman of the Ways and Means Committee can be a true National leader; for he is not elected by the Nation nor responsible to the Nation; he is elected by a District and is responsible to the District. If Mr. Cannon's District is opposed to tariff revision, he cannot be a revisionist; if it is opposed to expending money for a forest reserve, no matter how important to the Nation such a reserve may be, he cannot well vote for it and he is not likely to believe in it. With very rare exceptions, the Representative is and must be provincial. It may even be said that while he remains a Representative he ought to be provincial. For he is sent to the Congress to represent his province.

For these reasons, too, it is often the distinctive function of the President to take the initiative in legislation; to perceive the importance to the Nation of a measure which no individual member would perceive because it is National, not local, or, perceiving, would have no

power to get before the country, because he is a local, not a National, figure. This National quality in the President will make him sometimes more conservative, sometimes more radical, than the Congress, and generally more conservative than some Congressmen and more radical than others. It enabled Mr. Lincoln to realize the sentiment of the Middle West and hold back the Emancipation Proclamation against great pressure from the New England States until the Nation was ready to welcome and to enforce it. It enabled Mr. McKinley to hold the war spirits back from declaring war against Spain until the Eastern States were ready to second the demand which the West made weeks, if not months, before. It enabled Mr. Roosevelt to gauge the rising discontent with transportation conditions and in his Providence speech to demand a remedy more than three years before the Congress was ready to act upon a railway rate regulation bill. Mr. McKinley was criticised for having his ear to the ground. The President ought to have his ear to the ground, that he may listen to the tread of seventy million people, to know in what direction they are moving, and may guide them in the right direction. The Czar has his ear at the keyhole, and hears only the voice of the Bureaucracy; and because he cannot hear the people all Russia is in revolt.

What kind of a man, then, do we need for President?

First, a man of courage, who will enforce the laws alike against popular prejudice and private interests; second, a man of administrative ability, who understands men, has tact which enables him to get along with all sorts of men, power to win the loyalty of men, and so capability to supervise without directing in detail the immense business operations in which the country is engaged; and, third, a man with a broad horizon and with popular sympathies, who sees what are the needs of the Nation, what are its desires and what its perils, and who can interpret the needs, give expression to the desires, and warn against the perils, and can, in brief, give information to the Congress as to the state of the Union, and recommend measures to guard against the perils, satisfy the desires, and provide for the needs of the Nation. These measures the Congress can then consider and debate from the many points of view furnished by the representatives of many different constituencies, with conflicting opinions and interests.

The reader who believes that we have here correctly interpreted the function of the President may perhaps be interested to test by it the comparative merits of the following gentlemen, whom our correspondent tells us are being canvassed in Washington for the Presidency. We print their names here in alphabetical order, without even indicating by letter or emblem to which party they respectively belong. We do not put Mr. Roosevelt's name in the list, because we believe in the sincerity of Mr. Roosevelt's repeated declarations, and do not believe that there is any probability of any contingency which will lead him to become a candidate.

| | |
|---|---|
| William J. Bryan | William R. Hearst |
| Joseph G. Cannon | Charles E. Hughes |
| George B. Cortelyou | Robert M. La Follette |
| Charles W. Fairbanks | Richard Olney |
| Joseph W. Folk | Alton B. Parker |
| Joseph B. Foraker | Elihu Root |
| George Gray | Leslie M. Shaw |
| | William H. Taft |

❀

# The Railway Crisis

That the country is facing a crisis in its railway finances is the opinion of some of our ablest and most conservative bankers and financiers. The values of railway securities have fallen suddenly and alarmingly; it is reported that some necessary and important railway improvements have been stopped or curtailed because the promoters are in a state of uncertainty and alarm about the future; and it is known that one or two of our great railway systems, in order to supply their absolute and legitimate needs, have had to borrow funds at expensive rates of interest in foreign money markets, because American investors have lost their faith in railway stocks and bonds.

Various reasons are given for this serious condition of affairs. The railway managers ascribe it to the radical and reformatory policy of President Roosevelt; the shippers and investors assert that it results from the despotic and selfish policy of the railway managers, such as was revealed in the Inter-State Commerce Commission's investigation of Mr. Harriman; and Mr. Carnegie in a recent speech declared that " a few gamblers in Wall Street are the trouble."

Various remedies are proposed. A large number of State Legislatures think that freight and passenger rates fixed by lawmakers will cure the evils; State Socialists advocate Government ownership with renewed vigor; Mr. Morgan is reported to have cabled from Europe that the thing to do is to have some of the great bankers unite to "help the market;" and not a few of the railway managers, recognizing Mr. Roosevelt's great influence upon the American public, and thus upon American legislation, are urging him to call off the legislators, tell the people that all's well, and let the railway presidents and directors manage their affairs in the good, old-fashioned way—that is to say, upon the theory that a railway is not a public highway but a private business subject merely to the ordinary laws of supply and demand.

In the midst of this turmoil, this anxiety, this confusion of opinion, and this uncertainty regarding the facts, the proposal of Mr. Jacob H. Schiff ought to be welcomed everywhere. Mr. Schiff, who has, as a banker, very large and influential relations with American railways, urges an official conference of representative railway managers, appointed by the railways for the purpose, with the Inter-State Commerce Commission, representing the Government. "In this conference," says Mr. Schiff, "there could be a fair and frank discussion of all the proposals for railroad legislation of every kind, and it ought to be possible for such a body of men to agree upon a plan for legislation fair to all parties, which could receive the sanction of the President, of the people generally, and of stockholders in the railroads. This could be made the basis of legislation by Congress, and it should be of such a thorough nature as to make it unnecessary for individual States to do more than follow the lines laid down here."

As The Outlook has during the past few months made and reiterated a similar suggestion, we hardly need to say that we heartily indorse Mr. Schiff's proposal. It is clear that some form of Federal legislation is needed which will effectively protect the railways from unintelligent and inimical legislation on the part of the States, the shipper and traveler from the whims, selfishness, or dishonesty of individual railway despots, and the investor from the disasters which always follow personal quarrels carried on between ambitious and unscrupulous railway promoters in the too often foggy and impenetrable atmosphere of Wall Street.

We hope that the Schiff conference will be called, and we propose for its consideration and discussion a plan of Federal legislation which shall accomplish the following results:

1. The establishment of a Department of Railways, with a Secretary of Railways in the Cabinet.

2. Federal incorporation of all inter-State railways.

3. Pooling, traffic agreements, and mergers, under the supervision of the Department of Railways, to be made legal.

4. Capitalization of inter-State railways to be regulated and controlled by the Department of Railways.

5. Uniform system of accounting and absolute publicity of accounts under the inspection of a body of National Railway Examiners appointed and directed by the Secretary of Railways.

6. Tariffs and rates to be made by the railways, but on complaint of shippers in specific cases the reasonable and just rate to be fixed by the Department.

7. All accidents to be investigated and responsibility fixed by a Bureau of Railway Accidents within the Department.

8. Railway labor disputes to be investigated and all facts made public by the Department of Railways, and both railways and employees compelled to carry out strictly their mutual contracts and agreements.

Some such plan as this would protect the interests of the railway builder and manager, the railway investor, the railway laborer, the railway shipper, and the railway traveler—interests which now are so often conflicting and antagonistic.

❀

# Women and Politics

The women who are opposed to woman's suffrage would do well to reprint in a tract an article on "Women and Politics" by Caroline E. Stephen in the Nineteenth Century and After, reprinted in the Living Age (March 9, 1907). It is written in a spirit of calmness and womanly reserve which is in refreshing contrast to some of the unwomanly utterances which have been given forth by advocates upon the other side. The woman's suffrage question is two questions : one addressed to men, Ought the suffrage to be imposed on women without first ascertaining whether they desire it? the other addressed to women, Is it their duty to desire it? Each of these questions Miss Stephen states with great clearness and answers with great distinctness in the negative.

I. Some women regard suffrage as a privilege which they eagerly desire, or as a right which they vigorously and vehemently demand. Other women regard suffrage as they regard service in the militia or on the police or upon juries, as a part of the function of government from which they have been exempt in the past and wish to be exempt in the future. Miss Stephen presents the latter view with great clearness.

On behalf of a great though silent multitude of women, I desire to set forth some of the grounds on which we shrink from the proposed abolition of our present exemption from the office of electing members of Parliament. This change, if made without the serious attempt to ascertain the wishes of the women of England, may inflict upon them, against their will and without a hearing, a grave injustice.

Legislators ought not to impose the burden of the suffrage on women who think that exemption from it is a right of the sex, without first ascertaining which of the two opinions is prevalent among the women of the country, nor without considering which opinion is supported by the better reason. That a great many women do desire the continuance of this exemption and shrink from the proposed abolition of it is indisputable. That this is the present state of mind of an overwhelming majority of women we think is scarcely less indisputable. Any man who entertains doubts upon this question can get some light upon it by quietly and individually asking a score of women of his acquaintance, selected at hazard, whether they personally desire to vote. He may find one or two who will answer in the affirmative. He may find a few more who are seriously questioning whether they ought not to desire to vote. But he will find the majority either shrinking from assuming this new function or indifferent to it.

If he wishes to push his inquiries further, he will find that in several of the States are quiet organizations of women, not so demonstrative as the suffragists but quite as influential and more representative, who agree with Miss Stephen in protesting against the abolition of their traditional exemption from political duties; and now a similar organization has been formed in England. The defeat in the New York Assembly by a vote of 70 to 38 of the latest suffragist movement is in no small measure due to the effective protest against the proposed measure by the New York State Woman's Anti-Suffrage Association. Women who share Miss Stephen's reluctance to have the suffrage thrust upon them might well at least give to such associations, where they exist, the moral support of their names. This involves no publicity. For these quiet women hold no public meetings, enter into no public debates, make no public speeches, and depend almost wholly on the use of literature, on enlisting men as defenders of their cherished rights, and on protests before legislative committees against having unwelcome powers thrust upon them. The World, of London, very justly points out "the absurdity of shrieking against the brutal tyranny of withholding votes from women, when women in great and increasing numbers are protesting that they have no use for votes and consider themselves much better off without them."

Miss Stephen truly says that "it could hardly 'pass the wit of man' to devise some method by which the opinion of women could be ascertained." The wit of men in Massachusetts devised such a plan some years ago. In 1895 the women of that State were asked by the Legislature to vote on the question whether they wished the suffrage. Of the 575,000 voting women in the State only 22,209 cared enough for the suffrage to deposit in a ballot-box an affirmative answer to the question. That is, in round numbers, a trifle over ninety-six per cent. of the women of the State said by their silence, with Miss Stephen, "We shrink from the proposed abolition of our present exemption." The legislator has to consider, not whether he will refuse a prerogative to women who desire it, but whether he will impose an unauthorized duty upon women who shrink from accepting it. To impose the suffrage on a great class who do not desire to exercise it is to try an entirely new and very hazardous experiment in government.

II. Still, it is conceivable that this is a duty which women ought to assume, from which they ought not to shrink, and that it ought to be imposed upon them whether they will or no, as military duty is imposed on men of unmilitary temper, and jury duty on men who shrink from performing it. This question Miss Stephen also considers, and her statement of it appears to us to imply the true answer:

The real question, then, is whether our country will be best served by a continuation of the present immemorial distribution of functions, by which men undertake the actual management of what are emphatically called public affairs, while women are mainly occupied with private or domestic matters, each sex exercising the while a powerful influence on the way in which the other manages its own special business; or whether it would be a better plan that both sexes should indiscriminately attend to all business, whether public or private.

Miss Stephen goes on to say, with the quiet forcefulness which always attaches to a clear statement of an indisputable truth, that "there is a certain absurdity about the mere suggestion of men's taking any increased part in women's work;" that " what is in fact proposed is that women, while continuing to do all their own work, shall take ' an increased share in that of men." When women are told that it is their duty to demand the ballot, and the share in government which the ballot involves, the two questions which they have to ask of themselves are, on the one hand, Does time now hang so heavy on our hands that we ought to seek a new and public vocation for the sake of our own usefulness? and, on the other, Is the work of government so poorly done by our fathers, brothers, and husbands, and are we so much better fitted morally and intellectually to do that work, that we ought to step into the breach in order to correct the failures and follies of our male companions? To ask these questions is to answer them. The home, the school, the church, public and private charities, and social life, which is quite as vital to the well-being of the community as its political life, afford more opportunities for high and noble service than any woman has time and strength for. And, happily, there are few women so supercilious as to think that they must, despite their reluctance, undertake a share in the government of the State in order to save it from the misgovernment inflicted by their brothers.

III. There is one other argument for woman suffrage which may be tersely put thus: Women must have a share in the government in order that they may get justice from the government; women must be able to vote, and to vote together, in order to get for their sex what the sex wants and is entitled to. Miss Stephen treats this argument with scant respect—though with all it deserves—and, with true knowledge of woman's nature, points out a more excellent way to such as do not wish the suffrage for themselves, but think they ought to want it and to exercise it for their less fortunate sisters:

Anything like rivalry or jealousy between the sexes is too odious a thought to be dwelt on. But it seems necessary to remember that, were it possible for any such opposition to arise, women must of necessity fail. Our strength lies not in our power to oppose, but in our appeal to all that is best and tenderest in men, in our possession of a key to their reverence.

America has suffered much from the voting of section against section; much from the voting of race against race; and it has suffered locally from the voting of class against class and church against church. But neither sectional nor race nor class nor religious voting could inflict on the community so disastrous results as would follow from sex voting. The attempt to unite either sex in an endeavor to get an advantage out of the other sex by political action would be a more odious political combination than any of past history.

We repeat that we should like to see Miss Stephen's article reprinted for general circulation as a tract. We do not see how any fair-minded person, whatever his predilection, can well question her conclusion, as stated in her closing paragraph: " It may be that there are real needs, imperfectly visible to my eyes, for some further alteration of our traditional balance and adjustment of functions as between men and women. . . . But it cannot be right that such readjustment should be made or stimulated on any but the broadest grounds of national expediency, or without the hearty concurrence of the half of the nation most immediately concerned."

❋

# A False Messenger

The New Church Messenger, of Chicago, adopts as its motto, " Behold, I make all things new." It lives up to its motto by purporting to give its readers a report of an article in The Outlook based on a sermon by Dr. L. Mason Clarke, and in its report the Messenger makes both sermon and article so new that no reader would recognize either. It assumes that both preacher and editor denied the divinity of Jesus Christ, whereas both affirmed his divinity. It publishes sentences in quotation marks, saying that it is quoting from the preacher and the editor—sentences which are neither in the sermon nor in the editorial. There is nothing in either editorial or sermon which approximates these sentences in either spirit or phraseology. It is this sort of thing in journals which call themselves religious that makes men scoff at religion.

The New Church Messenger is a messenger of false tidings. We should be glad to have it tell its readers that The Outlook says so.

◉

# The Book of Life

Those who are disturbed lest modern critical study of the Bible shall diminish its authority will do well to read Professor J. H. Gardiner's discussion of "The Bible as Literature;"[1] a course of lectures of equal value to the student of the Old and New Testaments and of English literature. Mediæval thinking laid such overwhelming emphasis on the divine in Christ that Jesus of Nazareth was almost lost in a cloud of incense, and the sweetness, strength, and fellowship of one who bore our sins and was acquainted with our sorrows were so obscured that men lost some of the greatest things he came to bestow. The modern emphasis on the Jesus of the first three Gospels has not obscured the Jesus of the fourth Gospel and of the Apostolic epistles, but has brought him out of the mystery of the Godhead into the homes and fields and thronged streets where his human tenderness and his divine strength a : most sorely needed. In like manner the study of the Bible as literature, instead of lowering its power as revelation, has freshened and deepened the sense of its unique quality and authority, by treating it as the product of vital processes instead of a series of arbitrary acts of revelation.

Those who have feared that the study as literature of the sixty-six books bound together in the Bible, which came into being over a period of many centuries, from men of widely different temperaments, with varying moral standards and capacity for understanding spiritual things, would obliterate the unity of the great religious text-book of Christendom, will take heart again when they read the testimony of a dispassionate

[1] The Bible as English Literature. By J. H. Gardiner. Charles Scribner's Sons, New York.

2 A

critic to the wonderful harmony of fundamental thought which makes it possible to read these books as if they were chapters in one book. It is only five hundred years since Chaucer died, but how diverse and often irreconcilable have been the views of life presented in English literature since the author of the "Canterbury Tales" ended his pilgrimage! The Old Testament, on the other hand, was more than a thousand years in the making, and yet Professor Gardiner declares that the popular usage which speaks of the Bible as a single book is sound. The earliest materials, he reminds us, go back to the time when the people of Israel were just emerging from a nomadic life; songs, stories, and laws gradually coalesced in the hands of a long series of writers into something like connected histories; successive schools of priests and prophets gained a clearer perception of the nature of Jehovah and his relations to the chosen people, and changed the histories in some cases in purpose and contents until they came into the present form in the time of Persian sovereignty. The books of poetry came to be the expression of the Jews when they were struggling, with unconquerable faith, to preserve their church and nation. Prophecy reached its height with Amos, Hosea, and Isaiah, and then gradually lost its power. In the New Testament there are books written in a modern and mature language, under the Roman Empire. In twelve hundred years there had been brought together folk-songs, legends and myths, histories based on contemporary records, great bodies of laws reflecting important changes in civilization, highly developed schemes of liturgy and ecclesiastical law, proverbs, psalms, soaring prophecies, mystical visions, the "simple, everlasting stories and teachings of the gospels, the fiery and soaring arguments of St. Paul."

This varied literature reflects a long series of changes of thought, of government, of social condition; it was the product of men of many diverse types of spirit; it was Oriental, and came from the same civilization as the "Arabian Nights;" and yet the poetry throughout, unlike most Oriental poetry, is marked by the most extreme concreteness and objectivity of idea and of form; the books of wisdom never reason, in the modern sense of the word; the "religious ideas develop without any break which could make the pious Jew of the fourth century B.C. feel himself cut loose from ancestors of the tenth or fifteenth century B.C., whose religion and worship had close kinship to those of other desert tribes."

The seeds of this unity were sown in Old Testament times, in the gradual advance of the Jews to higher ideas of the nature of Jehovah; a definite, growing purpose directed the selection and molding of the material which went into the books of history. When the Bible finally took form, it reflected the background, the constantly changing conditions, the soil and sky and occupation, temperament and character, as clearly as the other great literatures reflect all the conditions, internal and external, of the peoples who created them; it was saturated with human nature from beginning to end, and it is primarily a revelation of man because its disclosure of God is made through its disclosure of the nature, the spiritual history and destiny of man.

This literature, not let down from heaven like the Koran, but growing out of the soil of human life, has wonderful unity not only of fundamental ideas, but of manner and style. It is as unlike all other Oriental literature in form as in idea. A large part of it is in narrative form, and is stamped throughout with "a simplicity and a limpid and vivid clearness which make it appeal to all sorts and conditions of men," while throughout its whole range it has "an undercurrent of earnestness and strong feeling;" the first qualities clothing even homely events with beauty and spiritual power, the second crystallizing deep feeling in strong rhythm and varied music. The characteristics of the poetry are concreteness and objectivity, with powerful rhythm and rich coloring of style. "The unsurpassed vividness of the Hebrew poetry and its unfailing hold on our imagination may be ascribed to this fact, that it always expressed emotions directly and concretely through sensations instead of describing them by words which are abstract and therefore pale. . . . Thus a literature which is able to express itself through these unalterable sensations has a permanence of power impossible to any literature which is phrased largely in abstractions and in inferences from these sensations."

The Wisdom books stand out from other writings of their class by reason of direct intuition instead of abstract reasoning, of telling terseness, and of commanding insight into human nature. In the Gospels there is the same vivid objectivity; the discourses of Christ deal with the solid facts of existence; secondary causes are never mentioned; "God watches over the sparrow just as he created the universe and established laws and ordinances for men to obey." St. Paul introduces a new manner and style, and often uses the methods of the abstract reasoner, but he sets forth new truths in the terms of the history of Israel. The prophecies, the most characteristic writings of the Hebrews, show the same grasp of solid fact, with profound seriousness and nobility of imagination; they are "phrased in the words of the things which men can see and hear and feel, but they are filled with the palpable breath of the things which lie beyond our present capacity to understand."

No one who does not know other literatures, and especially other Oriental literatures, can appreciate the extraordinary difference of note between the Bible and other literatures; its quiet, apparently unconscious assumption of authority, its definite and unhesitating attitude of command, its direct statement without any attempt to buttress its position by abstract reasoning, its simple narrative of unprecedented experiences and unusual events as if they were matters of common knowledge, its freedom from abstract statement, its marvelous concreteness. It habitually wears the air and uses the speech of revelation; it never explains, justifies, reasons; it is throughout a literature of intuition, insight, and vision anchored solidly in human experience and vitally bound up with historical events. It is, above all other books, the Book of Life, not only because it deals with the ultimate things of the soul, but because it is the book of the life of a race; bone of its bone and blood of its blood in its substance, but soaring far above the reach of its highest experiences in its revelation of God to man and of man to himself.

❀

# The Spectator

The Spectator recently made a winter trip in western New England. Together with a friend he traveled for the most part by trolley through a region where it will soon be possible to cover in that manner the entire route they took. This route ran from one State into two others, then back again and nearly across the first, continuing into a fourth by steam-cars the portion that in another year will be used entirely by trolley. It is not a densely inhabited region, according to the standard of the seaboard a hundred miles or so to the eastward. The possibilities of traffic would hardly justify a development of trolley lines to that extent by various local companies. These lines, however, were part of a great unified electric railway system, comprising both local and interurban features—a service made possible under the sagacious policy of one of the great steam railway companies of the country. This company has planned a vast secondary system of electric railways—"light railways," they call them in England. These braid themselves, so to speak, along the principal steam lines, and, at various points of vantage, radiate off into the more strictly rural regions. In this way the company is developing profitable new feeders for its main lines of traffic while providing its tributary communities with facilities for cheap and frequent intercommunication to an extent that would hardly be possible without the enormous financial resources of a giant corporation that operates on a great scale and plans with corresponding comprehensiveness.

❀

The Spectator and his companion had a deal of ground to cover in a limited time. So they particularly appreciated the frequency and regularity of the trolley-car movements. Indeed, their programme could otherwise hardly have been carried out, except by means of costly requisitions upon livery stables, entailing at least twice the time upon the road, and, in the frigid temperature of those days, with almost unbearable discomfort.

❀

Rural trolleying is a favorite summer-time diversion. But the city dwellers are few who know what it is to traverse a midwinter countryside by electric cars. Therefore they little realize how remarkable are the sociological changes that now are diffusing throughout whole counties and even larger sections the qualities of neighborliness lately limited to villages. Under the influence of institutions like the trolley, the rural free delivery of mails, the public library, the good roads movement, the automobile, and the telephone, the traditional stagnation of country life in New England has already very largely been dissipated. One notes an alertness of action and speech, a vivacity of manner, that from a social point of view seem highly significant. Little is seen of the yokel, the bumpkin, the "jay," in the regions touched by these enlightening institutions.

❀

In certain up-to-date modern developments the rural regions where these innovating things are to be found—either some or all of them—have the advantage of the great cities. In domestic circumstances "modern conveniences" have long been as characteristic of the country as of the city. In the more recent aspects of them, indeed, the large cities have suffered from the conservatism, the inertia, that makes addiction to the less desirable things a fixed habit. For instance, the country people and the residents of the smaller towns have very largely replaced malodorous kerosene by the cheerful, wholesome, and convenient electric light. But in their dwellings the greater portion of the residents of the larger cities still suffer under the infliction of the unhygienic gaslight. Likewise in their electric railway services the rural regions, the towns, and the minor cities have the advantage of metropolitan communities. In the winter the festal-seeming open car of the summer excursionist is replaced by something quite superior to the ordinary "box car" of the city. The electric car designed for rural and interurban service might be described as a sort of adolescent steam railway coach, with all the conveniences of the latter and some points decidedly in its favor—as in the excellent illumination and the electric heating.

❀

In the quietness, the snowy hush, of the midwinter landscape, the Spectator remarked an effect of snugness. Perhaps this came from the long strips of habitancy compressed between the great hills. With all their cold austerity, the hills—their rank almost that of mountains—had a brooding protectiveness of aspect; their huge uplifted solitudes made the valleys beneath seem all the more sociable. The feeling of snugness, of coziness, was also doubtless due to the service of the mountains in breaking the sweep of the winds. Snugness is incompatible with a raging wind. At such times a warm and tight-walled house may seem cozy; but a neighborhood, a stretch of countryside, never. Above on the uplands lay the "hill towns." How the winds must bluster up there! The late Charles Dudley Warner, born and bred in one of those towns, once told the Spectator that as a boy he felt the winter cold so intensely that he never got over the misery of it; the memory of that vast bleakness always made him shiver; he was glad enough to get away from those dreadful hill-top winters. Still, it was there that he had the supreme pleasure of "Being a Boy," that, reflected in his genial. summer-souled nature, has given a kindred delight to many hundreds whose boyhood remains beneath their husks of age.

❀

Throughout those days of winter trolleying the temperature kept well below zero. But in the valleys the keen air was dry, was bright with sunshine, and the cars were comfortably warm. The windows were densely frosted; for all that, could be seen through them, they might as well have been of ground glass. The most diligent scraping of the panes would have availed nothing. The frosted surface would have restored itself as quickly as the intrusive tide that returned upon each expulsive sweep of Dame Partington's broom. But one of the chief desires of the Spectator and his friend in their rural trolley-faring was to enjoy the landscape in its unfamiliar aspects. Fortunately, the Spectator had noted in advance the frosting of the windows. So he took the precaution of purchasing at a corner druggist's just before starting a dime's worth of glycerine. Its application proved a great success. Glycerine does not freeze or evaporate. Hence a little of it rubbed over the window-glass with some soft paper acted like magic. At first the glycerine was viscid. But the congealed humidity diluted it, and the frost coating vanished like magic, leaving a clear field for the vision. A little renewal now and then easily kept the landscape visible. The Spectator would have been pleased to pass his bottle around among his fellow-passengers, but these seemed to take no particular interest in the scenery. Doubtless it was all too familiar in their eyes. The glycerine proved a good investment. At the end of the three days there was still left at least seven and a half cents' worth.

❀

The Spectator found much and varied interest in those sections of four States—a scrap of New York besides portions of Massachusetts, Vermont, and Connecticut. He enjoyed contrasts of repeated transitions from brisk and sizable cities, with theaters and excellent hotels, into a rugged wilderness of mountains and woodlands; animated factory villages; reposing farmsteads; and the park-like domains and palatial country homes of multi-millionaires, snow-muffled and slumbrously awaiting the summer. There was also the historic interest: a famous revolutionary battlefield, with its imposing monumental shaft, a celebrated seat of learning nobly environed, the homes of poets classic in American literature—a region beloved by artists and rich in associations of song and story.

# THE NEXT PRESIDENT

## BY JOHN CALLAN O'LAUGHLIN

Correspondent of the Chicago Tribune

### SECOND PAPER

# DEMOCRATIC POSSIBILITIES

IT would take the seventh son of a seventh son to predict the nominee of the Republican party in the next Presidential campaign, but descent from a soothsayer is not necessary to forecast the man who will be selected by the Democratic party to lead it in that Titanic political struggle. William Jennings Bryan, of Nebraska, a little tarnished in the eyes of the South by the celebrated Government ownership speech he delivered at New York upon his return from a tour of the world, is the sole hope of the demoralized Democracy. He is a political phœnix soaring above the ashes of his free silver and anti-imperialistic theories. He has enjoyed the doubtful satisfaction of seeing a Republican President put into force the very principles for which he strenuously fought—National regulation of railways and prosecution of the trusts. He has been unfortunate in being ahead of the times, enunciating principles which the people at first failed to understand and approved only after education gave them light. Government ownership of railways may or may not come in the future; its fate will depend, without doubt, entirely upon the results of the enforcement of the new Inter-State Commerce Law. But Government ownership is not to-day a question of practical politics. The South has repudiated it. Its support would split the Democratic party. Were it not for the declaration he made in its behalf, Mr. Bryan would stand squarely before the people on old-line issues—greater control of the money power, which includes revision of the tariff, suppression of monopolies, and regulation of railways; preservation of State rights, honesty and economy in Federal administration, adoption of an income tax, etc. And some of these questions will be the prime issues of the Presidential campaign.

The Democratic party is suffering from sterility both in Presidential possibilities and campaign issues. Time and again I have heard prominent Democrats bemoan the fact that the Republicans were stealing their thunder. Take, for example, the tariff. They would like nothing better than to make the question of revision the paramount issue of the campaign. Yet the Republicans themselves, warned by the defeat of Congressman McCleary in Minnesota and the reduction in the vote of Congressman Dalzell of Pennsylvania, and others, are paving the way to a declaration in their platform that the Congress elected simultaneously with the President shall alter all those schedules which no longer benefit the people. Of course if Speaker Cannon be the nominee, the platform will contain no such declaration, or, if it does refer to revision, it will be in the same vague language as the plank of 1904. In such event the Democrats will be able to force a clean-cut fight on this issue. But if, on the other hand, a pledge for revision is made, and Secretary Taft or Secretary Root nominated, the Democrats must content themselves with observing their usual negative tactics, pointing to the non-fulfillment of the promise of 1904 and asking the people if it would not be the part of wisdom and prudence to confide the duty of revision to the party which consistently has urged it rather than to the party which upholds protection and would be

3

reluctant to modify even a few of the schedules which bear onerously upon the workingmen. The Democrats always have contended that the tariff is the "mother of trusts," and they assert that the remedies they have devised are the only certain cures for this great evil and the equally serious ones which it has produced. They ask, Who is there in the Republican ranks, outside of President Roosevelt, more thoroughly equipped to apply these remedies than Mr. Bryan? President Roosevelt has prosecuted the Standard Oil Trust, the Tobacco Trust, the Sugar Trust, the Paper Trust, the Turpentine Trust, and other combinations of capital. But the people have gained no advantage thereby; there has been no decrease in the cost of living, rather has there been an increase and a large one ; and the trusts have continued to flourish. A few years ago the President dissolved the Northern Securities Company, which controlled the Great Northern and Northern Pacific Railways. But is there any shipper in the region penetrated by these lines who does not know that the two roads are in as close agreement as to rates as they were before the Northern Securities Company was destroyed? And has not the Inter-State Commerce Commission been compelled to take notice of the situation and institute a new investigation? Did the dissolution of the Northern Securities Company cause E. H. Harriman to hesitate a moment in acquiring control of the Southern Pacific Railroad and various other railway and steamship lines so as to stop competition with and round out the Union Pacific system?

These are some of the questions in which the Democrats hope to interest the people; but, unfortunately from their point of view, a Republican President is doing all he can to settle them. They may claim that what he has done and is doing is inadequate; they will say that unless a Roosevelt succeed the Roosevelt now in power, the work of correction will fail and end; that additional remedies, which a Republican Congress will not authorize, besides the man, are necessary. Mr. Bryan, they say, is as strong in his way as Mr. Roosevelt in his, and would

compel the Democrats to grant him authority, as the President has forced the Republicans to give it to him.

But, after all, there is general appreciation in Democratic ranks of the fact that the President has strengthened considerably the position of the Republican party with respect to the trusts and railways, and no direct issue along this line can be created. Both parties will pledge themselves to correct the evils, the Republicans pointing to what they have done as an indication of what they will do, the Democrats relying upon promise and the efforts they have made to force the Republicans to observe the Anti-Trust Law. Something new is imperatively demanded. There has been a good deal of flirting during the Fifty-ninth Congress with the question of State rights. Usurpation by the Executive of the power of the States has been denounced in Congress, and the speeches have been sent broadcast over the land. But this issue is less Republican than Rooseveltian. Secretary of State Root made a speech in New York wherein he intended, so he says, merely to point out the dangers of centralization, but the Democrats will use it to convince the people that the Republican party is determined to override State rights. They conveniently overlook the fact that their support enabled the Administration to force the passage by Congress of the Railroad Rate Regulation Act, the Meat Inspection Act, and the Pure Food Act. All of these laws confide to the General Government greater power in connection with State affairs than ever has been granted in the past. To the disinterested observer it looks as though both parties were tarred with the same brush. While not in Congress, Mr. Bryan indorsed these measures and expressed regret at their inadequacy.

It is the hope of Democracy that fortune will cast an issue—a live issue—into its lap. It criticises John Sharp Williams, the minority leader in the House of Representatives, because he has failed to put the Republican party so palpably in an awkward position that the people would seek a change of masters. It finds fault with its representatives in the Senate and House who lacked the ability and the generalship to make campaign material out of the Railroad Rate Law, which was of Democratic origin. They had hoped for a scandal in connection with the construction of the Panama Canal. No scandal has yet developed. " Perhaps something underhand will be discovered before the election," was the hopeful observation of one Democratic leader.

It has been truly said that an issue is nothing without the man. Here again the Democrats are at a loss save for Mr. Bryan. It is almost pitiful to hear the leaders discuss the possibilities and then say with a sigh that Bryan is their only hope; they admit that he is not forcing himself upon them, that the logic of conditions is doing so. But I think Mr. Bryan is making the conditions logical. He is keeping himself before the people in every possible way, by speeches, by lectures, by letters, and by journalistic work of a spectacular character. His tour of the world was a good example of his methods. Before he started he arranged with a syndicate of papers throughout the country to publish his articles. I need not call attention to the character of his work, for that would be to precipitate controversy and perhaps call forth further criticism of Mr. Bryan's views, say from the English in India, who object to the way he wrote about Indian affairs. But it can be said for Mr. Bryan that he has been received by every ruler of Europe and the East; that he pleased the German Emperor immensely; that the Czar was delighted to have the opportunity to talk with such a man of affairs as the American statesman; that he charmed the King of England by his straightforwardness and simplicity; and that the speeches he made abroad were models of good taste and oratorical merit. In only one instance do I recall that he offended a foreign ruler, and that was President Loubet, of France. The interview he had with the President was reproduced in the New York American without the consent and to the great indignation of the French Executive. It was true that Mr. Bryan did not write the interview, but the American correspondent who was present, and who heard every word ex-

changed by the President and Mr. Bryan, did. At that time Mr. Bryan was being exploited by The American in anticipation of the coming Presidential campaign. It was all well enough to advertise Mr. Bryan, but it was in bad taste, to say the least, to violate the confidence of the head of the French Republic in order to do so.

There is not the slightest question that had Mr. Bryan remained abroad a year longer than he did, and when he came back delivered an innocuous speech, he would not only have been nominated, but in all probability elected. He appeals to the people far more than does any other possibility in the Democratic ranks or in the Republican party. But Mr. Bryan is stung by the consciousness that he made a tactical blunder in advocating Government ownership of railways when the country was not in the mood to listen to anything of the kind. The Republican party is squarely against Government ownership; it proposes to use Mr. Bryan's declaration as a bomb to destroy him should he be nominated. And yet Mr. Roosevelt, while insisting that Government ownership would be ruinous, contemplates further steps in railway regulation which will lead the Government nearer and nearer to the solution Mr. Bryan proposed. There is not a prominent Democratic leader, outside of Mr. Bryan himself, who believes that the time is ripe for advocacy of Government ownership. With the people, I am not so sure; at least they are tolerant. Since Mr. Bryan spoke in New York I have been in close touch with various sections of the country, and it is certain that the Nebraskan has lost nothing in the way of popularity. Wherever he has appeared he has been welcomed enthusiastically. In the South, politicians were inclined to treat him coolly because of his Government ownership speech; but public sentiment compelled them to shower him with attentions. Mr. Bryan has conciliated these men by declaring that his Government ownership views were individual and were not intended to bind the party or any other Democrat. He has not pledged himself to secure their incorporation into public law. In this matter he has responded to pressure with gratifying promptness and given hope to his friends that the obstinacy which in the past has marked his clinging to unattainable principles has been tempered by the winds of political adversity.

If Mr. Bryan wants the support of money—and what political candidate does not?—he must make it clear to the holders of this most important vote-getter that his Government ownership ideas will continue to remain his personal and not become his official views. I was talking the other day with a prominent Southern Democrat who believed firmly that the South would resent any attempt on the part of Mr. Bryan to secure the realization of his latest dream. The South has displayed in the past a most unselfish attitude with respect to the Presidency. It has been willing to support any one who seemed acceptable to the North and West. Bryan appealed to it in 1896 and again in 1900, and on both occasions it cast a solid vote for the Nebraska nominee. It was true to Judge Parker, with a single exception, in 1904. That exception was Missouri, which in 1900 gave Mr. Bryan a plurality of 37,831 and four years later put itself in the Roosevelt column by the substantial plurality of 25,137. To show the National popularity of Bryan over Parker it is only necessary to recall that the former received in 1900 1,350,000 votes more than Judge Parker did in 1904.

What makes Mr. Bryan's chances for the nomination the stronger is the fact that so many Democratic State conventions either have indorsed him or made complimentary references to his candidacy in resolutions they adopted. Of course it does not necessarily follow that the Democrats of the States in which these conventions were held must heed the expression. At the same time it is recognized that it will have a moral effect that should not be discounted upon the conventions that will meet next year to select delegates to the National Democratic Convention. The States which have indorsed Mr. Bryan or approved his candidacy since the last campaign are: Massachusetts, New York, Pennsylvania, and Delaware in the East; North Carolina, Arkansas, and Texas in the South; Indiana, Ohio, Illinois, Iowa, and Michigan in the Middle West; Wisconsin, North Dakota, South Dakota, Wyoming, Idaho, Montana, Utah, and Washington in the Northwest; and Nebraska, Colorado, and California in the Far West. New Mexico and Hawaii, two of the Territories, also have indorsed Mr. Bryan. This means that the Nebraskan already has pledged to his support twenty-three of the forty-six States of the Union. There are nine Southern States, besides those named, which unquestionably will instruct for his nomination. It is planned to have the New England States send uninstructed delegates to the Convention. Of course they will be expected to vote for Mr. Bryan. Mr. Hearst is organizing in the West, ostensibly intending to hold various State delegations for the Nebraskan. With Mr. Bryan so far in the lead, one hears rarely the name of any other Democrat mentioned for the nomination. Rather is heard a remark like this: " Well, at least Bryan is fundamentally a Democrat. We regret his vagaries, but at bottom he is all right." Or like this: " If Bryan should be defeated, he is the best man in the party to gloat over the result." Or like this: " If Bryan had been nominated in 1904, the Democrats would have stood a better chance of success. Looking back to that campaign, we doubt our own sanity in nominating Parker."

In spite of the strong grip of Mr. Bryan, there is no doubt that, if many of the political leaders could have their way, he would be put aside for one who in their opinion would be a stronger candidate. One Southern Democrat suggested the other day that an ideal ticket would be Judge George Gray, of Delaware, and Senator Charles A. Culberson, of Texas. Judge Gray is an admirable figure in American public life. That will be conceded both by Republicans and Democrats. For fourteen years he was a United States Senator. He served on the important committees of Foreign Relations and Judiciary. He affiliated with the Gold Democrats in 1896, and would appeal to the conservative financial interests. Just as he opposed Bryan on the silver issue, so he fought him on the question of territorial expansion—a question settled by the campaign of 1900, when it was Bryan's chief issue. He accepted an appointment as member of the Peace Commission which in Paris in 1898 negotiated the treaty with Spain whereby the independence of Cuba was secured and the United States acquired Porto Rico, Guam, and the Philippines. He is a member of the International Permanent Court of Arbitration under the Hague Convention, and has an international status which Bryan has been seeking. He was made a Judge of the United States Circuit Court of the Third Judicial Circuit in 1899. He would appeal to labor by reason of his memorable service as Chairman of the Anthracite Coal Commission which settled the serious dispute between the miners and operators of Pennsylvania in 1902. Of course Judge Gray is not as oratorical or as spectacular as is Mr. Bryan; but then it is certain that the Democratic candidate will not have a spectacular opponent, as Mr. Parker did in 1904. There would be many Democrats who would be disappointed should the Convention fail to put Bryan at the head of the ticket. But if the Nebraskan, unselfishly sinking personal ambition, should loyally support Judge Gray, the latter's chances for success would be excellent. Unfortunately, Mr. Bryan has gotten to the point where he feels that the Democratic party to win must win with him. He knows that if any other Democrat were to be placed in the White House, his chance of occupying it for four years would be slim. It is true that, if Judge Gray were elected, the Democrats could not expect the country to give him a second term. Judge Gray is only four years younger than Speaker Cannon. In 1909 he will be sixty-nine years of age. In 1913 he will be seventy-three, and it is hardly to be expected that his physical condition, taking into consideration the serious burden of the Presidency, would be such as to permit him to give that clear, sound, forceful attention to the Nation's affairs which the people and events would require. Mr. Bryan is twenty years younger than Judge Gray, and but for his fear of being eclipsed could afford to accept the Delaware statesman for the campaign of 1908, should a situa-

tion arise compelling it. Senator Culberson, of Texas, who has been mentioned as a running mate for Judge Gray, would arouse the South. He is an Alabamian by birth, a Virginian by education, and a Texan by adoption. His father was a member of Congress for twenty-two years. He himself served as Attorney-General and Governor of Texas, and since 1899 has occupied a seat in the Senate. He is a man of good judgment, sane and conservative, very different in temperament from his colleague, Senator Joseph Weldon Bailey, whose connection with Standard Oil companies has caused him such grave embarrassment in his Senatorial election. There is no question as to the ability of Senator Bailey. He is an orator of the first class. He is a Constitutional lawyer who ranks with Spooner and Foraker, of the Republican party. He has been the undisputed leader of the Democrats in the Senate since the death of Arthur Pue Gorman, of Maryland. Senator Bailey did some devious things in connection with the Railroad Rate Bill when it was pending in the Senate during the first session of the Fifty-ninth Congress. It was asserted that he and Senator Aldrich, of Rhode Island, understood each other, and that at the last moment a provision was to be slipped into the Railroad Rate Bill which would make the measure more acceptable to the railway interests. This talk, vague at first, became more pronounced as the session proceeded, and, followed as it has been by the public allegation that Bailey received money from one of the subsidiary concerns of the Standard Oil corporation, it definitely and finally removed the Texan Senator from all consideration as a Presidential possibility. It would not be at all surprising should Senator Bailey find his political actions looked on with suspicion in the future, and it is not likely that he will have the influence he has enjoyed in the past.

There is an occasional suggestion that Richard Olney, of Massachusetts, should be nominated by the Democratic Convention. Mr. Olney was Attorney-General and Secretary of State in the Cabinet of President Cleveland. One hears his voice occasionally raised in discussion of public policies or principles, his last utterance of this character being directed against the Japanese policy of President Roosevelt. Mr. Olney, like all other Democratic aspirants for office, is an ardent believer in States' rights. He supported this principle when he said that the Federal Government had no right to interfere in the school affairs of a State. But the expressions of Mr. Olney cannot be taken as evidence of any desire on his part to act as the standard-bearer of the Democratic party in the next campaign. The objection of age which has been made to Speaker Cannon would apply with greater force to Mr. Olney, because the latter is one year older than the presiding officer of the House of Representatives. Moreover, Mr. Olney pursued a policy in the Chicago labor trouble of a decade ago which would lose him the support of labor. To put it in the colloquial language of another one of the Democratic Presidential possibilities, " Olney is smudged with Clevelandism." It must be said, however, that, objectionable as Mr. Olney is to the Democratic leaders, his chance must be rated as better than that of Judge Parker. Probably neither will be mentioned in the next Democratic Convention.

The paths of many Presidential aspirants usually are as untraceable upon the political firmament as last year's comets upon the celestial horizon. Judge Parker could not to-day add a vote to or subtract a vote from any one who might be selected as the candidate of the Democratic party. It is no secret to those who were at the Democratic Convention in 1904 that Mr. Parker never was Mr. Bryan's candidate. In the last three hours of the Convention it became with Mr. Bryan " anybody to beat Judge Parker." Mr. Bryan made a determined effort to induce Joseph W. Folk, Governor of Missouri, but better known for his vigorous prosecution of St. Louis boodlers, to permit him to present his, Folk's, name to the Convention. If Mr. Bryan by any chance should fail to get the nomination in 1908, the probability is that he would use his influence in behalf of Governor Folk. There are two opinions as to Governor Folk's availability. He is not popular with the politicians

with whom he comes in contact. They recognize his intellectual force. He has some of the traits of President Roosevelt. He has a singleness of purpose which knows no modification until the result has been achieved. Unlike Mr. Roosevelt, he is not a man of varied interests. He does not write upon or discuss art, literature, or anything other than the subjects which directly concern his public duties. One Democrat of great influence said that he was nothing more than a public prosecutor. So at first was Mr. Cleveland. Mr. Folk stepped from the Circuit Attorneyship to the Governor's chair ; Mr. Cleveland became Mayor of Buffalo after his service as Assistant District Attorney and Sheriff, and then was elected Governor. As Governor Mr. Folk has done good work in " put ting on the lid." The saloons and racetracks have felt his hand, and the bucketshops are trembling. He is pushing a two-cent-per-mile railway fare. He has beaten every old-line politician in Missouri. He is not strictly Presidential timber, but he is a man, and he appeals to the people. He is said to have more of a reputation outside his State than he has in it. And yet he was elected Governor by a plurality of 30,000 at the time Roosevelt swept the State for President with a plurality of 25,000. It is said that Kansas would vote for him as enthusiastically as for Mr. Bryan. The South would back him strongly because he would be regarded by that section as a Southern candidate. He was born in Tennessee, and educated and married in that State. To labor throughout the country he is practically unknown. In spite of Governor Folk's achievements in Missouri, he will not be indorsed for the Presidency by that State. Mr. Bryan has been and still is the idol of Missouri. If a proposition now pending in the Missouri Legislature be made into law—and the chances are that it will be—there will be no possibility for a cut-and dried indorsement of Mr. Bryan or Mr. Folk or anybody else. The proposition contemplates the selection of delegates to the Convention by the direct vote of the people themselves. Governor Folk had recommended primaries for certain offices, but Senator Stone, who is one of his most ardent enemies, went still further and suggested that the primaries apply to all offices. The Governor has accepted Senator Stone's suggestion, and the probability is that it will be enacted into law. The people will then be called upon to vote at the proper time for Bryan delegates or Folk delegates. It is suggested that some division in the Missouri delegation will follow, and that either Mr. Bryan or Governor Folk will have to give way when the nomination is made.

Before I give in some detail the status politically of William Randolph Hearst, a really strong factor in Presidential politics in spite of his New York defeat, it seems desirable to dispose of the only remaining Southerner who has been suggested as a possibility. · I refer to John Sharp Williams, of Mississippi. As leader of the minority in the House of Representatives, Mr. Williams has done better work than his fellow-Democrats appreciate. He has been criticised for not being aggressive, but the votes at his command were not sufficient in number to enable him to wage a forceful campaign. An abortive attempt against his rule was made in the interest of Congressman Champ Clark, of Missouri. Mr. Clark disavowed any connection with the conspiracy, and ended the well-meant efforts of his friends by the statement that so long as Mr. Williams wanted the minority leadership he would be content to serve as one of his followers. Mr. Williams could get the support of many Democrats if he chose to scramble for the nomination. But he really and truly does not want it. He says modestly that he is not fitted for the Presidency, and he says it in a way that carries conviction. His aspirations are Senatorial, and he expects to be nominated and elected to the Upper House to succeed Senator Money.

Now as to William Randolph Hearst. Immediately after the election in New York last November, when it was established that the newspaper candidate had been beaten by more than fifty thousand votes, there were few men in the country willing to predict that he would have a chance for the Presidential nomination. Everybody who knows Mr. Hearst knows that he has only one ambition. That is

to be President. He has been willing to accept any other office, nay, to struggle for it, if he believed it would advance him a single step toward the goal upon which he has fixed his eyes. Mr. Hearst cares nothing for the Democratic party, as was shown by his willingness to wreck it to aid him in the achievement of his personal ambition. He formed the Independence League, and in New York used it as a lever to secure the nomination of the Democratic Convention at Buffalo for the Governorship of New York. Having put his foot upon a sounder plank, he was willing to let the Independence League flounder upon the rough sea upon which he had shipped it. He has denounced the "robber tariff," and yet, in a speech to farmers in upper New York, he favored protection. He has done splendid work in aiding the Government to prosecute the trusts, and yet the Hearst estate is proven to have underwritten the tobacco and other monopolies. He has denounced Chinese labor, but the Hearst estate in California has employed it.

If Mr. Hearst runs at all as a Presidential candidate, the chances are that it will be as an independent. He cannot hope to force the National Democratic party to make him its standard-bearer as he forced the New York Democracy to name him as its candidate. In the first place, rich as Mr. Hearst is, he has not money enough to accomplish this result, even if he wanted to do so. He admits having spent more than a quarter of a million dollars in his New York campaign, but competent politicians place his expenditure at nearer a million, basing this estimate upon information that he disbursed $600,000 in the organization of the Independence League in Illinois. Mr. Hearst has an Independence League in San Francisco, and its participation in the campaign resulted in the defeat of the Democratic ticket and the success of the Republican candidates. Friends of Mr. Hearst say that he would make a better running in a National campaign than he did in New York. They point to the fact that he is a rich man and can desire no more money; that his chain of newspapers make him a power to be reckoned with if he wanted power alone. But he does believe, they claim, that if he occupied the office of President he would be able to ameliorate the lot of the people to a far greater extent than any one else. He was defeated in New York, they allege, by his bitter enemy Senator McCarren, the Tammany leader in Brooklyn, who gave instructions to his followers to knife the head of the Democratic ticket. In spite of the fact that Mr. Hearst has denounced Mr. Taggart, Chairman of the Democratic National Committee, and other prominent Democratic leaders, he does not believe that they could effect his defeat if he were the Presidential candidate of the Democracy, as he believes Senator McCarren did in New York.

Mr. Hearst is a study in inconsistency. His treatment of Charles Murphy, the Tammany boss, shows his entire willingness to embrace to-day, for political purposes, a man whom he denounced a year ago as a fit subject for the penitentiary. If Mr. Taggart made overtures to Mr. Hearst, and would aid him in his Presidential aspirations, the New York American and other Hearst papers would, it is highly probable, cease editorial denunciation of the Indianian and cheerfully sing his praises. It is apparent from this that Mr. Hearst's principal enemies are those who dare to clash with his ambition. This brings up the question of Mr. Hearst's real feeling for Mr. Bryan. Mr. Hearst may find it expedient to declare for Mr. Bryan. If he does, the people of the country may as well understand that he does so simply because he believes he must. If he could overcome Mr. Bryan's tremendous popularity among the Democrats by some such manipulation as he practiced in New York, many of Mr. Bryan's best friends believe that he would do it.

Summing up the men and issues of the prospective Democratic campaign, it is not difficult to see whither the tide of affairs is drifting. Judge Gray would be classed among the Democrats as an ultra-conservative, of somewhat the same rank as Mr. Fairbanks and Mr. Cannon of the Republican party. Governor Folk would be accepted as an anti-corruptionist rather than as an advocate of great principles. Mr. Hearst would be looked upon as peculiarly the representative of discontent. Mr. Bryan takes place between Mr. Gray and Mr. Hearst, now that he has abandoned his advocacy of Government ownership of railways. The glaring radicalism of Mr. Hearst has benefited Mr. Bryan in making his radicalism seem conservative.

# DESECRATION

## BY HAROLD TROWBRIDGE PULSIFER

The solitary stillness of the wood,
The long deep silence of the morning calm,
The melody that nature understood,
When all the world lay cradled in His arm;
The solemn incense of the fragrant pine,
The half-heard music of a hidden choir,
The rhythm of a chant almost divine,
Sung underneath the starry altar-fire,
Has ended in the sullen sounding blows
Of crashing steel along the wooded aisle,
In blackened stumps above the winter snows,
In land that has forgotten how to smile;
A desert where the north wind sighing sweeps
Above the tomb in which the forest sleeps.

# EDWARD EVERETT HALE: A PRACTICAL IDEALIST.

## BY EDWARD EVERETT HALE, JR.

TO speak as a literary critic on the works of one's father offers a chance for much that is unbecoming. That chance comes to me sometimes in college classes, and I generally escape it by leaving the seat of judgment and becoming a historian. It does not seem just the thing for me to tell a class of college men that "The Man Without a Country" is one of the finest of our American short stories, or that it is not, but I can usually tell the fellows something about the way it came to be what it is. One does not have to lecture on the story to make them feel it, but they like to see that behind the story are a man and a life.

I am modern enough as a critic to believe that the literary work of a man who writes sincerely and readily for a good many years is a pretty fair index to his character. Doubtless the study of literature as the expression of personal character, or national, is not the only thing, but it is one of the elements of a useful criticism. And I often find in my studies of literature things that exhibit my father's character and interests and life as I remember them, or rather as they have left their impression on me in the many years that we have been intimate.

In his short stories the especial quality is a mixture of realism and phantasy. Whatever be its practical character, his best literary work always presents some idea that is curious, extravagant, quaint, impossible, strange, romantic, or something of the kind. His first striking story was of a clergyman who had a hired man who looked exactly like him, and whom he used to send in his place to all sorts of stupid public occasions, so that he himself could pursue quietly the really important things of life. His next story was of a man who had once wished he had no country, and who was forthwith put on board ship and kept for life

out of sight and hearing of the country he had had. "Ten Times One is Ten" represents the conversion of the world by a scheme that renders possible the wildest combinations of geography and ethnology. "In His Name" has the charm of romantic mediævalism. "The Brick Moon," "Crusoe in New York," are clearly by their very titles works of the fancy. So are half a hundred other of his writings at bottom; that is to say, in the means by which he chose to carry out what was not infrequently a serious purpose. There is a tradition that he used to say that a story was "substantially done" when he had thought what it was to be about. To his mind it was, for it had only to be written.

This writing, however, was not fanciful at all. It was very realistic. If his ideas were, as he said of something else, thoroughly absurd, they were also thoroughly practical. Everything, even of the most extraordinary character, had to be not only possible but plausible. These strange things, it appeared, had generally happened to intimate friends of his, or perhaps to people whom he knew personally. If not that, he had heard of them by word of mouth or read some mention of them in the newspapers. In fact, he used to assume that the reader was acquainted in some degree with the people concerned, so that he told of the most astonishing impossibilities much as he would have reminded any one of what had happened yesterday.

I do not know when he first read De Foe carefully, but I remember his great interest long since in that master of realism. I have no doubt that he thought him a much greater man than Richardson or Fielding. I never heard him say so, but I do not remember his ever speaking of the authors of "Clarissa" or "Tom Jones," nor were those books in the house. On the other hand, he often spoke with appreciation of

801

De Foe, assuring us that " Colonel Jack " was a fine piece of work, as it certainly is in the direction of interest to him.

This mingling of realism and extravagance was, of course, by no means a peculiarity of my father's. It was a fairly general characteristic of the short story writers of his time and some years before. The two elements are very noteworthy in Hawthorne, though not often mingled in one production. So with Poe, who more often realized the combination, as in " A Descent into the Maelstrom," for instance. " The Man Without a Country " is in this respect all of a piece with " The Diamond Lens " or " One of the Thirty Pieces." In American life, too, there is (or was) this mingling of the imaginative or the ideal or often extravagant fancy, and the realism that is practical and actual. It is not a matter of importance to point it out, but it serves as a way of getting together some of my recollections and impressions of my father, and accommodating them to the time of which he was a characteristic figure. I never try, nor have I ever tried, to form an impartial estimate of his powers. I never consider him or his life or his work from the standpoint of a student. I am always content that he should be a father and friend, seen at very short range, with all the advantages and possible inaccuracies of such seeing. But in spite of this general attitude ideas crystallize in one's mind, and I find this combination of powers, so marked in his writing, to be illustrated by a good deal that I remember in his life.

One thing that every one notices of him is a very wide range of interest which manifests itself in all sorts of ways. He did not like to be limited, sometimes even by fact. He was never entirely content with the realism of his own study, house, church, town ; he wanted larger impressions. Although a devoted Bostonian, yet, as with Burke, nothing less than " whole America "— or, more accurately, the whole world— would really do for him. It was a pleasure to him that wheat grown in Dakota would go and satisfy hunger on the banks of the Ganges. He liked to have to do with outlandish and out-of-the-way people and things. Mr. Cushing and

five Zuñi chiefs once came to our house to lunch. It was a curious sight to see these solemn gentlemen in paint and feathers sitting about in our every-day dining-room, dancing earnestly in the front hall, with uncouth cries, and carrying on religious rites in a circle on the parlor floor in front of the open fire. I am sure my father liked it much better than he would have liked even the Governor, the Bishop, the President of the College, or even more distinguished personages. I am sure we boys did. That dreadful dinner in " His Level Best," where a stray Swede, a Bohemian professor, a Dutch planter from Table Bay, a Japanese prince, Dr. South the minister, and a Brahmin gentleman, one of the first-fruits of the Serampore Mission, all dined with the Boothbys, together with two deaf and dumb dressmakers— that horrible feast never occurred at our house, at least not in my recollection, but that may have been out of regard for my dear mother, whose tastes were more consistently domestic. Still, though such things never really did take place, I'm sure my father would have been much pleased if they had, even if business had called him from the house so that he could not have enjoyed them himself.

Strictly speaking, perhaps, all this was no extravagance, but a feeling for a larger and more complete knowledge. Even as a boy he had had the same wide range of interest and the desire to get things into practical form. I used rather to wonder at his tales of his youth. We boys, as I recollect, did not have much intelligent curiosity. We were imaginative enough, and played vigorously in the nursery, the green parlor, or out in the yard, in many imaginary worlds of our own creation. But my father's anecdotes of his own childhood always impressed me as being different from our own way of looking at things. He used to try experiments in chemistry in the house in Hamilton Place, made electrical batteries that I believe he read about in " Harry and Lucy," and learned to set type in the printing office of the Advertiser. And it was so through life. His interests ranged widely, and he was curious to understand many things. He liked the sense of the remote and the adventurous; he also, as a rule, wanted to put his impressions and ideas into practical shape.

Whether this feeling for the romantic, the amusing, the extravagant even, were more than desire for flavor I cannot say. But flavor, as we may call it, is an important thing. He wanted life to be interesting. He wanted to know how and what it was, but he wanted it to be interesting. That, I take it, is the key to his historical method. He used often to talk to me of how important it was that a history should be interesting. If it were not interesting, people would not read it, so that it might as well not have been written. So he worked to have his history interesting, full of local color, lifelike. Yet he would often spend endless time in establishing accurately minute points—often far more time than I, who belonged to a more scholastic epoch, could think worth while. I presume there are errors in his historical writing, but they must be chiefly errors of judgment, or errors in matters that he did not consider important, for he certainly was unwearied in research about anything he did consider important. He would often spend a couple of hours and write a dozen letters to determine some very small point that came up in his mind, and if he could not find out at once he would remember it sometimes for years until he met with the person or book that could tell him.

In household affairs he was as characteristic as anywhere else. Thus, when we first went to Matunuck, he had the problem of arranging the household order of seven children between three years and seventeen. He at once conceived a military establishment, which he created and carried on with unwearied spirit and imagination from day to day by general orders which he read at breakfast. The system, though never ground in upon us, served excellently as a means of managing what might readily have become a horde of only slightly civilized savages. It was nothing very remarkable, and lasted only so long as it was needed, but so long it did last, and in its time gave the machinery necessary for carrying on the household, and yet

with a certain imaginative charm that, I fancy, we all appreciated.

We saw more of him at Matunuck than in Roxbury. In the city we had school in the morning, all sorts of occupations in the afternoon, and home lessons in the evening, while he was busy, too, morning, noon, and night, either (mysteriously to our minds) in the study, where we rarely went in earlier days, or at the church or elsewhere downtown. But at Matunuck, although he always had work to do for part of the day, and we often had excursions that took us off the place, yet we were more likely to do things together than in Boston, perhaps partly because there were more things that we could readily do together. He could not play baseball very well (he used to speak of cricket in his boyhood), nor could he well have joined many of our games in Roxbury, even had he had time. But in the summer he was as fond as we were of the woods and fields, the pond and the ocean. Of course, being at that time fifty and over, he enjoyed them in rather a different way. He liked to sketch and botanize, for instance, which in those years we rarely did. I do not remember ever to have seen him fishing, but the other things that we did he used to do, though as we grew older our more violent or vigorous sports had little charm for him. We would run races or play leap-frog on the beach after a bath, but he preferred to sit under the shelter with the other grown-ups, and hold sand congresses that appeared to us very staid.

He liked Matunuck partly because it rescued him from a too rigorous application of the larger life. When we first went there, there was no telegraph or telephone, no railway nearer than seven miles, no mail but four times a week, no friend's house save Mr. Weeden's and the neighboring farmers'. His passion for the ends of the earth, for having things touched by the extravagance of the remote, for having things out of the way and unfamiliar, was only one element in his make-up. He liked to think of such things, and now and then to experiment with them—for he was a great traveler—but he also liked to be at home and follow out his own destiny without being burst in upon by little boys from Dakota or little girls from the Ganges. He liked family occasions; he would look around the table with pleasure and say, "Only those God made here." You can see that, too, in his writings easily enough. The great charm of having a double was that one could live to one's self for a while—to one's self, and one's wife, and one's children. The enormous extravagance of the Brick Moon ends with the note of the charming life at Pigeon Cove—six families only, thirty-seven souls in all, including two babies born that summer, "a little world of our own." "Can it be possible that all human sympathies can thrive, and all human powers be exercised, and all human joys increase, if we live with all our might with the thirty or forty people next to us, telegraphing kindly to all other people, to be sure? Can it be possible that our passion for large cities, and large parties, and large theaters, and large churches, develops no faith nor hope nor love which would not find aliment and exercise in a little world of our own?"

For this breadth of range was also balanced by great sanity and common sense. He was a great philanthropist and great in his work in and with charitable organizations. But he would never have sent blankets to Africa while people were cold at home. He would never have neglected Boston for Borrioboola Gha; in fact, he was practically rather indifferent to Borrioboola Gha. Whether this was because of any thought-out system, or because his practical mind demanded that he should constantly be dealing with actual problems close at hand, I cannot say. He certainly did deal with the problems at hand, and, understanding very clearly that one man could not do everything, he left many problems of "the larger life" to others.

I think, however, that this feeling was often called forth, not by the pressure of the life at hand nor by any weakness of the appeal of far-away interests, but by the readiness with which such larger life drifted into formalism. He was always dead set against the machinery of life as machinery. The worst exaggerations of "His Level Best" and "My Double"

are only hardened, petrified forms of what might once have had vital energy. "Boards are made of wood," he used to say, meaning of course boards of management; "they are long and narrow." So in the beginning of "Ten Times One is Ten," the Harry Wadsworth Club as a formal organization gets no further than a discussion of name, covenant, and constitution. He was a Republican in politics, but I think that at heart he must have had much sympathy with the Jeffersonian view, that that government is best that gets on with as little governing as possible.

One may be curious as to just why formalism and machinery and observance and creed were distasteful to him. They are not in themselves necessarily uninteresting, certainly not to the historian. In religious matters where his feeling was strongest, I do not suppose that he disliked ritual as such. As I remember him, he always preached in a splendid silk gown in a high magnificent pulpit. He always liked to read the psalms responsively, either to Mr. Lang's fine improvisations on the organ opposite, or to the congregation standing up. He had a great love, I am sure, for the beauty of holiness. Why any hatred of formalism? Perhaps for this reason, that when any act has become formal, mechanical, petrified, whoever performs the act is in great danger of performing it to himself and not for another human creature or for the Lord God. And the personal intrusion into what was meant to be something else, that he could not stand. For him selfishness was sin.

He was not much given to analyzing or explaining. But I suppose he held that if a minister says a formal prayer or a formal creed, while he may really get out of himself, he is in great danger of not doing so. So with the secretary of a board for philanthropic activity: he may work as simply as the Lord Jesus worked in Galilee, but he is more than likely not to. And so with any one of the definite and regular forms and observances that are needed to carry on a larger life. One may doubtless do such things and still be genuine and loving and sympathetic—he could be so himself—but there was more than a chance that in the routine one would be bent on carrying out only the regular daily duty, thinking only of finishing up the work and getting off to enjoy one's self. And this sort of selfishness, or indeed any sort, will never do for him, for he really loves other people too much to have any sympathy with that temper which turns from others into self-absorption. He likes people and so is a great believer in human nature. I suppose that is one great reason for his being a Unitarian; not because he would deny the divinity of the Lord Jesus, but because he will not countenance the denial of the divinity of man. The great thing that makes people love him is that he loves them. Men and women are often interesting, but often they are not; they are often very tedious, very exasperating, very disgusting, terrible bores, terrible fools, and terrible wrecks. Still, they have not destroyed his confidence in them, and they never will. He believes in people, as in the people.

I suspect that gets to the bottom of it. He likes to be at Washington now, because he sees all sorts of people from all parts of the country and the world, because he touches life at so many sides or surfaces—a great many, of course, but still he does really touch it, and so lives freshly and genuinely. He likes to have the interests of life fresh—fresh and new and strange and unimagined before. He likes all those things. But then he is a realist; he wants things genuine. And they are genuine, as life always has been to him. That is perhaps the reason why at eighty-five he is as young as his sons or grandsons or great-grandsons.

# *THE IDAHO MURDER TRIAL*

## *BY LUKE GRANT*

FRANK STEUNENBERG, a respected citizen and former Governor of Idaho, was assassinated December 30, 1905. Almost at the threshold of his door he was literally blown to pieces by a bomb placed with such devilish ingenuity that a Russian Anarchist might well shudder at the thought of employing such an agent of destruction.

After more than twelve months' incarceration in an Idaho prison, the alleged murderers are about to be brought to trial. The eyes of the entire country are centered on Idaho. It is no ordinary murder trial. Important issues, some of them without a parallel in the history of the country, are involved. In a degree, the rights and liberties of American citizens are at stake, for the Supreme Court of the United States has in this case, according to the dissenting opinion of one of its own members, virtually legalized the crime of kidnapping, when committed by State officials.

Shall death on the gallows end the career of the leaders of the worst criminal conspiracy that can be conceived, or shall the lives of innocent men be sacrificed in the furtherance of a counter-conspiracy? Is the outcome of the trial to be the dramatic climax of a series of murders planned in wholesale fashion by men of power and influence in the world of labor, or will it result in disclosing a plot on the part of men influential in the world of finance to send to the gallows the leaders of those who have thwarted them in their plans? Those are the questions to be determined by an Idaho jury, and circumstantial evidence is not wanting to show either or both conspiracies.

Will the men be accorded a fair trial? Governor Gooding, of Idaho, says they will. "There is no question about a fair trial," he says. "No higher class of citizens can be found than those who live in Canyon County. They have no prejudice against any class of citizens, be they laborers or capitalists."

"It all depends on the jury," says an attorney for the defense. The same remark might be applied to a murder trial in Boston or New York, but it would not have the same significance.

Throughout the mining districts of the West class lines have been so sharply drawn that justice seems lost sight of. "Hang them on general principles" is the epitome of the feeling on one side, and "Get them off, right or wrong," is the feeling on the other side. The question of the guilt or innocence of the men seems to be incidental. Both sides have helped to create this feeling. The mine-owners and their representatives have been pictured as vultures watching over their prey. On the other hand, the Western Federation of Miners has been pictured as a lawless, anarchistic organization whose leaders have instigated a number of crimes that have shocked civilization.

In order to make clear the situation, it is necessary to take up the story at the beginning. Frank Steunenberg had few known enemies. He was elected Governor of Idaho as a Populist in 1897, largely by the votes of the miners whose accredited leaders are now on trial charged with complicity in his murder. During a strike in the Cœur d'Alene district in 1899 a mill at Wardner was blown up by a mob of union miners. The sheriff of the county sympathized with the strikers and made no effort to bring the ringleaders to justice. Governor Steunenberg was appealed to. The State militia was serving in the Philippines, and President McKinley sent Federal troops to the district. Lawlessness was put down by the most drastic measures. Men were arrested and thrown into a "bull-pen" in hundreds. Others were driven from the district by the military forces. Governor Steunenberg, "the union printer," was held responsible by the miners. The strike was forgotten by all except those directly interested. Other industrial conflicts had arisen between the mine-owners and the miners. Other acts of violence had been committed, and order had again been restored at the point of the bayonet. Steunenberg had returned to private life, and his connection with the strike had apparently been forgotten, when the country was shocked by the news of his assassination. It was a cruel, cold-blooded murder. A bomb had been placed under the gate leading to his residence in a little suburb of Caldwell, and so arranged that the victim in opening the gate fired the infernal machine that blew him into eternity.

The little town of Caldwell was stunned. Governor Gooding and other State officials hurried to Caldwell on a special train. Every train leaving the town was watched and every avenue of escape closely guarded. Harry Orchard was arrested and charged with the crime. He was one of the few men who was not known in the town and who could not give a satisfactory account of himself. A detective named McParland was called into the case. He was known as the man who unearthed the Mollie Maguire conspiracy in Pennsylvania years ago. Orchard is said to have confessed to McParland that he placed the bomb which killed Steunenberg. He said he was assisted by J. L. Simpkins, an organizer for the Western Federation of Miners. Simpkins escaped from the State, and has never been apprehended. In his confession (the details of which have never been fully made known) Orchard implicated Charles H. Moyer, President of the Western Federation of Miners, William D. Haywood, Secretary of the same organization, and George A. Pettibone, a former member of the union, who conducted a store in Denver in which it is alleged the bomb was manufactured.

That Orchard killed Steunenberg is not denied by attorneys for the defense. That much of his confession they admit. They deny, however, that he was the agent of the Western Federation of Miners, hired by its officials. Indeed, they doubt that Orchard ever made such a statement, for no one aside from the State authorities has seen the confession. That Orchard had a personal motive in killing Steunenberg the defense will endeavor to prove to the jury. At the time of the Cœur d'Alene troubles Orchard was working in that district. He was one of the strikers driven out by the troops. He had at the time a sixth interest in the Hercules Mine, which he had to dispose of for some $600. A few weeks previous to the assassination of Steunenberg, Orchard visited his old haunts in the Cœur d'Alene district.

He met his former associates who were interested with him in the Hercules Mine. That property had been developed, and was valued at $6,000,000. Orchard's former companions were rich, while he was virtually a wanderer on the face of the earth. He blamed Steunenberg for his condition, and in this frame of mind he went to Caldwell, determined to wreak vengeance on the man he held responsible. The murder of Steunenberg was the result. This is the theory of the defense.

That the State authorities of Idaho and Colorado are in league with the mine-owners to railroad to the gallows the leaders of the Western Federation of Miners is believed by many persons who cannot be accused of condoning murder. It is a serious charge, but certain events which followed the arrest and alleged confession of Orchard tend to give it a semblance of truth. Neither Moyer, Haywood, nor Pettibone was in Idaho at the time the murder was committed. That fact was well known to the authorities of both Idaho and Colorado. Under the law the men were not fugitives from justice, and could not be extradited. But the Idaho authorities were determined to get them regardless of law. The prosecuting attorney of Canyon County made affidavit that the men were in Idaho at the time of the murder. He knew that in doing so he was committing perjury, declares Attorney Darrow, counsel for the defendants, and Governor Gooding knew when he signed the requisition papers that the affidavit was false. Some apologies have been offered for the commission of these acts. One says that the Idaho statutes make accessories principals in a murder charge; another, that they were done to prevent habeas corpus proceedings in Colorado. The facts remain that the papers were signed, and that twelve armed deputies were hurried to Denver to secure the accused men. The requisition papers were presented to Governor McDonald, of Colorado, on February 15, 1906. He promptly honored them, although he knew the men wanted were not fugitives from justice, as claimed by the Idaho authorities. The men could have been arrested at any time during the next two days, but they were not. The fact that their extradition was sought was carefully kept a secret. Late Saturday night, February 17, when all courts were closed, the men were arrested and thrown into jail. They were given no opportunity of communicating with their attorneys, or even with their families. Early next morning they were placed on a special train and rushed to Boise, Idaho. The special train did not stop at stations, but changed engines at isolated points along the route. Once at their destination, the prisoners were placed in solitary confinement and treated as if they had already been convicted of, instead of being charged with, a crime. The theory of law was reversed, say friends of the accused, and the men were presumed to be guilty before they had even been indicted. It is a coincidence that Governor McDonald, who signed the warrants for the arrest of the men, and Pettibone, one of the defendants, were brought up together as boys, in the same town in Erie County, Pennsylvania.

The manner in which the accused men were taken from Colorado raised a storm of protest. It was declared that they had been kidnapped. Legal steps were at once taken to release them on habeas corpus proceedings. Suit was brought in the Supreme Court of Idaho. That tribunal decided that—

"One who commits a crime against the laws of a State, whether committed by him while in person on its soil, or absent in a foreign jurisdiction and acting through some other agency or medium, has no vested right of asylum in a sister State," and the fact " that a wrong is committed against him in the manner or method pursued in subjecting his person to the jurisdiction of the complaining State, and that such wrong is redressible either in the civil or criminal courts, can constitute no legal or just reason why he himself should not answer the charge against him when brought before the proper tribunal."

From the State Supreme Court the matter was carried to the United States District Court, with the same result. An appeal was taken to the Supreme Court of the United States, and it affirmed the decision of the lower court. The decision is interesting. It says:

If he [Pettibone] should be acquitted by the jury, then no question will remain as to a violation of the Constitution and laws of the United States by the methods adopted to secure his personal presence within the State of Idaho.

In another part it says:

It is true as contended by the petitioner that if he was not a fugitive from justice within the meaning of the Constitution, no warrant for his arrest could have been properly or legally issued by the Governor of Colorado. But it was not shown by proof before the Governor of Colorado that the petitioner alleged in the reqûisition papers to be a fugitive from justice was not one, nor was the jurisdiction of any court sitting in that State invoked to prevent his being taken out of the State and carried to Idaho. That he had no reasonable opportunity to present these facts before being taken from Colorado constitutes no legal reason why he should be discharged from the custody of the Idaho authorities.

In a dissenting opinion Justice McKenna said:

In the case at bar, the States through their officers are the offenders. They by an illegal exertion of power deprived the accused of a constitutional right. Kidnapping is a crime, pure and simple. It is difficult to accomplish; hazardous at every step. All the officers of the law are supposed to be on guard against it. But how is it when the law becomes the kidnapper? When the officers of the law, using its forms and exerting its powers, become abductors? This is not a distinction without a difference. It is another form of the crime of kidnapping, distinguished from that committed by an individual only by circumstances. If a State may say to one within her borders, " I will not inquire how you came here; I must execute my laws and remit you to proceedings against those who have wronged you," may she so plead against her own offense? May she claim that by mere physical presence of the accused within her borders, the accused person is within her jurisdiction deprived of his constitutional rights though he has been brought there by violence? Constitutional rights the accused in this case certainly did have, and valuable ones.

In his opinion Justice McKenna says that the right to resist removal from a State is not a right of asylum, but is the right to be free from molestation. He says:

It is the right of personal liberty in its most complete sense. . . . It is to be hoped that our criminal jurisprudence will not need for its efficient administration the destruction of either the right or the means to enforce it. The decision in the case at bar, as I view it, brings us perilously near both results.

But the manner in which the accused labor leaders were taken from Colorado is not the only evidence of a conspiracy on the part of the State authorities and mine-owners, say friends of the defendants. Confined with Orchard for a time in a prison in Boise was a man named Steve Adams. He was a member of the Western Federation, and was suspected of complicity in the Independence outrage and other murders in Colorado. He was said to have made a confession of his guilt. Adams secured his release on a writ of habeas corpus, and immediately went over to the side of the defense. He repudiated the alleged confession, declaring that it was all written out and that he was compelled to sign it on pain of death. He told some strange tales about the way in which the Orchard confession was secured. Adams was rearrested and charged with the murder of a "claim-jumper" in Shoshone County some years before. This the defense believes was done in the hope that he would be convicted and that he might be induced to testify against Moyer and Haywood on the promise of securing his own liberty. At each term of court the defense has been ready to proceed with the trial. The delays have been caused by the prosecution. If the State has proof of the guilt of the prisoners, why the delay in bringing them to trial? asks the defense. Why has it been necessary to keep the accused men confined for more than a year if the only witness against them had confessed before they were arrested?

What weight will the testimony of a confessed co-conspirator have with the jury? It has been charged by the miners that Orchard was a detective employed by the Cripple Creek Mine Owners' Association. The mine-owners deny this, and there is no proof that he was. Those who know him say that he is a desperate character, who might be hired to do murder by any one who paid him his price, whether miner or mine-owner. For years he has been known as the intimate friend of Haywood. At the time of his arrest he was wanted by the Colorado authorities on the charge of blowing up the railway station at Independence and causing the death of thirteen non-union miners. He is said to have confessed to that crime and to having committed twenty-six murders as the agent of the "inner circle" of the Western Federation of Miners.

The prisoners will have the advantage of the best legal talent that can be procured. E. F. Richardson, of Denver, known throughout the West as a lawyer of great ability, has associated with him in the case Clarence S. Darrow, of Chicago, whose famous argument to a jury in another conspiracy case in Oshkosh, Wisconsin, a few years ago resulted in an acquittal. That the men on trial in Idaho will require all the ability of their counsel to secure their liberty seems certain. Even should they be acquitted of the charge of planning the murder of Steunenberg, numerous murders committed in Colorado within the past few years are charged against them. There is strong circumstantial evidence that a conspiracy to commit wholesale murder actually existed as charged by the prosecution in this case. In addition to being implicated in the murder of Steunenberg, the leaders now in jail are accused, according to the alleged Orchard confession, of planning the murders of Lyte Gregory, a detective mysteriously killed in West Denver three years ago; Arthur Collins, superintendent of a mine at Telluride, shot through a window in his own home; Martin Gleason, superintendent of a mine in Cripple Creek, thrown down a shaft; Martin B. Walley, killed by the explosion of a bomb placed in a vacant lot through which Chief Justice Gabbert, of the Supreme Court, was accustomed to walk; the blowing up of the Independence railway platform, and a list of other crimes of the most revolting nature.

To comprehend the extent of this conspiracy it is necessary to know something of the history of the Western Federation of Miners. That history is a record of strikes, bloodshed, and lawlessness. It is true the lawlessness has not always been on the side of the miners, but they or their leaders have been responsible for much of it. Armed force has been advocated by its leaders since President Boyce in 1897 urged every union to organize a rifle club.. In a speech in a convention of the Industrial Workers of the World in Chicago in July, 1905, Haywood said that the American Federation

of Labor had some 2,000,000 members, while the Western Federation of Miners had 28,000, "but," he said, "with that small membership we can strike more terror to the hearts of the capitalists than can the American Federation of Labor." Terror they have struck, not only to the hearts of the capitalists, but to all who have in any way incurred their displeasure. A large majority of the men who compose the membership of the Western Federation differ but little from the men in other labor organizations. They are honest, hard-working miners, with as much respect for law and order as other citizens in the communities where they live. It should be understood that the Western Federation is not on trial, although some of its friends are anxious to have it appear that it is. It is the leaders who are accused of the crimes and atrocities which have made the organization a byword among labor unions. It may be said that the members are responsible for the leaders, but this is, perhaps, less true of the Western Federation than of any other labor organization in the country. The Western Federation is pledged to Socialism through its convention. Socialism is supposed to be the essence of democracy. The rank and file in the Socialist party are supposed to govern. But the Western Federation is a bureaucracy. It is ruled by a few individuals who have assumed absolute power. When the convention declared for Socialism in 1903, the question was never submitted to the membership for a vote. Privately the officials admit that it is doubtful if the membership as a whole would vote favorably on such a policy. So the visionaries who rule the organization did not give the membership a chance to defeat the revolutionary policy adopted by the convention. When the strike was ordered which led to the reign of lawlessness in 1903 and 1904, the members did not get a chance to vote on it. If they had, in all probability it would not have taken place. When the Western Federation withdrew from the American Federation of Labor some ten years ago, the step was taken by the officers. The membership had nothing to say about it. It is an open question to-day whether the membership, if given the opportunity, would not repudiate the whole policy and seek affiliation with the family of trade unions under the banner of the American Federation of Labor.

The abolition of the wage system and class hatred are constantly preached to the membership through the weekly publication of the union. " Labor produces all wealth ; wealth belongs to the producer thereof," is the motto emblazoned on the official paper and the working cards of the members. This saying may be interpreted in different ways. How far it is responsible for the pilfering of ore in high-grade mines is problematic, but. the mine-owners assert that since the Federation rule was broken in the Cripple Creek district they have saved $3,000,000 a year from that source alone. The truth of the statement may be questioned, however, since the mine-owners recently abolished the card system enforced for two years in the hope that the old miners who were deported might return.

The deportation by the State militia in 1903 of union miners from the Cripple Creek and Telluride districts has often been pictured as the most outrageous proceeding ever perpetrated by public officials under the guise of law. That innocent men were made to suffer there is no doubt. If it can be justified at all, it can be justified only on the ground of necessity which knows no law. But if that deportation, harsh as it may have been, is weighed against a former deportation of non-union men by a mob of union miners, armed with rifles ordered by union officials and paid for with union funds, it was humane in comparison. It was an application of the doctrine of force so consistently advocated by the leaders of the miners themselves, say the mine-owners. They were beaten at their own game, and their plaint was heard all over the country. Only two years previously an armed mob of miners, led by the president of the union, drove some one hundred non-union men over a rough mountain trail after having compelled them to throw away their shoes and march barefooted. Stragglers who fell behind were brutally beaten, and a few were shot and maimed for life.

It was not open lawlessness such as that described, however, that made the miners feared by those who opposed them. The open outbreaks were infrequent, and it was only during strikes that the atmosphere was charged with the spirit which makes mob violence possible. It was the secret murders that were a common occurrence that kept the whole community in dread. It is true that few, if any, of those murders have been brought home to men in a position of power in the union. Such men have on a few occasions been indicted and acquitted when brought to trial. This, perhaps, need not be wondered at when it is understood that juries were afraid to return a verdict of guilt. As an illustration, a watchman caught two union miners in the act of stealing ore. They were tried and acquitted. A short time afterward the watchman's house was blown up with dynamite.

When Sherman Bell filled the courtroom and surrounded the building with soldiers when some union miners were to be tried, it did not look like according men a fair trial by a jury of their peers ; but it can be shown that on other occasions an attorney defending union miners simply showed the affiliations of his clients and a union jury did the rest.

That an " inner circle " existed in the Western Federation of Miners is a matter of common belief. That the men in this " inner circle " are responsible for the crimes that have been committed against those who had incurred the displeasure of the union is also believed by many. Men prominent in organized labor circles in Denver and other cities privately shake their heads and say that " it looks bad," while they publicly denounce the manner in which Moyer and Haywood were taken from Colorado. Whether an " inner circle " exists, and whether Moyer and Haywood are members of it, are questions for an Idaho jury to determine when it has heard all the evidence. To the impartial observer it appears more than a coincidence that dozens of individuals who had troubles with the union met violent deaths. The mine-owners have resorted to many unscrupulous methods to discredit the miners' organization, but it is hardly conceivable that they would wantonly murder non-union men in their employ. It is hardly conceivable that they could have planned to blow up the station platform at Independence and kill the men who were helping them to operate their mines. Haywood pretends to believe that they did, but few will agree with him. The miners assert that when General Reardon, President of the Mine Owners' Association, learned of the result of the explosion he was heard to exclaim: "My God! we did not intend to kill anybody!"

When the militia raided the union headquarters in Victor, they found a number of group photographs of miners. Certain men in the groups were marked with a cross in lead pencil. Their names were written on the backs of the photographs. On one photograph were the names of five men. One was Charles McCormick, superintendent of the Vindicator mine. Another was Mel Beck. Both men were killed by a dynamite explosion when the fatal "accident" took place in the mine. A line was drawn through their names on the back of the photograph, which might indicate that the score had been settled. It is true that an official investigation showed that the machinery which operated the elevator in the shaft was in a defective condition. The elevator might have fallen, as was claimed by the union men and their friends, but the markings on the photographs looked suspicious. The miners say that the names were written on the photographs by detectives in the employ of the mine-owners, and left in convenient places for the militia to find them. As proof that the mine-owners have resorted to such tactics the miners cite the case against Sherman Parker, President of the miners' union of Cripple Creek. Parker was being tried for an attempt to wreck a train loaded with non-union miners, when a detective named McKinney, a witness for the mine-owners, admitted under cross-examination that he himself attempted to wreck the train, and was hired to do it by the Mine Owners' Association. He first tried to induce some of the miners to commit the crime, and, failing in that, he attempted it himself

with a view to shifting the blame on the union.

These things make it difficult to get at the truth in the whole affair. Whether the men about to be tried are convicted or acquitted of the crime with which they are charged, the more one studies the workings of the Western Federation of Miners, the more irresistibly is the impression borne home that the teachings of its officers are dangerous to the forces which make for law and order. Incendiary utterances against the Government and its constituted authorities are not likely to increase respect for the law. If the officers of the Western Federation are guiltless of all the crimes laid at their doors, they are at least guilty of teaching a doctrine that might easily incite weaker men to commit such crimes.

Important as are some of the issues in this trial, there is no occasion for the hysteria that is being manifested in certain quarters. Socialist papers and other radical publications are trying to make it appear that this is a death-struggle between organized labor and organized capital. It is nothing of the kind. It is a trial of men charged with one of the blackest murders ever committed in this country. If they are given a fair trial by a jury of their peers and found guilty, to say that their conviction means a deathblow to organized labor is worse than an insult to the organized wage-workers of the country. The labor movement rests on no such unsafe foundation. When Debs was sent to jail during the American Railway Union strike in 1894, the same hysterical writers and speakers declared it meant the death of organized labor. Debs served his sentence, and the American Railway Union was disrupted. The railway brotherhoods are to-day stronger than at any time in their history. The mere possibility of innocent men being hanged is serious to contemplate. It is also a serious matter that murders such as have been committed in the West can happen and the perpetrators escape unwhipped of justice. But the future of organized labor, even in the mining camps of the West, is not dependent on the result of the Moyer-Haywood trial.

# Comment on Current Books

**Among the Novels**

Mr. Oxenham's novels are less well known than they deserve to be, although two or three of them, such as " God's Prisoner " and " Barbe of Grand Bayou," have been praised by many judicious critics. In " The Long Road " he has exceeded his former work in human sympathy, quiet charm, and dramatic force. The story is of Siberia in the early days. The basis of the tale is found in a singular decree (an actual historical fact, we are told) by which a provincial governor ordered a man under his displeasure to move constantly from place to place, never to remain in one town longer than ten days. Stepan, this perpetual wanderer, builds a house on wheels, and with his wife and two children journeys from village to village, over the wild steppes —peddler, newsbearer, and friend of the peasants. In the summer the little family have idyllic days in the beautiful woods ; in the winter they suffer severe hardships and barely escape from wolves, cold, and starvation. One by one wife and children die, and there is left to Stepan only the hope of revenge on his persecutor. An opportunity offers, but his hand is held because a little girl, in name and appearance like his own little Katinka, turns aside his hatred. He disappears far into the northern wilds, living with savage beasts and Eskimos, passes through a period of insanity, but finally regains reason and faith in God, and with his now battered house on wheels resumes his rounds on the " long road," a sweet old man, beloved by children and by the poor. " While he lived he was an institution; when he died he became a legend." This simple story is told with not a few dramatic incidents, and with notable sincerity of feeling and unity of literary purpose. It is touching in its pathos, but always alive with action and character, so that it is never dolorous or depressing. For freshness of sentiment and vividness of narrative it seems to us unexcelled by any recent romance. (The Long Road. By John Oxenham. The Macmillan Company, New York. $1.50.)

In " The Turn of the Balance " Brand Whitlock bitterly arraigns the present system of administration of law in our country. Corruption, incompetence, neglect, fierce prejudice, and general injustice are its characteristics, according to this unrelievedly grim presentation. The worst of it is that there is no gleam of hope ; the few feeble efforts at reform undertaken by one of the young lawyers, who has a human feeling,

are utterly fruitless. The big, remorseless machine rolls on, crushing its victims. Punishment is not remedial. The lives of two . young offenders are traced to the bitter end—and all the effect of proffered help for them is to increase the horror of their ruin. The author shows a knowledge of the cruel and selfish phases of our civilization, but while his heart burns with indignation his eyes seem blinded to every ray of hope to be found in purity, righteousness, and sound judgment. Profoundly depressing is the effect of this story, yet the author surely must have been moved by a desire to better the conditions he describes with great power. Is nothing to be done? (The Turn of the Balance. By Brand Whitlock. The Bobbs-Merrill Company, Indianapolis, Ind. $1.50.)

Plot-stories are of late more abundant than novels of character-depiction. One of those now before us, Mr. Quiller-Couch's " Poison Island " (Charles Scribner's Sons, $1.50), has both elements, however, and one feels that the author really cares more for the people than for the plot. The story is of the type of Stevenson's " Treasure Island ; " thus, buried gold, ex-pirates, a boy with a secret chart, and a company voyaging in search of treasure are common to both stories. In the end Mr. Quiller-Couch springs some remarkable surprises on his reader, and the closing incidents are even so bizarre and unnatural that the reader suspects that the author is laughing in his sleeve at the credulity of romance-lovers. More consistent and better worked out as to plot is Mr. W. T. Eldridge's " Hilma " (Dodd, Mead & Co., New York, $1.50). This belongs in that class of which Anthony Hope's " Prisoner of Zenda " is the prototype. A brave and resourceful American is thrown into the dynastic plots of a petty imaginary nation in eastern Europe, and plots and counterplots develop in rapid and thrilling succession. One does not need to guess that the American foils the political villains who try to keep Princess Hilma from her throne, nor that he loves the beautiful young queen, and that both sacrifice love to duty. The tale is built up in a workmanlike way, and has a reasonable number of thrills and sudden turns. " Martin Hewitt, Investigator," is a new edition of a collection of detective stories in which Arthur Morrison (who, by the way, has done much better things than detective tales) almost avowedly imitates Conan Doyle. Martin is as clever as Sherlock, and some of these mysteries are capitally invented. (Harper & Brothers, New York, $1.25.) Somewhat similar in character but much cruder is "The Thinking Machine," by Jaques Futrelle (Dodd, Mead & Co., New York, $1.50). The author's ingenuity is great, but the element of probability is not always maintained.

In another story, Margaret Potter shows us the depth of social corruption in Russia among the nobility within the court circle. She writes intensely, and constructs a tragedy upon well-known and acknowledged foundations. The Princess Catharine, of noble mind and nature, lived a life corroded and crippled by the sins of those nearest to her. The touches of history involving Russia and Austria are introduced with dramatic effect, but we must warn readers that "The Princess" is immeasurably sad. An occult strain runs through the novel, managed with frankness and some skill. Ivan Gregoriev, writer of great symphonies, is permitted, after his death, to become the messenger of truth, the healing, ministering spirit to Catharine, and later to Vittoria, bringing to each wounded heart a knowledge of the meaning of existence, shadowy but real enough to them. (The Princess. By Margaret Potter. Harper & Brothers, New York. $1.50.)

Mr. Bullen's love of the sea and his conscientious realism in treating facts as facts, while often interpreting them in a poetic way, are so well known that he really did not need to preface this tale with the statement that it might be read without danger of acquiring false information about the sea or about the ways of its servants. As a story, strictly speaking, the book lacks proportion and construction; but as a picture of the sailor's life in port and on board ship, and a narrative of adventure and incident that might easily befall a boy apprentice, the book is capital, and will be relished by young readers. (Frank Brown, Sea Apprentice. By Frank T. Bullen, F.R.G.S. E. P. Dutton & Co., New York. $1.50.)

Mr. Owen Wister's humor is always genuine and racy, and in this little burlesque he fairly riots in absurd specimens of supersimplified spelling. This fantastic skit is immensely amusing at its outset, but becomes a little tedious before the end. (How Doth the Simple Spelling Bee. By Owen Wister. The Macmillan Company, New York. 50c.)

*Dampier's Voyages* A new and attractive edition in two volumes, with portrait, maps, and a brief sketch of Dampier's life by the editor, Mr. John Masefield. Dampier was not always a picturesque or lively writer, but he had a tremendous story of adventure, fighting, and discovery to tell, and, apart from the value of his "Voyages" as a historical record, there is in his faithful chronicle much that is human and vital. At his best, Admiral Smyth wrote, "the information flows as from a mind which possesses the mastery of its subject; he delights and instructs by the truth and discernment with which he narrates the incidents of a peculiar life." Buccaneer, naturalist, mariner, and thrice a circumnavigator of the globe, Dampier was emphatically a man of action, and in his way a thinker as well as a really great observer. (Dampier's Voyages. By Captain William Dampier. Edited by John Masefield. In 2 vols. E. P. Dutton & Co., New York. $7.50, net.)

*Eighteenth-Century Muck-Raking* Those misguided persons who read the New York Town Topics might enjoy these volumes. Their title, "The Real Louis XV.," indicates what one might expect. It is true that the period in which that monarch lived was emphatically one for the muck-raker, but Louis seemed fully equal to his time. The author has probably told his kind of story fairly well. But, if one must read scandal, and especially about this particular king, the more vivacious "Louis XV. et Sa Court," by Dumas *père*, is, we think, to be preferred. (The Real Louis Fifteenth. By Lieutenant-Colonel Andrew C. P. Haggard, D.S.O. In 2 vols. D. Appleton & Co., New York.)

*How It Works* A good title, this, for a book of clear, simple explanation of the operation of the practical mechanisms of the steam-engine, electric dynamos and motors, the telegraph, the wireless telegraph, talking-machines, heating and lighting apparatus, and much else. There are numerous diagrams. The book is not intended for technical students, but is especially adapted for young men interested in science and invention. For these and for the general reader the volume furnishes much that is practical and lucid. (How It Works. By Archibald Williams. Thomas Nelson & Sons, New York. $1.25.)

*Labor and Capital* This useful monograph in the form of a letter to "My Labor Friend," and written in a characteristically clear style, ought to find a wide reading in labor circles; but for this purpose it should be printed in cheaper form and circulated through the news companies. Professor Smith appears to us curiously to misinterpret the doctrine of the "single tax," which its advocates have repeatedly explained is a "tax" only in name; in reality it is a land rent, based on the idea that land is not a subject of private ownership but belongs to the entire community. (Labour and Capital. By Goldwin Smith, D.C.L. The Macmillan Company, New York. 50c., net.)

*Mr. Root's Achievement* If the rehabilitation of China is due to the efforts of John Hay more than to any other single agency, it may be also claimed that the increasing friendship between North and South America is due, more than to any other cause, to the efforts of Mr. Hay's successor as Secretary of State, the Hon. Elihu Root. Among Americans, past and present, in enhancing amity between ourselves and the nations to the south of us, Mr. Root has been prominent in word and deed. His most notable accomplishment so far was the circumnavigation of South America last summer in a Government vessel, paying official visits to Brazil, Uruguay, Argentina, Chile, Peru, Panama, and Colombia. Mr. Root refrained from visiting the remaining South American countries, Paraguay, Bolivia, and Ecuador, because the distance of their capitals from the seaboard made it impracticable with the time at his disposal. Everywhere the American Secretary of State was received in the spirit of the message which he carried, one of peace, friendship, and of strong desire for good understanding and mutual helpfulness. But his addresses were listened to not only with the respect due to his official rank in the Government, but also because of admiration for Elihu Root the man—for the masterful, individual force of mind and character which had forged to the fore as the leader of his profession in the Nation. To students of present-day politics the well-printed volume which comprises the text of Mr. Root's speeches in South America is invaluable. An interesting Latin atmosphere is given to those speeches by the inclusion of the addresses of introduction or reply from eminent South American statesmen. (Speeches Incident to the Visit of Secretary Root to South America, July 4 to September 30, 1906. Government Printing Office, Washington, D. C.)

*The Strang Etchings* The domain of art in general and of etchings in particular has received new and notable impulse by the work therein of William Strang. It is a satisfaction to all art-lovers that a collection of the Strang etchings has now been published, with an excellent prefatory account of them and their creator by Mr. Frank Newbolt. Like Mr. Newbolt, we would also call general attention to the striking quality of these pictures. If the etcher

illuminates Biblical scenes, his work has a marked dignity, a simple, rather somber reverence; in portraiture the technique of the etchings is ever to the fore; in the landscapes there is an individual note not to be lost; finally, in the book illustrations we see even more graphically the artist's imagination, firmness, and finality. (Etchings of William Strang, A. R. A. Charles Scribner's Sons, New York. $2.50, net.)

*Switzerland* The large page of this handsome volume enables the publishers to present in especially acceptable form Miss Jardine's interesting paintings, printed here, we rejoice to add, in colors attuned to nature and Swiss scenery rather than to startling art-color schemes, as has been the case occasionally with some recent books in which countries have been described by brush as well as pen. With very few exceptions these pictures can be cordially praised. We like also Mr. Rook's plan of treatment and division of his subject; he gives us neither an arid chronological history nor a descriptive guide-book, but takes up chapter by chapter for broad intelligent treatment such subjects as " Swiss Patriotism," " The Growth of a Republic," " The Swiss Government," " Popular Control," " Winter Sports," " The Swiss as Engineer." Each subject, whether serious or light, is treated in appropriate vein and with evidence of knowledge and discrimination. (Switzerland: The Country and Its People. By Clarence Rook. G. P. Putnam's Sons, New York. $5.)

*Vittoria Colonna* The love of friendship and the love of literature are frequently found together. The devotees of the latter are specially apt to have a fondness for the former. While prizing their hours of solitude and meditation, they find, when not really reclusive, their true ideal of society not in the world or in its crowds, but in intimate, responsive association with their close friends. We see this among men of letters of our own day, and it has always marked many literary personalities. It was particularly so during Renaissance times, with their humanistic point of view. One does not always realize the special, subtle appeal of that period of history as being specially due to the fact that it emphasized a time when the appreciation of friendship and poetry by men and women went hand in hand. This becomes evident when we recall some of the really important Renaissance characters— Reginald Pole, Juan de Valdés, Michelangelo, Sadoleto, Bembo, Ochino, Gaspara Stampa, Pompeo Colonna, above all, Vittoria Colonna, who was the friend of all the above named. The friendship which existed between her and Michelangelo, for instance, may take its place as a model for any such relation between man and woman. It seems strange that in the latest biography of Vittoria Colonna but twenty pages should be devoted to such a historic friendship. We also regret to find the inclusion of but one of Michelangelo's sonnets to Vittoria and one of his madrigals. Many of Vittoria's own sonnets, however, are included. They testify to her ideals of life, to her literary equipment, and to the literary forms of her time. For a woman whose character was clear and convincing her verse seems singularly stiff and conventional. Perhaps, however, it intensifies a certain quality of aloofness not surprising in one who took herself very seriously. But it was a sublime seriousness which distinguished her from the possibly more brilliant celebrated women of Italy. Those who have enjoyed Mr. Christopher Hare's "Famous Women of the Renaissance" and Mrs. Ady's more notable volumes on the women of the House of Este can appreciate the contrast between the sparkling and at times butterfly-like Este princesses, and the reserve, the solidity, the lofty and crystalline character of the Colonna princess. While this latest biography of Vittoria Colonna lacks some of the grace of Mrs. Ady's studies, it is a book full of charm and inspiration, one well reproducing the mellow Renaissance atmosphere enveloping the woman who has not unjustly been called the intellectual and moral leader of her time. As her latest biographer well says:

She was indeed a woman to be proud of—untouched by scandal, unspoiled by praise, incapable of any ungenerous action, unconvicted of one uncharitable word. . . . Here was a woman perfectly equipped for the journey of life, fully developed on all sides, whose religion being allied with intelligence was at once more powerful and more interesting; whose faith was as stimulating intellectually as it was spiritually satisfying; whom a wide culture and a great charity delivered from all narrowness of mind and heart.

(Vittoria Colonna. By Maud F. Jerrold. E. P. Dutton & Co., New York. $4, net.)

# Letters to The Outlook

## PROFESSOR FERNOW AND THE ADIRONDACKS

Theoretically, the State lands ought to be cared for under forestry principles—culling out the scrub and mature timber, planting profitable species, and bringing the woods to a condition which would yield the State a steady, even an increasing, income as the years roll up.

Practically, we are utterly unable to trust the politicians. The Adirondack logger cuts the best timber, takes no measure to replace it, and the chopping he leaves behind him is a waste. Cultivation by a real forester would improve the forest crop, not deteriorate it; but I do not know of one Adirondack tract of land that has not been "skinned" instead of "culled." There are now millions of feet of pulp logs lying on State land in the town of Wilmurt, cut down by pulp thieves whose work was sanctioned by bribe-taking game-wardens. The wardens, the timber-thieves, and the men who shared the bribe money are not yet punished, nor likely to be, though it is now two years since the saws did their work. If this could be done in spite of the State Constitution, what would be the result if the restriction was lifted ever so little?

Professor Fernow, a trained forester, was in charge of the Cornell College of Forestry at Axton, and I have been to some pains trying to understand why the experiment failed. It was a supreme opportunity to demonstrate "practical forestry," and the first thing, practically, done by the College was to enter into a contract by which it was obliged to deliver 49-inch hardwood, at two dollars a cord, in the yard of a wood alcohol factory, and hardwood logs at seven dollars a thousand, also delivered. It cost more to cut than the College got for it.

Here was Professor Fernow's great error. At the outset of the work, with 30,000 acres of Adirondack hardwood free of encumbrance, so-called practical forestry proved itself incapable of making a bargain equal to that of the ordinary Adirondack log jobber. This alone was enough to bring ridicule on "practical forestry." For sixteen years I lived within eighty rods of a wood alcohol factory whose owner has grown constantly wealthier making hardwood retort products—and this from only 4,000 acres of hardwood of the same kind as that controlled by the College. The College tried to demonstrate to just such a kind of man how to make forestry more profitable, more practical, and less wasteful!

The first chopping was made alongside the camp sites of summer people on Upper Saranac Lake. The campers came by thousands to the lake for the "woods," not for open choppings, however profitable they might be. Thus were antagonized the "summer people," who are less interested in forestry than in having a playground.

And, be it observed, Professor Fernow's idea was first to destroy completely the stand of trees on the College land, and then replace it with a new forest. Of course, forestry authorities, Gifford, for instance, say that it is better to remove a scrub forest completely, and plant to profitable varieties. But the State had more than seventy thousand acres of burnings and barrens which could have been planted without interfering with the "weed" trees. The College would have saved money by taking those waste lands instead of the forest, but it chose the best large tract of Adirondack land that was offered for sale—for destruction!

However, I am not sure that the College was free to choose just what Professor Fernow wanted. The Cornell tract was purchased from a pulp company, and pulp companies have proved themselves exceedingly powerful in Adirondack matters.

There is not a man in the State who has not reason for regretting the failure of this experiment, loggers most of all. The State needed some one to show how wastes and weed forests could be handled with present profit and future increase. But this "practical forestry" wasted the forest which it had, and looked seventy-five years into the future for its profit. (Beginnings of Professional Forestry in the Adirondacks, p. 6.)

A point that has not been covered by the storage reservoir opposition is the fact that by planting trees on the barrens and skinned lands of the Adirondacks every purpose desired by the reservoir advocates would be fulfilled—save one, the privilege of skinning the reservoir sites. It would cost less to plant the trees than it would to build cement dams, and every one of the objections urged against the reservoir ponds would be met; slimy overflows, destroyed forest, unsightly shore fronts, unhabitable shore fronts, would all be prevented by forest soil reservoirs, while the streams would be better regulated than by dams.

RAYMOND S. SPEARS.

Little Falls, New York.

## SHIP SUBSIDIES

There is one argument on the anti-subsidy side of the American shipping question which, while referred to in your article published in the number for March 9, was hardly given its due weight, for it is the controlling factor in the problem. The chief obstacle in the way of a resuscitation of the American merchant marine is the great cost of American-built ships. A freight steamer of moderate speed, having a carrying capacity of 6,000 tons, can be built in England on the Tyne at a cost of from $37 to $40 per ton, or say $240,000. Three years ago a contract could have been made to have such a steamer, ready for sea, for $150,000, or at the rate of $25 per ton, but in the interval there has been an advance in the cost both of labor and of materials. In this country the contract price for such a vessel would be from $80 to $90 per ton, or, on the lower basis, $480,000.

This difference in the initial cost has the effect of imposing the following handicap upon the American ship merchant. He has $240,000 of excess investment which must be taken care of before he can begin to compete on equal terms with his foreign competitors. The excess earning which must be made before conditions of equality are reached is represented by these items:

| | |
|---|---|
| Depreciation, 8 per cent.................. | $19,200 |
| Annual marine insurance, 7 per cent....... | 16,800 |
| Interest on investment, 5 per cent......... | 12,000 |
| | $48,000 |

In other words, the owner of the American-built vessel would be compelled to earn ten per cent. more upon his entire investment than would be necessary for the owner of the foreign-built vessel in order that each might receive equal returns. It is impossible successfully to carry on any large business operation when laboring under such a disability. The greater cost of maintenance is an insignificant circumstance. Fifty years ago the wages and keep on American merchant ships were twice what they were on British ships; but at that time our merchant craft cost less to build than the English vessels, and we had little difficulty in competing with transatlantic rivals. Give to American ship merchants, by the repeal of existing restrictive laws, the opportunity to buy low-cost vessels, and a quick and healthy restoration of the American merchant marine will take place. Those who demand subsidies assert that if such an opportunity were given our ship merchants, these would not take advantage of it; but that those who say this do not believe what they affirm is made evident by their vehement opposition to the repeal of our registration laws, a resistance which would not be shown if they were confident that our people would not purchase low-cost foreign-built vessels.

OSBORNE HOWES.

Boston, Massachusetts.

You can give added zest to any meal
by serving one or more of the famous

# Libby's
# Pickles, Preserves and Condiments

These delicious table delicacies are prepared from the finest of fruits and vegetables, in the spotless Libby Kitchens; and are absolutely pure.

Libby's Preserved Strawberries, Strawberry Jam, Currant Jelly, Tomato Catsup, Salad Dressing, Queen Olives, Gherkins, etc., are sold everywhere by grocers and delicatessen stores. Ask for Libby's and insist upon getting Libby's.

The new 84-page booklet, "How to Make Good Things to Eat," gives many delightful recipes for luncheons, dinners and evening spreads, that every housewife will appreciate. It is sent free on request.

## Libby, McNeill & Libby, Chicago.

ANALYSTS and Health Authorities strongly emphasize the fact that the Royal Baking Powder is always uniform in leavening strength. It always 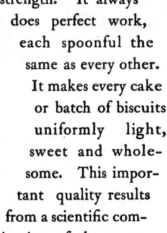 does perfect work, each spoonful the same as every other. It makes every cake or batch of biscuits uniformly light, sweet and wholesome. This important quality results from a scientific combination of the most highly refined ingredients, and no other powder possesses it. Many of the cheaper-made baking powders, imperfectly combined, have spoiled upon the hands of the grocers.

# THE TEXAS IDEA

## ity Government by a Board of Directors

### BY H. J. HASKELL

# CHOOL DAYS OF AN INDIAN

## BY CHARLES A. EASTMAN
### (OHIYESA)

### FIRST PAPER

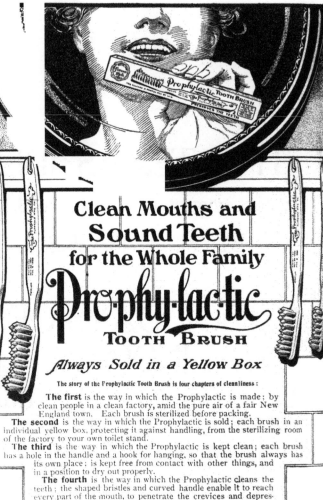

# Clean Mouths and
# Sound Teeth
## for the Whole Family

# Pro·phy·lac·tic
### TOOTH BRUSH

## *Always Sold in a Yellow Box*

The story of the Prophylactic Tooth Brush is four chapters of cleanliness :

**The first** is the way in which the Prophylactic is made : by clean people in a clean factory, amid the pure air of a fair New England town. Each brush is sterilized before packing.

**The second** is the way in which the Prophylactic is sold ; each brush in an individual yellow box, protecting it against handling, from the sterilizing room of the factory to your own toilet stand.

**The third** is the way in which the Prophylactic is kept clean ; each brush has a hole in the handle and a hook for hanging, so that the brush always has its own place ; is kept free from contact with other things, and in a position to dry out properly.

**The fourth** is the way in which the Prophylactic cleans the teeth ; the shaped bristles and curved handle enable it to reach every part of the mouth, to penetrate the crevices and depressions in and between the teeth which are the most vulnerable places for decay.

### Three Sizes ; Two Styles ; Three Textures

The texture of each brush is marked on each box—no need of handling bristles. The styles are : " PROPHYLACTIC " rigid handle, and " PROPHYLACTIC SPECIAL," new flexible handle. Three sizes : Adult's 35c., Youth's 25c., Child's 25c. Three textures : Soft, Medium, Hard.

Sold by druggists and dealers in toilet supplies everywhere. If your dealer does not sell the Prophylactic, we will deliver, postpaid, on receipt of price. Send for literature on teeth and their proper cleansing and preservation, and telling all about Prophylactic Tooth, Hair, and Nail Brushes.

FLORENCE MANUFACTURING COMPANY, 136 Pine St., FLORENCE, MASS.

**The Roosevelt-Harriman Correspondence**

The story of the Roosevelt-Harriman correspondence occupies eight columns of fine type in the New York dailies. All that is of real importance in this episode can be comprised in a paragraph of The Outlook. In 1904 the well informed had very little doubt that Mr. Roosevelt would be elected President, but a good deal of doubt whether Mr. Higgins could be elected Governor of New York. He was seriously handicapped by the unpopularity of his predecessor in office, Mr. Odell. The Federal campaign was going well with the Republican party, but not so the State campaign. The State Committee was without funds and could not get them. The President had very little anxiety as to his own election, but a good deal as to the election of Mr. Higgins. And the railway financiers had a good deal of anxiety as to Mr. Roosevelt's railway policies. He had already declared himself in favor of railway rate regulation, and they were desirous that he should confine it to such regulation as was possible under the then existing Elkins Law. Finally, Mr. Harriman was understood to be backing Mr. Odell in New York State politics, and desirous to see him vindicated, and his candidate, Mr. Black, sent to the United States Senate in place of Mr. Depew, whom therefore he was desirous of providing with a mission abroad. Such were the conditions when in October the President invited Mr. Harriman, "in view of the trouble over the State ticket in New York," to come on to Washington for lunch or dinner. He went. Exactly what took place at the interview is in dispute. Mr. Harriman reports that Mr. Roosevelt asked his help in raising funds for the National Committee. This Mr. Roosevelt emphatically denies; he avers that the

communication between them related exclusively to the State campaign, in which Mr. Harriman was intensely interested, because he regarded the attack on Mr. Higgins as an attack on himself and on his friend Mr. Odell. Mr. Harriman reports that Mr. Roosevelt promised that he would appoint Mr. Depew Ambassador to France; Mr. Roosevelt affirms that he declined to give any such assurances. Correspondence immediately following the election shows that Mr. Harriman desired to urge his railway views on the President before his Message should go to Congress. The President, while expressing willingness to confer with him on that subject, declared that the conference would be useless, since his mind was made up to urge further legislation and could not be changed. It is apparent that the interview between the President and Mr. Harriman was desired by Mr. Harriman to impress on the President his railway views, and by the President to impress on Mr. Harriman his views of the importance of electing Mr. Higgins. Mr. Harriman came back from the interview, and raised $200,000, giving one-quarter of it himself. He claims, without stating the grounds for his claim, that this sum added 50,000 to the Republican vote in New York City. If the differences in the reports of this interview given by Mr. Roosevelt and Mr. Harriman, respectively, involved an issue of veracity, we do not think, in view of recent revelations on the witness-stand, that the country would have any question about accepting Mr. Roosevelt's report. But a question of fact is not necessarily a question of veracity; and after a careful comparison of their conflicting reports, we are quite clear that the difference can be accounted for by a difference of interest and emphasis in their minds at the time, and a difference of recollection since. That the President wrote to Mr. Harriman explicitly saying that his visit to the White House would do exactly as well after the election as before it, is conclusive evidence, however, that there was no money-raising motive in the invitation. But Mr. Harriman has been in his political affiliations and experience so accustomed to the sordid use of money by both politicians and capitalists that it is quite probable that he could not understand the possibility of a more honorable motive. He is therefore entitled to whatever credit there may be in such a misunderstanding. Where one may legitimately choose between the hypothesis of a misunderstanding and that of a deliberate falsehood the misunderstanding is always the better hypothesis. We think it would have been stronger as well as more charitable if the President had adopted it instead of adopting the other.

❋            •

*Lessons of the Incident*  From this mass of correspondence and these contradictory recollections certain indisputable facts emerge ; and all the facts that are of real National importance are indisputable. Mr. Harriman did raise $200,000 on the eve of the election, report says from four subscribers including himself. This money was contributed in aid of a politician, Mr. Odell, who was in bad odor with the people of the State and the rank and file of his party, and to promote the interests of another politician, Mr. Depew, by securing either his re-election to the Senate or his appointment to a foreign mission. The money was all paid over to the State Committee, not to the National Committee, and was used presumably in the State campaign. There was no agreement or understanding, expressed or implied, that the President should modify his railway policy, and no such understanding is even intimated by Mr. Harriman. In fact, the President has not modified that policy, but has urged through Congress the railway rate regulation measure and has pushed forward investigation and prosecution of alleged millionaire lawbreakers, including Mr. Harriman himself. We do not see that there was any impropriety in Mr. Roosevelt's seeking a conference with Mr. Harriman—scarcely a day, never a week, goes by that he does not seek such conferences with leading men in their various departments—nor in his putting before Mr. Harriman, who was a Republican and a member of the National Convention which nominated Mr. Roosevelt, the needs of the New York State campaign, though in general the less a President mixes up in State politics the better. But the fact that four millionaires can afford to contribute $50,000 apiece to an election fund, and thus exercise financially as great an influence on the election as, say, twenty thousand ordinary citizens, furnishes an additional argument against the concentration of wealth in a democracy ; and the fact that four millionaires did make such a contribution lends emphasis to the demand that accounts of all campaign funds, all campaign contributions and contributors, and all campaign expenditures be kept and put on file where they will be accessible to the general public.

❋

*Federal Aid Averts the Railway Strike*  That the United States has not altogether neglected to use governmental instruments for averting industrial war is shown by the ending of the recent threatened strike on the part of trainmen and conductors of the railways west of Chicago. The threat of the strike was due to a demand on the part of the employees for a nine-hour labor day and a twelve per cent. increase in wages, to which the employers would concede only a ten-hour labor day and an increase of ten per cent. in wages. Fortunately for the country's peace and prosperity, both sides submitted the dispute to arbitration, under the Erdman Law, passed in 1898, by the terms of which the Chairman of the Inter-State Commerce Commission and the Commissioner of Labor were to use their best efforts towards conciliation. It is a satisfaction to record the fact that a settlement has been arranged by Chairman Knapp and Commissioner Neill. The men abandoned their demand for a nine-hour work-day, and the railways made an advance in wages over their previous proposition. It is said that the employees on these railways will now profit during the coming year by a total of over five million dollars, the number of men gaining by the advanced wage-scale being about fifty thousand. Both sides to the controversy have expressed themselves as satisfied with the solution accomplished by the Federal agents. On their part, Messrs. Knapp and Neill have testified to the spirit of fairness with which, in general, the differences have been treated. If a railway strike. unprecedented in extent, had occurred, the consequences both to capital and labor would, at any time, have been disastrous, but especially at this time of freight congestion in the West they would have been doubly felt. The country is to be congratulated, therefore, first, that so satisfactory a statute exists, and, secondly, that the parties to the recent dispute were swift to take advantage of it. The greatest gainer is the third party to the dispute, the public. The good effect of the present half-way measure ought to encourage Congress to follow the Canadian example and enact a still more effective law. The Canadian method of dealing with such conflicts is familiar to those who have followed the activities of the Dominion Department of Labor. The powers of the Department have been extended by a recent act.

❀

*The Canadian Way with Industrial War* As a consequence of a protracted strike in Alberta which threatened a fuel famine in that province and the neighboring province of Saskatchewan, the Parliament of Canada has passed a bill " To Aid in the Prevention and Settlement of Strikes and Lockouts in Coal Mines and on Public Service Utilities." The strike had been settled in November through the intervention of Mr. Mackenzie King, C.M.G., Deputy Minister of the Dominion Department of Labor; but hereafter, according to this Act, which was introduced upon his recommendation, until intervention and possible conciliation, such as he exercised, are

applied no such strike can be attempted. The Act prohibits, under penalty, the declaration of any strike or lockout in coal mines or on public service utilities until a Board of Conciliation and Investigation has examined the causes of the dispute. Upon application by either employer or employed, the Minister of Labor is obliged to appoint a Board of Conciliation and Investigation. The members of the Board are paid by the Government for their services. This Board shall consist of one representative of each of the disputants, and one chosen by these two. In case of a failure to choose any one of these, the Minister of Labor is to make the necessary appointment. The Board thus constituted is empowered to compel the attendance of witnesses, make personal examination of premises, and require the production of documents and books. It is the duty of the Board to attempt to effect a settlement of the differences and make such recommendations as, in its opinion, would lead to an adjustment of the difficulties on an equitable basis. Although the findings of the Board and its recommendations are not binding upon the parties, the inquiry will have made the public acquainted with the facts, and, if past experience may be trusted, public opinion can be expected to prevent the strike or lockout. An important provision of the Act is that which requires employers and employees to give at least thirty days' notice of an intended change affecting conditions of employment as to wages or hours ; and which also requires that pending an investigation the relation between the parties to the dispute shall remain unchanged. Attempts to cause lockouts or strikes contrary to the provisions of the Act are subject to heavy penalties. The fine for employers is from $100 to $1,000 and for employees $10 to $50 for each day of the illegal lockout or strike, respectively.

❀

*A Good Example* This act of the Canadian Legislature is a reasonable consequence of legislation in other years. The Dominion has shown a commendable fearlessness and foresight in attempting a practical solution of the industrial conflicts of our day. In 1900 a voluntary Conciliation Act was enacted, which has proved an effective means of settling many of the most serious strikes in the Dominion. In 1903 Canada went one step further in regard to industrial disputes on railways, providing machinery for compulsory investigation of a threatened or existing strike, though at that time no provision was made prohibiting a lockout or strike until such an investigation had taken place. In the present measure a still further advance has been made, providing not only machinery for compulsory investigation, but making it obligatory upon the parties to submit their differences to a full investigation before engaging in industrial warfare. The measure, moreover, is not confined to any one industry, but includes, as already mentioned, all public utilities, including mines, railways, steamships, telegraph and telephone lines, street railways, gas, electric light, water, and power works. What Canada has accomplished in promoting industrial conciliation has been repeatedly recommended to Congress by the highest authorities in our own land. The Commission appointed by the President in 1902 to pass upon the question of the controversy in connection with the strike in the anthracite regions of Pennsylvania expressed the belief " that the State and Federal Governments should provide the machinery for what may be called compulsory investigation of controversies when they arise." In his Message to Congress at the beginning of its recent session the President devoted considerable attention to the need of investigation of disputes between capital and labor, and, referring to the suggestion of the Anthracite Commission herein quoted, said : " This expression of belief is deserving of the favorable consideration of Congress and the enactment of its provisions into law." During the debate in the Canadian House of Commons frequent reference was made to these expressions of opinion by the President and by the Anthracite Coal Commission, and it is reasonable to infer that they added not a little to the weight of authority cited in support of the measure. In

seeking to advance the interests of her industries and people, Canada has not hesitated to profit by her knowledge of industrial conditions as they have shaped themselves in the United States. Our own country might well afford to follow Canada's example in the enactment of such legislation as is admitted by common experience and general consent to be in the interests of industrial peace.

❀

*The Chicago Election* On Tuesday of last week Mayor Dunne failed of reelection as Mayor of Chicago. His successful opponent was Mr. F. A. Busse, postmaster of Chicago by appointment of President Roosevelt. Mr. Busse's plurality was in excess of 13,000. At the same election the traction settlement ordinances opposed by Mayor Dunne were approved on a referendum vote by a majority of over 33,000. The campaign was full of bitter personalities and had many interesting features, not the least of which was the personal appearance in Chicago of Mr. Hearst with a special staff of cartoonists and editorial writers from New York to help wage the battle of Mayor Dunne. In the opinion of many it was the support of Mayor Dunne by Mr. Hearst that turned the tide against him. One of the campaign cries was, " Home rule *versus* Hearst rule." The Hearst papers were credited with causing Mayor Dunne's surprising change of front on the traction ordinances. These ordinances have heretofore been described in The Outlook. Briefly, they provide that the existing companies shall rehabilitate the properties and stand ready to sell to the city at an agreed valuation at any time on six months' notice. This plan of settlement had been worked out by Mr. Walter L. Fisher, as special traction counsel for Mayor Dunne, when it became evident to the " immediate municipal ownership " Mayor that municipalization could not be brought about during his present administration. Mayor Dunne approved this plan of settlement until the negotiations with the companies were all but concluded. Mr. Hearst himself last spring had approved the general plan of the settlement as outlined. But at the critical juncture the Hearst papers turned against the ordinances, and Mayor Dunne thereupon followed suit. In defense of their action they offered criticisms of the ordinances which the defenders of those measures said were inconsistent with the underlying plan of settlement concurred in by the critics at the outset. Mayor Dunne was renominated by the Democratic party after a bitter primary fight. Besides opposing the ordinances, he went back to the platform on which he had been elected two years ago—municipalization through condemnation proceedings. Had Mayor Dunne stood by the settlement ordinances worked out under his administration, it is quite possible that, in spite of his shortcomings, chief of which were vacillation and general administrative inefficiency, he might have been re-elected because of popular belief in his good intentions. The Republicans boldly championed the ordinances and promised a higher order of administrative efficiency. The election was one that presented many difficulties to independent voters, for to most of them neither Mr. Busse nor Mayor Dunne was satisfactory. Mr. Busse had long been an organization politician, and he was criticised on personal grounds. His friends claimed for him, however, that he was a politician who had generally done what the people wanted, and that he had been instrumental in bringing into public office many men of good records. An effective and in many ways unique campaign for the adoption of the ordinances was carried on by non-partisan organizations. One of them bore the name of the "Strap-hangers' League." The extremists both among the champions and the opponents of these ordinances contend that their adoption is a signal defeat for the municipal ownership movement. The moderate supporters of the settlement plan argue, however, that it offers the quickest and safest way to municipalization, and makes that policy possible just as soon as the people shall desire to embark upon it and can provide the funds to pay for the property, while providing in the meantime for immediate rehabilitation and improvement of service. In this matter it seems perfectly clear to us that the extremists are wrong and the moderates are right. What was defeated was not municipal ownership, but the particular brand of municipal operation which bore the name of Hearst.

❀

*A Political Scheme Nullified* — Again the cleverness of political tricksters has been their own undoing. The New York Court of Appeals, the highest court of the State, has declared unconstitutional and void the act of the last Legislature by which legislative districts were rearranged. The Court, in an opinion written by Judge Chase, gave as sufficient reason for the decision the conditions in two Senatorial districts—the Second and the Thirteenth. The Second was constituted by joining Queens County—which alone had a population more than sufficient to entitle it to a representative in the Senate—to Richmond County. The Thirteenth District, as created by the act, is, according to the Court, a "rambling territory;" its "many sides and various angles" are unwarranted by the Constitution. Both these districts are within the city of New York. In a very clear and sensible statement by Chief Justice Cullen, the Court points out that though the present Legislature is unconstitutionally composed, its acts will be valid. "We fully appreciate," says the Chief Justice, "that government should be prominently a practical thing;" therefore the present Legislature is declared a *de facto* Legislature, and each present member of it a *de jure* member. The next Legislature, however, must, according to the direction of the Court, be elected according to a new apportionment, or, if the present Legislature fails to make such a new apportionment, be elected according to that in force before the present unconstitutional one was made. The effect of the reapportionment act which the Court has condemned was to eliminate from the Legislature two of the most efficient of its members, and strengthen the hold of some of its least public-spirited. Already the gerrymander has proved in one respect futile; the attempt of Representative Wadsworth to overthrow State Senator Stevens resulted in his own defeat for Congress and the appointment of Mr. Stevens to be State Superintendent of Public Works. Now the whole gerrymander is made void. Of course those whose political power is weakened by this decision are among the opponents of Governor Hughes.

⚙

**The Prevention of War** Last week Mr. Root, Secretary of State, received from Baron Rosen, Russian Ambassador at Washington, a copy of the circular from the Russian Government, which issued the invitations to the coming Hague Conference, concerning the agreements and reservations made by the Governments invited. The original programme for the Conference was presented a year ago. It proposed as subjects for treatment :

1. Improvements in the settlement of international disputes by an international court.
2. Improvements relative to the laws' and customs of land warfare, especially as to (a) the opening of hostilities; (b) the rights of neutrals on land.
3. Improvements in the laws and customs of maritime warfare, especially as to (a) the bombardment of ports and towns by a naval force; (b) the laying of torpedoes; (c) the transformation of merchant vessels into warships; (d) the length of time to be granted to merchant ships in belligerent ports after the opening of hostilities; (e) the private property of belligerents at sea; (f) the rights and duties of neutrals, this covering the question of contraband, the rules applicable to belligerent vessels in neutral ports, and the capture of neutral merchant vessels.
4. Improvements in the adaptation to maritime warfare of the principles of the Geneva Convention of 1864.

All the Powers addressed have declared their general adherence to this programme, with two additions made by some of them : (1) the right to propose other subjects than the above, and (2) the right to refrain from discussing subjects which would lead to no practical result. The first of these two additional rights covers our Government's understood proposal to submit to the Conference the desirability of an agreement to limit the use of force in collecting ordinary public debts arising from contract. We hope and expect that our delegates will also propose the creation of a permanent international advisory parliamentary body;

no more important question could come before the Conference. The solution of all other questions should follow from it. The principle of international advisory legislation has already been applied to two subjects by the establishment of the Universal Postal Union and the International Agricultural Institute ; and in the case of the older body at least— the Postal Union—has already been justified. The subject next in importance is the first question on the Russian programme—a general international treaty in which the nations should agree to leave all subjects within certain defined limits to the Hague Court. Two nations, Sweden and Norway, have already agreed to submit all subjects to the Court, and have thus placed themselves deservedly in the forefront of international progress. Next in order, as removing one of the causes of war, should come the subject expected to be introduced by our delegates—the subject of international opinion as to what extent force may be used in collecting debts from a nation—namely, the Drago doctrine. Thus the subjects which have to do with preventing war rather than with its amelioration may take first place.

⚙

**The Amelioration of War** Among the subjects which deal with the amelioration of warfare, immediate attention will doubtless be given to those left unsettled by the first Hague Congress in 1899—the rights and duties of neutrals, the protection of private property at sea, and the bombardment of ports and towns by a naval force. As Mr. Hay pointed out in his circular note issued in 1904, the first of these subjects is of universal importance :

Its rightful disposition affects the interests and well-being of all the world. The neutral is something more than an onlooker. His acts of omission or commission may have an influence, indirect but tangible, on a war actually in progress, while, on the other hand, he may suffer from the exigencies of the belligerents. It is this phase of warfare which deeply concerns the world at large.

Concerning the protection of private property at sea, the American Government's position was well defined by the Joint Resolution passed in 1904; Congress then declared that there should be incorporated into the permanent law of civilized nations the principle of the exemption of all private property at sea, not contraband of war, from capture or destruction by belligerents. Among questions "unlikely to end in any practical issue," in the opinion of some Powers, that of limitation of armament finds first place. Despite the fact that, at Jean de Bloch's initiative, this very subject more than any other led to Russia's call for the first Hague Conference, her position to-day is somewhat changed. The admittance to the forthcoming Conference of many small States, where militarism does not oppress, makes Russia specially sensitive as to a possible adverse and (as she might think) unintelligent vote, the influence of which might restrict her freedom of action in restoring her army and navy to their normal strength, and in resuming her military position prior to the Japanese War. Be this as it may, the cart was really put before the horse when Russia proposed the subject of limitation of armament as the first to be examined in 1899, and the subject of arbitration the last. The special commission on limiting armament at that Conference did not go far with its labors before discovering that the moment had not yet arrived to limit military forces on land and sea by an international compact, and it referred the subject to the further study of the Powers, but at the same time unanimously declared that " a limitation of the military charges which now weigh upon the world is greatly to be desired in the interests of the material and moral welfare of mankind." It thus strengthened the opposition to any augmentation of militarism, for its influence has since forced Governments to justify, as they had not hitherto, every increase of armament. In 1907 the world recognizes what it did not fully recognize in 1899—that the way to arrive at peace is not by ameliorating war, but by preventing it. The adoption of arbitration as a means of settling international disputes should, of course, lead to gradual disarmament.

*The Pool-Room Disclosed*

The long-continued engagement of District Attorney Jerome in the Thaw trial has not prevented him from being active in other services to New York City. On the first of April the District Attorney's office made a raid on a pool-room, and the revelations furnish some startling figures as to the profits made by the syndicate which operated it. These amount, according to press reports, to eight millions a year. More interesting is the fact that these profits were shared in by an individual variously referred to as " T. G.," " T. Grady," " Tommy," " Sen. G." It has been pretty definitely intimated by the press that this " T. G." is a prominent member of Tammany Hall and a member of the State Senate ; at this writing there has come no denial of the identification from the Senator. If he is a member of the pool, he has been engaged in the violation of the laws of the State, and if so there is excellent authority for the doctrine that this is sufficient ground for his expulsion from the Senate ; for Mr. Roberts, the Utah polygamist, was expelled from the House of Representatives on the ground, entirely adequate it seems to us, that a man who is engaged in breaking the laws of the land is not a fit person to sit in the Legislature and help make the laws of the land. The facts brought to light by this raid ought to be sufficient to keep the ignorant and the innocent out of pool-rooms, and would be if it were not for the truth of the adage, " The fool and his money are soon parted." For a man who goes into a pool-room with the expectation of making money out of the pool deserves to be ranked in the first order of fools. A pool-room is a contrivance for enabling men to bet on horse races without attending the race ; that is, a contrivance for furnishing all the vices of horse-racing and none of its healthful interest. In the pool-room is a blackboard with the names of the horses engaged in the race. Above the name of each horse are written the odds which the pool will give to the individual bettor. If the reader will substitute for the letters below the names of horses, he will get a

8

little notion of the machinery of the pool-room:

| 10 to 1 | 4 to 1 | 1 to 1 | 6 to 1 | 3 to 1 |
| on | on | on | on | on |
| A | B | C | D | E |

10 to 1 means that the pool bets 10 to 1 that A will not win. The individual bettor pays his dollar and receives tickets or a ticket entitling him to ten dollars in case A wins. So of every other horse in the race; and there are sometimes a score of them. The reader will at once perceive that the individual bettor can only win on one horse—the horse that wins the race—though he may bet on other horses. The pool necessarily wins on all the others. Therefore, even if the game were always played fairly, the pool would be engaged in a very profitable business. But the game is not always played fairly, and the unfairness is always for the benefit of the pool. The manager of the pool has special advantages of knowing what horse is likely to win. More than that, he can enter into arrangements with jockeys and stablemen on the course, by which one horse will be made to lose though he is not the natural loser. To all the pool-rooms there comes a telegraphic or telephonic wire from the race-course so that the bettors in the room can be told how the race is progressing. As it progresses the excitement increases. The fools (and most of those in the pool-room are fools) lose their heads as well as their money; the manager never loses his head. To some of the pool-rooms there comes a private wire in a room above. Its messages are communicated to the manager. He knows the instant A has won the race—perhaps three or four minutes before the message comes over the other wire to the roomful. He is from time to time changing on the blackboard the odds which the pool will give. He changes the figures on B or C to 6 or 8 to 1. The fools, gulled by the larger odds, take the bet, and the pool thus possesses an additional opportunity to recoup itself out of bets on horses that have already lost for the payments which it must make on the horse which has already won. There are some additional complications in the pool-room which we do not think it necessary here to explain. We wish to make the statement so simple that the simple can understand it, in the hope that the proverb we have already quoted may be counteracted by another— "Surely in vain the net is spread in the sight of every bird."

❦

**Pennsylvania's Costly Capitol**

The Legislative Commission which is investigating the decoration and furnishing of the new Pennsylvania Capitol at Harrisburg has been in session for a month, with illuminating results. An article in The Outlook for January 26 described the beauty and splendor of the Capitol, and reported the charges of extravagance and graft made by State Treasurer William H. Berry. Mr. Berry expressed the firm conviction that the State had paid five million dollars more for the Capitol than it should have paid. The testimony taken by the Commission seems amply to bear out Mr. Berry's assertion. The contract for doing most of the decoration and furnishing of the building was awarded to one firm, Sanderson & Co.; though some of the decoration was done by the contractors who built the Capitol, Payne & Co. The actual work, however, as is usual in such cases, was done by numerous sub-contractors, each a specialist in a certain line. It is some of these sub-contractors who have furnished the most interesting evidence. The president of a Pittsburg company testified that it had furnished two mosaic frieze bands for the interior of the Capitol dome, for which it charged the contractor $7,224. The State paid the contractor for this work nearly $28,000, a price which gave him nearly 300 per cent. profit. The contract for the furnishings specified for the ornate chandeliers in the various rooms Baccarat glass, a product made only in France. The secretary of a glass company in Pittsburg testified that his company supplied all the glass under this specification, that it was manufactured in Pennsylvania, and that the price received for it was not quite $30,000. The price which the State paid was over $138,000. On this item the contractor's profit was about 360 per cent. Other items whose cost was testified to by the actual manufacturers were:

| | Sub-Contract-or's price to Contractor. | Contractor's price to State. | Contract-or's profit. |
|---|---|---|---|
| Woodwork in Governor's Suite | $16,089 | $94,208 | Nearly 500% |
| Woodwork in Senate Ante-rooms.......... | 6,145 | 62,486 | About 870% |
| Cup Rack in Barber Shop.... | 325 | 3,256 | About 900% |
| 38 Mahogany Clothes-Trees.. | 456 | 2,796 | About 513% |
| Desk in Lieuten-ant-Governor's Room.......... | 130 | 349 | About 151% |

*Curious Rules and Regulations* The methods which made such profits possible were pointed out in The Outlook's article on the Capitol. The famous "per foot" rule of computing the prices of furniture, woodwork, and miscellaneous decorations, and the "per pound" rule for chandeliers and bronze work, seem to have given the contractor practically unlimited opportunities for swelling his profits. The investigation has not yet revealed the proper process for determining the number of "feet" in an armchair, a clothes-tree, an umbrella-stand, or a bootblack-stand. In the case of one item, however, a mahogany table, it is clear from the bill how the thing is done. The number of "feet" charged for is the product of the length, the breadth, and the height of the table; the State, therefore, has had the pleasure of paying at the rate of $18.40 per cubic foot, not only for the mahogany of which the table is made, but for the air-space included within its outline. One of the most important discoveries of the Commission tends to explain why one bidder was awarded the entire contract for decorating and furnishing the building, although the bids of other firms on single items were much lower than those of the successful contractor. The Board of Public Grounds and Buildings, which had this part of the work in charge, passed a resolution that no bid should be considered except for the entire contract. Several witnesses have testified, however, that they knew nothing of this ruling until after their bids, on only one or at most a few items, had been made. The result of the investigation thus far has been to indi-

cate with increasing emphasis that the Capitol has cost the State much more than it is worth, on the most liberal valuation. It must be remembered, however, that neither the contractor, the architect, nor the members of the Public Buildings Board have been heard in their own defense. Until they are heard, judgment should be suspended; meanwhile, the evidence for the prosecution is intensely interesting.

*Ermete Novelli* "The man makes me cry; and yet I don't know a word of Italian." So muttered a man in a Novelli audience the other evening. A knowledge of Italian is not necessary to appreciate Signor Novelli's art. His realistic pantomime, his portrayal of passion, and the "business" of his admirable company need no language for expression, and repay attention from any one. During the past three weeks Ermete Novelli, new to the American stage, has been seen in sixteen plays. His versatility is remarkable. As a tragedian he disappoints, if we expect the reproduction of what we now are pleased to think traditional, due to long education by a Booth or an Irving. The Italian does not picture his Shakespearean heroes as nervous Americans or as intellectual Englishmen. He has the courage of his own convictions. Whether one agrees with the vigorous emphasis put upon certain features or not, his performance is always suggestive—and that, after all, is the highest merit of art. In his own way Signor Novelli is an absorbingly interesting actor in tragedy. But he is not as strong a tragedian as was his compatriot Salvini, and certainly does not rise to the lofty heights of the greatest English-speaking actors of our time. Signor Novelli is distinctly great in romantic drama and in comedy, where he can match any contemporary. Those sterling, if now to our taste rather florid, dramas, "Louis XI.," by Delavigne, and "Kean," by Dumas *père*, have rarely, if ever, had more impressive representations. It is especially, however, in such exquisite comedies as Shakespeare's "Taming of the Shrew" or Goldoni's "Burbero Benefico" that the stalwart Italian is notable. Underlying his astounding variety of facial expression, of gesture, of stage resource, of splendor of diction, is a very virile and sympathetic personality. In his every line independent and individual, Ermete Novelli leaves the auditor impressed by a red-blooded humanness, vitality, and reality. In sending us this actor of distinguished genius and finished art Italy has added to the debt America already owes her in the realm of æsthetic education.

❀

**Dr. Drummond**   Few Canadians were so widely known and so warmly appreciated in this country as Dr. William Henry Drummond, who died suddenly at Cobalt last week from the effects of a stroke of paralysis. Several years ago a dinner was given to Dr. Drummond in New York City which brought together an unusual number of writing men of position and quality, and was characterized by a still more unusual expression of admiration for the literary work of a singularly attractive writer and personal regard for him. Dr. Drummond was born in Ireland, spent a part of his boyhood among the hills of Donegal, but was brought to Canada at an early age and educated at the English High School in Montreal, at McGill University, and later at Bishop University in that city, graduating in medicine in 1884. He began the practice of his profession in the Province of Quebec, in a little community made up of Indians, half-breeds, Scotch-Irish Canadians, French habitants, and English. The locality and the people furnished him with the richest material for appeal to his sense of humor and pathos, and turned the country physician into a dialect poet of very unusual quality. He was, moreover, an athlete and an all-around out-of-door man; fond of sports, of hunting and fishing; and he acquired at first hand an intimate acquaintance with the woods and with the French-Canadian voyageurs and habitants. He was a poet by the gift of nature. Casual expressions from the people about him, such as "The wind, she blow, blow, blow!" used by a raftsman in describing a storm, gave him hints for his dialect poems. Many of them, like "Johnnie Couteau," are as widely known in the United States as in Canada. Four volumes contain Dr. Drummond's work in prose and verse, and much of this work is likely to survive for many years to come by reason of its closeness to life, its sincere feeling, its freedom and music. Dr. Drummond was, later in his career, Professor of Medical Jurisprudence in Bishop University, and was widely known as a reader and lecturer. His loyal nature, vigorous character, and the charm of his temperament will be long missed by the host of friends whom he had made.

❀

# State Control of Public Utilities

No question at the present time exceeds in importance the two questions—first, What ought to be the relation between the State and the corporations in a democracy? and, second, In a Federal democracy how shall the triple relation between the State, the Federal government, and the corporations be adjusted? The Public Service Commissions Bill in the New York State Legislature is of National interest because it throws light especially on the first of these questions. The discussion of it is important because it involves a consideration of principles applicable in any State of the Union.

To put into law a comprehensive plan for State control of all public utilities is the great undertaking attempted in the Public Service Commissions Bill. It might well be called the Hughes Bill; it was drafted to accord with Governor Hughes's recommendations. Last week, in two speeches, at Utica and Glens Falls, he appealed to the judgment of the people on behalf of the bill. The Outlook has already outlined it (see issues for the 16th and 23d of March). In the main the bill provides for the creation of two commissions which divide between them the responsibility for directing the operations and financial transactions of the railways, street railways, gas and electric companies, and indeed practically all public utilities within the State except telegraph and telephone companies. These commissions are required to act in accord with the Inter-State Commerce Commission.

Last week and the week before, the opponents of the bill directed their fire upon it at hearings before a legislative committee. At the same time newspapers have found their voice in criticism. The opponents of the bill consist of three classes : the officials of the public utilities involved ; conservatives who are concerned at the disregard which the bill shows for doctrines that they hold dear; and extreme radicals of the Hearst type who see in rigorous regulation a menace to more socialistic methods.

Their criticisms may be grouped as follows: First, objections are raised to certain details which, though of importance to New York State, are not of great National interest. Such, for instance, is the objection to the provision for meeting out of the resources of New York City the expense of that one of the two commissions which has charge of the district comprising the city itself. It is urged that since both commissions are State commissions with equal power, they both should be paid for from the State treasury.

More important is the objection raised against the alleged violation of the home rule principle. The commission which has charge of the utilities within the territory comprising New York City ought, it is said, to be a municipal, not a State, commission, and the members of it ought to be appointed not by the Governor but by the Mayor. This objection logically would require a separate commission for every city, would relegate all control of public utilities to local option, and would be fatal to unity of administration. It is true that such a commission must superintend activities carried on within the city; but the corporations which are engaged in those activities are creatures, not of the city, but of the State; the commission, therefore, should be created by the State and be held responsible to the State.

A vigorous objection is raised against the proposal to have the members of these commissions appointed by the Governor and subject to dismissal by the Governor. The really democratic plan, it is urged by the spokesman of Mr. Hearst, is to have these members elected by the people. This objection presented in the name of democracy would substitute for a democratic measure one essentially undemocratic. Theory and experience combine to teach that administrative officers should be appointed, not elected. If the Governor is, as he ought to be, held responsible for the administration of the laws, he should have full power to select such administrative officers. And experience has shown that an efficient commission of this kind is obtainable only by appointment. The Commissioners are to be chosen for their expert knowledge as well as for their executive ability. The people have no way of searching out such experts and of weighing their relative merits. This task ought to be given into the hands of a representative of the people, such as the Governor. In order to secure and protect competent men, the members of the commissions, it is urged by Mr. Joseph H. Choate as spokesman for the railways, should be subject to dismissal only by the Senate upon charges preferred by the Governor. If the Governor, however, is to be held responsible for the administration of the laws, he ought not to be denied the power to remove from office administrators in whom he has not confidence. Experience, moreover, shows that a cumbersome method of dismissal is a refuge for incompetency. The most democratic method is to put this power of selection and dismissal into the hands of the Governor, and then leave it to the people to determine what kind of a Governor it shall be to whom they will intrust this task.

An objection is raised against the bill because it has no elaborate provision to enable the judiciary to pass upon the reasonableness of the commissions' decisions. This is practically equivalent to a demand that ultimately all the work of the commissions should be intrusted to a court. As was brought out in the discussion over the Federal Railway Rate Regulation Bill, the courts themselves have held that the task intrusted to these commissions is one which belongs not to a judicial but to an administrative body. In the case of confiscatory acts the courts will intervene upon complaint, whether there be a provision for court review or not.

Very serious and plausible objection is raised against giving to these commissions power so drastic that they may find it possible, on the one hand, to require these corporations to incur vast expenses, and, on the other hand, to prohibit them from engaging in financial transactions which will enable them to meet the expenses laid upon them. For instance, the commissions are given power to prescribe the improvements which a railway should make in its permanent way and rolling stock, and then, on the other hand, it is empowered to prevent a railway from increasing its capitalization. These commissions, it is argued, may thus stand as overseer, and compel the railways as slaves to make bricks without straw— or even clay. Certainly great caution should be exercised in defining the powers of such a commission. In experiments of this kind it is better at first to give too little than to give too much power. But some power of destruction is inherent in all government. If that power is exercised destructively in this case, it will injure not merely a few railway managers but the whole commonwealth; and if the people wish to bring such destruction upon themselves, they can do so by a thousand other means as well as by means of these commissions. In fact, such commissioners as may be appointed by any Governor whom the people will choose are as likely to be solicitous for the welfare of investors and the public at large as most railway managers.

In some minor particulars this bill may be amended without injury. But as it stands it is a valuable contribution to the great question of corporation regulation by the State, and is well worthy the study of publicists, editors, and economists who are giving attention to this subject.

These fundamental principles implied in the bill are universally applicable :

Corporations engaging in inter-State commerce should be subject to Federal control.

Corporations engaging in business within the State should be subject to State control.

A commission created to supervise and regulate corporations has not legislative but administrative functions, and therefore should be appointed, not elected.

Its functions being administrative and not judicial, its actions should be subject to no judicial review except as constitutionally required.

The powers of such a commission should be carefully and clearly defined, but their extent should be determined not by past traditions but by present conditions.

# The Texas Idea

A page of experience is worth a volume of theory, although a little theory may often help to interpret experience.

Mr. H. J. Haskell, of the Kansas City Star, gives an account on another page of the municipal experiment in Texas that reinforces a theory of municipal government to which The Outlook has given occasional though somewhat hesitating expression. Iowa, Kansas, and South Dakota have recently passed laws providing for a system of municipal government based upon the Texas idea. In the light of this experience this plan of municipal government can no longer be considered a debatable theory; it is a practical and successful method which, in our judgment, ought to be widely followed throughout the country.

America has made a mistake in organizing its city governments upon the model presented by the Federal and State governments. It has been assumed that a city government must possess the three departments—legislative, executive, and judicial; that in the legislative department there must be local representation. There has been, therefore, always a municipal council, often two bodies, and the members have been elected, not by the city at large, but by wards or other political districts.

In fact, there is no real analogy between the city and the State, and no analogy at all between the city and the Nation. There is no occasion for local representation in a city government. The interest of one ward does not differ from that of any other ward, as the interest of one State differs from that of another State, or as the interest of one county sometimes differs from that of another county. The laws for the city are made by the Legislature of the State. There are, it is true, some relatively important city ordinances; but the chief work of law enforcement is, not to enforce these ordinances, but to enforce the laws of the State. The city is not a separate political entity. The work of a so-called city government is not primarily governing; certainly not primarily political. It is the work of a corporation carrying on an immense business, either directly by its own agencies, or indirectly through private enterprises employed for the purpose. This business includes such functions as providing water, seeing that the citizens are properly furnished with lights, making provision to guard against fires, establishing and maintaining public parks for popular health and recreation, watching against the approach of contagious disease, opening and paving the streets and maintaining them in good order, and the like. This is not legislative work, it is administrative work. In this work of administration all the citizens of the city are equally interested. It is a work which can be done by a few men better than by many; and by men having equally at heart the interests of all the city better than by men chosen by localities to represent localities. In the organization of such an administrative body the example furnished by individual enterprises is the one to be followed rather than the example furnished by political organizations.

All Boards of Aldermen and Councilmen should be abolished; all idea of elaborate legislative functions to be performed should be abandoned. A Board of Directors of the city should be elected, as there is elected a Board of Directors for a bank or a railway corporation. Possibly in the greatest cities, especially where there is a suburban population which is within the municipality, or where there are separate boroughs with separate ideals as in New York City, there should be provision for their representation in the Board; but with this possible exception the Board should be elected by the city at large. It should be a small Board, so small that the best men of the city could see it to be worth while to serve in it. And to this Board the entire administration of the city's business should be intrusted, as the entire business of a railway is intrusted to its Board of Directors.

❀

# Not Enemies but Friends

That there is a great deal of pain and sorrow in the world that is preventable is evident; that there is a steady diminution of disease and pain among men is probably demonstrable; but that pain and sorrow are wholly removable or essentially evil is a doctrine which misleads many from time to time, and which, in various forms, is commending itself to a host of men and women at this particular period. A pathetic fallacy underlies some modern thinking and some modern movements: the fallacy, as old as man, that the end of this present life is happiness; that every man and woman ought to attain happiness here and now; and that what is called the happy life is the successful one. According to this view, pain and sorrow and death are intruders at the feast—uninvited guests who enter to blight the joy and overshadow the festivity. This is a very inadequate and misleading conception of what men and women are here for. The instinct for happiness, the intuition that every human spirit ought to be happy, the passion for happiness which possesses many people, have their roots in a great and blessed fact; but the intuition and the passion are prophetic of what is to come when the discipline is ended, the school closed, this stage of education finished. No children are so unfortunate as those who are the victims of unintelligent affection; whose wills are never trained, whose purposes are never crossed, who never bear the yoke of discipline, and who are allowed to grow into men and women without self-control, or the ability to concentrate and direct their own powers. This evasion of the authority imposed on fathers and mothers is a prolific source of crime, disorder, and misery in this country. It is the untrained boy who becomes the lawless man; it is the undisciplined girl who wastes her life and makes the tragic mistake of supposing that the doing of one's own will is the road to happiness.

We are not in this world to be happy. We are here to be made strong for a happiness greater than that which we desire. We are not here to be at ease, to be protected and sheltered from discomfort, work, and anxiety, any more than a boy at a real school under a true master is to be allowed to shirk his lessons and waste his time. The school of life is so much vaster and the conception of human nature and human destiny that underlies it so much vaster than the dreams of most men and women that multitudes pass through it without any idea of what it all means, losing the wonder and glory of it in a feeble attempt to reconstruct it to meet their own wishes. Pain and sorrow and death are not only appointed for all men and women, but are among the greatest teachers, and therefore the best friends, of men and women. Pain is incidental to all birth and to every stage of growth. Sorrow must come wherever there are human affections; death, instead of being the specter of mediæval fancy, the terrible intruder of the Maeterlinck tragedy, is the angel of Watts's noble imagination: august, imperative, awful, but breathing beneficence from every fold of its garments. Pain is not to be treated as if it were an interference with normal living; it is as much one of the processes of living as the necessity of observing rules and learning lessons is a part of education in the school. Sorrow, instead of being feared as an enemy, ought to be accepted as a friend; for there is no surer way of taking the bitterness out of grief than by making sorrow at home in the house to which it has come. And as for death, who that has lived deeply and well has not had at times a vision of its beautiful service to the human soul? As Mr. Aldrich said, "It is the shadow that passes over the flower of life."

A sermon by Bishop McCormick, of Western Michigan, on "Pain and Sympathy," is full of the higher consolation which comes from clear vision and courageous acceptance, and brings out another of the many sides of sorrow and the immense place it fills in the mysterious training of life:

Nor can we forget, my brothers, that this cry is not only a challenge, a plaint, and a warning, but that it is also a plea for sympathy. "Is it nothing to you, all ye that pass by?" Ah! the apparent contrasts of life! This planet struck and scorched with sin and suffering, its Edens overgrown with thorns, its creatures become beasts of prey, its Perfect Man hanging in agony upon a cross; and those other worlds, lustrous, calm, splendid, whirling yonder through the depths of space. The half of a continent plague or famine smitten, and other lands aglow with pride and pomp and feasting. The hospital, with its moaning sufferers, its agony, its death-rattle, and the crowd that laughs by its doors. A soul singled out and sore stricken, and the chattering multitude that sweeps heedlessly along. O men and women, brothers, sisters, nurtured by the milk of human kindness, sharers of a common lot, is it nothing to you? To you, who at any moment may be swung from pole to pole, from light to darkness, the laugh suspended on your open lips to issue in a cry, the smile arrested to be frozen into horror: is it nothing to you, all ye that pass by? Thank God! it is already something: by and by it will be everything. The bypasser has become the bystander, and the bystander the sympathizer. Since Jerusalem sat solitary among the nations, since the Son of man was cursed upon the cross, and men laughed and mocked even on that awful Place of a Skull, sympathy has come. Men name it altruism; they may call it what they please, they may label it and its kindred virtues according to the latest scientific classifications. We know it to be Christianity; the charity of Christ, the Christ-born charity of all good Christian men. In the sympathy of the Saviour of mankind lies the secret and the source of all sympathy. From that fountain flows forth the ever-rising tide of brotherhood of man, the surging glory of the fatherhood of God. Because of Christ and Christly men, men are caring more and more. Strike here with calamity or pestilence and the nerves vibrate yonder, on the other side of the earth, and men there weep and pray and give and help. The priest and the Levite no longer pass by on the other side. Priest, Levite, and Samaritan, sinking all distinctions, are one in the relief of the wounded and the oppressed, all differences forgotten in a brotherhood of mercy. When we suffer, we know that many others are suffering with us. And, after all, there is much blessedness just here. Who can estimate in gold or gems the worth of loving sympathy, the uncommercial value of the pressure of a friend's hand?

# The Spectator

It was the eighteenth of January, and the Spectator found himself in Baltimore. The significance of the fact may not at once appear. But by some trick of memory it popped into the Spectator's head that morning that the eighteenth of January is the date of Poe's birth, and Baltimore his burial-place. To be sure, the poet was born in Boston, but incontestably he died in Baltimore; and where can one so fitly make obeisance to a man's memory as upon his tomb? The Spectator determined to devote the day to Poe—the more so as his conscience smote him because he had hitherto paid such small tribute to the good and great of his native land, for all his pilgrimages to the shrines of foreign men of letters. Barring an ineffectual search for the graves of Longfellow and Lowell amid the flowery mazes of Mount Auburn, and a brief visit to Sleepy Hollow, he could not recall one such pious quest. All a-fever with anxiety to make amends, he rose and prepared for the fray. There came back to him the words of an Englishman who had just completed a circular tour of the United States in six weeks. Said he, "What! you've not seen the grave of Edgar Allan Poe? It's unique, man, unique! Quite the rarest thing in America."

❀

The Spectator was not the only man in Baltimore that day who lay under the reproach of never having seen the Poe monument. Old Baltimoreans, Johns Hopkins professors, and policemen alike looked vaguely pained when appealed to for direction. "Oh, yes, certainly," they said. "He's buried somewhere about. The school-teachers put up a monument." The Spectator could have told them so much himself. He began to fear that the great fire might have wiped out the last visible trace of Poe. It was a young Englishwoman, a student in Johns Hopkins Medical School, who finally furnished a clue. "I believe," said she, "that you'll find it in the churchyard at Westminster Church."

❀

*At* Westminster Church? The Spectator put down the odd phrase to British idiom. But it wasn't that; it was precisely descriptive. When the Spectator found himself before the ugly red-brick front of Westminster Presbyterian Church, holding parley with the janitor through the cold bars of a locked iron gate, he understood. "No, sir, can't let you in. This isn't *my* churchyard. I'm the janitor of Westminster Church. It's not my business to show the graveyard of the *First* Church!" The Spectator cast a bewildered glance about. A high stone wall inclosed the church and the little plot of ground about it. "Where," said he, "*is* the First Church?" "Dunno," said the janitor shortly, and went inside and shut the door.

❀

To the house of his sole Baltimore acquaintance went the Spectator to be straightened out. She laughed at his tale of woe. "I'll get you in," said she, and straightway ran to don her wraps. Back she led the Spectator to the red church and the iron gate, and, while she made demonstrations to call the janitor, bade him press his nose against the bars and look attentively at the foundations. Baltimore churches are apt to have peculiar foundations; St. Paul's was based on a lottery, and Westminster, the Spectator now saw, had a unique underpinning of tombstones. Raised on tall brick piers, the building allowed the eye to stray beneath it where dim ranks of tottering tombstones glimmered weirdly out of the gloom. "If that be the graveyard of the First Church," gasped the Spectator, "pray, then, is the First Church a catacomb?" The Baltimorean smiled. "The old First has moved, and it looked for a time as if the graveyard, Poe and all, might be sold for building purposes. It was to save it from annihilation that Westminster Society agreed to build on the site. It's a makeshift, superimposing the church on the graveyard; but it was better than disturbing all those venerable tombs."

❀

"And Poe," the Spectator murmured with a shiver of repugnance. "Is he in there?" "In there? Yes; but luckily not in the cellarage. He is out in the sunshine behind the church." At this juncture the janitor appeared in response to the shakings at the gate. And sulky enough he looked when he recognized the Spectator. His answer was as short as before—the churchyard was not shown. "But," said the lady, firmly, "I have ancestors buried in that churchyard." The man hesitated. "What names?" said he. The lady mentioned two which fell meaningless upon the Spectator's Northern ear, but which bowed that janitor in the dust before her. Nowhere perhaps in all America is pride of birth stronger than in Maryland. Let those who, like the Spectator, aspire to drop a tear on the grave of Edgar Allan Poe see to it that they get themselves convoyed by Baltimoreans of lineage. For everybody "as is anybody" seems to have at least one family tie with the old graveyard at Westminster Church.

❦

The now respectful janitor led the way through the warm silence of the red-carpeted church, and so by the pulpit door out of that seemliness and peace upon a sight as wild, as melancholy, and withal as invincibly picturesque as the character of Poe himself. Surely the sickle can never have come upon the coarse, matted grass that riots over that singular, neglected plot. Out of the jungle of rank weeds and ranker ivy rose great family tombs in the style of ancient Egypt—huge pylons with the lotus bud topping the pillars that guarded the sealed doors, a pyramid or two full twenty feet high, and for the rest table-tombs leaning crazily on their ancient legs, and scores of tipsy or prostrate gravestones. The Spectator searched in vain on these venerable monuments for a date more than a century and a half old. Yet so cracked, so crumbling, so lichen-crusted were the stones, and weathered into so rich a chiaroscuro of black and yellow, that it was hard not to think of them as mellowing for four or five hundred years in the fogs of Old London.

❦

While the Spectator stooped his head to decipher the inscription on a worn old tomb, the janitor vouchsafed the fact that the records of the quaint little burial-place are lost. That is to say, since the

death of the old janitor nobody knows where the records are laid. Unless the half-obliterated inscriptions are soon recut, time will consign the inmates of these imposing tombs to the ranks of the unknown dead. The Baltimorean demurred. "Their descendants have no need of inscriptions to guide them," said she. "They will not forget. And are not a good many Baltimore families still interring here?" The janitor nodded, and, turning toward the church, pointed to the dim recess beneath it. "A tomb was opened just lately in there." He led the way into the cellar. There, quite close to the door of the modern furnace, he scraped away the coal from a deep-stained marble slab and showed us a ring by which it might be lifted to give access to the tomb beneath. The Spectator struggled to adjust his mind to admiration of this style of burial, but signally failed. As he peered about through the damp darkness of the place, noting how furnace pipes were forced to circumvent Egyptian vaults, and how the shadows bristled with gravestones, he could not help thinking how Poe would have liked the place, the eeriness, the mystery, the antiquity. And when outside he found the poet's corner and beheld the clean, clear-cut, modern little monument, he grieved. More than half a century has passed since Poe was laid to rest, and he had a right to all the dignity of crumbling stone, moss, lichen, and ivy. And, behold, the tardy assiduity of posterity has cheated him!

❦

The Spectator read that night in the "Sun paper," as Baltimoreans call their popular journal, that Richmond is preparing to put up a notable monument to the eccentric genius nourished to manhood within its walls. The Sun paper regretted that so little was done in Baltimore to honor the memory of Poe. It proposed, as indeed it has been proposed many times before, that a fund be raised to tidy up the old graveyard, erect a more fitting monument, and provide for the perpetual care of the poet's grave. But the Spectator does not like to think that modernizing hands will ever be laid upon the quaint disorder of the place.

# THE TEXAS IDEA

## CITY GOVERNMENT BY A BOARD OF DIRECTORS

### BY H. J. HASKELL

AN agent went from Milwaukee to Houston, Texas, recently, to look after back taxes on land. The taxes had been assessed against various persons owning indefinite interests, and the thing was in a tangle. The agent wanted to have the property reassessed against the real owners so that the back taxes could be cleared up.

He was familiar with the customary procedure. First, he expected to present a petition to the City Council setting forth the facts. This, of course, would be referred to a committee. The members would need to be seen individually, then would come the efforts to get them together. Political influences would be brought to bear, a favorable report would be obtained, and finally, after weeks of delay, the adjustment might be secured.

The lawyer whom he consulted was not impressed by the magnitude of the undertaking. He merely remarked that they might as well go over to the Mayor's office and settle it at once.

" Hold on," the agent replied, in surprise. " Before we see anybody, oughtn't we to get some influential business men here to go with us, so the adjustment will be made on a fair basis ? There's sometimes prejudice against an outside corporation—"

" You don't know what sort of a government we've got in Houston," the lawyer interrupted. " Pull doesn't go."

The doubting man from Milwaukee went to the Mayor's office. The lawyer made his explanations, the assessor was called in, figures were produced showing the assessments on adjoining property, and in an hour the intricate matter was practically disposed of. The agreement was then formally ratified by the Council.

That ended it. The business was transacted precisely as speedily and as equitably as it could have been done by any well-managed corporation.

And, indeed, it was a corporation that transacted it—the Corporation of Houston, managed by a board consisting of a chairman and four directors, Mayor and Aldermen, Houston calls them. In Galveston, the city that first tried the experiment, they are called frankly a Mayor-President * and Commissioners. The old name cf alderman is retained in Houston apparently only out of deference to the past.

These two towns are trying to work out a solution of the problem of municipal government along lines that are practically new in America. Having found the old form of government by municipal legislature a failure, they have not sought to abolish the council or even primarily to reform it. They have merely reduced it to such a size that its members may be held accountable, and then have given them the power essential to efficiency. In Galveston the emergency from the great hurricane of 1900 supplied the motive for the revolution. There was no such emergency in Houston But the Galveston system worked so efficiently that the sister city went to the Legislature two years ago for a charter to enable it to repeat the Galveston experiment.

It is quite conceivable, of course, that the crisis in storm-swept Galveston might have resulted in putting capable men in office who would have accomplished as much under the old form of government as has been accomplished under the new. But in Houston results quite comparable to those in Galveston have followed the adoption of the centralized scheme, and in Houston, as has been said, no great crisis called men to serve their city. The fact is that the more one examines the way municipal business is conducted in Houston, the more apparent it becomes that the city is proving the truth of Lord Salisbury's remark that three men around a table can settle any question—in this case even thè question of municipal efficiency.

The men in office now, with one exception, were seasoned politicians. They had held office before, without making any great mark. Mr. H. B. Rice, the Mayor, had served in the same capacity in the old régime. Mr. J. Z. Gaston, in charge of finance, and Mr. J. A. Thompson, at the head of the departments of sewerage, water, and health, were both members of the old Board of Aldermen when the new charter became effective. Mr. J. B. Marmion, in charge of the street and bridge department, had been City Recorder. Only Mr. James Appleby, head of the police and fire departments, was not known in politics, and his fire chief is an ex-alderman and ward politician, while his chief of police held that position under the old administration.

The increased efficiency to-day may be traced directly to the simplicity and centralization of the new plan of government, in which the Mayor and four Aldermen elected at large are left practically untrammeled to work out the city's salvation.

Take such a small matter as the prescriptions given by the city to the poor. Sometimes they had cost several hundred dollars a month. Rarely had they been less than $75. The Alderman in charge of the health department under the new system appointed a druggist as the clerk of his department and bought $100 worth of drugs. Since then the city has filled its own prescriptions at a cost of five cents each. The assistant health officer fitted up a surgical room where many patients are treated who formerly were sent to a hospital. The saving from these two economies amounts to from $100 to $150 a month.

This is not a large item, to be sure, though it amounts to something in a city of the size of Houston. The significant thing is that a competent city official was able to institute these economies without tedious delays and without the necessity of making concessions to "pull." Under the old system matters of this character would have been discussed at great length in the City Council—and Houston was fortunate in having a single House instead of two—aldermen would have been hauled about by druggists looking for city patronage, and very likely nothing would have been done.

Consider another instance. Several years ago the city erected a crematory, at an expense of $12,000, to dispose of its garbage and rubbish. The plant required a good deal of fuel and the services of three or four men. It frequently got out of order, and eventually was abandoned, though a watchman was retained, at an expense of sixty dollars a month, to look after it. The head of the Health Department under the new administration was not compelled to wait months for aldermanic committees to work out some remedial plan. There was a sewage pumping plant in the middle of the city. At a cost of $750 he rigged up a simple device for burning garbage adjacent to this plant. He connected the furnace with the stack of a pumping plant, thus securing sufficient draft to burn the garbage without additional fuel. The men at the pumping station were able to do the extra work necessary, so the bill for fuel and running expenses was practically eliminated. Observe, again, that this saving was accomplished in the manner of any well-conducted big business enterprise, and not after the fashion of city governments.

Observe, further, that "well conducted" is not a superfluous qualification. The city has had the opportunity to make a direct comparison of its efficiency with that of a corporation in handling its water plant. Under a former administration the city defeated by a vote of three to one a proposal that it own and operate its water-works. Confident of the business possibilities of the new charter, it reversed itself by a vote of four to one last year, and took charge of the plant in October. The old company's service had not been satisfactory. Since it was cheaper to pump from the Bayou than from the artesian wells that were supposed to furnish the supply, a considerable percentage of Bayou water was mixed with the pure water from the wells. Moreover, the fire pressure was often inadequate.

The city at once cut off the Bayou water, and began the installation of duplicate machinery. The average water pressure was increased about nine pounds, and adequate fire pressure was obtained. While wages of employees were increased slightly—about $3,600 a year—the salaries of the company's officials were dispensed with to the amount of $9,000 annually. The city is burning less coal than the old company, and the total expense of operating the more efficient plant is about $400 a month less than it was under private management.

Such specific instances as these are more significant, perhaps, than the dry facts that under the new charter the city, in less than two years, has reduced taxation from $2 on the hundred to $1.80, and that it has canceled the floating debt of nearly $300,000, while it has paid off nearly $200,000 more of indebtedness in the form of street-paving certificates, debts to the old water company, and the like.

Galveston has had a similar experience. In the last five years of commission government it has decreased its running expenses a third, has cleaned its streets, done much paving, put in sewers, improved its water plant, and become a well-ordered, prosperous town.

These like results in both cities are to be traced, as has been pointed out, to the abolition of the checks and balances which American municipalities copied from the Federal Government, which in turn had inherited them from parliamentary England, and to the centralization of authority and responsibility.

Formerly Houston was divided into six wards and there were two Aldermen from each ward. There was a multiplicity of other elective officers—half a dozen or more—besides the Aldermen. It was impossible to hold so many accountable for the conduct of their offices. Now the ward lines are abolished the four Aldermen are elected at large, and the other city officers are appointed by the

Mayor and may be removed by him at will—except the Comptroller, who is elected by the Council and to that body alone is responsible. If things go wrong, it is easy to fix the blame on the Mayor or one of his four assistants.

"If we should grow careless," a Houston man said, "and allow incompetent or dishonest men to be elected to the Council, we would at least have this advantage—it's easier to watch five thieves than fifteen."

But the thieves aren't likely to be elected. The new charter makes office-holding attractive to the competent man. By removing hampering restrictions that usually surround city officials, it enables him to get results. This is the direct testimony of such men as Mr. I. H. Kempner, President of the Texas Bank and Trust Company of Galveston, who is serving his city as Commissioner of Finance and Revenue. It is common sense, too.

This freedom from restriction is carried so far that the Houston charter, for instance, is more remarkable for the things it omits than for those it contains. You will search in vain in this pamphlet with the brick-colored covers for the scheme of government that is in actual operation.

You may know that the Mayor supervises the city engineering and legal departments; that one Alderman is in charge of finance, another of public health, another of streets, and a fourth of police and fire service. But you will find none of this information in the charter. It merely says that "the administration of the business affairs of Houston shall be conducted by a Mayor and four Aldermen," and that the Aldermen shall perform " such administrative duties as may be allotted by the Mayor."

In practice this plan has worked out on a business basis. The Mayor assigns the Aldermen to their departments at the beginning of his administration. In the conduct of the city affairs Mayor and Aldermen get together, talk things over, agree upon what should be done, and then ratify their agreements in formal and brief Council meetings. Theoretically the Council is always in session. Here is practically the British cabinet system, in which executive and legislative authority are combined. Readers of Bagehot who recall his comment on the effect of the responsibility of cabinet ministers in sobering their speeches and reducing promises to a basis of performance will be interested to note that an analogous result is produced under the centralized form of city government. The Council cannot afford to indulge in the customary buncombe.

This is admirably illustrated in the experience of Houston, where the city engineer says that the cost of running his office is about half as much as under the old order, for this reason : Under the old régime every Alderman, in order to make a showing for his own constituents, would get through the Council ordinances requiring the engineering department to prepare plans and specifications for vast amounts of work, with no expectation that the work would ever be actually performed. In one year his office prepared plans and specifications for more than three million dollars' worth of street improvements, when only $250,000 worth was actually done. So a needlessly large force of draughtsmen was required, and occasionally contracts were let on specifications perfunctorily prepared without expectation that they would be used, and the city's interests suffered. Now there is no temptation to play to the galleries. The city's Board of Directors knows how much work can be done. It has no object in calling for plans for more. It is responsible, not to the wards, but to the city as a whole.

This desire on the part of Aldermen to make a showing for their home wards is a familiar and sinister phenomenon in American cities. As a rule, the ward Alderman is much more interested in " getting things " for his constituents— street paving, lights, patronage, and what not—than he is in doing things for the city at large. So, too, he is apt to be unduly influenced by the aggressive " wide open " element in his ward, which by clever manipulation is often able to exercise a power out of all proportion to its real strength.

Galveston got rid of ward Aldermen in 1895, and elected its Aldermen at large. This brought better results. But

it was only after the commission form had gone into effect, and responsibility had been definitely and publicly located, that the worst dives were closed and the saloons and the disreputable element were brought under the control of the law.

In Houston gambling-houses were allowed to operate almost unmolested until the new system of government was introduced. Now these places have been practically suppressed. Formerly the saloons were open all day Sunday. Now they are open only after one o'clock in the afternoon. Although the Council has been criticised for failure to enforce the State law to the letter, many well-informed persons feel that it has gone as far as public sentiment sanctions.

That it commands the support of the public is indicated by the fact that more than a thousand persons recently petitioned the Mayor and the four Aldermen to become candidates for re-election. This is nearly a quarter of the voting population, for Houston, incidentally, disfranchises what it considers the irresponsible voter by requiring a receipt for a poll tax of $2.50 as a condition for casting the ballot. And only about 4,500 of a voting population of perhaps 12,000 go to the polls on election day.

With the experience of the average American municipality in mind, it might possibly be taken for granted that the majority of persons would agree that the centralization plan would generally result in increased efficiency, but that one insurmountable objection would occur to them. That's all very well, they would say, but what about franchise grabs ? Our present system, with its interminable debates and committee references, is cumbersome enough in the transaction of ordinary business; but at least it prevents—or makes less easy—the theft of valuable rights by public service corporations.

Houston, too, realized this difficulty, and this is the way it met it. The charter provides, in the first place, for the publication once a week for three consecutive weeks of the franchise ordinance. The publication is at the expense of the applicant. In the second place, it provides that the ordinance cannot become effective until thirty days after it shall have been signed by the Mayor. Lastly, on the petition of five hundred voters the Council is required to call a special election at which the franchise must be submitted to a popular vote. A majority vote is necessary to confirm the Council's grant.

In this way the rights of the city are as carefully safeguarded as they possibly could be even in municipalities where franchise ordinances are threshed over in two houses of the Council before they go to the Mayor. The city of St. Louis, it may be recalled, has a bicameral Council—under a requirement of the Missouri Constitution which thus sought to save the cities from themselves—and yet so remote was the city government from the people, so divided the responsibility, that both houses were regularly bought and sold until an alert and upright prosecutor, Joseph W. Folk, began sending the boodlers to the penitentiary.

Galveston and Houston do not insist that they have devised a perfect scheme of government, or one that could be advantageously adopted by other cities without modification. Indeed, there are striking, though minor, divergences between the charters of the two cities, Thus the Mayor-President and Commissioners of Galveston are paid small salaries (the Mayor-President $2,000 and the Commissioners $1,200 each), and they are not expected to give their entire time to the work. Their functions are like those of directors in a private corporation. They meet at night, discuss the city's affairs, and agree on a policy. The appointive heads of departments are held responsible for results. In Houston, on the other hand, the officials are paid larger salaries (the Mayor $4,000 and the Aldermen $2,400 each), and the charter requires them to give all their time to the work. It has been urged that the men whom the city needs for Aldermen cannot give up their entire time to the work for the salary offered, and that the Galveston plan in this respect is better for a city of, say, less than one hundred thousand inhabitants.

Again, it has been suggested that it would be better that the city elect five Aldermen, instead of four, and that the Aldermen elect the Mayor. A popular man with small business ability might be elected Mayor, as often happens in American cities. Whereas it is felt that the responsible board of managers of the city would be more apt to select its most capable member as its executive head. These, of course, are minor details which must be worked out in the light of fuller experience.

Meanwhile it is interesting to observe that the movement toward centralization is being widely discussed; that the officials of Galveston have been fairly swamped with letters of inquiry; that San Antonio and Fort Worth are considering the advisability of following the example of the two largest Texas cities, and that the officials of Topeka and of Kansas City, Kansas, have applied to the Kansas Legislature for permission to submit the commission form of government to a popular vote.

# IS MARS INHABITED?

## BY PERCIVAL LOWELL

Since 1840 the climate, conditions, and surface of Mars have been subjected to very careful examination by astronomers who have made this subject a special study, and have published from time to time maps giving pictorially the results of their observations. Of these special investigators, the leading ones are Schiaparelli, an Italian, and Percival Lowell, an American astronomer. The latter has had peculiar advantages for conducting such investigations in the possession of an observatory at Flagstaff, Arizona, where the peculiar clearness of the atmosphere, free alike from the smoky impurities of more populous regions and from the moisture common in the rainy regions, gives conditions especially favorable for this minuter study of the heavens. Here, to quote Mr. Lowell, " the stars shine out as they shone before the white man came." The investigations of these and other observers have brought to light on the surface of Mars a series of markings, the character of which precludes the idea that they are either rivers or chasms in the planet's surface, and warrants the supposition that they are areas of vegetation created and maintained by an artificial system of irrigation. If so, their existence would demonstrate that Mars is inhabited by intelligent beings, who are familiar with agricultural arts, possess the virtue of industry, and have some degree of what we would term scientific knowledge. To this conclusion the expert students of Mars have been brought by their studies, though they hold it more or less as a rational hypothesis rather than as a demonstrated fact. The only arguments against this hypothesis appear to us to be without weight—these, namely: first, that many astronomers who have lacked the special advantages of such observers as Schiaparelli and Lowell have not seen these markings; and, second, that it is not to be believed that any other world than our own can be inhabited. We suspect that the real reason for discrediting the conclusions of such observers as Mr. Lowell is this naïve egotism which persists in regarding man as the "lord of creation." The Copernican theory of astronomy put an end to the geocentric conception of the universe. If the not improbable hypothesis that Mars is inhabited by intelligent beings should be established, it would put an end to some of the semi-theological theories which we have inherited from a time when this world was thought to be the center of creation, the sun and stars a mechanism for supplying it with light, and man the supreme and only son of God, for whom the universe was all made. The reader who is interested to pursue further this topic will find the material in the very interesting recently published volume on " Mars and its Canals," by Percival Lowell, the author of the following article.—THE EDITORS.

PERHAPS no better response could be made to the request of the editor of The Outlook for an article on the habitation of Mars than by answering some of the questions that spontaneously arise on the subject in a reader's mind. For such a one is anxious to learn the evidence upon which the conclusion is based, that he may judge for himself of its cogency. To do this understandingly he must be satisfied on two points: of its value first and of its pertinency afterward. With regard to the first he is specially liable to be confused.

To a layman it seems sufficient that a man be an astronomer for his pronunciamento upon any astronomical matter to be regarded as authoritative, whatever the matter may be. But if the same layman will consider any other subject, such as law or medicine, he will recognize at once that to be skilled in one branch of his profession does not entitle a practitioner to expert opinion in another. One would hardly consult an aurist for an attack of typhoid fever, or a conveyancer for a point in criminal procedure. Yet to-day astronomy is itself quite as specialized, and a man whose occupation is celestial mechanics is not on that account an authority on planetary observation. Even in branches of the same profession it is surprising how often the mistake is made, and how in books on astronomy the writers will assert that the doctors disagree without so much as considering their respective qualifications to a diagnosis.

In no field is this more patent than in

that which deals with visual observation of the planets, partly because the workers are few, partly because the critics are mány. Only the other day I received a letter from an eminent astronomer, a doubter in print of the linearity of the canals, who, having just become aware of the importance of chromatic aberration in the matter, wrote suggesting my trying remedies for it, unaware that such remedies had been used first by Schiaparelli and then by me, for thirty years. After this, one willingly agrees with this astronomer's own words in another place —" If the reader ask about habitability of Mars, I can only reply that he knows as much about it as I do, and that is just nothing at all." In truth, the only astronomers capable of an opinion are those who have made special study of Mars. Now, the first point to be noted is the remarkable agreement between these astronomers, who are thus entitled to speak with authority on the subject, with regard to what they have depicted. Almost the only difference between them has been one of advance from the time of Beer and Mädler to the present day, as inspection of their maps will show.[1]

Undoubtedly the most important question we can ask about an observation, other than as to the man who made it, is the site of the observatory where it was made. For details are unmistakable in good air which wholly escape detection in a poor one. It is vital, therefore, to learn how the sites of observatories whose names are familiar to him compare with regard to what they will show. Now, a year and a half ago some tests were made at Flagstaff, Arizona, upon the number of stars visible in a certain region of the heavens which had been mapped first at the Naval Observatory in Washington and then at the Lick Observatory in California. The visibility of stars depends upon the character of the sky through which the rays coming to us must pass, the clearer and steadier the air the more stars being seen with a glass of a given aperture. To see stars of a magnitude fainter a glass of a

diameter half as big again must be used if the sky be the same in the two places. Now, the region examined yielded the following number of stars at the three observatories in question :

| | Size of aperture. | Number of stars. |
|---|---|---|
| Lowell Observatory... | 24-inch | 172 |
| Lick Observatory..... | 36-inch | 161 |
| Naval Observatory.... | 26-inch | 61 |

In other words, so much purer was the air at Flagstaff than at Mount Hamilton or Washington that more stars were visible with a 24-inch glass there than with a 36-inch one at the Lick, and nearly three times as many as could be detected with 26-inches at the Naval Observatory. The results were subsequently confirmed by photography of the region at Flagstaff. Now, the steadiness of the air which thus affects the stars affects still more the planets. The outcome, therefore, speaks impersonally for the credibility of the detail seen on the planets at the latter place. For Washington may be taken as a fair representative of observatories generally in the eastern United States and Europe.

Next comes the care with which the observations must be conducted. For denseness in the observer does not compensate for lack of vacuity in the air. Schiaparelli critically scanned and tested all his observations, and the present writer has studied the conditions of seeing side by side with the things seen. Knowledge of one's own eyes, study of the air-waves in their effect upon the telescopic image, investigation of apertures and eye-pieces, of interposed glasses to give monochromatic light, and of other researches too numerous and technical to repeat here, all go to a getting of the sharpest and most minute detail, and must be understood and practiced by one who would aspire to an opinion upon the facts.

Systematic study is no less imperative. Unless a man be of rare judgment and unusual acumen, a little knowledge here is as disastrous as in other vocations. Much of the skepticism on the subject is due directly to this cause. Many an observer has looked under poor conditions once or twice, seen nothing, and gone his way convinced that nothing was

---

[1] " Mars and its Canals " contains a number of these maps, which furnish the reader both ocular demonstration of the canals and also illustrate the progress which has been made since 1890 in discovering them.— THE EDITORS.

there, forgetful of the fact that if the thing were as easy as that it would not have waited so long for discovery. In truth, training here is as necessary as in anything else worth the finding out. The landsman cannot see what the sailor detects in a moment, and the Indian follows a trail where to the tenderfoot nothing is observable.

On the other hand, long-continued study helps to perfect both the observations themselves and 'the outcome to which they lead by intercomparison and summing up. Schiaparelli considered' that an observer should follow Mars for at least a cycle of oppositions, or, in other words, for fifteen years more or less, if he would know the planet; and the more the present writer has studied this interesting body, the more profitable he has found such study to be. The advances made since Schiaparelli's time are ample testimony to the amount there is yet to be learned about it.

Of the extent to which such systematic study is carried at Flagstaff it is enough to say that the planet has been kept under observation there now for twelve years, covering six oppositions—that is, six returns to proximity to the earth. At each of these favorable epochs Mars has been scanned for seven months or so, on end, as continuously as possible, and in that climate continuity of observation is possible. In 1903 there was a stretch of forty-six days when without a break the planet was visible every night. The drawings made of it in consequence number thousands—each a complete delineation of every marking to be seen upon its face. ' Such a mass of material furnish data not to be disputed save by an equal collection, and no other such collection exists.

Another matter should be mentioned in which a reader may go astray. Even good observers differ notably in their field of proficiency, because of two quite different qualities in the human eye. For an eye may be specially sensitive to light or specially perceptive of form, and the same eye rarely if ever has both capacities. Consequently a man who detects the difficult in faint stars or satellites is not only no authority for that reason on delicate detail, but is actually prevented by the constitution of his eye from seeing it, and is rendered all the more dangerous a guide to others from the fact that he is unaware of his limitation.

In passing on, now, by these stepping-stones of painstaking care to what they have revealed, I cannot in the transition do better than quote Schiaparelli's fine simplicity in refutation of his critics: "I am absolutely sure of what I have observed."

Under such research one set of markings presented by the planet's face is curious to a degree. It is the one most concerned with the subject of life. Over the map-like topography which the planet reveals unveiled to view, there is spread a fine reticulated network of lines. Each is straight or symmetrically curved and is of uniform character throughout its course, being of the same size from one end to the other. Some resemble strong pencil-marks, others show light as gossamer threads. But each is emphatically linear and of sharp definitiveness when the air is still. When the air is not still, the lines dilate, broadened into streaks just as a page of print violently shaken widens to a blur; and in this guise they are commonly seen at most observatories because of the disfigurement the images undergo in traversing our atmosphere. That such distortion is of our own air's fashioning I have had plenty of occasion to note. Unpossessed of measurable width, they are visible solely for their length; a seeming paradox that any one may verify by the-look of telegraph wires seen a long distance off. For to these they stand akin. From experiments made ,on such at Flagstaff it appears that we could see a line on Mars if it were only a mile wide.

The network starts near the edge of the polar caps, while its meshes lower down connect all the salient features of the great blue-green areas. Where the lines cross each other the junctions stand confessed of importance by small pinheads of spots. Instead of stopping at the dark areas, the lines have been found to lace them and thence to connect with others that carry the network up to the other polar cap. The consequence is that the planet's surface is triangulated as by a geodetic survey.

No part of it escapes the reticulation, whence all of it must be land.

Now, the geometricism of these lines shows at once that they cannot be cracks such as we see on the moon, nor rivers such as we know on earth. Their even size throughout precludes alike the one and the other supposition. Their amazing directness of direction equally negatives such a character. Nor is there any other natural phenomenon which will explain them. Unaccountable is their form and still more their interconnection on any purely natural hypothesis. They look to be of artificial creation; and, instead of giving up the ghost of the idea on closer and more critical investigation, the better they are seen the more perfectly do they carry out the character. It is not generally known and it is particularly telling that their geometric appearance grew on Schiaparelli as he continued to observe. His successive maps show strikingly how loth he was to credit his own eyesight, and how recognition of the wonderful method in these lines was gradually forced upon him by the lines themselves.

Not the least significant confession to their non-natural character is that critics who have not seen them are driven to denial of the correctness of the observations as the only refuge from acceptance of artificiality. But to deny from *a priori* prejudice what one has not seen and another has is like denying the existence of Paris because one has never been there.

Their appearance is not the end of the matter; their behavior is even more self-committal. To one who watches them month after month it becomes evident that these markings change. Where at first no lines were visible lines begin to appear. And this without regard to the planet's proximity to or remoteness from the earth. Indeed, the times when Mars is nearest are not, as a rule, the best for the detection of the lines, and this accounts for their having remained so long unseen. But to another circumstance they pay strict attention: the seasonal epoch of the planet's year. At certain Martian months they are conspicuous, at others the reverse. Now the dark areas with which they are associated are undoubtedly areas of vegetation. The fact that the lines traverse them shows that they cannot be seas, as was once thought, while other reasons, such as their own seasonal change, point to their being vegetation. A similar seasonal metamorphosis is undergone by the lines, and predicates a like character for them.

To appreciate how the links in a long chain of argument fit into one another to an articulate exposition of artificiality one must read the literature of the subject. Here it is possible only to point to a sign-post or two. For instance, one of the most telling things about the lines which are the much-talked-of "canals" is the course taken by their development. For this does not commence till the polar cap is well on its way in melting. The canals nearest to the cap proceed to darken first, then those next them take on tone, and so the evolution into conspicuousness progresses, the canals emerging, as it were, in turn according to latitudinal position. A wave of transformation sweeps thus silently down the disk. It is early summer when this metamorphosis occurs. Now we have assurance that the substance composing the caps is frozen water, because, first, it behaves like snow; second, there is no other substance known to us like it in look and character; and, third, the latest investigations by the writer, instead of the great cold formally supposed to be the Martian portion in consequence of the planet's distance from the sun, indicate a mean temperature of about 48° Fahrenheit. The development of the canals, then, waits on water and follows upon the unlocking of its winter's hoarding in the polar cap. But the way this occurs reveals something other than purely natural processes as cause. For the figure of the planet is such as to make of its surface a level surface, so that what is called, broadly speaking, water freed at one spot would not of itself, except in a very local way, seek another. It would be quite incapable of traveling of its own accord from the pole to the equator. Yet it does this surprising thing; and not only that, but pursues its course well over into the planet's other hemisphere. Twice each Martian year the singular phenomenon takes place, first from one pole and then six months later from the other. Nothing known to physics could cause it, for the flow takes place in defiance of the laws of gravity. So far as it can be measured, the flow advances down the latitudes with regular speed—fifty-two miles a day, or two miles an hour.

What, then, it will be asked, are these so-called canals? The best answer consists in pointing to the Nile. What we call the canals are narrow belts from ten to twenty miles wide on the average. They behave as strips of vegetation would, and such beyond much question is their character. Seen from space the Nile would look not otherwise. It, too, threading its way across a desert, fertilizes a ribbon of country which is some fifteen miles wide. Once each year it grows green after the fashion of the Martian canals, and then in due time lapses again to ocher. The river itself would escape detection from a Martian distance, and still more remain invisible if, as probably on Mars, the fertilizing conduit were smaller still. Canals, then, these lines may with propriety be called,

although there is no ground for supposing them to be of herculean description, any more than there would be for deeming the water supply of our cities to be indebted to anything larger than two-foot pipes, or an oasis in the Sahara to be the child of more than a tiny spring. It is the only explanation which is in accordance with the facts of observation concerning the lines themselves and the spots at their junctions, and it is furthermore the logical outcome of what research of the last few years has shown us to be the general physical condition of the planet. That life now habits Mars is the only rational deduction from the observations in our possession ; the only one which is warranted by the facts.

As to what the life habitant there may be like I should not pretend to say. As yet we lack sufficient data to infer. For just as it is unscientific to deny observations because we fear the seemingly startling conclusions to which they commit us, so it is not the province of science to speculate where observation is wanting, however interesting and even useful such speculation may be.

# CONSERVATISM IN THE UNITED STATES

## BY FRANKLIN K. LANE

*Inter-State Commerce Commissioner*

THOUSANDS of Americans sincerely believe that the United States is politically the most radical country on this round planet. Hardly a day passes lately without the publication of some alarming prophecy of the evil that will surely befall unless we mend our ways and utterly destroy those dangerous persons who by one means or another are seeking to change things. We have forsaken the gods of the elder days and are following after strange red gods of modern manufacture. Prosperity is to be destroyed and individual liberty and initiative are to be submerged in the rising sea of American radicalism. Woe is to be our portion and desolation will fall upon the land. And all this, indeed, because one man

favors the imposition of a tax on incomes, and another favors a tax on inheritances, and still one more would decrease the number of working children, and yet another would reduce street railway fares or curb illegal industrial combinations.

'There is nothing, to be sure, that stands between this country and any form of confiscatory policy that can be imagined excepting the letter of our laws and the spirit of our people. These, however, are quite sufficient.

This government is organically conservative. We could not, though we would, do violence to property rights without wrecking the government in substance and in form. The fundamental law of the Nation contains provisions more surely protecting property than are to be found in the laws of any other land. We have no doctrine that the king can do no wrong, or that the State can do no wrong. The right to property is a vital part of our organic law. The police powers of the State are broad, but this is necessarily so. There could be no government of any kind without such powers; they inhere in government itself.

Not only has this right to possess and enjoy property been anchored into the foundation stones of the Republic, but the people, if so disposed, have been deprived of the power to amend or alter the Constitution save by the most elaborate and almost impossible procedure. And to remove still further the danger of hasty and passionate expression, every legislative body, National, State, or municipal, is deprived of the power to convert its will into law without being subject to the check of the courts. Thus the Congress of the United States is less absolute than the Parliament of England or the Chambers of France.

These constitutional limitations upon the power of the people are our own; they are to be found nowhere else. Yet they apparently have no place in the thought or consideration of those alarmists who are somewhat monotonously declaiming upon the dangers of radicalism in the United States.

The American people themselves may be safely classed as the most conservative among the civilized peoples if we are to judge from their legislation. Things we call radical, other nations, older and perhaps soberer than ourselves, regard to-day as mere commonplaces. Many of the very ideas which alarm the conservatives of America are accepted and approved by conservatives elsewhere. And if those who speak in honest fear of present radical tendencies among our people will in all calmness review the proposals advanced by American statesmen, they will have difficulty in finding a single one which has not been debated in the parliaments of Europe and tested by one or more of those we call the great nations of the Old World. Tory statesmen of old England (whose policies did not spring, be it said, from fear of losing their seats) favored laws a full half-century ago which to the Americans of to-day seem perilous experiments. Germany's system of compulsory insurance and Great Britain's land policy in Ireland are, in point of paternalism, beyond the utmost bounds of any political programme seriously supported in America. It must be conceded that since the early years of our life we have done little to establish our right to pre-eminence in the world of political science, and it is difficult to refute the contention that other peoples have labored more zealously than ourselves to establish justice and equality under popular government and to perfect its forms. Not that we are indifferent to these things, but since the Civil War our minds have been obsessed by great material experiments and exploitations, and thus it has come about that we have permitted others to experiment for us in the political laboratory. We needed a secret ballot for many years, and one came to us at last from Australia—not by the direct route, however, but via Suez and across the Canadian border. So, too, its complement, the Purity of Elections Law, followed almost literally the Corrupt Practices Act of England. Our railway, factory, and other regulative measures of much prominence were born of foreign parents. Indeed, one has difficulty to find any so-called radical legislation which did not originate in some other land and take from ten to fifty years to cross the ocean. This is one industry in which the balance of trade has been altogether against us in recent times. We have imported some of the reform ideas of other lands, but have not been able to show a corresponding offset in the exportation of similar domestic products. One does not hear of any practical political reform, or even any economic theory, of American origin, causing debate in France, Switzerland, England, or New Zealand, excepting that in several foreign lands a much warmer reception has been given to Henry George's theory of taxation than has been extended to it in this country. Altogether, therefore, it would appear that the United States is not entitled to a seat on the Extreme Left in the Parliament of the Nations.

Patently, the fact that other peoples

may have found certain institutions or laws advantageous or beneficial is not a demonstration that we should incorporate them in our own system. Policies and measures may flourish and give rich returns in one land and produce naught but evil in another. The value of any piece of political machinery depends upon those who use it, their political upbringing, and the " set " of their natures. One need not, however, be either Socialist or dreamer because he proposes an Old World remedy for a New World symptom.

To those who see nothing in the political, social, or economic conditions now prevailing that calls for improvement, there must of course be something extremely absurd in any suggestion of new legislation. And so also to those who have adopted the easy philosophy that all political action is predestined to be futile. But to those who believe that the problems of a people change with the changes in the form and nature of their life, it would seem inevitable that they should feel a desire to see the machinery of society adapted as speedily and smoothly as possible to its new work. Hitherto we have had to meet but few of the problems of the more congested countries. The land has been rich enough to offer abundant opportunity to all. The distance between rich and poor has been so comparatively slight that it has been possible to step from one class into the other. Employer and employee have been neighbors and friends. We lived a narrow individualistic life—the life of the town-meeting, the church, and the farm. But who shall say that this old order is not passing or has not already passed away? Instead of the town, we have the great city in which one out of every twelve who die is buried by the municipality. Instead of the individual employer, we have the impersonal corporation. Instead of the individual employee, we have the sensitive, shrewdly directed labor union, representing perhaps a million men, with which to bargain. Instead of the farm whereon all was raised that the family needed, we have the farm which turns out a special product, and is entirely dependent upon the city for supplies. •Instead of the

single industry, we have the trust. Instead of competition, we have " community of interest "—extending across seas and around the world. Instead of the local railroad owned at home, we have the transcontinental system owned abroad. Instead of the little paper in the little town, we have the metropolitan daily reaching the remotest household. Instead of the country store, we have the mail order house. Instead of the boss, we have the syndicate. Big things have taken the place of small ones in all fields. We have become apparently interdependent to the fullest degree. This is not the work of government, nor has it been consciously effected. We thought at first that it was temporary; we know now that it means a mental as well as an industrial growth. Men think in continents where once they thought in villages, and in millions where once they thought in thousands. Men think, too, in relationships and not as solitary units. To this new order society and all its agencies must adapt itself.

The world, for it is a world movement, must deal with the new problems to which this spirit of combination and interdependence may give birth. They must be met in each land in a manner suited to the form of its government and the nature of its people. They are to be dealt with in the United States according to our laws and the temperament and ideals of our people. Again we are to be given an opportunity to prove the adaptability and the efficiency of a republican form of government. To find a way through—this is the statesman's problem; a way that will lead to peace and not contention, security and not shipwreck; a way that is not to be found by those who would substitute an artificial for a natural social order, nor yet by those who would deny to society the right more perfectly to express itself, its purposes and ambitions. There can be no peace and no security without maintenance of the law and a steady intent to do justice, and the dangerous class is composed of those, by whatsoever name they may be called, who, through ignorance, malice, or indifference, imperil all law by justifying or seeming to justify injustice.

# THE SCHOOL DAYS OF AN INDIAN

## BY CHARLES A. EASTMAN
### (OHIYESA)

## I. MY FIRST DAY IN SCHOOL

"**O**-HE-E-YE-SA!**" It was my name that rolled forth in a sonorous call· from a low log cabin which stood just around· a bend of the Big Sioux River in Dakota. The loop forms almost a complete circle, and the land within was heavily timbered with soft maple and elm trees ·which afforded some protection from the strong sweep of the prairie winds. The man who had built the cabin—it was his first house, and therefore he was proud of it —was tall and manly·looking. He stood in front of his pioneer home with a resolute face.

He had been accustomed to the buffalo-skin teepee all his life, until he opposed the white man and was defeated and made a prisoner of war at Davenport, Iowa. It was because of his meditations during those four years in a military prison that he had severed himself from his tribe and taken up a homestead. He declared that he would never join in another Indian outbreak, but would work with his hands for the rest of his life.

"I have hunted every day," he said, "for the support of my family. I sometimes chase the deer all day. One must work, and work hard, whether chasing the deer or planting corn. After all, the corn-planting is the surer provision."

These were my father's new views, and in this radical change of life he had persuaded a few other families to join him. They formed a little colony at Flandreau, on the Big Sioux River.

To be sure, his beginnings in civilization had not been attended with all the success that he had hoped for. One year the crops had been devoured by grasshoppers, and another year ruined by drought. But he was still satisfied that there was no alternative for the Indian. He was now anxious to have his boys learn the English language and something about books, for he could see that these were the " bow and arrows " of the white man. He had been into Manitoba that very summer, and with difficulty found and recovered me, his youngest son, from whom he had been separated ever since the outbreak of 1862.

He called once more, and at last a faint reply came from behind a swell of land. Soon the sounds of horses' hoofs were heard, and in another minute half a dozen wild ponies with a wild-looking boy upon the back of one of them came over the rise in a hot chase towards the cabin. The boy rider raised again and again his lariat over his head, until, panting, they halted before the door.

"Ohiyesa, I have said that you will have to go to school to learn the ways of the white man. It is time. You may take one of the ponies and ride over now to the school-house."

I remember quite well how I felt as I stood there with eyes fixed upon the ground.

"'And what am I to do at the school?" I asked finally, with much embarrassment.

"You will be taught the language of the white man, and also how to count your money and tell the prices of your horses and of your furs. The white teacher will first teach you the signs by which you can make out the words on their books. They call them A, B, C, and so forth. Old as I am, I have learned some of them."

The matter having been thus far explained, I was soon on my way to the little mission school, two miles distant

851

over the prairie. There was no clear idea in my mind as to what I had to do, but as I galloped along the road I turned over and over what my father had said, and the more I thought of it the less I was satisfied. Finally I said aloud:

"Why do we need a sign language, when we can both hear and talk?" And unconsciously I pulled on the lariat and the pony came to a stop. I suppose I was half curious and half in dread about this "learning white men's ways." Meanwhile the pony had begun to graze.

While thus absorbed in thought, I was suddenly startled by the yells of two other Indian boys and the noise of their ponies' hoofs. I pulled the pony's head up just as the two strangers also pulled up and stopped their panting ponies at my side. They stared at me for a minute, while I looked at them out of the corners of my eyes.

"Where are you going? Are you going to our school?" volunteered one of the boys at last.

To this I replied timidly: "My father told me to go to a place where the white men's ways are taught, and to learn the sign language."

"That's good—we are going there too! Come on, Red Feather, let's try another race! I think, if we had not stopped, my pony would have outrun yours. Will you race with us?" he continued, addressing me; and we all started our ponies at full speed.

I soon saw that the two strange boys were riding erect and soldier-like. "That must be because they have been taught to be like the white man," I thought. I allowed my pony a free start and leaned forward until the animal drew deep breaths, then I slid back and laid my head against the pony's shoulder, at the same time raising my quirt, and he leaped forward with a will! I yelled as I passed the other boys, and pulled up when I reached the crossing. The others stopped, too, and surveyed pony and rider from head to foot, as if they had never seen us before.

"You have a fast pony. Did you bring him back with you from Canada?" Red Feather asked. "I think you are the son of Many Lightnings, whom he brought home the other day," the boy added.

"Yes, this is my own pony. My uncle in Canada always used him to chase the buffalo, and he has ridden him in many battles." I spoke with considerable pride.

"Well, as there are no more buffalo to chase now, your pony will have to pull the plow like the rest. But if you ride him to school, you can join in the races. On the holy days the young men race horses, too." Red Feather and White Fish spoke both together, while I listened attentively, for everything was strange to me.

"What do you mean by the 'holy days'?" I asked.

"Well, that's another of the white people's customs. Every seventh day they call a 'holy day,' and on that day they go to a 'Holy House,' where they pray to their Great Mystery. They also say that no one should work on that day."

This definition of Sunday and church-going set me to thinking again, for I never knew before that there was any difference in the days.

"But how do you count the days, and how do you know what day to begin with?" I inquired.

"Oh, that's easy! The white men have everything in their books. They know how many days in a year, and they have even divided the day itself into so many equal parts; in fact, they have divided them again and again until they know how many times one can breathe in a day," said White Fish, with the air of a learned man.

"That's impossible," I thought, so I shook my head.

By this time we had reached the second crossing of the river, on whose bank stood the little mission school. Thirty or forty Indian children stood about, curiously watching the newcomers as we came up the steep bank. I realized for the first time that I was an object of curiosity, and it was not a pleasant feeling. On the other hand, I was considerably interested in the strange appearance of these school-children. They all had on some apology for white man's clothing, but their pantaloons belonged neither to the order *short* nor to the *long*. Their coats, some of them, met only half-way by the help of long strings. Others were lapped over in front, and held on by a string of some sort fastened round the body. Some of their hats were brimless and others without crowns, while most were fantastically painted. The hair of all the boys was cut short, and, in spite of the evidences of great effort to keep it down, it stood erect like porcupine quills. I thought, as I stood on one side and took a careful observation of the motley gathering, that if I had to look like these boys in order to obtain something of the white man's learning, it was time for me to rebel.

The boys played ball and various other games, but I tied my pony to a tree and then walked up to the school-house and stood there as still as if I had been glued to the wall. Presently the teacher came out and rang a bell, and all the children went in, but I waited for some time before entering, and then slid inside and took the seat nearest the door. I felt singularly out of place, and for the twentieth time wished my father had not sent me.

When the teacher spoke to me, I had not the slightest idea what he meant, so I did not trouble myself to make any demonstration, for fear of giving offense. Finally he asked in broken Sioux: "What is your name?" Evidently he had not been among the Indians long, or he would not have asked that question. It takes a tactician and a diplomat to get an Indian to tell his name! The poor man was compelled to give up the attempt and resume his seat on the platform.

He then gave some unintelligible directions, and, to my great surprise, the pupils in turn held their books open and talked the talk of a strange people. Afterward the teacher made some curious signs upon a blackboard on the wall, and seemed to ask the children to read them. To me they did not compare in interest with my bird's-track and fish-fin studies on the sands. I was something like a wild cub caught overnight, and appearing in the corral next morning with the lambs. I had seen nothing thus far to prove to me the good of civilization.

Meanwhile the children grew more

familiar, and whispered references were made to the "new boy's" personal appearance. At last he was called "Baby" by one of the big boys; but this was not meant for him to hear, so he did not care to hear. He rose silently and walked out. He did not dare to do or say anything in departing. The boys watched him as he led his pony to the river to drink and then jumped upon his back and started for home at a good pace. They cheered as he started over the hills: "Hoo-oo! hoo-oo! there goes the long-haired boy!"

When I was well out of sight of the school, I pulled in my pony and made him walk slowly home.

"Will going to that place make a man brave and strong?" I asked myself. "I must tell my father that I cannot stay here. I must go back to my uncle in Canada, who taught me to hunt and shoot and to be a brave man. They might as well try to make a buffalo build houses like a beaver as to teach me to be a white man," I thought.

It was growing late when at last I appeared at the cabin. "Why, what is the matter?" quoth my old grandmother, who had taken especial pride in me as a promising young hunter. Really, my face had assumed a look of distress and mental pressure that frightened the superstitious old woman. She held her peace, however, until my father returned.

"Ah," she said then, "I never fully believed in these new manners! The Great Mystery cannot make a mistake. I say it is against our religion to change the customs that have been practiced by our people ages back—so far back that no one can remember it. Many of the school-children have died, you have told me. It is not strange. You have offended Him, because you have made these children change the ways he has given us. I must know more about this matter before I give my consent." Grandmother had opened her mind in unmistakable terms, and the whole family was listening to her in silence.

Then my hard-headed father broke the pause. "Here is one Sioux who will sacrifice everything to win the wisdom of the white man! We have now entered upon this life, and there is no going back. Besides, one would be like a hobbled pony without learning to live like those among whom we must live."

During father's speech my eyes had been fixed upon the burning logs that stood on end in the huge mud chimney in a corner of the cabin. I didn't want to go to that place again; but father's logic was too strong for me, and the next morning I had my long hair cut, and started in to school in earnest.

I obeyed my father's wishes, and went regularly to the little day-school, but as yet my mind was in darkness. What has all this talk of books to do with hunting, or even with planting corn? I thought. The subject occupied my thoughts more and more, doubtless owing to my father's decided position on the matter; while, on the other hand, my grandmother's view of this new life was not encouraging.

I took the situation seriously enough, and I remember I went with it where all my people go when they want light— into the thick woods. I needed counsel, and human counsel did not satisfy me. I had been taught to seek the "Great Mystery" in silence, in the deep forest or on the height of the mountain. There were no mountains here, so I retired into the woods. I knew nothing of the white man's religion; I only followed the teaching of my ancestors.

When I came back, my heart was strong. I desired to follow the new trail to the end. I knew that, like the little brook, it must lead to larger and larger ones until it became a resistless river, and I shivered to think of it. But again I recalled the teachings of my people, and determined to imitate their undaunted bravery and stoic resignation. However, I was far from having realized the long, tedious years of study and confinement before I could begin to achieve what I had planned.

It was now twelve years since the Minnesota massacre, when the youngest son of Jacob Eastman, formerly called Many Lightnings, had been betrayed and led over the Canadian line. From that time his father had not seen or heard of him until he found him early that summer near Fort Ellice, Manitoba. Here was his family reunited at last under the new conditions, and he never lost an opportunity to impress upon the mind of his boy the importance of work and education. That youngest boy was myself.

It appears remarkable to me now that my father, thorough Indian as he was, should have had such deep and sound conceptions of a true civilization. But there is the contrast—my father's mother! whose faith in her people's philosophy and training could not be superseded by any other allegiance.

To her such a life as we lead to-day would be no less than sacrilege. "It is not a true life," she often said. "It is a sham. I cannot bear to see my boy live a made-up life!"

Ah, grandmother! you had forgotten one of the first principles of your own teaching, namely: "When you see a new trail, or a footprint that you do not know, follow it to the point of knowing."

"All I want to say to you," the old grandmother seemed to answer, "is this: Do not get lost on this new trail."

"I find," said my father to me, "that the white man has a well-grounded religion, and teaches his children the same virtues that our people taught to theirs. The 'Great Mystery' has shown to the red and white man alike the good and evil, from which to choose. I think the way of the white man is better than ours, because he is able to preserve on paper the things he does not want to forget. He records everything—the sayings of his wise men, the laws enacted by his counselors."

I began to be really interested in this curious scheme of living that my father was gradually unfolding to me out of his limited experience.

"The way of knowledge," he continued, "is like our old way in hunting. You begin with a mere trail—a footprint. If you follow that faithfully, it may lead you to a clearer trail—a track— a road. Later on there will be many tracks, crossing and diverging one from the other. Then you must be careful, for success lies in the choice of the right road. You must be doubly careful, for traps will be laid for you, of which the most dangerous is the spirit-water, that causes a man to forget his self-respect," he added, unwittingly giving to his aged mother material for her argument against civilization.

The general effect upon me of these discussions, which were logical enough on the whole, although almost entirely from the outside, was that I became convinced that my father was right.

My grandmother had to yield at last, and it was settled that I was to go to school at Santee Agency, Nebraska, where Dr. Alfred L. Riggs was then fairly started in the work of his great mission school, which has turned out some of the very best educated Sioux Indians. It was at that time the Mecca of the Sioux country; even though Sitting Bull and Crazy Horse were still at large, harassing soldiers and emigrants alike, and General Custer had just been placed in military command of the Dakota Territory.

# *A ROMANTIC BIOGRAPHY* [1]

THE story of Columbus has been told so often that at first thought there would seem to be little or no room for a new life of the great discoverer. But first thoughts are very likely to prove erroneous, and in point of fact Mr. Filson Young readily finds warrant for his biography. As is well known, the historians have been exceedingly busy with Columbus during the past few years, and as a result of their labors much that is surprising and not a little that is puzzling in his character and career have been brought to light. Reason has been found, for instance, for doubting the truthfulness of certain important statements he made regarding his ancestry and his achievements. It is hinted that he did not scruple to resort to forgery when forgery might serve h's purpose. And that he was treacherous and avaricious is suggested by the circumstance that he robbed a poor mariner of the reward promised to the man who should first sight land after the long voyage across the then unknown Atlantic. These and similar discoveries have naturally tended to dim the sun of his hitherto splendid reputation. But they have also been productive of an endless amount of controversy, interesting and instructive, no doubt, so far as the historians themselves are concerned, but leaving the general public very much in the dark respecting the manner of man Columbus really was.

For the general public, then, Mr. Young has written his book. Its purpose is not to add aught to the mass of controversial material accumulated by the recent investigators, but to take that material, extract from it the salient facts, and so present them that the uninformed reader can easily grasp their significance, and, what is more, will be stimulated to grasp it. This last is the really distinctive feature of Mr. Young's biography. He has striven to make his Columbus a very real figure moving in a very real world, a Columbus of the documents but also of flesh and blood, a Columbus whom we may not admire as unreservedly as was our wont before research turned its great white light on him, but a Columbus whom we understand, and with whom, understanding, we sympathize. In a word, from beginning to end his pages palpitate with feeling, with action, with life.

This effect is obtained by singularly audacious and original methods, methods so audacious and original, indeed, that the critic is hard put to peruse the work with an open mind and arrive at a fair verdict. If he be an adherent of the so-called scientific school of historical writing, he will be inclined to lose patience and disparage the biography; if, on the other hand, he be an enthusiastic disciple of the picturesque school, he will be tempted to overrate it. Mr. Young has, in effect, taken startling liberties with the established canons of historical writing. With the object of impressing upon his readers " that Christopher Columbus is not only a name, but that the human being whom we so describe did actually once live and walk

[1] Christopher Columbus and the New World of His Discovery. By Filson Young. With a Note on the Navigation of Columbus's First Voyage, by the Earl of Dunraven, K.G. Two Volumes. J. B. Lippincott Company, Philadelphia.

in the world; did actually sail and look upon seas where we may also sail and look; did stir with his feet the indestructible dust of this old earth, and center in himself, as we all do, the whole interest and meaning of the universe," he has clothed the known facts of Columbus's career in language the most romantic and dramatic, has sought to grasp the unknown facts by the aid of conjecture, and has at all times set the stage of action with striking and picturesque scenery.

His exordium prepares us for a book not cast along conventional lines. Instead of the usual introductory chapter dealing with the ancestry, birth, etc., of the hero, we have what is really a little essay on the emotions aroused in the mind of man by contemplation of the sea, an essay which finds its justification in Mr. Young's view-point of Columbus as owing his great achievement to the domination of an idea born of night watches on the vasty deep. Then follows, not in one chapter but in several, a bold reconstruction of that least-known period in the discoverer's life—the period of his infancy, youth, and early voyages. It is a period full of gaps from the documentary standpoint, and one which most biographers traverse hurriedly. But Mr. Young lingers, determined to make the most of the few bare facts available, and evidently hoping to give his readers some measure of understanding into the influences that went to shape Columbus's career, and it may be to account for the failings that modern research has so mercilessly exposed. Here, therefore, we find our author making liberal use of the gift of imagination with which he is richly endowed. Nor does he disdain the use of imagination when he comes to surer ground—to the years of sojourn in Portugal, of hope long deferred, of the discovery, of the successive voyages, and of the failures as a colonial administrator. There is space for but one quotation to illustrate the method pursued, a quotation from Mr. Young's account of the departure from Palos on the ever-memorable voyage to the unknown lands of the setting sun:

The time for meditations grows short. Lights are moving about in the town beneath; there is an unwonted midnight stir and bustle; the whole population is up and about, running hither and thither with lamps and torches through the starlit night. The tide is flowing; it will be high water before dawn; and with the first of the ebb the little fleet is to set sail. The stream of hurrying sailors and townspeople sets towards the church of Saint George, where mass is to be said and the Sacrament administered to the voyagers. The calls and shouts die away; the bell stops ringing; and the low muttering voice of the priest is heard beginning the Office. The light of the candles shines upon the gaudy roof and over the altar upon the wooden image of Saint George vanquishing the dragon, upon which the eyes of Christopher rested during some part of the service, and where to-day your eyes may rest also if you make that pilgrimage. The moment approaches; the bread and the wine are consecrated; there is a shuffling of knees and feet; then a pause. The clear notes of the bell ring out upon the warm, dusky silence—once, twice, thrice; the living God and the cold presence of dawn enter the church together. Every head is bowed; and for once at least every heart of that company beats in unison with the rest. And then the Office goes on, and the dark-skinned congregation streams up to the sanctuary and receives the Communion, while the blue light of dawn increases and the candles pale before the coming day. And then out again to the boats with shoutings and farewells, for the tide has now turned; hoisting of sails and tripping of anchors and breaking out of gorgeous ensigns; and the ships are moving! The Maria leads, with the sign of the Redemption painted on her mainsail, and the standard of Castile flying at her mizzen; and there is cheering from ships and from shore, and a faint sound of bells from the town of Huelva.

Thus, the sea being calm and a fresh breeze blowing off the land, did Christopher Columbus set sail from Palos at sunrise on Friday, the 3d of August, 1492.

No need to point out how strongly this smacks of the historical romance; and, the passage quoted being typical, such is the flavor of the work throughout. Not that Mr. Young shows himself at all times master of the romanticist's art. Occasionally there seems to be a straining after effect, and not infrequently there are crudities and floridities of diction that offend the more because of their unexpectedness. But, bearing in mind the fact that he achieves the exceedingly difficult task of bringing the man of the twentieth century into intimate touch with the man of the fifteenth, that he visualizes Columbus as few, if any, of his previous biographers have done, and that in addition to the gift of imagination he displays the scholar's passion for mastery of the facts; and bearing still more firmly in mind that he has written his book, not primarily for the special student, but for those readers—and their name is legion—to whom history profits nothing unless it be given a romantic setting, the judgment of candid criticism must be in his favor. At the same time, it is our opinion that he has pressed the theories of the picturesque school to a dangerous extreme, and he could have attained his purpose with even greater surety, and without any sacrifice of the dramatic elements of the story, by writing with more restraint.

## Comment on Current Books

**Beza**

The three hundredth anniversary of the death of the great reformer Beza was appropriately celebrated in Geneva recently by meetings which lasted three days and were addressed by eminent men. It is a satisfaction to students of history, especially of church history, that some of these discourses have now been printed and published with rare illustrations.[1] Among the discourses are those of Professor Doumergue, representing the Evangelical churches, and of Baron Schickler, representing the Reformed churches of France; of Professor Vuilleumier, of the University of Lausanne, and of Professor Borgeaud, the eminent historian and in especial the historian of the "Academy of Calvin," now the University of Geneva, as his recently published tome demonstrates.

**Birket Foster**

For many years, at least to the British public, the late Birket Foster seemed the water-color painter *par excellence*. He was not undeserving of this reputation. He combined, and often ideally, exactness of reproduction with pure poetic feeling. With this enviable equipment, his range of subjects was gratifyingly wide. It covered not only England, which he knew intimately from end to end, but also France, which he knew hardly less well, the Rhine, and Venice. The painter's lovable personality well matched his attractive pictures. It should be a satisfaction to Englishmen and also to many Americans to own the handsome just-published volume[2] in which they will find a wealth of charming illustrations, some of them in color, of very many of Foster's works. Mr. Cundall, one of the artist's oldest friends, furnishes some capital biographical and critical comment.

**Consular Jurisdiction in the Orient**

The appointment of Judge Wilfley to be the head of the new United States Court in China has called special attention to consular jurisdiction in the Orient. Judge Wilfley's court does not come under the jurisdiction of our Department of Justice. The court was created to take the place of consular courts. It is thus under the jurisdiction of our Department of State. Consular courts have been necessary in countries where governmental conditions have not afforded proper recourse to our citizens. In Japan, however, the conclusion of treaties ten years ago, recognizing the judicial autonomy of that country, ended the system of consular extraterritorial jurisdiction under which foreigners had been privileged to reside and trade there. Of course such a system demands peculiar qualifications on the part of our diplomatic and consular representatives. In general, the character of those representatives has been good. A number of flagrant exceptions to this rule in recent times, however, shows the desirability of having stricter courts of proceedings, which would also demand the service of men of greater attainments, efficiency, and character. Hence the institution of the United States Court for China. The difficulties already encountered by Judge Wilfley in presiding over that court, not only with those who come before him for trial but also with the Shanghai attorneys, make the publication of Dr. Hinckley's "American Consular Jurisdiction in the Orient"[1] peculiarly timely. Dr. Hinckley himself is a colleague of the officials of the new Chinese court. After reviewing historic forms of extraterritoriality and the list of our treaties with countries of the Orient, after summarizing American and foreign statutes establishing the system of consular courts, he discusses legal rights under such jurisdiction—among them, nationality, the rule of domicile, marriage, persons accused of crime, real property, taxation, commercial privileges, and the rights of missionaries. Appended to this are chapters on international tribunals, on the foreign settlements in China, and on the grounds for

---

1 Théodore de Bèze. Compte rendu publié par lar Société du Musée Historique de la Réformation. Imprimerie "Atar." Geneva, Switzerland.
2 Birket Foster, R.W.S. By H. M. Cundall, I.S.O, F.S.A. The Macmillan Company, New York. $6, net.

---

1 American Consular Jurisdiction in the Orient. By Frank E. Hinckley. W. H. Lowdermilk & Co., Washington, D. C.

relinquishing foreign jurisdiction. There follow the texts of various statutes, rules, and regulations, of great importance to students of international law. The work is amply indexed.

**The Electric Spirit** The author of these poems[1] brings to her work noticeable strength of thought and unusual feeling for rhythm. The title poem is addressed to the mysterious power only partly subdued to our uses, and expresses in highly poetic language the fantastic yet enduring quality of electric forces, whose " touch is flame " and whose " kiss is death." Among the verses that linger in the memory are " The City," " A Choice," " In a Hospital Ward," and " Love's Refuge."

### A CHOICE

Those who have fallen let others seek,
With soothing voice and lifting hand;
If God but give me leave to speak
One word of cheer to those who stand.

Let others with their love enfold
The feebler souls that cling to wrong;
I would but touch with steadying hold
The bitter burdens of the strong.

Great, patient souls, that make no plaint,
Till death reveals the weight they bore!
They close the ranks of those who faint,
And take their toils forevermore.

**Enameling** Mr. Henry H. Cunynghame has compiled a valuable volume[2] for that already valuable series, " The Connoisseur's Library." The volumes composing this library are models of book-making. Mr. Cunynghame has some surprising things to say to the general reader; for instance, the original of enamel work was not for the purpose of beautiful ornamentation, but for the preservation in a convenient manner of gems and metals which were supposed to possess various occult virtues. We are told about the various methods of enameling, such as the putting of enamels into cloisons or cavities scooped out of plates of copper, or of using them as a sort of paint, and putting them on in layers without metallic boundaries. The author then deals chronologically with enameling, distinguishing especially the work of the early Gauls and Byzantines.

**The Art Value of Furniture** There is a gratifyingly increasing appreciation of furniture and wood-carving as a distinct branch of art. Some American houses have been furnished with a really exquisite appreciation of the art value of furniture as well as of its utility. Collectors and others will welcome this hand-

some volume[1] descriptive of a wonderful collection of old furniture, wood-carvings, bindings, stained glass, and other objects of art. The interesting text is immensely reinforced by nearly two hundred illustrations.

**A History of Tapestry** Mr. J. Pierpont Morgan has just given to the Metropolitan Museum of Art, New York City, a notable series of Flemish-Burgundian tapestries, undoubtedly the most important gift of the kind ever made in America. The gift adds special interest to the publication of a sumptuous volume[2] on tapestry from the earliest times till the present day by Mr. W. G. Thomson. He has been very fortunate in being able to illustrate his own text. The pictures number over eighty, are in color and half-tone, on full-page plates and in the text. While the subject of tapestry interests every lover of decoration, it is not as appreciated as it should be. Its records throw valuable side-lights on history. In the present volume we find many more instances than are generally known, where national events have been commemorated and where sovereigns and princes have paved the way to negotiations and treaties desired by them by the timely gift of a costly tapestry. Finally, tapestries give us a wonderfully graphic idea of house construction and decoration, of folk and home life of old times. It seems strange that descriptions of this art should have been neglected in the field of English literature, but the greatly increasing interest in that art in our own day makes the publication of Mr. Thomson's book timely. It is, as well, in paper, print, binding, and weight of volume, a model publication.

**Lombardy** A book to be read in connection with Symonds's " Age of the Despots " has long been a desideratum—a clear and comprehensive account of North Italy from the Roman times down at least to the middle of the fourteenth century. Such a book is now at hand in Mr. Butler's " Lombard Communes."[3] In our time Lombardy is circumscribed within comparatively narrow limits, but when, in the year 568, the Lombards invaded Italy, the whole northern part of the peninsula was regarded by them as one homogeneous country. It is interesting to note in the development of subsequent history that the lakes—Como, Maggiore, and the rest—played a relatively small part, and it is equally interesting to note the very large part played by the cities of the plain, not

[1] The Electric Spirit and Other Poems. By Marion Couthouy Smith. The Gorham Press, Boston. $1.
[2] European Enamels. By Henry H. Cunynghame, C.B. G. P. Putnam's Sons, New York. $6.75, net.

[1] The Talbot J. Taylor Collection: Furniture, Wood-Carving, and Other Branches of the Decorative Arts. G. P. Putnam's Sons, New York. $6, net.
[2] A History of Tapestry: From the Earliest Times until the Present Day. By W. G. Thomson. G. F. Putnam's Sons, New York. $12, net.
[3] The Lombard Communes. By W. E. Butler. M.A. Charles Scribner's Sons, New York. $3.75, net.

only wealthier but also more democratic than were those of the hills and mountains. In no very picturesque phrase, but at the same time in easily understood language, Mr. Butler recounts the history of the City-States of Lombardy, the rule of the early bishops, the rights of the communes, the history of Milan, Lombardy's natural capital, the first and second Lombard Leagues, and the final struggles of the communes.

*A Notable Help to Students of International Law*

Our present Secretary of State is rapidly adding to his laurels. During the comparatively short time since Colonel Hay's death, Mr. Root has not only put the impress of his forceful personality upon the State Department, but has distinctly molded the currents of American political thought throughout the world. He has done this first of all by such notable speeches at home as his Hearst-destroying address last summer at Utica, and abroad by his series of epoch-making speeches in South America, but he may now mold the currents of political thought even more powerfully by means of the press. The American Society of International Law, of which he is the president, has begun the publication of "The American Journal of International Law," a quarterly. The first volume[1] is now before us. In his preface to the number Mr. Root calls attention to the increase of popular control over national conduct as the distinctive mark of contemporary political development of our time. This makes it constantly more important that in each country the great body of the people should have a just conception of their international rights and duties. Of course a principal means in bringing about this desirable condition is to promote popular habits of reading and thinking about international affairs. As Mr. Root says, "The more clearly and universally the people of a country realize the international obligations and duties of their country, the less likely they will be to resent the just demands of other countries that those obligations and duties be observed." Again, "The more familiar the people of a country are with the rules and customs of self-restraint and courtesy between nations, which long experience has shown to be indispensable for preserving the peace of the world, the greater will be the tendency to refrain from publicly discussing controversies with other countries in such a way as to hinder peaceful settlement by wounding sensibilities or arousing anger and prejudice on the other side." The true

basis of peace is certainly to be found in a just and considerate spirit among the people, and a means to this end is a familiarity with international law that will form and lead public opinion. The present number also includes articles by ex-Secretary of State Foster, Professor Moore, formerly First Assistant Secretary of State, Judge-Advocate-General Davis, Professor Hershey, of the University of Indiana, Professor Wilson, of Brown University, and other eminent authorities. The editorial comment covers a wide range of subject, and there is a chronicle of suggestive international events. Then comes a list of public documents relating to and the condensed text of judicial decisions involving questions of international law. Finally, there is a department of book reviews in which we note interesting notices of about forty books in about twenty pages. A supplement to the quarterly, of about one-quarter the thickness, published in the same form, admirable color of cover, paper and print, comprises certain official documents of note. The supplement is separately paged and sewed, and will be separately indexed in order that these original texts may be bound by themselves. The work as a whole is invaluable to the student of international law. To all members of the American Society of International Law the price is fifty cents a number; to non-members the price of single numbers is one dollar each.

*Panama Problems*

We are glad to see a new edition of General Abbot's valuable book.[1] It is in many ways the best compendium of information as to physical conditions, engineering natural difficulties, and the merits of different canal projects to be had anywhere. The book was originally published some two years ago, and to this revised edition a new chapter has been added carrying on the historical narrative since the transfer of the work to the United States; passages have also been introduced into other chapters with recent data regarding climate, hydraulic problems, and the new projects under way since the United States has begun its efforts. Thus the history of the enterprise throughout is covered and the technology and information of the book brought down to 1907.

*Pollaiuolo*

In their revolt against Roman sensuality the early Christians went so far as to revolt against sensuousness also. Their art took no account of the human form divine. They enveloped the body in draperies. They even conventionalized face, hands, and feet. Giotto was the first

---

[1] The American Journal of International Law. Vol. I. First Quarter. Published by the American Society of International Law, at the Waverly Press, Baltimore.

[1] Problems of the Panama Canal. By Brigadier-General Henry L. Abbot, United States Army, Retired. The Macmillan Company, New York. $2, net.

artist after the Greeks and Romans to give solidity and weight to the body, and Donatello the first to realize its superficial forms and to endow the nude with mind. But Pollaiuolo was the first fully to present the actual structure of muscle and bone, the actual movements of limb and joint. Though, curiously enough, Pollaiuolo was of all his contemporaries apparently the one least influenced by classic art, it may be claimed that he was also the one most genuinely to influence the art of his time. He certainly paved the way for Leonardo and Michelangelo. In his various Florentine studies Mr. Berenson has paid considerable attention to Pollaiuolo, it is true, but, strange as it may seem, no book exclusively dealing with that artist has heretofore been published. Fortunately, such a "find" in material comes to Miss Cruttwell's competent hands; her volume on the Robbias shows what she might be expected to do with it. Like that book, so the present[1] has permanent value. Practically for the first time, Pollaiuolo's place as painter, sculptor, draughtsman, designer, engraver, and goldsmith is definitely and popularly defined, and the attention of students is awakened as not before to Pollaiuolo's real influence and place in the history of art.

*Portuguese East Africa*  Mr. Maugham makes a valuable contribution in this book[2] to the not very easily obtainable existing stock of knowledge about Portuguese East Africa. He has been consul for Mozambique and other ports, he is evidently a keen sportsman, and it is equally evident that he has made some study of race characteristics, native superstitions, local dialects, and physical features of the country about which he writes. Photographs, mainly of large game and types of native races, add to the interest of the work.

*A Revolutionary Princess*  The daughter of an ancient Milanese house, Christina Belgiojoso-Trivulzio, was six years old when the abdication of Napoleon again gave North Italy to Austria. She matured in an atmosphere of political unrest and resentment, later to develop into actual revolution. Tall, pale, and beautiful to look at; melodramatic in manner, vain and erratic, of great fortune, thorough education, of rather masculine quality, of distinguished social position by birth, marriage, and environment, passionately patriotic, the Princess was an extraordinary figure. She had

marked genius for organization, whether in prosaic pioneer work necessary to establishing agricultural experiments on her own estates, which more than once had been sequestrated; in assembling the various social elements for her brilliant *salon*, or, finally and chiefly, as an indefatigable conspirator in collecting revolutionary forces together and in endowing them with something of her own enthusiasm. For hers was a real enthusiasm, although she was a hysterical woman who lived in hysterical times—at least the times were hysterical as she understood them. The times were also morally out of joint, and in drawing her portrait[1] Mr. Whitehouse has shown excellent taste and restraint. The Princess moved in circles where scandal was rife; wherever there has been "gabble" the biographer gives both his heroine and his readers the benefit of the doubt. The Princess's personal charm, together with her long connection with revolutionary and other movements and with the public men of her day, brought to her a circle of friends as varied as it was picturesque. Among them we find Cavour, Verdi, Bellini, Heine, Margaret Fuller, George Sand, Alfred de Musset, Thiers, and the good old Lafayette. To these in 1846 the Princess added the then poverty-stricken Louis Napoleon. She sought him out in his London lodgings and unfolded to him her plan to liberate Italy. Did he not think of it and her when, years later, he was a prime mover in that liberation? Mr. Whitehouse has given us not only an interesting biography but a vivacious history of the first three-quarters of the past century in leading to one of the greatest achievements of that century, the unification and liberation of Italy.

*The Russo-Japanese War and International Law*  The Russo-Japanese War affected international law in two ways. First, it aided in solving some disputed questions. Secondly, it gave rise to some new precedents. In either case, the war was an indication of the existing condition of international morality. Written exclusively from the standpoint of diplomacy and international law, a history of the war has been, of course, a desideratum ever since that war closed. It is a satisfaction, therefore, to chronicle the appearance of such a work in the stout, well-printed volume compiled by Dr. Hershey, Professor of Political Science and International Law in the University of Indiana.[2] After discussing the

1 Antonio Pollaiuolo. By Maud Cruttwell. Charles Scribner's Sons. New York. $2, net.
2 Portuguese East Africa. By R. C. F. Maugham. E. P. Dutton & Co., New York. $4.50, net.

1 A Revolutionary Princess, Christina Belgiojoso-Trivulzio; Her Life and Her Times, 1808-1871. By H. Remsen Whitehouse. E. P. Dutton & Co., New York. $3, net.
2 The International Law and Diplomacy of the Russo-Japanese War. By Amos S. Hershey, Ph.D. The Macmillan Company, New York. $3, net.

causes of the war and its outbreak, Professor Hershey treats of such subjects as the construction, sale, and exportation by neutrals of war-ships; of submarine boats and other vessels intended for belligerent service; of the rights of neutral merchantmen, especially the right of visit and search, and of the alleged right of seeking neutral prizes; of the rights and privileges of belligerent armed vessels in neutral ports and waters; of submarine mines; of wireless telegraphy; of contraband of war. Dr. Hershey also discusses our interpretation of international law and our conduct in respect to neutral rights and duties—the John Hay note and Chinese neutrality, for instance. He finally treats our relations with England as affected by the war. A chapter of special interest to army men has to do with Russian and Japanese warfare and on the relations of the belligerents with each other. As might be expected, the final chapter of this interesting and suggestive volume has the Treaty of Portsmouth as its subject; we might wish that the chapter had been longer. Of course the work is amply indexed.

# *Letters to The Outlook*

## *EDUCATIONAL EFFICIENCY IN THE SOUTH*

In an article in The Outlook for March 16 Robert W. Bruère asserts that Vanderbilt University and the Randolph-Macon Woman's College are the only two "institutions of higher learning south of Mason and Dixon's line whose entrance requirements are up to the standard adopted by the [Carnegie] Foundation;" this statement does injustice to at least one institution in the South, namely, Rollins College, at Winter Park, Florida.

Rollins College provides a four years' course of study covering one hundred and thirty-six points, *i.e.*, an average of seventeen recitations a week for eight semesters; and it requires for admission to the Freshman class four full years of preparatory work, covering the same number of points as in the college. For admission to the Freshman class in the classical course it requires seven years of language study, and for admission to the Freshman class of the scientific course four years of language study, together with Civil Government, English History, Elementary Astronomy, and Physical Geography, besides, in both courses, the usual amount of mathematical, English, and sub-preparatory work. It fully meets the requirements of the Carnegie Foundation. Several graduates of Rollins Academy have been admitted to the Freshman class of leading universities and colleges of the North, and several students in the College have been admitted *ad eundem* to advanced classes in these universities and colleges, where they have made Phi Beta Kappa rank. I may add that one of the recent graduates of the College is now serving as tutor in Columbia University, and a graduate of the Academy, who also took a portion of his college course here, as assistant professor in the Leland Stanford Junior University. A member of the present Senior class, who is also a graduate of the Academy, lately passed the Responsions examination and has been appointed to a Rhodes Scholarship at Oxford, England.

WM. F. BLACKMAN, President.

Rollins College, Winter Park, Florida,
Office of the President.

In Mr. Bruère's interesting article entitled "Educational Efficiency," in The Outlook, March 16, the following statement occurs:

Randolph-Macon Woman's College and Vanderbilt University are the only two other institutions of higher learning [Tulane University had just been mentioned] south of Mason and Dixon's line whose entrance requirements are up to the standard adopted by the [Carnegie] Foundation.

The language of this statement suggests that its source is to be found on page 25 of President Pritchett's report. The report itself is somewhat open to criticism at that point, but does not justify Mr. Bruère's more explicit putting of the case.

"South of Mason and Dixon's line" is not a rhetorical but a mathematical expression. That historic line coincides with the parallel of 39° 43' 26.3" north latitude. The latitude of Baltimore is 39° 17' north. Baltimore, therefore, is south of Mason and Dixon's line. It is the seat of two "institutions of higher learning" whose entrance requirements are fifteen points, while the "standard of the Foundation" is but fourteen points—Johns Hopkins University and the Woman's College of Baltimore. If Mr. Bruère holds to the form of his statement, he is bound to add these institutions to the three which he has named. The writer of such an able article cannot fail to see the importance of the correction asked.

JNO. B. VAN METER (Dean).

The Woman's College, Baltimore.

## WALT WHITMAN AGAIN

We were very much interested in a letter from James H. Ecob published in The Outlook March 2. The writer of the letter attacks Whitman in a most uncompromising manner. He accuses the bard of almost every act of indecency and of immorality in the catalogue. We have been students of Whitman for a couple of years, and we would be very grateful to Mr. Ecob if he will give us his authority for his assertions.

We have read Whitman's poems thoughtfully and seriously, and we have been unable to find anything but the loftiest and the purest spirit. We have searched the pages of his biographers, and they are unanimous in declaring that his life was sweet and wholesome. If Mr. Ecob knows of better authority for his accusations than John Addington Symonds, John Burroughs, and R. M. Bucke—Whitman's friends and biographers—we, as seekers after truth, wish he would enable us to extend our studies.

Mr. Ecob said that Whitman associated with the "toughs and bums" of the city. He associated with the common man—the man who labors from morning until night with his hands. He loved this common man; he understood him; and he wrote about him. Surely that cannot be such a serious crime, for he was following the example of the Great Leader, Christ.

"Not one honorable act or sentiment to his credit," is another statement made by his detractor. During the war Whitman gave his strength and the health of his future years to nursing his wounded brothers, whom he loved most tenderly. If he never did anything else, that one act cannot be wholly ignored. Opening a volume of Whitman at random, we chance to see this line, "There is no trade or employment but the young man following it may become a hero." Surely there is some good in that sentiment.

During the war Whitman contracted blood-poisoning, and he later suffered a stroke of paralysis. Perhaps these facts explain why he seemed "too idle and helpless to earn his own living."

John Burroughs, who knew him well, says of him: "That Whitman's life was a sane, temperate, manly one, free from excesses, free from perversions and morbidities of a mammonish, pampered, over-stimulated age, I do believe. Indeed, I may say I *know*. The one impression he never failed to make—physically, morally, intellectually—on young and old, women and men, was that of health, sanity, sweetness. He felt the ties of universal brotherhood as few felt it. It was not a theory with him, but a fact that shaped his life and colored his poems.

'Whoever degrades another degrades me, and the thought fired his imagination.'

Whitman, like other prophets, was misunderstood and scourged by his fellow-men; but he went on giving his message to the world undaunted. Listen to his courageous spirit:

"One effort more, my altar this bleak sand;
That Thou, O God, my life hast lighted,
With ray of light, steady, ineffable, vouchsafed of
　Thee,
Light rare, untellable, lighting the very light,
Beyond all signs, descriptions, languages;
For that, O God, be it my latest word, here on my
　knees,
Old, poor, and paralyzed, I thank Thee.
My hands, my limbs grow nerveless,
My brain feels rack'd, bewilder'd,
Let the old timbers part, I will not part,
I will cling fast to Thee, O God, though the waves
　buffet me,
Thee, Thee at least I know."

　　　　　　　　　　E. H. AND J. A. S.

Butte, Montana.

[Dr. Ecob's letter was a reply to the ions of The Outlook expressed in a review. It seemed to us that it was apparent that The Outlook entirely di with Dr. Ecob's position.—THE EDI

## A PATRIOTIC OBJECT

An organized effort is to be made to purchase, restore, and preserve the home of Francis Scott Key, author of the "Star-Spangled Banner," in Washington. It stands on the main street of old Georgetown in a dilapidated condition and covered with advertisements. Its present condition is disgraceful, and unless it is soon bought it must be torn down to make way for business. The owner is willing to wait a while and to sell at a reasonable price as his contribution towards the preservation of the mansion where Key lived at the time when the National anthem was written and for twenty years besides, and where all his children were born.

A society for the purchase and preservation of the house has just been incorporated in Washington, with Commissioner Macfarland as President; Admiral Dewey, Admiral Schley, Justice Barnard, and others, as Vice-Presidents; Francis Scott Key Smith, grandson of the poet, as Secretary; and W. D. Hoover, National Savings and Trust Company, as Treasurer. The society asks $25,000 for the purchase, repair, and maintenance of the Key home, and will give a certificate of membership, signed by the officers, to every member paying the modest dues of one dollar a year. Admiral Dewey, who the official adoption by the navy (wh followed by the army) of the "Star-S Banner" as the only National air to be played at all ceremonies, is taking a special interest in this undertaking.

85, NO. 16
287 Fourth Avenue, New York City
1430 Marquette Building, Chicago
PRICE TEN CENTS

# The Outlook

### Saturday, April 20, 1907

# THE YELLOW MAN'S BURDEN

## BY ARTHUR JUDSON BROWN

# SCHOOL DAYS OF AN INDIAN

## BY CHARLES A. EASTMAN
### (OHIYESA)
### SECOND PAPER

# HOW TO SEE ITALY

## BY AMY A. BERNARDY

SATURDAY, APRIL 20, 1907

**The Peace Congress in New York City**

On Monday of this week the first National Arbitration and Peace Congress of America convened in New York City. The preceding Sunday, however, had been fitly celebrated by a great gathering at Carnegie Hall, at which the Oratorio Society of New York furnished noble music. The meeting was addressed by Bishop Potter, of New York, Rabbi Hirsch, of Chicago, and Monsignor Lavelle, who represented Archbishop Farley. On Monday Mr. Andrew Carnegie, President of the Congress, presided at the opening conference, which was addressed by Mr. Root, Secretary of State, Governor Hughes, of New York State, and Mayor McClellan, of New York City. A letter from President Roosevelt to the delegates was also read. In the evening another great meeting was addressed by Baron d'Estournelles de Constant, President of the International Society of Conciliation, a French Senator, and a member of the Hague Court; Mr. Ernst Richard, President of the German-American Peace Society; Mr. Straus, Secretary of Commerce; Professor Münsterberg, representing Germany; Sir Robert Cranston, ex-Lord Mayor of Edinburgh, and Sir Robert Ball, of Cambridge University, representing Great Britain, and others. The most gratifying feature of the Conference so far has been the striking public interest shown. Such associations as the American Federation of Labor, the National Association of Manufacturers, the new Board of Trade and Transportation, the Brotherhoods of Locomotive Engineers and Firemen, the United Mine Workers of America, and other important bodies representing labor and capital, immediately announced their intention of taking part in the deliberations. The popular demand for seats at the meetings has been so great that a second series of conferences has had to be arranged. It is fortunate that a great supply of speakers has been provided for these meetings and for the banquets which are to follow. In addition to the above, addresses are expected from Earl Grey, Governor-General of Canada; the Rt. Hon. James Bryce, British Ambassador at Washington; President Eliot, of Harvard University; President Gompers, of the American Federation of Labor; the Hon. Seth Low, member of the first Hague Conference; Dr. John Rhys, of Oxford, and Vice-Chancellor Roberts, of Cambridge University; ex-Secretary of State Foster; Dr. Edward Everett Hale and Dr. Lyman Abbott; Mr. W. T. Stead, of the English Review of Reviews; J. M. W. van der Poorten Schwartz, the Dutch novelist, better known by his pseudonym Maarten Maartens; Sir Edward Elgar, the eminent composer; Mr. Moberly Bell, Manager of the London Times; Señor Diego Mendoza, of the University of Colombia; the Hon. W. J. Bryan, the Hon. Richard Bartholdt, and others. Meanwhile two or three times as many people as were expected have shown their interest in the peace movement by their presence.

❧

**The Carnegie Institute**

If the country were not so familiar with educational events of the first magnitude, the dedication of the Carnegie Institute in Pittsburg last week would have arrested attention as a fact of immense significance in current history. That it was such a fact no one who knows its scope, the need of education in this country, and the possible fruitfulness of the higher training will question. The Institute, which is not to be confused with the Carnegie Institution or the Carnegie Foundation, is planned on a great scale. Mr. Carnegie has already endowed it by gifts aggregating twenty-three millions of dollars. The group of buildings dedicated to literature, art, and science have as a background Schenley Park. The enlarged Institute, dedicated last week, contains a library, art galleries, museum, music hall, hall of sculpture, exhibition rooms, a lecture hall, and offices and executive rooms. The building is of marble, and the architectural and artistic effects are striking and expressive of their relation to the uses of the building. Guests from England, Germany, France, Belgium, Holland, and the United States included a large number of men distinguished in every profession and walk of life, and were so numerous as to constitute an audience in themselves. The exercises covered three days, the formal dedication taking place on the afternoon of Wednesday, April 10. The procession of guests, many of them in academic dress, passed from the Hotel Schenley through a double line of students which extended along the whole length of the parade. A letter from President Roosevelt, expressing his appreciation of the great work done by the founding of the Institute as tending to high individual efficiency, was read and was followed by a speech from Mr. Carnegie recalling the fact that eleven years ago he had handed over the Institute to Pittsburg as a bold experiment—a combination of library, art gallery, museum, and hall of music. The history of the establishment of the library system and of the development of the Institute was outlined, and the speaker declared that fortune came to him in Pittsburg, and that he had labored for Pittsburg; the Institute was built by a Pittsburger for Pittsburgers with Pittsburg money. The Institute is not only to promote art and literature, but will furnish a complete industrial education in its most modern form, both scientific and technical. There are to-day in the Institute nearly sixteen hundred students, and several thousand are awaiting admission. Mr. Carnegie said further:

There is room for many things of the spirit in our city. Things material are abundant, our mills and factories numerous, large, and prosperous; but things material, including money itself, should be only the foundation upon which are reared things

spiritual. Our mines of coal and iron have not completed their mission when transmuted into articles for use, and these into dollars. All is still upon the material plane. Not till the dollars are transmuted into service for others in one of the many forms best calculated to appeal to and develop those higher things of the moral, intellectual, and æsthetic domain has wealth completely justified its existence. Dollars are only dross until spiritualized, a means to an end; and miserable is the man, mean and squalid his life, who knows no better than to deaden his soul by mere possession, counting over the board which holds him down, or using his faculties in old age in augmenting the useless stuff that ministers not to any taste worthy of man.

Mr. Carnegie made special reference to the interest shown in the Institute by the German Emperor, who was represented by General von Löwenfeld, Secretary of State Möller, and other eminent men, and recognized the indebtedness of America to Germany as a teacher of the nations in industrial education. He spoke especially also of the congratulations sent by France and of the unpayable debt of America to that country. This great foundation, so comprehensive in its scope and novel in its combination of functions, is situated at a strategic point in one of the most active and powerful industrial communities in America.

❀

*Reconnoitering in Ohio* — Senator Foraker's speech in Canton, Ohio, last week, was the first shot fired in what is at present the most interesting preliminary skirmish of the Presidential campaign. This contest is of Senator Foraker's own choosing. He it was who suggested that a popular vote be taken to determine what men the Republicans of Ohio prefer for the Senatorship and the Presidency. The friends of Secretary Taft in Ohio accepted the challenge, and now the issue lies between them, on the one hand, and the Republican State machine, led by Senators Foraker and Dick, on the other. In the popular mind this has been interpreted as a struggle between Roosevelt Republicanism and machine politics. Of course, in view of the great popularity of the President in Ohio, as elsewhere, Senator Foraker has undertaken to avoid being put into the position of antagonizing Mr. Roosevelt. His first attack, therefore, had almost necessarily to assume the character of a defense. He first condemned the effort of a President to determine his successor. He quoted a published report which he interpreted as an assertion that Mr. Roosevelt was going to set limits to the discussion of Presidential candidates, and added : " I feel it a duty toward the President himself to enter for him, on my own motion, a disclaimer of all responsibility for such a publication." He, moreover, denied for himself participation in a rumored combination with financiers to oppose the President. Indeed, he declared that he had supported the President in all of the measures with which the President was identified, "except only three." These were joint Statehood for Arizona and New Mexico, railway rate regulation, and the Brownsville affair. Senator Foraker defended his course on all three subjects. He asserted his liberty, indeed his duty, to use, in his capacity as Senator, his own judgment, and his determination not to submit to the dictation or threats of any boss. As he brought his speech to a close he made this statement of political belief :

We can be proud, also, of the honor and integrity of the business men of this country. What they most need to-day is not so much an increased surveillance and guardianship of law as that liberty of action and trust and confidence in protection under the law which they have always heretofore enjoyed.

The protection of law-abiding corporations and the punishment of offending corporations, in which Mr. Foraker stated his faith, no one would oppose. What has given Mr. Roosevelt his leadership, however, has been his ability to express the determination of Americans that the Government shall be more than a big policeman ; that it shall rather be the agent of the people in controlling every power which, created for the public interest, is in danger of sacrificing the public interest for private purposes. To withstand this determination is not merely to oppose the chief policy of the President ; it is to dispute the popular will. Whether the popular will is misdirected is another matter. Senator Foraker has, by his speech, put himself among those who

attempt to frustrate, or to correct, this tendency in the Nation.

❦

**The Rhode Island Senatorial Deadlock** The Legislature of Rhode Island has not yet ended the Senatorial deadlock which began thirteen weeks ago. In this political struggle is involved the longer civic contest which has for years been waged in the State between democracy and a form of oligarchy. As is well known, membership in the Rhode Island Legislature is so apportioned that the small country towns, isolated and apathetic, hold the power. These little towns, strongholds of the native New England stock, are in the hands of the machine. At the head of the machine is the "blind boss," General Brayton. In the Senatorial contest the champion of those who would smash this machine is Colonel R. H. I. Goddard. Though a lifelong Republican, he has accepted the Democratic nomination. He has behind him, therefore, the Democratic party and such Republicans as are independent enough to withstand party pressure. The other two candidates are both avowedly Republicans. One, Mr. Wetmore, is a candidate to succeed himself. As Senator, he has left National affairs to his colleague, Mr. Aldrich. His kindly disposition has won him many friends ; but he has done nothing to end the scandalous conditions maintained by the State's system of rotten boroughs. Colonel S. P. Colt, the other Republican candidate, who is head of the Rubber Trust, has no qualification for the office. The only explanation for his candidacy is his great wealth. In brief, Senator Wetmore represents the older interests of the State who distrust manhood suffrage ; Colonel Colt represents the newer industrial life of the State and its moneyed interests. Together these two represent the forces working for the maintenance of present political conditions. Colonel Goddard, on the other hand, represents the forces of revolt, which means, in this case, that he represents not private but public interests. He comes from one of the oldest of New England families, he is irreproachable in character, is both respected and popular, and is a man of ability and experience. The situation is not only a comment upon the political enslavement of Rhode Island, but is also a severe criticism upon the method of leaving to the Legislature the election of Senators. The outcome, it has been remarked, "only one man can foresee, and he is blind."

❦

*Merit Triumphs in the Consular Service* — The first regular examination of candidates for consular appointments under the new system has just been held at Washington. By the law of April, 1906, Congress had finally graded the consular positions, and thereby made it practicable to extend to that branch of the civil service the principles embodied in the Civil Service Act of 1883. Thereupon the President, by executive order, declared that vacancies in the office of consul above the lowest class should be filled by promotion from the lower grades of the consular service, based upon ability and efficiency as shown in that service; and that vacancies in the lowest class of consuls should be filled (1) by promotion of vice and deputy consuls, or of consular clerks or agents who had been appointed to those offices *upon examination*, or (2) by appointments of candidates *who had passed a satisfactory examination*. The three examiners are the Secretary of State, or an officer of the Department of State designated by the President, the Chief of the Consular Bureau, and the Chief Examiner of the Civil Service Commission. The examinations just held were both oral and written. The object of the oral examination was to determine the character, disposition, address, manners, health, personal appearance, readiness, judgment, discretion, resourcefulness, accuracy of information, experience, and business capacity of the candidates. The written examination included one modern language other than English; the natural, industrial, and commercial resources and the commerce of the United States; political economy; the elements of international, commercial, and maritime law; American history, government, and insti-

tutions; the modern history of Europe, Latin America, and the Far East; geography and arithmetic. As an indication of the examination papers we quote the questions on political economy:

1. Define political economy. Name three great works on this subject.
2. Of what advantage to a consul is a knowledge of the principles of political economy?
3. State some of the principal reasons for taking at stated times a census of population and industries, especially with reference to manufactures and agriculture.
4. State some of the advantages of foreign exchange in canceling indebtedness between merchants of different countries. Why is exchange on London or New York preferable to exchange on smaller cities?
5. What are the principal reasons for the development of trade between different countries?

❦

*The First Examination Under the Reform Law* — Of course, future examination papers will be different in detail, and will not be published as these have been. The first papers are now made public in order to give the country an idea of the new system. Eighteen candidates were examined on the above subjects, and ten passed. The examinations were conducted by the civil service machinery. The change from the old spoils system will thus be realized. Under that system substantially all the consulates were held by persons named by the Senators, under the pressure of personal and political friendship. Unfortunately, the greatest pressure was often in favor of the most unfit candidate. It was supposed that there would be a great outburst of indignation from the spoilsmen concerning the change. On the contrary, it is gratifying to see how generally it has been accepted by some of the very men who formerly practically appointed the consuls. It would almost seem as if Senators and Representatives have become tired of the old plan, and feel a sense of relief at getting away from it, so long as every one is treated alike. By selecting from the competent young men, now *to* be obtained for the minor consulates, those who do the best work, and promoting them, an evenly competent body of consuls should result. The country needs more fully to comprehend this reform. When it does, three results should follow. First, the right kinds of candidates should be forthcoming. Secondly, they should be enabled to make proper preparation. Finally, before the end of the present Administration the new system should be so thoroughly established in popular regard that no succeeding Administration would dare to overturn it.

❋

*Railway Derailments Due to Malicious Obstruction*

In a statement of railway accidents made by the Inter-State Commerce Commission covering two years, derailments reported as due to malicious obstruction vary from 11 to 26 every three months, and the number of persons killed from 1 to 23. Last week two more attempts were made to wreck railway trains on the Pennsylvania system. In one case a fast train was flagged just in time by a farmer who had found a tie fastened to the track near a high bluff. In the other instance a switch was turned in the face of a fast freight. These events make more ominous the list of similar occurrences during the past eight weeks:

1. Flyer wrecked by withdrawal of fish-plates and bolts.
2. Eighteen-hour limited wrecked by same method near Steward. Nearly all the passengers were injured. Because of their all-steel construction the cars were not smashed.
3. Keystone Express wrecked near Wilmerding, the wreckers using the same methods; an engineer was killed and a number of passengers were hurt.
4. Attempt made on the Chicago Limited between Wilmerding and Turtle Creek.
5. Obstruction placed on freight track. Discovered after freight train had been derailed.
6. Pittsburg-Cleveland Express wrecked near Hudson, Ohio, by removal of fish-plates and spikes.
7. Obstruction piled on track at East Brady.

In every " successful " wreck the cars had hardly stopped rolling before robbers began their pillage. The company has offered an open reward of several thousand dollars for information that will lead to the conviction of the guilty; a large secret reward to the employees is also said to have been provided. In every case in which fish-plates and bolts have been removed the wreckers

have avoided disturbing the electrical connections between the rails, which of course, by setting the block signals at danger, would prevent the success of their fiendish endeavor—the most despicable form of murder, because, first, of its cowardice, second, of its incompatibility with any theory of pity, and, third, its wholesale threatening of life. In every way the Pennsylvania Company and the State of Pennsylvania should wage relentless war against this particular peril. It may be that the company may be forced to do as an English railway does, fence in its right of way, and treat every unauthorized person on any part of it as a trespasser. The Pennsylvania, running through a thickly populated country, could do what would be impossible in the case of one of the Western roads. But the duty of the State of Pennsylvania is no less clear. While by its law a successful attempt to wreck is murder, the attempt itself should be punishable far more severely than it now is, and the means of apprehending criminals should be made more effective. Yet at this very time an attempt is made to abolish the Pennsylvania State constabulary! Instead of abolishing it the State might well increase it both in numbers and in power.

❋

*The Water Storage Grab in New York State*

The annual meeting last week of the Association for the Protection of the Adirondacks called the attention of the citizens of New York State once more to the subject of its forest preserve. At the rate at which timber is being now removed from the State, without replanting, there will be none left in less than thirty years except what is protected by the Constitution in the forest preserve. Hence there should be encouragement of legislation to enlarge the State's holdings, and defeat of the bill now before the Legislature empowering the State to erect dams and store water on the public domain. The bill passed one Legislature because allowed no public hearing. As it involves a Constitutional amendment, however, it must pass a succeeding Legislature, the present body, and be submitted to the people at an ensuing election. Four benefits, it is claimed, would result from the amendment : (1) It would give to many cities and towns a clean and ample water supply throughout the year ; (2) it would permit the enlargement of the State canal system; (3) it would check freshets ; (4) it would bring into use millions of dollars' worth of water-power now going to waste. But these general benefits to the State could be obtained without touching the State domain, which, according to the Constitution, must "be forever kept as wild forest lands." Hence no Constitutional amendment is required. Power companies have attempted to mask their real aim by covering it with a general plan to purify and enlarge the facilities of the State water supply. The overwhelming sentiment of the State, we believe, opposes those who would acquire vested rights in the State's water-power, destroying, for the purposes of health, pleasure, and sport, practically every Adirondack lake. Medical testimony shows that the damming of water and its gradual drawing off during ·the dry season, creating mud flats, promotes disease. This has been shown in the history of the lakes so treated outside the State preserve. Moreover, the State may one day require the use of its Adirondack water, centralized in a few great reservoirs, for the domestic supply of its cities. The lakes of the watershed, an inestimable asset, belong to all the people. Why destroy them merely to gratify the financial ambition of the few?

❋

**Conserving Our Waterways as Natural Resources**

A humorist once said of the crooked Mississippi River that a steamer going south has been known to meet itself coming north, giving passing signals and narrowly escaping a collision with itself. In addition to this difficulty of navigation, the Mississippi has been notoriously and increasingly afflicted with sandbars during the low-water seasons. This is especially noticeable near its mouth; at present shipments to New Orleans by river must be transferred at Memphis and again at Vicksburg. But

the Mississippi has always been thus impeded. Half a century ago it was claimed that it swept into its lower reaches and the Gulf of Mexico four hundred million tons of sediment a year— twice the amount of material expected to be excavated in opening the Panama Canal. This sediment not only clogs the channel and floods the lowlands, but renders the current capricious. The two obstacles of crookedness and sandbars, together with railway competition, sufficiently account for the decline in Mississippi River steamboating. The last line of steamers operating a through service between St. Louis and New Orleans went out of business nine years ago. These several difficulties with river traffic caused Mr. James J. Hill, President of the Great Northern Railway, in a recent communication, to suggest the canalization of the Mississippi as the easiest and most obvious way of relief, first, from the natural obstacles, secondly, from the railway competition, and finally and especially from the transportation congestion from which, more than any other section, the Mississippi Valley region has been suffering. Canalization would reduce the present distance by water from St. Louis to New Orleans nearly one-half. A fifteen-foot channel from St. Louis to New Orleans might cost a hundred millions, but the necessity and importance of such a work are nevertheless to be carefully considered. Of all railway presidents Mr. Hill seems the most far-reaching in vision and fertile in resource. His testimony as to the need of a Mississippi canal was the more striking because it came from one interested in railways, in this country the apparently triumphant rivals of canals. The truth is that we need both. America must now follow the example of France, Germany, and Italy in the construction of inland waterways. Appropriately, in this connection, comes the official announcement from Washington of President Roosevelt's appointment of a Waterways Commission. Its members are to be the Hon. Theodore E. Burton, of Ohio, Chairman of the Rivers and Harbors Committee in the House of Representatives, who is to act as Chairman of the Commission; Senators Newlands, of Nevada, and Warner, of Missouri ;

Representative Bankhead, of Alabama; General Alexander Mackenzie, Chief of Engineers of the United States Army; Dr. W. J. McGee, the eminent geologist and anthropologist; and Messrs. F. H. Newell, Director of the United States Reclamation Service, Gifford Pinchot, United States Forester, and Herbert Knox Smith, Commissioner of Corporations. The Commission's duty will be to report a comprehensive plan for the improvement of our river systems. We do not always remember that the control of navigable waterways lies with the Federal Government and carries with it corresponding responsibilities and obligations. In emphasizing this fact President Roosevelt justly declares that our streams should be considered and conserved as great natural resources, and that the time has come for merging local projects and uses of the inland waters in a comprehensive plan to benefit the entire country. This has a particular and pressing application. As already emphasized by Mr. Hill, so President Roosevelt calls attention to the fact that our railways " are no longer able to move crops and manufactures rapidly enough to secure the prompt transaction of the business of the Nation, and there is small prospect of immediate relief." According to representative railway men, the products of the Northern interior States have doubled in ten years. But railway facilities have increased only an eighth. There is reason to doubt, says President Roosevelt, whether any railway development possible in the near future will suffice to keep transportation abreast of production. As he concludes, there appears, indeed, to be but one complete remedy—the development of a complementary system of transportation by water. If this attitude had been adopted twenty years ago, there might have been no congestion of freight to-day.

❦

*An Important Constitutional Question* Judge Speer, of the Circuit Court of the United States (Georgia), has rendered an interesting decision sustaining the constitutionality of the Federal law rendering common carriers engaged in inter-State commerce liable to their employees for damages. The English common-law rule that an employer is not liable for an injury suffered by one employee through the carelessness of another is thus set aside. The injustice of this common-law rule under modern conditions Judge Speer puts with great clearness and force. He shows that it has either been modified or set aside in England, Germany, Austria, France, Belgium, Holland, and other European countries. Founded upon reason when it was established, it has become unreasonable now. The engineer on the lightning express must blindly obey the orders given to him. Through the negligence of a fellow-servant over whose actions he has no control and of whose misconduct he has no knowledge, he may be in an instant hurled to death or mutilation indescribable. That the corporation should be exempt from damages because of his fellow-servant's misconduct or negligence is clearly unjust. But is it constitutional for the Federal Government to rectify this injustice? Judge Speer seems to us to show that a long course of judicial decisions establishes the constitutionality of such action. Commerce is not merely an exchange of goods; " in the advancement of society, labor, transportation, intelligence, care, and various mediums of exchange become commodities, and enter into commerce; the subject, the vehicle, the agent, and the various operations become the objects of commercial regulation." Such is the definition of commerce by the Supreme Court of the United States. The regulation of commerce, which is intrusted by the Constitution to the Federal Government, includes therefore the protection of passengers as well as of goods; the regulation of the instrumentalities by which the commerce is carried on, and therefore the regulation and the protection of the employees as well as of the passengers and the freight. It is under this recognized principle that Congress regulates the lights to be carried by all vessels in inland waters, whether engaged in commerce or not; that it establishes qualifications and conditions for masters, engineers, and pilots of vessels; that it has required safety appliances on all trains engaged in inter-State commerce, a requirement declared constitutional by the Supreme Court. We have no doubt that a certain class of writers will consider the action of Congress in prescribing the hours of labor and regulating the conditions of employment upon inter-State railways an unconstitutional extension of the Constitution into a new domain. We think that Judge Speer's opinion makes it clear that it is only the extension of a well-recognized principle over new conditions.

❀

*Japanese Rights in Public Schools* — The Outlook has expressed some doubt whether Congress can by treaty confer on Japanese residents the right to attend the public schools established and maintained in the several States. Professor William Draper Lewis, Dean of the Law Department of the University of Pennsylvania, in an article published in the American Law Register for February, and reprinted in pamphlet form, has discussed this question in very judicial spirit, and, as we must frankly say, removed the doubts that we entertained on this subject. The legislative power of Congress is specifically defined by the Constitution, and all powers not conferred on Congress are reserved to the several States; but the treaty-making powers are not specifically defined. Consequently " the treaty-making power of our Federal Government is not confined within the limits of the legislative power of that Government. That can be done by treaty which cannot be done by act of Congress." It is true that this treaty-making power is not absolutely unlimited. Limitation may be found in the expressed phraseology and perhaps in the necessary implications of the Constitution. Professor Lewis quotes the words of Judge Story : " A treaty to change the organization of the government or annihilate its sovereignty, to overturn its republican form or to deprive it of its constitutional powers, would be void, because it would destroy what it was designed to fulfill, the will of the people." But, subject to such limitations as are by expressed terms or by necessary implications in the Constitution put upon the treaty-making power

reposed in the President and the Senate, they may make any treaty which it is competent for the sovereign power of any free people to make. A treaty providing that the children of a particular race shall be privileged to attend such public schools as exist in the State does not violate any expressed terms or any necessary implications of the Constitution, and it is therefore a legitimate treaty and of supreme authority in all the States. The opposition of any State to such a treaty must be made through its Senators when the treaty is before the Senate for confirmation, and as no treaty can be confirmed without the assent of two-thirds of the members of the Senate present, the rights of the States are sufficiently protected. Whether in point of fact the treaty which we have made with Japan entitles the Japanese to claim an admission to the public schools of California is another and more doubtful question ; that it entitles them to claim the right to attend the same schools as white children we do not ourselves believe.

❀

*In the South : Child Labor and Compulsory Education* — Although the recent sessions of Southern Legislatures have produced no very radical laws, unless the railway rate laws of North Carolina and Alabama should be classed as such, several of the Southern States have made a record of progressive legislation. Child labor, which is an especially acute problem in the cotton-mill regions, has been the subject of considerable discussion and of some acts. Of these the North Carolina law is the most important. In that State the manufacturers have shown a spirit deserving of praise ; voluntarily they have promoted the passage of restrictive provisions. Heretofore no children under twelve could be employed, but children over that age were not especially protected. After 1907 no child under fourteen years of age can be employed in the mills on any day after eight o'clock P.M., and no child under thirteen can be employed night or day except in "apprenticeship capacity," then only upon condition that the child has attended school for four out of the preceding twelve months. An amendment shortening the hours of labor from sixty-six to sixty hours a week lacked only three votes of passage. In South Carolina and Alabama child labor bills were postponed until the second term of the Legislatures; in Arkansas and Tennessee amendments to the child labor law have been strongly advocated. It is evident that the cause of child labor legislation in the Southern States has been stimulated rather than hindered by the agitation for a National child labor law. As Mr. J. W. Bailey, of the North Carolina Child Labor Committee, has said in a letter to the press, which we find in the Biblical Recorder of that State, " there can be no satisfactory settlement of the child labor question apart from compulsory education." This fact has for some time been urged by manufacturers themselves. In North Carolina, for instance, where the organization of manufacturers worked in harmony with the Child Labor Committee, they advocated the passage of the compulsory education bill introduced at the instance of the State Superintendent. Through excessive caution the North Carolina Legislature failed to pass the bill in its original form, but it did pass a measure which allowed each school district the right to vote for compulsory school laws. In a State where the raising of taxes for school purposes has been made an object of an almost religious crusade, this application of the local option principle to the subject of compulsory education has better chance of success than it would have in a State where the local support of schools has become more traditional and perfunctory. In South Carolina, where the sentiment with regard to compulsory education has seemed sometimes almost hopelessly conservative, a compulsory education bill failed of passage by but a single vote. In Texas the subject of compulsory education has been earnestly agitated in the Legislature.

⊕

*In the South : Other Reform Measures* Southern Legislatures have also done much to foster the general movement of educational advance that has been notable of recent years in the South. In particular, North Carolina has been generous in its appropriations for educational institutions. The advance made may be suggested by contrasting the $25,000 appropriated in 1895 for the maintenance of the State University with the $70,000 appropriated for the same purpose this year. The General Assembly, as the Legislature is called in that State, has provided a new basis for secondary education by appropriating money to aid in the establishment of county high schools in co-operation with the counties themselves. The same body has initiated a reformatory system by chartering a reform and training school to which youthful criminals will be sent. Tennessee has also established a reformatory. In dealing with great corporations and with financial transactions there has been some drastic legislation. Concerning the railway bills we have already had occasion to speak. South Carolina and Alabama have now followed the lead of North Carolina and Georgia in abolishing the bucket-shops and prohibiting dealing in cotton futures, which has been a great source of demoralization. In labor matters there have been at least two effective measures. One, in South Carolina, establishes a ten-hour day for cotton and woolen mills; the reform was initiated by the manufacturers themselves, but was to be gradually introduced and not be finally effective until 1910; this the Legislature has put into effect for 1907. The other, in Alabama, in the form of an amendment to a bill appointing a jail inspector, provides for factory inspection. This amendment, it is interesting to note, was made by the Governor in accordance with the State Constitution, which gives to the Governor the right of suggesting amendments as an alternative to vetoing bills. In liquor legislation there has also been some very definite progress. In addition to the abolition of the State dispensary in South Carolina and a substitution of county option between no sale of liquor and sale by local dispensaries, Alabama has passed a local option law for counties and Tennessee has extended the local option provision to cities beyond five thousand population. As a result of the new measure in Tennessee, Knoxville, Clarksville, and Jackson have voted for no license.

❀

*Plans for the Cuban Elections*

In a statement addressed to Governor Magoon, of Cuba, last week, Secretary Taft expressed the decision of the Administration in regard to future Cuban elections. This decision was reached after consultations with leaders of the Liberal and Moderate parties. No elections can take place until after a census is taken. This is not merely his judgment, but that of an advisory committee composed of four Moderates, four Liberals, and three Americans. All the parties unite, he adds, in recommending that preliminary elections be held to test the electoral law and the tranquillity of the country. Beyond these two general recommendations, Secretary Taft's conclusions coincide with the proposals of neither party as a whole, but in part with those of each. With the omission · of details, the further points in the policy outlined by the Secretary of War are as follows: (1) That Cuba must be turned over to the Cuban Government as soon as the tranquillity of the country and the stability of the Government are assured ; (2) that no definite date should be set for the preliminary elections, but that such time should intervene between the completion of the census and the elections as to allow for compliance with the electoral law; (3) that the present local officials be continued in their *de facto* status until elections can be held, and that then both municipal and provincial elections be held as preliminary elections; (4) that within six months thereafter the national election should be held; (5) that, in accordance with the Cuban Constitution, one hundred days should elapse between the national election and the establishment of the new Government; (6) that this plan be made contingent upon the continuance of tranquillity through two elections; (7) that the plan, which has in substance the approval of President Roosevelt, be made public. Secretary Taft's statement contains nothing that is new in principle. It simply announces the method by which shall be carried out the purpose of the United States expressed in Mr. Taft's proclamation establishing the Provisional Government. In that document he said, "The Provisional Government . . . will be maintained only long enough to restore order and peace and public confidence and then to hold such elections as may be necessary to determine those persons upon whom the permanent government of the Republic should be devolved." It emphasizes the determination of the United States to leave the Cubans again to themselves, but to do so only after order is restored.

❀

*Lord Cromer's Resignation*

Among the imperial governors of the British Empire none stands in higher repute than the Earl of Cromer. His resignation of the office of what is practically the British Governor-Generalship in Egypt last week is therefore an event of historic moment, not only to England, but also to nations with similar problems beyond sea. Lord Cromer has long since been an example adopted as a standard by colonial governors of other nations. Two generations ago Egypt became practically independent of the Turkish Sultan. The land attracted foreign investments. Already there existed a system of "Capitulations" by which the more civilized nations were allowed to establish their consular courts and to exercise quasi-financial control. In 1877 the finances of Egypt necessitated a formal international inquiry. Captain Evelyn Baring, who had seen twenty-four years of English military and diplomatic service, was appointed a member of the International Commission of Inquiry. The following year he— then Major Baring—and M. de Blignières were made Comptrollers of Egypt. For four years thereafter Major Baring was Finance Minister in India. The period marked the effort of an oppressed people to throw off the yoke of a tyrannical and spendthrift Khedive, the rebellion of an unpaid army, and the English occupation. When Major Baring, now become Sir Evelyn Baring, returned as Agent—the office of chief British authority in Egypt—the Khedive's authority was gone and the country was in chaos. The new Agent left the nominal authority to the Khedive and his ministers, but appointed an assistant to each minister—an assistant who practically ruled the country under the Agent's direction. The new Agent reversed the age-long policy of privilege. This meant, first of all, justice at last to the hitherto practically enslaved fellahln. Sir Evelyn abolished forced labor; he developed irrigation; he mitigated taxation. The result was that the fellahln are now in the eyes of the law equal with the pashas themselves; that the establishment of vast works of water storage and irrigation in Egypt and the Sudan has doubled the opportunities of labor; finally, that the poorest Egyptian is now greatly benefited as a result of mitigation of taxation, for Sir Evelyn, now Lord Cromer, has never countenanced the establishment of tempting public works if with the same money he could lessen the burdens of taxation. He has ruggedly withstood popular acclaim at home in preferring the claims of the Egyptian taxpayer. In other words, the basis of Lord Cromer's policy has been sympathy with the Egyptian. He has looked at each question as much as possible from the Egyptian point of view, and he has been so obstinate in this as to call forth the criticism from a few jingo critics at home that "too much in Egypt is now subordinated to mere native prejudice." But, as one who knows him well says of him, he never forgot that he is in Egypt on behalf of the people of Egypt, that it is their revenues, their property, of which he was disposing. Even his annual reports have been largely addressed to the natives. A man who has had such insight into native character, who has had "the infinite capacity for taking pains," whose frankness equaled his courage, and whose patience equaled both, has made an ideal proconsul.

❀

*Russian Finances* At the opening session of the Russian Duma the Finance Minister boldly stated that, although the war with Japan had cost $1,300,000,000, yet the past year's income had exceeded the expenses by some $15,000,000. The deputies, independent or party, shrugged their shoul-

ders and were silent. They felt that impartial accounting might produce different figures. It is this conviction that has made Messrs. Aladin and Tschkaikovsky appeal to Americans not to give the Russian Government any financial aid; for loans made to the present Government in the face of the Duma's protests would inevitably be repudiated by the Duma did it ever overthrow the existing autocracy. The deputies of the Duma, if they are to establish a genuine representative government, must have control of the purse. This has been recognized by so eminent an authority as Count Witte. In October, 1905, before the issuance of the Emperor's manifesto, Count Witte was unable to negotiate a loan even in friendly France, for the good reason that the Russian people were in practical revolution. With the issuance of the Czar's manifesto, however, and the summoning of the Duma, enthusiasm among Russia's well-wishers throughout the world, and confidence in the financial power to be given to the Duma, were such that the clever Premier was able to borrow from Paris and London no less than $440,000,000. If, now, it is seen that the deputies are not to have complete power of the purse, it will be practically impossible for Russia to obtain a new loan, and this country would be about the last to which the Government would turn. Some years ago, in a time of great affluence, when Americans were subscribing freely for the Government bonds of various nations, and even for the loans of European cities, the Russian Government placed many million dollars' worth of bonds at our disposal. Of this, a small proportion was purchased by American life insurance companies, which, of course, had their own interests in Russia. But the New York Stock Exchange, it is said, has not registered a transaction in those bonds from that day to this, despite the silver vase which the Emperor sent to the listing committee as a token of his regard. The general gloomy outlook for financial help is perhaps the strongest possible argument to induce the Emperor and his advisers to grant to the deputies financial powers which are justly theirs. This was evident in the debate last week on the budget. The Finance Minister was studiously moderate in his plea for a new loan. He attributed Russia's financial difficulties to three causes—the costly war, the costlier revolution, and the great famine. He even declared that without consent of Parliament it would be impossible to increase the revenue by new taxes. Thus credit operations were necessitated. Far from agreeing to new taxation, ex-Minister Kuttler, one of the leaders of the Constitutional Democrats, assailed the present taxation system, direct and indirect. Though only eleven per cent. of the revenue is derived from direct taxes, he said, these taxes fall chiefly on the poor, two-thirds of the land tax being paid by the peasantry, while the city taxes are mainly paid by those who are not able to afford dwellings of their own, and live in rented houses and apartments. Furthermore, all of the indirect taxes bear with harshness on the poor. Nearly six hundred million dollars in revenue, he added, is derived from taxation of articles used almost exclusively by the poor, while less than two hundred million dollars is collected from articles of luxury. The speaker promised, nevertheless, on behalf of his party, that the Budget would be discussed on its merits, without any attempt needlessly to embarrass the Government. There is hope for any government when a spirit of reasonableness animates the leaders of opposing political factions. This, however, should only hasten the passing of complete control of the public purse from the autocracy to the democracy as represented by the people in their Parliament.

❀

**Two Kinds of College Spirit**  That college undergraduates have the privilege, which no other class of young men have, of disturbing the public peace at their own pleasure, is an obsolete tradition. Last week a number of Harvard students attempted to adhere to this tradition ; as a consequence they found themselves next day in court, and were fined like the ordinary "muckers" whom they despise. Moreover, the Judge called them " nothing but boys." It is

true the provocation was great. In the theater where the disturbance occurred a play was being performed which, as the Harvard Crimson says, presented " on the stage a composite picture of many of the worst features of American colleges, under the name of Harvard ;" and, what is still more exasperating, represented the customs and manners of Harvard undergraduates as not only immoral, but actually vulgar ! The offense was heightened by the fact that the leading actor was a Harvard man. If, however, the play misrepresented Harvard, the rowdyism of the objecting students misrepresented Harvard still more. This was demonstrated by the public apology read from the stage the next evening by the president of the senior class of Harvard. In the name of the presidents of the four undergraduate classes, he expressed to the actors and to the audience the regret of the " entire undergraduate body." It was an honorable proceeding, for which we do not believe there are many precedents. Unhappily, the play itself and the rowdies will do much to give a false impression of Harvard and of college life generally. The dignified apology will perhaps not be widely noted. It is, however, the brief speech of the senior class president that expresses, we believe, the normal spirit of American undergraduates in general, and Harvard undergraduates in particular.

❀

**" The Messiah " on the Plains of Kansas**  An interesting and significant musical event for a considerable district of the Middle West was the production, in Holy Week, of " The Messiah " at Lindsborg, Kansas. Lindsborg is a little town of two thousand inhabitants, in the Smoky Valley, not quite two hundred miles from Kansas City. It is a Swedish settlement, the seat of Bethany College—an institution with a thousand students. Twenty-five years ago the College authorities instituted the performance of Handel's most famous oratorio, which at once became an annual event, not only for the town, but for all the country around. This year fifteen special trains carried visitors to the five performances from

Kansas City and from other towns within a radius of two hundred miles. About fifteen thousand persons were thus enabled to attend. The oratorio was given by a chorus of six hundred voices, supported by an orchestra of sixty pieces. Two of the soloists were from Chicago. All the others who took part were either students in the College or residents of Lindsborg. In one instance three generations of a family sang in the chorus. The Mayor is a member, and the Cashier of the State Bank is in the orchestra. Indeed, it was found impossible to give the performance in Kansas City, largely because that would have necessitated transporting a good share of the townspeople, including children whose parents sing in the chorus. The oratorio is produced in a plain wooden auditorium, accommodating an audience of about three thousand persons, who sit on rude wooden benches. The chorus does really remarkable work, singing with extraordinary vigor and precision. The effect of such choruses as " Hallelujah " and " Worthy is the Lamb," thus sung, is overwhelming. Another musical festival is given at Lindsborg in October, and still another in December. That such performances should find generous and enthusiastic support on the plains of Kansas is a striking and important phenomenon. For one thing, it is a reminder that, although a country may be new, its inhabitants may have the traditions and the arts of an old civilization.

❀

*Arbor Day*  The dignity of Arbor Day has been enhanced by a circular issued from the Forest Service in the Department of Agriculture. The lesson of Arbor Day, it says, is the use and value of the tree in the life of the Nation. The diversion of setting out a few trees and the exercises by which school hours are enlivened should be regarded as a means to an end rather than the end itself—an intelligent and lasting impression in the mind of the child. While isolated trees along the country roadside or in the city streets please the eye and cool the air with refreshing shade, the true message of Arbor Day is found in the forest, where ·wood is grown to supply material for

houses, fuel, and industries, where the tree-protected soil is storing the waters for streams, to be used for quenching thirst, irrigating land, driving mills, or filling rivers deep so as to bear traffic. The forest is thus the producer and custodian of the necessaries of life. The science of forestry is based on the idea that exact knowledge makes it possible to co-operate with nature in bringing the forest to its fullest usefulness as a source of wood, as a protection to the soil, or as a natural reservoir. Arbor Day should be the occasion of imparting to children some simple forest laws ; the planting of a few trees, without reference to the forest's productive value and commercial utilities, is certainly but a small part of the day's work. The normal child always loves the forest. Its mystery fascinates. It is the home of wild life. As every child is a natural investigator, the forest is an object of prime curiosity. But on Arbor Day the child needs to begin the study of forestry economics. As practical object-lessons those suggested in the circular of the Forest Service are valuable. For instance, what child has not seen a muddy freshet ?—a sight common at this time of the year. The stream is discolored by earth gathered from the soil, and rushes with force where there has been no forest cover. An experiment is suggested with fine and coarse soils stirred quickly into a tumbler of water and then allowed to settle, as explaining how a stream continues muddy while it runs swiftly and how it clears again as it slackens on more level stages, dropping the soil to the bottom. Again, flowers and seeds of trees are suggested as subjects of investigation. Many early-flowering trees mature their seeds before the school year ends. It is interesting to note the adaptations by which the trees secure seed distribution ; as, for instance, by winds, stream-currents, birds, animals. Hence, the world of flower and seed conveys nature's purpose to renew the forest and carry it undepleted from one generation to another. Finally, the circular contains practical suggestions as to planting. If every school-teacher should follow out the ideas as outlined by the Forest Service, the whole Nation would be the gainer.

## Politics and Dust

The political field has been obscured during the last two weeks by a violent wind-storm and whirling clouds of dust set in motion from certain editorial offices. A kind of journalistic hysteria occasionally breaks out in this country, and for weeks at a time envelops editors and readers in a vast and elemental confusion, in which gigantic forms, shadowy but terrifying, appear and disappear. These sudden whirlwinds seem at the moment to have an almost cosmic significance and scope, but they subside as rapidly as they arise ; and then it appears that the only territory ravaged was that in the immediate neighborhood of the gentlemen whose temperamental tendency to excitement, combined with quick inventiveness, has set them in motion. During the past two weeks the awful specter in the whirlwind has been the President of the United States—dimly seen, now in one part of the country and now in another, very like the old pictures of Boreas—setting destructive currents of air in motion and ravaging the continent. Faithful readers of the New York Evening Post and the New York Sun, to take the nearest examples, who have kept a clear mind during these agitating days, have read columns of picturesque reports from Washington and other columns of lurid editorials, and with pained surprise have discovered only now and then a very unimportant fact in the cloud of surmise, report, and speculation. This kind of journalistic amusement is entertaining for a time, but becomes wearisome if kept up too long, and there is a grave danger that the sport may be carried to unconscionable lengths. A Presidential election will not occur until a year from next November. Three months of whirlwind of speech and tempest of agitation are all the country can stand ; the prospect of being ravaged by tempests for eighteen months is unendurable.

The Outlook urges its readers to preserve a quiet mind, a cool temper, and to observe carefully the phenomena of these storms, being confident that sane observation will entirely rob them of their terrors. It is well to call attention to three or four obvious facts which are to be obscured during the coming months :

The President of the United States must be judged by his own words and acts, not by the motives imputed to him by newspaper correspondents, nor by the rumors, surmises, and guesses printed in newspaper columns. One of the New York journals gravely printed on Thursday of last week the following despatch : "Washington, March 10, 1:30 A.M. It was impossible to arouse anybody at the White House at this hour." One would imagine that a great crisis was upon the Nation, and that lights were burning in anxious windows from the Atlantic to the Pacific awaiting news from Washington. As a matter of fact, nothing had happened except an outburst of journalistic hysteria in a few newspaper offices. Madness had seized a small group of editors, and had taken the curious but not unprecedented form of imputing madness to somebody else. This hallucination was fastened upon the President, who was supposed to be pacing the halls of the Presidential residence with stealthy or vociferous feet, declaiming against all opponents of his policies as traitors and convicts, and shrieking at the open windows that he was the victim of conspiracies. Meanwhile, mysterious lurid lights were to be observed in the back windows, and there was a rattle of chains in the basement. The only basis for this hallucination was the fact that the President had repeated a story which had reached him of a combination, backed by a large sum of money, to nominate as the next candidate for the Presidency a man opposed to his policies. Now, even the President is entitled to some consideration. The popular idea that he is a hired man at the call of all citizens to do their chores may have some basis in fact, but it does not describe all his functions. He is entitled to the right to be held responsible for his own opinions, words, and actions, and not for the opinions, words and actions of able and ingenious editors.

The President is also entitled to some interest in the things for which he cares, and to the common human desire that policies which he has inaugurated, and which he profoundly believes are necessary for the welfare of the country, should be continued under his successor. There is no reason why an American citizen who happens to live in the White House should be deaf, dumb, and blind. It would be highly improper for such a person to attempt to dictate the nomination of his successor; there is no evidence anywhere, outside certain editorial offices, that President Roosevelt has had any thought of doing this. He is a very frank man, and is in the habit of revealing his whole purpose. That he should desire a continuation of the great work he has undertaken is not only natural but wholesome for the country; that he should, if he chooses, express his preference for certain men who have his confidence is a matter entirely within his proper province; that he has attempted, by playing politics, by the use of appointments, or in any of the other ways familiar to politicians, to impose the man of his choice on the country, or on a convention, there is not the slightest evidence.

Nor, on the other hand, is the right of any American to criticise the President and oppose his policies to be questioned; nor is any man to be accused of treachery, bad faith, or lack of patriotism because he opposes these policies. Mr. Foraker has as much right to endeavor to hinder legislation looking to the regulation of railways as Mr. Roosevelt has to urge it. There is ample ground for honest difference of opinion on these great questions; and the interest of the country, which can be served only by their just and wise settlement, demands the utmost freedom of speech and the utmost fairness in reporting the positions and utterances of public men of all kinds. It is unjust and absurd to represent the President as cracking a whip over his party and driving it with set teeth to his own ends; and it is equally unwise and impertinent to denounce those who disagree with him on these vital points as being the servants of corrupt interests. The President and his critics are equally entitled to an open field and fair play, and the country will see that they get it.

The Presidential contest has opened prematurely. The present storms will subside, and peace will once more reign in aching and perturbed editorial breasts. The ogre whose form has loomed portentous through the storm will disappear, and the figure of Mr. Roosevelt—plainspoken, ardent, impetuous, but brave and frank—will again be seen in normal perspective and proportions. The Outlook urges its readers to pay attention, not to what the newspapers say, but to what they prove—to recall Dr. Johnson's famous letter to MacPherson, the author of Ossianic poems.

❋

# The Thaw Case

The most notorious and scandalous case in the recent history of American criminal law came to a lame and impotent conclusion last week, when the jury in the Thaw trial failed to agree upon a verdict. Seven of the jury are reported to have voted for Thaw's conviction, five for his acquittal. There was no dispute as to the facts during the trial, which for the sake of record may be briefly restated as follows:

Stanford White, one of the most gifted architects that this country has produced, a man of international reputation in his profession, unfortunately also a man who, like Benvenuto Cellini, chose certain of his associates from the dissipated and reckless classes of society, was shot to death last summer in a public theater by Harry K. Thaw. Thaw is a son of a very wealthy Pittsburg family, ill brought up, ill educated, with no profession and no business responsibilities, who has spent his life and the money supplied by his family in riotous living. He married a few years ago a young actress who has only the most trifling and mediocre standing in her profession, and who makes no pretense to the possession of a respectable character in accordance with the standards of the civilized world. Without apparent passion and without warning, Thaw approached White, and, in the presence of a crowd of witnesses, shot and killed him, alleging as the reason for his deed that White had outrageously wronged his (Thaw's) wife previous to his marriage to her. If this wrong was committed, no evidence was introduced by Thaw in the trial to show, nor has Thaw ever claimed, we believe, that he attempted by civil or criminal process to have Stanford White punished. It never has been denied, nor can it be denied, that the accused took the law into his own hands. Money was lavishly spent by the Thaw family to defend the indicted prisoner. A criminal lawyer of great newspaper reputation was brought on from California to conduct the case for the defense. By the introduction of expert testimony, voluminous statements, examinations and cross-examinations of witnesses who really had nothing to do with the case, by unseemly wrangles among a group of lawyers employed by the Thaw family, the case was dragged out over a period of nearly two months. There were only two grounds upon which an appeal was made to the jury to acquit the prisoner: first, that he was mentally irresponsible when he committed the deed; and, second, that he was mentally responsible but was acting a noble part in avenging outraged American womanhood.

The case was filled with bathos and mawkish sentimentality from beginning to end. Details of life and conduct of the degenerate actors in the tragedy were admitted in evidence and retailed to such an extent by sensational and reckless newspapers that the Federal Government seriously considered interfering with the passage of these papers through the mails. At the close of the trial some of the jury violated all precedents and the common and proper etiquette of the jury-room by giving to the press full details of the jury's disagreements and debates, which covered a period of nearly two days. One juror contributed to the New York Times, a newspaper which makes a somewhat pronounced profession of being a safeguard of decency in the community, a long serial article over his own name describing the deliberations of the jury. During the procedure of the trial Thaw, the indicted prisoner at the bar, was permitted by his counsel to give signed statements to the newspapers expressing his own opinion of the case, of his victim, of the prosecuting attorney, and even of the jury—statements which were prominently printed in many of the

newspapers. And, finally, the New York Journal, with characteristic effrontery, announced in huge type printed with colored ink twenty four hours before the jury had rendered its decision, that the verdict was ten for acquittal to two for conviction—a statement which proved to be contrary to the facts, and which, as the jury was locked up at the time, was a manifest falsehood.

This we believe to be a fair résumé of the history of the case. No intelligent American can think of it without chagrin. The only points of light which relieve the general darkness and misery of the story are found in the admirable charge of the presiding judge to the jury, the conscientious care with which the District Attorney performed his unwelcome task, and the resistance, by at least seven of the jury, of the appeal to vulgar sentimentality made by the chief counsel for the defense in behalf of the honor of a Tenderloin habitué who shoots down a man who he thinks has wronged him by wronging, three years before, the woman of questionable reputation who subsequently became his wife.

There will undoubtedly be a new trial, for it is clear to the mind of every intelligent layman that society must be protected against such individuals as Thaw by something more than a mere jury disagreement. There has been, during the last two or three years, a growing dissatisfaction among both lawyers and laymen with the procedure in criminal trials in this country. Readers of The Outlook will recall that the subject has been discussed at some length in our columns, notably in the articles by Judge Amidon, of North Dakota. The Thaw trial calls attention anew and in a very forceful way to the need of this reform. There should be a greater restriction of the kind and amount of evidence introduced, an enlargement of the powers of the presiding judge, and a much more thorough and severe regulation of newspaper comment and report during the progress of a capital case. If the Bar Association, as a result of the scandals of the Thaw trial, should take this question up and pursue it to some fruitful end, the trial may not have been entirely in vain.          *a*

# Foundations of Faith

Three recent books [1] indicate three different bases for our Christian faith: Mr. Campbell's "The New Theology," Sir Oliver Lodge's "The Experience of Faith," Adolf Harnack's "Christianity and History." The first is philosophical, the second scientific, the third historical. The first makes the foundation of Christian faith an *a priori* conception of the Infinite; the second, a study of human nature; the third, the historical development of Christianity. A comparison of these three books is interesting and instructive, because it suggests to the preacher three alternative methods for meeting the current skepticism.

Mr. Campbell bases faith on an assumption. "I start, then," he says, "with the assumption that the universe is God's thought about himself." And he defines God as "the all-controlling consciousness of the universe, as well as the infinite, unfathomable, and unknowable abyss of being beyond." How he knows that there is any such controlling consciousness, how he knows that the infinite and eternal energy from which all things proceed is a conscious energy, that it is one not many, that it is supremely good or supremely intellectual, not sometimes good and sometimes evil, sometimes wise and sometimes unwise, he does not tell us. He assumes that infinite perfection is at the heart of the universe. On this assumption he builds his whole theological system. Out of it he constructs, or to it he attempts to square, his conceptions of man, evil, Jesus Christ, the atonement, and the like. The inherent, essential, and ineradicable defect in this method is that it proceeds from the unknown to the known. It assumes that which the skeptic wants to have established; it takes for granted as true that which the agnostic declares we cannot know to be true. It may help to unify the beliefs of the believer (though,

in fact, we do not think that Mr. Campbell succeeds very well even in this endeavor), but it does little or nothing to establish belief in the mind of the unbeliever.

Sir Oliver Lodge starts with the study of man and of his ancestry. His first question is, What are you? And his answer, "I am a being alive and conscious upon this earth; a descendant of ancestors who rose by gradual processes from lower forms of animal life, and with struggle and suffering became men." With this as his starting-point, and with scientific evidence given for this account of man's ancestry, Sir Oliver Lodge proceeds to explain the development of conscience and of duty and service growing out of the conscience, the nature of sin as a violation of conscience, the reasons for believing that there are beings higher in the scale of existence than man, and so leads on to the evidence of an infinite spiritual power in the world working in man, through Christianity, for man's recovery from sin and improvement in virtue. This method has the advantage of beginning with the known and proceeding toward the unknown, of making clear the distinction between vital experience and intellectual speculation, of showing how far a better consciousness outside of ourselves—that is, God—enters into our experiences and modifies our lives. It has the disadvantage of beginning with man as he is—that is, with sinful man, with man who is confessedly abnormal. In other words, it enters upon the study of life through a study of diseased humanity.

Professor Harnack bases Christianity upon Jesus Christ. Christianity is a historical development of the race. It is by a study of that history that we are to know whether our Christian faith is true or not. It is, first of all, a spiritual and intellectual development. A study of this development makes it clear that it is due, primarily, to a great personality: "Without the strength and activity of an infinite personality, nothing great, nothing that would bring us further on our way, can be accomplished." Those who have taken part in this development have attributed their strength and inspiration to the Christ. This development

[1] The New Theology. By R. J. Campbell, M.A., Minister of the City Temple, London. The Macmillan Company.
The Substance of Faith Allied with Science: A Catechism for Parents and Teachers. By Sir Oliver Lodge. Principal of the University of Birmingham. Harper & Brothers.
Christianity and History. By Adolf Harnack. Translated with the Author's sanction by Thomas Bailey Saunders. The Macmillan Company.
3'

thus affords a historical demonstration of Christ's presence and power in the world's history, and " requires that the actual personality behind it should be honored as unique." This personality has been living and working in the world's history. It has not been a decaying influence, but a growing power; it has not been a sacred memory, but a real presence. The life of a risen Christ is revealed in the work which the living Christ and his followers have been accomplishing. Is it said that this faith in the living Christ rests upon the biography of Christ written in the Four Gospels, and that this biography has been rendered doubtful by historical criticism? The answer is that, while some details in that life have been made doubtful, the main events in the life, the essential lineaments in the personality, and the sense and spirit of his sayings, have been confirmed, not weakened, by historical criticism.

Professor Harnack's method of meeting modern skepticism, the method illustrated in the sermon of Dr. L. Mason Clarke mentioned in The Outlook of February 23, appears to us to be the method to be commended to the Christian ministry. It is far more effective than either the philosophical or the scientific method. There are comparatively few laymen who know what monistic idealism is, or would care about it if they did know; a theology built upon an abstract philosophy does not interest them. There are more men who know something of evolution, both as a biological and a sociological interpretation of life, but this is a matter of secondary interest to them. But there are no men who are not interested to know whether there is a power in the world which will help to overcome evil, to cure ignorance, to comfort in sorrow, to give strength to bear life's burdens, to disentangle the soul enmeshed in evil companions and evil habits, to take out the sting of remorse for the past, to inspire with aspirations of hope for the future—in a word, to redeem from sin. The answer to this question, which concerns every man, woman, and child in the minister's congregation, is to be found, not in monistic idealism, not in a doctrine of evolution, biological or sociological, but in the actual work of Jesus Christ and his disciples in the world's history. Christianity is its own best evidence.

❦

# The Spectator

One nipping cold day last winter the Spectator found himself in the business center of a notable New England region. It was a typical focus of New England prosperity. Set in a broad upland bowl rimmed by lofty hills, the city had ample room to expand. Around it were other industrial communities; also lakes, streams, fields, and woodlands. Two main thoroughfares, generously wide, crossed each other in the center of the place. Except in the business section the streets were magnificently elm-arched. Hundreds of comfortable homes spoke of a well-to-do community and very considerable affluence. At the intersection of the two great streets, about an attractive park-like space, a fine civic center had developed. Here stood the city hall, several churches, a large modern hotel, handsome office buildings (happily without sky-scraping pretensions), a theater, and two other monumental edifices. One was a public library, given to his native town by an eminent man who had made a large fortune in the West. The second was a museum of art and natural history, given by another big-hearted citizen, whose equally notable fortune was derived from home industries. The two institutions were under one administration. In the hotels and other public places the trustees had posted placards extending hospitable invitations to visiting strangers. Throughout the city were many factories—paper-mills, woolen-mills, enormous electric works, and other industries. All these things showed themselves almost at a glance—or at least in several successive glances—from the trolley-cars, in traversing the town. But the steam railway lines burrowed through the place, and gave their passengers no idea of its character.

❦

While walking along the main business thoroughfare the Spectator noticed a large new building on a side street. It was of three stories, built of red brick, plain and conspicuously substantial, but with an attractive aspect in its fine finish that implied public uses with some sort of every-day utility. " Boys' Club " was the legend upon a large projecting sign studded with electric lights. "It can't be that a boys' club has a building like that all to itself," remarked the Spectator's companion. " More likely it is the Young Men's Christian Association." They stepped down the street to make certain. Sure· enough, above the broad entrance was carved the same inscription, " Boys' Club." The illuminated sign was to attract boys from the street, as a candle draws moths. But here it was not to destruction.

❂

That evening the two friends visited the institution. It fairly hummed with young vitality. The interior was plain, neat, and durable, adapted to the requirements of very lively boys. A lot of " kids," all the way from eight years to twelve, were enjoying all sort of games of chance and skill in a large space on the right, and they were not at all silent about it ! But in the well-stocked reading-room on the left there was quiet for the many youngsters there, all absorbed in storing their minds and feeding their fresh and plastic imaginations. Down in the basement there was boisterous commotion from a perfect bowling-alley and two large courts for basket-ball— one for big boys and the other for little. Here also was a pleasant sense of warm humidity. It came from the bath where the boys who had finished their bowling òr ball-playing or their gymnastic exercise were luxuriating in hot showers, their nudity almost veiled by the misty vapor that filled the large room.

❂

Upstairs, again, in the wood-working department a beginning in "sloyd " led to the making of· useful things that the boys were proud of taking home as their finished handicraft : good, strong chairs, tables, etc. In two drawing classes under competent teachers many boys were studying mechanical draughtsmanship,

decorative design, and lettering for placards—every seat filled. In the music-room an orchestra class was practicing— a boy at the piano accompanying several boys with violins under direction of a teacher who played first violin. A good-sized room was used for various purposes, according to the evening in the week. One of the most appreciated gatherings here was on Saturday night, when boys would come to mend shoes for themselves and their families—a cobbler's shop as jolly as that of the old-time New England shoemaker. The third floor was chiefly devoted to a completely equipped gymnasium, with military drill at stated intervals. In an excellent audience-hall, with sloping floor and a good stage, entertainments and lectures were often given, and now and then there was a play by the boys. A feature of the institution was a savings bank, regularly operating under the laws of the State. The deposits already amounted to four hundred dollars. Very curiously, while the money was lent at three and one-half per cent., the depositors received four per cent. interest ! This came from the circumstance that no interest was paid on deposits under fifty cents. The many deposits running all the way from three to forty-nine cents made possible the extra half-cent in the rate. A little weekly newspaper, sold to outsiders for two cents and to members for one, brought in some revenue.

❂

The Spectator and his friend were immensely interested in what the club's young superintendent told them. His heart and soul were in the work. He had come to the city a few years before to take charge of the institution. He had expected to find something more developed than the mere rudiments of an organization that awaited his guidance. He was obliged to start at the very beginning. The movement gradually grew. It chanced that its progress was quietly watched by the same public-spirited citizen who gave the museum of art and natural history to the community. This gentleman, having become convinced that the Boys' Club was doing a most useful work, erected this fine building for it, at a cost of forty thousand dollars.

❀

The Spectator learned that the membership of the club was twelve hundred—nearly all poor boys, drawn from the large working population of the city, a population including numerous foreign nationalities. These boys were attracted from the street—often from cheerless homes and questionable diversions—to pleasant surroundings, where, with all the free sociability of their kind, they found wholesome and entertaining occupation. It was instructive to note in the members the significant changes in expression that registered the growth of the soul. The small boys, of course, had lately come into the club. Common to these was the rather suspicious, distrustful look of the " street Arab "—the semi-savage look that stamps the untrained child as akin to the young of wild animals. It was a period in life potent for either unlimited badness or goodness, as the die might fall. It was the purpose here to load the dice with good intent. Then, under the steadily exerted social fascination of the place, the disciplined exercise, the organized sports, the good reading, the manual training, the physical exercise, the accomplishments, there was evident a wonderful growth of character, betokened in the intelligently informed features, the clear and manly eyes lit with aroused ambition and steady purpose. " Every boy in the drawing classes holds down his seat, for he knows that if he is absent two nights in succession it will go to another boy who is waiting for it," said the superintendent. Instances of boys who had gone directly from their studies in the club into good places that stood ready for them in the great electric works and other manufacturing establishments were becoming numerous. Hence there was a growing consciousness that to take due advantage of the opportunities offered by the club meant a start in life that assured a future considerably beyond that of the ordinary wage-earning mechanic.

❀

In closing, the Spectator would say that the city here indicated is Pittsfield, Massachusetts ; the beneficent citizen, Mr. Zenas Crane, of the neighboring town of Dalton, and brother to the present junior Senator from Massachusetts, the Hon. Winthrop Murray Crane. To the many Outlook readers who have boys' clubs in their towns the Spectator would say, Do not neglect them, as too often they have been neglected and left unsupported. Give them your best encouragement ! They are good-citizenship factories of the highest efficiency. They reach precisely where they are most needed. They are immensely cheaper than a growing police force. Every new policeman stands for so much new lawbreaking, disorder, and crime to be prevented, suppressed, and punished. Practically every new lawbreaker, rowdy, and criminal is a young man gone wrong because he was a boy started wrong. The boys' clubs start the little fellows on the right road. They mean so much less evil in the new generation, less outlay for courts, prisons, and police. They also mean immense positive benefits—producers more competent and gainful, large additions to the common wealth and the common welfare.

## TRAILING ARBUTUS

### BY CHARLOTTE CHITTENDEN

O darling thing, beloved of spring,
From Earth you lie so near,
You send us up, from perfumed cup,
The news that Spring is here.
Your trailing gown, and faint pink crown,
Lie cushioned soft on moss.
If Spring, when new, should once miss you,
What could make good the loss ?

# THE YELLOW MAN'S BURDEN

## BY ARTHUR JUDSON BROWN

Author of "New Forces in Old China" and "The New Era in the Philippines"

UNDERLYING the political problem of the Far East and affecting it more profoundly than is commonly supposed is the lack of personal sympathy between the Oriental and Occidental. The chasm is deep and wide, and no small skill is required to bridge it. There appears to be a natural prejudice between men of different races. The terms Jew and Gentile, Greek and Barbarian, Roman and Enemy, testify to the age-old bitterness of this prejudice. Americans are prone to boast of their freedom from it, but their treatment of the negro, the Chinese, and more recently the Japanese in California, is painful evidence that they, too, are not exempt from this common failing of humanity. Is it surprising that a race antipathy which characterizes even the most enlightened and supposedly Christian people of the earth should exist on the part of proud and self-centered Asiatics?

This natural and deep-lying prejudice has been greatly aggravated by the aggressions of the white races. The author has discussed these at length elsewhere,[1] and space does not permit the recital here. Suffice it that nearly one-half of Asia, ten-elevenths of Africa, and practically all of the Island world are under nominally Christian governments; while some other countries have come so far under Western influences as to be from this view-point under almost the same conditions. However much we may be gratified by the fact, the methods by which it was achieved cannot be read by any fair-minded man without a feeling of mingled shame and indignation.

Commercially, too, the white man is ruthlessly aggressive. The products of the Western world are now to be found in almost every part of Asia and Africa. The old days of cheap living have passed away. The knowledge of modern inventions and of other foods and articles has created new wants, and an economic revolution of stupendous proportions is taking place.[1] Of this, too, the white man is considered the cause, and between the greed of some natives who hope to benefit by it and the resentment of others who are suffering from it, his position is one of increasing delicacy.

The resentment of the Asiatic is intensified by the conduct of many of the white men who seek his country. Traders and travelers have roamed through Asia and Africa for many years, and with the increasing facilities for inter-communication the number of these white men is rapidly increasing. While there are notable exceptions, it is notorious that their character as a class is bad.

The common attitude of these foreigners toward the natives is illustrated by the author of a recent book on Korea. He informs us that when the Korean sellers of curios became importunate, he "found the specific cure for their pestiferous attentions to be administered best in the shape of a little vigorous kicking." A sorcerer, who was making noisy incantations to exorcise a devil, so aggravated him that, "losing my temper and my reason altogether, I dropped his gongs and cymbals down a well, depositing him in it after them." When the poor inhabitants of a poverty-stricken village declined to sell him their scanty stock of chickens, "the grooms, the servants, and the interpreter at once tackled the mob, laying about them with their whips,

---

[1] "New Forces in Old China," Parts II. and III.

[1] For many facts on this subject see the author's article on Economic Changes in Asia, in the Century for March, 1904.

883

. . . and fowls and eggs were at once forthcoming."

The Siamese and Laos treat a foreigner with extreme courtesy, but it has not always been reciprocated. The "boy," as the Asiatic servant is universally called, whom we engaged in Bangkok for our trip through the northern jungles, unconsciously gave an illustration of the general conduct of white travelers in Siam. "Who is Master and what is he going to Laos for?" he was overheard asking before we started. "He is the father of all the missionaries in Laos," was a boatman's reply, "and is going to see them." Upon which the boy ejaculated in a tone of relief, "Oh, then he won't kick me and throw bottles at me!" And two weeks later he said to a friend, "Master must be a very holy man, for he hasn't beaten me or sworn at me at all!" What a side-light upon the conduct of the average foreign traveler! As white men, we felt humiliated that such treatment of a servant as is everywhere taken for granted in America should in Siam be regarded as so exceptional, though it was pleasant to know that the very fact that one was connected with the missionaries was deemed presumptive evidence that one was a gentleman. The incident is commended to the consideration of those critics who allege that the natives dislike the missionaries.

Almost every traveler in Siam exhausts his vocabulary in anathematizing the local magistrates because they do not immediately furnish him elephants and carriers. We know from experience how trying such delays are. At Utradit and Pre we lost valuable time on this account. At Paknampo we could not secure boatmen at all, and at Lakawn we should have been unable to get elephants if it had not been for the kindness of the agents of the British trading companies. And this though we had, in addition to a passport, a special letter of introduction from Prince Damrong, Minister of the Interior, directing all magistrates promptly to give us any assistance that we needed. Again we were ashamed when we found that some of the officials wondered that we did not curse them. They had evidently been accustomed to abuse in such circumstances.

But what were the facts? It was rice harvest, and all the men were in the fields. It was, moreover, just after the King's visit, the preparations for which had compelled men to neglect their own affairs for months. Would it have been reasonable for us to complain because it took several days to find the carriers we needed? As for elephants, each animal is owned by an individual who keeps it for his own use, and when he does not need it he hobbles it and turns it loose in the jungle. To secure an elephant for a traveler, therefore, means that an owner must be found who is either able or willing to stop his own work or to send a man two or three days into the jungle to hunt up one. Suppose an Asiatic were to enter an American town and peremptorily order the Mayor to furnish him immediately four saddle-horses and thirty men as carriers. Suppose the Mayor were courteously to reply, "It will be difficult for me to comply with your request, for it is harvest time and the men are all busy, while the only horses in town are kept by private individuals, who may need them themselves or who may not care to lend them to a stranger; but I shall have pleasure in doing the best I can." And suppose that, if the men and horses were not at once forthcoming, the Asiatic were to become insolent and abusive and threaten to have the Mayor severely punished. That is precisely what happens when the average foreigner travels in Asia. Only instead of kicking him out of doors, as an American official would do in such circumstances, the Oriental magistrate, knowing by bitter experience the trouble that the foreigner can make for him, meekly hastens to do his bidding, frequently being obliged to seize elephants needed by their owners, and to arrest men and forcibly compel them to leave their fields and families to bear heavy burdens for weary weeks under a hot sun. "Why shouldn't we hate the foreigners," they say—"those violent and angry men with white faces, who come from a country beyond the sea, who are always in a hurry, and who blaspheme their God as no Buddhist would ever dream of blaspheming his?"

Then the foreigner often offends the religious susceptibilities of the natives.

He excites the anger of a priest by tapping a god with a cane. He rouses a Moslem to murderous fury by entering a mosque without removing his shoes. In Siam it is a standing grievance that travelers steal the images of Buddha from the temples. What would be thought of a visitor in a Christian land who should carry off a communion vessel as a souvenir? When the religious convictions of a Buddhist people forbid the taking of life, the foreigner who shoots pigeons from the trees of the temple precincts simply stamps himself as a ruffian in the estimation of the monks.

Nor is the tension relieved by what the Oriental learns in other ways of Europe and America. China, Japan, India, and Siam have a vernacular press which does not fail to publish with savage satisfaction lurid accounts of our mobs and murders and social, financial, and political scandals. The Asiatic has learned to respect the purity of life and the unselfish labors of the missionaries, but he now knows that multitudes in the lands from which the missionaries come repudiate Christianity and sneer at the effort to preach it to other peoples. Chinese gentlemen visit America and are treated with shameful indignity. The Asiatic travels through Europe and America and goes back to tell his countrymen of our intemperance, our lust of gold, our municipal corruption.

And now we no longer confront a cringing heathenism, but an aroused and militant Asia which has awakened to a new consciousness of unity and power. The Japanese victory over Russia has intensified this spirit, so that to-day not only Japan, but China, India, and Turkey are aflame with the spirit of resistance to the white man's domination. British rule in Egypt has been of incalculable benefit to the people, but the fanatical hatred of the Moslem for all Christians is so fierce as to make him forget all the blessings that the Englishman has brought to him. He feels no gratitude whatever, and is ready at any time to break out in blindly furious rebellion. In India practically the same feeling exists. Whether or not Great Britain has done all for India that she ought to have done, the fact remains

that she has given India a peace and justice and security for life and property that the country had never known prior to British occupation. But the proud-spirited East Indian, even though he may admit these things, will nevertheless tell the traveler that he hates the Englishman. The reason is apparent: the Englishman is his conqueror. No people on earth like to be subjugated, and the attitude of the East Indians toward the white man is the attitude of a haughty, sensitive race rankling under the wound to their dignity involved in the dominance of a handful of white men whose treatment at best is condescending and at worst and more commonly is so contemptuous that a prominent hotel is forced to post the following notice: "Visitors will be good enough not to strike the servants; any complaints made against them will be attended to by the manager."

If we pass to China, we find that equally proud-spirited people chafing because foreigners occupy so many of their fine harbors, and because even in the capital itself, and almost under the shadow of the Palace of the Emperor, the Legations of Western nations are virtual fortifications, stored with provisions and munitions of war and garrisoned by foreign troops. The Roman Catholic priests add to this burden of hatred. They are not given to abusing the natives, but they so strongly espouse the cause of their converts in lawsuits and quarrels that often a magistrate dares not decide a case against a Catholic. Moreover, the priests so openly identify themselves with the political designs of their respected countries, usually, that officials and people alike fear as well as dislike them.

As travelers, traders, politicians, and priests combined greatly outnumber the Protestant missionaries, it will readily be seen that they, rather than the missionaries, fix the status of the foreigner in the public mind, and that they create against foreigners as a class an indiscriminate hostility that is exceedingly hard to overcome. The heartrending consequences in China have been painfully evident. Even in Siam, one of the last countries in Asia in which opposition to foreigners would normally be expected, for the people are naturally kindly and easy-going, dislike of foreigners is steadily growing, and, after the illustrations we have given, the reader will hardly wonder. The occurrences of the last few years have done much to increase this hostility all over Asia, and from present signs the coming years will do more.

Everywhere in the Far East "Asia for the Asiatic" is now the cry, and we must reckon with it. The myriads of Asia have awakened to the fear that the white man means them harm. The gulf between the Oriental and the Occidental is therefore becoming wider and deeper. The words "foreigner" and "native" are not literally appropriate, for there is no such gulf between the Chinese and the Korean, or between the Hindu and the Malay. In most of the cities of Siam there is an amazing mixture of different peoples—Siamese, Cambodians, Annamese, Burmese, Chinese—but they blend, about as Germans, Irish, English, and Scotch blend in an American city. The differences between them are infinitesimal as compared with those which separate the European and American from the Asiatic. The resultant condition must be frankly faced as a probably permanent and enlarging factor in our relations with the Far East.

Of all the foreigners in the Far East, the missionary is the one who most carefully adapts himself to the customs of the natives and who is animated by the strongest sympathy for them. But, unfortunately, the chasm between the foreigner and the native can never be wholly bridged even by the missionary. After he has shown all possible tact and made every practicable concession to the customs of the natives, the troublesome fact still remains that, as an intelligent native minister said to the author, "You are of another race. Your methods of living, your modes of thought and action, are not ours." Said a veteran missionary : "I know of no missionary who does not treat the natives kindly and who does not entertain a real love for the people. Our continuous aim has been to reach the heart. But I am much mistaken if there is not a great gulf fixed between all of us and the native people,

so that we do not come into their hearts and comprehend them, nor do they comprehend us."

A few illustrations will help to make this clear. Take the matter of scale of living. According to Mr. Bryan, the average annual income of a man in India is only $10 ; in China it is less than $50. It is simply impossible for the white man to descend to such physical conditions. He is the product of a totally different scale of living, and any attempt to descend to that of the native would simply wreck his health. Even when the Oriental is rich, his conceptions of comfort differ widely from ours, while of sanitation he knows nothing, except of course in Japan. The average school-boy in America sleeps in a better bedroom than the Emperor of China.

Then there is the question of personal privacy. The Anglo-Saxon values it, but the average Asiatic is comparatively indifferent to it. When we were traveling in Korea, our arrival at an interior village was the signal for almost the whole population to gather. The women, in particular, often neither clean nor free from vermin, would crowd about my wife, feel of her dress, try to pull out her hairpins, and lift up the edge of her skirt to examine her shoes, all the time keeping up a stream of questions and comments that excited the uproarious laughter of the crowd, which usually included men. Nor was relief found when refuge was taken in an inn or a house, for the Koreans would peer in at every door and window. Locks and curtains there were none, and if a blanket was hung up, eyes would presently be seen around the edges or glued to a crack in the wall. The people were good-natured and meant no offense, but most American women would hardly enjoy such curiosity. We do not forget that the street gamins and loafers of New York are apt to be insolently inquisitive when a strangely clad Oriental passes through the streets. But a Korean lady in America would not be subjected to such an experience as we have described. At any rate, she could more easily escape from prying eyes. Europeans and Americans have been bred to the idea that their house is their castle. The missionary, far from his native land

and surrounded by people of different customs, naturally values the privacy of his residence as the one bit of home in all the world that is left to him. But the natives are inquisitive, and they flock to his house in appalling numbers. They want to examine every part of it. With no idea of the value of time, they squat about it for hours, and if the owner objects they are bitterly offended. If he frequently has guests at his table, but confines his invitations to men of his own race, the natives think that they are discriminated against.

Then manner must be considered. The white man so instinctively feels that he is the lord of creation that it is hard for him, no matter how thoroughly Christian he may be, to get over the idea that men of a different color are his inferiors. Even well-meant kindness is apt to have an element of condescension in it. The missionary himself may not realize it, but the native is quick to detect it. The Anglo-Saxon is inclined to brusqueness. His tone is apt to be peremptory. He is always in a hurry. But the Oriental is polite, ceremonious, leisurely. He is very careful to respect "face," that mysterious but potent force in Asia. His manners more nearly resemble that extinct species, a gentleman of the old school.

The Oriental delights in exaggerations of the virtues of others, and in a correspondingly exaggerated depreciation of himself. It is said that a Chinese gentleman, wearing his finest gown of silk, called at a house where he happened to disturb a rat which was regaling itself out of a jar of oil standing on a beam over the door. In its sudden flight the rat upset the oil over the luckless visitor, ruining his fine raiment. While he was still pale with rage, his host appeared, and, after the customary greetings, the visitor accounted for his appearance in this wise: "As I was entering your honorable dwelling I frightened your honorable rat. While it was trying to escape it upset your honorable jar of oil over my poor and insignificant clothing. This explains the contemptible condition in which I find myself in your honorable presence." Could courtesy go further in trying to prevent the mortification of a host?

Probably a foreigner would hardly be equal to such a demand upon his politeness and self-control. But he will do well to familiarize himself with native customs and etiquette, and to be as tactful as possible in observing them. The ceremonies may appear absurd to him, but they are not absurd to the native, and the foreigner will only prejudice himself in native eyes by ignoring them. We know how we regard one in this country who tucks his napkin under his chin, eats with his knife, and drinks out of his saucer or finger-bowl. The Moslem has precisely the same opinion of a white man who enters a mosque without removing his shoes. The Chinese think no better of the American who promptly takes the seat farthest from the door, or who begins to drink his tea as soon as it is served. To look at a high Chinese official through glasses is to be wanting in proper respect, and the man who is forced to wear glasses all the time should be careful to explain, or he may give offense. To make a social call in China in a sedan chair with short handles creates something of the sensation that would be created in America if one were to make a social call in a hearse, because a short-handled sedan chair is employed at funerals to carry the spirit of the deceased. To send presents wrapped up in the wrong way or by the wrong kind of a messenger is to deprive them of their value to the recipient. To hold one's hands behind the back while talking to an Oriental is to be discourteous. To walk rapidly is to class one's self with coolies. To inquire of a Moslem about the health of his wife is to offer an unpardonable insult. To count the children of a household in Africa is to bring bad luck upon them. To jump quickly out of a gharry in India is, in the estimation of an East Indian lady or gentleman, as undignified as for a lady in New York to jump over a fence.

The Oriental seldom objects to Christianity as such. He usually has several religions already, and the coming of another does not itself arouse his antipathy. He probably knows that his race has more than once changed its faith, and that, too, without bloodshed or revolution. Indeed, Christianity in essential aspects appeals more readily to him than to an Anglo-Saxon, for Christ was an Oriental and the Bible is an Oriental book, abounding with ideas and expressions that an Oriental naturally understands better than we do. It is Christianity's identification with the foreigner that arouses the Asiatic's suspicion. It comes to him as the religion of the white man who is despoiling him of his territory, overthrowing or menacing, his national independence, upsetting all the economic conditions of his life, swaggering about his streets, robbing him of his goods, and insulting his women. Imagining that all white men are Christians, he blindly and furiously hates them all. This forms at once the most formidable obstacle and the most imperative need of the missionary.

The Government can help by greater care in selecting for consular and diplomatic posts in Asia men whose daily lives conform to those standards of uprightness which President Roosevelt inculcates and exemplifies in public life at home. Many of our representatives abroad are of this type, but there are exceptions. It is deplorable when, as in some lands to-day, this supposedly most Christian nation is officially represented among non-Christian peoples by men whom common fame charges with conduct that is beneath the level of respectable heathenism. And if the drunken and licentious agent is not employed in America by a reputable business house, why should he be employed as its agent in the Far East? Is it not reasonable to ask that governmental and commercial positions in Asia shall be given only to men whose lives are not inconsistent with those principles of righteousness upon which we pride ourselves at home?

But the main work of conciliation must be done by the churches in sending to Asia in increasing numbers missionaries who represent the spirit of Christ and the best types of our Western character and culture. This is precisely what the churches are doing, and more and more evident does it become that in this missionary effort is the only true solution of the Far Eastern question.

# A SUMMER MEMORY
## BY KATE TAYLOR KEMP

IT was on a July afternoon in 18— that I first saw the berry-woman. I was sitting idly on the steps of the quaint old house which we had taken for the summer. Before me lay the waters of Lake Champlain, while afar off rose the cool peaks of the Green Mountains, all purple and pink in the sunset glow. The afternoon had been a hot one, but a thunder-storm had cooled the air, and I had come out for a breath of the freshness. Sitting there face to face with the beauties of the scene, my thoughts had wandered far away to the time when all about was wilderness, and I quite lost sight of my surroundings in the vague dream of stalwart warriors, merry young squaws, and dusky little folk, in the life which my fancy pictured for them in the long ago.

But my dream was rudely shattered by a voice, shrill and unfamiliar. "I say, don't s'pose you want no berries, do you?" I looked up and saw seated in a rattletrap of a wagon a quaint figure of a little old woman. She was leaning eagerly towards me, and her face, shaded by a rusty black bonnet, was full of a bird-like alertness and curiosity. I rose, and, going down to the gate, began to question her as to her wares. As I approached she jumped lightly over the wheel, and, paying no attention to what I was saying, she grasped me cordially by the hand and went on rapidly, "I'm awful glad to see you; I don't generally come up this way, but they told me there was some city folks in the old Case house. and I reckoned I'd come and have a look at 'em, says I; won't do no harm even if I don't sell nothin'."

I laughed and said, "Let me see your berries; if they are nice, I shall be glad to take some." As I began to speak she had started to take a measure from under the old blanket which covered the box beneath the seat, but before I had finished she had turned, placed her hands firmly on her hips, and, looking me straight in the eye, said : "Now look here, you an' me's likely to do a lot of business together this summer ; you treat me right an' I'll treat you right. I ain't no skin, an' when I bring you berries *I bring you berries*, an' that's all there is to it. There ain't no *if* about it." "Very well," I said meekly, and bought my berries.

As she climbed into the wagon and settled herself, she said, "I'll be round again Tuesday, an' don't you buy of nobody else. I ain't comin' five miles jest for nothin', an' I'll bring 'em jest as long as they last. G'land !" And off she went.

True to her word, she came, and, without waiting to ask, took out a ten-quart basket, full of big, juicy berries, fresh and delicious. "There! I picked 'em jest for you. You can eat 'em' all. Your family's big an' you look good an' hearty ; now me, I don't care none for 'em in summer time. I like 'em put up in jars for winter, an' I tell you right now, I'm goin' to put up a lot by an' by, if I do have to get help pickin' 'em. I ain't going to sell my stomach empty, not for nobody."

A little child of perhaps six years sat holding the reins over the back of the old horse, and, wishing to get in a word myself, I said, "Do tell me your little girl's name." "Her name's Maria Jane Louise Ransome." "But you told me your name was Van Dusen." "So 'tis ; she is my great-gran'darter." "But, surely, *you* are not a great-grandmother!" I exclaimed in amazement, as her face, though lined and seamed, was still not that of an old woman. "I got three great-grandchildren," she said, proudly, "even if I don't look it. There! I can't stand talking here no longer. *I* got somethin' else to do," with a look at me which convicted me of being an idle person indeed.

As the summer drew along, I came to know my little berry-woman well, and used to watch for her arrival as one of the events of the day. She showed a great interest in the members of my family, and inquired as to the name and occupation of each one. "Now, who's that ?" she asked, abruptly, as my fair-haired Swedish nurse came towards us, leading the baby. My explanation was greeted with, "Oh, she's so fat, I thought she was related to you."

Her calls were evidently a source of much pleasure to her as well as to me, but one thing troubled her. She wanted to see my "man." Many were the questions which she asked as to his whereabouts, his occupation, looks, etc. For long her curiosity went unsatisfied, my husband's business keeping him elsewhere, but at last he joined us, and one morning soon after, my little woman drove up, with a look of serene satisfaction on her face. Her first words were accompanied by a nod of content. "Well, I seen him." "Whom ?" I asked, bewildered. "Your man ; they p'inted him out to me down street. Little feller, ain't he ?" He is nearly six feet. But with this all interest in him vanished.

During our many talks together I learned about her early marriage, her striving to make a home for herself and the "handful of children" who quickly came. How, after all these years, when the great-grandchildren numbered three, the little farm was being finally paid for in part by the proceeds of her sales of berries. Later, as I was driving one day, I overtook her, homeward bound, with her pails of freshly picked fruit, and, drawing up, I invited her to climb in and let me take her home. She accepted gratefully, and as she settled herself comfortably on the seat and took off her sunbonnet to cool her forehead, she remarked with a sigh of satisfaction, "Jest the minute I see them horses' heads over my shoulder, I said to my-self, ' *It's that woman.*' " A little later, when I helped her down at her door, she thanked me and said, "I do like you, you're so common." ·

This was almost the last time I saw her, for the berry season drew to a close and my drives took me seldom in that direction. It was but a chance acquaintance. Our paths lay far apart, and I have never seen her since that long-ago summer. But I can still in fancy see that bright, withered little face, and among my memories few give me greater pleasure than the evident sincerity of her "I do like you, you're so common."

# HOW TO SEE ITALY

## BY AMY A. BERNARDY

IT is said that a very particular housekeeper one day arrived in Venice, and the first thing she did was to write home as follows : " Oh, this dirty Venice ! I feel all the time as if I wanted to go around with a mop-pail and a scrubbing-brush and clean it up."

Mrs. Browning, on a similar occasion, wrote : " I have been between heaven and earth since our arrival at Venice. The heaven of it is ineffable ; never had I touched the skirts of so celestial a place. The beauty of the architecture, the silver trails of water between all that gorgeous color and carving, the enchanting silence, the music and the gondolas ! I mix all up together and maintain' that nothing is like it, nothing equal to it, not a second Venice in the world."

Moral : Try, if you can, to see Italy with the reverent and joyful spirit with which Mrs. Browning saw it. If you feel within you the possibility of sharing the housekeeper's views, don't go to Italy. Which second advice constitutes the serious problem of my subject. " How to see Italy " apparently implies a series of " do "—" do this," " do that," and so forth ; but it implacably presents itself instead arrayed in a series of " don't." Those to whom you would say " do ' are already so intelligent on the subject, and so conversant with its possibilities, that they need hardly be told how to treat it. These know. There are others who don't know, and who deserve some positive and some negative advice. There are, alas ! others yet who think they know, and who make your spirit groan. Never was I so much—so disagreeably, I mean—impressed as when, not long ago, I saw a group of American women, possibly well-to-do and otherwise civilized, come to the audience of the Pope in their traveling suits, with their Baedekers hardly concealed by their coats, and weather-beaten brown veils hanging from awry straw hats. They were " taking in " the Pope between the Vatican and possibly the Palatine. The good

890

old Pope blessed all, indiscriminately, but one could not help thinking that forgiveness was granted because they knew not what they were doing. Had I known those women, and met them at the bronze door, my advice would have been —don't. They no more really saw the Pope than if they had not seen him at all. They missed all the interest of the little drama—the preparation, the expectation of the event as a solemnity, not as a sight to be done ; the courtesy, the stateliness, the old-time flavor of it ; the suggestion of the black robes and the flowing veils, which are the rule, and which they ought to have worn in common decency, even if they were Protestants—yes, even if they had been atheists. They thought they knew all about it, and to this day probably they wonder why there was so little in it.

The daily increase in the rush of eastward travel increases sadly misconceptions and missteps of this kind. The superficial and businesslike and irreverent spirit of the age, and especially of the thriving democracy, is disastrous in connection with your Italy. If you can't get rid of it, leave Italy alone.

Don't, to begin with, feel in honor bound to make the eagle scream wherever you happen to be, and chiefly in the presence of the heraldic Zoo of the older world. Don't imagine that you are going to find America in Italy, and growl because American institutions don't thrive at the threshold of cathedrals, and the Adams Express sign doesn't hang at every village station. Don't imagine that on account of this diversity or deficiency Italy is worse off than America by any means, and that, when something strikes you abroad as odd or idiotic, the oddity or the other thing is all on the opposite side, and that it is always the other thing that is not " educated up " to you. Don't look for sky-scrapers on the Italian street and breakfast food on the Italian table, for mince pie at the *osteria* and ice-cream soda at the drug-store. Don't constantly keep thinking about the things mother used to make and the things you get used to at home. Don't read Marion Crawford and imagine that you are going to find his Italy in the real Italy; and don't think that Italy would be better run on the American plan. It is strange to the impartial observer to notice how sensitive, in fact how utterly intolerant, the American people are of foreign criticism about themselves, and with what magnificent liberality they bestow it upon others. You can't expect the people to do what suits you, since you volunteered to come; they never asked you. Leave off all thought of your personal habits and opinions and your national idiosyncrasies; hoist the banner of adaptability. It may be that Europe and Italy were originally intended to be some day civilized by America and populated by Americans; for the present, the natives are still there. Keep your mental Fourth of July firecrackers to yourself.

These, briefly and brutally, are the rudiments of your preparation. But you probably have still to overcome certain other traditional prejudices that consciously or unconsciously cloud the brain of the average American traveler to Italy. First, the bugaboo of malaria. Malaria exists no longer anywhere near the spots haunted by American tourists; the efficient work of the government and the landowners concerned has succeeded in relegating it to certain districts of the marshy, depopulated agricultural region of Maremma. One thing is certain, however, that if people would but court sickness with the same persistency in their own country that they do while traveling and sightseeing in the Latin lands, they could get malaria, typhoid fever, pneumonia, and I don't know what not in their own back yard in New York or in Omaha at much less trouble and expense than they incur in going abroad.

The same can be said of the water question. Everybody drinks natural water in Italy, and the water of Rome, and Naples, and other cities is as wholesome as any around the world. But the native also drinks wine at his meals, and mineral water, principally in summer. And the native does not eat a heavy American breakfast, which is absurd in the Italian climate; nor does he attempt indiscriminate sightseeing in the hot sun and in the cool churches, in a rush, on top of the heavy breakfast and after a hurried lunch washed down with a flood of iced water, which, however good to counteract the effects of steam heat, is dangerous when used against natural heat. Nor do the Italian ladies wear the lightest lingerie blouses with the heaviest traveling skirts and American walking boots or shoes, which even in their lightest description are far too heavy for the Italian street in summer.

Mosquitoes and insects generally are another of the alleged Italian nuisances. They are not dangerous or poisonous in any way, and at all events are milder than the New Jersey or New Hampshire specimens. Other small and inconvenient insects are but a part of the rush and dust of sightseeing, climbing, sitting, and generally moving about in all sorts of places. Choose good clean places to stay in, wear light wash-clothes, and you have solved the problem.

Bargaining and feeing must be met with equanimity. Besides, by this time the American traveler has learned to keep his money so close that the performance is less of a joy to the other party than to him. The shopkeeper still in many cases adheres to the traditional custom of asking a higher price than he intends to sell for, but the American's estimate of the relative value of money is generally so exact that he is hardly misled at all. In fact, the average traveler is rather apt to under-price things than otherwise. Needless to say, you do not bargain in the upper-class shops; their prices are high, but so is their standard, and you don't think of bargaining there any more than you would on Fifth Avenue or Regent Street. Besides, in all large cities there are minor shops with fixed prices, and department stores on the same plan. As for feeing, remember that the disaster is more apparent than real in Italy, just the reverse of what it is in New York. Your American messenger boy accepts a nickel but doesn't thank you for less than a quarter, while your Italian ragamuffin rejoices in the bounteous offering of one cent, and even if you have twenty-five objects of the kind to satisfy, the consequence is obvious. True, you fee ten people in Italy to one in New York, but in Italy the scrub-woman is not a *lady*, your driver doesn't refuse two cents for the purchase of a *sigaro*, and your porter doesn't think himself quite as good a citizen as you are, consequently he doesn't put quite so high a price upon the sacrifice of dignity entailed by his acceptance of your fee. Two or three cents call for a *grazie* with surprising frequency, and ten cents is often liberality. Besides, as F. Hopkinson Smith says, there are occasions in Italy when a smile is as good as a *soldo*. The trouble with too many travelers, especially women travelers, is that, on one side, having heard so much of the cheapness of Italy, they expect it to amount to almost nothingness; on the other, that too often, having money enough for three months, they expect to stretch it over six, and possibly nine. But the truth remains, generally, that you can rely upon getting more joy out of less money in Italy, if you only know how, than in almost any other part of the world.

To do so, however, you must be rich yourself in personal resources, in power of appreciation, in knowledge, in that virtue of detachment and abstraction from petty details which allows you to save your strength for contemplation and joy in the beauty of things around you. For now, having done our best to dispose of the minor material nuisances and molded our spirit to a feeling of superiority to events, we may pursue the higher interests of the proposed plan. First of all, give to a sensible preparation all the time that you can possibly spare. By this I don't mean what many people do—reading a certain number of handbooks on art, and proposing to exhaust your Baedeker, that wonderful help to the wise and great misleader of the unwary. Italy has been likened to the book of centuries. You don't take an encyclopædia to read from first to last page. Don't try to read all that the centuries have impressed upon their book. Don't attempt to cram churches and galleries, palaces and fortresses, catacombs with Renaissance, ancient

Roman with *barocco*, gardens with convents, a little of everything and nothing thoroughly. Make up your mind which attracts you most, whether pictures or architecture, nature or art. Going through galleries, try to see only some things, those that you have long known by fame and with which you are familiar already, or those that have some special attraction to your mind, and resist the temptation even to look upon the others. You wouldn't remember them, anyhow, after six months, and it is astonishing how much time, strength, and worry can be saved by a wise system of selection, how much clearness of ideas and depth of enjoyment are gained thus. In no case feel obliged to do Italy because others do it or as others do it. Stick to what is likely to appeal to you. No mistake in Italy is easier and more dangerous than this indiscriminate sightseeing, which soon becomes a burden to the body as well as to the mind, and leaves, even worse than a light impression, a blurred series of impressions on you, and the sense of weariness and of duty performed listlessly and joylessly. Have the courage of your own opinions. Don't pretend to be interested in the portraits of the Popes at St. Paul's when in your heart of hearts you know that you would rather drive to the Pincio, where the band plays while you sit in the sun and see the Queen pass by and smile. Don't go to the Popes because you'll never have a chance to see Italy again. Better see what you like if such is the case, disregarding completely, if necessary, the advice of friends and the trend of public opinion, which means the trend of conventionality. The flowers on the Lungarni in Florence or Pisa may have more to tell you than the frescoes in the palaces; sit and watch the flowers on the Lungarni. When you come to a place where you feel like tarrying a while, do so by all means, even if a hundred asterisks in your Baedeker clamor for your attention and maintain that you must enjoy something else. That hour of self-indulgence meanwhile will have revealed to you more of the real spirit of the place than any amount of cramming and hurrying through the conventional lines. Thus pursuing the elusive spirit of Italy with a soothed heart, after its own mood, having laid aside all dutiful mop-pail and scrubbing-brush ideas, you will be astonished to find how enjoyable is Italy with relaxation.

And let me add here that to the glamour of Florence and Rome, and to the accomplishment of the conventional tour, many another delight is sacrificed. Lots of people don't really begin to understand Rome who might grasp the tropical splendor and the Spanish or Saracen atmosphere of Sicily, or even more easily feel at home in the Riviera, with its brilliant mixture of natural beauty and Parisian elegance. If you seek old tradition and are attracted by millenary folk-lore, Abruzzo is the place for you. Romance of the Middle Ages hovers in the castles of Aosta even more than in the Tuscan strongholds. And if you have only a day to spend in Italy, or if you are tired and want only one impression, and that as different from all others as possible, see that you spend that day in Venice.

There seems to be a general feeling that northern Italy hardly deserves time and attention. *Error magnus, error deplorabilis.* From Genoa to Venice via Spezia, the brilliant military post; Parma, the city of Correggio; Milan, with possibly the *certosa* of Pavia and the frescoes of Mantua; Verona, the city of Juliet; Padua, Ferrara, and Treviso, makes one of the fullest and most comprehensive Italian trips, sufficiently harmonious and varied to be a delight from end to end. It begins with a suggestion and ends with a revelation. It might dawn upon you, meanwhile, that if Genoa had not the Van Dycks she would be noted as one of the wealthiest mercantile cities of Europe; that if Milan were not the city

of the Last Supper and the cathedral, we would realize that her institutions, organizations, modern conveniences, etc., are of the best that the twentieth century can furnish—for she is fully as up to date as New York, except that she retains some glamour of beauty and romance within the moats and walls of her castello. Let me also suggest the Adriatic coast, from Istria to Calabria, as the ideal coast of pastoral beauty and rugged grandeur, of mediæval legend and classic suggestion—Greek, Eastern, and Italian at one and the same time, pure, natural, undesecrated. To the old and experienced traveler a reminder: the ruins and dust-heaps of Italy are marvelously fecund of masterpieces, full of revelations. Seek henceforth in Genoa the renewed Loggia dei Mercanti; in Naples the Viceregal walls, the Castello in Milan. The Roman forum is teeming daily with new wonders, and in Florence the Uffizii are continually richer by several masterpieces.

Last but not least, to all, don't go to Italy by the northern route. The great rush of London, the dazzling Parisian brilliancy, the panoramic Swiss scenery, won't make a good background for your Italian impressions. Go by the southern lines, and if you want a preface to the vision of beauty, a communion with the spirit of rest, with the spirit of ages, with the gentle simplicity of life, stop off your transatlantic liner at the happy Azores, and then at Gibraltar, where the British, the Saracen, and the Latin soul are subdued in harmony among the flowers of the Alameda. That is the fittest introduction to Italy of the multiform spirit. Have your first glimpse of her from the blue sea, for she is a maritime land, the pearl of the Mediterranean.

# THE SCHOOL DAYS OF AN INDIAN

## BY CHARLES A. EASTMAN
### (OHIYESA)

## II. DISCOVERING A NEW WORLD

IT was in the fall of 1874 that I started from Flandreau, then only an Indian settlement, with a good neighbor of ours on his way to Santee. There were only a dozen houses or so at Sioux Falls, and the whole country was practically uninhabited, when we embarked in a home-made prairie schooner, on that bright September morning.

I had still my Hudson Bay flintlock gun, which I had brought down with me from Canada the year before. I took that old companion, with my shot-pouch and a well-filled powder-horn. All I had besides was a blanket and an extra shirt. I wore my hunting suit, which was a compromise between Indian attire and a frontiersman's outfit. I was about sixteen years old and small of my age.

Our first night on my way to school was at Hole-in-the-Hill, one of the most picturesque spots in the valley. Here I brought in a doe, which I had come upon in the tall grass of the river bottom. Peter shot several ducks, and we had a good supper. It seemed to me more like one of our regular fall hunts than like going away to school.

After supper I said, "I am going to set some of your traps, uncle."

"And I will go with you," replied Peter. "But before we go, we must have our prayer," and he took out his Bible and hymn-book printed in the Indian tongue.

It was all odd enough to me, for although my father did the same, I had not yet become thoroughly used to such things. Nevertheless, it was the new era for the Indian; and while we were still seated on the ground around the central fire of the Sioux teepee, and had just finished our repast of wild game, Peter read from the good book, and performed the devotional exercises of his teepee home, with quite as much zeal as if he were within four walls and surrounded by civilized things. I was very much impressed when this primitive Christian prayed that I might succeed in my new undertaking.

The next morning was frosty, and after an early breakfast we hurried to our traps. I got two fine minks and a beaver for my trouble, while Peter came home smiling with two otters and three beavers. I saw that he had something on his mind, but, like a true Indian, I held my peace. At last he broke the news to me—he had changed his mind about going to Santee agency!

I did not blame him—it was hard to leave such a trapper's paradise as this, alive with signs of otter, mink, and beaver. I said nothing, but thought swiftly. The temptation was strong to remain and trap too. That would please my grandmother; and I will confess here that no lover is more keen to do the right thing for the loved one than I was at that time to please my old grandmother.

The thought of my father's wish kept me on my true course. Leaving my gun with Peter, I took my blanket on my back and started for the Missouri on foot.

About this time I did some of the hardest thinking that I have ever done in my life. All day I traveled, and did not see any one until, late in the afternoon, descending into the valley of a stream, I came suddenly upon a solitary farm-house of sod, and was met by a white man—a man with much hair on his face.

894

I was hungry and thirsty as a moose in burned timber. I had some money that my father had given me—I hardly knew the different denominations; so I showed the man all of it, and told him by signs that he might take what he pleased if only he would let me have something to eat, and a little more to carry with me. As for lodging, I would not have slept in his house if he had promised me a war-bonnet!

While he was cordial—at any rate, after I exhibited my money—there was something about his manner that did not put me at my ease, and my wild instincts told me to keep an eye on him. But I was not alone in this policy, for his flock of four daughters and a son nearly put their necks out of joint in following my modest, shy movements.

When they invited me to sit down with them at the table, I felt uncomfortable, but hunger was stronger than my fears and modesty. The climax came when I took my seat on a rickety stool between the big, hairy man and one of his well-grown daughters. I felt not unlike a young blue heron just leaving the nest to partake of his first meal on an unsafe, swinging branch. I was entirely uncertain of my perch.

All at once, without warning, the man struck the table with the butt of his knife with such force that I jumped and was within an ace of giving a war-whoop. In spite of their taking a firm hold of the home-made table to keep it steady, the dishes were quivering, and the young ladies no longer able to maintain their composure. Severe glances from mother and father soon brought us calm, when it appeared that the blow on the table was merely a signal for quiet before saying grace. I pulled myself in, much as a turtle would do, and possibly it should be credited to the stoicism of my race that I scarcely ever ate a heartier meal.

After supper I got up and held out to the farmer nearly all the money I had. I did not care whether he took it all or not. I was grateful for the food, and money had no such hold on my mind as it has gained since. To my astonishment, he simply smiled, shook his head, and stroked his shaggy beard.

I was invited to join the family in the sod-house parlor, but owing to the severe nerve-shocks that I had experienced at the supper-table, I respectfully declined, and betook myself to the bank of the stream near by, where I sat down to meditate. Presently there pealed forth a peculiar, weird music, and the words of a strange song. It was music from a melodeon, but I did not then know what that was; and the tune was "Nearer, my God, to Thee." Strange as it sounded to me, I felt that there was something soothing and gentle about the music and the voices.

After a while curiosity led me back to the sod house, and I saw for the first time how the white woman pumps so much air into a box that when she presses on the top boards it howls convulsively. I forgot my bashfulness so far as to listen openly and enjoy the operation, wondering much how the white man puts a pair of lungs into a box, which is furnished with a whole set of black and white teeth, and when he sings to it, it appears to answer him. This is how the white people teach their children to do things, I thought.

Presently I walked over to a shed where the farmer seemed to be very busy with his son, earnestly hammering something with all their might in the midst of glowing fire and sparks. He had an old breaking-plow which he was putting into shape on his rude forge. With sleeves rolled up, face and hands blackened and streaming with sweat, I thought he looked not unlike a successful warrior just returned from the field of battle. His powerful muscles and the manly way in which he handled the iron impressed me tremendously. "I shall learn that profession if ever I reach the school and learn the white man's way," I thought.

I thanked the good man for his kind invitation to sleep within the sod walls with all his family, but signed to him that I preferred to sleep out-of-doors. I could see some distrust in his eyes, for his horses were in the open stable; and at that my temper rose, but I managed to control it. He had been kind to me, and no Indian will break the law of hospitality unless he has lost all the trails of his people. The man looked me over again carefully, and appeared satisfied; and I rolled myself up in my blanket among the willows, but every star that night seemed to be bent upon telling the story of the white man.

I slept little, and early the next morning I was awakened by the barking of the farmer's collie and the laughter of his daughters. I got up and came to the house. Breakfast was nearly ready, and every member of the family was on hand. After breakfast I once more offered my money, but was refused. I was glad. Then and there I loved civilization and renounced my wild life.

I took up my blanket and continued on my journey, which for three days was a lonely one. I had nothing with which to kill any game, so I stopped now and then at a sod house for food. When I reached the back hills of the Missouri, there lay before me a long slope leading to the river bottom, and upon the broad flat, as far as my eyes could reach, lay farm-houses and farms. Ah! I thought, this is the way of civilization, the basis upon which it rests! I desired to know that life.

Thirty miles from the school I met Dr. Riggs on the road, coming to the town of Yankton, and received some encouraging words from him, for he spoke the Sioux language very well. A little further on I met the Indian agent, Major Sears, a Quaker, and he, too, gave me a word of encouragement when he learned that I had walked a hundred and fifty miles to school. My older brother John, who was then assistant teacher and studying under Dr. Riggs, met me at the school and introduced me to my new life.

The bell of the old chapel at Santee summoned the pupils to school. Our principal read aloud from a large book and offered prayer. Although he conducted devotional exercises in the Sioux language, the subject matter was entirely strange, and the names he used were unintelligible to me. "Jesus" and "Jehovah" fell upon my ears as mere meaningless sounds.

I understood that he was praying to the "Great Mystery" that the work of the day might be blessed and their labor be fruitful. All this was new and very strange. A cold sweat came out upon me as I heard him ask the "Great Mystery" to be with us in that day's work in that school building. I thought it was too much to ask of him. I had been taught that the Supreme Being is only concerned with spirits, and that when one wishes to commune with him in nature he must be in a spiritual attitude, and must retire from human sound or influence, alone in the wilderness. Here for the first time I heard Him addressed openly in the presence of a house full of young men and young girls!

All the scholars were ordered to various rooms under different instructors, and I was left in the chapel with another long-haired young man. He was a Mandan from Fort Berthold—one of our ancient enemies: Not more than two years before that time my uncle had been on the war-path against this tribe and had brought home two Mandan scalps. He, too, was a new scholar, and looked as if he were about to come before the judge to receive his sentence. My heart at once went out to him, although the other pupils were all of my own tribe, the Sioux. I noticed that he had beautiful long hair arranged in two plaits, and in spite of his sad face he was noble-looking and appeared to great advantage, I thought, in contrast with the other pupils, whose hair was cut short and their garments not becoming to them at all. This boy, Alfred Mandan, became a very good friend of mine.

Dr. Riggs took me in hand and told me the rules of the school and what was expected of us. There was the chapel, which was used as a church every Sunday and as a school-house on week days. There was the Dakota Home for the girls' dormitory—a small, square frame building—and for the boys a long log house some two hundred yards from the chapel under the large cottonwood-trees.

Dr. Riggs said that I need not study any that first day, but could fill up the big bag he brought me with straw from the straw pile back of his barn. I carried it over to the log cabin, where the Doctor was before me and had provided a bunk or framework for my bed. I filled a smaller bag for a pillow, and, having received the sheets and blankets, I made my first white man's bed under his supervision. When it was done it looked clean and dignified enough for any one, I thought.

He said that I must make it every morning like that before going to school. " And for your wash, there is a tin basin or two on a bench just outside of the door, by the water-barrels." And so. it was. We had three barrels of Missouri River water, which we ourselves filled up every week, for we boys had to furnish our own water and wood, and were detailed in pairs for this work.

Dr. Riggs supplied axes for the wood-choppers, and barrels and pails for the water-carriers, also a yoke of large and gentle white oxen and a lumber-wagon. It. seems to me that I never was better acquainted with two animals than with these two! I have done some of my solemnest thinking behind them. The Missouri River was about two miles from our log house, with a wide stretch of bottom land intervening, partly cottonwood timber and partly open meadow with tall grass. I could take a nap, or dance a war-dance, if I cared to do so, while they were carrying me to wood or to water.

Dr. Riggs gave me a little English primer to study, also one or two books in the Dakota language, which I had learned to read in the day-school. There was a translation of the Psalms, and of the Pilgrim's Progress. I must confess that at that time I would have preferred one of grandmother's evening stories, or my uncle's account of his day's experiences in the chase. I thought it was the dullest hunting I had ever known!

Toward evening a company of three young men arrived from up the river—to all appearance full-fledged warriors. Ah, it was good to see the handsome white, blue, and red blankets worn by these stately Sioux youths! I had not worn one since my return from Canada. My brother got me a suit of clothes, and had some one cut my hair, which was already over my ears, as it had not been touched since the year before. I felt like a wild goose with its wings clipped.

Next morning the day pupils emerged in every direction from the woods and deep ravines where the Indians had made their temporary homes, while we, the

log-cabin boarders, came out in Indian file. The chapel bell was tolling as we reached the yard, when my attention was attracted to a pretty lass standing with her parents and Dr. Riggs near the Dakota Home. Then they separated and the father and mother came toward us, leaving the Doctor and the pretty Dakota maiden standing still. All at once the girl began to run toward her parents, screaming pitifully.

" Oh, I cannot, I cannot stay in the white man's house! I'll die, I'll die! Mamma! Mamma!"

The parents stopped and reasoned with the girl, but it was of no use. Then I saw them leading her back to the Dakota Home, in spite of her pleading and begging. The scene made my blood boil, and I suppressed with difficulty a strong desire to go to her aid.

How well I remember the first time we were called upon to recite! In the same primer class were Eagle-Crane, Kite, and their compatriot from up the river. For a whole week we youthful warriors were held up and harassed with words of three letters. Like raspberry bushes in the path, they tore, bled, and sweated us—those little words rat, cat, and so forth—until not a semblance of our native dignity and self-respect was left. And we were of just the age when the Indian youth is most on his dignity! Imagine the same fellows turned loose against Custer or Harney with anything like equal numbers and weapons, and those tried generals would feel like boys! We had been bred and trained to those things; but when we found ourselves within four walls and set to pick out words of three letters, we were like novices upon snow-shoes—often flat on the ground.

I hardly think I was ever tired in my life until those first days of boarding-school. All day things seemed to come and pass with a wearisome regularity, like walking railway ties—the step was too short for me. At times I felt something of the fascination of the new life, and again there would arise in me a dogged resistance, and a voice seemed to be saying, " It is cowardly to depart from the old things!"

Aside from repeating and spelling

words, we had to count and add imaginary amounts. We never had had any money to count, nor potatoes, nor turnips, nor bricks. Why, we valued nothing except honor; that cannot be purchased. It seemed now that everything must be measured in time or money or distance. And when the teacher placed before us a painted globe, and said that our world was like that—that upon such a thing our forefathers had roamed and hunted for untold ages, as it whirled and danced around the sun in space—I felt that my foothold was deserting me. All my savage training and philosophy was in the air, if these things were true.

Later on, when Dr. Riggs explained to us the industries of the white man, his thrift and forethought, we could see the reasonableness of it all. Economy is the able assistant of labor, and the two together produce great results. The systems and methods of business were of great interest to us, and especially the adoption of a medium of exchange.

The Doctor's own personality impressed us deeply, and his words of counsel and daily prayers, strange to us at first, in time found root in our minds. The world seemed gradually to unfold before me, and the desire to know all that the white man knows was the tremendous and prevailing thought in me, and was constantly growing upon me more and more.

I studied harder than most of the boys. Missionaries were poor, and the Government policy of education for the Indian had not then been developed. The white man in general had no use for the Indian. Sitting Bull and the Northern Cheyennes were still fighting in Wyoming and Montana, so that the outlook was not bright for me to pursue my studies among the whites, yet it was now my secret dream and ambition.

It was at Santee that I sawed my first cord of wood. Before long I had a little money of my own, for I sawed most of Dr. Riggs's own wood and some at the Dakota Home, besides other work for which I was paid. Although I could not understand or speak much English, at the end of my second year I could translate every word of my English studies into the native tongue, besides having

read all that was then published in the Sioux. I had caught up with boys who had two or three years the start of me, and was now studying elementary algebra and geometry.

One day Dr. Riggs came to me and said that he had a way by which he could send me to Beloit, Wisconsin, to enter the preparatory department of Beloit College. This was a great opportunity, and I grasped it eagerly, though I had not yet lost my old timidity about venturing alone among the white people.

I went to Beloit in September, 1876, two months after Custer's command had been annihilated by the Sioux. People were bitter against the Sioux in those days, and I think one of the local papers printed a story that I was a nephew of Sitting Bull, who had sent me there to study the white man's arts so that he might be better able to cope with them. When I went into the town, I was followed on the streets by gangs of little white savages, giving imitation warwhoops; but at the school they received me kindly.

The journey itself was an education. I had never before traveled by rail, nor seen a large town. Practically, I had not known what student life is, for here the young men worked with a regularity and earnestness that amazed me. I could understand simple sentences in English when slowly spoken, but I did not like to ask questions—that is not the Indian way—so I tried to reason everything out for myself, and discovered my mistakes later.

For one thing, I supposed then that every educated man must be highly religious and spiritual-minded. The chapel gatherings at each end of the day impressed me very much. Some of the professors appeared to me to be mysteriously endowed with more than human wisdom and experience, especially those whose heads were entirely bald. I supposed this to be a sign of something remarkable and holy.

Yet it was at Beloit College that my eyes were opened intelligently, for the first time, to the greatness and brilliancy of Christian civilization—the ideal civilization, as I then saw it prospectively—the development of every natural resource—the broad brotherhood of mankind—the blending of all languages and intermixture of all races under one religion. There must be no more warfare within our borders ; we must quit the trail for the breaking-plow, since pastoral life was the next thing for the Indian. So reasoning, I renounced finally my bow and arrows for the spade and pen;

I took off my soft moccasins and put on the rather heavy and clumsy but durable shoes. Every day of my life I put into use every English word that I knew. I was now eighteen years of age, well drilled in the philosophy of the Indian, alert and tireless in every faculty, and here for the first time I permitted myself to think and act as a white man.

# *THE FAMILY*

OF the three books[1] on which this article is based, " Sex and Society " is made up of a number of essays originally published independently, and has its unity in the fact that these essays have a common theme. Only incidentally does it treat of marriage and the family, and only in one chapter, and that on the adventitious character of a woman, does it deal to any considerable extent with modern woman or modern problems. Mrs. Parsons's book on " The Family " is offered avowedly as a text-book, " a pedagogic device for the university lecturers who are so commonly called upon to conduct elementary courses in sociology." It is scholarly, abounds with references to authorities and to text-books for the student's reading, but deals almost wholly with the family in its primitive forms. Only the last two chapters have anything of importance to say concerning the modern family—less than forty pages out of a volume of three hundred and sixty-four pages. In our judgment, it is wholly inadequate as a text-book for the study of the family, because it practically ignores the nature, origin, function, and laws of the modern Christian family, which is what the student most needs to comprehend. Helen Bosanquet's book on " The Family " is in form less scientific, but is in reality more so. It is divided into two parts of about equal length, the first dealing historically with the Family. Unlike Mrs. Parsons's volume, it brings this history down through

the Middle Ages to the present time. The second part of the book is devoted to the modern family, and is evidently based not merely upon second-hand information derived from other books, but upon a direct first-hand study of the modern family as it exists in England in different social circles ; and it treats the family, not as a mere physical organization, but as a vital, human, spiritual organization bound together by spiritual forces and working out spiritual results.

In the study of any organization we ask ourselves such questions as the following : What is this organization ? What is its origin ? What is its function ? What part does it play in the economy of life ? What are the laws of its nature, obedience to which will promote its health and welfare, disobedience to which will cause disease and perhaps death ? If it is a complex and perfected organization, what has been the history of its evolution, what its early forms ? The study of the family involves a consideration of these questions. We cannot, of course, in a brief article answer them ; we can only indicate illustratively the nature of the questions and suggest some of the answers.

Helen Bosanquet answers satisfactorily the first question : " What is a family, and what is its purpose ? No one will feel himself at a loss in answering the question ; man, woman, and child, and their conclusion, these in their combination form the Family, and the purpose of the combination is the mutual convenience and protection of all the members belonging to it." This is the family, and

[1] Sex and Society. By William I. Thomas. The University of Chicago Press, Chicago
The Family. By Elsie Parsons, Ph.D. G. P. Putnam's Sons, New York.
The Family. By Helen Bosanquet. The Macmillan Company, New York.

it exists in various forms. It may be a man and several women; that is, it may be a polygamous marriage; but throughout Christendom it is one man and one woman mated to each other with their child or children. The Christian family is monogamous.

What is the origin of this family—not out of what previous organization did the present family grow, but how is the specific family constructed? By marriage; and by this is meant, not a wedding ceremony, but, according to Mrs. Parsons, an agreement to live together until the birth of offspring. Professor Thomas's definition is better. It is an agreement to live together until the offspring have grown into a condition of independence of the parents. "Among mankind the longer dependence of children results in a correspondingly lengthened and intimate association of the parents, which we denominate marriage. For Westermarck is quite right in his view that children are not the result of marriage, but marriage is the result of children."

The answers to these two questions indicate the answer to the third—the function of the family. This is the birth, rearing, and training for manhood and womanhood of children. This is the most important function in life; therefore the family is the most important of all social organizations. For life has for its ultimate end nothing else than this—the creation of noble characters. Into the family the children are born; in the family they are prepared for their future careers; they grow up to manhood and womanhood; by marriage they form new families; in these new families new children are born and reared; the original father and mother, in the order of nature, live until the new family is launched, enjoy for a little while the pleasures which the grandchildren bring, without incurring the responsibilities of parenthood; then they die and leave the process to be repeated by future generations. To protect and promote this process of character-building, governments are organized, industry maintained, schools and churches supported. All other functions in life are subsidiary to this one essential function; all other organizations in life are to be tested by their efficacy in protecting and promoting this one essential function.

What are the laws of the family? What are the forces which unite this husband and wife, these parents and children, together, which if they be strengthened will promote the health and happiness of the family, which if they be weakened will tend to the disintegration and perhaps absolute dissolution of the family? No doubt the sexual passions are at the basis of the family organization, but they do not constitute this bond, for they may be and often are gratified outside the family. Doubtless there are economical advantages in the family organization. They are pointed out very clearly by Helen Bosanquet; but no one will suppose that the family is primarily an industrial corporation. Doubtless the bonds are reinforced somewhat by the laws of the land, still more by public opinion. There are families that are held together merely by the cost which legal separation would entail or by the social disgrace which would ensue upon the dissolution of the bond; but no observer of life can imagine that the family is held together simply by law, as the slave was held to his master in slavery, or by the force of an external public opinion. We have still to ask, What brought this law and this public opinion into existence?

The real bond which holds the family together is love, "the bond of perfectness." There is no spectrum that will analyze the white light of love into its various constituent elements, but we may safely say that family affection has features which distinguish it from other forms of affection; that the love of parents for children is something more than the compassion which the strong feel for the weak, and the love a husband and wife have for each other is something other than the love that either has for friends of the same sex. Without undertaking the difficult if not impossible analysis, we may at least say that this kind of love includes a feeling of chivalry on the part of the man for the woman, a feeling of trust and confidence on the part of the woman for the man, a guarding and protecting love in the parents for the children, and a loyal and filial love in the children for the parents.

This mysterious, undefinable, transcendent feeling, which binds the family together, which makes it possible for the family to fulfill its functions, and which has created for its support and the support of society the marriage laws and public opinion, is a love that is more than good nature, that is more than friendship; a love that takes not only for sickness and health, and for richer and poorer, but also for better and for worse; a love that " beareth all things, trusteth all things, hopeth all things, endureth all things." It is this love which holds together in the family members of very different individual characteristics and temperaments. It may be that Mr. Chesterton is paradoxical when he says that " the family is a good institution because it is uncongenial," but he is not at all paradoxical when he proceeds to illustrate this proposition: " It is exactly because our brother George is not interested in our religious difficulties, but is interested in the Trocadero Restaurant, that the family has something of the bracing qualities of the commonwealth. It is precisely because our uncle Henry does not approve of the theatrical ambitions of our sister Sarah that the family is like humanity. The men and women who, for good reasons and bad, revolt against the family are, for good reasons and bad, simply revolting against mankind."

There is no space here to indicate the evolution of the family or to consider what were its primitive forms. It must suffice to say that there is no indication that it has grown out of any previous condition of promiscuity; on the contrary, to quote from Helen Bosanquet, " as far back, then, as we can penetrate into the early history of the human race, we find the Family already existing, and we find the father as the protector and master of the Family."

These considerations, briefly as they are here stated, afford a sufficient reply to those who would seek a remedy for domestic unhappiness in the early dissolution of the marriage bond. The remedy for the ills of life is never fleeing

from them, but patiently enduring and ultimately overcoming them. They furnish a complete answer to the hypothetical suggestion of " trial marriages " made by Mrs. Parsons in her chapter on " Ethical Considerations." It is true that if we desire to maintain the Christian family, public opinion must demand the absolute chastity of both sexes until marriage; it is true that the alternative—disregard of chastity of both sexes before marriage—is not desirable or even tolerable; but her conclusion from these premises is extraordinary. We are not quite clear how Mrs. Parsons means her suggestion to be taken. If she means that trial marriages are desirable in the present state of society, her suggestion is as inconsistent with any scientific view of the family as it is repugnant to the moral instincts. If she means that, provided chastity before marriage cannot be made the social custom, trial marriages might advantageously be substituted for prostitution, it is as if she were to say, If honesty cannot be secured in business, it might be well to require the thief to return the stolen property after possessing it for a year. The conclusions induced by scientific study of the family are no less inconsistent with the plans of those *pseudo* reformers who would take children from their parents and give them at once to the keeping of expert nurses and teachers, and reduce the family to a merely industrial organization, and with the practice of those who, without adopting any theory, do in fact turn their children off to the care of nurses and governesses, and at the earliest practicable moment them out of the family to school. The school is an invaluable adjunct to the family; it is a wretched substitute for it—a truth which Helen Bosanquet puts very forcibly in a passage which we can only imperfectly represent by the following abstract:

Generally speaking, the child is valued in the home for what he is, while in the school he is valued in the main for what he is to be. . . . Who can question the incalculable benefit to a child, as indeed to all of us, however old, of feeling that his mere presence gives pleasure to some one, that some one really cares to know all his little secrets and fancies and troubles, and that there is some one with whom he lives in an equality of affection where differences of age and intellect are merged ? . . . The relation of the child to the home has in it far more of mutual service and reciprocity than is possible in the school. Children are naturally eager to share in the occupations and work of their elders, to do the things which "grown up" people do, and in any well-regulated family care is taken that this natural impulse of the child receives satisfaction and guidance. . . . The relation with the family is, normally, a permanent one. Hence, though it begins in absolute dependence of the child upon its parents, it gradually develops—at any rate among the majority of the people—into one of mutual support and assistance. The child knows from very early years that the time is coming when he will be expected to take his share in the responsibilities of the family; later on when he will himself be responsible for the maintenance of a family; and, later still, when his parents will look to him for some return of the care and support which he received from them as a child. . . . To every parent his own children are unique; they have their own characteristics in which he delights—partly, no doubt, because he thinks they come from him—and he does not want to see these obliterated. . . . *Per contra:* One of the principal lessons which the child has to learn at school is that of conforming to universal laws ; to feel that he has to play up to what is expected of a boy of his age, to overcome his own special difficulties or likings for the sake of promoting the work of the class.

The family is the oldest of all social organizations. As it is the oldest, so it is the most fundamental and the most important. Upon the family are built both the State and the Church. Whatever weakens the family ties and tends to the dissolution of the family weakens both the political and the religious bonds and tends to the dissolution of society. Whatever tends to lower its moral tone tends to corrupt society at its fountain head. Whatever makes for true, pure homes makes for a pure religion and an honorable State. And neither statesman nor ecclesiastic, however great his fame or high his position, equals in dignity and influence the fathers and the mothers, who are the first of sovereigns and the divinest of priests.

# *Comment on Current Books*

**The Life of a Courageous Woman** — More than fifty years ago the first book by Isabella Bird was published. Two generations have enjoyed her accounts of travels, but few people have known that she was from childhood a suffering invalid, at times quite incapacitated by acute pain. She exemplified Dr. Holmes's receipt for longevity. She had an incurable affliction of the spine, yet within her tiny, frail body were a strong spirit and a well-trained, insatiable mind. She made long journeys through America, Japan, India, and China, penetrating Tibet and riding across Persia. Little journeys in civilized countries counted for nothing in her experience. She was highly esteemed by expert travelers, and her observations, kept in voluminous note-books and letters, were regarded as of great value. She was made a member of the Royal Geographical Society and other scientific bodies, and while she did not consider herself a geographer, and was modest in the extreme, she added much to our stock of information regarding Oriental lands and people. The picture of her child life, in the cultivated atmosphere of her father's rectory, is very attractive. When she was grown to young womanhood, she and her sister were left alone and were congenial companions.

Her marriage to Dr. Bishop took place after her sister's death, when she was past middle life, and for five years she rested in the devotion of a man who is described as of lofty spirit and great usefulness. Upon his death the passion for travel seized Mrs. Bishop anew, and she made some of her most perilous journeys when she was nearly sixty years of age. The story of her life[1] has been written by a devoted friend, and is both a beautiful tribute to Mrs. Bishop's character and a fine estimate of her accomplishments. Upon her return from an extended tour in China she began to arouse the English public to the need of medical missions in the East, and was an ardent and effective advocate. She established three hospitals, containing 160 beds, in memory of Dr. Bishop and her sister, building them with money earned by her books. She formed decided opinions in regard to Oriental religions, quite different from those she held before she traveled. Mohammedanism, she said, was the most blighting, withering, degrading influence of any of the false creeds. " There is no resurrection power" in any Asiatic faith, she averred, nothing to arrest their further downward descent. Some of her

[1] The Life of Isabella Bird (Mrs. Bishop). By Anna M. Stoddart. E. P. Dutton & Co., New York. $5, net.

addresses were powerful because of the glimpses she gave of a personal·knowledge of the sort of sins that canker the Eastern world. Yet she was most broad-minded, recognizing the good in all religions. She had never belonged to that class who deblaterate against missions, as Robert Louis Stevenson said, but she had been awakened from her apathy in regard to them by what she actually saw and felt. A peculiarly lonely woman, she gathered devoted friends everywhere, and died surrounded by the loving care of those who were left of a large circle. Born in 1831, she died in 1904, after a remarkably active and interesting life, honored and loved in every land she had visited.

**Correggio** Correggio's works are in the highest sense original and complete. In the opinion of Correggio enthusiasts, Raphael's Madonnas and Michelangelo's prophets are not more distinguished in these respects. Mr. Berenson once said, "Centuries had to elapse before emotions so intense as those Correggio felt found expression in literature—in Shelley when he is at his best and in Keats when he is perfect." Another and certainly no less distinguished art critic, Signor Ricci, in discussing the same subject, harks back instead of coming forward in time, and quotes from Dante, in order to find words to carry a proper impression of that received by him from Correggio's works. While it may be useful to compare Titian with Shakespeare or Michelangelo with Milton, it is only confusing, says Correggio's latest biographer,[1] to use Shelley or Dante to help us to define what we mean by Correggio. Mr. Sturge Moore, therefore, sets himself to define the distinctive temper, address, inspiration, and quality of Correggio's work, its true proportions both within itself and in relation to other art. The result, though somewhat spun out in generalizations, is interesting, suggestive, and important, especially as coming from one who questions the value of the aims and methods of modern historical art criticism.

**Whistler** Four qualities specially distinguish Whistler's pictures. First, they are subtly but powerfully human. Secondly, they emphasize the casual note—a quality also characteristic of much of Mr. Sargent's work. Thirdly, they concentrate attention upon a single point of interest and yet combine with this the coincident recession of an apparently infinitely extended environment. Finally, they represent the restraint of everything not quite worthy of good taste ; as Whistler was·accustomed to

say, "A picture is finished when all trace of the means now used to bring about the end has disappeared." Hence he would obliterate every appearance of labor. These four characteristics express essential modernity. They and the tendencies exercised upon Whistler by America, England, France, Japan, become more evident if we glance at a series of illustrations of his pictures taken in chronological sequence, as in the latest book about the great painter and etcher. Whether regarded as a biographical sketch, a description of Whistler's works, or a critical study of his theory of art, Miss Cary's volume[1] merits attention both from the learned and the unlearned. The accomplished writer who has helped men and women to appreciate Rossetti has certainly not failed in attempting to help them to understand and appreciate Whistler. She is admirable alike in the selection of material and in the non-technical treatment of his inspiration. The book is beautifully printed, as its text merits.

**Lord Milner and South Africa** It is interesting to contrast the impressive opening of the first Transvaal Parliament with the criticisms made by British Conservatives on the terms of the peace of Vereeniging, which closed the Boer War. There was then serious question as to whether the conquerors should allow the Boers to possess rifles for their own protection, and as to whether the Dutch language was to be recognized in the law courts and public schools whenever the Boers desired it. Both concessions have now been amply justified by considerations of practical convenience and of sound policy. A book essential to a full understanding of the causes which led to the Boer War and of the events of that war is Mr. Basil Worsfold's " Lord Milner's Work in South Africa from 1897-1902," [2] the first period of that able High Commissioner's administration. Interest in this well-printed publication is heightened by the author's long study of British colonies, particularly those of South Africa, and also by the fact that the book contains hitherto unpublished information.

**Heroines of French Society** An exhaustless mine of treasure to writers is found in the annals of French society. Mrs. Bearne, a student of the subject, has made an entertaining, gossipy book[3] about four of these heroines who lived during the Revolution and the years immediately preceding and following it. Quite dif-

[1] Correggio. By T. Moore. Charles Scribner's Sons, New York. $2, net.

[1] The Works of James McNeill Whistler. A Study by Elisabeth Luther Cary. Moffat, Yard & Co. $4, net.
[2] Lord Milner's Work in South Africa. By W. Basil Worsfold. E. P. Dutton & Co., New York. $4.50, net.
[3] Heroines of French Society. By Mrs. Bearne. E. P. Dutton & Co.. New York. $3, net.

ferent in character, influence, and purpose, these four make an interesting group. They figured in the old Court, in the Revolution, the Empire, and the Restoration. Madame Le Brun, of humble birth, unhappy domestic life, but strong in religious principle and passionately devoted to her great art, lived to an honored and loved old age, having passed many years in England, exiled from her beloved France. She has left beautiful memorials both of her genius and of her personality. La Marquise de .Montagu, of exalted family, lived the life of a saint in the midst of corrupt social conditions. She endured with heroic fortitude long years of terror, poverty, and humiliation, and was, as her biographer says, a mixture of *grande dame* and saint. Her life as an exile was shadowed and unhappy. In Madame Tallien a greater change is seen. Early influenced by revolutionary theories, both socially and morally, she gave herself up to promoting. her ideas, regardless of .religion or conventional restraint. Her generous nature and her great talents, however, won for her a place in the affections of her countrymen. In later life she married the Prince de Chimay, and renounced her errors, regretting her indiscretions in a truly French manner. Of Madame de Genlis much has been written, yet many episodes in her life remain mysterious. Ambitious, complaisant, yet marvelously strong on the proprieties, she wrote several books expounding her extraordinary notions in regard to education, which seem preposterous in these days. Mrs. Bearne writes fluently, and opens here and there a door through which the lover of personal anecdote and gossip can get glimpses of characteristic French court society.

**The Adriatic Side of Italy** If this large volume[1] could be divided into four small ones, the work would prove practical and valuable to travelers. For their use the volume is too large. For the use of stay-at-home travelers, however, the volume should make quick appeal. It contains much information, clearly and compactly put. Nevertheless, we wish that the author's manner were more vivacious, and that the color of the history described were as equally evident as its outline. Mr. Jackson's province, of course, embraces Venice, but, in view of the many histories and descriptions of Venice, he has done wisely, we think, to omit it from a book portly enough without it. It is a satisfaction to

those who know Italy to feel that at last such too little described regions as the Friuli, for instance, have been brought to the reader's attention.

**Leonardo da Vinci's Thoughts on Art and Life** One reason why the Italian Renaissance was notable was because of its union of the rational and the mystical. In art, probably the most perfect expression of this union was reached by Leonardo da Vinci. It is a satisfaction to note that in his introductory essay to the opening volume[1] of the altogether exquisite "Humanist's Library" Mr. Lewis Einstein lays particular emphasis on this feature of the Renaissance in general, and particularly on Leonardo's contribution to it. The volume comprises a selection from Leonardo's note-books, translated by Mr. Maurice Baring. It appropriately follows Mr. McCurdy's equally admirable selection and translation, on which The Outlook commented recently.

**Political Phrases** A novel reference-book and one which fills distinctively a field of its own is this "Dictionary of Political Phrases and Allusions."[2] It is of English origin, and naturally relates almost solely to English affairs. Its general character may be indicated by three or four titles which appear on a page to which we open. These are: Jameson Raid Inquiry, Jesse Collings Amendment (*see* Three Acres and a Cow), Jingo, Jewish Disabilities, Juvenile Court Bill, 1906. To any one having occasion to refer to British acts of legislation or to catchwords of British politics the usefulness of this volume is obvious.

**Three Acres and Liberty** By means of alluring photographs, interesting figures, and much compiling, the author of this book,[3] Bolton Hall, makes us feel that we need not be tied to a desk—but, like a freed horse, "trot off" if we will. A little bit of land, not too far from the city, if intelligently cultivated, he declares, will support a family, and give them a life far more wholesome than they could ever have in the crowded city. Intensive cultivation is the password now, and if any one wishes to know all about roseate possibilities, let him read this book. Long ago we were told that "Ten Acres" were "enough." Now we are more modest, and find liberty in Three Acres.

---

[1] The Shores of the Adriatic: The Italian Side. By F. Hamilton Jackson, R.B.A. E. P. Dutton & Co., New York. $6. net.

[1] Leonardo da Vinci's Thoughts on Art and Life. The Humanist's Library. Lewis Einstein, Editor. The Merrymount Press, Boston.
[2] A Dictionary of Political Phrases and Allusions. By Hugh Montgomery and Philip G. Cambray. E. P. Dutton & Co., New York. $2 net.
[3] Three Acres and Liberty. By Bolton Hall. Assisted by R. F. Powell. The Macmillan Company, New York. $1.75, net.

The Quarterly 189X

'OLD DOC' HITCHCOCK
BY BURGES JOHNSON

"Intelligence needs no learnin's"

## More EGG-O-SEE was eaten during the past year than all other flaked foods combined.

Never before in the history of a food, have the American people given such a sweeping endorsement of merit, as has been accorded EGG-O-SEE.

There is more actual proof of the real value of EGG-O-SEE in this unqualified testimony of the people than in all the claims we might make.

EGG-O-SEE is made from the choicest selected White Wheat; in the largest, cleanest and most economically operated Pure Food Mills in the World, by the famous EGG-O-SEE Process. Thus we are enabled to give the people a large package of delicious food for only 10 cents.

If you are not already one of the great army of EGG-O-SEE users, begin today. Buy a package of your Grocer and be convinced.

### Warm in a Pan before Serving
In Canada the price of EGG-O-SEE is 15c, two packages for 25c.

## FREE "-back to nature" book

How to get well, keep well by natural means—bathing, exercise, food, etc.,—and how to use EGG-O-SEE for every meal in the week is told in our expensively prepared booklet, "-back to nature," sent free. We are glad to send it. You will be glad to get it.

### EGG-O-SEE CEREAL COMPANY
914 AMERICAN SAVINGS BANK BLDG., CHICAGO, ILL.

❀

**Peace and Forcible Disarmament**

The city of New York is now in the throes of disarming by force hundreds of citizens who prefer to settle their disputes by the use of weapons of war instead of by an appeal to the courts. It is a curious and striking coincidence that this practical demonstration of the recognized barbarism of shooting and stabbing men in order to obtain one's rights or to avenge fancied or real injuries should come just at the time of the gathering of the great Peace Congress. A week ago last Sunday in a public park a young Italian shot another Italian because of a fancied insult. Two unarmed policemen, with excellent records for bravery and faithfulness, attempted to arrest the would-be murderer and were shot by him. One of the officers died on the operating-table immediately after the encounter, leaving a young wife and child. The circumstances of his death were so pathetic as to call public attention to the fact, which has aroused widespread public indignation, that there have been in New York in recent months numerous assaults with deadly weapons among the lower classes of Italian immigrants. There is on the statute-book a law forbidding under severe penalties the carrying of concealed weapons, but it has not been very vigorously enforced. Upon the death of Policeman Sechler the Police Commissioner and the City Magistrates determined to bring this law into the fullest operation. In ten days literally hundreds of men were arrested for carrying revolvers or dirks, and heavily fined or imprisoned. The major part of these offenders were Italians, probably because the Italian of this class in his own country has been accustomed to settle his personal difficulties by attacking his enemy himself, instead of appealing to the courts for protection or redress. But there was no racial discrimination on the part of the authorities, and the overwhelming majority of our Italian citizens, who are peaceable and law-abiding, heartily approve of this crusade to establish arbitration, or the processes of the law, in place of personal combat or private war. It is not straining a point to indicate the very close analogy between this situation in New York City and the international situation. Public opinion in New York overwhelmingly demands the abolition of armed conflicts and the maintenance of peace and good order in her streets; we cannot have the abolition of international wars and the maintenance of international peace without a similar international public opinion. New York has established courts (that is to say, arbitration conferences) with full authority to settle all questions of disagreement, civil and criminal, between her citizens, and if it were not for these courts citizens would be compelled to resort to personal combat and vigilance committees, as they did in the pioneer days of the Western frontier; international combats, that is to say war, will continue until the nations establish an international court with requisite authority to settle international disputes. But in New York there are still ill-educated, selfish, or vicious men who insist on fighting in spite of the courts, and it is therefore necessary for the courts in turn to insist upon the forcible disarmament of these citizens who interfere with the peace of the city; so it will be necessary for the peace-loving nations of the world to authorize their international court to disarm vicious or recalcitrant nations. But, again, the New York courts cannot forcibly disarm robbers, murderers, or violators of the peace without a body of well-trained and brave men who are themselves skilled in the use of arms—

905-909

that is to say, the police ; so it will be necessary for the nations of the world to maintain suitable navies and armies which shall constitute the police force of the international court, and which shall under its direction maintain peace. About eight thousand policemen are necessary to maintain peace in New York City.· Eighty thousand, however, would be not only absolutely unnecessary for this purpose, but would themselves be a menace to peace and freedom as well as a great burden on the taxpayer. The advocate of international peace who appeals for the total abolition of all armies and navies advocates the destruction of the instruments by means of which law may maintain peace. It is nevertheless true that with the establishment of an international court the armies and navies of the world may be and ought to be very much reduced in numbers and in cost.

❦

*Education in the South*　In preceding years it has been the custom of members of the Conference for Education in the South to gather at some Southern center of population. Not the least, therefore, of its effects has been the impression it has made directly upon a number of important Southern communities. So beneficial have been these public meetings that city after city has invited the Conference for the sake of the benefit it would receive. This year, however, this custom has been suspended. Instead of gathering in a city, the members assembled for the Tenth Annual Conference at the Hotel Carolina, Pinehurst, North Carolina, and devoted their time, not to popular gatherings at all, but solely to mutual consultation. There were many addresses, of course, and reports of them were published ; but they were addressed primarily, not to the public, but to the members of the Conference. As an organized body the Conference this year was put to a severe test. It missed the inspiration and the elevating influence of Mr. Robert C. Ogden's personality. For years Mr. Ogden has been President of the Conference. His strong hand has been felt in its organization, and his pacific spirit has won for the Conference

the friendship of many who had been distrustful. This year, unhappily, Mr. Ogden has been forced by ill health to abandon many of his activities, and could not attend the Conference. He was nevertheless re-elected President. He will, of course, be saved from the burdens which have heretofore fallen upon him by virtue of his official position. In spite of his absence, the gathering was large, and, as the members of the Conference expressed it in a telegraphic message to Mr. Ogden, his spirit ruled.

❦

*Among Southern Farmers*　Two lines of development were clearly indicated in the addresses and consultations. The first is the extension of secondary or high schools, for which a steadily increasing appropriation is made in almost every one of the Southern States. The reports from State Superintendents, to which an entire session was given, were most interesting and encouraging. The second is the prominence given to agriculture in the educational system of the South. Governor Terrell, of Georgia, for instance, in his admirable address laid emphasis on the recently enacted law which establishes in each of the eleven Congressional districts in that State an agricultural high school to work in harmony with and subsidiary to the State agricultural college. All but one of the addresses on the last day of the Conference were devoted to the general subject of improvement in agricultural conditions. The most impressive of these addresses was given by Dr. Seaman A. Knapp, of the United States Department of Agriculture. He stated that while eighty-five per cent. of the people of the South must get their living by rural pursuits, the present productivity of the soil in the Southern States is only $160 per man as against $1,000 per man in the State of Iowa. The fundamental problem before the Southern farmer is how he may make his land more productive and more profitable. Dr. Knapp has devised and put into operation in two States a system of local co-operative demonstration work, supported by the National Government, and Dr. Buttrick, of the

General Education Board, stated that funds would be provided for the establishment of these demonstration farms in the other Southern States. Dr. Knapp gave this suggestive outline of the process of changing the environment of a farmer :

First, the farmer is selected to conduct a simple and inexpensive demonstration. Second, a contract is drawn with the United States Department of Agriculture, by which he agrees to follow certain instructions. Third, better seed is furnished him, and his name is published in the papers. Fourth, each month when the Government's Field Agent goes to inspect his Demonstration, many of his neighbors are invited; consequently, he will almost unconsciously improve his farm so as to be ready for company, and cultivate all of his crops better. Fifth, a report of his extra crop is made in the county papers. His neighbors talk about it and want to buy seed. Sixth, he sells the seed of his crop at a high price; his neighbors ask him how he produced it; he is invited to address public assemblies; he has become a man of note and a leader of the people, and cannot return to his old ways. Soon there is a body of such men; a township, a county, and finally a State is transformed.

❦

*A Novel Idea*  The address of Captain Richmond Pearson Hobson, of Alabama, contained what is perhaps the most novel suggestion presented during the Conference. Captain Hobson believes that it is the duty and the privilege of all members of Congress to afford definite aid in the education of their constituents, and has already arranged to carry his belief into effect so far as his own district is concerned. The statement of his plan was received with great interest. On the first of May Captain Hobson will start, with at least four Government experts, on an eleven-day tour of his district, each of the five members of the party to deliver brief addresses in three or four places each day. One of his companions will be an expert on road-making, one an expert on soils, one an expert forester, and one from the Department of Education. The addresses of each of these will be simple and filled with definite information, and it is hoped that most of the voters in the district will be reached. Captain Hobson also proposes to avail himself of the National resources for the making of a mile of perfect roadway in his district, as

an object-lesson for the local highway commissioners. He further proposes to secure the printing of some, if not all, of these speeches in the Congressional Record, to the end that it may be sent, under the franking law, to all the voters in the district; and he believes that other Congressmen will find the plan of such interest and value that they will follow in his footsteps. Another idea proposed by Captain Hobson was the preparation by leading educators of short addresses applicable to local conditions, with the idea that all candidates for office should be provided with these brief, practical addresses, to the end that the subject of education may become an issue in every campaign, local, State, or National, and that the best thought of the leading educators shall be disseminated among all the people. An afternoon session of the Conference was devoted to the work of women. The presiding officer, Mrs. Patterson, won the enthusiastic approval of the audience by keeping the numerous speakers within their time limit, and the speakers themselves, who reported the progress of volunteer educational work in practically every State in the South, were notably successful in compressing a volume of important information into the very limited time devoted to each address. Great progress has been made during the past two years in the development and the co-ordination of the volunteer educational associations, which have for their object the enlargement of school facilities and the development of educational sentiment throughout the South.

❦

*The Mutual Life Election*  The long-drawn-out canvass of the vote for trustees in the Mutual Life Insurance Company has come to an end. The "administration" ticket is elected by a vote of nearly three to one over the ticket proposed by the International Policy-holders' Committee; an average vote of about one hundred and eighty-six thousand is reported for the names on the successful ticket, an average vote of about sixty-five thousand for the unsuccessful candidates. Charges of extensive fraud in the securing of votes have been made against the management of the Company by the managers of the International Committee; and it is announced that the election will be contested in the courts. The Company, on the other hand, asserts that if there is a legal contest it will be made simply for the sake of thwarting and annoying the management manifestly chosen by the great majority of policy-holders. The elected ticket was put in nomination by the present officials of the Mutual; and the new Board will, it is to be presumed, continue the principles and methods of administration which have been followed by the Company since its reorganization as a result of the revelations of the Armstrong Committee. It w.ll be remembered that four members of the International Policy-holders' Committee—General Benjamin F. Tracy, Judge George Gray, Mr. H. N. Higginbotham, and Mr. Alfred M. Shook—were nominated on the "administration" ticket; and that the action of the Company's officials in naming them was denounced by the International Committee as a trick. It is announced by President Peabody, of the Mutual, that three of these men have consented to serve, and that Judge Gray has declined on account of pressing public duties. In deciding to commit their interests for another year into the hands of the present managers of the Company, the Mutual policy-holders have taken the course which The Outlook recommended throughout the campaign. They have preferred to continue in control a management which had been purged of its objectionable elements by its reorganization, and which, in the persons of many of its members, had wide experience in life insurance business, rather than to elect a Board composed of men who, however honorable and able, were certainly unknown and untried in the insurance field. In so doing, The Outlook believes that the policy-holders have done wisely. But an even more important duty lies before them. They must make the trustees of the Company feel their responsibility to them, and appreciate that the Company belongs to the policy-holders and that they will be held to account for their stewardship. If the officials and the trustees fail in their duty to the policy-holders, the policy-holders must see to it at the next election that they are replaced. Whether it is possible for the policy-holders, scattered throughout this country and others, and having nothing in common but their relation to the Company, to exert this influence and accomplish these ends, under the present law or under any practical revision of it, is a serious question which only the future can solve. On the answer to this question, in our opinion, rests the determination whether the mutual company is a legitimate and proper form of organization for the life insurance business. The canvass of the vote in this election has lasted almost exactly four months. The canvass in the case of the New York Life Insurance Company is not yet ended. The expense to the policy-holders has been very large. It is a pertinent question for the State Insurance Department and the Legislature whether the insurance law or the management of the department should not be amended to obviate this delay and this expense.

❦

**A Well-Planned Struggle with Vice** Almost every evil in America has an organized foe. However prevalent some forms of vice may be, it is well to remember that they do not flourish unmolested. One of these forms of vice in the city of New York is the so-called Raines Law hotel. Its intelligent and persistent antagonist is the Committee of Fourteen for the Suppression of the Raines Law Hotel in New York. According to the law which was fathered by State Senator John Raines, no persons can sell liquor on Sunday except such as take out a hotel license; on the other hand, any man can take out a hotel license who complies with certain provisions prescribing the number of rooms that his resort shall contain. Consequently, keepers of public bars who desire to avoid raids or blackmail for selling liquor on Sunday have been in the habit of attaching to their saloons the prescribed number of rooms in order to make them eligible for hotel licenses. These saloon-keepers, however, finding no economic demands for such accommodations as they provide, and being disinclined to allow these rooms to remain empty and unremunerative, have for the most part yielded to the temptation to allow, and indeed to promote, the illicit use of the rooms. Because these infamous places have the guise of restaurants and hotels, they are peculiarly effective lures for young men and traps for young women. How disreputable they are can be illustrated by contrast from a single case. On the outskirts of New York City, in the midst of a German population, a German and his wife kept a beer garden. Their patrons wanted their beer on Sunday, just as most Americans want their tea and coffee. So this honest couple added the requisite rooms to their place and obtained a hotel license. No one, however, under any circumstances, could rent a room from them. They preferred to lose the interest of the money invested in those rooms rather than allow their place to become like other Raines Law hotels. Against these noisome resorts the Committee of Fourteen is making a carefully planned fight. Organized at the City Club in January, 1905, it began by undertaking to change the liquor tax law. The first bill it promoted was so delayed in the Legislature that when passed it was rendered ineffective; the second, after it became law, was adjudged unconstitutional. Finally a measure introduced at the instance of the Committee became law. Under this, licenses can be granted only to those places which the building authorities in a city or town report as complying with the hotel laws. This measure has reduced the number of Raines Law hotels in New York City by about fifty per cent. Many of the places, however, which failed to obtain hotel licenses have continued in their nefarious business. To meet this exigency the Committee is working in two directions. By means of an Executive Secretary, Mr. F. H. Whitin, with an office at 27 East Twenty-second Street, New York City, it is, first, lending its assistance to State officers and local agencies in the enforcement of the law; second, it is persuading business interests involved to discountenance the illegal resorts. It has now the support of the largest brewers and surety companies. A brewing company advances the money for most of the places in which its beer is sold, and takes a mortgage; a surety company usually furnishes the bond required by the license. Proprietors of places to which the Committee object on account of their disreputable character have already learned that they have lost the financial support of the brewers and cannot obtain the requisite bonds from the surety companies. Without having any special theories or doctrines to promulgate, the Committee is thus striking at a known and universally recognized evil. It ought to have the good will and the necessary financial support of the citizens of New York.

❦

**For the Protection of Young Women**  Every big exposition is not only an embodiment of social health; it is also a center of attraction for human parasites. There is no reason to believe that the Jamestown Exposition will be an exception. There is no viler class of persons than that which preys upon young women. It is therefore well for all young women who intend to visit the Jamestown Exposition to know that there is an organized body, known as the Exposition Travelers' Aid Committee, already in existence, to protect them from these enemies. The headquarters of the Committee are at 238 East Forty-eighth Street, New York City, and at 26 Plume Street, Norfolk, Virginia. Those who go with friends need advice only in case they become separated from their friends. They will receive it if they call at the Young Women's Christian Association Building on the grounds. There they can be restored to their friends, or find safe conduct to their boarding-places. Young women who are planning to go alone, with the expectation of earning their way, ought, however, to be on their guard. The Committee makes the statement, for their benefit, that they should be prepared to meet necessary expenses of not less than three dollars a day; that they ought to avoid competing with negro labor, which is used almost exclusively in the South; and that they can receive various kinds of assistance from the Committee. It offers to give any girl information about routes and about boarding-places, and to investigate advertisements or other offers of employment, if she will write to the New York headquarters ; and if she writes to the Norfolk headquarters, giving the date, time, and train (or boat) by which she will arrive, and a description of some noticeable point in her personal appearance (as her hat) for identification, the Committee will see that she is met and directed on her way. Further information can be obtained from the Committee. Of course the Committee will be able to use contributions; and such can be sent to the treasurer, Miss Katharine L. Potter, at the New York address. There are a number of organizations co-operating in the work of this Committee. Among these may be mentioned the Young Women's Christian Association, the Council of Jewish Women, the Association of Catholic Charities, and the Girls' Friendly Society. A similar committee was active during the St. Louis and Portland Expositions, and helped many young women in the midst of serious dangers. A similar work in Jamestown will undoubtedly be similarly justified.

⊕

***Women's Work for Women***  What this Committee undertakes to do in the special exigency of an exposition has been done and is being done regularly for young women traveling under usual conditions. This has been, for instance, a part of the regular work of the Young Women's Christian Association of New York. In that big city, where any one can easily be lost in the human wilderness, the unsuspicious and unprotected girl is in constant danger. Conditions of living and of working put upon many a young girl, whose instincts are sound, a downward pressure which is nearly if not quite irresistible. The Association finds for such safe homes, gives them advice, and even supplies industrial training which will free them in part from their state of economic helplessness. The office is at 7 East Fifteenth Street. The Girls' Friendly Society is likewise engaged in this task of protecting young women. It is de-

voted exclusively to giving personal oversight to girls to save them from ruin. It originated in England thirty-two years ago, and was established in this country two years later. It is now declared to be the largest and most widely spread of all the societies for women and girls in existence. It is carried on by communicants of the Episcopal Church. The only qualification for membership, however, is comprised in the rule : "No girl who has not borne a virtuous character to be admitted as a member ; such character being lost, the member to forfeit her card." Personal oversight is systematized. For example, a young girl belonging to a branch of the Society in Scotland starts for America. One of the active workers of the Society, called an Associate, writes to inform the so-called "Commendation Associate" in the port for which the steamer sails ; this Scotch girl is then met on her arrival. If she is going to work, for instance, in a shoe factory in Massachusetts, the Associate who meets her writes to the Commendation Associate in Massachusetts. So the Society keeps a watch over every such emigrating member. In one case a respectable English girl was thus saved from falling into the hands of an aunt in America who kept a notorious house ; in another case a very attractive English girl, who had spent most of her life in an institution and had little knowledge of the world, traveled under the Commendation system by way of Liverpool, Montreal, and New York to Ohio with but ninepence in her pocket and without the slightest misadventure. The central office in America is at the Church Missions House, New York City. The work that such organizations as the Girls' Friendly Society, the Young Women's Christian Association, and the Exposition Travelers' Aid Committee is doing ought to be widely known and generously supported.

⊕

***No Government Guarantee***  Purchasers of food products and drugs will profit if they note an announcement made last week by Secretary Wilson, of the Department of Agriculture. The housekeeper who buys a can of vegetables, or a bottle of syrup, or any other prepared article for the table, is likely to misunderstand the statement on the label that the preparation is "guaranteed under the Food and Drugs Act, June 30, 1906." This does not mean that the United States guarantees the purity of the article, or even that it is what the label declares it to be. The United States makes no guarantee whatever concerning it. " On the contrary," says the Secretary, " the statement means that the manufacturer of the article guarantees it to be pure, free from adulteration, and that he warrants every fact stated on the label to be true. It is the guarantee of the manufacturer, not the guarantee of the Government." If a dealer is found selling an impure or falsely labeled article, he is liable to punishment unless he can show a guarantee from the manufacturer. If he can show such a guarantee, then the manufacturer is held responsible. For this purpose the Department of Agriculture allows every manufacturer to file a general guarantee; it then assigns him a serial number for the purpose of identification. This guarantee and number, therefore, are signs, not of the Government's sanction, but of the manufacturer's responsibility. In spite of this fact, certain manufacturers are issuing advertisements which assert that the guarantee or the serial number stamps their products with the approval of the Government. " Such advertising . . . must be stopped," declared the Secretary, "and stopped at once, or I will do a little advertising myself in behalf of the people." In explanation of this statement he continued :

I am thinking if this outrageous misrepresentation does not cease that the Department will publish a list bearing the names of the manufacturers who are indulging in this campaign of deception. In this list the Department will state that it has not analyzed the products represented by the advertisements, and hence has no actual knowledge of their purity or impurity, but that it advises the consuming public to judge the purity or impurity of the products according to the false representations made concerning the guaranty. In other words, manufacturers who will deceive the public about the guaranty will lie about the quality of their product.

This warning to advertisers is also a warning to housekeepers. Meats and meat products are examined by Government inspectors ; no meats or meat products can enter inter-State commerce without having been passed by these officials representing the Government; but, although for the purpose of enforcing the law specimens of food and drugs will be examined by the Bureau of Chemistry, those products which are labeled to accord with the Pure Food and Drugs Act have not been inspected and passed by the Government. Every advertisement which gives the impression that under the Pure Food and Drugs Act the product named bears the Government approval ought to be read as a notice that that product had better be avoided.

❀

**Technicalities and Justice**    On December 30, 1903, the Iroquois Theater fire in Chicago caused the death of nearly six hundred persons. The coroner's jury found several flagrant violations of the city theater ordinance, compliance with which would have saved many lives. Indictments were returned against persons considered responsible for the faulty conditions existing in the theater at the time of the fire, among them Mr. Will J. Davis, manager of the theater and president of the company that owned it. Mr. Davis was brought to trial only last month, or more than three years after the indictment. The proceedings were had in Danville, Judge Kimbrough, of the Circuit Court, presiding. A change of venue had been taken from Chicago on the ground that a fair trial could not be had in that city. After all this delay, the case was not heard upon its merits. Judge Kimbrough ordered a verdict for the defendant solely on the ground of the invalidity, in two respects, of the city ordinance recited in the indictment. Judge Kavanaugh, of Chicago, had previously refused to accept the same reasons as ground for quashing the indictment. Dean John H. Wigmore, of the Northwestern University Law School, in an editorial note in the April number of the Illinois Law Review, makes the proceedings in this case the text for comment on the shortcomings of our judicial system, which he characterizes as " a system of antiquated pedantry, unfitted to do the work that is required of it." All of the features which mark the failure even to reach a trial of fact in the Iroquois case, he says, are barren traditions of technicality, at war with good sense. It is this general lack of direct, modern, practical, working sense which he finds to be the depressing feature of our criminal procedure to-day. Dean Wigmore does not undertake to dispute the judge's interpretation of the law in the Iroquois case, although it is obvious that he does not agree with it. But he does assert that if the administration of the criminal law is what it is declared to be in that case, " then it is a travesty on our ideals—a worn-out, dilapidated temple of justice—the sooner torn down and rebuilt the better. The time has come for us," he adds, " to stand outside of it, to forsake our professional nooks and corners, to look at the structure in the bright, healthy light of common sense, and to ask whether it is not now a plain anachronism, ripe for a thorough renovation." Judge Kimbrough held the Chicago theater ordinance invalid because, in his opinion, it failed to impose expressly any personal duty upon the defendant, and because it applied to only a part of the city territory. As to the first objection, Dean Wigmore recites various provisions of the ordinance, calling for specific things to be done, which were not done, and also the following : " Any person, firm, company, or corporation, who violates, disobeys, omits, neglects, or refuses to comply with . . . the execution of any of the provisions of this ordinance shall be subject to a fine . . . and every such person, firm, company, or corporation shall be deemed guilty of a separate offense for every day such violation shall continue." Mr. Wigmore evidently deems it absurd that this language does not apply to the manager of the theater and the president of the company. The idea that an ordinance designed to safeguard life in the crowded amusement centers of a great city must also be made applicable to all parts of the city or be held invalid is also regarded as at war with common sense. The decision of Judge Kimbrough turned upon a question of interpretation of an ordinance. So far as the people

were concerned, that decision is final. There can be no appeal to the Supreme Court. In view of all the features of the situation, Dean Wigmore regards it as unfortunate that a verdict of acquittal was ordered, when the trial judge might have entered a *nolle prosequi*, and thus have afforded the prosecution an opportunity to have the question of law raised elsewhere, especially in view of the fact that another judge of concurrent jurisdiction had already ruled differently on the same point of law.

❀

**Real Preparation for the Ministry**
As a sign of the fact that theological seminaries have been waking to the necessity of making themselves schools for the training of active ministers, a change, recently announced, in the curriculum of the Yale Divinity School is worthy of note. Traditionally, theological seminaries have emphasized linguistic and metaphysical studies. Some history and a course in so-called homiletics have usually served to supply intellectual perspective and a little practical knowledge. Gradually in recent years historical courses have been supplanting dogmatics ; and practical experience in church work has been made more and more accessible to divinity students. It is in line with this movement that the change in the Yale Divinity School has been made. Hereafter, in place of the single three-year course of study, there are to be three courses : one will proceed from the historical point of view, the second from the philosophical, and the third from the practical. The first course will be practically the same as that now offered; and will be the only one in which Hebrew will be required. What may be called the philosophical course will emphasize modern science, psychology, and Christian theology. The practical course will emphasize sociology, philanthropy, legal principles, and the practical problems involved in applying the spirit of Christianity to modern life. Elective studies will enable a student in any one of these courses to get some benefit from the other two. Too long the standards of the divinity schools, at least in America, have been those of the teacher

of theology, rather than those of the active minister; too long theological professors have been teaching as if their dearest aim was to make their students like themselves. While medical students have been studying to be, not medical professors, but physicians and surgeons; while law students have been studying to be, not professors of law, but lawyers; theological students have been studying as if they were all to be theological pedagogues. The practice of adopting what may be called clinical methods in theological seminaries is now evident; it has come tardily; it is welcome.

❀

**Dr. Hamlin**    When a clergyman notable in his profession remains in charge of a church for two decades, exercising a real influence in the community, the fact is worthy of note. It is particularly worthy of note when it happens in the National Capital. Because of the changes and chances of political life, a considerable proportion of Washington's population is necessarily migratory and transient. There is special need there for the ministrations of virile and vigorous but tactful ministers of the Gospel, those who know how to adapt themselves to all sorts and conditions of men and women. A clergyman of this kind was Teunis S. Hamlin, who died suddenly last week. For over twenty years he was the honored pastor of the Presbyterian Church of the Covenant, the beautiful Romanesque bell-tower of which is a distinguishing feature of the northwestern part of the city. The congregation of this church has been notable, not only because it has always numbered among its elders and trustees distinguished statesmen like John W. Foster and John Hay, but also because it has represented every branch of official and social Washington life. President Harrison was a regular attendant at the services of this church, and was Dr. Hamlin's warm friend. Indeed, Dr. Hamlin seemed to have a genius for making quick acquaintanceships which often ripened into lasting friendships. With his wide sympathies, his talent for detecting and emphasizing the color, humor, and pathos of life, he found his work first in broadening men humanly that he might lift them spiritually. Thus, however intellectually and spiritually interesting his sermons, the hearer always felt, first of all, a very human heart behind them. Such work in such a community cannot die. The very character of the congregation to which Dr. Hamlin preached and the community in which he lived means that he preached by deed and word to a National audience.

❀

# Child Labor in the South

An interesting debate is brought to a close in our columns this week between Dr. A. J. McKelway, of Georgia, and Captain E. A. Smyth, of South Carolina, on the question of child labor in Southern cotton-mills. The discussion between these gentlemen only strengthens the opinion of The Outlook that some form of Federal legislation is needed to control, if not to abolish, the evils connected with the employment of children in the factories and mines of the country. We cannot even depend upon State statistics for accurate information upon this vital subject. Captain Smyth is an officer of an important manufacturing corporation in his State; Dr. McKelway is Assistant Secretary of the National Child Labor Committee. How is it that these two authorities differ by many thousands in their estimates of the number of young children engaged in exhausting labor in South Carolina and the Southern States?

Obviously, it is because there are no trustworthy current official statements published by the State of South Carolina that a bewildered world is thus left to choose among the estimates of Mr. Smyth, Dr. McKelway, and the figures collected seven years ago by the Federal Census Bureau. South Carolina has no State Department of Labor, no Bureau of Labor Statistics, no State factory inspector, no compulsory education law, no truant officers or comprehensive school enrollment, no school census, and no State census of industrial workers in the long interim between the periods of the Federal census. In the absence of current data such as would be at hand if all these departments of the State were regularly publishing the results of their labors, the public cannot be blamed for accepting with reserve the estimates and opinions of an advocate speaking from within a corporation which employs children under fourteen years of age.

Captain Smyth attempts to excuse South Carolina by accusing Maine, New Hampshire, and Rhode Island of permitting children twelve and thirteen years of age to work in their mills. Far be it from The Outlook to hold up New England mill conditions as perfect models for the rest of the world ; but these New England States to which Captain Smyth applies his *tu quoque* argument have established regulations and safeguards which it appears hopeless to expect in the near future in South Carolina. In New Hampshire children of twelve years are permitted to work in the mills only during the vacations of the public schools, no child under fourteen years can be employed at any occupation when the public schools are in session, and no. child under sixteen years may be employed during school sessions unless he can read and write English. Similar regulations, differing only in detail, prevail in Vermont. In New Hampshire the total number of illiterate children, ten to fourteen years of age, reported in 1900 by the United States Census was 557, in Vermont 287, while in South Carolina the number was 51,536. Comment upon these appalling figures would be more than useless. Delaware, Maine, New Jersey, Pennsylvania, and Rhode Island, all cotton-manufacturing States, have fixed the age for beginning to work in factories at fourteen years, and all these have State officials to enforce the law and supply the public with authentic information. In South Carolina nominally no child under the age of twelve years can be employed in a cotton-mill. But an orphan or any widowed mother or any disabled father may take oath before a magistrate or a county clerk that children at any age are dependent upon their own earnings, and the children are thereafter free to work until 8 P.M. Any child of twelve years or more may, so far as the law is concerned, work all night.

Louisiana, Maryland, Kentucky, and Tennessee, all have departments of Factory Inspection. Why not South Carolina ? North Carolina has a Bureau of Labor Statistics. Why not South Carolina ? Kentucky and Tennessee have established fourteen years as the age limit for boys and girls in mills, and Louisiana has set the same limit for girls. Why not South Carolina ? Kentucky ends the working day at 7 P.M. for all children under sixteen years of age in mills and mines, and Alabama for all children under thirteen years in mills. Why not South Carolina ? The New York Legislature has just passed a bill, which the Governor will undoubtedly sign, providing that no child under sixteen shall work more than eight hours a day, and that those eight hours shall be between eight o'clock in the morning and five o'clock in the afternoon. It is, perhaps, too much to say, Why not South Carolina ? but we can at least hold up the example to that State.

Let South Carolina establish the fourteenth birthday as the earliest date for beginning to work, and require the child to prove its assertion that it is fourteen years old by showing the physical stature and the school record of a normal child of that age. Let South Carolina establish a Bureau of Labor Statistics and a Department of Factory Inspection authorized to inspect factories by day and by night and to prosecute all violations of the law, publishing in a monthly bulletin of labor, as New York does, the records of these investigations. Let South Carolina provide, as Massachusetts has provided, for a State industrial census, independent of the Federal Census. Let South Carolina, by statute, establish the eight-hour day for all working children under the age of sixteen years, as Illinois and New York have done. And let South Carolina establish a compulsory education law, as all the States of the Union but eleven have done. It is safe to predict that when these changes become known as accomplished facts, adverse criticism of the attitude of the people of South Carolina towards the children of their State will cease. There is only one way in which the Southern States can silence this adverse criticism, and that is by adopting and maintaining as high standards of dealing with child labor as are successfully maintained in other parts of the civilized world.

What these standards are may be found presented in a compact and telling form in a "Handbook of Child Labor" compiled by Miss Josephine Goldmark, Assistant Secretary of the National Consumers' League. The League, which has accomplished remarkable results in the amelioration of the too often wretched conditions in which women and children work, has performed no one single service of more value than the publication of this significant tabulation of practical and successful legislation in behalf of child workers.

❁

# Justice through Peace

We do not recall any series of meetings, non-political, which have moved the city of New York as profoundly as the Peace Congress, of which we give an account on another page. This Congress at once marks the extent of public sentiment in behalf of peace and gives to it expression and added impulse.

Peace sentiment is not new. Absolute non-resistance has had its advocates ever since the beginning of the Christian era. Not to go further back in history, it has been maintained by the Society of Friends, in the main with great consistency and under great difficulties, since the middle of the seventeenth century. But it has never made any headway. The Society of Friends has not been a growing organization; and while its doctrine of the Inner Light has been taken up by other Christian bodies, this is not true to any extent of its doctrine of non-resistance. It is quite safe to say that the sentiment for international peace has made more progress in the last ten years than in the thousand years preceding. Why?

This is partly due to the general moral development of the race, especially in the humanitarian virtues; partly to the effect of long-continued presentation of the horrors of war and the glories of peace by a small body of advocates whose persistence neither argument, ridi-

cule, nor indifference could silence; partly to a change in war methods, intensifying its horrors and robbing it of much of its romance. But more than all these causes combined has been the definite proposal of a rational substitute for war as a means of securing justice between nations. This substitute for war is judicial procedure—the submission of the controversy to the decision of an impartial tribunal. This method has long since been adopted by all civilized nations for private war as a means of settling individual disputes; by the framers of our Constitution it was adopted for the settlement of all disputes among the several States of the Union. By the Hague Conference of 1899 it was adopted as a method of settling disputes among nations. This is not the same as international arbitration, which method had preceded the Hague Court for something like a century. In arbitration the Court is created after the dispute has arisen; in judicial procedure it is a permanent body: in arbitration the tribunal is bi-partisan, with an umpire to decide between the partisans; in judicial procedure it is non-partisan: in arbitration only the specific controversy is settled; in judicial procedure a permanent principle is generally established, which operates to prevent a similar dispute in the future: arbitration is adapted to settle controversies which can be settled by a conference; judicial procedure is equally adapted to settle those which can be determined only by determining an absolute principle of justice. The creation of an international tribunal to establish justice among the nations, by substituting the appeal to reason for the appeal to force, has given to the peace sentiment a power which the plea for non-resistance to injustice never had and never could have. The war against war was ineffective; the demand for an international tribunal to do justice between the nations is proving invincible.

The objection to war is not the loss of life it causes. The American railways maimed and killed more in a single year than all that were killed, wounded, and missing from the Russian army in the greatest battle of modern times; but we do not propose to abolish the railways, only to regulate them. It is not the pain which war causes. It is better to suffer pain than to suffer injustice. It is not even the base passions which war excites. It is at least conceivable that men might learn to fight without passion, influenced only by a love of liberty or a stern sense of justice. So apparently Washington fought. The objection to war is that it wholly fails of its avowed purpose; that never in a single instance in human history has it accomplished the object for which it is supposed to be intended; and that it never can accomplish that object. Charles Sumner's definition of war is recognized by the authorities of to-day as a classic: "War is a public armed contest between nations, under the sanction of international law, to establish justice between them." This is something which war never has done and never can do. A trial of strength can never determine which of the contestants is right; it can only determine which of the two is the stronger. This is sometimes a very important question; it may even be the more important of the two. But the two are not the same. The American Revolution did not determine that it is not just that one community should tax another community without giving it representation; it determined that Great Britain had not the power to tax America. The Civil War did not determine that under the United States Constitution a State had no right to secede; it determined that under the existing conditions in 1861 a very powerful combination of States had not the power to secede. The defeat of Aguinaldo did not prove that America ought to maintain its sovereign authority over the Philippines; it proved that America had the power to maintain that sovereignty.

When injustice is attempted and there is no other recourse provided, war may be justified. It may be a duty to submit to injustice; it may be a duty to resist it; which is the duty depends on a variety of considerations. Frederick Douglass, a boy of seventeen, was regarded by his master as unruly; he was leased out to a neighboring planter who had a reputation for "breaking in unruly niggers;" fought the new master and

conquered, and was not broken in. There was no tribunal to which he could appeal for justice; for had he appealed to the court he would have been sent back to the master to be flogged. There is no question that the world is far better for his successful resistance. A tribunal existed in America for the settlement of controversies between the States. The secessionists might have submitted their claim of a constitutional right to secede to that tribunal. But they did not; and when they opened war to accomplish the secession, there was nothing left but either to fight or to surrender the life of the united Nation. If the North had followed Horace Greeley's non-resistant course and "let the erring sisters go in peace," there would have been a century of border warfare between the two sections instead of a short, sharp, and decisive war of four years, resulting in a free and united Nation. The world is no more inclined to accept the doctrine of non-resistance to-day than it was a hundred years ago. The peace sentiment of which this Congress was an expression is not a sentiment of non-resistance. It is a sentiment in favor of substituting the appeal to reason and conscience for the appeal to force, and so changing the issues between the nations from the question, Which of two contestants is the stronger? to the question, Which of the two has justice on its side? The remedy for war which the ancient Hebrew prophet pointed out centuries ago the world has at last taken up: "Out of Zion shall go forth the law, and the word of the Lord from Jerusalem. And he shall judge among the nations, and shall rebuke many people; and they shall beat their swords into plowshares, and their spears into pruning-hooks: nation shall not lift up sword against nation, neither shall they learn war any more." Why shall they not learn war any more? Because they have learned to listen to the divine voice speaking through the universal conscience, and to seek the triumph of right reason, not the triumph of brute force. The nations will still resist evil and demand righteousness; but they will do this by the force of arguments in a court of justice, not by force of arms on a field of battle.

# Berea College

No one who has looked into the faces of the students at Berea, or has gone into the homes from which the white students come in the mountains of Kentucky, Tennessee, and the Virginias, or who knows the condition of that mountain population of more than two million, the menace of its ignorance, the great possibilities of its education, will doubt the pressing need of the College or the imperative call to which it is responding. No one who knows its faculty, its history, or what Dr. Frost has given up to be its President for fifteen years, the story of his work of educational adaptation and upbuilding, the breadth of his view, the missionary spirit which has penetrated the mountains in every direction, the courage with which he has fought for Berea's open door " to all young people of good moral character," the good sense and justice with which he has endeavored, by the assistance of his trustees, to solve the great problems, will withhold confidence and support from Berea in a crisis the like of which it is probable no other college has ever been compelled to face.

For Berea has not only been fighting in Kentucky, in season and out of season, in the courts, through the public press, by personal agitation, to maintain its right to admit colored students as a Northern or European school would do, but it has now to meet shortsighted and baseless criticism from men who ought to be its devoted friends and supporters. The letter which Mr. William Lloyd Garrison published a few weeks ago was a remarkable illustration of misinformation. Berea College, he declared, was founded by men who recognized neither race nor sex distinctions, and who welcomed black and white, male and female, on the same footing. When Dr. Frost became President, he maintained the radical traditions of Berea; but gradually rumors of dissatisfaction from the colored people of the neighborhood reached the North. It was declared that the proportion of colored students was being reduced and white mountaineers given the preference of admission. Then, after a time, came the proposal to prohibit by State law the co-education of the races. Mr. Garrison fails to report that the College resisted, but the hostile legislation triumphed, and the colored students were distributed among other institutions. The belief is current among some friends of the College, according to Mr. Garrison, that insufficient effort was made to block the law of separation. He declares that if a division had to be made, the colored students should have remained and new quarters been sought for the whites. " Better that the institution dedicated to equal rights by its founders should stand untenanted than flourish as a monument to subserviency."

Mr. Garrison's history was speedily corrected by the son of the founder of Berea College and the President of its Alumni Association. John A. R. Rogers, out of the inspiration of whose faith and works Berea came, died last July, having told the story of the early history of the institution in a book published before his death. He was a clergyman in Illinois, a graduate of Oberlin, specially interested in Kentucky because teachers and colporteurs among Oberlin students had reported that the capacity of the people of the mountain section of the State was far in advance of their educational opportunities, He persuaded a friend to go into the State and open a school for the mountaineers; and when this friend withdrew at the last moment, Dr. Rogers went himself, leaving a comfortable home and sacrificing many personal advantages, precisely as did Dr. Frost fifteen years ago. He was an abolitionist of the Birney rather than of the Garrison type, eager for abolition by legal means. He found in eastern Kentucky a valiant group of Southern anti-slavery men like the Rev. John G. Fee and General Cassius M. Clay.

Mr. Rogers, who corrects Mr. Garrison's statements, was present when the first colored pupil came to Berea, which was then an academy. After serious discussion, the trustees decided in favor of admitting him. Later many colored students came. Mr. Rogers is of opinion that only small sums were contributed to the funds of the College for the benefit of the colored race alone, and the assumption that the donations for many years were for their benefit, alone or particularly, is not borne out by the facts. "From the start of the recent agitation colored students have assumed a proprietary interest in the College, which they neither had particularly nor for their race." Berea was never essentially a negro college, but it has done more for the negro since the law of separation was enacted than was demanded even by the moral code.

Mr. Rogers's letter is supplemented by a statement from Dr. Frost, notable for its dispassionate recitation of facts, its candor, and its transparent loyalty to both races and to the College. The founders, he recalls, did not consider it wise to admit colored pupils. Ten years later, when emancipation had been proclaimed, they were admitted on equal terms, and they continued to attend freely until the State interfered. Two reasons took Dr. Frost to Berea: the desire to place character above race, and the belief that the largest hope of the New South lay in the education of the people of the mountains. When he went to Berea, through ineffective management, the white students had largely fallen off; their attendance was brought up until the proportion between white and colored students in the College was about the same as between the white and colored people in the State. When the Legislature of Kentucky, by law, compelled the separate education of the two races, there were nine hundred and seventy-seven students in Berea College, of whom one hundred and seventy-four were colored, and the institution had never been more prosperous or contented. Those who have been in its atmosphere will not forget with what fine idealism and sound judgment the relations of the two races were kept harmonious and unassailably proper. One by one, all other mixed schools in the South had been given up. When the law was proposed in Kentucky against the co-education of the races in private schools, Berea College interposed every possible obstacle, by discussion and protest, against its passage.

But the bill became a law, and the trustees at Berea were compelled to face an actual situation. They looked at it from every point of view. They carefully considered keeping the colored students and sending away the white. Their anxiety to do the right thing was known to all men who had any relations with them. They finally decided that the white students who came from the mountains, for whom the College was the only accessible institution of its class, and who were far more numerous than the colored students, must be taken care of at Berea, while the colored students could be distributed among other schools. One hundred have been sent to Fisk University, Knoxville College, Hampton, and other good schools, although this has involved a terrible drain on the limited resources of the College. The College is still fighting the law which has separated its students, and hopes that, for the sake of the principle, it will be set aside in the courts; but the fact remains that, for the present at least, the dominant sentiment of the South is against co-education of the races, not only in the public schools but in all schools. Instead of making a barren protest, as Mr. Garrison suggests, Berea is dealing with the situation with the breadth of view and the practical sagacity of men who have the sense of loyalty both to the ideal and to the demands of reality. Berea has not surrendered any principle nor abandoned any faith. It stands by its motto, "God hath made of one blood all nations of men;" but it does not propose to abdicate its work or lose its opportunity with two races because, for the time being, sectional and local sentiment make its former solution of the problem impossible.

It is the one institution which adequately provides for the education of a great white population whose training is of supreme importance to the country; for the negro, on the other hand, there are many admirable schools; and Berea now proposes, not to add to the number of colored colleges, but to care for its colored students by establishing a school for the training of agriculturists, artisans, housekeepers, and teachers for the public colored schools. In a word, the College proposes to attempt to provide for both its white and colored students advantages equivalent to those they had before the separation. To do this it will be necessary to set up a separate establishment especially adapted to the colored people. This is not merely to meet a sentiment but to meet a need, for with Berea closed the negroes of Kentucky are more destitute of educational guidance than those of any other State. An " adjustment fund " of $400,000 is therefore called for at once. Such a sudden demand upon a college already overburdened constitutes a grave crisis, such as would be brought about by the burning of buildings or destruction by an earthquake. It is a situation which will awaken the intense interest of Berea's former friends, and which should call new friends to its aid.

In view of the misrepresentation to which the noble work of Berea College and the inspiring personality of its missionary President, Dr. Frost, are now being subjected, it is well to bear in mind the words of Bishop Lawrence spoken at a recent meeting in behalf of the College in Boston : " We want to keep ourselves on a level keel, and not yield to the popular opinion that the races are drawing apart. Who knows how soon they may be drawn together again ? We want to be patient, charitable towards all. There is not yet any agreement among the best people on these matters. The South is not solid, the North is not solid. . . . I congratulate Berea that there may still be a helpful connection between its white and colored departments in the way of encouragement, management, and helpfulness." Berea needs and deserves, by reason of its great services to both races in the past, and the courage, patience, and sagacity with which it is meeting a grave crisis, the faith and the practical support of its friends, and of the friends of the negro and the mountaineers, as it has never had them before.

# THE PEACE CONGRESS

## BY A STAFF CORRESPONDENT

LAST week's great event in America was the Peace Congress in New York City.

In every respect it surpassed expectation. First of all, in numbers. Delegates registered by the thousand. The best hall in the metropolis proved inadequate. Overflow and additional meetings were held in other halls and in churches. For the first time in the history of great conferences, two banquets were necessary at the close, taking place coincidentally, with some of the same speakers passing from one to the other, no hotel accommodations being sufficient for the function if all applicants were to be housed in one place. Even with this doubling the issuance of tickets had to be stopped.

Secondly, the Congress was the first really National peace meeting in America. In comparison, previous peace congresses have been sectional. But at last week's over thirty-five States were represented by their Governors or their representatives, by members of State tribunals and State Legislatures, and by Mayors of important cities. The Federal Government was represented by members of the Hague Court, of the Supreme, Circuit, and District Courts, and of Congress. Thus the resultant body was a peculiarly representative official gathering.

To America's everlasting credit, the world's first Peace Society was founded in this country—in New York City, by David Low Dodge, in 1815. Though the first International Peace Congress was held in London, an American, Elihu Burritt, was the chief inspiring force for the following International Congresses, and of them all, that in Boston, in 1904, had the largest attendance. The function of National peace congresses for America has been in great measure performed by the Mohonk Arbitration Conferences. At one of them, a decade ago, Dr. Edward Everett Hale showed how arbitration could settle disputes, and the Conference put itself on record : " The feasibility of arbitration as a substitute for war is now demonstrated." But the apostle of peace, whom all delight to honor, did not stop there. He told his hearers that

The possibility of a central tribunal, existing as a permanent tribunal, to adjudicate in questions among nations, can no longer be called the dream of a Utopia. . . . It would certainly happen that, as questions arose, nations would begin to submit them to such a tribunal, at first timidly, but eventually with confidence. The bare existence of an impartial tribunal would carry with it a power impossible to overestimate.

With such prophetic words was born the idea now incorporated in the international court at The Hague. The idea was increasingly emphasized at succeeding Mohonk meetings, and the movement was the more significant because the Conference became representative of more widely separated parts of the country, a gathering representing a greater variety of types and also now including official representatives from Chambers of Commerce and other trade organizations.

The ideal of peace and righteousness carries with it an element of the religious. Some churches have availed themselves of the opportunity presented, and have observed the Sunday before Christmas as "Peace Sunday." This feature was again emphasized last week. On Sunday many sermons had for their text "The Prince of Peace." Delegates even spoke in some churches, notable meetings occurring in the Christian Science temples in New York City and Boston. The Sunday night service in Carnegie Hall united many men of many faiths. They were addressed by Protestant, Roman Catholic, and Jewish clergymen. Thus the First National Arbitration and Peace Congress began with a religious note. Händel's "Glory to God in the Highest, Peace on Earth, Good Will towards Men" and Mendelssohn's "How Lovely are the Messengers that Bring us the Gospel of Peace," made hearers feel themselves embarked upon what is also a religious movement.

Another marked feature was the prominence given to the education of the young in the principles of peace. Women's meetings have long become a recognized adjunct of the annual Civil Service Conventions and other National conferences, and the women's meeting last week was a very important aid. No National conference seems to have

so definitely recognized as did this the importance of enlisting not only young people but even children in a particular movement. The leaders of the Conference, however, appreciated the change taking place in our school and college text-books on history. Ever since the publication of Green's "History of the English People" war details have been increasingly minimized. Schoolboys now see in truer perspective the heroes of war as compared with the heroes of peace—poets, scientists, inventors, philosophers, philanthropists, statesmen. There was a recent vote in France on the question, "Who is our greatest man?" Most people, certainly most outsiders, might suppose that Napoleon would have the majority vote. Instead, he actually came seventh on the list; Pasteur was first and Victor Hugo next. A similar change is taking place in this country. Last week's "Young People's Meeting" was the most enthusiastic of any; its climax was reached when the children saluted the flag of peace. At this meeting of children, Baron d'Estournelles de Constant, the eminent French Senator and member of the Hague Court, began to speak to the children in his own language. He asked them a question and waited for an answer. It was not forthcoming. With a shrug, he requested a reply. He then wanted to know if they understood French. There came a few naïve cries of "Oui!" which seemed to amuse the orator. He then protested that it was selfish of the children to force him to speak in English! He was thus able to point a moral on the differences in languages. He declared that misunderstandings were often brought about by such small things as a lack of knowledge of languages, and even wars resulted. Hence, children should know at least one language besides their own. Baron d'Estournelles won the hearts of all the young people as he cleverly led their minds to the contemplation of the ideal of the Congress. With justifiable satisfaction he explained later: "When I go home, I shall say to the old people, 'I do not care what you think; I have seen the children, and *they know*.'" The lesson to us is evident: success attends any altruistic movement which is made to educate and appeal to the sympathies of the young.

Still another striking feature of the Congress lay in the prominent place given to the representatives of labor and commerce, a feature comprised in two meetings, addressed by prominent leaders of the various industries. The general position was well taken by Mr. Samuel Gompers, President of the American Federation of Labor :

Not as workers will we permit ourselves to be shot down in order to conquer the markets of barbarians and savages. I know of no gathering of labor in the last twenty-five years which has not declared itself unequivocally for international brotherhood and peace.

A final and chief feature of interest lay in the notably practical character of the vast majority of speakers and listeners. The Congress was no " collection of cranks and fools," as a hard-headed man of affairs dubbed it in passing the hall, without looking in to verify his statement. Neither was it a collection of white-blooded, weak-kneed theorists, feebly appreciating the actual conditions that govern individual passions and national prejudices. As one glanced around, there were the faces of great captains of industry, of practical leaders of labor, of men who bulk large in commercial enterprises, of trusted political leaders. Nor was the Congress any mere anti-war affair: its business was positive, not negative ; it was to affirm the necessity of substituting reason for passion. There was a general sentiment that it ought to emphasize, not " rainbows " or distant Utopias, but only practical plans certain of realization, and of realization, too, not in the far future, but in this very coming summer by action at The Hague.

So much for the Congress as a whole and its tendencies. But men are more interesting than movements. Behind every movement one finds some man, some distinct, masterful personality. While all the members of the Congress were united on general principles, the more interesting speakers had each some individual idea to present—for instance, Secretary Root's deprecation of diplomatic and not judicial attitude in the Hague Court and the consequent necessity of making it permanent, Mr. Bartholdt's scheme of an International Congress, Baron d'Estournelles's plan of international conciliation, Mr. Carnegie's notion of an international police, and Mr. Bryan's demand that money should be made contraband of war.

Chief among the speakers was, of course, the public-spirited citizen who had summoned the Congress, Mr. Carnegie, its President ; its " Little Father," as he was affectionately called. He certainly was its Little Father and Santa Claus in one. To him is due the gratitude of all who believe in international amity. Who so well as an American would have generously provided for the material well-being of his guests and friends here, and commanded the erection of a Palace of Peace at The Hague ? Who so well as a Scot could have presided over the sessions with unfailing humor and the pithy expression of acute opinion ?

For instance, Mr. Root, Secretary of State, was introduced by Mr. Carnegie as " something more than the President's right hand." Mr. Root's address was practically a state paper, and hence was read from notes. He proclaimed what had hitherto been only surmised— first, that, in our Government's opinion, the question of limiting armaments ought to be discussed at the next Hague Conference. The Government, therefore, reserves the right to present this, and, as well, the subject of limiting the use of force for the collection of ordinary contract debts due by one Government to the citizens of another. Mr. Root then pointed out the great obstacle to arbitration—a fear that the tribunals selected would not be impartial, because arbitrators are thought often to act diplomatically rather than judicially.

We need for arbitrators, not distinguished public men concerned in all the international questions of the day, but judges interested only in the question appearing on the record before them. Plainly, this end is to be attained by the establishment of a court of permanent judges.

Of all the speakers, none had juster claim to recognition than the Hon. Richard Bartholdt, member of Congress from Missouri. He was the author in 1904 of the resolution under which President

Roosevelt issued the call for a second Hague Conference, afterwards deferring to the Emperor of Russia, the original summoner for the Conference of 1899, who desired to issue the call for the second Conference. Mr. Bartholdt's resolution formed the basis of Mr. Hay's letter to the nations signatory to the first Hague Conference, thus defining in a timely way the American Government's attitude on a number of pending international questions. Secondly, his influence in the Interparliamentary Union, where he is President of the American group, has been of commanding importance. Two years ago he defined his plan for an International Congress. He would have the Interparliamentary Union form the Lower House and the Hague Conference the Upper House.

Americans have hitherto regarded Mr. Bryan necessarily from a National point of view, but people, independent of nationality, may now regard him as an international statesman. Last week he suggested that in time of war money-lenders shall not be allowed to wax fat by loans, taking advantage of a nation's weakness and urging it to continue hostilities. A loan by the citizens of a neutral nation, he pointed out, is practically a loan by the nation itself, and should be objected to as much as furnishing shot and shell.

Baron d'Estournelles de Constant was apparently the most hard-worked member of the Congress. He spoke several times every day. But he did not speak too often. His speeches were always sympathetically acclaimed. He has abandoned the diplomatic career, which he is well fitted to adorn, and is devoting himself, at every sacrifice, to spread abroad throughout the world the doctrines of arbitration, but especially of conciliation. He brought to the Congress, as did no other, the rich background of experience from his membership in the Hague Court, and from the wider activity represented by his presidency of the "Conciliation Internationale," a society deservedly reaching out its ramifications to the ends of the earth. The practical ideal towards which Baron d'Estournelles strives is certainly not to ameliorate war, it is not even so much to prevent war by international courts and congresses as,

by far-seeing methods of conciliation, to remove the sources of any international disputes or misunderstandings. To this end, among other means, he has organized parliamentary excursions. He took two hundred members of the French Parliament to London, and engineered a return visit of as many English parliamentarians. What was the result ? The Anglo-French compact, by which two mighty nations agreed to bury their exasperating differences of a century, and outline their spheres of activity which now do *not* overlap ! As the head of the French parliamentary group of arbitration, Baron d'Estournelles has received at Paris the visits of large delegations from the Dutch, Danish, Norwegian, and Swedish Parliaments, and is attempting to induce further similar social interchanges in the justified hope that only amity, peace, and greater international justice will result.

While these ideals are becoming by such methods appreciably nearer of realization, their coming will indeed be hastened if the recommendations of the Congress are realized—the opening of the Hague Court to all nations, the evolution of the Hague Conferences into a more permanent and comprehensive International Union, with representatives from all the nations, meeting periodically to insure regularly and systematically the efficient co-operation of the Powers in the development and application of international law ; a general arbitration treaty providing for the settlement of disputes not to be adjusted by diplomacy ; in the case of disputes not included in an arbitration treaty, the contending parties, before resorting to force, to invoke the services of an international commission of inquiry, or the mediation of friendly Powers ; in time of war the protection of private property at sea, and at all times the limitation of armaments.

Thus the Peace Congress did not "end in smoke," as some skeptics prophesied it would. If the ideas suggested at it demonstrated that peoples are generally ahead of their governments, the resolutions adopted were rational enough to appeal to any critic. They fitly define the atmosphere of the Congress—an enthusiasm for justice.

E. F. B.

# THE GATES OF NEW YORK

## BY ROBERT W. BRUÈRE

ESS than thirty years ago tunnels beneath the rivers of Manhattan were declared engineering impossibilities; now fourteen tubes are building beneath the East and Hudson Rivers. Twenty-five years ago electric traction was considered impracticable; to-day all the railways about New York are installing their initial electric zone. Electric traction has become eminently practicable, and with electric traction have come the subways, the tunnels, and the sub-surface terminal yards.

In February, 1888, Frank Julian Sprague, of Milford, Connecticut, equipped and put into operation in Richmond, Virginia, the first successful electric trolley road in the world. In the following year, 1889, Sir W. Arrol and E. W. Moir, Englishmen, set up on American ground the first great cylindrical tunnel shield, after the designs of the distinguished English engineer, James Henry Greathead. It is thanks to these epoch-making inventions of Greathead and Sprague that the railways and the people are at present opening the gates of New York.

The congestion of traffic in New York has increased with unexpected rapidity during the last ten years. When in 1870 the municipality decided to build the Brooklyn Bridge, it was confidently believed that bridges and ferries would be adequate to the growing traffic of the city. In 1883, when the Brooklyn Bridge was opened to the public, sanguine prophets declared that the structure would be used by as many as ten thousand people every day. At the time this estimate was considered extravagant, but in 1902 the Board of Rapid Transit Railroad Commissioners announced that one hundred and twenty millions of people, or a daily average of about three hundred and thirty thousand, had crossed the bridge in that year. The traffic on the rivers has grown in proportion. It is said that the lower East River has reached the limit of its traffic-bearing capacity. These facts only serve to illustrate the extraordinary rapidity with which the population of Manhattan has grown. At the present time every foot of ground from Battery Park to the Bronx is pre-empted by workshops, stores, and dwellings. There is no longer room on the surface of the narrow island for long bridge approaches, nor for surface terminal yards. The development of the terminal facilities of New York, it has long been clear, would have to take place, not on the surface, but under ground.

The key to the problem presented by the growing numbers of people, now approaching three-quarters of a million, who daily enter and pass out of New York, and by the congestion of the city's population, was the decision of the railways, compelled in the first instance by legislative enactment of the State of New York, to replace steam by electricity as their motive power. This substitution has in every case determined the peculiar character of the improvements under way—has, in fact, made these improvements possible. Without electricity, the sub-surface yards under construction by the New York Central, by the Pennsylvania, and by the so-called McAdoo companies, as well as the tunnels themselves, would have been impracticable. The experience of the public in the Park Avenue tunnels of the New York Central has alone demonstrated the danger and inconvenience that are inseparable from sub-surface travel through coal gas and smoke. To the evolution of the electric motor into an economical locomotive, more than

THE NEW YORK CENTRAL YARDS BEFORE THE IMPROVEMENTS WERE BEGUN

to any other single factor, the opening of
the gates of Manhattan is due.

If one enters the New York Central
yards, the site of the proposed Pennsylvania station, or the terminals of the
McAdoo tunnels, one sees hundreds of
men busy in removing, with compressed
air drills and dynamite, and huge, der-
rick-suspended steam shovels, millions
of cubic yards of stone and silt. All
the tracks of the new terminals are to be
laid beneath the street level, and all
switching and repairing are to take place
in subterranean chambers. At first
glance the necessity of making these
unprecedented excavations appears to
involve an extravagant expenditure of
labor and money. When it is considered, however, that the space beneath
the ground is to be occupied by what
will virtually be the basement floors of
huge steel buildings, and that in no instance will there be less than two stories
underground, it will be apparent that
the gain in total area in a city where
ground values are so high as they are in
New York must constitute a very large,
if indeed not a perfect, compensation
for the cost of excavation.

The simplest illustration of this fact
is found in the remodeled New York
Central terminal. The terminal yards
are being constructed at two levels, both
of which are below the level of the city

streets. All the suburban trains will
enter the station at an approximate
depth of thirty-five feet below the street;
all the express and through trains on a
suspended yard, resembling the second
floor of an office building, built of steel
and concrete, immediately overhanging
the suburban tracks, and fifteen feet
below street level. Above the express
level, in turn, south of Forty-fifth Street,
will rise the new buildings of the station,
including a great new office building, a
considerable portion of which has been
leased by the Federal Post-Office Department, while from Forty-fifth Street north-
ward all of the streets which are at present broken by the New York Central
surface yards will be restored to city
traffic. The municipal highways will be
carried on steel and concrete viaducts
across the inoffensive sub-surface yards.
This admirable restoration, made possible
by the use of electricity, is, from the point
of view of the neighboring residents, possibly the most delightful feature of the
present plans.

The engineers in charge of the work
of excavation and reconstruction have
proceeded with a swiftness and surety
that, to a layman, are little short of marvelous. When their work of lowering
the yards began, the engineers had to
conduct their operations within a narrow,
four-track space immediately south of

THE NEW YORK CENTRAL YARDS AS THEY WILL LOOK IN 1910
" The municipal highways will be carried on steel and concrete viaducts across the inoffensive sub-surface yards "

the Park Avenue tunnels, without interfering with the movement of more than six hundred daily trains. As their work has advanced, and a section of the new approach to the Grand Central Station has been electrified, the number of daily trains has almost doubled, and yet the engineers have proceeded with the reconstruction of the roadway and yards with clock-like regularity, and without interfering with the movement of the trains. To understand how this feat is being accomplished, one needs to descend into the yards at Fifty-seventh Street, the southern terminus of the Park Avenue tunnels, from which point southward the present work of excavation is progressing. The tunnels make provision for four tracks only, and the trains that pass through them formerly occupied but a four-track space between them and the confines of the yards proper. When the reconstruction is finished, these four tracks will spread out into six, almost immediately upon issuing from the tunnel. In order to secure room for the two additional tracks, the engineers had to remove vast quantities of rock both to the right and to the left of the old roadway, and to penetrate beneath the sidewalks and under the foundations of the buildings along both sides of Park Avenue. All buildings along this avenue below Fifty-seventh Street have been underpinned with steel and concrete retaining walls, so that the yards, along the entire distance of contact with the municipal highway, now have the appearance of one of New York's subway tunnels with its top removed. This preliminary work having been accomplished, the total area within the new walls was divided into three parts. To the left of the old tracks, as one looks southward, the first excavation was begun. Crowded between the wall and the frequently passing trains, that at intervals crushed out the life of an insufficiently alert workman, the engineers blasted out space for two tracks. When these tracks were completed, a part of the traffic moving to and from the tunnels was diverted to them, and the work of excavation transferred to the western side of the old roadbed. When this western section is in its turn completed, what traffic cannot be carried over the eastern section will be diverted from the old roadbed to it, and the engineers will go on to remove the huge ridge of stone that now stretches like a fossilized leviathan down between the two excavations.

While this work has been progressing, the engineers have been lowering and reconstructing the yards themselves into two levels, corresponding to the floors

FIRST EXCAVATIONS FOR THE ENLARGED NEW YORK CENTRAL YARDS
Breaking ground and rock within a narrow space

of the station which have already been described. When their work is done, on the street level there will be a network of bridges which will carry the city highways. Fifteen feet below will be the express terminal, providing room for twenty tracks: and yet twenty feet below this will be the suburban terminal with its fifteen tracks. To the east of these terminals will stretch the yards proper, the dimensions of which have been greatly increased through the purchase by the railways of all the property bounded on the north by Forty-fifth Street and on the east by Lexington Avenue, from which upwards of two hundred buildings have been removed. The area of the old terminal yards was about twenty-three acres, all of which was at street level; the total acreage of the reconstructed yards will be about sixty-five acres, twenty-four of which will be on the suburban level and forty on the express level, leaving the street level clear. There were about ten miles of track in the old terminal; in the new terminal, two miles will be devoted to the suburban service, nearly four miles to the express service, with about twenty-two miles on both levels, for storage, express, mail, etc.,

making a total of more than twenty-seven miles.

At the beginning of this account I said that the electrification of the roads was the key to the new improvements; and, indeed, both from the scientific and industrial points of view, this substitution of one motive power for another is by far the most significant, if not the most picturesque, feature of the enterprise. Into the question of the comparative values of alternating and direct currents, of overhead trolley and third-rail transmission, of reciprocating and turbine engines, it is not possible here to enter. It may, however, be said in passing that, with the object of harmonizing all the larger electrical installations in the vicinity of New York, the New York Central and the Pennsylvania have adopted an eleven-thousand-volt, three-phase alternating current for the high-pressure transmission lines between the central power stations and the sub-stations, and a six-hundred-volt direct current for the low-pressure conductors from the sub-stations to the feeders of the third rail. Moreover, the great power stations which the New York Central is erecting at Port Morris and Yonkers, and which may be considered typical of all the new installations, are to be equipped with great turbine engines similar to those which have been installed in the latest Cunard steamers—the Lusitania and the Carmania—each of which will be capable of developing forty thousand horse-power.

But these features of the improvements are not the ones which strike the eye of the layman who is passing through the yards. What he first observes on entering the completed section of the New York Central terminal is the very ingeniously guarded third rail and the splendidly compact and powerful electric locomotives that, within the initial electric zone, are to do the work of the steam locomotives that have hitherto brought the long-distance trains into the station. The suburban trains within the initial electric zone will be equipped similarly to those at present in use in our subways and upon our elevated roads. In these trains many of the cars are furnished with motors like the trolley-cars on the surface roads, and the train, containing many units of locomotion, that is, containing a number of motors, has a highly increased initial acceleration—gets under way more rapidly than a train of equal weight drawn by

a single engine. This equipment of individual cars with motors—called the multiple unit system, and also, by the way, the product of the inventive genius of Sprague—is, of course, impracticable beyond the electric zone. It would be folly, for instance, to have the Pullman and day coaches which are to travel across the continent loaded down with electrical apparatus that could not be used thirty-two miles beyond New York. Hence arises the necessity of electrical locomotives to bring the coaches of through trains into the city from the outer limits of the electric zone. The powerful electric locomotives and the guarded third rail are, at least from the layman's point of view, the most curious and interesting products of the present improvements.

One of the obvious difficulties presented by the introduction into a crowded and busy terminal of a third rail carrying a current of six hundred volts is the danger of accident due to the exposure of the rail itself. It was necessary to devise some means to protect men and property from the live third rail, and this was satisfactorily accomplished by Vice-President W. J. Wilgus, who has general charge of the New York

THE NEW YORK CENTRAL YARDS AT A LATER STAGE OF CONSTRUCTION

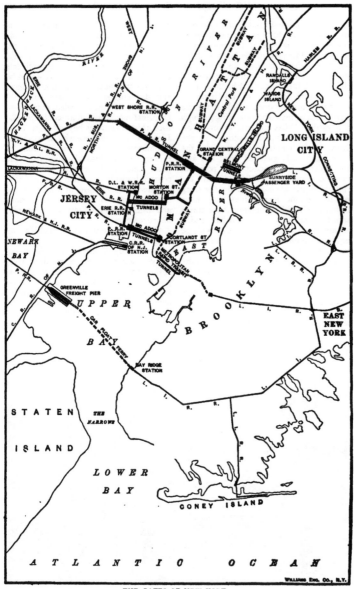

THE GATES OF NEW YORK

Central improvements. In his device a seventy-pound bull-head rail is used. The upper part of the rail is covered first by a porcelain insulating casing, which is in turn inclosed in a heavy wooden shield whose cross section looks like a diminutive gambrel roof. The only part of the rail not covered is that beneath this insulating hood, which it is almost impossible to come in contact with without such deliberate action as is exerted by the springs that press the contact shoe of the motors against it. The rail is supported by cast-iron pedestals shaped like the neck of a goose, so as to avoid interference with the movement of the contact shoe. As a result of this arrangement, the rail is not only protected from rain and snow, but from the stumbling bodies of men who might inadvertently or through carelessness fall upon it.

No precaution, however, is adequate to guard against the caprices of human curiosity. With this thought in mind, I asked the engineer who was guiding me through the yard whether any freak accident had occurred since the new third rail had been installed.

"Only one," he replied, "and we got out of that cheap at the cost of some thousands of dollars."

Then he told me that the men whom the road employed on the excavation and construction work were newly imported Italians. For many months they had lived in intimate daily relations with the steam-engines that went to and fro in the yards. When the first section of the new equipment was completed, and the trains began to move through the yards without the assistance either of steam-engines or of any other apparent motive power, the Italians were puzzled. "You might have seen them," said my guide, "almost any day gathering in groups and talking confidentially to one another about the mystery that had fallen among them. After a time the most adventuresome member of the gang decided that he had located the deviltry in the third rail, and he determined to make an investigation. He was walking across the yard one afternoon, a crowbar in one hand and a spade in the other. When no one was looking, he thrust his spade under the hood of the third rail. Immediately there was a flash of fire. He howled and ran, dropping his crowbar as he went. The

THE GREAT TURBINE ENGINES AT PORT MORRIS WHICH GENERATE ELECTRICITY FOR THE NEW YORK CENTRAL TRAINS

crowbar somehow got caught between the third rail and the track. A short circuit was established, and the electric fire spread across the entire electrified section of the yards. Submerged transmission cables were destroyed, fuses were everywhere burned out, and property worth some thousands of dollars was ruined. The meddler ran howling across the yards as if the very devil were indeed after him, and jumped over the edge of one of our deepest excavations. He was taken to the hospital with a broken leg. I hear that he has recovered since, but we have seen nothing further of him. As for the remainder of the gang, they were so thoroughly demoralized with fright that it took days to get them back to steady work. It was a costly accident, but it served a good purpose. There has been no loss of life or of property through trifling with the third rail since."

The electric locomotive looks as though two tenders had been detached from their engines and joined, back to back, by a box-like cabin. Both tenders are engines, and together are capable of developing 2,200 horse-power. In swiftness of acceleration and in ultimate speed the electric locomotive has surpassed the best type of steam-engine as a drawer of moderately heavy passenger trains. It derives its power by shoe-contact with the under side of the third rail, already described. Besides doing away with the smoke and gas generated by a steam-engine, it has the further advantage that, being a double-header, it is always in position to go forward, thus obviating the use of turn-tables, and making for economy both in yard space and in labor. It has been tested in all weathers and under all conditions that arise in practice, and has proved itself perfectly efficient.

Only less important from the point of view of the transportation problem of New York than Sprague's invention is the invention of the English engineer Greathead, for it may be justly said that without the shield which he devised the great tunnels beneath the Hudson and East Rivers would have remained impossible. The story of the

ERECTING A SECTION OF THE TUNNEL LINING

manner in which Greathead's inventive genius was brought to bear upon the traction problem of New York is an exceedingly romantic one. As early as 1879 a company of enterprising gentlemen concluded that tunnels must sooner or later supplant bridges as highways between Manhattan and the mainland. They decided that the best way to open the gates of New York was to burrow beneath the Hudson to the Jersey shore. With this object in view, they sank a brick shaft on the New Jersey side, and started to tunnel eastward. Their work

workers, making their progress impossible. Undaunted, they decided to drive a temporary entrance or heading into the silt, from which to construct their tunnel tubes. This was accomplished by erecting, outside the air-lock, two rings formed of wrought-iron plates and angles, six feet four inches in diameter, four feet long, and bolted together. Then they ran a series of similar rings, each two feet six inches wide, and each succeeding one increasing about one foot six inches in diameter, until with the eleventh ring they reached the full diameter of the

THE CURVE AT GREENWICH AND CHRISTOPHER
STREETS IN THE EAST-BOUND McADOO TUNNEL

was watched with curiosity by all the world, for they were the first to attempt the construction of a great tunnel with the exclusive assistance of compressed air. When they had gone twenty-three feet below tide-level, they built an air-lock into their brick shaft, from which they hoped the tunnel could be started. They decided to begin the break-up for the tunnel by opening the earth outward and timbering the roof of their excavation, while the sand or the rock or the silt of which it was composed was being removed and lifted to the surface. But the compressed air blew its way through the silt and permitted the water from the river above to filter down upon the

projected tunnel. With the aid of compressed air, which held up the silt and water at the face of this improvised tunnel, they began their work of excavation and started the construction, within a thin iron casing, of a tubular wall of brick, the material of which their permanent tunnel was to be made. They had not gone far, however, when one of the rings of the improvised temporary tunnel, which led from the air-lock to the tube of brick, yielded to the pressure of the compressed air. The tunnel was flooded and wrenched out of shape by the inrushing water, and twenty men were drowned. The company attempted by many other fruitless experiments to

continue their work, but in 1882 they gave up their project under the conviction that subaqueous construction beneath so deep and heavy a river as the Hudson was impossible.

In the meantime the population of Manhattan had grown so rapidly that what these pioneers had foreseen as a probable necessity had become a real one. In 1889 an English company, realizing that a sub-Hudson tunnel would be a valuable investment, consulted Sir B. Baker and Mr. James Henry Greathead. These gentlemen examined the abortive tubes beneath the Hudson, decided to substitute cast iron for brick as the permanent material of the tunnel, and devised a shield for its construction,

those that are being used in the construction of the fourteen tunnels at present under way beneath the Hudson and the East Rivers.

In looking at the Greathead shield one feels himself in the presence not so much of an instrument of steel as of a material embodiment of an idea. When the shield is set to work beneath the river, it represents the accumulated intelligence of the many men who have worked upon the problem of subaqueous construction for generations. In appearance the shield resembles a great drum built of heavy steel plates. In the drumhead, called the diaphragm, there are doors for the passage of workmen and the withdrawal of mud and rock and silt.

ELECTRIC LOCOMOTIVE ON THE NEW YORK CENTRAL

which was the first of its kind to be built in any part of the world. The construction of this shield was intrusted to Mr. E. W. Moir, who is at the present time vice-president of the concern that is building the great Pennsylvania tunnels under the East River. From the point of view of tunnel construction, it is of little consequence that the funds of the English company were soon exhausted, and that the tunnel beneath the Hudson was not completed by them. The shield which Mr. Moir constructed from Greathead's design was the most perfect realization of an idea which had been evolving in the minds of engineers since Brunel, the Frenchman, constructed the first crude shield for the tunnel which he built beneath the Thames in the early part of the last century, and it has served as the pattern·for all the shields that have been built since, as well as for

The upper drum rim is a cutting edge, which, when the shield is driven forward by hydraulic jacks, goes through the material in front like a biscuit-cutter, and holds up the river bed above while the biscuit of mud and silt is removed. The barrel of the drum, extending backward over the completed portion of the tunnel tube, forms the true shield for the men who set up the tunnel proper, ring by ring, within its protecting circumference. The bottom of the drum is at the same time the head of the completed tunnel tube, and is supplied with air-locks, through which workmen enter into the construction chamber within the shield. Immediately back of the drum-head there is a huge revolving crane called an "erector," also Greathead's invention, equipped with a muzzle like the jaws of an ant, which picks up the heavy sections of the tunnel rings, and, lifting them,

TWIN TUBES OF THE PENNSYLVANIA TUNNEL IN PLACE UNDER THE RIVER

holds them in place while the workmen bolt them together.

Few experiences are more impressive than a descent into one of the tunnels. You drop sixty feet or more beneath the surface of the ground to the level of the tunnel opening. If you chance to be entering the Pennsylvania tunnel, let us say, that has been driven at Thirty-second Street from the west side of Eleventh Avenue six thousand one hundred feet to the great shaft in Weehawken, you first pass through a long, circular cavern of rock which has been blasted out with

dynamite without the aid of the shield. As you advance towards the river you come to the subaqueous section in which the shield was used. Here your path is crossed by a circular diaphragm, a great steel disc dotted with doors, and twenty-three feet high. At a little round window in one of these doors you see through the glass the eyes of a man. After some minutes. with a rush of steam, the door swings open, and a gang of men troop out. Now you enter this door with your guide, and find yourself in a small chamber, with benches at either side, like a compartment of a diminutive European railway coach. Your guide puts his hand on a lever above his head. There is a whistling of wind as the compressed air rushes in. The sensation reminds you of a weird tale by Poe. "Blow out your eardrums!" the guide shouts, as he looks anxiously at you. You try to seem unafraid, but the hollow sound of your guide's voice, and the wild whirl in your head, fill your mind with fantastic and uncouth imagery. It is a relief when

THE CORTLANDT STREET TERMINAL OF THE McADOO TUNNELS
From the architect's drawing

the door ahead of you swings open and you see the long, dim vista of the tunnel ahead. You enter into what appears to be the hollow carcass of a monstrous serpent, whose ribs stretch before you, round after round, apparently without end. Yet not very far away the bed of the river is flowing like a stream of black lava through a door in the shield, and the " sand-hogs," as tunnel workers are called, are loading it into little cars that stand on a track laid on the floor of the tunnel.

And now your guide explains to you the mystery of the compressed air. It is the air, driven at a pressure of thirty pounds to the square inch against it, that holds the fluid bed of the river in check. Often the men work in a pocket in front of the shield, and while they work the compressed air holds up the face of the excavation, blows out the water, and keeps the silt dry. But here is the danger. The pressure of the river varies with its depth—that is, with the length of the column of water that rises from the excavation to the surface of the stream ; the pressure of the air is uniform at all points of the face of the excavation, and can therefore balance the pressure of the river only at a single point. Where the tunnel is twenty-three feet in diameter. the difference in the pressure of the river at the upper part of the shield and at the lower part may be as much as nine to eleven pounds. Now, ordinarily, the pressure of the air is made to balance the maximum pressure of the river at the bottom of the shield. So long, therefore, as the face of the excavation is composed of fairly compact material, everything goes well. But let the shield be driven into a stratum of over-liquid silt or quicksand, and the face of the excavation at the top of the shield is pretty sure to give way. Then the air "blows out" with a burst, its pressure within the shield is rapidly reduced, the equilibrium between it and the river is overcome, and the water rushes in like a hungry monster. Against this emergency a safety curtain is erected within the tunnel tube, but frequently enough the men cannot outdistance the river in their rush to cover, and thus many a good life has been lost.

But your guide will assure you that the men like their work. The engineer who conducted me through the tunnel told me how, when the two Pennsylvania tubes were approaching the line that separates New Jersey from New York, there was great rivalry between the forces in each of them to cross the border first. Day and night the men in either tube could hear the shouts and

THE PENNSYLVANIA TERMINAL AT EIGHTH AVENUE AND THIRTY-FOURTH STREET
From a model

the singing of their neighbors beneath the river, and the cry of triumph that went up when the men in the southern tube won the race.

As you make your way out of the tunnel back into the open air, you feel that you have been in the presence not so much of a work of giants as of heroes. Every day the men who enter the tunnels take their lives in their hands, and the delight which they experience in their work is due to their consciousness of participation in an enterprise the successful conclusion of which will bring a boon to humanity.

I have dwelt upon the Pennsylvania tunnel and the New York Central sub-surface yards because they are typical of the major improvements now under way. If the reader will turn to the accompanying map of New York, he will see the larger scope of the works that are changing the metropolis from one of the most awkward and difficult of access to perhaps the most ample and convenient terminal in the world. Under the Hudson, westward from Thirty-second Street run the two great twenty-three-foot tunnels of the Pennsylvania, already in part described. Further south, at Christopher and again at Cortlandt Street, are the four so-called McAdoo tunnels, which, it is announced, are to be used by the Erie, the Lackawanna, the Central Railroad of New Jersey, and by the suburban trains of the Interborough-Metropolitan Rapid Transit Company. From Battery Park, in Manhattan, to Joralemon Street, in Brooklyn, stretches the splendid tunnel built for the use of the Metropolitan Company by the city. Eastward from Thirty-fourth Street four Pennsylvania tunnels plunge beneath the East River to East Avenue in Long Island City. And above all these, in the reefs of Blackwell's Island, east of Forty-second Street, lie the two Belmont tunnel tubes. These tunnels, with their magnificent terminals at Morton and Cortlandt Streets, together with the great New York Central and Pennsylvania sub-surface

yards, constitute the most important contributions which have thus far been made to the solution of New York's transportation problem.

But other improvements are in process of execution by the railways that will be hardly less important in their ultimate effect upon the commerce of the city, and to these I shall give a concluding word. Across the Hudson, at Greenville, on the long peninsula that stretches down between New York and Newark Bays, the Pennsylvania has for several years been building a freight yard which, when it is completed, will accommodate forty thousand cars. This yard is supplemented by a lighterage pier two thousand feet long, extending out into the water of New York Bay, and with three float bridges, equipped with the most modern and ingenious electrical machinery for the transfer of freight trains to the barges that carry them across to Bay Ridge in Long Island. At Bay Ridge another freight yard with lighterage piers and bridges has been laid out; and at Sunnyside, between Jackson and Morton Avenues in Long Island City, the Pennsylvania has just begun the excavation of what will be possibly the largest yard devoted to the exclusive use of the passenger service in the country. This Sunnyside yard, like the New York Central and Pennsylvania yards in Manhattan, will lie below the level of the city streets, which will be carried across it on steel viaducts or under it in tunnels, and its business will be transacted entirely by electricity. When completed, this yard will contain forty-five miles of track, capable of accommodating a few more than two thousand coaches. Finally, to the north of these yards a bridge has been planned that will carry traffic across Ward's and Randall's Islands to Port Morris in the Bronx. These Long Island terminals, if they will not be among the most conspicuous, are destined to be among the most useful, of the new gates of New York.

# ART AND DEMOCRACY

## SECOND PAPER

HARE AND HOUNDS
By H. M. Walcott
Bought from the Daniel G. Reid Purchase Fund in 1906

## AN ART ASSOCIATION FOR THE PEOPLE

### BY ELLA BOND JOHNSTON

WHEREVER people are wanting more beauty in public life, and are trying to do something, at first hand, to bring the pleasure of art to all the people of a community, the story of the Art Association of Richmond, Indiana, ought to be interesting and helpful. It attempts a democratic art movement which is thus far unique.

The Association is ten years old. A few citizens started it, and a few have been its vital force ; but the number has grown steadily. In its first organiza-

tion this Association brought together all the forces in the town that could be helpful in maintaining a public art movement. These forces have held together for ten years, and been so successful in arousing a community interest in beauty and art that " The Richmond Story " has become an inspiration to other towns. The Association is now an incorporated body, and is acquiring by purchase and donation a permanent collection of works of art. It numbers on its Board of Directors the Superintendent of the Public Schools, the Super-

THE OFFICE OF THE SCHOOL CONVERTED INTO A GALLERY

THE ARRANGEMENT OF THE CORRIDOR

visor of Drawing and two other public school teachers, two newspaper men, a lawyer, four local artists, a merchant, a college professor, the town's most distinguished citizen, and, of course, several enthusiastic club-women.

Such an organization, with so many influences co-operating for its success, will grow and live in a small city where a more exclusive art club would fail. What can be done in Richmond, with its population of twenty-five thousand, can be done in any city where are found a few people willing to work hard and

make much personal sacrifice for the sake of a cause.

The leaders of this Art Association believe that beauty is an essential part of life, and that " art should not be for the ·few, any more than education or freedom is for the few." For ten years they have held annual Art Exhibits of a high order of merit, with doors open *free* to all the people of the town.

The expenses are met, in part, by the fifty-cent annual dues of a large membership, and five-dollar subscriptions from interested citizens. For the past four years the Common Council of the town deemed the art exhibit of sufficient civic importance to justify the appropriation from the town treasury of one hundred dollars for the Annual Exhibition expense fund. This is a significant and encouraging fact for those who believe that the people ought to have public beauty at public expense.

Last year we came near losing this hundred dollars from the Council. A new State law governing cities makes no provision for expending public money for such purposes. When the appropriation was proposed in Council, each member spoke in favor of it, and heartily commended the good work of the Art Association. The Mayor said it would be his duty to veto it, but that he would give ten dollars out of his own pocket to help make up the hundred.

At this uncertain stage of the proceedings the City Attorney appeared on the scene and made an unusual speech of some length. He said in part: "There has been nothing done in this city that has been of such great and widespread benefit as the annual art exhibits of the last ten years. The project deserves the support and backing of the city. It is a matter that is above the law. The *people* of Richmond want you to give this hundred dollars, and the people are greater than the law. You are justified in making this appropriation by the nature of the cause. All our people are enabled to see, without charge, examples of art such as are shown only in the finest galleries of the world. No one makes any money out of the exhibit; it is not a private matter. It is of broad influence and benefit, and deserves your support."

The appropriation was made by the unanimous vote of the Council.

GARFIELD SCHOOL

The public school-house in which the art exhibitions are held

When the history of the new democratic civilization we dream of is written, which will take some account of the souls of men, it ought to be recorded as one of the early symptoms that in the Hoosier town of Richmond, early in the twentieth century, the Common Council spent two hours one hot night in June, when business was pressing, discussing the value of a free art exhibit and appropriating money from the public treasury for its support.

From all these sources we have been successful each year in obtaining a fund that has equaled the expense and. sometimes exceeded it by a sum large enough to purchase a picture for the Association. This would not be true were it not for the generous donation of the building in which the exhibitions are held, which is—wonderful to relate—a school-house; just a public school-house. However, in this case, it is a beautiful building, centrally located, and admirably adapted for exhibition purposes.

The use of this building, with lights and janitor service, is given free to the Art Association by a Superintendent and School Board who believe in the educational value of art exhibits, and in the school as the educational center of a community; who believe, with President Eliot, of Harvard, that "the main object in every school should be, not to provide the children with the means of earning a livelihood, but to show them how to live a happy and worthy life, inspired by ideals which exalt and dignify both labor and pleasure. To see beauty and to love it is to possess large securities for such a life."

We think we have successfully demonstrated that school-houses are possible art galleries, and might be used in all communities for such purpose.

Our exhibitions are held in June. The building is turned over to us on Saturday before the last week of school, and the private view for members is held on the following Tuesday evening. What happens in those few days is a fairy tale of the transformation of a school-house into an art gallery, with its twelve rooms and two large corridors entirely filled with exhibits.

We shake up our "enchanted rug"

vigorously, and the desks are all removed from the rooms, false walls are put up, blackboards are covered with suitable background materials, draperies are hung, and in every way the building is made as attractive as possible. This actual labor of preparing the building and installing the exhibits is done by the janitor force of the schools and about fifty members of the Association, whom we call "The Faithful." This is not a small task when you consider that the insurance list covering the whole amount of exhibits each year generally foots up to one hundred thousand dollars. The teachers of the building sit in the furnace-room, in the basement, to finish their school reports, and smilingly say that they are willing to do so for the sake of the cause.

Believing that a beautiful ideal suitably and adequately rendered is art, whether it be on canvas, in clay, metal, or whatsoever, and, fortunately, not being hampered by precedents or traditions, this Association displays, along with paintings and sculpture, examples of handicraft in the various mediums and materials.

The catalogue of the last annual exhibition shows a collection of one hundred and fifty paintings by well-known American artists, prominent among whom are H. M. Walcott, Miss Ahrens, Thomas Anshutz, Mr. Breckenridge, Mary Cassatt, Thomas Eakins, Childe Hassam, Robert Henri, Edward Redfield, Horatio Walker, etc.; a group of fifteen pieces of sculpture; a notable exhibit of one hundred etchings by Cameron, Rembrandt, Seymour Haden, Whistler, Fisher, Dürer, Pennell, Helleu, etc., mostly loaned by the Library of Congress; a room of sketches and original drawings for illustration by some of the foremost American illustrators; a rare display of artistic photography, showing work from forty photographers, including the well-known Photo-Secessionists; five hundred and fifty pieces of handicraft in pottery, metals, books, leather, and textiles; an exhibit of paintings and carbon photographs belonging to the public schools; and the work of the drawing and manual training departments.

We have found American painters

much interested in our art movement, and more than generous in responding to our invitation to exhibit their pictures in Richmond. As a special inducement in obtaining really good paintings, we have annually the Daniel G. Reid Purchase Fund of five hundred dollars, given us by a former Richmond man, to be used for the purchase of a painting exhibited in the annual exhibition. We have had the fund four years, and with it have purchased and added to our permanent collection the following paintings: "The Duet," Henry Mosler; "Late Afternoon, Litchfield Hills," Ben Foster; "Old Pastures," Leonard Ochtman; and "Hare and Hounds," H. M. Walcott. These names speak for themselves, and the fact that we own them speaks something at least of what we have learned to appreciate.

These four pictures, with nine others which we bought with the surplus expense fund, and one which was purchased for us by a woman's club, make up our collection of fourteen really good paintings—an encouraging beginning for the collection we hope some day to see hanging in a beautiful public gallery in Richmond—if some good angel who knows

A VARIETY OF RAFFIA AND GRASS NOVELTIES

THE ANTIQUE CORNER

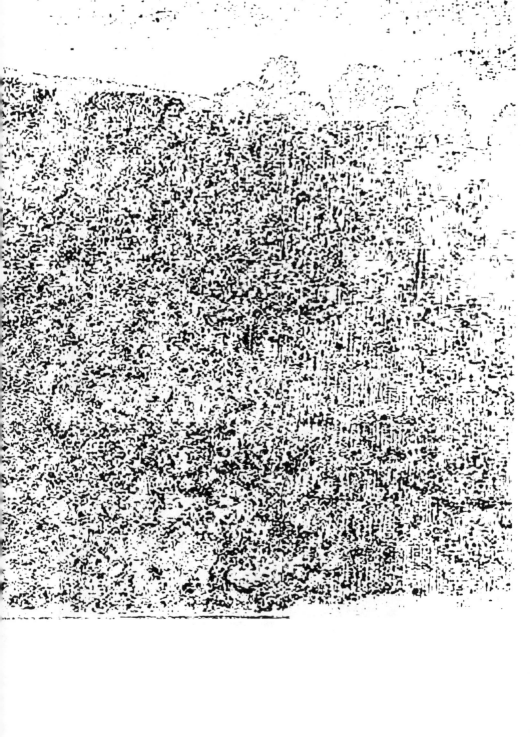

understanding: It is needless to say that they come again dragging along wondering and sometimes unwilling parents. In this way all sorts of people get to the exhibition, who would have little chance in their lives for the enjoyment of art if it were not brought thus freely to them.

We sometimes call the Art Exhibit our most beautiful public charity. It is gratifying to find how many people want to help a cause that is for the benefit of every one in the community. Our florists send plants and cut flowers to beautify the building, a piano company of the town each year during the exhibition gives a complimentary concert to the Association, the city band and orchestra play without charge when invited to do so, and our daily papers always give us any amount of courteous and helpful publicity.

This interesting of the whole community makes the assertion really seem true that " this annual exhibition has become a democratic festival."

It is difficult to estimate the educational influence of these exhibitions. One noticeable result is the progress the Richmond painters have made in their work. It cannot be said that these artists are without honor in their own town. Their work always hangs in the exhibition, and the citizens take a genuine interest in it. This opportunity for ex-

hibiting their own pictures and for studying the work of other artists has been the inspiration of their progress during the past ten years. In such native development among groups of artists elsewhere throughout our country, in a similar appreciative atmosphere, lies the beginning of hope for a truly American art. Are not ideals of beauty held in common, a common knowledge of the principles of artistic expression, a common wonder and joy and appreciation for a work of art, all necessary to that art atmosphere so essential to the development of a national art ?

The close association of the public schools with the exhibition has been the opportunity for better school-room decoration. Three of the best landscapes in our last exhibition were bought by schools. Most of the school buildings have paintings secured at the exhibitions. Among these are a Forsyth, an Albright, a Walter Palmer, a Carlton Wiggins, etc.

Through the exhibitions our people have become acquainted with American painters and craftsmen. The standard of taste in Richmond has been elevated ; at least we have been set thinking about things beautiful.

The display of handicrafts is changing our ideals of beauty in all those environing things which we must see and use and think about in the daily life. Our citizens generally are more alive to the

ONE OF THE CLASS-ROOMS TURNED INTO AN ART GALLERY

need of preserving the natural beauty of the town's situation, and adding to it parks and boulevards, and they are learning that beauty has not only a spiritual value, but also a value in dollars and cents.

We have discovered from studying landscape painting that, having eyes, we yet did not see the beauty of our own familiar landscape. We are learning to see.

In our third annual exhibition we had on display a landscape, "The Whitewater Valley," painted by T. C. Steele. It was a scene in our own river valley some miles below us. We ought to have been familiar with it. The Board wanted to buy the picture, but did not have money enough. So we tried to interest people in it, in the hope that they might like it well enough to help out with the money. Their comments were interesting. They all seemed to think that it ought to be all right if Mr. Steele painted it. Most of them said it was beautiful. Some of them frankly thought it was not. But

they invariably said, "I never saw anything in nature that looks like that." It was true, they had not. We might have given them that famous retort, "Don't you wish you could!" but we did not feel that way, and thought we could afford to wait. We got the money, and bought the picture, and waited. Each year it hangs in our exhibition, and each year many come to say, "We have seen for ourselves." "The shadows in the Whitewater Valley are more purple and the atmosphere more hazy than the artist dared to paint them." So we have learned what Browning meant when he wrote, "We love first, when we see them painted, things we have passed, perhaps a hundred times, nor cared to see."

Books have been written about how to look at pictures. We have had the rare opportunity of observing how the same people *do* look at pictures year after year—our neighbors, friends, and acquaintances. We know what they feel, think, and say.

The unconscious joy of the children,

THE WHITEWATER VALLEY
By T. C. Steele
Owned by the Richmond Art Association

the keen, wide-awake interest of boys and young men, the gush of the girls, the critical attitude of students, the despair of the foreign traveled, the appreciation of real art-lovers, the tears of sensitive, hungry souls, and the growth in intelligent appreciation of all of these, make the effort for the art exhibit seem worth while.

We hope to keep this democratic art movement alive in Richmond for twenty-five years, that a generation of children may grow up under its influence. Perhaps by that time we can know the full value of such influence and can write a book about how people look at pictures.

Art holds out to well-ordered human beings legitimate and infinite sources of happiness. The works of art brought by the Art Association furnish to our people a high kind of pleasure which otherwise would be left out of their lives. It is *something* to have made that possible in one small city.

# "THOUGHTS FROM THE DISH-PAN"
## THE STORY OF A STUDENT COOK

THE Japanese question is in temporary abeyance, but it is nevertheless a coming problem. There are in the immediate vicinity of Los Angeles alone fifteen thousand Japanese of varying grades, from the coolie to the most enlightened student. The former class is not proportionately numerous, as in the case with the Chinese. The larger part of them are here as higher-class servants, merchants, or as students in our schools.

There are two daily newspapers and two weekly magazines published in the Japanese language in Los Angeles, and clubs without number. There is even a Woman's Club. Nearly all the churches are doing mission work among them, and a Buddhist temple is soon to be built by them.

In business the Japanese are meeting the Greeks on their own ground with their own weapons. Los Angeles has been a real-estate battle-ground for several years, and the agents are looking with dismay at the little brown men. On a conspicuous street corner is a huge signboard stating, in Japanese characters, that the Japanese Investment Company will build a modern steel and brick structure of five stories, and those who wish to secure offices must apply early. This company has been incorporated, and although a young affair, has already made money in city and country investments. It is unique in that not only are the leading and more influential Japanese concerned in it, but any common laborer who can pay in five dollars each month may become a shareholder in the profits.

Already in Los Angeles the Japanese control enough land to come into competition with white men as growers of small fruits, and especially numerous are the little strawberry farms. The investment company already spoken of is about to buy one thousand acres not far from the city, which is to be divided into small farms, with a Jap in control of each. A village with houses for the laborers and business offices for the officers will be the center of the industrial plan.

This all shows the Jap as a money-maker. I think, in a general way, this remarkable people may be divided into two classes, the commercial and the student. Under the head of the latter comes my cook, who may serve as a fair type. When Kanaya came to us, I was struck with his rather unusual face—eyes that expressed a great deal of feeling, and quite unlike the usual slant and expressionless Oriental eye. During the mutual cross-examination one of the conditions expressed was that he should have time each day to study. This we promised, for we were in despair as to our kitchen, and willing to promise anything.

Kanaya arrived, and became a member of our household. He proved to be a very good servant in many ways, although there are days when not only genius burns, but also the roast and muffins. However, we learned to respect his moods, for when he really walks on earth he is good, unfailingly courteous unless his very sensitive feelings are hurt, faithful, honest, and a good cook.

Going into his room one day to see about a needed change, I found Carlyle's Life of Schiller, Goethe, Quick's Educational Reformers, and among his Japanese books were Lives of Buddha, Confucius, and Christ. He is making a study of comparative religions. He tells me that Buddhism is much more in line with the philosophical mind of the Japanese students, but Christianity is more in harmony with progress, and therefore better suited for the present needs of Japan, besides being simpler and better understood by the common people.

If I have guests, and a new or interesting subject is introduced when Kanaya is in the room, it is with the greatest difficulty that he withdraws, and afterward I am catechised as to what was meant. Of course one learns to know that the curiosity of these people is not intended as an impertinence, but is a part of their thirst for knowledge, and inasmuch as they do not belong to the servant class in their own country, they have not learned the attitude of servants, as this is interpreted in white countries.

Kanaya is able to quote glibly from the poets, from Petrarch to Poe, and as glibly from the philosophers, beginning with the earliest reasoning day.

Of course there is a little vanity about it, but it is not surprising that he is proud of his ability to read and understand in English this class of literature. He seems to be equally at home among painters ; Turner, Sir Joshua Reynolds, Rembrandt, Watts, and their methods are at his tongue's end. He himself can paint charmingly and with great feeling. For instance, a rose in the garden will appeal to him, and he paints it as he sees it, not in the flat but artistic way of the Japanese, but the *real* rose.

Kanaya is a great reader of the newspapers, especially if any question concerning his beloved Japan is discussed. When a traveler asserted that an outsider was not allowed in the public schools of Japan and also could not buy property, he told me that the American people had a great many "mis-notions" about his country. The schools are not free to the Japanese themselves; the government having required all its money for war and defense, it demands school fees of the people, which they gladly pay. Koreans, Chinese, and "Indes" are allowed in the schools, and the fact that there are no white children is probably because the foreigners have never wanted to study in the Japanese language and with Japanese methods. As for buying property, the country is so exceedingly small that if the rich Americans should come in and buy the mines and other valuable property, they could soon buy up the Empire.

The greatest motive in Kanaya's life is to do something for Japan, either on social or patriotic lines, or perhaps write some great thing. His present life is merely a preparation. Apropos of the kitchen work, he said to me that the only thing that ennobled it was that it had to be done. He painted a picture for me and signed his poet name, which was written in two characters, one standing for "pine-tree" and the other for the sound that the wind makes in the branches of the pine-tree ; which, being explained, was that the pine-tree stands for Japan, and the sound of the wind is his own voice, which will sometime sound through Japan, and, like the wind, no one will know where it comes from or where it goes—it is enough to know that he has sung for Japan.

One evening an officer in the German army, a young English gentleman, and a very successful young American were dining with us. I noticed that Kanaya was listening very intently to the conversation as he was serving the table. After all the guests had gone he came in from the kitchen and asked if he could read a "few thoughts from the dish-pan," which proved to be something like this, that the lack of seeming success and heredity does not make or unmake the man—he is the man only who proves himself one by meeting a sordid life bravely. He carried the thought out in careful and elaborate English—the old thought that "a man's a man for a' that."

Another "dish-pan thought" I found written in a book in which I wrote the daily menu and orders for the grocer and butcher: "He lingers between heaven and earth; now he seeks the pleasure of the earth, which grasps his heart with mysterious hand. The world is sweet and the world he loves, yet his spirit, the inner self, aspires for the higher sphere. Then he turns, as if whispered to by an unknown power. He seems to possess two separate selves: in his worldly character one would find a Godly spot; and in his best, too, one would not claim for him to be pure."

Carlyle is Kanaya's favorite philosopher, and there are days when he fancies that he is like Carlyle, and consequently it is rather a distinction to be so absorbed and melancholy that he forgets the baking-powder!

The love of beauty with the Japanese is a passion which dwarfs everything else in their nature, unless it is patriotism. The daily lectures on beauty and poetry were interspersed with politics. The unexplained granting of the franchise to the negro and withholding it from the yellow man he cannot understand. The seemingly universal repulsion that the white man has for the black, even more than for the yellow, he naïvely ascribes to the fact that they are a little more hideous than the yellow man.

Any new word or phrase of mine was subject to immediate analysis. We were in the throes of a very annoying gas famine, and I flippantly remarked that we were "up against it," meeting of course the usual "What iss that?" I was in a hurry, and dismissed it with a brief definition: "Oh, up against it is when you can't get anything for love or money." Later in the day I found written in a book in beautiful handwriting, "Up against it: when you can not get anything for love or money." My sins of slang had found me out, and I feel a great responsibility now that I may be unconsciously writing a Japanese-English dictionary.

Kanaya deplores the talk of war, and says Japan has all it can do to fill up its depleted treasury and take care of the educational problem without making war; after some years it may be different, but not now. He adds innocently, "The Japanese are late in coming out [sic], and all the other countries have taken everything, but we will be felt."

Kanaya's father is a teacher in Japan, and was one of the first to study the sciences and philosophies of other lands, although he could not read them in the original. He is also a landowner, and rents his land in small farms to other Japanese. It was against his father's wishes that Kanaya came to this country, and so he has never asked his father for financial aid, although there have been times when he has lived on five cents a day. He tells me that he could have secured a very profound education in his own country; it is not because they can not get a good education in their own country, ah, no, not at all, but it is good discipline for their minds and characters to come to this land. Although not expressed, he rather implies that contact with a freer, ruder, and more material people is an excellent thing for the artist, dreamer, and philosopher of his land.

Are there any farming people in the world quite like them? Kanaya tells me that during the rainy season or on feast days the farmers meet at one another's houses and write a poem or paint a picture—not a long poem but a little one, expressing the thought as the picture does, in a few lines. Kanaya calls the people who live in the country "farmers," but this is too heavy a word to my mind to describe these little men who cultivate rice and live in bamboo houses.

At Christmas time we decided we would give Kanaya books, and the various members of the family, moved by the same impulse, bought him books appropriate to his remarkable taste. It was rather a new experience buying your cook Marcus Aurelius, Emerson, and a volume of Lamb's Essays; and, to our dismay, not only had he read these books, but he had them already in his library!

To live for Japan and to die for Japan is the sole ambition of this little brown man. I am very much of the opinion that we are all like the Irish gardener who called a Japanese a Chinaman, which the Japanese resented, and said to Mike, "I see that you do not understand the difference between a material and a spiritual civilization."

# "OLD DOC" HITCHCOCK

## CREATOR of a SYSTEM of PHYSICAL EDUCATION

### BY BURGES JOHNSON

SOME honest old pessimist now and again tells us that a college education is not what it was in his day. In that golden time noses were held to the grindstone and there was no frittering away of opportunity—no such devotion to athletics, nor the carnage of the football field, nor dancing nor drinking nor debt. Our earnest old friend remembers the better part, and perhaps sees something of a rainbow in the mist that obscures his memory. Every generation has its studious sons, and it is doubtless true that in those days before the sixties concentration on a few matters gave a thoroughness of mastery that later student-minds lack. But the happy-go-lucky spirits of that day—the boys who went to college only because they were sent—and the roystering lads and the thoughtless ones—were they given no chance of betterment? The athletic field and the gymnasium as an outlet for exuberance did not exist, nor the training-table with its object-lesson in healthy living. And, good Pessimist, what of those studious ones held to the grindstone till thousands laid the foundation of a lifetime's ill health, weak-eyed, anæmic, hollow-chested?

Things were not so perfect then in the student world, nor so bad now as one will discern if he but adjust the lenses in his glasses; some of our older educators have lived to see and to recognize the two extremes, over-attention to the mind and over-attention to the body; and one of the men who has done most, in his shrewdly wise way, to swing the pendulum toward a common-sense center is Dr. Edward Hitchcock, the central figure of this sketch.

In the year 1859, William A. Stearns, D.D., President of Amherst College, delivered a notable address to his trustees in which the idea was "impressively set forth that without the support of well-developed bodily powers and functions the mental faculties could not reach their full development," from which conclusion he developed the theory that "students should receive discipline in the care of their bodies as well as of their intellects, and that the government of the college should give a proper attention to physical health, as well as to the culture of those powers for which departments were ordinarily created and endowments made." Axiomatic enough, no doubt, in these days, but one must bear in mind that some fifty years of progress in pedagogy have elapsed since that address was delivered.

President Stearns was then in the sixth year of his administration—a man of prominence in the State, and of wide renown as an educator. He had been a resident of Cambridge, and for a number of years a member of the State Board of Education. The presidency of Amherst was a position, perhaps, of greater comparative prominence then, before the distended universities of to-day had outgrown their neighbors. Only thirty-eight years before, Amherst had sprung, Minerva-like, fully armed from the head of Williams College, departing, however, from the classic parallel in that she took the head with her; and the parent was at this time only just recovered from the shock. State universities were few and in their infancy, and the Nation looked almost wholly to New England for theories on education. The pronouncement of President Stearns, therefore, came from a high pulpit and found a wide audience. Doubtless the time was ripe for it—certainly the times needed it. In Amherst there had occurred during the first of the Stearns administration "the sad deaths of two promising young men, the breaking down in health of others just at the end of their college courses, and there existed a general apathy in regard to bodily health"—this in a country college where a beautiful hill-top location and pure air made for physical development. Si . ฆฆ.฿e conditions pre- ฆu among student bo̶d̶i̶e̶s elsewhere.

So the seed fell at a good time upon ready soil. The trustees of the College were impressed. One among their number, Dr. Nathan Allen, of Lowell, in a paper read twenty years ago before the American Academy of Medicine, wrote in reminiscence: "This appeal produced at once a strong impression on the Board of Trustees. The writer having for years made a special study of physiology in its application to education and health, and fully appreciating the importance of good health to students in college, was prepared to second President Stearns's appeal and to enter heartily into the work."

Columbus did not invent the theory of the earth's rotundity—he merely acted upon it; Edward Hitchcock did not invent the idea of physical education, and full credit is due President Stearns and Dr. Allen for the impetus given a great idea, the discovery of which might. upon conscientious research, be thrown back to classic times. However that may be, in 1859 the trustees of Amherst blazed a new path for American colleges by creating a Department of Physical Education and Hygiene. The catalogue of the following year described the innovation as follows:

Its design is to secure healthful daily exercise and recreation to all of the students; to instruct them in the use of the vocal organs, movements of the body, and manners, as connected with oratory; and to teach them, both theoretically and practically, the laws of health. This daily physical training is a part of the regular college course. The professor is an educated physician, and has not only a general oversight of the health of the College, but the students have the privilege of consulting him without charge. While the gymnasium will furnish opportunities for the highest physical training, the required exercises will be such as can be performed without undue effort or risk of injury.

Among the duties of this professorship, as outlined by Dr. Allen and approved by the whole Board, the following are of particular interest:

To have a general oversight of the health of the students, and to give such instruction on the subject as may be deemed expedient, . . . under the direction of the faculty, like all other studies.

To give lectures, from time to time, on hygiene, physical culture, and other topics pertaining to the laws of health, including some general knowledge of anatomy and physiology. . . .

All the students shall be required to attend on its [the gymnasium's] exercises for half an hour, designated for the purpose, at least four days in the week. . . .

While it may not be expedient to mark the gradation of attainment as in the intellectual branches, yet regularity, attention, and docility should be carefully noted, so as to have their proper weight in the deportment column of the student's general position.

The instructor ought to be a member of the faculty, and give in to it his marks and occasional accounts, and receive directions as other officers of the College are accustomed to do.

Here was a broad enough foundation, surely, for the use of the right builder. Dr. J. W. Hooker, of New Haven, a recent graduate of Yale College and Medical School, was the first incumbent of the chair. Ill health forced his resignation but a few months later, and his death soon followed. In the meantime a generous friend of the College supplied funds for the housing of the department, and in 1860 there was built the Barrett Gymnasium, the first building of its kind to be erected in America. Over the door of it were graven these words, spoken by Professor Owen, of the British Museum:

Such are the dominating powers with which we, and we alone, are gifted !

I say gifted, for the surpassing organization was no work of ours.

It is He that hath made us, not we ourselves. This frame is a temporary trust, for the uses of which we are responsible to the Maker.

Oh ! you who possess it in the supple vigor of lusty youth, think well what it is that He has committed to your keeping. Waste not its energies; dull them not by sloth; spoil them not by pleasures ! The supreme work of creation has been accomplished that you might possess a body—the sole erect—of all animal bodies the most free, and for what? for the service of the soul.

Strive to realize the conditions of the possession of this wonderful structure. Think what it may become—the Temple of the Holy Spirit! Defile it not. Seek, rather, to adorn it with all meek and becoming gifts, with that fair furniture, moral and intellectual, which it is our inestimable privilege to acquire through the teachings and examples and ministrations of this Seat of Sound Learning and Religious Education.

To this new department, on which the eyes of the educational world were focused, the trustees called young Dr. Edward Hitchcock. He came as a full professor, with his department uniquely housed in a building of its own; he faced the untried proposition that physical as well as mental training was within the province of the College, and that therefore attention to such training on the part of the student must be reckoned as a part of required work; and that proficiency therein must receive credit toward the earning of a degree. It was necessary for the young doctor to build upon this basis a working system.

Dr. Hitchcock was then thirty-three years old. He was born in Amherst on May 23, 1828, a son of Professor Edward Hitchcock, who afterward became President of the College. He fitted for Amherst at the Amherst Academy and Williston Seminary, and graduated in 1849. Then followed a full course at the Harvard Medical School. Among his college classmates were William J. Rolfe, the Shakespearean scholar, and President Julius H. Seelye.

At the time of this call he had recently left an instructorship at Williston and was studying comparative anatomy in London as a private pupil of Sir Richard Owen, Curator of the British Museum. With the best technical training his day could provide, with a fine physique, with high moral ideals, and with enthusiasm, Dr. Hitchcock became a part of Amherst College.

It is not the purpose of this article to write of that institution save only in so far as it chanced to be the scene of Edward Hitchcock's labors. The small colleges of New England have been and still are a power for good in the world to an extent which no man may measure. It is a common and justifiable claim on the part of these institutions that with them the relation between graduate and Alma Mater is an unusually personal and intimate one. Forty-nine successive classes of Amherst students have "sat under" Dr. Hitchcock—nearly five thousand of his "boys," graduate and non-graduate, of whom forty-one hundred are living to-day in every part of the world. Every one of them he has known by name; more than that, he has known each man's chest expansion, and his "pull-up," and some forty other listed and intimate physical details, and has rejoiced with him over every least showing of gain; but, more than that, through all these years he has believed that he held retainer as personal counsel for every troubled student before the high court of college government. Many cases has he pleaded there, while many seemingly hopeless ones never got to court as a result of a shrewd, searching, kindly talk in that little office in the "gym." Cases of actual want or need he has always felt belonged to his special department. His tact found a way where pride seemed insurmountable; and various foreign lads, from Bulgaria to Japan, who trusted themselves in a confiding way to this great Republic, expecting to gather food and clothing and an education as freely as manna was gathered by the Israelites of old, never had their ideals shattered because of Dr. Hitchcock. Physician of soul as well as of body he has been, yet any measure here of the value of his stated work can never take into full account that other side. Dr. Edward Hitchcock of the college catalogue may be appreciated to some extent; "Old Doc," who heads the faculty list in the hearts of thousands of living, working citizens, is beyond any possible appraisal.

We have wandered too soon in this paper from the "founding of a system of physical education." Dr. Hitchcock saw no paths marked out for him. Common sense was his chief guide. A letter written a few weeks ago by the old Doctor summarizes in his own words much that has already been said:

When a six or eight year old boy, I well remember the oak grove in rear of chapel, in which were a crude walk, a running walk, wide enough for only one man to travel on; three swings of differing height and capacity; a vaulting bar, iron quoits, and a game that we called "loggerheads," which consisted in pitching a club—very much like an Indian club—at a stake. This apparatus was in charge of a society which was kept up by volunteer subscriptions.

The use of this was allowed only out of study hours—eight to nine in the morning, twelve to two at noon, and five to six at night, and after supper till eight o'clock, and woe to the man who was seen there at any other hour, day or night. There was also a rude hut called a bath-house, where we could draw water from the well and put it in a tank over our heads, and get a cold shower-bath.

Perhaps half of the students as they felt disposed made use of these appurtenances in the warm and pleasant weather.

This was about the status of physical education here till President Stearns's day, beginning say 1855 or 6. At this time everything centered in high scholarship and attaining high rank, and students put all their time and energies into book cramming and watching for exhibition and commencement appointments. As a result many of the so-called best men in college failed in health and were obliged to leave college, and two brilliant fellows died, one on Commencement Day, apparently from over study.

This was a starter, with Dr. Stearns, for a Department of Physical Education and Hygiene; and with a committee consisting of Henry Ward Beecher, Dr. Nathan Allen, and Dr. Ebeneeser Alden, the movement got under way and into the old Gym. Dr. Hooker, of New Haven, was appointed the first professor. . . . I went ahead with much of what he had planned, and we made quite a show in gymnastic and military drill. And I added all anthropometric measurements, and more minute care and direction for the individual health of the students, and the study of the biggest, smallest, strongest, and weakest man was entered into eagerly, and has kept up until now. . . . Much of my work has been of the scientific style and not the stuff to make a magazine article of.

In a report to the trustees, after twenty years' experience in the department, Dr. Hitchcock wrote:

One of the first duties I felt called upon to perform after your appointment to this professorship was to prepare blanks for several anthropometric observations of the students of college. This I did partly to enable the students to learn by yearly comparison of themselves how they were getting on as regards the physical man. The ulterior object, however, was to help ascertain what are the data or constants of the typical man, and especially the college man. I have conceived no theory on the subject, and have instituted but very few generalizations; but my desire has been to compile carefully and put on record as many of these observations as pos-

sible for comparison and verification of statistical work in this same direction by many other persons in America and Europe.

In the fall of 1861 I took measurement of all the college students in seven particulars, and have faithfully made these examinations of almost every sound man since connected with the College up to the present date. The measurements are made of the Freshmen soon after entering, and are repeated upon them near the end of each year of the course. Thus every man who goes through college has been observed five times.

The anthropometric tables, of which this was the beginning, have been elaborated and faithfully kept up by the department for nearly half a century, entailing the tabulation of millions of figures, with results of great value to the individual student and to science in general. Again in the same report he says :

There are a few members of your Board who may remember some performances preliminary to the establishment of this branch of the College curriculum about twenty-one years ago, when in Village Church, upon an elevated platform, before a large and interested audience, Dr. Winship exhibited himself as able to lift with his hands and shoulders immense weights. The hardware stores in town were levied upon to loan their casks of nails and spikes, the old iron of the College cellar was brought out, and all to enable Dr. Winship to show how much he could lift. And these feats, remarkable as they surely were, were then considered as indications of health, and held up to the students as the means for the true hygiene of college life. Soon the Gymnasium was equipped with apparatus, not the lightest of which were one-hundred-pound dumb-bells, and apparatus by which a young man could be induced to try and lift a ton; and the dumb-bells for class exercises weighed ten pounds each. But at this time it was the prediction of Dr. Dio Lewis that we soon should adopt the lighter dumb-bells for exercise and discard the immense in muscular effort, which has proved true, for now we use bells that weigh two pounds to the pair, and the original lifting-machines are in the pile of scrap-iron.

The idea of physical culture has too often been that great muscular development is the only essential element in it, and the fact is indeed true that the really well man is muscularly strong. And for valetudinarians, for those who are able to give very much of their time, means, and thought for their own health, who can give a large share of their energy and thought to self-culture and preservation, without doubt the muscular system is the principal one to be attended to. But the problem to be solved by us has been what arrangement of required muscular exercise and recreation combined is the best for our students as a whole. In what way can we best help them to keep body and mind working harmoniously and effectually together? How shall the man physically be made efficient so that the intellectual, moral, and spiritual may at the same time secure its full development?

In order that our students be in the best condition for work it seems demanded that the muscles be not trained to their highest powers. For the most healthful and intellectual men are not those who have the most muscular power. They are often well-developed men, it is true, and of excellent physical inheritance, but they are not *muscle* men.

Physical culture as expressed to Amherst College students by the experience of the past twenty years means something besides, something in addition to, muscular exercise. It includes cleanliness of skin, attention to stomach and bowels, relaxation from daily mental work, freedom from certain kinds of petty discipline, but with so much requirement and restraint as will give coherence, respect, and stability to the methods of maintaining health and the men employing them.

In the above is embodied one of the first important truths discovered in Dr. Hitchcock's laboratory—old Barrett Gym.

In a publication of the Massachusetts State Board of Health in 1879 is this quotation from the Doctor—of surprising interest to his old boys:

While a necessary uniformity and periodicity are maintained, yet the elasticity of young nature is not so curbed that the student must act with the monotony of a machine, or with the absolute precision of the manual of arms, day by day, week by week, and year by year. For not only is this exercise of value to favor the chemical changes which accompany muscular activity; but it is desired, at the same time, to give the mind and spirits opportunity to escape, for the half-hour, from scientific and literary restraints and occupation, and enjoy the liberty of rational animal life; to allow the animal powers and sensibilities a chance for " full play;" to induce the material and social nature to such use and recreation as shall compensate its repression while engaged in the absorbing occupation of close study; or, in short, to compel the intellectual to rest while the material shall work. Hence a much greater latitude of noise, shouting, and freedom is allowed in connection with the exercises than would be expected by a schoolmaster of gymnastics, or a drill-master; and it is allowed as an important element or safety-valve of the system. Professor W. S. Tyler, in speaking of this matter, says: " If I were asked to specify what I consider to be the most marked characteristic and distinctive excellence of the Amherst gymnastics, I should say that it is the union of recreation and amusement with exercise; of the

7

voluntary and spontaneous with the required and the prescribed; in a word, of play with work."

Can it be that those joyous class-mutinies, when order became riot and the gym floor clanged to hurtling dumb-bells, were but part of old Doc's system, and were entered as evidence in staid official reports? " Gentlemen, gentlemen!" his resonant tones would finally ring out, " haven't ye kicked up your hind legs 'bout long enough?"

There were not lacking immediate results to encourage the department. Says a State report;

The statistics of this department show some interesting facts in reference to the duration of sickness among the students of the College. Dr. Edward Jarvis says that the average amount of time lost on account of sickness by each laborer in Europe is from 19 to 20 days each year; and in the Massachusetts Board of Health Report for 1872 it is estimated that, for that year, 13 days' labor was lost by sickness for each productive person in the Commonwealth. The returns of Amherst College sick list for term-time give 2.64 days as an annual average of time lost to every student, and of 11.36 days to each sick student, for 17 years. . . . A decrease in the amount of sickness during the course is an important feature in the health of the College. Taking the number on the sick list in the freshman year as 1,000, the number for the sophomore year is represented by 912; for the junior year by 759; and for the senior year by 575.

This is the reverse of what had occurred among students thirty, forty, and fifty years before, according to an authority of that time, and the reverse of what was to be expected. Moreover, the records were soon showing splendid and unexpected results. Of the first five thousand items of measurement taken, 77 per cent. showed a distinct increase during the college course. These items indicated every possible form of bodily development.

The department was no longer an experiment. It was popular with the students, and elicited everywhere favorable comment. At the end of twenty years over fifty large institutions in the country had either adopted some regular system of physical culture or were making preparations to that end. Said President Eliot, of Harvard: " It is to Amherst College that the colleges of the country are indebted for a demonstration of the proper mode of organizing the department of physical culture."

In 1876 the Japanese Government sent to Amherst her Vice-Minister of Education to study and report upon this matter, and the following year the Emperor requested President Seelye to select and send to Japan a man able to introduce the system to the Government schools; in prompt response Dr. George A. Leland, "class captain" of '74, went over and spent three years at the work, to the great satisfaction of the Japanese.

But Dr. Leland could not carry abroad, nor could institutions at home imitate, "Old Doc's" lectures to freshmen on hygiene. You will have noticed provision for such a course in the outline of the department prepared by the trustees in 1860. From that day to this they have not failed. The same shrewd knowledge of student nature that led the Doctor to encourage an apparent unlicense in the gymnasium gave to these homely, intimate talks a humorous freedom that insured a full roll of attendance. But under the coating of the pill was something that made for moral and physical health—facts for college men ; yet in how many colleges even to-day does the curriculum provide for such general instruction ?

Such has been the life-work of Dr. Edward Hitchcock. The sphere has been so limited in one aspect, and the results are now so much a part of accepted fact, that one might almost question his right to a place among *creative* Americans. But discovery breeds discovery. The study of the various problems having to do with physical education goes forward from a hundred centers that first drew inspiration from the old Barrett Gymnasium. More is yet to come out of Amherst. Compulsory gymnasium work no longer solves the problems of the current day and generation. Democracy of sport is the next achievement sought, as opposed to the super-training of nine or eleven men, and the enforced grand-stand idleness and homage of several hundred fellow-students. Whatever be your attitude toward college athletics, it is worth following to a conclusion, this line of thought that is engaging the attention of the Amherst College government to-day. Thousands of dollars are raised annually by the students in our colleges of their own effort, all working together, and the greater part of it is spent to provide high-priced professional training for a very few, and, what is more, for a selected few who are probably the least in need of physical development. If such skilled training is a good and desirable thing, should not every student have a right to a share in it—or, more, should he not be directed to partake of its benefits ? To-day at Amherst in the fall and spring the new gymnasium never resounds to hurtling clubs and dumb-bells, but instead hundreds of young men are undergoing an enforced daily period of actual athletic training, each man according to his capacity, on Pratt Athletic Field. What this may lead to belongs to some future account of the work of Dr. Paul Phillips, Dr. Hitchcock's young associate; yet it will not be another story, for "Old Doc" is still at the helm, and his spirit of enthusiasm and scientific investigation is being passed down like the mantle of Elijah. The inspiration, not the bondage, of tradition carries the work quietly forward.

"I wish you could see us between the hours of three and six P.M.," writes "Old Doc," in a letter that seems to carry with it the peculiar emphatic earnestness of his tones; and he adds, "We are getting great comfort, joy, and good out of the swimming pool and squash court which Messrs. Pratt and Schiff have given us."

It has been a hard task for one of "Old Doc's" boys to write with restraint and deliberation of the Doctor's contribution to the world of scientific knowledge. Inquiry shows that he has been honored on every side by his fellow-investigators; that the American Association for the Advancement of Physical Education, of which he was a founder, has lately dined in his honor, and passed glowing resolutions; that he is grouped with Sargent, of Harvard, the Crown Prince of Sweden, Angelo Mosso, of Italy, and Professor Schmidt, of Germany, in the honor-list of that society; that the list of his writings comprises eight pages of titles; and that degrees and trusteeships have attached to his name. He has more than earned all of these honors.

But to us who know him the mention of "Old Doc" calls to mind none of these things. We see a wiry, brisk old man, with snow-white hair and beard, who gives us a firm, welcoming hand-clasp and a glance from keen, kindly eyes. Perhaps we last saw him tramping up and down the sidelines at some intercollegiate game, greeting and being greeted. Or, better still, he sat in his office at Commencement time where a stream of graduates came to seek him ; you heard them, man after man, ahead of you—"Guess you don't remember me, Old Doc ; I'm Jones, of 'sixty-blank ; got a boy in college now." "He's a good boy, Jones, a good boy. Better deportment than his father had, but I'm glad to see ye !" An incisive voice for a man whose eightieth birthday occurs next month, a firm mental grasp of affairs for a teacher who has faced forty-nine successive classes. Jones of 'sixty-blank went back to his home in the West well satisfied, though he bore but that one memory of Commencement time.

Of what importance to-day are the contributions to science compared to the mere inspiration of the old man's presence there on College Hill? Such an article as this is for you who have not known him ; but to you who have, one can easily imagine the message he would send, and hear the very tones of his voice : "I love every one of ye—let me hear how you're getting along !"

## THE YEAR'S CHILD

### BY MARY BALDWIN

Spring wandered lightly through a city street
Where many crowded and impatient feet
Jostled and drifted, pressing ever on ;
Until a presence, vague as coming dawn
Or some forgotten, half-hid melody
That shyly lurks beyond the conscious ken,
Spread newness o'er the frayed-out souls of men,
Trailed from afar a sense of unsung song,
And lured to life old faded hopes that long
Had lain inert. Ah, but it seemed to me
A little child, in passing, plucked my sleeve,
Slipped trusting hand in mine, nor asked my leave
To cling with arms that knew their right to cling, —
The sweet, unanswerable right of Spring.

BIBI LALOUETTE

"He was the son of Lalouette; who kept a pension near the Rue Dauphine, at which Whistler, Legros, Fantin, and others used to take their meals in those early days."—Whistler's Etchings, by Frederick Wedmore

# WHISTLER AS AN ETCHER

## BY FREDERICK KEPPEL

### ILLUSTRATED WITH REPRODUCTIONS OF ETCHINGS AND DRY-POINTS BY WHISTLER

IN introducing the subject of Whistler as an etcher I cannot do so better than by citing the opinion of the man whom I believe to be the best living authority on the subject. I mean Joseph Pennell, the American artist and critic, who was the stanch friend of Whistler to the end, and who, in collaboration with his distinguished wife, is now writing a biography of the master which must prove to be the standard for all time to come, although other biographies are also in preparation. "There is no man so fit for the sea as a sailor," and there is no man so competent to write on the etchings of Whistler as is a brother etcher, who not only knows a fine etching when he sees it, but goes beyond the intelligent outsider by also knowing just why, from a technical and constructive point of view, the etching is so signally good. Mr. Pennell's superlatives in writing of Whistler's etchings are not the words of some irresponsible enthusiast, but the words of a recognized critical authority.

Here, then, is a condensed extract of what Mr. Pennell has written in a London magazine on the subject of Whis-

PORTRAIT OF WHISTLER BY PAUL RAJON

THE FORGE. DRY-POINT DONE IN FRANCE, 1861

tler's etchings : " Whistler was the greatest etcher and the most accomplished lithographer who ever lived. All his work is alike perfect. It has only been produced under different circumstances, and is an attempt to render different effects or situations. Therefore the methods vary, but the results are always the same—great. The greatest, the most

admit it. But for those of us of the younger generation it is impossible to understand the compulsion. Because he was so serious, because he was so honest and strong, they (the critics) think he must have been a fraud. He was the most intensely American of Americans. But though Whistler passed almost all his life in England and but a

PART OF A LETTER WRITTEN BY WHISTLER IN 1878
In it he offers his famous Carlyle portrait as security for a loan of one hundred and fifty pounds

perfect, as a whole, that any etcher has ever accomplished." After the death of Whistler in 1903 Mr. Pennell also wrote of him, in the North American Review: " The greatest artist of modern times is dead. These are strong words, and I mean them to be. No one since Velasquez and Rembrandt has had such an effect on the art of the world. He knew he was making great art. He was so sure of it that, even during his lifetime, he compelled an unwilling public to

few years in France, he followed American affairs with the feelings and the emotions of a patriot. No tribute that can be bestowed upon him by the United States will be too great for his glory."

I quote liberally from Mr. Pennell because I heartily concur with his opinions on this subject. Artists are supposed to be, in general, jealous of one another ; but the intimate intercourse of Mr. and Mrs. Pennell with Whistler shows us a beautiful example of absolute

OLD HUNGERFORD BRIDGE, LONDON.  ETCHED ABOUT 1863

"The reflections in the water are exquisite, and in the far distance the buildings down the river are indicated with great subtlety of touch."—The Art of J. McNeill Whistler, by T. R. Way

loyalty to a great man, just because they knew so well how great an artist he was; and although very few people could avoid quarreling with him. With the Pennells "the King could do no wrong," and I remember that when Whistler (as was his habit) arrived an hour or so late for dinner at their house in London, not a word of reproach from hostess or host was ever expressed or implied; although we cannot blame the French servant, Augustine, when, on admitting the honored guest upon such an occasion, she would shake her finger at him and say, "*Ah, Monsieur Veestlaire, vous avez gâtt mon diner, vous savez!*" A dozen of such dinners might have been spoiled without a word or a look of reproach from one or other of the two accomplished art critics who had invited their hero to dine.

I must relate a quaint incident to illustrate this immense admiration of one artist for the work of another.

Having shaken hands with Mr. Pennell on arriving at his house, I said to him: "You have a hand like Whistler's, very delicate and frail, but your hand is bigger than his because you are a much bigger man." To this Mr. Pennell, willfully misunderstanding me, exclaimed: "A *bigger* man than Whistler—oh, I wish to heaven I were!"

The mere list of books or of detached articles on Whistler is already a long one, and more are forthcoming. Even writers who scorned his work during the years when he was producing it have now rushed in to proclaim that he was a great master. This state of things had already begun before his death, and Whistler, who was always an aggressive and valiant fighter, used to say to critics of this sort: "If you now find my works to be masterpieces, why were not these same things masterpieces long years ago when you neglected them totally or when you ridiculed them?"

The serious student of the best original etchings is often confronted with a dangerous obstacle in the form of the deceiving counterfeits which have been fabricated on the masterworks of the art. Rembrandt's etchings were shamefully and shamelessly copied by dishonest anonymous etchers even during

his own lifetime and by later forgers for two centuries, and within the last fifty years some deceiving counterfeits have been made of the etchings of such masters as Méryon, Millet, and Seymour Haden. But no man has ever successfully counterfeited an etching by Whistler—for the good reason that no man could. The master's exquisitely delicate and intensely personal style and touch stand hopelessly above and beyond the reach of the counterfeiter. If such a falsification were attempted, by the etching process, the result would surely remind us of Dickens's description of the wig of Mrs. Sairey Gamp, which was so visibly an imitation of natural human hair "that it could hardly be called false." Yet even with this protection to collectors, based on Whistler's unattainable superiority of style and technique, there is still some danger that passably good imitations of the etchings might be made by some mechanical process founded on photography, although such imitations would be speedily detected by any expert.

James McNeill Whistler was born on the 10th of July, 1834, in Worthen Street, Lowell, Massachusetts, and he died at Chelsea, London, on the 17th of July, 1903. He really was baptized with the name of James Abbot, but he repudiated the latter name and substituted for it the maiden name of his mother. His father, Major George.W. Whistler, was an eminent engineer in the United States army, and it was he who was the real designer and constructor of the first Russian railway, which runs from St. Petersburg to Moscow, although (as so often happens) he was by no means the chief beneficiary from his own work. Major Whistler, having lost his first wife—who left him one daughter, now Lady Seymour Haden—married Miss McNeill, a Southern lady, who was the mother of our artist. At the age of ten young Whistler was living in St. Petersburg with his father and mother, and I must quote an extract from his mother's diary of that time, which shows us how true it is that "the child's the father of the man." She writes: "While visiting the Czar's palace we were allowed, as a special favor, to see some pictures of feathered fowl which were made by Peter the Great. I thought they were beautiful— *but our Jimmie had the impudence to laugh at them.*" ·Poor fellow I he continued to laugh at the productions of other artists all his life long. Later we find Whistler a cadet at West Point. That was about fifty years ago, yet his name is still a potent memory there. His engaging personality and bright wit made him a favorite among his comrades, but he was so refractory and so little amenable to discipline that the authorities had to dismiss him. Long years afterward he gave his own whimsical version of this dismissal : " I would have been a United States' officer to-day except for a difference of opinion between the authorities and myself ; they maintained that silicon was a mineral, while I insisted that it wa's a gas."

While on the tempting subject of Whistler's witticisms, I must relate one of his latest and least known :· During his last visit to Paris he was making a call on a lady of exalted rank, and she said to him, " You are well acquainted with King Edward of England." " Well, no," said Whistler, " not personally." " Why," said the lady, " his Majesty was speaking to me in London recently, and he said he knew you well." " Oh," said Whistler, " that was only his *brag.*"

Whistler's very first etching was, characteristically enough, the cause of storms and tempests ; and then began his life-long habit, which recalls to us the prophecy concerning Ishmael of old, " His hand shall be against every man, and every man's hand against him." After his dismissal from West Point he found employment in the Bureau of Engraving at Washington, where the director instructed him to etch a plate for the United States Coast Survey. He had no chance to make a work of art of this first plate, for it was a slavishly accurate picture of one part of the coast line and was destined for the guidance of mariners. The young Whistler etched this uncongenial subject very accurately, although in a perfunctory and " tight " manner, but he " let himself go " by decorating the sky of Uncle Sam's formal plate with· a series of fantastic little heads which were spun from his own

imagination. The bureaucratic authorities were shocked, the plate was confiscated, and the too imaginative young etcher was cashiered.

At about the age of twenty Whistler drifted to Paris, and it was there that the budding master first " found himself." Paris, indeed, has for long years been the mother and the nurse of artists. Among the French, art in any form is a very serious matter indeed ; while, in comparison, both in England and America art is generally looked on as a trifling, non-essential, outside matter, and one that any educated person may notice or not, as he thinks fit. In this it may be compared to the religion of some of us—a sentimental, idealistic emotion, and one that we may take on if we are in the humor, or lay off if our humor drifts the other way.

The incurable refractory bent which so often caused trouble to Whistler as a man was altogether favorable to his development as an artist. It was simply impossible for his independent nature to shut his eyes and tamely swallow rules and methods which were not of his own making. It was this *intransigeant* spirit, combined with his own inherent genius, that made him the thoroughly original master that he was. He was a master in a double sense— first, through his great pictures, and, secondly, through the dominating influence which these pictures exercised on so many other artists throughout the civilized world. Many of these men would fiercely deny that they were imitating Whistler ; but they *were*, whether they knew it or not. Thus, when a recent exhibition of new etchings was held in London, the Saturday Review, in noticing it, said that these etchings were " mainly penny-Whistlers," and, just because they were more or less gross imitations of the style and method of the master, they were of no more value artistically than a child's penny whistle.

It was in Paris, at the·age of twenty-five and in the year 1859, that Whistler published his first series of etchings—the " French Set," as it is now called. There were thirteen in the set. and the price for it was fifty francs— or ten dollars. Happy were the few

WEARY. A DRY-POINT, DATED 1863

"Of all the portraits, however, that entitled "Weary," a beautiful study of a girl lying back in a chair, every line expressing fatigue, nd the portrait of Florence Le land, with its perfect grace of line and pose, are perhaps the most completely satisfying."—The Art of J. McNeill Whistler, by T. R. Way.

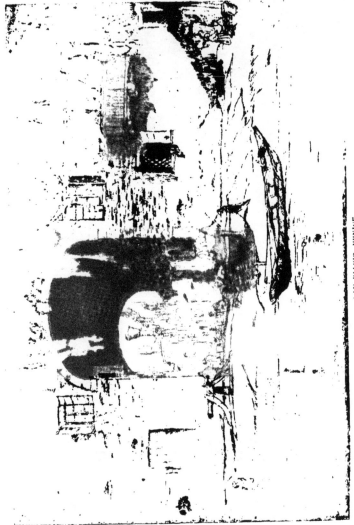

SAN BIAGIO, VENICE

THE ADAM AND EVE TAVERN, OLD CHELSEA. DONE ABOUT 1879

"One of the most interesting, I think, of all his coppers is the Adam and Eve Tavern, in which the earlier manner is being broken away from and his final method is taking its place, both the styles harmonizing perfectly."—Joseph Pennell

enlightened Frenchmen who invested fifty francs in the modest little portfolio of the young and unknown etcher. If they or "their heirs, administrators, and assigns" still possess them, they may have the satisfaction of knowing that they could sell them at nearly a hundred times the price which they originally cost. The "French Set" included some veritable masterpieces—such as the "Kitchen," the "Mustard Woman," the "Vieille aux Loques," and the "Street in Saverne," which last-named print must be about the first of Whistler's magnificent series of night scenes, or nocturnes as he called them. At about the same period he produced the "Rag Shop" and the two charming portraits of French children, "Bibi Lalouette" and "Bibi Valentin."

From Paris Whistler went to London and made his home with Sir Seymour Haden, who was then an eminent surgeon, but who afterward attained to much wider fame as an etcher of landscapes. It was while he was living there with his half-sister and—shall we say, his *half*-brother-in-law, that Whistler etched most of the magnificent plates which are known as the "Thames Set." It consisted of sixteen etchings, and although he did very beautiful things in later years, my own conviction is that the Thames Set includes several of his supreme achievements. This opinion is fortified by that of Mr. Pennell. In writing of one of them, the "Black Lion Wharf," he calls it "one of the greatest engraved plates that has been produced in modern times," and he adds, "I would even say that it is the greatest etching of modern times were it not for the fact that it is but one of a set." Mr. Pennell goes on to commend other prints of the series, such as the "Forge" and the "Lime-burner," and he adds, "This series alone is enough to win immortality for any man."

Mere verbal description of a picture cannot be otherwise than unsatisfying, but, fortunately for Americans in general and for New Yorkers in particular, probably the very best collection of Whistler's etchings which exists is on free exhibition to every one in New York. It can be visited at the Lenox Library, where

the very competent curator, Mr. Frank Weitenkampf, will show to visitors the magnificent collection which was formed by the late Samuel P. Avery and donated by him to the Public Library. No amount of money could duplicate it to-day; this could be done only in one way, and that is the way by which Napoleon Bonaparte enriched the gallery of the Louvre. He first conquered nearly all of the nations of Europe (England excepted), and he then carried off their finest art treasures to Paris. But this high-handed operation can never be repeated, and Mr. Avery was a man of peace; he made his living by buying and selling paintings, but whenever he bought a picture for himself it was pretty sure to be a simple etching in black and white and not a painting in oil colors. He already knew Whistler when the latter was a merry, harum-scarum young fellow in Paris, who took little care of the masterpieces he was producing. In those early and happy-go-lucky years Whistler would etch some great plate, and, not having the money to pay for the printing of a sufficient edition of proofs from it, he would pay for perhaps half a dozen. Then the etched copper would drift into the mysterious limbo whither all lost things disappear and whence they never return, or else—as plates of copper cost money—Whistler would have the surface of the plate planed off and use the old copper for a new etching. It was in these early years that Mr. Avery got possession of such rarities as the dry-point portraits of Riault the wood-engraver, and of "Joe," the latter a beautiful portrait of a young girl. These two prints are now absolutely unprocurable, as is many another of which the noble-hearted Samuel P. Avery has made a free gift for the use of his fellow-citizens in New York and for the whole Nation.

When, in 1886, the distinguished London art critic and enthusiastic collector, Mr. Frederick Wedmore, undertook the making of a descriptive catalogue of Whistler's etchings, his first move was to call on the master himself. Whistler approved of the project, but said, in effect: "I can show you very little, but if you really wish to make

THE DOORWAY, VENICE

" Much richer in effect and with more elaboration of detail than is usual in this series is ' The Doorway.' A beautiful view of what has once been a palace. . . . The fine architecture of the exterior, with the rich drapery of the windows, is very beautifully indicated, and the water in the foreground is wonderfully transparent."—The Art of J. McNeill Whistler, by T. R. Way

such a book you must first of all cross the Atlantic Ocean, go to New York, seek out Mr. Avery, and he can let you examine the material for your catalogue." All of this was done, and in the introduction to his book Mr. Wedmore (who was working in London and writing for Englishmen) quaintly writes—without mentioning America or New York at all—" Mr. Avery, when Mr. Keppel took me to see him in East Thirty-eighth Street, put at my disposal everything he knew."

After twenty years of useful service Mr. Wedmore's book is likely to be partly superseded by the exhaustive catalogue which is now in preparation by some enthusiastic gentlemen of New York. They are leaving no stone unturned in the course of their researches, and the result must be a book of great value.

Most of the plates of the Thames Set were etched in the year 1859, but—" O fools and blind !"—no publisher would touch them until twelve years later, in the year 1871. All this is only a modern repetition of the action of the ancient people, who first persecuted and stoned their prophets and afterwards built sepulchers in their honor.

The copper plates of the sixteen Thames etchings were destroyed years ago, so that no more proofs from them can ever be printed; but how these beautiful things could have remained neglected for twelve years is still an unaccountable thing.

Besides the two sets of etchings already mentioned other sets were to follow, but in addition to these Whistler continued to produce detached etchings of high artistic value. About the year 1870 his method underwent a radical change. He temporarily discarded etching proper—where the lines of the plate are corroded or " bitten " with an acid—and took up dry-point, a process in which the copper plate is worked upon direct and without any " biting." Whistler's dry-points are characterized by extreme delicacy and refinement. Of necessity they are very rare, because a plate thus prepared wears out very quickly in the printing. In the case of some very delicately cut dry-points not more than half a dozen fine proofs can be obtained. Whistler was equally

master of the dry-point method whether he was making portraits such as those of the Leyland family or depicting some fascinating and elusive view of the Thames at London, the river that he loved so faithfully.

One of his Thames views deserves special mention because it was, in style, the precursor of the two magnificent " Venice Sets " which were to follow. I mean the " Adam and Eve Tavern, Old Chelsea." It was etched, not dry-pointed, and was wrought in a manner then new to him, but which he afterward continued to practice to the end of his life. In the " Adam and Eve " the innovation is the short and broken character of the lines. In it, as well as in the succeeding Venice etchings, the result is an effect of the most charming vivacity and freshness. Whistler hated dullness in every form. The man, the artist, the writer, was never dull. Whistler *couldn't* be ! After the Venice etchings came views in Holland and in France, as well as a series of little plates depicting war-ships on the occasion of Queen Victoria's jubilee. These latest plates of his are still almost unknown to the public. For many years before his death he printed his own proofs because no outside printer could satisfy him, and after he died his heiress and her advisers decided that never again should a proof from any plate of his be printed by another hand. I think that this was a most pious and wise decision, made to do honor to the memory of the fastidious and exquisite artist.

It is a comfort to know that the greater part of Whistler's works are owned in America, and in America we have the most serious and most accomplished students of the master. I must here relate an extraordinary illustration of this : Mr. Charles L. Freer, of Detroit, whose precious collection of Whistler's works will be given to the Nation, was examining, at his home, some unfinished trial proofs of Whistler's lithographs. In Mr. Freer's company was an accomplished professional artist. Mr. Freer pointed out to him what he thought to be a slightly false line in one of the prints. " Pooh !" said the artist, " Whistler will never trouble himself to correct a trifle like that." " But I am *sure*,"

NOCTURNE PALACES, VENICE

said Mr. Freer, "that Whistler will never allow that line to remain as it now is." When the lithograph was definitely published, the defective line had been corrected by the master, although he had heard not a word about the matter.

It may be an audacious thing for me to venture to say, but I think Whistler made a mistake when, late in life, he adopted the system of cutting off every shred of margin from his proofs—except a little tab which he left in one spot below and which bore his mystical signature in the form of a sort of butterfly. This leaves the composition itself unprotected from any little accidental abrasion of the edges, and the sight of the etching when the margins are all cut away has the same unpleasant effect on me as has the sight of the finger-tips of a person who has the little vice of biting his nails. However, Whistler's taste was very apt to be most refined and correct. His "Propositions," on the small dimensions to which an etching should be limited, are here reprinted from his famous book, "The Gentle Art of Making Enemies;" and I agree with it all except his pronouncement that the four blank margins of the print should be mercilessly cut away.

### PROPOSITIONS BY MR. WHISTLER

I. That in Art it is criminal to go beyond the means used in its exercise.

II. That the space to be covered should always be in proper relation to the means used for covering it.

III. That in etching, the means used, or the instrument employed, being the finest possible point, the space to be covered should be small in proportion.

IV. That all attempts to overstep the limits insisted upon by such proportions are inartistic thoroughly, and tend to reveal the paucity of the means used, instead of concealing the same, as required by Art in its refinement.

V. That the huge plate, therefore, is an offense—its undertaking an unbecoming display of determination and ignorance—its accomplishment a triumph of unthinking earnestness and uncontrollable energy—endowments of the "duffer."

VI. That the custom of "Remarque" emanates from the amateur, and reflects his foolish facility beyond the border of his picture, thus testifying to his unscientific sense of its dignity.

VII. That it is odious.

VIII. That, indeed, there should be no margin on the proof to receive such "Remarque."

IX. That the habit of margin, again, dates from the outsider, and continues with the collector in his unreasoning connoisseurship—taking curious pleasure in the quantity of paper.

X. That, the picture ending where the frame begins, and in the case of etching the white mount being inevitably, because of its color, the frame, the picture thus extends itself irrelevantly through the margin to the mount.

XI. That wit of this kind would leave six inches of raw canvas between the painting and its gold frame, to delight the purchaser with the quality of the cloth.

Of the illustrations which accompany this article the earliest in order of chronology is "The Forge," a plate done in France in the year 1861, although it was included in the Thames Set. Mr. Wedmore calls the Forge "an audacious dry-point," and Mr. Pennell calls it "a dry-point, excessively rare." The "Old Hungerford Bridge," though not dated, was done about the year 1862. It looks like a very simple little picture, but no man save Whistler could have depicted the scene so truly. The "Weary" is dated 1863. For extreme delicacy Whistler himself never surpassed it. This dry point is now very scarce. The three Venetian illustrations, "The Doorway," "San Biagio," and the "Nocturne Palaces," date from about the year 1880. Rajon's excellent portrait of Whistler represents him at about the age of fifty. Finally, the letter written by Whistler shows us that even a man of genius may be (the slang phrase is the most expressive) *hard up.* On that occasion the artist sought to obtain the loan of a trifling sum of money, and offered as security his great painted portrait of Thomas Carlyle, the picture which is now the pride of the city of Glasgow.

Knowing, as I do, that The Outlook is widely read by "all sorts and conditions of men" (except the bad ones!), the present article will be read by many people who have not yet acquainted themselves with the technical methods of the etcher—what to expect from the process and what not to expect. To all such readers I would say that they can find a detailed description of the etching process, and of the other processes used by engravers, in The Outlook for November 24, 1906, where, in an article on Sir Seymour Haden (pages 762–763) I have endeavored to explain these technicalities.

It was greatly his own fault that for long years Whistler did not win the recognition which was his due. He loved to paint, he loved to etch, he loved to joke, and sometimes to joke very wickedly, but, above all, he loved to quarrel. This very costly pastime of his wrought its inevitable consequences; many well-meaning and influential people who would gladly have been his friends were driven into the ranks of his enemies, and even so peaceable a person as the present writer has been forced into more than one battle royal with him. But now that he has gone to the Silent Land—whither we must all follow him—these frailties of his are already fading from our memories, while " the immortal part of him "grows greater and brighter; and it will continue so to grow unless some still greater artist shall arise to push him from his pedestal. And even if such an unlikely thing should ever happen, still there never can be another Whistler.

# AT TWILIGHT—MY SON AND I
### BY KARL JUNKER

The autumn twilight wraps us round,
   And shadows stretch across the room;
Old heart and youthful life are bound
   Together in the silent gloom.
Your parted lips I cannot see,
   But on my hand your kisses fall
Like soft white flowers of Tuscany
   Dropped on some hoary Roman wall.
We speak of deep and peaceful things;
   With earth-wide sweep, our thought explores
The deeds of old forgotten kings,
   The world of men, its creeds and laws.
Whenever in the passing day
   My spirit's powers have highly dreamed,
Each evening at your feet I lay
   Such blossoms as my thought has gleaned.
You listen, and I scarcely care
   Whether you grasp the whole of it;
The touch of lips and wavy hair
   Pleases me more than scholar's wit.
You give me love; I teach you lore;
   To each a gift, for each a joy;
And stronger, closer than before
   Is knit the bond 'twixt man and boy.

LIEUTENANT-COLONEL GEORGE W. GOETHALS
Chairman and Chief Engineer of the Canal Commission

# THE NEW CANAL COMMISSION

## BY HENRY S. BROWN

IN making his latest reorganization of the Panama Canal Commission, President Roosevelt has taken two important steps as to personnel and one as to policy. He has generally selected for the work young and robust men, who might be expected to withstand the strain incident to anxiety and climate, and live to see the project completed; he has guarded against the interruption of the work through the sudden and unexpected withdrawal of the engineering head; and he has turned the execution largely over to the engineering corps of the United States Army, reversing the course he had hitherto followed of giving the important management to civilians.

One of the reasons given by John F. Stevens, the brilliant Western mountain-railway builder, for desiring to be relieved of the position of chief engineer was the fear that he might not be able to continue at the work until its completion, on account of failing health. Mr. Stevens is nearly fifty-four years old, and less than two years on the Isthmus had served to shake his own superb self-confidence that had already been ample to cope with some of the most difficult and strenuous work of conquering mountains on the Rocky division of the Great Northern Railroad. Added to this was the feeling on the part of Mr. Stevens that he could earn more than double his salary following his profession in the States. The retirement from his post as Chief Engineer of John F. Wallace, who had preceded Mr. Stevens, had

MAJOR WILLIAM L. SIBERT

given the canal project a backset, and, in view of the fact that on two occasions the men on whom the Government depended for the completion of the work had decided to sever their connection and there was no alternative but to let them go, President Roosevelt decided that there must be some other arrangement, which would give him younger men and at the same time insure the Government against being without a Chief Engineer to carry on the work.

Thus it was that the happy expedient was hit upon not only of drafting for the work an army engineer in the prime of life and with ripe experience to his credit, but of giving him two assistants or associates from the engineer corps. This of course carried with it the plan of placing the work under the supervision of that branch of the service which has had as glorious a record in war and peace as any arm of the United States forces. For the army engineers stand without reproach after more than a century of service. Whether it be building a pontoon bridge across the Rappahannock at Fredericksburg under fire, building great fortifications on the coast, relieving sudden distress from floods, or turning a turbulent river into a navigable stream for a thousand miles, the engineers have acquitted themselves with credit and honor. The engineers have had the expenditure actually of billions of dollars, and few of these dollars have gone astray. Only at rare intervals has an officer of the corps gone wrong, and

PHOTOGRAPH BY HARRIS-EWING

MAJOR DAVID GAILLARD

Lieutenant-Colonel Goethals, the new head of the Commission, has had very extensive experience in harbor and canal work. He will have had fifteen years of active service before he reaches the retirement age of sixty-four. Indeed, Lieutenant-Colonel Goethals for the last three or four years has made a very careful and complete study of the Panama project. As a member of the General Staff of the army he sat almost constantly at the elbow of Secretary Taft when important questions came up on which the Secretary would have to pass. Unlike the Secretary, Lieutenant-Colonel Goethals has been consistently a lock canal man. He believed that was the best type, and he stuck out for that when the board of foreign and American experts declared in favor of the sea-level type. He therefore takes with him to the Isthmus a mind thoroughly saturated with the project, and familiarity with handling large enterprises. Lieutenant-Colonel Goethals's most important work has been in connection with the fortifications, harbor improvements, etc., around Newport, Narragansett Bay, and Long Island Sound. While in charge of these works he built all the defenses on the

then it has been his associates who have exposed him and seen justice meted out.

It is really, comparatively speaking, a young man's Commission. The active engineers are all less than fifty years of age. Lieutenant-Colonel George W. Goethals, the Chairman of the Commission, is forty-nine years of age; Major David Du B. Gaillard is forty-eight, and Major William L. Sibert is forty-seven. Harry Harwood Rousseau, Civil Engineer of the United States Navy, who is appointed to the Commission in the place of Rear-Admiral Endicott, retired, is but thirty-six years of age. Of the other important members of the Commission, Colonel William C. Gorgas is fifty-three years of age, and has been on the Isthmus almost continuously since the property of the Panama Canal Company was transferred to the United States. Joseph Clay Stiles Blackburn, of Kentucky, who has been appointed not for the purpose of attending to work at Panama so much as for expounding President Roosevelt's policies before Congress, is sixty-nine years of age; and Jackson Smith, the Commissioner who is charged with supplying the labor on the Canal, is comparatively a young man.

PHOTOGRAPH BY CLINEDINST

COLONEL WILLIAM C. GORGAS

MR. JACKSON SMITH

southeast coast of Massachusetts and Rhode Island, improved the harbors of Hyannis, Nantucket, New Bedford, Vineyard Haven, Fall River, Newport, Block Island, Great Salt Pond Harbor, Point Judith, Woods Hole Channel. He also had charge of the construction of the Shelter Harbor at Point Judith, Rhode Island.

Another very important task which Lieutenant-Colonel Goethals carried to success was the improvement of the Tennessee River below Chattanooga. At a place known as the " Suck," which began thirteen miles below Chattanooga and extended down the stream nine miles, the river formed a series of rapids separated by pools formed by bars of gravel and boulders. The work consisted in removing the obstructions, building a canal fourteen and one-half miles long, seventy to one hundred feet wide, and six feet deep, with a series of nine locks sixty by three hundred feet, and an aqueduct nine hundred feet long and sixty feet wide.

Lieutenant-Colonel Goethals is an engineer of great originality and imagination, and he also possesses to a great degree patience and equal temperament and capacity for hard work. It is freely

predicted for him that he will make the entire canal force on the Isthmus follow his leadership loyally, because he has singular facility for getting out the very best of the men who are employed under him.

Major Gaillard is an expert in wave action and in concrete construction. This will make him especially valuable at Panama, because knowledge of such things is needed. Major Gaillard conducted an elaborate system of experiments at Duluth, where he was in charge of the construction of great piers by the Government. This officer saw actual engineering work as assistant to Colonel Black, who was in charge of the river and harbor improvements in Florida. He was later appointed one of the United States Commissioners on the Mexican Boundary Survey. He had service at Fortress Monroe, and later was placed in charge of the aqueduct work at Washington, D C., and was a member of the board of officers which decided upon the completion of the Washington tunnel. He saw active service during the Spanish War as Colonel of the Third Volunteer Engineers. He has for several years been a member of the Army General

EX-SENATOR J. C. S. BLACKBURN

Staff, and has recently been stationed in Cuba as assistant to the chief of staff of the United States forces there.

Major Sibert has been almost exclusively employed on engineering construction since he completed a special course in engineering at the school at Willet's Point, following his graduation at West Point. He has for several years had complete charge of the improvements on the rivers around Pittsburg. He is a specialist in the construction of locks and dams, and, like his two associates, brings special qualifications to the work.

One incident which occurred a few months ago will show the methods under which Major Sibert is likely to act if an unexpected emergency should arise. A heavy freshet caused by rainfall and melting snow swept down the Alleghany last winter. The river is in Major Sibert's field of operations. A government dam at Springdale encountered the water, and the river threatened to overflow the one-million-dollar glass plant and cause its destruction. Without a moment's hesitation and without for a moment considering appealing to Washington, owing to the precious time that would be lost, Major Sibert blew up an $80,000 dam and saved the glass plant. His course was approved heartily by his superior.

Civil Engineer Rousseau, the youngest man on the Commission, is an engineering product of the Rensselaer Polytechnic Institute. which has produced many famous engineers. It is a high compliment to Mr. Rousseau that he should be placed in the responsible position of the Bureau of Yards and Docks of the United States Navy, with the rank and pay of a rear-admiral, and also be the fourth man on the Commission, with a salary of $14,000 a year. Mr. Rousseau has lately been on service at the Mare Island Navy-Yard, where his work of applying the jetty principle by means of timber bulkheads for clearing and keeping open the channel to Mare Island Straits has been commended.

The appointment of ex-Senator J. S. C. Blackburn to the Commission came as a surprise. Mr. Blackburn has been a Kentucky politician of the old school, and seems to have attracted President Roosevelt's gratitude for the rather sensational move he made toward the determination, in the last session of Congress, of the Brownsville matter. It had been determined by the Republican managers that they would not make any concessions to President Roosevelt in ordering the investigation. Senator Blackburn introduced a resolution which declared that this investigation was not designed to inquire into the legality of the President's acts in dismissing the battalion of colored troops. This forced the Republicans into agreeing to a new resolution which went even further than Mr. Blackburn's, because it added that the Senate in making this investigation would question neither the legality nor the justice of the President's acts. Mr. Blackburn was appointed Panama Canal Commissioner without his knowledge. He retired to private life on March 4, and while he knows practically nothing about engineering, he will be a considerable aid to the President in using his influence with Southern members in Congress. Mr. Blackburn is a fluent speaker, a dashing campaigner, and for many years he has been a total abstainer, although hailing from the land of toddy. Mr. Blackburn for twenty-eight years served the people of the Blue Grass State in Washington—ten years in the House and eighteen years in the Senate. When he retired from the Senate, he was the leader of the Democratic party in that chamber.

Colonel Gorgas and Mr. Smith, who have been made full-fledged Commissioners, have for several years been actively connected with the Canal enterprise, Colonel Gorgas in perfecting the sanitation of the canal zone, and Mr. Smith in supplying the labor needed for the construction of the Canal.

ROBERT LOUIS STEVENSON
From the bas-relief by Augustus Saint-Gaudens

# WILL O' THE MILL

## BY ROBERT LOUIS STEVENSON

### WITH AN INTRODUCTION BY HAMILTON W. MABIE

IT is easy to imagine the whimsical enjoyment, half wistful, half humorous, which Stevenson would get out of the endeavors of his friends and critics to set him in his place among English writers. Is he one of the immortals, or will he join, in the end, the group of those variously gifted men who climbed well up the slope of Olympus, but failed to reach the summit? It is always difficult and, for the most part, idle to attempt to pass final judgment on an artist who has dealt with the vital stuff of our own age and used the language of our own brief hour. In the case of Stevenson there is added the complication of a vivid personality and a career so full of vitality, courage, and a certain chivalry of spirit that no critic with a soul can utterly disregard it ; and critics without souls are like judges who know all the points of procedure, but have no grasp of the principles of law and no insight into its equities. Stevenson faced death so long and with such a fine scorn that, like Lanier, his splendid audacity is as much a part of him as his genius.

That he had a touch of genius is beyond question; whether its energy was great enough to vitalize his work against the insidious erosion of time and change is uncertain, and he was so cunning an artificer that one sometimes suspects him of concealing the absence of an imperative impulse to create by the immense and delicate adroitness which was part of his equipment. No man—not even Flaubert or de Maupassant—studied the art of writing with more eager and tireless zeal. He practiced a great profession, but he knew every device of the trade as well. One feels at times as if his invention eclipsed his originality. He could secure large effects, but he was also master of all the tricks of the craft; and he must have been sorely tempted at times to try them on the unsophisticated. It has been said recently by an acute critic of the age that the twentieth will never understand the nineteenth century, because the nineteenth century took itself seriously. Stevenson had a strain of heroism in his nature, and he was a tireless worker, but it is doubtful if he always took himself seriously; he was an artist to his finger-tips, but he was not always in dead earnest. In his most characteristic and individual work he was not quite serious. If "Treasure Island" is to be counted his most graphic piece of narrative and "Kidnapped" his most thoroughly constructed and spirited romance, "Prince Otto" and "Providence and the Guitar" must be regarded as the most Stevensonian, so to speak, of the works of his hand. In these fascinating tales his talent comes close to genius, and falls short only because these stories do not strike root deep in the soil of life, but, like the reputed miracles of Hindu jugglers, take shape by the touch of a magical skill. One would not change them nor have them other than they are; but in their rococo charm, their gay escape from the dull world of reality, their beguiling detachment, they register not only exquisite accomplishment, but definite limitation. One cannot re-read them without recalling that expressive phrase about the attitude of the artist toward the world which brought such a storm of criticism on Stevenson years ago.

In one of his ingenious and unconventional chapters on the art of writing this significant passage appears: "The conjurer juggles with two oranges, and our pleasure in beholding him springs from this, that neither is for an instant overlooked or sacrificed. So with the writer. His pattern, which is to please the supersensual ear, is yet addressed, throughout and first of all, to the demands of logic. Whatever be the obscurities, whatever the intricacies, of the argument, the neatness of the fabric must not suffer, or the artist has been proved unequal to his design. And, on the other hand, no form of words must be selected, no knot must be tied among the phrases, unless knot and word be precisely what is wanted to forward and illuminate the argument; for to fail in this is to swindle in the game." Stevenson always played the game according to the rules; but one wishes at times that he had forgotten the game altogether. A great many very dull or pretentious people take themselves seriously, and when one thinks of Mr. Hall Caine and Miss Corelli, one rejoices that Stevenson laid so light a hand on his themes. In spite of the unholy alliance between seriousness and dullness, however, it remains true that art is fundamentally serious and that its masters, however they may delight in the magic of it, are at heart in earnest. The impression that Stevenson sometimes amuses himself and diverts us by keeping two oranges in the air at the same time is due in some measure to his self-consciousness ; the ultimate freshness of the inimitable and the unconscious comes only in whiffs from his work. The artist must always carry a little mirror in his hand—to borrow the favorite phrase of an eminent Dutch actor of the day ; but the audience must never get a chance reflection from it.

No sooner does one ask these questions about Stevenson and entertain these doubts than he dismisses them as he recalls the eager spirit, the vivid temperament, the superb courage, the unique talent, the steadfast and unappeasable artistic conscience of the author of " Will o' the Mill."

H. W. M.

### THE PLAIN AND THE STARS

THE Mill where Will lived with his adopted parents stood in a falling valley between pine woods and great mountains. Above, hill after hill soared upwards until they soared out of the depth of the hardiest timber, and stood naked against the sky. Some way up, a long gray village lay like a seam or a rag of vapor on a wooded hillside ; and when the wind was favorable, the sound of the church bells would drop down, thin and silvery, to Will. Below, the valley grew ever steeper and steeper, and at the same time widened out on either hand ; and from an eminence beside the mill it was possible to see its whole length and away beyond it over a wide plain, where the river turned and shone, and moved on from city to city on its voyage towards the sea. It chanced that over this valley there lay a pass into a neighboring kingdom, so that, quiet and rural as it was, the road that ran along beside the river was a high thoroughfare between two splendid and powerful societies. All through the summer, traveling-carriages came crawling up, or went plunging briskly downwards past the mill, and as it happened that the other side was very much easier of ascent, the path was not much frequented, except by people going in one direction ; and of all the carriages that Will saw go by, five-sixths were plunging briskly downwards and only one-sixth crawling up. Much more was this the case with foot-passengers. All the light-footed tourists, all the peddlers laden with strange wares, were tending downward like the river that accompanied their path. Nor was this all ; for when

Will was yet a child a disastrous war arose over a great part of the world. The newspapers were full of defeats and victories, the earth rang with cavalry hoofs, and often for days together and for miles around the coil of battle terrified good people from their labors in the fields. Of all this, nothing was heard for a long time in the valley ; but at last one of the commanders pushed an army over the pass by forced marches, and for three days horse and foot, cannon and tumbril, drum and standard, kept pouring downward past the mill. All day the child stood and watched them on their passage—the rhythmical stride, the pale, unshaven faces tanned about the eyes, the discolored regimentals and the tattered flags, filled him with a sense of weariness, pity, and wonder ; and all night, long after he was in bed, he could hear the cannon pounding and the feet trampling, and the great armament sweeping onward and downward past the mill. No one in the valley ever heard the fate of the expedition, for they lay out of the way of gossip in those troublous times ; but Will saw one thing plainly—that not a man returned. Whither had they all gone ? Whither went all the tourists and peddlers with strange wares ? whither all the brisk barouches with servants in the dicky ? whither the water of the stream, ever coursing downward and ever renewed from above ? Even the wind blew oftener down the valley, and carried the dead leaves along with it in the fall. It seemed like a great conspiracy of things animate and inanimate ; they all went downward, fleetly and gayly downward, and only he, it seemed, remained behind, like a stock upon the wayside. It sometimes made him glad when he noticed how the fishes kept their heads up stream. They, at least, stood faithfully by him while all else were posting downward to the unknown world.

One evening he asked the miller where the river went.

"It goes down the valley," answered he, "and turns a power of mills—six-score mills, they say from here to Unterdeck—and it none the wearier after all. And then it goes out into the lowlands, and waters the great corn country, and runs through a sight of fine cities (so they say) where kings live all alone in great palaces, with a sentry walking up and down before the door. And it goes under bridges with stone men upon them, looking down and smiling so curious at the water, and living folks leaning their elbows on the wall and looking over too. And then it goes on and on, and down through marshes and sands, until at last it falls into the sea, where the ships are that bring parrots and tobacco from the Indies. Ay, it has a long trot before it as it goes singing over our weir, bless its heart!"

"And what is the sea?" asked Will.

"The sea!" cried the miller. "Lord help us all, it is the greatest thing God made! That is where all the water in the world runs down into a great salt lake. There it lies, as flat as my hand and as innocent-like as a child; but they do say when the wind blows it gets up into water-mountains bigger than any of ours, and swallows down great ships bigger than our mill, and makes such a roaring that you can hear it miles away upon the land. There are great fish in it five times bigger than a bull, and one old serpent as long as our river and as old as all the world, with whiskers like a man, and a crown of silver on her head."

Will thought he had never heard anything like this, and he kept on asking question after question about the world that lay away down the river, with all its perils and marvels, until the old miller became quite interested himself, and at last took him by the hand and led him to the hill-top that overlooks the valley and the plain. The sun was near setting, and hung low down in a cloudless sky. Everything was defined and glorified in golden light. Will had never seen so great an expanse of country in his life; he stood and gazed with all his eyes. He could see the cities, and the woods and fields, and the bright curves of the river, and far away to where the rim of the plain trenched along the shining heavens. An overmastering emotion seized upon the boy, soul and body; his heart beat so thickly that he could not breathe; the scene swam before his eyes; the sun seemed to wheel round and round, and throw off, as it turned, strange shapes which disappeared with the rapidity of thought, and were succeeded by others. Will covered his face with his hands and burst into a violent fit of tears; and the poor miller, sadly disappointed and perplexed, saw nothing better for it than to take him up in his arms and carry him home in silence.

From that day forward Will was full of new hopes and longings. Something kept tugging at his heartstrings; the running water carried his desires along with it as he dreamed over its fleeting surface; the wind, as it ran over innumerable tree-tops, hailed him with encouraging words; branches beckoned downward; the open road, as it shouldered round the angles and went turning and vanishing faster and faster down the valley, tortured him with its solicitations. He spent long whiles on the eminence, looking down the river-shed and abroad on the flat lowlands, and watched the clouds that traveled forth upon the sluggish wind and trailed their purple shadows on the plain; or he would linger by the wayside, and follow the carriages with his eyes as they rattled downward by the river. It did not matter what it was; everything that went that way, were it cloud or carriage, bird or brown water in the stream, he felt his heart flow out after it in an ecstasy of longing.

We are told by men of science that all the ventures of mariners on the sea, all that countermarching of tribes and races that confounds old history with its dust and rumor, sprang from nothing more abstruse than the laws of supply and demand, and a certain natural instinct for cheap rations. To any one thinking deeply this will seem a dull and pitiful explanation. The tribes that came swarm ing out of the North and East, if they were indeed pressed onward from behind by others were drawn at the same time by the magnetic influence of the South and West. The fame of other lands had reached them ; the name of the eternal city rang in their ears ; they were not colonists, but pilgrims ; they traveled towards wine and gold and sunshine, but their hearts were set on something higher. That divine unrest, that old stinging trouble of humanity that makes all high achievements and all miserable failure, the same that spread wings with Icarus, the same that sent Columbus into the desolate Atlantic, inspired and supported these barbarians on their perilous march. There is one legend which profoundly represents their spirit, of how a flying party of these wanderers encountered a very old man shod with iron. The old man asked them whither they were going ; and they answered with one voice, "To the Eternal City !" He looked upon them gravely ; " I have sought it," he said, " over the most part of the world. Three such pairs as I now carry on my feet have I worn out upon this pilgrimage, and now the fourth is growing slender underneath my steps. And all this while I have not found the city." And he turned and went his own way alone, leaving them astonished.

And yet this would scarcely parallel the intensity of Will's feeling for the plain. If he could only go far enough out there, he felt as if his eyesight would be purged and clarified, as if his hearing would grow more delicate, and his very breath would come and go with luxury. He was transplanted and withering where he was ; he lay in a strange country and was sick for home. Bit by bit, he pieced together broken notions of the world below : of the river, ever moving and growing until it sailed forth into the majestic ocean ; of the cities full of brisk and beautiful people, playing fountains, bands of music and marble palaces, and lighted up at night from end to end with artificial stars of gold ; of the great churches, wise universities, brave armies, and untold money lying stored in vaults ; of the high-flying vice that moved in the sunshine, and the stealth and swiftness

of midnight murder. I have said he was sick as if for home : the figure halts. He was like some one lying in twilit, formless pre-existence, and stretching out his hands lovingly towards many-colored, many-sounding life. It was no wonder he was unhappy—he would go and tell the fish : they were made for their life, and wished for no more than worms and running water, and a hole below a falling bank ; but he was differently designed, full of desires and aspirations, itching at the fingers, lusting with the eyes, whom the whole variegated world could not satisfy with aspects. The true life, the true bright sunshine, lay far out upon the plain. And O ! to see this sunlight once before he died, to move with a jocund spirit in a golden land ! to hear the trained singers and sweet church bells, and see the holiday gardens ! " And O fish !" he would cry, " if you would only turn your noses down stream. you could swim so easily into the fabled waters and see the vast ships passing over your head like clouds, and hear the great water hills making music over you all day long !" But the fish kept looking patiently in their own direction, until Will hardly knew whether to laugh or cry.

Hitherto the traffic on the road had passed by Will like something seen in a picture : he had perhaps exchanged salutations with a tourist, or caught sight of an old gentleman in a traveling cap at a carriage window ; but for the most part it had been a mere symbol, which he contemplated from apart and with something of a superstitious feeling. A time came at last when this was to be changed. The miller, who was a greedy man in his way, and never forewent an opportunity of honest profit, turned the mill-house into a little wayside inn, and, several pieces of good fortune falling in opportunely, built stables and got the position of post master on the road. It now became Will's duty to wait upon people, as they sat to break their fasts in the little arbor at the top of the mill garden ; and you may be sure that he kept his ears open, and learned many new things about the outside world as he brought the omelet or the wine. Nay, he would often get into conversation with single guests, and, by adroit questions and polite attention, not only gratify his own curiosity, but win the goodwill of the travelers. Many complimented the old couple on their serving-boy; and a professor was eager to take him away with him, and have him properly educated in the plain. The miller and his wife were mightily astonished and even more pleased. They thought it a very good thing that they should have opened their inn. "You see," the old man would remark, "he has a kind of talent for a publican; he never would have made anything else!" And so life wagged on in the valley, with high satisfaction to all concerned except Will. Every carriage that left the inn door seemed to take a part of him away with it; and when people jestingly offered him a lift, he could with difficulty command his emotion. Night after night he would dream that he was awakened by flustered servants, and that a splendid equipage waited at the door to carry him down into the plain; night after night; until the dream, which had seemed all jollity to him at first, began to take on a color of gravity, and a nocturnal summons and waiting equipage occupied a place in his mind as something to be both feared and hoped for.

One day, when Will was about sixteen, a fat young man arrived at sunset to pass the night. He was a contented-looking fellow, with a jolly eye, and carried a knapsack. While dinner was preparing, he sat in the arbor to read a book; but as soon as he had begun to observe Will, the book was laid aside; he was plainly one of those who prefer living people to people made of ink and paper. Will, on his part, although he had not been much interested in the stranger at first sight, soon began to take a great deal of pleasure in his talk, which was full of good-nature and good sense, and at last conceived a great respect for his character and wisdom. They sat far into the night; and about two in the morning Will opened his heart to the young man, and told him how he longed to leave the valley and what bright hopes he had connected with the cities of the plain. The young man whistled and then broke into a smile.

"My young friend," he remarked, "you are a very curious little fellow, to be sure, and wish a great many things which you will never get. Why, you would feel quite ashamed if you knew how the little fellows in these fairy cities of yours are all after the same sort of nonsense, and keep breaking their hearts to get up into the mountains. And let me tell you, those who go down into the plains are a very short while there before they wish themselves heartily back again. The air is not so light nor so pure; nor is the sun any brighter. As for the beautiful men and women, you would see many of them in rags and many of them deformed with horrible disorders; and a city is so hard a place for people who are poor and sensitive that many choose to die by their own hand."

"You must think me very simple," answered Will. "Although I have never been out of this valley, believe me, I have used my eyes. I know how one thing lives on another; for instance, how the fish hangs in the eddy to catch his fellows; and the shepherd, who makes so pretty a picture carrying home the lamb, is only carrying it home for dinner. I do not expect to find all things right in your cities. That is not what troubles me; it might have been that once upon a time; but although I live here always, I have asked many questions and learned a great deal in these last years, and certainly enough to cure me of my old fancies. But you would not have me die like a dog and not see all that is to be seen, and do all that a man can do, let it be good or evil? you would not have me spend all my days between this road here and the river, and not so much as make a motion to be up and live my life?—I would rather die out of hand," he cried, "than linger on as I am doing."

"Thousands of people," said the young man, "live and die like you, and are none the less happy."

"Ah!" said Will, "if there are thousands who would like, why should not one of them have my place?"

It was quite dark; there was a hanging lamp in the arbor which lit up the table and the faces of the speakers; and along the arch the leaves upon the trellis stood out illuminated against the night sky, a pattern of transparent green upon a dusky purple. The fat young man rose, and, taking Will by the arm, led him out under the open heavens.

"Did you ever look at the stars?" he asked, pointing upwards.

"Often and often," answered Will.

"And do you know what they are?"

"I have fancied many things."

"They are worlds like ours," said the young man. "Some of them less; many of them a million times greater; and some of the least sparkles that you see are not only worlds, but whole clusters of worlds turning about each other in the midst of space. We do not know what there may be in any of them; perhaps the answer to all our difficulties, or the cure of all our sufferings; and yet we can never reach them; not all the skill of the craftiest of men can fit out a ship for the nearest of these our neighbors, nor would the life of the most aged suffice for such a journey. When a great battle has been lost or a dear friend is dead, when we are hipped or in high spirits, there they are unweariedly shining overhead. We may stand down here, a whole army of us together, and shout until we break our hearts, and not a whisper reaches them. We may climb the highest mountain, and we are no nearer them. All we can do is to stand down here in the garden and take off our hats; the starshine lights upon our heads, and where mine is a little bald, I dare say you can see it glisten in the darkness. The mountain and the mouse. That is like to be all we shall ever have to do with Arcturus or Aldebaran. Can you apply a parable?" he added, laying his hand upon Will's shoulder. "It is not the same thing as a reason, but usually vastly more convincing."

Will hung his head a little, and then raised it once more to heaven. The stars seemed to expand and emit a sharper brilliancy; and as he kept turning his eyes higher and higher, they seemed to increase in multitude under his gaze.

"I see," he said, turning to the young man. "We are in a rat-trap."

"Something of that size. Did you ever see a squirrel turning in a cage? and another squirrel sitting philosophically over his nuts? I needn't ask you which of them looked more of a fool."

## THE PARSON'S MARJORY

After some years the old people died, both in one winter, very carefully tended by their adopted son, and very quietly mourned when they were gone. People who had heard of his roving fancies supposed he would hasten to sell the property, and go down the river to push his fortunes. But there was never any sign of such an intention on the part of Will. On the contrary, he had the inn set on a better footing, and hired a couple of servants to assist him in carrying it on; and there he settled down, a kind, talkative, inscrutable young man, six feet three in his stockings, with an iron constitution and a friendly voice. He soon began to take rank in the district as a bit of an oddity; it was not much to be wondered at from the first, for he was always full of notions, and kept calling the plainest common sense in question; but what most raised the report upon him was the odd circumstance of his courtship with the parson's Marjory.

The parson's Marjory was a lass about nineteen, when Will would be about thirty; well enough looking, and much better educated than any other girl in that part of the country, as became her parentage. She held her head very high, and had already refused several offers of marriage with a grand air, which had got her hard names among the neighbors. For all that she was a good girl, and one that would have made any man well contented.

Will had never seen much of her; for although the church and parsonage were only two miles from his own door, he was never known to go there but on Sundays. It chanced, however, that the parsonage fell into disrepair, and had to be dismantled; and the parson and his daughter took lodgings for a month or so, on very much reduced terms, at Will's inn. Now, what with the inn, and the mill, and the old miller's savings, our friend was a man of substance; and besides that, he had a name for good temper and shrewdness, which make a capital portion in marriage; and so it was currently gossiped, among their ill-wishers, that the parson and his daughter had not chosen their temporary lodging with their eyes shut. Will was about the last man in the world to be cajoled or frightened into marriage. You had only to look into his eyes, limpid and still like pools of water, and yet with a sort of clear light that seemed to come from within, and you would understand at once that here was one who knew his own mind, and would stand to it immovably. Marjory herself was no weakling by her looks, with strong, steady eyes and a resolute and quiet bearing. It might be a question whether she was not Will's match in steadfastness, after all, or which of them would rule the roast in marriage. But Marjory had never given it a thought, and accompanied her father with the most unshaken innocence and unconcern.

The season was still so early that Will's customers were few and far between; but the lilacs were already flowering, and the weather was so mild that the party took dinner under the trellis, with the noise of the river in their ears and the woods ringing about them with the songs of birds. Will soon began to take a particular pleasure in these dinners. The parson was rather a dull companion, with a habit of dozing at table; but nothing rude or cruel ever fell from his lips. And as for the parson's daughter, she suited her surroundings with the best grace imaginable; and whatever she said seemed so pat and pretty that Will conceived a great idea of her talents. He could see her face, as she leaned forward, against a background of rising pine woods; her eyes shone peaceably; the light lay around her hair like a kerchief; something that was hardly a smile rippled her pale cheeks, and Will could not contain himself from gazing on her in an agreeable dismay. She looked, even in her quietest moments, so complete in herself, and so quick with life down to her finger-tips and the very skirts of her dress, that the remainder of created things became no more than a blot by comparison; and if Will glanced away from her to her surroundings, the trees looked inanimate and senseless, the clouds hung in heaven like dead

things, and even the mountain tops were disenchanted. The whole valley could not compare in looks with this one girl.

Will was always observant in the society of his fellow-creatures; but his observation became almost painfully eager in the case of Marjory. He listened to all she uttered, and read her eyes, at the same time, for the unspoken commentary. Many kind, simple, and sincere speeches found an echo in his heart. He became conscious of a soul beautifully poised upon itself, nothing doubting, nothing desiring. clothed in peace. It was not possible to separate her thoughts from her appearance. The turn of her wrist, the still sound of her voice, the light in her eyes, the lines of her body, fell in tune with her grave and gentle words, like the accompaniment that sustains and harmonizes the voice of the singer. Her influence was one thing, not to be divided or discussed, only to be felt with gratitude and joy. To Will, her presence recalled something of his childhood, and the thought of her took its place in his mind beside that of dawn, of running water, and of the earliest violets and lilacs. It is the property of things seen for the first time, or for the first time after long, like the flowers in spring, to reawaken in us the sharp edge of sense and that impression of mystic strangeness which otherwise passes out of life with the coming of years; but the sight of a loved face is what renews a man's character from the fountain upwards.

One day after dinner Will took a stroll among the firs; a grave beatitude possessed him from top to toe, and he kept smiling to himself and the landscape as he went. The river ran between the stepping-stones with a pretty wimple; a bird sang loudly in the wood; the hill-tops looked immeasurably high, and as he glanced at them from time to time seemed to contemplate his movements with a beneficent but awful curiosity. His way took him to the eminence which overlooked the plain; and there he sat down upon a stone, and fell into deep and pleasant thought. The plain lay abroad with its cities and silver river; everything was asleep, except a great eddy of birds which kept rising and falling and going round and round in the blue air. He repeated Marjory's name aloud, and the sound of it gratified his ear. He shut his eyes, and her image sprang up before him, quietly luminous and attended with good thoughts. The river might run forever; the birds fly higher and higher till they touched the stars. He saw it was empty bustle after all; for here, without stirring a foot, waiting patiently in his own narrow valley, he also had attained the better sunlight.

The next day Will made a sort of declaration across the dinner-table, while the parson was filling his pipe.

"Miss Marjory," he said, "I never knew any one I liked so well as you. I am mostly a cold, unkindly sort of man; not from want of heart, but out of strangeness in my way of thinking; and people seem far away from me. 'Tis as if there were a circle round me, which kept every one out but you; I can hear the others talking and laughing; but you come quite close. Maybe, this is disagreeable to you?" he asked.

Marjory made no answer.

"Speak up, girl," said the parson.

"Nay, now," returned Will, "I wouldn't press her, parson. I feel tongue-tied myself, who am not used to it; and she's a woman, and little more than a child, when all is said. But for my part, as far as I can understand what people mean by it, I fancy I must be what they call in love. I do not wish to be held as committing myself; for I may be wrong; but that is how I believe things are with me. And if Miss Marjory should feel any otherwise on her part, mayhap she would be so kind as shake her head."

Marjory was silent, and gave no sign that she had heard.

"How is that, parson?" asked Will.

"The girl must speak," replied the parson, laying down his pipe. "Here's our neighbor who says he loves you, Madge. Do you love him, ay or no?"

"I think I do," said Marjory, faintly.

"Well, then, that's all that could be wished!" cried Will, heartily. And he took her hand across the table, and held it a moment in both of his with great satisfaction.

"You must marry," observed the parson, replacing his pipe in his mouth.

9

"Is that the right thing to do, think you?" demanded Will.

"It is indispensable," said the parson.

"Very well," replied the wooer.

Two or three days passed away with great delight to Will, although a bystander might scarce have found it out. He continued to take his meals opposite Marjory, and to talk with her and gaze upon her in her father's presence; but he made no attempt to see her alone, nor in any other way changed his conduct towards her from what it had been since the beginning. Perhaps the girl was a little disappointed, and perhaps not unjustly; and yet if it had been enough to be always in the thoughts of another person, and so pervade and alter his whole life, she might have been thoroughly contented. For she was never out of Will's mind for an instant. He sat over the stream, and watched the dust of the eddy, and the poised fish, and straining weeds; he wandered out alone into the purple even, with all the blackbirds piping round him in the wood; he rose early in the morning, and saw the sky turn from gray to gold, and the light leap upon the hill-tops; and all the while he kept wondering if he had never seen such things before, or how it was that they should look so different now. The sound of his own mill-wheel, or of the wind among the trees, confounded and charmed his heart. The most enchanting thoughts presented themselves unbidden in his mind. He was so happy that he could not sleep at night, and so restless that he could hardly sit still out of her company. And yet it seemed as if he avoided her rather than sought her out.

One day, as he was coming home from a ramble, Will found Marjory in the garden picking flowers, and as he came up with her, slackened his pace and continued walking by her side.

"You like flowers?" he said.

"Indeed, I love them dearly," she replied. "Do you?"

"Why, no," said he, "not so much. They are a very small affair, when all is done. I can fancy people caring for them greatly, but not doing as you are just now."

"How?" she asked, pausing and looking up at him.

"Plucking them," said he. "They are a deal better off where they are, and look a deal prettier, if you go to that."

"I wish to have them for my own," she answered, "to carry them near my heart, and keep them in my room. They tempt me when they grow here; they seem to say, 'Come and do something with us;' but once I have cut them and put them by, the charm is laid; and I can look at them with quite an easy heart."

"You wish to possess them," replied Will, "in order to think no more about them. It's a bit like killing the goose with the golden eggs. It's a bit like what I wished to do when I was a boy. Because I had a fancy for looking out over the plain, I wished to go down there—where I couldn't look out over it any longer. Was not that fine reasoning? Dear, dear, if they only thought of it, all the world would do like me; and you would let your flowers alone, just as I stay up here in the mountains." Suddenly he broke off sharp. "By the Lord!" he cried. And when she asked him what was wrong, he turned the question off and walked away into the house with rather a humorous expression of face.

He was silent at table; and after the night had fallen and the stars had come out overhead, he walked up and down for hours in the courtyard and garden with an uneven pace. There was still a light in the window of Marjory's room; one little oblong patch of orange in a world of dark-blue hills and silver starlight. Will's mind ran a great deal on the window; but his thoughts were not very lover-like. "There, she is in her room," he thought, "and there are the stars overhead—a blessing upon both!" Both were good influences in his life; both soothed and braced him in his profound contentment with the world. And what more should he desire with either? The fat young man and his counsels were so present to his mind that he threw back his head, and, putting his hands before his mouth, shouted aloud to the populous heavens. Whether from the position of his head or the sudden strain of the exertion, he seemed to see a momentary shock among the stars, and a diffusion of frosty light pass from one to another along the sky. At the same instant, a corner of the blind was lifted up and lowered again at once. He laughed a loud ho-ho! "One and another!" thought Will. "The stars tremble, and the blind goes up. Why, before Heaven, what a great magician I must be! Now if I were only a fool, should not I be in a pretty way?" And he went off to bed, chuckling to himself, "If I were only a fool!"

The next morning, pretty early, he saw her once more in the garden, and sought her out.

"I have been thinking about getting married," he began abruptly; "and after having turned it all over, I have made up my mind it's not worth while."

She turned upon him for a single moment; but his radiant, kindly appearance would, under the circumstances, have disconcerted an angel, and she looked down again upon the ground in silence. He could see her tremble.

"I hope you don't mind," he went on, a little taken aback. "You ought not. I have turned it all over, and upon my soul there's nothing in it. We should never be one whit nearer than we are just now, and, if I am a wise man, nothing like so happy."

"It is unnecessary to go round about with me," she said. "I very well remember that you refused to commit yourself; and now that I see you were mistaken, and in reality have never cared for me, I can only feel sad that I have been so far misled."

"I ask your pardon," said Will stoutly; "you do not understand my meaning. As to whether I have ever loved you or not, I must leave that to others. But for one thing, my feeling is not changed; and for another, you may make it your boast that you have made my whole life and character something different from what they were. I mean what I say; no less. I do not think getting married is worth while. I would rather you went on living with your father, so that I could walk over and see you once or maybe twice a week, as people go to church, and then we should both be all the happier between whiles. That's my notion. But I'll marry you if you will," he added.

"Do you know that you are insulting me," she broke out.

"Not I, Marjory," said he; "if there is anything in a clear conscience, not I. I offer all my heart's best affections; you can take it or want it, though I suspect it's beyond either your power or mine to change what has once been done, and set me fancy-free. I'll marry you, if you like; but I tell you again and again, it's not worth while, and we had best stay friends. Though I am a quiet man, I have noticed a heap of things in my life. Trust in me, and take things as I propose; or, if you don't like that, say the word, and I'll marry you out of hand."

There was a considerable pause, and Will, who began to feel uneasy, began to grow angry in consequence.

"It seems you are too proud to say your mind," he said. "Believe me, that's a pity. A clean shrift makes simple living. Can a man be more downright or honorable to a woman than I have been? I have said my say, and given you your choice. Do you want me to marry you? or will you take my friendship, as I think best? or have you had enough of me for good? Speak out, for the dear God's sake! You know your father told you a girl should speak her mind in these affairs."

She seemed to recover herself at that, turned without a word, walked rapidly through the garden, and disappeared into the house, leaving Will in some confusion as to the result. He walked up and down the garden, whistling softly to himself. Sometimes he stopped and contemplated the sky and hill-tops; sometimes he went down to the tail of the weir and sat there, looking foolishly in the water. All this dubiety and perturbation was so foreign to his nature and the life which he had resolutely chosen for himself, that he began to regret Marjory's arrival. "After all," he thought, "I was as happy as a man need be. I could come down here and watch my fishes all day long if I wanted; I was as settled and contented as my old mill."

Marjory came down to dinner, looking very trim and quiet; and no sooner were all three at table than she made her father a speech, with her eyes fixed upon her plate, but showing no other sign of embarrassment or distress.

"Father," she began, "Mr. Will and I have been talking things over. We see that we have each made a mistake about our feelings, and he has agreed, at my request, to give up all idea of marriage, and be no more than my very good friend, as in the past. You see, there is no shadow of a quarrel, and indeed I hope we shall see a great deal of him in the future, for his visits will always be welcome in our house. Of course, father, you will know best, but perhaps we should do better to leave Mr. Will's house for the present. I believe, after what has passed, we should hardly be agreeable inmates for some days."

Will, who had commanded himself with difficulty from the first, broke out upon this into an inarticulate noise, and raised one hand with an appearance of real dismay, as if he were about to interfere and contradict. But she checked him at once, looking up at him with a swift glance and an angry flush upon her cheek.

"You will perhaps have the good grace," she said, "to let me explain these matters for myself."

Will was put entirely out of countenance by her expression and the ring of her voice. He held his peace, concluding that there were some things about this girl beyond his comprehension, in which he was exactly right.

The poor parson was quite crestfallen. He tried to prove that this was no more than a true lovers' tiff, which would pass off before night; and when he was dislodged from that position, he went on to argue that where there was no quarrel there could be no call for a separation; for the good man liked both his entertainment and his host. It was curious to see how the girl managed them, saying little all the time, and that very quietly, and yet twisting them round her finger and insensibly leading them wherever she would by feminine tact and generalship. It scarcely seemed to have been her doing—it seemed as if things had merely so fallen out—that she and her father took their departure that same afternoon in a farm-cart, and went farther down the valley, to wait, until their own house was ready for them, in another hamlet. But Will had been observing closely, and was well aware of her dexterity and resolution. When he found himself alone, he had a great many curious matters to turn over in his mind. He was very sad and solitary, to begin with. All the interest had gone out of his life, and he might look up at the stars as long as he pleased, he somehow failed to find support or consolation. And then he was in such a turmoil of spirit about Marjory. He had been puzzled and irritated at her behavior, and yet he could not keep himself from admiring it. He thought he recognized a fine, perverse angel in that still soul which he had never hitherto suspected ; and though he saw it was an influence that would fit but ill with his own life of artificial calm, he could not keep himself from ardently desiring to possess it. Like a man who has lived among shadows and now meets the sun, he was both pained and delighted.

As the days went forward he passed from one extreme to another ; now pluming himself on the strength of his determination, now despising his timid and silly caution. The former was perhaps the true thought of his heart, and represented the regular tenor of the man's reflections ; but the latter burst forth from time to time with an unruly violence, and then he would forget all consideration, and go up and down his house and garden or walk among the fir woods like one who is beside himself with remorse. To equable, steady-minded Will this state of matters was intolerable ; and he determined, at whatever cost, to bring it to an end. So, one warm summer afternoon he put on his best clothes, took a thorn switch in his hand, and set out down the valley by the river. As soon as he had taken his determination, he had regained at a bound his customary peace of heart, and he enjoyed the bright weather and the variety of the scene without any admixture of alarm or unpleasant eagerness. It was nearly the same to him how the matter turned out. If she accepted him, he would have to marry her this time,

which perhaps was all for the best. If she refused him, he would have done his utmost, and might follow his own way in the future with an untroubled conscience. He hoped, on the whole, that she would refuse him ; and then, again, as he saw the brown roof which sheltered her, peeping through some willows at an angle of the stream, he was half inclined to reverse the wish, and more than half ashamed of himself for this infirmity of purpose.

Marjory seemed glad to see him, and gave him her hand without affectation or delay.

" I have been thinking about this marriage," he began.

" So have I," she answered. " And I respect you more and more for a very wise man. You understood me better than I understood myself ; and I am now quite certain that things are all for the best as they are."

" At the same time— " ventured Will.

" You must be tired," she interrupted. " Take a seat and let me fetch you a glass of wine. The afternoon is so warm ; and I wish you not to be displeased with your visit. You must come quite often ; once a week, if you can spare the time ; I am always so glad to see my friends."

" Oh, very well," thought Will to himself. " It appears I was right, after all." And he paid a very agreeable visit, walked home again in capital spirits, and gave himself no further concern about the matter.

For nearly three years Will and Marjory continued on these terms, seeing each other once or twice a week without any word of love between them ; and for all that time I believe Will was nearly as happy as a man can be. He rather stinted himself the pleasure of seeing her ; and he would often walk half-way over to the parsonage, and then back again, as if to whet his appetite. Indeed, there was one corner of the road, whence he could see the church spire wedged into a crevice of the valley between sloping fir woods, with a triangular snatch of plain by way of background, which he greatly affected as a place to sit and moralize in before returning homewards ; and the peasants got so much into the habit of finding him there in the twilight that they gave it the name of " Will o' the Mill's Corner."

At the end of the three years Marjory played him a sad trick by suddenly marrying somebody else. Will kept his countenance bravely, and merely remarked that, for as little as he knew of women, he had acted very prudently in not marrying her himself three years before. She plainly knew very little of her own mind, and, in spite of a deceptive manner, was as fickle and flighty as the rest of them. He had to congratulate himself on an escape, he said, and would take a higher opinion of his own wisdom in consequence. But at heart he was reasonably displeased, moped a good deal for a month or two, and fell away in flesh, to the astonishment of his serving-lads.

It was perhaps a year after this marriage that Will was awakened late one night by the sound of a horse galloping on the road, followed by precipitate knocking at the inn door. He opened his window and saw a farm servant, mounted and holding a led horse by the bridle, who told him to make what haste he could and go along with him; for Marjory was dying, and had sent urgently to fetch him to her bedside. Will was no horseman, and made so little speed upon the way that the poor young wife was very near her end before he arrived. But they had some minutes' talk in private, and he was present and wept very bitterly while she breathed her last.

### DEATH

Year after year went away into nothing, with great explosions and outcries in the cities on the plain: red revolt springing up and being suppressed in blood, battle swaying hither and thither, patient astonomers in observatory towers picking out and christening new stars, plays being performed in lighted theaters, people being carried into hospitals on stretchers, and all the usual turmoil and agitation of men's lives in crowded centers. Up in Will's valley only the winds and seasons made an epoch; the fish hung in the swift stream, the birds circled overhead, the pine-tops rustled underneath the stars, the tall hills stood

over all; and Will went to and fro, minding his wayside inn, until the snow began to thicken on his head. His heart was young and vigorous; and if his pulses kept a sober time, they still beat strong and steady in his wrists. He carried a ruddy stain on either cheek like a ripe apple; he stooped a little, but his step was still firm; and his sinewy hands were reached out to all men with a friendly pressure. His face was covered with those wrinkles which are got in open air, and which, rightly looked at, are no more than a sort of permanent sunburning. Such wrinkles heighten the stupidity of stupid faces, but to a person like Will, with his clear eyes and smiling mouth, only give another charm by testifying to a simple and easy life. His talk was full of wise sayings. He had a taste for other people, and other people had a taste for him. When the valley was full of tourists in the season, there were merry nights in Will's arbor; and his views, which seemed whimsical to his neighbors, were often enough admired by learned people out of towns and colleges. Indeed, he had a very noble old age, and grew daily better known; so that his fame was heard of in the cities of the plain; and young men who had been summer travelers spoke together in cafés of Will o' the Mill and his rough philosophy. Many and many an invitation, you may be sure, he had; but nothing could tempt him from his upland valley. He would shake his head and smile over his tobacco-pipe with a deal of meaning. " You come too late," he would answer. " I am a dead man now; I have lived and died already. Fifty years ago you would have brought my heart into my mouth; and now you do not even tempt me. But that is the object of long living, that man should cease to care about life." And again: " There is only one difference between a long life and a good dinner: that, in the dinner, the sweets come last." Or, once more: " When I was a boy I was a bit puzzled, and hardly knew whether it was myself or the world that was curious and worth looking into. Now, I know it is myself, and stick to that."

He never showed any symptoms of

frailty, but kept stalwart and firm to the last; but they say he grew less talkative towards the end, and would listen to other people by the hour in an amused and sympathetic silence. Only, when he did speak, it was more to the point and more charged with old experience. He drank a bottle of wine gladly; above all, at sunset on the hill-top or quite late at night under the stars in the arbor. The sight of something attractive and unattainable seasoned his enjoyment, he would say; and he professed he had lived long enough to admire a candle all the more when he could compare it with a planet.

One night, in his seventy-second year, he awoke in bed, in such uneasiness of body and mind that he arose and dressed himself and went out to meditate in the arbor. It was pitch dark, without a star; the river was swollen, and the wet woods and meadows loaded the air with perfume. It had thundered during the day, and it promised more thunder for the morrow. A murky, stifling night for a man of seventy-two! Whether it was the weather or the wakefulness, or some little touch of fever in his old limbs, Will's mind was besieged by tumultuous and crying memories. His boyhood, the night with the fat young man, the death of his adopted parents, the summer days with Marjory, and many of those small circumstances which seem nothing to another and are yet the very gist of a man's own life to himself—things seen, words heard, looks misconstrued—arose from their forgotten corners and usurped his attention. The dead themselves were with him, not merely taking part in this thin show of memory that defiled before his brain, but revisiting his bodily senses as they do in profound and vivid dreams. The fat young man leaned his elbows on the table opposite; Marjory came and went with an apronful of flowers between the garden and the arbor; he could hear the old parson knocking out his pipe or blowing his resonant nose. The tide of his consciousness ebbed and flowed; he was sometimes half asleep and drowned in his recollections of the past; and sometimes he was broad awake, wondering at himself. But about the middle of the night he was startled by the voice of the dead miller calling to him out of the house as he used to do on the arrival of custom. The hallucination was so perfect that Will sprang from his seat and stood listening for the summons to be repeated; and as he listened he became conscious of another noise besides the brawling of the river and the ringing in his feverish ears. It was like the stir of the horses and the creaking of harness, as though a carriage with an impatient team had been brought up upon the road before the courtyard gate. At such an hour, upon this rough and dangerous pass, the supposition was no better than absurd; and Will dismissed it from his mind, and resumed his seat upon the arbor chair; and sleep closed over him again like running water. He was once again awakened by the dead miller's call, thinner and more spectral than before; and once again he heard the noise of an equipage upon the road. And so thrice and four times the same dream, or the same fancy, presented itself to his senses; until at length, smiling to himself as when one humors a nervous child, he proceeded towards the gate to set his uncertainty at rest.

From the arbor to the gate was no great distance, and yet it took Will some time; it seemed as if the dead thickened around him in the court, and crossed his path at every step. For, first, he was suddenly surprised by an overpowering sweetness of heliotropes; it was as if his garden had been planted with this flower from end to end, and the hot, damp night had drawn forth all their perfumes in a breath. Now the heliotrope had been Marjory's favorite flower, and since her death not one of them had ever been planted in Will's ground.

"I must be going crazy," he thought. "Poor Marjory and her heliotropes!"

And with that he raised his eyes towards the window that had once been hers. If he had been bewildered before, he was now almost terrified; for there was a light in the room; the window was an orange oblong as of yore; and the corner of the blind was lifted and let fall as on the night when he stood and shouted to the stars in his perplexity.

The illusion only endured an instant; but it left him somewhat unmanned, rubbing his eyes and staring at the outline of the house and the black night behind it. While he thus stood, and it seemed as if he must have stood there quite a long time, there came a renewal of the noises on the road ; and he turned in time to meet a stranger, who was advancing to meet him across the court. There was something like the outline of a great carriage discernible on the road behind the stranger, and above that a few black pine-tops, like so many plumes.

"Master Will?" asked the newcomer, in brief military fashion.

"That same, sir," answered Will. "Can I do anything to serve you?"

"I have heard you much spoken of, Master Will," returned the other; "much spoken of, and well. And though I have both hands full of business, I wish to drink a bottle of wine with you in your arbor. Before I go I shall introduce myself."

Will led the way to the trellis, and got a lamp lighted and a bottle uncorked. He was not altogether unused to such complimentary interviews, and hoped little enough from this one, being schooled by many disappointments. A sort of cloud had settled on his wits and prevented him from remembering the strangeness of the hour. He moved like a person in his sleep; and it seemed as if the lamp caught fire and the bottle came uncorked with the facility of thought. Still, he had some curiosity about the appearance of his visitor, and tried in vain to turn the light into his face; either he handled the lamp clumsily, or there was a dimness over his eyes, but he could make out little more than a shadow at table with him. He stared and stared at this shadow, as he wiped out the glasses, and began to feel cold and strange about the heart. The silence weighed upon him, for he could hear nothing now, not even the river, but the drumming of his own arteries in his ears.

"Here's to you," said the stranger, roughly.

"Here is my service, sir," replied Will, sipping his wine, which somehow tasted oddly.

"I understand you are a very positive fellow," pursued the stranger.

Will made answer with a smile of some satisfaction and a little nod.

"So am I," continued the other; "and it is the delight of my heart to tramp on people's corns. I will have nobody positive but myself; not one. I have crossed the whims, in my time, of kings and generals and great artists. And what would you say," he went on, "if I had come up here on purpose to cross yours?"

Will had it on his tongue to make a sharp rejoinder; but the politeness of an old innkeeper prevailed; and he held his peace and made answer with a civil gesture of the hand.

"I have," said the stranger. "And if I did not hold you in a particular esteem, I should make no words about the matter. It appears you pride yourself on staying where you are. You mean to stick by your inn. Now I mean you shall come for a turn with me in my barouche; and before this bottle's empty, so you shall."

"That would be an odd thing, to be sure," replied Will, with a chuckle. "Why, sir, I have grown here like an old oak-tree; the Devil himself could hardly root me up; and for all I perceive you are a very entertaining old gentleman, I would wager you another bottle you lose your pains with me."

The dimness of Will's eyesight had been increasing all this while; but he was somehow conscious of a sharp and chilling scrutiny which irritated and yet overmastered him.

"You need not think," he broke out suddenly, in an explosive, febrile manner that startled and alarmed himself, "that I am a stay-at-home because I fear anything under God. God knows I am tired enough of it all; and when the time comes for a longer journey than ever you dream of, I reckon I shall find myself prepared."

The stranger emptied his glass and pushed it away from him. He looked down for a little, and then, leaning over the table, tapped Will three times upon the forearm with a single finger. "The time has come!" he said, solemnly.

An ugly thrill spread from the spot he

touched. The tones of his voice were dull and startling, and echoed strangely in Will's heart.

"I beg your pardon," he said, with some discomposure. "What do you mean?"

"Look at me, and you will find your eyesight swim. Raise your hand; it is dead-heavy. This is your last bottle of wine, Master Will, and your last night upon the earth."

"You are a doctor?" quavered Will.

"The best that ever was," replied the other; "for I cure both mind and body with the same prescription. I take away all pain and I forgive all sins; and where my patients have gone wrong in life, I smooth out all complications and set them free again upon their feet."

"I have no need of you," said Will.

"A time comes for all men, Master Will," replied the doctor, "when the helm is taken out of their hands. For you, because you were prudent and quiet, it has been long of coming, and you have had long to discipline yourself for its reception. You have seen what is to be seen about your mill; you have sat close all your days like a hare in its form; but now that is at an end, and," added the doctor, getting on his feet, "you must arise and come with me."

"You are a strange physician," said Will, looking steadfastly upon his guest.

"I am a natural law," he replied, "and people call me Death."

"Why did you not tell me so at first?" cried Will. "I have been waiting for you these many years. Give me your hand, and welcome."

"Lean upon my arm," said the stranger, "for already your strength abates. Lean on me heavily as you need; for though I am old, I am very strong. It is but three steps to my carriage, and there all your trouble ends. Why, Will," he added, "I have been yearning for you as if you were my own son; and of all the men that ever I came for in my long days, I have come for you most gladly. I am caustic, and sometimes offend people at first sight; but I am a good friend at heart to such as you."

"Since Marjory was taken," returned Will, "I declare before God you were the only friend I had to look for."

So the pair went arm-in-arm across the courtyard.

One of the servants awoke about this time and heard the noise of horses pawing before he dropped asleep again; all down the valley that night there was a rushing as of a smooth and steady wind descending towards the plain; and when the world rose next morning, sure enough Will o' the Mill had gone at last upon his travels.

# RESURGAM

## BY GEORGIANA WOOD ADAMS

When grief has wrapped my spirit in a shroud,
  And the tense parting with a hope is past,
  Let me not molder where the tears fall fast,
Or swell the ranks of any useless crowd;

Nor let the stoic rule my darkened room
  With his stern silences, or seal the way
  Of agony with granite, as did they
Who locked the living fast within a tomb;

Nor let me in those solitudes find rest
  Where poetry's enchantments break in prose,
  Where parts are played by waiting—nor dispose
These willful hands too humbly on my breast.

Ah no! But bear me up those mighty steeps
  Which from the Valley of the Shadow rise,
  In time for one more stirring enterprise,
Not dead, but as a warrior who sleeps.

# Letters to The Outlook

## CHILD LABOR IN THE SOUTH

Captain Ellison A. Smyth's letter to The Outlook of March 30 on "Child Labor in the South" calls for a brief reply, as he questions both my knowledge of the conditions and the spirit of fairness in my article of February 16 on the same subject. I shall not enter into another discussion of the conflicting estimates as to the number of children employed in the Southern mills. The Government investigation, which the National Child Labor Committee earnestly advocated and the manufacturing interests vehemently opposed, ought to determine which is right. I simply call attention to the fact that the same manufacturers report over 200,000 operatives to their trade journal and 123,000 to the census department the same year, and I have taken the larger figure as nearer the truth from my own knowledge. For instance, I have actually seen in one cigar factory in Tampa, Florida, more children at work than the manufacturers report—nineteen in all—for all the cigar factories in the State.

With regard to my statement that "the same class and quality of goods made in the South and in the East bring a considerably lower price when made in the South, through the bad reputation that Southern mills have won for the indifferent product of unskilled, that is, child, labor," Captain Smyth says: "Indisputable proof could be furnished that the statement is wide of the facts and grossly incorrect." The Hon. Murphy Candler, of the Georgia Senate, a practical cotton manufacturer, made the statement on the floor of the Senate, and challenged contradiction from his manufacturer colleagues, that Southern cotton goods brought from two to three cents a pound less than the same quality of goods from Eastern mills. The Hon. W. A. Covington, member of the Georgia House of Representatives, told me that a mill with which he was connected was ordered by its Northern selling agents to conceal the fact that its goods were made in Georgia, as they had been passing them off as Eastern goods. On March 21 of this year Mr. Garrett Andrews, of Chattanooga, who was chosen to represent the Tennessee manufacturers in their opposition to the passage of a nine-hour law for children under sixteen, said before the legislative committee, in my hearing, that the same cotton goods brought one and a half cents a pound less in the South than when manufactured in the North, arguing that Tennessee manu-

facturers should not be put at a further disadvantage with their Northern competitors. I do not deny that individual Southern mills have earned a better reputation, and therefore get better prices.

At an address at Cooper Union, February 16, 1905, I said: "I was told not long ago by a leading dealer in cotton-mill machinery that a spooler had been put upon the market with adjustable legs for small help." Says Captain Smyth in his letter to The Outlook: "I first alluded to the statement of Spargo in his book, 'The Bitter Cry of the Children,' on the authority of Dr. A. J. McKelway, that the spinning-frames in the Southern cotton-mills had adjustable legs, so as to be lowered to the floor for the convenience of the small children. I clearly demonstrated the absurdity of this statement, and the ignorance of conditions and the spirit of unfairness that prompted it." Captain Smyth should consider Captain Sigsbee's proverb, "It is better to know than to think." If he will turn to Draper's "Textile Texts," edition of 1901, page 183, he will find the advertisement of a spooler with the following description: "Another important feature of our construction is the use of adjustable legs in the frame so that the height of the machine may be suited to the operative. Small help is used in some mills and full-grown help in others. The motions required in spooling are very fatiguing if the spindles are not at a proper height for easy manipulation, and this height necessarily varies with the height of the attendant."

Captain Smyth seems inclined to boast that the present child labor law in South Carolina was enacted "largely through the influence of the manufacturers themselves." Captain Smyth will not deny that the law was a compromise measure, that it began with a ten-year age limit, gradually increasing to a twelve-year age limit, that the hours are sixty-six a week, which means twelve hours a day for the first five days of the week, and that children of any age who are unfortunate enough to be orphans or the children of dependent parents are allowed to work in the mills. So that to-day a six-year-old orphan or the child of a disabled father is allowed, by law, to work twelve hours a day in the South Carolina cotton-mills. Nor will Captain Smyth deny that during the session of the Legislature of South Carolina in January he argued before the committee against raising the age limit to fourteen years and against the immediate reduction of the hours to sixty a week for children. I have his argument before me as I write.

A. J. McKelway.

Atlanta, Georgia.

### TOUGALOO UNIVERSITY

A company of about thirty gentlemen and ladies from the North, including ministers and business men, recently made, at their own expense, a tour of some of the schools of the American Missionary Association in the South—Fisk at Nashville, Straight at New Orleans, Piedmont at Demorest, Georgia, Atlanta Theological Seminary, Talladega at Talladega, Alabama, Le Moyne at Memphis, Tennessee, and · Tougaloo at Tougaloo, Mississippi.

The last-named school is differently situated from the others, being in the country seven miles from Jackson, the capital of the State. It is on the main line of travel, but not on the main line of travelers, for there is no town there, and the fast through trains do not stop. One must usually take a slower train from Jackson or some point North. Tougaloo, consequently, has few visitors and its work is not so well known as it deserves to be.

It was, then, an occasion of no small moment when this company of visitors descended from their special car on March 4, and spent some hours in making acquaintance with the school and its work. Arriving at noon, the afternoon session afforded but little opportunity of seeing the best work of the school, but the opportunity was well employed, and the visitors expressed themselves as much pleased with what they saw in the way of accomplishment and impressed with what they saw in the way of the necessities of the school, particularly in the equipment of the industrial departments and the condition of Strieby Hall, the latter being only partially ready for its intended and sorely needed use as an assembly and recitation building for the academy.

An occasion of special interest was the dedication of the new dormitory for the boys, for which they have waited so long. The building bears the name of Galloway Hall, after Bishop Galloway, of the Methodist Church, a steadfast friend of the school and of the race for which the school was established, an eminent citizen of the State, and a wise and devoted Christian leader. It was a matter of great regret that the Bishop could not be present at the dedication. He had not returned from Florida and Cuba, where he had been spending some months for the recovery of his health, impaired by his labors to the point of extreme danger. The dedicatory address was delivered in the church by the Rev. Dr. De Witt S. Clarke, of Salem, Massachusetts. Other brief addresses followed from the visitors and some gentlemen from Jackson, who manifested by their presence and words their interest and sympathy with the work of the school. It was a happy feature of the day that representatives of the North and the South should thus come together.

In the evening the usual mid-year concert was given by the University Chorus, numbering over one hundred, composed of the students of the college and academy. Then the visitors went to their car to be taken on their way to other schools.

Those who were visited cannot say what impression was left on the minds of the visitors, but they testify to the great enjoyment and benefit which they themselves received from even the few hours of such companionship, from the hearty words of appreciation, and the breath of an unaccustomed and bracing life thus breathed upon them. It is rarely that the colored students are made to feel in such a way the personal interest of men and women of Christian culture and large practical success in life. Such a visit means far more to them than the pleasant occupation of a day. It brings a new sense of being part of the world represented by such friends, an addition to the sense of fellowship in an experience where fellowship is not very abundant, a widening of their horizon, and an ennobling of their estimate of life and of their own work and possibilities.

C. H.

### AMERICAN RHODES SCHOLARS: A LETTER FROM THE SECRETARY OF THE TRUSTEES.

I am told that statements have appeared in the American press to the effect that the American Rhodes scholars have failed to give satisfaction here, have distinguished themselves in nothing except athletics, and compare unfavorably with Rhodes scholars from elsewhere. I would ask you of your courtesy to allow me to contradict these statements. My position as Oxford Secretary to the Rhodes Trustees brings me into touch both with the colleges and the Rhodes scholars themselves, and gives me a quite special opportunity for knowing the facts. It is difficult to speak in terms of results, for the simple reason that few of the men—indeed, only some half-dozen out of eighty—have as yet arrived at the examinations which are to provide those results. Relying, however, partly on the few results to which we can already point, partly on reports which I have received from college tutors, and partly on my own observations, I have no hesitation in saying that the American Rhodes scholars as a body are regarded by the colleges and the university as a valuable addition to Oxford life, that they are recognized as being at once able and strenuous, and that in respect neither of ability nor of strenuous endeavor do they yield anything to their brother Rhodes scholars from elsewhere. To represent them as successful only in athletics is absurd. One or two certainly have done extremely well in the athletic line; others have been useful college performers at football, lawn-tennis, or rowing. But their real contribution to the life of Oxford has not been athletic distinction, but a sense of purpose, and a certain freshness of intellectual interest. I do not pretend that all the American Rhodes scholars have been equally able, or even equally strenuous. Who would expect that? I speak of them in the only way that I can—as a whole, and on the average. Up to the present, as I have already explained, we have few actual examination results to which to point. Those, however, to which we can point are distinctly encouraging.

Five Americans took the final honor examination for the B.A. degree last June. Of these five three took the examination a year before the usual time, allowing themselves rather less than one year instead of the normal two years in which to prepare for it. The results were as follows: 2 First Classes, 1 Second, 1 Fourth, and 1 failure. In addition, one American Rhodes scholar took the B.C.L. degree, and another the B.Sc. This last is a distinction at least equivalent to a first class in a final honor school. By any one who understands the conditions these results can only be regarded as eminently creditable. Two of the Americans, I may add, have within the last six months been appointed demonstrators at the University Museum, one (Mr. J. A. Brown, of New Hampshire) under the Wykeham Professor of Physics, the other (Mr. H. A. Hinds, of North Dakota) under the Professor of Geology. These last appointments are unquestionably among the one or two leading distinctions won by Rhodes scholars of any nationality.

I have received reports from many college tutors which, along with some inevitable differences, agree in their appreciation of the spirit in which the American Rhodes scholars as a whole approach their work, and of the general influence which they exercise upon the life of their colleges. I close my letter with a few words quoted from a letter which I have received from the President of Magdalen College, who is the present Vice-Chancellor of the University: "I am glad to hear that you are writing to some of the American papers refuting the statements which have appeared over there that we are not satisfied with the Rhodes scholars, and that we think they have failed to distinguish themselves here except in athletics. My acquaintance with them is not, indeed, very large or long, for they have not been very long here, and I am of course very much preoccupied; but I have, as it happens, seen something of them both in my college and at other colleges, and of course I hear and note a good deal about them in other ways. Giving my impressions for what they are worth, I should certainly say that they are an intellectual class; and I can say with confidence that if the system had only brought to Oxford some few whom I have come across here, it would have gone far to justify itself on intellectual grounds. I do not think I ought to attempt to say more at present. We must remember that the system is, after all, still very young."

F. J. WYLIE,
Oxford Secretary to the Rhodes Trustees.

## TUSKEGEE

Rather disturbed and unsettled conditions in the South, so far as the race is concerned, have made me feel that it is my duty to remain South during the greater part of the year; this I have done. I have spent my time at the school, and in traveling and speaking to mixed audiences of both races in various parts of the South. I feel that I have in this way accomplished great good, and I am quite sure, by reason of the work of many broad and patriotic white and colored men, that the relations at present are much more satisfactory and settled; but the time I have spent in this way has prevented my getting into the Northern and Western States in the way I usually do, for the purpose of getting contributions for the work of Tuskegee Institute. The result is that we are much more in need of funds for current expenses than usual.

The President of one of the State universities in the South recently said to a friend: "Say to Professor Washington that I wish he could spend the next six or eight months or longer, if possible, speaking in the South. He is needed badly here now. I feel that the sentiment is growing better, and he knows what to say to help further this good feeling."

Our needs are in two directions: first, fifty-dollar scholarships with which to pay the tuition of students through school; and, second, money with which to increase our endowment fund so it will not be necessary to spend so much of my time away from the school collecting money for its current expenses.

Any money, whether in large or small sums, sent for these purposes will be of great help to our work, and highly appreciated.

BOOKER T. WASHINGTON,
Principal.

### A PLEA FOR UNCONSCIOUS SLAVES

Please permit me to dissent from the ably written editorial in The Outlook for April 6 on "Women and Politics." I seriously question the right of withholding the ballot from women, even if a large majority of them shrink from assuming political and civic responsibilities. To my mind, those who thus shrink afford thereby but evidences of their psychological enthralldom. As a class, women have not yet awakened to the fact that they are really free or can be free, that they have in themselves the possibility of as much independent existence as the other sex enjoys. Now, is it right to withhold from the thoroughly emancipated woman the right to govern herself, simply because her backward sisters, even though they may be in the majority, shrink from exercising the political prerogatives that of a right belong to the new womanhood? Miss Stephen, whom you quote, seems to think that the bestowal of the ballot upon women will work injustice or hardship upon those of the sex who shrink. from political duty. Is it necessary or imperative, however, that the timid woman, the overly feminine woman, the psychologically unemancipated woman, avail herself of her prerogative of voting? We condone more or less political passivity in men. Why should we not do so cheerfully in the case of women, remembering that they have been sorely oppressed for ages and that they should not be expected one and all, therefore, to rise at once to the full stature of perfectly free womanhood? The fully emancipated woman wants the ballot. By all means let her have it, and let us wait as patiently as possible for the fuller development of the woman who is still ever and anon casting her eyes backward to that retarded frontier of social advance where she dwelt so long in subjection to the authority of man. Shall we deny to the enlightened, intelligent woman who wants to govern herself, the right that in the United States is granted to the ignorant foreigner and the lowly negro? Is it right that the college-bred and cultivated negro woman of some Northern city should have no voice in the government, while the negro criminal of the South is a voter? Is it right that the intelligent women of whatever race or color should have no right to express a choice as to who shall be the Mayor of their city, the Governor of their State, or the President of the United States, while ignorant, irresponsible men, in spite of the Australian ballot system, are voted by the party boss?

In my opinion, running the government is in this age no more the work of men than it is of women. The designations *women's work* and *men's work* are but marks of a psychological lagging behind the times. Division of occupations on a basis of sex has long ago begun to break down. A woman lawyer pleads, and pleads ably, cases at law; while a man does the cleaning and scrubbing in the apartment-house where the woman lawyer lives. A woman administers the finances of Kansas City, Kansas, while men bake our bread.

As for the danger of a contest in politics between the sexes, such a thing is in my opinion an imp ossibility, for the real welfare of the two sexes is one and the same thing. If there does arise a struggle having reference to sex privileges, it will not be a struggle between the sexes, but a struggle between two parties made up of both sexes, one party recognizing the right, and, yea, the expediency too—for citizens inherit both from mother and father—the right and the expediency of the fullest freedom for woman, consistent with her health and morals; while in the other party will be found those whose mental processes are impeded by some vestige of the long bygone ages, when woman was the mere slave and creature of man, those who are possessed perhaps of some of the spirit that made it possible for a mediæval church council to debate the question as to whether women had souls.

Some women, having risen to the full stature of the new, freer womanhood, demand the ballot. They should have it. The English, the American woman, the woman in every enlightened country in this advanced twentieth century, has as much moral right to vote as has man; and England and the United States will continue to be democracies but in name as long as their women are denied equal political rights with men.

RAYMOND V. PHELAN.

Department of Economics and Sociology,
Miami University, Ohio.

# Index to Volume Eighty-five of The Outlook

## January 5 to April 27, 1907 (Four Months)

## CONTRIBUTED ARTICLES :